Collins
Canadian
English
Dictionary

Collins
Canadian
English
Dictionary

Collins

HarperCollins books may be purchased for educational, business, or
sales promotional use through our Special Markets Department.

HarperCollins Publishers Ltd
2 Bloor Street East, 20th Floor
Toronto, Ontario, Canada
M4W 1A8

www.collinsdictionaries.ca

Cataloguing in Publication Data is available upon request.

OPM 9 8 7 6 5 4 3 2 1

Printed and bound in the United States

CONTENTS

EDITORIAL STAFF

PREFACE

Collins Canadian English Dictionary presents comprehensive coverage of **today's** language in a clear, accessible format.

For this new edition, the editors have been able to consult the **Bank of English®**, a unique computer-based collection of over 524 million words of written and spoken English. Analysis of this data enables the editors to give the user the most up-to-date information about how English is written and spoken today. The dictionary now contains new items such as *bioterrorism, globalization, ringtone* and *satnav*, and new senses of words such as *bookmark, fusion,* and *hit*.

The **Canadian English Dictionary** also gives in-depth coverage of Canadian English, and reflects its uniqueness and variety. Entries such as *Kabloona, parkade* and *tupik* are included, in addition to many of the variant forms found in Canada.

As well as defining a wide variety of words, this dictionary contains many other features which are designed to be helpful to the user. For example, a simple phonetic respelling is given for pronunciations which could cause difficulty. All irregular spelling forms are shown. Labels inform the user if a word is, for instance, slang, rare, or literary. To make all this and other information easy to find, the layout of the pages is clear and uncluttered.

All these features make **Collins Canadian English Dictionary** an easy-to-use and indispensable guide to today's English.

USING THE DICTIONARY

Main Entry Words
printed in large bold type, e.g.
abbey
All main entry words, including abbreviations and combining forms, in one alphabetical sequence, e.g.
abbreviate
ABC
abdicate
abdomen

Variant Spellings
shown in full, e.g.
adrenalin, adrenaline

Pronunciations
given in square brackets for words that are difficult or confusing; the word is respelt as it is pronounced, with the stressed syllable in bold type, e.g.
aegis [**ee**-jiss]

Parts of Speech
shown in italics as an abbreviation, e.g.
ablaze *adj*
When a word can be used as more than one part of speech, the change of part of speech is shown after a lozenge, e.g.
mock *v* make fun of, mimic. ◆ *n* imitation.
Parts of speech may be combined for some words, e.g.
alone *adj, adv* without anyone or anything else.

Cross References
shown in small capital letters, e.g.
deshabille *n* same as DISHABILLE.

Irregular Spellings   or confusing forms of verbs, nouns, adjectives, and adverbs shown in bold type, e.g.

begin *v* **-ginning, -gan, -gun.**
regret *v* **-gretting, -gretted.**
anniversary *n, pl* **-ries.**
angry *adj* **-grier, -griest.**
well *adv* **better, best.**

Meanings   separated by semicolons, e.g.

casual *adj* appearing unconcerned; (of work or workers) occasional; shallow or superficial; for informal wear; happening by chance.

Phrases and Idioms   included immediately after the meanings of the entry word, e.g.

head *n* ... *adj* ... *v* ... **go to someone's head** make someone drunk or conceited. **head over heels** very much in love.

Related Words   shown in the same paragraph as the main entry word, e.g.

absurd *adj* incongruous or ridiculous. **absurdly** *adv* **absurdity** *n*
Note: where the meaning of a related word is not given, it may be understood from the main entry word, or from another related word.

Compounds   shown in alphabetical order at the end of the paragraph, e.g.

ash *n* ... **ashtray** *n* receptacle for tobacco ash and cigarette butts. **Ash Wednesday** first day of Lent.

ABBREVIATIONS USED IN THE DICTIONARY

AD	anno Domini	*Meteorol*	Meteorology
adj	adjective	*Mil*	Military
adv	adverb	*n*	noun
Anat	Anatomy	*N*	North
Archit	Architecture	*Naut*	Nautical
Astrol	Astrology	*NZ*	New Zealand
Aust	Australia(n)	*Obs*	Obsolete
BC	before Christ	*Offens*	Offensive
Biol	Biology	*orig.*	originally
Brit	British	*Photog*	Photography
Canad	Canadian	*pl*	plural
Chem	Chemistry	*prep*	preposition
conj	conjunction	*pron*	pronoun
E	East	*Psychol*	Psychology
e.g.	for example	®	Trademark
esp.	especially	*RC*	Roman Catholic
etc.	et cetera	*S*	South
fem	feminine	*S Afr*	South Africa(n)
foll.	followed	*Scot*	Scottish
Geom	Geometry	*sing*	singular
Hist	History	*US*	United States
interj	interjection	*usu.*	usually
Lit	Literary	*v*	verb
masc	masculine	*W*	West
Med	Medicine	*Zool*	Zoology

DICTIONARY

— A a —

a *adj* indefinite article, used before a noun mentioned for the first time.

AA Alcoholics Anonymous; Automobile Association.

aardvark *n* S African anteater with long ears and snout.

AB able-bodied seaman; Alberta.

aback *adv* **taken aback** startled or disconcerted.

abacus [ab-a-cuss] *n* beads on a wire frame, used for doing calculations.

abalone [ab-a-lone-ee] *n* edible shellfish yielding mother-of-pearl.

abandon *v* desert or leave (one's wife, children, etc.); give up (hope etc.) altogether. ♦ *n* freedom from inhibition. **abandoned** *adj* deserted; uninhibited. **abandonment** *n*

abase *v* humiliate, degrade (oneself). **abasement** *n*

abashed *adj* embarrassed and ashamed.

abate *v* diminish in strength. **abatement** *n*

abattoir [ab-a-twahr] *n* slaughterhouse.

abbess *n* nun in charge of a convent.

abbey *n* dwelling place of, or a church belonging to, a community of monks or nuns.

abbot *n* head of an abbey of monks.

abbr., abbrev. abbreviation.

abbreviate *v* shorten (a word) by omitting some letters. **abbreviation** *n* shortened form of a word or words.

ABC *n* alphabet; rudiments of a subject.

abdicate *v* give up (the throne or a responsibility). **abdication** *n*

abdomen *n* part of the body containing the stomach and intestines. **abdominal** *adj*

abduct *v* carry off, kidnap. **abduction** *n* **abductor** *n*

Aberdeen Angus *n* breed of cattle, orig. Scottish.

aberration *n* deviation from what is normal; mental lapse. **aberrant** *adj* showing aberration. **aberrance** *n*

abet *v* **abetting, abetted** assist or encourage in wrongdoing. **abettor** *n*

abeyance *n* state of not being in use.

abhor *v* **-horring, -horred** dislike strongly. **abhorrence** *n* **abhorrent** *adj* hateful, loathsome.

abide *v* endure, put up with; *Obs* stay or dwell, e.g. *abide with me.* **abiding** *adj* lasting. **abide by** *v* obey (the law, rules, etc.).

ability *n, pl* **-ties** competence, power; talent.

abject *adj* utterly miserable; lacking all self-respect. **abjectly** *adv*

abjure *v* deny or renounce on oath. **abjuration** *n*

ablative [ab-lat-iv] *n* case of nouns in Latin and other languages, indicating source, agent, or instrument of action.

ablaze *adj* burning fiercely.

able *adj* capable, competent. **ably** *adv* **able-bodied** *adj* strong and healthy.

ablutions *pl n* act of washing.

abnegate *v* give up, renounce. **abnegation** *n*

abnormal *adj* not normal or usual. **abnormally** *adv* **abnormality** *n*

aboard *adv, prep* on, in, onto, or into a ship, train, or aircraft.

abode *n* home, dwelling.

abolish *v* do away with. **abolition** *n* **abolitionist** *n* person who wishes to do away with something, esp. slavery.

abominate *v* detest or hate. **abominable** *adj* detestable, very bad. **abominably** *adv* **abomination** *n* **abominable snowman** large apelike creature said to inhabit the Himalayas.

aborigine [ab-or-rij-in-ee], **aboriginal** *n* original inhabitant of a country or region, esp. **(A-)** Australia. **aboriginal** *adj*

abort *v* terminate (a pregnancy) prematurely; give birth to a dead fetus; end prematurely and unsuccessfully. **abortion** *n* operation to terminate a pregnancy; *Informal* something grotesque. **abortionist** *n* person who performs abortions, esp. illegally. **abortive** *adj* unsuccessful.

abound *v* be plentiful; overflow. **abounding** *adj*

about prep concerning, on the subject of; in or near a place. ◆ adv nearly, approximately; nearby. **about to** intending to; on the point of, e.g. *about to give up hope*. **about turn** v Mil turn to face the opposite direction. **about-turn** n turn to the opposite direction; complete change of attitude.

above adv, prep over or higher than; greater than; superior to. **above board** in the open, honestly.

abracadabra n supposedly magic word.

abrade v rub or scrape away.

abrasion n scraped area on the skin. **abrasive** adj harsh and annoying in manner; causing abrasion. ◆ n substance for cleaning or polishing by rubbing.

abreast adj side by side. **abreast of** up to date with.

abridge v shorten by using fewer words. **abridgment, abridgement** n

abroad adv to or in a foreign country; at large.

abrogate v cancel (a law or agreement) formally. **abrogation** n

abrupt adj sudden, unexpected; blunt and rude. **abruptly** adv **abruptness** n

abs pl n Informal abdominal muscles.

abscess n inflamed swelling containing pus.

abscond v leave secretly.

abseil [ab-sale] v descend a vertical cliff by using a rope fixed at a higher point.

absent adj not present; lacking; inattentive. ◆ v keep (oneself) away. **absently** adv **absence** n being away; lack. **absentee** n person who should be present but is not. **absenteeism** n persistent absence from work or school. **absent-minded** adj inattentive or forgetful. **absent-mindedly** adv

absinthe n potent green aniseed-flavoured liqueur.

absolute adj complete and utter; not limited, unconditional; pure, e.g. *absolute alcohol*. **absolutely** adv completely. ◆ interj certainly, yes. **absolutism** n government by a ruler with unrestricted power.

absolve v declare to be free from blame or sin. **absolution** n

absorb v soak up (a liquid); take in; engage the interest of (someone). **absorption** n **absorbent** adj able to absorb liquid. **absorbency** n

abstain v choose to refrain; choose not to vote. **abstainer** n **abstention** n abstaining, esp. from voting. **abstinence** n abstaining, esp. from drinking alcohol. **abstinent** adj

abstemious [ab-steem-ee-uss] adj sparing in the consumption of food or alcohol. **abstemiously** adv **abstemiousness** n

abstract adj existing as a quality or idea rather than a material object; theoretical; (of art) using patterns of shapes and colours rather than realistic likenesses. ◆ n summary; abstract work of art; abstract word or idea. ◆ v remove; summarize. **abstracted** adj preoccupied.

abstruse adj not easy to understand.

absurd adj incongruous or ridiculous. **absurdly** adv **absurdity** n

abundant adj plentiful. **abundantly** adv **abundance** n

abuse n prolonged ill-treatment of someone; insulting comments; wrong use. ◆ v use wrongly; ill-treat violently; speak harshly and rudely to. **abuser** n **abusive** adj **abusively** adv **abusiveness** n

abut v **abutting, abutted** adjoin, border on. **abutment** n end support of a bridge or arch.

abysmal adj Informal extremely bad, awful. **abysmally** adv

abyss n very deep hole or chasm.

AC alternating current.

a/c account.

acacia [a-kay-sha] n tree or shrub with yellow or white flowers.

academy n, pl -mies society to advance arts or sciences; institution for specialized training; Scot secondary school. **academic** adj of an academy or university; of theoretical interest only. ◆ n lecturer or researcher at a university. **academically** adv **academician** n member of an academy.

acanthus n prickly plant; ornamental carving in the shape of an acanthus leaf.

accede v consent or agree (to); take up (an office or position).

accelerate v (cause to) move faster.

acceleration n **accelerator** n pedal in a motor vehicle to increase speed.

accent n distinctive style of pronunciation of a local, national, or social group; mark over a letter to show how it is pronounced; stress on a syllable or musical note. ◆ v place emphasis on.

accentuate v stress, emphasize. **accentuation** n

accept v receive willingly; consider to be true; agree to. **acceptance** n **acceptable** adj satisfactory; tolerable. **acceptably** adv **acceptability** n

access n means of or right to approach or enter. ◆ v obtain (data) from a computer. **accessible** adj easy to approach or enter. **accessibility** n

accession n taking up of an office or position.

accessory n, pl -ries supplementary part or object; person involved in a crime although not present when it is committed.

accident n mishap, usu. one causing injury or death; event happening by chance. **accidental** adj happening by accident. ◆ n Music symbol indicating that a sharp, flat, or natural note is not a part of the key signature. **accidentally** adv

acclaim v applaud, praise. ◆ n applause. **acclamation** n acclaim; election without opposition to a public position.

acclimatize v adapt to a new climate or environment. **acclimatization** n

accolade n award, honour, or praise; award of knighthood.

accommodate v provide with lodgings; have room for; do a favour for; get used to (something). **accommodating** adj obliging. **accommodation** n house or room for living in.

accompany v -nying, -nied go along with; occur with; provide a musical accompaniment for. **accompaniment** n something that accompanies; Music supporting part that goes with a solo. **accompanist** n

accomplice n person who helps another to commit a crime.

accomplish v manage to do; finish. **accomplished** adj expert, proficient. **accomplishment** n personal ability or skill; completion.

accord n agreement, harmony. ◆ v fit in with.

accordance n **in accordance with** in conformity with.

according adv **according to** as stated by; in conformity with. **accordingly** adv in an appropriate manner; consequently.

accordion n portable musical instrument played by moving the two sides apart and together, and pressing a keyboard or buttons to produce the notes. **accordionist** n

accost v approach and speak to.

account n report, description; business arrangement making credit available; record of money received and paid out with the resulting balance; person's money held in a bank; importance, value. ◆ v judge to be. **on account of** because of. **accountable** adj responsible to someone or for something. **accountability** n

accounting n skill or practice of maintaining and auditing business accounts. **accountant** n person who maintains and audits business accounts. **accountancy** n

accoutrements [ak-koo-trem-ments] pl n clothing and equipment.

accredited adj authorized, officially recognized.

accretion [ak-kree-shun] n gradual growth; something added.

accrue v -cruing, -crued increase gradually. **accrual** n

accumulate v gather together in increasing quantity. **accumulation** n **accumulative** adj **accumulator** n rechargeable electric battery.

accurate adj exact, correct. **accurately** adv **accuracy** n

accursed adj under a curse; detestable.

accusative n grammatical case indicating the direct object.

accuse v charge with wrongdoing; blame. **accused** n, adj **accuser** n **accusing** adj **accusation** n **accusatory** adj

accustom v make used to. **accustomed** adj usual; used (to); in the habit (of).

ace n playing card with one spot on it; Informal expert; Tennis unreturnable serve. ◆ adj Informal excellent.

acerbic [ass-**sir**-bik] adj harsh or bitter. **acerbity** n

acetate [**ass**-it-tate] n Chem salt or ester of acetic acid; (also **acetate rayon**) synthetic textile fibre.

acetic [ass-**see**-tik] adj of or involving vinegar. **acetic acid** colourless liquid used to make vinegar.

acetone [**ass**-it-tone] n colourless liquid used as a solvent.

acetylene [ass-**set**-ill-een] n colourless flammable gas used in welding metals.

ache n dull continuous pain. ◆ v be in or cause continuous pain.

achieve v gain by hard work or ability. **achievement** n something accomplished.

Achilles heel [ak-**kill**-eez] n small but fatal weakness. **Achilles tendon** cord connecting the calf to the heel bone.

achromatic adj colourless; Music with no sharps or flats.

acid n Chem one of a class of compounds, corrosive and sour when dissolved in water, that combine with a base to form a salt; Slang LSD. ◆ adj containing acid; sour-tasting; sharp or sour in manner. **acidic** adj **acidify** v **acidity** n **acidulous** adj sharp; caustic. **acid rain** rain containing acid from atmospheric pollution. **acid test** conclusive test of value.

acknowledge v admit, recognize; indicate recognition of (a person); say one has received. **acknowledgment, acknowledgement** n

acme [**ak**-mee] n highest point of achievement or excellence.

acne [ak-nee] n pimply skin disease.

acolyte n follower or attendant; Christianity person who assists a priest.

aconite n poisonous plant with hoodlike flowers; poison obtained from this plant.

acorn n nut of the oak tree.

acoustic adj of sound and hearing; (of a musical instrument) not electronically amplified. **acoustics** n science of sounds. ◆ pl features of a room or building determining how sound is heard within it. **acoustically** adv

acquaint v make familiar, inform. **acquainted** adj **acquaintance** n person known; personal knowledge.

acquiesce [ak-wee-**ess**] v accept without complaining. **acquiescence** n **acquiescent** adj

acquire v gain, get. **acquirement** n **acquisition** n act of getting; thing acquired. **acquisitive** adj eager to gain material possessions. **acquisitiveness** n

acquit v -quitting, -quitted declare innocent; conduct (oneself) in a particular way. **acquittal** n

acre n measure of land, 4840 square yards. **acreage** [**ake**-er-rij] n land area in acres.

acrid [ak-rid] adj pungent, bitter.

acrimony [ak-rim-mon-ee] n bitterness of speech or manner. **acrimonious** adj

acrobat n person skilled in gymnastic feats requiring agility and balance. **acrobatic** adj **acrobatics** pl n acrobatic feats.

acronym n word formed from the initial letters of other words, such as NATO.

acropolis [a-**crop**-pol-liss] n citadel of an ancient Greek city.

across adv, prep from side to side (of); on or to the other side (of). **across the board** applying equally to all.

acrostic n word puzzle in which the first or last letters of each line spell a word or saying.

acrylic n, adj (synthetic fibre, paint, etc.) made from acrylic acid. **acrylic acid** strong-smelling corrosive liquid.

act n thing done; law or decree; section of a play or opera; one of several short performances in a show; pretended attitude. ◆ v do something; behave in a particular way; perform in a play, film, etc. **act of God** unpredictable natural event. **acting** n art of an actor. ◆ adj temporarily performing the duties of. **actor, actress** n person who acts in a play, film, etc.

actinium n radioactive chemical element.

action n process of doing; thing done; operating mechanism; lawsuit; minor battle. **actionable** adj giving grounds for a lawsuit. **action replay** rerun of an event on a television tape.

active adj busy, energetic; moving, working; Grammar (of a verb) in a form indicating that the subject is performing the action, e.g. *threw* in *Kim threw the ball.* **actively** *adv* **activity** *n* active behaviour; leisure pursuit. **activate** *v* make active. **activation** *n* **activator** *n* **activist** *n* person who works energetically to achieve political or social goals. **activism** *n*

actual *adj* existing in reality. **actually** *adv* really, indeed. **actuality** *n*

actuary *n, pl* **-aries** statistician who calculates insurance risks.

actuate *v* activate (a device). **actuation** *n*

acuity [ak-kew-it-ee] *n* keenness of vision or thought.

acumen [ak-yew-men] *n* ability to make good judgments.

acupuncture *n* medical treatment involving the insertion of needles at various points on the body. **acupuncturist** *n*

acute *adj* severe or intense; keen, shrewd; sharp, sensitive; (of an angle) less than 90°. ◆ *n* accent (´) over a letter to indicate the quality or length of its sound, as in *café.* **acutely** *adv* **acuteness** *n*

ad *n Informal* advertisement.

AD anno Domini.

adage [ad-ij] *n* wise saying, proverb.

adagio [ad-dahj-yo] *adv Music* slowly and gracefully.

adamant *adj* inflexibly determined. **adamantly** *adv*

Adam's apple *n* projecting lump of thyroid cartilage at the front of the throat.

adapt *v* alter for new use or new conditions. **adaptable** *adj* **adaptability** *n* **adaptation** *n* adapting; thing produced by adapting something. **adaptor, -er** *n* device for connecting several electrical appliances to one socket.

add *v* combine (numbers or quantities); join (to something); say further.

addendum *n, pl* **-da** an addition; appendix to a book etc.

adder *n* any of various harmless American snakes.

addict *n* person who is unable to stop taking drugs; *Informal* person devoted to something. **addicted** *adj* **addiction** *n* **addictive** *adj* causing addiction.

addition *n* adding; thing added. **in addition** besides, as well. **additional** *adj* **additionally** *adv* **additive** *n* something added, esp. to foodstuffs.

addle *v* make rotten or muddled.

address *n* place where a person lives; direction on a letter; location; formal public speech. ◆ *v* mark the destination, as on an envelope; speak to; give attention to (a problem, task, etc.). **addressee** *n* person addressed.

adduce *v* cite as proof.

adenoids [ad-in-oidz] *pl n* mass of tissue at the back of the nose. **adenoidal** *adj* having a nasal voice caused by swollen adenoids.

adept *adj, n* very skilful (person).

adequate *adj* sufficient, enough; not outstanding. **adequately** *adv* **adequacy** *n*

adhere *v* stick to; be devoted to. **adherence** *n* **adherent** *n* devotee, follower. **adhesion** *n* adhering; abnormal sticking together of parts of the body, as after surgery.

adhesive *adj* able to stick to things. ◆ *n* substance used to stick things together.

ad hoc *adj, adv* for a particular occasion only.

adieu [a-dew] *interj* farewell, goodbye.

ad infinitum *adv Latin* endlessly.

adipose *adj* of fat, fatty.

adj. adjective.

adjacent *adj* near or next to; having a common boundary; *Geom* (of a side in a right-angled triangle) lying between a specified angle and the right angle.

adjective *n* word that adds information about a noun or pronoun. **adjectival** *adj*

adjoin *v* be next to. **adjoining** *adj*

adjourn *v* close (a court) at the end of a session; postpone temporarily; *Informal* go elsewhere. **adjournment** *n*

adjudge *v* declare (to be).

adjudicate *v* decide on (a dispute); judge (a competition). **adjudication** *n* **adjudicator** *n*

adjunct *n* subordinate or additional person or thing.

adjure *v* command to do; appeal earnestly.

adjust *v* adapt to new conditions; alter slightly so as to be suitable. **adjustable** *adj* **adjuster** *n* **adjustment** *n*

adjutant [aj-oo-tant] n army officer in charge of routine administration.

ad-lib v -libbing, -libbed improvise a speech etc. without preparation. ◆ n improvised remark.

admin n *Informal* administration.

administer v manage (business affairs); dispense (justice); give (medicine or treatment).

administrate v manage (an organization). **administration** n **administrative** adj **administrator** n

admiral n highest naval rank.

admire v regard with esteem and approval. **admirable** adj **admirably** adv **admiration** n **admirer** n **admiring** adj **admiringly** adv

admissible adj allowed to be brought in as evidence in court.

admission n permission to enter; entrance fee; confession.

admit v -mitting, -mitted confess, acknowledge; concede the truth of; allow in. **admittance** n permission to enter. **admittedly** adv it must be agreed (that).

admixture n mixture; ingredient.

admonish v reprove sternly. **admonition** n **admonitory** adj

ad nauseam [ad naw-zee-am] adv *Latin* to a boring extent.

ado n fuss, trouble.

adobe [ad-oh-bee] n sun-dried brick.

adolescence n period between puberty and adulthood. **adolescent** n, adj (person) between puberty and adulthood.

adopt v take (someone else's child) as one's own; take up (a plan or principle). **adoption** n **adoptive** adj related by adoption.

adore v love intensely; worship. **adorable** adj **adoration** n **adoring** adj **adoringly** adv

adorn v decorate, embellish. **adornment** n

ADP automatic data processing.

adrenal [ad-reen-al] adj near the kidney. **adrenal glands** glands covering the top of the kidneys.

adrenalin, adrenaline n hormone secreted by the adrenal glands in response to stress.

adrift adj, adv drifting; without clear purpose.

adroit adj quick and skilful. **adroitly**

adv **adroitness** n

adsorb v (of a gas or vapour) condense and form a thin film on a surface. **adsorbent** adj **adsorption** n

ADT Atlantic Daylight Time.

adulation n uncritical admiration.

adult adj fully grown, mature. ◆ n adult person or animal. **adulthood** n

adulterate v make impure by addition. **adulteration** n

adultery n, pl -teries sexual unfaithfulness of a husband or wife. **adulterer, adulteress** n **adulterous** adj

adumbrate v give a faint indication of. **adumbration** n

adv. adverb.

advance v go or bring forward; further (a cause); propose; lend (a sum of money). ◆ n forward movement; improvement; loan. ◆ pl approaches to a person with the hope of starting a romantic or sexual relationship. ◆ adj previous. **in advance** ahead. **advanced** adj at a late stage in development; not elementary. ◆ n green flashing traffic signal that allows left turn. **advancement** n promotion.

advantage n more favourable position or state; benefit or profit; *Tennis* point scored after deuce. **take advantage of** use (an opportunity); use (a person) unfairly. **advantageous** adj **advantageously** adv

advent n arrival; (A-) season of four weeks before Christmas. **Adventist** n member of a Christian sect that believes in the imminent return of Christ.

adventitious adj added or appearing accidentally.

adventure n exciting and risky undertaking or exploit. **adventurer, adventuress** n person who seeks adventures; person who unscrupulously seeks money or power. **adventurous** adj

adverb n word that adds information about a verb, adjective, or other adverb. **adverbial** adj **adverbially** adv

adversary [ad-verse-er-ree] n, pl -saries opponent or enemy.

adverse adj antagonistic or hostile; unfavourable. **adversely** adv **adversity** n affliction or hardship.

advertise v present or praise (goods or services) to the public in order to encourage sales; make (a vacancy, event, etc.) known publicly. **advertisement** *n* public announcement to sell goods or publicize an event. **advertiser** *n* **advertising** *adj, n*

advice *n* recommendation as to what to do. **advise** *v* offer advice to; notify (someone). **adviser, -or** *n* **advisable** *adj* prudent, sensible. **advisability** *n* **advisory** *adj* giving advice. **advised** *adj* considered, thought-out, e.g. *ill-advised*. **advisedly** *adv* deliberately.

advocaat *n* liqueur with a raw egg base.

advocate *v* propose or recommend. ◆ *n* person who publicly supports a cause; *Scot* barrister. **advocacy** *n*

adze *n* tool with an arched blade set at right angles to the handle.

aegis [ee-jiss] *n* sponsorship, protection.

aeolian harp [ee-oh-lee-an] *n* musical instrument that produces sounds when the wind passes over its strings.

aeon *n* same as EON.

aerate *v* put gas into (a liquid), as when making a fizzy drink. **aeration** *n*

aerial *adj* in, from, or operating in the air; relating to aircraft. ◆ *n* metal pole or wire for receiving or transmitting radio or TV signals.

aerie *n* same as EYRIE.

aerobatics *pl n* stunt flying. **aerobatic** *adj*

aerobics *pl n* exercises designed to increase the amount of oxygen in the blood. **aerobic** *adj*

aerodrome *n* small airport.

aerodynamics *pl n* (study of) air flow, esp. around moving solid objects. **aerodynamic** *adj*

aerofoil *n* part of an aircraft, such as the wing, designed to give lift.

aerogram *n* airmail letter on a single sheet of paper that seals to form an envelope.

aeronautics *n* study or practice of aircraft flight. **aeronautical** *adj*

aeroplane *n Brit* airplane.

aerosol *n* pressurized can from which a substance can be dispensed as a fine spray.

aerospace *n* earth's atmosphere and space beyond.

aesthetic, esthetic [iss-thet-ik] *adj* relating to the appreciation of art and beauty. **aesthetics, esthetics** *n* study of art, beauty, and good taste. **aesthetically, esthetically** *adv* **aesthete, esthete** [eess-theet] *n* person who has or affects an extravagant love of art. **aestheticism, estheticism** *n*

aether *n* same as ETHER.

aetiology *n* same as ETIOLOGY.

afar *adv* from or at a great distance.

affable *adj* friendly and easy to talk to. **affably** *adv* **affability** *n*

affair *n* event or happening; sexual relationship outside marriage; thing to be done or attended to. ◆ *pl* personal or business interests; matters of public interest.

affect[1] *v* act on, influence; move (someone) emotionally. **affecting** *adj* moving the feelings. **affection** *n* fondness or love. **affectionate** *adj* loving. **affectionately** *adv*

affect[2] *v* put on a show of; wear or use by preference. **affectation** *n* show, pretence. **affected** *adj* full of affectation; pretended.

affianced [af-fie-anst] *adj Old-fashioned* engaged to be married.

affidavit [af-fid-dave-it] *n* written statement made on oath.

affiliate *v* (of a group) link up with a larger group. **affiliation** *n*

affinity *n, pl* **-ties** close connection or liking; close resemblance; chemical attraction.

affirm *v* assert, declare; uphold or confirm (an idea or belief). **affirmation** *n* **affirmative** *n, adj* (word or phrase) indicating agreement. **affirmative action** provision of special opportunities in employment for a disadvantaged group.

affix *v* attach or fasten. ◆ *n* word or syllable added to a word to change its meaning.

afflict *v* give pain or grief to. **affliction** *n*

affluent *adj* wealthy. **affluence** *n*

afford *v* have enough money to buy; be able to spare (the time etc.); give or supply. **affordable** *adj*

afforest *v* plant trees on. **af-forestation** *n*

affray *n* noisy fight, brawl.

affront *v, n* insult.

Afghan *adj* of Afghanistan or its language. **Afghan hound** large slim dog with long silky hair.

aficionado [af-fish-yo-nah-do] *n*, *pl* -dos enthusiastic fan of something or someone.

afield *adv*, *adj* **far afield** far away.

aflame *adv*, *adj* burning.

afloat *adv*, *adj* floating; at sea.

afoot *adv*, *adj* happening, in operation.

aforesaid *adj* referred to previously.

aforethought *adj* premeditated, e.g. *with malice aforethought*.

Afr. Africa(n).

afraid *adj* frightened; regretful.

afresh *adv* again, anew.

African *adj* of Africa. ◆ *n* person from Africa. **African violet** house plant with pink or purple flowers and hairy leaves.

Afrikaans *n* language used in S Africa, related to Dutch.

Afrikaner *n* White S African whose mother tongue is Afrikaans.

Afro *n*, *pl* -ros frizzy bushy hair style.

Afro- *combining form* African, e.g. *Afro-Caribbean*.

aft *adv* at or towards the rear of a ship or aircraft.

after *prep* following in time or place; in pursuit of; in imitation of. ◆ *conj* at a later time than. ◆ *adv* at a later time.

afters *pl n Brit* dessert.

afterbirth *n* material expelled from the womb after childbirth.

aftercare *n* support given to a person discharged from a hospital or prison; regular care required to keep something in good condition.

aftereffect *n* effect occurring some time after its cause.

afterglow *n* glow left after a source of light has gone; pleasant feeling left after an enjoyable experience.

afterlife *n* life after death.

aftermath *n* aftereffects collectively.

afternoon *n* time between noon and evening.

aftershave *n* lotion applied to the face after shaving.

afterthought *n* idea occurring later; something added later.

afterwards, afterward *adv* later.

Ag *Chem* silver.

again *adv* once more; in addition.

against *prep* in opposition or contrast to; in contact with; in readiness for.

agape *adj* (of the mouth) wide open; (of a person) very surprised.

agaric *n* fungus with gills on the underside of the cap, such as a mushroom.

agate [ag-git] *n* semiprecious form of quartz with striped colouring.

age *n* length of time a person or thing has existed; time of life; latter part of human life; period of history; long time. ◆ *v* **ageing** or **aging**, **aged** make or grow old. **aged** *adj* [ay-jid] old; [rhymes with **raged**] having the age of. **ageing, aging** *n*, *adj* **ageless** *adj* apparently never growing old; timeless. **age-old** *adj* very old.

agenda *n* list of things to be dealt with, esp. at a meeting.

agent *n* person acting on behalf of another; person or thing producing an effect. **agency** *n* organization providing a service; business or function of an agent; *Old-fashioned* power or action by which something happens. **agent general** diplomat who represents a Canadian province.

agent provocateur [azh-on prov-vok-at-**tur**] *n*, *pl* **agents provocateurs** [azh-on prov-vok-at-**tur**] person employed by the authorities to tempt people to commit illegal acts and so be discredited or punished.

agglomerate *v* gather into a mass. ◆ *n* confused mass; rock consisting of fused volcanic fragments. ◆ *adj* formed into a mass. **agglomeration** *n*

agglutinate *v* stick with or as if with glue. **agglutination** *n*

aggrandize *v* make greater in size, power, or rank. **aggrandizement** *n*

aggravate *v* make worse; *Informal* annoy. **aggravating** *adj* **aggravation** *n*

aggregate *v* gather into a mass. ◆ *adj* gathered into a mass; total or final. ◆ *n* total; rock consisting of a mixture of minerals; sand or gravel used to make concrete. **aggregation** *n*

aggression *n* unprovoked attack; hostile behaviour. **aggressive** *adj* full of anger or hostility; forceful or determined. **aggressively** *adv* **aggressiveness** *n* **aggressor** *n*

aggrieved *adj* upset and angry.

aggro n Slang aggression.

aghast adj amazed or shocked.

agile adj nimble, quick-moving; mentally quick. **agilely** adv **agility** n

agitate v disturb or excite; stir or shake (a liquid); stir up public opinion for or against something. **agitation** n **agitator** n

aglow adj glowing.

AGM annual general meeting.

agnostic n person who believes that it is impossible to know whether God exists. ◆ adj of agnostics. **agnosticism** n

ago adv in the past.

agog adj eager or curious.

agony n, pl **-nies** extreme physical or mental pain. **agonize** v (cause to) suffer agony; worry greatly. **agonizing** adj **agony column** newspaper or magazine feature offering advice on personal problems.

agoraphobia n fear of open spaces. **agoraphobic** n, adj

agrarian adj of land or agriculture. **agrarianism** n

agree v **agreeing, agreed** be of the same opinion; consent; reach a joint decision; be consistent; (foll. by with) be suitable to one's health or digestion. **agreeable** adj willing; pleasant. **agreeably** adv **agreement** n agreeing; contract.

agriculture n raising of crops and livestock. **agricultural** adj **agriculturalist** n

agronomy [ag-ron-om-mee] n science of soil management and crop production. **agronomist** n

aground adv onto the bottom of shallow water.

ague [aig-yew] n periodic fever with shivering.

ahead adv in front; forwards.

ahoy interj shout used at sea to attract attention.

AI artificial insemination; artificial intelligence.

aid v, n help, support.

aide n assistant.

aide-de-camp [aid-de-kom] n, pl **aides-de-camp** [aid-de-kom] military officer serving as personal assistant to a senior.

AIDS acquired immunodeficiency syndrome, a viral disease that destroys the body's ability to fight infection.

ail v trouble, afflict; be ill. **ailing** adj sickly. **ailment** n illness.

aileron [ale-er-on] n movable flap on an aircraft wing which controls rolling.

aim v point (a weapon or missile) or direct (a blow or remark) at a target; propose or intend. ◆ n aiming; intention, purpose. **aimless** adj without purpose. **aimlessly** adv

ain't Not standard am not; is not; are not; has not; have not.

air n mixture of gases forming the earth's atmosphere; space above the ground, sky; breeze; tune; quality or manner. ◆ pl affected manners. ◆ v expose to air to dry or ventilate; make known publicly. **on the air** in the act of broadcasting on radio or television. **airy** adj well-ventilated; jaunty, nonchalant. **airily** adv **airiness** n **airless** adj stuffy. **airing** n exposure to air for drying or ventilation; exposure to public debate. **air base** centre from which military aircraft operate. **air bed** inflatable mattress. **airborne** adj carried by air; (of aircraft) in flight. **air brake** brake worked by compressed air. **airbrush** n atomizer spraying paint by compressed air. **air conditioning** system that controls the temperature and humidity of the air in a building. **aircraft** n any machine that flies, such as an airplane. **aircraft carrier** warship from which aircraft operate. **airfield** n place where aircraft can land and take off. **air force** branch of the armed forces responsible for air warfare. **air gun** gun discharged by the force of compressed air. **airlift** n transport of troops or cargo by aircraft when other routes are blocked. ◆ v transport by airlift. **airline** n company providing scheduled flights for passengers and cargo. **airliner** n large passenger aircraft. **airlock** n air bubble obstructing the flow of liquid in a pipe; airtight chamber. **airmail** n system of sending mail by aircraft; mail sent in this way. **airman, airwoman** n member of the air force. **airplane** n powered flying vehicle with fixed wings. **airplay** n broadcast performances (of a record) on radio. **airport** n airfield for civilian aircraft, with facilities for aircraft maintenance and passengers. **air raid** attack by aircraft. **airship** *n* lighter-than-air flying machine with means of propulsion. **airsick** *adj* nauseated from travelling in an aircraft. **airspace** *n* atmosphere above a country, regarded as its territory. **airstrip** *n* strip of ground where aircraft can take off and land. **airtight** *adj* not allowing the passage of air. **airworthy** *adj* (of aircraft) fit to fly. **airworthiness** *n*

Airedale *n* large rough-coated terrier dog.

aisle [rhymes with **mile**] *n* passageway separating seating areas in a church, theatre, etc., or row of shelves in a supermarket.

ajar *adj, adv* (of a door) partly open.

akimbo *adv* **with arms akimbo** with hands on hips and elbows outwards.

akin *adj* similar, related.

Al *Chem* aluminum.

alabaster *n* soft white translucent stone.

à la carte *adj, adv* (of a menu) having dishes individually priced.

alack *interj Obs* cry of grief or sorrow.

alacrity *n* speed, eagerness.

à la mode *adj* fashionable.

alarm *n* sudden fear caused by awareness of danger; warning sound; device that gives this; alarm clock. ◆ *v* frighten. **alarming** *adj* **alarmist** *n* person who alarms others needlessly. **alarm clock** clock which sounds at a set time to wake someone up.

alas *adv* unfortunately, regrettably.

albatross *n* large sea bird with very long wings.

albeit *conj* although.

Alberta *see* Canadian Provincial Facts p630.

albino *n, pl* **-nos** person or animal with white skin and hair and pink eyes. **albinism** *n*

album *n* book with blank pages for keeping photographs or stamps in; long-playing record.

albumen *n* egg white.

albumin, albumen *n* protein found in blood plasma, egg white, milk, and muscle. **albuminous** *adj*

alchemy *n* medieval form of chemistry concerned with trying to turn base metals into gold and to find the elixir of life. **alchemist** *n*

alcohol *n* colourless flammable liquid present in intoxicating drinks; intoxicating drinks generally. **alcoholic** *adj* of alcohol. ◆ *n* person addicted to alcohol. **alcoholism** *n* addiction to alcohol.

alcove *n* recess in the wall of a room.

aldehyde *n* one of a group of chemical compounds derived from alcohol by oxidation.

alder *n* tree related to the birch.

alderman *n* member of a municipal council.

ale *n* kind of beer.

aleatory *adj* dependent on chance.

alert *adj* watchful, attentive. ◆ *n* warning of danger. ◆ *v* warn of danger; make (someone) aware of (a fact). **on the alert** watchful. **alertness** *n*

alfalfa *n* kind of plant used as fodder.

alfresco *adv, adj* in the open air.

algae [al-jee] *pl n* plants which live in or near water and have no true stems, leaves, or roots.

algebra *n* branch of mathematics using symbols to represent numbers. **algebraic** *adj*

ALGOL *n Computers* computer programming language designed for mathematical and scientific purposes.

Algonquin, Algonkin *n* a member of a North American Indian people formerly living along the St Lawrence and Ottawa Rivers in Canada.

algorithm *n* logical arithmetical or computational procedure for solving a problem.

alias *adv* also known as, e.g. *William Bonney, alias Billy the Kid.* ◆ *n* false name.

alibi *n* plea of being somewhere else when a crime was committed; *Informal* excuse.

alien *adj* foreign; repugnant (to); from another world. ◆ *n* foreigner; being from another world. **alienate** *v* cause to become hostile. **alienation** *n*

alight¹ *v* step out of (a vehicle); land.

alight² *adj* burning; lit up.

align [a-**line**] *v* place in a line; make or bring (a person or group) into agreement with the policy of another. **alignment** *n*

alike *adj* like, similar. ◆ *adv* in the same way.

alimentary *adj* of nutrition.

alimentary canal food passage in the body.

alimony n allowance paid under a court order to a separated or divorced spouse.

A-line adj (of a skirt) slightly flared.

aliquot adj of or denoting an exact divisor of a number. ◆ n exact divisor.

alive adj living, in existence; lively. **alive to** aware of. **alive with** swarming with.

alkali [alk-a-lie] n substance which combines with acid and neutralizes it to form a salt. **alkaline** adj **alkalinity** n **alkaloid** n any of a group of organic compounds containing nitrogen.

all adj whole quantity or number (of). ◆ adv wholly, entirely; (in the score of games) each. ◆ n whole; everything, everyone. **all in** adj exhausted; (of wrestling) with no style prohibited. ◆ adv with all expenses included. **all right** adj adequate, satisfactory; unharmed. ◆ interj expression of approval or agreement. **all-rounder** n person with ability in many fields. **all-terrain vehicle** motor vehicle with large tires for travel over rough land.

Allah n name of God in Islam.

allay v reduce (fear or anger) or relieve (pain or grief).

allege v state without proof. **alleged** adj **allegedly** adv **allegation** n thing alleged.

allegiance n loyalty to a person, country, or cause.

allegory n, pl **-ries** story with an underlying meaning as well as the literal one. **allegorical** adj **allegorically** adv **allegorize** v

allegretto adv Music fairly quickly.

allegro adv Music in a brisk lively manner.

allergy n, pl **-gies** extreme sensitivity to a substance, which causes the body to react to any contact with it. **allergic** adj having or caused by an allergy; Informal having an aversion (to), e.g. allergic to work. **allergen** [al-ler-jen] n substance capable of causing an allergic reaction.

alleviate v lessen (pain or suffering). **alleviation** n

alley n narrow street or path; long narrow enclosure in which tenpin bowling or skittles is played.

alliance n state of being allied; formal relationship between countries or groups for a shared purpose.

alligator n reptile of the crocodile family, found in the southern US and China.

alliteration n use of the same sound at the start of consecutive words. **alliterative** adj

allocate v allot or assign. **allocation** n

allophone n Canadian whose native language is neither French nor English.

allot v **-lotting, -lotted** assign as a share or for a particular purpose. **allotment** n distribution; portion allotted; small piece of public land rented to grow vegetables on.

allotrope n any of two or more physical forms in which an element can exist. **allotropic** adj

allow v permit; acknowledge (a point or claim); set aside. **allow for** take into account. **allowable** adj **allowance** n amount of money given at regular intervals; amount permitted. **make allowances for** be lenient towards (someone) because he or she has special problems; take into account.

alloy n mixture of two or more metals. ◆ v mix (metals).

allspice n spice made from the berries of a tropical American tree.

allude v (foll. by to) refer indirectly to. **allusion** n indirect reference. **allusive** adj

allure v entice or attract. ◆ n attractiveness. **allurement** n **alluring** adj

alluvium n fertile soil deposited by flowing water. **alluvial** adj

ally n, pl **-lies** country or person having an agreement to support another. ◆ v **-lying, -lied. ally oneself with** join as an ally. **allied** adj

alma mater n one's former school, university, or college.

almanac n yearly calendar with detailed information on anniversaries, phases of the moon, etc.

almighty adj having absolute power; Informal very great. ◆ n **the Almighty** God.

almond n edible oval-shaped nut which grows on a small tree.

almoner n person who distributes alms.

almost *adv* very nearly.

alms [ahmz] *pl n Old-fashioned* gifts to the poor. **almshouse** *n* formerly, a house financed by charity, offering accommodation to the poor.

aloe *n* plant with fleshy spiny leaves.
♦ *pl* bitter drug made from aloe leaves.

aloft *adv* in the air; in a ship's rigging.

alone *adj, adv* without anyone or anything else.

along *prep* over part or all the length of. ♦ *adv* forward; in company with others, e.g. *come along for the ride.* **alongside** *adv, prep* beside.

aloof *adj* distant or haughty in manner. **aloofness** *n*

alopecia [al-loh-pee-sha] *n* loss of hair.

aloud *adv* in an audible voice.

alpaca *n* Peruvian llama; its wool; cloth made from this.

alpenstock *n* iron-tipped staff used by climbers.

alphabet *n* set of letters used in writing a language. **alphabetical** *adj* in the conventional order of the letters of an alphabet. **alphabetically** *adv* **alphabetize** *v* put in alphabetical order.

alpine *adj* of high mountains; (**A-**) of the Alps, a high mountain range in S central Europe. ♦ *n* mountain plant.

already *adv* before this time; sooner than expected.

Alsatian *n* large wolflike dog.

also *adv* in addition; too. **also-ran** *n* loser in a race, competition, or election.

alt. *combining form Informal* alternative: *alt. rock.*

Alta. Alberta.

altar *n* raised structure on which sacrifices are offered and religious rites are performed; table used for Communion in Christian churches. **altarpiece** *n* work of art above and behind the altar in some Christian churches.

alter *v* make or become different. **alteration** *n*

altercation *n* heated argument.

alter ego *n* second self; very close friend.

alternate *v* (cause to) occur by turns. ♦ *adj* occurring by turns; every second one of a series, e.g. *alternate Fridays.*

alternately *adv* **alternation** *n*

alternative *n* one of two choices.
♦ *adj* able to be done or used instead of something else; (of medicine, lifestyle, etc.) not conventional. **alternatively** *adv* **alternator** *n* electric generator for producing alternating current. **alternating current** electric current that reverses direction at frequent regular intervals.

although *conj* despite the fact that.

altimeter [al-tim-it-er] *n* instrument that measures altitude.

altitude *n* height above sea level.

alto *n, pl* **-tos** *Music* short for CONTRALTO; (singer with) the highest adult male voice; instrument with the second-highest pitch in its group.

altogether *adv* entirely; on the whole; in total.

altruism *n* unselfish concern for the welfare of others. **altruist** *n* **altruistic** *adj* **altruistically** *adv*

aluminum, aluminium *n* light nonrusting silvery-white metal.

alumnus [al-lumm-nuss] *n, pl* **-ni** [-nie] graduate of a college. **alumna** [al-lumm-na] *n fem, pl* **-nae** [-nee]

always *adv* at all times; for ever.

alyssum *n* garden plant with small yellow or white flowers.

am *v* see BE.

AM amplitude modulation.

a.m. before noon.

amalgam *n* blend or combination; alloy of mercury and another metal.

amalgamate *v* combine or unite. **amalgamation** *n*

amanuensis [am-man-yew-en-siss] *n, pl* **-ses** [-seez] person who writes from dictation.

amaranth *n* imaginary flower that never fades; lily-like plant with red, green, or purple flowers.

amaryllis *n* lily-like plant with large red or white flowers.

amass *v* collect or accumulate.

amateur *n* person who performs a sport or activity as a pastime rather than as a profession; person unskilled in something. ♦ *adj* not professional. **amateurish** *adj* lacking skill. **amateurishly** *adv*

amatory *adj* relating to romantic or sexual love.

amaut, amowt *n* a hood on an

Eskimo woman's parka for carrying a child.

amaze v surprise greatly, astound. **amazing** adj **amazingly** adv **amazement** n

Amazon n legendary female warrior; tall strong woman. **Amazonian** adj

ambassador n senior diplomat who represents his or her country in another country. **ambassadorial** adj **ambassadorship** n

amber n yellowish translucent fossil resin. ♦ adj brownish-yellow.

ambergris [am-ber-greece] n waxy substance secreted by the sperm whale, used in making perfumes.

ambidextrous adj able to use both hands with equal ease.

ambience n atmosphere of a place. **ambient** adj surrounding.

ambiguous adj having more than one possible meaning; uncertain. **ambiguously** adv **ambiguity** n

ambit n limits or boundary.

ambition n desire for success; something so desired, goal. **ambitious** adj **ambitiously** adv **ambitiousness** n

ambivalence [am-biv-a-lenss] n state of feeling two conflicting emotions at the same time. **ambivalent** adj **ambivalently** adv

amble v walk at a leisurely pace. ♦ n leisurely walk or pace.

ambrosia n Myth food of the gods; anything delightful to taste or smell. **ambrosial** adj

ambulance n motor vehicle designed to carry the sick or injured.

ambush n act of waiting in a concealed position to make an attack; attack from a concealed position. ♦ v attack from a concealed position.

ameliorate [am-meal-yor-rate] v make (something) better. **amelioration** n **ameliorative** adj

amen interj so be it: used at the end of a prayer.

amenable adj likely or willing to cooperate. **amenability** n

amend v correct or improve (something). **amendment** n

amends pl n **make amends for** compensate for.

amenity n, pl -**ties** useful or enjoyable facility.

American adj of the United States of America or the North, Central, or South American continents. ♦ n American person. **Americanism** n expression or custom peculiar to people in the US.

amethyst [am-myth-ist] n bluish-violet variety of quartz used as a gemstone.

amiable adj friendly, pleasant-natured. **amiably** adv **amiability** n

amicable adj friendly. **amicably** adv

amid, amidst prep in the middle of, among. **amidships** adv at or towards the middle of a ship.

amino acid [am-mean-oh] n organic compound found in protein.

amiss adv wrongly, badly. ♦ adj wrong, faulty. **take something amiss** be offended by something.

amity n friendship.

ammeter n instrument for measuring electric current.

ammonia n pungent alkaline gas containing hydrogen and nitrogen; solution of this in water.

ammonite n fossilized spiral shell of an extinct sea creature.

ammunition n any projectile that can be fired from or as a weapon; facts that can be used in an argument.

amnesia n loss of memory. **amnesiac** adj, n

amnesty n, pl -**ties** general pardon for offences against a government.

amniocentesis n, pl -**ses** removal of amniotic fluid to test for possible abnormalities in a fetus.

amniotic fluid n fluid surrounding a fetus in the womb.

amoeba [am-mee-ba] n, pl -**bae**, -**bas** microscopic single-celled animal able to change its shape.

amok adv **run amok** run about in a violent frenzy.

among, amongst prep in the midst of; in the group or number of; to each of, e.g. divide it among yourselves.

amoral [aim-mor-ral] adj without moral standards. **amorality** n

amorous adj feeling, showing, or relating to sexual love. **amorously** adv **amorousness** n

amorphous adj without distinct shape.

amortize v pay off (a debt) gradually by periodic transfers to a sinking fund.

amortization n

amount n extent or quantity. ◆ v (foll. by to) be equal or add up to.

amour n (illicit) love affair.

amp n ampere; Informal amplifier.

ampere [am-pair] n unit of electric current.

ampersand n the character (&), meaning and.

amphetamine [am-fet-am-in] n drug used as a stimulant.

amphibian n animal that lives on land but breeds in water; vehicle that can travel both on land and water. amphibious adj living or operating on land and in water.

amphitheatre n open oval or circular building with tiers of seats rising round an arena.

amphora n, pl -phorae, -phoras two-handled ancient Greek or Roman jar.

ample adj more than sufficient; large. amply adv

amplify v -fying, -fied increase the strength of (a current or sound signal); explain in more detail; increase the size or effect of. amplification n amplifier n device used to amplify a current or sound signal.

amplitude n greatness of extent; breadth or scope. amplitude modulation method of sending information by varying the size of the peaks and troughs of the carrier wave to suit the input signal.

ampoule n small sealed glass vessel containing liquid for injection.

amputate v cut off (a limb etc.) for medical reasons. amputation n

amuck adv same as AMOK.

amulet n something carried or worn as a charm against evil.

amuse v entertain or divert; cause to laugh or smile. amusing adj amusement n state of being amused; something that amuses.

an adj form of (a) used before vowels, and sometimes before h. e.g. an hour.

anabolic steroid n synthetic steroid hormone used by athletes to stimulate muscle growth.

anachronism [an-nak-kron-iz-zum] n person or thing placed in the wrong historical period or seeming to belong to another time. anachronistic adj

anaconda n large S American snake which kills by constriction.

anaemia n same as ANEMIA.

anaesthetic n, adj same as ANESTHETIC.

anagram n word or phrase made by rearranging the letters of another word or phrase.

anal [ain-al] adj of the anus.

analgesic [an-nal-jeez-ik] n, adj (drug) relieving pain. analgesia n absence of pain.

analogy [an-nal-a-jee] n, pl -gies similarity in some respects; comparison made to show such a similarity. analogical adj analogically adv analogue [an-nal-log] n something that is analogous to something else. ◆ adj displaying information by means of a dial. analogous [an-nal-log-uss] adj similar in some respects.

analysis [an-nal-liss-iss] n, pl -ses [-seez] separation of a whole into its components for study and interpretation; psychoanalysis. analyse [an-nal-lize] v make an analysis of (something); psychoanalyse. analyst [an-nal-list] n person skilled in analysis. analytical, analytic adj analytically adv

anarchy [an-ark-ee] n lawlessness and disorder; lack of government in a state. anarchic adj anarchism n doctrine advocating the abolition of government. anarchist n person who believes in anarchism. anarchistic adj

anathema [an-nath-im-a] n detested person or thing.

anatomy n, pl -mies science of the structure of the body; physical structure; person's body, e.g. a delicate part of his anatomy; detailed analysis. anatomical adj anatomically adv anatomist n expert in anatomy.

ancestor n person from whom one is descended; forerunner. ancestral adj ancestry n lineage or descent.

anchor n heavy hooked device attached to a boat by a cable and dropped overboard to fasten the ship to the sea bottom. ◆ v fasten with or as if with an anchor. anchorage n place where boats can be anchored. anchorman n broadcaster in a central studio who links up and presents items from outside camera units and other studios; last person to compete in a relay team.

anchorite *n* religious recluse.

anchovy [an-**chov**-ee] *n, pl* **-vies** small strong-tasting fish.

ancient *adj* dating from very long ago; very old. ◆ *n* person who lived long ago.

ancillary *adj* auxiliary, supplementary; subsidiary.

and *conj* in addition to; as a consequence; then, afterwards.

andante [an-**dan**-tay] *adv Music* moderately slowly.

andiron *n* iron stand for supporting logs in a fireplace.

androgynous *adj* having both male and female characteristics.

android *n* robot resembling a human.

anecdote *n* short amusing account of an incident. **anecdotal** *adj*

anemia, anaemia [an-**neem**-ee-a] *n* deficiency in the number of red blood cells. **anemic, anaemic** *adj* having anemia; pale and sickly; lacking vitality.

anemometer *n* instrument for recording wind speed.

anemone [an-**nem**-on-ee] *n* plant with white, purple, or red flowers.

aneroid barometer *n* device for measuring air pressure, consisting of a partially evacuated chamber in which variations in pressure cause a pointer on the lid to move.

anesthetic, anaesthetic [an-niss-**thet**-ik] *n, adj* (substance) causing loss of sensation. **anesthesia, anaesthesia** [an-niss-**theez**-ee-a] *n* loss of sensation. **anesthetist, anaesthetist** [an-**neess**-thet-ist] *n* doctor trained to administer anaesthetics. **anesthetize, anaesthetize** *v*

aneurysm, aneurism [an-**new**-riz-zum] *n* permanent swelling of a blood vessel.

anew *adv* once more; in a different way.

angel *n* spiritual being believed to be an attendant or messenger of God; very kind person. **angelic** *adj* **angelically** *adv*

angelica [an-**jell**-ik-a] *n* aromatic plant; its candied stalks, used in cookery.

Angelus [an-**jell**-uss] *n* (in the Roman Catholic Church) prayers recited in the morning, at midday, and in the evening; bell signalling the times of these prayers.

anger *n* fierce displeasure; extreme annoyance; rage, wrath. ◆ *v* make (someone) angry. **angry** *adj* full of anger; inflamed, e.g. *an angry wound*. **angrily** *adv*

angina [an-**jine**-a] *n* heart disorder causing sudden severe chest pains (also **angina pectoris**).

angle¹ *n* space between or shape formed by two lines or surfaces that meet; divergence between these, measured in degrees; corner; point of view. ◆ *v* bend or place (something) at an angle.

angle² *v* fish with a hook and line; try to get by hinting. **angler** *n* **angling** *n*

Anglican *n, adj* (member) of the Church of England. **Anglicanism** *n*

anglicize *v* make English in outlook, form, etc. **Anglicism** *n* expression or custom peculiar to the English.

Anglo- *combining form* English or British, e.g. *Anglo-French*. **Anglo** *n* an English-speaking person.

Anglo-Saxon *n* member of any of the W Germanic tribes which settled in England from the fifth century AD; language of the Anglo-Saxons. ◆ *adj* of the Anglo-Saxons or their language.

angora *n* variety of goat, cat, or rabbit with long silky hair; hair of the angora goat or rabbit; cloth made from this hair.

Angostura Bitters *pl n* ® bitter tonic, used as a flavouring in alcoholic drinks.

angst *n* feeling of anxiety.

angstrom *n* unit of length used to measure wavelengths.

anguish *n* great mental or physical pain. **anguished** *adj*

angular *adj* (of a person) lean and bony; having angles; measured by an angle. **angularity** *n*

anhydrous *adj Chem* containing no water.

aniline *n* colourless oily liquid obtained from coal tar and used for making dyes, plastics, and explosives.

animadversion *n* criticism or censure.

animal *n* living creature having specialized sense organs and the power of voluntary motion, esp. one other than a human being;

quadruped. ◆ *adj* of animals; sensual, physical.

animate *v* give life to; enliven; motivate; make a cartoon film of. ◆ *adj* having life. **animated** *adj* **animation** *n* life, vigour; technique of making cartoon films. **animator** *n*

animism *n* belief that natural objects possess souls. **animist** *n*, *adj* **animistic** *adj*

animosity *n*, *pl* **-ties** hostility, hatred.

animus *n* hatred, animosity.

anion [an-eye-on] *n* ion with negative charge.

anise [an-niss] *n* plant with liquorice-flavoured seeds.

aniseed *n* liquorice-flavoured seeds of the anise.

ankle *n* joint between the foot and leg. **anklet** *n* ornamental chain worn round the ankle.

annals *pl n* yearly records of events.

anneal *v* toughen (metal or glass) by heating and slow cooling.

annelid *n* worm with a segmented body, such as an earthworm.

annex *v* seize (territory); take (something) without permission; join or add (something) to something larger. ◆ *n* extension to a building; nearby building used as an extension. **annexation** *n*

annihilate *v* destroy utterly. **annihilation** *n*

anniversary *n*, *pl* **-ries** date on which something occurred in a previous year; celebration of this.

anno Domini *adv Latin* (indicating years numbered from the supposed year of the birth of Christ) in the year of our Lord.

annotate *v* add notes to (a written work). **annotation** *n*

announce *v* make known publicly; proclaim. **announcement** *n* **announcer** *n* person who introduces radio or television programmes.

annoy *v* irritate or displease. **annoyance** *n*

annual *adj* happening once a year; lasting for a year. ◆ *n* plant that completes its life-cycle in a year; book published each year. **annually** *adv*

annuity *n*, *pl* **-ties** fixed sum paid every year.

annul *v* **-nulling, -nulled** make

(something, esp. a marriage) invalid. **annulment** *n*

annular [an-new-lar] *adj* ring-shaped.

Annunciation *n Christianity* angel Gabriel's announcement to the Virgin Mary of her conception of Christ.

anode *n Electricity* positive electrode in a battery, valve, etc.

anodyne *n* something that relieves pain or distress. ◆ *adj* relieving pain or distress.

anoint *v* smear with oil as a sign of consecration.

anomaly [an-nom-a-lee] *n*, *pl* **-lies** something that deviates from the normal, irregularity. **anomalous** *adj*

anon *adv Obs* in a short time, soon.

anon. anonymous.

anonymous *adj* by someone whose name is not known; having no known name. **anonymously** *adv* **anonymity** *n*

anorak *n* waterproof hooded jacket.

anorexia *n* psychological disorder characterized by fear of becoming fat and refusal to eat (also **anorexia nervosa**). **anorexic** *adj, n*

another *adj, pron* one more; a different (one).

answer *v* give an answer (to); respond or react; be responsible to (a person). ◆ *n* reply to a question, request, letter, etc.; solution to a problem; reaction or response. **answerable** *adj* (foll. by *for* or *to*) responsible for or accountable to. **answering machine** device for answering a telephone automatically and recording messages.

ant *n* small insect living in highly organized colonies. **anteater** *n* mammal which feeds on ants by means of a long sticky tongue. **ant hill** mound built by ants around their nest.

antagonist *n* opponent or adversary. **antagonism** *n* open opposition or hostility. **antagonistic** *adj* **antagonize** *v* arouse hostility in, annoy.

Antarctic *n* the Antarctic area around the South Pole. *adj* of this region.

ante *n* player's stake in poker. ◆ *v* **-teing, -ted** *or* **-teed.** place (one's stake) in poker.

ante- *prefix* before in time or position, e.g. *antedate, antechamber*.

antecedent *n* thing coming before something else. ◆ *adj* preceding.

antedate *v* precede in time.

antediluvian *adj* of the time before the biblical Flood; old-fashioned.

antelope *n* deerlike mammal with long legs and horns.

antenatal *adj* during pregnancy, before birth.

antenna *n, pl* **-nae** insect's feeler; *pl* **-nas** aerial.

anterior *adj* to the front; earlier.

anteroom *n* small room leading into a larger one, often used as a waiting room.

anthem *n* song of loyalty, esp. to a country; piece of music for a choir, usu. set to words from the Bible.

anther *n* part of a flower's stamen containing pollen.

anthology *n, pl* **-gies** collection of poems or other literary pieces by various authors. **anthologist** *n*

anthracite *n* hard coal burning slowly with little smoke or flame but intense heat.

anthrax *n* dangerous disease of cattle and sheep, communicable to humans.

anthropoid *adj* like a human. ◆ *n* ape, such as a chimpanzee, resembling a human.

anthropology *n* study of human origins, institutions, and beliefs. **anthropological** *adj* **anthropologist** *n*

anthropomorphic *adj* attributing human form or personality to a god, animal, or object. **anthropomorphism** *n*

anti- *prefix* against, opposed to, e.g. *anti-war*; opposite to, e.g. *anticlimax*; counteracting, e.g. *antifreeze*.

anti-aircraft *adj* for defence against aircraft attack.

antibiotic *n* chemical substance capable of destroying bacteria. ◆ *adj* of antibiotics.

antibody *n, pl* **-bodies** protein produced in the blood, which destroys bacteria.

anticipate *v* foresee and act in advance of; look forward to; expect. **anticipation** *n* **anticipatory** *adj*

anticlimax *n* disappointing conclusion to a series of events.

anticlockwise *adv, adj* in the opposite direction to the rotation of the hands of a clock.

antics *pl n* absurd acts or postures.

anticyclone *n* area of moving air of high pressure in which the winds rotate outwards.

antidote *n* substance that counteracts a poison.

antifreeze *n* liquid added to water to lower its freezing point, used in automobile radiators.

antigen [an-tee-jen] *n* substance, usu. a toxin, causing the blood to produce antibodies.

antihero *n, pl* **-roes** central character in a book, film, etc. who lacks the traditional heroic virtues.

antihistamine *n* drug used to treat allergies.

antimacassar *n* cloth put over a chair-back to prevent soiling.

antimony [an-tim-mon-ee] *n* brittle silvery-white metallic element.

antipathy [an-tip-a-thee] *n* dislike, hostility. **antipathetic** *adj*

antiperspirant *n* substance used to reduce or prevent sweating.

antiphon *n* hymn sung in alternate parts by two groups of singers.

antipodes [an-tip-pod-deez] *pl n* any two places diametrically opposite one another on the earth's surface. **the Antipodes** Australia and New Zealand. **antipodean** *adj*

antipyretic *adj* reducing fever. ◆ *n* drug that reduces fever.

antique *n* object of an earlier period, valued for its beauty, workmanship, or age. ◆ *adj* made in an earlier period; old-fashioned. **antiquarian** *adj* of or relating to antiquities or rare books. **antiquary** *n* student or collector of antiques or ancient works of art. **antiquated** *adj* out-of-date. **antiquity** *n* great age; ancient times; object dating from ancient times.

antiracism *n* policy of challenging racism and promoting racial tolerance.

antirrhinum *n* two-lipped flower of various colours.

anti-Semitism *n* prejudice against Jews. **anti-Semitic** *adj*

antiseptic *adj* preventing infection by killing germs. ◆ *n* antiseptic substance.

antisocial *adj* avoiding the company of other people; (of behaviour) harmful to society.

antistatic *adj* reducing the effects of static electricity.

antithesis [an-tith-iss-iss] *n, pl* **-ses** [-

seez] exact opposite; placing together of contrasting ideas or words to produce an effect of balance. **antithetical** adj

antitoxin n (serum containing) an antibody that acts against a toxin.

antler n branching horn of male deer.

antonym n word that means the opposite of another.

anus [ain-uss] n opening at the end of the alimentary canal, through which feces are discharged.

anvil n heavy iron block on which a smith hammers metal into shape.

anxiety n, pl -ties state of being anxious.

anxious adj worried and tense; intensely desiring. **anxiously** adv

any adj, pron one or some, no matter which. ◆ adv at all, e.g. it isn't any worse. **anybody** pron anyone. **anyhow** adv anyway. **anyone** pron any person; person of any importance. **anything** pron **anyway** adv at any rate, nevertheless; in any manner. **anywhere** adv in, at, or to any place.

Anzac n (in World War 1) a soldier serving with the Australian and New Zealand Army Corps.

aorta [eh-or-ta] n, pl -tas, -tae main artery of the body, carrying oxygen-rich blood from the heart. **aortal** adj

apace adv Lit swiftly.

apart adv to or in pieces; to or at a distance; individual, distinct.

apartheid n former official government policy of racial segregation in S Africa.

apartment n set of rooms for living in which are part of a larger building.

apathy n lack of interest or enthusiasm. **apathetic** adj **apathetically** adv

ape n tailless monkey such as the chimpanzee or gorilla; stupid, clumsy, or ugly man. ◆ v imitate. **apish** adj

aperient [ap-peer-ee-ent] adj mildly laxative. ◆ n mild laxative.

aperitif [ap-per-rit-teef] n alcoholic drink taken before a meal.

aperture n opening or hole.

apex n highest point.

APEX Advance Purchase Excursion: reduced fare for journeys booked a specified period in advance.

aphasia n disorder of the central nervous system that affects the ability to speak and understand words.

aphid [eh-fid], **aphis** [eh-fiss] n small insect which sucks the sap from plants.

aphorism n short wise saying. **aphoristic** adj

aphrodisiac [af-roh-diz-zee-ak] adj arousing sexual desire. ◆ n aphrodisiac substance.

apiary [ape-yar-ee] n, pl -ries place where bees are kept. **apiculture** n breeding and care of bees.

apiece adv each, e.g. they were given two apples apiece.

aplomb [ap-plom] n calm self-possession.

apocalypse n end of the world; event of great destruction. **the Apocalypse** book of Revelation, last book of the New Testament. **apocalyptic** adj

Apocrypha [ap-pok-rif-fa] pl n **the Apocrypha** collective name for the 14 books of the Old Testament which are not accepted as part of the Hebrew scriptures. **apocryphal** adj (of a story) of questionable authenticity.

apogee [ap-oh-jee] n point of the moon's or a satellite's orbit farthest from the earth; highest point.

apology n, pl -gies expression of regret for wrongdoing; (foll. by for) poor example of; formal written defence of a cause. **apologetic** adj making an apology. **apologetically** adv **apologetics** n branch of theology concerned with the reasoned defence of Christianity. **apologist** n person who formally defends a cause. **apologize** v make an apology.

apophthegm [ap-poth-em] n short wise saying.

apoplexy n Med stroke. **apoplectic** adj of apoplexy; Informal furious.

apostasy [ap-poss-stass-ee] n, pl -sies abandonment of one's religious faith or other belief. **apostate** [ap-poss-state] n, adj

a posteriori [eh poss-steer-ee-or-rye] adj Logic involving reasoning from effect to cause.

Apostle n one of the twelve disciples chosen by Christ to preach the Gospel; (a-) ardent supporter of a cause or movement. **apostolic** adj

apostrophe [ap-poss-trof-fee] n punctuation mark (') showing the omission of a letter or letters in a word (e.g. *don't*) or forming the possessive (e.g. *Jill's coat*); digression from a speech to address an imaginary or absent person or thing.

apothecary *n, pl* **-caries** *Obs* pharmacist.

apotheosis [ap-poth-ee-oh-siss] *n, pl* **-ses** [-seez] elevation to the rank of a god; perfect example.

appal *v* **-palling, -palled** dismay, terrify. **appalling** *adj* dreadful, terrible.

apparatus *n* equipment for a particular purpose.

apparel [ap-par-rel] *n Old-fashioned* clothing.

apparent *adj* readily seen, obvious; seeming as opposed to real. **apparently** *adv*

apparition *n* ghost or ghostlike figure.

appeal *v* make an earnest request; be attractive; request a review of a lower court's decision by a higher court. ◆ *n* earnest request; attractiveness; request for a review of a lower court's decision by a higher court. **appealing** *adj*

appear *v* become visible or present; seem; be seen in public. **appearance** *n* sudden arrival of someone or something; way a person or thing looks.

appease *v* pacify (a person) by yielding to his or her demands; satisfy or relieve (a feeling). **appeasement** *n*

appellant *n* person who makes an appeal to a higher court.

appellation *n* name, title.

append *v* join on, add. **appendage** *n* thing joined on or added.

appendicitis *n* inflammation of the appendix.

appendix *n, pl* **-dixes, -dices** separate additional material at the end of a book; *Anat* short closed tube attached to the large intestine.

appertain *v* (foll. by *to*) belong to; be connected with.

appetite *n* desire or inclination, esp. for food or drink. **appetizer** *n* thing eaten or drunk to increase the appetite. **appetizing** *adj* stimulating the appetite. **appetizingly** *adv*

applaud *v* show approval of by clapping one's hands; approve strongly. **applause** *n* approval shown by clapping one's hands.

apple *n* round firm fleshy fruit that grows on trees. **apple-pie order** *Informal* perfect order. **apple polish** *Informal* seek favour by using flattery.

appliance *n* device with a specific function.

appliqué [ap-plee-kay] *n* kind of decoration in which one material is cut out and attached to another.

apply *v* **-plying, -plied** make a formal request; put to practical use; put onto a surface; be relevant or appropriate. **apply oneself** concentrate one's efforts. **applicable** *adj* relevant. **applicably** *adv* **applicability** *n* **applicant** *n* person who applies for something. **application** *n* formal request; act of applying something to a particular use; concentrated effort; act of putting something onto a surface. **applied** *adj* (of a skill, science, etc.) put to practical use.

appoint *v* assign to a job or position; fix or decide, e.g. *appoint a time*; equip or furnish. **appointment** *n* arrangement to meet a person; act of placing someone in a job; the job itself. ◆ *pl* fixtures or fittings.

apportion *v* divide out in shares. **apportionment** *n*

apposite *adj* suitable, apt. **appositeness** *n* **apposition** *n* grammatical construction in which two nouns or phrases referring to the same thing are placed one after another without a conjunction, as in *my son the doctor*.

appraise *v* estimate the value or quality of. **appraisal** *n*

appreciate *v* value highly; be aware of and understand; be grateful for; rise in value. **appreciable** *adj* enough to be noticed. **appreciably** *adv* **appreciation** *n* act of appreciating. **appreciative** *adj* feeling or showing appreciation.

apprehend *v* seize, arrest; understand. **apprehension** *n* dread, anxiety; arrest; understanding. **apprehensive** *adj* fearful or anxious.

apprentice *n* someone working for a skilled person for a fixed period in order to learn his or her trade. ◆ *v* take or place (someone) as an apprentice. **apprenticeship** *n*

apprise *v* make aware (of).

appro *n* **on appro** *Informal* on

approval.

approach v come near or nearer (to); make a proposal or suggestion to; begin to deal with (a matter). ◆ n approaching or means of approaching; approximation. **approachable** adj **approachability** n

approbation n approval.

appropriate adj suitable, fitting. ◆ v take for oneself; put aside for a particular purpose. **appropriately** adv **appropriateness** n **appropriation** n

approve v consider good or right; authorize, agree to. **approval** n favourable opinion; consent. **on approval** (of goods) with an option to be returned without payment if unsatisfactory.

approx. approximate(ly).

approximate adj almost but not quite exact. ◆ v come close to; be almost the same as. **approximately** adv **approximation** n

appurtenance n minor or additional feature.

Apr. April.

après-ski [ap-ray-skee] n social activities after a day's skiing.

apricot n yellowish-orange juicy fruit like a small peach. ◆ adj yellowish-orange.

April n fourth month of the year. **April fool** victim of a practical joke played on April 1 (**April Fools' Day**).

a priori [eh pry-or-rye] adj involving reasoning from cause to effect.

apron n garment worn over the front of the body to protect the clothes; part of a stage in front of the curtain; area at an airport or hangar for manoeuvring and loading aircraft.

apropos [ap-prop-poh] adj, adv appropriate(ly). **apropos of** with regard to.

apse n arched or domed recess, esp. in a church.

apt adj having a specified tendency; suitable; quick to learn. **aptly** adv **aptness** n **aptitude** n natural ability.

aqualung n mouthpiece attached to air cylinders, worn for underwater swimming.

aquamarine n greenish-blue gemstone. ◆ adj greenish-blue.

aquaplane n board on which a person stands to be towed by a motorboat. ◆ v ride on an aquaplane; (of a motor vehicle) skim uncontrollably on a thin film of water.

aquarium n, pl **aquariums**, **aquaria** tank in which fish and other underwater creatures are kept; building containing such tanks.

aquatic adj living in or near water; done in or on water. **aquatics** pl n water sports.

aquatint n print like a watercolour, produced by etching copper.

aqua vitae [ak-wa vee-tie] n Obs brandy.

aqueduct n structure carrying water across a valley or river.

aqueous adj of, like, or containing water.

aquiline adj of or like an eagle; (of a nose) curved like an eagle's beak.

Ar Chem argon.

Arab n member of a Semitic people originally from Arabia. ◆ adj of the Arabs. **Arabic** n language of the Arabs. ◆ adj of Arabic, Arabs, or Arabia.

arabesque [ar-ab-besk] n ballet position in which one leg is raised behind and the arms are extended; elaborate ornamental design.

arable adj suitable for growing crops on.

arachnid [ar-rak-nid] n eight-legged invertebrate, such as a spider, scorpion, tick, or mite.

Aran adj (of sweaters etc.) knitted in a complicated pattern traditional to the Aran Islands, usu. with natural unbleached wool.

arbiter n person empowered to judge in a dispute; person with influential opinions about something. **arbitrary** adj based on personal choice or chance, rather than reason. **arbitrarily** adv **arbitrate** v settle (a dispute) by arbitration. **arbitration** n hearing and settling of a dispute by an impartial referee chosen by both sides. **arbitrator** n

arboreal [ahr-bore-ee-al] adj of or living in trees.

arboretum [ahr-bore-ee-tum] n, pl -ta place where rare trees or shrubs are cultivated.

arboriculture n cultivation of trees or shrubs.

arbour n glade sheltered by trees.

arc n part of a circle or other curve; luminous discharge of electricity across a small gap between two electrodes. ◆ v form an arc.

arcade n row of arches on pillars; covered passageway, usu. lined with shops; set of arches.

arcane adj mysterious and secret.

arch[1] n curved structure supporting a bridge or roof; something curved; curved lower part of the foot. ◆ v (cause to) form an arch. **archway** n passageway under an arch.

arch[2] adj superior, knowing; coyly playful. **archly** adv **archness** n

arch- combining form chief, principal, e.g. archenemy.

archaeology, archeology n study of ancient cultures from their physical remains. **archaeological, archeological** adj **archaeologist, archeologist** n

archaic [ark-kay-ik] adj ancient; out-of-date. **archaically** adv **archaism** [ark-kay-iz-zum] n archaic word or phrase. **archaistic** adj

archangel [ark-ain-jell] n chief angel.

archbishop n chief bishop.

archdeacon n priest ranking just below a bishop. **archdeaconry** n

archdiocese n diocese of an archbishop.

archery n art or sport of shooting with a bow and arrow. **archer** n

archetype [ark-ee-type] n original model; perfect specimen. **archetypal** adj

archiepiscopal adj of an archbishop.

archipelago [ark-ee-pel-a-go] n, pl -gos group of islands; sea full of small islands. **archipelagic** adj

architect n person qualified to design and supervise the construction of buildings. **architecture** n style of building; designing and construction of buildings. **architectural** adj

architrave n Archit beam that rests on columns; moulding round a doorway or window.

archive [ark-ive] n (often pl.) collection of records or documents; place where these are kept. **archival** adj **archivist** [ark-iv-ist] n person in charge of archives.

Arctic n the Arctic area around the North Pole. adj of this region; (a-)

Informal very cold. **arctic hare** large hare with white fur in winter. **arctic willow** low-growing shrub of Canadian Tundra.

ardent adj passionate; eager, zealous. **ardently** adv **ardency** n **ardour** n passion; enthusiasm, zeal.

arduous adj hard to accomplish, strenuous. **arduously** adv **arduousness** n

are[1] v see BE.

are[2] n unit of measure, 100 square metres.

area n part or region; size of a two-dimensional surface; subject field; small sunken yard giving access to a basement.

arena n seated enclosure for sports events; area of a Roman amphitheatre where gladiators fought; sphere of intense activity.

aren't are not.

areola n, pl -lae, -las small circular area, such as the coloured ring around the human nipple.

argon n inert gas found in the air.

argot [ahr-go] n slang or jargon.

argue v -guing, -gued try to prove by giving reasons; debate; quarrel, dispute. **arguable** adj **arguably** adv **argument** n point presented for or against something; discussion; quarrel. **argumentation** n process of reasoning methodically. **argumentative** adj given to arguing.

aria [ah-ree-a] n elaborate song for solo voice, esp. one from an opera.

arid adj parched, dry; uninteresting. **aridity** n

aright adv rightly.

arise v arising, arose, arisen come about; come into notice; get up.

aristocracy n, pl -cies highest social class; government by this class. **aristocrat** n member of the aristocracy. **aristocratic** adj **aristocratically** adv

arithmetic n calculation by or of numbers. ◆ adj of arithmetic. **arithmetical** adj **arithmetically** adv

ark n Bible boat built by Noah, which survived the Flood; (A-) Judaism chest containing the writings of Jewish Law.

arm[1] n upper limb from the shoulder to the wrist; sleeve of a garment; side of a chair. **armful** n as much as an arm can hold. **armchair** n upholstered chair with side supports for the arms. **armhole** n opening in a garment through which the arm passes. **armpit** n hollow under the arm at the shoulder.

arm² v supply with weapons; prepare (a bomb etc.) for use. **arms** pl n weapons; military exploits; heraldic emblem. **armament** n military weapons; preparation for war.

armada n large number of warships.

armadillo n, pl **-los** small S American mammal covered in strong bony plates.

Armageddon n Bible final battle between good and evil at the end of the world; catastrophic conflict.

armature n revolving structure in an electric motor or generator, wound with coils carrying the current.

armistice [arm-miss-stiss] n suspension of fighting.

armour, armor n metal clothing formerly worn to protect the body in battle; metal plating of tanks, warships, etc. **armourer, armorer** n maker, repairer, or keeper of arms or armour. **armoury, armory** n place where weapons are stored. **armorial** adj relating to heraldry.

army n, pl **-mies** military force that fights on land; great number.

aroma n pleasant smell. **aromatic** adj

aromatherapy n massage with fragrant oils to relieve tension.

arose v past tense of ARISE.

around prep, adv on all sides (of); from place to place (in); somewhere in or near; approximately.

arouse v awaken; stimulate, make active.

arpeggio [arp-**pej**-ee-oh] n, pl **-gios** Music notes of a chord played or sung in quick succession.

arr. arranged (by); arrival; arrive(d).

arraign [ar-**rain**] v indict (a person) on a charge; accuse. **arraignment** n

arrange v plan; agree; put in order; adapt (music) for performance in a certain way. **arrangement** n

arrant adj utter, downright.

arras n tapestry wall-hanging.

array n impressive display or collection; orderly arrangement, esp. of troops; Poetic rich clothing. ◆ v arrange in order; dress in rich clothing.

arrears pl n money owed. **in arrears** late in paying a debt.

arrest v take (a person) into custody; stop the movement or development of; catch and hold (the attention). ◆ n act of taking a person into custody; slowing or stopping. **arresting** adj attracting attention, striking.

arrive v reach a place or destination; happen, come; Informal be born; Informal attain success. **arrival** n arriving; person or thing that has just arrived.

arrogant adj proud and overbearing. **arrogantly** adv **arrogance** n

arrogate v claim or seize without justification.

arrow n pointed shaft shot from a bow; arrow-shaped sign or symbol used to show direction. **arrowhead** n pointed tip of an arrow.

arrowroot n nutritious starch obtained from the root of a W Indian plant.

arse n Taboo buttocks or anus. **arsehole** n Taboo anus; stupid or annoying person.

arsenal n place where arms and ammunition are made or stored.

arsenic n toxic grey element; highly poisonous compound of this. **arsenical** adj

arson n crime of intentionally setting property on fire. **arsonist** n

art n creation of works of beauty, esp. paintings or sculpture; works of art collectively; skill. ◆ pl nonscientific branches of knowledge. **artful** adj cunning, wily. **artfully** adv **artfulness** n **artist** n person who produces works of art, esp. paintings or sculpture; person skilled at something; artiste. **artiste** n professional entertainer such as a singer or dancer. **artistic** adj **artistically** adv **artistry** n artistic skill. **artless** adj free from deceit or cunning; natural, unpretentious. **artlessly** adv **artlessness** n **arty** adj Informal having an affected interest in art.

artefact, artifact n something made by man.

arteriosclerosis [art-ear-ee-oh-skler-oh-siss] n hardening of the arteries.

artery n, pl **-teries** one of the tubes

carrying blood from the heart; major
road or means of communication.
arterial adj of an artery; (of a route)
major.

artesian well [art-**teez**-yan] n well
bored vertically so that the water is
forced to the surface by natural
pressure.

arthritis n painful inflammation of a
joint or joints. **arthritic** adj, n

arthropod n animal, such as a spider
or insect, with jointed limbs and a
segmented body.

artichoke n thistle-like plant with a
flower cooked as a vegetable.

article n item or object; written piece
in a magazine or newspaper; clause in
a document; Grammar any of the
words the, a, or an. **articled** adj bound
by a written contract, e.g. an articled
clerk.

articulate adj able to express oneself
clearly and coherently; Zool having
joints; (of speech) clear, distinct. ◆ v
speak or say clearly and coherently.
articulately adv **articulated** adj
jointed. **articulation** n

artifice n clever trick; cleverness, skill.
artificer [art-**tiff**-iss-er] n craftsman.
artificial adj man-made, not occurring
naturally; made in imitation of
something natural; not sincere.
artificial insemination introduction of
semen into the womb by means other
than sexual intercourse. **artificial
intelligence** branch of computer
science aiming to produce machines
which can imitate intelligent human
behaviour. **artificial respiration**
method of restarting a person's
breathing after it has stopped.
artificially adv **artificiality** n

artillery n large-calibre guns; branch
of the army who use these.

artisan n skilled worker, craftsman.

arum lily [**air**-rum] n plant with a
white funnel-shaped leaf surrounding
a spike of flowers.

as conj while, when; in the way that;
that which, e.g. do as you are told;
since, seeing that; for instance. ◆ adv,
conj used to indicate amount or extent
in comparisons, e.g. he is as tall as
you. ◆ prep in the role of, being, e.g.
as a mother, I am concerned.

As Chem arsenic.

asafoetida n strong-smelling plant

resin used as a spice in Eastern
cookery.

a.s.a.p. as soon as possible.

asbestos n fibrous mineral which does
not burn. **asbestosis** n lung disease
caused by inhalation of asbestos fibre.

ascend v go or move up. **ascension** n
ascending. **ascent** n ascending;
upward slope. **ascendant** adj
dominant or influential. ◆ n **in the
ascendant** increasing in power or
influence. **ascendancy** n condition of
being dominant.

ascertain v find out definitely.
ascertainable adj **ascertainment** n

ascetic [ass-**set**-tik] n person who
abstains from worldly pleasures and
comforts. ◆ adj abstaining from
worldly pleasures and comforts.
ascetically adv **asceticism** n

ascorbic acid [ass-**core**-bik] n vitamin
C.

ascribe v attribute, as to a particular
origin. **ascribable** adj **ascription** n

aseptic [eh-**sep**-tik] adj germ-free.

asexual [eh-**sex**-yew-al] adj without
sex. **asexually** adv

ash[1] n powdery substance left when
something is burnt. ◆ pl remains after
burning, esp. of a human body after
cremation. **ashen** adj pale with shock.
ashtray n receptacle for tobacco ash
and cigarette butts. **Ash Wednesday**
first day of Lent.

ash[2] n tree with grey bark.

ashamed adj feeling shame.

ashlar n square block of hewn stone
used in building.

ashore adv towards or on land.

ashram n religious retreat where a
Hindu holy man lives.

Asian adj of the continent of Asia or
any of its peoples or languages. ◆ n
person from Asia or a descendant of
one. **Asiatic** adj

aside adv to one side; out of other
people's hearing, e.g. he took me aside
to tell me his plans. ◆ n remark not
meant to be heard by everyone
present.

asinine [**ass**-in-nine] adj stupid, idiotic.
asininity n

ask v say or write (something) in a
form that requires an answer; make a
request or demand; invite.

askance [ass-**kanss**] adv **look askance**

at look at with an oblique glance; regard with suspicion.

askew *adv, adj* to one side, crooked.

aslant *adv, prep* at a slant (to), slanting (across).

asleep *adj* sleeping; (of limbs) numb.

asp *n* small poisonous snake.

asparagus *n* plant whose shoots are cooked as a vegetable.

aspect *n* feature or element; appearance or look; position facing a particular direction.

aspen *n* kind of poplar tree.

asperity [ass-per-rit-ee] *n* roughness of temper.

aspersion *n* **cast aspersions on** make derogatory remarks about.

asphalt *n* black hard tarlike substance used for road surfaces etc. ◆ *v* cover with asphalt.

asphodel *n* plant with clusters of yellow or white flowers.

asphyxia [ass-fix-ee-a] *n* suffocation. **asphyxiate** *v* suffocate. **asphyxiation** *n*

aspic *n* savoury jelly used to coat meat, eggs, fish, etc.

aspidistra *n* plant with long tapered leaves.

aspirate *Phonetics v* pronounce with an *h* sound. ◆ *n* an *h* sound.

aspire *v* (foll. by *to*) yearn (for), hope (to do or be). **aspirant** *n* person who aspires. **aspiration** *n* strong desire or aim.

aspirin *n* drug used to relieve pain and fever; tablet of this.

ass *n* donkey; stupid person.

assagai *n* same as ASSEGAI.

assail *v* attack violently. **assailant** *n*

assassin *n* person who murders a prominent person. **assassinate** *v* murder (a prominent person). **assassination** *n*

assault *n* violent attack. ◆ *v* attack violently. **assault course** series of obstacles used in military training.

assay *n* analysis of a substance, esp. a metal, to ascertain its purity. ◆ *v* make such an analysis.

assegai *n* slender spear used in S Africa.

assemble *v* collect or congregate; put together the parts of (a machine). **assemblage** *n* collection or group; assembling. **assembly** *n* assembling;

assembled group. **assembly line** sequence of machines and workers in a factory assembling a product.

assent *n* agreement or consent. ◆ *v* agree or consent.

assert *v* declare forcefully; insist upon (one's rights etc.). **assert oneself** speak and act forcefully. **assertion** *n* **assertive** *adj* **assertively** *adv*

assess *v* judge the worth or importance of; estimate the value of (income or property) for taxation purposes. **assessment** *n* **assessor** *n*

asset *n* valuable or useful person or thing. ◆ *pl* property that a person or firm can sell, esp. to pay debts.

asseverate *v* declare solemnly.

assiduous *adj* diligent and persevering. **assiduously** *adv* **assiduity** *n*

assign *v* appoint (someone) to a job or task; allot (a task); attribute. **assignation** [ass-sig-nay-shun] *n* assigning; secret arrangement to meet. **assignment** *n* assigning; task assigned.

assimilate *v* learn and understand (information); absorb or be absorbed or incorporated. **assimilable** *adj* **assimilation** *n*

assist *v* give help or support. **assistance** *n* **assistant** *n* helper. ◆ *adj* junior or deputy.

assizes *pl n* court sessions formerly held in each county of England and Wales.

associate *v* connect in the mind; mix socially. ◆ *n* partner in business; friend or companion. ◆ *adj* having partial rights or subordinate status, e.g. *associate member.* **association** *n* associating; society or club.

assonance *n* rhyming of vowel sounds but not consonants, as in *time* and *light.* **assonant** *adj*

assorted *adj* consisting of various types mixed together. **assortment** *n* assorted mixture.

assuage [ass-wage] *v* relieve (pain, grief, thirst, etc.).

assume *v* take to be true without proof; pretend, e.g. *I assumed indifference;* take upon oneself, e.g. *he assumed command.* **assumption** *n* assuming; thing assumed. **assumptive** *adj*

assure v promise or guarantee; convince; make (something) certain; insure against loss of life. **assured** adj confident; certain to happen. **assuredly** adv definitely. **assurance** n assuring or being assured.

AST Atlantic Standard Time.

aster n plant with daisy-like flowers.

asterisk n star-shaped symbol (*) used in printing to indicate a footnote etc. ◆ v mark with an asterisk.

astern adv at or towards the stern of a ship; backwards.

asteroid n any of the small planets that orbit the sun between Mars and Jupiter.

asthma [ass-ma] n illness causing difficulty in breathing. **asthmatic** adj, n

astigmatism [eh-stig-mat-tiz-zum] n inability of a lens, esp. of the eye, to focus properly. **astigmatic** adj

astir adj out of bed; in motion.

astonish v surprise greatly. **astonishment** n

astound v overwhelm with amazement. **astounding** adj

astrakhan n dark curly fleece of lambs from Astrakhan in Russia; fabric resembling this.

astral adj of stars; of the spirit world.

astray adv off the right path.

astride adv, prep with a leg on either side (of).

astringent adj severe or harsh; causing contraction of body tissue; checking the flow of blood from a cut. ◆ n astringent substance. **astringency** n

astrolabe n instrument formerly used to measure the altitude of stars and planets.

astrology n study of the alleged influence of the stars, planets, and moon on human affairs. **astrologer** n **astrological** adj

astronaut n person trained for travelling in space.

astronautics n science and technology of space flight. **astronautical** adj

astronomy n scientific study of heavenly bodies. **astronomer** n **astronomical** adj of astronomy; very large. **astronomically** adv

astrophysics n science of the physical and chemical properties of stars,

planets, etc. **astrophysical** adj **astrophysicist** n

astute adj perceptive or shrewd. **astutely** adv **astuteness** n

asunder adv into parts or pieces.

asylum n refuge or sanctuary; old name for a mental hospital.

asymmetry n lack of symmetry. **asymmetrical, asymmetric** adj

asymptote [ass-im-tote] n straight line closely approached by but never met by a curve.

at prep indicating position in space or time; towards; engaged in; in exchange for, e.g. it's selling at two pounds; indicating the cause of an emotion, e.g. shocked at his rudeness.

atavism [at-a-viz-zum] n recurrence of a trait present in distant ancestors. **atavistic** adj

ataxia n lack of muscular coordination. **ataxic** adj

ate v past tense of EAT.

atheism [aith-ee-iz-zum] n belief that there is no God. **atheist** n **atheistic** adj

atherosclerosis n, pl -ses disease in which deposits of fat cause the walls of the arteries to thicken.

athlete n person trained in or good at athletics. **athletic** adj physically fit or strong; of an athlete or athletics. **athletics** pl n track and field sports such as running, jumping, throwing, etc. **athletically** adv **athleticism** n

athwart prep across. ◆ adv transversely.

atigi n a type of parka worn by the Inuit.

atlas n book of maps.

atmosphere n mass of gases surrounding a heavenly body, esp. the earth; prevailing tone or mood (of a place etc.); unit of pressure. **atmospheric** adj **atmospherics** pl n radio interference due to electrical disturbance in the atmosphere.

atoll n ring-shaped coral island enclosing a lagoon.

atom n smallest unit of matter which can take part in a chemical reaction; very small amount. **atomic** adj of atoms; of or using atomic bombs or atomic energy. **atomic bomb, atom bomb** bomb in which the energy is provided by nuclear fission. **atomic**

energy nuclear energy. **atomic number** number of protons in the nucleus of an atom. **atomic weight** ratio of the mass per atom of an element to one twelfth of the mass of a carbon atom. **atomize** v reduce to atoms or small particles. **atomizer** n device for discharging a liquid in a fine spray.

atonal [eh-tone-al] adj (of music) not written in an established key. **atonality** n

atone v make amends (for sin or wrongdoing). **atonement** n

atop prep on top of.

atrium n, pl **atria** upper chamber of either half of the heart; central hall extending through several storeys of a modern building; main courtyard of an ancient Roman house.

atrocious adj extremely cruel or wicked; horrifying or shocking; Informal very bad. **atrociously** adv **atrocity** n wickedness; act of cruelty.

atrophy [at-trof-fee] n, pl -**phies** wasting away of an organ or part. ◆ v -**phying**, -**phied** (cause to) waste away.

attach v join, fasten, or connect; attribute or ascribe, e.g. he attaches great importance to his looks. **attached** adj (foll. by to) fond of. **attachment** n

attaché [at-tash-shay] n specialist attached to a diplomatic mission. **attaché case** flat rectangular briefcase for papers.

attack v launch a physical assault (against); criticize; set about (a job or problem) with vigour; affect adversely. ◆ n act of attacking; sudden bout of illness. **attacker** n

attain v achieve or accomplish (a task or aim); reach. **attainment** n accomplishment. **attainable** adj **attainability** n

attar n fragrant oil made from roses.

attempt v try, make an effort. ◆ n effort or endeavour.

attend v be present at; look after; pay attention; apply oneself (to). **attendance** n attending; number attending. **attendant** n person who assists, guides, or provides a service. ◆ adj accompanying. **attention** n concentrated direction of the mind; consideration; care; alert position in military drill. **attentive** adj giving

attention; considerably helpful. **attentively** adv **attentiveness** n

attenuate v weaken; make or become thin. **attenuation** n

attest v affirm the truth of, be proof of. **attestation** n

attic n space or room within the roof of a house.

attire n fine or formal clothes. ◆ v clothe.

attitude n way of thinking and behaving; posture of the body.

attorney n person legally appointed to act for another, esp. a lawyer.

attract v arouse the interest or admiration of; draw (something) closer by exerting a force on it. **attraction** n power to attract; something that attracts. **attractive** adj **attractively** adv **attractiveness** n

attribute v (usu. foll. by to) regard as belonging to or produced by. ◆ n quality or feature representative of a person or thing. **attributable** adj **attribution** n **attributive** adj Grammar (of an adjective) preceding the noun modified.

attrition n constant wearing down to weaken or destroy, e.g. war of attrition.

attune v adjust or accustom (a person or thing).

atypical [eh-tip-ik-al] adj not typical.

Au Chem gold.

aubergine [oh-bur-zheen] n Brit eggplant.

aubrietia [aw-bree-sha] n trailing plant with purple flowers.

auburn adj, n (of hair) reddish-brown.

auction n public sale in which articles are sold to the highest bidder. ◆ v sell by auction. **auctioneer** n person who conducts an auction.

audacious adj recklessly bold or daring; impudent. **audaciously** adv **audacity** n

audible adj loud enough to hear. **audibly** adv **audibility** n

audience n group of spectators or listeners; formal interview.

audio adj of sound or hearing; of or for the transmission or reproduction of sound. **audiovisual** adj (esp. of teaching aids) involving both sight and hearing.

audit n official examination of business accounts. ◆ v examine (business accounts) officially. **auditor** n

audition n test of a performer's ability for a particular role or job. ♦ v test or be tested in an audition.

auditorium n, pl **-toriums, -toria** building for public gatherings or meetings.

auditory adj of or relating to hearing.

au fait [oh fay] adj French fully informed; expert.

Aug. August.

auger n carpenter's tool for boring holes.

aught pron Old-fashioned anything.

augment v increase or enlarge. **augmentation** n

au gratin [oh grat-tan] adj covered and cooked with breadcrumbs and sometimes cheese.

augur v be a sign of (future events). **augury** n foretelling of the future; omen.

august adj dignified and imposing.

August n eighth month of the year.

auk n northern sea bird with short wings and black-and-white plumage.

aunt n father's or mother's sister; uncle's wife. **auntie, aunty** n Informal aunt. **Aunt Sally** figure used in fairgrounds as a target; target of abuse or criticism.

au pair n young foreign woman who does housework in return for board and lodging.

aura n distinctive air or quality of a person or thing.

aural adj of or using the ears or hearing. **aurally** adv

aureole, aureola n halo.

au revoir [oh rev-vwahr] interj French goodbye.

auricle n upper chamber of the heart; outer part of the ear.

aurochs n, pl **aurochs** recently extinct European wild ox.

aurora n, pl **-ras, -rae** bands of light sometimes seen in the sky in polar regions. **aurora australis** aurora seen near the South Pole. **aurora borealis** aurora seen near the North Pole.

auscultation n listening to the internal sounds of the body, usu. with a stethoscope, to help with diagnosis.

auspices [aw-spiss-siz] pl n **under the auspices of** with the support and approval of.

auspicious adj showing signs of future success, favourable. **auspiciously** adv

Aussie n, adj Informal Australian.

austere adj stern or severe; ascetic; severely simple or plain. **austerely** adv **austerity** n

Australasian n, adj (person) from Australia, New Zealand, and neighbouring islands.

Australian n, adj (person) from Australia.

autarchy [aw-tar-kee] n absolute power or autocracy.

autarky [aw-tar-kee] n policy of economic self-sufficiency.

authentic adj known to be real, genuine. **authentically** adv **authenticity** n **authenticate** v establish as genuine. **authentication** n

author n writer of a book etc.; originator or creator. **authoress** n fem **authorship** n

authority n, pl **-ties** power to command or control others; (often pl.) person or group having this power; expert in a particular field. **authoritarian** n, adj (person) insisting on strict obedience to authority. **authoritative** adj recognized as being reliable, e.g. the authoritative book on Shakespeare; possessing authority. **authoritatively** adv **authorize** v give authority to; give permission for. **authorization** n

autism n Psychiatry disorder, usu. of children, characterized by lack of response to people and limited ability to communicate. **autistic** adj

auto- combining form self-, e.g. autobiography.

autobiography n, pl **-phies** account of a person's life written by that person. **autobiographical** adj **autobiographically** adv

autocrat n absolute ruler; dictatorial person. **autocratic** adj **autocratically** adv **autocracy** n government by an autocrat.

autocross n motor-racing over a rough course.

Autocue n ® electronic television prompting device displaying a speaker's script, unseen by the audience.

autogiro, autogyro n, pl **-ros** self-propelled aircraft resembling a helicopter but with an unpowered rotor.

autograph *n* handwritten signature of a (famous) person. ♦ *v* write one's signature on or in.

automate *v* make (a manufacturing process) automatic.

automatic *adj* (of a device) operating mechanically by itself; (of a process) performed by automatic equipment; done without conscious thought; (of a firearm) self-loading. ♦ *n* self-loading firearm; vehicle with automatic transmission. **automatic transmission** transmission system in a motor vehicle in which the gears change automatically. **automatically** *adv*

automation *n* use of automatic devices in industrial production.

automaton *n* robot; person who acts mechanically.

automobile *n* motor vehicle designed to carry a small number of people.

autonomy *n* self-government. **autonomous** *adj*

autopsy *n, pl* **-sies** examination of a corpse to determine the cause of death.

autoroute *n* expressway.

autosuggestion *n* process in which a person unconsciously influences his or her own behaviour or beliefs.

autumn *n* fall. **autumnal** *adj* **autumnally** *adv*

auxiliary *adj* secondary or supplementary; supporting. ♦ *n, pl* **-ries** person or thing that supplements or supports. **auxiliary verb** verb used to form the tense, voice, or mood of another, such as *will* in *I will go*.

avail *v* be of use or advantage (to). ♦ *n* use or advantage, esp. in *to no avail*. **avail oneself of** make use of.

available *adj* obtainable or accessible. **availability** *n*

avalanche *n* mass of snow or ice falling down a mountain; sudden overwhelming quantity of anything.

avant-garde [av-ong-gard] *n* group of innovators, esp. in the arts. ♦ *adj* innovative and progressive.

avarice [av-a-riss] *n* greed for wealth. **avaricious** *adj*

avast *interj Naut* stop.

avatar *n Hinduism* appearance of a god in animal or human form.

Ave. Avenue.

avenge *v* take revenge in retaliation for (harm done) or on behalf of (a person harmed). **avenger** *n*

avenue *n* wide street; road between two rows of trees; way of approach.

aver [av-vur] *v* **averring, averred** state to be true. **averment** *n*

average *n* typical or normal amount or quality; result obtained by adding quantities together and dividing the total by the number of quantities. ♦ *adj* usual or typical; calculated as an average. ♦ *v* calculate the average of; amount to as an average.

averse *adj* (usu. foll. by *to*) disinclined or unwilling. **aversion** *n* strong dislike; person or thing disliked.

avert *v* turn away; ward off.

avg. average.

aviary *n, pl* **aviaries** large cage or enclosure for birds.

aviation *n* art of flying aircraft. **aviator** *n*

avid *adj* keen or enthusiastic; greedy (for). **avidly** *adv* **avidity** *n*

avocado *n, pl* **-dos** pear-shaped tropical fruit with a leathery green skin and yellowish-green flesh.

avocation *n Old-fashioned* occupation; hobby.

avocet *n* long-legged wading bird with a long slender upward-curving bill.

avoid *v* refrain from; prevent from happening; keep away from. **avoidable** *adj* **avoidance** *n*

avoirdupois [av-er-de-poise] *n* system of weights based on pounds and ounces.

avow *v* state or affirm; admit openly. **avowal** *n* **avowed** *adj* **avowedly** *adv*

avuncular *adj* friendly, helpful, and caring towards someone younger.

await *v* wait for; be in store for.

awake *adj* not sleeping; alert. ♦ *v* **awaking, awoke, awoken** emerge or rouse from sleep; (cause to) become alert.

awaken *v* awake. **awakening** *n* start of a feeling or awareness.

award *v* give (something, such as a prize) formally. ♦ *n* something awarded, such as a prize.

aware *adj* having knowledge,

informed. **awareness** n

awash adv washed over by water.

away adv from a place, e.g. go away; to another place, e.g. put that gun away; out of existence, e.g. fade away; continuously, e.g. laughing away. ◆ adj not present; distant, e.g. two miles away; Sport played on an opponent's ground.

awe n wonder and respect mixed with dread. ◆ v fill with awe. **awesome** adj inspiring awe; Slang excellent or wonderful. **awestruck** adj filled with awe.

awful adj very bad or unpleasant; Obs inspiring awe; Informal very great. **awfully** adv in an unpleasant way; Informal very.

awhile adv for a time.

awkward adj clumsy or ungainly; embarrassed; difficult to use, handle, or deal with; inconvenient. **awkwardly** adv **awkwardness** n

awl n pointed tool for piercing wood, leather, etc.

awning n canvas roof supported by a frame to give protection against the weather.

awoke v past tense of AWAKE. **awoken** v past participle of AWAKE.

AWOL adj Mil absent without leave.

awry [a-rye] adv, adj with a twist to one side, askew; amiss.

axe n tool with a sharp blade for felling trees or chopping wood; Informal dismissal from employment etc. ◆ v Informal dismiss (employees), restrict (expenditure), or terminate (a project).

axil n angle where the stalk of a leaf joins a stem.

axiom n generally accepted principle; self-evident statement. **axiomatic** adj containing axioms; self-evident.

axis n, pl **axes** (imaginary) line round which a body can rotate or about which an object or geometrical figure is symmetrical; one of two fixed lines on a graph, against which quantities or positions are measured. **axial** adj **axially** adv

axle n shaft on which a wheel or pair of wheels turn.

ayatollah n Islamic religious leader in Iran.

aye, ay interj yes. ◆ n affirmative vote

or voter.

azalea [az-**zale**-ya] n garden shrub grown for its showy flowers.

azimuth n arc of the sky between the zenith and the horizon; horizontal angle of a bearing measured clockwise from the north.

Aztec n, adj (person) of the Indian race ruling Mexico before the Spanish conquest in the 16th century.

azure adj, n (of) the colour of a clear blue sky.

B b

BA Bachelor of Arts.

baa v baaing, baaed make the cry of a sheep. ◆ n cry made by a sheep.

babble v talk excitedly or foolishly; (of streams) make a low murmuring sound. ◆ n incoherent or foolish talk.

babe n baby.

babel [**babe**-el] n confused mixture of noises or voices.

babiche n thongs or lacings of rawhide.

baboon n large monkey with a pointed face and a long tail.

baby n, pl **-bies** very young child or animal; Slang sweetheart. ◆ adj comparatively small of its type. **babyish** adj **baby beef** young beef animal; its meat. **baby carriage** small hand-pushed carriage for a baby. **baby-sit** v take care of a child while the parents are out. **baby-sitter** n

baccarat [back-a-rah] n card game involving gambling.

bacchanalia pl n drunken revelry or orgy.

bachelor n unmarried man; person who holds the lowest university degree.

bacillus [bass-ill-luss] n, pl **-li** [-lie] rod-shaped bacterium.

back n rear part of the human body, from the neck to the pelvis; part or side of an object opposite the front; part of anything less often seen or used; Ball games defensive player or position. ◆ v (cause to) move backwards; provide money for (a person or enterprise); bet on the success of; (foll. by *onto*) have the back facing towards. ◆ *adj* situated behind; owing from an earlier date. ◆ *adv* at, to, or towards the rear; to or towards the original starting point or condition. **backer** *n* person who gives financial support. **backing** *n* support; musical accompaniment for a pop singer. **backward** *adj* directed towards the rear; retarded in physical, material, or intellectual development. **backwardness** *n* **backwards** *adv* towards the rear; with the back foremost; in the reverse of the usual direction. **back bacon** sweet pickled bacon cut from the loin. **backbencher** *n* Member of Parliament who does not hold office in the government or opposition. **backbiting** *n* spiteful talk about an absent person. **backbone** *n* spinal column; strength of character. **backchat** *n Informal* answering back, esp. impudently. **backcloth, backdrop** *n* painted curtain at the back of a stage set. **backdate** *v* make (a document) effective from an earlier date. **backfire** *v* (of a plan) fail to have the desired effect; (of an engine) make a loud noise like an explosion. **back forty** area of farm most remote from a farmhouse; any remote area. **background** *n* events or circumstances that help to explain something; person's social class, education, or experience; space behind the chief figures in a picture. **backhand** *n Tennis etc* stroke played with the back of the hand facing the direction of the stroke. **backhanded** *adj* sarcastic, e.g. *a backhanded compliment*. **backhouse** outhouse. **backlash** *n* sudden and adverse reaction. **backlog** *n* accumulation of things to be dealt with. **backpack** *n* rucksack. **backside** *n Informal* buttocks. **backslide** *v* relapse into former bad habits. **backslider** *n* **backstage** *adv, adj* behind the stage in a theatre. **backstroke** *n* swimming stroke performed on the back. **backtrack** *v* return by the same route by which one has come; retract or reverse one's opinion or policy. **back up** *v* support. **backup** *n* support or reinforcement; reserve or substitute. **backwash** *n* water washed backwards by the motion of a boat; repercussion. **backwater** *n* isolated or backward place or condition. **backwoods** *pl n*

remote sparsely populated area.
backgammon *n* game played with counters and dice.
bacon *n* salted or smoked pig meat.
bacteria *pl n, sing* **-rium** large group of microorganisms, many of which cause disease. **bacterial** *adj* **bacteriology** *n* study of bacteria. **bacteriologist** *n*
bad *adj* **worse, worst** of poor quality; lacking skill or talent; harmful; immoral or evil; naughty or mischievous; rotten or decayed; severe or unpleasant. **badly** *adv* **badness** *n* **badlands** *pl n* barren, rocky region in western N America.
bade *v* a past tense of BID.
badge *n* emblem worn to show membership, rank, etc.
badger *n* nocturnal burrowing mammal with a black and white head. ◆ *v* pester or harass.
badinage [bad-in-nahzh] *n* playful and witty conversation.
badminton *n* game played with a racket and shuttlecock, which is hit over a high net.
baffle *v* perplex or puzzle. **bafflement** *n*
bag *n* flexible container with an opening at one end; *Offens* ugly or bad-tempered woman. ◆ *pl Informal* (foll. by *of*) lots of. ◆ *v* **bagging, bagged** put into a bag; (cause to) bulge; capture or kill. **baggy** *adj* (of clothes) hanging loosely. **bagman** *n Informal* person who solicits money for a political party.
bagatelle *n* something of little value; board game in which balls are struck into holes.
baggage *n* suitcases packed for a journey.
bagpipes *pl n* musical wind instrument with reed pipes and an inflatable bag.
bail[1] *n Law* money deposited with a court as security for a person's reappearance in court. ◆ *v* pay bail for (a person).
bail[2], **bale** *v* (foll. by *out*) remove (water) from (a boat). **bail out, bale out** *v Informal* help (a person or organization) out of a predicament; make an emergency parachute jump from an aircraft.

bailey *n* outermost wall or court of a castle.

bailiff *n* sheriff's officer who serves writs and summonses; court official; landlord's agent.

bairn *n Scot* child.

bait *n* piece of food on a hook or in a trap to attract fish or animals. ◆ *v* put a piece of food on or in (a hook or trap); persecute or tease.

baize *n* woollen fabric used to cover billiard and card tables.

bake *v* cook by dry heat as in an oven; make or become hardened by heat. **baker** *n* person whose business is to make or sell bread, cakes, etc. **baker's dozen** thirteen. **bakery** *n, pl* **-eries** place where bread, cakes, etc. are baked or sold. **baking powder** powdered mixture used in baking instead of yeast.

bakeapple *n* cloudberry.

Balaclava, Balaclava helmet *n* close-fitting woollen hood that covers the ears and neck.

balalaika *n* guitar-like musical instrument with a triangular body.

balance *n* stability of mind or body; state of being in balance; harmony in the parts of a whole; something that remains; difference between the credits and debits of an account; weighing device. ◆ *v* weigh on a balance; remain steady; equalize in weight, amount, etc.; consider or compare.

balcony *n, pl* **-nies** platform on the outside of a building with a rail along the outer edge; upper tier of seats in a theatre or cinema.

bald *adj* having little or no hair on the scalp; (of a tire) having a worn tread; without unnecessary words. **balding** *adj* becoming bald. **baldness** *n* **bald prairie** part of prairie without trees.

balderdash *n* stupid talk.

bale¹ *n* large bundle of hay or goods tightly bound together. ◆ *v* make or put into bales.

bale² *v* same as BAIL².

baleful *adj* vindictive or menacing. **balefully** *adv*

balk, baulk *v* be reluctant to (do something); thwart or hinder.

Balkan *adj* of any of the countries of the Balkan Peninsula: Romania, Bulgaria, Albania, Greece, the former Yugoslavia, and the European part of Turkey.

ball¹ *n* round or nearly round object, esp. one used in games; single delivery of the ball in a game. ◆ *pl Taboo slang* testicles; nonsense. ◆ *v* form into a ball. **ball bearings** steel balls between moving parts of a machine to reduce friction. **ball cock** device with a floating ball and a valve for regulating the flow of water. **ballpoint, ballpoint pen** *n* pen with a tiny ball bearing as a writing point.

ball² *n* formal social function for dancing. **ballroom** *n*

ballad *n* narrative poem or song; slow sentimental song.

ballast *n* substance, such as sand, used to stabilize a ship when it is not carrying cargo.

ballet *n* classical style of expressive dancing based on conventional steps; theatrical performance of this. **ballerina** *n* female ballet dancer.

ballistics *n* study of the flight of projectiles, such as bullets. **ballistic missile** missile guided automatically in flight but which falls freely at its target.

balloon *n* inflatable rubber bag used as a plaything; large bag inflated with air or gas, designed to carry passengers in a basket underneath. ◆ *v* fly in a balloon; swell or increase rapidly in size. **balloonist** *n*

ballot *n* method of voting secretly; actual vote or paper indicating a person's choice. ◆ *v* **-loting, -loted** vote or ask for a vote from. **ballot box**

ballyhoo *n* exaggerated fuss.

balm *n* aromatic substance used for healing and soothing; anything that comforts or soothes.

balmy *adj* **balmier, balmiest** (of weather) mild and pleasant; same as BARMY.

baloney *n Informal* nonsense.

balsa [bawl-sa] *n* tropical American tree that yields light wood.

balsam *n* soothing ointment; flowering plant.

baluster *n* set of posts supporting a rail. **balustrade** *n* ornamental rail supported by balusters.

bamboo *n* tall treelike tropical grass

with hollow stems.

bamboozle v Informal cheat or mislead; confuse, puzzle.

ban v **banning, banned** prohibit or forbid officially. ◆ n official prohibition.

banal [ban-nahl] adj ordinary and unoriginal. **banality** n

banana n yellow crescent-shaped fruit.

band[1] n group of musicians playing together; group of people having a common purpose; community of Canadian Indians recognized by federal government. **bandsman** n **bandstand** n roofed outdoor platform for a band. **band together** v unite.

band[2] n strip of material, used to hold objects together; Physics range of frequencies or wavelengths between two limits.

bandage n piece of material used to cover a wound. ◆ v cover with a bandage.

bandanna, bandana n large brightly coloured handkerchief.

b. and b., B and B bed and breakfast.

bandit n robber, esp. a member of an armed gang. **banditry** n

bandoleer, bandolier n shoulder belt for holding cartridges.

bandwagon n **climb, jump on the bandwagon** join a party or movement that seems assured of success.

bandy adj **-dier, -diest** having legs curved outwards at the knees. ◆ v **-dying, -died** exchange (words) in a heated manner; circulate (a name, rumour, etc.).

bane n person or thing that causes misery or distress. **baneful** adj

bang n short loud explosive noise; hard blow or loud knock. ◆ v hit or knock, esp. with a loud noise; close (a door) noisily. ◆ adv with a sudden impact; precisely.

banger n Slang sausage; Informal old decrepit automobile; firework that explodes loudly.

bangle n bracelet worn round the arm or the ankle.

banish v send (someone) into exile; dismiss from one's thoughts. **banishment** n

banisters pl n railing supported by posts on a staircase.

banjo n, pl **-jos, -joes** guitar-like

instrument with a circular body.

bank[1] n institution offering services, such as the safekeeping and lending of money; any supply, store, or reserve. ◆ v deposit (cash or cheques) in a bank. **banker** n manager or owner of a bank. **banking** n **banknote** n piece of paper money. **bank on** v rely on.

bank[2] n raised mass, esp. of earth; sloping ground at the side of a river. ◆ v form into a bank; cause (an aircraft) or (of an aircraft) to tip to one side on turning

bank[3] n row of switches, keys, etc. on a machine.

bankrupt n person declared by a court to be unable to pay his or her debts. ◆ adj financially ruined. ◆ v make bankrupt. **bankruptcy** n

banner n long strip of cloth displaying a slogan, advertisement, etc.; placard carried in a demonstration or procession.

bannisters pl n same as BANISTERS.

banns pl n public declaration, esp. in a church, of an intended marriage.

banquet n elaborate formal dinner.

banshee n (in Irish folklore) female spirit whose wailing warns of impending death.

bantam n small chicken. ◆ adj Sport under 15 years of age. **bantamweight** n boxer weighing up to 118lb (professional) or 54 kg (amateur).

banter v tease jokingly. ◆ n teasing or joking conversation.

Bantu n group of languages of Africa.

banyan n Indian tree whose branches grow down into the soil forming additional trunks.

baptism n Christian religious ceremony in which a person is immersed in or sprinkled with water as a sign of purification and acceptance into the Church. **baptismal** adj **baptize** v perform baptism on.

Baptist n member of a Protestant denomination that believes in adult baptism by immersion.

bar[1] n rigid length of metal, wood, etc.; solid, usu. rectangular block, of any material; anything that obstructs or prevents; counter or room where drinks are served; heating element in an electric fire; Music group of beats repeated throughout a piece of music.

◆ *v* **barring, barred** secure with a bar; ban or forbid; obstruct. ◆ *prep* (also **barring**) except for. **the bar** lawyers collectively. **barman, barmaid** *n*

bar² *n* unit of atmospheric pressure.

barachois *n* (in the Atlantic Provinces) a shallow lagoon formed by a sand bar.

barb *n* point facing in the opposite direction to the main point of a fish-hook etc.; cutting remark. **barbed** *adj* **barbed wire** strong wire with protruding sharp points.

barbarian *n* member of a primitive or uncivilized people. **barbaric** *adj* cruel or brutal. **barbarism** *n* condition of being backward or ignorant. **barbarity** *n* state of being barbaric or barbarous; vicious act. **barbarous** *adj* uncivilized; brutal or cruel.

barbecue *n* grill on which food is cooked over hot charcoal, usu. outdoors; outdoor party at which barbecued food is served. ◆ *v* cook (food) on a barbecue.

barber *n* person who cuts men's hair.

barbiturate *n* drug used as a sedative.

bard *n* *Lit* poet. **the Bard** William Shakespeare.

bare *adj* unclothed; without the natural or usual covering; unembellished, simple; just sufficient. ◆ *v* uncover. **barely** *adv* only just. **bareness** *n* **bareback** *adj, adv* (of horse-riding) without a saddle. **barefaced** *adj* shameless.

bargain *n* agreement establishing what each party will give, receive, or perform in a transaction; something bought or offered at a low price. ◆ *v* negotiate the terms of an agreement. **bargain for** *v* anticipate or take into account.

barge *n* flat-bottomed boat used to transport freight. ◆ *v* *Informal* push violently. **barge in, into** *v* interrupt rudely.

barista *n* person who makes and sells coffee in a coffee bar.

baritone *n* (singer with) the second lowest adult male voice.

barium [bare-ee-um] *n* soft white metallic element.

bark¹ *n* loud harsh cry of a dog. ◆ *v* (of a dog) make its typical cry; shout in an angry tone.

bark² *n* tough outer layer of a tree.

barley *n* tall grasslike plant cultivated for grain.

barmy *adj* **-mier, -miest** *Slang* insane.

barn *n* large building on a farm used for storing grain. **barnstorm** *v* tour rural districts putting on shows or making speeches in a political campaign.

barnacle *n* shellfish that lives attached to objects under water.

barometer *n* instrument for measuring atmospheric pressure.

baron *n* member of the lowest rank of nobility; powerful businessman. **baroness** *n fem* **baronial** *adj*

baronet *n* commoner who holds the lowest hereditary British title.

baroque [bar-rock] *n* highly ornate style of art and architecture from the late 16th to the early 18th century. ◆ *adj* extremely complicated, rich, and elaborate.

barque [bark] *n* sailing ship, esp. one with three masts.

barrack *v* criticize loudly or shout against (a team or speaker).

barracks *pl n* building used to accommodate military personnel.

barracuda [bar-rack-kew-da] *n* predatory tropical sea fish.

barrage [bar-rahzh] *n* continuous delivery of questions, complaints, etc.; continuous artillery fire; artificial barrier across a river.

barrel *n* cylindrical container with rounded sides and flat ends; tube in a firearm through which the bullet is fired. **barrel organ** musical instrument played by turning a handle.

barren *adj* (of land) unable to support the growth of crops, fruit, etc.; (of a woman or female animal) incapable of producing offspring. **barrenness** *n* **Barren Lands, Grounds** sparsely inhabited Tundra region in Canada.

barricade *n* barrier, esp. one erected hastily for defence. ◆ *v* erect a barricade across (an entrance).

barrier *n* anything that prevents access or progress.

barrister *n* lawyer who pleads in court.

barrow¹ *n* wheelbarrow; movable stall, used esp. by street vendors.

barrow² n mound of earth placed over a prehistoric tomb.

barter v trade (goods) in exchange for other goods. ◆ n trade by the exchange of goods.

basalt [bass-awlt] n dark volcanic rock. **basaltic** adj

bascule n drawbridge that operates by a counterbalanced weight.

base¹ n bottom or supporting part of anything; fundamental part; centre of operations, organization, or supply; starting point. ◆ v (foll. by on or upon) use as a basis (for); (foll. by at or in) station, post, or place. **baseless** adj **basement** n partly or wholly underground storey of a building.

base² adj dishonourable or immoral; of inferior quality.

baseball n N American team game played with a bat and ball; ball used for this.

bash Informal ◆ v hit violently or forcefully. ◆ n heavy blow.

bashful adj shy or modest. **bashfully** adv **bashfulness** n

basic adj of or forming a base or basis; elementary or simple. **basics** pl n fundamental principles, facts, etc. **basically** adv

BASIC n computer programming language that uses common English words.

basil n aromatic herb used in cooking.

basilica n rectangular church with a rounded end and two aisles.

basilisk n legendary serpent said to kill by its breath or glance.

basin n round open container; sink for washing the hands and face; sheltered area of water where boats may be moored; catchment area of a particular river.

basis n, pl **-ses** fundamental principles etc. from which something is started or developed.

bask v lie in or be exposed to (pleasant warmth).

basket n container made of interwoven strips of wood or cane. **basketwork** n

basketball n team game similar to netball; ball used for this.

Basque n, adj (member or language) of a people living in the W Pyrenees in France and Spain.

bas-relief n sculpture in which the figures stand out slightly from the background.

bass¹ [base] n (singer with) the lowest adult male voice. ◆ adj of the lowest range of musical notes.

bass² n edible sea fish.

basset hound n smooth-haired dog with short legs and long ears.

bassoon n large woodwind instrument.

basswood n tall shade tree with heart-shaped leaves.

bastard n person born of parents not married to each other; Offens obnoxious or despicable person. **bastardize** v debase or corrupt.

baste¹ v moisten (meat) during cooking with hot fat.

baste² v sew with loose temporary stitches.

bastion n projecting part of a fortification; thing or person regarded as defending a principle.

bat¹ n any of various types of club used to hit the ball in certain sports. ◆ v **batting, batted** strike with or as if with a bat.

bat² n nocturnal mouselike flying animal.

batch n group of people or things dealt with at the same time.

bated adj **with bated breath** in suspense or fear.

bath n large container in which to wash the body; act of washing in such a container. ◆ pl public swimming pool. ◆ v wash in a bath. **bathroom** n room with a bath, sink, and usu. a toilet.

bathe v swim in open water; apply liquid to (the skin or a wound) in order to cleanse or soothe; (foll. by in) fill (with), e.g. bathed in sunlight. **bather** n

bathos [bay-thoss] n sudden change in speech or writing from a serious subject to a trivial one.

bathyscaph, bathyscaphe n deep-sea diving vessel for observation.

batik [bat-teek] n process of printing fabric using wax to cover areas not to be dyed; fabric printed in this way.

baton n thin stick used by the conductor of an orchestra; short bar transferred in a relay race; policeman's truncheon.

battalion n army unit consisting of three or more companies.

batten[1] n strip of wood fixed to something, esp. to hold it in place. **batten down** v secure with a batten.

batten[2] **batten on** v thrive at the expense of (someone else).

batter[1] v hit repeatedly. **battering ram** large beam used to break down fortifications.

batter[2] n mixture of flour, eggs, and milk, used in cooking.

battery n, pl **-teries** device that produces electricity in a flashlight, radio, etc.; group of heavy guns operating as a single unit; series of cages for intensive rearing of poultry.

battle n fight between large armed forces; conflict or struggle. ◆ v struggle. **battle-axe** n Informal domineering woman; large heavy axe. **battleship** n heavily armoured warship.

battlement n wall with gaps for shooting through.

batty adj **-tier, -tiest** Slang crazy.

bauble n trinket of little value.

baulk v same as BALK.

bauxite n claylike substance from which aluminum is obtained.

bawdy adj **bawdier, bawdiest** (of writing etc.) containing humorous references to sex. **bawdiness** n

bawl v shout or weep noisily.

bay[1] n wide curving coastline.

bay[2] n recess in a wall; area in which vehicles may park or unload.

bay[3] v (of a hound or wolf) howl in deep prolonged tones.

bay[4] n Mediterranean laurel tree. **bay leaf** dried leaf of a laurel, used in cooking.

bay[5] adj, n reddish-brown (horse).

bayonet n sharp blade fixed to the end of a rifle. ◆ v **-neting, -neted** stab with a bayonet.

bazaar n sale in aid of charity; market area, esp. in Eastern countries.

bazooka n rocket launcher that fires a projectile capable of piercing armour.

BBC British Broadcasting Corporation.

BC before Christ; British Columbia.

be v, present sing, 1st person **am**, 2nd person **are**, 3rd person **is**, present pl **are**, past sing, 1st person **was**, 2nd person **were**, 3rd person **was**, past pl **were**, present participle **being**, past participle **been** exist or live; used as a linking between the subject of a sentence and its complement, e.g. John is a musician; forms the progressive present tense, e.g. the man is running; forms the passive voice of all transitive verbs, e.g. a good film is being shown on television tonight.

beach n area of sand or pebbles on a shore. ◆ v run or haul (a boat) onto a beach. **beachhead** n beach captured by an attacking army on which troops can be landed.

beacon n fire or light on a hill or tower, used as a warning.

bead n small ball of plastic etc., pierced for threading on a string to form a necklace etc.; small drop of moisture. **beaded** adj **beading** n strip of moulding used for edging furniture. **beady** adj small, round, and glittering, e.g. beady eyes.

beagle n small hunting dog with short legs and drooping ears.

beak n projecting horny jaws of a bird; Slang nose. **beaky** adj

beaker n large drinking cup; lipped glass container used in laboratories.

beam n broad smile; ray of light; narrow flow of electromagnetic radiation or particles; long thick piece of wood, metal, etc., used in building. ◆ v smile broadly; divert or aim (a radio signal, light, etc.) in a certain direction.

bean n seed or pod of various plants, eaten as a vegetable or used to make coffee etc.

bear[1] v **bearing, bore, borne** support or hold up; bring, e.g. to bear gifts; (**born** in passive use) give birth to; produce as by natural growth; tolerate or endure; hold in the mind; show or be marked with; move in a specified direction. **bearable** adj **bearer** n **bear out** v show to be truthful.

bear[2] n large heavy mammal with a long shaggy coat. **bearskin** n tall fur helmet worn by some British soldiers.

beard n hair growing on the lower parts of a man's face. **bearded** adj

bearing n relevance (to); part of a machine that supports another part, esp. one that reduces friction; person's general social conduct. ◆ *pl* sense of one's own relative position.

beast *n* large wild animal; brutal or uncivilized person. **beastly** *adj* unpleasant or disagreeable.

beat *v* **beating, beat, beaten** *or* **beat.** hit hard and repeatedly; move (wings) up and down; throb rhythmically; stir or mix vigorously; overcome or defeat. ◆ *n* regular throb; assigned route, as of a policeman; basic rhythmic unit in a piece of music. **beater** *n* **beat up** *v* injure (someone) by repeated blows or kicks.

beatify [bee-at-if-fie] *v* **-fying, -fied** *RC Church* declare (a dead person) to be among the blessed in heaven. **beatific** *adj* displaying great happiness. **beatification** *n* **beatitude** *n* supreme blessedness.

beau [boh] *n, pl* **beaus, beaux** dandy.

Beaufort scale *n* scale for measuring the speed of wind.

beauty *n, pl* **-ties** combination of all the qualities of a person or thing that delight the senses and mind; very attractive woman; *Informal* something outstanding of its kind. **beautiful** *adj* possessing beauty; very pleasant. **beautifully** *adv* **beautify** *v* make or become beautiful. **beautification** *n* **beautician** *n* person whose profession is to give beauty treatments.

beaver *n* amphibious rodent with a big flat tail; (B-) Beaver Scout. **beaver away** *v* work industriously. **beaver lodge** rounded structure of mud, sticks, and stones built by beavers as a den. **Beaver Scout** member of a junior branch of the Boy Scouts.

becalmed *adj* (of a sailing ship) motionless through lack of wind.

became *v* past tense of BECOME.

because *conj* on account of the fact that. **because of** on account of.

beck *n* **at someone's beck and call** subject to someone's slightest whim.

beckon *v* summon with a gesture.

become *v* **-coming, -came, -come** come to be; (foll. by *of*) happen to; suit. **becoming** *adj* attractive or pleasing; appropriate or proper.

bed *n* piece of furniture on which to sleep; garden plot; bottom of a river, lake, or sea; layer of rock. ◆ *v* **bedding, bedded** have sexual intercourse with. **go to bed with** have sexual intercourse with. **bedding** *n* sheets and covers that are used on a bed. **bed down** *v* go to or put into a place to sleep or rest. **bedpan** *n* shallow bowl used as a toilet by bedridden people. **bedridden** *adj* confined to bed because of illness or old age. **bedrock** *n* solid rock beneath the surface soil; basic facts or principles. **bedroom** *n* **bedsit, bedsitter** *n* furnished sitting room with a bed.

bedevil [bid-dev-ill] *v* **-illing, -illed** harass or torment.

bedlam *n* noisy confused situation.

bedraggled *adj* untidy, wet, or dirty.

bee *n* insect that makes wax and honey. **beehive** *n* structure in which bees live. **beeswax** *n* wax secreted by bees, used in polishes etc.

beech *n* European tree with a smooth greyish bark.

beef *n* flesh of a cow, bull, or ox. ◆ *v* *Informal* complain. **beefy** *adj* like beef; *Informal* strong and muscular; *Informal* fleshy, obese. **beefalo** *n* cross between bison and other cattle. **beefeater** *n* yeoman warder at the Tower of London.

been *v* past participle of BE.

beep *n* high-pitched sound, like that of an automobile horn. ◆ *v* (cause to) make this noise. **beeper** *n*

beer *n* alcoholic drink brewed from malt and hops. **beery** *adj* **beer parlour** tavern.

beet *n* plant with an edible root and leaves. **beetroot** *n* type of beet plant with a dark red root.

beetle *n* insect with a hard wing cover on its back. ◆ *v* *Informal* scuttle or scurry.

befall *v* *Old-fashioned* happen to (someone).

befit *v* be appropriate or suitable for. **befitting** *adj*

before *conj* earlier than the time when; rather than. ◆ *prep* preceding in space or time; in the presence of; in preference to. ◆ *adv* at an earlier time, previously; in front. **beforehand** *adv* in advance.

befriend *v* be a friend to.

beg *v* **begging, begged** solicit (for money or food), esp. in the street; ask formally or humbly. **beggar** n

began v past tense of BEGIN.

beget v -getting, -got or -gat, -gotten or -got. cause or create; father.

begin v -ginning, -gan, -gun start; bring or come into being. **beginner** n person who has just started learning to do something. **beginning** n

begonia n tropical plant with waxy flowers.

begrudge v grudge.

beguile [big-gile] v cheat or mislead; charm or amuse. **beguiling** adj

begun v past participle of BEGIN.

behalf n **on behalf of** in the interest of or for the benefit of.

behave v act or function in a particular way; conduct (oneself) properly. **behaviour, behavior** n

behead v remove the head from.

beheld v past of BEHOLD.

behest n order or earnest request.

behind prep at the back of; responsible for or causing; supporting. ◆ adv in or to a position further back; remaining after someone's departure; in arrears; late. ◆ n Informal buttocks.

behold v Old-fashioned look (at). **beholder** n

beholden adj indebted or obliged.

behove v Old-fashioned be necessary or fitting for.

beige adj pale brown.

being v present participle of BE. ◆ n existence; something that exists or is thought to exist; human being.

belabour, belabor v attack verbally or physically.

belated adj late or too late. **belatedly** adv

belch v expel wind from the stomach noisily through the mouth; expel or be expelled forcefully, e.g. smoke belched from the factory. ◆ n act of belching.

beleaguered adj besieged; surrounded or beset.

belfry n, pl -fries part of a tower where bells are hung.

belie v show to be untrue.

belief n trust or confidence; opinion; principle etc. accepted as true; religious faith. **believe** v accept as true or real; think, assume, or suppose; (foll. by in) be convinced of the truth

or existence of. **believable** adj **believer** n

belittle v treat as having little value or importance.

bell n hollow, usu. metal, cup-shaped instrument that emits a ringing sound when struck; device that rings or buzzes as a signal.

belladonna n (drug obtained from) deadly nightshade.

belle n beautiful woman.

bellicose adj warlike.

belligerent adj hostile and aggressive; engaged in war. ◆ n person or country engaged in war. **belligerence** n

bellow v make a low deep cry like that of a bull; shout in a loud deep voice. ◆ n loud deep roar.

bellows pl n instrument for pumping a stream of air into something.

belly n, pl -lies part of the body of a vertebrate which contains the intestines; stomach; front, lower, or inner part of something. ◆ v -lying, -lied (cause to) swell out. **bellyful** n Slang more than one can tolerate.

belong v (foll. by to) be the property of; (foll. by to) be a part of; have a proper or usual place. **belongings** pl n personal possessions.

beloved adj dearly loved. ◆ n person dearly loved.

below prep, adv at or to a position lower than, under.

belt n band of cloth, leather, etc., worn usu. around the waist; long narrow area; circular strip of rubber that drives moving parts in a machine; area where a specific thing is found. ◆ v fasten with a belt; Slang hit very hard.

bemoan v express sorrow or dissatisfaction about.

bemused adj puzzled or confused.

bench n long seat; judge or magistrate sitting in court; long narrow work table. **bencher** n governing member of a provincial law society. **bench mark** mark on a fixed object, used as a reference point in surveying; criterion by which to measure something.

bend v bending, bent (cause to) form a curve; (often foll. by down) etc.) incline the body. ◆ n curved part. ◆ pl Informal decompression sickness. **bendy** adj

beneath adv, prep below; not worthy of.

Benedictine n, adj (monk or nun) of the order of Saint Benedict.

benediction n prayer for divine blessing.

benefit n something helpful, beneficial, or advantageous; payment made by a government to a poor, ill, or unemployed person. ◆ v -fiting, -fited do or receive good. **beneficial** adj advantageous. **beneficiary** n person who gains or benefits. **benefactor, benefactress** n someone who supports a person or institution by giving money. **benefaction** n **beneficent** [bin-eff-iss-ent] adj charitable or generous. **beneficence** n

benevolent adj kind and helpful. **benevolently** adv **benevolence** n

benighted adj ignorant or uncultured.

benign [bin-nine] adj showing kindliness; (of a tumour) not malignant. **benignly** adv

bent v past of BEND. ◆ adj curved; Slang dishonest. ◆ n personal inclination or aptitude. **bent on** determined to pursue (a course of action).

bento, bento box n thin lightweight box divided into compartments, which contain small separate dishes comprising a Japanese meal.

benzene n flammable poisonous liquid used as a solvent, fuel, etc.

bequeath v dispose of (property) as in a will. **bequest** n legal gift of money or property by someone who has died.

berate v scold harshly.

bereaved adj having recently lost someone close through death. **bereavement** n

bereft adj (foll. by of) deprived.

beret [ber-ray] n round flat close-fitting brimless cap.

bergamot n small Asian tree with sour pear-shaped fruit.

beriberi n tropical disease caused by vitamin B deficiency.

berry n, pl -ries small soft stoneless fruit.

berserk adj **go berserk** become violent or destructive.

berth n bunk in a ship or train; place assigned to a ship at a mooring. ◆ v dock (a vessel).

beryl n hard transparent mineral.

beseech v -seeching, -sought or -seeched. ask (someone) earnestly.

beset v trouble or harass constantly.

beside prep at, by, or to the side of; as compared with. **beside oneself** overwhelmed or overwrought. **besides** adv, prep in addition.

besiege v surround with military forces; overwhelm, as with requests.

besom n broom made of twigs.

besotted adj infatuated.

besought v past of BESEECH.

bespeak v indicate or suggest. **bespoke** adj (of clothes) made to the customer's specifications.

best adj most excellent of a particular group etc. ◆ adv in a manner surpassing all others. ◆ n most outstanding or excellent person, thing, or group in a category. **best man** groom's attendant at a wedding. **best seller** book or other product that has sold in great numbers.

bestial adj brutal or savage; of or like a beast. **bestiality** n

bestir v cause (oneself) to become active.

bestow v present (a gift) or confer (an honour). **bestowal** n

bestride v have or put a leg on either side of.

bet n agreement that money will be paid to someone who correctly predicts the outcome of an event; stake risked. ◆ v **betting, bet** or **betted**. make or place (a bet); Informal predict (an outcome).

betel [bee-tl] n Asian climbing plant, the leaves and nuts of which can be chewed.

bête noire [bet nwahr] n, pl **bêtes noires** person or thing that one particularly dislikes.

betide v happen (to).

betoken v indicate or signify.

betray v hand over or expose (one's nation etc.) treacherously to an enemy; disclose (a secret or confidence) treacherously; reveal unintentionally. **betrayal** n **betrayer** n

betrothed adj engaged to be married. **betrothal** n

better adj more excellent than others; improved or fully recovered in health. ♦ adv in a more excellent manner; in or to a greater degree. ♦ pl n one's superiors. ♦ v improve upon.

between prep at a point intermediate to two other points in space, time, etc.; indicating a linked relation or comparison; indicating alternatives. ♦ adv between one thing and another.

betwixt prep, adv Old-fashioned between.

bevel n slanting edge. ♦ v -elling, -elled cut a bevel on (a piece of timber etc.).

beverage n drink. **beverage room** tavern.

bevy n, pl **bevies** flock or group.

bewail v express great sorrow over.

beware v be on one's guard (against).

bewilder v confuse utterly. **bewildering** adj **bewilderment** n

bewitch v attract and fascinate; cast a spell over. **bewitching** adj

beyond prep at or to a point on the other side of; outside the limits or scope of. ♦ adv at or to the far side of something.

bi- combining form twice or two, e.g. bifocal.

biannual adj occurring twice a year. **biannually** adv

bias n mental tendency, esp. prejudice; diagonal cut across the weave of a fabric; Bowls weight on one side of a bowl that causes it to run in a curve. ♦ v -asing, -ased or -assing, -assed cause to have a bias. **biased, biassed** adj

bib n piece of cloth or plastic worn under a child's chin to protect his or her clothes when eating; upper front part of dungarees etc.

Bible n sacred writings of the Christian and Jewish religions; (b-) book regarded as authoritative. **biblical** adj

bibliography n, pl -phies list of books on a subject; list of sources used in a book etc. **bibliographer** n

bibliophile n person who collects or is fond of books.

bibulous adj addicted to alcohol.

bicarbonate n salt of carbonic acid. **bicarbonate of soda** powder used in baking or as medicine.

bicentenary n, pl -naries 200th anniversary.

biceps n large muscle in the upper arm.

bicker v argue over petty matters.

bicultural adj having or relating to two cultures, esp. English and French.

bicycle n vehicle with two wheels, one behind the other, pedalled by the rider.

bid v **bidding, bade, bidden** offer (a sum of money) in an attempt to buy something; (past bid) say (a greeting etc.); command. ♦ n offer of a sum of money; attempt. **bidder** n **biddable** adj obedient. **bidding** n command.

bide v **bide one's time** wait patiently for an opportunity.

bidet [bee-day] n low basin for washing the genital area.

biennial adj occurring every two years. ♦ n plant that completes its life cycle in two years.

bier n stand on which a coffin rests before burial.

bifocals pl n pair of spectacles with each lens in two parts, the upper for distance and the lower for reading.

big adj **bigger, biggest** of considerable size, height, number, or capacity; important through having wealth etc.; elder; generous, magnanimous. ♦ adv on a grand scale. **Bigfoot** n legendary hairy, human-like monster in Pacific NW of N America. **big shot, bigwig** n Informal important person.

bigamy n crime of marrying a person while still legally married to someone else. **bigamist** n **bigamous** adj

bigot n person who is intolerant, esp. regarding religion or race. **bigoted** adj **bigotry** n

bijou [bee-zhoo] adj small but tasteful.

bike n Informal bicycle or motorcycle.

bikini n woman's brief two-piece swimming costume.

bilateral adj affecting or undertaken by two parties.

bile n bitter yellow fluid secreted by the liver. **bilious** adj sick, nauseous.

bilge n Informal nonsense; ship's bottom, where dirty water collects.

bilingual adj speaking, or written in, two languages. **bilingualism** adj

bill¹ n statement of money owed for goods or services supplied; draft of a proposed new law; piece of paper money; poster; list of events, such as a theatre programme. ◆ v send or present a bill to; advertise by posters.

bill² n bird's beak.

billabong n Aust stagnant pool in an intermittent stream.

billet v -leting, -leted assign a lodging to (a soldier). ◆ n civilian accommodation for a soldier.

billet-doux [bill-ee-doo] n, pl **billets-doux** love letter.

billhook n tool with a hooked blade, used for chopping etc.

billiards n game played on a table with balls and a cue.

billion n one thousand million; formerly, one million million. **billionth** adj

billow n large sea wave. ◆ v rise up or swell out.

billy, billycan n, pl -lies, -lycans metal can or pot for cooking on a camp fire.

bimbo n Slang attractive but empty-headed young person, esp. a woman.

bin n container for garbage or for storing grain, coal, etc.

binary [bine-a-ree] adj composed of two parts; Math, computers of or expressed in a counting system with only two digits, 0 and 1.

bind v binding, bound make or become secure with or as if with a rope; place (someone) under obligation; enclose and fasten (the pages of a book) between covers. ◆ n Informal annoying situation. **binder** n firm cover for holding loose sheets of paper together. **binding** n book cover; strip of cloth used as edging.

bindweed n flowering plant that twines around a support.

binge n Informal bout of excessive eating or drinking.

bingo n gambling game in which numbers are called out and covered by the players on their individual cards.

binoculars pl n telescope made for both eyes. **binocular** adj involving both eyes.

binomial n, adj (mathematical expression) consisting of two terms.

bio- combining form life or living organisms, e.g. biology.

biochemistry n study of the chemistry of living things. **biochemist** n

biodegradable adj capable of being decomposed by natural means.

biography n, pl -phies account of a person's life by another. **biographical** adj **biographer** n

biology n study of living organisms. **biological** adj **biologist** n

bionic adj having a part of the body that is operated electronically.

biopsy n, pl -sies examination of tissue from a living body.

bioterrorism n use of viruses, bacteria, etc., by terrorists. **bioterrorist** n

biped [bye-ped] n animal with two feet.

biplane n airplane with two sets of wings.

birch n tree with thin peeling bark; birch rod or twigs used, esp. formerly, for flogging offenders.

bird n creature with feathers and wings, the female of which lays eggs; Slang young woman.

birdie n Golf score of one stroke under par for a hole.

biretta n stiff square cap worn by the Catholic clergy.

birth n childbirth; act of being born; ancestry. **give birth to** v bear (offspring). **birth control** any method of contraception. **birthday** n anniversary of the day of one's birth. **birthmark** n blemish on the skin formed before birth. **birthright** n privileges or possessions that someone is entitled to as soon as he or she is born.

biscuit n small cake of bread made with soda or baking powder; Brit cookie or thin cracker.

bisect v divide into two equal parts.

bisexual adj sexually attracted to both men and women. **bisexuality** n

bishop n clergyman who governs a diocese; piece at chess. **bishopric** n diocese or office of a bishop.

bismuth n pinkish-white metallic element.

bison n, pl -son large hairy animal of the cattle family.

bistro n, pl -tros small restaurant.

bit¹ n small piece, portion, or quantity. **a bit** rather, somewhat. **bit by bit**

gradually.

bit² *n* metal mouthpiece on a bridle; cutting or drilling part of a tool.

bit³ *v* past tense of BITE.

bit⁴ *n* smallest unit of information held in a computer's memory, either 0 or 1.

bitch *n* female dog, fox, or wolf; *Offens* spiteful woman. ◆ *v Informal* complain or grumble. **bitchy** *adj* **bitchiness** *n*

bite *v* **biting, bit, bitten** cut off, puncture, or tear as with the teeth or fangs; take firm hold of or act effectively upon. ◆ *n* act of biting; wound or sting inflicted by biting; snack. **biter** *n* **biting** *adj* piercing or keen; sarcastic.

bitter *adj* having a sharp unpleasant taste; showing or caused by hostility or resentment; extremely cold. ◆ *n* beer with a slightly bitter taste. ◆ *pl* bitter-tasting alcoholic drink. **bitterly** *adv* **bitterness** *n*

bittern *n* wading bird like a heron.

bivalve *n* marine mollusc with a double shell.

bivouac *n* temporary camp in the open air. ◆ *v* **-acking, -acked** camp in a bivouac.

bizarre *adj* odd or unusual.

blab *v* **blabbing, blabbed** reveal (secrets) indiscreetly; chatter thoughtlessly.

black *adj* of the darkest colour, like jet or coal; (**B-**) dark-skinned; without hope; angry or resentful, e.g. *black looks*; unpleasant in a macabre manner, e.g. *black comedy*. ◆ *n* darkest colour; (**B-**) member of a dark-skinned race, esp. of African origin; complete darkness. ◆ *v* make black. **blackness** *n* **blacken** *v* make or become black; defame or slander. **blackball** *v* exclude from a group. **blackbird** *n* common American or European thrush. **blackboard** *n* hard black surface used for writing on with chalk. **blackhead** *n* small black spot on the skin. **blacklist** *n* list of people or organizations considered untrustworthy etc. **black magic** magic used for evil purposes. **blackmail** *n* act of attempting to extort money by threats. ◆ *v* (attempt to) obtain money by blackmail. **black market** illegal trade in goods or currencies. **black out** *v* extinguish (lights); lose consciousness or memory

temporarily. **blackout** *n* extinguishing of all light as a precaution against an air attack; momentary loss of consciousness or memory. **black sheep** person who is regarded as a disgrace by his or her family. **blacksmith** *n* person who works iron with a furnace, anvil, etc.

bladder *n* sac in the body where urine is held; hollow bag which may be filled with air or liquid.

blade *n* cutting edge of a weapon or tool; thin flattish part of a propeller, oar, etc.; leaf of grass.

blame *v* consider (someone) responsible for. ◆ *n* responsibility for something that is wrong. **blameless** *adj* **blameworthy** *adj* deserving blame.

blanch *v* become pale; prepare (vegetables etc.) by plunging them in boiling water.

blancmange [blam-**monzh**] *n* jelly-like dessert made with milk.

bland *adj* dull and uninteresting. **blandly** *adv*

blandishments *pl n* persuasive flattery.

blank *adj* not written on; showing no interest, feeling, or understanding. ◆ *n* empty space; cartridge containing no bullet. **blankly** *adv* **blank verse** unrhymed verse.

blanket *n* thick covering for a bed; concealing cover, as of snow. ◆ *v* cover as with a blanket.

blare *v* sound loudly and harshly. ◆ *n* loud harsh noise.

blarney *n* flattering talk.

blasé [**blah**-zay] *adj* indifferent or bored through familiarity.

blaspheme *v* speak disrespectfully of (God or sacred things). **blasphemy** *n* **blasphemous** *adj* **blasphemer** *n*

blast *n* explosion; sudden strong gust of air or wind; sudden loud sound, as of a trumpet. ◆ *v* blow up (a rock etc.) with explosives. **blastoff** *n* launching of a rocket.

blatant [**blay**-tant] *adj* glaringly obvious. **blatantly** *adv*

blaze¹ *n* strong fire or flame; very bright light. ◆ *v* burn or shine brightly.

blaze² *n* mark made on a tree to indicate a route.

blazer *n* lightweight jacket, esp. in the colours of a school etc.

blazon v proclaim publicly.

bleach v make or become white or colourless. ◆ n bleaching agent.

bleak adj exposed and barren; offering little hope.

bleary adj -rier, -riest with eyes dimmed, as by tears or tiredness. **blearily** adv

bleat v, n (utter) the plaintive cry of a sheep, goat, or calf.

bleed v **bleeding, bled** lose blood; draw blood from (a person or animal); Informal obtain money by extortion.

bleep n short high-pitched sound made by an electrical device. ◆ v make a bleeping sound.

blemish n defect or stain. ◆ v spoil or tarnish.

blench v shy away, as in fear.

blend v mix or mingle (components); look good together. ◆ n mixture. **blender** n kitchen appliance for mixing food or liquid at high speed.

bless v make holy by means of a religious rite; call upon God to protect; endow with health, talent, etc. **blessed** adj holy. **blessing** n prayer for God's favour; happy event.

blew v past tense of BLOW[1].

blight n withering plant disease; person or thing that spoils or prevents growth. ◆ v frustrate or disappoint. **blighter** n Informal irritating person.

blimp n small airship.

blind adj unable to see; unable or unwilling to understand; not determined by reason, e.g. blind hatred. ◆ v deprive of sight; deprive of good sense, reason, or judgment. ◆ n covering for a window; something that serves to conceal the truth. **blinders** pl n leather flaps on a horse's bridle to prevent sideways vision. **blindly** adv **blindness** n **blindfold** v prevent (a person) from seeing by covering the eyes. ◆ n piece of cloth used to cover the eyes. **blind trust** arrangement in which a public official's personal wealth is managed by another person.

blink v close and immediately reopen (the eyes); shine intermittently. ◆ n act of blinking. **on the blink** Slang not working properly.

blip n small light which flashes on and off regularly on equipment such as a radar screen.

bliss n perfect happiness. **blissful** adj **blissfully** adv

blister n small bubble on the skin; swelling, as on a painted surface. ◆ v (cause to) have blisters. **blistering** adj (of weather) very hot; (of criticism) extremely harsh.

blithe adj casual and indifferent. **blithely** adv

blitz n violent and sustained attack by aircraft; intensive attack or concerted effort. ◆ v attack suddenly and intensively.

blizzard n blinding storm of wind and snow.

bloated adj swollen up with liquid or gas.

bloater n salted smoked herring.

blob n soft mass or drop; indistinct or shapeless form.

bloc n people or countries combined by a common interest.

block n large solid piece of wood, stone, etc.; large building of offices, apartments, etc.; group of buildings enclosed by intersecting streets; obstruction or hindrance; Slang person's head. ◆ v obstruct or impede by introducing an obstacle. **blockage** n **blockhead** n stupid person. **block heater** electrical device for keeping engine of motor vehicle warm. **block letter** plain capital letter.

blockade n action that prevents goods from reaching a place. ◆ v impose a blockade on.

blog n short for WEBLOG

bloke n Informal man.

blonde, (masc**) blond** adj, n fair-haired (person).

blood n red fluid that flows around the body; race or ancestry. **in cold blood** done deliberately. **bloodless** adj **bloody** adj covered with blood; marked by much killing. ◆ adj, adv Slang extreme or extremely. ◆ v stain with blood. **bloody-minded** adj deliberately unhelpful. **blood bath** massacre. **bloodhound** n large dog used for tracking. **bloodshed** n slaughter or killing. **bloodshot** adj (of eyes) inflamed. **blood sport** sport involving the killing of animals. **bloodstream** n flow of blood round the body. **bloodsucker** n animal that sucks blood; *Informal* person who extorts money from other people. **bloodthirsty** *adj* taking pleasure in violence.

bloom *n* blossom on a flowering plant; youthful or healthy glow. ◆ *v* bear flowers; be in a healthy glowing condition.

blossom *n* flowers of a plant. ◆ *v* (of plants) flower; come to a promising stage.

blot *n* spot or stain; something that spoils or stains. ◆ *v* **blotting, blotted** cause a blemish in or on; soak up (ink) by using blotting paper. **blotter** *n* **blot out** *v* darken or hide completely. **blotting paper** soft absorbent paper for soaking up ink.

blotch *n* discoloured area or stain. **blotchy** *adj*

blotto *adj Slang* extremely drunk.

blouse *n* woman's shirtlike garment.

blow¹ *v* **blowing, blew, blown** (of air, the wind, etc.) move; move or be carried as if by the wind; expel (air etc.) through the mouth or nose; cause (a musical instrument) to sound by forcing air into it; burn out (a fuse etc.); *Slang* spend (money) freely. **blower** *n* **blowy** *adj* windy. **blow-dry** *v* style (the hair) with a hand-held dryer. **blowout** *n* sudden loss of air in a tire; escape of oil or gas from a well; *Slang* filling meal. **blow up** *v* explode; fill with air; *Informal* enlarge (a photograph); *Informal* lose one's temper.

blow² *n* hard hit; sudden setback; attacking action.

blown *v* past participle of BLOW¹.

blowzy, blowsy *adj* fat, untidy, and red-faced.

blubber *v* sob without restraint. ◆ *n* fat of whales, seals, etc.

bludgeon *n* short thick club. ◆ *v* hit with a bludgeon; force or bully.

blue *n* colour of a clear unclouded sky; short for BLUE LINE. ◆ *pl* feeling of depression; sad slow music like jazz. ◆ *adj* **bluer, bluest** of the colour blue; depressed; pornographic. **out of the blue** unexpectedly. **bluish** *adj* **bluebell** *n* flower with blue bell-shaped flowers. **bluebottle** *n* large fly with a dark-blue body. **blue-collar** *adj* denoting manual industrial workers. **blue jay** N American bird with bright blue

feathers. **blue line** *Ice hockey* either of two blue lines drawn midway between the centre of the rink and each goal. **blueprint** *n* photographic print of a plan; description of how a plan is expected to work.

bluff¹ *v* pretend to be confident in order to influence (someone). ◆ *n* act of bluffing.

bluff² *n* steep cliff or bank. ◆ *adj* good-naturedly frank and hearty.

blunder *n* clumsy mistake. ◆ *v* make a blunder; act clumsily.

blunderbuss *n* obsolete gun with a wide muzzle.

blunt *adj* lacking sharpness; (of people, speech, etc.) straightforward or uncomplicated. ◆ *v* make less sharp. **bluntly** *adv*

blur *v* **blurring, blurred** make or become vague or less distinct. ◆ *n* something vague, hazy, or indistinct. **blurry** *adj*

blurb *n* promotional description, as on the jacket of a book.

blurt *v* (foll. by *out*) utter suddenly and involuntarily.

blush *v* become red in the face, esp. from embarrassment or shame. ◆ *n* reddening of the face.

bluster *v* speak loudly or in a bullying way. ◆ *n* empty threats or protests. **blustery** *adj* (of weather) rough and windy.

BO *Informal* body odour.

boa constrictor *n* large snake that kills its prey by crushing.

boar *n* uncastrated male pig; wild pig.

board *n* long flat piece of wood; smaller flat piece of rigid material for a specific purpose, e.g. *ironing board*; group of people who administer a company, trust, etc.; meals provided for money. ◆ *pl* wooden barrier around the surface of an ice hockey rink. ◆ *v* go aboard (a train, airplane, etc.); cover with boards; receive meals and lodgings in return for money. **on board** on or in a ship, airplane, etc. **boarder** *n* pupil who lives at school during the school term. **boarding** *n Ice hockey* illegal bodycheck of a player into the boards. **boarding house** private house that provides meals and accommodation for paying guests. **boardroom** *n* room where the board of a company meets.

boast v speak too proudly about one's talents, etc.; possess (something to be proud of). ◆ n boasting statement. **boastful** adj

boat n small vehicle for travelling across water. **boater** n flat straw hat. **boating** n **boatswain, bo's'n, bosun** [boh-sn] n ship's officer in charge of the equipment.

bob¹ v **bobbing, bobbed** move up and down repeatedly. ◆ n short abrupt movement.

bob² n hair style in which the hair is cut level with the chin. ◆ v **bobbing, bobbed** cut (the hair) in a bob.

bobbin n reel on which thread is wound.

bobble n small ball of material, usu. for decoration.

bobby n, pl -**bies** Informal policeman.

bobsleigh n sledge used for racing. ◆ v ride on a bobsleigh.

bode v be an omen of (good or ill).

bodice n upper part of a dress.

bodkin n blunt large-eyed needle.

body n, pl **bodies** entire physical structure of an animal or human; trunk or torso; corpse; group regarded as a single entity; main part of anything; woman's one-piece undergarment. **bodily** adj relating to the body. ◆ adv by taking hold of the body. **bodycheck** Sport n use of the body to block an opposing player. ◆ v make a bodycheck. **bodyguard** n person or group of people employed to protect someone. **bodywork** n outer shell of a motor vehicle.

Boer n descendant of the Dutch settlers in S Africa.

bog n wet spongy ground; Slang toilet. **boggy** adj **bog down** v **bogging, bogged** impede physically or mentally.

bogan n sluggish side stream.

bogey n something that worries or annoys; Golf score of one stroke over par on a hole.

boggle v be surprised, confused, or alarmed.

bogus [boh-guss] adj not genuine.

bogy n, pl -**gies** same as BOGEY.

bohemian n, adj (person) leading an unconventional life.

boil¹ v (cause to) change from a liquid to a vapour so quickly that bubbles are formed; cook by the process of boiling. ◆ n state or action of boiling. **boiler** n piece of equipment which provides hot water.

boil² n red pus-filled swelling on the skin.

boisterous adj noisy and lively. **boisterously** adv

bold adj confident and fearless; immodest or impudent. **boldly** adv **boldness** n

bole n tree trunk.

bolero n, pl -**ros** short open jacket; traditional Spanish dance.

bollard n short thick post used to prevent the passage of motor vehicles.

boloney n same as BALONEY.

Bolshevik n Russian Communist. **bolshie, bolshy** adj Informal difficult or rebellious.

bolster v support or strengthen. ◆ n long narrow pillow.

bolt n sliding metal bar for fastening a door etc.; metal pin which screws into a nut; flash (of lightning). ◆ v fasten with a bolt; eat hurriedly; run away suddenly. **bolt upright** stiff and rigid. **bolt hole** place of escape.

bomb n container fitted with explosive material. ◆ v attack with bombs; move very quickly. **the bomb** nuclear bomb. **bomber** n aircraft that drops bombs; person who throws or puts a bomb in a particular place. **bombard** v attack with heavy gunfire or bombs; attack verbally, esp. with questions. **bombardment** n **bombshell** n shocking or unwelcome surprise.

bombastic adj using pompous language.

bona fide [bone-a fide-ee] adj real or genuine.

bonanza n sudden good luck or wealth.

bond n something that binds or fastens; feeling of friendship etc., that unites two people or a group of people. ◆ pl something that restrains or imprisons; written or spoken agreement; Finance certificate of debt issued to raise funds. ◆ v bind. **bonded** adj

bondage n slavery.

bone n any of the hard parts in the body that form the skeleton. ◆ v remove the bones from (meat for cooking etc.). **boneless** adj **bony** adj having many bones; thin or emaciated. **bone-dry** adj completely dry. **bone-idle** adj extremely lazy.

bonfire n large outdoor fire.

bongo n, pl **-gos**, **-goes** small drum played with the fingers.

bonhomie [bon-om-ee] n happy friendliness.

bonk v Informal have sex with; hit. **bonking** n

bonnet n Brit hood of automobile; hat which ties under the chin.

bonny adj **-nier**, **-niest** Scot beautiful.

bonsai n, pl **-sai** ornamental miniature tree or shrub.

bonspiel n curling match.

bonus n something given, paid, or received above what is expected.

boo interj shout of disapproval. ◆ v **booing**, **booed** shout 'boo' to show disapproval.

boob n Slang foolish mistake; female breast.

booby n, pl **-bies** foolish person. **booby prize** prize given for the lowest score in a competition. **booby trap** hidden bomb primed to be set off by an unsuspecting victim; trap for an unsuspecting person, intended as a joke.

boogie v Informal dance quickly to pop music.

book n number of printed pages bound together between covers; written work; number of tickets, stamps, etc. fastened together. ◆ pl record of transactions of a business or society. ◆ v reserve (a place, passage, etc.) in advance; record the name of (a person) in a book or on a list. **booklet** n thin book with paper covers. **book-keeping** n systematic recording of business transactions. **bookmaker** n person whose occupation is taking bets. **bookworm** n person devoted to reading.

bookmark v Computers store (a website) so that one can return to it easily.

boom¹ v make a loud deep echoing sound; prosper vigorously and rapidly. ◆ n loud deep echoing sound; rapid increase; period of high economic growth.

boom² n pole to which the foot of a sail is attached; pole carrying an overhead microphone; barrier across a waterway.

boomerang n curved wooden missile which returns to the thrower. ◆ v (of a plan) recoil unexpectedly.

boon n something beneficial.

boondoggle n Informal unnecessary work.

boor n rude or insensitive person. **boorish** adj

boost n encouragement or help; increase. ◆ v improve; increase. **booster** n small additional injection of a vaccine.

boot¹ n shoe that covers the whole foot and the lower part of the leg; Brit trunk of automobile; Informal kick. ◆ v Informal kick; start up (a computer). **bootee** n baby's soft shoe.

boot² n to boot in addition.

booth n small partly enclosed cubicle; stall where goods are sold.

bootleg v **-legging**, **-legged** make, carry, or sell (illicit goods). ◆ adj produced, distributed, or sold illicitly. **bootlegger** n

booty n, pl **-ties** valuable articles obtained as plunder.

booze v, n Informal (consume) alcoholic drink. **boozy** adj **boozer** n Informal person who is fond of drinking; pub. **booze-up** n Informal drinking spree.

bop v **bopping**, **bopped** Informal dance to pop music.

borax n white mineral used in making glass.

border n dividing line between regions; band around or along the edge of something. ◆ v provide with a border; be nearly the same as, e.g. his stupidity borders on madness.

bore¹ v make (a hole) with a drill etc. ◆ n (diameter of) the hollow of a gun barrel.

bore² v make weary by being dull or repetitious. ◆ n dull or repetitious person or thing. **boredom** n

bore³ n tidal wave in a narrow estuary.

bore⁴ v past tense of BEAR¹.

boreal adj northern.

born v a past participle of BEAR¹. ◆ adj possessing certain qualities from birth, e.g. a born musician.

borne v a past participle of BEAR[1].

boron n chemical element used in hardening steel.

borough n town or district with its own council.

borrow v obtain (something) temporarily; adopt (ideas etc.) from another source. **borrower** n

borstal n prison for young criminals.

borzoi n tall dog with a long silky coat.

bosh n Informal empty talk, nonsense.

bosom n chest of a person, esp. the female breasts. ◆ adj very dear, e.g. a bosom friend.

boss[1] n person in charge of or employing others. ◆ v **boss around, about** be domineering towards. **bossy** adj

boss[2] n raised knob or stud.

botany n study of plants. **botanical, botanic** adj **botanist** n

botch v spoil through clumsiness. ◆ n (also **botch-up**) badly done piece of work.

both adj, pron two considered together.

bother v take the time or trouble; give annoyance or trouble to; pester. ◆ n trouble, fuss, or difficulty. **bothersome** adj

bottle n container for holding liquids. ◆ v put in a bottle. **bottleneck** n narrow stretch of road where traffic is held up. **bottle up** v restrain (powerful emotion).

bottom n lowest, deepest, or farthest removed part of a thing; buttocks. ◆ adj lowest or last. **bottomless** adj

botulism n severe food poisoning.

boudoir [boo-dwahr] n woman's bedroom or private sitting room.

bougainvillea n climbing plant with red or purple flowers.

bough n large branch of a tree.

bought v past of BUY.

boulder n large rounded rock.

boulevard n wide street; grass strip between sidewalk and road.

bounce v (of a ball etc.) rebound from an impact; Slang (of a cheque) be returned uncashed owing to a lack of funds in the account. ◆ n act of rebounding; springiness; Informal vitality or vigour. **bouncer** n person employed at a disco etc. to remove

unwanted people. **bouncing** adj vigorous and robust.

bound[1] v past of BIND. ◆ adj destined or certain; obliged.

bound[2] v move forwards by jumps. ◆ n jump upwards or forwards.

bound[3] v form a boundary of. ◆ pl n limit, e.g. his ignorance knows no bounds. **boundary** n dividing line that indicates the farthest limit.

bound[4] adj going or intending to go towards, e.g. homeward bound.

bounty n, pl -ties generosity; generous gift or reward. **bountiful, bounteous** adj

bouquet n bunch of flowers; aroma of wine.

bourbon [bur-bn] n whiskey made from corn.

bourgeois [boor-zhwah] adj, n Offens middle-class (person).

bout n period of activity or illness; boxing or wrestling match.

boutique n small clothes shop.

bovine adj relating to cattle; rather slow and stupid.

bow[1] v lower (one's head) or bend (one's knee or body) as a sign of respect or shame; comply or accept. ◆ n movement made when bowing.

bow[2] n knot with two loops and loose ends; long stick stretched with horsehair for playing stringed instruments; weapon for shooting arrows. **bow-legged** adj bandy.

bow[3] n front end of a ship.

bowdlerize v remove words regarded as indecent from (a play etc.). **bowdlerization** n

bowel n intestine, esp. the large intestine. ◆ pl innermost part.

bower n shady leafy shelter.

bowl[1] n round container with an open top; hollow part of an object.

bowl[2] n large heavy ball. ◆ pl game played on smooth grass with wooden bowls. ◆ v Cricket send (a ball) towards the batsman. **bowler** n **bowling** n game in which bowls are rolled at a group of pins.

bowler n stiff felt hat with a rounded crown.

box[1] n container with a flat base and sides; separate compartment in a theatre, stable, etc.; Informal television. ◆ v put into a box. **box office** place

box 47 **breach**

where theatre or cinema tickets are sold.

box² v fight (an opponent) in a boxing match. **boxer** n man who participates in the sport of boxing; medium-sized dog similar to a bulldog. **boxing** n sport of fighting with the fists. **boxer shorts, boxers** men's underpants shaped like shorts but with a front opening.

box³ n evergreen tree with shiny leaves.

boy n male child. **boyish** adj **boyhood** n **boyfriend** n woman's male companion.

boycott v refuse to deal with or engage in. ◆ n instance of boycotting.

Br Chem bromine.

bra n woman's undergarment for supporting the breasts.

brace n object fastened to something to straighten or support it; appliance of metal bands and wires for correcting uneven teeth; pair, esp. of game birds. ◆ pl Brit suspenders. ◆ v steady or prepare (oneself) for something unpleasant; strengthen or fit in with a brace. **bracing** adj refreshing and invigorating.

bracelet n ornamental chain for the wrist.

bracken n large fern.

bracket n pair of characters used to enclose a section of writing; group falling within certain defined limits; support fixed to a wall. ◆ v -eting, -eted put in brackets; class together.

brackish adj (of water) slightly salty.

bract n leaf at the base of a flower.

brag v bragging, bragged speak arrogantly and boastfully. **braggart** n

Brahman, Brahmin n member of the highest Hindu caste.

braid v interweave (hair, thread, etc.). ◆ n length of hair, etc. that has been braided; narrow ornamental tape of woven silk etc.

Braille n system of writing for the blind, consisting of raised dots interpreted by touch.

brain n soft mass of nervous tissue in the head; intellectual ability. ◆ v hit (someone) hard on the head. **brainless** adj stupid. **brainy** adj Informal clever. **brainchild** n idea produced by creative thought.

brainwash v force (a person) to change his or her beliefs, esp. by methods based on isolation, pain, sleeplessness, etc. **brainwave** n sudden idea.

braise v stew slowly in a covered pan.

brake n device for slowing or stopping a vehicle. ◆ v slow down or stop by using a brake.

bramble n prickly shrub that produces blackberries.

bran n husks of cereal grain.

branch n secondary stem of a tree; offshoot or subsidiary part of something larger or more complex. ◆ v (of stems, roots, etc.) grow and diverge (from another part). **branch out** v expand one's interests.

brand n particular product; particular kind or variety; identifying mark burnt onto the skin of an animal. ◆ v mark with a brand; denounce or stigmatize. **brand-new** adj absolutely new.

brandish v wave (a weapon etc.) in a threatening way.

brandy n, pl -dies alcoholic spirit distilled from wine.

brash adj self-confident and aggressive. **brashness** n

brass n alloy of copper and zinc; group of wind instruments made of brass. **brassy** adj like brass, esp. in colour; insolent or brazen.

brassiere n bra.

brat n unruly child.

bravado n showy display of self-confidence.

brave adj having or showing courage, resolution, and daring. ◆ n North American Indian warrior. ◆ v confront with resolution or courage. **bravery** n

bravo interj well done!

brawl n rough fight. ◆ v fight noisily.

brawn n physical strength; pressed meat from the head of a pig or calf. **brawny** adj

bray v (of a donkey) utter its loud harsh sound. ◆ n donkey's loud harsh sound.

brazen adj shameless and bold. **brazenly** adv

brazier [bray-zee-er] n container for burning charcoal or coal.

breach n breaking of a promise etc.; gap or break. ◆ v break (a promise etc.); make a gap in.

bread n food made of baked flour and water; Slang money. **breadwinner** n person whose earnings support a family.

breadth n extent of something from side to side.

break v **breaking, broke, broken** separate or become separated into two or more pieces; damage or become damaged so as to be inoperative; fail to observe (an agreement etc.); disclose or be disclosed, e.g. he broke the news; bring or come to an end, e.g. the good weather broke at last; weaken or be weakened, as in spirit; cut through or penetrate; improve on or surpass, e.g. break a record; (of the male voice) become permanently deeper at puberty. ◆ n act or result of breaking; gap or interruption in continuity; Informal fortunate opportunity. **breakable** adj **breakage** n **breaker** n large wave. **break camp** v leave one's camping place. **break down** v cease to function; yield to strong emotion; analyse. **breakdown** n act or instance of breaking down; nervous breakdown; analysis. **break even** v make neither a profit nor a loss. **break-in** n illegal entering of a building, esp. by thieves. **breakneck** adj fast and dangerous. **break off** v sever or detach; end (a relationship etc.). **break out** v begin or arise suddenly. **breakthrough** n important development or discovery. **break trail** v force a path through snow or bush. **break-up** n thawing of ice in lakes and rivers in springtime. **break up** v (cause to) separate; (of a relationship) come to an end; (of a school) close for the holidays. **breakwater** n wall that extends into the sea to protect a harbour or beach from the force of waves.

breakfast v, n (eat) the first meal of the day.

breast n either of the two soft fleshy milk-secreting glands on a woman's chest; chest. ◆ v meet at breast level, e.g. she breasted the finishing line. **breaststroke** n swimming stroke performed on the front.

breath n taking in and letting out of air during breathing; air taken in and let out during breathing. **breathless**

adj **breathtaking** adj causing awe or excitement. **breathe** v take in oxygen and give out carbon dioxide; whisper. **breather** n Informal short rest. **breathing** n

Breathalyzer n ® device for estimating the amount of alcohol in the breath. **breathalyze** v

bred v past of BREED.

breech n buttocks; part of a firearm behind the barrel. **breech delivery** birth of baby with the feet or buttocks appearing first.

breeches pl n trousers extending to just below the knee.

breed v **breeding, bred** produce new or improved strains of (domestic animals or plants); bear (offspring); produce or be produced, e.g. breed trouble. ◆ n group of animals etc. within a species; kind or sort. **breeder** n **breeding** n result of good upbringing or training.

breeze n gentle wind. ◆ v move quickly or casually. **breezy** adj windy; casual or carefree.

brethren pl n Old-fashioned (used in religious contexts) brothers.

breve n long musical note.

breviary n, pl **-aries** book of prayers to be recited daily by a Roman Catholic priest.

brevity n shortness.

brew v make (beer, ale, etc.) by steeping, boiling, and fermentation; prepare (a drink) by infusing; be impending or forming. ◆ n beverage produced by brewing. **brewer** n **brewery** n company that brews beer etc.; place where beer etc. is brewed.

briar n wild rose with long thorny stems.

bribe n anything offered or given to someone to gain favour, influence, etc. ◆ v give (someone) a bribe. **bribery** n

bric-a-brac n miscellaneous small ornamental objects.

brick n (rectangular block of) baked clay used in building. ◆ v build, enclose, or fill with bricks. **bricklayer** n person who builds with bricks.

bride n woman who has just been or is about to be married. **bridal** adj **bridegroom** n man who has just been or is about to be married. **bridesmaid** n girl who attends a bride at her wedding.

bridge¹ n structure for crossing a river etc.; platform from which a ship is steered or controlled; upper part of the nose; dental plate with artificial teeth that is secured to natural teeth; piece of wood supporting the strings of a violin etc. ◆ v build a bridge over (something). **bridgehead** n fortified position at the end of a bridge nearest the enemy.

bridge² n card game based on whist.

bridle n headgear for controlling a horse. ◆ v show anger or indignation; restrain. **bridle path** path suitable for riding horses.

brief adj short in duration. ◆ n condensed statement or written synopsis; set of instructions. ◆ pl men's or women's underpants. ◆ v give information and instructions to (a person). **briefly** adv **briefcase** n small flat case for carrying papers, books, etc.

brier n same as BRIAR.

brig n two-masted square-rigged ship.

brigade n army unit smaller than a division; group of people organized for a certain task. **brigadier** n high-ranking army officer.

brigand n bandit.

brigantine n two-masted sailing ship.

bright adj emitting or reflecting much light; (of colours) intense; clever. **brightly** adv **brightness** n **brighten** v

brilliant adj shining with light; splendid; extremely clever. **brilliance, brilliancy** n

brim n projecting edge of a hat; upper rim of a cup etc. ◆ v **brimming, brimmed** be full to the brim.

brimstone n Obs sulfur.

brindled adj brown streaked with another colour.

brine n salt water. **briny** adj very salty. **the briny** Informal the sea.

bring v **bringing, brought** carry, convey, or take to a designated place or person; cause to happen; Law put forward (charges) officially. **bring about** v cause to happen. **bring down** v present (a budget) in a legislature. **bring off** v succeed in achieving. **bring out** v publish or have (a book) published; reveal or cause to be seen. **bring up** v rear (a child); mention;

vomit (food).

brink n edge of a steep place.

brisk adj lively and quick. **briskly** adv

brisket n beef from the breast of a cow.

bristle n short stiff hair. ◆ v (cause to) stand up like bristles; show anger. **bristly** adj

Brit n Informal British person.

British adj of Great Britain or the British Commonwealth. ◆ pl n people of Great Britain.

British Columbia see Canadian Provincial Facts p630.

brittle adj hard but easily broken. **brittleness** n

broach v introduce (a topic) for discussion; open (a bottle or barrel).

broad adj having great breadth or width; not detailed; extensive, e.g. broad support; vulgar or coarse; strongly marked, e.g. a broad Yorkshire accent. **broadly** adv **broaden** v **broadband** n telecommunication transmission technique using a wide range of frequencies. **broad-minded** adj tolerant. **broadside** n strong verbal or written attack; Naval firing of all the guns on one side of a ship at once.

broadcast n programme or announcement on radio or television. ◆ v transmit (a programme or announcement) on radio or television; make widely known. **broadcaster** n **broadcasting** n

brocade n rich woven fabric with a raised design.

broccoli n type of cabbage with greenish flower heads.

brochure n booklet that contains information about a product or service.

brogue¹ n sturdy walking shoe.

brogue² n strong accent, esp. Irish.

broil v grill.

broke v past tense of BREAK. ◆ adj Informal having no money.

broken v past participle of BREAK. ◆ adj fractured or smashed; (of the speech of a foreigner) imperfectly spoken, e.g. broken English. **brokenhearted** adj overwhelmed by grief.

broker n agent who buys or sells shares, securities, etc.

brolly n, pl **-lies** Informal umbrella.

bromide n chemical compound used

in medicine and photography.

bromine n toxic liquid element.

bronchus [bronk-uss] n, pl **bronchi** [bronk-eye] either of the two branches of the windpipe. **bronchial** adj **bronchitis** n inflammation of the bronchi.

bronco n, pl -cos wild or partially tamed pony.

brontosaurus n very large plant-eating four-footed dinosaur.

bronze n alloy of copper and tin; statue, medal, etc. made of bronze. ◆ adj made of, or coloured like, bronze. ◆ v (of the skin) make or become brown.

brooch n ornament with a pin for attaching to clothes.

brood n number of birds produced at one hatching; all the children of a family. ◆ v think long and morbidly. **broody** adj moody and sullen; (of a hen) wishing to hatch eggs.

brook¹ n small stream.

brook² v bear or tolerate.

broom n long-handled sweeping brush; yellow-flowered shrub. **broomstick** n handle of a broom.

broth n soup, usu. containing vegetables.

brothel n house where men pay to have sex with prostitutes.

brother n boy or man with the same parents as another person; member of a male religious order. **brotherly** adj **brotherhood** n fellowship; association, such as a trade union. **brother-in-law** n brother of one's husband or wife; husband of one's sister.

brought v past of BRING.

brow n forehead; eyebrow; top of a hill.

browbeat v frighten (someone) with threats.

brown n colour of earth or wood. ◆ adj of the colour brown. ◆ v make or become brown. **brownish** adj **browned-off** adj Informal bored and depressed.

Brownie Guide, Brownie n junior Girl Guide.

browse v look through (a book or articles for sale) in a casual manner; nibble on young shoots or leaves. ◆ n instance of browsing; shoots and leaves used as food by wild animals.

browser n Computers software package that enables a user to read hypertext, esp. on the Internet.

bruise n discoloured area on the skin caused by an injury. ◆ v cause a bruise on. **bruiser** n strong tough person.

brunch n Informal breakfast and lunch combined.

brunette n girl or woman with brown hair.

brunt n main force or shock of a blow, attack, etc.

brush¹ n device made of bristles, wires, etc. used for cleaning, painting, etc.; brief unpleasant encounter; fox's tail. ◆ v apply, remove, clean, etc. with a brush; touch lightly and briefly. **brush off** v Slang dismiss or ignore (someone). **brush up** v refresh one's knowledge of (a subject).

brush² n thick growth of shrubs.

brusque adj blunt or curt in manner or speech. **brusquely** adv **brusqueness** n

Brussels sprout n vegetable like a tiny cabbage.

brute n brutal person; animal other than man. ◆ adj wholly instinctive or physical, like that of an animal; without reason. **brutish** adj of or like an animal. **brutal** adj cruel and vicious. **brutally** adv **brutality** n **brutalize** v

BSc Bachelor of Science.

BSE bovine spongiform encepha-lopathy.

bubble n ball of air in a liquid. ◆ v form bubbles; move or flow with a gurgling sound. **bubbly** adj excited and lively; full of bubbles. **bubble over** v express an emotion freely.

bubonic plague [bew-bonn-ik] n acute infectious disease characterized by swellings.

buccaneer n pirate.

buck¹ n male of certain animals, such as the deer and hare. ◆ v (of a horse etc.) jump with legs stiff and back arched. **buck up** v make or become more cheerful.

buck² n Slang dollar.

buck³ n **pass the buck** Informal shift blame or responsibility onto someone else.

bucket n open-topped round container with a handle. **bucketful** n

bucket down v -eting, -eted rain heavily.

buckle n metal clasp for fastening a belt or strap. ◆ v fasten or be fastened with a buckle; (cause to) bend out of shape through pressure or heat. **buckle down** v apply oneself with determination.

buckram n coarse stiffened cloth.

buckshee adj Slang free.

buckteeth pl n projecting upper front teeth. **buck-toothed** adj

buckwheat n small black grain used for making flour.

bucolic [bew-koll-ik] adj rustic.

bud n swelling on a tree or plant that develops into a leaf or flower. ◆ v **budding, budded** produce buds; develop or grow, e.g. a budding actor.

Buddhism n eastern religion founded by Buddha. **Buddhist** n, adj

buddleia n shrub with purple or yellow flowers.

buddy n, pl **-dies** Informal friend.

budge v move slightly.

budgerigar n small brightly coloured Aust. bird.

budget n financial plan for a period of time; money allocated for a specific purpose. ◆ v -eting, -eted plan the expenditure of (money or time). ◆ adj cheap. **budgetary** adj

budgie n Informal short for BUDGERIGAR.

buff[1] adj dull yellowish-brown. ◆ v rub with soft material. **in the buff** Informal naked.

buff[2] n Informal expert on a given subject.

buffalo n type of cattle; bison. **buffalo jump** (formerly) place where bison were stampeded over a cliff.

buffer n something that lessens shock or protects from damaging impact, circumstances, etc.

buffet[1] [buff-ay] n refreshment bar; meal at which guests serve themselves.

buffet[2] [buff-it] v -feting, -feted knock against or about.

buffoon n clown or fool. **buffoonery** n

bug n small insect; Informal minor illness; small mistake in a computer program; concealed microphone. ◆ v **bugging, bugged** Informal irritate (someone); conceal a microphone in (a room or phone).

bugbear n thing that causes obsessive anxiety.

bugger n Taboo slang unpleasant or difficult person or thing; person who practises buggery. ◆ v Slang tire; practise buggery with. **buggery** n anal intercourse.

bugle n instrument like a small trumpet. **bugler** n

build v **building, built** make, construct, or form by joining parts or materials. ◆ n shape of the body. **builder** n **building** n structure with walls and a roof. **build-up** n gradual increase. **built-up** adj having many buildings.

bulb n glass part of an electric lamp; onion-shaped root which grows into a flower or plant. **bulbous** adj round and fat.

bulge n swelling on a normally flat surface; sudden increase in number. ◆ v swell outwards. **bulging** adj

bulimia n disorder characterized by compulsive overeating followed by vomiting.

bulk n great size or volume; main part. **in bulk** in large quantities. **bulky** adj

bulkhead n partition in a ship or airplane.

bull[1] n male of some animals, such as cattle, elephants, and whales. **bullock** n castrated bull. **bulldog** n sturdy thickset dog with a broad head and a muscular body. **bulldozer** n powerful tractor for moving earth. **bulldoze** v **bullfight** n public show in which a matador kills a bull. **bull's-eye** n central disc of a target.

bull[2] n papal decree.

bull[3] n Informal complete nonsense.

bullet n small piece of metal fired from a gun.

bulletin n short official report or announcement.

bullion n gold or silver in the form of bars.

bully n, pl **-lies** person who hurts, persecutes, or intimidates a weaker person. ◆ v **-lying, -lied** hurt, intimidate, or persecute (a weaker person).

bulrush n tall stiff reed.

bulwark n wall used as a fortification; person or thing acting as a defence.

bum¹ n Slang buttocks or anus.

bum² n Informal person who avoids work, idler.

bumble v speak, do, or move in a clumsy way. **bumbling** adj, n

bumblebee n large hairy bee.

bump v knock or strike with a jolt; travel in jerks and jolts. ◆ n (dull thud from) an impact or collision; raised uneven part. **bumper** n bar on the front and back of a vehicle to protect against damage. ◆ adj unusually large or abundant. **bump off** v Informal murder.

bumph, bumf n Informal official documents or forms.

bumpkin n awkward simple country person.

bumptious adj offensively self-assertive.

bun n small round cake; hair gathered into a bun shape.

bunch n number of things growing, fastened, or grouped together; group, e.g. a bunch of boys. ◆ v group or be grouped together in a bunch.

bundle n number of things gathered loosely together. ◆ v cause to go roughly or unceremoniously. **bundle up** v make into a bundle.

bung n stopper for a cask etc. ◆ v (foll. by up) Informal close with a bung.

bungalow n one-storey house.

bungle v spoil through incompetence. **bungler** n **bungling** adj, n

bunion n inflamed swelling on the big toe.

bunk¹ n narrow shelflike bed. **bunk bed** one of a pair of beds constructed one above the other.

bunk² n same as BUNKUM.

bunk³ n **do a bunk** Slang leave a place without telling anyone.

bunker n sandy hollow on a golf course; underground shelter; large storage container for coal etc.

bunkum n nonsense.

bunny n, pl **-nies** child's word for a rabbit.

Bunsen burner n gas burner used in laboratories.

bunting n decorative flags.

buoy n floating marker anchored in the sea. ◆ v prevent from sinking; encourage or hearten. **buoyant** adj able to float; cheerful or resilient.

buoyancy n

bur n same as BURR¹.

burble v make a bubbling sound; talk quickly and excitedly.

burden¹ n heavy load; something difficult to cope with. ◆ v put a burden on; oppress. **burdensome** adj

burden² n theme of a speech etc.

bureau n, pl **-reaus**, **-reaux** office that provides a service; writing desk with shelves and drawers.

bureaucracy n, pl **-cies** an administrative system based on complex rules and procedures; excessive adherence to complex procedures. **bureaucrat** n **bureaucratic** adj

burgeon v develop or grow rapidly.

burgh n Scottish borough.

burglar n person who enters a building to commit a crime, esp. theft. **burglary** n **burglarize** v

burgundy n type of French wine. ◆ adj dark purplish-red.

burial n burying of a dead body.

burlesque n artistic work which satirizes a subject by caricature.

burly adj **-lier**, **-liest** (of a person) broad and strong.

burn¹ v **burning**, **burnt** or **burned**. be or set on fire; destroy or be destroyed by fire; damage, injure, or mark by heat; feel strong emotion; to record data on (a compact disc). ◆ n injury or mark caused by fire or exposure to heat. **burning** adj intense; urgent.

burn² n Scot small stream.

burnish v make smooth and shiny by rubbing.

burp v, n Informal belch.

burr¹ n head of a plant with prickles or hooks.

burr² n soft trilling sound given to the letter (r) in some English dialects; whirring sound.

burrow n hole dug in the ground by a rabbit etc. ◆ v dig holes in the ground.

bursar n treasurer of a school, college, or university. **bursary** n scholarship.

burst v **bursting**, **burst** (cause to) break open or apart noisily and suddenly; come or go suddenly and forcibly; be full to the point of breaking open. ◆ n instance of breaking open suddenly; sudden and violent outbreak or occurrence. **burst**

into v give vent to (an emotion) suddenly.

bury v **burying, buried** place in a grave; place in the earth and cover with soil; conceal or hide.

bus n large motor vehicle for carrying passengers. ◆ v **bussing, bussed** travel or transport by bus.

busby n, pl **-bies** tall fur hat worn by certain soldiers.

bush n dense woody plant, smaller than a tree; wild uncultivated part of a country. **bushed** adj tired out; mentally disturbed from living in isolation. **bushy** adj (of hair) thick and shaggy. **bushbaby** n small tree-living mammal with large eyes. **bush pilot** pilot who flies in northern or remote areas.

bushel n unit of measure equal to eight gallons.

business n purchase and sale of goods and services; commercial establishment; trade or profession; proper concern or responsibility; affair, e.g. *it's a dreadful business*. **businesslike** adj **businessman, businesswoman** n

busker n street entertainer. **busk** v act as a busker.

bust[1] n woman's bosom; sculpture of the head and shoulders.

bust[2] *Informal* ◆ v **busting, bust** or **busted.** break; (of the police) raid (a place) or arrest (someone). ◆ adj broken. **go bust** become bankrupt.

bustle[1] v hurry with a show of activity or energy. ◆ n energetic and noisy activity. **bustling** adj

bustle[2] n *Hist* cushion worn by women to hold out their dress below the waist at the back.

busy adj **busier, busiest** actively employed; full of activity. ◆ v **busying, busied** keep (someone) busy. **busily** adv **busybody** n meddlesome or nosy person.

but conj contrary to expectation; in contrast; other than; without it happening. ◆ prep except. ◆ adv only. **but for** were it not for.

butane [bew-tane] n gas used for fuel.

butch adj *Slang* markedly or aggressively masculine.

butcher n person who sells the meat

of slaughtered animals; brutal murderer. ◆ v slaughter (animals) for meat; kill (people) brutally or indiscriminately. **butchery** n

butler n chief male servant.

butt[1] n thick end of something; unused end of a cigar or cigarette.

butt[2] n person or thing that is the target of ridicule.

butt[3] v strike with the head or horns. **butt in** v interrupt a conversation.

butt[4] n large cask.

butte n steep, often flat-topped hill in W Canada.

butter n edible fatty solid made from cream by churning. ◆ v put butter on. **buttery** adj **butter tart** small tart with sugar and butter filling. **butter up** v flatter.

buttercup n small yellow flower.

butterfingers n *Informal* person who drops things by mistake.

butterfly n insect with brightly coloured wings; swimming stroke in which both arms move together in a forward circular action.

buttermilk n sourish milk that remains after the butter has been separated from milk.

butterscotch n hard brittle toffee.

buttock n either of the two fleshy masses that form the human rump.

button n small hard object sewn to clothing to fasten it; knob that operates a piece of equipment when pressed. ◆ v fasten with buttons. **buttonhole** n slit in a garment through which a button is passed; flower worn on a lapel. ◆ v detain (someone) in conversation.

buttress n structure to support a wall. ◆ v support with a buttress.

buxom adj (of a woman) healthily plump and full-bosomed.

buy v **buying, bought** acquire by paying money for; bribe; *Slang* accept as true. ◆ n thing acquired through payment. **buyer** n customer; person employed to buy merchandise.

buzz n rapidly vibrating humming sound; *Informal* sense of excitement. ◆ v make a humming sound; be filled with an air of excitement. **buzzer** n **buzz around** v move around quickly and busily. **buzz word** jargon word which becomes fashionably popular.

buzzard *n* bird of prey of the hawk family.

by *adv* near; past. ◆ *prep* used to indicate the person responsible for a creative work, e.g. *an opera by Verdi*; used to indicate a means used, e.g. *I go home by bus*; past; not later than; during; near; placed between measurements, e.g. *a plank fourteen inches by seven.* **by and by** presently. **by and large** in general.

bye, bye-bye *interj Informal* goodbye.

by-election *n* election held during parliament to fill a vacant seat.

bygone *adj* past or former.

bylaw, bye-law *n* rule made by a local authority.

bypass *n* main road built to avoid a city; operation to divert blood flow away from a damaged part of the heart. ◆ *v* go round or avoid.

by-product *n* secondary or incidental product of a process.

bystander *n* person present but not involved.

byte *n Computers* group of bits processed as one unit of data.

byway *n* side road.

byword *n* person or thing regarded as a perfect example of something.

C c

C *Chem* carbon; Celsius; centigrade.

c. cent; century; circa; copyright.

Ca *Chem* calcium.

ca. circa.

CAA Canadian Automobile Association.

cab *n* taxi; enclosed driver's compartment on a train, truck, etc. **cabbie** *n Informal* taxi driver.

cabal [kab-**bal**] *n* small group of political plotters; secret plot.

cabaret [kab-a-ray] *n* dancing and singing show in a nightclub.

cabbage *n* vegetable with a large head of green leaves.

caber *n* tree trunk tossed in competition at Highland games.

cabin *n* compartment in a ship or aircraft; small hut. **cabin cruiser** motorboat with a cabin.

cabinet *n* piece of furniture with drawers or shelves; (C-) committee of senior government ministers. **cabinet-maker** *n* person who makes fine furniture.

cable *n* strong thick rope; bundle of wires that carries electricity or telegraph messages; telegram sent abroad. ◆ *v* send (a message) to (someone) by cable. **cable car** vehicle pulled up a steep slope by a moving cable. **cable television** television service conveyed by cable to subscribers.

caboodle *n* **the whole caboodle** *Informal* the whole lot.

cacao [kak-**kah**-oh] *n* tropical tree with seed pods from which chocolate and cocoa are made.

cache [**kash**] *n* hiding place, esp. for supplies and provisions; hidden store of weapons or treasure.

cachet [**kash**-shay] *n* prestige, distinction; distinctive mark.

cackle *v* laugh or chatter shrilly; (of a hen) squawk with shrill broken notes. ◆ *n* cackling noise.

cacophony [kak-**koff**-on-ee] *n* harsh discordant sound. **cacophonous** *adj*

cactus *n, pl* **-tuses, -ti** fleshy desert plant with spines but no leaves.

cad *n Old-fashioned* dishonourable man. **caddish** *adj*

cadaver [kad-**dav**-ver] *n* corpse. **cadaverous** *adj* deathly pale; gaunt.

caddie, caddy *n, pl* **-dies** person who carries a golfer's clubs. ◆ *v* **-dying, -died** act as a caddie.

caddis fly *n* insect whose larva (**caddis worm**) lives underwater in a protective case of sand and stones.

caddy *n, pl* **-dies** small box for tea.

cadence [**kade**-enss] *n* rise and fall in the pitch of a voice; close of a musical phrase.

cadenza *n* complex passage for a soloist in a piece of music.

cadet *n* young person training for the armed forces or police.

cadge *v* get (something) from someone by taking advantage of his or her generosity. **cadger** *n*

cadmium *n* bluish-white metallic element used in alloys.

cadre [**kah**-der] *n* (member of) a group of selected trained people forming the core of a military unit, Communist Party, etc.

caecum [**seek**-um] *n, pl* **-ca** pouch at the beginning of the large intestine.

Caesarean section [see-**zair**-ee-an] *n* surgical incision into the womb to deliver a baby.

caesium *n* same as CESIUM.

café *n* small or inexpensive restaurant serving light refreshments. **cafeteria** *n* self-service restaurant.

caffeine *n* stimulant found in tea and coffee.

caftan *n* same as KAFTAN.

cage *n* enclosure of bars or wires, for keeping animals or birds; enclosed platform of an elevator, esp. in a mine. **caged** *adj* kept in a cage.

cagey *adj* **cagier, cagiest** not frank; wary. **caginess** *n*

cagoule [kag-**gool**] *n* lightweight hooded waterproof jacket.

cahoots *pl n* **in cahoots** *Informal* conspiring together.

cairn *n* mound of stones erected as a memorial or marker. **cairn terrier** small rough-haired terrier.

cairngorm *n* yellow or brownish quartz gemstone.

caisson [**kay**-son] *n* watertight chamber used to carry out construction work under water.

cajole *v* persuade by flattery. **cajolery** *n*

cake *n* sweet food baked from a mixture of flour, eggs, etc.; flat compact mass. ◆ *v* form into a hardened mass or crust.

calabash *n* type of large gourd.

calamine *n* pink powder consisting chiefly of zinc oxide, used in skin lotions and ointments.

calamity *n, pl* **-ties** disaster. **calamitous** *adj*

calcify *v* **-fying, -fied** harden by the depositing of calcium salts. **calcification** *n*

calcium *n* silvery-white metallic element found in bones, teeth, limestone, and chalk.

calculate *v* solve (a problem) mathematically; estimate; plan deliberately. **calculable** *adj* **calculating** *adj* selfishly scheming. **calculation** *n* **calculator** *n* small electronic device for making calculations.

calculus *n, pl* **-luses** branch of mathematics dealing with infinitesimal changes to a variable number or quantity; *Pathol* stone.

Caledonian *adj* of Scotland.

calendar *n* chart showing a year divided into months, weeks, and days; system for determining the beginning, length, and division of years; schedule of events or appointments.

calendula *n* marigold.

calf¹ *n, pl* **calves** young cow, bull, elephant, whale, or seal; leather made from calf skin. **calve** *v* give birth to a calf. **calf love** adolescent infatuation.

calf² *n, pl* **calves** back of the leg between the ankle and knee.

calibre [**kal**-lib-ber] *n* ability, personal worth; diameter of the bore of a gun or of a shell or bullet. **calibrate** *v* mark the scale or check the accuracy of (a measuring instrument); measure the calibre of. **calibration** *n*

calico *n, pl* **-coes, -co** plain white cotton cloth.

caliph *n Hist* Muslim ruler.

call *v* name; shout to attract attention; telephone; ask to come; (often foll. by on) visit; arrange (a meeting, strike, etc.). ◆ *n* shout; animal's or bird's cry; telephone communication; visit; summons or invitation; need, demand. **caller** *n* **calling** *n* vocation or profession. **call box** *Brit* telephone booth. **call for** *v* need, demand. **call off** *v* cancel. **call up** *v* summon to serve in the armed forces; evoke.

calligraphy *n* (art of) beautiful handwriting. **calligrapher** *n*

calliper *n* (usu. pl.) metal splint for the leg; instrument for measuring diameters.

callisthenics *pl n* light keep-fit exercises. **callisthenic** *adj*

callous *adj* showing no concern for other people's feelings. **calloused** *adj* covered in calluses. **callously** *adv* **callousness** *n*

callow *adj* immature and inexperienced.

callus *n, pl* **-luses** area of thick hardened skin.

calm *adj* not showing or feeling agitation or excitement; not ruffled by the wind; windless. ◆ *n* peaceful state. ◆ *v* make or become calm. **calmly** *adv*

calmness n

calorie n unit of heat; unit of measurement for the energy value of food. **calorific** adj of calories or heat.

calumny n, pl **-nies** slander.

calypso n, pl **-sos** West Indian song with improvised topical lyrics.

calyx n, pl **calyxes, calyces** outer leaves that protect the bud of a flower.

cam n device which converts rotary motion to to-and-fro motion. **camshaft** n part of an engine consisting of a rod to which cams are fixed.

camaraderie n comradeship.

camber n slight upward curve to the centre of a surface.

cambric n fine white-linen fabric.

camcorder n combined portable video camera and recorder.

came v past tense of COME.

camel n humped mammal of Asia and Africa. ◆ adj fawn-coloured.

camellia [kam-**meal**-ya] n evergreen ornamental shrub with roselike white, pink, or red flowers.

Camembert [kam-**mem**-bare] n soft creamy French cheese.

cameo n, pl **cameos** brooch or ring with a profile head carved in relief; small, brief part in a film or television play performed by a well-known actor or actress.

camera n apparatus used for taking photographs. **in camera** in private. **cameraman** n photographer, esp. for television or cinema.

camisole n woman's bodice-like garment.

camomile n aromatic plant, used to make herbal tea.

camouflage [kam-**moo**-flahzh] n use of natural surroundings or artificial aids to conceal or disguise something. ◆ v conceal or disguise by camouflage.

camp[1] n (place for) temporary lodgings consisting of tents, huts, or cabins; group supporting a particular doctrine. ◆ v stay in a camp. **camper** n

camp[2] adj Informal homosexual; consciously artificial or affected. **camp it up** Informal behave in a camp way.

campaign n series of coordinated activities designed to achieve a goal. ◆ v conduct or take part in a campaign.

campanology n art of ringing bells. **campanologist** n

campanula n plant with blue or white bell-shaped flowers.

camphor n aromatic crystalline substance used medicinally and in mothballs. **camphorated** adj

campion n white or pink wild flower.

campus n, pl **-puses** grounds of a college or university.

can[1] v, past **could** be able; be allowed.

can[2] n metal container for liquid or foods. ◆ v **canning, canned** put (something) in a can. **canned** adj preserved in a can; (of music etc.) prerecorded. **cannery** n factory where food is canned.

Canada Day July 1st, anniversary of establishment of Confederation in 1867.

Canada goose large greyish-brown N American goose.

Canada jay N American bird with grey, white-tipped feathers.

Canadarm n extension of spacecraft to fetch and deploy objects.

Canadian n, adj (native) of Canada. **Canadianize** v make or become Canadian.

canal n artificial watercourse; duct in the body.

canapé [kan-nap-pay] n small piece of bread or toast spread with a savoury topping.

canary n, pl **-ries** small yellow songbird often kept as a pet.

canasta n card game like rummy, played with two packs.

cancan n lively high-kicking dance performed by a female group.

cancel v **-celling, -celled** postpone indefinitely; cross out; mark (a cheque or stamp) to prevent reuse. **cancellation** n **cancel out** v counterbalance or neutralize.

cancer n serious disease caused by a malignant growth or tumour; malignant growth or tumour. **cancerous** adj

candela [kan-**dee**-la] n unit of luminous intensity.

candelabrum n, pl **-bra** ornamental candleholder for several candles.

candid adj frank and outspoken. **candidly** adv

candidate n person seeking a job or

position; person taking an examination. **candidacy, candidature** n

candle n stick of wax enclosing a wick, which is burned to produce light. **candlestick** n holder for a candle. **candlewick** n cotton fabric with a tufted surface.

candour, candor n frankness.

candy n, pl **-dies** shaped piece of food consisting mainly of sugar. **candied** adj coated with sugar. **candyfloss** n light fluffy mass of spun sugar on a stick. **candy-striped** adj having coloured stripes on a white background.

cane n stem of the bamboo or similar plant; slender walking stick; flexible rod used to beat someone. ◆ v beat with a cane.

canine [kay-nine] adj of or like a dog. **canine tooth** sharp pointed tooth between the incisors and the molars.

canister n metal container.

canker n ulceration or ulcerous disease; something that spreads and corrupts. ◆ v infect or become infected with canker. **cankerous** adj

cannabis n drug obtained from the hemp plant.

cannelloni pl n tubular pieces of pasta filled with meat etc.

cannibal n person who eats human flesh; animal that eats others of its own kind. **cannibalism** n **cannibalize** v use parts from (one machine) to repair another.

cannon¹ n large gun on wheels. **cannonade** n continuous heavy gunfire. **cannonball** n heavy metal ball fired from a cannon.

cannon² n billiard stroke in which the cue ball hits two balls successively. ◆ v make this stroke; rebound, collide.

cannot can not.

canny adj **-nier, -niest** shrewd and cautious. **cannily** adv

canoe n light narrow boat propelled by a paddle or paddles. **canoeing** n **canoeist** n

canola n rapeseed oil.

canon¹ n Church law or decree; general rule or principle; set of writings accepted as genuine. **canonical** adj **canonize** v declare (a person) officially to be a saint.

canonization n

canon² n priest serving in a cathedral.

canoodle v Slang kiss and cuddle.

canopy n, pl **-pies** covering above a throne, bed, etc.; any large or wide covering. **canopied** adj

cant¹ n insincere talk; specialized vocabulary of a particular group.

cant² v, n tilt or slope.

can't can not.

cantaloupe, cantaloup n kind of melon with sweet orange flesh.

cantankerous adj bad-tempered.

cantata [kan-tah-ta] n musical work consisting of arias, duets, and choruses.

canteen n restaurant attached to a workplace; case of cutlery.

canter n horse's gait between a trot and a gallop. ◆ v (cause to) move at a canter.

canticle n short hymn with words from the Bible.

cantilever n beam or girder fixed at one end only.

canto [kan-toe] n, pl **-tos** main division of a long poem.

canton n political division of a country, esp. Switzerland.

cantonment [kan-toon-ment] n military camp.

cantor n man employed to lead services in a synagogue.

Canuck n, adj Informal Canadian.

canvas n heavy coarse cloth used for sails and tents, and for painting on; a painting on canvas.

canvass v try to get votes or support (from); determine the opinions of (people) by conducting a survey. ◆ n canvassing.

canyon n deep steep-sided valley.

cap n soft close-fitting covering for the head; small lid; small explosive device used in a toy gun. ◆ v **capping, capped** cover or top with something; select (a player) for a national team; impose an upper limit on (a tax); outdo.

capable adj (foll. by of) having the ability or skill to do something; competent and efficient. **capably** adv **capability** n

capacity n, pl **-ties** ability to contain, absorb, or hold; maximum amount that can be contained or produced;

physical or mental ability; position or function. **capacious** *adj* roomy.

capacitance *n* (measure of) the ability of a system to store electric charge.

capacitor *n* device for storing electric charge.

caparisoned [kap-**par**-riss-sond] *adj* magnificently decorated.

cape¹ *n* short cloak.

cape² *n* large piece of land jutting into the sea.

capelin [kap-**ill**-in] *n* small food fish of the N Atlantic and Pacific.

caper¹ *n* high-spirited prank. ◆ *v* skip or dance about.

caper² *n* pickled flower bud of a Mediterranean shrub used in sauces.

capercaillie, capercailzie [kap-per-**kale**-yee] *n* large black European grouse.

capillary [kap-**pill**-a-ree] *n*, *pl* **-laries** very fine blood vessel.

capital *n* chief town of a country; accumulated wealth; wealth used to produce more wealth; large letter, as used at the beginning of a name or sentence; top part of a pillar. ◆ *adj* involving or punishable by death; chief or principal; *Old-fashioned* excellent. **capitalism** *n* economic system based on the private ownership of industry. **capitalist** *adj* based on or supporting capitalism. ◆ *n* supporter of capitalism; person who owns capital. **capitalize** *v* convert into or provide with capital; write or print (text) in capital letters. **capitalize on** *v* take advantage of (a situation).

capitation *n* charge or grant of a fixed amount per person.

capitulate *v* surrender on agreed terms. **capitulation** *n*

capon [**kay**-pon] *n* castrated cock fowl fattened for eating.

cappuccino [kap-poo-**cheen**-oh] *n*, *pl* **-nos** coffee with steamed milk.

caprice [kap-**reess**] *n* whim. **capricious** *adj* changeable. **capriciously** *adv*

capsicum *n* kind of pepper used as a vegetable or as a spice.

capsize *v* overturn accidentally.

capstan *n* rotating cylinder on which a rope etc. is wound.

capsule *n* soluble case containing a dose of medicine; seed vessel of a plant; detachable crew compartment of a spacecraft.

captain *n* leader of a team or group; commander of a ship or civil aircraft; middle-ranking naval officer; junior officer in the armed forces. ◆ *v* be captain of. **captaincy** *n*

caption *n* title or explanation accompanying an illustration. ◆ *v* provide with a caption.

captious *adj* tending to make trivial criticisms. **captiously** *adv* **captiousness** *n*

captivate *v* fascinate or enchant. **captivating** *adj* **captivation** *n*

captive *n* person kept in confinement. ◆ *adj* kept in confinement; (of an audience) unable to leave. **captivity** *n*

captor *n* person who captures a person or animal.

capture *v* take prisoner; gain control over; succeed in representing (something elusive) artistically. ◆ *n* capturing.

capybara *n* very large S American rodent.

car *n* motor vehicle designed to carry a small number of people; passenger compartment of a cable car, elevator, etc.; railway carriage. **car park** area or building reserved for parking cars.

carafe [kar-**raff**] *n* glass bottle for serving water or wine.

caramel *n* chewy candy made from sugar and milk; burnt sugar used for colouring and flavouring food. **caramelize** *v* turn into caramel.

carapace *n* hard upper shell of tortoises and crustaceans.

carat *n* unit of weight of precious stones; measure of the purity of gold in an alloy.

caravan *n* group travelling together for safety in the East; *Brit* large enclosed vehicle for living in, able to be towed by an automobile or horse.

caraway *n* plant whose seeds are used as a spice.

carbide *n* compound of carbon with a metal.

carbine *n* light automatic rifle.

carbohydrate *n* any of a large group of energy-producing compounds in food, such as sugars and starches.

carbolic, carbolic acid *n* disinfectant derived from coal tar.

carbon n nonmetallic element occurring as charcoal, graphite, and diamond, found in all organic matter. **carbonate** n salt or ester of carbonic acid. **carbonated** adj containing carbon dioxide. **carbonize** v turn into carbon as a result of heating; coat with carbon. **carbon copy** copy made with carbon paper; very similar person or thing. **carbon dioxide** colourless gas exhaled by people and animals. **carbonic acid** weak acid formed from carbon dioxide and water. **carbon paper** paper covered with a dark waxy pigment, used to make a duplicate of something as it is typed or written.

Carborundum n ® compound of silicon and carbon, used for grinding and polishing.

carboy n large bottle with a protective casing.

carbuncle n inflamed boil; rounded garnet cut without facets.

carburetor n device which mixes gasoline and air in an internal-combustion engine.

carcass, carcase n dead body or skeleton of an animal.

carcinogen n substance producing cancer. **carcinogenic** adj **carcinoma** n malignant tumour.

card[1] n piece of thick stiff paper or cardboard used for identification, reference, or sending greetings or messages; one of a set of cards with a printed pattern, used for playing games; small rectangle of stiff plastic for use as a credit card or banker's card; Old-fashioned witty or eccentric person. ◆ pl any card game, or card games in general. **cardboard** n thin stiff board made from paper pulp. **cardsharp, cardsharper** n professional card player who cheats.

card[2] n machine or tool for combing wool before spinning.

cardiac adj of the heart. **cardiograph** n instrument which records heart movements. **cardiogram** n record of heart movements. **cardiology** n study of the heart and its diseases. **cardiologist** n **cardiovascular** adj of the heart and the blood vessels.

cardigan n knitted jacket.

cardinal n one of the high-ranking clergymen of the RC Church who elect the Pope and act as his counsellors. ◆ adj chief, principal; deep red. **cardinal number** number denoting quantity but not order in a group, for example one, two, or three. **cardinal point** one of the four main points of the compass.

care v be concerned; have regard or liking for; have a desire for; look after. ◆ n serious attention; protection or supervision; worry, anxiety; caution. **careful** adj **carefully** adv **carefulness** n **careless** adj **carelessly** adv **carelessness** n **carefree** adj without worry or responsibility. **caretaker** n person employed to look after a place. **careworn** adj showing signs of worry.

careen v tilt over to one side.

career n profession or occupation; course through life. ◆ v rush in an uncontrolled way. **careerist** n person who seeks advancement by any possible means.

caress n gentle affectionate touch or embrace. ◆ v touch gently and affectionately.

caret [kar-rett] n symbol (ʌ) showing the place in written or printed matter where something is to be inserted.

cargo n, pl -goes goods carried by a ship, aircraft, etc. **cargo pants, trousers** pl n loose trousers with a large pocket on each leg.

caribou n N American reindeer.

caricature n likeness of a person which exaggerates features for comic effect. ◆ v portray by a caricature.

caries [care-reez] n tooth decay.

carillon [kar-rill-yon] n set of bells played by keyboard or mechanically; tune played on this.

carmine adj vivid red.

carnage n slaughter.

carnal adj of a sexual or sensual nature. **carnal knowledge** sexual intercourse.

carnation n cultivated plant with fragrant white, pink, or red flowers.

carnival n festive period with processions and entertainment.

carnivore n flesh-eating animal. **carnivorous** adj

carob n Mediterranean tree with edible pods used as a chocolate substitute.

carol n joyful religious song sung at Christmas. ◆ v -olling, -olled sing carols; sing joyfully.

carotid [kar-**rot**-id] *adj, n* (of) one of the two arteries supplying blood to the head.

carouse *v* have a merry drinking party. **carousal** *n* merry drinking party.

carousel [kar-roo-**sell**] *n* revolving conveyor; merry-go-round.

carp[1] *n* freshwater fish.

carp[2] *v* complain or find fault.

carpel *n* female reproductive organ of a flowering plant.

carpenter *n* person who makes or repairs wooden structures. **carpentry** *n*

carpet *n* heavy fabric for covering a floor. ♦ *v* **carpeting, carpeted** cover with a carpet. **on the carpet** *Informal* being reprimanded.

carpus *n, pl* **-pi** set of eight small bones forming the wrist.

carriage *n* one of the sections of a train for passengers; person's bearing; four-wheeled horse-drawn vehicle; moving part of a machine that supports and shifts another part; act or cost of conveying goods. **carriageway** *n* part of a road along which traffic passes in one direction.

carrier *n* person or thing that carries something; person or animal that does not show symptoms of a disease but can transmit it to others. **carrier pigeon** homing pigeon used for carrying messages.

carrion *n* dead and rotting flesh.

carrot *n* long tapering orange root vegetable; incentive. **carroty** *adj* reddish.

carry *v* **-rying, -ried** take (something) from one place to another, transport; have on one's person; transmit; have as a penalty or result; bear (the head, body, etc.) in a specified manner; win acceptance for (a bill or motion); (of sound) travel over a distance. **carryall** *n* large strong travelling bag. **carry on** *v* continue or persevere; *Informal* fuss unnecessarily. **carry out** *v* perform or complete.

cart *n* open two-wheeled horse-drawn vehicle for carrying goods or passengers. ♦ *v* carry in a cart; carry with effort. **carthorse** *n* large heavily built horse. **cartwheel** *n* sideways somersault supported by the arms

with the legs outstretched; large spoked wheel of a cart.

carte blanche *n French* complete authority.

cartel *n* association of competing firms formed to fix prices.

cartilage [kar-**till**-ij] *n* firm elastic tissue forming part of the skeleton. **cartilaginous** *adj*

cartography *n* map making. **cartographer** *n* **cartographic** *adj*

carton *n* container made of cardboard or waxed paper.

cartoon *n* humorous or satirical drawing; sequence of these telling a story; film made by photographing a series of drawings which give the illusion of movement when projected; preliminary sketch for a painting. **cartoonist** *n*

cartridge *n* casing containing an explosive charge for a firearm; sealed container of film, tape, etc.; unit in the pick-up of a record player holding the stylus. **cartridge paper** strong thick paper.

carve *v* cut; form (an object or design) by cutting, esp. in stone or wood; slice (meat) into pieces. **carving** *n*

caryatid [kar-ree-**at**-id] *n* supporting column in the shape of a female figure.

Casanova *n* promiscuous man.

cascade *n* waterfall; something that flows or falls like a waterfall. ♦ *v* fall in cascades.

case[1] *n* instance or example; matter for discussion; condition or state of affairs; set of arguments for an action or cause; person attended to by a doctor, solicitor, or social worker; lawsuit; grounds for a lawsuit; *Grammar* form of a noun, pronoun, or adjective showing its relation to other words in the sentence. **in case** so as to allow for eventualities.

case[2] *n* container or protective covering; container and its contents. ♦ *v Slang* inspect (a building) with the intention of burgling it. **case-harden** *v* harden (an iron alloy) by carbonizing the surface. **case-hardened** *adj* made callous by experience.

casement *n* window that is hinged on one side.

cash *n* banknotes and coins. ♦ *v* obtain

cash for. **cash in on** v Informal gain profit or advantage from. **cash register** till that displays and adds the prices of the goods sold.

cashew n edible tropical American nut.

cashier[1] n person responsible for handling cash in a bank or shop.

cashier[2] v dismiss with dishonour from the armed forces.

cashmere n fine soft wool; fabric made from this.

casing n protective case or covering.

casino n, pl **-nos** public building or room where gambling is done.

cask n barrel for holding alcoholic drink.

casket n small box for valuables; coffin.

cassava n flour obtained from the roots of a tropical American plant, used to make tapioca.

casserole n covered dish in which food is cooked and served; food cooked in this way. ◆ v cook in a casserole.

cassette n plastic case containing a reel of film or magnetic tape.

cassock n long tunic worn by a clergyman.

cassowary n, pl **-waries** large flightless bird of Australia and New Guinea.

cast n actors in a play or film collectively; something shaped by a mould while molten; mould used to shape something; rigid casing to help set a broken bone; quality or nature; slight squint in the eye. ◆ v **casting**, **cast** select (actors) to play parts in a play or film; give (a vote); let fall, shed; shape (molten material) in a mould; throw with force; direct (a glance). **castaway** n shipwrecked person. **casting vote** deciding vote used by the chairman when the votes on each side are equal. **cast-iron** adj made of a hard but brittle type of iron; rigid or unchallengeable. **cast-off** adj, n discarded (garment).

castanets pl n two small curved pieces of hollow wood clicked together in the hand, used esp. by Spanish dancers.

caste n one of the hereditary classes into which Hindu society is divided; social rank.

castellated adj having battlements.

caster sugar n Brit finely ground white sugar.

castigate v criticize or scold severely. **castigation** n

castle n large fortified building; rook in chess.

castor n small swivelled wheel fixed to a piece of furniture to allow it to be moved easily.

castor oil n oil obtained from an Indian plant, used as a lubricant and purgative.

castrate v remove the testicles of; deprive of vigour or masculinity. **castration** n

casual adj appearing unconcerned; (of work or workers) occasional; shallow or superficial; for informal wear; happening by chance. **casually** adv

casualty n, pl **-ties** person killed or injured in an accident or war; anything lost or destroyed.

casuistry n reasoning that is misleading or oversubtle. **casuist** n

cat n small domesticated furry mammal; related wild mammal, such as the lion or tiger; Informal spiteful woman. **catty** adj Informal spiteful. **catkin** n drooping flower spike of certain trees. **catcall** n derisive whistle or cry. **catgut** n strong cord used to string musical instruments. **catnap** v, n doze. **cat's paw** person used as a tool by another. **catwalk** n narrow pathway or platform.

cataclysm [kat-a-kliz-zum] n violent upheaval; disaster, such as an earthquake. **cataclysmic** adj

catacombs [kat-a-kooms] pl n underground burial place consisting of tunnels with recesses for tombs.

catafalque [kat-a-falk] n raised platform on which a body lies in state before or during a funeral.

catalepsy n trancelike state in which the body is rigid. **cataleptic** adj

catalogue n book containing details of items for sale; systematic list of items. ◆ v make such a list; enter (an item) in a catalogue.

catalyst n substance that speeds up a chemical reaction without itself changing. **catalyse** v speed up (a chemical reaction) by a catalyst.

catalysis n **catalytic** adj

catamaran n boat with twin parallel hulls.

catapult n Brit slingshot; device used to launch aircraft from a warship. ◆ v launch as if from a catapult.

cataract n eye disease in which the lens becomes opaque; opaque area of an eye; waterfall.

catarrh [kat-**tar**] n inflammation of a mucous membrane causing a flow of mucus. **catarrhal** adj

catastrophe [kat-**ass**-trof-fee] n great and sudden disaster. **catastrophic** adj

catch v **catching, caught** seize or capture; surprise, e.g. catch someone red-handed; hit unexpectedly; be in time for; see or hear by chance or with difficulty; contract (a disease); understand; entangle or become entangled; check (one's breath) suddenly; begin to burn. ◆ n catching; thing caught; device that fastens; Informal concealed or unforeseen difficulty. **catch it** Informal be punished. **catching** adj infectious. **catchy** adj (of a tune) pleasant and easily remembered. **catchment area** area served by a particular school or hospital. **catch on** v Informal become popular; understand. **catch out** v Informal trap (someone) in an error or lie. **catch phrase, catchword** n well-known and frequently used phrase. **catch 22** inescapable dilemma.

catechism [kat-ti-kiz-zum] n doctrine of a Christian Church in a series of questions and answers.

category n, pl **-ries** class or group. **categorical** adj absolute or unconditional. **categorically** adv **categorize** v put in a category. **categorization** n

cater v provide what is needed, esp. food or services. **caterer** n

caterpillar n wormlike larva of a moth or butterfly; ® endless track, driven by cogged wheels, used to propel a heavy vehicle.

caterwaul v wail, yowl.

catharsis [kath-**thar**-siss] n, pl **-ses** relief of strong suppressed emotions. **cathartic** adj

cathedral n principal church of a diocese.

Catherine wheel n rotating firework.

catheter [kath-it-er] n tube inserted into a body cavity to drain fluid.

cathode n negative electrode, by which electrons leave a circuit. **cathode rays** stream of electrons from a cathode in a vacuum tube.

catholic adj (of tastes or interests) covering a wide range. ◆ n, adj (C-) (member) of the Roman Catholic Church. **Catholicism** n

cattle pl n domesticated cows, bulls, or oxen.

Caucasoid adj of the light-skinned racial group of mankind.

caucus n, pl **-cuses** local committee or faction of a political party; political meeting to decide future plans.

caught v past of CATCH.

cauldron n large pot used for boiling.

cauliflower n type of cabbage with an edible white flower head.

caulk v stop up (cracks, esp. in a ship) with filler.

causal adj of or being a cause; of cause and effect. **causally** adv **causality, causation** n relationship of cause and effect.

cause n aim or principle supported by a person or group; something that produces an effect; reason or motive. ◆ v be the cause of.

cause célèbre [kawz sill-**leb**-ra] n, pl **causes célèbres** [kawz sill-**leb**-ra] controversial legal case or issue.

causeway n raised road or path across water or marshland.

caustic adj capable of burning by chemical action; sarcastic or cutting. ◆ n caustic substance. **caustically** adv

cauterize v burn (body tissue) with heat or a chemical to treat a wound. **cauterization** n

caution n attention to safety; warning. ◆ v warn. **cautionary** adj warning. **cautious** adj showing caution. **cautiously** adv

cavalcade n procession of people on horseback or in cars.

cavalier adj arrogant, offhand. ◆ n (C-) supporter of Charles I in the English Civil War.

cavalry n, pl **-ries** mounted troops.

cave n large hole in a hill or cliff. **caving** n sport of exploring caves. **cave in** v collapse inwards; give in. **caveman** n prehistoric cave dweller.

caveat [kav-vee-at] n warning.

cavern n large cave. **cavernous** adj

caviar, caviare n salted sturgeon roe.

cavil v -illing, -illed make petty objections. ◆ n petty objection.

cavity n, pl -ties hole; decayed area in a tooth.

cavort v prance, caper.

caw n cry of a crow, rook, or raven. ◆ v make this cry.

cayenne pepper, cayenne n hot red spice made from capsicum seeds.

cayman n, pl -mans S American reptile similar to an alligator.

CB Citizens' Band.

CBC Canadian Broadcasting Corporation.

CBE Commander of the Order of the British Empire.

cc cubic centimetre(s).

Cd Chem cadmium.

CD compact disc.

CD-ROM compact disc read-only memory.

CDT Central Daylight Time.

cease v bring or come to an end. **ceaseless** adj **ceaselessly** adv **ceasefire** n order to stop firing; temporary truce.

cedar n large evergreen tree; its wood.

cede v surrender (territory or legal rights).

cedilla n hooklike symbol placed under a letter c to show that it is pronounced s, not k.

ceilidh [kay-lee] n informal social gathering for singing and dancing, esp. in Scotland.

ceiling n inner upper surface of a room; upper limit set on something.

celandine n wild plant with yellow flowers.

celebrate v hold festivities to mark (a happy event, anniversary, etc.); perform (a religious ceremony). **celebrated** adj famous. **celebration** n **celebrant** n person who performs a religious ceremony. **celebrity** n famous person; fame.

celeriac [sill-ler-ee-ak] n kind of celery with a large turnip-like root.

celerity [sill-ler-rit-tee] n swiftness.

celery n vegetable with crisp juicy edible stalks.

celestial adj heavenly; of the sky.

celibate adj unmarried or abstaining from sex, esp. because of a religious vow of chastity. ◆ n celibate person. **celibacy** n

cell n smallest unit of an organism that is able to function independently; small room for a prisoner, monk, or nun; small compartment; small group operating as the core of a larger organization; device which generates electrical energy from a chemical reaction. **cellular** adj of or consisting of cells; woven with an open texture. **cell phone, cellular phone** telephone operating by radio communication via a network of transmitters each serving a small area.

cellar n underground room for storage; stock of wine.

cello [chell-oh] n, pl -los low-pitched instrument of the violin family. **cellist** n

Cellophane n ® thin transparent cellulose sheeting used as wrapping.

celluloid n plastic formerly used to make photographic film; cinema or films generally.

cellulose n main constituent of plant cell walls, used in making plastics, paper, etc.

Celsius adj of the temperature scale in which water freezes at 0° and boils at 100°.

Celt [kelt] n person who speaks a Celtic language. **Celtic** [kel-tik or sel-tik] n group of languages including Gaelic and Welsh. ◆ adj of the Celts or their languages.

cement n fine grey powder mixed with water and sand to make mortar or concrete; adhesive; material used to fill teeth. ◆ v join, bind, or cover with cement; make (a relationship) stronger.

cemetery n, pl -teries burial ground not attached to a church.

cenotaph n monument honouring soldiers who died in a war.

censer n container for burning incense.

censor v ban or cut parts of (a film, book, etc.) considered obscene or otherwise unacceptable. ◆ n official employed to examine and censor films, books, etc. **censorship** n **censorial** adj **censorious** adj harshly critical.

censure *n* severe disapproval. ◆ *v* criticize severely.

census *n, pl* **-suses** official count, esp. of population.

cent *n* hundredth part of a monetary unit such as the dollar.

centaur *n* mythical creature resembling a horse with the head, arms, and torso of a man.

centenary [sen-teen-a-ree] *n, pl* **-naries** 100th anniversary. **centenarian** *n* person at least 100 years old. **centennial** *n* centenary.

centigrade *adj* same as CELSIUS.

centigram, centigramme *n* hundredth part of a gram.

centilitre *n* hundredth part of a litre.

centimetre *n* hundredth part of a metre.

centipede *n* small wormlike creature with many legs.

central *adj* of, at, or forming the centre; main or principal. **centrally** *adv* **centrality** *n* **centralism** *n* principle of central control of a country or organization. **centralize** *v* bring under central control. **centralization** *n* **central heating** system for heating a building from one central source of heat.

centre, center *n* middle point or part; place for a specified activity; political party or group favouring moderation; *Sport* player who plays in the middle of the field. ◆ *v* move towards, put, or be at the centre. **centrist** *n, adj* (person) favouring political moderation. **centrifugal** *adj* moving away from the centre. **centrifuge** *n* machine which separates substances by centrifugal force. **centripetal** *adj* moving towards the centre. **centre on** *v* have as a main theme.

centurion *n* Roman officer commanding 100 men.

century *n, pl* **-ries** period of 100 years; cricket score of 100.

CEO chief executive officer.

cephalopod [seff-a-loh-pod] *n* sea mollusc with a head and tentacles, such as the octopus.

ceramic *n* hard brittle material made by firing clay; object made of this. ◆ *pl* art of producing ceramic objects. ◆ *adj*

made of ceramic; of ceramics.

cereal *n* grass plant with edible grain, such as wheat or rice; this grain; breakfast food made from this grain.

cerebral [ser-rib-ral] *adj* of the brain; intellectual. **cerebrum** *n* main part of the human brain.

ceremony *n, pl* **-nies** formal act or ritual; formally polite behaviour. **ceremonial** *adj, n* **ceremonially** *adv* **ceremonious** *adj* **ceremoniously** *adv*

cerise [ser-reess] *adj* cherry-red.

certain *adj* sure, without doubt; reliable or unerring; some but not much. **certainly** *adv* **certainty** *n* state of being sure; thing sure to happen.

certificate *n* official document stating the details of a birth, death, etc.

certify *v* **-fying, -fied** declare formally or officially; declare (someone) legally insane. **certifiable** *adj* **certification** *n*

certitude *n* confidence, certainty.

cerulean [ser-rule-ee-an] *adj* of a deep blue colour.

cervix *n, pl* **cervixes, cervices** narrow entrance of the womb; neck. **cervical** [ser-vik-kl *or* ser-vie-kl] *adj*

cesium, caesium *n* silvery-white metallic element used in photocells.

cessation *n* ceasing.

cesspool, cesspit *n* covered tank or pit for sewage.

cetacean [sit-tay-shun] *n, adj* (member) of the whale family.

cf. compare.

CFC chlorofluorocarbon.

CFL Canadian Football League.

CGI computer-generated image(s).

ch. chapter; church.

chafe *v* make or become sore or worn by rubbing; make or be impatient or annoyed.

chafer *n* large beetle.

chaff *n* grain husks; chopped hay and straw used to feed cattle; light-hearted teasing. ◆ *v* tease good-naturedly.

chagrin [shag-grin] *n* annoyance and embarrassment. ◆ *v* annoy and embarrass.

chain *n* flexible length of connected metal links; connected series of things or events; group of shops, hotels, etc. owned by one firm; unit of length equal to 22 yards. ◆ *v* confine or fasten with or as if with a chain. **chain reaction** series of events, each of which causes the next. **chain-smoke** *v* smoke (cigarettes) continuously. **chain-smoker** *n*

chair *n* seat with a back, for one person; official position of authority; person holding this; professorship. ◆ *v* preside over (a meeting). **chair lift** series of chairs on a cable for carrying people, esp. skiers, up a slope. **chairman, chairperson, chairwoman** *n* person who presides over a meeting.

chaise [shaze] *n* light horse-drawn carriage.

chaise longue [long] *n* sofa with a back and single armrest.

chalcedony [kal-sed-don-ee] *n*, *pl* **-nies** variety of quartz.

chalet *n* kind of Swiss wooden house; house like this, used as a holiday home.

chalice [chal-liss] *n* large goblet.

chalk *n* soft white rock consisting of calcium carbonate; piece of this, often coloured, used for drawing and writing on blackboards. ◆ *v* mark with chalk. **chalky** *adj*

challenge *v* invite (someone) to take part in a contest or fight; call (something) into question; order (someone) to stop and be identified; be difficult but stimulating to. ◆ *n* act of challenging. **challenged** *adj* disabled as specified: *physically challenged; mentally challenged.* **challenger** *n*

chamber *n* hall used for formal meetings; legislative or judicial assembly; compartment or cavity; *Obs* bedroom. ◆ *pl* set of rooms used as offices by a barrister. **chamberlain** *n* official who manages the household of a king or nobleman. **chambermaid** *n* woman employed to clean bedrooms in a hotel. **chamber music** classical music to be played by a small group of players. **chamber pot** bowl for urine, formerly used in bedrooms.

chameleon [kam-meal-yon] *n* small lizard that changes colour according to its surroundings.

chamfer [cham-fer] *v* bevel the edge of.

chamois [sham-wah] *n*, *pl* **-ois** small mountain antelope; [sham-ee] soft leather; [sham-ee] cloth of this.

chamomile [kam-mo-mile] *n* same as CAMOMILE.

champ[1] *v* chew noisily; be impatient.

champ[2] *n* short for CHAMPION.

champagne *n* sparkling white French wine.

champion *n* overall winner of a competition; someone who defends a person or cause. ◆ *v* support. ◆ *adj* excellent. **championship** *n*

chance *n* likelihood; opportunity; risk, gamble; unpredictable element that causes things to happen one way rather than another. ◆ *v* risk; happen by chance. ◆ *adj* accidental. **chancy** *adj* risky.

chancel *n* part of a church containing the altar and choir.

chancellor *n* state or legal officer of high rank; head of a university. **chancellorship** *n*

Chancery *n* division of the British High Court of Justice.

chandelier [shan-dill-eer] *n* hanging branched holder for lights.

chandler *n* dealer, esp. in ships' supplies.

change *n* becoming different; variety or novelty; different set; balance received when the amount paid is more than the cost of a purchase; coins of low value. ◆ *v* make or become different; interchange or exchange; exchange (money) for its equivalent in a smaller denomination or different currency; put different clothes or coverings on; leave one vehicle and board another. **changeable** *adj* changing often. **changeling** *n* child believed to have been exchanged by fairies for another.

channel *n* band of broadcasting frequencies; means of access or communication; broad strait connecting two areas of sea; course along which a river, shipping, etc. moves; groove. ◆ *v* **-nelling, -nelled** direct or convey through a channel.

chant *v* sing or utter (a psalm or slogan). ◆ *n* rhythmic or repetitious slogan; psalm with a short simple melody.

chanter *n* (on bagpipes) pipe on which the melody is played.

chaos *n* complete disorder. **chaotic** *adj* **chaotically** *adv*

chap *n* Informal man or boy.

chapatti, chapati *n* (in Indian

cookery) flat thin unleavened bread.

chapel *n* place of worship with its own altar, within a church; similar place of worship in a large house or institution; Nonconformist place of worship; section of a trade union in the print industry.

chaperone [**shap**-per-rone] *n* older person who accompanies and supervises a young person. ◆ *v* act as a chaperone to.

chaplain *n* clergyman attached to a chapel, military body, or institution. **chaplaincy** *n*

chaplet *n* garland for the head.

chapped *adj* (of the skin) raw and cracked, through exposure to cold.

chapter *n* division of a book; period in a life or history; branch of a society or club; group of canons of a cathedral.

char¹ *v* **charring, charred** blacken by partial burning.

char² *Brit informal* ◆ *n* charwoman. ◆ *v* **charring, charred** work as a charwoman.

char³ *n* *Brit slang* tea.

character *n* combination of qualities distinguishing an individual; moral strength; reputation, esp. good reputation; person represented in a play, film, or story; notable or eccentric person; letter, numeral, or symbol used in writing or printing. **characteristic** *n* distinguishing feature or quality. ◆ *adj* distinguishing. **characteristically** *adv* **characterize** *v* be a characteristic of; describe the character of. **characterization** *n*

charade [shar-**rahd**] *n* absurd pretence. ◆ *pl* game in which one team acts out a word, which the other team has to guess.

charcoal *n* black substance formed by partially burning wood.

charge *v* ask as a price; enter a debit against (a person or an account); accuse formally; assign a task to; make a rush or sudden attack (upon); fill (a battery) with electricity; fill or load. ◆ *n* price charged; formal accusation; attack or rush; command or exhortation; custody; person or thing entrusted to someone's care; amount of electricity stored in a battery. **in charge** in command. **chargeable** *adj* **charger** *n* device for charging an accumulator; horse used in battle.

chargé d'affaires [shar-zhay daf-**fair**] *n, pl* **chargés d'affaires** head of a diplomatic mission in the absence of an ambassador or in a small or unimportant mission.

chariot *n* two-wheeled horse-drawn vehicle used in ancient times in wars and races. **charioteer** *n* chariot driver.

charisma [kar-**rizz**-ma] *n* person's power to attract people. **charismatic** [kar-rizz-**mat**-ik] *adj*

charity *n, pl* **-ties** organization that helps those in need; giving of help, such as money or food, to those in need; help given; kindly attitude towards people. **charitable** *adj* **charitably** *adv*

charlady *n* same as CHARWOMAN.

charlatan [**shar**-lat-tan] *n* person who claims expertise that he or she does not have.

charleston *n* lively dance of the 1920s.

charm *n* attractiveness; trinket worn on a bracelet; magic spell. ◆ *v* attract or delight; protect or influence as if by magic; influence by personal charm. **charmer** *n* **charming** *adj* attractive.

charnel house *n* building or vault for the bones of the dead.

chart *n* information shown in the form of a diagram, graph, or table; map to aid navigation. ◆ *v* plot the course of; make a chart of. **the charts** *Informal* weekly list of best-selling pop records.

charter *n* document granting or demanding certain rights; constitution of an organization; hire of transport for private use. ◆ *v* hire by charter; grant a charter to. **chartered** *adj* officially qualified to practise a profession, e.g. *chartered accountant*.

chartreuse [shar-**trerz**] *n* sweet-smelling green or yellow liqueur.

charwoman *n* woman employed as a cleaner.

chary [**chair**-ee] *adj* **-rier, -riest** cautious. **charily** *adv*

chase¹ *v* run after quickly in order to catch or drive away; *Informal* hurry; *Informal* try energetically to obtain. ◆ *n* chasing or pursuit. **chaser** *n* drink drunk after another of a different kind.

chase² *v* engrave (metal).

chasm [**kaz**-zum] *n* deep crack or ravine in the earth.

chassis [shass-ee] n, pl -sis frame, wheels, and mechanical parts of a motor vehicle.

chaste adj refraining from sex outside marriage or altogether; (of style) simple. **chastely** adv **chastity** n

chasten [chase-en] v correct by punishment; subdue.

chastise v scold severely; punish by beating. **chastisement** n

chasuble [chazz-yew-bl] n long sleeveless outer vestment worn by a priest while celebrating Mass.

chat v **chatting, chatted** talk in an easy familiar way. ◆ n easy familiar talk. **chatty** adj **chattily** adv

chateau [shat-toe] n, pl -teaux, -teaus French castle or country house.

chatelaine [shat-tell-lane] n esp. formerly, mistress of a large house or castle.

chattels pl n movable possessions.

chatter v talk about trivial matters rapidly and continuously; (of the teeth) rattle with cold or fear. ◆ n idle talk. **chatterbox** n person who chatters incessantly.

chauffeur n person employed to drive a car. **chauffeuse** n fem

chauvinism [show-vin-iz-zum] n irrational belief that one's own race, group, or sex is superior; fanatical patriotism. **chauvinist** n, adj **chauvinistic** adj

cheap adj low in price; of poor quality; of little value; mean, despicable. **cheaply** adv **cheapen** v make cheap; degrade. **cheapskate** n Informal miserly person.

cheat v act dishonestly to gain profit or advantage; deprive (someone) unfairly. ◆ n person who cheats; fraud or deception.

check v examine or investigate; stop or hinder; verify. ◆ n examination or investigation; stoppage or restraint; US cheque; pattern of squares or crossing lines; Chess position of a king under attack. **check in** v register one's arrival. **checkmate** n Chess winning position in which an opponent's king is under attack and unable to escape; utter defeat. ◆ v Chess place (an opponent's king) in checkmate; defeat. **check out** v pay the bill and leave a hotel; examine; Informal have a look at.

checkout n counter in a supermarket, where customers pay. **checkup** n general (medical) examination.

checker n piece used in Chinese checkers. ◆ pl game played on chessboard with flat, round pieces. **checkered** adj marked in squares; marked by varied fortunes, e.g. a checkered career.

Cheddar n smooth firm cheese.

cheek n side of the face below the eye; Informal impudence. ◆ v Informal speak impudently to. **cheeky** adj impudent. **cheekily** adv **cheekiness** n

cheep n young bird's high-pitched cry. ◆ v utter a cheep.

cheer v applaud with shouts; (often foll. by up) make or become happy or hopeful. ◆ n shout of applause. **cheerful, cheery** adj **cheerfully, cheerily** adv **cheerfulness** n **cheerless** adj gloomy.

cheerio interj Brit informal goodbye.

cheese n food made from coagulated milk curd; shaped block of this. **cheesy** adj **cheeseburger** n hamburger with cheese on it. **cheesecake** n dessert with a crumb base and a cream cheese filling; Slang photographs of scantily clad women. **cheesecloth** n loosely woven cotton cloth. **cheesed off** bored or annoyed.

cheetah n swift spotted African animal of the cat family.

chef n cook in a restaurant.

chef-d'oeuvre [shay-durv] n, pl **chefs-d'oeuvre** masterpiece.

chemical n substance used in or resulting from a reaction involving changes to atoms or molecules. ◆ adj of chemistry or chemicals. **chemically** adv

chemise [shem-meez] n woman's loose-fitting slip or dress.

chemistry n science of the composition, properties, and reactions of substances. **chemist** n specialist in chemistry; Brit pharmacist.

chemotherapy n treatment of disease by chemical means.

chenille [shen-neel] n (fabric of) thick tufty yarn.

cheque n written order to one's bank to pay money from one's account.

chequer n same as CHECKER.

cherish v care for; hold dear; cling to

(an idea or feeling).

cheroot [sher-**root**] n cigar with both ends cut flat.

cherry n, pl **-ries** small red or black fruit with a stone; tree bearing this. ◆ adj deep red.

cherub n angel, often represented as a winged child; sweet child. **cherubic** [cher-**rew**-bik] adj

chervil n herb with an aniseed flavour.

chess n game of skill for two players with 16 pieces each on a checkered board (**chessboard**) of 64 squares. **chessman** n piece used in chess.

chest n front of the body, from the neck to the belly; large strong box. **chest of drawers** piece of furniture consisting of drawers in a frame.

chesterfield n sofa with high padded sides and back.

chestnut n reddish-brown edible nut; tree bearing this; horse of a reddish-brown colour; Informal old joke. ◆ adj reddish-brown.

cheval glass [shev-**val**] n full-length mirror mounted to swivel within a frame.

chevron [**shev**-ron] n V-shaped pattern, esp. denoting rank.

chew v grind (food etc.) between the teeth. **chewy** adj requiring chewing. **chewing gum** flavoured gum that is chewed but not swallowed.

chianti [kee-**ant**-ee] n dry red Italian wine.

chiaroscuro [kee-ah-roh-**skew**-roh] n, pl **-ros** distribution of light and shade in a picture.

chic [**sheek**] adj stylish or elegant. ◆ n stylishness.

chick n young bird. **chickadee** n small N American bird with a dark crown. **chickpea** n edible pealike seed of an Asian plant. **chickweed** n weed with small white flowers.

chicken n domestic fowl; flesh of this used as food; Slang coward. ◆ adj cowardly. **chicken feed** Slang trifling amount of money. **chicken out** v Informal fail to do something through cowardice. **chickenpox** n infectious disease with an itchy rash.

chicory n, pl **-ries** plant whose leaves are used in salads; root of this plant, used as a coffee substitute.

chide v **chiding**, **chided** or **chid**, **chid**

or **chidden**. rebuke.

chief n head of a group of people. ◆ adj principal, foremost. **chiefly** adv mainly; especially. **chieftain** n leader of a tribe.

chiffon [**shif**-fon] n gauzy fabric.

chignon [**sheen**-yon] n knot of hair worn at the back of the head.

chihuahua [chee-**wah**-wah] n tiny short-haired dog.

chilblain n inflammation on the fingers or toes, caused by exposure to cold.

child n, pl **children** young human being; son or daughter. **childhood** n **childish** adj immature; of or like a child. **childishly** adv **childless** adj **childlike** adj simple or innocent. **childbirth** n giving birth to a child. **child's play** very easy task.

chile, chili n small hot-tasting red or green pepper used in cooking.

chill n feverish cold; unpleasant coldness. ◆ v make or become cold. ◆ adj cold. **chill out** Informal ◆ vb to relax, esp. after energetic dancing at a rave. **chilly** adj cold; unfriendly. **chilliness** n

chime n bell or set of bells; sound of this. ◆ v ring or be rung; produce (sounds) or indicate (the time) by chiming; be in agreement.

chimera [kime-**meer**-a] n illusory hope; fabled monster with a lion's head, goat's body, and serpent's tail.

chimney n hollow vertical structure for carrying away smoke or steam. **chimneypot** n short pipe on the top of a chimney. **chimney sweep** person who cleans soot from chimneys.

chimp n Informal short for CHIMPANZEE.

chimpanzee n intelligent ape of central W Africa.

chin n part of the face below the mouth.

china n fine earthenware or porcelain; cups, saucers, etc.

chinchilla n S American rodent with soft grey fur; its fur.

Chinese adj of China or its people. ◆ n, pl **-ese** person from China; any of the languages of China.

chink[1] n cleft or crack.

chink[2] n light ringing sound. ◆ v make this sound.

chinook n warm wind during winter

in western N America.

chintz *n* printed cotton fabric with a glazed finish.

chip *n* very thin slice of potato fried till crunchy; *Brit* French fried potato; tiny wafer of a semiconductor forming an integrated circuit; counter used to represent money in gambling; small piece broken off; mark left where a small piece has broken off. ◆ *v* **chipping, chipped** break small pieces from. **have a chip on one's shoulder** *Informal* bear a grudge. **chip in** *v* *Informal* contribute (money); interrupt with a remark.

chipboard *n* thin board made of compressed wood particles.

chipmunk *n* small striped N American squirrel.

chipolata *n* *Brit* small sausage.

chiropodist [kir-**rop**-pod-ist] *n* person who treats minor foot complaints. **chiropody** *n*

chiropractic [kire-oh-**prak**-tik] *n* system of treating bodily disorders by manipulation of the spine. **chiropractor** *n*

chirp, chirrup *v* (of a bird or insect) make a short high-pitched sound. ◆ *n* this sound. **chirpy** *adj* *Informal* cheerful and lively.

chisel *n* metal tool with a sharp end for shaping wood or stone. ◆ *v* **-elling, -elled** carve with a chisel.

chit *n* note or memorandum.

chitchat *n* chat or gossip.

chitterlings *pl n* pig's intestines cooked as food.

chivalry *n* courteous and considerate behaviour, esp. towards women; medieval system and principles of knighthood. **chivalrous** *adj*

chive *n* herb with a mild onion flavour.

chivvy *v* **-vying, -vied** *Informal* urge to do something.

chlorine *n* yellowish-green pungent gaseous element. **chlorinate** *v* disinfect or purify (esp. water) with chlorine. **chlorination** *n* **chloride** *n* compound of chlorine.

chlorofluorocarbon *n* any of various gaseous compounds of chlorine, fluorine, and carbon, used in refrigerators and aerosol propellants, some of which cause a breakdown of ozone in the earth's atmosphere.

chloroform *n* strong-smelling liquid formerly used as an anesthetic. ◆ *v* make unconscious with chloroform.

chlorophyll *n* green colouring matter in plants, which helps them convert sunlight into energy.

chock *n* block or wedge used to prevent a heavy object from moving. **chock-full, chock-a-block** *adj* completely full.

chocolate *n* food made from cacao seeds; candy or drink made from this. ◆ *adj* dark brown.

choice *n* choosing; opportunity or power of choosing; thing or person chosen; possibilities from which to choose. ◆ *adj* of superior quality.

choir *n* organized group of singers, esp. in church; part of a church occupied by the choir.

choke *v* hinder or stop the breathing of (a person) by squeezing or blocking the windpipe; have trouble in breathing; block or clog up. ◆ *n* device controlling the amount of air that is mixed with the fuel in a gasoline engine. **choker** *n* tight-fitting necklace. **choke back** *v* suppress (anger, tears, etc.).

cholera [**kol**-ler-a] *n* dangerous infectious disease characterized by vomiting and diarrhea.

choleric *adj* bad-tempered.

cholesterol [kol-**lest**-er-oll] *n* fatty substance found in animal tissue.

chomp *v* chew noisily.

choose *v* **choosing, chose, chosen** select from a number of alternatives; decide (to do something). **choosy** *adj* *Informal* fussy, hard to please.

chop¹ *v* **chopping, chopped** cut with a blow from an axe or knife; cut into pieces; hit (an opponent) with a sharp blow. ◆ *n* sharp blow; slice of meat, usu. with a rib. **chopper** *n* small axe; *Informal* helicopter. **choppy** *adj* (of the sea) fairly rough.

chop² *v* **chopping, chopped. chop and change** change one's mind repeatedly.

chops *pl n* *Informal* jaws or cheeks.

chopsticks *pl n* pair of thin sticks used to eat with by the Chinese and Japanese.

chop suey *n* Chinese-style dish of chopped meat and vegetables fried in soy sauce.

choral adj of or for a choir.

chorale [kor-**rahl**] n slow stately hymn tune.

chord n simultaneous sounding of three or more musical notes; *Math* straight line joining two points on a curve.

chore n routine task.

choreography n steps and movements of a dance. **choreographer** n **choreographic** adj

chorister n singer in a choir.

chortle v chuckle gleefully. ◆ n gleeful chuckle.

chorus n, pl -ruses large choir; group of singers or dancers who perform together; part of a song repeated after each verse; something expressed by many people at once. ◆ v **chorusing**, **chorused** sing or say together. **in chorus** in unison.

chose v past tense of CHOOSE. **chosen** v past participle of CHOOSE.

choux pastry [shoo] n very light pastry made with eggs.

chow[1] n thick-coated dog with a curled tail, orig. from China.

chow[2] n Informal food.

chowder n thick soup containing clams or fish.

chow mein n Chinese dish consisting of chopped meat or vegetables fried with noodles.

Christ n Jesus, regarded by Christians as the Messiah.

christen v baptize; give a name to; use for the first time. **christening** n

Christendom n all Christian people or countries.

Christian n person who believes in and follows Christ. ◆ adj relating to Christ or Christianity; kind or good. **Christianity** n religion based on the life and teachings of Christ. **Christian name** person's first name. **Christian Science** religious system which emphasizes spiritual healing.

Christmas n annual festival on Dec. 25 commemorating the birth of Christ; period around this time. **Christmassy** adj **Christmas Day** Dec. 25. **Christmas Eve** Dec. 24. **Christmas tree** evergreen tree or imitation of one, decorated as part of Christmas celebrations.

chromatic adj of colour or colours; *Music* (of a scale) proceeding by semitones. **chromatically** adv

chromatography n separation and analysis of the components of a substance by slowly passing it through an adsorbing material.

chrome, chromium n metallic element used in steel alloys and for electroplating.

chromosome n microscopic gene-carrying body in the nucleus of a cell.

chronic adj lasting a long time; habitual, e.g. *a chronic smoker*; Informal very bad. **chronically** adv

chronicle n record of events in chronological order. ◆ v record in or as if in a chronicle. **chronicler** n

chronology n, pl -gies list or arrangement of events in order of occurrence. **chronological** adj **chronologically** adv

chronometer n timepiece designed to be accurate in all conditions.

chrysalis [**kriss**-a-liss] n insect in the stage between larva and adult, when it is in a cocoon.

chrysanthemum n garden plant with bright showy flowers.

chub n freshwater fish of the carp family.

chubby adj -bier, -biest plump. **chubbiness** n

chuck[1] v Informal throw; Informal give up, reject; touch (someone) affectionately under the chin.

chuck[2] n cut of beef from the neck to the shoulder; device that holds a workpiece in a lathe or a tool in a drill. **chuck wagon** wagon carrying cooking supplies for men working in the open.

chuckle v laugh softly. ◆ n soft laugh.

chug n short dull sound, as of an engine. ◆ v **chugging**, **chugged** operate or move with this sound.

chum Informal ◆ n close friend. ◆ v **chumming**, **chummed**. **chum up with** form a close friendship with. **chummy** adj

chump n Informal stupid person.

chunk n thick solid piece; considerable amount. **chunky** adj thick and short; with thick pieces.

church n building for public Christian worship; (C-) particular Christian denomination; (C-) Christians collectively; clergy. **churchgoer** n person who attends church regularly. **churchyard** n grounds round a church, used as a graveyard.

churlish adj surly and rude.

churn n machine in which cream is shaken to make butter; large container for milk. ◆ v stir (cream) vigorously or make butter in a churn; move about violently. **churn out** v Informal produce (things) rapidly in large numbers.

chute [shoot] n steep channel down which things may be slid; waterfall or rapids; Informal short for PARACHUTE.

chutney n pickle made from fruit, vinegar, and spices.

CIA US Central Intelligence Agency.

cicada [sik-kah-da] n large insect that makes a high-pitched drone.

cicatrix [sik-a-trix] n, pl **-trices** scar.

CID Brit Criminal Investigation Department.

cider n drink made from apples.

cigar n roll of cured tobacco leaves for smoking. **cigarette** n shredded tobacco in a thin paper cylinder for smoking.

cilantro n a plant widely cultivated for its aromatic seeds and leaves, used in flavouring food, etc.

cinch [sinch] n Informal easy task; certainty.

cinder n piece of incombustible material left after burning coal.

cine camera n camera for taking moving pictures.

cinema n place for showing films; films collectively. **cinematic** adj **cinematography** n technique of making films. **cinematographer** n

cineraria n garden plant with daisy-like flowers.

cinnamon n spice obtained from the bark of an Asian tree.

cipher [sife-er] n system of secret writing; unimportant person.

circa [sir-ka] prep Latin about, approximately.

circle n perfectly round geometric figure, line, or shape; group of people sharing an interest or activity; Theatre section of seats above the main level of the auditorium. ◆ v move in a circle; surround. **circlet** n circular ornament worn on the head. **circular** adj round; moving in a circle. ◆ n letter or notice

for general distribution. **circularity** n **circulate** v send, go, or move around. **circulation** n flow of blood around the body; number of copies of a newspaper or magazine sold; sending or moving around. **circulatory** adj

circuit n complete round or course; complete path through which an electric current can flow; periodical journey around a district, as made by judges; motor-racing track. **circuitous** [sir-kew-it-uss] adj roundabout, indirect. **circuitry** [sir-kit-tree] n electrical circuit(s).

circumcise v cut off the foreskin of. **circumcision** n

circumference n boundary of a specified area or shape, esp. of a circle; distance round this.

circumflex n accent (^) over a vowel to show that it is pronounced in a particular way.

circumlocution n indirect expression. **circumlocutory** adj

circumnavigate v sail right round. **circumnavigation** n

circumscribe v restrict; draw a line round. **circumscription** n

circumspect adj cautious, prudent. **circumspectly** adv **circumspection** n

circumstance n (usu. pl.) occurrence or condition that accompanies or influences a person or event. **circumstantial** adj (of evidence) strongly suggesting something but not proving it; detailed.

circumvent v avoid or get round (a difficulty etc.). **circumvention** n

circus n, pl **-cuses** (performance given by) a travelling company of acrobats, clowns, performing animals, etc.

cirrhosis [sir-roh-siss] n liver disease.

cirrus n, pl **-ri** high wispy cloud.

cisco [siss-ko] n, pl **-coes** N American whitefish.

cistern n water tank.

citadel n fortress in a city.

cite v quote; bring forward as proof. **citation** n

citizen n native or naturalized member of a state or nation; inhabitant of a city or town. **citizenship** n **Citizens' Band** range of radio frequencies for private communication by the public.

citric acid n weak acid found in citrus fruits.

citrus fruit n juicy, sharp-tasting fruit such as an orange, lemon, or lime.

city n, pl **-ties** large or important town. **the City** area of London as a financial centre.

civet [siv-vit] n spotted catlike African mammal; musky fluid from its glands used in perfume.

civic adj of a city or citizens. **civics** pl n study of the rights and responsibilities of citizenship.

civil adj relating to the citizens of a state as opposed to the armed forces or the Church; polite. **civilly** adv **civility** n politeness. **civilian** n, adj (person) not belonging to the armed forces. **civil service** public service. **civil servant** public servant. **civil war** war between people of the same country.

civilize v bring out of barbarism into a state of civilization; refine. **civilization** n high level of human cultural and social development; particular society which has reached this level.

civvies pl n Slang civilian clothes.

Cl Chem chlorine.

clack n sound made by two hard objects striking together. ◆ v (cause to) make this sound.

clad v a past of CLOTHE.

cladding n material used for the outside facing of a building etc.

claim v assert; demand as a right; call for or need. ◆ n assertion; demand for something as due; right; thing claimed. **claimant** n

clairvoyance n power of perceiving things beyond the natural range of the senses. **clairvoyant** n, adj

clam n edible shellfish with a hinged shell. ◆ v **clamming, clammed. clam up** Informal refuse to talk.

clamber v climb with difficulty.

clammy adj **-mier, -miest** unpleasantly moist and sticky. **clamminess** n

clamour n loud protest; loud persistent outcry or noise. ◆ v make a loud outcry or noise. **clamorous** adj **clamour for** v demand noisily.

clamp n tool with movable jaws for holding things together tightly. ◆ v fasten with a clamp. **clamp down on** v become stricter about; suppress.

clan n group of families with a common ancestor; close group. **clannish** adj (of a group) tending to

exclude outsiders.

clandestine adj secret, furtive.

clang n loud ringing sound. ◆ v (cause to) make this sound. **clanger** n Informal conspicuous mistake.

clangour n loud continuous clanging sound. **clangorous** adj

clank n harsh metallic sound. ◆ v (cause to) make this sound.

clap[1] v **clapping, clapped** applaud by striking the palms of one's hands sharply together; put quickly or forcibly. ◆ n act or sound of clapping; sharp abrupt sound, esp. of thunder. **clapped out** Slang worn out. **clapper** n piece of metal inside a bell, which causes it to sound when struck against the side. **clapperboard** n pair of hinged boards clapped together during filming to aid synchronizing sound and picture. **claptrap** n empty words.

clap[2] n Slang gonorrhea.

claret [klar-rit] n dry red wine from Bordeaux.

clarify v **-fying, -fied** make or become clear. **clarification** n

clarinet n keyed woodwind instrument with a single reed. **clarinettist** n

clarion n obsolete high-pitched trumpet; its sound. **clarion call** rousing appeal.

clarity n clearness.

clash v come into conflict; (of events) coincide; (of colours) look unattractive together; (cause to) make a clashing sound. ◆ n conflict; loud harsh noise, esp. of things striking together.

clasp n device for fastening things; firm grasp or embrace. ◆ v grasp or embrace firmly; fasten with a clasp.

class n social group of a particular rank; system of dividing society into such groups; group of people or things sharing a common characteristic; group of pupils or students taught together; standard of quality; Informal excellence or elegance. ◆ v place in a class. **classy** adj Informal stylish, elegant. **classify** v arrange in classes; designate (information) as officially secret. **classifiable** adj **classification** n

classic adj typical; of lasting significance because of excellence;

characterized by simplicity and purity of form. ◆ *n* author, artist, or work of art of recognized excellence. ◆ *pl* study of ancient Greek and Roman literature and culture. **classical** *adj* traditional and standard; *Music* denoting serious art music; of or influenced by ancient Greek and Roman culture. **classically** *adv* **classicism** *n* artistic style showing regularity of form and emotional restraint. **classicist** *n*

clatter *n* rattling noise. ◆ *v* (cause to) make a rattling noise.

clause *n* part of a sentence, containing a verb; section in a legal document.

claustrophobia *n* abnormal fear of confined spaces. **claustrophobic** *adj*

clavichord *n* early keyboard instrument.

clavicle *n* collarbone.

claw *n* sharp hooked nail of a bird or beast; similar part, such as a crab's pincer. ◆ *v* tear with claws or nails.

clay *n* fine-grained earth, soft when moist and hardening when baked, used to make bricks and pottery. **clayey** *adj* **clay pigeon** baked clay disc hurled into the air as a target for shooting.

claymore *n* two-edged broadsword formerly used by Scottish Highlanders.

CLC Canadian Labour Congress.

clean *adj* free from dirt or impurities; morally sound; without obscenity; not yet used; complete, e.g. *a clean break*; smooth and regular. ◆ *v* free from dirt. ◆ *adv Not standard* completely. **come clean** *Informal* confess. **cleaner** *n* **cleanly** *adv* **cleanliness** *n* **cleanse** *v* make clean. **cleanser** *n*

clear *adj* free from doubt or confusion; plain, distinct; transparent; free from darkness or obscurity, bright; free from obstruction; (of weather) free from clouds; without blemish or defect; (of money) net. ◆ *adv* clearly; completely; out of the way, e.g. *stand clear of the gates.* ◆ *v* make or become clear; pass by or over without touching; acquit; make as profit. **clearly** *adv* **clearness** *n* **clearance** *n* clearing; official permission. **clearing** *n* area cleared of trees. **clear off** *v Informal* go away. **clear out** *v* empty; *Informal* go away. **clear-sighted** *adj* perceptive.

cleat *n* wedge; piece of wood or iron with two projecting ends round which

ropes are fastened.

cleave[1] *v* **cleaving, cleft, cleaved** or **clove, cleft, cleaved** or **cloven.** split apart. **cleavage** *n* space between a woman's breasts, as revealed by a low-cut dress; division, split. **cleaver** *n* heavy butcher's knife.

cleave[2] *v* cling or adhere.

clef *n Music* symbol at the beginning of a stave to show the pitch.

cleft *n* split or indentation. ◆ *v* a past of CLEAVE[1]. **in a cleft stick** in a very difficult position.

clematis *n* climbing plant with showy flowers.

clement *adj* (of weather) mild. **clemency** *n* mercy.

clementine *n* small orange citrus fruit.

clench *v* close (one's teeth or fist) firmly together; grasp firmly.

clerestory [clear-store-ee] *n, pl* **-ries** row of windows at the top of a wall above an adjoining roof.

clergy *n* priests and ministers as a group. **clergyman** *n*

cleric *n* member of the clergy.

clerical *adj* of clerks or office work; of the clergy.

clerk *n* employee in an office, bank, or court who keeps records, files, and accounts.

clever *adj* intelligent, quick at learning; showing skill. **cleverly** *adv* **cleverness** *n*

cliché [klee-shay] *n* hackneyed expression or idea. **clichéd** *adj*

click *n* short slight sound. ◆ *v* (cause to) make this sound; *Informal* become suddenly clear; *Informal* (of two people) get on well; *Slang* be a success. Also: **click on** *Computers* to select a particular function by pressing a button on a mouse.

client *n* person who uses the services of a professional; customer. *Computers* a program or work station that requests data from a server. **clientele** [klee-on-tell] *n* clients collectively.

cliff *n* steep rock face, esp. along the sea shore. **cliffhanger** *n* film, game, etc. which is exciting and full of suspense because its outcome is uncertain.

climate *n* prevalent weather conditions of an area. **climatic** *adj*

climax *n* most intense point of an

experience, series of events, or story; orgasm. ◆ v reach a climax. **climactic** adj

climb v go up or ascend; rise. ◆ n place to be climbed. **climber** n **climb down** v retreat from an opinion or position.

clime n Lit region or its climate.

clinch v settle (an argument or agreement) decisively. ◆ n clinching. **clincher** n Informal something decisive.

cling v **clinging, clung** hold fast or stick closely. **clingfilm** n thin polythene wrapping.

clinic n place in which outpatients receive medical advice or treatment; private or specialized hospital. **clinical** adj of a clinic; scientifically detached. **clinically** adv

clink[1] n light sharp metallic sound. ◆ v (cause to) make such a sound.

clink[2] n Slang prison.

clinker n fused coal residues from a fire or furnace.

clinker-built adj (of a boat) made of overlapping planks.

clip[1] v **clipping, clipped** cut with shears or scissors; Informal hit sharply. ◆ n short extract of a film; Informal sharp blow. **clippers** pl n tool for clipping. **clipping** n something cut out, esp. an article from a newspaper.

clip[2] n device for attaching or holding things together. ◆ v **clipping, clipped** attach or hold together with a clip.

clipper n fast commercial sailing ship.

clique [kleek] n small exclusive group. **cliqueish** adj

clitoris [klit-or-iss] n small sexually sensitive part of the female genitals. **clitoral** adj

cloak n loose sleeveless outer garment. ◆ v cover or conceal. **cloakroom** n room where coats may be left temporarily.

clobber v Informal batter; defeat utterly.

cloche [klosh] n cover to protect young plants; woman's close-fitting hat.

clock n instrument for showing the time; device with a dial for recording or measuring. **clockwise** adv, adj in the direction in which the hands of a clock rotate. **clock in** or **on**, **out** or **off** v register arrival at or departure from

work on an automatic time recorder. **clock up** v reach (a total). **clockwork** n mechanism similar to that of a clock, as in a wind-up toy.

clod n lump of earth; stupid person. **cloddish** adj

clog v **clogging, clogged** block. ◆ n wooden-soled shoe.

cloisonné [klwah-**zon**-nay] n design made by filling in a wire outline with coloured enamel.

cloister n covered pillared arcade, usu. in a monastery. **cloistered** adj sheltered.

clone n group of organisms or cells reproduced asexually from a single plant or animal; Informal person who closely resembles another. ◆ v produce as a clone.

close[1] v shut; prevent access to; finish; bring or come nearer together. ◆ n end. **closed shop** place of work in which all workers must belong to a particular trade union.

close[2] adj near; intimate; careful, thorough; oppressive or stifling; secretive; compact, dense. ◆ adv closely or tightly. ◆ n street closed at one end; courtyard or quadrangle. **closely** adv **closeness** n **close season** period when it is illegal to kill certain kinds of game and fish. **close shave** Informal narrow escape. **close-up** n photograph or film taken at very close range.

closet n cupboard; small private room. ◆ adj private or secret. ◆ v **closeting, closeted** shut away in private, esp. for conference.

closure n closing or being closed; a resolution of a significant event or relationship in a person's life.

clot n soft thick lump formed from liquid; Informal fool. ◆ v **clotting, clotted** form clots.

cloth n woven fabric.

clothe v **clothing, clothed** or **clad** put clothes on; provide with clothes. **clothes** pl n articles of dress. **clothing** n clothes collectively.

cloud n mass of condensed water vapour floating in the sky; floating mass of smoke, dust, etc. ◆ v make or become cloudy; confuse; make gloomy or depressed. **cloudless** adj **cloudy** adj full of clouds; (of liquid) opaque. **cloudberry** n creeping plant with yellowish fruit. **cloudburst** n heavy fall of rain.

clout Informal ♦ n blow; influence, power. ♦ v hit.

clove¹ n dried flower bud of a tropical tree, used as a spice; segment of a bulb of garlic.

clove² v a past tense of CLEAVE¹. **clove hitch** knot used to fasten a rope to a spar.

cloven v a past participle of CLEAVE¹. **cloven hoof** divided hoof of a sheep, goat, etc.

clover n plant with three-lobed leaves. **in clover** in luxury.

clown n comic entertainer in a circus; amusing person; stupid person. ♦ v perform as a clown; behave foolishly. **clownish** adj

cloy v sicken by an excess of something sweet or pleasurable.

club n association of people with common interests; building used by such a group; thick stick used as a weapon; bat or stick used in some games; playing card of the suit marked with black three-leaved symbols. ♦ v **clubbing, clubbed** strike with a club. **club together** v combine resources for a common purpose.

club foot n congenitally deformed foot.

cluck n low clicking noise made by a hen. ♦ v make this noise.

clue n something that helps to solve a mystery or puzzle. **not have a clue** be completely baffled. **clueless** adj stupid.

clump¹ n cluster or mass. ♦ v form into a clump.

clump² v walk or tread heavily. ♦ n dull heavy tread.

clumsy adj -sier, -siest lacking skill or physical coordination; badly made or done. **clumsily** adv **clumsiness** n

clung v past of CLING.

clunk n dull metallic sound. ♦ v make such a sound.

cluster n small close group. ♦ v (cause to) form a cluster.

clutch¹ v grasp tightly; try to seize. ♦ n tight grasp; device enabling two revolving shafts to be connected and disconnected.

clutch² n set of eggs laid at the same time; brood of chickens.

clutter v strew objects about (a place)

in disorder. ♦ n disordered heap or mass of objects.

cm centimetre(s).

Co Chem cobalt.

CO Commanding Officer.

Co. Company; County.

co- prefix together; joint or jointly, e.g. coproduction.

c/o care of; Book-keeping carried over.

coach n long-distance bus; railway carriage; large four-wheeled horse-drawn carriage; trainer, tutor. ♦ v train or teach.

coagulate [koh-ag-yew-late] v change from a liquid to a semisolid mass. **coagulation** n **coagulant** n substance causing coagulation.

coal n black mineral consisting mainly of carbon, used as fuel. **coalfield** n area rich in coal.

coalesce [koh-a-less] v come together, merge. **coalescence** n

coalition [koh-a-lish-un] n temporary alliance, esp. between political parties.

coarse adj rough in texture; unrefined or indecent. **coarsely** adv **coarseness** n **coarsen** v **coarse fish** Brit any freshwater fish not of the salmon family.

coast n sea shore. ♦ v move by momentum, without the use of power. **coastal** adj **coaster** n small ship; small mat placed under a glass. **coastguard** n organization which aids shipping and prevents smuggling; member of this. **coastline** n outline of a coast.

coat n long outer garment with sleeves; animal's fur or hair; covering layer. ♦ v cover with a layer. **coating** n covering layer. **coat of arms** heraldic emblem of a family or institution.

coax v persuade gently; manipulate carefully and patiently.

coaxial [koh-ax-ee-al] adj (of a cable) transmitting by means of two concentric conductors separated by an insulator.

cob n thickset type of horse; male swan; stalk of an ear of corn; round loaf of bread.

cobalt n metallic element; deep blue pigment made from it.

cobber n Aust informal mate; used as a term of address between men.

cobble v put together roughly. ♦ n (also **cobblestone**) round stone used for paving. **cobbler** n shoe mender.

cobra n venomous hooded snake of Asia and Africa.

cobweb n spider's web.

cocaine n addictive drug used as a narcotic and local anesthetic.

coccyx [kok-six] n, pl **coccyges** [kok-sije-eez] bone at the base of the spinal column.

cochineal n scarlet dye obtained from a Mexican insect.

cock n male bird, esp. of the domestic fowl; stopcock; hammer of a gun. ◆ v draw back (the hammer of a gun) to firing position; lift and turn (part of the body). **cockerel** n young cock. **cock-a-hoop** adj in high spirits. **cock-and-bull story** improbable story. **cockeyed** adj Informal askew; absurd.

cockade n rosette or feather worn on a hat as a badge.

cockatoo n crested parrot of Australia or the East Indies.

cockatrice [kok-a-triss] n mythical animal like a small dragon.

cockchafer n large flying beetle.

cocker spaniel n small breed of spaniel.

cockle n edible bivalve mollusc.

Cockney n native of the East End of London; Cockney dialect.

cockpit n pilot's compartment in an aircraft; driver's compartment in a racing car.

cockroach n beetle-like insect which is a household pest.

cocksure adj overconfident.

cocktail n mixed alcoholic drink; appetizer of seafood or mixed fruits.

cocky adj **cockier**, **cockiest** conceited and overconfident. **cockily** adv **cockiness** n

cocoa n powder made from the seed of the cacao tree; drink made from this powder.

coconut n large hard fruit of a type of palm tree; edible flesh of this fruit. **coconut matting** coarse matting made from the fibrous husk of the coconut.

cocoon n silky sheath of a chrysalis; protective covering. ◆ v wrap or protect as if in a cocoon.

cod n large food fish of the North Atlantic.

COD cash on delivery.

coda [kode-a] n final part of a musical composition.

coddle v overprotect or pamper.

code n system of letters, symbols, or prearranged signals by which messages can be communicated secretly or briefly; set of principles or rules. ◆ v put into code. **codify** [kode-if-fie] v organize (rules or procedures) systematically. **codification** n

codeine [kode-een] n drug used as a painkiller.

codex n, pl **codices** volume of manuscripts of an ancient text.

codger n Informal old man.

codicil [kode-iss-ill] n addition to a will.

coeducation n education of boys and girls together. **coeducational** adj

coefficient n Math number or constant placed before and multiplying a quantity.

coelacanth [seel-a-kanth] n primitive marine fish.

coeliac disease [seel-ee-ak] n disease which hampers digestion of food.

coerce [koh-urss] v compel or force. **coercion** n **coercive** adj

coeval [koh-eev-al] adj, n contemporary.

coexist v exist together, esp. peacefully despite differences. **coexistence** n

C of E Church of England.

coffee n drink made from the roasted and ground seeds of a tropical shrub; beanlike seeds of this shrub. ◆ adj light brown. **coffee table** small low table.

coffer n chest for valuables. ◆ pl store of money.

cofferdam n watertight enclosure pumped dry to enable construction work to be done.

coffin n box in which a corpse is buried or cremated.

cog n one of a series of teeth on the rim of a gearwheel; unimportant person in a big organization.

cogent [koh-jent] adj forcefully convincing. **cogency** n **cogently** adv

cogitate [koj-it-tate] v think deeply, ponder. **cogitation** n

cognac [kon-yak] n French brandy.

cognate adj related, akin.

cognition *n* act or experience of knowing or acquiring knowledge. **cognitive** *adj*

cognizance *n* knowledge, perception. **cognizant** *adj*

cognoscenti [kon-yo-**shen**-tee] *pl n* connoisseurs.

cohabit *v* live together as husband and wife without being married. **cohabitation** *n*

cohere *v* stick together; be logically connected and consistent. **coherence** *n* **coherent** *adj* capable of intelligible speech; logical and consistent. **coherently** *adv* **cohesion** *n* tendency to unite. **cohesive** *adj*

cohort *n* band of associates; tenth part of a Roman legion.

coiffure *n* hairstyle. **coiffeur, coiffeuse** *n* hairdresser.

coil *v* wind or be wound in loops; move in a winding course. ◆ *n* something coiled; single loop of this; *Brit* contraceptive device inserted in the womb.

coin *n* piece of metal money; metal currency collectively. ◆ *v* invent (a word or phrase). **coin it in** *Informal* make money rapidly. **coinage** *n* coining; coins collectively; word or phrase coined.

coincide *v* happen at the same time; agree or correspond exactly. **coincidence** *n* occurrence of simultaneous or apparently connected events; coinciding. **coincident** *adj* **coincidental** *adj* **coincidentally** *adv*

coir *n* coconut husk fibre.

coition [koh-**ish**-un], **coitus** [koh-it-uss] *n* sexual intercourse. **coital** *adj*

coke¹ *n* solid fuel left after gas has been distilled from coal.

coke² *n* *Slang* cocaine.

col *n* high mountain pass.

cola *n* soft drink flavoured with an extract from the nuts of a tropical tree.

colander *n* perforated bowl for straining or rinsing foods.

cold *adj* lacking heat; lacking affection or enthusiasm; (of a colour) giving an impression of coldness; *Slang* unconscious, e.g. *out cold.* ◆ *n* lack of heat; illness characterized by catarrh and sneezing. **coldly** *adv* **coldness** *n* **cold-blooded** *adj* having a body temperature that varies with that of the surroundings; callous or cruel. **cold cream** creamy preparation for softening and cleansing the skin. **cold feet** *Slang* fear. **cold-shoulder** *v* treat (someone) with indifference. **cold war** political hostility between countries without actual warfare.

coleslaw *n* salad dish of shredded raw cabbage in a dressing.

coley *n* codlike food fish of the N Atlantic.

colic *n* severe pains in the stomach and bowels. **colicky** *adj*

colitis [koh-**lie**-tiss] *n* inflammation of the colon.

collaborate *v* work with another on a project; cooperate with an enemy invader. **collaboration** *n* **collaborative** *adj* **collaborator** *n*

collage [kol-**lahzh**] *n* art form in which various materials or objects are glued onto a surface; picture made in this way.

collapse *v* fall down or in suddenly; fail completely; fold compactly. ◆ *n* act of collapsing; sudden failure or breakdown. **collapsible** *adj*

collar *n* part of a garment round the neck; band put round an animal's neck; cut of meat from an animal's neck; band round a pipe, rod, or shaft. ◆ *v* *Informal* seize, arrest; catch in order to speak to; take for oneself. **collarbone** *n* bone joining the shoulder blade to the breast bone.

collate *v* compare carefully. **collation** *n* collating; light meal.

collateral *n* security pledged for the repayment of a loan.

colleague *n* fellow worker, esp. in a profession.

collect¹ *v* gather or be gathered together; accumulate (stamps etc.) as a hobby; fetch. **collected** *adj* calm and controlled. **collection** *n* collecting; things collected. **collector** *n* **collective** *adj* of or done by a group, combined. ◆ *n* group of people working together on an enterprise and sharing the benefits from it. **collectively** *adv*

collect² *n* short prayer.

colleen *n* *Irish* girl.

college *n* place of higher education; group of people of the same profession or with special duties. **collegiate** *adj*

collide v crash together violently; conflict. **collision** n

collie n silky-coated sheepdog.

colliery n, pl **-lieries** coal mine. **collier** n coal miner; coal ship.

collocate v (of words) occur together regularly. **collocation** n

colloid n suspension of particles in a solution.

collop n small slice of meat.

colloquial adj suitable for informal speech or writing. **colloquialism** n colloquial expression.

colloquy n, pl **-quies** conversation or conference.

collusion n secret agreement for a fraudulent purpose. **collude** v act in collusion.

collywobbles pl n Slang nervousness; upset stomach.

cologne n perfumed toilet water.

colon[1] n punctuation mark (:).

colon[2] n part of the large intestine connected to the rectum.

colonel n senior commissioned army or air-force officer.

colonnade n row of columns.

colony n, pl **-nies** group of people who settle in a new country but remain subject to their parent state; territory occupied by a colony; group of people or animals of the same kind living together. **colonial** adj, n (inhabitant) of a colony. **colonialism** n policy of acquiring and maintaining colonies. **colonist** n settler in a colony. **colonize** v make into a colony. **colonization** n

colophon n publisher's emblem.

Colorado beetle n black-and-yellow beetle that is a serious pest of potatoes.

coloration n colouring.

colossal adj huge.

colossus n, pl **-si**, **-suses** huge statue; huge or important person.

colostomy n, pl **-mies** operation to form an opening from the colon onto the surface of the body, for emptying the bowel.

colour n appearance of things as a result of reflecting light; paint or pigment; complexion. ◆ pl flag; Sport badge or symbol denoting membership of a team. ◆ v apply or give colour to; influence or distort; blush. **Coloured** adj Offensive non-White; (in S Africa) of mixed race. **colourful** adj with bright or varied colours; vivid or distinctive. **colourfully** adv **colourless** adj **colour-blind** adj unable to distinguish between certain colours.

colt n young male horse.

columbine n garden flower with five spurred petals.

column n pillar; vertical arrangement of numbers; long narrow formation of troops; vertical division of a newspaper page; regular feature in a newspaper. **columnist** n journalist writing a regular feature for a newspaper.

coma n state of deep unconsciousness. **comatose** adj in a coma; sound asleep.

comb n toothed implement for arranging the hair; cock's crest; honeycomb. ◆ v use a comb on; search with great care.

combat v **-bating**, **-bated**, n fight. **combatant** n **combative** adj

combine v join together. ◆ n association of people or firms for a common purpose. **combination** n combining; people or things combined; set of numbers that opens a special lock. ◆ pl one-piece undergarment with long sleeves and legs. **combine harvester** machine which reaps and threshes grain in one operation.

combustion n process of burning. **combustible** adj burning easily.

come v **coming**, **came**, **come** move towards a place, arrive; occur; be available; reach a specified point or condition; originate (from); become. **come across** v meet or find by accident; (foll. by as) give an impression (of being). **comeback** n Informal return to a former position; retort. **comedown** n decline in status; disappointment. **comeuppance** n Informal deserved punishment.

comedy n, pl **-dies** humorous play, film, or programme. **comedian**, **comedienne** n entertainer who tells jokes.

comely adj **-lier**, **-liest** Old-fashioned good-looking.

comestibles pl n food.

comet n heavenly body with a long luminous tail.

comfort n physical ease or wellbeing; relief from suffering; person or thing that brings ease. ♦ v give comfort to. **comfortable** adj giving comfort; free from pain; Informal well-off financially. **comfortably** adv **comforter** n

comfrey n tall plant with bell-shaped flowers.

comfy adj -fier, -fiest Informal comfortable.

comic adj humorous, funny; relating to comedy. ♦ n comedian; magazine consisting of strip cartoons. **comical** adj amusing. **comically** adv

comma n punctuation mark (,).

command v order; have authority over; deserve and get; look down over. ♦ n authoritative instruction that something must be done; authority to command; knowledge, mastery; military or naval unit with a specific function. **commandant** n officer commanding a military group. **commandeer** v seize for military use. **commander** n military officer in command of a group or operation; middle-ranking naval officer. **commander-in-chief** n supreme commander. **commandment** n divine command.

commando n, pl -dos, -does (member of) a military unit trained for swift raids in enemy territory.

commemorate v honour the memory of. **commemoration** n **commemorative** adj

commence v begin. **commencement** n

commend v praise; recommend; entrust. **commendable** adj **commendably** adv **commendation** n

commensurable adj measurable by the same standard. **commensurability** n

commensurate adj corresponding in degree, size, or value.

comment n remark; gossip; explanatory note. ♦ v make a comment or comments. **commentary** n spoken accompaniment to a broadcast or film; explanatory notes. **commentate** v provide a commentary. **commentator** n

commerce n buying and selling, trade; dealings. **commercial** adj of commerce; (of television or radio) paid for by advertisers; having profit as the main aim. ♦ n television or radio advertisement. **commercialize** v make commercial. **commercialization** n

commiserate v (foll. by with) express pity or sympathy (for). **commiseration** n

commissar n official responsible for political education in Communist countries.

commissariat n military department in charge of food supplies.

commission n order for a piece of work, esp. a work of art; duty or task given to someone; percentage paid to a salesperson for each sale made; group of people appointed to perform certain duties; committing; Mil rank or authority officially given to an officer; delegated authority. ♦ v place an order for; Mil give a commission to; grant authority to. **out of commission** not working. **commissioner** n appointed official in a government department; member of a commission.

commissionaire n uniformed doorman at a hotel, theatre, etc.

commit v -mitting, -mitted perform (a crime or error); pledge to a cause or course of action; send (someone) to prison or hospital. **committal** n sending of someone for trial, etc. **commitment** n dedication to a cause; responsibility that hinders freedom of action.

committee n group of people appointed to perform a specified service or function.

commode n seat with a compartment holding a chamber pot; chest of drawers.

commodious adj roomy.

commodity n, pl -ities article of trade.

commodore n senior naval or air-force officer; president of a yacht club.

common adj occurring often; belonging to two or more people; public, general; low-class. ♦ n area of grassy land belonging to a community. ♦ pl ordinary people; (C-) House of Commons. **commonly** adv **commoner** n Brit person who does not belong to the nobility. **common-law** adj (of a relationship) regarded as marriage through being long-standing. **Common Market** European Union. **commonplace** adj ordinary,

everyday. ◆ n trite remark. **common sense** sound practical understanding.
commonwealth n republic; (C-) federation of independent states that used to be ruled by Great Britain.
commotion n noisy disturbance.
commune[1] n group of people living together, sharing property and responsibilities. **communal** adj shared. **communally** adv
commune[2] v (foll. by with) experience strong emotion (for). **communion** n sharing of thoughts or feelings; (C-) Christian ritual of sharing consecrated bread and wine; religious group with shared beliefs and practices.
communicate v make known, reveal (information, thoughts, or feelings); (of rooms) have a connecting door. **communicable** adj (of a disease) able to be passed on. **communicant** n person who receives Communion. **communication** n communicating; thing communicated. ◆ pl means of travelling or sending messages. **communicative** adj willing to talk.
communiqué [kom-**mune**-ik-kay] n official announcement.
communism n doctrine that all property and means of production should be shared by the people; (C-) political and social system of state control of the economy and society in some countries. **communist** n, adj
community n, pl -**ties** all the people living in one district; group having shared interests or origins; society, the public. **community centre** building used by a community for activities.
commute v travel daily to and from work; reduce (a sentence) to a less severe one. **commuter** n person who commutes to and from work. **commutator** n device used to change alternating electric current into direct current.
compact[1] adj closely packed; neatly arranged; concise, brief. ◆ n small flat case containing a mirror and face powder. ◆ v pack closely together. **compactly** adv **compactness** n **compact disc** small digital audio disc on which the sound is read by an optical laser system.
compact[2] n agreement, contract.
companion n person who associates with or accompanies another.

companionable adj friendly. **companionship** n
companionway n ladder linking the decks of a ship.
company n, pl -**nies** business firm; group of actors; small unit of troops; crew of a ship; companionship; gathering of people; guest or guests; associates.
compare v examine (things) to find the resemblances or differences; declare to be like; be worthy of comparison. **comparable** adj **comparability** n **comparative** adj relative; involving comparison; Grammar denoting the form of an adjective or adverb indicating more. ◆ n Grammar comparative form of a word. **comparatively** adv **comparison** n
compartment n separate section; section of a railway carriage.
compass n instrument for showing direction, with a needle that points north; range. ◆ pl hinged instrument for drawing circles.
compassion n pity, sympathy. **compassionate** adj
compatible adj able to exist, work, or be used together. **compatibility** n
compatriot n fellow countryman or countrywoman.
compeer n equal, companion.
compel v -**pelling**, -**pelled** force (to be or do). **compelling** adj convincing; arousing strong interest.
compendium n, pl -**diums**, -**dia** selection of different table games in one container. **compendious** adj brief but inclusive.
compensate v make amends to (someone), esp. for injury or loss; (foll. by for) cancel out a bad effect. **compensation** n **compensatory** adj
compère n Brit person who presents a stage, radio, or television show. ◆ v be the compère of.
compete v take part in (a contest or competition); strive (to achieve something or be successful).
competition n competing; event in which people compete; people against whom one competes. **competitive** adj **competitor** n
competent adj having sufficient skill or knowledge. **competently** adv

competence n

compile v collect and arrange (information), esp. to form a book. **compilation** n **compiler** n

complacent adj self-satisfied. **complacently** adv **complacency** n

complain v express resentment or displeasure; state that one is suffering from pain or illness. **complaint** n complaining; mild illness. **complainant** n plaintiff.

complaisant [kom-**play**-zant] adj obliging, willing to please. **complaisance** n

complement n thing that completes something; complete amount or number; Grammar word or words added after a verb to complete the meaning. ◆ v make complete. **complementary** adj

complete adj thorough; perfect in quality or kind; finished; having all the necessary parts. ◆ v finish; make whole or perfect. **completely** adv **completeness** n wholeness. **completion** n finishing.

complex adj made up of parts; complicated. ◆ n whole made up of parts; group of unconscious feelings that influences behaviour. **complexity** n

complexion n natural appearance of the skin of the face; character.

complicate v make or become complex or difficult to deal with. **complication** n

complicity n fact of being an accomplice, esp. in a crime.

compliment n expression of praise. ◆ pl formal greetings. ◆ v praise. **complimentary** adj expressing praise; free of charge.

compline n last service of the day in the Roman Catholic Church.

comply v **-plying, -plied** act in accordance (with a rule, order, or request). **compliance** n **compliant** adj

component n part of a whole. ◆ adj being a component.

comport v behave (oneself) in a specified way.

compose v put together; be the component parts of; create (music or literature); arrange in order; calm (oneself). **composer** n

composite adj made up of separate parts.

composition n way that something is put together or arranged; musical work; essay; act of composing.

compositor n person who arranges type for printing.

compos mentis adj Latin sane.

compost n decayed plants used as a fertilizer.

composure n calmness.

compote n fruit stewed in syrup.

compound¹ n, adj (thing, esp. chemical) made up of two or more combined parts or elements. ◆ v combine or make by combining; intensify, make worse.

compound² n fenced enclosure containing buildings.

comprehend v understand. **comprehensible** adj **comprehension** n **comprehensive** adj of broad scope, fully inclusive.

compress v squeeze together; condense. ◆ n pad applied to stop bleeding or cool inflammation. **compressible** adj **compression** n **compressor** n device that compresses a gas.

comprise v be made up of.

compromise [kom-**prom**-mize] n settlement reached by concessions on each side. ◆ v settle a dispute by making concessions; put in a dishonourable position.

comptroller n (in titles) financial controller.

compulsion n irresistible impulse; compelling or being compelled. **compulsive** adj **compulsively** adv **compulsory** adj required by rules or laws, obligatory.

compunction n feeling of guilt.

compute v calculate, esp. using a computer. **computation** n **computer** n electronic machine that stores and processes data. **computerize** v equip with a computer; perform or operate by computer. **computerization** n

comrade n fellow member of a union or socialist political party; companion. **comradeship** n

con¹ Informal ◆ v **conning, conned** deceive or swindle (someone) by gaining his or her trust. ◆ n such a deception or swindle.

con² n pros and cons see PRO¹.

concatenation n linked series of events.

concave adj curving inwards. **concavity** n

conceal v cover and hide; keep secret. **concealment** n

concede v admit to be true; grant as a right; acknowledge defeat in (a contest or argument).

conceit n too high an opinion of oneself; Lit far-fetched or clever comparison. **conceited** adj

conceive v imagine or think; form in the mind; become pregnant. **conceivable** adj imaginable or possible. **conceivably** adv

concentrate v fix one's attention or efforts (on); bring or come together in large numbers in one place; make (a substance) stronger. ◆ n concentrated substance. **concentration** n concentrating; concentrated substance. **concentration camp** prison camp for civilian prisoners, esp. in Nazi Germany.

concentric adj having the same centre.

concept n abstract or general idea. **conceptual** adj of or based on concepts. **conceptualize** v form a concept of.

conception n general idea; act of conceiving.

concern n anxiety; something that concerns a person; business or firm. ◆ v worry; involve or interest; be relevant or important to. **concerned** adj interested or involved; anxious. **concerning** prep about, regarding.

concert n musical entertainment. **in concert** working together; (of musicians) performing live. **concerted** adj done together.

concertina n small musical instrument similar to an accordion. ◆ v -naing, -naed collapse or fold up like a concertina.

concerto [kon-**chair**-toe] n, pl -tos, -ti large-scale composition for a solo instrument and orchestra.

concession n grant; reduction in price for a specified category of people; conceding; thing conceded; land division in township survey. **concessionary** adj **concession road** one of a series of roads separating

concessions in township.

conch n marine mollusc with a large spiral shell; its shell.

concierge [kon-see-**airzh**] n (in France) caretaker of an apartment block.

conciliate v overcome the hostility of. **conciliation** n **conciliator** n **conciliatory** adj

concise adj brief and to the point. **concisely** adv **concision, conciseness** n

conclave n secret meeting; private meeting of cardinals to elect a new pope.

conclude v decide by reasoning; end, finish; arrange or settle finally. **conclusion** n decision or opinion; ending; outcome. **conclusive** adj ending doubt, convincing. **conclusively** adv

concoct v make by combining ingredients; make up (a story or plan). **concoction** n

concomitant adj accompanying.

concord n state of peaceful agreement, harmony. **concordance** n similarity or consistency; index of words in a book. **concordant** adj agreeing.

concourse n large open public place where people can gather; crowd.

concrete n mixture of sand, gravel, and cement, used in building. ◆ adj made of concrete; particular, specific; real or solid, not abstract.

concubine [kon-**kew**-bine] n woman living with a man as his wife, but not married to him; secondary wife in polygamous societies. **concubinage** n

concupiscence [kon-**kew**-piss-enss] n lust. **concupiscent** adj

concur v -curring, -curred agree, be in accord. **concurrence** n **concurrent** adj **concurrently** adv at the same time.

concussion n brain injury caused by a blow or fall. **concuss** v affect with concussion.

condemn v express disapproval of; sentence; doom; declare unfit for use. **condemnation** n **condemnatory** adj

condense v express in fewer words; concentrate, make more dense; turn from gas into liquid. **condensation** n **condenser** n Electricity capacitor.

condescend v behave patronizingly

towards; do something as if it were beneath one's dignity. **condescension** n

condiment n seasoning for food.

condition n particular state of being; necessary requirement for something else to happen; restriction or qualification; state of health, physical fitness; ailment. ◆ pl circumstances. ◆ v accustom; make fit or healthy; subject to a condition. **on condition that** only if. **conditional** adj dependent on circumstances. **conditioner** n thick liquid used when washing to make hair or clothes feel softer.

condo n, pl **-dos** informal a condominium building or apartment.

condole v express sympathy (with someone). **condolence** n

condom n rubber sheath worn on the penis or in the vagina during sexual intercourse to prevent conception or infection.

condominium n apartment building in which each apartment is individually owned.

condone v overlook or forgive (an offence or wrongdoing).

condor n large vulture of S America.

conducive adj (foll. by to) likely to produce (a result).

conduct n behaviour; management. ◆ v carry out; behave (oneself); direct (musicians) by moving the hands or a baton; lead, guide; transmit (heat or electricity). **conduction** n transmission of heat or electricity. **conductive** adj able to conduct heat or electricity. **conductivity** n **conductor** n person who conducts musicians; (fem **conductress**) official on a bus who collects fares; official on a passenger train; something that conducts electricity or heat.

conduit [kon-dew-it] n channel or tube for fluid or cables.

cone n hollow or solid object with a circular base, tapering to a point; scaly fruit of a conifer tree.

coney n same as CONY.

confabulation, Informal **confab** n conversation.

confection n any sweet food; elaborate article of clothing. **confectioner** n maker or seller of confectionery. **confectionery** n candies and cakes.

confederate n member of a confederacy; accomplice. ◆ v unite in a confederacy. ◆ adj united, allied. **confederacy** n union of states or people for a common purpose. **confederation** n alliance of political units; (C-) federation of Canada inaugurated in 1867.

confer v **-ferring, -ferred** discuss together; give. **conference** n meeting for discussion. **conferment** n formal giving.

confess v admit (a fault or crime); admit to be true; declare (one's sins) to God or a priest, in hope of forgiveness. **confession** n confessing; thing confessed. **confessional** n small stall in which a priest hears confessions. **confessor** n priest who hears confessions.

confetti n small bits of coloured paper thrown at weddings.

confidant n person confided in. **confidante** n fem

confide v (foll. by in) tell (something) in confidence (to); entrust. **confidence** n trust; self-assurance; something confided, secret. **in confidence** as a secret. **confidence game** same as CON[1]. **confident** adj feeling or showing self-assurance. **confidently** adv **confidential** adj private or secret; entrusted with another's secret affairs. **confidentially** adv **confidentiality** n

configuration n arrangement of parts; shape.

confine v keep within bounds; restrict the free movement of. **confines** pl n boundaries, limits. **confinement** n being confined; period of childbirth.

confirm v prove to be true; reaffirm or strengthen; administer the rite of confirmation to. **confirmation** n confirming; something that confirms; Christianity rite which admits a baptized person to full church membership. **confirmed** adj long-established in a habit.

confiscate v seize (property) by authority. **confiscation** n

conflagration n great destructive fire.

conflate v combine or blend into a whole. **conflation** n

conflict n disagreement; struggle or fight. ◆ v be incompatible.

confluence n place where two rivers join. **confluent** adj

conform v comply with accepted standards, rules, or customs; be like or in accordance with. **conformist** n person who conforms, esp. excessively. **conformity** n

confound v bewilder; confuse. **confounded** adj Informal damned.

confront v come or bring face to face with. **confrontation** n serious argument.

confuse v mix up, mistake (one thing) for another; perplex or disconcert; make unclear. **confusion** n

confute v prove wrong.

conga n dance performed by a number of people in single file; large single-headed drum played with the hands.

congeal v (of a liquid) coagulate, solidify.

congenial adj pleasant, agreeable; of similar disposition or tastes. **congenially** adv **congeniality** n

congenital adj (of a condition) existing from birth. **congenitally** adv

conger n large sea eel.

congested adj too full; clogged or blocked. **congestion** n

conglomerate n large corporation comprising many companies; mass composed of several different things. ♦ v form into a mass. ♦ adj made up of several different things. **conglomeration** n

congratulate v express one's pleasure to (a person) at his or her good fortune or success. **congratulations** pl n **congratulatory** adj

congregate v gather together in or as a crowd. **congregation** n assembled group of worshippers. **congregational** adj **Congregationalism** n Protestant denomination in which each church is self-governing. **Congregationalist** n, adj

congress n formal meeting for discussion; (C-) federal parliament of the US. **congressional** adj **Congressman, Congresswoman** n member of the US Congress.

congruent adj agreeing or corresponding; Geom identical in shape and size. **congruence** n

conic adj of a cone. **conical** adj cone-shaped.

conifer n cone-bearing tree, such as the fir or pine. **coniferous** adj

conjecture n, v guess. **conjectural** adj

conjoined twins pl n the technical name for SIAMESE TWINS

conjugal [kon-jew-gal] adj of marriage.

conjugate [kon-jew-gate] v give the inflections of (a verb). **conjugation** n complete set of inflections of a verb.

conjunction n combination; simultaneous occurrence of events; part of speech joining words, phrases, or clauses.

conjunctivitis n inflammation of the membrane covering the eyeball and inner eyelid. **conjunctiva** n this membrane.

conjure v perform tricks that appear to be magic. **conjure up** v produce as if by magic. **conjurer, -or** n

conk n Slang head or nose. **conk out** v Informal (of a machine) break down.

conker n Informal horse chestnut.

connect v join together; associate in the mind. **connection, connexion** n association; link or bond; opportunity to transfer from one public vehicle to another; influential acquaintance. **connective** adj

conning tower n raised observation tower containing the periscope on a submarine.

connive v (foll. by at) give assent to (wrongdoing) by ignoring it; conspire. **connivance** n

connoisseur [kon-noss-sir] n person with special knowledge of the arts, food, or drink.

connote v imply in addition to the literal meaning. **connotation** n

connubial [kon-new-bee-al] adj of marriage.

conquer v defeat; overcome; take (a place) by force. **conqueror** n **conquest** n conquering; person or thing conquered.

consanguineous adj related by birth. **consanguinity** n

conscience n sense of right or wrong as regards thoughts and actions. **conscientious** adj painstaking; governed by conscience. **conscientious objector** person who refuses to serve in the armed forces on

moral or religious grounds.
conscientiously adv

conscious adj alert and awake; aware;
deliberate, intentional. **consciously**
adv **consciousness** n

conscript v enrol (someone) for
compulsory military service. ◆ n
conscripted person. **conscription** n

consecrate v make sacred; dedicate
to a specific purpose. **consecration** n

consecutive adj in unbroken
succession. **consecutively** adv

consensus n general agreement.

consent n permission, agreement. ◆ v
permit, agree (to).

consequence n result, effect;
importance. **consequent** adj resulting.
consequently adv therefore; as a
result. **consequential** adj important.

conservative adj opposing change;
cautious; conventional in style; (**C-**) of
or supporting the Progressive
Conservative Party, the most
conservative of the three main political
parties. ◆ n one who wishes to
preserve political institutions against
change; one opposed to hasty
changes or innovations; (**C-**) supporter
or member of the Progressive
Conservative Party. **conservatism** n

conservatoire [kon-serv-a-twahr] n
school of music.

conservatory n, pl **-ries** greenhouse;
conservatoire.

conserve v protect from harm, decay,
or loss; preserve (fruit) with sugar. ◆ n
fruit preserved by cooking in sugar.
conservancy n environmental
conservation. **conservation** n
protection of natural resources and the
environment; conserving.
conservationist n

consider v be of the opinion that;
think about; be considerate of; discuss;
examine. **considerable** adj fairly large;
much. **considerably** adv **considerate**
adj thoughtful towards others.
considerately adv **consideration** n
careful thought; fact that must be
considered; kindness; payment for a
service. **considering** prep taking (a
specified fact) into account.

consign v deposit; entrust; address or
deliver (goods). **consignment** n
shipment of goods.

consist v **consist in** have as its main or

only feature. **consist of** be made up
of.

consistency n, pl **-cies** degree of
thickness or smoothness; being
consistent. **consistent** adj unchanging,
constant; in agreement. **consistently**
adv

console[1] v comfort in distress.
consolation n consoling; person or
thing that consoles.

console[2] n panel of controls for
electronic equipment; cabinet for a
television or audio equipment;
ornamental wall bracket; part of an
organ containing the pedals, stops,
and keys.

consolidate v make or become
stronger or more stable; combine into
a whole. **consolidation** n

consommé [kon-som-may] n thin
clear meat soup.

consonant n speech sound made by
partially or completely blocking the
breath stream; letter representing this.
◆ adj (foll. by with) agreeing (with).
consonance n

consort v (foll. by with) keep
company (with). ◆ n husband or wife
of a monarch.

consortium n, pl **-tia** association of
business firms.

conspectus n survey or summary.

conspicuous adj clearly visible;
striking. **conspicuously** adv

conspire v plan a crime together in
secret; act together as if by design.
conspiracy n conspiring; plan made
by conspiring. **conspirator** n
conspiratorial adj

constable n police officer of the
lowest rank. **constabulary** n police
force of an area.

constant adj continuous; unchanging;
faithful. ◆ n unvarying quantity;
something unchanging. **constantly**
adv **constancy** n

constellation n group of stars.

consternation n anxiety, dismay, or
confusion.

constipation n difficulty in
defecating. **constipated** adj having
constipation.

constituent n member of a
constituency; component part. ◆ adj
forming part of a whole. **constituency**
n area represented by a Member of

Parliament; voters in such an area.

constitute v form, compose.
constitution n principles on which a state is governed; physical condition; structure. **constitutional** adj of a constitution; in accordance with a political constitution. ◆ n walk taken for exercise. **constitutionally** adv

constrain v force, compel; restrain or confine. **constraint** n compulsion or restraint; forced unnatural manner.

constrict v make narrower or tighter, esp. by squeezing. **constriction** n **constrictive** adj **constrictor** n large snake that squeezes its prey to death; muscle that constricts.

construct v build or put together. **construction** n constructing; thing constructed; interpretation; *Grammar* way in which words are arranged in a sentence, clause, or phrase. **constructive** adj (of advice, criticism, etc.) useful and helpful. **constructively** adv

construe v **-struing, -strued** interpret; analyse grammatically.

consul n official representing a state in a foreign country; one of the two chief magistrates in ancient Rome. **consular** adj **consulate** n position or offices of a consul. **consulship** n

consult v go to for information or advice. **consultant** n *Brit* specialist doctor with a senior position in a hospital; specialist who gives professional advice. **consultancy** n work or position of a consultant. **consultation** n (meeting for) consulting. **consultative** adj giving advice.

consume v eat or drink; use up; destroy; obsess. **consumer** n person who buys goods or uses services. **consumption** n consuming; amount consumed; *Old-fashioned* tuberculosis. **consumptive** adj, n (person) having tuberculosis.

consummate v [kon-sume-mate] make (a marriage) legal by sexual intercourse; complete or fulfil. ◆ adj [kon-**sum**-mit] supremely skilled; perfect. **consummation** n

cont. continued.

contact n communicating; touching; useful acquaintance; connection between two electrical conductors in a circuit. ◆ v get in touch with. **contact**

lens lens fitting over the eyeball to correct defective vision.

contagion n passing on of disease by contact; contagious disease; spreading of a harmful influence. **contagious** adj spreading by contact, catching.

contain v hold or be capable of holding; consist of; control, restrain. **container** n receptacle used to hold something; large standard-sized box for transporting cargo by truck or ship. **containment** n prevention of the spread of something harmful.

contaminate v pollute, make impure; make radioactive. **contaminant** n contaminating substance. **contamination** n

contemplate v think deeply (about); consider as a possibility; gaze at. **contemplation** n **contemplative** adj **contemplatively** adv

contemporary adj present-day, modern; living or occurring at the same time. ◆ n, pl **-raries** person or thing living at the same time or of approximately the same age as another. **contemporaneous** adj

contempt n attitude of scornful disregard; open disrespect for the authority of a court. **contemptible** adj deserving contempt. **contemptuous** adj showing contempt. **contemptuously** adv

contend v (foll. by *with*) deal with; assert; compete. **contender** n competitor. **contention** n disagreement or dispute; point asserted in argument. **contentious** adj causing dispute; quarrelsome.

content[1] n meaning or substance of a book etc.; amount of a substance in a mixture. ◆ pl what something contains; list of chapters at the front of a book.

content[2] adj satisfied with things as they are. ◆ v make (someone) content. ◆ n peace of mind. **contented** adj **contentment** n

contest n competition or struggle. ◆ v dispute; fight or compete for. **contestant** n

context n circumstances of an event or fact; words before and after a word or passage that contribute to its meaning. **contextual** adj

contiguous adj very near or touching. **contiguity** n

continent[1] *n* one of the earth's large masses of land. **the Continent** *Brit* mainland of Europe. **continental** *adj* **continental breakfast** light breakfast of rolls, coffee, etc.

continent[2] *adj* able to control one's urination and defecation; sexually chaste. **continence** *n*

contingent *adj* (foll. by *on*) dependent on (something uncertain). ◆ *n* group of people, esp. soldiers, that is part of a larger group. **contingency** *n* something that may happen.

continue *v* **-tinuing, -tinued** (cause to) remain in a condition or place; carry on (doing something); resume. **continual** *adj* constant; frequently recurring. **continually** *adv* **continuance** *n* continuing. **continuation** *n* continuing; part added. **continuity** *n* smooth development or sequence. **continuous** *adj* continuing uninterrupted. **continuously** *adv*

continuo *n, pl* **-tinuos** *Music* continuous bass part, usually played on a keyboard instrument.

continuum *n, pl* **-tinua, -tinuums** continuous series.

contort *v* twist out of normal shape. **contortion** *n* **contortionist** *n* performer who contorts his or her body to entertain.

contour *n* outline; (also **contour line**) line on a map joining places of the same height.

contra- *prefix* against or contrasting, e.g. *contraflow*.

contraband *adj, n* smuggled (goods).

contraception *n* prevention of pregnancy by artificial means. **contraceptive** *n* device used or pill taken to prevent pregnancy. ◆ *adj* preventing pregnancy.

contract *n* formal agreement. ◆ *v* make a formal agreement (to do something); make or become smaller or shorter; catch (an illness). **contraction** *n* **contractor** *n* firm that supplies materials or labour, esp. for building. **contractual** *adj*

contradict *v* declare the opposite of (a statement) to be true; be at variance with. **contradiction** *n* **contradictory** *adj*

contralto *n, pl* **-tos** (singer with)

lowest female voice.

contraption *n* strange-looking device.

contrapuntal *adj Music* of or in counterpoint.

contrary *adj* opposed, completely different; perverse. ◆ *n* complete opposite. ◆ *adv* in opposition. **contrarily** *adv* **contrariness** *n* **contrariwise** *adv* conversely.

contrast *n* striking difference; something showing this. ◆ *v* compare or be compared in order to show differences; (foll. by *with*) be very different (from). **contrastive** *adj*

contravene *v* break (a rule or law). **contravention** *n*

contretemps [kon-tra-tahn] *n, pl* **-temps** embarrassing minor disagreement.

contribute *v* give to a common purpose or fund; (foll. by *to*) help (something) to occur. **contribution** *n* **contributor** *n* **contributory** *adj*

contrite *adj* guilty and regretful. **contritely** *adv* **contrition** *n*

contrive *v* make happen; invent and construct. **contrivance** *n* device; plan; contriving. **contrived** *adj* planned, artificial.

control *n* power to direct something; curb or check; standard of comparison in an experiment. ◆ *pl* instruments used to operate a machine. ◆ *v* **-trolling, -trolled** have power over; limit or restrain; regulate. **controllable** *adj* **controller** *n*

controversy *n, pl* **-sies** fierce argument or debate. **controversial** *adj* causing controversy.

contumacy [kon-tume-mass-ee] *n* obstinate disobedience. **contumacious** [kon-tume-may-shuss] *adj*

contumely [kon-tume-mill-ee] *n* scornful or insulting treatment.

contusion *n* bruise.

conundrum *n* riddle.

conurbation *n* large urban area formed by the growth and merging of towns.

convalesce *v* recover health after an illness or operation. **convalescence** *n* **convalescent** *adj, n*

convection *n* transmission of heat in liquids or gases by the circulation of currents. **convector** *n* heater which emits hot air.

convene v gather or summon for a formal meeting. **convener, -or** n person who calls a meeting.

convenient adj suitable or opportune; easy to use; nearby. **conveniently** adv **convenience** n quality of being convenient; convenient thing; Brit public lavatory. **convenience store** small shop open long hours.

convent n building where nuns live; school run by nuns.

convention n widely accepted view of proper behaviour; formal agreement; assembly. **conventional** adj (slavishly) following the accepted customs; customary; (of weapons or warfare) not nuclear. **conventionally** adv **conventionality** n

converge v move towards the same point. **convergence** n

conversant adj **conversant with** having knowledge of.

converse[1] v have a conversation. **conversation** n informal talk. **conversational** adj **conversationalist** n person with a specified ability at conversation.

converse[2] adj, n opposite or contrary. **conversely** adv

convert v change in form, character, or function; cause to change in opinion or belief. ◆ n converted person. **conversion** n (thing resulting from) a converting or being converted. **converter, -or** n **convertible** adj capable of being converted. ◆ n automobile with a folding or removable roof.

convex adj curving outwards. **convexity** n

convey v communicate (information); carry, transport. **conveyance** n Old-fashioned vehicle; transfer of the legal title to property. **conveyancing** n branch of law dealing with the transfer of ownership of property. **conveyor belt** continuous moving belt for transporting things, esp. in a factory.

convict v declare guilty. ◆ n person serving a prison sentence. **conviction** n firm belief; instance of being convicted.

convince v persuade by evidence or argument. **convincing** adj **convincingly** adv

convivial adj sociable, lively.

conviviality n

convoke v call together. **convocation** n convoking; large formal meeting.

convoluted adj coiled, twisted; (of an argument or sentence) complex and hard to understand. **convolution** n

convolvulus n twining plant with funnel-shaped flowers.

convoy n group of vehicles or ships travelling together.

convulse v (of muscles) undergo violent spasms; Informal be overcome (with laughter or rage). **convulsion** n violent muscular spasm. ◆ pl uncontrollable laughter. **convulsive** adj **convulsively** adv

cony n, pl **conies** rabbit; rabbit fur.

coo v **cooing, cooed** (of a dove or pigeon) make a soft murmuring sound. ◆ n cooing sound.

cooee interj call to attract attention.

cook v prepare (food) by heating; (of food) be cooked; Informal falsify (accounts etc.). ◆ n person who cooks food. **cooker** n apparatus for cooking heated by gas or electricity; apple suitable for cooking. **cookery** n art of cooking. **cookie** n small flat or slightly raised cake. **cook up** v Informal devise (a story).

cool adj moderately cold; calm and unemotional; indifferent or unfriendly; Informal sophisticated or excellent; Informal (of a large sum of money) without exaggeration, e.g. a cool ten thousand. ◆ v make or become cool. ◆ n coolness; Slang calmness, composure. **coolly** adv **coolness** n **coolant** n fluid used to cool machinery while it is working. **cooler** n container for making or keeping things cool; Slang prison.

coolie n Old-fashioned offens unskilled Oriental labourer.

coomb, coombe n valley.

coop n cage or pen for poultry. **coop up** v confine in a restricted place.

co-op n cooperative society; shop run by one.

cooper n person who makes or repairs barrels or casks.

cooperate v work or act together. **cooperation** n **cooperative** adj willing to cooperate; (of an enterprise) owned and managed collectively. ◆ n cooperative organization.

co-opt v add (someone) to a group by the agreement of the existing members. **co-option** n

coordinate v bring together and cause to work together efficiently. ◆ n Math any of a set of numbers defining the location of a point. ◆ pl garments designed to be worn together. **coordination** n **coordinator** n

coot n small black water bird.

cop Slang ◆ n policeman. ◆ v copping, copped. **cop it** get into trouble or be punished. **cop out** v avoid taking responsibility or committing oneself.

cope¹ v deal successfully (with).

cope² n large ceremonial cloak worn by some Christian priests.

coping n sloping top row of a wall. **coping stone**

copious [kope-ee-uss] adj abundant, plentiful. **copiously** adv

copper¹ n soft reddish-brown metal; copper or bronze coin; large metal container used to boil water. **copper-bottomed** adj financially reliable. **copperplate** n fine handwriting style.

copper² n Slang policeman.

coppice, copse n dense growth of small trees and undergrowth.

copra n dried oil-yielding kernel of the coconut.

copulate v have sexual intercourse. **copulation** n

copy n, pl copies thing made to look exactly like another; single specimen of a book etc.; material for printing. ◆ v copying, copied make a copy of; act or try to be like another. **copyright** n exclusive legal right to reproduce and control a book, work of art, etc. ◆ v take out a copyright on. ◆ adj protected by copyright. **copywriter** n person who writes advertising copy.

coquette n woman who flirts. **coquettish** adj **coquetry** n

coracle n small round boat of wicker covered with skins.

coral n hard substance formed from the skeletons of very small sea animals. ◆ adj made of coral; orange-pink.

corbel n stone or timber support projecting from a wall.

cord n thin rope or thick string; cordlike structure in the body; corduroy. ◆ pl corduroy trousers. ◆ adj (of fabric) ribbed.

cordial adj warm and friendly; strong, e.g. cordial dislike. ◆ n drink with a fruit base. **cordially** adv **cordiality** n

cordite n explosive used in guns and bombs.

cordon n chain of police, soldiers, etc. guarding an area; fruit tree grown as a single stem. **cordon off** v form a cordon round.

cordon bleu [bluh] adj (of cookery or cooks) of the highest standard.

corduroy n cotton fabric with a velvety ribbed surface.

core n central part of certain fruits, containing the seeds; essential part. ◆ v remove the core from.

co-respondent n person with whom someone being sued for divorce is claimed to have committed adultery.

corgi n short-legged sturdy dog.

coriander n plant with aromatic seeds and leaves used for flavouring.

cork n thick light bark of a Mediterranean oak; piece of this used as a stopper. ◆ v stop up with a cork. **corkage** n restaurant's charge for serving wine bought elsewhere. **corkscrew** n tool for extracting corks from bottles.

corm n bulblike underground stem of certain plants.

cormorant n large dark-coloured long-necked sea bird.

corn¹ n tall plant bearing kernels on cobs enclosed in husks; grain of this plant used for food or fodder; cereal grass or grain; Slang something unoriginal or oversentimental. **corny** adj Slang unoriginal or oversentimental. **cornflakes** pl n breakfast cereal of toasted corn flakes. **cornflour** n finely ground corn. **cornflower** n plant with blue flowers.

corn² n painful hard skin on the foot or toe.

cornea [korn-ee-a] n, pl -neas, -neae transparent membrane covering the eyeball. **corneal** adj

corned beef n beef preserved in salt.

cornelian n reddish semiprecious stone.

corner n area or angle where two converging lines or surfaces meet; place where two streets meet; sharp bend in a road; remote or inaccessible place; Sport free kick or shot from the

corner of the field. ◆ v (of a vehicle) turn a corner; force into a difficult or inescapable position; obtain a monopoly of. **cornerstone** n indispensable part or basis.

cornet n brass instrument similar to the trumpet; cone-shaped ice-cream wafer.

cornice [korn-iss] n decorative moulding round the top of a wall.

cornucopia [korn-yew-kope-ee-a] n great abundance; symbol of plenty, consisting of a horn overflowing with fruit and flowers.

corolla n petals of a flower collectively.

corollary [kor-oll-a-ree] n, pl -laries idea, fact, or proposition which is the natural result of something else.

corona [kor-rone-a] n, pl -nas, -nae ring of light round the moon or sun.

coronary [kor-ron-a-ree] adj of the arteries surrounding the heart. ◆ n, pl -naries coronary thrombosis. **coronary thrombosis** condition in which the flow of blood to the heart is blocked by a blood clot.

coronation n ceremony of crowning a monarch.

coroner n official responsible for the investigation of violent, sudden, or suspicious deaths.

coronet n small crown.

corpora n plural of CORPUS.

corporal[1] adj of the body. **corporal punishment** physical punishment, such as caning.

corporal[2] n noncommissioned officer below sergeant.

corporation n large business or company; city or town council; Informal large paunch. **corporate** adj relating to business corporations; shared by a group.

corporeal [kore-pore-ee-al] adj physical or tangible.

corps [kore] n, pl corps military unit with a specific function; organized body of people.

corpse n dead body.

corpulent adj fat or plump. **corpulence** n

corpus n, pl corpora collection of writings, esp. by a single author.

corpuscle n red or white blood cell.

corral n enclosure for cattle or horses. ◆ v -ralling, -ralled put in a corral.

correct adj free from error, true; in accordance with accepted standards. ◆ v put right; indicate the errors in; rebuke or punish. **correctly** adv **correctness** n **correction** n correcting; alteration correcting something. **corrective** n, adj (thing) intended or tending to correct.

correlate v place or be placed in a mutual relationship. ◆ n either of two things mutually related. **correlation** n **correlative** adj, n

correspond v be consistent (with); be similar (to); communicate (with) by letter. **corresponding** adj **correspondingly** adv **correspondence** n communication by letters; letters so exchanged; relationship or similarity. **correspondent** n writer of letters; person employed by a newspaper etc. to report on a special subject or from a foreign country.

corridor n passage in a building or train; strip of land or air space providing access through foreign territory.

corrigendum [kor-rij-end-um] n, pl -da thing to be corrected.

corroborate v support (a fact or opinion) by giving proof. **corroboration** n **corroborative** adj

corrode v eat or be eaten away by chemical action. **corrosion** n **corrosive** adj

corrugate v fold into alternate grooves and ridges. **corrugated** adj **corrugation** n

corrupt adj open to or involving bribery; morally wrong; (of a text or data) made unreliable by errors or alterations. ◆ v make corrupt. **corruptly** adv **corruption** n **corruptible** adj

corsage [kor-sahzh] n small bouquet worn on the bodice of a dress.

corsair n pirate; pirate ship.

corset n close-fitting undergarment worn to support the torso.

cortege [kor-tayzh] n funeral procession.

cortex n, pl -tices Anat outer layer of the brain or other internal organ. **cortical** adj

cortisone n steroid hormone used to treat various diseases.

corundum n hard mineral used as an

abrasive.

coruscate v sparkle. **coruscation** n

corvette n lightly armed escort warship.

cos Math cosine.

cosh n heavy blunt weapon. ◆ v hit with a cosh.

cosine [koh-sine] n (in trigonometry) ratio of the length of the adjacent side to that of the hypotenuse in a right-angled triangle.

cosmetic n preparation used to improve the appearance of a person's skin. ◆ adj improving the appearance only.

cosmic adj of the whole universe. **cosmic rays** electromagnetic radiation from outer space.

cosmonaut n Russian name for ASTRONAUT.

cosmopolitan adj composed of people or elements from many countries; having lived and travelled in many countries. ◆ n cosmopolitan person. **cosmopolitanism** n

cosmos n the universe. **cosmology** n study of the origin and nature of the universe. **cosmological** adj

Cossack n member of a S Russian people famous as horsemen.

cosset v **cosseting, cosseted** pamper or pet.

cost n amount of money, time, labour, etc. required for something. ◆ pl expenses of a lawsuit. ◆ v **costing, cost** have as its cost; involve the loss or sacrifice of; (past **costed**) estimate the cost of. **costly** adj expensive; involving great loss or sacrifice. **costliness** n

costive adj having or causing constipation.

costume n style of dress of a particular place or time, or for a particular activity; clothes worn by an actor or performer. **costumier** n maker or seller of costumes. **costume jewellery** inexpensive artificial jewellery.

cosy adj **-sier, -siest** snug and warm; intimate, friendly. ◆ n, pl **cosies** cover to keep a teapot etc. hot. **cosily** adv **cosiness** n

cot n Brit child's bed with high sides; small portable bed.

coterie [kote-er-ee] n exclusive group, clique.

cotoneaster [kot-tone-ee-**ass**-ter] n garden shrub with red berries.

cottage n small house in the country. **cottage cheese** soft mild white cheese. **cottage industry** craft industry in which employees work at home. **cottage pie** dish of minced meat topped with mashed potato.

cotter n pin or wedge used to secure machine parts.

cotton n white downy fibre covering the seeds of a tropical plant; thread or cloth made of this. **cottony** adj **cotton batting, cotton wool** fluffy cotton used for surgical dressings etc. **cotton on (to)** v Informal understand.

cotyledon [kot-ill-ee-don] n first leaf of a plant embryo.

couch n piece of upholstered furniture for seating more than one person. ◆ v express in a particular way.

couchette [koo-shett] n bed converted from seats in a train.

couch grass n quickly spreading grassy weed.

cougar [koo-gar] n puma.

cough v expel air from the lungs abruptly and noisily. ◆ n act or sound of coughing; illness which causes coughing.

could v past tense of CAN[1].

couldn't could not.

coulee [koo-lay] n ravine cut by water in western N America.

coulomb [koo-lom] n unit of electric charge.

coulter [kole-ter] n blade at the front of a plowshare.

council n group meeting for discussion or consultation; local governing body of a town or county. **councillor** n member of a council.

counsel n advice or guidance; barrister or barristers. ◆ v **-selling, -selled** give guidance to; urge or recommend. **counsellor** n

count[1] v say numbers in order; find the total of; be important; regard as; take into account. ◆ n number reached by counting; counting; Law one of a number of charges. **countless** adj too many to be counted. **count on** v expect; rely on.

count[2] n European nobleman. **countess** n fem

countdown n counting backwards to zero of the seconds before an event.

countenance n (expression of) the face. ◆ v support or tolerate.

counter[1] n long flat surface in a bank or shop, on which business is transacted; small flat disc used in board games.

counter[2] v oppose, retaliate against. ◆ adv in the opposite direction; in direct contrast. ◆ n opposing or retaliatory action.

counter- combining form used with many main words to mean: against, opposite, e.g. counterbalance; retaliatory, rival, e.g. counter-revolution, counterclaim.

counteract v neutralize or act against. **counteraction** n

counterattack v, n attack in response to an attack.

counterbalance n weight or force balancing or neutralizing another. ◆ v act as a counterbalance to.

counterblast n aggressive response to a verbal attack.

counterfeit adj fake, forged. ◆ n fake, forgery. ◆ v fake, forge.

counterfoil n Brit part of a cheque or receipt kept as a record.

countermand v cancel (a previous order).

counterpane n bed covering.

counterpart n person or thing corresponding to another.

counterpoint n Music technique of combining melodies.

counterpoise n, v counterbalance.

counterproductive adj having an effect opposite to the one intended.

countersign v sign (a document already signed by another) as confirmation.

countersink v drive (a screw) into a shaped hole so that its head is below the surface.

countertenor n male alto.

country n, pl **-tries** nation; nation's territory; nation's people; rural areas as opposed to town. **countrified** adj rustic in manner or appearance. **country and western** popular music based on N American White folk music. **countryman, countrywoman** n compatriot; person who lives in the country. **countryside** n rural areas.

county n, pl **-ties** division of a country.

coup [koo] n successful action; coup d'état.

coup de grace [koo de grahss] n final or decisive action.

coup d'état [koo day-tah] n sudden violent overthrow of a government.

coupé [koo-pay] n sporty automobile with two doors and a sloping fixed roof.

couple n two people who are married or romantically involved; two partners in a dance or game. ◆ v connect, associate; Lit have sexual intercourse. **a couple** a pair; Informal a few. **couplet** n two consecutive lines of verse, usu. rhyming and of the same metre. **coupling** n device for connecting things, such as railway carriages.

coupon n piece of paper entitling the holder to a discount or gift; detachable order form; football pools entry form.

courage n ability to face danger or pain without fear. **courageous** adj **courageously** adv

coureur de bois [koo-rir-di-bwah] n, pl **coureurs de bois** [koo-rir] French Canadian or Métis woodsman.

courgette n Brit zucchini.

courier n person who looks after and guides travellers; person paid to deliver urgent messages.

course n series of lessons or medical treatment; onward movement in space or time; direction or route of movement; area where golf is played or a race is run; any of the successive parts of a meal; continuous layer of masonry at one level in a building; mode of conduct or action; natural development of events. ◆ v (of liquid) run swiftly; hunt with hounds that follow the quarry by sight and not scent. **of course** naturally.

court n body which decides legal cases; place where it meets; marked area for playing a racket game; courtyard; residence, household, or retinue of a sovereign. ◆ v Old-fashioned try to win (someone) as a spouse; try to win (someone's favour); invite, e.g. court disaster. **courtier** n attendant at a royal court. **courtly** adj ceremoniously polite. **courtliness** n **courtship** n courting of an intended spouse or mate. **court martial** court

for trying naval or military offences.
court shoe woman's low-cut shoe without straps or laces. **courtyard** n paved space enclosed by buildings or walls.

courtesan [kor-tiz-**zan**] n Hist mistress or high-class prostitute.

courtesy n, pl -**sies** politeness, good manners; courteous act. **courtesy of, by courtesy of** by permission of. **courteous** adj polite. **courteously** adv

cousin n child of one's uncle or aunt.

cove n small bay or inlet.

coven [kuv-ven] n meeting of witches.

covenant [kuv-ven-ant] n formal agreement, esp. to make an annual (charitable) payment. ◆ v agree (to pay) by a covenant.

cover v place or spread or be placed or spread over; screen or conceal; travel over; protect from loss or risk by insurance; keep a gun aimed at; include; report (an event) for a newspaper; be enough to pay for. ◆ n anything which covers; outside of a book or magazine; pretext or disguise; shelter or protection; insurance. **coverage** n amount or extent covered. **coverlet** n bed cover.

covert adj secret, concealed. ◆ n thicket giving shelter to game birds or animals. **covertly** adv

covet v **coveting, coveted** long to possess (what belongs to someone else). **covetous** adj **covetousness** n

covey [kuv-vee] n small flock of grouse or partridge.

cow[1] n mature female of cattle and of certain other animals, such as the elephant or whale. **cowboy** n ranch worker who herds and tends cattle, usu. on horseback; Informal unscrupulous worker.

cow[2] v intimidate, subdue.

coward n person who lacks courage. **cowardly** adj **cowardice** n lack of courage.

cower v cringe or shrink in fear.

cowl n loose hood; monk's hooded robe; cover on a chimney to increase ventilation.

cowling n cover on an engine.

cowrie n brightly marked sea shell.

cowslip n fragrant wild primrose.

cox n coxswain. ◆ v act as cox of (a boat).

coxswain [kok-sn] n person who steers a rowing boat.

coy adj affectedly shy or modest. **coyly** adv **coyness** n

coyote [koy-**ote**-ee] n prairie wolf of N America.

coypu n beaver-like aquatic rodent, bred for its fur.

cozen v cheat or trick.

CP Canadian Pacific.

CPU Computers central processing unit.

Cr Chem chromium.

crab n edible shellfish with ten legs, the first pair modified into pincers.

crab apple n small sour apple.

crabbed adj (of handwriting) hard to read; (also **crabby**) bad-tempered.

crack v break or split partially; break with a sharp noise; (cause to) make a sharp noise; break down or yield under strain; hit suddenly; tell (a joke); solve (a code or problem); (of the voice) become harsh or change pitch suddenly. ◆ n narrow gap; sudden sharp noise; sharp blow; Informal gibe or joke; Slang pure highly addictive form of cocaine. ◆ adj Informal excellent, first-rate, e.g. a crack shot.

cracker n thin dry biscuit; decorated cardboard tube, pulled apart with a bang, containing a paper hat and a motto or toy; small explosive firework. **crackers** adj Slang crazy. **cracking** adj first-class. **crackdown** n severe disciplinary or repressive measure. **crack down on** v take severe measures against. **crackpot** adj, n Informal eccentric (person).

crackle v make small sharp popping noises. ◆ n crackling sound. **crackling** n crackle; crisp skin of roast pork.

cradle n baby's bed on rockers; place where something originated; supporting structure. ◆ v hold gently as if in a cradle.

craft[1] n skilled trade; skill or ability; cunning. **crafty** adj skilled in deception. **craftily** adv **craftiness** n **craftsman, craftswoman** n skilled worker. **craftsmanship** n

craft[2] n, pl **craft** boat, ship, aircraft, or spaceship.

crag n steep rugged rock. **craggy** adj

cram v **cramming, crammed** force into too small a space; fill too full; study hard just before an examination.

cramp *n* painful muscular contraction; clamp for holding masonry or timber together. ◆ *v* confine or restrict.

crampon *n* spiked plate strapped to a boot for climbing on ice.

cranberry *n* sour edible red berry.

crane *n* machine for lifting and moving heavy weights; wading bird with long legs, neck, and bill. ◆ *v* stretch (one's neck) to see something.

crane fly *n* long-legged insect with slender wings.

cranium *n, pl* -niums, -nia skull. **cranial** *adj*

crank *n* arm projecting at right angles from a shaft, for transmitting or converting motion; *Informal* eccentric person. ◆ *v* start (an engine) with a crank. **cranky** *adj* eccentric; bad-tempered. **crankshaft** *n* shaft driven by a crank.

cranny *n, pl* -nies small opening, chink.

crape *n* same as CREPE.

craps *n* gambling game played with two dice.

crash *n* collision involving a vehicle or vehicles; sudden loud smashing noise; financial collapse. ◆ *v* (cause to) collide violently with a vehicle, a stationary object, or the ground; (cause to) make a loud smashing noise; (cause to) fall with a crash; collapse or fail financially. ◆ *adj* requiring or using great effort to achieve results quickly, e.g. *a crash course*. **crash helmet** protective helmet worn by a motorcyclist. **crash-land** *v* land (an aircraft) in an emergency, causing it damage. **crash-landing** *n*

crass *adj* grossly stupid. **crassly** *adv* **crassness** *n*

crate *n* large wooden container for packing goods.

crater *n* bowl-shaped cavity made by the impact of a meteorite or an explosion; mouth of a volcano.

cravat *n* man's scarf worn like a tie.

crave *v* desire intensely; beg or plead for. **craving** *n*

craven *adj* cowardly.

craw *n* bird's crop; animal's stomach.

crawfish *n* same as CRAYFISH.

crawl *v* move on one's hands and knees; move very slowly; act in a servile manner; be or feel as if covered with crawling creatures. ◆ *n* crawling motion or pace; overarm swimming stroke. **crawler** *n*

crayfish *n* edible freshwater shellfish like a lobster.

crayon *n* stick or pencil of coloured wax or clay. ◆ *v* draw or colour with a crayon.

craze *n* short-lived fashion or enthusiasm. **crazed** *adj* demented; (of porcelain) having fine cracks. **crazy** *adj Informal* ridiculous; (foll. by *about*) very fond (of); insane. **craziness** *n* **crazy paving** paving made of irregularly shaped slabs of stone.

creak *v, n* (make) a harsh squeaking sound. **creaky** *adj*

cream *n* fatty part of milk; something, esp. a food or cosmetic, resembling cream in consistency; best part (of something). ◆ *adj* yellowish-white. ◆ *v* beat to a creamy consistency; (foll. by *off*) take the best part from. **creamy** *adj* **cream cheese** soft white cheese.

crease *n* line made by pressing; *Hockey* small area in front of goal net. ◆ *v* make, develop creases.

create *v* bring into being; appoint to a new rank or position; *Slang* make an angry fuss. **creation** *n* **creative** *adj* imaginative or inventive. **creativity** *n* **creator** *n*

creature *n* person, animal, or being.

crèche *n* day nursery for very young children.

credence [kreed-enss] *n* belief in the truth or accuracy of a statement.

credentials *pl n* document giving evidence of the bearer's identity or qualifications.

credible *adj* believable; trustworthy. **credibly** *adv* **credibility** *n*

credit *n* system of allowing customers to take goods and pay later; reputation for trustworthiness in paying debts; money at one's disposal in a bank account; side of an account book on which sums are entered; (source or cause of) praise or approval; influence or reputation based on the good opinion of others; belief or trust. ◆ *pl* list of people responsible for the production of a film, programme, or record. ◆ *v* **crediting, credited** enter as a credit in an account; (foll. by *with*) attribute (to); believe. **creditable** *adj* praiseworthy. **creditably** *adv*

creditor n person to whom money is owed. **credit card** card allowing a person to buy on credit.

credulous adj too willing to believe. **credulity** n

creed n statement or system of (Christian) beliefs or principles.

creek n narrow inlet or bay; small stream.

creel n wicker basket used by anglers.

creep v creeping, crept move with stealthy slow movements; crawl with the body near to the ground; (of a plant) grow along the ground or over a surface. ◆ n Slang obnoxious or servile person. ◆ pl feeling of fear or disgust. **creeper** n creeping plant. **creepy** adj Informal causing a feeling of fear or disgust.

cremate v burn (a corpse) to ash. **cremation** n **crematorium** n building where corpses are cremated.

crenellated adj having battlements. **crenellation** n

creole n language developed from a mixture of languages; (C-) native-born W Indian or Latin American of mixed European and African descent.

creosote n dark oily liquid distilled from coal tar and used for preserving wood. ◆ v treat with creosote.

crepe [krayp] n fabric or rubber with a crinkled texture; very thin pancake. **crepe paper** paper with a crinkled texture.

crept v past of CREEP.

crepuscular adj of or like twilight.

crescendo [krish-end-oh] n, pl -dos gradual increase in loudness, esp. in music.

crescent n (shape of) the moon as seen in its first or last quarter; crescent-shaped street.

cress n plant with strong-tasting leaves, used in salads.

crest n top of a mountain, hill, or wave; tuft or growth on a bird's or animal's head; heraldic device used on a coat of arms, notepaper, and elsewhere. **crested** adj **crestfallen** adj disheartened.

cretin n person afflicted with physical and mental retardation caused by a thyroid deficiency; Informal stupid person. **cretinous** adj

cretonne n heavy printed cotton

fabric used in furnishings.

crevasse n deep open chasm, esp. in a glacier.

crevice n narrow fissure or crack.

crew n people who man a ship or aircraft; group of people working together; Informal any group of people. ◆ v serve as a crew member on. **crew cut** man's closely cropped haircut.

crewel n fine worsted yarn used in embroidery.

crib n child's bed usu. with barred sides; barred rack used for fodder; plagiarism; translation or list of answers used by students, often illicitly. ◆ v cribbing, cribbed confine in small space; copy (someone's work) dishonestly. **crib death** unexplained death of a baby while asleep.

cribbage n card game for two to four players.

crick n muscle spasm or cramp, esp. in the back or neck. ◆ v cause a crick in.

cricket[1] n outdoor game played with bats, a ball, and wickets by two teams of eleven. **cricketer** n

cricket[2] n chirping insect like a grasshopper.

crime n unlawful act; unlawful acts collectively; Informal disgraceful act. **criminal** n person guilty of a crime. ◆ adj of crime. **criminally** adv **criminality** n **criminology** n study of crime. **criminologist** n

crimp v fold or press into ridges.

crimson adj deep red.

cringe v flinch or shrink; behave in a servile or timid way.

crinkle v, n wrinkle, twist, or fold.

crinoline n hooped petticoat.

cripple n person who is lame or disabled. ◆ v make a cripple of (someone); damage (something).

crisis n, pl -ses crucial stage; time of acute trouble or danger.

crisp adj fresh and firm; dry and brittle; clean and neat; (of weather) cold but invigorating; brisk and lively. ◆ n Brit potato chip. **crisply** adv **crispness** n **crispy** adj **crispbread** n thin dry biscuit.

crisscross v move in, mark with, or consist of a crosswise pattern. ◆ adj (of lines) crossing in different directions.

criterion n, pl -ria standard of

judgment.

critic *n* professional judge of any of the arts; person who finds fault. **critical** *adj* very important or dangerous; seriously ill; fault-finding; discerning; of a critic or criticism. **critically** *adv* **criticism** *n* fault-finding; evaluation of a work of art. **criticize** *v* find fault with. **critique** *n* critical essay.

croak *v* (of a frog or crow) give a low hoarse cry; utter or speak with a croak. ◆ *n* low hoarse cry. **croaky** *adj* hoarse.

crochet [kroh-shay] *n* handicraft like knitting, done with a single hooked needle. ◆ *v* do or make such work.

crock *n* earthenware jar or pot; *Informal* old or decrepit person or thing. **crockery** *n* earthenware or china dishes.

crocodile *n* large amphibious tropical reptile; line of children walking two by two. **crocodile tears** insincere grief.

crocus *n, pl* **-cuses** small plant with yellow, white, or purple flowers in spring.

croft *n* small farm worked by the occupier in Scotland. **crofter** *n*

croissant [krwah-son] *n* rich flaky crescent-shaped roll.

crone *n* witchlike old woman.

crony *n, pl* **-nies** close friend.

crook *n Informal* criminal; bent or curved part; hooked pole. **crooked** *adj* bent or twisted; set at an angle; *Informal* dishonest.

croon *v* hum, sing, or speak in a soft low tone. **crooner** *n*

crop *n* cultivated plant; season's total yield of produce; group of things appearing at one time; hunting whip; pouch in a bird's gullet; short haircut. **crop-top** *n* short T-shirt or vest that reveals the wearer's midriff. ◆ *v* **cropping, cropped** cut short; produce or harvest as a crop; (of animals) feed on (grass etc.). **cropper** *n* **come a cropper** *Informal* have a disastrous failure or heavy fall. **crop up** *v Informal* happen unexpectedly.

croquet [kroh-kay] *n* game in which balls are hit through hoops.

croquette [kroh-kett] *n* fried cake of potato, meat, or fish.

crosier *n* same as CROZIER.

cross *v* move or go across (something); meet and pass; draw a cross or lines through (something); mark with lines across; place (one's arms or legs) crosswise; make the sign of the cross on (oneself); thwart or oppose; interbreed or cross-fertilize. ◆ *n* structure, symbol, or mark of two intersecting lines; such a structure of wood as a means of execution; representation of the Cross as an emblem of Christianity; mixture of two things; affliction. ◆ *adj* angry, in a bad mood; lying or placed across. **the Cross** *Christianity* the cross on which Christ was crucified. **crossing** *n* place where a street etc. may be crossed; place where things cross; journey across water. **crossly** *adv* **crossness** *n* **crossbar** *n* horizontal bar across goalposts or on a bicycle. **crossbow** *n* bow fixed across a wooden stock. **crossbred** *adj* bred from two different types of animal or plant. **crossbreed** *n* crossbred animal or plant. **cross-country** *adj, adv* by way of open country or fields. **cross-examine** *v* question (a witness in court) to check his or her testimony. **cross-examination** *n* **cross-eyed** *adj* with eyes turning inwards. **cross-fertilize** *v* fertilize (an animal or plant) from one of a different kind. **cross-fertilization** *n* **crossfire** *n* gunfire crossing another line of fire. **cross-ply** *adj* (of a tire) having the fabric cords in the outer casing running diagonally. **cross-purposes** *pl n* **at cross-purposes** misunderstanding each other. **cross-reference** *n* reference within a text to another part. **crossroads** *n* place where roads intersect. **cross section** (diagram of) a surface made by cutting across something; representative sample. **crosswalk** *n* place marked where pedestrians may cross a road. **crosswise** *adj, adv* transverse(ly); in the shape of a cross. **crossword puzzle** *n* puzzle in which words suggested by clues are written into a grid of squares.

crotch *n* fork between the legs.

crotchety *adj Informal* bad-tempered.

crouch *v* bend low with the legs and body close. ◆ *n* this position.

croupier [kroop-ee-ay] *n* person who collects bets and pays out winnings at a gambling table.

crouton *n* small piece of fried or

toasted bread served in soup.

crow[1] n large black bird with a harsh call. **as the crow flies** in a straight line. **crow's feet** wrinkles at the corners of the eyes. **crow's nest** lookout platform high on a ship's mast.

crow[2] v (of a cock) utter a shrill squawking sound; boast of one's superiority; (of a baby) utter cries of pleasure. ◆ n cock's cry.

crowbar n iron bar used as a lever.

crowd n large group of people or things; particular group of people. ◆ v flock together; fill.

crown n monarch's headdress; wreath for the head; highest point of something arched or curved; artificial cover for a broken or decayed tooth; former British coin worth twenty-five pence. ◆ v put a crown on the head of (someone) to proclaim him or her monarch; form or put on the top of; put the finishing touch to (a series of events); *Informal* hit on the head. **the Crown** power of the monarchy. **crown corporation** business owned by a government but run like a private company. **crown prince, crown princess** heir to the throne.

cruces n a plural of CRUX.

crucial adj very important, critical. **crucially** adv

crucible n pot in which metals are melted.

crucify v -fying, -fied put to death by fastening to a cross; treat cruelly; *Informal* ridicule publicly. **crucifix** n model of Christ on the Cross. **crucifixion** n crucifying. **the Crucifixion** *Christianity* crucifying of Christ; representation of this. **cruciform** adj cross-shaped.

crude adj rough and simple; tasteless or vulgar; in an unrefined state. **crudely** adv **crudity** n

cruel adj delighting in others' pain; causing pain or suffering. **cruelly** adv **cruelty** n

cruet n small container for salt, pepper, etc. at table.

cruise n voyage for pleasure. ◆ v sail about for pleasure; (of a vehicle, aircraft, or ship) travel at a moderate and economical speed. **cruiser** n motorboat with a cabin; fast warship.

crumb n small fragment of bread or other dry food; small bit.

crumble v break into fragments; fall apart or decay. ◆ n pudding of stewed fruit with a crumbly topping. **crumbly** adj

crummy adj -mier, -miest *Slang* inferior; squalid.

crumpet n round soft yeast cake eaten buttered; *Slang* sexually attractive women collectively.

crumple v crush and crease; collapse. **crumpled** adj

crunch v crush (food) noisily with the teeth; (cause to) make a crisp or brittle sound. ◆ n crunching sound; *Informal* critical moment. **crunchy** adj

crupper n strap that passes from the back of a saddle under a horse's tail.

crusade n medieval Christian war to recover the Holy Land from the Muslims; vigorous campaign in favour of a cause. ◆ v take part in a crusade. **crusader** n

crush v compress so as to break, injure, or crumple; break into small pieces; defeat utterly. ◆ n dense crowd; *Informal* infatuation; drink made by crushing fruit.

crust n hard outer part of something, esp. bread. ◆ v cover with or form a crust. **crusty** adj having a crust; irritable.

crustacean n hard-shelled, usu. aquatic animal with several pairs of legs, such as the crab or lobster.

crutch n staff with a rest for the armpit, used by a lame person; support; crotch.

crux n, pl **cruxes, cruces** crucial or decisive point.

cry v **crying, cried** shed tears; call or utter loudly; appeal urgently (for). ◆ n, pl **cries** fit of weeping; loud utterance; urgent appeal. **crybaby** n person who cries too readily.

cryogenics n branch of physics concerned with very low temperatures. **cryogenic** adj

crypt n vault, esp. one under a church. **cryptic** adj obscure in meaning. **cryptically** adv **cryptogram** n message in code. **cryptography** n art of writing in and deciphering codes.

cryptogam n plant that reproduces by spores, not seeds.

crystal n glasslike mineral; very clear and brilliant glass; tumblers, vases, etc. made of such glass; (single grain of a) symmetrically shaped solid formed naturally by some substances. ◆ adj bright and clear. **crystalline** adj of or like crystal or crystals; clear. **crystallize** v make or become definite; form into crystals; preserve (fruit) in sugar. **crystallization** n

CST Central Standard Time.

CTV Canadian Television (Network Ltd.).

Cu Chem copper.

cu. cubic.

cub n young of certain mammals, such as the lion; (C-) Cub Scout. ◆ v **cubbing, cubbed** give birth to (cubs). **Cub Scout** member of a junior branch of the Boy Scouts.

cubbyhole n small enclosed space or room.

cube n solid with six equal square sides; product obtained by multiplying a number by itself twice. ◆ v find the cube of (a number); cut into cubes. **cubic** adj having three dimensions; cube-shaped. **cubism** n style of art in which objects are represented by geometrical shapes. **cubist** n, adj **cube root** number whose cube is a given number.

cubicle n enclosed part of a large room, screened for privacy.

cuckold n man whose wife has committed adultery. ◆ v make a cuckold of.

cuckoo n migratory bird with a characteristic two-note call, which lays its eggs in the nests of other birds. ◆ adj Informal crazy.

cucumber n long green-skinned fleshy fruit used in salads.

cud n partially digested food which a ruminant brings back into its mouth to chew again. **chew the cud** reflect or ponder.

cuddle v hug fondly; nestle. ◆ n fond hug. **cuddly** adj

cudgel n short thick stick used as a weapon.

cue¹ n signal to an actor or musician to begin speaking or playing; signal or reminder. ◆ v **cueing, cued** give a cue to (someone).

cue² n long tapering stick used in billiards, snooker, or pool. ◆ v **cueing, cued** strike (a ball) with a cue.

cuff¹ n end of a sleeve. **off the cuff** Informal impromptu. **cuff link** one of a pair of decorative fastenings for shirt cuffs.

cuff² v strike with an open hand. ◆ n blow with an open hand.

cuisine [quiz-**zeen**] n style of cooking.

cul-de-sac n road with one end blocked off.

culinary adj of the kitchen or cookery.

cull v gather, select; remove or kill (inferior or surplus animals) from a herd. ◆ n culling.

culminate v reach the highest point or climax. **culmination** n

culottes pl n women's flared trousers cut to look like a skirt.

culpable adj deserving blame. **culpability** n

culprit n person guilty of an offence or misdeed.

cult n specific system of worship; devotion to a person, idea, or activity; popular fashion.

cultivate v prepare (land) to grow crops; grow (plants); develop or improve (something); try to develop a friendship with (someone). **cultivated** adj cultured or well-educated. **cultivation** n

culture n ideas, customs, and art of a particular society; particular society; developed understanding of the arts; cultivation of plants or rearing of animals; growth of bacteria for study. **cultural** adj **cultured** adj showing culture. **cultured pearl** pearl artificially grown in an oyster shell.

culvert n drain under a road or railway.

cumbersome adj awkward or unwieldy.

cumin, cummin n aromatic seeds of a Mediterranean plant, used in cooking.

cummerbund n broad sash worn round the waist.

cumulative [kew-myew-la-tiv] adj increasing steadily.

cumulus [kew-myew-luss] n, pl -li cloud shaped in heaped-up rounded masses.

cuneiform [kew-nif-form] n ancient system of writing using wedge-shaped characters. ◆ adj written in cuneiform.

cunning *adj* clever at deceiving; ingenious. ◆ *n* cleverness at deceiving; ingenuity. **cunningly** *adv*

cup *n* small bowl-shaped drinking container with a handle; contents of a cup; cup-shaped trophy given as a prize; hollow rounded shape; mixed drink with fruit juice or wine as a base. ◆ *v* **cupping, cupped** form (one's hands) into the shape of a cup; hold in cupped hands. **cupful** *n*

cupboard *n* piece of furniture or recess with a door, for storage.

cupidity [kew-**pid**-it-ee] *n* greed for wealth or possessions.

cupola [kew-**pol**-la] *n* domed roof or ceiling.

cur *n* mongrel dog; contemptible person.

curaçao [kew-rah-so] *n* orange-flavoured liqueur.

curare [kew-**rah**-ree] *n* poisonous resin of a S American tree, used as a muscle relaxant in medicine.

curate *n* clergyman who assists a parish priest. **curacy** [kew-rah-see] *n* work or position of a curate.

curative *adj* able to cure. ◆ *n* something curative.

curator *n* person in charge of a museum or art gallery. **curatorship** *n*

curb *n* check or restraint; edge of sidewalk. ◆ *v* restrain.

curd *n* coagulated milk. **curdle** *v* turn into curd, coagulate.

cure *v* heal (an ailment or problem); restore to health; preserve by salting, smoking, or drying. ◆ *n* restoration to health; medical treatment; remedy or solution. **curable** *adj*

curet, curette *n* surgical instrument for scraping tissue from body cavities. ◆ *v* **-retting, -retted** scrape with a curet. **curettage** *n*

curfew *n* law ordering people to stay indoors after a specific time at night; time set as a deadline by such a law.

curie *n* standard unit of radioactivity.

curio [kew-ree-oh] *n, pl* **-rios** strange or rare thing valued as a collector's item.

curious *adj* eager to know; eager to find out private details; unusual or peculiar. **curiously** *adv* **curiosity** *n* eagerness to know; eagerness to find out private details; strange or rare

thing.

curium [kew-ree-um] *n* artificial radioactive element produced from plutonium.

curl *v* twist (hair) or (of hair) be twisted into coils; twist into a spiral or curve. ◆ *n* coil of hair; spiral or curved shape. **curly** *adj* **curling** *n* game like bowls, played with heavy stones on ice.

curlew *n* long-billed wading bird.

curmudgeon *n* bad-tempered or mean person.

currant *n* dried grape; small round berry, such as a redcurrant.

current *adj* of the immediate present; most recent, up-to-date; commonly accepted. ◆ *n* flow of water or air in one direction; flow of electricity; general trend. **currently** *adv* **currency** *n* money in use in a particular country; state of being current.

curriculum *n, pl* **-la, -lums** specified course of study. **curriculum vitae** [vee-tie] outline of someone's educational and professional history, prepared for job applications.

curry[1] *n, pl* **-ries** dish of meat or vegetables in a hot or mild spicy sauce. ◆ *v* **-rying, -ried** prepare (food) with curry powder. **curry powder** mixture of spices for making curry.

curry[2] *v* **-rying, -ried** groom (a horse) with a currycomb. **curry favour** ingratiate oneself, esp. with one's superiors. **currycomb** *n* ridged comb for grooming a horse.

curse *v* say profane or obscene things (to); utter a curse against. ◆ *n* profane or obscene expression, usu. of anger; call to a supernatural power for harm to come to a person; affliction, misfortune. **cursed** *adj* hateful.

cursive *n, adj* (handwriting) done with joined letters.

cursor *n* movable point of light that shows a specific position on a visual display unit.

cursory *adj* hasty and superficial. **cursorily** *adv*

curt *adj* (of speech) impolitely brief. **curtly** *adv* **curtness** *n*

curtail *v* cut short; restrict. **curtailment** *n*

curtain *n* piece of cloth hung at a window or opening as a screen;

hanging cloth separating the audience and the stage in a theatre; end of a scene or act, marked by the fall or closing of the curtain; thing(s) forming a barrier or screen. ◆ v conceal with a curtain; provide with curtains.

curtsy, curtsey n, pl -sies, -seys woman's gesture of respect made by bending the knees and bowing the head. ◆ v -sying, -sied or -seying, -seyed make a curtsy.

curve n continuously bending line with no straight parts. ◆ v bend into or move in a curve. **curvy** adj **curvaceous** adj Informal (of a woman) having a shapely body. **curvature** n state or degree of being curved. **curvilinear** adj consisting of or bounded by a curve.

cushion n bag filled with soft material, to make a seat more comfortable; something that provides comfort or absorbs shock. ◆ v protect from injury or shock; lessen the effects of.

cushy adj **cushier, cushiest** Informal easy, e.g. a cushy job.

cusp n pointed end, esp. on a tooth; Astrol division between houses or signs of the zodiac.

cuss Informal ◆ n curse, oath; annoying person. ◆ v swear (at). **cussed** [kuss-id] adj Informal obstinate.

custard n dish or sauce made of sweetened milk thickened with eggs or cornflour.

custody n guardianship; imprisonment prior to being tried. **custodial** adj **custodian** n person in charge of a public building or museum collection.

custom n long-established activity or action; usual habit; regular use of a shop or business. ◆ pl duty charged on imports or exports; government department which collects these; area at a port, airport, or border where baggage and freight are examined for dutiable goods. **customary** adj usual; established by custom. **customarily** adv **customer** n person who buys goods or services. **custom-built, custom-made** adj made to the specifications of an individual customer.

cut v **cutting, cut** open up, penetrate, wound, or divide with a sharp instrument; divide; intersect; trim or shape by cutting; abridge; reduce; Informal snub (a person); Informal absent oneself from (classes). ◆ n stroke or incision made by cutting; piece cut off; reduction; abridgment; style in which hair or a garment is cut; Informal share, esp. of profits. **cutter** n person or tool that cuts; any of various small fast boats. **cutting** n piece cut from a plant for rooting or grafting; article cut from a newspaper or magazine; passage cut through high ground for a road or railway. ◆ adj keen, piercing; (of a remark) hurtful. **cut in** v interrupt; obstruct another vehicle in overtaking it. **cutthroat** adj fierce or relentless. ◆ n murderer.

cutaneous [kew-**tane**-ee-uss] adj of the skin.

cute adj appealing or attractive; Informal clever or shrewd. **cutely** adv **cuteness** n

cuticle [kew-tik-kl] n skin at the base of a fingernail or toenail.

cutlass n short curved one-edged sword.

cutlery n knives, forks, and spoons, used for eating. **cutler** n maker or seller of cutlery.

cutlet n small piece of meat grilled or fried.

cuttlefish n sea mollusc like a squid.

CV curriculum vitae.

cwt. hundredweight.

cyanide n extremely poisonous chemical compound.

cyanosis n blueness of the skin, caused by a deficiency of oxygen in the blood.

cyber- combining form computers e.g. cyberspace.

cybernetics n branch of science in which electronic and mechanical systems are studied and compared to biological systems.

cyberspace n place said to contain all the data stored in computers.

cyclamen [sik-la-men] n plant with red, pink, or white flowers having turned-back petals.

cycle n bicycle; motorcycle; recurrent series of events; time taken for one such series. ◆ v ride a cycle. **cyclic, cyclical** adj occurring in cycles. **cyclist** n person who rides a cycle.

cyclone n violent wind moving

clockwise round a central area. **cyclonic** adj

cyclotron n apparatus which accelerates charged particles by means of a strong vertical magnetic field.

cygnet n young swan.

cylinder n solid or hollow body with straight sides and circular ends; chamber within which the piston moves in an internal-combustion engine. **cylindrical** adj

cymbal n percussion instrument consisting of a brass plate which is struck against another or hit with a stick.

cynic [sin-ik] n person who believes that people always act selfishly. **cynical** adj **cynically** adv **cynicism** n

cynosure [sin-oh-zyure] n centre of attention.

cypher n same as CIPHER.

cypress n evergreen tree with very dark foliage.

cyst [sist] n (abnormal) sac in the body containing fluid or soft matter. **cystic** adj **cystitis** [siss-tite-iss] n inflammation of the bladder.

cytology [site-ol-a-jee] n study of plant and animal cells. **cytological** adj **cytologist** n

czar [zahr] n same as TSAR.

D d

d Physics density.

D Chem deuterium.

d. died; Brit old penny.

dab[1] v **dabbing, dabbed** pat lightly; apply with short tapping strokes. ◆ n small amount of something soft or moist; light tap or stroke. **dab hand** Informal person who is particularly good at something.

dab[2] n small flatfish.

dabble v deal in something superficially; splash about. **dabbler** n

dace n small freshwater fish.

dachshund n dog with a long body and short legs.

dactyl n metrical foot of three syllables, one long followed by two short. **dactylic** adj

dad n Informal father.

daddy n, pl **-dies** Informal father.

daddy-longlegs n Informal crane fly.

dado [day-doe] n, pl **-does, -dos** lower part of an interior wall that is decorated differently from the upper part.

daffodil n spring plant with yellow trumpet-shaped flowers.

daft adj informal foolish or crazy.

dagger n short stabbing weapon with a pointed blade.

dago [day-go] n Offens Spanish or other Latin person.

daguerreotype [dag-gair-oh-type] n type of early photograph produced on chemically treated silver.

dahlia [day-lya] n garden plant with showy flowers.

daily adj occurring every day or every weekday. ◆ adv every day. ◆ n, pl **-lies** daily newspaper; Brit informal charwoman.

dainty adj **-tier, -tiest** delicate or elegant. **daintily** adv

daiquiri [dak-eer-ee] n iced drink containing rum, lime juice, and sugar.

dairy n, pl **dairies** place for the processing or sale of milk and its products. ◆ adj of milk or its products.

dais [day-iss] n raised platform in a hall.

daisy n, pl **-sies** flower with a yellow centre and white petals.

Dalai Lama n chief lama and (until 1959) ruler of Tibet.

dale n valley.

dally v **-lying, -lied** dawdle; (foll. by with) amuse oneself (with). **dalliance** n flirtation.

Dalmatian n large dog with a white coat and black spots.

dam[1] n barrier built across a river to create a lake; lake created by this. ◆ v **damming, dammed** restrict by a dam.

dam[2] n female parent of an animal.

damage v harm. ◆ n injury or harm to a person or thing; Informal cost, e.g. what's the damage? ◆ pl money to be paid as compensation for injury or loss.

damask n fabric with a pattern woven into it, used for tablecloths etc.

dame n Slang woman; (D-) title of a woman who has been awarded the OBE or another order of chivalry.

damn *interj Slang* exclamation of annoyance. ◆ *adv, adj* (also **damned**) *Slang* extreme or extremely. ◆ *v* declare to be bad or worthless; swear (at); (of God) condemn to hell; prove (someone) guilty, e.g *damning evidence*. **damnable** *adj* annoying. **damnably** *adv* **damnation** *n*

damp *adj* slightly wet. ◆ *n* slight wetness, moisture. ◆ *v* make damp; (foll. by *down*) reduce the force of (feelings or actions). **damply** *adv* **dampness** *n* **dampen** *v* damp. **damper** *n* depressing influence; movable plate to regulate the draft in a fire; pad in a piano that deadens the vibration of each string.

damsel *n Obs* young woman.

damson *n* small blue-black plumlike fruit.

dance *v* move the feet and body rhythmically in time to music; perform (a particular kind of dance); skip or leap; move rhythmically. ◆ *n* social meeting arranged for dancing; series of steps and movements in time to music. **dancer** *n*

D and C *Surgery* dilat(at)ion and curettage: an operation in which the neck of the womb is stretched and the lining of the womb is scraped, for example to remove diseased tissue.

dandelion *n* yellow-flowered wild plant.

dander *n* **get one's dander up** *Slang* become angry.

dandle *v* move (a child) up and down on one's knee.

dandruff *n* loose scales of dry dead skin shed from the scalp.

dandy *n, pl* **-dies** man who is greatly concerned with the elegance of his appearance. ◆ *adj* **-dier, -diest** *Informal* very good or fine. **dandified** *adj*

danger *n* state of being vulnerable to injury or loss; person or thing that may cause injury; likelihood that something unpleasant will happen. **dangerous** *adj* **dangerously** *adv*

dangle *v* hang freely; display as an enticement.

dank *adj* unpleasantly damp and chilly.

daphne *n* shrub with small bell-shaped flowers.

dapper *adj* (of a man) neat in appearance and slight in build.

dappled *adj* marked with spots of a different colour. **dapple-grey** *n* horse having a grey coat with spots of a different colour.

dare *v* be courageous enough to try (to do something); challenge to do something risky. ◆ *n* challenge. **daring** *adj* willing to take risks. ◆ *n* courage to do dangerous things. **daringly** *adv* **daredevil** *adj, n* reckless (person).

daren't dare not.

dark *adj* having little or no light; (of a colour) reflecting little light; (of hair or skin) brown or black; gloomy or sinister; secret, e.g. *keep it dark*. ◆ *n* absence of light; night. **darkly** *adv* **darkness** *n* **darken** *v* **dark horse** person who reveals unexpected talents. **darkroom** *n* darkened room for processing film.

darling *n* much-loved person; favourite, e.g. *the darling of the gossip columns*. ◆ *adj* beloved.

darn[1] *v* mend (a garment) with a series of interwoven stitches. ◆ *n* patch of darned work.

darn[2] *interj, adv, adj, v Euphemistic* damn.

dart *n* small narrow pointed missile that is thrown or shot, esp. in the game of darts; sudden quick movement; tuck made in dressmaking. ◆ *pl* indoor game in which darts are thrown at a circular numbered board (**dartboard**). ◆ *v* move or throw quickly and suddenly.

Darwinism *n* theory of the origin of animal and plant species by evolution. **Darwinian, Darwinist** *adj, n*

dash *v* move hastily; throw or strike violently; frustrate (someone's hopes). ◆ *n* sudden quick movement; small amount; mixture of style and courage; punctuation mark (-) showing a change of subject; longer symbol used in Morse code. **dashing** *adj* lively; stylish. **dashboard** *n* instrument panel in an automobile, boat, or aircraft.

dastardly *adj* mean and cowardly.

data *n* series of observations, measurements, or facts; numbers, digits, etc. operated on by a computer. **database** *n* store of information that can be easily handled by a computer. **data capture** process for converting information into a form

that can be handled by a computer.
data processing series of operations performed on data, esp. by a computer, to extract or interpret information.

date¹ *n* specified day of the month; particular day or year when an event happened; *Informal* appointment, esp. with a person of the opposite sex; *Informal* this person. ◆ *v* mark with the date; assign a date of occurrence to; (foll. by *from*) originate from (a date), e.g. *this house dates from the 16th century*; make or become old-fashioned. **dated** *adj*

date² *n* dark-brown sweet-tasting fruit of the date palm. **date palm** tall palm grown in tropical regions for its fruit.

dative *n* (in certain languages) the form of the noun that expresses the indirect object.

daub *v* smear or spread clumsily.

daughter *n* female child; woman who comes from a certain place or is connected with a certain thing, e.g. *daughter of the church.* **daughterly** *adj* **daughter-in-law** *n, pl* **daughters-in-law** son's wife.

daunt *v* intimidate or dishearten. **daunting** *adj* **dauntless** *adj* fearless.

dauphin [daw-fin] *n* (formerly) eldest son of the king of France.

davenport *n* small writing table with drawers; large couch.

davit [dav-vit] *n* crane, usu. one of a pair, at a ship's side, for lowering and hoisting boats.

Davy lamp *n* miner's lamp designed to prevent it from igniting gas.

dawdle *v* be slow or lag behind; waste time. **dawdler** *n*

dawn *n* daybreak; beginning (of something). ◆ *v* begin to grow light; begin to develop or appear; (foll. by *on* or *upon*) become apparent (to).

day *n* period of 24 hours; period of light between sunrise and sunset; part of a day occupied with regular activity, esp. work; period or point in time; day of special observance; time of success. **daybreak** *n* time in the morning when light first appears. **daydream** *n* pleasant fantasy indulged in while awake. ◆ *v* indulge in idle fantasy. **daydreamer** *n* **daylight** *n* light from the sun. **day release** system in which workers go to college one day a week.

day-to-day *adj* routine.

daze *v* stun, esp. by a blow or shock. ◆ *n* state of confusion or shock.

dazzle *v* impress greatly; blind temporarily by sudden excessive light. ◆ *n* bright light that dazzles. **dazzling** *adj* **dazzlingly** *adv*

dB, db decibel(s).

DC direct current.

DCM Distinguished Conduct Medal.

DD Doctor of Divinity.

D-day *n* day selected for the start of some operation, esp. the Allied invasion of Europe in 1944.

DDT kind of insecticide.

de- *prefix* indicating: removal, e.g. *deforest*; reversal, e.g. *decode*; departure, e.g. *decamp*.

deacon *n Christianity* ordained minister ranking immediately below a priest; (in some Protestant churches) lay official who assists the minister. **deaconess** *n fem*

dead *adj* no longer alive; no longer in use; numb, e.g. *my leg has gone dead*; complete, e.g. *a dead stop*; *Informal* very tired; (of a place) lacking activity. ◆ *n* period during which coldness or darkness is most intense, e.g. *the dead of night*. ◆ *adv* extremely; suddenly, e.g. *stop dead.* **the dead** dead people. **dead beat** *Informal* exhausted. **dead set against** completely opposed to. **deaden** *v* make less sensitive or lively; make less resonant. **deadly** *adj* **-lier, -liest** likely to cause death; *Informal* extremely boring. ◆ *adv* extremely. **deadly nightshade** plant with poisonous black berries. **deadbeat** *n Informal* lazy useless person. **dead end** road with one end blocked off; situation in which further progress is impossible. **deadhead** *Informal* person who does not pay on a bus, to get into a sports game, etc.; *Slang* dull, unenterprising person; *Informal* train, bus, etc. travelling empty; log sticking out of water and hindering navigation. **dead heat** tie for first place between two participants in a contest. **dead letter** law or rule that is no longer enforced. **deadline** *n* time limit. **deadlock** *n* point in a dispute at which further progress is impossible. ◆ *v* bring to a deadlock. **deadpan** *adj, adv* showing no expression. **dead reckoning** method of establishing one's position using the distance and direction travelled. **dead weight** heavy weight.

deaf *adj* unable to hear. **deaf to** refusing to listen to or take notice of. **deafen** *v* make deaf, esp. temporarily. **deafness** *n*

deal¹ *n* transaction or agreement; treatment, e.g. *a fair deal*; large amount. ◆ *v* **dealing, dealt** [delt] distribute; inflict (a blow) on; *Cards* give out (cards) to the players. **dealer** *n* **dealings** *pl n* transactions or business relations. **deal in** *v* engage in commercially. **deal with** *v* take action on; be concerned with.

deal² *n* plank of fir or pine wood.

dean *n* chief administrative official of a college or university faculty; chief administrator of a cathedral. **deanery** *n* office or residence of a dean; parishes of a dean.

dear *n* someone regarded with affection. ◆ *adj* beloved; costly. **dearly** *adv* **dearness** *n*

dearth [dirth] *n* inadequate amount, scarcity.

death *n* permanent end of all functions of life in a person or animal; instance of this; ending, destruction. **deathly** *adj, adv* like death, e.g. *deathly quiet, deathly pale.* **death duty** *Brit* tax paid on property left at death. **death's-head** *n* human skull or a representation of one. **deathtrap** *n* place or vehicle considered very unsafe. **deathwatch beetle** beetle that bores into wood and makes a tapping sound.

deb *n* Informal debutante.

debacle [day-bah-kl] *n* disastrous collapse or defeat.

debar *v* exclude or bar.

debase *v* lower in value, quality, or character. **debasement** *n*

debate *n* a discussion. ◆ *v* discuss, esp. in a formal assembly; consider (a course of action). **in debate** in doubt, uncertain. **debatable** *adj* not absolutely certain.

debenture *n* long-term bond, bearing fixed interest, issued by a company or a government agency.

debilitate *v* weaken. **debilitation** *n* **debility** *n* weakness, infirmity.

debit *n* acknowledgment of a sum

owing by entry on the left side of an account. ◆ *v* **debiting, debited** record as a debit; charge with a debit.

debonair *adj* suave; carefree.

debouch *v* move out from a narrow place to a wider one.

debrief *v* receive a report from (a soldier, diplomat, etc.) after an event. **debriefing** *n*

debris [deb-ree] *n* fragments of something destroyed.

debt *n* something owed, esp. money; state of owing something. **debtor** *n*

debunk *v* Informal expose the pretensions or falseness of.

debut [day-byoo] *n* first public appearance of a performer. **debutante** [day-byoo-tont] *n* young upper-class woman making her first formal appearance in society.

Dec. December.

deca- combining form ten.

decade *n* period of ten years.

decadence [dek-a-denss] *n* state of deterioration of morality or culture. **decadent** *adj*

decaffeinated [dee-kaf-fin-ate-id] *adj* (of tea or coffee) with caffeine removed.

decagon *n* geometric figure with ten sides. **decagonal** *adj*

decahedron [dek-a-hee-dron] *n* solid figure with ten sides.

Decalogue *n* the Ten Commandments.

decamp *v* depart secretly or suddenly.

decant *v* pour (a liquid) from one container to another; rehouse (people) while their homes are being refurbished. **decanter** *n* stoppered bottle for wine or spirits.

decapitate *v* behead. **decapitation** *n*

decarbonize *v* remove carbon from (an internal-combustion engine). **decarbonization** *n*

decathlon *n* athletic contest with ten events.

decay *v* rot; become weaker or more corrupt. ◆ *n* process of decaying; state brought about by this process.

decease *n* Formal death. **deceased** *adj Formal* dead. ◆ *n* **the deceased** person who has recently died.

deceive *v* mislead by lying; be unfaithful to (one's sexual partner). **deceiver** *n* **deceit** *n* behaviour intended to deceive. **deceitful** *adj*

decelerate *v* slow down.
deceleration *n*

December *n* twelfth month of the year.

decennial *adj* lasting for ten years; happening every ten years.

decent *adj* of an acceptable standard or quality; polite or respectable; fitting or proper; conforming to conventions of sexual behaviour; *Informal* kind. **decently** *adv* **decency** *n*

decentralize *v* reorganize into smaller local units. **decentralization** *n*

deception *n* deceiving; something that deceives, trick. **deceptive** *adj* likely or designed to deceive. **deceptively** *adv* **deceptiveness** *n*

deci- *combining form* one tenth.

decibel *n* unit for measuring the intensity of sound.

decide *v* (cause to) reach a decision; settle (a contest or question). **decided** *adj* unmistakable; determined. **decidedly** *adv* **decision** *n* judgment, conclusion, or resolution; act of making up one's mind; firmness of purpose. **decisive** *adj* indisputable, e.g. *a decisive win*; having the ability to make (quick) decisions. **decisively** *adv* **decisiveness** *n*

deciduous *adj* (of a tree) shedding its leaves annually.

decimal *n* fraction written in the form of a dot followed by one or more numbers. ◆ *adj* relating to or using powers of ten; expressed as a decimal. **decimalize** *v* change (a system or number) to the decimal system. **decimalization** *n* **decimal currency** system of currency in which the units are parts or powers of ten. **decimal point** dot between the unit and the fraction of a number in the decimal system. **decimal system** number system with a base of ten, in which numbers are expressed by combinations of the digits 0 to 9.

decimate *v* destroy or kill a large proportion of. **decimation** *n*

decipher *v* decode; make out the meaning of (poor handwriting). **decipherable** *adj*

deck *n* area of a ship that forms a floor; similar area in a bus; platform that supports the turntable and pick-up of a record player. ◆ *v* decorate.
deck chair folding chair made of canvas over a wooden frame. **decking** *n* wooden platform in a garden. **deck out** *v* dress (oneself) or decorate (a room).

declaim *v* speak loudly and dramatically; protest loudly. **declamation** *n* **declamatory** *adj*

declare *v* state firmly and forcefully; announce officially; acknowledge for tax purposes. **declaration** *n* **declaratory** *adj*

decline *v* become smaller, weaker, or less important; say that one is unwilling to give, accept, or do (something); *Grammar* list the inflections of (a noun, pronoun, or adjective). ◆ *n* gradual deterioration; movement downwards; diminution. **declension** *n Grammar* changes in the form of nouns, pronouns, or adjectives to show case, number, and gender.

declivity *n*, *pl* **-ties** downward slope. **declivitous** *adj*

declutch *v* disengage the clutch of a motor vehicle.

decoct *v* extract the essence from (a substance) by boiling. **decoction** *n*

decode *v* convert from code into ordinary language. **decoder** *n*

décolleté [day-kol-tay] *adj* (of a woman's garment) having a low neckline.

decompose *v* be broken down through chemical or bacterial action. **decomposition** *n*

decompress *v* free from pressure; return (a diver) to normal atmospheric pressure. **decompression** *n*

decongestant *n* drug that relieves nasal congestion.

decontaminate *v* render harmless by the removal of poisons, radioactivity, etc. **decontamination** *n*

decor [day-core] *n* decorative scheme of a room or house.

decorate *v* ornament; paint or wallpaper (a room); award a (military) medal to. **decoration** *n* **decorative** *adj* **decorator** *n*

decorous [dek-a-russ] *adj* polite, calm, and sensible in behaviour. **decorously** *adv* **decorousness** *n* **decorum** [dik-core-um] *n* decorous behaviour.

decoy n person or thing used to lure someone into danger; image of a bird or animal, used to lure game within shooting range. ◆ v lure into danger by means of a decoy.

decrease v diminish. ◆ n lessening; amount by which something has been diminished.

decree n law made by someone in authority; court judgment. ◆ v order by decree.

decrepit adj weakened or worn out by age or long use. **decrepitude** n

decry v -crying, -cried express disapproval of.

dedicate v commit (oneself or one's time) wholly to a special purpose or cause; inscribe or address (a book etc.) to someone as a tribute. **dedicated** adj devoted to a particular purpose or cause. **dedication** n

deduce v reach (a conclusion) by reasoning from evidence. **deducible** adj

deduct v subtract.

deduction n deducting; something that is deducted; deducing; conclusion reached by deducing. **deductive** adj

deed n something that is done; legal document.

deem v have as an opinion.

deep adj extending or situated far down, inwards, backwards, or sideways; of a specified dimension downwards, inwards, or backwards; coming from or penetrating to a great depth; difficult to understand; of great intensity; (foll. by in) immersed (in); (of a colour) strong or dark; low in pitch. **the deep** Poetic the sea. **deeply** adv profoundly or intensely. **deepen** v **deepfreeze** n same as FREEZER.

deer n, pl **deer** hoofed mammal with antlers in the male. **deerstalker** n cloth hat with peaks back and front and earflaps.

deface v spoil the surface or appearance of. **defacement** n

de facto adv in fact. ◆ adj existing in fact, whether legally recognized or not.

defame v attack the good reputation of. **defamation** n **defamatory** [dif-fam-a-tree] adj

default n failure to do something; Computers instruction to a computer to select a particular option unless the user specifies otherwise. ◆ v fail to fulfil an obligation. **in default of** in the absence of.

defeat v overcome; thwart. ◆ n defeating or being defeated. **defeatism** n ready acceptance of defeat. **defeatist** n, adj

defecate v discharge waste from the body through the anus. **defecation** n

defect n imperfection. ◆ v desert one's cause or country to join the opposing forces. **defective** adj having a flaw. **defection** n **defector** n

defence esp US, **defense** n resistance to attack; plea in support of something; a country's military resources; defendant's case in a court of law. **defenceless** adj

defend v protect from harm or danger; support in the face of criticism, esp. by argument; represent (a defendant) in court; protect (a title) against a challenge. **defendant** n person accused of a crime. **defender** n **defensible** adj capable of being defended because believed to be right. **defensibility** n **defensive** adj intended for defence; overanxious to protect oneself against (threatened) criticism. **defensively** adv

defer[1] v -ferring, -ferred delay (something) until a future time. **deferment, deferral** n

defer[2] v -ferring, -ferred (foll. by to) comply with the wishes (of). **deference** n compliance with the wishes of another; respect. **deferential** adj **deferentially** adv

deficient adj lacking some essential; inadequate in quality or quantity. **deficiency** n lack; state of being deficient. **deficit** n amount by which a sum of money is too small.

defile[1] v desecrate. **defilement** n

defile[2] n narrow pass or valley.

define v describe the nature of; state precisely the meaning of; show clearly the outline of. **definable** adj **definite** adj firm, clear, and precise; having precise limits; known for certain. **definitely** adv **definition** n statement of the meaning of a word or phrase; quality of being clear and distinct. **definitive** adj providing an unquestionable conclusion; being the best example of something.

deflate v (cause to) collapse through the release of gas; take away the conceit from; *Economics* cause deflation of (an economy). **deflation** n *Economics* reduction in economic activity resulting in lower output and investment; feeling of sadness following excitement. **deflationary** adj

deflect v (cause to) turn aside from a course. **deflection** n **deflector** n

deflower v *Lit* deprive (a woman) of her virginity.

defoliate v deprive (a plant) of its leaves. **defoliant** n **defoliation** n

deforest v clear of trees. **deforestation** n

deform v cause to be misshapen; make ugly. **deformation** n **deformity** n

defraud v take away money, rights, etc. from (a person) by fraud.

defray v provide money for (costs or expenses).

defrock v deprive (a priest) of priestly status.

defrost v make or become free of frost or ice; thaw (frozen food) by removing it from a freezer.

deft adj quick and skilful in movement. **deftly** adv **deftness** n

defunct adj no longer existing or operative.

defuse v remove the triggering device from (an explosive device); remove the tension from (a situation).

defy v **-fying, -fied** resist openly and boldly; elude, esp. in a baffling way, e.g. *defy description*. **defiance** n open resistance to authority or opposition. **defiant** adj

degenerate adj having deteriorated to a lower mental, moral, or physical level. ◆ n degenerate person. ◆ v become degenerate. **degeneracy** n degenerate behaviour. **degeneration** n

degrade v reduce to dishonour or disgrace; reduce in status or quality; *Chem* decompose into smaller molecules. **degradation** n

degree n stage in a scale of relative amount or intensity; academic award given by a university or college on successful completion of a course; unit of measurement for temperature or angles.

dehumanize v deprive of human qualities; make (an activity) mechanical or routine. **dehumanization** n

dehydrate v cause to lose water; deprive the body of (someone) of water. **dehydration** n

de-ice v free of ice. **de-icer** n

deify [day-if-fie] v **-fying, -fied** treat or worship as a god. **deification** n

deign [dane] v think it worthy of oneself (to do something), condescend.

deity [day-it-ee] n, pl **-ties** god or goddess; state of being divine.

déjà vu [day-zhah voo] n feeling of having experienced before something that is actually happening now.

dejected adj in low spirits. **dejectedly** adv **dejection** n

de jure adv, adj according to law.

deke *Ice hockey* n feigned move which draws an opponent out of position. ◆ v feign a move.

delay v put off to a later time; slow up or cause to be late. ◆ n act of delaying; interval of time between events.

delectable adj very attractive. **delectation** n *Formal* great pleasure.

delegate n person chosen to act for others, esp. at a meeting. ◆ v entrust (duties or powers) to another person; appoint as a delegate. **delegation** n group of people appointed as delegates; delegating.

delete v remove (something written or printed). **deletion** n

deleterious [del-lit-eer-ee-uss] adj harmful, injurious.

deliberate adj carefully thought out in advance; careful and unhurried. ◆ v consider (something) deeply. **deliberately** adv **deliberation** n **deliberative** adj for the purpose of deliberating, e.g. *a deliberative assembly*.

delicate adj fine or subtle in quality or workmanship; having a fragile beauty; (of a taste etc.) pleasantly subtle; easily damaged; requiring tact. **delicately** adv **delicacy** n being delicate; something particularly good to eat.

delicatessen n shop selling imported or unusual foods, already cooked or prepared.

delicious *adj* very appealing, esp. to taste or smell. **deliciously** *adv*

delight *n* great pleasure. ◆ *v* please greatly; (foll. by *in*) take great pleasure (in). **delightful** *adj* **delightfully** *adv*

delimit *v* mark or prescribe the limits of. **delimitation** *n*

delineate [dill-lin-ee-ate] *v* show by drawing; describe in words. **delineation** *n*

delinquent *n* someone, esp. a young person, who repeatedly breaks the law. ◆ *adj* repeatedly breaking the law. **delinquency** *n*

delirium *n* state of excitement and mental confusion, often with hallucinations; violent excitement. **delirious** *adj* **deliriously** *adv*

deliver *v* carry (goods etc.) to a destination; hand over; aid in the birth of; release or rescue; present (a speech etc.); strike (a blow) suddenly. **deliverance** *n* rescue from danger or captivity. **delivery** *n* act of delivering; something that is delivered; act of giving birth to a child; style, esp. in public speaking.

dell *n* small wooded hollow.

Delphic *adj* ambiguous, like the ancient Greek oracle at Delphi.

delphinium *n* plant with spikes of blue flowers.

delta *n* fourth letter of the Greek alphabet; flat area at the mouth of some rivers where the main stream splits up into several tributaries.

delude *v* deceive. **delusion** *n* mistaken idea or belief; state of being deluded. **delusive** *adj*

deluge [del-lyooj] *n* great flood of water; torrential rain; overwhelming number. ◆ *v* flood; overwhelm.

de luxe *adj* rich or sumptuous; superior in quality.

delve *v* research deeply or intensively (for information).

demagogue *n* political agitator who appeals to the prejudice and passions of the mob. **demagogic** *adj* **demagogy** *n*

demand *v* ask for forcefully; require as just, urgent, etc.; claim as a right. ◆ *n* forceful request; *Economics* willingness and ability to purchase goods and services. ◆ *pl* something that requires special effort or sacrifice. **demanding** *adj* requiring a lot of time or effort.

demean *v* lower (someone) in dignity, character, or status.

demeanour *n* way a person behaves.

demented *adj* mad. **dementedly** *adv* **dementia** [dim-men-sha] *n* state of serious mental deterioration.

demerara sugar *n* brown crystallized cane sugar.

demerit *n* flaw, disadvantage.

demesne [dim-mane] *n* land surrounding a house; *Law* possession of one's own property or land.

demi- *combining form* half.

demijohn *n* large bottle with a short neck, often encased in wicker.

demilitarize *v* remove the military forces from. **demilitarization** *n*

demimonde *n* (esp. in the 19th century) class of women considered to be outside respectable society, because of promiscuity; group considered not wholly respectable.

demise *n* *Formal* death; eventual failure (of something successful).

demo *n* *Informal* demonstration, organized expression of public opinion.

demob *v* *Informal* demobilize. **demobilize** *v* release from the armed forces. **demobilization** *n*

democracy *n, pl* **-cies** government by the people or their elected representatives; state governed in this way; social equality. **democrat** *n* advocate of democracy; (D-) member or supporter of the Democratic Party in the US. **democratic** *adj* connected with democracy; upholding democracy; (D-) of the Democratic Party, the more liberal of the two main political parties in the US. **democratically** *adv*

demography *n* study of human populations. **demographer** *n* **demographic** *adj*

demolish *v* tear down or break up (buildings); put an end to (an argument etc.). **demolition** *n*

demon *n* evil spirit; person extremely skilful in or devoted to a given activity. **demonic** *adj* **demoniacal, demoniac** *adj* appearing to be possessed by a devil; frenzied. **demoniacally** *adv* **demonology** *n* study of demons.

demonstrate *v* show or prove by

reasoning or evidence; reveal the existence of; display and explain the workings of; show support or protest by public parades or rallies. **demonstrable** adj able to be proved. **demonstrably** adv **demonstration** n organized expression of public opinion; explanation or experiment showing how something works; proof. **demonstrative** adj tending to express one's feelings unreservedly. **demonstratively** adv **demonstrator** n person who demonstrates machines, products, etc.; person who takes part in a public demonstration.

demoralize v undermine the morale of. **demoralization** n

demote v reduce in status or rank. **demotion** n

demur v -murring, -murred show reluctance. **without demur** without objecting.

demure adj quiet, reserved, and rather shy. **demurely** adv **demureness** n

den n home of a wild animal; small secluded room in a home; place where people indulge in criminal or immoral activities, e.g. den of iniquity.

denationalize v transfer (an industry) from public to private ownership. **denationalization** n

denature v change the nature of; make (alcohol) unfit to drink.

denigrate v criticize unfairly. **denigration** n **denigrator** n

denim n hard-wearing cotton fabric. ◆ pl jeans made of denim.

denizen n inhabitant.

denominate v give a specific name to. **denomination** n group having a distinctive interpretation of a religious faith; grade or unit of value, measure, etc. **denominational** adj **denominator** n divisor of a fraction.

denote v be a sign of; have as a literal meaning. **denotation** n

denouement [day-noo-mon] n final outcome or solution, esp. in a play or book.

denounce v speak violently against; give information against. **denunciation** n open condemnation.

dense adj closely packed; difficult to see through; stupid. **densely** adv **density** n degree to which something

is filled or occupied; Physics measure of the compactness of a substance, expressed as its mass per unit volume.

dent n hollow in a surface, as made by a blow. ◆ v make a dent in.

dental adj of or relating to the teeth or dentistry. **dental floss** waxed thread used to remove food particles from between the teeth. **dentine** [den-teen] n calcified tissue comprising the bulk of a tooth. **denture** n artificial tooth. ◆ pl set of artificial teeth.

dentist n person qualified to practise dentistry. **dentistry** n branch of medicine concerned with the teeth and gums.

denude v (foll. by of) remove the covering or protection from.

deny v -nying, -nied declare to be untrue; refuse to give or allow; refuse to acknowledge. **deniable** adj **denial** n denying; statement that something is not true.

deodorize v remove or disguise the smell of. **deodorant** n substance applied to the body to mask the smell of perspiration.

dep. department; departure.

depart v leave; differ. **departed** adj Euphemistic dead. **the departed** dead people. **departure** n

department n specialized division of a large organization; major subdivision of the administration of a government. **departmental** adj **department store** large shop selling many kinds of goods.

depend v (foll. by on or upon) put trust (in); be influenced or determined (by); rely (on) for income or support. **dependable** adj **dependably** adv **dependability** n **dependant** n person who depends on another for financial support. **dependence** n state of being dependent. **dependency** n territory subject to a state on which it does not border; overreliance on another person or a drug. **dependent** adj depending on a person or thing for support.

depict v give a picture of; describe in words. **depiction** n

deplete v use up; reduce in number. **depletion** n

deplore v express or feel strong disapproval of. **deplorable** adj very bad.

deploy v organize (troops or resources) into a position ready for immediate action. **deployment** n

depopulate v cause to be reduced in population. **depopulation** n

deport v remove forcibly from a country. **deport oneself** behave oneself in a specified manner. **deportation** n **deportee** n

deportment n manner in which a person behaves.

depose v remove from an office or position of power; Law make a statement on oath.

deposit v put down; entrust for safekeeping, esp. to a bank; lay down naturally. ♦ n entrusting of money to a bank; money entrusted; money given in part payment or as security; accumulation of sediments, minerals, etc. **depositary** n person to whom something is entrusted for safety. **depositor** n **depository** n store for furniture etc.

deposition n Law sworn statement of a witness used in court in his or her absence; deposing; depositing; something deposited.

depot [**dee**-poh or **dep**-oh] n building used for storage; building for the storage and servicing of buses or railway engines; bus or railway station.

deprave v make morally bad. **depravity** n moral corruption.

deprecate v express disapproval of, protest against. **deprecation** n **deprecatory** adj

depreciate v decline in value or price; criticize. **depreciation** n **depreciatory** adj

depredation n plundering.

depress v lower the spirits of (someone); lower (prices or wages); push down. **depressing** adj **depressingly** adv **depressant** n drug which reduces nervous activity. **depression** n mental state in which a person has feelings of gloom and inadequacy; economic condition in which there is a lot of unemployment and low output and investment; area of low air pressure; sunken place. **depressive** adj tending to cause depression.

deprive v (foll. by of) prevent from

(possessing or enjoying). **deprivation** n **deprived** adj lacking adequate living conditions, education, etc.

depth n distance downwards, backwards, or inwards; intensity of emotion; profundity of character or thought; intensity of colour. **depth charge** bomb used to attack submarines by exploding at a preset depth of water.

depute v appoint (someone) to act on one's behalf. **deputation** n body of people appointed to represent others. **deputize** v act as a deputy. **deputy** n person appointed to act on behalf of another.

derail v cause (a train) to go off the rails. **derailment** n

derange v make insane; throw into disorder. **derangement** n

derby n, pl **-bies** sporting event between teams from the same area; bowler hat. **the Derby** annual horse race run at Epsom Downs.

deregulate v remove regulations or controls from. **deregulation** n

derelict adj deserted or abandoned; falling into ruins. ♦ n social outcast, vagrant. **dereliction** n wilful neglect (of duty); state of being abandoned.

deride v speak of or treat with contempt or ridicule. **derision** n **derisive** adj mocking or scornful. **derisory** adj so small or inadequate that it is not worth serious consideration.

de rigueur [de rig-**gur**] adj required by fashion.

derive v (foll. by from) draw or be drawn (from) in origin. **derivation** n **derivative** adj, n

dermatitis n inflammation of the skin.

dermatology n branch of medicine concerned with the skin. **dermatologist** n

derogatory [dir-**rog**-a-tree] adj intentionally offensive.

derrick n simple crane; framework erected over an oil well.

dervish n member of a Muslim religious order noted for a frenzied whirling dance.

descant n Music tune played or sung above a basic melody.

descend v move down (a slope etc.); move to a lower level, pitch, etc.; (foll.

by *to*) stoop to (unworthy behaviour); (foll. by *on*) visit unexpectedly. **be descended from** be connected by a blood relationship to. **descendant** *n* person or animal descended from an individual, race, or species. **descendent** *adj* descending. **descent** *n* act of descending; downward slope; derivation from an ancestor.

describe *v* give an account of (something or someone) in words; trace the outline of (a circle etc.). **description** *n* statement that describes something or someone; sort, e.g *reptiles of every description*. **descriptive** *adj* **descriptively** *adv*

descry *v* **-scrying, -scried** catch sight of; discover by looking carefully.

desecrate *v* violate the sacred character of (an object or place). **desecration** *n*

desegregate *v* end racial segregation in. **desegregation** *n*

desert[1] *n* region that has little or no vegetation because of low rainfall.

desert[2] *v* abandon (a person or place) without intending to return; *Mil* abscond from (a post or duty) with no intention of returning. **deserter** *n* **desertion** *n*

deserts *pl n* **get one's just deserts** get the punishment one deserves.

deserve *v* be entitled to or worthy of. **deserved** *adj* rightfully earned. **deservedly** *adv* **deserving** *adj* worthy, esp. of praise or help.

deshabille *n* same as DISHABILLE.

desiccate *v* remove most of the water from. **desiccation** *n*

design *v* work out the structure or form of (something), as by making a sketch or plans; plan and make artistically; intend for a specific purpose. ◆ *n* preliminary drawing; arrangement or features of an artistic or decorative work; art of designing; intention, e.g. *by design*. **designedly** *adv* by intention. **designer** *n* person who draws up original sketches or plans from which things are made. ◆ *adj* designed by a well-known designer; fashionable or trendy, e.g. *designer stubble*. **designing** *adj* crafty, cunning.

designate [dez-zig-nate] *v* give a name to; select (someone) for an office or duty. ◆ *adj* appointed but not yet in office. **designation** *n* name.

desire *v* long for. ◆ *n* strong feeling of wanting something; sexual appetite; person or thing desired. **desirable** *adj* worth having; arousing sexual desire. **desirability** *n* **desirous of** [diz-zire-uss] having a desire for.

desist *v* (foll. by *from*) stop or abstain (from).

desk *n* piece of furniture with a writing surface and usually drawers; service counter in a public building; section of a newspaper covering a specific subject, e.g. *the news desk*. **desktop** *adj* denoting a computer system small enough to use at a desk.

desolate *adj* uninhabited and bleak; without hope. ◆ *v* lay waste; make (a person) very sad. **desolation** *n*

despair *n* total loss of hope. ◆ *v* lose hope.

despatch *v*, *n* same as DISPATCH.

desperado *n*, *pl* **-does, -dos** reckless person ready to commit any violent illegal act.

desperate *adj* careless of danger, as from despair; (of an action) undertaken as a last resort; having a great need or desire. **desperately** *adv* **desperation** *n*

despise *v* look down on with contempt. **despicable** *adj* worthy of being despised. **despicably** *adv*

despite *prep* in spite of.

despoil *v* *Formal* plunder. **despoliation** *n*

despondent *adj* dejected or depressed. **despondently** *adv* **despondency** *n*

despot *n* person in power who acts tyrannically. **despotic** *adj* **despotism** *n* tyrannical government or behaviour.

dessert *n* sweet course served at the end of a meal. **dessertspoon** *n* spoon between a tablespoon and a teaspoon in size.

destination *n* place to which someone or something is going.

destine [dess-tin] *v* set apart (for a certain purpose).

destiny *n*, *pl* **-nies** future destined for a person or thing; (**D-**) the power that predetermines the course of events.

destitute *adj* totally impoverished. **destitution** *n*

destroy *v* ruin; put an end to; kill (an

animal). **destroyer** n small heavily armed warship; person or thing that destroys. **destructible** adj **destruction** n destroying or being destroyed; cause of ruin. **destructive** adj causing destruction; intending to discredit someone, without positive suggestions, e.g. *destructive criticism.* **destructively** adv

desuetude [diss-**syoo**-it-tude] n condition of not being in use.

desultory [**dez**-zl-tree] adj changing fitfully from one thing to another; random. **desultorily** adv

detach v disengage and separate. **detachable** adj **detached** adj standing apart; showing no emotional involvement. **detachment** n aloofness; small group of soldiers.

detail n item that is considered separately; unimportant item; treatment of particulars; *Chiefly mil* (personnel) assigned a specific duty. ◆ v list fully.

detain v delay (someone); hold (someone) in custody. **detainee** n **detainment** n

detect v notice; discover the existence or presence of. **detectable** adj **detection** n **detective** n policeman or private agent who investigates crime. **detector** n instrument used to find something, e.g. *smoke detector.*

detente [day-**tont**] n easing of tension between nations.

detention n imprisonment; form of punishment in which a pupil is detained after school.

deter v -terring, -terred discourage (someone) from doing something by instilling fear or doubt. **deterrent** n something that deters; weapon, esp. nuclear, to deter attack by another nation. ◆ adj tending to deter.

detergent n chemical cleansing agent. ◆ adj having cleansing power.

deteriorate v become worse. **deterioration** n

determine v settle (an argument or a question) conclusively; find out the facts about (something); fix in scope, extent, etc.; make a decision to do something. **determinant** n factor that determines. **determinate** adj definitely limited or fixed. **determination** n condition of being determined or resolute; act of determining.

determined adj firmly decided, unable to be persuaded. **determinedly** adv **determiner** n *Grammar* word that determines the object to which a noun phrase refers, such as *all.* **determinism** n theory that human choice is not free, but decided by past events. **determinist** n, adj

detest v dislike intensely. **detestable** adj **detestation** n

dethrone v remove from a throne or deprive of high position.

detonate v cause (an explosive device) to explode or (of an explosive device) explode. **detonation** n **detonator** n small amount of explosive, or a device, used to set off an explosion.

detour n deviation from a direct route or course of action.

detox v, n *Informal* (undergo) treatment to rid the body of poisonous substances.

detract v (foll. by *from*) lessen the value of, diminish. **detractor** n

detriment n disadvantage or damage. **detrimental** adj **detrimentally** adv

detritus [dit-**trite**-uss] n loose mass of stones or silt worn away from rocks, debris. **detrital** adj

de trop [de **troh**] adj not wanted; in the way.

deuce [**dyewss**] n *Tennis* score of forty all; playing card or dice with two spots.

deuterium n isotope of hydrogen twice as heavy as the normal atom.

Deutschmark [**doytch**-mark], **Deutsche Mark** [**doytch**-a] n a former monetary unit of Germany.

devalue v -valuing, -valued reduce the exchange value of (a currency); reduce the value of (something or someone). **devaluation** n

devastate v damage (a place) severely or destroy it. **devastated** adj shocked and extremely upset. **devastation** n

develop v grow or bring to a later, more elaborate, or more advanced stage; come or bring into existence; improve the value or change the use of (land); treat (a photographic plate or film) to produce a visible image. **developer** n person who develops property; chemical used to develop

photographs or films. **development** n
developing country poor or
nonindustrial country that is seeking to
develop its resources by
industrialization.

deviate v differ from others in belief
or thought; turn aside from a course
of action. **deviation** n **deviant** n, adj
(person) deviating from what is
considered acceptable behaviour.
deviance n

device n machine or tool used for a
specific task; scheme or trick.

devil n evil spirit; person regarded as
wicked; person, e.g. *poor devil*; person
regarded as daring; *Informal*
something difficult or annoying. ♦ v
-**illing, -illed** prepare (food) with a
highly flavoured spiced mixture; do
routine literary work, esp. for a lawyer
or author. **the Devil** *Christianity* chief
spirit of evil and enemy of God. ♦
devilish adj of or like the devil. ♦ adv
(also **devilishly**) *Informal* extremely.
devilment n mischievous conduct.
devilry n reckless fun; wickedness.
devil-may-care adj happy-go-lucky.
devil's advocate person who takes an
opposing or unpopular point of view
for the sake of argument.

devious adj not sincere or
straightforward; indirect. **deviously**
adv **deviousness** n

devise v work out (something) in
one's mind.

devoid adj (foll. by *of*) destitute (of) or
free (from).

devolve v (foll. by *on, upon,* or *to*)
pass (power or duties) or (of power or
duties) be passed to a successor or
substitute **devolution** n transfer of
authority from a central government
to regional governments.

devote v apply or dedicate to some
cause. **devoted** adj feeling loyalty or
devotion. **devotedly** adv **devotee**
[dev-vote-tee] n person ardently
enthusiastic about something; zealous
follower of a religion. **devotion** n
strong affection for or loyalty to a
cause or person; religious zeal or piety.
♦ pl prayers. **devotional** adj

devour v eat up greedily; engulf and
destroy; read or look at avidly.
devouring adj

devout adj deeply religious. **devoutly**
adv

dew n drops of water condensed on a
cool surface at night from vapour in
the air. **dewy** adj

dewclaw n nonfunctional claw on a
dog's leg.

dewlap n loose fold of skin hanging
under the throat in dogs, cattle, etc.

dexterity n skill in using one's hands;
mental quickness. **dexterous** adj
dexterously adv

dextrose n glucose occurring in fruit,
honey, and the blood of animals.

dg decigram.

diabetes [die-a-beet-eez] n disorder
in which an abnormal amount of urine
containing an excess of sugar is
excreted. **diabetic** n, adj

diabolic adj of the devil; extremely
cruel. **diabolical** adj *Informal* extremely
bad. **diabolically** adv **diabolism** n
devil worship.

diaconate n position or period of
office of a deacon. **diaconal** adj

diacritic n sign above or below a
letter or character to indicate phonetic
value or stress.

diadem n *Old-fashioned* crown.

diaeresis n, pl -**ses** same as DIERESIS.

diagnosis [die-ag-no-siss] n, pl -**ses** [-
seez] discovery and identification of
diseases from the examination of
symptoms. **diagnose** v **diagnostic** adj

diagonal adj from corner to corner;
slanting. ♦ n diagonal line. **diagonally**
adv

diagram n sketch demonstrating the
form or workings of something.
diagrammatic adj **diagrammatically**
adv

dial n face of a clock or watch;
graduated disc on a measuring
instrument; control on a radio or
television used to change the station;
numbered disc on the front of some
telephones. ♦ v **dialling, dialled** try to
establish a telephone connection with
(someone) by operating the dial or
buttons on a telephone.

dialect n form of a language spoken
in a particular area. **dialectal** adj

dialectic n logical debate by question
and answer to resolve differences
between two views. **dialectical** adj

dialogue n conversation between two
people; discussion between
representatives of two nations or

groups. **dialogue box** n small window on a computer screen prompting the user to enter information.

dialysis [die-al-iss-iss] n Med filtering of blood through a membrane to remove waste products.

diamanté [die-a-man-tee] adj decorated with artificial jewels.

diameter n (length of) a straight line through the centre of a circle or sphere. **diametric, diametrical** adj of a diameter; completely opposed, e.g. the diametric opposite. **diametrically** adv

diamond n usually colourless, exceptionally hard precious stone; Geom figure with four sides of equal length forming two acute and two obtuse angles; playing card marked with red diamond-shaped symbols. **diamond wedding** sixtieth anniversary of a wedding.

diaper n piece of absorbent material fastened round a baby's lower torso to absorb urine and feces.

diaphanous [die-af-fan-ous] adj fine and almost transparent.

diaphragm [die-a-fram] n muscular partition that separates the abdominal cavity and chest cavity; contraceptive device placed over the neck of the womb.

diarrhea, diarrhoea [die-a-ree-a] n frequent discharge of abnormally liquid feces.

diary n, pl -ries (book for) a record of daily events, appointments, or observations. **diarist** n

diatribe n bitter critical attack.

dibble n small hand tool used to make holes in the ground for seeds or plants.

dice n, pl **dice** small cube each of whose sides has a different number of spots (1 to 6), used in games of chance. ◆ v cut (food) into small cubes. **dice with death** take a risk. **dicey** adj Informal dangerous.

dichotomy [die-kot-a-mee] n, pl -mies division into two opposed groups or parts.

dicky[1] n, pl **dickies** false shirt front. **dicky-bird** n child's word for a bird.

dicky[2] adj **dickier, dickiest** Informal shaky or weak, e.g. a dicky heart.

Dictaphone n ® tape recorder for

recording dictation for subsequent typing.

dictate v say aloud for another person to transcribe; give (commands) authoritatively. ◆ n authoritative command; guiding principle. **dictation** n **dictator** n ruler who has complete power; tyrannical person. **dictatorship** n **dictatorial** adj like a dictator, tyrannical. **dictatorially** adv

diction n manner of pronouncing words and sounds.

dictionary n, pl -aries book that consists of an alphabetical list of words with their meanings; reference book listing terms and giving information about a particular subject.

dictum n, pl -tums, -ta formal statement; popular saying.

did v past tense of DO.

didactic adj intended to instruct. **didactically** adv

diddle v Informal swindle.

didn't did not.

die[1] v **dying, died** (of a person, animal, or plant) cease all biological activity permanently; (of something inanimate) cease to exist or function. **be dying for** Informal be eager for. **die-hard** n person who resists change.

die[2] n shaped block used to cut or form metal; casting mould.

dieresis [die-air-iss-iss] n, pl -ses [-seez] mark (¨) placed over a vowel to show that it is pronounced separately from the preceding one, as in Noël.

diesel n diesel engine; vehicle driven by a diesel engine; Informal diesel oil. **diesel engine** internal-combustion engine in which oil is ignited by compression. **diesel oil** fuel obtained from petroleum distillation.

diet[1] n food that a person or animal regularly eats; specific allowance of food, to control weight or for health reasons. ◆ v follow a special diet so as to lose weight. ◆ adj (of food or drink) suitable for eating with a weight-reduction diet. **dietary** adj **dietary fibre** fibrous substances in fruit and vegetables that aid digestion. **dieter** n **dietetic** adj prepared for special dietary requirements. **dietetics** pl n study of food intake and preparation. **dietician** n person who specializes in dietetics.

diet² n parliament of some countries.

differ v be unlike; disagree. **difference** n state or quality of being unlike; disagreement; remainder left after subtraction. **different** adj unlike; unusual. **differently** adv

differential adj of or using a difference; *Math* involving differentials. ◆ n factor that differentiates between two comparable things; *Math* slight difference between values in a scale; difference between rates of pay for different types of labour. **differential calculus** branch of calculus concerned with derivatives and differentials. **differential gear** mechanism in a road vehicle that allows one driving wheel to rotate faster than the other when cornering. **differentiate** v perceive or show the difference (between); make (one thing) distinct from other such things; *Math* determine the derivative of (a function or variable). **differentiation** n

difficult adj requiring effort or skill to do or understand; not easily pleased. **difficulty** n

diffident adj lacking self-confidence. **diffidence** n **diffidently** adv

diffract v cause to undergo diffraction. **diffraction** n *Physics* deviation in the direction of a wave at the edge of an obstacle in its path; formation of light and dark fringes by the passage of light through a small aperture.

diffuse v spread in all directions. ◆ adj widely spread; lacking conciseness. **diffusely** adv **diffusion** n

dig v **digging**, **dug** (often foll. by *up*) cut into, break up, and turn over or remove (earth etc.), esp. with a spade; (foll. by *out* or *up*) find by effort or searching; (foll. by *in* or *into*) thrust or jab. ◆ n act of digging; thrust or poke; cutting remark; archaeological excavation. ◆ pl *Informal* lodgings. **digger** n

digest v subject to a process of digestion; absorb mentally. ◆ n methodical compilation of information, often a condensed one. **digestible** adj **digestion** n process of breaking down food into easily absorbed substances. **digestive** adj

digit [dij-it] n finger or toe; numeral from 0 to 9. **digital** adj displaying information as numbers rather than

with a dial, e.g. *digital clock*. **digital recording** sound-recording process that converts audio or analogue signals into a series of pulses. **digitally** adv **digitate** adj (of leaves) shaped like a hand; (of animals) having digits.

digitalis n drug made from foxglove leaves, used as a heart stimulant.

dignity n, pl **-ties** serious, calm, and controlled behaviour or manner; quality of being worthy of honour; sense of self-importance. **dignify** v **-fying**, **-fied** give dignity to. **dignitary** n person of high official position.

digress v depart from the main subject in speech or writing. **digression** n **digressive** adj

dike n same as DYKE.

dilapidated adj (of a building) fallen into ruin. **dilapidation** n

dilate v make or become wider or larger. **dilation**, **dilatation** n

dilatory [dill-a-tree] adj tending or intended to waste time.

dildo n, pl **-dos** object used as a substitute for an erect penis.

dilemma n situation offering a choice between two equally undesirable alternatives.

dilettante [dill-it-tan-tee] n person whose interest in a subject, esp. art, is superficial rather than serious. **dilettantism** n

diligent adj careful and persevering in carrying out duties; carried out with care and perseverance. **diligently** adv **diligence** n

dill n sweet-smelling herb used for flavouring.

dilly-dally v **-lying**, **-lied** *Informal* dawdle or waste time.

dilute v make (a liquid) less concentrated, esp. by adding water; make (a quality etc.) weaker in force. **dilution** n

diluvial, **diluvian** adj of a flood, esp. the great Flood described in the Old Testament.

dim adj **dimmer**, **dimmest** badly illuminated; not clearly seen; mentally dull. ◆ v **dimming**, **dimmed** make or become dim. **take a dim view of** disapprove of. **dimly** adv **dimness** n **dimmer** n device for dimming an electric light.

dime n coin of Canada and the US,

worth ten cents.

dimension n aspect or factor, e.g. a new dimension to politics. ◆ pl scope or extent; measurement of the size of something in a particular direction.

diminish v make or become smaller, fewer, or less. **diminution** n

diminutive adj very small. ◆ n word or affix which implies smallness or unimportance.

diminuendo n Music gradual decrease in loudness.

dimple n small natural dent, esp. in the cheeks or chin. ◆ v produce dimples by smiling.

din n loud discordant confused noise. ◆ v **dinning, dinned** instil (something) into someone by constant repetition.

dinar [dee-nahr] n monetary unit of various Balkan, Middle Eastern, and North African countries.

dine v eat dinner. **diner** n person eating a meal; small cheap restaurant. **dining car** railway coach in which meals are served. **dining room** room where meals are eaten.

ding-dong n sound of a bell; Informal violent exchange of blows or words.

dinghy [ding-ee] n, pl **-ghies** small boat, powered by sails, oars, or an outboard motor.

dingle n small wooded dell.

dingo n, pl **-goes** wild dog of Australia.

dingy [din-jee] adj **-gier, -giest** dirty-looking, dull. **dinginess** n

dinkum adj Aust & NZ informal genuine or right.

dinky adj **-kier, -kiest** Informal small and neat.

dinner n main meal of the day, taken either in the evening or at midday; official banquet. **dinner jacket** man's semiformal evening jacket, usu. black.

dinosaur n extinct prehistoric reptile, often of gigantic size.

dint n **by dint of** by means of.

diocese [die-a-siss] n district under the jurisdiction of a bishop. **diocesan** adj

diode n semiconductor device for converting alternating current to direct current.

dioptre [die-op-ter] n unit for measuring the refractive power of a lens.

dioxide n oxide containing two oxygen atoms per molecule.

dip v **dipping, dipped** plunge quickly or briefly into a liquid; slope downwards; switch (automobile headlights) from the main to the lower beam; lower briefly. ◆ n act of dipping; brief swim; liquid chemical in which farm animals are dipped to rid them of insects; depression, esp. in a landscape; creamy mixture into which pieces of food are dipped before being eaten. **dip into** v read passages at random from (a book or journal).

diphtheria [dif-theer-ya] n contagious disease producing fever and difficulty in breathing and swallowing.

diphthong n union of two vowel sounds in a single compound sound.

diploma n document conferring a qualification or recording successful completion of a course of study.

diplomacy n conduct of the relations between nations by peaceful means; tact or skill in dealing with people. **diplomat** n official engaged in diplomacy. **diplomatic** adj of or relating to diplomacy; tactful in dealing with people. **diplomatically** adv

dipper n ladle used for dipping; kind of river bird.

dipsomania n compulsive craving for alcohol. **dipsomaniac** n, adj

diptych [dip-tik] n painting on two hinged panels.

dire adj desperate or urgent; indicating disaster.

direct adj (of a route) shortest, straight; without anyone or anything intervening; honest, frank. ◆ adv in a direct manner. ◆ v conduct or control the affairs of; give orders with authority to (a person or group); tell (someone) the way to a place; address (a letter, package, remarks, etc.); provide guidance to (actors, cameramen, etc.) in (a play or film). **directly** adv in a direct manner; at once. ◆ conj as soon as. **directness** n **direction** n course along which a person or thing moves, points, or lies; management or guidance. ◆ pl instructions for doing something or for reaching a place. **directional** adj **directive** n order. **director** n person or thing that directs or controls; member of the governing board of a business etc.; person responsible for the artistic and technical aspects of the making of a film etc. **directorial** *adj* **directorship** *n* **directorate** *n* board of directors; position of director. **directory** *n* book listing names, addresses, and telephone numbers of individuals and firms; *Computers* area of a disk containing the names and locations of the files it currently holds.

dirge *n* slow sad song of mourning.

dirigible [dir-rij-jib-bl] *adj* able to be steered. ◆ *n* airship.

dirk *n* dagger, formerly worn by Scottish Highlanders.

dirndl *n* (dress with) full gathered skirt.

dirt *n* unclean substance, filth; loose earth or soil; obscene speech or writing; *Informal* scandal, harmful gossip. **dirt track** racetrack made of packed earth or cinders.

dirty *adj* **dirtier, dirtiest** covered or marked with dirt; unfair or dishonest; obscene; displaying dislike or anger, e.g. *a dirty look.* ◆ *v* **dirtying, dirtied** make dirty. **dirtiness** *n*

dis- *prefix* indicating: reversal, e.g. *disconnect*; negation or lack, e.g. *dissimilar, disgrace*; removal or release, e.g. *disembowel.*

disable *v* make ineffective, unfit, or incapable. **disabled** *adj* lacking one or more physical powers, such as the ability to walk. **disablement** *n* **disability** *n* condition of being physically or mentally impaired; something that disables someone.

disabuse *v* (foll. by *of*) rid (someone) of a mistaken idea.

disadvantage *n* unfavourable circumstance, thing, or situation. **disadvantageous** *adj* **disadvantaged** *adj* socially or economically deprived.

disaffected *adj* having lost loyalty to or affection for someone or something. **disaffection** *n*

disagree *v* **-greeing, -greed** have different opinions; fail to correspond; (foll. by *with*) cause physical discomfort (to), e.g. *curry disagrees with me.* **disagreement** *n*

disagreeable *adj* (of a person) bad-tempered or disobliging; unpleasant. **disagreeably** *adv*

disallow *v* reject as untrue or invalid.

disappear *v* cease to be visible; cease to exist. **disappearance** *n*

disappoint *v* fail to meet the expectations or hopes of. **disappointment** *n* feeling of being disappointed; person or thing that disappoints.

disapprobation *n* disapproval.

disapprove *v* (foll. by *of*) consider wrong or bad. **disapproval** *n*

disarm *v* deprive of weapons; win the confidence or affection of; (of a nation) decrease the size of one's armed forces. **disarmament** *n* **disarming** *adj* removing hostility or suspicion. **disarmingly** *adv*

disarrange *v* throw into disorder.

disarray *n* confusion and lack of discipline; extreme untidiness.

disaster *n* occurrence that causes great distress or destruction; project etc. that fails. **disastrous** *adj* **disastrously** *adv*

disavow *v* deny connection with or responsibility for (something). **disavowal** *n*

disband *v* (cause to) cease to function as a group or unit.

disbelieve *v* reject as false; (foll. by *in*) have no faith (in). **disbelief** *n*

disburse *v* pay out. **disbursement** *n*

disc *n* flat circular object; gramophone record; *Anat* circular flat structure in the body, esp. between the vertebrae; *Computers* same as DISK. **disc jockey** person who introduces and plays pop records on a radio programme or at a disco.

discard *v* get rid of (something or someone) as useless or undesirable.

discern *v* see or be aware of (something) clearly. **discernible** *adj* **discerning** *adj* having or showing good judgment. **discernment** *n*

discharge *v* release, allow to go; dismiss (someone) from duty or employment; fire (a gun); pour forth, emit; meet the demands of (an obligation etc.); relieve oneself of (a responsibility or debt). ◆ *n* something that is discharged; dismissal from duty or employment; emission.

disciple [diss-**sipe**-pl] *n* follower of the doctrines of a teacher, esp. Jesus Christ.

discipline n practice of imposing strict rules of behaviour on other people; ability to behave and work in a controlled manner; branch of learning. ◆ v (attempt to) improve the behaviour of (oneself or another) by training or rules; punish. **disciplinarian** n person who practises strict discipline. **disciplinary** adj

disclaim v deny (responsibility for or knowledge of something). **disclaimer** n repudiation, denial.

disclose v make known; allow to be seen. **disclosure** n

disco n, pl -cos occasion at which people dance to pop records; place where such dances are held; mobile equipment for providing music for a disco.

discolour v change in colour, stain. **discoloration** n

discomfit v make uneasy or confused. **discomfiture** n

discomfort n inconvenience, distress, or mild pain.

discommode v cause inconvenience to. **discommodious** adj

disconcert v disturb the confidence or self-possession of.

disconnect v undo or break the connection between (two things); stop the supply of (electricity or gas) of. **disconnected** adj (of speech or ideas) not logically connected. **disconnection** n

disconsolate adj sad beyond comfort. **disconsolately** adv

discontent n lack of contentment, as with one's lot in life. **discontented** adj **discontentedly** adv

discontinue v -uing, -ued come or bring to an end. **discontinuous** adj characterized by interruptions. **discontinuity** n lack of smooth or unbroken development.

discord n lack of agreement or harmony between people; harsh confused sounds. **discordant** adj **discordance** n

discotheque n full name for DISCO.

discount v leave (something) out of account as being unreliable, prejudiced, or irrelevant; deduct (an amount) from the price of something. ◆ n deduction from the full price of something.

discourage v deprive of the will to persist in something; oppose by expressing disapproval. **discouragement** n

discourse n conversation; formal treatment of a subject in speech or writing. ◆ v (foll. by on) speak or write (about) at length.

discourteous adj showing bad manners. **discourteously** adv **discourtesy** n

discover v be the first to find or to find out about; learn about for the first time; find after study or search. **discoverer** n **discovery** n act of discovering; person, place, or thing that has been discovered.

discredit v damage the reputation of (someone); cause (an idea) to be disbelieved or distrusted. ◆ n (something that causes) damage to someone's reputation. **discreditable** adj bringing discredit.

discreet adj careful to avoid embarrassment, esp. by keeping confidences secret; unobtrusive. **discreetly** adv

discrepancy n, pl -cies variation between facts, figures, or claims.

discrete adj separate or distinct.

discretion [diss-kresh-on] n quality of behaving in a discreet way; freedom or authority to make judgments and to act as one sees fit. **discretionary** adj

discriminate v (foll. by against or in favour of) single out a particular person or group for special disfavour or favour; (foll. by between or among) recognize or understand the difference (between). **discriminating** adj showing good taste and judgment. **discrimination** n **discriminatory** adj based on prejudice.

discursive adj passing from one topic to another.

discus n disc-shaped object with a heavy middle, thrown in sports competitions.

discuss v consider (something) by talking it over; treat (a subject) in speech or writing. **discussion** n

disdain n feeling of superiority and dislike. ◆ v refuse with disdain. **disdainful** adj **disdainfully** adv

disease n illness, sickness. **diseased** adj

disembark v (cause to) land from a ship, aircraft, or bus. **disembarkation** n

disembodied adj lacking a body; seeming not to be attached to or coming from anyone.

disembowel v **-elling, -elled** remove the entrails of.

disenchanted adj disappointed and disillusioned (with something). **disenchantment** n

disenfranchise v deprive (a person) of the right to vote or or of other rights of citizenship.

disengage v release from a connection. **disengagement** n

disentangle v release from entanglement or confusion. **disentanglement** n

disfavour n disapproval or dislike.

disfigure v spoil the appearance or shape of. **disfigurement** n

disfranchise v same as DISENFRANCHISE.

disgorge v vomit; discharge (contents).

disgrace n condition of shame, loss of reputation, or dishonour; shameful person or thing. ♦ v bring shame upon (oneself or others). **disgraceful** adj **disgracefully** adv

disgruntled adj sulky or discontented. **disgruntlement** n

disguise v change the appearance or manner in order to conceal the identity of (someone or something); misrepresent (something) in order to obscure its actual nature or meaning. ♦ n mask, costume, or manner that disguises; state of being disguised.

disgust n great loathing or distaste. ♦ v sicken, fill with loathing.

dish n shallow container used for holding or serving food; portion or variety of food; short for DISH AERIAL; Informal attractive person. **dish aerial** aerial consisting of a concave disc-shaped reflector. **dishcloth** n cloth for washing dishes. **dish out** v Informal distribute. **dish up** v Informal serve (food).

dishabille [diss-a-beel] n state of being partly dressed.

dishearten v weaken or destroy the hope, courage, or enthusiasm of.

dishevelled adj (of a person's hair, clothes, or general appearance) disordered and untidy.

dishonest adj not honest or fair. **dishonestly** adv **dishonesty** n

dishonour v treat with disrespect. ♦ n lack of respect; state of shame or disgrace; something that causes a loss of honour. **dishonourable** adj **dishonourably** adv

disillusion v destroy the illusions or false ideas of. ♦ n (also **disillusionment**) state of being disillusioned.

disincentive n something that acts as a deterrent.

disinclined adj unwilling or reluctant. **disinclination** n

disinfect v rid of harmful germs, esp. by chemical means. **disinfectant** n substance that destroys harmful germs. **disinfection** n

disinformation n false information intended to mislead.

disingenuous adj not sincere. **disingenuously** adv

disinherit v Law deprive (an heir) of inheritance. **disinheritance** n

disintegrate v break up into fragments. **disintegration** n

disinter v **-terring, -terred** dig up; reveal, make known.

disinterested adj free from bias or involvement. **disinterest** n

disjointed adj having no coherence; disconnected.

disk n Computers storage device, consisting of a stack of plates coated with a magnetic layer, which rotates rapidly as a single unit.

dislike v consider unpleasant or disagreeable. ♦ n feeling of not liking something or someone.

dislocate v displace (a bone or joint) from its normal position; disrupt or shift out of place. **dislocation** n

dislodge v remove (something) from a previously fixed position.

disloyal adj not loyal, deserting one's allegiance. **disloyalty** n

dismal adj causing gloom; Informal of poor quality. **dismally** adv

dismantle v take apart piece by piece.

dismay v fill with alarm or depression. ♦ n alarm mixed with sadness.

dismember v remove the limbs of; cut to pieces. **dismemberment** n

dismiss v remove (an employee) from

a job; allow (someone) to leave; put out of one's mind; (of a judge) state that (a case) will not be brought to trial. **dismissal** n **dismissive** adj contemptuous.

dismount v get off a horse or bicycle.

disobey v neglect or refuse to obey. **disobedient** adj **disobedience** n

disobliging adj unwilling to help.

disorder n state of untidiness and disorganization; public violence or rioting; an illness. **disordered** adj untidy. **disorderly** adj very untidy, disorganized; uncontrolled, unruly.

disorganize v disrupt the arrangement or system of. **disorganization** n

disorientate, disorient v cause (someone) to lose his or her bearings. **disorientation** n

disown v deny any connection with (someone).

disparage v speak contemptuously of. **disparagement** n

disparate adj utterly different in kind. **disparity** n

dispassionate adj uninfluenced by emotion. **dispassionately** adv

dispatch v send off to a destination or to perform a task; carry out (a duty or a task) with speed; Old-fashioned kill. ◆ n official communication or report, sent in haste; report sent to a newspaper by a correspondent. **dispatch rider** motorcyclist who carries dispatches.

dispel v **-pelling, -pelled** disperse or drive away.

dispense v distribute in portions; prepare and distribute (medicine); administer (the law etc.). **dispensable** adj not essential. **dispensation** n act of dispensing; exemption from an obligation; administrative system. **dispenser** n **dispensary** n place where medicine is dispensed. **dispense with** v do away with; manage without.

disperse v scatter over a wide area; (cause to) leave a gathering. **dispersal, dispersion** n

dispirit v make downhearted.

displace v move from the usual location; remove from office. **displacement** n **displaced person** person forced from his or her home or country, esp. by war or revolution.

display v make visible or noticeable. ◆ n act of displaying; something displayed; exhibition.

displease v annoy. **displeasure** n

disport v **disport oneself** indulge oneself in pleasure.

dispose v place in a particular way. **disposable** adj designed to be thrown away after use; available for use if needed, e.g. disposable assets. **disposal** n getting rid of something. **at one's disposal** available for use. **disposed** adj willing (to do something); inclined as specified (towards someone or something), e.g. well disposed. **disposition** n person's usual temperament; tendency; arrangement. **dispose of** v throw away; give or sell to another; deal with (a problem, etc.); kill.

dispossess v (foll. by of) deprive (someone) of (a possession). **dispossession** n

disproportion n lack of proportion or equality. **disproportionate** adj **disproportionately** adv

disprove v show (an assertion or claim) to be incorrect.

dispute n disagreement between workers and their employers; argument. ◆ v argue about (something); doubt the validity of; fight over possession of. **disputation** n Formal argument.

disqualify v **-fying, -fied** debar from a contest; make ineligible. **disqualification** n

disquiet n feeling of anxiety. ◆ v make (someone) anxious. **disquietude** n anxiety, uneasiness.

disregard v give little or no attention to. ◆ n lack of attention.

disrepair n condition of being worn out or in poor working order.

disrepute n loss or lack of good reputation. **disreputable** adj having or causing a bad reputation.

disrespect n lack of respect. **disrespectful** adj **disrespectfully** adv

disrobe v undress.

disrupt v interrupt the progress of. **disruption** n **disruptive** adj

dissatisfied adj not pleased, disappointed. **dissatisfaction** n

dissect v cut open (a dead body) to examine it; examine critically and minutely. **dissection** n

dissemble v conceal one's real motives or emotions by pretence.

disseminate v scatter about. **dissemination** n

dissent v disagree; *Christianity* reject the doctrines of an established church. ◆ n disagreement; *Christianity* separation from an established church. **dissension** n **dissenter** n

dissertation n written thesis, usu. required for a higher university degree; long formal speech.

disservice n bad turn or wrong.

dissident n person who disagrees, esp. with the government. ◆ adj disagreeing. **dissidence** n

dissimilar adj not alike, different. **dissimilarity** n

dissimulate v conceal one's real feelings by pretence. **dissimulation** n

dissipate v waste or squander; scatter. **dissipated** adj showing signs of overindulging in alcohol and other pleasures. **dissipation** n

dissociate v regard or treat as separate. **dissociate oneself from** deny or break a connection with. **dissociation** n

dissolute adj leading an immoral life.

dissolve v (cause to) become liquid; bring to an end; dismiss (a meeting, Parliament, etc.); collapse emotionally. **dissolution** n destruction by breaking up and dispersing; termination of a meeting, assembly, or legal relationship.

dissonance n discordant combination of sounds; lack of agreement or consistency. **dissonant** adj

dissuade v deter (someone) by persuasion from a course of action, policy, etc. **dissuasion** n

distaff n rod on which wool, flax, etc. is wound for spinning. **distaff side** female side of a family.

distance n space between two points; state of being apart; distant place; remoteness in manner. **distance oneself from** separate oneself mentally from. **distant** adj far apart; separated by a specified distance; remote in manner. **distantly** adv

distaste n dislike, aversion. **distasteful** adj offensive.

distemper¹ n highly contagious

disease of animals, esp. dogs.

distemper² n paint mixed with water, glue, etc., which is used for painting walls.

distend v expand by pressure from within. **distension** n

distil v **-tilling, -tilled** subject to or obtain by distillation; give off (a substance) in drops; extract the essence of. **distillation** n process of evaporating a liquid and condensing its vapour; (also **distillate**) concentrated essence. **distiller** n person or company that makes spirits. **distillery** n place where alcoholic drinks are made by distillation.

distinct adj not the same; clearly seen, heard, or recognized; clear and definite, e.g. *a distinct possibility of rain*. **distinctly** adv **distinction** n act of distinguishing; distinguishing feature; state of being different; special honour, recognition, or fame. **distinctive** adj easily recognizable. **distinctively** adv **distinctiveness** n

distinguish v (foll. by *between* or *among*) make, show, or recognize a difference (between or among); be a distinctive feature of; perceive. **distinguishable** adj **distinguished** adj noble or dignified in appearance; highly respected.

distort v alter or misrepresent (facts); twist out of shape. **distortion** n

distract v draw the attention of (a person) away from something; confuse, trouble; entertain. **distraction** n

distrait [diss-**tray**] adj absent-minded or abstracted.

distraught [diss-**trawt**] adj extremely anxious or agitated.

distress n extreme unhappiness or worry; great physical pain; financial trouble. ◆ v upset badly. **distressed** adj much troubled; in financial difficulties. **distressing** adj **distressingly** adv

distribute v hand out or deliver (leaflets, etc.); share (something) among the members of a particular group. **distribution** n act of distributing; arrangement or spread of anything over an area, period of time, etc. **distributor** n wholesaler who distributes goods to retailers in a specific area; device in a gasoline engine that sends the electric current to the spark plugs.

district n area of land regarded as an administrative or geographical unit.

distrust v regard as untrustworthy. ◆ n suspicion or doubt. **distrustful** adj

disturb v intrude on; disarrange; worry, make anxious. **disturbance** n **disturbing** adj **disturbingly** adv **disturbed** adj Psychiatry emotionally upset, troubled, or maladjusted.

disunite v cause disagreement among. **disunity** n

disuse n condition of being unused. **disused** adj

ditch n narrow channel dug in the earth for drainage or irrigation. ◆ v Slang abandon.

dither v be uncertain or indecisive. ◆ n state of indecision or agitation. **ditherer** n **dithery** adj

ditto n, pl **-tos** the same. ◆ adv in the same way.

ditty n, pl **-ties** short simple poem or song.

diuretic [die-yoor-et-ik] n drug that increases the flow of urine.

diurnal [die-urn-al] adj happening during the day or daily.

divan n backless sofa or couch; low backless bed.

dive v **diving, dived** plunge headfirst into water; (of a submarine or diver) submerge under water; fly in a steep nose-down descending path; move quickly in a specified direction; (foll. by in or into) start (doing something) enthusiastically. ◆ n act of diving; steep nose-down descent; Slang disreputable bar or club. **diver** n person who works or explores underwater; person who dives for sport. **dive bomber** military aircraft designed to release bombs during a dive.

diverge v separate and go in different directions; deviate (from a prescribed course). **divergence** n **divergent** adj

divers adj Old-fashioned various.

diverse adj having variety; different in kind. **diversity** n quality of being varied; range of difference. **diversify** v **diversification** n

divert v change the direction of (traffic); distract the attention of; entertain. **diversion** n something that

distracts someone's attention; an entertainment. **diversionary** adj

divest v strip (of clothes); dispossess or deprive.

divide v separate into parts; share or be shared out in parts; (cause to) disagree; keep apart, be a boundary between; calculate how many times (one number) can be contained in (another). ◆ n division, split. **dividend** n sum of money representing part of the profit made, paid by a company to its shareholders; bonus. **divider** n screen used to divide a room into separate areas. ◆ pl n compasses with two pointed arms, used for measuring or dividing lines.

divine adj of God or a god; godlike; Informal splendid. ◆ v discover (something) by intuition or guessing. **divinely** adv **divination** n art of discovering future events, as though by supernatural powers. **divinity** n theology; state of being divine; god. **divining rod** forked twig said to move when held over ground in which water or metal is to be found.

division n act of dividing or sharing out; one of the parts into which something is divided; difference of opinion; mathematical operation of dividing. **divisional** adj of a division in an organization. **divisible** adj **divisibility** n **divisive** [div-vice-iv] adj tending to cause disagreement. **divisor** n number to be divided into another number.

divorce n legal ending of a marriage; separation, esp. one that is total. ◆ v separate or be separated by divorce; remove or separate. **divorcé, divorcée** n person who is divorced.

divulge v make known, disclose. **divulgence** n

Dixie n southern states of the US.

dizzy adj **-zier, -ziest** having or causing a whirling sensation; mentally confused. ◆ v **-zying, -zied** make dizzy. **dizzily** adv **dizziness** n

DJ disc jockey; dinner jacket.

dl decilitre.

dm decimetre.

DNA n deoxyribonucleic acid, the main constituent of the chromosomes of all living things.

do v **does, doing, did, done** perform or complete (a deed or action); be suitable, suffice; provide, serve, e.g. *this place doesn't do lunch on Sundays*; make tidy, elegant, or ready, e.g *do one's hair*; improve, e.g. *that hat does nothing for you*; find the answer to (a problem or puzzle); cause or produce, e.g. *complaints do nothing to help*; give or render, e.g *do me a favour*; work at, esp. as a course of study or a job; travel (a distance); *Informal* cheat or rob; used to form questions, e.g. *do you agree?*; used to intensify positive statements and commands, e.g. *I do like your new house, do hurry!*; used to form negative statements and commands, e.g. *do not leave me here alone!*; used to replace an earlier verb, e.g. *he likes you as much as I do.* ◆ *n, pl* **dos, do's** *Informal* festive gathering or party. **do away with** *v* kill; get rid of. **do-it-yourself** *n* practice of constructing and repairing things oneself, esp. as a hobby. **do up** *v* fasten; renovate. **do with** *v* find useful or benefit from. **do without** *v* manage without.

Doberman, Doberman pinscher *n* large slender dog with a glossy black-and-tan coat.

docile *adj* (of a person or animal) easily managed. **docilely** *adv* **docility** *n*

dock[1] *n* enclosed area of water where ships are loaded, unloaded, or repaired. ◆ *v* moor or be moored at dock; link (two spacecraft) or (of two spacecraft) be linked together in space. **docker** *n* person employed in the loading or unloading of ships. **dockyard** *n* place with docks and equipment where ships are built or repaired.

dock[2] *v* deduct (an amount) from (a person's wages); remove part of (an animal's tail) by cutting through the bone.

dock[3] *n* enclosed space in a court of law where the accused person sits or stands.

dock[4] *n* weed with broad leaves.

docket *n* piece of paper accompanying a package or other delivery, stating contents, delivery instructions, etc. ◆ *v* fix a docket to (a package etc.).

doctor *n* person licensed to practise medicine; person who has been

awarded a doctorate. ◆ *v* make different in order to deceive; poison or drug (food or drink); *Informal* castrate or sterilize (a cat, dog, etc.). **doctoral** *adj* **doctorate** *n* highest academic degree in any field of knowledge.

doctrine [dock-trin] *n* body of teachings of a religious, political, or philosophical group; principle or body of principles that is taught or advocated. **doctrinal** *adj* of or related to doctrine. **doctrinaire** *adj* stubbornly insistent on the application of a theory without regard to practicality.

document *n* piece of paper, booklet, etc. providing information, esp. of an official nature. ◆ *v* record or report (something) in detail; support (a claim) with evidence. **documentation** *n*

documentary *n, pl* **-ries** film or television programme presenting the facts about a particular subject. ◆ *adj* of or based on documents.

dodder *v* move unsteadily. **dodderer** *n* **doddery** *adj*

dodecagon [doe-**deck**-a-gon] *n* geometric figure with twelve sides.

dodge *v* avoid (a blow, being seen, etc.) by moving suddenly; evade by cleverness or trickery. ◆ *n* plan contrived to deceive; sudden evasive movement. **dodger** *n* **dodgy** *adj* *Informal* difficult or dangerous; untrustworthy.

Dodgem *n* ® electrically propelled vehicle driven and bumped against similar vehicles in a rink at a funfair.

dodo *n, pl* **dodos, dodoes** large flightless extinct bird.

doe *n* female deer, hare, or rabbit.

does *v* third person singular of the present tense of DO.

doesn't does not.

doff *v* take off or lift (one's hat) as a mark of respect.

dog *n* domesticated four-legged meat-eating mammal occurring in many different breeds; any other member of the dog family, such as the dingo or coyote; male of animals of the dog family; *Informal* fellow, chap, e.g. *you lucky dog!* ◆ *v* **dogging, dogged** follow (someone) closely; trouble or plague. **go to the dogs** go to ruin physically or morally. **let sleeping dogs lie** leave things undisturbed.

dogged [**dog**-gid] *adj* obstinately determined. **doggedly** *adv* **doggedness** *n* **doggy, doggie** *n* child's word for a dog. **dogcart** *n* light horse-drawn two-wheeled vehicle. **dog collar** collar for a dog; *Informal* clerical collar. **dog-eared** *adj* (of a book) having pages folded down at the corner; shabby or worn. **dogfight** *n* close-quarters combat between fighter aircraft; any rough fight. **dogfish** *n* small shark. **doghouse** *n* kennel. **in the doghouse** *Informal* in disfavour. **dogleg** *n* sharp bend. **dog rose** wild rose with pink or white flowers. **dogsbody** *n Informal* person who carries out menial tasks for others. **dogsled** *n* sled drawn by dogs. **dog-tired** *adj Informal* exhausted.

doge [**doje**] *n* (formerly) chief magistrate of Venice or Genoa.

doggerel *n* poorly written, usually comic verse.

doggo *adv* **lie doggo** *Informal* hide and keep quiet.

dogma *n* doctrine or system of doctrines proclaimed by authority as true. **dogmatic** *adj* (of a statement or opinion) forcibly asserted as if unchallengeable; (of a person) prone to making such statements. **dogmatically** *adv* **dogmatism** *n*

doily *n, pl* **-lies** decorative mat of lace or lacelike paper, laid on plates.

doldrums *pl n* depressed state of mind; state of inactivity.

dole *n Informal* money received from the state while out of work. ◆ *v* (foll. by *out*) distribute (something), esp. in small portions.

doleful *adj* dreary or mournful. **dolefully** *adv* **dolefulness** *n*

doll *n* small model of a human being, used as a toy; *Slang* girl or young woman, esp. a pretty one.

dollar *n* standard monetary unit of Canada, the US, and various other countries.

dollop *n Informal* semisolid lump.

dolly *n, pl* **-lies** child's word for a doll; wheeled support on which a camera may be moved.

dolman sleeve *n* sleeve that is very wide at the armhole and tapers to a tight wrist.

dolmen *n* prehistoric monument consisting of a horizontal stone supported by vertical stones.

dolomite *n* mineral consisting of calcium magnesium carbonate.

dolorous *adj* causing or involving pain or sorrow.

dolphin *n* sea mammal of the whale family, with a beaklike snout.

dolt *n* stupid person. **doltish** *adj*

domain *n* field of knowledge or activity; land under one ruler or government.

dome *n* rounded roof built on a circular base; something shaped like this. **domed** *adj*

domestic *adj* of the home or family; home-loving; (of an animal) bred or kept as a pet or for the supply of food; of one's own country or a specific country, e.g. *domestic and foreign affairs.* ◆ *n* household servant. **domestically** *adv* **domesticity** *n* **domesticate** *v* bring or keep (wild animals or plants) under control or cultivation; accustom (someone) to home life. **domestication** *n* **domestic science** study of household skills.

domicile [**dom**-miss-ile] *n* person's regular dwelling place. **domiciliary** *adj*

dominant *adj* having authority; main or chief, e.g. *the dominant topic of the day.* **dominance** *n*

dominate *v* control or govern; tower above (surroundings); be the most important of (a particular set of people or things). **domination** *n*

domineering *adj* acting arrogantly or tyrannically.

Dominican *n* friar or nun of an order founded by Saint Dominic. ◆ *adj* of the Dominican order.

dominion *n* rule or authority; land governed by one ruler or government; formerly, self-governing division of the British Empire.

domino *n, pl* **-noes** small rectangular block marked with dots, used in dominoes. ◆ *pl* game in which dominoes with matching halves are laid together.

don[1] *v* **donning, donned** put on (clothing).

don[2] *n Brit* member of the teaching staff at a university or college; Spanish gentleman or nobleman. **donnish** *adj* resembling a university don.

donate v give (something), esp. to a charity. **donation** n act of donating; a contribution. **donor** n Med person who gives blood, organs, etc. for use in the treatment of another person; person who makes a donation.

done v past participle of DO.

doner kebab n grilled minced lamb served in a split slice of unleavened bread.

donkey n long-eared member of the horse family. **donkey jacket** man's thick hip-length jacket with a waterproof panel across the shoulders. **donkey's years** Informal a long time. **donkey-work** n groundwork; drudgery.

don't do not.

doodle v draw aimlessly. ♦ n shape or picture drawn aimlessly.

doom n death or a terrible fate. ♦ v destine or condemn to death or a terrible fate. **doomsday** n Christianity day on which the Last Judgment will occur; any dreaded day.

door n hinged or sliding panel for closing the entrance to a room, cupboard, etc.; entrance. **doormat** n mat, placed at an entrance, for wiping dirt from shoes; Informal person who offers little resistance to ill-treatment. **doorway** n opening into a building or room.

dope n Slang illegal drug, usu. cannabis; drug, esp. one administered to a racehorse etc. to affect its performance; Informal slow-witted person; confidential information. ♦ v administer a drug to. **dopey, dopy** adj half-asleep; Slang silly.

dormant adj temporarily quiet, inactive, or not being used. **dormancy** n

dormer (window) n window that projects from a sloping roof.

dormitory n, pl -ries large room, esp. at a school, containing several beds.

dormouse n small rodent resembling a mouse with a furry tail.

dorsal adj of or on the back.

dory n, pl -ries spiny-finned sea fish.

dose n specific quantity of a medicine taken at one time; Informal something unpleasant to experience. ♦ v administer a dose to (someone). **dosage** n size of a dose.

doss v **doss down** Brit slang sleep, esp. on a makeshift bed. **dosshouse** n Brit slang cheap lodging house for homeless people.

dossier [doss-ee-ay] n collection of papers with information about a subject or person.

dot n small round mark; shorter symbol used in Morse code. ♦ v dotting, dotted mark with a dot; scatter or intersperse. **on the dot** at exactly the arranged time. **dotty** adj Slang slightly mad. **dottiness** n

dote v **dote on** love to an excessive or foolish degree. **dotage** [dote-ij] n feebleness of mind as a result of old age. **dotard** [dote-ard] n person who is feeble-minded through old age.

double adj as much again in size, strength, number, etc.; composed of two equal or similar parts; designed for two users; folded in two. ♦ adv twice over, twofold. ♦ n twice the number, amount, size, etc.; duplicate or counterpart, esp. a person who closely resembles another. ♦ pl game between two pairs of players. ♦ v make or become twice as much; bend or fold (material etc.); play two parts; turn sharply. **at the double** quickly or immediately. **doubly** adv **double agent** spy employed simultaneously by two opposing sides. **double bass** stringed instrument, largest and lowest member of the violin family. **double chin** fold of fat under the chin. **double cream** thick cream with a high fat content. **double-cross** v cheat or betray. ♦ n instance of double-crossing. **double-dealing** n treacherous or deceitful behaviour. **double-decker** n bus with two passenger decks one on top of the other; Informal sandwich made from three slices of bread with two fillings. **double Dutch** Informal incomprehensible talk, gibberish. **double glazing** two panes of glass in a window, fitted to reduce heat loss. **double take** (esp. in comedy) delayed reaction by a person to a remark or situation. **double talk** deceptive or ambiguous talk.

double entendre [doob-bl on-tond-ra] n word or phrase that can be interpreted in two ways, esp. with one meaning that is rude.

doublet [dub-lit] n (formerly) man's close-fitting jacket, with or without sleeves.

doubloon n former Spanish gold coin.

doubt n uncertainty about the truth, facts, or existence of something; unresolved difficulty or point. ◆ v be inclined to disbelieve (a fact or story); distrust or be suspicious of (a person). **doubter** n **doubtful** adj unlikely; feeling doubt. **doubtfully** adv **doubtless** adv certainly; probably.

douche [doosh] n (instrument for applying) a stream of water directed onto or into the body for cleansing or medical purposes. ◆ v cleanse or treat by means of a douche.

dough n thick mixture of flour and water or milk, used for making bread; Slang money. **doughnut** n small cake of sweetened dough cooked in hot fat.

doughty [dowt-ee] adj -tier, -tiest hardy or resolute.

dour [doo-er] adj sullen and unfriendly. **dourness** n

douse [rhymes with **mouse**] v drench with water or other liquid; put out (a light).

dove n bird with a heavy body, small head, and short legs; Politics person opposed to war. **dovecote, dovecot** n structure for housing pigeons. **dovetail** n joint containing wedge-shaped tenons. ◆ v fit together neatly.

dowager n widow possessing property or a title obtained from her husband.

dowdy adj -dier, -diest shabby or old-fashioned. **dowdily** adv **dowdiness** n

dowel n wooden or metal peg that fits into two corresponding holes to join two adjacent parts.

dower n life interest in a part of her husband's estate allotted to a widow by law.

down[1] prep from a higher to a lower position in or on; at a lower or further level or position on, in, or along. ◆ adv at or to a lower position or level; used to indicate lowering or destruction, e.g. knock down; used with several verbs to indicate intensity or completion, e.g. calm down; immediately, e.g. cash down; on paper, e.g. write this down; lower in price; from an earlier to a later time. ◆ adj depressed, sad. ◆ v Informal drink, esp. quickly. **have a down on** Informal bear ill will towards. **down under** Informal Australia or New Zealand. **downward** adj descending from a higher to a lower level, condition, or position. ◆ adv downwards. **downwards** adv from a higher to a lower place, level, etc. **down-and-out** adj without any means of livelihood. ◆ n person who is destitute and, often, homeless. **downbeat** adj Informal gloomy; relaxed. **downcast** adj dejected; directed downwards. **downfall** n sudden loss of position or reputation; cause of this. **downgrade** v reduce in importance or value. **downhearted** adj sad and discouraged. **downhill** adj going or sloping down. ◆ adv towards the bottom of a hill. **download** v transfer (data) from the memory of one computer to that of another. **downpour** n heavy fall of rain. **downright** adj, adv extreme(ly). **downstairs** adv to or on a lower floor. ◆ n lower or ground floor. **down-to-earth** adj sensible or practical. **downtown** n the central or lower part of a city, especially the main commercial area. **downtrodden** adj oppressed and lacking the will to resist.

down[2] n soft fine feathers or hair. **downy** adj

downs pl n rolling upland, esp. in the chalk areas of S England.

Down's syndrome n genetic disorder characterized by a flat face, slanting eyes, and mental retardation.

dowry n, pl -ries property brought by a woman to her husband at marriage.

dowse [rhymes with **cows**] v search for underground water or minerals using a divining rod.

doxology n, pl -gies short hymn of praise to God.

doyen [doy-en] n senior member of a group, profession, or society. **doyenne** [doy-en] n fem

doze v sleep lightly or intermittently. ◆ n short sleep. **dozy** adj drowsy; Informal stupid. **doze off** v fall into a light sleep.

dozen adj, n twelve. **dozenth** adj, n

Dr Doctor; Drive.

drab adj drabber, drabbest dull or dingy; dreary. **drabness** n

drachma n, pl **-mas, -mae** a former monetary unit of Greece.

draconian adj harsh or severe.

draft[1] n preliminary outline of a book, speech, etc.; written order for payment of money by a bank; US selection for compulsory military service. ◆ v write a preliminary outline of a book, speech, etc.; detach (personnel) from one place to another; US select for compulsory military service.

draft[2], **draught** n current of air, esp. in an enclosed space; act of pulling a load by a vehicle or animal; portion of liquid to be drunk, esp. medicine; instance of drinking. **drafty** adj exposed to drafts of air. **draftsman** n person employed to prepare detailed scale drawings of machinery, buildings, etc. **draftsmanship** n **draft beer** beer stored in a cask.

drag v **dragging, dragged** pull with force, esp. along the ground; trail on the ground; (foil. by along or to) bring (oneself or someone else) with effort or difficulty; (foil. by on or out) last, prolong, or be prolonged tediously; search (a river) with a dragnet or hook. ◆ n person or thing that slows up progress; Informal tedious person or thing; Slang women's clothes worn by a man. **dragnet** n net used to scour the bottom of a pond or river, when searching for something. **drag race** race in which specially built automobiles or motorcycles are timed over a measured course.

dragon n mythical fire-breathing monster with a scaly body, wings, claws, and a long tail; Informal fierce woman. **dragonfly** n, pl **-flies** brightly coloured insect with a long slender body and two pairs of wings.

dragoon n heavily armed cavalryman. ◆ v coerce or force.

drain n pipe or channel that carries off water or sewage; cause of continuous diminution of resources or energy. ◆ v draw off or remove liquid from; flow away or filter off; drink the entire contents of (a glass or cup); make constant demands on (resources, energy, etc.); exhaust (someone) physically and emotionally. **drainage** n process of draining; system of drains.

drake n male duck.

dram n small amount of spirits, esp. whisky; one sixteenth of an ounce.

drama n a work to be performed by actors; art of the writing or production of plays; situation that is highly emotional, turbulent, or tragic. **dramatic** adj of or like drama; striking or effective. **dramatically** adv **dramatist** n playwright. **dramatize** v put into dramatic form; express (something) in a dramatic or exaggerated way. **dramatization** n

drank v past tense of DRINK.

drape v cover with material, usu. in folds; place casually and loosely. ◆ n curtain. **draper** n Brit dealer in fabrics and sewing materials. **drapery** n fabric or clothing arranged and draped; fabrics and cloth collectively. ◆ pl curtains.

drastic adj sudden and extreme.

draught n same as DRAFT[2]. ◆ pl Brit checkers.

draw v **drawing, drew, drawn** depict or sketch (a figure, picture, etc.) in lines, with a pencil or pen; cause (a person or thing) to move out, as from a drawer, holster, etc.; move in a specified direction; arouse the interest or attention of; formulate or derive, e.g. draw conclusions; take from a source, e.g. draw money from the bank; (of two teams or contestants) finish a game with an equal number of points. ◆ n raffle or lottery; contest or game ending in a tie; event, act, etc., that attracts a large audience. **drawer** n boxlike container in a chest, table, etc., made for sliding in and out. ◆ pl Old-fashioned undergarment worn below the waist. **drawing** n picture or plan made by means of lines on a surface; art of making drawings. **drawing pin** short tack with a broad smooth head. **drawing room** Old-fashioned room where visitors are received and entertained. **drawback** n disadvantage. **drawbridge** n bridge that may be raised to prevent access or to enable vessels to pass. **draw out** v extend; encourage (a person) to talk freely. **drawstring** n cord run through a hem around an opening, so that when it is pulled tighter, the opening closes. **draw up** v (of a vehicle) come to a halt; formulate and write out (a contract).

drawl *v* speak slowly, esp. prolonging the vowel sounds. ◆ *n* drawling manner of speech.

drawn *v* past participle of DRAW. ◆ *adj* haggard, tired, or tense in appearance.

dray *n* low cart used for carrying heavy loads.

dread *v* anticipate with apprehension or terror. ◆ *n* great fear. **dreadful** *adj* extremely bad; extreme. **dreadfully** *adv*

dreadlocks *pl n* hair worn in the Rastafarian style of tightly curled strands.

dream *n* mental activity, usu. an imagined series of events, occurring during sleep; cherished hope; *Informal* something wonderful. ◆ *v* **dreaming, dreamt** or **dreamed**. experience (a dream); (foll. by *of* or *about*) have an image (of) or fantasy (about); (foll. by *of*) consider the possibility (of). **dreamer** *n* **dreamy** *adj* vague or impractical; *Informal* wonderful. **dreamily** *adv*

dreary *adj* **drearier, dreariest** dull or boring. **drearily** *adv* **dreariness** *n*

dredge[1] *v* remove (silt or mud) from (a river bed etc.). **dredger** *n* boat fitted with machinery for dredging.

dredge[2] *v* sprinkle (food) with flour etc.

dregs *pl n* solid particles that settle at the bottom of some liquids; most despised elements, e.g. *the dregs of society*.

drench *v* make completely wet. **drenching** *n*

dress *n* one-piece garment for a woman or girl, consisting of a skirt and bodice and sometimes sleeves; complete style of clothing. ◆ *v* put clothes on; put on formal clothes; apply protective covering to (a wound); arrange or prepare. **dressing** *n* sauce for salad; covering for a wound. **dressing-down** *n Informal* severe scolding. **dressing gown** robe worn before dressing. **dressing room** room used for changing clothes, esp. backstage in a theatre. **dressy** *adj* (of clothes) elegant. **dressiness** *n* **dress circle** first gallery in a theatre. **dressmaker** *n* person who makes clothes for women. **dressmaking** *n* **dress rehearsal** last rehearsal of a play, using costumes, lighting, etc., as

for the first night.

dressage [dress-ahzh] *n* training of a horse to perform manoeuvres in response to the rider's body signals.

dresser[1] *n* set of shelves, usu. with cupboards, for storing or displaying dishes.

dresser[2] *n Theatre* person employed to assist actors with their costumes.

drew *v* past tense of DRAW.

drey *n* squirrel's nest.

dribble *v* (allow to) flow in drops; allow saliva to trickle from the mouth; propel (a ball) by repeatedly tapping it with the foot, hand, or a stick. ◆ *n* small quantity of liquid falling in drops. **dribbler** *n*

dried *v* past of DRY.

drier *adj* comparative of DRY. ◆ *n* same as DRYER.

driest *adj* superlative of DRY.

drift *v* be carried along by currents of air or water; move aimlessly from one place or activity to another. ◆ *n* something piled up by the wind or current, such as a snowdrift; general movement or development; main point of an argument or speech. **drifter** *n* person who moves aimlessly from place to place or job to job. **driftwood** *n* wood floating on or washed ashore by the sea.

drill[1] *n* tool or machine for boring holes; strict and often repetitious training; *Informal* correct procedure. ◆ *v* pierce, bore, or cut (a hole) in (material) (as if) with a drill; teach by rigorous exercises and training.

drill[2] *n* machine for sowing seed in rows; small furrow for seed.

drill[3] *n* hard-wearing cotton cloth.

drily *adv* same as DRYLY.

drink *v* **drinking, drank, drunk** swallow (a liquid); consume alcohol, esp. to excess. ◆ *n* liquid suitable for drinking; portion of liquid for drinking; alcohol or its habitual or excessive consumption. **drinkable** *adj* **drinker** *n* **drink in** *v* pay close attention to. **drink to** *v* drink a toast to.

drip *v* **dripping, dripped** fall or let fall in drops. ◆ *n* falling of drops of liquid; sound made by falling drops; *Informal* weak or foolish person; *Med* apparatus for the administration of a solution drop by drop into a vein. **drip-dry** *adj* denoting clothing that will dry free of creases if hung up when wet.

dripping n fat that comes from meat while it is being cooked.

drive v driving, drove, driven guide the movement of (a vehicle); transport or be transported in a vehicle; goad into a specified state; push or propel; Sport hit (a ball) very hard and straight. ◆ n journey in a driven vehicle; road for vehicles, esp. a private road leading to a house; united effort towards a common goal, e.g. an investment drive; energy, ambition, or initiative; Psychol motive or interest, e.g sex drive; means by which force, motion, etc. is transmitted in a mechanism. **driver** n person who drives a vehicle; Golf club used for tee shots. **drive at** v Informal intend or mean, e.g. what are you driving at? **drive-in** adj, n (denoting) a public facility used by patrons in their automobiles.

drivel n foolish talk. ◆ v -elling, -elled speak foolishly.

drizzle n very light rain. ◆ v rain lightly. **drizzly** adj

droll adj quaintly amusing. **drolly** adv **drollery** n

dromedary [drom-mid-er-ee] n, pl -daries camel with a single hump.

drone¹ n male bee.

drone² v, n (make) a monotonous low dull sound. **drone on** v talk for a long time in a monotonous tone.

drool v (foll. by over) show excessive enthusiasm (for); allow saliva to flow from the mouth.

droop v sag, as from weakness. **droopy** adj

drop v dropping, dropped (allow to) fall vertically; decrease in amount, strength, or value; mention casually; discontinue (an activity). ◆ n small quantity of liquid forming a round shape; very small quantity of liquid; act of falling; decrease in amount or value; vertical distance that anything may fall. ◆ pl liquid medication applied drop by drop. **droplet** n **droppings** pl n feces of certain animals, such as rabbits or birds. **drop in, by** v pay someone a casual visit. **drop off** v grow smaller or less; Informal fall asleep. **dropout** n person who rejects conventional society; person who fails

to complete a course of study. **drop out** v abandon or withdraw from (a school, job, etc.).

dropsy n illness in which watery fluid collects in the body.

dross n scum formed on the surfaces of molten metals; worthless matter.

drought n prolonged shortage of rainfall.

drove¹ v past tense of DRIVE.

drove² n moving herd of livestock; moving crowd of people. **drover** n person who drives sheep or cattle.

drown v die or kill by immersion in liquid; forget (one's sorrows) temporarily by drinking alcohol; drench thoroughly; render (a sound) inaudible by making a loud noise.

drowse v be sleepy, dull, or sluggish. **drowsy** adj **drowsily** adv **drowsiness** n

drubbing n utter defeat, as in a contest.

drudge n person who works hard at wearisome menial tasks. ◆ v toil at such tasks. **drudgery** n

drug n substance used in the treatment or prevention of disease; chemical substance, esp. a narcotic, taken for the effect it produces. ◆ v drugging, drugged administer a drug to (a person or animal) in order to induce sleepiness or unconsciousness; mix a drug with (food or drink). **drugstore** n pharmacy where a wide variety of goods is available.

Druid n member of an ancient order of Celtic priests. **Druidic, Druidical** adj

drum n percussion instrument sounded by striking a skin stretched across the opening of a hollow cylinder; cylindrical object or container. ◆ v drumming, drummed play (music) on a drum; tap rhythmically or regularly. **drummer** n **drum into** v instil into (someone) by constant repetition. **drumstick** n stick used for playing a drum; lower joint of the leg of a cooked fowl. **drum up** v obtain (support) by canvassing.

drunk v past participle of DRINK. ◆ adj intoxicated with alcohol to the extent of losing control over normal functions; overwhelmed by a strong influence or emotion. ◆ n person who is drunk. **drunkard** n person who is frequently or habitually drunk. **drunken** adj drunk; caused by or

relating to alcoholic intoxication.
drunkenly *adv* **drunkenness** *n*

dry *adj* **drier, driest** *or* **dryer, dryest**
lacking moisture; having little or no
rainfall; *Informal* thirsty; (of wine) not
sweet; uninteresting, e.g. *a dry book*;
(of humour) subtle and sarcastic;
prohibiting the sale of alcohol, e.g. *a
dry area.* ◆ *v* **drying, dried** make or
become dry; preserve (food) by
removing the moisture. **dryly** *adv*
dryness *n* **dryer** *n* apparatus for
removing moisture. **dry-clean** *v* clean
(clothes etc.) with a solvent other than
water. **dry-cleaner** *n* **dry-cleaning** *n*
dry out *v* make or become dry; (cause
to) undergo treatment for alcoholism
or drug addiction. **dry rot** crumbling
and drying of timber, caused by
certain fungi. **dry run** *Informal*
rehearsal.

dryad *n* wood nymph.

DSc Doctor of Science.

dual *adj* relating to or denoting two;
twofold. **duality** *n* **dual carriageway**
Brit road on which traffic travelling in
opposite directions is separated by a
central strip of turf or concrete.

dub¹ *v* **dubbing, dubbed** give (a
person or place) a name or nickname.

dub² *v* **dubbing, dubbed** provide (a
film) with a new soundtrack, esp. in a
different language; provide (a film or
tape) with a soundtrack.

dubbin *n* greasy preparation applied
to leather to soften and waterproof it.

dubious [dew-bee-uss] *adj* feeling or
causing doubt. **dubiously** *adv* **dubiety**
[dew-by-it-ee] *n*

ducal [duke-al] *adj* of a duke.

ducat [duck-it] *n* former European
gold or silver coin.

duchess *n* woman who holds the rank
of duke in her own right; wife or
widow of a duke.

duchy *n, pl* **duchies** territory of a duke
or duchess.

duck¹ *n* water bird with short legs,
webbed feet, and a broad blunt bill;
female of this bird; flesh of this bird,
used as food; *Cricket* score of nothing.
duckling *n* young duck.

duck² *v* move (the head or body)
quickly downwards, to escape
observation or to dodge a blow;
plunge suddenly into water; *Informal*

dodge or escape (a duty etc.).

duct *n* tube, pipe, or canal by means
of which a fluid or gas is conveyed;
bodily passage conveying secretions or
excretions. **ductile** *adj* (of metal) able
to be shaped into sheets or wires;
easily influenced. **ductility** *n*

dud *Informal* ◆ *n* person or thing that
proves ineffectual. ◆ *adj* bad or useless.

dude *n US informal* man, chap; *Old-
fashioned* dandy.

dudgeon *n* **in high dudgeon** angry.

due *adj* expected or scheduled to be
present or arrive; owed as a debt;
fitting, proper. ◆ *n* something that is
owed, required, or due. ◆ *pl* charges
for membership of a club or
organization. ◆ *adv* directly or exactly,
e.g. *due north.* **due to** attributable to
or caused by.

duel *n* formal prearranged combat
with deadly weapons between two
people, to settle a quarrel. ◆ *v*
duelling, duelled fight in a duel.

duenna *n* (esp. in Spain) elderly
woman acting as chaperone to a
young woman.

duet *n* piece of music for two
performers.

duffel, duffle *n* coat made of heavy
woollen cloth.

duffer *n Informal* dull or incompetent
person.

dug¹ *v* past of DIG.

dug² *n* teat or udder.

dugong *n* whalelike mammal found in
tropical waters.

dugout *n* canoe made by hollowing
out a log; (at a sports ground) covered
bench where managers and
substitutes sit; *Mil* covered excavation
dug to provide shelter.

duke *n* nobleman of the highest rank;
prince or ruler of a small principality or
duchy. **dukedom** *n*

dulcet [dull-sit] *adj* (of a sound)
soothing or pleasant.

dulcimer *n* tuned percussion
instrument consisting of a set of
strings stretched over a sounding
board and struck with hammers.

dull *adj* uninteresting; stupid; (of a
pain) not acute or intense; (of
weather) not bright or clear; lacking in
spirit; (of a blade) lacking sharpness.
◆ *v* make or become dull. **dullness** *n*

dully adv **dullard** n dull or stupid person.

duly adv in a proper manner; at the proper time.

dumb adj lacking the power to speak; silent; Informal stupid. **dumbly** adv **dumbness** n **dumbbell** n exercising weight consisting of a short bar with a heavy ball or disc at either end.

dumbfounded adj speechless with amazement. **dumb show** meaningful gestures without speech.

dumdum n soft-nosed bullet that expands on impact and inflicts extensive wounds.

dummy n, pl -mies figure representing the human form, used for displaying clothes etc.; copy of an object, often lacking some essential feature of the original; Slang stupid person. ◆ adj imitation or substitute. **dummy run** practice, rehearsal.

dump v drop or let fall heavily or in a mass; Informal abandon (something or someone) carelessly; dispose of (nuclear waste); market (goods) in bulk and at low prices, esp. abroad. ◆ n place where waste materials are dumped; Informal dirty unattractive place; Mil place where weapons or supplies are stored. **down in the dumps** in a state of depression. **dumpy** adj short and plump.

dumpling n small ball of dough cooked and served with stew; round pastry case filled with fruit.

dun adj brownish-grey.

dunce n person who is stupid or slow to learn.

dunderhead n slow-witted person.

dune n mound or ridge of drifted sand.

dung n excrement of animals.

dungarees pl n trousers with a bib attached.

dungeon n underground prison cell.

dunk v dip (a cookie etc.) into liquid before eating it; submerge (something) in liquid.

duo n, pl **duos** pair of performers; Informal pair of closely connected people.

duodecimal adj reckoned in twelves or twelfths.

duodenum [dew-oh-**deen**-um] n, pl -na, -nums first part of the small

intestine, just below the stomach. **duodenal** adj

dupe v deceive or cheat. ◆ n person who is easily deceived.

duple adj Music having two beats in a bar.

duplex adj twofold. ◆ n house divided into two separate dwellings; either dwelling.

duplicate adj copied exactly from an original. ◆ n exact copy. ◆ v make a replica of; do again (something that has already been done). **duplication** n **duplicator** n

duplicity n deception or double-dealing.

durable adj long-lasting. **durables, durable goods** pl n goods that require infrequent replacement. **durability** n

duration n length of time that something lasts.

duress n compulsion by use of force or threats.

during prep throughout or within the limit of (a period of time).

dusk n time just before nightfall, when it is almost dark. **dusky** adj dark in colour; shadowy. **duskiness** n

dust n dry fine powdery material, such as particles of dirt. ◆ v remove dust from (furniture) by wiping; sprinkle (something) with dust or some other powdery substance. **duster** n cloth used for dusting. **dusty** adj covered with dust. **dustbin** n Brit garbage can. **dustbowl** n dry area in which the surface soil is exposed to wind erosion. **dust jacket, cover** removable paper cover used to protect a book. **dustman** n Brit garbage collector. **dustpan** n short-handled hooded shovel into which dust is swept from floors.

Dutch adj of the Netherlands, its inhabitants, or their language. **go Dutch** Informal share the expenses on an outing. **Dutch courage** false courage gained from drinking alcohol.

duty n, pl -ties task that a person is bound to perform for moral or legal reasons; government tax, esp. on imports. **on duty** at work. **dutiable** adj (of goods) requiring payment of duty. **dutiful** adj showing or resulting from a sense of duty. **dutifully** adv

duvet [**doo**-vay] n quilt filled with

down or artificial fibre.

DVT deep-vein thrombosis.

dwarf n, pl **dwarfs, dwarves** undersized person; (in folklore) small ugly manlike creature, often possessing magical powers. ◆ adj denoting an animal or plant much below the average size for a species. ◆ v cause (someone or something) to seem small by being much larger.

dwell v **dwelling, dwelt** or **dwelled.** live as a permanent resident. **dweller** n **dwelling** n place of residence. **dwell on, upon** v think, speak, or write at length about.

dwindle v grow less in size, intensity, or number.

dye n staining or colouring substance; colour produced by dyeing. ◆ v **dyeing, dyed** colour or stain (fabric, hair, etc.) by the application of dye. **dyer** n **dyed-in-the-wool** adj uncompromising or unchanging in attitude or opinion.

dying v present participle of DIE¹.

dyke n wall built to prevent flooding; ditch; Slang lesbian.

dynamic adj characterized by force of personality, ambition, and energy; of or concerned with energy or forces that produce motion. **dynamically** adv **dynamism** n forcefulness of an energetic personality.

dynamics n branch of mechanics concerned with the forces that change or produce the motions of bodies.

dynamite n high-explosive mixture containing nitroglycerin; Informal spectacular or potentially dangerous person or thing. ◆ v mine or blow (something) up with dynamite.

dynamo n, pl **-mos** device for converting mechanical energy into electrical energy.

dynasty n, pl **-ties** sequence of hereditary rulers. **dynastic** adj

dysentery n infection of the intestine causing severe diarrhea.

dysfunction n Med disturbance or abnormality in the function of an organ or part.

dyslexia n disorder causing impaired ability to read. **dyslexic** adj

dysmenorrhea, dysmenorrhoea n painful menstruation.

dyspepsia n indigestion. **dyspeptic** adj

dystrophy [diss-trof-fee] n wasting of the body tissues, esp. the muscles.

E e

E East(ern).

e- prefix electronic e.g. e-mail.

each adj, pron every (one) taken separately.

eager adj showing or feeling great desire, keen. **eagerly** adv **eagerness** n

eagle n large bird of prey with keen eyesight; Golf score of two strokes under par for a hole. **eaglet** n young eagle.

ear¹ n organ of hearing, esp. the external part of it; sensitivity to musical or other sounds. **earache** n pain in the ear. **eardrum** n thin piece of skin inside the ear which enables one to hear sounds. **earmark** v set (something) aside for a specific purpose. ◆ n distinguishing mark. **earphone** n receiver for a radio etc., held to or put in the ear. **earring** n ornament for the lobe of the ear. **earshot** n hearing range.

ear² n head of corn.

earl n British nobleman ranking next below a marquess. **earldom** n

early adj, adv **-lier, -liest** before the expected or usual time; in the first part of a period; in a period far back in time.

earn v obtain by work or merit; (of investments etc.) gain (interest). **earnings** pl n money earned.

earnest¹ adj serious and sincere. **in earnest** seriously. **earnestly** adv

earnest² n part payment given in advance, esp. to confirm a contract.

earth n planet that we live on; land, the ground; soil; fox's hole; wire connecting an electrical apparatus with the earth. ◆ v connect (a circuit) to earth. **earthen** adj made of baked clay or earth. **earthenware** n pottery made of baked clay. **earthly** adj conceivable or possible, e.g. no earthly reason. **earthy** adj coarse or crude; of or like earth. **earthquake** n violent vibration of the earth's surface. **earthwork** n fortification made of

earth. earthworm *n* worm which burrows in the soil.

earwig *n* small insect with a pincer-like tail.

ease *n* freedom from difficulty, discomfort, or worry; rest or leisure, e.g. *at one's ease.* ◆ *v* give bodily or mental ease to; lessen (severity, tension, pain, etc.); move carefully or gradually.

easel *n* frame to support an artist's canvas or a blackboard.

east *n* part of the horizon where the sun rises; eastern lands or the orient. ◆ *adj* on, in, or near the east; (of the wind) from the east. ◆ *adv* in, to, or towards the east. **easterly** *adj, adv* to the east; (of a wind) from the east. **eastern** *adj* of, in, or from the east. **eastward** *adj, adv* **eastwards** *adv* **East Coast** Atlantic Coast of N America.

Easter *n* Christian spring festival commemorating the Resurrection of Jesus Christ. **Easter egg** chocolate egg given at Easter.

easy *adj* **easier, easiest** not needing much work or effort; free from pain, care, or anxiety; easy-going. **easily** *adv* **easiness** *n* **easy chair** comfortable armchair. **easy-going** *adj* relaxed in attitude, tolerant.

eat *v* **eating, ate, eaten** take (food) into the mouth and swallow it; (foll. by *away* or *up*) destroy; have a meal. **eatable** *adj* fit for eating.

eau de Cologne [oh de kol-**lone**] *n French* light perfume.

eaves *pl n* overhanging edges of a roof.

eavesdrop *v* **-dropping, -dropped** listen secretly to a private conversation. **eavesdropper** *n* **eavesdropping** *n*

ebb *v* (of tide water) flow back; become weaker. ◆ *n* flowing back of the tide. **at a low ebb** in a state of weakness.

ebony *n, pl* **-onies** hard black wood. ◆ *adj* deep black.

ebullient *adj* overflowing with enthusiasm. **ebullience** *n*

eccentric *adj* odd or unconventional; (of circles) not having the same centre. ◆ *n* unconventional person. **eccentrically** *adv* **eccentricity** *n* unconventional behaviour; odd habit.

ecclesiastic *adj* (also **ecclesiastical**) of the Christian Church or clergy. ◆ *n* clergyman.

ECG electrocardiogram; electrocardiograph.

echelon [**esh**-a-lon] *n* level of power or responsibility; *Mil* formation in which units follow one another but are spaced out sideways to allow each a line of fire ahead.

echo *n, pl* **-oes** repetition of sounds by reflection of sound waves off a surface; close imitation. ◆ *v* **-oing, -oed** repeat or be repeated as an echo; imitate closely. **echo sounder** sonar. **echo sounding** use of sonar to navigate.

éclair *n* finger-shaped pastry filled with cream and covered with chocolate.

éclat [ake-**lah**] *n* brilliant success; splendour.

eclectic *adj* selecting from various ideas or sources. **eclecticism** *n*

eclipse *n* temporary obscuring of one heavenly body by another. ◆ *v* surpass or outclass. **ecliptic** *n* apparent path of the sun.

eclogue *n* short poem on a rural theme.

ecological *adj* of ecology; intended to protect the environment. **ecologically** *adv* **ecology** *n* study of the relationships between living things and their environment. **ecologist** *n*

e-commerce, ecommerce *n* business transactions done on the Internet.

economy *n, pl* **-mies** system of interrelationship of money, industry, and employment in a country; careful management of resources to avoid waste. **economic** *adj* of economics; profitable. **economics** *n* social science concerned with the production and consumption of goods and services. ◆ *pl* financial aspects. **economical** *adj* not wasteful, thrifty. **economically** *adv* **economist** *n* specialist in economics. **economize** *v* limit or reduce waste.

ecosystem *n* system involving interactions between a community and its environment.

ecru *adj* greyish-yellow.

ecstasy *n* state of intense delight; *Slang* powerful drug that can produce hallucinations. **ecstatic** *adj* **ecstatically** *adv*

ectoplasm *n Spiritualism* substance that supposedly is emitted from the body of a medium during a trance.

ECU European Currency Unit.

ecumenical *adj* of the Christian Church throughout the world, esp. with regard to its unity.

eczema [ek-sim-a] *n* skin disease causing intense itching.

Edam *n* round Dutch cheese with a red rind.

eddy *n, pl* **eddies** small whirling movement in air, water, etc. ◆ *v* **eddying, eddied** move in eddies.

edelweiss [ade-el-vice] *n* alpine plant with white flowers.

Eden *n Bible* garden in which Adam and Eve were placed at the Creation; place of delight or contentment.

edge *n* border or line where something ends or begins; cutting side of a blade; sharpness of tone. ◆ *v* provide an edge or border for; push (one's way) gradually. **have the edge on** have an advantage over. **on edge** nervous or irritable. **edgeways** *adv* with the edge forwards or uppermost. **edging** *n* anything placed along an edge. **edgy** *adj* nervous or irritable.

edible *adj* fit to be eaten. **edibility** *n*

edict [ee-dikt] *n* order issued by an authority.

edifice [ed-if-iss] *n* large building.

edify [ed-if-fie] *v* **-fying, -fied** improve morally by instruction. **edification** *n*

edit *v* prepare (a book, film, etc.) for publication or broadcast. **edition** *n* form in which something is published; number of copies of a new publication printed at one time. **editor** *n* person who edits; person in overall charge of a newspaper or magazine. **editorial** *adj* of editing or editors. ◆ *n* newspaper article stating the opinion of the editor.

EDT Eastern Daylight Time.

educate *v* teach; provide schooling for. **education** *n* **educational** *adj* **educationally** *adv* **educationalist** *n* expert in the theory of education. **educative** *adj* educating.

Edwardian *adj* of the reign of King Edward VII of Great Britain and Ireland (1901–10).

EEG electroencephalogram.

eel *n* snakelike fish.

eerie *adj* uncannily frightening or disturbing. **eerily** *adv*

efface *v* remove by rubbing; make (oneself) inconspicuous. **effacement** *n*

effect *n* change or result caused by someone or something; overall impression; condition of being operative, e.g. *the law comes into effect next month.* ◆ *pl* property; lighting, sounds, etc. to accompany a film or a broadcast. ◆ *v* cause to happen, accomplish. **effective** *adj* producing a desired result; impressive; operative. **effectively** *adv* **effectual** *adj* successful in producing a desired result. **effectually** *adv*

effeminate *adj* (of a man) displaying characteristics thought to be typical of a woman. **effeminacy** *n*

effervescent *adj* (of a liquid) giving off bubbles; (of a person) lively and enthusiastic. **effervescence** *n*

effete [if-feet] *adj* feeble.

efficacious *adj* producing the intended result, effective. **efficacy** *n*

efficient *adj* functioning effectively with little waste of effort. **efficiently** *adv* **efficiency** *n*

effigy [ef-fij-ee] *n, pl* **-gies** image or likeness of a person.

efflorescence *n* flowering.

effluent *n* liquid discharged as waste. **effluence** *n* something that flows out. **effluvium** *n, pl* **-via** unpleasant smell, as decaying matter or gaseous waste.

effort *n* physical or mental exertion; attempt. **effortless** *adj*

effrontery *n* brazen impudence.

effusion *n* unrestrained outburst. **effusive** *adj* openly emotional. **effusively** *adv* **effusiveness** *n*

EFTA European Free Trade Association.

e.g. for example.

egalitarian *adj* upholding the equality of all people. ◆ *n* person who holds egalitarian beliefs. **egalitarianism** *n*

egg[1] *n* oval or round object laid by the females of birds and other creatures, containing a developing embryo; hen's egg used as food; (also **egg cell**) ovum. **egghead** *n Informal* intellectual person. **eggplant** *n* plant bearing egg-shaped purple fruit eaten as a vegetable.

egg[2] *v* **egg on** encourage or incite, esp. to do wrong.

eglantine *n* sweetbrier.

ego *n, pl* **egos** self-esteem; the self of an individual person. **egoism, egotism** *n* excessive concern for one's own interests; excessively high opinion of oneself. **egoist, egotist** *n* **egoistic, egotistic** *adj* **egocentric** *adj* self-centred.

egregious [ig-**greej**-uss] *adj* outstandingly bad.

egress [**ee**-gress] *n* way out; departure.

egret [**ee**-grit] *n* lesser white heron.

eider *n* Arctic duck. **eiderdown** *n* quilt (orig. stuffed with eider feathers).

eight *adj, n* one more than seven. ◆ *n* eight-oared boat; its crew. **eighth** *adj, n* (of) number eight in a series. **eighteen** *adj, n* eight and ten. **eighteenth** *adj, n* **eighty** *adj, n* eight times ten. **eightieth** *adj, n*

eisteddfod [ice-**sted**-fod] *n* Welsh festival with competitions in music and other performing arts.

either *adj, pron* one or the other (of two); each of two. ◆ *conj* used preceding two or more possibilities joined by *or*. ◆ *adv* likewise, e.g. *I don't eat meat and he doesn't either.*

ejaculate *v* eject (semen); utter abruptly. **ejaculation** *n*

eject *v* force out, expel. **ejection** *n* **ejector** *n*

eke *v* **eke out** make (a supply) last by frugal use; make (a living) with difficulty.

elaborate *adj* with a lot of fine detail. ◆ *v* expand upon. **elaboration** *n*

élan [ale-**an**] *n* style and vigour.

eland [**eel**-and] *n* large antelope of southern Africa.

elapse *v* (of time) pass by.

elastic *adj* resuming normal shape after distortion; adapting easily to change. ◆ *n* tape or fabric containing interwoven strands of flexible rubber. **elasticity** *n*

elate *v* fill with high spirits or pride. **elation** *n*

elbow *n* joint between the upper arm and the forearm; part of a garment that covers this. ◆ *v* shove or strike with the elbow. **elbow grease** vigorous physical labour. **elbowroom** *n* sufficient room to move freely.

elder[1] *adj* older. ◆ *n* older person; (in certain Protestant Churches) lay officer. **elderly** *adj* (fairly) old. **eldest** *adj* oldest.

elder[2] *n* small tree with white flowers and black berries.

El Dorado [el dor-**rah**-doe] *n* fictitious country rich in gold.

eldritch *adj Scot* weird, uncanny.

elect *v* choose by voting; decide (to do something). ◆ *adj* appointed but not yet in office, e.g. *president elect.* **election** *n* choosing of representatives by voting; act of choosing. **electioneer** *v* be active in a political election. **elective** *adj* chosen by election; optional. **elector** *n* someone who has the right to vote in an election. **electoral** *adj* **electorate** *n* people who have the right to vote.

electricity *n* form of energy associated with stationary or moving electrons or other charged particles; electric current or charge. **electric** *adj* produced by, producing, transmitting, or powered by electricity; exciting or tense. **electrics** *pl n* electric appliances. **electric chair** *US* chair in which criminals who have been sentenced to death are electrocuted. **electric cord** flexible insulated cable that conducts electricity. **electrical** *adj* using or concerning electricity. **electrician** *n* person trained to install and repair electrical equipment. **electrify** *v* **-fying, -fied** adapt for operation by electric power; charge with electricity; startle or excite intensely. **electrification** *n*

electro- *combining form* operated by or caused by electricity. **electrocardiograph** *n* instrument for recording the electrical activity of the heart. **electrocardiogram** *n* tracing produced by this. **electrodynamics** *n* branch of physics concerned with the interactions between electrical and mechanical forces. **electroencephalograph** [ill-lek-tro-en-sef-a-loh-graf] *n* instrument for recording the electrical activity of the brain. **electroencephalogram** *n* tracing produced by this. **electromagnet** *n* magnet containing a coil of wire through which an electric current is passed. **electromagnetic** *adj* **electromagnetism** *n* **electroplate** *v* coat with silver etc. by electrolysis.

electrocute v kill or injure by electricity. **electrocution** n.

electrode n conductor through which an electric current enters or leaves a battery, vacuum tube, etc.

electrolysis [ill-lek-troll-iss-iss] n conduction of electricity by an electrolyte, esp. to induce chemical change; destruction of living tissue such as hair roots by an electric current.

electrolyte n solution or molten substance that conducts electricity. **electrolytic** adj

electron n elementary particle in all atoms that has a negative electrical charge. **electronic** adj (of a device) dependent on the action of electrons; (of a process) using electronic devices. **electronic mail** see E-MAIL. **electronics** n technology concerned with the development of electronic devices and circuits. **electron microscope** microscope that uses electrons, rather than light, to produce a magnified image. **electron volt** unit of energy used in nuclear physics.

elegant adj tasteful in dress, style, or design; graceful. **elegance** n

elegy [el-lij-ee] n, pl **-egies** mournful poem, esp. a lament for the dead. **elegiac** adj mournful.

element n component part; substance which cannot be separated into other substances by ordinary chemical techniques; distinguishable section of a social group, e.g. liberal elements in Polish society; heating wire in an electric kettle, stove, etc. ◆ pl basic principles of something; weather conditions, esp. wind, rain, and cold. **in one's element** in a situation where one is happiest. **elemental** adj fundamental; of primitive natural forces or passions. **elementary** adj simple and straightforward.

elephant n huge four-footed thick-skinned animal with ivory tusks and a long trunk. **elephantine** adj unwieldy, clumsy. **elephantiasis** [el-lee-fan-tie-a-siss] n disease with hardening of the skin and enlargement of the legs etc.

elevate v raise in rank or status; lift up. **elevation** n raising; scale drawing of one side of a building; height above sea level. **elevator** n cage raised or lowered in a vertical shaft to transport people or goods.

eleven adj, n one more than ten. ◆ n Sport team of eleven people. **eleventh** adj, n (of) number eleven in a series. **elevenses** n Informal light mid-morning snack.

elf n, pl **elves** (in folklore) small mischievous fairy. **elfin** adj small and delicate.

elicit v draw out (information) from someone.

elide v omit (a vowel or syllable) from a spoken word. **elision** n

eligible adj qualified to be chosen; desirable as a spouse. **eligibility** n

eliminate v get rid of. **elimination** n

elite [ill-eet] n most powerful, rich, or gifted members of a group. **elitism** n belief that society should be governed by a small group of superior people. **elitist** n, adj

elixir [ill-ix-er] n liquid medicine in syrup.

Elizabethan adj of the reign of Elizabeth I of England (1558–1603).

elk n large deer of N Europe and Asia.

ellipse n oval shape. **elliptical** adj oval-shaped; (of speech or writing) obscure or ambiguous.

ellipsis [ill-lip-siss] n, pl **-ses** omission of letters or words in a sentence.

elm n tree with serrated leaves.

elocution n art of speaking clearly in public.

elongate [eel-long-gate] v make or become longer. **elongation** n

elope v run away secretly to get married. **elopement** n

eloquence n fluent powerful use of language. **eloquent** adj **eloquently** adv

else adv otherwise; besides; instead. **elsewhere** adv in or to another place.

elucidate v make (something difficult) clear, explain. **elucidation** n

elude v baffle; escape from by cleverness or quickness. **elusive** adj difficult to catch or remember.

elver n young eel.

elves n plural of ELF.

emaciated [im-mace-ee-ate-id] adj abnormally thin. **emaciation** n

e-mail n (also **electronic mail**) sending of messages between computer terminals. ◆ v communicate in this way.

emanate [em-a-nate] v issue, proceed from a source. **emanation** n

emancipate v free from social, political, or legal restraints. **emancipation** n

emasculate v deprive of power. **emasculation** n

embalm v preserve (a corpse) from decay by the use of chemicals etc.

embankment n man-made ridge that carries a road or railway or holds back water.

embargo n, pl **-goes** order stopping the movement of ships; legal stoppage of trade; ban. ♦ v **-going, -goed** put an embargo on.

embark v board a ship or aircraft; (foll. by on or upon) begin (a new project). **embarkation** n

embarrass v cause to feel self-conscious or ashamed. **embarrassed** adj **embarrassment** n

embassy n, pl **-sies** offices or official residence of an ambassador; ambassador and his staff.

embattled adj having a lot of difficulties.

embed v **-bedding, -bedded** fix firmly in something solid.

embellish v decorate; embroider (a story). **embellishment** n

ember n glowing piece of wood or coal in a dying fire.

embezzle v steal money that has been entrusted to one. **embezzlement** n **embezzler** n

embitter v make bitter. **embitterment** n

emblazon [im-blaze-on] v decorate with bright colours; proclaim or publicize.

emblem n object or representation that symbolizes a quality, type, or group. **emblematic** adj

embody v **-bodying, -bodied** be an example or expression of; comprise, include. **embodiment** n

embolden v encourage (someone).

embolism n blocking of a blood vessel by a blood clot or air bubble.

emboss v mould or carve a raised design on.

embrace v clasp in the arms, hug; accept (an idea) eagerly; comprise. ♦ n act of embracing.

embrasure n door or window having splayed sides so that the opening is larger on the inside; opening like this in a fortified wall, for shooting through.

embrocation n lotion for rubbing into the skin to relieve pain.

embroider v decorate with needlework; make (a story) more interesting with fictitious detail. **embroidery** n

embroil v involve (a person) in problems. **embroilment** n

embryo [em-bree-oh] n, pl **-bryos** unborn creature in the early stages of development; something at an undeveloped stage. **embryonic** adj at an early stage. **embryology** n

emend v remove errors from. **emendation** n

emerald n bright green precious stone. ♦ adj bright green.

emerge v come into view; (foll. by from) come out of; become known. **emergence** n **emergent** adj

emergency n, pl **-cies** sudden unforeseen occurrence needing immediate action. ♦ adj for use in an emergency, e.g. emergency exit.

emeritus [im-mer-rit-uss] adj retired, but retaining an honorary title, e.g. emeritus professor.

emery n hard mineral used for smoothing and polishing. **emery board** cardboard strip coated with crushed emery, for filing the nails.

emetic [im-met-ik] n substance that causes vomiting. ♦ adj causing vomiting.

emigrate v go and settle in another country. **emigrant** n **emigration** n

émigré [em-mig-gray] n someone who has left his native country for political reasons.

eminent adj distinguished, well-known. **eminently** adv **eminence** n position of superiority or fame; (E-) title of a cardinal.

emir [em-meer] n Muslim ruler. **emirate** n his country.

emissary n, pl **-saries** agent sent on a mission by a government.

emit v **emitting, emitted** give out (heat, light, or a smell); utter. **emission** n

emollient adj softening, soothing. ♦ n substance which softens or soothes something.

emolument n Formal payment for work, salary.

emoticon (i-**mote**-i-kon) n Computers symbol depicting a smile or other facial expression, used in e-mail.

emotion n strong feeling. **emotional** adj readily affected by or appealing to the emotions. **emotive** adj tending to arouse emotion.

empathy n power of imaginatively entering into and understanding another's feelings.

emperor n ruler of an empire. **empress** n fem

emphasis n, pl -**ses** special importance given to something, such as an idea; stress on a word or phrase in speech. **emphasize** v **emphatic** adj showing emphasis. **emphatically** adv

emphysema [em-fiss-**see**-ma] n condition in which the air sacs of the lungs are grossly enlarged, causing breathlessness.

empire n group of territories under the rule of one state or person; large organization that is directed by one person or group.

empirical adj relying on experiment or experience, not on theory. **empirically** adv **empiricism** n doctrine that all knowledge derives from experience. **empiricist** n

emplacement n prepared position for a gun.

employ v hire (a person); provide work or occupation for; use. ♦ n state of being employed, e.g. in someone's employ. **employee** n **employer** n **employment** n state of being employed; work done by a person to earn money.

emporium n Old-fashioned large general shop.

empower v enable, authorize.

empress n see EMPEROR.

empty adj -**tier**, -**tiest** containing nothing; unoccupied; without purpose or value; (of words) insincere. ♦ v -**tying**, -**tied** make or become empty. **empties** pl n empty boxes, bottles, etc. **emptiness** n

emu n large Aust. flightless bird with long legs.

emulate v attempt to equal or surpass by imitating. **emulation** n

emulsion n light-sensitive coating on photographic film; type of water-based paint. ♦ v paint with emulsion paint. **emulsify** v -**fying**, -**fied** make into an emulsion. **emulsifier** n

enable v provide (a person) with the means, opportunity, or authority (to do something).

enact v establish by law; represent as in a play. **enactment** n

enamel n glasslike coating applied to metal etc. to preserve the surface; hard white coating on a tooth. ♦ v -**elling**, -**elled** cover with enamel.

enamoured adj inspired with love.

en bloc adv French as a body or a whole, all together.

encamp v set up in a camp. **encampment** n

encapsulate v abridge; enclose as in a capsule.

encephalitis [en-sef-a-**lite**-iss] n inflammation of the brain.

encephalogram n short for ELECTROENCEPHALOGRAM.

enchant v bewitch or delight. **enchantment** n **enchanter** n **enchantress** n fem

encircle v form a circle around. **encirclement** n

enclave n part of a country entirely surrounded by foreign territory.

enclose v surround completely; include along with something else. **enclosure** n

encomium n, pl -**miums**, -**mia** formal expression of praise.

encompass v surround; include comprehensively.

encore interj again, once more. ♦ n extra performance due to enthusiastic demand.

encounter v meet unexpectedly; be faced with. ♦ n unexpected meeting; contest.

encourage v inspire with confidence; spur on. **encouragement** n

encroach v intrude gradually on a person's rights or land. **encroachment** n

encrust v cover with a layer of something.

encumber v hamper or burden. **encumbrance** n impediment.

encyclical [en-**sik**-lik-kl] n letter sent by the Pope to all bishops.

encyclopedia, encyclopaedia *n* book or set of books containing facts about many subjects, usually in alphabetical order. **encyclopedic, encyclopaedic** *adj* comprehensive.

end *n* furthest point or part; limit; last part of something; act of bringing or coming to a finish; fragment; *Lit* death; destruction; purpose; *Sport* either of the two defended areas of a playing field. ◆ *v* bring or come to a finish. **make ends meet** have just enough money for one's needs. **ending** *n* **endless** *adj* **endways** *adv* having the end forwards or upwards.

endanger *v* put in danger.

endear *v* cause to be liked. **endearing** *adj* **endearment** *n* affectionate word or phrase.

endeavour *v* try. ◆ *n* effort.

endemic *adj* present within a localized area or peculiar to a particular group of people.

endive *n* curly-leaved plant used in salads.

endocrine *adj* relating to the glands which secrete hormones directly into the bloodstream.

endogenous [en-**dodge**-in-uss] *adj* originating from within.

endorse *v* give approval to; sign the back of (a cheque); record a conviction on (a driving licence). **endorsement** *n*

endow *v* provide permanent income for. **endowed with** provided with. **endowment** *n*

endure *v* bear (hardship) patiently; last for a long time. **endurable** *adj* **endurance** *n* act or power of enduring.

enema [**en**-im-a] *n* medicine injected into the rectum to empty the bowels.

enemy *n, pl* **-mies** hostile person or nation, opponent.

energy *n, pl* **-gies** capacity for intense activity; capacity to do work and overcome resistance; source of power, such as electricity. **energy drink** soft drink supposed to boost the drinker's energy levels. **energetic** *adj* **energetically** *adv* **energize** *v* give vigour to.

enervate *v* weaken, deprive of vigour. **enervation** *n*

enfant terrible [on-**fon** ter-**reeb**-la]

n, pl **enfants terribles** *French* clever but unconventional or indiscreet person.

enfeeble *v* weaken. **enfeeblement** *n*

enfold *v* cover by wrapping something around; embrace.

enforce *v* impose obedience (to a law etc.); impose (a condition). **enforceable** *adj* **enforcement** *n*

enfranchise *v* grant (a person) the right to vote. **enfranchisement** *n*

engage *v* take part, participate; involve (a person or his or her attention) intensely; employ (a person); bring (a mechanism) into operation; *Mil* begin a battle with. **engaged** *adj* pledged to be married; in use. **engagement** *n* **engaging** *adj* charming.

engender *v* produce, cause to occur.

engine *n* any machine which converts energy into mechanical work; railway locomotive. **engineer** *n* person trained in any branch of engineering. ◆ *v* plan in a clever manner; design or construct as an engineer. **engineering** *n* profession of applying scientific principles to the design and construction of engines, automobiles, buildings, or machines.

English *n* language of Britain, the US, Canada, most parts of the Commonwealth, and certain other countries. ◆ *adj* relating to England. **the English** the people of England. **English muffin** light round yeast cake.

engrave *v* carve (a design) onto a hard surface; fix deeply in the mind. **engraver** *n* **engraving** *n* print made from an engraved plate.

engross [en-**groce**] *v* occupy the attention of (a person) completely.

engulf *v* cover or surround completely.

enhance *v* increase in quality, value, or attractiveness. **enhancement** *n*

enigma *n* puzzling thing or person. **enigmatic** *adj* **enigmatically** *adv*

enjoin *v* order (someone) to do something.

enjoy *v* receive pleasure from; have or experience something, e.g. *enjoy excellent health*. **enjoy oneself** have a good time. **enjoyable** *adj* **enjoyment** *n*

enlarge *v* make or grow larger; (foll. by *on* or *upon*) speak or write about in greater detail. **enlargement** n

enlighten v give information to. **enlightenment** n

enlist v enter the armed forces; obtain the support of. **enlistment** n

enliven v make lively or cheerful.

en masse adv French in a group, all together.

enmesh v entangle.

enmity n, pl -ties ill will, hatred.

ennoble v make noble, elevate. **ennoblement** n

ennui [on-**nwee**] n boredom, dissatisfaction.

enormous adj very big, vast. **enormity** n, pl -ties great wickedness; gross offence; Informal great size.

enough adj as much or as many as necessary. ◆ n sufficient quantity. ◆ adv sufficiently; just adequately.

en passant [on pass-on] adv French in passing, by the way.

enquire v same as INQUIRE. **enquiry** n

enrapture v fill with delight.

enrich v improve in quality; make rich.

enrol v -rolling, -rolled (cause to) become a member. **enrolment** n

en route adv French on the way.

ensconce v settle firmly or comfortably.

ensemble [on-**som**-bl] n all the parts of something taken together; complete outfit of clothes; company of actors or dancers; Music group of musicians playing together.

enshrine v cherish or treasure.

ensign n naval flag; banner; US naval officer.

ensilage n process of storing green fodder in a silo; silage.

enslave v make a slave of (someone). **enslavement** n

ensnare v catch in or as if in a snare.

ensue v come next, result.

en suite adv French as part of a set or single unit.

ensure v make certain or sure; make safe or protect.

entail v bring about or impose inevitably.

entangle v catch or involve in or as if in a tangle. **entanglement** n

entente [on-**tont**] n friendly understanding between nations.

enter v come or go in; join; become

involved or take part (in); record (an item) in a journal etc.; begin, e.g. enter upon a new career. **entrance** n way into a place; act of entering; right of entering. **entrant** n person who enters a university, contest, etc. **entry** n, pl -tries entrance; entering; item entered in a journal etc.

enteric [en-**ter**-ik] adj intestinal. **enteritis** [en-ter-**rite**-iss] n inflammation of the intestine, causing diarrhea.

enterprise n company or firm; bold or difficult undertaking; boldness and energy. **enterprising** adj full of boldness and initiative.

entertain v amuse; receive as a guest; consider (an idea). **entertainer** n **entertainment** n

enthral [en-**thrawl**] v -thralling, -thralled hold the attention of. **enthralling** adj **enthralment** n

enthusiasm n eagerness. **enthuse** v (cause to) show enthusiasm. **enthusiast** n ardent supporter of something. **enthusiastic** adj **enthusiastically** adv

entice v attract by exciting hope or desire, tempt. **enticement** n

entire adj complete; unbroken or undivided. **entirely** adv **entirety** n

entitle v give a right to; give a title to. **entitlement** n

entity n, pl -ties separate distinct thing.

entomology n study of insects. **entomological** adj **entomologist** n

entourage [on-**toor**-ahzh] n group of people who assist an important person.

entrails pl n intestines; innermost parts of something.

entrance[1] n see ENTER.

entrance[2] v delight; put into a trance.

entreat v ask earnestly. **entreaty** n, pl -ties earnest request.

entrée [on-**tray**] n right of admission; main course of a meal; dish served before a main course.

entrench v establish firmly; establish in a fortified position with trenches. **entrenchment** n

entrepreneur n business person who attempts to make a profit by risk and initiative.

entropy [en-**trop**-ee] n Formal lack of

organization.

entrust v put into the care or protection of.

entwine v twist together or around.

enumerate v name one by one. **enumeration** n

enunciate v pronounce clearly; proclaim. **enunciation** n

envelop v enveloping, enveloped wrap up, enclose. **envelopment** n

envelope n folded gummed paper cover for a letter.

environment [en-**vire**-on-ment] n external conditions and surroundings in which people, animals, or plants live. **environmental** adj **environmentalist** n person concerned with the protection of the natural environment.

environs pl n surrounding area, esp. of a town.

envisage v visualize; conceive of as a possibility.

envoy n messenger; diplomatic minister ranking below an ambassador.

envy v -vying, -vied grudge (another's good fortune, success, or qualities). ◆ n bitter contemplation of another's good fortune. **enviable** adj arousing envy. **envious** adj full of envy.

enzyme n any of a group of complex proteins that act as catalysts in specific biochemical reactions.

Eolithic adj of the early part of the Stone Age.

eon, aeon [**ee**-on] n immeasurably long period of time.

epaulette n shoulder ornament on a uniform.

ephemeral adj short-lived.

epic n long poem, book, or film about heroic events or actions. ◆ adj very impressive or ambitious.

epicentre n point on the earth's surface immediately above the origin of an earthquake.

epicure n person who enjoys good food and drink. **epicurism** n **epicurean** adj devoted to sensual pleasures, esp. food and drink. ◆ n epicure. **epicureanism** n

epidemic n widespread occurrence of a disease; rapid spread of something.

epidermis n outer layer of the skin.

epidural [ep-pid-**dure**-al] adj, n (of)

spinal anesthetic injected to relieve pain during childbirth.

epiglottis n thin flap that covers the opening of the larynx during swallowing.

epigram n short witty remark or poem. **epigrammatic** adj

epigraph n quotation at the start of a book; inscription.

epilepsy n disorder of the nervous system causing loss of consciousness and sometimes convulsions. **epileptic** n person who has epilepsy. ◆ adj of or having epilepsy.

epilogue n short speech or poem at the end of a literary work, esp. a play.

Epiphany n Christian festival held on January 6 commemorating the manifestation of Christ to the Magi.

episcopal [ip-**piss**-kop-al] adj of or governed by bishops. **episcopalian** n member of an episcopal Church. ◆ adj advocating Church government by bishops.

episode n incident in a series of incidents; section of a serialized book, television programme, etc. **episodic** adj occurring at irregular intervals.

epistemology [ip-iss-stem-**ol**-a-jee] n study of the source, nature, and limitations of knowledge.

epistle n letter, esp. of an apostle. **epistolary** adj

epitaph n commemorative inscription on a tomb; commemorative speech.

epithet n descriptive word or name.

epitome [ip-**pit**-a-mee] n typical example. **epitomize** v be the epitome of.

epoch [**ee**-pok] n period of notable events. **epoch-making** adj extremely important.

eponymous [ip-**pon**-im-uss] adj after whom a book, play, etc. is named.

equable [**ek**-wab-bl] adj even-tempered. **equably** adv

equal adj identical in size, quantity, degree, etc.; having identical rights or status; evenly balanced; (foll. by to) having the necessary ability (for). ◆ n person or thing equal to another. ◆ v equalling, equalled be equal to. **equally** adv **equality** n state of being equal. **equalize** v make or become equal; reach the same score as one's opponent. **equalization** n equal

opportunity nondiscrimination as to sex, race, etc. in employment.

equanimity n calmness of mind.

equate v make or regard as equivalent. **equation** n mathematical statement that two expressions are equal; act of equating.

equator n imaginary circle round the earth, equidistant from the poles. **equatorial** adj

equerry [ek-kwer-ee] n, pl -ries officer who acts as an attendant to a member of a royal family.

equestrian adj of horses and riding.

equidistant adj equally distant.

equilateral adj having equal sides.

equilibrium n, pl -ria steadiness or stability.

equine adj of or like a horse.

equinox n time of year when day and night are of equal length. **equinoctial** adj

equip v equipping, equipped provide with what is needed. **equipment** n set of tools or devices used for a particular purpose; equipping.

equipoise n perfect balance.

equity n, pl -ties fairness; legal system, founded on the principles of natural justice, that supplements common law. ♦ pl interest of ordinary shareholders in a company. **equitable** adj fair, just. **equitably** adv

equivalent n something having the same function as something else. ♦ adj equal in value; having the same meaning or result. **equivalence** n

equivocal adj ambiguous; deliberately misleading; of doubtful character or sincerity. **equivocally** adv **equivocate** v use equivocal words to mislead people. **equivocation** n

ER Queen Elizabeth.

era n period of time considered as distinctive.

eradicate v destroy completely. **eradication** n

erase v rub out; remove. **eraser** n object for erasing something written. **erasure** n erasing; place or mark where something has been erased.

ere prep, conj Poetic before.

erect v build; set up. ♦ adj upright; (of the penis, clitoris, or nipples) rigid as a result of sexual excitement. **erectile** adj capable of becoming erect from

sexual excitement. **erection** n

erg n unit of work or energy.

ergonomics n study of the relationship between workers and their environment. **ergonomic** adj

ergot n fungal disease of cereal; dried fungus used in medicine.

ermine n stoat in northern regions; its white winter fur.

erode v wear away. **erosion** n

erogenous [ir-roj-in-uss] adj sexually sensitive or arousing.

erotic adj relating to sexual pleasure or desire. **eroticism** n **erotica** n sexual literature or art.

err v Formal make a mistake. **erratum** n, pl -ta error in writing or printing. **erroneous** adj incorrect, mistaken **error** n something considered to be incorrect.

errand n short trip to do something for someone.

errant adj behaving in a manner considered to be unacceptable.

erratic adj irregular or unpredictable. **erratically** adv

ersatz [air-zats] adj made in imitation, e.g. ersatz coffee.

erstwhile adj former.

erudite [air-rude-ite] adj having great academic knowledge. **erudition** n

erupt v eject (steam, water, or volcanic material) violently; (of a blemish) appear on the skin; burst forth suddenly and violently. **eruption** n

erysipelas n acute skin infection causing purplish patches.

escalate v increase in extent or intensity. **escalation** n

escalator n moving staircase.

escalope [ess-kal-lop] n thin slice of meat, esp. veal.

escape v get free (of); avoid, e.g. escape attention; (of a gas, liquid, etc.) leak gradually; be forgotten by, e.g. the figure escapes me. ♦ n act of escaping; means of relaxation or relief **escapade** n mischievous adventure. **escapee** n person who has escaped. **escapism** n taking refuge in fantasy to avoid unpleasant reality. **escapologist** n entertainer who specializes in freeing himself or herself from confinement. **escapology** n

escarpment n steep face of a ridge or

mountain.

eschew [iss-**chew**] v abstain from, avoid.

escort n people or vehicles accompanying another person for protection or as an honour; person who accompanies a person of the opposite sex to a social event. ◆ v act as an escort to.

escudo [ess-**kyoo**-doe] n, pl **-dos** a former monetary unit of Portugal.

escutcheon n shield with a coat of arms. **blot on one's escutcheon** stain on one's honour.

Eskimo n Derogatory a term formerly used for Inuit.

esoteric [ee-so-**ter**-rik] adj understood by only a small number of people with special knowledge.

ESP extrasensory perception.

esp. especially.

espadrille [ess-pad-**drill**] n light canvas shoe with a braided cord sole.

espalier [ess-**pal**-yer] n shrub or fruit tree trained to grow flat; trellis for this.

esparto n, pl **-tos** grass used for making rope etc.

especial adj Formal special. **especially** adv particularly.

Esperanto n universal artificial language.

espionage [ess-pyon-**ahzh**] n spying.

esplanade n wide open road used as a public promenade.

espouse v adopt or give support to (a cause etc.). **espousal** n

espresso n, pl **-sos** strong coffee made by forcing steam or boiling water through ground coffee beans.

esprit [ess-**pree**] n spirit, liveliness. **esprit de corps** [de **core**] pride in and loyalty to a group.

espy v espying, espied catch sight of.

Esq. esquire.

esquire n courtesy title placed after a man's name.

essay n short literary composition; short piece of writing on a subject done as an exercise by a student. ◆ v attempt. **essayist** n

essence n most important feature of a thing which determines its identity; concentrated extract obtained by distillation, e.g. vanilla essence.

essential adj vitally important;

fundamental. ◆ n something essential. **essentially** adv

EST Eastern Standard Time.

establish v set up on a permanent basis; make secure or permanent in a certain place, job, etc.; prove; cause to be accepted. **establishment** n act of establishing; commercial or other institution. **the Establishment** group of people having authority within a society.

estate n landed property; large area of property development, esp. of new houses or factories; property of a deceased person. **estate agent** Brit real estate agent. **estate car** Brit station wagon.

esteem v think highly of; judge or consider. ◆ n high regard.

ester n Chem compound produced by the reaction between an acid and an alcohol.

esthetic n, adj see AESTHETIC.

estimate v calculate roughly; form an opinion about. ◆ n approximate calculation; opinion; statement from a workman etc. of the likely charge for a job. **estimable** adj worthy of respect. **estimation** n judgment, opinion.

estranged adj no longer living with one's spouse; having lost someone's affection and loyalty. **estrangement** n

estuary n, pl **-aries** mouth of a river.

ETA estimated time of arrival.

etc. et cetera.

et cetera [et **set**-ra] n, v and the rest, and others; or the like. **etceteras** pl n miscellaneous extra things or people.

etch v wear away or cut the surface of (metal, glass, etc.) with acid; imprint vividly (on someone's mind). **etching** n

eternal adj without beginning or end; unchanging. **eternally** adv **eternity** n infinite time; timeless existence after death. **eternity ring** ring given as a token of lasting affection.

ether n colourless sweet-smelling liquid used as an anesthetic; region above the clouds. **ethereal** [eth-**eer**-ee-al] adj extremely delicate.

ethic n moral principle. ◆ pl code of behaviour; study of morals. **ethical** adj **ethically** adv

ethnic adj relating to a people or group that shares a culture, religion, or language; belonging or relating to such a group, esp. one that is a minority group in a particular place. **ethnic cleansing** practice, by the dominant ethnic group in an area, of removing other ethnic groups by expulsion or extermination. **ethnology** n study of human races. **ethnological** adj **ethnologist** n

ethos [eeth-oss] n distinctive spirit and attitudes of a people, culture, etc.

ethyl [eth-ill] adj of, consisting of, or containing the hydrocarbon group C_2H_{15}. **ethylene** n poisonous gas used as an anesthetic and as fuel.

etiolate [ee-tee-oh-late] v become pale and weak; *Botany* whiten through lack of sunlight.

etiology n study of the causes of diseases.

etiquette n conventional code of conduct.

étude [ay-tewd] n short musical composition for a solo instrument, esp. intended as a technical exercise.

etymology n, pl -**gies** study of the sources and development of words. **etymological** adj **etymologist** n

EU European Union.

eucalyptus, eucalypt n tree, mainly grown in Australia, that provides timber and gum.

Eucharist [yew-kar-ist] n Christian sacrament commemorating Christ's Last Supper; consecrated elements of bread and wine. **Eucharistic** adj

eugenics [yew-jen-iks] n study of methods of improving the human race.

eulogy n, pl -**gies** speech or writing in praise of a person. **eulogize** v praise (a person or thing) highly in speech or writing.

eunuch n castrated man, esp. (formerly) a guard in a harem.

euphemism n inoffensive word or phrase substituted for one considered offensive or upsetting. **euphemistic** adj **euphemistically** adv

euphony n, pl -**nies** pleasing sound. **euphonious** adj pleasing to the ear. **euphonium** n brass musical instrument, tenor tuba.

euphoria n sense of elation. **euphoric** adj

Eurasian adj of Europe and Asia; of

mixed European and Asian parentage. ◆ n person of Eurasian parentage.

eureka [yew-reek-a] interj exclamation of triumph at finding something.

European n, adj (person) from Europe. **European Union** association of a number of European nations for trade, etc.

Eustachian tube n passage leading from the ear to the throat.

euthanasia n act of killing someone painlessly, esp. to relieve his or her suffering.

evacuate v send (someone) away from a place of danger; empty. **evacuation** n **evacuee** n

evade v get away from or avoid; elude. **evasion** n **evasive** adj not straightforward, e.g. *an evasive answer.* **evasively** adv

evaluate v find or judge the value of. **evaluation** n

evanescent adj quickly fading away. **evanescence** n

evangelical adj of or according to gospel teaching; of certain Protestant sects which maintain the doctrine of salvation by faith. ◆ n member of an evangelical sect. **evangelicalism** n

evangelist n writer of one of the four gospels; travelling preacher. **evangelism** n teaching and spreading of the Christian gospel. **evangelize** v preach the gospel. **evangelization** n

evaporate v change from a liquid or solid to a vapour; disappear. **evaporation** n **evaporated milk** thick unsweetened canned milk.

eve n evening or day before some special event; period immediately before an event. **evensong** n evening prayer.

even adj flat or smooth; (foll. by *with*) on the same level (as); constant; calm; equally balanced; divisible by two. ◆ adv equally; simply; nevertheless. ◆ v make even.

evening n end of the day or early part of the night; concluding period.

event n anything that takes place; actual outcome; contest in a sporting programme. **eventful** adj full of exciting incidents. **eventing** n riding competitions, usually involving cross-country, jumping, and dressage. **eventual** adj ultimate. **eventually** adv

eventuality n possible event.

ever adv at any time; always.

evergreen n, adj (tree or shrub) having leaves throughout the year.

everlasting adj **evermore** adv all time to come.

every adj each without exception; all possible. **everybody** pron every person. **everyday** adj usual or ordinary. **everyone** pron every person. **everything** pron **everywhere** adv in all places.

evict v legally expel (someone) from his or her home. **eviction** n

evidence n ground for belief or disbelief; matter produced before a lawcourt to prove or disprove a point. ◆ v demonstrate, prove. **in evidence** on display. **evident** adj easily noticed or understood. **evidently** adv **evidential** adj of, serving as, or based on evidence. **evidentially** adv

evil n wickedness; wicked deed. ◆ adj morally bad; harmful; very unpleasant. **evilly** adv **evildoer** n wicked person.

evince v make evident.

eviscerate v disembowel. **evisceration** n

evoke v call or summon up (a memory, feeling, etc.). **evocation** n **evocative** adj

evolve v develop gradually; (of an animal or plant species) undergo evolution. **evolution** n gradual change in the characteristics of living things over successive generations, esp. to a more complex form. **evolutionary** adj

ewe n female sheep.

ewer n large jug with a wide mouth.

ex n Informal former wife or husband.

ex- prefix out of, outside, from, e.g. exodus; former, e.g. ex-wife.

exacerbate [ig-zass-er-bate] v make (pain, emotion, or a situation) worse. **exacerbation** n

exact adj correct and complete in every detail; precise, as opposed to approximate. ◆ v demand (payment or obedience). **exactly** adv precisely, in every respect. **exactness, exactitude** n **exacting** adj making rigorous or excessive demands.

exaggerate v regard or represent as greater than is true; make greater or more noticeable. **exaggeratedly** adv **exaggeration** n

exalt v praise highly; elevate in rank. **exaltation** n feeling of great joy; act of praising highly.

exam n short for EXAMINATION.

examine v inspect carefully; test the knowledge of; formally question someone on oath. **examination** n examining; test of a candidate's knowledge or skill. **examinee** n **examiner** n

example n specimen typical of its group; person or thing worthy of imitation; punishment regarded as a warning to others.

exasperate v cause great irritation to. **exasperation** n

excavate v unearth buried objects from (a piece of land) methodically to learn about the past; make (a hole) in solid matter by digging. **excavation** n **excavator** n large machine used for digging.

exceed v be greater than; go beyond (a limit).

excel v **-celling, -celled** be superior to; be outstandingly good at something. **excellent** adj very good. **excellence** n **Excellency** n title used to address a high-ranking official, such as an ambassador.

except prep (sometimes foll. by for) other than, not including. ◆ v not include. **except that** with the exception that. **excepting** prep except. **exception** n thing that is excluded from or does not conform to the general rule. **exceptional** adj not ordinary; much above the average.

excerpt n passage taken from a book, speech, etc.

excess n state or act of exceeding the permitted limits; immoderate amount; amount by which a thing exceeds the permitted limits. **excessive** adj **excessively** adv

exchange v give or receive (something) in return for something else. ◆ n act of exchanging; thing given or received in place of another; centre in which telephone lines are interconnected; Finance place where securities or commodities are traded; Finance transfer of sums of money of equal value between different currencies. **exchangeable** adj

Exchequer n Brit government department in charge of state money.

excise[1] *n* tax on goods produced for the home market.

excise[2] *v* cut out or away. **excision** *n*

excite *v* arouse to strong emotion; arouse or evoke (an emotion); arouse sexually. **excitement** *n* **excitable** *adj* easily excited. **excitability** *n*

exclaim *v* speak suddenly, cry out. **exclamation** *n* **exclamation mark** punctuation mark (!) used after exclamations. **exclamatory** *adj*

exclude *v* leave out of consideration; keep out, leave out. **exclusion** *n* **exclusive** *adj* catering for a privileged minority; not shared; excluding everything else. ◆ *n* story reported in only one newspaper. **exclusively** *adv* **exclusiveness, exclusivity** *n*

excommunicate *v* exclude from membership and the sacraments of the Church. **excommunication** *n*

excoriate *v* censure severely; strip skin from. **excoriation** *n*

excrement *n* waste matter discharged from the body.

excrescence *n* lump or growth on the surface of an animal or plant.

excrete *v* discharge (waste matter) from the body. **excretion** *n* **excreta** [ik-**skree**-ta] *n* excrement. **excretory** *adj*

excruciating *adj* agonizing; very intense. **excruciatingly** *adv*

exculpate *v* free from blame or guilt.

excursion *n* short journey, esp. for pleasure.

excuse *n* explanation offered to excuse (a fault etc.). ◆ *v* put forward a reason or justification for (a fault etc.); forgive (a person) or overlook (a fault etc.); make allowances for; exempt; allow to leave. **excusable** *adj*

ex-directory *adj* not listed in a telephone directory by request.

execrable [**eks**-sik-rab-bl] *adj* of very poor quality.

execute *v* put (a condemned person) to death; perform (a plan or action); produce (a work of art); render (a legal document) effective, as by signing. **execution** *n* **executioner** *n* person employed to execute criminals. **executor, executrix** *n* person appointed to perform the instructions of a will.

executive *n* person or group in an administrative position; branch of government responsible for carrying out laws etc. ◆ *adj* having the function of carrying out plans, orders, laws, etc.

exegesis [eks-sij-jee-siss] *n, pl* **-ses** explanation of a text, esp. of the Bible.

exemplar *n* example; person or thing to be copied, model. **exemplary** *adj* being a good example; serving as a warning.

exemplify *v* **-fying, -fied** be an example of; show an example of. **exemplification** *n*

exempt *adj* not subject to an obligation etc. ◆ *v* release from an obligation etc. **exemption** *n*

exequies [**eks**-sik-wiz] *pl n* funeral rites.

exercise *n* activity to train the body or mind; set of movements or tasks designed to improve or test a person's ability; performance of a function. ◆ *v* take exercise or perform exercises; make use of, e.g. *to exercise one's rights*.

exert *v* use (influence, authority, etc.) forcefully or effectively. **exert oneself** make a special effort. **exertion** *n*

exeunt [**eks**-see-unt] *Latin* they go out: used as a stage direction.

ex gratia [eks **gray**-sha] *adj* given as a favour where no legal obligation exists.

exhale *v* breathe out. **exhalation** *n*

exhaust *v* tire out; use up; discuss (a subject) thoroughly. ◆ *n* gases ejected from an engine as waste products; pipe through which an engine's exhaust fumes pass. **exhaustion** *n* extreme tiredness; exhausting. **exhaustive** *adj* comprehensive. **exhaustively** *adv*

exhibit *v* show (a quality); display to the public. ◆ *n* object exhibited to the public; *Law* document or object produced in court as evidence. **exhibitor** *n* **exhibition** *n* public display of art, skills, etc.; exhibiting. **exhibitionism** *n* compulsive desire to draw attention to oneself; compulsive desire to display one's genitals in public. **exhibitionist** *n*

exhilarate *v* make lively and cheerful. **exhilaration** *n*

exhort *v* urge earnestly. **exhortation** *n*

exhume [ig-**zyume**] *v* dig up

(something buried, esp. a corpse). **exhumation** n

exigency n, pl **-cies** urgent demand or need. **exigent** adj

exiguous adj scanty, meagre.

exile n prolonged, usu. enforced, absence from one's country; person banished or living away from his or her country. ◆ v expel from one's country.

exist v have being or reality; eke out a living; live. **existence** n **existent** adj

existential adj of or relating to existence, esp. human existence. **existentialism** n philosophical movement stressing the personal experience and responsibility of the individual, who is seen as a free agent. **existentialist** adj, n

exit n way out; going out; actor's going off stage. ◆ v go out; go offstage: used as a stage direction.

exocrine adj relating to a gland, such as the sweat gland, that secretes externally through a duct.

exodus [eks-so-duss] n departure of a large number of people. **the Exodus** departure of the Israelites from Egypt.

ex officio [eks off-**fish**-ee-oh] adv, adj Latin by right of position or office.

exonerate v free from blame or a criminal charge. **exoneration** n

exorbitant adj (of prices, demands, etc.) excessive, immoderate. **exorbitantly** adv

exorcize v (attempt to) expel (evil spirits) by prayers and religious rites. **exorcism** n **exorcist** n

exotic adj having a strange allure or beauty; originating in a foreign country. ◆ n non-native plant. **exotically** adv **exotica** pl n (collection of) exotic objects.

expand v make or become larger; spread out; (foll. by on) enlarge (on); become more relaxed, friendly, and talkative. **expansion** n **expanse** n uninterrupted wide area. **expansive** adj friendly and talkative; wide or extensive.

expatiate [iks-**pay**-shee-ate] v (foll. by on) speak or write at great length (on). **expatiation** n

expatriate [eks-**pat**-ree-it] n person living outside his or her native country. ◆ adj living outside one's native

country. **expatriation** n

expect v regard as probable; look forward to, await; require as an obligation. **expectation** n act or state of expecting; something looked forward to; attitude of anticipation or hope. **expectancy** n something expected on the basis of an average, e.g. life expectancy; feeling of anticipation. **expectant** adj expecting or hopeful; pregnant. **expectantly** adv

expectorate v spit out (phlegm etc.). **expectoration** n **expectorant** n medicine that helps to bring up phlegm from the respiratory passages.

expedient [iks-**pee**-dee-ent] n something that achieves a particular purpose. ◆ adj suitable to the circumstances, appropriate. **expediency** n

expedite v hasten the progress of. **expedition** n organized journey, esp. for exploration; people and equipment comprising an expedition; pleasure trip or excursion. **expeditionary** adj relating to an expedition, esp. a military one. **expeditious** adj prompt, speedy.

expel v **-pelling, -pelled** dismiss from a school etc. permanently; drive out with force. **expulsion** n

expend v spend, use up. **expendable** adj able to be sacrificed to achieve an objective. **expenditure** n something expended, esp. money; amount expended. **expense** n cost; (cause of) spending. ◆ pl charges, outlay incurred. **expensive** adj high-priced.

experience n direct personal participation; particular incident, feeling, etc. that a person has undergone; accumulated knowledge. ◆ v participate in; be affected by (an emotion). **experienced** adj skilful from extensive participation.

experiment n test to provide evidence to prove or disprove a theory; attempt at something new. ◆ v make an experiment. **experimental** adj **experimentally** adv **experimentation** n

expert n person with extensive skill or knowledge in a particular field. ◆ adj skilful or knowledgeable. **expertise** [eks-per-**teez**] n special skill or knowledge.

expiate v make amends for. **expiation** n

expire v finish or run out; *Lit* die; breathe out. **expiration** n **expiry** n end, esp. of a contract period.

explain v make clear and intelligible; account for. **explanation** n **explanatory** adj

expletive [iks-**plee**-tiv] n swearword.

explicable adj able to be explained. **explicate** v *Formal* explain. **explication** n

explicit adj precisely and clearly expressed; shown in realistic detail. **explicitly** adv

explode v burst with great violence, blow up; react suddenly with emotion; increase rapidly; show (a theory etc.) to be baseless. **explosion** n **explosive** adj tending to explode. ◆ n substance that causes explosions.

exploit v take advantage of for one's own purposes; make the best use of. ◆ n notable feat or deed. **exploitation** n **exploiter** n

explore v travel into (unfamiliar regions), esp. for scientific purposes; investigate. **exploration** n **exploratory** adj **explorer** n

expo n *Informal* exposition, large public exhibition.

exponent n person who advocates an idea, cause, etc.; skilful performer, esp. a musician. **exponential** adj *Informal* very rapid. **exponentially** adv

export n selling or shipping of goods to a foreign country; product shipped or sold to a foreign country. ◆ v sell or ship (goods) to a foreign country. **exporter** n

expose v uncover or reveal; make vulnerable, leave unprotected; subject (a photographic film) to light. **expose oneself** display one's sexual organs in public. **exposure** n exposing; lack of shelter from the weather, esp. the cold; appearance before the public, as on television.

exposé [iks-**pose**-ay] n bringing of a crime, scandal, etc. to public notice.

exposition n see EXPOUND.

expostulate v (foll. by *with*) reason (with), esp. to dissuade. **expostulation** n

expound v explain in detail. **exposition** n explanation; large public exhibition.

express v put into words; show (an emotion); indicate by a symbol or formula; squeeze out (juice etc.). ◆ adj explicitly stated; (of a purpose) particular; of or for rapid transportation of people, mail, etc. ◆ n fast train or bus stopping at only a few stations. ◆ adv by express delivery. **expression** n expressing; word or phrase; showing or communication of emotion; look on the face that indicates mood; *Math* variable, function, or some combination of these. **expressionless** adj **expressive** adj

expressionism n early 20th-century artistic movement which sought to express emotions rather than represent the physical world. **expressionist** n, adj

expropriate v deprive an owner of (property). **expropriation** n

expunge [iks-**sponge**] v delete, erase, blot out.

expurgate [**eks**-per-gate] v remove objectionable parts from (a book etc.).

exquisite adj of extreme beauty or delicacy; intense in feeling. **exquisitely** adv

extant adj still existing.

extemporize v speak, perform, or compose without preparation.

extend v increase in size or scope; draw out or be drawn out, stretch; last for a certain time; (foll. by *to*) include; offer, e.g. *extend one's sympathy*. **extendable** adj **extension** n continuation or additional part of a building etc.; additional telephone connected to the same line as another; extending. **extensive** adj covering a large area; very great in effect, e.g. *extensive damage*. **extensor** n muscle that extends a part of the body. **extent** n length, area, or size of something.

extenuate v make (an offence or fault) less blameworthy. **extenuation** n

exterior n part or surface on the outside; outward appearance. ◆ adj of, on, or coming from the outside.

exterminate v destroy (animals or people) completely. **extermination** n **exterminator** n

external adj of, situated on, or coming from the outside. **externally** adv

extinct adj having died out; (of a volcano) no longer liable to erupt. **extinction** n

extinguish v put out (a fire or light); remove or destroy entirely. **extinguisher** n

extirpate [eks-ter-pate] v destroy utterly.

extol v **-tolling, -tolled** praise highly.

extort v get (something) by force or threats. **extortion** n **extortionate** adj (of prices) excessive.

extra adj additional; more than usual. ◆ n additional person or thing; something for which an additional charge is made; Films actor hired for crowd scenes. ◆ adv unusually or exceptionally.

extra- prefix outside or beyond an area or scope, e.g. extrasensory, extraterritorial.

extract v pull out by force; remove; derive; copy out (an article, passage, etc.) from a publication. ◆ n something extracted, such as a passage from a book etc.; preparation containing the concentrated essence of a substance, e.g. beef extract. **extraction** n **extractor** n

extradite v send (an accused person) back to his or her own country for trial. **extradition** n

extramural adj connected with but outside the normal courses of a university or college.

extraneous [iks-train-ee-uss] adj irrelevant.

extraordinary adj very unusual; (of a meeting) specially called to deal with a particular subject. **extraordinarily** adv

extrapolate [iks-trap-a-late] v infer (something not known) from the known facts; Math estimate (a value of a function or measurement) beyond the known values by the extension of a curve. **extrapolation** n

extrasensory adj **extrasensory perception** supposed ability to obtain information other than through the normal senses.

extravagant adj spending money excessively; going beyond reasonable limits. **extravagance** n **extravaganza** n elaborate and lavish entertainment, display, etc.

extreme adj of a high or the highest degree or intensity; immoderate; severe; farthest or outermost. ◆ n either of the two limits of a scale or range. **extreme sport** sport with a high risk of injury or death. **extremely** adv **extremist** n person who favours immoderate methods. ◆ adj holding extreme opinions. **extremity** n, pl **-ties** farthest point; extreme condition, as of misfortune. ◆ pl hands and feet.

extricate v free from complication or difficulty. **extrication** n

extrovert adj lively and outgoing; concerned more with external reality than inner feelings. ◆ n extrovert person.

extrude v squeeze or force out. **extrusion** n

exuberant adj high-spirited; growing luxuriantly. **exuberance** n

exude v make apparent by mood or behaviour, e.g. exude confidence; ooze out as sweat or sap.

exult v be joyful or jubilant. **exultation** n **exultant** adj

eye n organ of sight; (often pl.) ability to see; external part of an eye; attention, e.g. his new shirt caught my eye; ability to judge or appreciate, e.g a good eye for detail; one end of a sewing needle; dark spot on a potato from which a stem grows; small area of calm at the centre of a hurricane. ◆ v **eyeing** or **eying, eyed** look at carefully or warily. **eyeless** adj **eyelet** n small hole for a lace or cord to be passed through; ring that strengthens this. **eyeball** n ball-shaped part of the eye. **eyebrow** n line of hair on the bony ridge above the eye. **eyeglass** n lens for aiding defective vision. **eyelash** n short hair that grows out from the eyelid. **eyelid** n fold of skin that covers the eye when it is closed. **eyeliner** n cosmetic used to outline the eyes. **eye-opener** n Informal something startling or revealing. **eye shadow** coloured cosmetic worn on the upper eyelids. **eyesight** n ability to see. **eyesore** n ugly object. **eyetooth** n canine tooth. **eyewash** n Informal nonsense. **eyewitness** n person who was present at an event and can describe what happened.

eyrie n nest of an eagle; high isolated place.

F f

f *Music* forte.

F Fahrenheit; farad; *Chem* fluorine.

fable *n* story with a moral; legend; lie. **fabled** *adj* made famous in legend.

fabric *n* knitted or woven cloth; framework or structure. **fabricate** *v* make or build; make up (a story or lie). **fabrication** *n* **fabricator** *n*

fabulous *adj Informal* excellent; astounding; told of in fables. **fabulously** *adv*

façade [fas-**sahd**] *n* front of a building; (false) outward appearance.

face *n* front of the head; facial expression; distorted expression; front or main side; dial of a clock; exposed area of coal or ore in a mine; dignity, self-respect; outward appearance. ◆ *v* look or turn towards; be opposite; be confronted by; provide with a surface. **faceless** *adj* impersonal, anonymous. **facing** *n* lining or covering for decoration or reinforcement. ◆ *pl* contrasting collar and cuffs on a jacket. **face-lift** *n* operation to tighten facial skin, to remove wrinkles. **face-saving** *adj* maintaining dignity or self-respect. **face up to** *v* accept (an unpleasant fact or reality). **face value** apparent worth or meaning.

facet *n* surface of a cut gem; aspect.

facetious [fas-**see**-shuss] *adj* funny or trying to be funny, esp. at inappropriate times. **facetiousness** *n*

facia *n, pl* **-ciae** same as FASCIA.

facial *adj* of the face. ◆ *n* beauty treatment for the face.

facile [**fas**-sile] *adj* superficial and showing lack of real thought.

facilitate *v* make easy. **facilitation** *n*

facility *n, pl* **-ties** ability to do things easily or well. ◆ *pl* means or equipment for an activity.

facsimile [fak-**sim**-ill-ee] *n* exact copy.

fact *n* event or thing known to have happened or existed; provable truth. **facts of life** details of sex and reproduction. **factual** *adj*

faction *n* (dissenting) minority group within a larger body; dissension. **factious** *adj* of or producing factions.

factitious *adj* artificial.

factor *n* element contributing to a result; *Math* one of the integers multiplied together to give a given number; level on a scale, e.g *factor 15 suntan cream.* **factorial** *n* product of all the integers from one to a given number. **factorize** *v* calculate the factors of (a number).

factory *n, pl* **-ries** building where goods are manufactured.

factotum *n* person employed to do all sorts of work.

faculty *n, pl* **-ties** physical or mental ability; department in a university or college.

fad *n* short-lived fashion; whim. **faddy, faddish** *adj*

fade *v* (cause to) lose brightness, colour, or strength; vanish slowly. **fade-in, -out** *n* gradual increase or decrease, as of vision or sound in a film or broadcast.

faeces *pl n* same as FECES.

fag¹ *n Informal* boring task; *Brit* young public schoolboy who does menial chores for a senior boy. ◆ *v* (often foll. by *out*) *Informal* tire; do menial chores in a public school.

fag² *n Offens* male homosexual.

faggot *n Offens* male homosexual.

Fahrenheit [**far**-ren-hite] *adj* of a temperature scale with the freezing point of water at 32° and the boiling point at 212°.

faïence [fie-**ence**] *n* tin-glazed earthenware.

fail *v* be unsuccessful; stop operating; be or judge to be below the required standard in a test; disappoint or be useless to (someone); omit or be unable to do (something); go bankrupt. ◆ *n* instance of not passing an exam or test. **without fail** definitely; regularly. **failing** *n* weak point. ◆ *prep* in the absence of. **failure** *n* act or instance of failing; unsuccessful person or thing.

fain *adv Obs* gladly.

faint *adj* lacking clarity, brightness, or volume; lacking conviction or force; feeling dizzy or weak. ◆ *v* lose consciousness temporarily. ◆ *n* temporary loss of consciousness.

fair¹ *adj* unbiased and reasonable; light in colour; beautiful; quite good; unblemished; (of weather) fine. ◆ *adv* fairly; absolutely. **fairly** adv as deserved, reasonably; moderately; to a great degree. **fairness** n **fairway** n Golf smooth area between the tee and the green.

fair² n travelling entertainment with stalls and machines to ride on, etc.; exhibition of commercial or industrial products. **fairground** n open space used for a fair.

Fair Isle n intricate multicoloured knitted pattern.

fairy n, pl **fairies** imaginary small creature with magic powers; Offens male homosexual. **fairy godmother** person who helps in time of trouble. **fairyland** n **fairy light** small coloured light used as decoration. **fairy tale, story** story about fairies or magic; unbelievable story or explanation.

fait accompli [fate ak-kom-plee] n French something already done that cannot be altered.

faith n strong belief, esp. without proof; religion; complete confidence or trust; allegiance to a person or cause. **faithful** adj loyal; firm in support; accurate. **faithfully** adv **faithless** adj disloyal.

fake v cause (something) to appear real or more valuable by fraud; pretend to have (an illness, emotion, etc.). ◆ n person, thing, or act that is not genuine. ◆ adj not genuine. **faker** n

fakir [fay-keer] n member of any Islamic religious order; Hindu holy man.

falcon n small bird of prey. **falconry** n art of training falcons; sport of hunting with falcons. **falconer** n

fall v **falling, fell, fallen** drop from a higher to a lower place through the force of gravity; collapse to the ground; decrease in number or quality; slope downwards; die in battle; be captured; pass into a specified condition; (of the face) take on a sad expression; yield to temptation; occur. ◆ n falling; thing or amount that falls; decrease in value or number; decline in power or influence; season between summer and winter; capture or overthrow. ◆ pl waterfall. **fall for** v fall in love with; be taken in by. **fall guy** Informal victim of a confidence trick; scapegoat. **fallout** n

radioactive particles spread as a result of a nuclear explosion.

fallacy n, pl **-cies** false belief; unsound reasoning. **fallacious** adj

fallible adj liable to error. **fallibility** n

Fallopian tube n either of a pair of tubes through which egg cells pass from the ovary to the womb.

fallow¹ adj (of land) plowed but left unseeded to regain fertility.

fallow² adj **fallow deer** reddish-brown deer with white spots in summer.

false adj not true or correct; not genuine but intended to seem so; deceptive or misleading. **falsely** adv **falseness, falsity** n **falsehood** n quality of being untrue; lie. **falsify** v **-fying, -fied** alter fraudulently. **falsification** n

falsetto n, pl **-tos** voice pitched higher than one's natural range.

falter v lose power momentarily; be unsure; utter hesitantly; move unsteadily.

fame n state of being widely known or recognized. **famed** adj famous.

familiar adj well-known; acquainted; too friendly; intimate, friendly. ◆ n friend; demon supposed to attend a witch. **familiarly** adv **familiarity** n **familiarize** v acquaint fully with a particular subject. **familiarization** n

family n, pl **-lies** group of parents and their children; one's spouse and children; one's children; group descended from a common ancestor; group of related objects or beings. ◆ adj suitable for parents and children together. **familial** adj **family planning** control of the number of children in a family, esp. through contraception.

famine n severe shortage of food.

famished adj very hungry.

famous adj very well-known. **famously** adv Informal excellently.

fan¹ n hand-held or mechanical object used to create a current of air for ventilation or cooling. ◆ v **fanning, fanned** blow or cool with a fan; spread out like a fan. **fanbase** n body of admirers of a particular pop singer, sports team, etc. **fan belt** belt that drives a cooling fan in an automobile engine.

fan² n Informal devotee of a pop star, sport, or hobby.

fanatic n person who is excessively enthusiastic about something. **fanatical** adj **fanatically** adv **fanaticism** n

fancy adj **-cier, -ciest** elaborate, not plain; (of prices) higher than usual. ◆ n, pl **-cies** sudden irrational liking or desire; uncontrolled imagination. ◆ v **-cying, -cied** have a wish for; picture in the imagination; suppose; Brit informal be sexually attracted to. **fancy oneself** Informal have a high opinion of oneself. **fanciful** adj not based on fact; excessively elaborate. **fancifully** adv **fancy dress** party costume representing a historical figure, animal, etc. **fancy-free** adj not in love.

fandango n, pl **-gos** lively Spanish dance.

fanfare n short loud tune played on brass instruments.

fang n snake's tooth which injects poison; long pointed tooth.

fantasy n, pl **-sies** far-fetched idea; imagination unrestricted by reality; daydream; fiction with a large fantasy content. **fantasize** v indulge in daydreams. **fantasia** n musical composition of an improvised nature. **fantastic** adj Informal very good; unrealistic or absurd; strange or difficult to believe. **fantastically** adv

FAQ Computers frequently asked question or questions.

far adv **farther** or **further, farthest** or **furthest** at, to, or from a great distance; at or to a remote time; very much. ◆ adj remote in space or time. **Far East** East Asia. **far-fetched** adj hard to believe. **Far North** the Arctic.

farad n unit of electrical capacitance.

farce n boisterous comedy; ludicrous situation. **farcical** adj ludicrous. **farcically** adv

fare n charge for a passenger's journey; passenger; food provided. ◆ v get on (as specified), e.g. we fared badly. **farewell** interj goodbye. ◆ n act of saying goodbye and leaving.

farinaceous adj mealy, starchy.

farm n area of land for growing crops or rearing livestock. ◆ v cultivate (land); rear (stock). **farmer** n **farmhouse** n **farm out** v send (work) to be done by others. **farmstead** n farm and its buildings. **farmyard** n

farrago [far-**rah**-go] n, pl **-gos, -goes** jumbled mixture of things.

farrier n person who shoes horses.

farrow n litter of pigs. ◆ v (of a sow) give birth.

fart Taboo ◆ n emission of gas from the anus. ◆ v break wind.

farther, farthest adv, adj see FAR.

farthing n former British coin equivalent to a quarter of a penny.

farthingale n Obs hoop worn under skirts.

fascia [**fay**-shya] n, pl **-ciae** flat surface above a shop window; outer surface of a dashboard.

fascinate v attract and interest strongly; make motionless from fear or awe. **fascinating** adj **fascination** n

fascism [**fash**-iz-zum] n right-wing political system characterized by state control and extreme nationalism. **fascist** adj, n

fashion n style in clothes, esp. the latest style; manner of doing something. ◆ v form or make into a particular shape. **fashionable** adj currently popular. **fashionably** adv

fast¹ adj (capable of) acting or moving quickly; done in or lasting a short time; allowing rapid movement; (of a clock) showing a time later than the correct time; dissipated; firmly fixed; steadfast. ◆ adv quickly; tightly, firmly; soundly, deeply. **fast food** food, such as hamburgers, prepared and served very quickly. **fast-track** adj taking the quickest but most competitive route to success e.g. fast-track executives. ◆ v speed up the progress of (a project or person).

fast² v go without food, esp. for religious reasons. ◆ n period of fasting.

fasten v make or become firmly fixed or joined; close by fixing in place or locking; (foll. by on) direct (one's attention) towards. **fastener, fastening** n device that fastens.

fastidious adj very fussy about details; easily disgusted. **fastidiously** adv **fastidiousness** n

fastness n fortress, safe place.

fat n extra flesh on the body; oily substance obtained from animals or plants. ◆ adj **fatter, fattest** having excess flesh on the body; containing much fat; thick; profitable. **fatness** n

fatten v (cause to) become fat. **fatty** adj containing fat. **fathead** n Informal fool. **fat-headed** adj

fatal adj causing death or ruin. **fatally** adv **fatality** n death caused by an accident or disaster.

fatalism n belief that all events are predetermined and man is powerless to change his destiny. **fatalist** n **fatalistic** adj

fate n power supposed to predetermine events; inevitable fortune that befalls a person or thing. **fated** adj destined; doomed to death or destruction. **fateful** adj having important, usu. disastrous, consequences.

father n male parent; man who originates or founds something; title of some priests; (F-) God. ◆ pl ancestors. ◆ v be the father of (offspring). **fatherhood** n **fatherless** adj **fatherly** adj **father-in-law** n father of one's husband or wife. **fatherland** n one's native country.

fathom n unit of measurement of the depth of water, equal to six feet. ◆ v understand. **fathomable** adj **fathomless** adj too difficult to fathom.

fatigue [fat-eeg] n physical or mental exhaustion caused by exertion; weakening of a material due to stress; soldier's nonmilitary duty. ◆ v tire out.

fatuous adj foolish. **fatuously** adv **fatuity** n

faucet n valve with handle, plug etc. to regulate or stop flow of fluid.

fault n responsibility for something wrong; mistake; defect or flaw; Geology break in layers of rock; Tennis, squash, etc. invalid serve. ◆ v criticize or find mistakes in. **at fault** guilty of error. **find fault with** seek out minor imperfections in. **to a fault** excessively. **faulty** adj **faultily** adv **faultless** adj **faultlessly** adv

faun n (in Roman legend) rural god with goat's horns and legs.

fauna n, pl **-nas**, **-nae** animals of a given place or time.

faux pas [foe pah] n, pl **faux pas** social blunder.

favour n goodwill, approval; act of goodwill or generosity; partiality. ◆ v prefer; regard or treat with especial kindness; support or advocate; Informal resemble. **favourable** adj encouraging; giving consent; useful or beneficial. **favourably** adv **favourite** n preferred person or thing; Sport competitor expected to win. ◆ adj most liked. **favouritism** n practice of unfairly favouring one person or group.

fawn[1] n young deer. ◆ adj light yellowish-brown.

fawn[2] v (foll. by on) seek attention from (someone) by being obsequious; (of a dog) try to please by a show of extreme affection.

fax n electronic system for sending facsimiles of documents by telephone; document sent by this system. ◆ v send by this system.

FBI US Federal Bureau of Investigation.

FC Football Club.

Fe Chem iron.

fealty n Obs subordinate's loyalty to his ruler or lord.

fear n distress or alarm caused by impending danger or pain; cause of this. ◆ v be afraid of (something or someone); feel anxiety about (something). **fearful** adj feeling fear; causing fear; Informal very unpleasant. **fearfully** adv **fearless** adj **fearlessly** adv **fearsome** adj terrifying.

feasible adj able to be done, possible. **feasibly** adv **feasibility** n

feast n lavish meal; periodic religious celebration; something extremely pleasing. ◆ v eat a feast; (foll. by on) enjoy eating (something); give a feast to; delight.

feat n remarkable, skilful, or daring action.

feather n one of the barbed shafts forming the plumage of birds. ◆ v fit or cover with feathers; turn (an oar) edgeways. **feather in one's cap** achievement one can be pleased with. **feather one's nest** make one's life comfortable. **feathered** adj **feathery** adj **featherbedding** n overprotection. **featherweight** n boxer weighing up to 126lb (professional) or 57kg (amateur); insignificant person or thing.

feature n prominent or distinctive part; part of the face, such as the eyes; special article in a newspaper or magazine; main film in a cinema programme. ◆ v have as a feature or be a feature in; give prominence to.

featureless *adj*

Feb. February.

febrile [**fee**-brile] *adj* feverish.

February *n* second month.

feces, faeces [**fee**-seez] *pl n* waste matter discharged from the anus. **fecal, faecal** *adj*

feckless *adj* irresponsible.

fecund *adj* fertile. **fecundity** *n*

fed *v* past of FEED. **fed up** *Informal* bored, dissatisfied.

federal *adj* of a system in which power is divided between one central government and several regional governments; of the central government of a federation. **federalism** *n* **federalist** *n* **federate** *v* unite in a federation. **federation** *n* union of several states, provinces, etc.; association.

fedora [fid-**or**-a] *n* man's soft hat with a brim.

fee *n* charge paid to be allowed to do something; payment for professional services.

feeble *adj* lacking physical or mental power; unconvincing. **feebleness** *n* **feebly** *adv* **feeble-minded** *adj* mentally deficient.

feed *v* **feeding, fed** give food to; give (something) as food; eat; supply or prepare food for; supply (what is needed). ◆ *n* act of feeding; food, esp. for babies or animals; *Informal* meal. **feeder** *n* baby's bib; road or railway line linking outlying areas to the main traffic network. **feedback** *n* information received in response to something done; return of part of the output of an electrical circuit or loudspeaker to its source.

feel *v* **feeling, felt** have a physical or emotional sensation of; become aware of or examine by touch; believe. ◆ *n* act of feeling; way something feels; impression; sense of touch; instinctive aptitude. **feeler** *n* organ of touch in some animals; remark made to test others' opinion. **feeling** *n* emotional reaction; intuitive understanding; opinion; sympathy, understanding; ability to experience physical sensations; sensation experienced. ◆ *pl* emotional sensitivities. **feel like** wish for, want.

feet *n* plural of FOOT.

feign [fane] *v* pretend.

feint[1] [faint] *n* sham attack or blow meant to distract an opponent. ◆ *v* make a feint.

feint[2] [faint] *n* narrow lines on ruled paper.

feisty *adj* 1 *Inf* lively, resilient, and self-reliant. 2 irritable.

feldspar *n* hard mineral that is the main constituent of igneous rocks.

felicity *n, pl* **-ties** happiness; appropriate expression or style. **felicitate** *v* congratulate. **felicitation** *n* **felicitous** *adj*

feline *adj* of cats; catlike. ◆ *n* animal of the cat family.

fell[1] *v* past tense of FALL.

fell[2] *v* knock down; cut down (a tree).

fell[3] *adj* Old-fashioned fierce, terrible. **one fell swoop** single action.

fell[4] *n* (in N England) a mountain, hill, or moor.

felloe *n* (segment of) the rim of a wheel.

fellow *n* Informal man or boy; comrade or associate; person in the same group or condition; member of a learned society or the governing body of a college. ◆ *adj* in the same group or condition. **fellowship** *n* sharing of aims or interests; group with shared aims or interests; feeling of friendliness; college research post.

felon *n* person guilty of a felony. **felony** *n, pl* **-nies** serious crime. **felonious** *adj*

felspar *n* same as FELDSPAR.

felt[1] *v* past of FEEL.

felt[2] *n* matted fabric made by bonding fibres by pressure. **felt-tip pen** pen with a writing point made from pressed fibres.

fem. feminine.

female *adj* of the sex which bears offspring; (of plants) producing fruits. ◆ *n* female person or animal.

feminine *adj* of women; having qualities traditionally regarded as suitable for, or typical of, women; belonging to a particular class of grammatical inflection in some languages. **femininity** *n* **feminism** *n* advocacy of equal rights for women. **feminist** *n, adj*

femme fatale [fam fat-**tahl**] *n, pl* **femmes fatales** alluring woman who causes men distress.

femur [fee-mer] n thighbone. **femoral** adj of the thigh.

fen n low-lying flat marshy land.

fence n barrier of posts linked by wire or wood, enclosing an area; Slang dealer in stolen property. ♦ v enclose with or as if with a fence; fight with swords as a sport; avoid a question. **fencing** n sport of fighting with swords; material for making fences. **fencer** n

fend v **fend for oneself** provide for oneself. **fend off** v ward off.

fender n part of an automobile bodywork surrounding the wheels; soft but solid object hung over a ship's side to prevent damage when docking; low metal frame in front of a fireplace.

feng shui (fung shway) n Chinese art of deciding the best design of a building, etc., in order to bring good luck.

fennel n fragrant plant whose seeds, leaves, and root are used in cookery.

fenugreek n Mediterranean plant grown for its pungent seeds.

feral adj wild.

ferment n commotion, unrest. ♦ v undergo or cause to undergo fermentation. **fermentation** n reaction in which an organic molecule splits into simpler substances, esp. conversion of sugar to alcohol.

fern n flowerless plant with fine fronds.

ferocious adj fierce, violent. **ferocity** n

ferret n tamed polecat used to catch rabbits or rats. ♦ v **ferreting, ferreted** hunt with ferrets; search around. **ferret out** v find by searching.

ferric, ferrous adj of or containing iron.

ferris wheel n large vertical fairground wheel with hanging seats for riding in.

ferrule n metal cap to strengthen the end of a stick.

ferry n, pl **-ries** boat for transporting people and vehicles. ♦ v **-rying, -ried** carry by ferry; convey (goods or people). **ferryman** n

fertile adj capable of producing young, crops, or vegetation; highly productive. **fertility** n **fertilize** v provide (an animal or plant) with

sperm or pollen to bring about fertilization; supply (soil) with nutrients. **fertilization** n **fertilizer** n

fervent, fervid adj intensely passionate and sincere. **fervently** adv **fervour** n intensity of feeling.

fescue n pasture and lawn grass with stiff narrow leaves.

festal adj festive.

fester v form or cause to form pus; rot, decay; become worse.

festival n organized series of special events or performances; day or period of celebration. **festive** adj of or like a celebration. **festivity** n, pl **-ties** joyful celebration, merriment. ♦ pl celebrations.

festoon v hang decorations in loops.

feta n white salty Greek cheese.

fetch v go after and bring back; be sold for; Informal deal (a blow). **fetching** adj attractive. **fetch up** v Informal arrive or end up.

fete, fête [fate] n gala, bazaar, etc., usu. held outdoors. ♦ v honour or entertain regally.

fetid adj stinking.

fetish n form of behaviour in which sexual pleasure is derived from looking at or handling an inanimate object; thing with which one is excessively concerned; object believed to have magical powers. **fetishism** n **fetishist** n

fetlock n projection behind and above a horse's hoof.

fetter n chain or shackle for the foot. ♦ pl restrictions. ♦ v restrict; bind in fetters.

fettle n state of health or spirits.

fetus [fee-tuss] n, pl **-tuses** embryo of a mammal in the later stages of development. **fetal** adj

feud n long bitter hostility between two people or groups. ♦ v carry on a feud.

feudalism n medieval system in which vassals held land from a lord, and in return worked and fought for him. **feudal** adj of or like feudalism.

fever n (illness causing) high body temperature; nervous excitement. **fevered** adj **feverish** adj suffering from fever; in a state of nervous excitement. **feverishly** adv

few adj not many. **a few** a small

number. **good few, quite a few** several.

fey *adj* whimsically strange; clairvoyant.

fez *n, pl* **fezzes** brimless tasselled cap, orig. from Turkey.

ff *Music* fortissimo.

fiancé [fee-on-say] *n* man engaged to be married. **fiancée** *n fem*

fiasco *n, pl* **-cos, -coes** ridiculous or humiliating failure.

fiat [fee-at] *n* arbitrary order; official permission.

fib *n* trivial lie. ◆ *v* **fibbing, fibbed** tell a fib. **fibber** *n*

fibre *n* thread that can be spun into yarn; threadlike animal or plant tissue; fibrous material in food; strength of character; essential substance or nature. **fibrous** *adj* **fibreboard** *n* board made of compressed plant fibres. **fibreglass** *n* material made of fine glass fibres. **fibre optics** transmission of information by light along very thin flexible fibres of glass.

fibroid [fibe-royd] *n* benign tumour derived from fibrous connective tissue. **fibrositis** [fibe-roh-**site**-iss] *n* inflammation of muscle tissue, causing pain and stiffness.

fibula [fib-yew-la] *n, pl* **-lae, -las** slender outer bone of the lower leg. **fibular** *adj*

fiche [feesh] *n* sheet of film for storing publications in miniaturized form.

fickle *adj* changeable, inconstant. **fickleness** *n*

fiction *n* literary works of the imagination, such as novels; invented story. **fictional** *adj* **fictionalize** *v* turn into fiction. **fictitious** *adj* not genuine; of or in fiction.

fiddle *n* violin; *Informal* dishonest action or scheme. ◆ *v* play the violin; move or touch something restlessly; falsify (accounts). **fiddling** *adj* trivial. **fiddly** *adj* awkward to do or use. **fiddlehead** *n* edible coiled tip of young fern frond.

fidelity *n* faithfulness; accuracy in detail; quality of sound reproduction.

fidget *v* move about restlessly. ◆ *n* person who fidgets. ◆ *pl* restlessness. **fidgety** *adj*

fiduciary [fid-yew-sheer-ee] *adj* relating to a trust or trustee. ◆ *n, pl* -aries trustee.

fief [feef] *n Hist* land granted by a lord in return for war service.

field *n* enclosed piece of agricultural land; marked off area for sports; area rich in a specified natural resource; sphere of knowledge or activity; place away from the laboratory or classroom where practical work is done; all the competitors in a competition; all the competitors except the favourite; battlefield; area over which electric, gravitational, or magnetic force is exerted; background, as of a flag. ◆ *v Sport* catch and return (a ball); *Sport* send a (player or team) on to the field; *Sport* play as a fielder; deal with (a question) successfully. **fielder** *n Sport* player whose task is to field the ball. **field day** day or time of exciting activity. **field events** throwing and jumping events in athletics. **field glasses** binoculars. **field marshal** army officer of the highest rank. **field sports** hunting, shooting, and fishing. **fieldwork** *n* investigation made in the field as opposed to those made in the classroom or the laboratory.

fiend [feend] *n* evil spirit; cruel or wicked person; *Informal* person devoted to something, e.g. *fresh-air fiend*. **fiendish** *adj* cruel; *Informal* cunning; *Informal* very difficult. **fiendishly** *adv*

fierce *adj* wild; intense; turbulent. **fiercely** *adv* **fierceness** *n*

fiery [fire-ee] *adj* **fierier, fieriest** consisting of or like fire; easily angered; (of food) very spicy.

fiesta *n* religious festival, carnival.

fife *n* small high-pitched flute.

fifth, fifteen, fifteenth, fifty, fiftieth *n, adj* see FIVE.

fig *n* soft pear-shaped fruit; tree bearing it.

fight *v* **fighting, fought** struggle (against) in battle or physical combat; struggle to overcome someone or obtain something; carry on (a battle or struggle); make (a way) by fighting. ◆ *n* aggressive conflict between two (groups of) people; quarrel or contest; resistance; boxing match. **fighter** *n* boxer; determined person; aircraft designed to destroy other aircraft. **fight off** *v* repulse; struggle to avoid.

figment *n* **figment of one's**

figure　　　　　157　　　　　**find**

imagination imaginary thing.

figure n numerical symbol; amount expressed in numbers; bodily shape; well-known person; representation in painting or sculpture of a human form; diagram or illustration; set of movements in dancing or skating; *Math* any combination of lines, planes, points, or curves. ◆ v consider, conclude; (usu. foll. by *in*) be included (in); calculate. **figure of speech** expression in which words do not have their literal meaning. **figurative** adj (of language) abstract, imaginative, or symbolic. **figuratively** adv **figurine** n statuette. **figurehead** n nominal leader; carved bust at the bow of a ship. **figure out** v solve.

filament n fine wire in a light bulb that gives out light; fine thread.

filbert n hazelnut.

filch v steal (small amounts).

file[1] n box or folder used to keep documents in order; documents in a file; information about a person or subject; line of people one behind the other; *Computers* organized collection of related material. ◆ v place (a document) in a file; place (a legal document) on official record; bring a lawsuit, esp. for divorce; walk or march in a line.

file[2] n tool with a roughened blade for smoothing or shaping. ◆ v shape or smooth with a file. **filings** pl n shavings removed by a file.

filial adj of or befitting a son or daughter.

filibuster v obstruct legislation by making long speeches. ◆ n act of filibustering; person who filibusters.

filigree n delicate ornamental work of gold or silver wire. ◆ adj made of filigree.

fill v make or become full; occupy completely; plug (a gap); satisfy (a need); hold and perform the duties of (a position); appoint to (a job or position). **one's fill** sufficient for one's needs or wants. **filler** n substance that fills a gap or increases bulk. **filling** n substance that fills a gap or cavity, esp. in a tooth. ◆ adj (of food) substantial and satisfying. **filling station** garage selling gasoline, oil, etc.

fillet n boneless piece of meat or fish. ◆ v **filleting, filleted** remove the bones from.

fillip n something that adds stimulation or enjoyment.

filly n, pl **-lies** young female horse.

film n sequence of images projected on a screen, creating the illusion of movement; story told in such a sequence of images; thin strip of light-sensitive cellulose used to make photographic negatives and transparencies; thin sheet or layer. ◆ v photograph with a movie or video camera; make a film of (a scene, story, etc.); cover or become covered with a thin layer. ◆ adj connected with cinema. **filmy** adj very thin, delicate. **film strip** set of pictures on a strip of film, projected separately as slides.

filter n material or device permitting fluid to pass but retaining solid particles; device that blocks certain frequencies of sound or light; traffic signal that allows vehicles to turn either left or right while the main signals are at red. ◆ v pass slowly or faintly; remove impurities from (a substance) with a filter. **filtrate** n filtered gas or liquid. ◆ v remove impurities with a filter. **filtration** n

filth n disgusting dirt; offensive material or language. **filthy** adj **filthily** adv **filthiness** n

fin n projection from a fish's body enabling it to balance and swim; vertical tailplane of an aircraft.

finagle [fin-**nay**-gl] v get or achieve by craftiness or trickery.

final adj at the end; having no possibility of further change, action, or discussion. ◆ n deciding contest in a competition. ◆ pl last examinations in an educational course. **finally** adv **finality** n **finalist** n competitor in a final. **finalize** v put into final form. **finale** [fin-**nah**-lee] n concluding part of a dramatic performance or musical work.

finance v provide or obtain funds for. ◆ n management of money; (provision of) funds. ◆ pl money resources. **financial** adj **financially** adv **financier** n person involved in large-scale financial business. **financial year** twelve-month period used for financial calculations.

finch n small songbird with a stout bill.

find v **finding, found** discover by

chance; discover by search or effort; become aware of; consider to have a particular quality; experience (a particular feeling); *Law* pronounce (the defendant) guilty or not guilty; provide, esp. with difficulty. ◆ *n* person or thing found, esp. when valuable. **finder** *n* **finding** *n* conclusion from an investigation. **find out** *v* gain knowledge of; detect (a crime, deception, etc.).

fine¹ *adj* very good; in good health; acceptable; thin or slender; in small particles; subtle or abstruse, e.g. *a fine distinction*; of delicate workmanship; (of weather) clear and dry. **finely** *adv* **fineness** *n* **finery** *n* showy clothing. **fine art** art produced to appeal to the sense of beauty. **fine-tune** *v* make small adjustments to (something) so that it works really well.

fine² *n* payment imposed as a penalty. ◆ *v* impose a fine on.

finesse [fin-ness] *n* delicate skill; subtlety and tact.

finger *n* one of the four long jointed parts of the hand; part of a glove that covers a finger; quantity of liquid in a glass as deep as a finger is wide. ◆ *v* touch or handle with the fingers. **fingering** *n* technique of using the fingers in playing a musical instrument. **fingerboard** *n* part of a stringed instrument on which the fingers are placed. **fingerprint** *n* impression of the ridges on the tip of the finger. ◆ *v* take the fingerprints of (someone).

finial *n Archit* ornament at the apex of a gable or spire.

finicky *adj* excessively particular, fussy; overelaborate.

finis *n Latin* end: used at the end of a book.

finish *v* bring to an end, stop; use up; bring to a desired or completed condition; put a surface texture on (wood, cloth, or metal); defeat or destroy. ◆ *n* end; death or defeat; surface texture.

finite [fine-ite] *adj* having limits in space, time, or size.

fiord *n* same as FJORD.

fir *n* pyramid-shaped tree with needle-like leaves and erect cones.

fire *n* state of combustion producing heat, flames, and smoke; uncontrolled destructive burning; burning coal or wood, or a gas or electric device, used to heat a room; shooting of guns; intense passion, ardour. ◆ *v* operate (a weapon) so that a bullet or missile is released; *Informal* dismiss from employment; excite; bake (ceramics etc.) in a kiln. **firearm** *n* rifle, pistol, or shotgun. **firebrand** *n* person who causes unrest. **firebreak** *n* strip of cleared land to stop the advance of a fire. **firebug** *n Informal* person who deliberately starts fires. **firedamp** *n* explosive gas, composed mainly of methane, formed in mines. **fire department** organized body of people whose job it is to put out fires. **fire drill** rehearsal of procedures for escape from a fire. **fire engine** vehicle with apparatus for extinguishing fires. **fire escape** metal staircase or ladder down the outside of a building for escape in the event of fire. **firefly** *n* beetle that glows in the dark. **fireguard** *n* protective grating in front of a fire. **fire hall** building housing a fire department. **fire irons** tongs, poker, and shovel for tending a domestic fire. **fireman** *n* member of a fire department. **fireplace** *n* recess in a room for a fire. **firepower** *n Mil* amount a weapon or unit can fire. **fire station** building where fire-fighting vehicles and equipment are stationed. **firewall** *n Computers* computer that prevents unauthorized access to a computer network from the Internet. **firework** *n* device containing chemicals that is ignited to produce spectacular explosions and coloured sparks. ◆ *pl* show of fireworks; *Informal* outburst of temper. **firing squad** group of soldiers ordered to execute an offender by shooting.

firkin *n* small cask.

firm¹ *adj* not soft or yielding; securely in position; definite; determined, resolute. ◆ *adv* in an unyielding manner, e.g. *hold firm*. ◆ *v* make or become firm. **firmly** *adv* **firmness** *n*

firm² *n* business company.

firmament *n Lit* sky, heavens.

first *adj* earliest in time or order; graded or ranked above all others. ◆ *n* person or thing coming before all others; outset, beginning; first-class honours degree at university; lowest forward gear in a motor vehicle. ◆ *adv* before anything else; for the first time. **firstly** *adv* **first aid** immediate medical assistance given in an emergency. **first-class** *adj* of the highest quality; excellent. **first-hand** *adj, adv* (obtained) directly from the original source. **first mate, officer** officer of a merchant ship second in command to the captain. **first ministers** Canadian prime minister and provincial premiers. **First Nations** Canadian aboriginal communities. **First Peoples** Indian, Inuit, and Métis in Canada. **first person** *Grammar* category of verbs and pronouns used by a speaker to refer to himself or herself. **first-rate** *adj* excellent. **first-strike** *adj* (of a nuclear missile) for use in an opening attack to destroy enemy weapons.

firth *n* narrow inlet of the sea.

fiscal *adj* of government finances, esp. taxes.

fish *n, pl* **fish, fishes** cold-blooded vertebrate with gills, that lives in water; its flesh as food. ◆ *v* try to catch fish; try to catch fish in (a specified place); (foll. by *for*) grope for and find with difficulty; (foll. by *for*) seek indirectly. **fisherman** *n* person who catches fish for a living or for pleasure. **fishery** *n, pl* **-eries** area of the sea used for fishing. **fishy** *adj* of or like fish; *Informal* suspicious or questionable. **fish finger** oblong piece of fish covered in breadcrumbs. **fish meal** dried ground fish used as animal feed or fertilizer. **fishmonger** *n Brit* seller of fish. **fishnet** *n* open mesh fabric resembling netting. **fishwife** *n* coarse scolding woman.

fishplate *n* metal plate joining one rail to the next on a track.

fission *n* splitting; *Biol* asexual reproduction involving a division into two or more equal parts; splitting of an atomic nucleus with the release of a large amount of energy. **fissionable** *adj* **fissile** *adj* capable of undergoing nuclear fission; tending to split.

fissure [fish-er] *n* long narrow cleft or crack.

fist *n* clenched hand. **fisticuffs** *pl n* fighting with the fists.

fistula [fist-yew-la] *n* long narrow ulcer.

fit¹ *v* **fitting, fitted** be appropriate or suitable for; be of the correct size or shape (for); adjust so as to make appropriate; try (clothes) on and note any adjustments needed; make competent or ready; correspond with the facts or circumstances. ◆ *adj* appropriate; in good health; worthy or deserving. ◆ *n* way in which something fits. **fitness** *n* **fitter** *n* person skilled in the installation and adjustment of machinery; person who fits garments. **fitting** *adj* appropriate, suitable. ◆ *n* accessory or part; trying on of clothes for size. ◆ *pl* furnishings and accessories in a building. **fitment** *n* detachable part of the furnishings of a room. **fit in** *v* give a place or time to; belong or conform. **fit out** *v* provide with the necessary equipment.

fit² *n* sudden attack or convulsion, such as an epileptic seizure; sudden short burst or spell.

fitful *adj* occurring in irregular spells. **fitfully** *adv*

five *adj, n* one more than four. **fives** *n* ball game resembling squash but played with bats or the hands. **fifth** *adj, n* (of) number five in a series. **fifth column** group secretly helping the enemy. **fifteen** *adj, n* five and ten. **fifteenth** *adj, n* **fifty** *adj, n* five times ten. **fiftieth** *adj, n*

fix *v* make or become firm, stable, or secure; repair; place permanently; settle definitely; direct (the eyes etc.) steadily; *Informal* unfairly influence the outcome of. ◆ *n Informal* difficult situation; ascertaining of the position of a ship by radar etc.; *Slang* injection of a narcotic drug. **fixed** *adj* **fixedly** [fix-id-lee] *adv* steadily. **fixation** *n* preoccupation, obsession. **fixated** *adj* obsessed. **fixative** *n* liquid used to preserve or hold things in place. **fixer** *n* solution used to make a photographic image permanent; *Slang* person who arranges things. **fixture** *n* permanently fitted piece of household equipment; person whose presence seems permanent; sports match or the date fixed for it. **fix up** *v* arrange; provide (with).

fizz *v* give off small bubbles; make a hissing or bubbling noise. ◆ *n* hissing or bubbling noise; releasing of small bubbles of gas by a liquid; effervescent drink. **fizzy** *adj*

fizzle v make a weak hissing or bubbling sound. **fizzle out** v Informal come to nothing, fail.

fjord [fee-**ord**] n long narrow inlet of the sea between cliffs, esp. in Norway.

flab n Informal unsightly body fat.

flabbergast v amaze utterly.

flabby adj -bier, -biest loose or limp; having flabby flesh. **flabbiness** n

flaccid [**flas**-sid] adj soft and limp. **flaccidity** n

flag[1] n piece of cloth attached to a pole as an emblem or signal. ◆ v **flagging, flagged** mark with a flag or sticker; (often foll. by down) signal (a vehicle) to stop by waving the arm. **flagpole, flagstaff** n pole for a flag. **flagship** n admiral's ship; most important product of an organization.

flag[2] v **flagging, flagged** lose enthusiasm or vigour.

flag[3], **flagstone** n flat paving-stone. **flagged** adj paved with flagstones.

flagellate [**flaj**-a-late] v whip. **flagellation** n **flagellant** n person who whips himself, esp. in religious penance.

flageolet [flaj-a-**let**] n small instrument like a recorder.

flagon n wide bottle for wine or cider; narrow-necked jug for liquid.

flagrant [**flayg**-rant] adj openly outrageous. **flagrantly** adv **flagrancy** n

flail v wave about wildly; beat or thrash. ◆ n tool formerly used for threshing grain by hand.

flair n natural ability; stylishness.

flak n anti-aircraft fire; Informal adverse criticism.

flake n small thin piece, esp. chipped off something. ◆ v peel off in flakes. **flaky** adj **flake out** v Informal collapse from exhaustion.

flambé [**flahm**-bay] v **flambéing, flambéed** cook or serve (food) in flaming brandy.

flamboyant adj very bright and showy; behaving in a very noticeable, extravagant way. **flamboyance** n

flame n luminous burning gas coming from burning material. ◆ v burn brightly; become bright red. **old flame** Informal former sweetheart.

⸻enco n, pl -cos rhythmical ⸻ ⸻ance accompanied by a ⸻d vocalist; music for this dance.

flamingo n, pl -gos, -goes large pink wading bird with a long neck and legs and a curved bill.

flammable adj easily set on fire. **flammability** n

flan n egg custard with caramelized topping; Brit open sweet or savoury tart.

flange n projecting rim or collar. **flanged** adj

flank n part of the side between the hips and ribs; side of a body of troops. ◆ v be at or move along the side of.

flannel n soft woollen fabric for clothing; small piece of cloth for washing the face and hands; Informal evasive talk. ◆ pl trousers made of flannel. ◆ v -nelling, -nelled Informal talk evasively. **flannelette** n cotton imitation of flannel.

flap v **flapping, flapped** move back and forwards or up and down. ◆ n action or sound of flapping; piece of something attached by one edge only; Informal state of excitement or panic.

flapjack n thin pancake.

flare v blaze with a sudden unsteady flame; Informal (of temper, violence, or trouble) break out suddenly; (of a skirt or trousers) become wider towards the hem. ◆ n sudden unsteady flame; signal light. ◆ pl flared trousers. **flared** adj (of a skirt or trousers) becoming wider towards the hem.

flash n sudden burst of light or flame; sudden occurrence (of intuition or emotion); very short time; brief unscheduled news announcement; Photog small bulb that produces an intense flash of light. ◆ v (cause to) burst into flame; (cause to) emit light suddenly or intermittently; move very fast; come rapidly (to mind or view); Informal display ostentatiously; Slang expose oneself indecently. ◆ adj (also **flashy**) vulgarly showy. **flasher** n Slang man who exposes himself indecently. **flashing** n watertight material used to cover joins in a roof. **flashback** n scene in a book, play, or film, that shows earlier events. **flash flood** sudden short-lived flood. **flashlight** n small portable battery-powered lamp. **flash point** critical point beyond which a situation will inevitably erupt into violence; lowest temperature at which vapour given off by a liquid can ignite.

flask n vacuum flask; flat bottle for carrying alcoholic drink in the pocket; narrow-necked bottle.

flat[1] adj **flatter**, **flattest** level and horizontal; even, smooth; (of a tire) deflated; outright; fixed; without variation or emotion; (of a battery) with no electrical charge; (of a drink) no longer fizzy; Music below the true pitch. ◆ adv in or into a flat position; exactly; completely, absolutely; Music too low in pitch. ◆ n flat surface; Music symbol lowering the pitch of a note by a semitone; punctured automobile tire; level ground; mudbank exposed at low tide. **flat out** with maximum speed or effort. **flatly** adv **flatness** n **flatten** v **flatfish** n sea fish, such as the sole, which has a flat body. **flat racing** horse racing over level ground with no jumps.

flat[2] n Brit apartment.

flatter v praise insincerely; show to advantage; make (a person) appear more attractive in a picture than in reality. **flatterer** n **flattery** n

flatulent adj suffering from, or caused by, excess gas in the intestines. **flatulence** n

flaunt v display (oneself or one's possessions) arrogantly.

flautist [flaw-tist] n flute player.

flavour n distinctive taste; distinctive characteristic or quality. ◆ v give flavour to. **flavouring** n substance used to flavour food. **flavourless** adj

flaw n blemish; mistake that makes a plan or argument invalid. **flawed** adj **flawless** adj

flax n plant grown for its stem fibres and seeds; its fibres, spun into linen thread. **flaxen** adj (of hair) pale yellow.

flay v strip the skin off, esp. by whipping; criticize severely.

flea n small wingless jumping bloodsucking insect. **flea market** market for cheap goods. **fleapit** n Informal shabby cinema or theatre.

fleck n small mark, streak, or speck. ◆ v speckle.

fled v past of FLEE.

fledged adj (of young birds) able to fly; (of people) fully trained. **fledgling**, **fledgeling** n young bird. ◆ adj new,

inexperienced.

flee v **fleeing**, **fled** run away (from).

fleece n sheep's coat of wool; sheepskin used as a lining for coats etc. ◆ v defraud or overcharge. **fleecy** adj made of or like fleece.

fleet[1] n number of warships organized as a unit; number of vehicles under the same ownership.

fleet[2] adj swift in movement. **fleeting** adj rapid and soon passing. **fleetingly** adv

flesh n soft part of a human or animal body; Informal excess fat; meat of animals as opposed to fish or fowl; thick soft part of a fruit or vegetable; human body as opposed to the soul. ◆ adj yellowish-pink. **in the flesh** in person, actually present. **one's own flesh and blood** one's family. **fleshly** adj carnal; worldly. **fleshy** adj plump; like flesh. **flesh wound** wound affecting only superficial tissue.

fleur-de-lis, **fleur-de-lys** [flur-de-lee] n, pl **fleurs-de-lis**, **fleurs-de-lys** heraldic lily with three petals.

flew v past tense of FLY[1].

flex v bend. ◆ n Brit electric cord. **flexible** adj easily bent; adaptable. **flexibly** adv **flexibility** n **flexitime** n system permitting variation in starting and finishing times of work.

flibbertigibbet n flighty gossiping person.

flick v touch or strike lightly. ◆ n tap or quick stroke. ◆ pl Slang the cinema. **flick knife** knife with a spring-loaded blade which shoots out when a button is pressed. **flick through** v look at (a book or magazine) quickly or idly.

flicker v shine unsteadily or intermittently; move quickly to and fro. ◆ n unsteady brief light; brief faint indication.

flier n see FLY[1].

flight[1] n act or manner of flying through the air; journey by air; group of birds or aircraft flying together; aircraft flying on a scheduled journey; set of stairs between two landings; stabilizing feathers or plastic fins on an arrow or dart. **flightless** adj (of certain birds or insects) unable to fly. **flight deck** crew compartment in an airliner; runway deck on an aircraft carrier. **flight recorder** electronic device in an aircraft storing information about its flight.

flight² *n* act of running away.

flighty *adj* **flightier, flightiest** frivolous and fickle.

flimsy *adj* **-sier, -siest** not strong or substantial; thin; unconvincing, weak. **flimsily** *adv* **flimsiness** *n*

flinch *v* draw back or wince, as from pain. **flinch from** *v* shrink from.

fling *v* **flinging, flung** throw, send, or move forcefully or hurriedly. ◆ *n* spell of self-indulgent enjoyment; brief romantic or sexual relationship. **fling oneself into** (start to) do with great vigour.

flint *n* hard grey stone; piece of this; small piece of an iron alloy producing a spark when struck, as in a cigarette lighter. **flinty** *adj* cruel; of or like flint.

flip *v* **flipping, flipped** flick; turn (something) over; *Slang* fly into an emotional state (also **flip one's lid**). ◆ *n* snap or tap; alcoholic drink containing beaten egg. ◆ *adj Informal* flippant. **flipper** *n* limb of a sea animal adapted for swimming; one of a pair of paddle-like rubber devices worn on the feet to help in swimming. **flip-flop** *n* rubber-soled sandal held on by a thong between the big toe and the next toe. **flip side** less important side of a record. **flip through** *v* look at (a book or magazine) quickly or idly.

flippant *adj* treating serious things lightly. **flippantly** *adv* **flippancy** *n*

flirt *v* behave amorously without emotional commitment; consider lightly, toy (with). ◆ *n* person who flirts. **flirtation** *n* **flirtatious** *adj*

flit *v* **flitting, flitted** move lightly and rapidly; *Informal* depart hurriedly and secretly. ◆ *n* act of flitting.

flitch *n* side of bacon.

flitter *v, n* same as FLUTTER.

float *v* rest on the surface of liquid; move lightly and freely; move about aimlessly; launch (a company); offer for sale on the stock market; allow (a currency) to fluctuate against other currencies. ◆ *n* inflatable object used to help people to swim; indicator on a fishing line that moves when a fish bites; small delivery vehicle; motor vehicle carrying a tableau in a parade; sum of money used for minor expenses or to provide change. **floating** *adj* moving about, changing,

e.g. *floating population*; (of a voter) not committed to one party. **flotation** *n* launching or financing of a business enterprise.

flocculent *adj* like tufts of wool.

flock¹ *n* number of animals of one kind together; large group of people; *Christianity* congregation. ◆ *v* gather in a crowd.

flock² *n* very small tufts of wool giving a raised pattern on wallpaper; wool or cotton waste used as stuffing.

floe *n* sheet of floating ice.

flog *v* **flogging, flogged** beat with a whip, stick, etc.; *Slang* sell. **flogging** *n*

flood *n* overflow of water onto a normally dry area; large amount of water; rising of the tide. ◆ *v* cover or become covered with water; fill to overflowing; come in large numbers or quantities. **floodgate** *n* gate used to control the flow of water. **floodlight** *n* lamp that casts a broad intense beam of light. ◆ *v* **-lighting, -lit** illuminate by floodlight.

floor *n* lower surface of a room; level of a building; flat bottom surface; (right to speak in) a legislative hall. ◆ *v* *Informal* disconcert or defeat; knock down. **floored** *adj* covered with a floor. **flooring** *n* material for floors. **floor show** entertainment in a nightclub.

floozy *n, pl* **-zies** *Slang* disreputable woman.

flop *v* **flopping, flopped** bend, fall, or collapse loosely or carelessly; *Informal* fail. ◆ *n* flopping movement; *Informal* failure. **floppy** *adj* hanging downwards, loose. **floppiness** *n* **floppy disk** *Computers* flexible magnetic disk that stores information.

flora *n* plants of a given time or place. **floral** *adj* consisting of or decorated with flowers.

floret [flaw-ret] *n* small flower forming part of a composite flower head.

floribunda *n* type of rose whose flowers grow in large clusters.

florid *adj* with a red or flushed complexion; ornate.

florin *n* former British coin equivalent to ten pence.

florist *n* seller of flowers.

floss *n* fine silky fibres.

flotilla *n* fleet of small ships; small

fleet.

flotsam n floating wreckage. **flotsam and jetsam** odds and ends; homeless or vagrant people.

flounce¹ v go with emphatic movements. ◆ n flouncing movement.

flounce² n ornamental ruffle on a garment.

flounder¹ v move with difficulty, as in mud; behave or speak in a bungling or hesitating manner.

flounder² n edible flatfish.

flour n powder made by grinding grain, esp. wheat. ◆ v sprinkle with flour. **floury** adj **flouriness** n

flourish v be active, successful, or widespread; be at the peak of development; be at the peak of development; wave (something) dramatically. ◆ n dramatic waving motion; ornamental curly line in writing; extravagant action or part. **flourishing** adj

flout [rhymes with **out**] v deliberately disobey (a rule, law, etc.).

flow v (of liquid) move in a stream; (of blood or electricity) circulate; proceed smoothly; hang loosely; be abundant. ◆ n act, rate, or manner of flowing; continuous stream or discharge. **flow chart** diagram showing a sequence of operations in a process.

flower n part of a plant that produces seeds; plant grown for its colourful flowers; best or finest part. ◆ v produce flowers, bloom; come to prime condition. **in flower** with flowers open. **flowered** adj decorated with a floral design. **flowery** adj decorated with a floral design; (of language or style) elaborate. **flowerbed** n piece of ground for growing flowers on.

flown v past participle of FLY¹.

fl. oz. fluid ounce(s).

flu n short for INFLUENZA.

fluctuate v change frequently and erratically. **fluctuation** n

flue n passage or pipe for smoke or hot air.

fluent adj able to speak or write with ease; spoken or written with ease. **fluently** adv **fluency** n

fluff n soft fibres; down; Informal mistake. ◆ v make or become soft and light; Informal make a mistake. **fluffy** adj

fluid n liquid. ◆ adj able to flow or change shape easily. **fluidity** n **fluid ounce** one twentieth of a pint.

fluke¹ n accidental stroke of luck. **fluky** adj

fluke² n flat triangular point of an anchor; lobe of a whale's tail.

fluke³ n parasitic worm.

flume n narrow sloping channel for water.

flummox v perplex or bewilder.

flung v past of FLING.

flunk v Informal fail.

flunky, flunkey n, pl **flunkies, flunkeys** manservant who wears a livery; servile person.

fluorescence n emission of light from a substance bombarded by particles, such as electrons, or by radiation. **fluorescent** adj **fluoresce** v exhibit fluorescence.

fluoride n compound containing fluorine. **fluoridate** v add fluoride to (water) as protection against tooth decay. **fluoridation** n

fluorine n toxic yellow gas, most reactive of all the elements.

fluorspar n mineral consisting of calcium fluoride.

flurry n, pl **-ries** sudden commotion; squall or gust of rain, wind, or snow. ◆ v **-rying, -ried** fluster.

flush¹ v blush; send water through (a toilet or pipe) so as to clean it; elate. ◆ n blush; rush of water; excitement or elation.

flush² adj level with the surrounding surface; Informal having plenty of money.

flush³ n (in card games) hand all of one suit.

flush⁴ v drive out of a hiding place.

fluster v make nervous or upset. ◆ n nervous or upset state.

flute n wind instrument consisting of a tube with sound holes and a mouth hole in the side; decorative groove; tall thin wineglass. **fluted** adj having decorative grooves.

flutter v wave rapidly; flap the wings; move quickly and irregularly; (of the heart) beat abnormally quickly. ◆ n flapping movement; nervous agitation; Informal small bet; abnormally fast heartbeat.

fluvial [flew-vee-al] adj of rivers.

flux *n* constant change or instability; flow or discharge; substance mixed with metal to assist in fusion.

fly[1] *v* **flying, flew, flown** move through the air on wings or in an aircraft; control the flight of; float, flutter, display, or be displayed in the air; transport or be transported by air; move quickly or suddenly; (of time) pass rapidly; flee. ◆ *n, pl* **flies** (often pl.) fastening at the front of trousers; flap forming the entrance to a tent. ◆ *pl* space above a stage, used for storage. **flyer, flier** *n* small advertising leaflet; aviator. **flyleaf** *n* blank leaf at the beginning or end of a book. **flyover** *n Brit* road passing over another by a bridge. **flywheel** *n* heavy wheel regulating the speed of a machine.

fly[2] *n, pl* **flies** two-winged insect, esp. the housefly. **flyblown** *adj* covered with bluebottle eggs. **flycatcher** *n* small insect-eating songbird. **flyfishing** *n* fishing with an artificial fly as a lure. **flypaper** *n* paper with a sticky poisonous coating, used to kill flies. **flyweight** *n* boxer weighing up to 112lb (professional) or 51kg (amateur).

flying *adj* hurried, brief. **flying boat** aircraft fitted with floats instead of landing wheels. **flying buttress** *Archit* buttress supporting a wall by an arch. **flying colours** conspicuous success, e.g. *pass with flying colours*. **flying fish** fish with winglike fins used for gliding above the water. **flying fox** large fruiteating bat. **flying saucer** unidentified disc-shaped flying object, supposedly from outer space. **flying squad** small group of police, soldiers, etc., ready to act quickly. **flying start** very good start.

FM frequency modulation.

foal *n* young of a horse or related animal. ◆ *v* give birth to a foal.

foam *n* mass of small bubbles on a liquid; frothy saliva; light spongelike solid used for insulation, packing, etc. ◆ *v* produce foam. **foamy** *adj*

fob[1] *n* short watch chain; small pocket in a waistcoat.

fob[2] *v* **fobbing, fobbed** (foll. by *off*) pretend to satisfy (a person) with lies or excuses; sell or pass off (something inferior) as valuable.

fo'c's'le *n* same as FORECASTLE.

focus *v* **-cusing, -cused** *or* **-cussing, -cussed** adjust one's eyes or an instrument so that an image becomes clear; concentrate (on). ◆ *n, pl* **-cuses, -ci** [-sye] point at which light or sound waves converge; state of an optical image when it is clearly defined; state of an instrument producing such an image; centre of interest or activity. **focus group** group of people gathered by a market-research company to discuss and assess a product or service. **focal** *adj* of or at a focus.

fodder *n* feed for livestock.

foe *n* enemy, opponent.

foetid *adj* same as FETID.

foetus *n, pl* **-tuses** same as FETUS.

fog *n* mass of condensed water vapour in the lower air, often greatly reducing visibility. ◆ *v* **fogging, fogged** cover with steam. **foggy** *adj* **foghorn** *n* large horn sounded to warn ships in fog.

fogy, fogey *n, pl* **-gies, -geys** oldfashioned person.

foible *n* idiosyncrasy.

foil[1] *v* ruin (someone's plan).

foil[2] *n* metal in a thin sheet; anything which sets off another thing to advantage.

foil[3] *n* light slender flexible sword tipped with a button.

foist *v* (usu. foll. by *on*) force or impose on.

fold[1] *v* bend so that one part covers another; interlace (the arms); *Lit* clasp (in the arms); *Cooking* mix gently; *Informal* fail. ◆ *n* folded piece or part; mark, crease, or hollow made by folding. **folder** *n* piece of folded cardboard for loose papers.

fold[2] *n* enclosure for sheep; church or its members.

foliage *n* leaves. **foliate** *adj* having leaves; leaflike. **foliation** *n* process of producing leaves.

folio *n, pl* **-lios** sheet of paper folded in half to make two leaves of a book; book made up of such sheets; page number.

folk *n* people in general; race of people; *Informal* folk music. ◆ *pl* relatives. **folksy** *adj* simple and unpretentious. **folk dance** traditional country dance. **folklore** *n* traditional beliefs and stories of a people. **folk song** song handed down among the common people; modern song like this. **folk singer**

follicle n small cavity in the body, esp. one from which a hair grows.

follow v go or come after; be a logical or natural consequence of; keep to the course or track of; act in accordance with; accept the ideas or beliefs of; understand; have a keen interest in. **follower** n disciple or supporter. **following** adj about to be mentioned; next in time. ♦ n group of supporters. ♦ prep as a result of. **follow up** v investigate; do a second, often similar, thing after (a first). **follow-up** n something done to reinforce an initial action.

folly n, pl -lies foolishness; foolish action or idea; useless extravagant building.

foment [foam-ent] v encourage or stir up (trouble). **fomentation** n

fond adj tender, loving; unlikely to be realized, e.g. a fond hope; indulgent. **fond of** having a liking for. **fondly** adv **fondness** n

fondant n (sweet made from) flavoured paste of sugar and water.

fondle v caress.

fondue n Swiss dish typically of a hot melted cheese sauce into which pieces of bread are dipped.

font n bowl in a church for baptismal water.

fontanelle n soft membranous gap between the bones of a baby's skull.

food n what one eats, solid nourishment. **foodie** n Informal gourmet. **foodstuff** n substance used as food.

fool[1] n person lacking sense or judgment; person made to appear ridiculous; Hist jester, clown. ♦ v deceive (someone). **foolish** adj unwise, silly, or absurd. **foolishly** adv **foolishness** n **foolery** n foolish behaviour. **fool around** v act or play irresponsibly or aimlessly. **foolproof** adj unable to fail.

fool[2] n dessert of puréed fruit mixed with cream.

foolhardy adj recklessly adventurous. **foolhardiness** n

foolscap n size of paper, 13 or 13.5

by 16 or 17 inches (33 or 44 by 41 or 43 centimetres).

foot n, pl **feet** part of the leg below the ankle; unit of length of twelve inches (0.3048 metre); lowest part of anything; unit of poetic rhythm; Obs infantry. **foot the bill** pay the entire cost. **footage** n amount of film used. **foot-and-mouth disease** infectious viral disease of sheep, cattle, etc. **footbridge** n bridge for pedestrians. **footfall** n sound of a footstep. **foothills** pl n hills at the foot of a mountain. **foothold** n small place giving a secure grip for the foot; secure position from which progress may be made. **footlights** pl n lights across the front of a stage. **footloose** adj free from ties. **footman** n male servant in livery. **footnote** n note printed at the foot of a page. **footprint** n mark left by a foot. **footsore** adj having sore or tired feet. **footstep** n step in walking; sound made by walking. **footstool** n low stool used to rest the feet on while sitting. **footwear** n anything worn to cover the feet. **footwork** n skilful use of the feet, as in sport or dancing.

football n game played by two teams, each side attempting to kick, pass, or carry a ball across a goal line in order to score points; rugby; Brit soccer. **footballer** n **football pools** Brit form of gambling on the results of football matches.

footing n secure grip by or for the feet; basis, foundation; relationship between people.

footsie n Informal flirtation involving the touching together of feet.

fop n man excessively concerned with fashion. **foppish** adj

for prep intended to be received or used by; in order to help or benefit; representing, e.g. speaking for the opposition; because of, e.g. I could not see for the fog; over a span of (time or distance); in the direction of, e.g. heading for the border; at a cost of; in favour of, e.g. vote for me. ♦ conj because. **for it** Informal liable for punishment.

forage [for-ridge] v search about (for). ♦ n food for cattle or horses.

foray n brief raid or attack; first attempt or new undertaking.

forbear v cease or refrain (from doing something). **forbearance** n tolerance, patience. **forbearing** adj

forbid v refuse to allow. **forbidden** adj **forbidding** adj severe.

force n strength or power; compulsion; *Physics* influence tending to produce a change in a physical system; mental or moral strength; person or thing with strength or influence; vehemence or intensity; group of people organized for a particular task or duty; body of troops, police, etc. ◆ v compel, make (someone) do something; acquire or produce through effort, strength, etc.; propel or drive; break open; impose or inflict; cause to grow at an increased rate; strain to the utmost. **in force** having legal validity; in great numbers. **forced** adj compulsory; false or unnatural; due to an emergency. **forceful** adj emphatic; effective. **forcefully** adv **forcefulness** n **forcible** adj involving physical force or violence; strong and emphatic. **forcibly** adv

forceps pl n surgical pincers.

ford n shallow place where a river may be crossed. ◆ v cross (a river) at a ford. **fordable** adj

fore adj in, at, or towards the front. ◆ n front part. **to the fore** in a conspicuous position.

fore- prefix before in time or rank, e.g. *forefather*; at the front, e.g. *forecourt*.

fore-and-aft adj located at both ends of a ship.

forearm[1] n arm from the wrist to the elbow.

forearm[2] v prepare beforehand.

forebear n ancestor.

foreboding n feeling that something bad is about to happen.

forecast v **-casting, -cast** or **-casted**. predict (weather, events, etc.). ◆ n prediction.

forecastle [foke-sl] n raised front part of a ship.

foreclose v take possession of (property bought with borrowed money which has not been repaid). **foreclosure** n

forecourt n courtyard or open space in front of a building.

forefather n ancestor.

forefinger n finger next to the thumb.

forefront n most active or conspicuous position; very front.

forego v same as FORGO.

foregoing adj going before, preceding. **foregone conclusion** inevitable result.

foreground n part of a view, esp. in a picture, nearest the observer.

forehand adj (of a stroke in tennis, squash, etc.) made with the palm of the hand forward. ◆ n such a stroke.

forehead n part of the face above the eyebrows.

foreign adj not of, or in, one's own country; relating to or connected with other countries; unfamiliar, strange; in an abnormal place or position, e.g. *foreign matter*. **foreigner** n

foreland n headland.

forelock n lock of hair falling over the forehead.

foreman n person in charge of a group of workers; leader of a jury.

foremast n mast nearest the bow of a ship.

foremost adj, adv first in time, place, or importance.

forename n first name.

forenoon n morning.

forensic [for-ren-sik] adj used in or connected with courts of law. **forensic medicine** use of medical knowledge for the purposes of the law.

foreplay n sexual stimulation before intercourse.

forerunner n person or thing that goes before, precursor.

foresee v see or know beforehand. **foreseeable** adj

foreshadow v show or indicate beforehand.

foreshore n part of the shore between high- and low-tide marks.

foreshorten v represent (an object) in a picture as shorter than it really is in accordance with perspective.

foresight n ability to anticipate and provide for future needs.

foreskin n fold of skin covering the tip of the penis.

forest n large area with a thick growth of trees. **forested** adj **forestry** n science of planting and caring for trees. **forester** n person skilled in forestry.

forestall v prevent or guard against in advance.

foretaste n early limited experience of something to come.

foretell v tell or indicate beforehand.

forethought n thoughtful planning for future events.

forever adv without end; at all times; Informal for a long time.

forewarn v warn beforehand.

foreword n preface.

forfeit [for-fit] n thing lost or given up as a penalty for a fault or mistake. ◆ v lose as a forfeit. ◆ adj lost as a forfeit. **forfeiture** n

forgather v assemble.

forge¹ n place where metal is worked, smithy; furnace for melting metal. ◆ v make a fraudulent imitation of (something); shape (metal) by heating and hammering it; create (an alliance etc.).

forge² v advance steadily. **forge ahead** v take the lead.

forgery n, pl -**ries** something forged; act of making a fraudulent imitation. **forger** n

forget v -**getting**, -**got**, -**gotten** fail to remember; neglect; leave behind by mistake. **forgetful** adj tending to forget. **forgetfulness** n **forget-me-not** n plant with clusters of small blue flowers.

forgive v cease to blame or hold resentment against, pardon. **forgiveness** n

forgo v do without, give up.

forgot v past tense of FORGET. **forgotten** v past participle of FORGET.

fork n tool for eating food, with prongs and a handle; large similarly-shaped tool for digging or lifting; point where a road, river, etc. divides into branches; one of the branches. ◆ v branch; take one or other branch at a fork in the road; pick up, dig, etc. with a fork. **forked** adj **fork-lift truck** vehicle with a forklike device at the front which can be raised or lowered to move loads. **fork out** v Informal pay.

forlorn adj forsaken and unhappy. **forlorn hope** hopeless enterprise. **forlornly** adv

form n shape or appearance; mode in which something appears; type or kind; printed document with spaces for details; physical or mental condition; previous record of an athlete, racehorse, etc.; class in school; procedure or etiquette; bench; hare's nest. ◆ v give a (particular) shape to or take a (particular) shape; come or bring into existence; make or be made; train; acquire or develop; be an element of. **formless** adj **formation** n forming; thing formed; structure or shape; arrangement of people or things acting as a unit. **formative** adj shaping; of or relating to development.

formal adj of or characterized by established conventions of ceremony and behaviour; of or for formal occasions; stiff in manner; organized; symmetrical. **formally** adv **formality** n requirement of custom or etiquette; necessary procedure without real importance. **formalize** v make official or formal.

formaldehyde [for-mal-de-hide] n colourless pungent gas used to make formalin. **formalin** n solution of formaldehyde in water, used as a disinfectant or a preservative for biological specimens.

format n size and shape of a publication; style in which something is arranged. ◆ v -**matting**, -**matted** arrange in a format.

former adj of an earlier time, previous. **the former** first mentioned of two. **formerly** adv

Formica n ® kind of laminated sheet used to make heat-resistant surfaces.

formic acid n acid derived from ants and many plants.

formidable adj difficult to overcome or manage; extremely impressive. **formidably** adv

formula n, pl -**las**, -**lae** group of numbers, letters, or symbols expressing a scientific or mathematical rule; set form of words used in religion, law, etc.; method or rule for doing or producing something; specific category of vehicle in motor racing. **formulaic** adj **formulate** v plan or describe precisely and clearly. **formulation** n

fornicate v have sexual intercourse

without being married. **fornication** n **fornicator** n

forsake v -saking, -sook, -saken withdraw support or friendship from; give up, renounce.

forsooth adv Obs indeed.

forswear v renounce or reject.

forsythia [for-syth-ee-a] n shrub with yellow flowers in spring.

fort n fortified building or place. **hold the fort** Informal keep things going during someone's absence.

forte[1] [for-tay] n thing at which a person excels.

forte[2] adv Music loudly.

forth adv forwards, out, or away.

forthcoming adj about to appear or happen; available; (of a person) communicative.

forthright adj outspoken.

forthwith adv at once.

fortieth adj, n see FOUR.

fortify v -fying, -fied make (a place) defensible, as by building walls; strengthen; add alcohol to (wine) to make sherry or port; add vitamins etc. to (food). **fortification** n

fortissimo adv Music very loudly.

fortitude n calm and patient courage in adversity or pain.

fortnight n two weeks. **fortnightly** adv, adj

FORTRAN n Computers programming language for mathematical and scientific purposes.

fortress n large fort or fortified town.

fortuitous [for-tyew-it-uss] adj happening by (lucky) chance. **fortuitously** adv **fortuity** n

fortunate adj having good luck; occurring by good luck. **fortunately** adv

fortune n luck, esp. when favourable; power regarded as influencing human destiny; wealth. ◆ pl person's destiny. **fortune-teller** n person who claims to predict the future of others.

forty adj, n see FOUR.

forty-ninth parallel n Informal border between Canada and the US.

forum n meeting or medium for open discussion or debate.

forward adj directed or moving ahead; in, at, or near the front; presumptuous; well developed or advanced; relating to the future. ◆ n attacking player in various team games, such as football or hockey. ◆ v send (a letter etc.) on to an ultimate destination; advance or promote. ◆ adv forwards. **forwardly** adv **forwardness** n **forwards** adv towards or at a place further ahead in space or time; towards the front.

fossil n hardened remains of a prehistoric animal or plant preserved in rock. **fossilize** v turn into a fossil; become out-of-date or inflexible. **fossilization** n **fossil fuel** fuel, like coal and oil, found in the remains of prehistoric organisms.

foster v bring up (a child not one's own); promote the growth or development of. ◆ adj of or involved in fostering a child.

fought v past of FIGHT.

foul adj loathsome or offensive; stinking or dirty; (of language) obscene or vulgar; unfair. ◆ n Sport violation of the rules. ◆ v make dirty or polluted; make or become entangled or clogged; Sport commit a foul against (an opponent). **fall foul of** come into conflict with. **foully** adv **foulness** n **foul-mouthed** adj (habitually) using foul language. **foul play** unfair conduct, esp. involving violence.

found[1] v past of FIND.

found[2] v establish or bring into being; lay the foundation of; (foll. by on or upon) have a basis (in). **founder** n **foundation** n basis or base; act of founding; institution supported by an endowment; cosmetic used as a base for make-up. ◆ pl part of a building or wall below the ground.

found[3] v cast (metal or glass) by melting and setting in a mould; make (articles) by this method. **founder** n **foundry** n place where metal is melted and cast.

founder v break down or fail; (of a ship) sink; stumble or fall.

foundling n abandoned infant.

fount n Lit fountain; source; set of printing type of one style and size.

fountain n pool or structure from which a jet or water spurts; jet of water; source. **fountainhead** n source. **fountain pen** pen supplied with ink from a container inside it.

four adj, n one more than three. ♦ n (crew of) four-oared rowing boat. **on all fours** on hands and knees. **fourth** adj, n (of) number four in a series. ♦ n quarter. **fourthly** adv **foursome** n group of four people. **fourteen** adj, n four and ten. **fourteenth** adj, n **forty** adj, n four times ten. **fortieth** adj, n **fourth dimension** time. **fourth estate** the press. **four-letter word** short obscene word referring to sex or excrement. **four-poster** n bed with four posts supporting a canopy.

fowl n domestic cock or hen; any bird used for food or hunted as game. ♦ v hunt wild birds. **fowler** n

fox n reddish-brown bushy-tailed animal of the dog family; its fur; cunning person. ♦ v Informal perplex or deceive. **foxy** adj **foxglove** n tall plant with purple or white flowers. **foxhole** n Mil small pit dug for protection. **foxhound** n dog bred for hunting foxes. **fox terrier** small short-haired terrier. **foxtrot** n ballroom dance with slow and quick steps; music for this.

foyer [foy-ay] n entrance hall in a theatre, cinema, or hotel.

fracas [frak-ah] n, pl **-cas** noisy quarrel.

fraction n numerical quantity that is not a whole number; fragment, piece; Chem substance separated by distillation. **fractional** adj **fractionally** adv

fractious adj easily angered.

fracture n breaking, esp. of a bone. ♦ v break.

fragile adj easily broken or damaged; in a weakened physical state. **fragility** n

fragment n piece broken off; incomplete piece. ♦ v break into pieces or parts. **fragmentary** adj **fragmentation** n

fragrant adj sweet-smelling. **fragrantly** adv **fragrance** n pleasant smell; perfume, scent.

frail adj physically weak; easily damaged. **frailty** n

frame n structure giving shape or support; enclosing case or border, as round a picture; person's build; individual exposure on a strip of film; individual game of snooker in a match. ♦ v put into a frame; put together, construct; put into words; Slang incriminate (a person) on a false charge. **frame of mind** mood, attitude. **frame-up** n Slang false incrimination. **framework** n supporting structure.

franc n standard monetary unit of Switzerland.

franchise n right to vote; authorization to sell a company's goods.

Franciscan n, adj (friar or nun) of a Christian religious order founded by St Francis of Assisi.

francization n practice of making French the main language in the workplace, esp. in Quebec.

Franco- combining form of France or the French.

Francophone n native speaker of French.

frangipani [fran-jee-pah-nee] n fragrant tropical American shrub.

frank adj honest and straightforward; outspoken or blunt. ♦ v put a mark on (a letter) to allow it delivery. ♦ n official mark on a letter allowing delivery. **frankly** adv **frankness** n

frankfurter n smoked sausage.

frankincense n aromatic gum resin burned as incense.

frantic adj distracted with rage, grief, joy, etc.; hurried and disorganized. **frantically** adv

fraternal adj of a brother, brotherly. **fraternally** adv **fraternity** n group of people with shared interests, aims, etc.; brotherhood; male social club at college. **fraternize** v associate on friendly terms. **fraternization** n **fratricide** n crime of killing one's brother; person who does this.

Frau [rhymes with **how**] n German title, equivalent to Mrs. **Fräulein** [froy-line] n German title, equivalent to Miss.

fraud n (criminal) deception, swindle; person who acts in a deceitful way. **fraudulent** adj **fraudulence** n

fraught [frawt] adj tense or anxious. **fraught with** involving, filled with.

fray[1] v make or become ragged at the edge; become strained.

fray[2] n noisy quarrel or conflict.

frazzle n Informal exhausted state.

freak n abnormal person or thing;

person who is excessively enthusiastic about something. ◆ *adj* abnormal. **freakish** *adj* **freak out** *v Slang* (cause to) be in a heightened emotional state.

freckle *n* small brown spot on the skin. **freckled** *adj* marked with freckles.

free *adj* **freer, freest** able to act at will, not compelled or restrained; not subject (to); independent; provided without charge; generous, lavish; not in use; (of a person) not busy; not fixed or joined. ◆ *v* **freeing, freed** release, liberate; remove (obstacles, pain, etc.) from; make available or usable. **freely** *adv* **freedom** *n* being free. **freebooter** *n* pirate. **free fall** part of a parachute descent before the parachute opens. **free-for-all** *n Informal* brawl. **freehand** *adj* drawn without guiding instruments. **free hand** unrestricted freedom to act. **freehold** *n* tenure of land for life without restrictions. **freeholder** *n* **free house** *Brit* public house not bound to sell only one brewer's products. **freelance** *adj, n* (of) self-employed person doing specific pieces of work for various employers. **freeloader** *n Slang* habitual scrounger. **Freemason** *n* member of a secret fraternity pledged to help each other. **free-range** *adj* kept or produced in natural conditions. **freeway** *n* highway. **freewheel** *v* travel downhill on a bicycle without pedalling.

-free *adj combining form* without, e.g. *a trouble-free journey.*

freesia *n* plant with fragrant tubular flowers.

freeze *v* **freezing, froze, frozen** change from a liquid to a solid by the reduction of temperature, as water to ice; preserve (food etc.) by extreme cold; (cause to) be very cold; become motionless with fear, shock, etc.; fix (prices or wages) at a particular level; ban the exchange or collection of (loans, assets, etc.). ◆ *n* period of very cold weather; freezing of prices or wages. **freezer** *n* insulated cabinet for cold-storage of perishable foods. **freeze-dry** *v* preserve (food) by rapid freezing and drying in a vacuum. **freeze-up** *n* freezing of watercourses and wetlands during fall and winter.

freight [**frate**] *n* commercial transport of goods; cargo transported; cost of this. ◆ *v* send by freight. **freighter** *n* ship or aircraft for transporting goods.

French *n* language of France. ◆ *adj* of France, its people, or their language. **French bread** white bread in a long thin crusty loaf. **French dressing** salad dressing of oil and vinegar. **French fries** thin strips of potato, fried. **French horn** brass wind instrument with a coiled tube. **French polish** shellac varnish for wood. **French window** window extending to floor level, used as a door.

frenetic [**frin-net-ik**] *adj* uncontrolled. **frenetically** *adv*

frenzy *n, pl* **-zies** violent mental derangement; wild excitement. **frenzied** *adj* **frenziedly** *adv*

frequent *adj* happening often; habitual. ◆ *v* visit habitually. **frequently** *adv* **frequency** *n* rate of occurrence; *Physics* number of times a wave repeats itself in a given time.

fresco *n, pl* **-coes, -cos** watercolour painting done on wet plaster on a wall.

fresh *adj* newly made, acquired, etc.; novel, original; most recent; further, additional; (of food) not preserved; (of water) not salty; (of weather) invigorating; not tired; *Informal* impudent. **freshly** *adv* **freshness** *n* **freshen** *v* **freshman, fresher** *n* first-year student.

fret[1] *v* **fretting, fretted** be worried. **fretful** *adj* irritable.

fret[2] *n* small bar on the fingerboard of a guitar etc. **fret saw** fine saw with a narrow blade, used for fretwork. **fretwork** *n* decorative carving in wood.

Freudian [**froy-dee-an**] *adj* of or relating to the psychoanalyst Sigmund Freud or his theories.

friable [**fry-a-bl**] *adj* easily crumbled. **friability** *n*

friar *n* member of a male Roman Catholic religious order. **friary** *n* house of friars.

fricassee *n* stewed meat served in a thick sauce.

friction *n* rubbing; resistance met with by a body moving over another; clash of wills or personalities. **frictional** *adj*

Friday n sixth day of the week. **Good Friday** Friday before Easter.

fridge n short for REFRIGERATOR.

fried v past of FRY[1].

friend n person whom one knows well and likes; supporter; **(F-)** Quaker. **friendly** adj showing or expressing liking; not hostile, on the same side. - **friendly** combining form good or easy for the person or thing specified, e.g. user-friendly. **friendly fire** n Military firing by one's own side, esp when it harms one's own personnel. **friendliness** n **friendless** adj **friendship** n

Friesian [free-zhan] n Brit Holstein.

frieze [freeze] n ornamental band on a wall.

frigate [frig-it] n medium-sized fast warship.

fright n sudden fear or alarm; sudden alarming shock; Informal grotesque person. **frighten** v scare or terrify; force (someone) to do something from fear. **frightening** adj **frightful** adj horrifying; Informal very great. **frightfully** adv

frigid [frij-id] adj (of a woman) sexually unresponsive; very cold; excessively formal. **frigidly** adv **frigidity** n

frill n gathered strip of fabric attached at one edge. ◆ pl superfluous decorations or details. **frilled** adj **frilly** adj

fringe n hair cut short over the forehead; ornamental edge of hanging threads, tassels, etc.; outer edge; less important parts of an activity or group. ◆ v decorate with a fringe. ◆ adj (of theatre) unofficial. **fringed** adj **fringe benefit** benefit given in addition to a regular salary.

frippery n, pl -peries useless ornamentation; trivia.

frisk v move or leap playfully; Informal search (a person) for concealed weapons etc. **frisky** adj lively or high-spirited. **friskily** adv

frisson [frees-sonn] n shiver of fear or excitement.

fritter n piece of food fried in batter.

fritter away v waste.

frivolous adj not serious or sensible; enjoyable but trivial. **frivolously** adv **frivolity** n

frizz v form (hair) into stiff wiry curls. **frizzy** adj

frizzle v cook or heat until crisp and shrivelled.

frock n dress. **frock coat** man's skirted coat as worn in the 19th century.

frog n smooth-skinned tailless amphibian with long back legs used for jumping. **frog in one's throat** phlegm on the vocal cords, hindering speech. **frogman** n swimmer with a rubber suit and breathing equipment for working underwater. **frogmarch** v force (a resisting person) to move by holding his arms. **frogspawn** n jelly-like substance containing frog's eggs.

frolic v -icking, -icked run and play in a lively way. ◆ n lively and merry behaviour. **frolicsome** adj playful.

from prep indicating the point of departure, source, distance, cause, change of state, etc.

frond n long leaf or leaflike part of a fern, palm, or seaweed.

front n fore part; position directly before or ahead; seaside promenade; battle line or area; Meteorol dividing line between two different air masses; outward aspect; Informal cover for another, usu. criminal, activity; group with a common goal. ◆ v face (onto); be the presenter of (a television show). ◆ adj of or at the front. **frontal** adj **frontage** n façade of a building. **frontispiece** n illustration facing the title page of a book. **front bench** parliamentary leaders of the government or opposition. **front-bencher** n **frontrunner** n Informal person regarded as most likely to win a race, election, etc.

frontier n area of a country bordering on another.

frost n white frozen dew or mist; atmospheric temperature below freezing point. ◆ v become covered with frost. **frosted** adj (of glass) having a rough surface to make it opaque; covered with frosting. **frosting** n sugar icing. **frosty** adj characterized or covered by frost; unfriendly. **frostily** adv **frostiness** n **frostbite** n destruction of tissue, esp. of the fingers or ears, by cold. **frostbitten** adj **frost boil** bulge in road caused by freezing.

froth n mass of small bubbles. ◆ v

foam. **frothy** adj

frown v wrinkle one's brows in worry, anger, or thought; look disapprovingly (on). ◆ n frowning expression.

frowsy adj **-sier, -siest** unkempt.

froze v past tense of FREEZE. **frozen** v past participle of FREEZE.

fructify v **-fying, -fied** (cause to) bear fruit. **fructification** n

frugal [froo-gl] adj thrifty, sparing; meagre and inexpensive. **frugally** adv **frugality** n

fruit n part of a plant containing seeds, esp. if edible; any plant product useful to man; (often pl.) result of an action or effort. ◆ v bear fruit. **fruiterer** n person who sells fruit. **fruitful** adj useful or productive. **fruitfully** adv **fruition** [froo-ish-on] n fulfilment of something worked for or desired. **fruitless** adj useless or unproductive. **fruitlessly** adv **fruity** adj of or like fruit; (of a voice) mellow; *Informal* mildly bawdy. **fruit machine** coin-operated gambling machine.

frump n dowdy woman. **frumpy** adj

frustrate v upset or anger; hinder or prevent. **frustrated** adj **frustrating** adj **frustration** n

fry[1] v **frying, fried** cook or be cooked in fat or oil. ◆ n, pl **fries** dish of fried food; social occasion at which fried food is eaten.

fry[2] pl n young fishes. **small fry** young or insignificant people.

ft. foot; feet.

fuchsia [fyew-sha] n ornamental shrub with hanging flowers.

fuddle v cause to be intoxicated or confused. **fuddled** adj

fuddy-duddy n, pl **-dies**, adj *Informal* old-fashioned (person).

fudge[1] n soft caramel-like candy.

fudge[2] v avoid making a firm statement or decision.

fuel n substance burned or treated to produce heat or power; something that intensifies (a feeling etc.). ◆ v **fuelling, fuelled** provide with fuel.

fug n hot stale atmosphere. **fuggy** adj

fugitive [fyew-jit-iv] n person who flees, esp. from arrest or pursuit. ◆ adj fleeing; transient.

fugue [fyewg] n musical composition in which a theme is repeated in different parts.

fulcrum n, pl **-crums, -cra** pivot about which a lever turns.

fulfil v **-filling, -filled** bring about the achievement of (a desire or promise); carry out (a request or order); do what is required. **fulfilment** n **fulfil oneself** v achieve one's potential.

full adj containing as much or as many as possible; abundant in supply; having had enough to eat; plump; complete, whole; (of a garment) of ample cut; (of a sound or flavour) rich and strong. ◆ adv completely; directly; very. **fully** adv **fullness** n **in full** without shortening. **full-blooded** adj vigorous or enthusiastic. **full-blown** adj fully developed. **full moon** phase of the moon when it is visible as a fully illuminated disc. **full-scale** adj (of a plan) of actual size; using all resources. **full stop** punctuation mark (.) at the end of a sentence and after abbreviations.

fulmar n Arctic sea bird.

fulminate v (foll. by *against*) criticize angrily. **fulmination** n

fulsome adj insincerely excessive.

fumble v handle awkwardly; say awkwardly.

fume v be very angry; give out smoke or vapour; treat with fumes. ◆ n (usu. pl.) pungent smoke.

fumigate [fyew-mig-gate] v disinfect with fumes. **fumigation** n

fun n enjoyment or amusement. **make fun of** mock. **funny** adj comical, humorous; odd. **funny bone** part of the elbow where the nerve is near the surface. **funnily** adv

function n purpose something exists for; way something works; large or formal social event; *Math* quantity whose value depends on the varying value of another; series of operations done by a computer. ◆ v operate or work; (foll. by *as*) fill the role of. **functional** adj of or as a function; practical rather than decorative; in working order. **functionary** n official.

fund n stock of money for a special purpose; supply or store. ◆ pl money resources. ◆ v provide money to. **funding** n

fundamental adj essential or primary; basic. **fundamentals** pl n basic rules or facts. **fundamentally** adv **fundamentalism** n literal or strict

interpretation of a religion.
fundamentalist n, adj

funeral n ceremony of burying or cremating a dead person. **funerary** adj of or for a funeral. **funereal** [fyew-neer-ee-al] adj gloomy.

funfair n entertainment with machines to ride on and stalls.

fungus n, pl -gi, -guses plant without leaves, flowers, or roots, such as a mushroom or mould. **fungal, fongous** adj **fungicide** n substance that destroys fungi.

funicular [fyew-nik-yew-lar] n cable railway on a mountainside or cliff.

funk[1] n style of dance music with a strong beat. **funky** adj (of music) passionate or soulful.

funk[2] Informal ◆ n nervous or fearful state. ◆ v avoid (doing something) through fear.

funnel n cone-shaped tube for pouring liquids into a narrow opening; chimney of a ship or locomotive. ◆ v -nelling, -nelled (cause to) move through or as if through a funnel.

fur n soft hair of a mammal; animal skin with the fur left on; garment made of this; whitish coating on the tongue or inside a kettle. ◆ v cover or become covered with fur. **furry** adj **furrier** n dealer in furs.

furbish v smarten up.

furious adj very angry; violent or unrestrained. **furiously** adv

furl v roll up and fasten (a sail, umbrella, or flag).

furlong n eighth of a mile.

furlough [fur-loh] n leave of absence from military duty.

furnace n enclosed chamber containing a very hot fire.

furnish v fit up (a house or room) with furniture; (foll. by with) supply, provide. **furnishings** pl n furniture, carpets, and fittings. **furniture** n large movable articles such as chairs and wardrobes.

furore [fyew-ror-ee] n very excited or angry reaction.

furrow n trench made by a plow; groove. ◆ v make or become wrinkled; make furrows in.

further adv in addition; to a greater distance or extent. ◆ adj additional; more distant. ◆ v assist the progress of. **furthest** adv to the greatest distance or extent. ◆ adj most distant. **furtherance** n **furthermore** adv besides. **furthermost** adj most distant.

furtive adj sly and secretive. **furtively** adv

fury n, pl -ries wild anger; uncontrolled violence.

furze n gorse.

fuse[1] n cord containing an explosive for detonating a bomb.

fuse[2] v join or combine; melt with heat; unite by melting; (cause to) fail as a result of a blown fuse. ◆ n safety device for electric circuits, containing a wire that melts and breaks the connection when the circuit is overloaded. **fusible** adj **fusion** n melting; product of fusing; combination of two atoms with release of energy; popular music blending styles, esp. jazz and funk. ◆ adj of a style of cooking that combines traditional Western techniques and ingredients with those used in Eastern cuisine.

fuselage [fyew-zill-lahzh] n body of an aircraft.

fusilier [fyew-zill-leer] n soldier of certain regiments. **fusillade** [fyew-zill-lade] n continuous discharge of firearms; outburst of criticism, questions, etc.

fuss n needless activity or worry; complaint or objection; great display of attention. ◆ v make a fuss. **fussy** adj inclined to fuss; overparticular; overelaborate. **fussily** adv **fussiness** n

fusty adj -tier, -tiest stale-smelling; behind the times. **fustiness** n

futile [fyew-tile] adj unsuccessful or useless. **futility** n

futon [foo-tonn] n Japanese padded quilt, laid on the floor as a bed.

future n time to come; what will happen; prospects. ◆ adj yet to come or be; of or relating to time to come; (of a verb tense) indicating that the action specified has not yet taken place. **futuristic** adj of a design appearing to belong to some future time.

fuzz[1] n mass of fine or curly hairs or fibres. **fuzzy** adj of, like, or covered with fuzz; blurred or indistinct; (of hair) tightly curled. **fuzzily** adv **fuzziness** n

fuzz² n Slang police(man).

G g

g gram(s); (acceleration due to) gravity.

gab n, v **gabbing, gabbed** Informal talk or chatter. **gift of the gab** eloquence. **gabby** adj Informal talkative.

gabardine, gaberdine n strong twill cloth used esp. for raincoats.

gabble v speak rapidly and indistinctly. ◆ n rapid indistinct speech.

gable n triangular upper part of a wall between sloping roofs. **gabled** adj

gad v **gadding, gadded. gad about, around** go around in search of pleasure. **gadabout** n pleasure-seeker.

gadfly n fly that bites cattle; constantly annoying person.

gadget n small mechanical device or appliance. **gadgetry** n gadgets.

Gael [gayl] n Gaelic-speaker. **Gaelic** [gal-lik] n Celtic language of Ireland and the Scottish Highlands. ◆ adj of the Gaels or their language.

gaff¹ n stick with an iron hook for landing large fish. ◆ v hook or land (a fish) with a gaff.

gaff² n **blow the gaff** Slang divulge a secret.

gaffe n social blunder.

gaffer n old man; Informal boss.

gag¹ v **gagging, gagged** stop up the mouth of (a person) with cloth etc.; deprive of free speech; retch; choke. ◆ n cloth etc. put into or tied across the mouth.

gag² n Informal joke.

gaga [gah-gah] adj Slang senile; crazy.

gage n thing given as security; formerly, something thrown down as a challenge to combat.

gaggle n flock of geese; Informal disorderly crowd.

gaiety n cheerfulness; merrymaking. **gaily** adv merrily; colourfully.

gain v acquire or obtain; win in competition; increase or improve; reach; (of a watch or clock) be or become too fast. ◆ n profit; increase or improvement. **gainful** adj useful or profitable. **gainfully** adv **gain on, upon** v get nearer to or catch up with.

gainsay v **-saying, -said** deny or contradict.

gait n manner of walking.

gaiter n cloth or leather covering for the lower leg.

gala [gah-la] n festival; competitive sporting event.

galaxy n, pl **-axies** system of stars; gathering of famous people. **galactic** adj

gale n strong wind; Informal loud outburst.

gall¹ [gawl] n Informal impudence; bitter feeling. **gall bladder** sac attached to the liver, storing bile. **gallstone** n hard growth in the gall bladder or its ducts.

gall² [gawl] n sore caused by chafing. ◆ v make sore by rubbing; annoy.

gall³ [gawl] n abnormal outgrowth on a tree or plant.

gallant adj brave and noble; (of a man) attentive to women. **gallantly** adv **gallantry** n

galleon n large three-masted sailing ship of the 15th–17th centuries.

gallery n, pl **-ries** room or building for displaying works of art; balcony in a church, theatre, etc.; long narrow room for a specific purpose, e.g. shooting gallery; passage in a mine.

galley n kitchen of a ship or aircraft; Hist ship propelled by oars, usu. rowed by slaves. **galley proof** printer's proof in long slip form. **galley slave** slave forced to row in a galley; Informal drudge.

Gallic adj French; of ancient Gaul.

gallium n soft grey metallic element used in semiconductors.

gallivant v go about in search of pleasure.

gallon n liquid measure of eight pints, equal to 4.55 litres.

gallop n horse's fastest pace; galloping. ◆ v **galloping, galloped** go or ride at a gallop; move or progress rapidly.

gallows n wooden structure used for hanging criminals.

Gallup poll n public opinion poll carried out by questioning a cross section of the population.

galore adv in plenty, e.g. presents galore.

galoshes pl n waterproof overshoes.

galumph v Informal leap or move about clumsily.

galvanic adj of or producing an electric current generated by chemical means; Informal stimulating or startling. **galvanize** v stimulate into action; coat (metal) with zinc.

gambit n opening line or move intended to secure an advantage; Chess opening move involving the sacrifice of a pawn.

gamble v play games of chance to win money; act on the expectation of something. ◆ n risky undertaking; bet or wager. **gambler** n **gambling** n

gamboge [gam-**boje**] n gum resin used as a yellow pigment and purgative.

gambol v -**bolling**, -**bolled** jump about playfully, frolic. ◆ n frolic.

game n amusement or pastime; contest for amusement; single period of play in a contest; scheme or trick; animals or birds hunted for sport or food; their flesh. ◆ v gamble. ◆ adj brave; willing. **gamer** n person who plays computer games. **gamely** adv **gaming** n gambling. **gamekeeper** n person employed to breed game and prevent poaching. **gamesmanship** n art of winning by cunning practices without actually cheating.

gamete [gam-**eet**] n Biol reproductive cell.

gamine [gam-**een**] n slim boyish young woman.

gamma n third letter of the Greek alphabet. **gamma ray** electromagnetic ray of shorter wavelength and higher energy than x-rays.

gammon n cured or smoked ham.

gamut n whole range or scale (of music etc.).

gander n male goose; Informal quick look.

gang n (criminal) group; organized group of workmen. **gangland** n criminal underworld. **gang up** v form an alliance (against).

gangling adj lanky and awkward.

ganglion n group of nerve cells; small harmless tumour.

gangplank n portable bridge for boarding or leaving a ship.

gangrene n decay of body tissue as a result of disease or injury interrupting blood supply. **gangrenous** adj

gangster n member of a criminal gang.

gangway n passage between rows of seats; gangplank.

gannet n large sea bird; Slang greedy person.

gantry n, pl -**tries** structure supporting something such as a crane or rocket.

gaol [jayl] n same as JAIL.

gap n break or opening; interruption or interval; divergence or difference. **gappy** adj

gape v stare in wonder; open the mouth wide; be or become wide open. **gaping** adj

garage n building used to house automobiles; place for the refuelling and repair of automobiles. ◆ v put or keep an automobile in a garage.

garb n clothes. ◆ v clothe.

garbage n waste matter. **garbage can** large usu. cylindrical container for household rubbish. **garbage collector** person whose job is to collect household rubbish.

garble v jumble (a story etc.).

garden n piece of land for growing flowers, fruit, or vegetables. ◆ pl ornamental park. ◆ v cultivate a garden. **gardener** n **gardening** n **garden centre** place selling plants and gardening equipment.

gardenia [gar-**deen**-ya] n large fragrant white waxy flower; shrub bearing this.

gargantuan adj huge.

gargle v wash the throat with (a liquid) by breathing out slowly through the liquid. ◆ n act or sound of gargling; liquid used for gargling.

gargoyle n waterspout carved in the form of a grotesque face, esp. on a church.

garish adj crudely bright or colourful. **garishly** adv **garishness** n

garland n wreath of flowers worn or hung as a decoration. ◆ v decorate with garlands.

garlic n pungent bulb of a plant of the onion family, used in cooking.

garment n article of clothing.

garner v collect or store.

garnet n red semiprecious stone.

garnish v decorate (food). ◆ n decoration for food.

garret n attic in a house.

garrison n troops stationed in a town or fort; fortified place. ◆ v station troops in.

garrotte n Spanish method of execution by strangling; cord or wire used for this. ◆ v kill by this method.

garrulous adj talkative. **garrulously** adv **garrulity** n

garter n band worn round the leg to hold up a sock or stocking.

gas n, pl **gases** or **gasses**. airlike substance that is not liquid or solid; fossil fuel in the form of a gas, used for heating; gaseous anesthetic; gasoline; Informal idle talk, boasting. ◆ v **gassing, gassed** poison or render unconscious with gas; Informal talk idly or boastfully. **gassy** adj filled with gas. **gaseous** adj of or like gas. **gasbag** n Informal person who talks too much. **gas chamber** airtight room which is filled with poison gas to kill people or animals. **gasholder, gasometer** [gas-som-it-er] n large tank for storing gas. **gas mask** mask with a chemical filter to protect the wearer against poison gas.

gash v make a long deep cut in. ◆ n long deep cut.

gasket n piece of rubber etc. placed between two metal surfaces to act as a seal.

gasoline n inflammable liquid obtained from petroleum, used as fuel in internal-combustion engines. **gasoline bomb** incendiary device consisting of a bottle filled with gasoline.

gasp v draw in breath sharply or with difficulty; utter breathlessly. ◆ n convulsive intake of breath.

gastric adj of the stomach. **gastritis** n inflammation of the stomach.

gastroenteritis n inflammation of the stomach and intestines.

gastronomy n art of good eating. **gastronomic** adj

gastropod n mollusc, such as a snail, with a single flattened muscular foot.

gate n movable barrier, usu. hinged, in a wall or fence; opening with a gate; any entrance or way in; (entrance money paid by) those attending a sporting event. **gate-crash** v enter (a party) uninvited. **gatehouse** n building at or above a gateway.

gateway n entrance with a gate; means of access, e.g. Bombay, gateway to India.

gâteau [gat-toe] n, pl **-teaux** [-toes] Brit rich elaborate cake.

gather v assemble; increase gradually; collect gradually; learn from information given; draw (material) into small tucks or folds; pick or harvest. **gathers** pl n gathered folds in material. **gathering** n assembly.

gauche [gohsh] adj socially awkward. **gaucheness** n **gaucherie** n awkwardness; gauche act.

gaucho [gow-choh] n, pl **-chos** S American cowboy.

gaudy adj **gaudier, gaudiest** vulgarly bright or colourful. **gaudily** adv **gaudiness** n

gauge [gayj] v measure the amount or condition of; estimate or judge. ◆ n scale or standard of measurement; measuring instrument; distance between the rails of a railway track.

gaunt adj lean and haggard; (of a place) desolate or bleak. **gauntness** n

gauntlet[1] n heavy glove with a long cuff. **throw down the gauntlet** offer a challenge.

gauntlet[2] n **run the gauntlet** be forced to run between, and be struck by, two rows of men, as a former military punishment; be exposed to criticism or unpleasant treatment.

gauze n transparent loosely-woven fabric; fine wire mesh. **gauzy** adj

gave v past tense of GIVE.

gavel [gahv-el] n small hammer banged on a table by a judge, auctioneer, or chairman to call for attention.

gavotte n old formal dance; music for this.

gawk v Slang stare stupidly. **gawky** adj clumsy or awkward. **gawkiness** n

gawp v Slang stare stupidly.

gay adj homosexual; carefree and merry; colourful. ◆ n homosexual. **gayness** n homosexuality.

gaze v look fixedly. ◆ n fixed look.

gazebo [gaz-zee-boh] n, pl **-bos**, **-boes** summerhouse with a good view.

gazelle n small graceful antelope.

gazette n official publication containing announcements. **gazetteer**

n (part of) a book that lists and describes places.

gazump *v* raise the price of a house after verbally agreeing it with (a prospective buyer).

GB Great Britain.

gear *n* set of toothed wheels connecting with another or with a rack to change the direction or speed of transmitted motion; mechanism for transmitting motion by gears; setting of a gear to suit engine speed, e.g. *first gear*; clothing or belongings; equipment. ◆ *v* adapt (one thing) to fit in with another. **in, out of gear** with the gear mechanism engaged or disengaged. **gearbox** *n* case enclosing a set of gears in a motor vehicle. **gear up** *v* prepare for an activity.

gecko *n*, *pl* **geckos**, **geckoes** small tropical lizard.

geese *n* plural of GOOSE.

geezer *n Informal* (old or eccentric) man.

Geiger counter [**guy**-ger] *n* instrument for detecting and measuring radiation.

geisha [**gay**-sha] *n*, *pl* **-sha**, **-shas** (in Japan) professional female companion for men.

gel [**jell**] *n* jelly-like substance. ◆ *v* **gelling**, **gelled** form a gel; *Informal* take on a definite form.

gelatin [**jel**-at-tin], **gelatine** *n* substance made by boiling animal bones; edible jelly made of this. **gelatinous** [**jel**-at-in-uss] *adj* of or like jelly.

geld *v* castrate. **gelding** *n* castrated horse.

gelid [**jel**-lid] *adj* very cold.

gelignite *n* type of dynamite used for blasting.

gem *n* precious stone or jewel; highly valued person or thing.

gen *n Informal* information. **gen up on** *v* **genning**, **genned** *Informal* make or become fully informed about.

gendarme [**zhahn**-darm] *n* member of the French police force.

gender *n* state of being male or female, sex; *Grammar* classification of nouns in certain languages as masculine, feminine, or neuter.

gene [**jean**] *n* part of a cell which determines inherited characteristics.

genealogy [jean-ee-**al**-a-gee] *n*, *pl* **-gies** (study of) the history and descent of a family or families. **genealogical** *adj* **genealogist** *n*

genera [**jen**-er-a] *n* plural of GENUS.

general *adj* common or widespread; of or affecting all or most; not specific; including or dealing with various or miscellaneous items; highest in authority or rank, e.g. *general manager*; true in most cases. ◆ *n* very senior army officer. **generally** *adv* **generality** *n* general principle; state of being general. **generalize** *v* draw general conclusions; speak in generalities; make widely known or used. **generalization** *n* **general delivery** post office department where a traveller's letters are kept until called for. **general election** election in which representatives are chosen for every constituency. **general practitioner** nonspecialist doctor serving a local area.

generate *v* produce or bring into being. **generative** *adj* capable of producing. **generator** *n* machine for converting mechanical energy into electrical energy.

generation *n* all the people born about the same time; average time between two generations (about 30 years); generating.

generic [jin-**ner**-ik] *adj* of a class, group, or genus. **generically** *adv*

generous *adj* free in giving; free from pettiness; plentiful. **generously** *adv* **generosity** *n*

genesis [**jen**-iss-iss] *n*, *pl* **-eses** [-iss-eez] beginning or origin.

genetic [jin-**net**-tik] *adj* of genes or genetics. **genetics** *n* study of heredity and variation in organisms. **geneticist** *n* **genetic engineering** alteration of the genetic structure of an organism for a particular purpose. **genetic fingerprinting** use of a person's unique DNA pattern for identification.

genial [**jean**-ee-al] *adj* cheerful and friendly. **genially** *adv* **geniality** *n*

genie [**jean**-ee] *n* (in fairy tales) a servant who appears by magic and grants wishes.

genital *adj* of the sexual organs or reproduction. **genitals**, **genitalia** [jen-it-**ail**-ya] *pl n* external sexual organs.

genitive *adj*, *n* (of) the grammatical

case indicating possession or association.

genius [jean-yuss] *n* (person with) exceptional ability in a particular field.

genocide [jen-no-side] *n* murder of a race of people.

genre [zhahn-ra] *n* style of literary, musical, or artistic work.

gent *Informal* ◆ *n* gentleman. ◆ *pl* men's public lavatory.

genteel *adj* affectedly proper and polite. **genteelly** *adv*

gentian [jen-shun] *n* mountain plant with deep blue flowers.

gentile *adj, n* non-Jewish (person).

gentle *adj* mild or kindly; not rough or severe; gradual; easily controlled, tame; noble or well-born. **gentleness** *n* **gently** *adv* **gentleman** *n* polite well-bred man; man of high social position; polite name for a man. **gentlemanly** *adj* **gentlewoman** *n fem*

gentry *n* people just below the nobility in social rank. **gentrification** *n* taking-over of a traditionally working-class area by middle-class incomers. **gentrify** *v*

genuflect *v* bend the knee as a sign of reverence or deference. **genuflection, genuflexion** *n*

genuine *adj* not fake; sincere. **genuinely** *adv* **genuineness** *n*

genus [jean-uss] *n, pl* **genera** group into which a family of animals or plants is divided; kind, type.

geocentric *adj* having the earth as a centre; measured as from the earth's centre.

geode *n* cavity lined with crystals within a rock.

geography *n* study of the earth's physical features, climate, population, etc. **geographer** *n* **geographical, geographic** *adj* **geographically** *adv*

geology *n* study of the earth's origin, structure, and composition. **geological** *adj* **geologically** *adv* **geologist** *n*

geometry *n* branch of mathematics dealing with points, lines, curves, and surfaces. **geometric, geometrical** *adj* **geometrically** *adv*

geopolitics *n* study of the effect of the geographical position of a country on its politics; global politics. **geopolitical** *adj*

georgette [jor-jet] *n* fine silky fabric.

Georgian *adj* of the time of any of the kings of Britain called George, esp. 1714–1830; of or from Georgia.

geostationary *adj* (of a satellite) orbiting so as to remain over the same point of the earth's surface.

geothermal *adj* of or using the heat in the earth's interior.

geranium *n* cultivated plant with red, pink, or white flowers.

gerbil [jer-bill] *n* burrowing desert rodent of Asia and Africa.

geriatrics *n* branch of medicine dealing with old age and its diseases. **geriatric** *adj, n* old (person).

germ *n* microbe, esp. one causing disease; beginning from which something may develop; simple structure that can develop into a complete organism. **germicide** *n* substance that kills germs. **germicidal** *adj*

german *adj* having the same parents, e.g. *brother-german*; being a first cousin, e.g. *cousin-german*.

German *adj* of Germany. ◆ *n* person from Germany; language of Germany, Austria, and parts of Switzerland. **German measles** contagious disease accompanied by a cough, sore throat, and red spots. **German shepherd dog** Alsatian.

germane *adj* **germane to** relevant to.

germinate *v* (cause to) sprout or begin to grow. **germination** *n* **germinal** *adj* of or in the earliest stage of development.

gerrymandering *n* division of voting constituencies in order to give an unfair advantage to one party.

gerund [jer-rund] *n* noun formed from a verb, such as *living*.

Gestapo *n* secret state police of Nazi Germany.

gestation *n* (period of) carrying of babies in the womb during pregnancy; developing of a plan or idea in the mind.

gesticulate *v* make expressive movements of the hands and arms. **gesticulation** *n*

gesture *n* movement to convey meaning; thing said or done to show one's feelings. ◆ *v* gesticulate.

get *v* **getting, got** obtain or receive;

bring or fetch; contract (an illness); (cause to) become as specified, e.g. *get wet*; understand; (often foll. by *to*) come (to) or arrive (at); go on board (a plane, bus, etc.); persuade; *Informal* annoy; *Informal* have the better of; be revenged on; receive a broadcast signal; prepare (a meal). **get across** *v* (cause to) be understood. **get at** *v* gain access to; imply or mean; criticize. **getaway** *adj, n* (used in) escape. **get by** *v* manage in spite of difficulties. **get off** *v* (cause to) avoid the consequences of, or punishment for, an action. **get off with** *v Informal* start a romantic or sexual relationship with. **get over** *v* recover from. **get through** *v* (cause to) succeed; contact by telephone; use up (money or supplies). **get through to** *v* make (a person) understand. **get-up** *n Informal* costume. **get up to** *v* be involved in.

geyser [geez-er] *n* spring that discharges steam and hot water; *Brit* domestic gas water heater.

ghastly *adj* -lier, -liest *Informal* very unpleasant; deathly pale; *Informal* horrible. **ghastliness** *n*

ghat *n* (in India) steps leading down to a river; mountain pass.

ghee [gee] *n* (in Indian cookery) clarified butter.

gherkin *n* small pickled cucumber.

ghetto *n, pl* -tos, -toes slum area inhabited by a deprived minority. **ghetto-blaster** *n Informal* large portable cassette-recorder.

ghillie *n* same as GILLIE.

ghost *n* disembodied spirit of a dead person; faint trace. ♦ *v* ghostwrite. **ghostly** *adj* **ghost town** deserted town. **ghostwrite** *v* write (a book or article) on behalf of another person who is credited as the author. **ghostwriter** *n*

ghoul [gool] *n* person with morbid interests; demon that eats corpses. **ghoulish** *adj*

GI *n Informal* US soldier.

giant *n* mythical being of superhuman size; very large person or thing. ♦ *adj* huge. **giantess** *n fem*

gibber [jib-ber] *v* speak rapidly and unintelligibly. **gibberish** *n* rapid unintelligible talk.

gibbet [jib-bit] *n* gallows.

gibbon [gib-bon] *n* agile tree-dwelling ape of S Asia.

gibbous *adj* (of the moon) more than half but less than fully illuminated.

gibe [jibe] *v, n* same as JIBE[1].

giblets [jib-lets] *pl n* gizzard, liver, heart, and neck of a fowl.

giddy *adj* -dier, -diest feeling unsteady on one's feet, as if about to faint; scatter-brained. **giddily** *adv* **giddiness** *n*

gift *n* present; natural talent. ♦ *v* present with. **gifted** *adj* talented.

gig[1] *n* single performance by pop or jazz musicians. ♦ *v* gigging, gigged play gigs.

gig[2] *n* light two-wheeled horse-drawn carriage.

gigantic *adj* enormous.

giggle *v* laugh nervously or foolishly. ♦ *n* such a laugh. **giggly** *adj*

gigolo [jig-a-lo] *n, pl* -los man paid by an older woman to be her escort or lover.

gigot *n* leg of lamb or mutton.

gild *v* gilding, gilded *or* gilt. put a thin layer of gold on; make falsely attractive. **gilt** *adj* gilded. ♦ *n* thin layer of gold used as decoration. **gilt-edged** *adj* denoting government stocks on which interest payments and final repayment are guaranteed.

gill [jill] *n* liquid measure of quarter of a pint, equal to 0.142 litres.

gillie *n* (in Scotland) attendant for hunting or fishing.

gills [gillz] *pl n* breathing organs in fish and other water creatures.

gimbals *pl n* set of pivoted rings which allow nautical instruments to remain horizontal at sea.

gimcrack [jim-krak] *adj* showy but cheap; shoddy.

gimlet [gim-let] *n* small tool with a screwlike tip for boring holes in wood. **gimlet-eyed** *adj* having a piercing glance.

gimmick *n* something designed to attract attention or publicity. **gimmickry** *n* **gimmicky** *adj*

gin[1] *n* alcoholic drink flavoured with juniper berries.

gin[2] *n* machine for separating seeds from raw cotton; wire noose used to trap small animals.

ginger *n* root of a tropical plant, used

as a spice; light orange-brown colour.

gingery adj **ginger ale, beer** fizzy ginger-flavoured soft drink.

gingerbread n moist cake flavoured with ginger. **ginger group** group within a larger group that agitates for a more active policy. **ginger snap** hard ginger-flavoured cookie.

gingerly adv cautiously. ◆ adj cautious.

gingham n cotton cloth, usu. checked or striped.

gingivitis [jin-jiv-**vite**-iss] n inflammation of the gums.

ginkgo [**gink**-go] n, pl -**goes** ornamental Chinese tree.

ginseng [**jin**-seng] n (root of) a plant believed to have tonic and energy-giving properties.

Gipsy n, pl -**sies** same as GYPSY.

giraffe n African ruminant mammal with a spotted yellow skin and long neck and legs.

gird v **girding, girded** or **girt**. put a belt round; secure with or as if with a belt; surround. **gird (up) one's loins** prepare for action.

girder n large metal beam.

girdle[1] n woman's elastic corset; belt; Anat encircling structure or part. ◆ v surround or encircle.

girl n female child; young woman. **girlhood** n **girlish** adj **girlie** adj Informal featuring photographs of naked or scantily clad women. **girlfriend** n girl or woman with whom a person is romantically or sexually involved; female friend.

giro [**jire**-oh] n, pl -**ros** Brit system of transferring money within a post office or bank directly from one account to another; Informal social security payment by giro cheque.

girt v past of GIRD.

girth n measurement round something; band round a horse to hold the saddle in position.

gist [jist] n substance or main point of a matter.

give v **giving, gave, given** present (something) to another person; transfer in exchange or payment; grant or provide; utter or emit; perform or do, e.g. give an interview; organize or host; sacrifice or devote; concede; yield or break under

pressure. ◆ n resilience or elasticity.

give away v donate as a gift; reveal; hand over (a bride) formally to her husband in a marriage ceremony. **giveaway** n unintentional disclosure. ◆ adj very cheap or free. **give in** v admit defeat. **give off** v emit. **give out** v distribute; emit; come to an end or fail. **give over** v set aside for a specific purpose; Informal cease. **give up** v acknowledge defeat; abandon.

gizzard n part of a bird's stomach.

glacé [**glass**-say] adj crystallized or candied.

glacier n slow-moving mass of ice formed by accumulated snow. **glacial** adj of ice or glaciers; very cold; unfriendly. **glaciated** adj covered with or affected by glaciers. **glaciation** n

glad adj **gladder, gladdest** pleased and happy; causing happiness. **glad to** very willing to (do something). **the glad eye** Informal an inviting or seductive glance. **gladly** adv **gladness** n **gladden** v make glad. **glad rags** Informal best clothes.

glade n open space in a forest.

gladiator n (in ancient Rome) man trained to fight in arenas to provide entertainment.

gladiolus n, pl -**lus**, -**li**, -**luses** garden plant with sword-shaped leaves.

glamour n alluring charm or fascination. **glamorous** adj alluring. **glamorize** v

glance n quick look. ◆ v look quickly. **glancing** adj hitting at an oblique angle. **glance off** v strike and be deflected off (an object) at an oblique angle.

gland n organ that produces and secretes substances in the body. **glandular** adj

glanders n contagious disease of horses.

glare v stare angrily; be unpleasantly bright. ◆ n angry stare; unpleasant brightness. **glaring** adj conspicuous; unpleasantly bright. **glaringly** adv

glasnost n policy of openness and accountability, developed in the USSR in the 1980s.

glass n hard brittle, usu. transparent substance made by melting sand; objects made of glass; tumbler; its contents; mirror; barometer. ◆ pl spectacles. **glassy** *adj* like glass; expressionless. **glassiness** *n* **glasshouse** *n* greenhouse; *Informal* army prison. **glass wool** fine glass fibres used for insulating.

glaucoma *n* eye disease.

glaze *v* fit or cover with glass; cover with a glassy substance; become glassy. ◆ *n* transparent coating; substance used for this. **glazier** *n* person who fits windows with glass.

gleam *n* small beam or glow of reflected light; brief or faint indication. ◆ *v* shine. **gleaming** *adj*

glean *v* gather (facts etc.) bit by bit; gather (the useful remnants of a crop) after harvesting. **gleaner** *n*

glebe *n* land belonging to a parish church.

glee *n* triumph and delight; musical composition for three or more unaccompanied voices. **gleeful** *adj* **gleefully** *adv*

glen *n* deep narrow valley.

glib *adj* **glibber, glibbest** fluent but superficial. **glibly** *adv* **glibness** *n*

glide *v* move easily and smoothly; (of an aircraft) move without the use of engines. ◆ *n* smooth easy movement. **glider** *n* aircraft without an engine which floats on air currents. **gliding** *n* sport of flying gliders.

glimmer *v* shine faintly, flicker. ◆ *n* faint gleam; faint indication.

glimpse *n* brief or incomplete view. ◆ *v* catch a glimpse of.

glint *v* gleam brightly. ◆ *n* bright gleam.

glissando *n* *Music* slide between two notes in which all intermediate notes are played.

glisten *v* gleam by reflecting light.

glitch *n* sudden malfunction in an electronic system.

glitter *v* shine with bright flashes; be showy. ◆ *n* sparkle or brilliance; shiny powder used as decoration.

gloaming *n* twilight.

gloat *v* (often foll. by *over*) look (at) or think (of) with smug pleasure.

glob *n* rounded mass of thick fluid.

globe *n* sphere with a map of the earth on it; spherical object. **the globe** the earth. **global** *adj* worldwide; total or comprehensive. **globalization** *n* process by which a company, etc.,

expands to operate internationally. **global warming** increase in the planet's temperature believed to be caused by the greenhouse effect. **globally** *adv* **globetrotter** *n* habitual worldwide traveller. **globetrotting** *n*, *adj*

globule *n* small round drop. **globular** *adj*

globulin *n* simple protein found in living tissue.

glockenspiel *n* percussion instrument consisting of small metal bars played with hammers.

gloom *n* melancholy or depression; darkness. **gloomy** *adj* **gloomily** *adv*

glory *n*, *pl* **-ries** praise or honour; splendour; praiseworthy thing; adoration or worship. ◆ *v* **-rying, -ried** (foll. by *in*) take great pleasure in. **glorify** *v* make (something) seem more important than it is; praise; worship (God). **glorification** *n* **glorious** *adj* brilliantly beautiful; delightful; having or full of glory. **gloriously** *adv* **glory hole** *Informal* untidy cupboard or storeroom. **glory in** *v* triumph or exalt.

gloss[1] *n* surface shine or lustre; paint or cosmetic giving a shiny finish. **glossy** *adj* smooth and shiny; (of a magazine) printed on shiny paper. **glossily** *adv* **glossiness** *n* **gloss over** *v* (try to) cover up or pass over (an error).

gloss[2] *n* explanatory comment added to the text of a book. ◆ *v* add glosses to.

glossary *n*, *pl* **-ries** list of special or technical words with definitions.

glottis *n*, *pl* **-tises, -tides** vocal cords and the space between them. **glottal** *adj*

glove *n* covering for the hand with individual sheaths for each finger and the thumb. **gloved** *adj* covered by a glove. **glove compartment** small storage area in the dashboard of an automobile.

glow *n* light produced by a great heat; brightness of complexion; feeling of wellbeing. ◆ *v* produce a steady light without flames; shine; have a feeling of wellbeing or satisfaction; (of a colour) look warm. **glow-worm** *n* insect giving out a green light.

glower [rhymes with **power**] *v*, *n*

scowl.

gloxinia *n* tropical plant with large bell-shaped flowers.

glucose *n* kind of sugar found in fruit.

glue *n* natural or synthetic sticky substance used as an adhesive. ◆ *v* **glueing** *or* **gluing, glued** fasten with glue; (foll. by *to*) pay full attention to, e.g. *her eyes were glued to the TV*. **gluey** *adj* **glue-sniffing** *n* inhaling of glue fumes for intoxicating or hallucinatory effects.

glum *adj* **glummer, glummest** sullen or gloomy. **glumly** *adv*

glut *n* excessive supply. ◆ *v* **glutting, glutted** feed or fill to excess; oversupply.

gluten [gloo-ten] *n* protein found in cereal grain.

glutinous [gloo-tin-uss] *adj* sticky or gluey.

glutton[1] *n* greedy person; person with a great capacity for something. **gluttonous** *adj* **gluttony** *n*

glutton[2] *n* wolverine.

glycerin, glycerine *n* colourless sweet liquid used widely in chemistry and industry.

glycerol *n* technical name for GLYCERIN (E).

GM genetically modified.

gm gram.

GMT Greenwich Mean Time.

gnarled *adj* rough, twisted, and knobbly.

gnash *v* grind (the teeth) together in anger or pain.

gnat *n* small biting two-winged fly.

gnaw *v* **gnawing, gnawed, gnawed** *or* **gnawn**. bite or chew steadily; (foll. by *at*) cause constant distress (to).

gneiss *n* coarse-grained metamorphic rock.

gnome *n* imaginary creature like a little old man.

gnomic [no-mik] *adj* of pithy sayings.

Gnosticism *n* religious movement believing in intuitive spiritual knowledge. **Gnostic** *n, adj*

GNP Gross National Product.

gnu [noo] *n* oxlike S African antelope.

go *v* **going, went, gone** move to or from a place; depart; make regular journeys; function; be, do, or become as specified; contribute to a result, e.g. *it just goes to show*; be allotted to a specific purpose or recipient; be sold; blend or harmonize; fail or break down; elapse; be got rid of; attend; reach or exceed certain limits, e.g. *she's gone too far this time*; be acceptable; carry authority. ◆ *n* attempt; verbal attack; turn; *Informal* energy or vigour. **make a go of** be successful at. **go back on** *v* break (a promise etc.). **go-between** *n* intermediary. **go for** *v* choose; attack; apply to equally. **go-getter** *n* energetically ambitious person. **go-go dancer** scantily-dressed erotic dancer. **go off** *v* explode; ring or sound; *Informal* stop liking; *Informal* become stale or rotten. **go out** *v* go to social events; be romantically involved (with); be extinguished. **go over** *v* examine or check. **go-slow** *n* deliberate slowing of work-rate as an industrial protest. **go through** *v* suffer or undergo; examine or search.

goad *v* provoke (someone) to take action, usu. in anger. ◆ *n* incentive; spiked stick for driving cattle.

goal *n* *Sport* posts through which the ball or puck has to be propelled to score; *Sport* score made in this way; aim or purpose. **goalie** *n* *Informal* goalkeeper. **goalkeeper** *n* player whose task is to stop shots entering the goal. **goalpost** *n* one of the two posts supporting the crossbar of a goal. **move the goalposts** change the aims of an activity to ensure the desired result.

goat *n* sure-footed ruminant animal. **get someone's goat** *Slang* annoy someone. **goatee** *n* small pointed beard.

gob *n* lump of a soft substance; *Slang* mouth.

gobbet *n* lump, esp. of food.

gobble[1] *v* eat hastily and greedily.

gobble[2] *n* rapid gurgling cry of the male turkey. ◆ *v* make this noise.

gobbledegook, gobbledygook *n* unintelligible (official) language.

goblet *n* drinking cup.

goblin *n* (in folklore) small malevolent creature.

goby *n, pl* **-by, -bies** small spiny-finned fish.

god *n* spirit or being worshipped as having supernatural power; object of worship, idol; **(G-)** (in monotheistic religions) the Supreme Being, creator and ruler of the universe. **goddess** *n fem* **the gods** top balcony in a theatre. **godlike** *adj* **godly** *adj* devout or pious. **godliness** *n* **god-fearing** *adj* pious and devout. **godforsaken** *adj* desolate or dismal. **godsend** *n* something unexpected but welcome.

godetia *n* garden plant with showy flowers.

godparent *n* person who promises at a person's baptism to look after his or her religious upbringing. **godchild** *n* child for whom a person stands as godparent. **goddaughter** *n* **godfather** *n* male godparent; head of a criminal, esp. Mafia, organization. **godmother** *n* **godson** *n*

goggle *v* stare with wide-open eyes. **goggles** *pl n* protective spectacles.

going *n* departure; condition of the ground for walking or riding over; rate of travel. ◆ *adj* thriving; current or accepted; available. **going-over** *n, pl* **goings-over** *Informal* investigation or examination; scolding or thrashing. **goings-on** *pl n* mysterious or unacceptable events.

goitre [goy-ter] *n* swelling of the thyroid gland in the neck.

go-kart *n* small low-powered racing car.

gold *n* yellow precious metal; jewellery or coins made of this. ◆ *adj* made of gold; deep yellow. **gold-digger** *n Informal* woman who uses her sexual attractions to get money from a man. **goldeye** *n* edible N American fish, often smoked. **goldfinch** *n* kind of finch, the male of which has yellow-and-black wings. **goldfish** *n* orange fish kept in ponds or aquariums. **gold leaf** thin gold sheet used for gilding. **gold medal** medal given to the winner of a competition or race.

golden *adj* made of gold; gold-coloured; very successful or promising. **golden eagle** large mountain eagle of the N hemisphere. **golden handshake** *Informal* payment to a departing employee. **golden mean** middle course between extremes. **golden rule** important principle. **golden wedding** fiftieth wedding anniversary.

golf *n* outdoor game in which a ball is struck with clubs into a series of holes.

◆ *v* play golf. **golfer** *n*

golliwog *n* soft black-faced male doll.

gonad *n* organ producing reproductive cells, such as a testicle or ovary.

gondola *n* long narrow boat used in Venice; suspended cabin of a cable car, airship, etc. **gondolier** *n* person who rows a gondola.

gone *v* past participle of GO. **goner** *n Informal* person or thing beyond help or recovery.

gong *n* rimmed metal disc that produces a note when struck; *Slang* medal.

gonorrhea, gonorrhoea [gon-or-**ree**-a] *n* venereal disease with a discharge from the genitals.

good *adj* **better, best** giving pleasure; kindly; commendable; morally excellent; talented; well-behaved; beneficial; valid; reliable; financially sound; complete or full. ◆ *n* benefit; positive moral qualities. ◆ *pl* merchandise; property. **as good as** virtually. **for good** permanently. **goodness** *n* **goodly** *adj* considerable. **goody** *n, pl* **-dies** enjoyable thing; *Informal* hero in a book or film. **goody-goody** *adj, n* smugly virtuous (person). **good-for-nothing** *adj, n* irresponsible or worthless (person). **Good Samaritan** person who helps another in distress. **goodwill** *n* kindly feeling; popularity and good reputation of a business.

goodbye *interj, n* expression used on parting.

gooey *adj* **gooier, gooiest** *Informal* sticky and soft.

goof *Informal* ◆ *n* mistake. ◆ *v* make a mistake.

goon *n Informal* stupid person; hired thug.

goose *n, pl* **geese** web-footed bird like a large duck; female of this bird. **goose flesh, pimples** bristling of the skin due to cold or fright. **goose-step** *v* march with the legs high and without bending the knees.

gooseberry *n* edible yellowy-green berry; *Informal* unwanted single person accompanying a couple.

gopher [go-fer] *n* N American burrowing rodent.

gore[1] *n* blood from a wound.

gore² v pierce with horns.

gorge n deep narrow valley. ◆ v eat greedily. **make one's gorge rise** cause feelings of disgust.

gorgeous adj strikingly beautiful or attractive; Informal very pleasant. **gorgeously** adv

gorgon n terrifying or repulsive woman.

Gorgonzola n sharp-flavoured blue-veined Italian cheese.

gorilla n largest of the apes, found in Africa.

gormless adj Informal stupid.

gorse n prickly yellow-flowered shrub.

gory adj **gorier**, **goriest** horrific or bloodthirsty; involving bloodshed.

goshawk n large hawk.

gosling n young goose.

gospel n unquestionable truth; **(G-)** any of the first four books of the New Testament.

gossamer n filmy cobweb; very fine fabric.

gossip n idle talk, esp. about other people; person who engages in gossip. ◆ v **gossiping**, **gossiped** engage in gossip. **gossipy** adj

got v past of GET. **have got** possess. **have got to** be required to.

Gothic adj (of architecture) of or in the style common in Europe from the 12th–16th centuries, with pointed arches; of or in an 18th-century literary style characterized by gloom and the supernatural; in a heavy ornate script typeface.

gouache n (painting using) watercolours mixed with glue.

Gouda n mild-flavoured Dutch cheese.

gouge [gowj] v scoop or force out; cut (a hole or groove) in (something). ◆ n chisel with a curved cutting edge; hole or groove.

goulash [goo-lash] n rich stew seasoned with paprika.

gourd [goord] n fleshy fruit of a climbing plant; its dried shell, used as a container.

gourmand [goor-mand] n person who is very keen on food and drink.

gourmet [goorm-may] n connoisseur of food and drink.

gout [gowt] n disease causing inflammation of the joints.

govern v rule, direct, or control; exercise restraint over (temper etc.). **governable** adj **governance** n governing. **governess** n woman teacher in a private household. **government** n executive policy-making body of a state; the state and its administration; system by which a country or state is ruled. **governmental** adj **Government House** residence of Canadian governor general or lieutenant governor. **governor** n official governing a province or state; senior administrator of a society, institution, or prison. **governor general** representative of the Crown in a Commonwealth dominion.

gown n woman's long formal dress; surgeon's overall; official robe worn by judges, clergymen, etc.

goy n Slang Jewish word for a non-Jew.

GP general practitioner.

GPS Global Positioning System: a satellite-based navigation system.

grab v **grabbing**, **grabbed** grasp suddenly, snatch. ◆ n sudden snatch.

grace n beauty and elegance; polite, kind behaviour; goodwill or favour; delay granted; courtesy or decency; short prayer of thanks for a meal; **(G-)** title of a duke, duchess, or archbishop. ◆ v add grace to; honour. **graceful** adj **gracefully** adv **graceless** adj **gracious** adj kind and courteous; condescendingly polite; elegant. **graciously** adv **grace note** Music note ornamenting a melody.

grade n place on a scale of quality, rank, or size; mark or rating; class in school. ◆ v arrange in grades; assign a grade to. **make the grade** succeed. **gradation** n (stage in) a series of degrees or steps; arrangement in stages.

gradient n (degree of) slope.

gradual adj occurring, developing, or moving in small stages. **gradually** adv

graduate n person with a degree or diploma. ◆ v receive a degree or diploma; change by degrees; mark (a container etc.) with units of measurement. **graduation** n

graffiti [graf-fee-tee] pl n words or drawings scribbled or sprayed on walls etc.

graft¹ n shoot of a plant set in the

stalk of another; surgical transplant of skin or tissue. ◆ v insert (a plant shoot) in another stalk; transplant (living tissue) surgically.

graft² Informal ◆ n hard work; obtaining of money by misusing one's position. ◆ v work hard. **grafter** n

grail n same as HOLY GRAIL.

grain n seedlike fruit of a cereal plant; cereal plants in general; small hard particle; arrangement of fibres, as in wood; texture or pattern resulting from this; very small amount. **go against the grain** be contrary to one's natural inclination. **grainy** adj

gram, gramme n metric unit of mass equal to one thousandth of a kilogram.

grammar n branch of linguistics dealing with the function, and order of words; book on the rules of grammar; use of words. **grammarian** n **grammatical** adj according to the rules of grammar. **grammatically** adv **grammar school** esp. formerly, a secondary school providing an education with a strong academic bias.

gramophone n record player.

grampus n, pl **-puses** sea mammal.

gran n Informal grandmother.

granary n, pl **-ries** building for storing threshed grain.

grand adj large or impressive; imposing; dignified or haughty; Informal excellent; (of a total) final; chief. ◆ n grand piano; Slang thousand pounds or dollars. **grandchild** n child of one's child. **granddaughter** n female grandchild. **grandfather** n male grandparent. **grandfather clock** tall standing clock with a pendulum and wooden case. **grandmother** n female grandparent. **grandparent** n parent of one's parent. **grand piano** large harp-shaped piano with the strings set horizontally. **grand slam** see SLAM. **grandson** n male grandchild. **grandstand** n terraced block of seats giving the best view at a sports ground.

grandeur n magnificence; nobility or dignity.

grandiloquent adj using pompous language. **grandiloquence** n

grandiose adj imposing; pretentiously grand. **grandiosity** n

grange n country house with farm buildings.

granite [gran-nit] n very hard igneous rock often used in building.

granivorous adj feeding on grain or seeds.

granny, grannie n Informal grandmother. **granny apartment** apartment in or added to a house, suitable for an elderly parent.

grant v give formally; consent to fulfil (a request); admit. ◆ n sum of money provided by a government for a specific purpose, such as education. **take for granted** accept as true without proof; take advantage of without due appreciation.

granule n small grain. **granular** adj of or like grains. **granulated** adj (of sugar) in coarse grains.

grape n small juicy green or purple berry, eaten raw or used to produce wine, raisins, currants, or sultanas. **grapevine** n grape-bearing vine; Informal unofficial way of spreading news.

grapefruit n large round yellow citrus fruit.

graph n drawing showing the relation of different numbers or quantities plotted against a set of axes.

graphic adj vividly descriptive; of or using drawing, painting, etc. **graphics** pl n diagrams, graphs, etc., esp. as used on a television programme or computer screen. **graphically** adv

graphite n soft black form of carbon, used in pencil leads.

graphology n study of handwriting. **graphologist** n

grapnel n tool with several hooks, used to grasp or secure things.

grapple v come to grips with (a person); try to cope with (something difficult). **grappling iron** grapnel.

grasp v grip something firmly; understand. ◆ n grip or clasp; understanding; total rule or possession. **grasping** adj greedy or avaricious.

grass n common type of plant with jointed stems and long narrow leaves, including cereals and bamboo; lawn; pasture land; Slang marijuana. ◆ v cover with grass. **grassy** adj **grasshopper** n jumping insect with long hind legs. **grass roots** ordinary members of a group, as distinct from its leaders. **grassroots** adj **grass widow** wife whose husband is absent for a time.

grate[1] n framework of metal bars for holding fuel in a fireplace. **grating** n framework of metal bars covering an opening.

grate[2] v rub into small bits on a rough surface; scrape with a harsh rasping noise; annoy. **grater** n **grating** adj harsh or rasping; annoying.

grateful adj feeling or showing thanks. **gratefully** adv **gratefulness** n

gratify v -fying, -fied satisfy or please; indulge (a desire or whim). **gratification** n

gratis adv, adj free, for nothing.

gratitude n feeling of being thankful for a favour or gift.

gratuitous [grat-**tyoo**-it-uss] adj unjustified, e.g. gratuitous violence; given free. **gratuitously** adv

gratuity [grat-**tyoo**-it-ee] n, pl -ties money given for services rendered, tip.

grave[1] n hole for burying a corpse. **gravestone** n stone marking a grave. **graveyard** n cemetery.

grave[2] adj serious and worrying; serious and solemn. **gravely** adv

grave[3] [rhymes with halve] n accent (`) over a vowel to indicate a special pronunciation.

gravel n mixture of small stones and coarse sand. **gravelled** adj covered with gravel. **gravelly** adj covered with gravel; rough-sounding.

graven [**grave**-en] adj carved or engraved.

gravid [**grav**-id] adj Med pregnant.

gravitate v be influenced or drawn towards; Physics move by gravity. **gravitation** n **gravitational** adj

gravity n, pl -ties force of attraction of one object for another, esp. of objects to the earth; seriousness or importance; solemnity.

gravy n, pl -vies juices from meat in cooking; sauce made from these.

gray adj US same as GREY.

grayling n fish of the salmon family.

graze[1] v feed on grass. **grazier** n person who feeds cattle for market.

graze[2] v touch lightly in passing; scratch or scrape the skin. ♦ n slight scratch or scrape.

grease n soft melted animal fat; any thick oily substance. ♦ v apply grease to. **greasy** adj **greasiness** n **grease gun** appliance for injecting oil or grease into machinery. **greasepaint** n theatrical make-up.

great adj large in size or number; extreme; important; pre-eminent; Informal excellent. **great-** prefix one generation older or younger than, e.g. great-grandfather. **greatly** adv **greatness** n **greatcoat** n heavy overcoat. **Great Dane** very large graceful dog.

greave n piece of armour for the shin.

grebe n diving water bird.

Grecian [**gree**-shan] adj of ancient Greece.

greed n excessive desire for something, such as food or money. **greedy** adj **greedily** adv **greediness** n

Greek n language of Greece; person from Greece. ♦ adj of Greece, the Greeks, or the Greek language.

green adj of a colour between blue and yellow; covered with grass or plants; unripe; of or concerned with environmental issues; envious or jealous; immature or gullible. ♦ n colour between blue and yellow; area of grass kept for a special purpose; (G-) person concerned with environmental issues. ♦ pl green vegetables. **greenness** n **greenish**, **greeny** adj **greenery** n vegetation. **green belt** protected area of open country around a town. **greengage** n sweet green plum. **greengrocer** n Brit shopkeeper selling vegetables and fruit. **greenhorn** n novice. **greenhouse** n glass building for rearing plants. **greenhouse effect** rise in the temperature of the earth caused by heat absorbed from the sun being unable to leave the atmosphere. **green light** signal to go; permission to proceed with something. **greenroom** n room for actors when offstage. **greenshank** n large European sandpiper. **green thumb** skill in gardening.

greet v meet with expressions of welcome; receive in a specified manner; be immediately noticeable to. **greeting** n

gregarious adj fond of company; (of

animals) living in flocks or herds.

gremlin *n* imaginary being blamed for mechanical malfunctions.

grenade *n* small bomb thrown by hand or fired from a rifle. **grenadier** *n* soldier of a regiment formerly trained to throw grenades.

grenadine [gren-a-**deen**] *n* syrup made from pomegranates, used in cocktails.

grew *v* past tense of GROW.

grey *adj* of a colour between black and white; (of hair) partly turned white. ◆ *n* colour between black and white; grey or whitish horse. **greyness** *n* **grey matter** *Informal* brains. **greyish** *adj*

greyhound *n* swift slender dog used in racing.

grid *n* network of horizontal and vertical lines, bars, etc.; national network of electricity supply cables.

griddle *n* flat iron plate for cooking.

gridiron *n* frame of metal bars for grilling food; N American football field.

grief *n* deep sadness. **grieve** *v* (cause to) feel grief. **grievance** *n* real or imaginary cause for complaint. **grievous** *adj* very severe or painful; very serious.

griffin *n* mythical monster with an eagle's head and wings and a lion's body.

grill *n* device on a cooker that radiates heat downwards; grilled food; gridiron. ◆ *v* cook under a grill; question relentlessly. **grilling** *n* relentless questioning.

grille, grill *n* grating over an opening.

grilse [grills] *n* salmon on its first return from the sea to fresh water.

grim *adj* **grimmer, grimmest** harsh and unpleasant; stern; disagreeable. **grimly** *adv* **grimness** *n*

grimace *n* ugly or distorted facial expression of pain, disgust, etc. ◆ *v* make a grimace.

grime *n* ingrained dirt. ◆ *v* make very dirty. **grimy** *adj* **griminess** *n*

grin *v* **grinning, grinned** smile broadly, showing the teeth. ◆ *n* broad smile.

grind *v* **grinding, ground** crush or rub to a powder; smooth or sharpen by friction; scrape together with a harsh noise; (foll. by *down*) treat harshly so

as to prevent resistance. ◆ *n Informal* hard or tedious work. **grind out** *v* produce in a routine or uninspired manner. **grindstone** *n* stone used for grinding.

grip *n* firm hold or grasp; way in which something is grasped; control or understanding; travelling bag; handle. ◆ *v* **gripping, gripped** grasp or hold tightly; hold the interest or attention of. **gripping** *adj*

gripe *v Informal* complain persistently. ◆ *n* sudden intense bowel pain; *Informal* complaint.

grisly *adj* **-lier, -liest** horrifying.

grist *n* grain for grinding. **grist to one's mill** something which can be turned to advantage.

gristle *n* cartilage in meat. **gristly** *adj*

grit *n* rough particles of sand; courage; (G-) *Informal* member or supporter of Liberal Party. ◆ *pl* meal consisting of coarsely ground grain. ◆ *v* **gritting, gritted** spread grit on (an icy road); clench or grind (the teeth). **gritty** *adj* **grittiness** *n*

grizzle *v Informal* whine or complain.

grizzled *adj* grey-haired.

grizzly *n, pl* **-zlies** (also **grizzly bear**) large American bear.

groan *n* deep sound of grief or pain; *Informal* complaint. ◆ *v* utter a groan; *Informal* complain.

groat *n Hist* fourpenny piece.

grocer *n* shopkeeper selling foodstuffs. **grocery** *n, pl* **-ceries** business or premises of a grocer. ◆ *pl* goods sold by a grocer.

grog *n* spirit, usu. rum, and water.

groggy *adj* **-gier, -giest** *Informal* faint, shaky, or dizzy.

groin *n* place where the legs join the abdomen; edge made by the intersection of two vaults.

grommet *n* ring or eyelet; *Med* tube inserted in the ear to drain fluid from the middle ear.

groom *n* person who looks after horses; bridegroom; officer in a royal household. ◆ *v* make or keep one's clothes and appearance neat and tidy; brush or clean a horse; train (someone) for a future role.

groove *n* long narrow channel in a surface. ◆ *v* cut groove(s) in.

grope *v* feel about or search

uncertainly. **groping** n

gross adj outrageously wrong; vulgar; repulsively fat; total, without deductions. ◆ n twelve dozen. ◆ v make as total revenue before deductions. **grossly** adv **grossness** n

grotesque [grow-**tesk**] adj strangely distorted or bizarre; ugly. ◆ n grotesque person or thing; artistic style mixing distorted human, animal, and plant forms. **grotesquely** adv

grotto n, pl **-toes**, **-tos** small picturesque cave.

grotty adj **-tier**, **-tiest** Informal nasty or in bad condition.

grouch Informal ◆ v grumble. ◆ n grumble; persistent grumbler. **grouchy** adj

ground[1] n surface of the earth; soil; area used for a specific purpose, e.g. *rugby ground*; position in an argument or controversy. ◆ pl enclosed land round a house; reason or motive; coffee dregs. ◆ v ban an aircraft or pilot from flying; run (a ship) aground; instruct in the basics; base. **groundless** adj without reason. **grounding** n basic knowledge of a subject. **groundnut** n peanut. **groundsheet** n waterproof sheet put on the ground under a tent. **groundsman** n person employed to maintain a sports ground or park. **groundswell** n rapidly developing general feeling. **groundwork** n preliminary work.

ground[2] v past of GRIND.

group n number of people or things regarded as a unit; small band of musicians or singers. ◆ v place or form into a group.

grouper n large edible sea fish.

grouse[1] n stocky game bird; its flesh.

grouse[2] v complain. ◆ n complaint.

grout n thin mortar. ◆ v fill up with grout.

grove n small group of trees.

grovel [**grov**-el] v **-elling**, **-elled** behave humbly in order to win a superior's favour; crawl on the floor.

grow v growing, grew, grown develop physically; (of a plant) exist; cultivate (plants); increase in size or degree; originate; become gradually, e.g. *it was growing dark*. **growth** n growing; increase; something grown

or growing; tumour. **grown-up** adj, n adult. **grow up** v mature.

growl v make a low rumbling sound; say in a gruff manner. ◆ n growling sound.

groyne n wall built out from the shore to control erosion.

grub n legless insect larva; Slang food. ◆ v grubbing, grubbed dig out or uproot; dig up the surface of (soil); search.

grubby adj **-bier**, **-biest** dirty. **grubbiness** n

grudge v be unwilling to give or allow. ◆ n resentment.

gruel n thin porridge.

gruelling adj exhausting or severe.

gruesome adj causing horror and disgust.

gruff adj rough or surly in manner or voice. **gruffly** adv **gruffness** n

grumble v complain; rumble. ◆ n complaint; rumble. **grumbler** n **grumbling** adj, n

grumpy adj **grumpier**, **grumpiest** bad-tempered. **grumpily** adv **grumpiness** n

grunge n style of rock music with a fuzzy guitar sound; deliberately untidy and uncoordinated fashion style.

grunt v (esp. of pigs) make a low short gruff sound. ◆ n pig's sound; gruff noise.

Gruyère [grew-**yair**] n hard yellow Swiss cheese with holes.

gryphon n same as GRIFFIN.

GST Goods and Services Tax.

G-string n small strip of cloth covering the genitals and attached to a waistband.

GT gran turismo, used of a sports automobile.

guano [**gwa**-no] n dried sea-bird manure.

guarantee n formal assurance, esp. in writing, that a product will meet certain standards; something that makes a specified condition or outcome certain. ◆ v **-teeing**, **-teed** ensure; give a guarantee; secure against risk etc. **guarantor** n person who gives or is bound by a guarantee.

guard v watch over to protect or to prevent escape. ◆ n person or group that guards; official in charge of a train; protection; screen for enclosing anything dangerous; posture of defence in sports such as boxing or fencing. ◆ pl (**G-**) regiment with ceremonial duties. **guardsman** n member of the Guards. **guarded** adj cautious or noncommittal. **guardedly** adv **guard against** v take precautions against.

guardian n keeper or protector; person legally responsible for a child, mentally ill person, etc. **guardianship** n

guava [**gwah**-va] n yellow-skinned tropical American fruit.

gudgeon n small European freshwater fish.

Guernsey [**gurn**-zee] n breed of dairy cattle; (**g-**) seaman's knitted sweater.

guerrilla, guerilla n member of an unofficial armed force fighting regular forces.

guess v estimate or draw a conclusion without proper knowledge; estimate correctly by guessing; suppose. ◆ n estimate or conclusion reached by guessing. **guesswork** n process or results of guessing.

guest n person entertained at another's house or at another's expense; invited performer or speaker; customer at a hotel or restaurant. **guesthouse** n boarding house.

guff n Slang nonsense.

guffaw n crude noisy laugh. ◆ v laugh in this way.

guide n person who shows the way; adviser; book of instruction or information; device for directing motion; (**G-**) member of an organization for girls equivalent to the Scouts. ◆ v act as a guide for; control, supervise, or influence. **guidance** n leadership, instruction, or advice. **guided missile** missile whose flight is controlled electronically. **guide dog** dog trained to lead a blind person. **guideline** n set principle for doing something.

guild n organization or club; Hist society of men in the same trade or craft.

guilder n a former monetary unit of the Netherlands.

guile [gile] n cunning or deceit. **guileful** adj **guileless** adj

guillemot [gil-lee-mot] n black-and-

white diving sea bird.

guillotine n machine for beheading people; device for cutting paper or sheet metal; method of preventing lengthy debate in parliament by fixing a time for taking the vote. ◆ v behead by guillotine; limit debate by the guillotine.

guilt n fact or state of having done wrong; remorse for wrongdoing. **guiltless** adj innocent. **guilty** adj responsible for an offence or misdeed; feeling or showing guilt. **guiltily** adv

guinea n former British monetary unit worth 21 shillings (1.05 pounds); former gold coin of this value. **guinea fowl** bird related to the pheasant. **guinea pig** tailless S American rodent; Informal person used for experimentation.

guise [rhymes with **size**] n false appearance.

guitar n six-stringed instrument played by plucking or strumming. **guitarist** n

gulch n deep narrow valley in western N America.

gulf n large deep bay; chasm; large difference in opinion or understanding.

gull n long-winged sea bird.

gullet n muscular tube through which food passes from the mouth to the stomach.

gullible adj easily tricked. **gullibility** n

gully n, pl **-lies** channel cut by running water.

gulp v swallow hastily; gasp. ◆ n gulping; thing gulped.

gum[1] n firm flesh in which the teeth are set. **gummy** adj toothless.

gum[2] n sticky substance obtained from certain trees; adhesive; gumdrop; chewing gum; gumtree. ◆ v **gumming, gummed** stick with gum. **gummy** adj **gumboots** pl n Wellington boots. **gumdrop** n hard jelly-like candy. **gumtree** n eucalypt tree.

gumption n Informal resourcefulness; courage.

gun n weapon with a metal tube from which missiles are fired by explosion; device from which a substance is ejected under pressure. ◆ v **gunning, gunned** cause (an engine) to run at high speed. **jump the gun** see JUMP. **gunner** n artillery soldier. **gunnery** n use or science of large guns. **gunboat** *n* small warship. **gun dog** dog used to retrieve game. **gun down** *v* shoot (a person). **gun for** *v* seek or pursue vigorously. **gunman** *n* armed criminal. **gunmetal** *n* alloy of copper, tin, and zinc. ◆ *adj* dark grey. **gunpowder** *n* explosive mixture of potassium nitrate, sulfur, and charcoal. **gunrunning** *n* smuggling of guns and ammunition. **gunrunner** *n* **gunshot** *n* shot or range of a gun.

gunge *n Informal* sticky unpleasant substance. **gungy** *adj*

gunny *n* strong coarse fabric used for sacks.

gunwale, gunnel [gun-nel] *n* top of a ship's side.

guppy *n, pl* **-pies** small colourful aquarium fish.

gurgle *v, n* (make) a bubbling noise.

Gurkha *n* person, esp. a soldier, belonging to a Hindu people of Nepal.

guru *n* Indian spiritual teacher; leader or adviser.

gush *v* flow out suddenly and profusely; express admiration effusively. ◆ *n* sudden copious flow; effusiveness. **gusher** *n* spurting oil well.

gusset *n* piece of material sewn into a garment to strengthen it.

gust *n* sudden blast of wind. ◆ *v* blow in gusts. **gusty** *adj*

gusto *n* enjoyment or zest.

gut *n* intestine; short for CATGUT *Informal* fat stomach. ◆ *pl* internal organs; *Informal* courage. ◆ *v* **gutting, gutted** remove the guts from; (of a fire) destroy the inside of (a building). ◆ *adj* basic or instinctive, e.g. *gut reaction*. **gutsy** *adj Informal* courageous; vigorous or robust, e.g. *a gutsy performance*. **gutted** *adj Informal* disappointed and upset.

gutter *n* shallow trough for carrying off water from a roof or roadside. ◆ *v* (of a candle) burn unsteadily, with wax running down the sides. **the gutter** degraded or criminal environment. **guttering** *n* material for gutters. **gutter press** newspapers that rely on sensationalism.

guttural [gut-ter-al] *adj* (of a sound) produced at the back of the throat; (of a voice) harsh-sounding.

guy[1] *n Informal* man or boy; *Brit* effigy of Guy Fawkes burnt on Nov. 5th (**Guy Fawkes Day**).

guy[2] *n* rope or chain to steady or secure something. **guyrope** *n*

guzzle *v* eat or drink greedily.

gybe [jibe] *v* (of a fore-and-aft sail) swing suddenly from one side to the other; (of a boat) change course by gybing.

gym *n* short for GYMNASIUM or GYMNASTICS.

gymkhana [jim-kah-na] *n* horse-riding competition.

gymnasium *n* large room with equipment for physical training. **gymnast** *n* expert in gymnastics. **gymnastic** *adj* **gymnastics** *pl n* exercises to develop strength and agility.

gynecology, gynaecology [guy-nee-kol-la-jee] *n* branch of medicine dealing with diseases and conditions specific to women. **gynecological, gynaecological** *adj* **gynecologist, gynaecologist** *n*

gypsophila *n* garden plant with small white flowers.

gypsum *n* chalklike mineral used to make plaster of Paris.

Gypsy *n, pl* **-sies** member of a travelling people found throughout Europe.

gyrate [jire-rate] *v* rotate or spiral about a point or axis. **gyration** *n* **gyratory** *adj* gyrating.

gyrocompass *n* compass using a gyroscope.

gyroscope [jire-oh-skohp] *n* disc rotating on an axis that can turn in any direction, used to keep navigation instruments steady. **gyroscopic** *adj*

H h

H *Chem* hydrogen.

habeas corpus [hay-bee-ass kor-puss] *n* writ ordering a prisoner to be brought before a court.

haberdasher *n Brit* dealer in small articles used for sewing. **haberdashery** *n*

habit *n* established way of behaving; addiction to a drug; costume of a nun or monk; woman's riding costume. **habitual** adj done regularly and repeatedly. **habitually** adv **habituate** v accustom. **habituation** n **habitué** [hab-it-yew-ay] n frequent visitor to a place.

habitable adj fit to be lived in. **habitant** n (descendant of) original French settler. **habitat** n natural home of an animal or plant. **habitation** n dwelling place; occupation of a dwelling place.

hacienda [hass-ee-end-a] n ranch or large estate in Latin America.

hack¹ v cut or chop (at) violently; utter a harsh dry cough **hacker** n Slang computer enthusiast, esp. one who breaks into the computer system of a company or government.

hack² n horse kept for riding; Informal (inferior) writer or journalist. **hackwork** n dull repetitive work.

hackles pl n hairs or feathers on the back of the neck of some animals and birds, which are raised in anger.

hackney carriage n taxi; coach or carriage for hire.

hackneyed [hak-need] adj (of language) stale or trite because of overuse.

hacksaw n small saw for cutting metal.

had v past of HAVE.

haddock n large edible sea fish.

Hades [hay-deez] n Greek myth underworld home of the dead.

hadj n same as HAJJ.

haematic adj same as HEMATIC.

haemoglobin n same as HEMOGLOBIN.

haemophilia n same as HEMOPHILIA.

haemorrhage n same as HEMORRHAGE.

haemorrhoids pl n same as HEMORRHOIDS.

haft n handle of an axe, knife, or dagger. ◆ v provide with a haft.

hag n ugly old woman; witch. **hag-ridden** adj distressed or worried.

haggard adj looking tired and ill.

haggis n Scottish dish made from sheep's offal, oatmeal, suet, and onion.

haggle v bargain or wrangle over a price.

hagiology n, pl **-gies** literature about the lives of the saints. **hagiography** n writing of this.

hail¹ n (shower of) small pellets of ice; large amount of words, missiles, blows, etc. ◆ v fall as or like hail. **hailstone** n

hail² v greet; call (out to); acclaim, acknowledge. **hail from** v come originally from.

hair n threadlike growth on the skin; such growths collectively, esp. on the head. **hairy** adj covered with hair; Slang dangerous or exciting. **hairiness** n **hairdo** n style in which a person's hair is cut and arranged. **hairdresser** n person who cuts and styles hair. **hairline** n margin of hair at the top of the forehead. ◆ adj very fine or narrow. **hairpin** n U-shaped wire used to hold the hair in place. **hairpin bend** U-shaped bend in the road. **hair-raising** adj terrifying. **hairsplitting** n making of petty distinctions. **hairspring** n very fine spring in a watch or clock.

hajj n pilgrimage a Muslim makes to Mecca. **hajji** n Muslim who has made a pilgrimage to Mecca.

hake n edible fish of the cod family.

halal n meat from animals slaughtered according to Muslim law.

halberd n spear with an axe blade.

halcyon [hal-see-on] adj peaceful and happy. **halcyon days** time of peace and happiness.

hale adj robust, healthy, e.g. hale and hearty.

half n, pl **halves** either of two equal parts; Informal half-pint; half-price ticket. ◆ adj incomplete. ◆ adv to the extent of half; partially. **half-baked** adj Informal poorly planned. **half-breed** n half-caste. **half-brother, -sister** n brother or sister related through one parent only. **half-caste** n person with parents of different races. **half-cocked** adj **go off half-cocked** fail because of inadequate preparation. **half-hearted** adj unenthusiastic. **half-life** n time taken for half the atoms in radioactive material to decay. **half-nelson** n hold in wrestling in which one wrestler's arm is pinned behind his back by his opponent. **half note** musical note half the length of a whole note. **halfpenny** [hayp-nee] n former British coin worth half an old penny. **half-pipe** large U-shaped ramp used for skateboarding, snowboarding, etc.

half-timbered adj having an exposed wooden frame filled in with plaster.

half-time n Sport interval between two halves of a game. **halftone** n illustration showing lights and shadows by means of very small dots. **halfway** adv, adj at or to half the distance. **halfwit** n feeble-minded person.

halibut n large edible flatfish.

halitosis n bad-smelling breath.

hall n (entrance) passage; large room or building belonging to a particular group or used for a particular purpose; large country house.

hallelujah [hal-ee-loo-ya] interj exclamation of praise to God.

hallmark n mark indicating the standard of tested gold and silver; distinguishing feature. ♦ v stamp with a hallmark.

hallo interj same as HELLO.

hallowed adj regarded as holy.

Hallowe'en n October 31, the eve of All Saints' Day.

hallucinate v seem to see something that is not really there. **hallucination** n experience of seeming to see something that is not really there. **hallucinatory** adj **hallucinogen** n drug that causes hallucinations.

halo [hay-loh] n, pl -loes, -los disc of light round the head of a sacred figure; ring of light round the sun or moon.

halogen [hal-oh-jen] n Chem any of a group of nonmetallic elements including chlorine and iodine.

halt v stop. ♦ n temporary stop; minor railway station without a building. **halting** adj hesitant, e.g. halting speech.

halter n strap around a horse's head with a rope to lead it with. **halterneck** n top or dress with a strap fastened at the back of the neck.

halve v cut in half; reduce to half; share.

halves n plural of HALF.

halyard n rope for raising a ship's sail or flag.

ham n smoked or salted meat from a pig's thigh; Informal amateur radio operator; Informal actor who overacts. ♦ v hamming, hammed. **ham it up** Informal overact. **ham-fisted, -handed**

adj clumsy.

hamburger n flat round piece of minced beef, often served in a bread roll.

hamlet n small village.

hammer n tool with a heavy head, used to drive in nails, beat metal, etc.; part of a gun which causes the bullet to be fired; metal ball on a wire, thrown as a sport; auctioneer's mallet; striking mechanism in a piano. ♦ v strike (as if) with a hammer; Informal defeat. **hammer and tongs** with great effort or energy. **hammerhead** n shark with a wide flattened head. **hammertoe** n condition in which the toe is permanently bent at the joint.

hammock n hanging bed made of canvas or net.

hamper[1] v make it difficult for (someone or something) to move or progress.

hamper[2] n large basket with a lid; selection of food and drink packed as a gift.

hamster n small rodent with a short tail and cheek pouches.

hamstring n tendon at the back of the knee. ♦ v make it difficult for someone to take any action.

hand n end of the arm beyond the wrist; style of writing; applause; pointer on a dial; manual worker; cards dealt to a player in a card game; unit of four inches used to measure horses. ♦ v pass or give. **at hand, on hand, to hand** nearby. **hand in glove** in close association. **hands down** easily. **have a hand in** be involved in. **lend a hand** help. **out of hand** beyond control. **handful** n the amount that can be held in the hand; small quantity or number; Informal person or thing that is difficult to control. **handbag** n purse. **handbill** n small printed notice. **handbook** n small reference or instruction book. **handcuff** n one of a linked pair of metal rings used for securing a prisoner. ♦ v put handcuffs on **handheld** adj 1 (of a computer) small enough to be held in the hand. ♦ n 2 computer small enough to be held in the hand. **handicraft** n objects made by hand. **handiwork** n work of a particular person. **hand-out** n thing given free; written information given out at a talk etc. **hands-on** *adj* involving practical experience of equipment. **handstand** *n* act of supporting the body on the hands in an upside-down position. **handwriting** *n* (style of) writing by hand.

handicap *n* any physical or mental disability; something that makes progress difficult; contest in which the competitors are given advantages or disadvantages in an attempt to equalize their chances; disadvantage or advantage given. ♦ *v* make it difficult for (someone) to do something.

handkerchief *n* small square of fabric used to wipe the nose.

handle *n* small lever used to open and close a door, etc.; part of an object that is held so that it can be used. ♦ *v* hold, feel, or move with the hands; control or deal with. **handler** *n* person who controls an animal. **handlebars** *pl n* curved metal bar used to steer a cycle.

handsome *adj* attractive in appearance; large or generous, e.g. *a handsome reward.*

handy *adj* **handier, handiest** convenient, useful; good at manual work. **handily** *adv* **handiness** *n* **handyman** *n* man skilled at odd jobs.

hang *v* **hanging, hung** attach or be attached at the top with the lower part free, *past* **hanged** suspend or be suspended by the neck until dead; fasten to a wall; droop. **get the hang of** *Informal* understand. **hanger** *n* curved piece of wood or hook for hanging clothes on. **hang back** *v* hesitate. **hangdog** *adj* sullen, dejected. **hang-glider** *n* glider with a light framework from which the pilot hangs in a harness. **hang-gliding** *n* **hangman** *n* person who executes people by hanging. **hangover** *n* aftereffects of drinking too much alcohol. **hang-up** *n* *Informal* emotional or psychological problem. **hang up** *v* end a telephone call.

hangar *n* large shed for storing aircraft.

hank *n* coil or skein, esp. of yarn.

hanker *v* (foll. by *after*) long for.

hanky, hankie *n, pl* **hankies** *Informal* handkerchief.

hanky-panky *n* *Informal* illicit sexual relations.

hansom *n* formerly, a two-wheeled horse-drawn cab for hire.

haphazard *adj* not organized or planned. **haphazardly** *adv*

hapless *adj* unlucky.

happen *v* occur, take place; do by chance. **happening** *n* occurrence, event.

happy *adj* **-pier, -piest** glad or content; lucky or fortunate; willing. **happily** *adv* **happiness** *n* **happy-go-lucky** *adj* carefree and cheerful.

hara-kiri *n* Japanese ritual suicide by disembowelment.

harangue *v* address angrily. ♦ *n* angry speech.

harass *v* annoy or trouble constantly. **harassed** *adj* **harassment** *n*

harbinger [har-binge-er] *n* person or thing that announces the approach of something.

harbour *n* sheltered port. ♦ *v* give shelter or protection to; maintain secretly in the mind.

hard *adj* firm, solid, or rigid; difficult; requiring a lot of effort; unkind or unfeeling; difficult to bear; (of water) containing calcium salts which stop soap lathering freely; (of a drug) strong and addictive. ♦ *adv* with great energy or effort; carefully; intensely. **hard of hearing** slightly deaf. **hard up** *Informal* short of money. **harden** *v* **hardness** *n* **hardship** *n* suffering; difficult circumstances. **hard-bitten** *adj* tough. **hardboard** *n* thin stiff board made of compressed sawdust and woodchips. **hard-boiled** *adj* (of eggs) boiled until solid; *Informal* tough, unemotional. **hard copy** computer output printed on paper. **hard-core** *adj* (of pornography) showing sexual acts in explicit detail. **hard-headed** *adj* shrewd, practical. **hard-hearted** *adj* unfeeling, unkind. **hard sell** aggressive sales technique. **hardware** *n* metal tools or implements; machinery used in a computer system; military weapons. **hardwood** *n* wood of a deciduous tree such as oak or ash.

hardly *adv* scarcely or not at all; with great difficulty.

hardy *adj* **-dier, -diest** able to stand difficult conditions. **hardiness** *n*

hare *n* animal like a large rabbit, with

longer legs and ears. ◆ v run fast.
harebell n blue bell-shaped flower.
harebrained adj foolish or impractical.
harelip n split in the upper lip.
harem n (apartments of) a Muslim
man's wives and concubines.
haricot [har-rik-oh] n white bean
which can be dried.
hark v Old-fashioned listen. **hark back**
v return (to an earlier subject).
harlequin n stock comic character,
with a diamond-patterned costume
and mask. ◆ adj in varied colours.
harlot n Obs prostitute.
harm v injure physically, mentally, or
morally. ◆ n physical, mental, or moral
injury. **harmful** adj **harmless** adj
harmony n, pl -nies peaceful
agreement and cooperation;
combination of notes to make a
pleasing sound. **harmonious** adj
harmoniously adv **harmonic** adj of
harmony; harmonious. **harmonics** n
science of musical sounds. **harmonize**
v fit in or go well with each other.
harmonization n **harmonica** n mouth
organ. **harmonium** n small organ.
harness n equipment for attaching a
horse to a cart or plow; set of straps
fastened round someone's body to
attach something, e.g. a parachute
harness. ◆ v put a harness on; control
(something) in order to use its energy.
harp n large triangular stringed
instrument played with the fingers.
harpist n **harp on about** v talk about
continuously.
harpoon n barbed spear attached to a
rope used for hunting whales. ◆ v
spear with a harpoon.
harpsichord n stringed keyboard
instrument.
harpy n, pl -pies cruel or grasping
woman.
harridan n shrewish (old) woman.
harrier n cross-country runner.
harrow n implement used to break up
clods of soil. ◆ v draw a harrow over.
harrowing adj very distressing.
harry v -rying, -ried keep asking
(someone) to do something, pester.
harsh adj unpleasant to the senses;
severe or cruel. **harshly** adv **harshness**
n
hart n adult male deer.
hartebeest n large African antelope.

harum-scarum adj reckless.
harvest n (season for) the gathering of
crops; crops gathered. ◆ v gather (a
ripened crop). **harvester** n
has v third person singular of the
present tense of HAVE. **has-been** n
Informal person who is no longer
popular or successful.
hash n dish of diced meat and
vegetables; Informal hashish. **make a
hash of** Informal mess up or destroy.
hashish [hash-eesh] n drug made
from the hemp plant, taken for its
intoxicating effects.
hasp n clasp which fits over a staple
and is secured by a bolt or padlock,
used as a fastening.
hassle Informal ◆ n trouble or
difficulty; nuisance. ◆ v cause
annoyance or trouble to.
hassock n cushion for kneeling on in
church.
haste n speed or hurry. **make haste**
hurry or rush. **hasten** v (cause to)
increase speed. **hasty** adj (too) quick.
hastily adv
hat n covering for the head, often with
a brim, usually worn to give protection
from the weather. **keep something
under one's hat** keep something
secret. **hat trick** any three successive
achievements, esp. in sport.
hatch[1] v (cause to) emerge from an
egg; devise (a plot or plan). **hatchery**
n place for hatching eggs.
hatch[2] n (hinged door covering) an
opening in a floor or wall; opening in
the wall between a kitchen and a
dining area; door in an aircraft or
spacecraft. **hatchback** n automobile
with a single lifting door in the rear.
hatchway n opening in the deck of a
ship.
hatchet n small axe. **bury the hatchet**
make peace. **hatchet job** malicious
verbal or written attack. **hatchet man**
Informal person carrying out
unpleasant tasks for an employer.
hate v dislike intensely; be unwilling
(to do something). ◆ n intense dislike;
person or thing that is hated. **hateful**
adj causing or deserving hate. **hatred**
n intense dislike.
haughty adj -tier, -tiest proud,
arrogant. **haughtily** adv **haughtiness** n
haul v pull or drag with effort. ◆ n

amount gained by effort or theft. **long haul** something that takes a lot of time and effort to achieve. **haulage** n (charge for) transporting goods. **haulier** n firm or person that transports goods by road.

haunch n human hip or fleshy hindquarter of an animal.

haunt v visit in the form of a ghost; remain in the thoughts or memory of. ◆ n place visited frequently. **haunted** adj visited by ghosts; worried. **haunting** adj extremely beautiful or sad.

haute couture [oat koo-**ture**] n French high fashion.

hauteur [oat-**ur**] n haughtiness.

have v **has, having, had** hold, possess; experience or be affected with; be obliged (to do); Slang cheat or outwit; receive, take, or obtain; cause to be done; give birth to; used to form past tenses (with a past participle), e.g. I have gone, I had gone. **have it out** Informal settle by argument. **have on** v Informal trick or tease.

haven n place of safety.

haversack n canvas bag carried on the back or shoulder.

havoc n disorder and confusion.

haw n hawthorn berry.

hawk[1] n bird of prey with short rounded wings and a long tail; supporter or advocate of warlike policies. **hawkish, hawklike** adj **hawk-eyed** adj having extremely good eyesight.

hawk[2] v offer (goods) for sale in the street or door-to-door. **hawker** n

hawser n large rope used on a ship.

hawthorn n thorny shrub or tree.

hay n grass cut and dried as fodder. **hay fever** allergic reaction to pollen or dust. **haystack** n large pile of stored hay. **haywire** adj **go haywire** Informal not function properly.

hazard n risk, danger. ◆ v put at danger; venture (a guess). **hazardous** adj

haze n mist, often caused by heat. **hazy** adj misty; vague.

hazel n bush producing nuts. ◆ adj (of eyes) greenish-brown. **hazelnut** n

H-bomb n hydrogen bomb.

he pron male person or animal; person or animal of unspecified sex.

He Chem helium.

head n upper or front part of the body, containing the sense organs and the brain; upper or most forward part of anything; aptitude, intelligence; chief of a group or organization; person or animal considered as a unit; white froth on beer; headline or title; Informal headache. ◆ adj chief, principal. ◆ v be at the top or front of; lead, direct; move (in a particular direction); provide with a heading; hit (a ball) with the head. **go to someone's head** make someone drunk or conceited. **head over heels** very much in love. **not make head nor tail of** not understand. **off one's head** Slang insane. **header** n action of striking a ball with the head; headlong dive. **heading** n title written or printed at the top of a page. **heads** adv Informal with the side of a coin which has a portrait of a head on it uppermost. **heady** adj intoxicating or exciting. **headache** n continuous pain in the head; cause of worry or annoyance. **headboard** n vertical board at the head of a bed. **head-hunter** n person who sets out to recruit someone from another company for a particular job. **headland** n area of land jutting out into the sea. **headlight** n powerful light on the front of a vehicle. **headline** n news summary in large type in a newspaper. ◆ pl main points of a news broadcast. **headlong** adv head foremost; with haste. **head-on** adj, adv front foremost; direct(ly) and uncompromising(ly). **headphones** pl n two small loudspeakers held against the ears by a strap. **headquarters** pl n centre from which operations are directed. **head start** advantage in a competition. **headstone** n gravestone. **headstrong** adj self-willed; obstinate. **headway** n progress. **headwind** n wind blowing against the course of an aircraft or ship.

heal v make or become well. **healer** n **health** n normal good condition of someone's body; toast drunk in a person's honour. **healthy** adj having good health; of or producing good health; functioning well, sound. **healthily** adv **health food** natural food, organically grown and free from additives.

heap n pile of things lying one on top of another; large quantity. ◆ v gather into a pile; (foll. by on) give abundantly (to).

hear v **hearing, heard** perceive (a sound) by ear; listen to; learn or be informed; Law try (a case). **hear! hear!** exclamation of approval or agreement. **hearer** n **hearing** n ability to hear; trial of a case. **within hearing** close enough to be heard.

hearken v Obs listen.

hearsay n gossip; rumour.

hearse n funeral vehicle used to carry a casket.

heart n organ which pumps blood round the body; centre of emotions and affections; tenderness; enthusiasm or courage; central or most important part; figure representing a heart; playing card of the suit marked with the figure of a heart. **break someone's heart** cause someone great grief. **by heart** from memory. **set one's heart on something** greatly desire something. **take to heart** get upset about. **hearten** v make cheerful, encourage. **heartless** adj cruel. **hearty** adj friendly, enthusiastic; substantial; nourishing. **heartily** adv **heartache** n intense anguish. **heart attack** sudden severe malfunction of the heart. **heartbeat** n one complete pulsation of the heart. **heartbreak** n intense grief. **heartburn** n pain in the chest caused by indigestion. **heart failure** sudden stopping of the heartbeat. **heartfelt** adj felt sincerely. **heart-rending** adj causing great sorrow. **heart-throb** n Slang very attractive person.

hearth n floor of a fireplace; home.

heat n state of being hot; energy transferred as a result of a difference in temperature; hot weather; intensity of feeling; preliminary eliminating contest in a competition; readiness to mate in some female animals. ◆ v make hot. **heated** adj angry. **heatedly** adv **heater** n

heath n area of open uncultivated land; low-growing evergreen shrub.

heathen n person not believing in an established religion, pagan. ◆ adj of or relating to heathen peoples.

heather n shrub with small bell-shaped flowers growing on heaths and mountains.

heave v lift with effort; throw (something heavy); utter (a sigh); rise and fall; vomit. ◆ n act of heaving.

heaven n home of God; place or state of bliss. **the heavens** sky. **heavenly** adj wonderful or divine; of or like heaven; of or occurring in space.

heavy adj **-vier, -viest** of great weight; great in degree or amount; dense; difficult or severe; sorrowful; (of a situation) serious. **heavily** adv **heaviness** n **heavy industry** large-scale production of raw material or machinery. **heavy metal** very loud rock music featuring guitar riffs. **heavyweight** n boxer weighing over 175lb (professional) or 81kg (amateur).

Hebrew n ancient language of the Hebrews; its modern form, used in Israel; member of an ancient Semitic people. ◆ adj of this language or people.

heckle v interrupt (a public speaker) with questions, taunts, and comments. **heckler** n

hectare n one hundred ares or 10 000 square metres (2.471 acres).

hectic adj rushed or busy.

hector v bully.

hedge n row of bushes forming a barrier or boundary. ◆ v be evasive; (foll. by against) protect oneself from (loss). **hedgerow** n bushes forming a hedge. **hedge sparrow** small brownish songbird.

hedgehog n small mammal with a protective covering of spines.

hedonism n doctrine that pleasure is the most important thing in life. **hedonist** n **hedonistic** adj

heed v pay close attention to. **heedless** adj **heedless of** taking no notice of.

heel[1] n back part of the foot; part of a shoe supporting the heel; Slang contemptible person. ◆ v make or replace the heel of.

heel[2] v lean to one side.

hefty adj **heftier, heftiest** large, heavy, or strong.

hegemony [hig-em-on-ee] n political domination.

Hegira n Mohammed's flight from Mecca to Medina in 622 AD.

heifer [hef-fer] *n* young cow.

height *n* distance from base to top; distance above sea level; highest degree or topmost point. **heighten** *v* make or become higher or more intense.

heinous *adj* evil and shocking.

heir *n* person entitled to inherit property or rank. **heiress** *n fem* **heirloom** *n* object that has belonged to a family for generations.

held *v* past of HOLD[1].

helicopter *n* aircraft lifted and propelled by rotating overhead blades. **heliport** *n* airport for helicopters.

heliotrope *n* plant with purple flowers. ♦ *adj* light purple.

helium [heel-ee-um] *n* very light colourless odourless gas.

helix [heel-iks] *n, pl* **helices, helixes** spiral. **helical** *adj*

hell *n* home of the wicked after death; place or state of wickedness, suffering, or punishment. **hell for leather** at great speed. **hellish** *adj* **hell-bent** *adj* intent.

Hellenic *adj* of the (ancient) Greeks or their language.

hello *interj* expression of greeting or surprise.

helm *n* tiller or wheel for steering a ship.

helmet *n* hard hat worn for protection.

help *v* make something easier, better, or quicker for (someone); improve (a situation); refrain from, e.g. *I can't help laughing.* ♦ *n* assistance or support. **help oneself** serve oneself; *Informal* steal something. **helper** *n* **helpful** *adj* **helping** *n* single portion of food. **helpless** *adj* weak or incapable. **helplessly** *adv* **helpline** *n* telephone line set aside for callers to contact an organization for help with a problem. **helpmate, -meet** *n* companion and helper; husband or wife.

helter-skelter *adj* haphazard and careless. ♦ *adv* in a haphazard and careless manner. ♦ *n* high spiral slide at a fairground.

hem *n* border of cloth, folded under and stitched down. ♦ *v* **hemming, hemmed** provide with a hem. **hem in** *v* surround and prevent from moving. **hemline** *n* level to which the hem of a skirt hangs.

hematic, haematic *adj* relating to or containing blood **hematology, haematology** *n* study of blood.

hemisphere *n* half of a sphere, esp. the earth. **hemispherical** *adj*

hemlock *n* poison derived from a plant with spotted stems and small white flowers; evergreen of pine family.

hemoglobin, haemoglobin [hee-moh-**globe**-in] *n* protein found in red blood cells which carries oxygen.

hemophilia, haemophilia *n* hereditary illness in which the blood does not clot. **hemophiliac** *n*

hemorrhage, haemorrhage [hem-or-ij] *n* heavy bleeding. ♦ *v* bleed heavily.

hemorrhoids, haemorrhoids [hem-or-oydz] *pl n* swollen veins in the anus (also **piles**).

hemp *n* Asian plant; its fibre, used to make canvas and rope; narcotic drug obtained from hemp.

hen *n* female domestic fowl; female of any bird. **henpecked** *adj* (of a man) dominated by his wife.

hence *adv* for this reason; from this time. **henceforward, henceforth** *adv* from now on.

henchman *n* attendant or follower.

henna *n* reddish dye made from a shrub or tree. ♦ *v* dye the hair with henna.

henry *n, pl* **-ry, -ries, -rys** unit of electrical inductance.

hepatic *adj* of the liver. **hepatitis** *n* inflammation of the liver.

heptagon *n* figure with seven sides.

heptathlon *n* athletic contest involving seven events.

her *pron* refers to a female person or animal or anything personified as feminine when the object of a sentence or clause. ♦ *adj* of, belonging to, or associated with her.

herald *n* person who announces important news; forerunner. ♦ *v* announce or signal the approach of. **heraldry** *n* study of coats of arms and the histories of families. **heraldic** *adj*

herb *n* plant used for flavouring in cookery, and in medicine. **herbal** *adj* **herbalist** *n* person who grows or specializes in the use of medicinal herbs. **herbaceous** *adj* (of a plant) soft-stemmed. **herbaceous border** flower bed that contains perennials rather than annuals. **herbicide** *n* chemical which destroys plants. **herbivore** *n* animal that feeds on plants. **herbivorous** [her-biv-or-uss] *adj*

herculean [her-kew-lee-an] *adj* requiring great strength or effort.

herd *n* group of animals feeding and living together; large crowd of people. ♦ *v* collect into a herd. **herdsman** *n* man who looks after a herd of animals.

here *adv* in, at, or to this place or point. **hereabouts** *adv* near here. **hereafter** *n* life after death. ♦ *adv* in the future. **hereby** *adv* by means of or as a result of this. **herein** *adv* in this place, matter, or document. **herewith** *adv* with this.

heredity [hir-red-it-ee] *n* passing on of characteristics from one generation to another. **hereditary** *adj* passed on genetically from one generation to another; passed on by inheritance.

heresy [herr-iss-ee] *n*, *pl* **-sies** opinion contrary to accepted opinion or belief. **heretic** [herr-it-ik] *n* person who holds unorthodox opinions. **heretical** [hir-ret-ik-al] *adj*

heritage *n* possessions, traditions, or conditions passed from one generation to another.

hermaphrodite [her-maf-roe-dite] *n* person, animal, or plant that has both male and female reproductive organs.

hermetic *adj* sealed so as to be airtight. **hermetically** *adv*

hermit *n* person living in solitude, esp. for religious reasons. **hermitage** *n* dwelling of a hermit.

hernia *n* protrusion of (part of) an organ through the lining of the surrounding body cavity.

hero *n*, *pl* **heroes** principal character in a film, book, play, etc.; man greatly admired for exceptional qualities or achievements. **heroine** *n fem* **heroic** *adj* courageous; of, like, or befitting a hero. **heroics** *pl n* extravagant behaviour. **heroically** *adv* **heroism** [herr-oh-izz-um] *n*

heroin *n* highly addictive drug derived from morphine.

heron *n* long-legged wading bird. **heronry** *n* place where herons breed.

herpes [her-peez] *n* any of several inflammatory skin diseases, including shingles and cold sores.

Herr [hair] *n*, *pl* **Herren** German title of address equivalent to Mr.

herring *n* important food fish of northern seas. **herringbone** *n* pattern of zigzag lines.

hertz *n*, *pl* **hertz** *Physics* unit of frequency.

hesitate *v* be slow or uncertain in acting; pause during speech; be reluctant (to do something). **hesitation** *n* **hesitant** *adj* undecided or wavering. **hesitantly** *adv* **hesitancy** *n*

hessian *n* coarse jute cloth.

heterodox *adj* not orthodox.

heterogeneous [het-er-oh-jean-ee-uss] *adj* composed of diverse elements. **heterogeneity** *n*

heterosexual *n*, *adj* (person) sexually attracted to members of the opposite sex. **heterosexuality** *n*

heuristic [hew-rist-ik] *adj* involving learning by investigation.

hew *v* **hewing, hewed, hewed** or **hewn.** chop or cut with an axe; carve from a substance.

hexagon *n* figure with six sides. **hexagonal** *adj*

hey *interj* expression of surprise or for catching attention.

heyday *n* time of greatest success.

Hg *Chem* mercury.

hiatus [hie-ay-tuss] *n*, *pl* **-tuses, -tus** break in continuity.

hibernate *v* (of an animal) pass the winter as if in a deep sleep. **hibernation** *n*

Hibernia *n Poetic* Ireland. **Hibernian** *adj*

hibiscus *n*, *pl* **-cuses** tropical plant with large brightly coloured flowers.

hiccup, hiccough *n* spasm of the breathing organs with a sharp coughlike sound. ♦ *v* make a hiccup or hiccups.

hick *n Informal* unsophisticated country person.

hickory *n*, *pl* **-ries** N American nut-bearing tree; its tough wood.

hide[1] *v* **hiding, hid, hidden** conceal or obscure (oneself or an object); keep secret. ♦ *n* place of concealment, esp. for a bird-watcher. **hide-out** *n* hiding place.

hide² *n* skin of an animal. **hiding** *n* *Slang* thrashing. **hidebound** *adj* restricted by petty rules.

hideous [hid-ee-uss] *adj* ugly, revolting. **hideously** *adv*

hierarchy [hire-ark-ee] *n, pl* **-chies** system of people or things arranged in a graded order. **hierarchical** *adj*

hieroglyphic [hire-oh-gliff-ik] *adj* of a form of writing using picture symbols, as used in ancient Egypt. ◆ *n* (also **hieroglyph**) symbol representing an object, idea, or sound; symbol that is difficult to decipher.

hi-fi *n* set of high-quality sound-reproducing equipment. ◆ *adj* short for HIGH-FIDELITY.

higgledy-piggledy *adv, adj* in confusion.

high *adj* tall, of greater than average height; far above ground or sea level; being at its peak; greater than usual in intensity or amount; of great importance, quality, or rank; (of a sound) acute in pitch; *Informal* under the influence of alcohol or drugs; (of food) slightly decomposed. ◆ *adv* at or to a high level. **highly** *adv* **highly strung** nervous and easily upset. **Highness** *n* title used to address or refer to a royal person. **High Arctic** regions of Canada, esp. northern islands, within the Arctic Circle. **highbrow** *n* intellectual or scholar. ◆ *adj* appealing to highbrows. **High Church** belonging to a section within the Anglican church stressing the importance of ceremony and ritual. **higher education** education at colleges, universities, and polytechnics. **high-fidelity** *adj* able to reproduce sound with little or no distortion. **high-flown** *adj* (of ideas or speech) grand and elaborate. **high-handed** *adj* overbearing and dogmatic. **highlands** *pl n* area of relatively high ground. **highlight** *n* outstanding part or feature; light-toned area in a painting or photograph; lightened streak in the hair. ◆ *v* give emphasis to. **high-rise** *adj* (of a building) having many storeys. **high tea** *Brit* early evening meal consisting of a cooked dish, bread, cakes, and tea. **high-tech** *adj* same as HI-TECH. **high time** latest possible time. **highway** *n* main road for fast-moving traffic. **highwayman** *n*

formerly, robber, usually on horseback, who robbed travellers at gunpoint.

hijack *v* seize control of (a vehicle or aircraft) while travelling. **hijacker** *n*

hike *v* walk a long way (for pleasure) in the country; (foll. by *up*) pull (up) or raise. **hiker** *n*

hilarious *adj* very funny. **hilariously** *adv* **hilarity** *n*

hill *n* raised part of the earth's surface, less high than a mountain; incline or slope. **hilly** *adj* **hillock** *n* small hill. **hillbilly** *n US* unsophisticated country person.

hilt *n* handle of a sword or knife.

him *pron* refers to a male person or animal when the object of a sentence or clause.

hind¹ *adj* **hinder, hindmost** situated at the back.

hind² *n* female deer.

hinder *v* obstruct the progress of. **hindrance** *n*

Hinduism *n* dominant religion of India which involves the worship of many gods and a belief in reincarnation. **Hindu** *n* person who practises Hinduism. ◆ *adj* of Hinduism. **Hindi** *n* language of N central India.

hinge *n* device for holding together two parts so that one can swing freely. ◆ *v* fit a hinge to; (foll. by *on*) depend (on).

hint *n* indirect suggestion; piece of advice; small amount. ◆ *v* suggest indirectly.

hinterland *n* land lying behind a coast or near a city, esp. a port.

hip¹ *n* either side of the body below the waist and above the thigh.

hip² *n* fruit of the rose bush.

hip-hop *n* pop-culture movement originating in the 1980s, comprising rap music, graffiti, and break dancing.

hippie *n* (esp. in the late 1960s) person whose behaviour and dress imply a rejection of conventional values.

hippo *n, pl* **-pos** *Informal* hippopotamus.

hippodrome *n* music hall, variety theatre, or circus.

hippopotamus *n, pl* **-muses, -mi** large African mammal with thick wrinkled skin, living in rivers.

hippy *n, pl* **-pies** same as HIPPIE.

hire *v* obtain temporary use of by payment; employ for wages. ◆ *n* act of hiring; payment for the use of something. **hireling** *n* person who works only for wages. **hire-purchase** *n Brit* instalment plan.

hirsute [her-suit] *adj* hairy.

his *pron, adj* (something) belonging to him.

Hispanic *adj* of Spain or a Spanish-speaking country.

hiss *n* sound like that of a long *s* (as an exclamation of contempt). ◆ *v* utter a hiss; show derision or anger towards.

histamine [hiss-ta-meen] *n* substance released by the body tissues, causing allergic reactions.

histogram *n* statistical graph in which the frequency of values is represented by vertical bars of varying heights and widths.

histology *n* study of the tissues of an animal or plant.

history *n, pl* **-ries** (record or account of) past events and developments; study of these; record of someone's past; play that depicts historical events. **historian** *n* writer of history. **historic** *adj* famous or significant in history. **historical** *adj* based on history; occurring in the past. **historically** *adv*

histrionic *adj* excessively dramatic. **histrionics** *pl n* melodramatic behaviour.

hit *v* **hitting, hit** strike forcefully; come into violent contact with; affect adversely; reach (a point or place). ◆ *n* impact or blow; success; *Computers* single visit to a website. **hitter** *n* **hit it off** *Informal* get on well together. **hit the trail, road** *Informal* set out on a journey. **hit man** hired assassin. **hit on** *v* think of (an idea). **hit-or-miss** *adj* haphazard.

hitch *v* fasten with a loop or hook; pull up with a jerk; *Informal* obtain (a lift) by hitchhiking. ◆ *n* slight difficulty. **hitchhike** *v* travel by obtaining free lifts. **hitchhiker** *n*

hi-tech *adj* using sophisticated technology.

hither *adv* to or towards this place. **hitherto** *adv* until this time.

HIV human immunodeficiency virus.

hive *n* structure in which bees live. **hive of activity** place where people are very busy. **hive off** *v* separate from a larger group.

hives *n* disease causing itchy red or whitish patches on the skin.

HM Her (*or* His) Majesty.

HMCS Her (*or* His) Majesty's Canadian Ship.

HMS Her (*or* His) Majesty's Service *or* Ship.

hoard *n* store hidden away for future use. ◆ *v* gather or accumulate. **hoarder** *n*

hoarding *n* large board for displaying advertisements.

hoarfrost *n* white ground frost.

hoarse *adj* (of a voice) rough and unclear; having a rough and unclear voice. **hoarsely** *adv* **hoarseness** *n*

hoary *adj* **hoarier, hoariest** grey or white (with age); very old.

hoax *n* deception or trick. ◆ *v* deceive or play a trick upon. **hoaxer** *n*

hob *n* flat top part of a cooker.

hobble *v* walk lamely; tie the legs of (a horse) together.

hobby *n, pl* **-bies** activity pursued in one's spare time. **hobbyhorse** *n* favourite topic; toy horse.

hobgoblin *n* mischievous goblin.

hobnail *n* large-headed nail for boot soles.

hobnob *v* **-nobbing, -nobbed** (foll. by *with*) socialize (with).

hobo *n, pl* **-bos** tramp or vagrant.

hock¹ *n* joint in the leg of a horse or similar animal corresponding to the human ankle.

hock² *n* white German wine.

hock³ *v Informal* pawn. **in hock** pawned; in debt.

hockey *n* team game played on a field with a ball and curved sticks; ice hockey.

hocus-pocus *n* trickery.

hod *n* open wooden box attached to a pole, for carrying bricks or mortar; type of coal scuttle.

hoe *n* long-handled tool used to loosen soil or to weed. ◆ *v* scrape or weed using a hoe.

hog *n* castrated male pig; *Informal* greedy person. ◆ *v* **hogging, hogged** *Informal* take more than one's share of. **hogshead** *n* large cask. **hogwash** *n Informal* nonsense.

Hogmanay n (in Scotland) New Year's Eve.

hoi polloi n the ordinary people.

hoist v raise or lift up. ◆ n device for lifting things.

hoity-toity adj Informal haughty.

hold[1] v **holding, held** keep or support in or using the hands or arms; consider to be as specified, e.g. who are you holding responsible?; maintain in a specified position or state; have the capacity for; Informal wait, esp. on the telephone; own, possess; keep possession of; reserve (a room etc.); restrain or keep back; not use; cause to take place, e.g. hold a meeting; (cause to) remain committed to (a promise etc.); believe. ◆ n act or method of holding; influence; something held onto for support. **holder** n **holding** n property, such as land or stocks and shares. **holdall** n Brit carryall. **hold-up** n armed robbery; delay.

hold[2] n cargo compartment in a ship or aircraft.

hole n area hollowed out in a solid; opening or hollow; animal's burrow; Informal unattractive place; Informal difficult situation; Golf place into which the ball is to be played. ◆ v make holes in; hit (a golf ball) into a hole. **holey** adj

holiday n time spent away from home for rest or recreation; day or other period of rest from work or studies.

holism n consideration of the complete person in the treatment of disease. **holistic** adj

hollow adj having a hole or space inside; (of sounds) as if echoing in a hollow place; without any real value or worth. ◆ n cavity; dip in the land. ◆ v form a hollow in.

holly n evergreen tree with prickly leaves and red berries.

hollyhock n tall garden plant with spikes of colourful flowers.

holocaust n destruction or loss of life on a massive scale.

hologram n three-dimensional photographic image.

holograph n document handwritten by the author.

holography n science of using lasers to produce holograms.

Holstein n breed of black-and-white dairy cattle.

holster n leather case for a pistol, hung from a belt.

holy adj **-lier, -liest** of or associated with God or a deity; devout or virtuous. **holiness** n **holier-than-thou** adj self-righteous. **Holy Communion** Christianity service in remembrance of the death and resurrection of Jesus Christ. **Holy Grail** (in medieval legend) the bowl used by Jesus Christ at the Last Supper. **Holy Spirit, Ghost** Christianity one of the three aspects of God. **Holy Week** Christianity week before Easter.

homage n show of respect or honour towards something or someone.

home n place where one lives; institution to care for the elderly, infirm, etc. ◆ adj of one's home, birthplace, or native country. ◆ adv to or at home. ◆ v (foll. by in on) direct or be directed onto (a point or target). **at home** at ease. **bring home to** make clear to. **home and dry** Informal safe or successful. **homeless** adj having nowhere to live. ◆ pl n people who have nowhere to live. **homelessness** n **homely** adj unattractive; Brit simple, ordinary, and comfortable. **homeward** adj, adv **homewards** adv **home-brew** n beer made at home. **home-made** adj made at home or on the premises. **home page** Computers introductory information about a website with hyperlinks to further pages. **home plate** Baseball base where hitter bats. **homesick** adj depressed by absence from home. **homesickness** n **homestead** n house with outbuildings, esp. on a farm; Hist land assigned to a N American settler. **homesteader** n **home truths** unpleasant facts told to a person about himself or herself. **homework** n school work done at home.

homeopathy [home-ee-**op**-ath-ee] n treatment of disease by small doses of a drug that produces symptoms of the disease in healthy people. **homeopath** n person who practises homeopathy. **homeopathic** [home-ee-oh-**path**-ik] adj **homeopathically** adv

homicide n killing of a human being; person who kills another. **homicidal** adj

homily n, pl **-lies** speech telling people how they should behave.

hominid n man or any extinct forerunner of man.

homo- combining form same, e.g. homosexual.

homogeneous [home-oh-**jean**-ee-uss] adj formed of similar parts. **homogeneity** n **homogenize** v make homogeneous; break up fat globules in (milk or cream) to distribute them evenly.

homograph n word spelt the same as another.

homologous [hom-**ol**-log-uss] adj having a related or similar position or structure.

homonym n word with the same spelling or pronunciation as another, but with a different meaning.

homophobia n hatred or fear of homosexuals. **homophobic** adj

homophone n word with the same pronunciation as another.

Homo sapiens [hoe-moh **sap**-ee-enz] n human beings as a species.

homosexual n, adj (person) sexually attracted to members of the same sex. **homosexuality** n

hone v sharpen.

honest adj not cheating, lying, or stealing; genuine or sincere; gained or earned fairly. **honestly** adv **honesty** n quality of being honest; plant with silvery seed pods.

honey n sweet edible fluid made by bees from nectar; term of endearment. **honeycomb** n waxy structure of hexagonal cells in which honey is stored. **honeydew melon** melon with yellow skin and sweet pale flesh. **honeymoon** n holiday taken by a newly married couple. **honeysuckle** n climbing shrub with sweet-smelling flowers.

honk n sound made by an automobile horn; sound made by a goose. ◆ v (cause to) make this sound.

honour, honor n personal integrity; (award given out of) respect; pleasure or privilege. ◆ pl rank or mark of the highest academic standard in a university degree course. ◆ v give praise and attention to; give an award to (someone) out of respect; keep (a promise); accept or pay (a cheque or bill). **do the honours** act as host or hostess by pouring drinks or giving out food. **honourable, honorable** adj **honourably, honorably** adv **honorary** adj held or given only as an honour; holding a position or giving one's services without pay. **honorific** adj showing respect.

hood[1] n head covering, often part of a coat etc.; folding roof of a convertible automobile or a baby carriage; metal cover over a vehicle's engine. ◆ v cover (as if) with a hood. **hooded** adj (of a garment) having a hood; (of eyes) having heavy eyelids that appear to be half closed.

hood[2] n Slang hoodlum.

hoodlum n Slang lawless youth.

hoodoo n, pl **-doos** (person or thing that brings) bad luck.

hoodwink v trick or deceive.

hoof n, pl **hooves, hoofs** horny casing of the foot of a horse, deer, etc. **hoof it** Informal walk.

hoo-ha n fuss or commotion.

hook n curved piece of metal or plastic used to hang, hold, or pull something; short swinging punch. ◆ v fasten or catch (as if) with a hook. **hooked** adj shaped like a hook; caught; (foll. by on) Slang addicted (to). **hooker** n Slang prostitute. **hook-up** n linking of radio or television stations. **hookworm** n parasitic worm with hooked mouth parts.

hookah n oriental pipe in which smoke is drawn through water and a long tube.

hooligan n rowdy young person. **hooliganism** n

hoop n rigid circular band, used esp. as a child's toy or for animals to jump through in the circus. **be put through the hoops** go through an ordeal. **hooped** adj

hoopla n fairground game in which hoops are thrown over objects in an attempt to win them.

hooray interj same as HURRAH.

hoot n sound of an automobile horn; owl's cry or similar sound; cry of derision; Informal amusing person or thing. ◆ v jeer or yell contemptuously at (someone); sound (an automobile horn); Informal laugh. **hooter** n device that hoots; Slang nose.

Hoover n ® vacuum cleaner. ◆ v (h-) vacuum.

hooves n a plural of HOOF.

hop¹ v hopping, hopped jump on one foot; move in short jumps; *Informal* move quickly. ◆ n instance of hopping; short journey, esp. by air; *Informal* dance.

hop² n climbing plant with green conelike flowers used to give beer a bitter flavour. ◆ pl the dried flowers.

hope v want (something) to happen or be true. ◆ n expectation of something desired; thing that gives cause for hope or is desired. **hopeful** adj having, expressing, or inspiring hope. ◆ n person considered to be on the brink of success. **hopefully** adv in a hopeful manner; it is hoped. **hopeless** adj

hopper n container for storing things such as grain or sand.

hopscotch n children's game of hopping in a pattern drawn on the ground.

horde n large crowd.

horizon n apparent line that divides the earth and the sky. ◆ pl limits of scope, interest, or knowledge.

horizontal adj flat and level with the ground or with a line considered as a base. ◆ n horizontal plane, position, or line. **horizontally** adv

hormone n substance secreted by certain glands which stimulates certain organs of the body; synthetic substance with the same effect. **hormonal** adj

horn n one of a pair of bony growths on the heads of animals such as cows and antelopes; substance of which this is made; wind instrument with a tube or pipe of brass fitted with a mouthpiece; device on a vehicle sounded as a warning. **horned** adj **horny** adj of or like horn; *Slang* sexually aroused. **hornbeam** n tree with smooth grey bark. **hornbill** n bird with a bony growth on its large beak. **hornpipe** n (music for) a lively solo dance, traditionally associated with sailors.

hornblende n mineral containing aluminum, calcium, sodium, magnesium, and iron.

hornet n large wasp with a severe sting.

horology n art or science of clock-making and measuring time.

horoscope n prediction of a person's future based on the positions of the planets, sun, and moon at his or her birth; diagram of the positions of these at a particular time and place.

horrendous adj horrific.

horror n (thing or person causing) terror or hatred. **horrible** adj disagreeable; causing horror. **horribly** adv **horrid** adj unpleasant or disagreeable; *Informal* unkind. **horrify** v cause feelings of horror in; shock. **horrific** adj particularly horrible.

hors d'oeuvre [or durv] n appetizer served before a main meal.

horse n four-footed animal with hooves, a mane, and a tail, used for riding and pulling carts, etc.; piece of gymnastic equipment used for vaulting over. **straight from the horse's mouth** from the most reliable source. **horsy** adj devoted to horses; like a horse. **horse about, around** v *Informal* play roughly or boisterously. **horse chestnut** tree with broad leaves, white or pink flowers, and large brown shiny nuts. **horsefly** n large bloodsucking fly. **horsehair** n hair from the tail or mane of a horse. **horse laugh** harsh boisterous laugh. **horseman, horsewoman** n rider on a horse. **horseplay** n rough or rowdy behaviour. **horsepower** n unit of power (equivalent to 745.7 watts), used to measure the power of an engine. **horseradish** n plant with a strong-tasting root, used to make a sauce. **horseshoe** n protective U-shaped piece of iron nailed to a horse's hoof, often regarded as a symbol of good luck.

horticulture n art or science of cultivating gardens. **horticultural** adj **horticulturist** n

hosanna interj exclamation of praise to God.

hose¹ n flexible tube for conveying liquid or gas. ◆ v water with a hose. **hoser** n *Slang* beer-drinking country dweller.

hose² n stockings, socks, and tights. **hosiery** n stockings, socks, etc. collectively.

hospice [hoss-piss] n nursing home

for the terminally ill.

hospital *n* institution for the care and treatment of sick or injured people. **hospitalize** *v* send or admit for care in a hospital. **hospitalization** *n*

hospitality *n* friendliness in welcoming strangers or guests. **hospitable** *adj* welcoming.

host¹ *n* person who entertains another as a guest; place or country providing the facilities for an event; compère of a show; animal or plant on which a parasite lives. ◆ *v* be the host of. **hostess** *n* woman who welcomes guests.

host² *n* large number.

Host *n Christianity* bread used in Holy Communion.

hostage *n* person who is illegally held prisoner until certain demands are met by other people.

hostel *n* building providing accommodation at a low cost for particular categories of people, such as homeless people.

hostelry *n, pl* **-ries** *Obs* tavern.

hostile *adj* unfriendly; of an enemy; (foll. by *to*) opposed (to). **hostility** *n* unfriendly and aggressive feelings or behaviour. ◆ *pl* acts of warfare.

hot *adj* **hotter, hottest** having a high temperature; giving or feeling heat; (of a temper) quick to flare up; (of a competition) intense; recent or new; liked very much, e.g. *a hot favourite*; spicy; *Slang* stolen. **in hot water** *Informal* in trouble. **hotly** *adv* **hotness** *n* **hotting** *n Informal* practice of stealing fast automobiles and putting on a show of skilful but dangerous driving. **hot air** *Informal* empty talk. **hotbed** *n* any place encouraging a particular activity, e.g. *a hotbed of vice*. **hot-blooded** *adj* passionate or excitable. **hot dog** hot sausage (esp. a frankfurter) in a bread roll. **hotfoot** *v, adv Informal* (go) as fast as possible. **hotheaded** *adj* hasty, having a hot temper. **hothouse** *n* heated greenhouse. **hot line** direct telephone link for emergency use. **hotplate** *n* heated metal surface on an electric cooker; portable device for keeping food warm.

hotchpotch *n* jumbled mixture.

hotel *n* commercial establishment providing lodging and meals. **hotelier** *n* owner or manager of a hotel.

Hottentot *n* member of a race of people of southern Africa, now nearly extinct.

hound *n* hunting dog. ◆ *v* pursue relentlessly.

hour *n* twenty-fourth part of a day; sixty minutes; time of day; appointed time. ◆ *pl* period regularly appointed for work or business. **hourly** *adj, adv* (happening) every hour; frequent(ly). **hourglass** *n* device with two glass compartments, containing a quantity of sand that takes an hour to trickle from the top section to the bottom one.

houri *n Islam* any of the beautiful nymphs of paradise.

house *n* building used as a dwelling; building for some specific purpose, e.g. *schoolhouse*; law-making body or the hall where it meets; family or dynasty; business firm; theatre audience or performance. ◆ *v* give accommodation to; cover or contain. **get on like a house on fire** *Informal* get on very well together. **on the house** *Informal* provided free by the management. **housing** *n* (providing of) houses; protective case or covering of a machine. **house arrest** confinement to one's home rather than to prison. **houseboat** *n* stationary boat used as a home. **housebreaker** *n* burglar. **housecoat** *n* woman's long loose robelike garment for casual wear. **household** *n* all the people living in a house. **householder** *n* person who owns or rents a house. **housekeeper** *n* person employed to run someone else's household. **housekeeping** *n* (money for) running a household. **housemaid** *n* female servant who does housework. **house-train** *v* train (a domestic animal) to urinate and defecate outside. **house-warming** *n* party to celebrate moving into a new home. **housewife** *n* woman who runs her own household. **housework** *n* work of running a house, such as cleaning, cooking, and shopping.

House music, House *n* kind of disco music based on funk, with fragments of other recordings edited in electronically.

hovel *n* small dirty dwelling.

hover *v* (of a bird etc.) remain

suspended in one place in the air; loiter; be in a state of indecision.

hovercraft *n* vehicle which can travel over both land and sea on a cushion of air.

how *adv* in what way; by what means; in what condition; to what degree.

however *adv* nevertheless; by whatever means; no matter how.

howdah *n* canopied seat on an elephant's back.

howitzer *n* cannon firing shells at a steep angle.

howl *v* utter a long loud cry. ◆ *n* such a cry; loud burst of laughter. **howler** *n* *Informal* stupid mistake.

hoyden *n* wild or boisterous girl, tomboy.

HP, hp hire-purchase; horsepower.

HQ headquarters.

HRH Her (*or* His) Royal Highness.

HTML hypertext markup language: text description language used on the Internet.

hub *n* centre of a wheel, through which the axle passes; central point of activity.

hubbub *n* confused noise of many voices, uproar.

hubby *n*, *pl* **-bies** *Informal* husband.

hubris [**hew-briss**] *n* pride.

huckster *n* person using aggressive methods of selling.

huddle *n* small group; *Informal* impromptu conference. ◆ *v* heap or crowd closely together; hunch (oneself) as through cold.

hue *n* colour.

hue and cry *n* public outcry.

huff *n* passing mood of anger or resentment. ◆ *v* blow or puff heavily. **huffy** *adj* **huffily** *adv*

hug *v* **hugging, hugged** clasp tightly in the arms, usually with affection; keep close to. ◆ *n* tight or fond embrace.

huge *adj* very big. **hugely** *adv* very much.

huh *interj* exclamation of derision, bewilderment, or inquiry.

hula *n* native dance of Hawaii.

Hula-Hoop *n* ® plastic hoop swung round the body by wriggling the hips.

hulk *n* body of an abandoned ship; *Offens* large or unwieldy person or thing. **hulking** *adj* unwieldy.

hull *n* main body of a boat; leaves round the stem of a strawberry, raspberry, or similar fruit; shell or husk of a fruit or seed. ◆ *v* remove the hulls from (fruit or seeds).

hullabaloo *n*, *pl* **-loos** loud confused noise or clamour.

hum *v* **humming, hummed** make a low continuous vibrating sound; sing with closed lips; *Slang* be very active. ◆ *n* humming sound. **hummingbird** *n* very small N American bird whose powerful wings make a humming noise as they vibrate.

human *adj* of, concerning, or typical of people. ◆ *n* human being. **humanity** *n* human nature; mankind; kindness or mercy. ◆ *pl* study of literature, philosophy, and the arts. **human being** man, woman, or child. **humanly** *adv* by human powers or means. **humanize** *v* make human or humane. **humankind** *n* mankind.

humane *adj* kind or merciful. **humanely** *adv*

humanism *n* belief in human effort rather than religion. **humanist** *n* **humanitarian** *n*, *adj* (person) with the interest of mankind at heart.

humble *adj* conscious of one's failings; modest, unpretentious; unimportant. ◆ *v* cause to become humble; humiliate. **humbly** *adv*

humbug *n* boiled candy flavoured with peppermint; nonsense; person or thing that deceives people.

humdinger *n* *Slang* excellent person or thing.

humdrum *adj* commonplace and dull.

humerus [**hew-mer-uss**] *n*, *pl* **-eri** bone from the shoulder to the elbow.

humid *adj* (of the weather) damp and warm. **humidity** *n* **humidify** *v* **humidifier** *n* device for increasing the amount of water vapour in the air in a room.

humiliate *v* lower the dignity or hurt the pride of. **humiliating** *adj* **humiliation** *n*

humility *n* quality of being humble.

hummock *n* hillock.

humour *n* ability to say or perceive things that are amusing; situations, speech, or writings that are humorous; state of mind, mood; *Obs* fluid in the body. ◆ *v* be kind and indulgent to.

humorous adj **humorously** adv

humorist n person who acts, speaks, or writes in a humorous way.

hump n normal or deforming lump, esp. on the back; hillock; Informal fit of sulking. ◆ v Slang carry or heave. **humpback** n person with an abnormal curvature of the spine. **humpbacked** adj **hump-back bridge** road bridge with a sharp slope on either side.

humus [hew-muss] n decomposing vegetable and animal mould in the soil.

hunch n Informal feeling or suspicion not based on facts. ◆ v draw (one's shoulders) up or together. **hunchback** n humpback.

hundred adj, n ten times ten. **hundredth** adj, n (of) number one hundred in a series. **hundredfold** adj, adv **hundredweight** n unit of weight of 112 lbs (50.8 kg).

hung v past of HANG ◆ adj (of a jury) unable to decide; (of a parliament) with no clear majority. **hung over** Informal suffering the effects of a hangover.

hunger n discomfort or weakness from lack of food; lack of food that causes suffering or death, e.g. refugees dying of hunger; desire or craving. ◆ v (foll. by for) want very much. **hungry** adj desiring food. **hungrily** adv **hunger strike** refusal of all food, as a means of protest.

hunk n large piece; Slang sexually attractive man.

hunt v seek out (animals) to kill or capture for sport or food; search (for). ◆ n act or instance of hunting; (party organized by) hunting wild animals for sport. **hunter** n man or animal that seeks out and kills or captures game; horse or dog bred for hunting. **huntress** n Obs woman who seeks out and kills or captures game. **huntsman** n man in charge of a pack of hounds; man who hunts.

hurdle n light barrier for jumping over; problem or difficulty. ◆ pl race involving hurdles. ◆ v jump over (something). **hurdler** n person who races over hurdles.

hurdy-gurdy n, pl **-dies** mechanical musical instrument, such as a barrel organ.

hurl v throw or utter violently.

hurling, hurley n Irish game resembling hockey.

hurly-burly n loud confusion.

hurrah, hurray interj exclamation of joy or applause.

hurricane n very strong, often destructive wind or storm. **hurricane lamp** kerosene lamp with a glass covering.

hurry v **-rying, -ried** (cause to) move or act in great haste. ◆ n haste; eagerness. **hurriedly** adv

hurt v **hurting, hurt** cause physical or mental pain to; wound the feelings of; Informal feel pain. ◆ n physical or mental pain or suffering. **hurtful** adj

hurtle v move rapidly or violently.

husband n woman's partner in marriage. ◆ v use economically. **husbandry** n farming; management of resources.

hush v make or be silent. ◆ n stillness or quietness. **hush-hush** adj Informal secret. **hush up** v suppress information about.

husk n outer covering of certain seeds and fruits. ◆ v remove the husk from.

husky[1] adj **huskier, huskiest** hoarse or dry in the throat; Informal big and strong. **huskily** adv

husky[2] n, pl **huskies** Arctic sledge dog with a thick coat and a curled tail.

hussar [hoo-zar] n Hist lightly armed cavalry soldier.

hussy n, pl **-sies** brazen or promiscuous woman.

hustings pl n proceedings at a parliamentary election.

hustle v push about, jostle; Slang (of a prostitute) solicit. ◆ n lively activity or bustle.

hut n small house or shelter.

hutch n cage for small pet animals.

hyacinth n sweet-smelling spring flower which grows from a bulb.

hyaena n same as HYENA.

hybrid n offspring of two plants or animals of different species; anything of mixed ancestry. ◆ adj of mixed ancestry.

hydra n mythical many-headed water serpent; any persistent problem; freshwater polyp.

hydrangea n ornamental shrub with clusters of pink, blue, or white flowers.

hydrant n outlet from a water main

with a nozzle for a hose.

hydrate n chemical compound of water with another substance.

hydraulic adj operated by pressure forced through a pipe by a liquid such as water or oil. **hydraulics** n study of the mechanical properties of fluids as they apply to practical engineering. **hydraulically** adv

hydro n hydroelectric power; electricity as supplied to residence, business, etc.; (H-) hydroelectric power company.

hydro- combining form water; hydrogen.

hydrocarbon n compound of hydrogen and carbon.

hydrochloric acid n strong colourless acid used in many industrial and laboratory processes.

hydrodynamics n science concerned with the mechanical properties of fluids.

hydroelectric adj of the generation of electricity by the use of water.

hydrofoil n fast light vessel with its hull raised out of the water on one or more pairs of fins.

hydrogen n light flammable colourless gaseous element which combines with oxygen to form water. **hydrogen bomb** atom bomb of enormous power in which energy is released by the fusion of hydrogen nuclei to give helium nuclei. **hydrogen peroxide** colourless liquid used as a hair bleach and as an antiseptic.

hydrolysis [hie-**drol**-iss-iss] n decomposition of a chemical compound reacting with water.

hydrometer [hie-**drom**-it-er] n device for measuring the relative density of a liquid.

hydropathy n method of treating disease by the use of large quantities of water both internally and externally.

hydrophobia n fear of water; rabies.

hydroplane n light motorboat which skims the water.

hydroponics n science of cultivating plants in water without using soil.

hydrotherapy n Med treatment of certain diseases by exercise in water.

hydrous adj containing water.

hyena, hyaena n scavenging doglike mammal of Africa and S Asia.

hygiene n principles and practice of health and cleanliness; study of these principles. **hygienic** adj **hygienically** adv

hymen n membrane covering the opening of a girl's vagina, which breaks before puberty or at the first occurrence of sexual intercourse.

hymn n Christian song of praise sung to God or a saint. **hymnal** adj of hymns. ◆ n (also **hymn book**) book of hymns.

hype n intensive or exaggerated publicity or sales promotion. ◆ v promote (a product) using intensive or exaggerated publicity.

hyper adj Informal overexcited.

hyper- prefix over, above, excessively, e.g. hyperactive, hypercritical.

hyperbola [hie-**per**-bol-a] n curve produced when a cone is cut by a plane at a steeper angle to its base than its side.

hyperbole [hie-**per**-bol-ee] n deliberate exaggeration for effect. **hyperbolic** adj

hyperlink Computers ◆ n link from a hypertext file that gives users instant access to related material in another file.

hypermarket n huge self-service store.

hypersensitive adj unduly vulnerable emotionally or physically.

hypersonic adj having a speed of at least five times the speed of sound.

hypertension n abnormally high blood pressure.

hyphen n punctuation mark (-) indicating that two words or syllables are connected. **hyphenate** v join with a hyphen. **hyphenated** adj having two words or syllables joined by a hyphen. **hyphenation** n

hypnosis n artificially induced state of relaxation in which the mind is more than usually receptive to suggestion. **hypnotic** adj of or (as if) producing hypnosis. **hypnotism** n **hypnotist** n **hypnotize** v induce hypnosis in (someone).

hypo- prefix below, less than, e.g. hypocrite, hypodermic.

hypoallergenic adj (of cosmetics) not likely to cause an allergic reaction.

hypochondria n undue

preoccupation with one's health.
hypochondriac *n*

hypocrisy [hip-ok-rass-ee] *n, pl* **-sies**
(instance of) pretence of having
standards or beliefs that are contrary
to one's real character or actual
behaviour. **hypocrite** [hip-oh-krit] *n*
person who pretends to be what he or
she is not. **hypocritical** *adj*
hypocritically *adv*

hypodermic *adj, n* (denoting) a
syringe or needle used to inject a drug
beneath the skin.

hypotension *n* abnormally low blood
pressure.

hypotenuse [hie-pot-a-news] *n* side
of a right-angled triangle opposite the
right angle.

hypothermia *n* condition in which a
person's body temperature is reduced
to a dangerously low level.

hypothesis [hie-poth-iss-iss] *n, pl* **-ses**
[-seez] suggested but unproved
explanation of something.
hypothetical *adj* based on assumption
rather than fact or reality.
hypothetically *adv*

hysterectomy *n, pl* **-mies** surgical
removal of the womb.

hysteria *n* state of uncontrolled
excitement, anger, or panic. **hysterical**
adj **hysterically** *adv* **hysterics** *pl n*
attack of hysteria.

Hz hertz.

I i

I *pron* used by a speaker or writer to
refer to himself or herself as the
subject of a verb.

iambic *adj* (of poetry) written in
metrical units formed of one long and
one short syllable.

IBA Independent Broadcasting
Authority.

Iberian *adj* of Iberia, the peninsula of
Spain and Portugal.

ibex [ibe-eks] *n* wild goat with large
backward-curving horns.

ibid. (referring to a book, passage, etc.
previously cited) in the same place.

ibis [ibe-iss] *n* wading bird with long
legs.

ice *n* frozen water; *Brit* portion of ice

cream. ◆ *v* become covered with ice;
cover with icing; cool with ice. **break
the ice** create a relaxed atmosphere,
esp. between people meeting for the
first time. **iced** *adj* served very cold;
covered with icing. **icy** *adj* very cold;
covered with ice; aloof and unfriendly.
icily *adv* **iciness** *n* **ice age** period
when much of the earth's surface was
covered in glaciers. **iceberg** *n* large
floating mass of ice. **ice bridge** road
of ice across a frozen watercourse or
harbour. **ice cap** mass of ice
permanently covering an area. **ice
cream** sweet creamy frozen food. **ice
cube** small square block of ice added
to a drink to cool it. **ice floe** sheet of
floating ice. **ice hockey** team game
like hockey played on ice with a puck.
ice lolly flavoured ice on a stick. **ice
pick** axe-like tool for breaking ice. **ice
skate** boot with a steel blade fixed to
the sole, to enable the wearer to glide
over ice. **ice-skate** *v* **ice-skater** *n*

ichthyology [ik-thi-ol-a-jee] *n*
scientific study of fish.

icicle *n* tapering spike of ice hanging
where water has dripped.

icing *n* mixture of sugar and water etc.
used to cover and decorate cakes.
icing sugar finely ground sugar for
making icing.

icon *n* picture of Christ or another
religious figure, venerated in the
Orthodox Church; picture on a
computer screen representing a
computer function that can be
activated by moving the cursor over it.

iconoclast *n* person who attacks
established principles or ideas.
iconoclastic *adj*

id *n Psychoanalysis* the mind's
instinctive unconscious energies.

idea *n* plan or thought formed in the
mind; thought of something, e.g. *the
idea horrified her*; opinion.

ideal *n* conception of something that
is perfect; perfect person or thing.
◆ *adj* most suitable; perfect. **ideally**
adv **idealism** *n* tendency to seek
perfection in everything. **idealist** *n*
idealistic *adj* **idealize** *v* regard or
portray as perfect. **idealization** *n*

idem *pron, adj Latin* the same: used to
refer to a book, article, etc. already
quoted.

identical *adj* exactly the same.

identically *adv*

identify *v* **-fying, -fied** prove or recognize as being a certain person or thing; understand and sympathize with a person or group because one regards oneself as being similar or similarly situated; treat as being the same. **identifiable** *adj* **identification** *n*

Identikit *n* ® set of pictures of parts of faces that can be built up to form a likeness of a person wanted by the police.

identity *n, pl* **-ties** state of being a specified person or thing; individuality or personality; state of being the same.

ideogram, ideograph *n* picture, symbol, etc. representing an object rather than the sounds of its name.

ideology *n, pl* **-gies** body of ideas and beliefs of a group, nation, etc. **ideological** *adj* **ideologist** *n*

idiocy *n, pl* **-cies** utter stupidity.

idiom *n* group of words which when used together have a different meaning from the component words, e.g. *raining cats and dogs*; way of expression natural or peculiar to a language or group. **idiomatic** *adj* **idiomatically** *adv*

idiosyncrasy *n, pl* **-sies** personal peculiarity of mind, habit, or behaviour.

idiot *n* foolish person; mentally retarded person. **idiotic** *adj* utterly stupid. **idiotically** *adv*

idle *adj* not doing anything; not being used; lazy; useless, e.g. *idle thoughts*. ◆ *v* (esp. foll. by *away*) waste (time); (of an engine) run slowly with the gears disengaged. **idleness** *n* **idler** *n* **idly** *adv*

idol [ide-ol] *n* image of a god as an object of worship; object of excessive devotion. **idolatry** [ide-ol-a-tree] *n* worship of idols; excessive devotion or reverence. **idolater** *n* **idolatrous** *adj* **idolize** *v* love or admire excessively.

idyll [id-ill] *n* scene or time of peace and happiness; description in literature of a picturesque or charming scene or episode, esp. of country life. **idyllic** *adj* **idyllically** *adv*

i.e. that is to say.

if *conj* on the condition or supposition that; whether; even though. ◆ *n* uncertainty or doubt, e.g. *I won't have*

any ifs or buts. **iffy** *adj* Informal doubtful, uncertain.

igloo *n, pl* **-loos** dome-shaped Inuit house of snow and ice.

igneous [ig-nee-uss] *adj* (of rocks) formed as molten rock cools and hardens.

ignite *v* catch fire or set fire to. **ignition** *n* system that ignites the fuel-air mixture to start an engine; igniting.

ignoble *adj* dishonourable. **ignobly** *adv*

ignominy [ig-nom-in-ee] *n* humiliating disgrace. **ignominious** *adj* **ignominiously** *adv*

ignoramus *n, pl* **-muses** ignorant person.

ignore *v* refuse to notice, disregard deliberately **ignorance** *n* lack of knowledge. **ignorant** *adj* lacking knowledge; rude through lack of knowledge of good manners. **ignorantly** *adv*

iguana *n* large tropical American lizard.

ileum *n* lower part of the small intestine. **ileac** *adj*

ilk *n* of that ilk of the same type.

ill *adj* not in good health; bad, evil; unfavourable, e.g. *an ill omen*. ◆ *n* evil, harm. ◆ *adv* badly; hardly, with difficulty, e.g. *I can ill afford the expense*. **ill at ease** uncomfortable, unable to relax. **illness** *n* **ill-advised** *adj* badly thought out; unwise. **ill-disposed** *adj* (often foll. by *towards*) unfriendly or unsympathetic. **ill-fated** *adj* doomed or unlucky. **ill-gotten** *adj* obtained dishonestly. **ill-health** *n* condition of being unwell. **ill-mannered** *adj* rude. **ill-treat** *v* treat cruelly. **ill will** unkind feeling.

illegal *adj* against the law. **illegally** *adv* **illegality** *n*

illegible *adj* unable to be read or deciphered.

illegitimate *adj* born to parents not married to each other; unlawful. **illegitimacy** *n*

illicit *adj* illegal; forbidden or disapproved of by society.

illiterate *adj* unable to read or write; uneducated, ignorant. **illiteracy** *n*

illogical *adj* unreasonable; not logical. **illogicality** *n*

illuminate *v* light up; make clear,

explain; decorate with lights; *Hist* decorate (a manuscript) with designs of gold and bright colours.
illumination *n* **illuminating** *adj* helping to explain.

illusion *n* deceptive appearance or belief. **illusionist** *n* conjurer. **illusory** *adj* false.

illustrate *v* explain by use of examples; provide (a book or text) with pictures; be an example of. **illustration** *n* picture or diagram; example. **illustrative** *adj* **illustrator** *n*

illustrious *adj* famous and distinguished.

image *n* mental picture of someone or something; impression people have of a politician, organization, etc.; simile or metaphor; representation of a person or thing in art or literature; optical counterpart, as in a mirror; double, copy. ◆ *v* make an image of; reflect. **imagery** *n* images collectively, esp. in literature.

imagine *v* form a mental image of; think, believe, or guess. **imaginable** *adj* **imaginary** *adj* existing only in the imagination. **imagination** *n* ability to make mental images of things not present; creative mental ability. **imaginative** *adj* **imaginatively** *adv*

imago [im-may-go] *n*, *pl* **imagoes**, **imagines** [im-**maj**-in-ees] sexually mature adult insect.

imam *n* leader of prayers in a mosque; title of some Islamic leaders.

IMAX ® (**eye**-max) *n* film projection process which produces an image ten times larger than standard.

imbalance *n* lack of proportion.

imbecile [**imb**-ess-eel] *n* idiot. ◆ *adj* idiotic. **imbecility** *n*

imbibe *v* drink (esp. alcohol); *Lit* absorb (ideas etc.).

imbroglio [imb-**role**-ee-oh] *n*, *pl* **-ios** confusing and complicated situation.

imbue *v* **-buing**, **-bued** (usu. foll. by *with*) fill or inspire with (ideals or principles).

IMF International Monetary Fund.

imitate *v* take as a model; mimic or copy. **imitation** *n* copy of an original; imitating. **imitative** *adj* **imitator** *n*

immaculate *adj* completely clean or tidy; completely flawless. **immaculately** *adv*

immanent *adj* present within and throughout something. **immanence** *n*

immaterial *adj* not important, not relevant.

immature *adj* not fully developed; lacking wisdom or stability because of youth. **immaturity** *n*

immediate *adj* occurring at once; next or nearest in time, space, or relationship. **immediately** *adv* **immediacy** *n*

immemorial *adj* having existed or happened for longer than anyone can remember. **immemorially** *adv*

immense *adj* huge or vast. **immensely** *adv* **immensity** *n*

immerse *v* plunge (something) into liquid; involve deeply, e.g. *I immersed myself in my work.* **immersion** *n* immersing. **immersion heater**, **immerser** *n* electric heater contained in a domestic hot-water tank.

immigrant *n* person who comes to a foreign country in order to settle there. **immigration** *n*

imminent *adj* about to happen. **imminently** *adv* **imminence** *n*

immobile *adj* unable to move; not moving. **immobility** *n* **immobilize** *v* make unable to move or work.

immoderate *adj* excessive or unreasonable.

immolate *v* kill as a sacrifice. **immolation** *n*

immoral *adj* morally wrong, corrupt; sexually depraved or promiscuous. **immorality** *n*

immortal *adj* living forever; famed for all time. ◆ *n* immortal being; person whose fame will last for all time. **immortality** *n* **immortalize** *v*

immune *adj* protected against a specific disease; secure (against); exempt (from). **immunity** *n* ability to resist disease; freedom from prosecution, tax, etc. **immunize** *v* make immune to a disease. **immunization** *n*

immunodeficiency *n* deficiency in or breakdown of a person's immune system.

immunology *n* study of immunity. **immunological** *adj* **immunologist** *n*

immure *v* *Lit* imprison.

immutable [im-**mute**-a-bl] *adj* unchangeable. **immutability** *n*

imp n demon; mischievous child.

impact n strong effect; collision. ◆ v press firmly against or into. **impaction** n

impair v weaken or damage. **impaired** adj Law influenced by alcohol while driving a motor vehicle. **impairment** n

impala [imp-ah-la] n southern African antelope.

impale v pierce with a sharp object. **impalement** n

impalpable adj imperceptible to the touch; difficult to understand.

impart v communicate (information); give, e.g. impart flavour.

impartial adj not favouring one side or the other. **impartially** adv **impartiality** n

impassable adj (of a road etc.) impossible to travel over or through.

impasse [am-pass] n situation in which progress is impossible.

impassioned adj full of emotion.

impassive adj showing no emotion, calm. **impassivity** n

impatient adj irritable at any delay or difficulty; restless to have or do something. **impatiently** adv **impatience** n

impeach v charge with a serious crime against the state. **impeachment** n

impeccable adj without fault, excellent. **impeccably** adv

impecunious adj penniless.

impedance [imp-eed-anss] n Electricity measure of the opposition to the flow of an alternating current.

impede v hinder in action or progress. **impediment** n something that makes action, speech, or progress difficult. **impedimenta** pl n objects impeding progress, esp. baggage or equipment.

impel v -pelling, -pelled drive (a person) to do something.

impending adj (esp. of something bad) about to happen.

impenetrable adj impossible to get through; impossible to understand.

imperative adj extremely urgent, vital; Grammar denoting a mood of verbs used in commands. ◆ n Grammar imperative mood.

imperceptible adj too slight or gradual to be noticed. **imperceptibly** adv

imperfect adj having faults or mistakes; not complete; Grammar denoting a tense of verbs describing continuous, incomplete, or repeated past actions. ◆ n Grammar imperfect tense. **imperfection** n

imperial adj of an empire or emperor; majestic; denoting weights and measures formerly official in Britain, Canada, and other countries of the Commonwealth. **imperialism** n rule by one country over many others. **imperialist** n, adj

imperil v -illing, -illed endanger.

imperious adj used to being obeyed, domineering.

impersonal adj not influenced by emotion; lacking human warmth or personality; Grammar (of a verb) without a personal subject, as in it is snowing. **impersonality** n

impersonate v pretend to be (another person); imitate the mannerisms of (someone). **impersonation** n **impersonator** n

impertinent adj rude. **impertinently** adv **impertinence** n

imperturbable adj calm, not excitable. **imperturbability** n

impervious adj not letting (water etc.) through; not influenced by (a feeling, argument, etc.).

impetigo [imp-it-tie-go] n contagious skin disease.

impetuous adj done or acting without thought, rash. **impetuously** adv **impetuosity** n

impetus [imp-it-uss] n, pl -tuses impulse; force with which a body moves.

impinge v encroach (upon), affect or restrict.

impious [imp-ee-uss] adj showing a lack of respect or reverence.

impish adj mischievous.

implacable adj not to be appeased; unyielding. **implacably** adv **implacability** n

implant v fix firmly in the mind; insert or embed. ◆ n Med anything implanted in the body, such as a tissue graft. **implantation** n

implement n tool or instrument. ◆ v carry out (instructions etc.). **implementation** n

implicate v show to be involved, esp. in a crime. **implication** n something implied.

implicit adj expressed indirectly; absolute, e.g. implicit belief. **implicitly** adv

implore v beg desperately.

imply v -plying, -plied indicate by hinting, suggest; mean.

impolitic adj unwise, ill-advised.

imponderable n, adj (something) impossible to assess.

import v bring in (goods) from another country. ◆ n something imported; meaning; importance. **importation** n **importer** n

important adj of great significance or value; famous, powerful. **importance** n

importunate adj persistent in making demands. **importune** v persist in demands. **importunity** n

impose v force the acceptance of; take unfair advantage of. **imposing** adj impressive. **imposition** n unreasonable demand, burden.

impossible adj incapable of being done or experienced; absurd or unreasonable. **impossibly** adv **impossibility** n

impostor n person who cheats or swindles by pretending to be someone else.

impotent [imp-a-tent] adj powerless; (of a man) incapable of sexual intercourse. **impotence** n **impotently** adv

impound v take legal possession of, confiscate.

impoverish v make poor or weak. **impoverishment** n

impracticable adj incapable of being put into practice.

impractical adj not sensible.

imprecation n curse.

impregnable adj impossible to break into. **impregnability** n

impregnate v spread all through; make pregnant. **impregnation** n

impresario n, pl -ios person who runs theatre performances, concerts, etc.

impress v affect strongly, usu. favourably; stress or emphasize; imprint or stamp. **impression** n (strong or favourable) effect; vague idea; impersonation for entertainment; mark made by pressing.

impressionable adj easily influenced.

impressionism n art style that gives a general effect or mood rather than form or structure. **impressionist** n **impressionistic** adj

impressive adj making a strong impression, esp. through size, importance, or quality.

imprimatur [imp-rim-ah-ter] n official approval to print a book.

imprint n mark made by printing or stamping; publisher's name and address on a book. ◆ v produce (a mark) by printing or stamping.

imprison v put in prison. **imprisonment** n

improbable adj unlikely. **improbability** n

impromptu adv, adj without preparation, improvised.

improper adj indecent; incorrect or irregular; (of a fraction) with a numerator larger than the denominator, as in $5/3$.

impropriety [imp-roe-**pry**-a-tee] n, pl -ties improper behaviour.

improve v make or become better. **improvement** n

improvident adj not planning for future needs. **improvidence** n

improvise v make use of materials at hand; make up (a piece of music, speech, etc.) as one goes along. **improvisation** n

impudent adj cheeky. **impudently** adv **impudence** n

impugn [imp-**yoon**] v call in question, cast doubt on.

impulse n sudden urge to do something; short electrical signal passing along a wire or nerve or through the air. **on impulse** suddenly and without planning. **impulsive** adj tending to act without thinking first. **impulsively** adv

impunity [imp-**yoon**-it-ee] n **with impunity** without punishment or unpleasant consequences.

impure adj having unwanted substances mixed in; immoral or obscene. **impurity** n

impute v attribute responsibility to. **imputation** n

in prep inside, within; during; at the end of (a period of time); indicating a state, situation, or manner; into. ◆ adv in or into a particular place; at one's home or place of work; in office or power; in fashion. ◆ adj fashionable.

inability n lack of means or skill to do something.

inaccurate adj not correct. **inaccuracy** n

inadequate adj not enough; not good enough. **inadequacy** n

inadvertent adj unintentional. **inadvertently** adv

inalienable adj not able to be taken away, e.g. an inalienable right.

inane adj senseless or silly. **inanity** n

inanimate adj not living.

inanition n exhaustion or weakness, as from lack of food.

inappropriate adj not suitable.

inarticulate adj unable to express oneself clearly or well.

inasmuch as conj seeing that, because.

inaugurate v open or begin the use of, esp. with ceremony; formally establish (a new leader) in office. **inaugural** adj **inauguration** n

inauspicious adj unlucky, suggesting an unfavourable outcome.

inboard adj (of a boat's engine) inside the hull.

inborn adj existing from birth.

inbred adj produced as a result of inbreeding; inborn or ingrained.

inbreeding n breeding from closely related individuals.

inbuilt adj present from the start.

Inc. (of a company) incorporated.

incalculable adj impossible to estimate, very great.

in camera adv in private session.

incandescent adj glowing with heat; (of artificial light) produced by a glowing filament. **incandescence** n

incantation n ritual chanting of magic words or sounds. **incantatory** adj

incapable adj (foll. by of) lacking the ability to; helpless.

incapacitate v deprive of strength or ability, disable. **incapacity** n

incarcerate v imprison. **incarceration** n

incarnate adj possessing human form; typified, e.g. stupidity incarnate. **incarnation** n **Incarnation** n Christianity God's coming to earth in human form as Jesus Christ.

incendiary [in-**send**-ya-ree] adj (of bombs etc.) designed to cause fires. ◆ n, pl -aries bomb designed to cause fires; fire raiser or arsonist.

incense[1] v make very angry.

incense[2] n substance that gives off a sweet perfume when burned; its smoke.

incentive n something that encourages effort or action.

inception n beginning.

incessant adj never stopping. **incessantly** adv

incest n sexual intercourse between two people too closely related to marry. **incestuous** adj

inch n unit of length equal to one twelfth of a foot or 2.54 centimetres. ◆ v move very slowly.

inchoate [in-**koe**-ate] adj just begun and not yet properly developed.

incidence n extent, degree, or frequency of occurrence.

incident n (memorable) event; public disturbance.

incidental adj occurring as a minor part of or accompaniment to something else; happening by chance. **incidentally** adv **incidental music** background music for a film or play.

incinerate v burn to ashes. **incineration** n **incinerator** n furnace for burning rubbish.

incipient adj just starting to appear or happen.

incise v cut into with a sharp tool. **incision** n **incisive** adj direct and forceful. **incisor** n cutting tooth.

incite v stir up or provoke. **incitement** n

incivility n, pl -ties rudeness.

inclement adj (of weather) bad. **inclemency** n

incline v lean, slope; (cause to) have a certain disposition or tendency. ◆ n slope. **inclination** n liking, tendency, or preference; slope; degree of deviation from the horizontal or vertical.

include v have as (part of) the contents; put in as part of a set or group. **inclusion** n **inclusive** adj including everything. **inclusively** adv

incognito [in-kog-**nee**-toe] adv, adj under an assumed identity. ◆ n, pl -tos false identity.

incoherent adj (of speech) unclear

and impossible to understand.
incoherence n **incoherently** adv

income n amount of money earned from work, investments, etc. **income tax** personal tax levied on annual income.

incoming adj about to arrive; about to come into office.

incommode v inconvenience.

incommodious adj cramped.

incommunicado adj, adv deprived of communication with other people.

incomparable adj beyond comparison. **incomparably** adv

incompatible adj inconsistent or conflicting. **incompatibility** n

incompetent adj lacking the necessary ability to do something. **incompetence** n

inconceivable adj impossible to imagine.

inconclusive adj not giving a final decision or result.

incongruous adj inappropriate or out of place. **incongruously** adv **incongruity** n

inconsequential adj unimportant.

inconsiderable adj relatively small; insignificant.

inconstant adj liable to change one's loyalties or opinions.

incontinent adj not able to control one's bladder or bowels. **incontinence** n

incontrovertible adj impossible to deny or disprove.

inconvenience n trouble or difficulty. ◆ v cause trouble or difficulty to. **inconvenient** adj

incorporate v include or be included as part of a larger unit. **incorporation** n

incorporeal adj without bodily existence.

incorrigible adj beyond reform. **incorrigibility** n

incorruptible adj impossible to bribe or corrupt; honest; not subject to decay.

increase v make or become greater in size, number, etc. ◆ n rise in number, size, etc.; amount by which something increases. **increasingly** adv more and more.

incredible adj unbelievable; Informal marvellous, amazing. **incredibly** adv

incredulous adj not willing or able to believe something. **incredulity** n

increment n increase in money or value, esp. a regular salary increase. **incremental** adj

incriminate v make (someone) seem guilty of a crime. **incriminating** adj **incrimination** n

incubate [in-cube-ate] v (of birds) hatch eggs by sitting on them; grow (bacteria); (of bacteria) remain inactive in an animal or person before causing disease. **incubation** n **incubator** n heated enclosed apparatus for rearing premature babies; apparatus for artificially hatching eggs.

incubus [in-cube-uss] n, pl **-bi, -buses** demon believed to have sex with sleeping women; nightmare.

inculcate v fix in someone's mind by constant repetition. **inculcation** n

incumbent adj it is incumbent on it is the duty of. ◆ n person holding a particular office or position. **incumbency** n

incur v **-curring, -curred** bring (something unpleasant) upon oneself.

incurable adj not able to be cured. **incurably** adv

incurious adj showing no curiosity or interest.

incursion n sudden brief invasion; inroad.

indebted adj owing gratitude for help or favours; owing money. **indebtedness** n

indecent adj morally or sexually offensive; unsuitable or unseemly, e.g indecent haste. **indecently** adv **indecency** n **indecent assault** sexual attack which does not include rape. **indecent exposure** showing of one's genitals in public.

indecipherable adj impossible to read.

indeed adv really, certainly. ◆ interj showing surprise, doubt, etc.

indefatigable adj never getting tired. **indefatigably** adv

indefensible adj not justifiable; unable to be defended. **indefensibly** adv

indefinite adj without exact limits, e.g. an indefinite period; vague. **indefinite article** Grammar the word a or an. **indefinitely** adv

indelible *adj* impossible to erase or remove; producing indelible marks. **indelibly** *adv*

indelicate *adj* embarrassing, tasteless. **indelicacy** *n*

indemnify *v* **-ifying, -ified** give indemnity to; compensate. **indemnification** *n*

indemnity *n, pl* **-ties** insurance against loss or damage; compensation for loss or damage suffered.

indent *v* start (a line of writing) further from the margin than the other lines; order (goods) using a special order form. **indentation** *n* dent in a surface or edge.

indenture *n* contract, esp. one binding an apprentice to his employer.

independent *adj* free from the control or influence of others; separate; financially self-reliant; capable of acting for oneself or on one's own. ♦ *n* politician who does not belong to any party. **independently** *adv* **independence** *n*

in-depth *adj* detailed or thorough.

indescribable *adj* too intense or extreme for words. **indescribably** *adv*

indeterminate *adj* uncertain in extent, amount, or nature. **indeterminacy** *n*

index *n, pl* **indexes**, *Math* **indices** [in-diss-eez] alphabetical list of names or subjects dealt with in a book; file or catalogue used to find things; pointer or indicator; *Math* exponent. ♦ *v* provide (a book) with an index; enter in an index; make index-linked. **index finger** finger next to the thumb. **index-linked** *adj* (of pensions, wages, etc.) rising or falling in line with the cost of living.

Indian *n, adj* (person) from India; (person) descended from the original inhabitants of the American continents. **Indian summer** period of warm sunny weather in fall.

India rubber *n* eraser.

indicate *v* be a sign or symptom of; point out; state briefly; (of a measuring instrument) show a reading of. **indication** *n* **indicative** [in-dik-a-tiv] *adj* suggesting, e.g. *clouds indicative of rain*; *Grammar* denoting a mood of verbs used to make a statement. **indicator** *n* something

acting as a sign or indication; flashing light on a vehicle showing the driver's intention to turn; dial or gauge.

indict [in-dite] *v* formally accuse of a crime. **indictable** *adj* **indictment** *n*

indifferent *adj* showing no interest or concern; of poor quality or low standard. **indifference** *n* **indifferently** *adv*

indigenous [in-dij-in-uss] *adj* born in or natural to a country.

indigent *adj* so poor as to lack necessities. **indigence** *n*

indigestion *n* (discomfort or pain caused by) difficulty in digesting food. **indigestible** *adj*

indignation *n* anger caused by something unfair or wrong. **indignant** *adj* feeling or showing indignation. **indignantly** *adv*

indignity *n, pl* **-ties** embarrassing or humiliating treatment.

indigo *n* deep violet-blue; dye of this colour.

indirect *adj* done or caused by someone or something else; not by a straight route. **indirect object** *Grammar* person or thing indirectly affected by an action, such as *Sue* in *I bought Sue a book*. **indirect speech** report that gives the content of what someone said but not the actual words.

indiscreet *adj* incautious or tactless in revealing secrets. **indiscreetly** *adv* **indiscretion** *n*

indiscriminate *adj* chosen or choosing without thought or care.

indispensable *adj* impossible to do without.

indisposed *adj* unwell or ill; unwilling. **indisposition** *n*

indisputable *adj* without doubt. **indisputably** *adv*

indissoluble *adj* permanent.

indium *n* soft silver-white metallic element.

individual *adj* characteristic of or meant for a single person or thing; separate or distinct; distinctive, unusual. ♦ *n* single person or thing. **individually** *adv* singly. **individualism** *n* principle of living one's life in one's own way. **individualist** *n* **individualistic** *adj* **individuality** *n* distinctive character or personality.

indoctrinate v teach (someone) to accept a doctrine or belief uncritically. **indoctrination** n

Indo-European adj, n (of) a family of languages spoken in most of Europe and much of Asia, including English, Russian, and Hindi.

indolent adj lazy. **indolence** n

indomitable adj too strong to be defeated or discouraged. **indomitably** adv

indoor adj inside a building. **indoors** adv

indubitable [in-dew-bit-a-bl] adj beyond doubt, certain. **indubitably** adv

induce v persuade; cause; Med bring on (labour) by the use of drugs etc. **inducement** n something that encourages someone to do something.

induct v formally install someone, esp. a clergyman, in office.

induction n reasoning process by which general conclusions are drawn from particular instances; process by which electrical or magnetic properties are produced by the proximity of an electrified or magnetic object; formal installing of a person into office. **inductance** n **inductive** adj **induction coil** transformer for producing high voltage from a low voltage. **induction course** training course to help familiarize someone with a new job.

indulge v allow oneself pleasure, e.g. indulge in daydreaming; allow (someone) to have or to do everything he or she wants. **indulgence** n something allowed because it gives pleasure; act of indulging oneself or someone else; favourable or tolerant treatment. **indulgent** adj **indulgently** adv

industrial adj of, used in, or employed in industry. **industrialize** v develop large-scale industry in (a country or region). **industrial action** action such as a strike or work-to-rule, by which workers can protest about their conditions. **industrial estate** Brit industrial park. **industrial park** area of land set aside for factories and warehouses. **industrial relations** relations between management and workers.

industry n, pl -tries manufacture of goods; branch of this, e.g. the publishing industry; quality of working hard. **industrious** adj hard-working.

inebriate adj, n habitually drunk (person). **inebriated** adj drunk. **inebriation** n drunkenness.

inedible adj not fit to be eaten.

ineffable adj too great for words. **ineffably** adv

ineffectual adj having no effect or an inadequate effect.

ineligible adj not qualified for or entitled to something.

ineluctable adj impossible to avoid.

inept adj clumsy, lacking skill. **ineptitude** n

inequitable adj unfair.

ineradicable adj impossible to remove.

inert adj without the power of motion or resistance; chemically unreactive. **inertly** adv **inertness** n

inertia n feeling of unwillingness to do anything; Physics property by which a body remains still or continues to move unless a force is applied to it. **inertial** adj

inescapable adj unavoidable.

inestimable adj too great to be estimated. **inestimably** adv

inevitable adj unavoidable, sure to happen. ♦ n something inevitable. **inevitably** adv **inevitability** n

inexorable adj relentless; unavoidable. **inexorably** adv

inexpert adj lacking skill.

inexplicable adj impossible to explain. **inexplicably** adv

in extremis adv Latin in great difficulty; at the point of death.

inextricable adj impossible to escape from; impossible to disentangle or separate.

infallible adj never wrong; always successful. **infallibly** adv **infallibility** n

infamous [in-fam-uss] adj well-known for something bad. **infamously** adv **infamy** n

infant n very young child. **infancy** n early childhood; early stage of development. **infantile** adj childish.

infanticide n murder of an infant; person guilty of this.

infantry n foot soldiers.

infatuate v inspire with intense

unreasonable passion. **infatuated** *adj* **infatuation** *n*

infect *v* affect with a disease; affect with a feeling. **infection** *n* **infectious** *adj* (of a disease) spreading without actual contact; spreading from person to person, e.g. *infectious laughter.*

infer *v* **-ferring, -ferred** work out from evidence. **inference** *n*

inferior *adj* lower in position, status, or quality. ◆ *n* person of lower position or status. **inferiority** *n*

infernal *adj* of hell; *Informal* irritating. **infernally** *adv*

inferno *n, pl* **-nos** intense raging fire.

infertile *adj* unable to produce offspring; (of soil) barren, not productive. **infertility** *n*

infest *v* inhabit or overrun in unpleasantly large numbers. **infestation** *n*

infidel *n* person with no religion; person who rejects a particular religion, esp. Christianity or Islam.

infidelity *n, pl* **-ties** sexual unfaithfulness to one's husband, wife, or lover.

infield *n Baseball* area covered by the home plate and three bases.

infighting *n* quarrelling within a group.

infiltrate *v* enter gradually and secretly. **infiltration** *n* **infiltrator** *n*

infinite [in-fin-it] *adj* without any limit or end. **infinitely** *adv*

infinitesimal *adj* extremely small.

infinitive [in-fin-it-iv] *n Grammar* form of a verb not showing tense, person, or number, such as *to sleep.*

infinity *n* endless space, time, or number.

infirm *adj* physically or mentally weak. **infirmity** *n*

infirmary *n, pl* **-ries** hospital.

inflame *v* make angry or excited. **inflamed** *adj* (of part of the body) red and swollen because of infection. **inflammation** *n* inflamed part of the body. **inflammatory** *adj* likely to provoke anger.

inflammable *adj* easily set on fire.

inflate *v* expand by filling with air or gas; cause economic inflation in. **inflatable** *adj* able to be inflated. ◆ *n* plastic or rubber object which can be inflated.

inflation *n* increase in prices and fall in the value of money; inflating. **inflationary** *adj*

inflection, inflexion *n* change in the pitch of the voice; *Grammar* change in the form of a word to show grammatical use.

inflexible *adj* obstinate or unyielding; fixed and unalterable. **inflexibly** *adv* **inflexibility** *n*

inflict *v* impose (something unpleasant) on. **infliction** *n*

inflorescence *n Botany* arrangement of flowers on a stem.

influence *n* effect of one person or thing on another; (person with) the power to have such an effect. ◆ *v* have an effect on. **influential** *adj* **influentially** *adv*

influenza *n* viral disease causing muscle pains, fever, and catarrh.

influx *n* arrival or entry of many people or things; a flowing in.

info *n Informal* information.

inform *v* tell; give incriminating information to the police. **informant** *n* person who gives information. **information** *n* what is told, knowledge. **informative** *adj* giving useful information. **information technology** use of computers and electronic technology to store and communicate information. **informer** *n* person who informs to the police.

informal *adj* relaxed and friendly; appropriate for everyday life or use. **informally** *adv* **informality** *n*

infra dig *adj Informal* beneath one's dignity.

infrared *adj* of or using rays below the red end of the visible spectrum.

infrastructure *n* basic facilities, services, and equipment needed for a country or organization to function properly.

infringe *v* break (a law or agreement). **infringement** *n*

infuriate *v* make very angry.

infuse *v* fill with (an emotion or quality); soak to extract flavour. **infusion** *n* infusing; liquid obtained by infusing.

ingenious [in-jean-ee-uss] *adj* clever at contriving; cleverly contrived. **ingeniously** *adv* **ingenuity** [in-jen-new-it-ee] *n*

ingénue [an-jay-new] *n* naive or inexperienced young woman, esp. as a role played by an actress.

ingenuous [in-jen-new-uss] *adj* unsophisticated and trusting. **ingenuously** *adv*

ingest *v* take (food or drink) into the body. **ingestion** *n*

inglorious *adj* shameful.

ingot *n* oblong block of cast metal.

ingrained *adj* (of a habit etc.) deep-rooted; (of dirt) deeply fixed.

ingratiate *v* bring (oneself) into favour (with). **ingratiating** *adj* **ingratiatingly** *adv*

ingredient *n* component of a mixture or compound.

ingress *n* act or right of entering.

ingrowing *adj* (of a toenail) growing abnormally into the flesh.

inhabit *v* **-habiting**, **-habited** live in. **inhabitable** *adj* **inhabitant** *n*

inhale *v* breathe in (air, smoke, etc.). **inhalation** *n* **inhalant** [in-**hale**-ant] *n* medical preparation inhaled to help breathing problems. **inhaler** *n* container for an inhalant.

inherent *adj* existing as an inseparable part. **inherently** *adv*

inherit *v* **-heriting**, **-herited** receive (money etc.) from someone who has died; receive (a characteristic) from parents etc.; receive from predecessors. **inheritance** *n* **inheritor** *n*

inhibit *v* **-hibiting**, **-hibited** restrain (an impulse or desire); hinder or prevent (action). **inhibition** *n* feeling of fear or embarrassment that stops one from behaving naturally. **inhibited** *adj*

inhospitable *adj* not hospitable, unfriendly; difficult to live in, harsh.

inhuman *adj* cruel or brutal; not human.

inhumane *adj* cruel or brutal. **inhumanity** *n*

inimical *adj* unfavourable or hostile. **inimically** *adv*

inimitable *adj* impossible to imitate, unique. **inimitably** *adv*

iniquity *n, pl* **-ties** great injustice; wickedness; sin. **iniquitous** *adj*

initial *adj* first, at the beginning. ♦ *n* first letter, esp. of someone's name. ♦ *v* **-tialling**, **-tialled** sign with one's initials. **initially** *adv* originally.

initiate *v* begin or set going; admit (someone) into a closed group; instruct in the basics of something. ♦ *n* initiated person. **initiation** *n* **initiator** *n* **initiatory** *adj*

initiative *n* first step, commencing move; ability to act independently.

inject *v* put (a fluid) into the body with a syringe; introduce (a new element), e.g. *he injected some humour into the scene.* **injection** *n*

injudicious *adj* showing poor judgment, unwise.

injunction *n* court order not to do something.

injure *v* hurt physically or mentally; damage. **injury** *n* physical hurt; damage. **injury time** *Sport* time added at the end of a match to compensate for time spent treating injured players. **injurious** *adj*

injustice *n* unfairness; unfair treatment or action.

ink *n* coloured liquid used for writing or printing. ♦ *v* mark or cover with ink. **inky** *adj* dark or black; stained with ink.

inkling *n* slight idea or suspicion.

inlaid *adj* set in another material so that the surface is smooth; made like this, e.g. *an inlaid table.*

inland *adj, adv* in or towards the interior of a country, away from the sea.

in-laws *pl n* relatives by marriage.

inlay *n* inlaid substance or pattern.

inlet *n* narrow piece of water extending from the sea into the land; valve etc. through which liquid or gas enters.

in loco parentis [par-**rent**-iss] *Latin* in place of a parent.

inmate *n* person living in an institution such as a prison.

inmost *adj* furthest inside, most secret.

inn *n* hotel; *Brit* pub or small hotel, esp. in the country. **innkeeper** *n*

innards *pl n Informal* internal organs; working parts.

innate *adj* being part of someone's nature, inborn.

inner *adj* happening or located within; of the mind or spirit, e.g. *inner peace.* **innermost** *adj* **inner city** parts of a city near the centre, esp. when seen as poor or violent.

innings n Sport player's or side's turn of batting; spell or turn.

innocent adj not guilty of a crime; without experience of evil; harmless. ◆ n innocent person, esp. a child. **innocently** adv **innocence** n

innocuous adj harmless. **innocuously** adv

innovate v introduce new ideas or methods. **innovation** n **innovative** adj **innovator** n

innuendo n, pl **-does** indirect accusation.

innumerable adj too many to be counted. **innumerably** adv

innumerate adj having no understanding of mathematics or science. **innumeracy** n

inoculate v protect against disease by injecting with a vaccine. **inoculation** n

inoperable adj Med unable to be operated on without risk.

inopportune adj badly timed.

inordinate adj excessive.

inorganic adj not having the characteristics of living organisms; of or denoting chemical substances that do not contain carbon. **inorganically** adv

inpatient n patient who stays in a hospital for treatment.

input n resources put into a project etc.; data fed into a computer. ◆ v **-putting, -put** enter (data) in a computer.

inquest n official inquiry, esp. into a sudden death.

inquire v seek information or ask about. **inquirer** n **inquiry** n question; investigation.

inquisition n thorough investigation; Hist (I-) organization within the Catholic Church for suppressing heresy. **inquisitor** n **inquisitorial** adj

inquisitive adj too curious about other people's business. **inquisitively** adv

inquorate adj without enough people present to make a quorum.

inroads pl n make inroads into start affecting or reducing, e.g my gambling has made inroads into my savings.

insalubrious adj likely to cause ill-health.

insane adj mentally ill; stupidly

irresponsible. **insanely** adv **insanity** n

insanitary adj dirty or unhealthy.

insatiable [in-**saysh**-a-bl] adj impossible to satisfy.

inscribe v write or carve words on. **inscription** n words inscribed.

inscrutable adj mysterious or enigmatic; incomprehensible. **inscrutably** adv **inscrutability** n

insect n small invertebrate animal with six legs, a segmented body, and usu. two or four wings. **insecticide** n substance for killing insects. **insectivorous** adj insect-eating.

insecure adj anxious or uncertain; not safe or firm.

inseminate v implant semen into. **insemination** n

insensate adj without sensation, unconscious; unfeeling.

insensible adj unconscious; without feeling; not aware; imperceptible. **insensibility** n

insensitive adj unaware of or ignoring other people's feelings. **insensitivity** n

insert v put inside or between. ◆ n something inserted. **insertion** n

inset adj decorated with something inserted. ◆ n small map or diagram within a larger one.

inshore adj close to the shore. ◆ adj, adv towards the shore.

inside prep in or to the interior of. ◆ adj of or on the inside; by or from someone within an organization, e.g inside information. ◆ adv in or into the inside; Slang in prison. ◆ n inner side, surface, or part. ◆ pl Informal stomach and bowels. **inside out** with the interior facing outwards; thoroughly. **insider** n member of a group who has exclusive knowledge about it.

insidious adj subtle or unseen but dangerous. **insidiously** adv

insight n clear understanding.

insignia [in-**sig**-nee-a] n, pl **-nias, -nia** badge or emblem of honour or office.

insignificant adj not important. **insignificance** n

insincere adj pretending what one does not feel. **insincerely** adv **insincerity** n

insinuate v suggest indirectly; work oneself into a position by gradual manoeuvres. **insinuation** n

insipid adj lacking spirit or flavour.

insipidity *n*

insist *v* demand or state firmly.
insistent *adj* making persistent
demands; demanding attention.
insistently *adv* **insistence** *n*

in situ *adv, adj Latin* in its original
position.

insofar as *adv* to the extent that.

insole *n* inner sole of a shoe or boot.

insolent *adj* arrogantly rude.
insolence *n* **insolently** *adv*

insoluble *adj* incapable of being
solved; incapable of being dissolved.

insolvent *adj* unable to pay one's
debts. **insolvency** *n*

insomnia *n* sleeplessness. **insomniac** *n*

insouciant *adj* carefree and
unconcerned. **insouciance** *n*

inspect *v* check closely or officially.
inspection *n* **inspector** *n* person who
inspects; high-ranking police officer.

inspire *v* fill with enthusiasm,
stimulate; arouse (an emotion).
inspiration *n* good idea; creative
influence or stimulus. **inspirational** *adj*

instability *n* lack of steadiness or
reliability.

install *v* put in and prepare
(equipment) for use; formally place (a
person) in a position or rank.
installation *n* installing; equipment in-
stalled; place containing equipment
for a particular purpose, e.g. *radar
installation.*

instalment *n* any of the portions of a
thing presented or a debt paid in
successive parts. **instalment plan**
system of purchase by which the
buyer pays for goods by instalments.

instance *n* particular example. ◆ *v*
mention as an example. **for instance**
for example.

instant *n* very brief time; particular
moment. ◆ *adj* immediate; (of foods)
requiring little preparation. **instantly**
adv at once.

instantaneous *adj* happening at
once. **instantaneously** *adv*

instead *adv* as a replacement or
substitute.

instep *n* part of the foot forming the
arch between the ankle and toes; part
of a shoe etc. covering this.

instigate *v* cause to happen, bring
about. **instigation** *n* **instigator** *n*

instil *v* -stilling, -stilled introduce (an

idea etc.) gradually in someone's
mind. **instilment** *n*

instinct *n* inborn tendency to behave
in a certain way. **instinctive** *adj*
instinctively *adv*

institute *n* organization set up for a
specific purpose, esp. teaching or
research. ◆ *v* start or establish.

institution *n* large important
organization such as a university or
bank; hospital etc. for people with
special needs; long-established
custom. **institutional** *adj*
institutionalize *v* make unable to cope
with life outside an institution.

instruct *v* order to do something;
teach (someone) how to do
something; brief (a solicitor or
barrister). **instruction** *n* order;
teaching. ◆ *pl* information on how to
do or use something. **instructive** *adj*
informative or helpful. **instructor** *n*

instrument *n* tool used for particular
work; object played to produce a
musical sound; measuring device to
show height, speed, etc.; *Informal*
person used by another. **instrumental**
adj helping to cause; played by or
composed for musical instruments.
instrumentalist *n* player of a musical
instrument. **instrumentation** *n* set of
instruments in an automobile etc.;
arrangement of music for instruments.

insubordinate *adj* not submissive to
authority. **insubordination** *n*

insufferable *adj* unbearable.

insular *adj* not open to new ideas,
narrow-minded; of or like an island.
insularity *n*

insulate *v* prevent or reduce the
transfer of electricity, heat, sound, etc.
by surrounding or lining with
nonconductive material; isolate or set
apart. **insulation** *n* **insulator** *n*

insulin [in-syoo-lin] *n* hormone
produced by the pancreas which
controls the amount of sugar in the
blood.

insult *v* behave rudely to, offend. ◆ *n*
insulting remark or action. **insulting**
adj

insuperable *adj* impossible to
overcome. **insuperability** *n*
insuperably *adv*

insupportable *adj* incapable of being
tolerated; indefensible.

insurance *n* agreement by which one

makes regular payments to a company who pay an agreed sum if damage, loss, or death occurs; money paid by or for insurance; means of protection. **insure** v protect by insurance. **insurance policy** contract of insurance.

insurgent adj in revolt. ♦ n rebel. **insurgence** n revolt.

insurrection n rebellion.

intact adj not damaged in any way.

intaglio [in-**tah**-lee-oh] n, pl -**lios**, -**li** (gem carved with) an engraved design.

intake n thing or quantity taken in; opening through which fluid or gas enters an engine, pipe, etc.

integer n positive or negative whole number or zero.

integral adj being an essential part of a whole. ♦ n Math sum of a large number of very small quantities.

integrate v combine into a whole; amalgamate (a religious or racial group) into a community. **integration** n **integrated circuit** tiny electronic circuit on a silicon chip.

integrity n honesty; quality of being sound or whole.

integument n natural covering such as skin or rind.

intellect n power of thinking and reasoning. **intellectual** adj of or appealing to the intellect; clever or intelligent. ♦ n intellectual person. **intellectually** adv

intelligent adj able to understand, learn, and think things out quickly; (of a computerized device) able to initiate or modify action in the light of ongoing events. **intelligently** adv **intelligence** n quality of being intelligent; collection of secret information; people or department collecting military information.

intelligentsia n intellectual or cultured classes in a society.

intelligible adj understandable. **intelligibility** n

intemperate adj uncontrolled; drinking alcohol to excess; extreme. **intemperance** n

intend v propose or plan (something or to do something); have as one's purpose.

intense adj of great strength or degree; deeply emotional. **intensity** n

intensify v -**fying**, -**fied** make or become more intense. **intensification** n

intensive adj using or needing concentrated effort or resources. **intensively** adv

intent n intention. ♦ adj paying close attention. **intently** adv **intentness** n **intent on** determined to.

intention n something intended. **intentional** adj deliberate. **intentionally** adv

inter [in-**ter**] v -**terring**, -**terred** bury (a corpse). **interment** n burial (of a corpse).

inter- prefix between or among, e.g. intercontinental.

interact v act on or in close relation with each other. **interaction** n **interactive** adj

interbreed v breed within a related group.

intercede v plead in favour of; mediate. **intercession** n **intercessor** n

intercept v seize or stop in transit. **interception** n

interchange v (cause to) exchange places. ♦ n highway junction. **interchangeable** adj

inter-city adj (of a passenger service) travelling fast between cities.

intercom n internal communication system with loudspeakers.

intercontinental adj travelling between or linking continents.

intercourse n act of having sex; communication or dealings between people or groups.

interdict, interdiction n formal order forbidding something.

interdisciplinary adj involving more than one academic discipline.

interest n desire to know or hear more about something; hobby or subject that one enjoys; (often pl.) advantage, e.g. in one's own interests; sum paid for use of borrowed money; right or share. ♦ v arouse the interest of. **interested** adj feeling or showing interest; involved in or affected by. **interesting** adj **interestingly** adv

interface n area where two things interact or link; circuit linking a computer and another device.

interfere v try to influence other

people's affairs where one is not involved or wanted; clash (with); *Euphemistic* abuse sexually. **interfering** *adj* **interference** *n* interfering; *Radio* interruption of reception by atmospherics or unwanted signals.

interferon *n* protein that stops the development of an invading virus.

interim *adj* temporary.

interior *n* inside; inland region. ♦ *adj* inside, inner; mental or spiritual.

interject *v* make (a remark) suddenly or as an interruption. **interjection** *n*

interlace *v* join by lacing or weaving together.

interlay *v* insert (layers) between.

interlink *v* connect together.

interlock *v* join firmly together. ♦ *adj* closely knitted.

interlocutor [in-ter-**lok**-yew-ter] *n* person who takes part in a conversation.

interloper [**in**-ter-lope-er] *n* person in a place or situation where he or she has no right to be.

interlude *n* short rest or break in an activity or event.

intermarry *v* (of families, races, or religions) become linked by marriage. **intermarriage** *n*

intermediate *adj* coming between two points or extremes. **intermediary** *n* person trying to create agreement between others; messenger.

intermezzo [in-ter-**met**-so] *n, pl* **-zos, -zi** short piece of music, esp. one performed between the acts of an opera.

interminable *adj* seemingly endless because boring. **interminably** *adv*

intermingle *v* mix together.

intermission *n* interval between parts of a play, film, etc.

intermittent *adj* occurring at intervals. **intermittently** *adv*

intern *v* imprison, esp. during a war. ♦ *n* trainee doctor in a hospital. **internment** *n* **internee** *n* person who has been interned.

internal *adj* of or on the inside; within a country or organization; spiritual or mental. **internally** *adv* **internal-combustion engine** engine powered by the explosion of a fuel-and-air mixture within the cylinders.

international *adj* of or involving two

or more countries. ♦ *n* game or match between teams of different countries; player in such a match. **internationally** *adv*

internecine *adj* mutually destructive or ruinous.

Internet *n* large international computer network.

interplanetary *adj* of or linking planets.

interplay *n* action and reaction of two things upon each other.

interpolate [in-ter-**pole**-ate] *v* insert (a comment or passage) in (a conversation or text). **interpolation** *n*

interpose *v* insert between or among things; say as an interruption. **interposition** *n*

interpret *v* explain the meaning of; convey the meaning of (a poem, song, etc.) in performance; translate orally from one language into another. **interpretation** *n* **interpreter** *n*

interprovincial *adj* between or involving two or more provinces.

interregnum *n, pl* **-nums, -na** interval between reigns.

interrogate *v* question closely. **interrogation** *n* **interrogative** *adj* questioning. ♦ *n* word used in asking a question, such as *how* or *why*. **interrogator** *n*

interrupt *v* break into (a conversation etc.); temporarily stop (a process or activity). **interruption** *n*

intersect *v* (of roads or lines) meet and cross; divide by passing across or through. **intersection** *n*

interspersed *adj* scattered among, between, or on.

interstate *adj* *US* between or involving two or more states.

interstellar *adj* between or among stars.

interstice [in-ter-**stiss**] *n* small crack or gap between things.

intertwine *v* twist together or entwine.

interval *n* time between two particular moments or events; break between parts of a play, concert, etc.; difference in pitch between notes. **at intervals** repeatedly; with spaces left between.

intervene *v* involve oneself in a situation, esp. to prevent conflict; happen so as to stop something.

intervention n

interview n formal discussion, esp. between a job-seeker and employer; questioning of a well-known person about his or her career, views, etc., by a reporter. ♦ v have an interview with. **interviewee** n **interviewer** n

interwar adj of or during the period 1919–39.

interweave v weave together.

intestate adj not having made a will. **intestacy** n

intestine n (usu. pl.) lower part of the alimentary canal between the stomach and the anus. **intestinal** adj

intimate[1] adj having a close personal relationship; private; (of knowledge) extensive and detailed; Euphemistic having sexual relations; having a friendly quiet atmosphere. ♦ n intimate friend. **intimately** adv **intimacy** n

intimate[2] v hint or suggest; announce. **intimation** n

intimidate v subdue or influence by frightening. **intimidation** n **intimidating** adj

into prep to the inner part of; to the middle of; (up) against; used to indicate the result of a change, e.g. he turned into a monster; Math used to indicate division, e.g. three into six is two; Informal interested in.

intolerable adj more than can be endured. **intolerably** adv

intolerant adj narrow-minded or bigoted. **intolerance** n

intonation n sound pattern produced by variations in the voice.

intone v speak or recite in an unvarying tone of voice.

intoxicate v make drunk; excite to excess. **intoxicant** n, adj (drink) capable of intoxicating. **intoxication** n

intractable adj (of a person) difficult to influence; (of a problem or illness) hard to solve or cure.

intranet n Computers internal network that makes use of Internet technology.

intransigent adj refusing to change one's attitude. **intransigence** n

intransitive adj (of a verb) not taking a direct object.

intrauterine adj within the womb.

intravenous [in-tra-vee-nuss] adj into a vein. **intravenously** adv

intrepid adj fearless or bold.

intrepidity n

intricate adj involved or complicated; full of fine detail. **intricately** adv **intricacy** n

intrigue v make interested or curious; plot secretly. ♦ n secret plotting; secret love affair. **intriguing** adj

intrinsic adj part of the basic nature of. **intrinsically** adv

introduce v present (someone) by name (to another person); present (a radio or television programme); bring forward for discussion; bring into use; insert. **introduction** n introducing; preliminary part or treatment; presentation of one person to another. **introductory** adj preliminary.

introspection n examination of one's own thoughts and feelings. **introspective** adj

introvert n person concerned more with his or her thoughts and feelings than with external reality. **introverted** adj **introversion** n

intrude v come in or join in without being invited. **intruder** n **intrusion** n **intrusive** adj

intuition n instinctive knowledge or insight without conscious reasoning. **intuitive** adj **intuitively** adv

Inuit n member of the aboriginal race inhabiting N Canada, Greenland, Alaska, and E Siberia; their language.

Inuk n a member of any Inuit people.

Inuktitut [in-nook-ti-toot] n language of Inuit, Eskimo.

inundate v flood; overwhelm. **inundation** n

inure v accustom, esp. to hardship or danger.

invade v enter (a country) by military force; enter in large numbers; disturb (privacy etc.). **invader** n

invalid[1] n disabled or chronically ill person. ♦ v dismiss from active service because of illness etc. **invalidity** n

invalid[2] adj having no legal force; (of an argument etc.) not valid because based on a mistake. **invalidate** v make or show to be invalid.

invaluable adj priceless.

invasion n act of invading; intrusion.

invective n abusive speech or writing.

inveigh [in-vay] v (foll. by against) criticize (something) harshly.

inveigle v coax or entice.

inveiglement n

invent v think up or create (something new); make up (a story, excuse, etc.). **invention** n something invented; ability to invent. **inventive** adj resourceful; creative. **inventiveness** n **inventor** n

inventory [in-ven-tree] n, pl **-tories** detailed list of goods or furnishings.

inverse adj opposite, inverted; Math linking two variables in such a way that one increases as the other decreases. **inversely** adv

invert v turn upside down or inside out. **inversion** n **inverted commas** raised commas in writing to show where speech begins and ends.

invertebrate n animal with no backbone.

invest v spend (money, time, etc.) on something with the expectation of profit. **investment** n money invested; something invested in. **investor** n **invest in** v buy. **invest with** v give (power or rights) to.

investigate v inquire into; examine. **investigation** n **investigative** adj **investigator** n

investiture n formal installation of a person in an office or rank.

inveterate adj deep-rooted; confirmed in a habit or practice. **inveteracy** n

invidious adj likely to cause resentment. **invidiously** adv

invigilate [in-vij-il-late] v supervise examination candidates. **invigilator** n

invigorate v give energy to or refresh.

invincible adj unconquerable. **invincibly** adv **invincibility** n

inviolable adj that must not be broken or violated.

inviolate adj unharmed, unaffected.

invisible adj not able to be seen. **invisibly** adv **invisibility** n

invite v request the company of; ask politely for; attract, e.g. *the plan invited criticism.* ◆ n Informal invitation. **inviting** adj **invitation** n

in vitro adj (of a biological process) happening outside the body in an artificial environment.

invoice v, n (send) a bill for goods or services supplied.

invoke v put (a law or penalty) into operation; prompt or cause (a certain feeling); call on (a god) for help, inspiration, etc. **invocation** n

involuntary adj not done consciously; unintentional. **involuntarily** adv

involve v include as a necessary part; affect; implicate (a person); make complicated. **involved** adj complicated; concerned in. **involvement** n

invulnerable adj not able to be wounded or harmed.

inward adj internal; situated within; spiritual or mental. ◆ adv (also **inwards**) towards the inside or middle. **inwardly** adv

iodine n bluish-black element used in medicine, photography, and dyeing. **iodize** v treat with iodine.

ion n electrically charged atom. **ionic** adj **ionize** v change into ions. **ionization** n **ionosphere** n region of ionized air in the upper atmosphere which reflects radio waves.

iota [eye-oh-ta] n ninth letter in the Greek alphabet; very small amount.

IOU n signed paper acknowledging debt.

IPA International Phonetic Alphabet.

ipso facto adv Latin by that very fact.

IQ intelligence quotient.

IRA Irish Republican Army.

irascible adj easily angered. **irascibly** adv **irascibility** n

irate adj very angry.

ire n Lit anger.

iridescent adj having shimmering changing colours like a rainbow. **iridescence** n

iris n circular membrane of the eye containing the pupil; plant with sword-shaped leaves and showy flowers.

Irish adj of Ireland. **Irish coffee** hot coffee mixed with whiskey and topped with cream.

irk v irritate. **irksome** adj tiresome.

iron n metallic element widely used for structural and engineering purposes; tool made of iron; appliance used, when heated, to press clothes or fabric; metal-headed golf club. ◆ pl fetters or chains. ◆ adj made of iron; inflexible, e.g. *an iron will.* ◆ v smooth (clothes or fabric) with an iron. **iron out** v settle (a problem) through discussion. **Iron Age** era when iron tools were used. **ironing** n clothes to be ironed. **ironing board** long cloth-covered board, usu. with folding legs, on which to iron clothes.

ironic, ironical adj using irony. **ironically** adv

ironmonger n Brit shopkeeper or shop dealing in hardware. **ironmongery** n

ironstone n rock consisting mainly of iron ore; tough durable earthenware.

irony n, pl **-nies** mildly sarcastic use of words to imply the opposite of what is said; event or situation the opposite of that expected.

irradiate v subject to or treat with radiation. **irradiation** n

irrational adj not based on logical reasoning.

irredeemable adj not able to be reformed, improved, or corrected; not able to be recovered, bought back, or converted into coin.

irreducible adj impossible to put in a reduced or simpler form.

irrefutable adj impossible to deny or disprove.

irregular adj not regular or even; unconventional; (of a word) not following the typical pattern of formation in a language. **irregularly** adv **irregularity** n

irrelevant adj not connected with the matter in hand. **irrelevantly** adv **irrelevance** n

irreparable adj not able to be repaired. **irreparably** adv

irreproachable adj blameless, faultless. **irreproachably** adv

irresistible adj too attractive or strong to resist. **irresistibly** adv

irrespective of prep without taking account of.

irreverence n lack of due respect; disrespectful remark or act. **irreverent** adj

irrevocable adj not possible to change or undo. **irrevocably** adv

irrigate v water by artificial channels or pipes. **irrigation** n

irritate v annoy or anger; cause (a body part) to itch or become inflamed. **irritable** adj easily annoyed. **irritably** adv **irritant** n, adj (person or thing) causing irritation. **irritation** n

irrupt v enter forcibly or suddenly.

irruption n

is v third person singular present tense of BE.

isinglass [ize-ing-glass] n kind of gelatine obtained from some freshwater fish.

Islam n Muslim religion teaching that there is one God and that Mohammed is his prophet; Muslim countries and civilization. **Islamic** adj

island n piece of land surrounded by water. **islander** n person who lives on an island.

isle n island. **islet** n little island.

isobar [ice-oh-bar] n line on a map connecting places of equal barometric pressure. **isobaric** adj

isolate v place apart or alone; Chem obtain (a substance) in uncombined form. **isolation** n **isolationism** n policy of not participating in international affairs. **isolationist** n, adj

isomer [ice-oh-mer] n substance whose molecules contain the same atoms as another but in a different arrangement. **isomeric** adj **isomerism** n

isometric adj having equal dimensions; relating to muscular contraction without movement; (of a three-dimensional drawing) having three equally inclined axes and drawn to scale in every direction. **isometrics** pl n system of isometric exercises.

isosceles triangle [ice-soss-ill-eez] n triangle with two sides of equal length.

isotherm [ice-oh-therm] n line on a map connecting points of equal mean temperature.

isotope [ice-oh-tope] n one of two or more atoms with the same number of protons in the nucleus but a different number of neutrons.

issue n topic of interest or discussion; question requiring a decision; particular edition of a magazine or newspaper; outcome or result; Law children. ◆ v make (a statement etc.) publicly; officially supply (with); send out or distribute; publish. **take issue** disagree.

isthmus [iss-muss] n, pl **-muses** narrow strip of land connecting two areas of land.

it pron refers to a nonhuman, animal,

plant, or inanimate object; refers to the thing mentioned or being discussed; used as the subject of impersonal verbs, e.g. *it is snowing*; *Informal* crucial or ultimate point. **its** *adj* belonging to it. **it's** it is; it has. **itself** *pron* emphatic form of IT.

IT information technology.

italic *adj* (of printing type) sloping to the right. **italics** *pl n* this type, now used for emphasis etc. **italicize** *v* put in italics.

itch *n* skin irritation causing a desire to scratch; restless desire. ◆ *v* have an itch. **itchy** *adj*

item *n* single thing in a list or collection; piece of information. **itemize** *v* put on a list; make a list of.

iterate *v* repeat. **iteration** *n*

itinerant *adj* travelling from place to place.

itinerary *n, pl* **-aries** detailed plan of a journey; route.

IUD intrauterine device: coil-shaped contraceptive fitted into the womb.

IVF in vitro fertilization.

ivory *n, pl* **-ries** hard white bony substance forming the tusks of elephants. ◆ *adj* yellowish-white. **ivory tower** remoteness from the realities of everyday life.

ivy *n, pl* **ivies** climbing evergreen plant.

J j

jab *v* **jabbing, jabbed** poke roughly. ◆ *n* quick short punch; *Informal* injection.

jabber *v* talk excitedly or incoherently.

jacaranda *n* tropical tree with sweet-smelling wood.

jacinth *n* reddish-orange precious stone.

jack *n* device for raising an automobile or other heavy object; playing card with a picture of a pageboy; *Bowls* small white ball aimed at by the players; socket in electrical equipment into which a plug fits; flag flown at the bow of a ship, showing nationality. **jack up** *v* lift with a jack.

jackal *n* doglike wild animal of Asia and Africa.

jackass *n* male of the ass; fool.

laughing jackass same as KOOKABURRA.

jackboot *n* high military boot.

jackdaw *n* black-and-grey bird of the crow family.

jacket *n* short coat; outer paper cover on a hardback book; skin of a baked potato.

jackknife *n* large clasp knife; dive with a sharp bend at the waist in mid-air. ◆ *v* (of a tractor-trailer) go out of control so that the trailer swings round at a sharp angle to the cab.

jackpot *n* large prize or accumulated stake that may be won in a game. **hit the jackpot** be very successful through luck.

Jacobean [jak-a-bee-an] *adj* of the reign of James I of England.

Jacobite *n* supporter of the exiled Stuarts after the overthrow of James II of England.

Jacquard [jak-ard] *n* fabric in which the design is incorporated into the weave.

Jacuzzi [jak-oo-zee] *n* ® circular bath with a device that swirls the water.

jade *n* ornamental semiprecious stone, usu. dark green. ◆ *adj* bluish-green.

jaded *adj* tired and unenthusiastic.

jag¹ *n* sharp or ragged projection; *Informal* injection. **jagged** [jag-gid] *adj*

jag² *n* spree or drinking bout.

jaguar *n* large S American spotted cat.

jail *n* building for confinement of criminals or suspects. ◆ *v* send to jail. **jailer** *n* **jailbird** *n Informal* person who is or has often been in jail.

jalopy [jal-lop-ee] *n, pl* **-lopies** *Informal* old automobile.

jam¹ *n* spread made from fruit boiled with sugar.

jam² *v* **jamming, jammed**. pack tightly into a place; crowd or congest; make or become stuck; *Radio* block (another station) with impulses of equal wavelength. ◆ *n* hold-up of traffic; *Informal* awkward situation. **jam on** *v* apply (brakes) fiercely. **jam-packed** *adj* filled to capacity. **jam session** informal rock or jazz performance.

jamb *n* side post of a door or window frame.

jamboree *n* large rally of Scouts; large celebration.

Jan. January.

jangle *v* (cause to) make a harsh

ringing noise; (of nerves) be upset or irritated.

janitor n caretaker of a school or other building.

January n first month of the year.

japan n very hard varnish, usu. black. ◆ v **-panning, -panned.** cover with this varnish.

jape n Old-fashioned joke or prank.

japonica n shrub with red flowers.

jar¹ n wide-mouthed container, usu. cylindrical and made of glass.

jar² v **jarring, jarred.** have a disturbing or unpleasant effect on; (cause to) vibrate suddenly or violently. ◆ n jolt or shock.

jardinière n ornamental plant pot.

jargon n specialized technical language of a particular subject.

jasmine n shrub with sweet-smelling yellow or white flowers.

jasper n red, yellow, dark green, or brown variety of quartz.

jaundice n disease marked by yellowness of the skin. **jaundiced** adj (of an attitude or opinion) bitter or cynical; having jaundice.

jaunt n short journey for pleasure. ◆ v make such a journey.

jaunty adj **-tier, -tiest.** sprightly and cheerful; smart. **jauntily** adv

javelin n light spear thrown in sports competitions.

jaw n one of the bones in which the teeth are set; lower part of the face below the mouth; Slang long chat. ◆ v Slang have a long chat.

jay n bird of crow family in Europe and N America.

jaywalking n crossing the road in a careless or dangerous manner. **jaywalker** n

jazz n rhythmic music of African-American origin. **jazzy** adj flashy or showy. **jazz up** v make more lively.

jealous adj fearful of losing a partner or possession to a rival; envious; resulting from jealousy, e.g. jealous rage. **jealously** adv **jealousy** n

jeans pl n casual denim trousers.

Jeep n ® four-wheel-drive motor vehicle.

jeer v scoff. ◆ n cry of derision.

Jehovah n God.

jejune adj simple or naive; dull or boring.

jell v take on a definite form; form a gel.

jelly n, pl **-lies.** fruit-flavoured dessert set with gelatine; jam made from fruit juice and sugar. **jellied** adj prepared in a jelly.

jellyfish n small jelly-like sea animal.

jemmy n, pl **-mies.** short steel crowbar used by burglars.

jenny n, pl **-nies.** female ass; female wren.

jeopardy n danger. **jeopardize** v place in danger.

jerboa n small mouselike African rodent with long hind legs.

jeremiad n long lamenting complaint.

jerk n sharp or abruptly stopped movement; sharp pull; Slang contemptible person. ◆ v move or throw with a jerk. **jerky** adj sudden or abrupt. **jerkily** adv **jerkiness** n

jerkin n sleeveless jacket.

jerry-built adj built badly using flimsy materials.

jerry can n flat-sided can for carrying gasoline etc.

jersey n knitted jumper; machine-knitted fabric; (J-) breed of cow.

Jerusalem artichoke n small yellowish-white root vegetable.

jest n, v joke. **jester** n joker; Hist professional clown at court.

Jesuit [jezz-yoo-it] n member of the Society of Jesus, a Roman Catholic order. **jesuitical** adj crafty through using oversubtle reasoning.

jet¹ n aircraft driven by jet propulsion; stream of liquid or gas, esp. one forced from a small hole; nozzle from which gas or liquid is forced; burner on a gas fire. ◆ v **jetting, jetted.** travel by jet aircraft. **jet lag** fatigue caused by crossing time zones in an aircraft. **jet propulsion** propulsion by thrust provided by a jet of gas or liquid. **jet-propelled** adj **jet set** rich and fashionable people who travel the world for pleasure.

jet² n hard black mineral. **jet-black** adj glossy black.

jetsam n goods thrown overboard to lighten a ship and later washed ashore.

jettison v **-soning, -soned.** abandon; throw overboard.

jetty *n, pl* **-ties**. small pier.

Jew *n* person whose religion is Judaism; descendant of the ancient Hebrews. **Jewish** *adj* **Jewry** *n* Jews collectively. **jew's-harp** *n* musical instrument held between the teeth and played by plucking a metal strip with one's finger.

jewel *n* precious stone; special person or thing. **jeweller** *n* dealer in jewels. **jewellery** *n*

jib¹ *v* **jibbing, jibbed** (of a horse, person, etc.) stop and refuse to go on. **jib at** *v* object to (a proposal etc.).

jib² *n* projecting arm of a crane or derrick; triangular sail set in front of a mast.

jibe¹ *n* insulting remark. ◆ *v* make insulting remarks.

jibe² *v Informal* be consistent.

jiffy *n, pl* **-fies** *Informal* very short period of time.

jig *n* type of lively dance; music for it; device that holds a component in place for cutting etc. ◆ *v* **jigging, jigged**. make jerky up-and-down movements.

jigger *n* small glass for spirits.

jiggery-pokery *n Informal* trickery or mischief.

jiggle *v* move up and down with short jerky movements.

jigsaw *n* machine fret saw ; (also **jigsaw puzzle**) picture cut into interlocking pieces, which the user tries to fit together again.

jihad *n* Islamic holy war against unbelievers.

jilt *v* leave or reject (one's lover).

jingle *n* short catchy song used to advertise a product; gentle ringing sound. ◆ *v* make a jingling sound.

jingoism *n* aggressive nationalism. **jingoist** *n* **jingoistic** *adj*

jinks *pl n* **high jinks** boisterous merrymaking.

jinni *n, pl* **jinn**. spirit in Muslim mythology.

jinx *n* person or thing bringing bad luck. ◆ *v* be or put a jinx on.

jitters *pl n* worried nervousness. **jittery** *adj* nervous.

jiujitsu *n* same as JUJITSU.

jive *n* lively dance of the 1940s and '50s. ◆ *v* dance the jive.

job *n* task to be done; occupation or paid employment; *Informal* difficult task; *Informal* crime, esp. robbery. **jobbing** *adj* doing individual jobs for payment. **jobless** *adj, pl n* unemployed (people). **job lot** assortment sold together. **job sharing** splitting of one post between two people working part-time.

jockey *n* (professional) rider of racehorses. ◆ *v* **jockey for position** manoeuvre to obtain an advantage.

jockstrap *n* belt with a pouch to support the genitals, worn by male athletes.

jocose [joke-**kohss**] *adj* humorous.

jocular *adj* joking; fond of joking. **jocularly** *adv* **jocularity** *n*

jocund [jok-kund] *adj Lit* cheerful.

jodhpurs *pl n* riding breeches, stretchy or loose-fitting above the knee but tight below.

jog *v* **jogging, jogged**. run at a gentle pace, esp. for exercise; nudge slightly. ◆ *n* jogging. **jogger** *n* **jogging** *n*

joggle *v* move to and fro in jerks; shake.

Johnny Canuck *n Informal* a Canadian; Canada.

joie de vivre [jwah de **veev**-ra] *n French* enjoyment of life.

join *v* come or bring together; become a member (of); come into someone's company; take part (in). ◆ *n* place of joining. **joined-up** *adj* integrated by an overall strategy: *joined-up government*. **join up** *v* enlist in the armed services.

joiner *n* maker of finished woodwork. **joinery** *n* joiner's work.

joint *adj* shared by two or more. ◆ *n* place where bones meet but can move; junction of two or more parts or objects; piece of meat for roasting; *Slang* house or place, esp. a disreputable bar or nightclub; *Slang* cannabis cigarette. ◆ *v* divide meat into joints. **out of joint** dislocated; disorganized. **jointed** *adj* **jointly** *adv* **joint-stock company** firm whose capital is jointly owned by shareholders.

jointure *n* property settled on a wife for her use after her husband's death.

joist *n* horizontal beam that helps support a floor or ceiling.

jojoba [hoe-**hoe**-ba] *n* shrub whose

seeds yield oil used in cosmetics.

joke n thing said or done to cause laughter; amusing or ridiculous person or thing. ◆ v make jokes. **jokey** adj **jokingly** adv **joker** n person who jokes; Slang fellow; extra card in a pack, counted as any other in some games.

jolly adj -lier, -liest. full of good humour; involving a lot of fun. ◆ v -lying, -lied. **jolly along** try to keep (someone) cheerful by flattery or coaxing. **jolliness** n **jollity** n **jollification** n merrymaking.

jolt n sudden jerk or bump; unpleasant surprise or shock. ◆ v move or shake with jolts; shock.

jonquil n fragrant narcissus.

josh v Slang joke or tease.

joss stick n stick of incense giving off a sweet smell when burnt.

jostle v knock or push against; compete.

jot n very small amount. ◆ v jotting, jotted. write briefly; make a note of. **jotter** n notebook. **jottings** pl n notes jotted down.

joual n French Quebec working-class dialect.

joule [jool] n Physics unit of work or energy.

journal n daily newspaper or other periodical; daily record of events. **journalese** n superficial and clichéd writing, as found in newspapers. **journalism** n writing in or editing of periodicals. **journalist** n **journalistic** adj

journey n act or process of travelling from one place to another. ◆ v travel.

journeyman n qualified craftsman employed by another.

joust Hist n combat with lances between two mounted knights. ◆ v fight on horseback using lances.

jovial adj happy and cheerful. **jovially** adv **joviality** n

jowl n lower jaw; fatty flesh hanging from the lower jaw. ◆ pl n cheeks.

joy n feeling of great delight or pleasure; cause of this feeling. **joyful** adj **joyless** adj **joyous** adj extremely happy and enthusiastic. **joyriding** n driving for pleasure, esp. in a stolen vehicle. **joyride** n **joystick** n Informal control device for an aircraft or computer.

JP Justice of the Peace.

JPEG (jay-peg) Computing standard compressed file format used for pictures. picture held in this file format.

Jr Junior.

jubilant adj feeling or expressing great joy. **jubilantly** adv **jubilation** n

jubilee n special anniversary, esp. 25th (golden jubilee) or 50th (silver jubilee).

Judaism n religion of the Jews, having only one God and based on the teachings of the Old Testament and the Talmud. **Judaic** adj

judder v vibrate violently. ◆ n violent vibration.

judge n public official who hears cases and passes sentence in a court of law; person who decides the result of a competition. ◆ v act as a judge; decide the result of a (competition); appraise critically; consider something to be the case. **judgment, judgement** n opinion reached after careful thought; sentence of a court; faculty of judging. **judgmental, judgemental** adj

judicature n administration of justice; body of judges.

judicial adj of or by a court or judge; showing or using judgment. **judicially** adv

judiciary n system of courts and judges.

judicious adj well-judged, sensible. **judiciously** adv

judo n modern sport derived from jujitsu, where the opponent must be defeated using the minimum physical effort.

jug n container for liquids, with a handle and small spout; its contents; Slang prison. **jugged hare** Brit hare stewed in an earthenware pot.

juggernaut n large heavy truck; any irresistible destructive force.

juggle v throw and catch (several objects) so that most are in the air at the same time; manipulate (figures, situations, etc.) to suit one's purposes. **juggler** n

jugular vein n one of three large veins of the neck returning blood from the head.

juice n liquid part of vegetables, fruit, or meat; fluid secreted by an organ of the body; *Informal* gasoline. **juicy** *adj* succulent; interesting.

jujitsu *n* Japanese art of wrestling and self-defence.

juju *n* W African magic charm.

jujube *n* chewy candy of flavoured gelatine.

jukebox *n* automatic coin-operated record player.

Jul. July.

julep *n* sweet alcoholic drink.

julienne *n* clear soup containing thinly shredded vegetables.

July *n* seventh month of the year.

jumble *v* mix in a disordered way. ◆ *n* confused heap or state; articles for a jumble sale. **jumble sale** sale of miscellaneous second-hand items.

jumbo *adj Informal* very large. **jumbo jet** large jet airliner.

jump *v* leap or spring into the air using the leg muscles; leap over (an obstacle); move quickly and suddenly; jerk with surprise; increase suddenly; pass over or miss out (intervening material); change the subject abruptly; come off (tracks, rails, etc.); *Informal* attack without warning; *Informal* pass through a (red traffic light). ◆ *n* jumping; obstacle to be jumped; sudden nervous jerk; sudden rise in prices; break in continuity. **jump the gun** act prematurely. **jump the queue** not wait one's turn. **jumpy** *adj* nervous. **jump at** *v* accept (a chance etc.) gladly. **jumper cables** electric cables to connect a discharged automobile battery to an external battery to aid starting an engine. **jump jet** fixed-wing jet that can take off and land vertically. **jump on** *v* criticize suddenly and forcefully. **jump suit** one-piece garment of trousers and top.

jumper *n* sweater or pullover.

junction *n* place where routes, railway lines, or roads meet; point where traffic can leave or enter a highway; join.

juncture *n* point in time, esp. a critical one.

June *n* sixth month of the year.

jungle *n* tropical forest of dense tangled vegetation; tangled mass; place of intense struggle for survival.

junior *adj* of lower standing; younger.
◆ *n* junior person.

juniper *n* evergreen shrub with berries yielding oil.

junk¹ *n* discarded or useless objects; *Informal* rubbish; *Slang* narcotic drug, esp. heroin. **junkie** *n Slang* drug addict. **junk food** snack food of low nutritional value. **junk mail** unsolicited mail advertising goods and services.

junk² *n* flat-bottomed Chinese sailing vessel.

junket *n* excursion by public officials paid for from public funds; dessert made of milk set with rennet. **junketing** *n*

junta *n* group of military officers holding power in a country after a revolution.

Jupiter *n* Roman chief of the gods; largest of the planets.

juridical *adj* of law or the administration of justice.

jurisdiction *n* right or power to administer justice and apply laws; extent of this right or power.

jurisprudence *n* science or philosophy of law.

jurist *n* expert in law.

jury *n*, *pl* **-ries**. group of people sworn to deliver a verdict in a court of law. **juror, juryman, jurywoman** *n*

just *adv* very recently; exactly; barely; at this instant; merely, only; really.
◆ *adj* fair or impartial in action or judgment; proper or right; well-founded. **justly** *adv* **justness** *n*

justice *n* quality of being just; fairness; judicial proceedings; judge or magistrate. **justice of the peace** person who is authorized to act as a judge in a local court of law.

justify *v* **-fying, -fied**. prove right or reasonable; show to be free from blame or guilt; align (text) so the margins are straight. **justifiable** *adj* **justifiably** *adv* **justification** *n*

jut *v* **jutting, jutted**. stick out.

jute *n* fibre of certain plants, used for rope, canvas, etc.

juvenile *adj* young; suitable for young people; immature and rather silly. ◆ *n* young person or child. **juvenilia** *pl n* works produced in an author's youth. **juvenile delinquent** young person guilty of a crime.

juxtapose v put side by side.
  juxtaposition n

K k

K kelvin; *Chem* potassium; *Informal* thousand(s).

Kabloona n a person who is not of Inuit ancestry, esp. a White person.

Kaffir [**kaf-**fer] n S *Afr offens obs* a Black African.

kaftan n long loose Eastern garment; woman's dress resembling this.

kail n same as KALE.

kaiser [**kize-**er] n *Hist* German or Austro-Hungarian emperor.

Kalashnikov n Russian-made automatic rifle.

kale n cabbage with crinkled leaves.

kaleidoscope n tube-shaped toy containing loose pieces of coloured glass reflected by mirrors so that various symmetrical patterns form when the tube is twisted. **kaleidoscopic** adj

kamik n a traditional Inuit boot made of caribou hide or sealskin.

kamikaze [kam-mee-**kah-**zee] n (in World War II) Japanese pilot who performed a suicide mission. ◆ adj (of an action) undertaken in the knowledge that it will kill or injure the person performing it.

kangaroo n, pl -**roos**. Aust. marsupial which moves by jumping with its powerful hind legs. **kangaroo court** unofficial court set up by a group to discipline its members.

kaolin n fine white clay used to make porcelain and in some medicines.

kapok n fluffy fibre from a tropical tree, used to stuff cushions etc.

kaput [kap-**poot**] adj *Informal* ruined or broken.

karaoke [kar-a-oh-kee] n kind of entertainment in which members of the public sing well-known songs over a prerecorded backing tape.

karate n Japanese system of unarmed combat using blows with feet, hands, elbows, and legs.

karma n *Buddhism Hinduism* person's actions affecting his or her fate for his or her next reincarnation.

karoo n S *Afr* high arid plateau.

kasbah n citadel of N African town.

kayak n Inuit canoe made of sealskins stretched over a frame; fibreglass or canvas-covered canoe of this design.

kbyte *Computers* kilobyte.

kebab n dish of small pieces of meat grilled on skewers.

kedge n small anchor. ◆ v move (a ship) by hauling on a cable attached to a kedge.

kedgeree n dish of fish with rice and eggs.

keel n main lengthways timber or steel support along the base of a ship. **keel over** v turn upside down; *Informal* collapse suddenly.

keen¹ adj eager or enthusiastic; intense or strong; intellectually acute; (of the senses) capable of recognizing small distinctions; sharp; cold and penetrating; competitive. **keenly** adv **keenness** n

keen² v wail over the dead. ◆ n funeral lament.

keep v **keeping**, **kept**. have or retain possession of; take temporary charge of; store; look after or maintain; stay (in, on, or at a place or position); detain (someone); support financially; continue or persist; remain good. ◆ n cost of food and everyday expenses; central tower of a castle. **keeper** n person who looks after animals in a zoo; person in charge of a museum or collection; short for GOALKEEPER.

keeping n care or charge. **in , out of keeping with** appropriate or inappropriate for. **keep fit** exercises designed to promote physical fitness. **keepsake** n gift treasured for the sake of the giver. **keep up** v maintain at the current level. **keep up with** maintain a pace set by (someone).

keg n small metal beer barrel.

kelp n large brown seaweed.

kelvin n SI unit of temperature. **Kelvin scale** temperature scale starting at absolute zero (-273.15° Celsius).

ken n range of knowledge. ◆ v **kenning, kenned** or **kent** *Scot* know.

kendo n Japanese sport of fencing using wooden staves.

kennel n hutlike shelter for a dog. ◆ pl place for breeding, boarding, or training dogs.

kepi *n* French military cap with a flat top and horizontal peak.

kept *v* past of KEEP.

keratin *n* fibrous protein found in the hair and nails.

kerb *n* Brit curb.

kerchief *n* piece of cloth worn over the head or round the neck.

kerfuffle *n* Informal commotion.

kermes [kur-meez] *n* red dyestuff obtained from dried insects.

kernel *n* inner seed of a nut or fruit stone; central and essential part of something.

kerosene *n* paraffin oil distilled from petroleum or coal and shale and used as fuel, solvent, etc.

kestrel *n* small falcon.

ketch *n* two-masted sailing ship.

ketchup *n* thick cold sauce, usu. of tomatoes.

kettle *n* container with a spout and handle used for boiling water. **a different kettle of fish** a different matter entirely.

kettledrum *n* large metal drum with a brass bottom.

key *n* device for operating a lock by moving a bolt; device turned to wind a clock, operate a machine, etc.; any of a set of levers or buttons pressed to operate a piano, typewriter, etc.; *Music* set of related notes; list of explanations of codes, symbols, etc.; something crucial in providing an explanation or interpretation; means of achieving a desired end. ◆ *adj* of great importance. ◆ *v* (foll. by *to*) adjust to. **keyed up** very excited or nervous. **key in** *v* keyboard.

keyboard *n* set of keys on a piano, typewriter, etc.; musical instrument played using a keyboard. ◆ *v* enter (text) using a keyboard.

keyhole *n* opening for inserting a key into a lock.

keynote *n* dominant idea of a speech etc.; basic note of a musical key.

keystone *n* central stone of an arch which locks others in position.

kg kilogram(s).

KGB *n* formerly, the Soviet secret police.

khaki *adj* dull yellowish-brown. ◆ *n* hard-wearing fabric of this colour used for military uniforms.

kHz kilohertz.

kibbutz *n, pl* **kibbutzim**. communal farm or factory in Israel.

kibosh *n* **put the kibosh on** *Slang* put a stop to.

kick *v* drive, push, or strike with the foot; score with a kick; (of a gun) recoil when fired; *Informal* object or resist; *Informal* free oneself of (an addiction). ◆ *n* thrust or blow with the foot; recoil; *Informal* excitement or thrill. **kickback** *n* money paid illegally for favours done. **kick off** *v* start a game of football; *Informal* begin. **kick out** *v* expel forcibly. **kick-start** *v* start a motorcycle engine by kicking a pedal. **kick up** *v* *Informal* create (a fuss).

kid[1] *n* *Informal* child; young goat; leather made from the skin of a kid.

kid[2] *v* **kidding, kidded** *Informal* tease or deceive (someone).

kidnap *v* **-napping, -napped**. seize and hold (a person) to ransom. **kidnapper** *n*

kidney *n* either of the pair of organs which filter waste products from the blood to produce urine; animal kidney used as food. **kidney bean** reddish-brown kidney-shaped bean, edible when cooked.

kill *v* cause the death of; *Informal* cause (someone) pain or discomfort; put an end to; pass (time). ◆ *n* act of killing; animals or birds killed in a hunt. **killer** *n* **killing** *Informal* ◆ *adj* very tiring; very funny. ◆ *n* sudden financial success. **killjoy** *n* person who spoils others' pleasure.

kiln *n* oven for baking, drying, or processing pottery, bricks, etc.

kilo *n* short for KILOGRAM(ME).

kilo- *combining form* one thousand, e.g. *kilolitre*.

kilobyte *n* *Computers* 1000 or 1024 units of information.

kilogram, kilogramme *n* one thousand grams.

kilohertz *n* one thousand hertz.

kilometre, kilometer *n* one thousand metres.

kilowatt *n* *Electricity* one thousand watts.

kilt *n* knee-length pleated tartan skirt worn orig. by Scottish Highlanders. **kilted** *adj*

kimono [kim-**moan**-no] *n, pl* -**nos.** loose wide-sleeved Japanese robe, fastened with a sash; European dressing gown like this.

kin *n* (also **kinsfolk**) person's relatives collectively. **kinship** *n*

kind[1] *adj* considerate, friendly, and helpful. **kindness** *n* **kindly** *adj* -**lier,** -**liest.** having a warm-hearted nature; pleasant or agreeable. ◆ *adv* in a considerate way; please, e.g. *will you kindly be quiet!.* **kindliness** *n* **kind-hearted** *adj*

kind[2] *n* class or group having common characteristics; essential nature or character. **in kind** (of payment) in goods rather than money; with something similar. **kind of** to a certain extent.

kindergarten *n* class or school for children of about four to six years old.

kindle *v* set (a fire) alight; (of a fire) start to burn; arouse or be aroused. **kindling** *n* dry wood or straw for starting fires.

kindred *adj* having similar qualities; related. ◆ *n* person's relatives collectively.

kine *pl n Obs* cows or cattle.

kinetic [kin-**net**-ik] *adj* relating to or caused by motion.

king *n* male ruler of a monarchy; ruler or chief; best or most important of its kind; most important piece in chess; playing card with a picture of a king on it. **kingly** *adj* **kingship** *n* **kingdom** *n* state ruled by a king or queen; division of the natural world. **king-size, king-sized** *adj Informal* larger than standard size.

kingfisher *n* small bird with a bright plumage that dives for fish.

kingpin *n* most important person in an organization.

kink *n* twist or bend in rope, wire, hair, etc.; *Informal* quirk in personality. **kinky** *adj* full of kinks; *Slang* given to deviant or unusual sexual practices.

kiosk *n* small booth selling drinks, cigarettes, newspapers, etc.; public telephone box.

kip *n, v* **kipping, kipped** *Informal* sleep.

kipper *n* cleaned, salted, and smoked herring.

kirk *n Scot* church.

Kirsch *n* brandy made from cherries.

kismet *n* fate or destiny.

kiss *v* touch with the lips in affection or greeting; join lips with a person in love or desire. ◆ *n* touch with the lips. **kisser** *n Slang* mouth or face. **kiss of life** mouth-to-mouth resuscitation.

kit *n* outfit or equipment for a specific purpose; set of pieces of equipment sold ready to be assembled. **kitbag** *n* bag for a soldier's or traveller's belongings. **kit out** *v* **kitting, kitted.** provide with clothes or equipment needed for a particular activity.

kitchen *n* room used for cooking. **kitchenette** *n* small kitchen. **kitchen garden** garden for growing vegetables, herbs, etc.

kite *n* light frame covered with a thin material flown on a string in the wind; large hawk with a forked tail.

kith *n* **kith and kin** friends and relatives.

kitsch *n* vulgarized or pretentious art or literature with popular sentimental appeal.

kitten *n* young cat. **kittenish** *adj* lively and flirtatious.

kittiwake *n* type of seagull.

kitty *n, pl* -**ties.** communal fund for buying drinks etc.; pool in certain gambling games.

kiwi *n NZ* flightless bird with a stout beak and no tail; *Informal* a New Zealander. **kiwi fruit** edible fruit with a fuzzy brown skin and green flesh.

klaxon *n* loud horn used on emergency vehicles as a warning signal.

kleptomania *n* compulsive tendency to steal. **kleptomaniac** *n*

klick *n Informal* kilometre.

km kilometre(s).

knack *n* skilful way of doing something; innate ability.

knacker *n* buyer of old horses for killing.

knapsack *n* soldier's or traveller's bag worn strapped on the back.

knave *n* jack at cards; *Obs* rogue. **knavish** *adj* **knavery** *n* dishonest behaviour.

knead v work (flour) into dough using the hands; squeeze or press with the hands.

knee n joint between thigh and lower leg; part of a garment covering the knee; lap. ◆ v **kneeing, kneed**. strike or push with the knee. **kneecap** n bone in front of the knee. ◆ v shoot in the kneecap. **kneejerk** adj (of a reply or reaction) automatic and predictable.

kneel v **kneeling, kneeled** or **knelt**. fall or rest on one's knees.

knell n sound of a bell, esp. at a funeral or death; portent of doom.

knew v past tense of KNOW.

knickerbockers pl n loose-fitting short trousers gathered in at the knee.

knickers pl n woman's or girl's undergarment covering the lower trunk and having legs or leg holes.

knick-knack n trifle or trinket.

knife n, pl **knives**. cutting tool or weapon consisting of a sharp-edged blade with a handle. ◆ v cut or stab with a knife.

knight n honorary title given to a man by the British sovereign; Hist man who served his lord as a mounted armoured soldier; chess piece shaped like a horse's head. ◆ v award a knighthood to. **knighthood** n **knightly** adj

knit v **knitting, knitted** or **knit**. make (a garment) by interlocking a series of loops in wool or other yarn; draw (one's eyebrows) together; join closely together. **knitter** n **knitting** n **knitwear** n knitted clothes, such as sweaters.

knob n rounded projection, such as a switch on a radio; rounded handle on a door or drawer; small amount of butter. **knobbly** adj covered with small bumps.

knock v give a blow or push to; rap sharply with the knuckles; make or drive by striking; Informal criticize adversely; (of an engine) make a regular banging noise as a result of a fault. ◆ n blow or rap; knocking sound. **knocker** n metal fitting for knocking on a door. **knock about, around** v travel or wander; hit or kick brutally. **knockabout** adj (of comedy) boisterous. **knock back** v Informal drink quickly; cost; reject or refuse.

knock down v reduce the price of. **knockdown** adj (of a price) very low. **knock-knees** pl n legs that curve in at the knees. **knock off** v take (a specified amount) off a price; Informal make or do (something) hurriedly or easily; Informal cease work; Informal steal. **knock out** v render (someone) unconscious; Informal overwhelm or amaze; defeat in a knockout competition. **knockout** n blow that renders an opponent unconscious; competition from which competitors are progressively eliminated; Informal overwhelmingly attractive person or thing. **knock up** v Slang make pregnant; Brit informal waken.

knoll n small rounded hill.

knot n fastening made by looping and pulling tight strands of string, cord, or rope; tangle, as of hair; small cluster or huddled group; round lump or spot in timber; unit of speed used by ships, equal to one nautical mile per hour. ◆ v **knotting, knotted**. tie with or into a knot. **knotty** adj full of knots; puzzling or difficult.

know v **knowing, knew, known**. be aware of; be or feel certain of the truth of (information etc.); be acquainted with; have a grasp of or understand (a skill or language). **in the know** Informal informed or aware. **knowable** adj **knowing** adj cunning or shrewd. **knowingly** adv shrewdly; deliberately. **know-all** n Offens person who acts as if knowing more than other people. **know-how** n Informal ingenuity, aptitude, or skill.

knowledge n facts or experiences known by a person; state of knowing; specific information on a subject. **knowledgeable, knowledgable** adj well-informed.

knuckle n bone at the finger joint; knee joint of a calf or pig. **near the knuckle** Informal approaching indecency. **knuckle-duster** n metal appliance worn on the knuckles to add force to a blow. **knuckle under** v yield or submit.

KO knockout.

koala n tree-dwelling Aust. marsupial with dense grey fur.

kohl n cosmetic powder used to darken the edges of the eyelids.

kohlrabi [kole-rah-bee] n, pl **-bies**.

type of cabbage with an edible stem.

kokanee [koh-**kah**-nee] *n* salmon of N American lakes.

kookaburra *n* large Aust. kingfisher with a cackling cry.

kopeck *n* monetary unit of the former Soviet republics, one hundredth of a rouble.

kopje, koppie *n S Afr* small hill.

Koran *n* sacred book of Islam.

kosher [**koh**-sher] *adj* conforming to Jewish religious law, esp. (of food) to Jewish dietary law; *Informal* authentic. ◆ *n* kosher food.

kowtow *v* touch one's forehead to the ground in deference; be humble and servile (towards).

kph kilometres per hour.

kraal *n S* African village surrounded by a strong fence.

kraken *n* mythical Norwegian sea monster.

Kremlin *n* central government of Russia and, formerly, of the Soviet Union.

krill *n, pl* **krill**. small shrimplike sea creature.

krypton *n* colourless gas present in the atmosphere and used in fluorescent lights and lasers.

kudos [**kyoo**-doss] *n* fame or credit.

kulak *n Hist* independent well-to-do Russian peasant.

kümmel *n* German liqueur flavoured with caraway seeds.

kumquat *n* citrus fruit resembling a tiny orange.

kung fu *n* Chinese martial art combining hand, foot, and weapon techniques.

kW kilowatt.

kWh kilowatt-hour.

L l

l litre.

L large; Latin; learner (driver).

laager *n S Afr* camp defended by a circle of wagons.

lab *n Informal* short for LABORATORY.

label *n* piece of card or other material fixed to an object to show its ownership, destination, etc. ◆ *v*

-**elling**, -**elled** give a label to.

labia *pl n, sing* **labium** four liplike folds of skin forming part of the female genitals. **labial** [**lay**-bee-al] *adj* of the lips; pronounced with the lips.

laboratory *n, pl* -**ries** building or room designed for scientific research or for the teaching of practical science.

laborious *adj* involving great prolonged effort. **laboriously** *adv*

labour *n* physical work or exertion; workers in industry; final stage of pregnancy, leading to childbirth. ◆ *v* work hard; stress to excess or too persistently; be at a disadvantage because of a mistake or false belief. **laboured** *adj* uttered or done with difficulty. **labourer** *n* person who labours, esp. someone doing manual work for wages.

labrador *n* large retriever dog with a yellow or black coat.

laburnum *n* ornamental tree with yellow hanging flowers.

labyrinth [**lab**-er-inth] *n* network of tortuous passages, maze; interconnecting cavities in the internal ear. **labyrinthine** *adj*

lace *n* delicate decorative fabric made from threads woven into an open weblike pattern; cord drawn through eyelets and tied. ◆ *v* fasten with laces; thread a cord or string through holes in something; add a small amount of alcohol or drug to (food or drink). **lacy** *adj* fine, like lace. **lace-ups** *pl n* shoes which fasten with laces.

lacerate [**lass**-er-rate] *v* tear (flesh) jaggedly; wound (feelings). **laceration** *n*

lachrymose *adj* tearful; sad.

lack *n* shortage or absence of something needed or wanted. ◆ *v* need or be short of (something).

lackadaisical *adj* lacking vitality and purpose; lazy and careless in a dreamy way.

lackey *n* servile follower; uniformed male servant.

lacklustre *adj* lacking vitality.

laconic *adj* using only a few words, terse. **laconically** *adv*

lacquer *n* hard varnish for wood or metal; clear sticky substance sprayed onto the hair to hold it in place. ◆ *v* apply lacquer to.

lacrimal, lachrymal *adj* of tears or the glands which produce them.

lacrosse *n* sport in which teams catch and throw a ball using long sticks with a pouched net at the end, in an attempt to score goals.

lactation *n* secretion of milk by female mammals to feed young. **lactic** *adj* of or derived from milk. **lactose** *n* white crystalline sugar found in milk.

lacuna [lak-kew-na] *n, pl* **-nae, -nas** gap or missing part, esp. in a document or series.

lad *n* boy or young fellow.

ladder *n* frame of two poles connected by horizontal steps used for climbing; line of stitches that have come undone in a stocking or tights. ◆ *v* have or cause to have such a line of undone stitches.

laden *adj* loaded; burdened.

la-di-da, lah-di-dah *adj Informal* affected or pretentious.

ladle *n* spoon with a long handle and a large bowl, used for serving soup etc. ◆ *v* serve out liquid with a ladle.

lady *n, pl* **-dies** polite term of address for a woman; woman regarded as having characteristics of good breeding or high rank; (**L-**) title of some women of rank. **Our Lady** the Virgin Mary. **lady-in-waiting** *n, pl* **ladies-in-waiting** female servant of a queen or princess. **ladykiller** *n Informal* man who is or thinks he is irresistible to women. **ladylike** *adj* well-mannered.

ladybug *n* small red beetle with black spots.

lag[1] *v* **lagging, lagged** go too slowly, fall behind. ◆ *n* delay between events. **laggard** *n* person who lags behind.

lag[2] *v* **lagging, lagged** wrap (a boiler, pipes, etc.) with insulating material. **lagging** *n* insulating material.

lager *n* light-bodied type of beer.

lagoon *n* saltwater lake enclosed by an atoll or separated by a sandbank from the sea.

laid *v* past of LAY[1]. **laid-back** *adj Informal* relaxed.

lain *v* past participle of LIE[2].

lair *n* resting place of an animal.

laird *n* Scottish landowner.

laissez-faire [less-ay-fair] *n* principle of nonintervention, esp. by a government in commercial affairs.

laity [lay-it-ee] *n* people who are not members of the clergy.

lake[1] *n* expanse of water entirely surrounded by land. **lakeside** *n*

lake[2] *n* red pigment.

lam *v* **lamming, lammed** *Slang* beat or hit.

lama *n* Buddhist priest in Tibet or Mongolia. **lamasery** *n* monastery of lamas.

lamb *n* young of sheep; its meat; innocent or helpless creature. ◆ *v* (of sheep) give birth to a lamb or lambs. **lambskin** *n* **lambswool** *n*

lambaste, lambast *v* beat or thrash; reprimand severely.

lambent *adj Lit* (of a flame) flickering softly.

lame *adj* having an injured or disabled leg or foot; (of an excuse) unconvincing. ◆ *v* make lame. **lamely** *adv* **lameness** *n* **lame duck** person or thing unable to cope without help.

lamé [lah-may] *n, adj* (fabric) interwoven with gold or silver thread.

lament *v* feel or express sorrow (for). ◆ *n* passionate expression of grief; song of grief. **lamentable** *adj* deplorable. **lamentation** *n* **lamented** *adj* grieved for.

laminate *v* make (a sheet of material) by bonding together two or more thin sheets; cover with a thin sheet of material. ◆ *n* laminated sheet. **laminated** *adj* **lamination** *n*

lamp *n* device which produces light from electricity, oil, or gas. **lampblack** *n* pigment made from soot. **lamppost** *n* post supporting a lamp in the street. **lampshade** *n*

lampoon *n* humorous satire ridiculing someone. ◆ *v* satirize.

lamprey *n* eel-like fish with a round sucking mouth.

lance *n* long spear used by a mounted soldier. ◆ *v* pierce (a boil or abscess) with a lancet. **lancer** *n* formerly, cavalry soldier armed with a lance. **lance corporal** lowest noncommissioned rank in the army.

lanceolate *adj* narrow and tapering to a point at each end.

lancet *n* pointed two-edged surgical knife; narrow window in the shape of a pointed arch.

land n solid part of the earth's surface; ground, esp. with reference to its type or use; rural or agricultural area; property consisting of land; country or region. ♦ v come or bring to earth after a flight, jump, or fall; go or take from a ship at the end of a voyage; come to or touch shore; come or bring to some point or condition; *Informal* obtain; take (a hooked fish) from the water; *Informal* deliver (a punch). **landed** adj possessing or consisting of lands. **landed immigrant** former name for Canadian permanent resident. **landless** adj **landward** adj nearest to or facing the land. **land up** v arrive at a final point or condition.

landau [lan-daw] n four-wheeled carriage with a folding hood.

landfall n ship's first landing after a voyage.

landing n floor area at the top of a flight of stairs; bringing or coming to land; (also **landing stage**) place where people or goods go onto or come off a boat.

landlocked adj completely surrounded by land.

landlord, landlady n person who rents out land, houses, etc.; owner or manager of a pub or boarding house.

landlubber n person who is not experienced at sea.

landmark n prominent object in or feature of a landscape; event, decision, etc. considered as an important development.

landscape n extensive piece of inland scenery seen from one place; picture of it. ♦ v improve natural features of (a piece of land).

landslide n (also **landslip**) falling of soil, rock, etc. down the side of a mountain; overwhelming electoral victory.

lane n narrow road; area of road for one stream of traffic; specified route followed by ships or aircraft; strip of a running track or swimming pool for use by one competitor.

language n system of sounds, symbols, etc. for communicating thought; particular system used by a nation or people; system of words and symbols for computer programming.

languid adj lacking energy or enthusiasm. **languidly** adv

languish v suffer neglect or hardship; lose or diminish in strength or vigour; pine (for). **languishing** adj

languor [lang-ger] n laziness or weariness; dreamy relaxation; oppressive stillness. **languorous** adj

lank adj (of hair) greasy and limp; lean and tall. **lanky** adj ungracefully tall and thin. **lankiness** n

lanolin n grease from sheep's wool used in ointments etc.

lantern n light in a transparent protective case. **lantern jaw** long thin jaw. **lantern-jawed** adj

lanthanum n silvery-white metallic element. **lanthanide series** class of 15 elements chemically related to lanthanum.

lanyard n short cord worn round the neck to hold a knife or whistle; *Naut* short rope.

lap[1] n part between the waist and knees of a person when sitting. **lapdog** n small pet dog. **laptop** adj (of a computer) small enough to fit on a user's lap.

lap[2] n single circuit of a racecourse or track; stage of a journey; overlap. ♦ v **lapping, lapped** overtake an opponent so as to be one or more circuits ahead; enfold or wrap around.

lap[3] v **lapping, lapped** (of waves) beat softly against (a shore etc.). **lap up** v drink by scooping up with the tongue; accept (information or attention) eagerly.

lapel [lap-pel] n part of the front of a coat or jacket folded back towards the shoulders.

lapidary adj of stones, esp. gemstones.

lapis lazuli [lap-iss lazz-yoo-lie] n bright blue gemstone.

lapse n temporary drop in a standard, esp. through forgetfulness or carelessness; instance of bad behaviour by someone usually well-behaved; break in occurrence or usage. ♦ v drop in standard; end or become invalid, esp. through disuse; (of time) slip away; abandon religious faith. **lapsed** adj

lapwing n plover with a tuft of feathers on the head.

larboard adj, n *Old-fashioned* port (side of a ship).

larceny n, pl **-nies** theft.

larch n deciduous coniferous tree.

lard n soft white fat obtained from a pig. ◆ v insert strips of bacon in (meat) before cooking; decorate (speech or writing) with strange words unnecessarily.

larder n storeroom for food.

large adj great in size, number, or extent. **at large** in general; free, not confined. **largely** adv **largish** adj **large-scale** adj extensive.

largesse, largess [lar-**jess**] n generous giving, esp. of money.

largo adv Music in a slow and dignified manner.

lariat n lasso.

lark¹ n small brown songbird, skylark.

lark² n Informal harmless piece of mischief; unnecessary activity or job. **lark about** v play pranks.

larkspur n plant with spikes of blue, pink, or white flowers with spurs.

larva n, pl **-vae** insect in an immature stage, often resembling a worm. **larval** adj

larynx n, pl **larynges** part of the throat containing the vocal cords. **laryngeal** adj **laryngitis** n inflammation of the larynx.

lasagne, lasagna [laz-**zan**-ya] n pasta in wide flat sheets; dish made from layers of lasagne, meat, vegetables, etc.

lascivious [lass-**iv**-ee-uss] adj lustful. **lasciviously** adv

laser [**lay**-zer] n device that produces a very narrow intense beam of light, used for cutting very hard materials and in surgery etc.

lash¹ n eyelash; sharp blow with a whip. ◆ v hit with a whip; (of rain or waves) beat forcefully against; attack verbally, scold; flick or wave sharply to and fro. **lash out** v make a sudden physical or verbal attack; Informal spend (money) extravagantly.

lash² v fasten tightly with cord etc.

lashings pl n Brit informal large amount.

lass, lassie n girl.

lassitude n physical or mental weariness.

lasso [lass-**oo**] n, pl **-sos, -soes** rope with a noose for catching cattle and horses. ◆ v **-soing, -soed** catch with a lasso.

last¹ adj, adv coming at the end or after all others; most recent(ly). ◆ adj only remaining. ◆ n last person or thing. **lastly** adv finally. **last-ditch** adj done as a final resort. **last post** army bugle-call played at sunset or funerals. **last straw** small irritation or setback that, coming after others, is too much to bear. **last word** final comment in an argument; most recent or best example of something.

last² v continue; be sufficient for (a specified period of time); remain fresh, uninjured, or unaltered. **lasting** adj

last³ n model of a foot on which shoes and boots are made or repaired.

latch n fastening for a door with a bar and lever; lock which can only be opened from the outside with a key. ◆ v fasten with a latch. **latchkey** n key for a latch. **latch onto** v become attached to (a person or idea).

late adj arriving or occurring after the normal or expected time; towards the end of (a period of time); being at an advanced time; recently dead; recent; former. ◆ adv after the normal or expected time; at a relatively advanced age; recently. **lately** adv not long since. **lateness** n **latecomer** n

lateen sail n triangular sail on a long yard hoisted to the head of a mast.

latent adj hidden and not yet developed. **latency** n

lateral [**lat**-ter-al] adj of, at, to, or from the side. **laterally** adv

latex n milky sap found in some plants, esp. the rubber tree, used in making rubber and glue.

lath n thin strip of wood used to support plaster, tiles, etc.

lathe n machine for turning wood or metal while it is being shaped.

lather n froth of soap and water; frothy sweat; Informal state of agitation. ◆ v make frothy; rub with soap until lather appears.

Latin n language of the ancient Romans. ◆ adj of or in Latin; of a people whose language derives from Latin. **Latin America** parts of South and Central America whose official language is Spanish or Portuguese. **Latin American** n, adj

latitude n angular distance measured in degrees N or S of the equator; scope for freedom of action or thought. ◆ pl regions considered in relation to their distance from the equator. **latitudinal** adj

latitudinarian adj liberal, esp. in religious matters.

latrine n toilet in a barracks or camp.

latter adj second of two; near or nearer the end; more recent. **latterly** adv **latter-day** adj modern.

lattice [lat-iss] n framework of intersecting strips of wood, metal, etc.; gate, screen, etc. formed of such a framework. **latticed** adj

laud v praise or glorify. **laudable** adj praiseworthy. **laudably** adv **laudatory** adj praising or glorifying.

laudanum [lawd-a-num] n opium-based sedative.

laugh v make inarticulate sounds with the voice expressing amusement, merriment, or scorn; utter or express with laughter. ◆ n laughing; manner of laughing; Informal person or thing causing amusement. **laughable** adj ludicrous. **laughter** n sound or action of laughing. **laughing gas** nitrous oxide as an anesthetic. **laughing stock** object of general derision. **laugh off** v treat (something serious) lightly.

launch¹ v put (a ship or boat) into the water, esp. for the first time; begin (a campaign, project, etc.); put a new product on the market; send (a missile or spacecraft) into space or the air. ◆ n launching. **launcher** n **launch into** v start doing something enthusiastically. **launch out** v start doing something new.

launch² n large open motorboat.

launder v wash and iron (clothes and linen); make (illegally obtained money) seem legal by passing it through foreign banks or legitimate businesses. **laundry** n, pl -**dries** place for washing clothes and linen, esp. as a business; clothes etc. for washing or which have recently been washed. **Laundromat** n ® shop with coin-operated washing and drying machines.

laureate [lor-ee-at] adj **poet laureate** poet appointed by the British sovereign to write poems on important occasions.

laurel n glossy-leaved shrub, bay tree. ◆ pl wreath of laurel, an emblem of victory or merit.

lava n molten rock thrown out by volcanoes, which hardens as it cools.

lavatory n, pl -**ries** toilet.

lavender n shrub with fragrant flowers. ◆ adj bluish-purple. **lavender water** light perfume made from lavender.

lavish adj great in quantity or richness; giving or spending generously; extravagant. ◆ v give or spend generously. **lavishly** adv

law n rule binding on a community; system of such rules; Informal police; general principle deduced from facts. **lawful** adj allowed by law. **lawfully** adv **lawless** adj breaking the law, esp. in a violent way. **lawlessly** adv **lawlessness** n **law-abiding** adj adhering to the laws. **law-breaker** n **lawsuit** n court case brought by one person or group against another.

lawn¹ n area of tended and mown grass. **lawn mower** machine for cutting grass. **lawn tennis** tennis, esp. when played on a grass court.

lawn² n fine linen or cotton fabric.

lawyer n professionally qualified legal expert.

lax adj not strict. **laxity** n **laxly** adv

laxative n, adj (medicine) having a loosening effect on the bowels.

lay¹ v **laying**, **laid** cause to lie; set in a particular place or position; arrange (a table) for a meal; put forward (a plan, argument, etc.); attribute (blame); (of a bird or reptile) produce eggs; devise or prepare; place (a bet). **lay waste** devastate. **lay-by** n Brit stopping place for traffic beside a road. **lay off** v dismiss staff during a slack period. **lay-off** n **lay on** v provide or supply. **lay out** v arrange or spread out; prepare (a corpse) for burial; Informal spend money, esp. lavishly; Slang knock unconscious. **layout** n arrangement, esp. of matter for printing or of a building.

lay² v past tense of LIE². **layabout** n lazy person, loafer.

lay³ adj of or involving people who are not clergymen; nonspecialist. **layman** n ordinary person.

lay⁴ n short narrative poem designed

to be sung.

layer n single thickness of some substance, as a stratum or coating on a surface; laying hen. ◆ v form a layer. **layered** adj

layette n clothes for a newborn baby.

lay figure n jointed figure of the body used by artists; nonentity.

laze v be idle or lazy. ◆ n lazing.

lazy adj **lazier, laziest** not inclined to work or exert oneself; done in a relaxed manner with little effort; (of a movement) slow and gentle. **lazily** adv **laziness** n **lazybones** n Informal lazy person.

lb pound (weight).

lea n Poetic meadow.

leach v remove or be removed from a substance by a liquid passing through it.

lead¹ v **leading, led** guide or conduct; cause to feel, think, or behave in a certain way; control or direct; be the most important person or thing in; be, go, or play first; (of a road, path, etc.) go towards; pass or spend (one's life); result in. ◆ n first or most prominent place; example or leadership; amount by which a person or group is ahead of another; clue; length of leather or chain attached to a dog's collar to control it; principal role or actor in a film, play, etc.; cable bringing current to an electrical device. ◆ adj acting as a leader or lead. **leading** adj **leading question** question worded to prompt the answer desired. **lead-in** n introduction to a subject.

lead² n soft heavy grey metal; (in a pencil) graphite; lead weight on a line, used for sounding depths of water. **leaded** adj (of windows) made from many small panes of glass held together by lead strips. **leaden** adj heavy or sluggish; dull grey; made from lead.

leader n person who leads or guides others; (also **leading article**) article in a newspaper expressing editorial views. **leadership** n

leaf n, pl **leaves** flat usu. green blade attached to the stem of a plant; single sheet of paper in a book; very thin sheet of metal; extending flap on a table. **leafy** adj **leafless** adj **leaf mould** rich soil composed of decayed leaves. **leaf through** v turn pages without reading them.

leaflet n sheet of printed matter for distribution; small leaf.

league¹ n association promoting the interests of its members; association of sports clubs organizing competitions between its members; Informal class or level.

league² n Obs measure of distance, about three miles.

leak n hole or defect that allows the escape or entrance of liquid, gas, radiation, etc.; liquid etc. that escapes or enters; disclosure of secrets. ◆ v let fluid etc. in or out; (of fluid etc.) find its way through a leak; disclose secret information. **leakage** n leaking; gradual escape or loss. **leaky** adj

lean¹ v **leaning, leant** or **leaned.** rest against; bend or slope from an upright position; tend (towards). **leaning** n tendency. **lean on** v Informal threaten or intimidate; depend on for help or advice. **lean-to** n shed built against an existing wall.

lean² adj thin but healthy-looking; (of meat) lacking fat; unproductive. ◆ n lean part of meat. **leanness** n

leap v **leaping, leapt** or **leaped.** make a sudden powerful jump. ◆ n sudden powerful jump; abrupt increase, as in costs or prices. **leapfrog** n game in which a player vaults over another bending down. **leap year** year with February 29th as an extra day.

learn v **learning, learnt** or **learned.** gain skill or knowledge by study, practice, or teaching; memorize (something); find out. **learned** adj erudite, deeply read; showing much learning. **learner** n **learning** n knowledge got by study.

lease n contract by which land or property is rented for a stated time by the owner to a tenant. ◆ v let or rent on lease. **leasehold** adj held on lease. **leaseholder** n

leash n lead for a dog.

least adj smallest; superlative of LITTLE. ◆ n smallest one. ◆ adv in the smallest degree.

leather n material made from specially treated animal skins. ◆ adj made of leather. ◆ v beat or thrash. **leathery** adj like leather, tough.

leave¹ v **leaving, left** go away from; discontinue membership of; allow to remain, accidentally or deliberately; cause to be or remain in a specified state; permit; deposit; entrust; bequeath. **leave out** v exclude or omit.

leave² n permission to be absent from work or duty; period of such absence; permission to do something; formal parting.

leaven [lev-ven] n yeast; influence that produces a gradual change. ◆ v raise with leaven; spread through and influence (something).

lecher n lecherous man. **lechery** n

lecherous [letch-er-uss] adj (of a man) having or showing excessive sexual desire. **lecherously** adv **lecherousness** n

lectern n sloping reading desk, esp. in a church.

lecture n informative talk to an audience on a subject; lengthy rebuke or scolding. ◆ v give a talk; reprove. **lecturer** n **lectureship** n appointment as a lecturer.

ledge n narrow shelf sticking out from a wall; shelflike projection from a cliff etc.

ledger n book of debit and credit accounts of a firm.

lee n sheltered part or side; side away from the wind. **leeward** adj, n (on) the lee side. ◆ adv towards this side. **leeway** n room for free movement within limits.

leech n species of bloodsucking worm; person who lives off others.

leek n vegetable of the onion family with a long bulb and thick stem.

leer v look or grin at in a sneering or suggestive manner. ◆ n sneering or suggestive look or grin.

leery adj Informal suspicious (of).

lees pl n sediment of wine.

left¹ adj denotes the side that faces west when the front faces north; opposite to right. ◆ n left hand or part; Politics people supporting socialism rather than capitalism. ◆ adv on or towards the left. **leftist** n, adj (person) of the political left. **left-handed** adj more adept with the left hand than with the right. **left-wing** adj socialist; belonging to the more radical part of a political party.

left² v past of LEAVE¹.

leftover n unused portion of food or material.

leg n one of the limbs on which a person or animal walks, runs, or stands; part of a garment covering the leg; structure that supports, such as one of the legs of a table; stage of a journey; Sport (part of) one game or race in a series. **pull someone's leg** tease someone. **leggy** adj long-legged. **legless** adj without legs; Slang very drunk. **leggings** pl n covering of leather or other material for the legs; close-fitting trousers for women or children.

legacy n, pl -cies thing left in a will; thing handed down to a successor.

legal adj established or permitted by law; relating to law or lawyers. **legally** adv **legalize** v make legal. **legalization** n **legality** n

legate n messenger or representative, esp. from the Pope. **legation** n diplomatic minister and his staff; official residence of a diplomatic minister.

legatee n recipient of a legacy.

legato [leg-ah-toe] adv Music smoothly.

legend n traditional story or myth; traditional literature; famous person or event; stories about such a person or event; inscription. **legendary** adj famous; of or in legend.

legerdemain [lej-er-de-main] n sleight of hand; cunning deception.

legible adj easily read. **legibility** n **legibly** adv

legion n large military force; large number; association of veterans; infantry unit in the Roman army. **legionary** adj, n **legionnaire** n member of a legion. **legionnaire's disease** serious bacterial disease similar to pneumonia.

legislate v make laws. **legislation** n legislating; laws made. **legislative** adj **legislator** n maker of laws. **legislature** n body of persons that makes, amends, or repeals the laws of a state.

legitimate adj authorized by or in accordance with law; fairly deduced; born to parents married to each other. ◆ v make legitimate. **legitimately** adv **legitimacy** n **legitimize** v make legitimate, legalize. **legitimization** n

Lego n ® construction toy of plastic bricks fitted together by studs.

legume n pod of a plant of the pea or bean family. ♦ pl peas or beans. **leguminous** adj (of plants) pod-bearing.

lei n (in Hawaii) garland of flowers.

leisure n time for relaxation or hobbies. **at one's leisure** when one has time. **leisurely** adj deliberate, unhurried. ♦ adv slowly. **leisured** adj with plenty of spare time. **leisure centre** building with facilities such as a swimming pool, gymnasium, and café.

leitmotif [lite-mote-eef] n Music recurring theme associated with a person, situation, or thought.

lemming n rodent of arctic regions, reputed to run into the sea and drown during mass migrations.

lemon n yellow acid fruit that grows on trees; Slang useless or defective person or thing. ♦ adj pale-yellow. **lemonade** n lemon-flavoured soft drink, often fizzy. **lemon curd** creamy spread made of lemons, butter, etc. **lemon sole** edible flatfish.

lemur n nocturnal animal like a small monkey, found on Madagascar.

lend v **lending, lent** give the temporary use of; provide (money) temporarily, often for interest; add (a quality or effect), e.g. her presence lent beauty to the scene. **lend itself to** be suitable for. **lender** n

length n extent or measurement from end to end; duration; quality of being long; piece of something narrow and long. **at length** in full detail; at last. **lengthy** adj very long or tiresome. **lengthily** adv **lengthen** v make or become longer. **lengthways, lengthwise** adj, adv

lenient [lee-nee-ent] adj tolerant, not strict or severe. **leniency** n **leniently** adv

lenity n, pl -**ties** mercy or clemency.

lens n, pl **lenses** piece of glass or similar material with one or both sides curved, used to converge or diverge light rays in cameras, spectacles, telescopes, etc.; transparent structure in the eye that focuses light.

lent v past of LEND.

Lent n period from Ash Wednesday to Easter Eve. **Lenten** adj of, in, or suitable for Lent.

lentil n small edible seed of a leguminous Asian plant.

lento adv Music slowly.

leonine adj like a lion.

leopard n large spotted carnivorous animal of the cat family. **leopardess** n fem

leotard n tight-fitting garment covering most of the body, worn by acrobats, dancers, etc.

leper n person suffering from leprosy; despised person.

lepidoptera pl n order of insects with four wings covered with fine gossamer scales, as moths and butterflies. **lepidopterous** adj **lepidopterist** n person who studies or collects butterflies or moths.

leprechaun n mischievous elf of Irish folklore.

leprosy n disease attacking the nerves and skin, resulting in loss of feeling in the affected parts. **leprous** adj

lesbian n homosexual woman. ♦ adj of homosexual women. **lesbianism** n

lese-majesty [lezz-maj-est-ee] n treason; taking of liberties against people in authority.

lesion n structural change in an organ of the body caused by illness or injury; injury or wound.

less adj smaller in extent, degree, or duration; not so much; comparative of LITTLE. ♦ n smaller part or quantity; lesser amount. ♦ adv to a smaller extent. ♦ prep after deducting, minus. **lessen** v make or become smaller or not as much. **lesser** adj not as great in quantity, size, or worth.

lessee n person to whom a lease is granted.

lesson n single period of instruction in a subject; content of this; experience that teaches; portion of Scripture read in church.

lessor n person who grants a lease.

lest conj so as to prevent any possibility that; for fear that.

let[1] v **letting, let** allow, enable, or cause; allow to escape; grant use of for rent, lease; used as an auxiliary to express a proposal, command, threat, or assumption. **let alone** not to mention. **let down** v disappoint; lower; deflate. **letdown** n disappointment. **let off** v excuse from (a duty or punishment); fire or explode (a weapon); emit (gas, steam, etc.). **let on** v Informal reveal (a secret). **let out** v emit; release. **let up** v diminish or stop. **let-up** n lessening.

let² n hindrance; Tennis minor infringement or obstruction of the ball requiring a replay of the point.

lethal adj deadly.

lethargy n sluggishness or dullness; abnormal lack of energy. **lethargic** adj **lethargically** adv

letter n alphabetical symbol; written message, usu. sent by post; strict meaning (of a law etc.). ◆ pl n literary knowledge or ability. **lettered** adj learned. **lettering** n **letter bomb** explosive device in a parcel or letter that explodes when it is opened. **letter box** slot in a door through which letters are delivered; box in a street or post office where letters are posted. **letterhead** n printed heading on stationery giving the sender's name and address.

lettuce n plant with large green leaves used in salads.

leucocyte [loo-koh-site] n white blood corpuscle.

leukemia, leukaemia [loo-**kee**-mee-a] n disease caused by uncontrolled overproduction of white blood corpuscles.

levee¹ n natural or artificial river embankment; landing-place.

levee² n formal reception for visitors, orig. held by a sovereign on rising.

level adj horizontal; having an even surface; of the same height as something else; equal to or even with (someone or something else); not going above the top edge of (a spoon etc.). ◆ v -elling, -elled make even or horizontal; make equal in position or status; direct (a gun, accusation, etc.) at; raze to the ground. ◆ n horizontal line or surface; device for showing or testing if something is horizontal; position on a scale; standard or grade; flat area of land. **on the level** Informal honest or trustworthy. **level crossing** point where a railway line and road cross. **level-headed** adj not apt to be carried away by emotion.

lever n rigid bar pivoted about a fulcrum to transfer a force with

mechanical advantage; bar used to move a heavy object or to open something; handle pressed, pulled, etc. to operate machinery; means of exerting pressure to achieve an aim. ◆ v prise or move with a lever. **leverage** n action or power of a lever; influence.

leviathan [lev-**vie**-ath-an] n sea monster; anything huge or formidable.

Levis pl n ® denim jeans.

levitation n raising of a solid body into the air supernaturally. **levitate** v rise or cause to rise into the air.

levity n, pl -ties inclination to make a joke of serious matters.

levy [lev-vee] v levying, levied impose and collect (a tax); raise (troops). ◆ n, pl levies imposition or collection of taxes; enrolling of troops; amount or number levied.

lewd adj lustful or indecent. **lewdly** adv **lewdness** n

lexicon n dictionary; vocabulary of a language. **lexical** adj relating to the vocabulary of a language. **lexicographer** n writer of dictionaries. **lexicography** n

liable adj legally obliged or responsible; given to or at risk from a condition. **liability** n state of being liable; financial obligation; hindrance or disadvantage.

liaise v establish and maintain communication (with). **liaison** n communication and cooperation between groups; secret or adulterous relationship.

liana n climbing plant in tropical forests.

liar n person who tells lies.

lib n Informal short for LIBERATION.

libation [lie-**bay**-shun] n drink poured as an offering to the gods.

libel n published statement falsely damaging a person's reputation. ◆ v -belling, -belled defame falsely. **libellous** adj defamatory.

liberal adj having political views that favour progress and reform; generous in behaviour or temperament; tolerant; abundant; (of education) designed to develop general cultural interests. ◆ n person who has liberal ideas or opinions. **liberally** adv **liberalism** n belief in democratic

reforms and individual freedom.
liberality *n* generosity. **liberalize** *v* make (laws, a country, etc.) less restrictive. **liberalization** *n* **Liberal Party** major political party with viewpoints between those of the Progressive Conservative Party and the New Democratic Party.

liberate *v* set free. **liberation** *n* **liberator** *n*

libertarian *n* believer in freedom of thought and action. ◆ *adj* having such a belief.

libertine [lib-er-teen] *n* morally dissolute person.

liberty *n, pl* **-ties** freedom; act or comment regarded as forward or socially unacceptable. **at liberty** free; having the right. **take liberties** be presumptuous.

libido [lib-ee-doe] *n, pl* **-dos** life force; emotional drive, esp. of sexual origin. **libidinous** *adj* lustful.

library *n, pl* **-braries** room or building where books are kept; collection of books, records, etc. for consultation or borrowing. **librarian** *n* keeper of or worker in a library. **librarianship** *n*

libretto *n, pl* **-tos, -ti** words of an opera. **librettist** *n*

Librium *n* ® drug used as a tranquillizer.

lice *n* a plural of LOUSE.

licence *n* document giving official permission to do something; formal permission; excessive liberty; disregard of conventions for effect, e.g. *poetic licence*. **license** *v* grant a licence to. **licensed** *adj* **licensee** *n* holder of a licence, esp. to sell alcohol. **licence number** numbers and letters displayed on a vehicle to identify it. **licence plate** plate mounted on front and back of motor vehicle showing the licence number.

licentiate *n* person licensed as competent to practise a profession.

licentious *adj* sexually immoral, dissolute. **licentiously** *adv*

lichen *n* small flowerless plant forming a crust on rocks, trees, etc.

licit *adj* lawful, permitted.

lick *v* pass the tongue over; touch lightly or flicker round; *Slang* defeat. ◆ *n* licking; small amount (of paint etc.); *Informal* fast pace.

licorice *n* same as LIQUORICE.

lid *n* movable cover; short for EYELID.

lie[1] *v* **lying, lied** make a deliberately false statement. ◆ *n* deliberate falsehood. **white lie** untruth said without evil intent.

lie[2] *v* **lying, lay, lain** place oneself or be in a horizontal position; be situated; be or remain in a certain state or position; exist or be found. ◆ *n* way something lies. **lie-down** *n* rest. **lie in** *v* remain in bed late into the morning. **lie-in** *n* long stay in bed in the morning.

lied [leed] *n, pl* **lieder** *Music* setting for voice and piano of a romantic poem.

lief *adv Obs* gladly, willingly.

liege [leej] *n* lord; vassal or subject. ◆ *adj* bound to give or receive feudal service; faithful.

lien *n* right to hold another's property until a debt is paid.

lieu [lyew] *n* **in lieu of** instead of.

lieutenant [lef-ten-ant] *n* junior officer in the army or navy; main assistant. **lieutenant governor** representative of the Crown in a province.

life *n, pl* **lives** state of living beings, characterized by growth, reproduction, and response to stimuli; period between birth and death or between birth and the present time; amount of time something is active or functions; way of living; biography; liveliness or high spirits; living beings collectively. **lifeless** *adj* dead; inert; dull. **lifelike** *adj* **lifelong** *adj* lasting all of a person's life. **life belt, jacket** buoyant device to keep afloat a person in danger of drowning. **life cycle** series of changes undergone by each generation of an animal or plant. **lifeline** *n* means of contact or support; rope used in rescuing a person in danger. **life science** any science concerned with living organisms, such as biology, botany, or zoology. **lifestyle** *n* particular attitudes, habits, etc. **life-support** *adj* (of equipment or treatment) necessary to keep a person alive. **lifetime** *n* length of time a person is alive.

lift *v* move upwards in position, status, volume, etc.; revoke or cancel; take (plants) out of the ground for harvesting; disappear; make or become more cheerful. ◆ *n* lifting; *Brit* elevator; ride in an automobile etc. as a passenger; *Informal* feeling of cheerfulness. **liftoff** *n* moment a rocket leaves the ground.

ligament *n* band of tissue joining bones.

ligature *n* link, bond, or tie; *Printing* two or more joined letters.

light[1] *n* electromagnetic radiation by which things are visible; source of this, lamp; anything that lets in light, such as a window; mental vision; light part of a photograph etc.; means of setting fire to; understanding. ◆ *pl* traffic lights. ◆ *adj* bright; (of a colour) pale. ◆ *v* **lighting, lighted** or **lit**. ignite; illuminate or cause to illuminate. **lighten** *v* make less dark. **lighting** *n* apparatus for supplying artificial light; use of artificial light in theatres, films, etc. **light bulb** glass part of an electric lamp. **lighthouse** *n* tower with a light to guide ships. **light year** *Astronomy* distance light travels in one year, about six million million miles.

light[2] *adj* not heavy, weighing relatively little; relatively low in strength, amount, density, etc.; not serious or profound; not clumsy; easily digested; carrying light arms or equipment; (of industry) producing small goods, using light machinery. ◆ *adv* with little equipment or luggage. ◆ *v* **lighting, lighted** or **lit** (esp. of birds) settle after flight; come (upon) by chance. **lightly** *adv* **lightness** *n* **lighten** *v* make less heavy or burdensome; make more cheerful or lively. **light-fingered** *adj* liable to steal. **light-headed** *adj* feeling faint, dizzy; frivolous. **light-hearted** *adj* carefree. **lightweight** *n, adj* (person) of little importance. ◆ *n* boxer weighing up to 135lb (professional) or 60kg (amateur).

lighter[1] *n* device for lighting cigarettes etc.

lighter[2] *n* flat-bottomed boat for unloading ships.

lightning *n* visible discharge of electricity in the atmosphere. ◆ *adj* fast and sudden.

lights *pl n* lungs of animals as animal food.

ligneous *adj* of or like wood.

lignite [lig-nite] *n* woody textured rock used as fuel.

like[1] *adj* resembling; similar; characteristic of. ◆ *prep* in the manner of; such as. ◆ *adv* in the manner of. ◆ *pron* similar thing. **liken** *v* compare. **likeness** *n* resemblance; portrait. **likewise** *adv* in a similar manner.

like[2] *v* find enjoyable; be fond of; prefer, choose, or wish. **likable, likeable** *adj* **liking** *n* fondness; preference.

likely *adj* probable; tending or inclined; promising. ◆ *adv* probably. **not likely** *Informal* definitely not. **likelihood** *n* probability.

lilac *n* shrub bearing pale mauve or white flowers. ◆ *adj* light purple.

Lilliputian [lil-lip-pew-shun] *adj* tiny.

lilt *n* pleasing musical quality in speaking; jaunty rhythm; graceful rhythmic motion. **lilting** *adj*

lily *n, pl* **lilies** plant which grows from a bulb and has large, often white, flowers.

limb *n* arm or leg; wing; main branch of a tree.

limber *adj* supple. **limber up** *v* loosen stiff muscles by exercising.

limbo[1] *n, pl* **-bos** supposed region intermediate between Heaven and Hell for the unbaptized; unknown intermediate place or state.

limbo[2] *n, pl* **-bos** West Indian dance in which dancers lean backwards to pass under a bar.

lime[1] calcium compound used as a fertilizer or in making cement. **limelight** *n* glare of publicity. **limestone** *n* sedimentary rock used in building.

lime[2] *n* small green citrus fruit. **lime-green** *adj* greenish-yellow.

lime[3] *n* linden tree.

limerick [lim-mer-ik] *n* nonsensical humorous verse of five lines.

limey *n Slang* British person.

limit *n* ultimate extent, degree, or amount of something; boundary or edge. ◆ *v* **-iting, -ited** restrict or confine. **limitation** *n* **limitless** *adj* **limited company** company whose shareholders' liability is restricted.

limousine *n* large luxurious automobile.

limp[1] *adj* without firmness or stiffness.

limply adv

limp² v walk lamely. ◆ n limping gait.

limpet n shellfish which sticks tightly to rocks.

limpid adj clear or transparent; easy to understand. **limpidity** n

linchpin n pin to hold a wheel on its axle; essential person or thing.

linctus n, pl **-tuses** syrupy cough medicine.

linden n large deciduous tree with heart-shaped leaves and fragrant yellowish flowers, the lime.

line n long narrow mark; indented mark or wrinkle; continuous length without breadth; row of words; queue of people; boundary or limit; mark on a sports ground showing divisions of a field or track; string or wire for a particular use; telephone connection; wire or cable for transmitting electricity; shipping company; railway track; course or direction of movement; class of goods; prescribed way of thinking; field of interest or activity; ancestors collectively. ◆ pl words of a theatrical part; school punishment of writing out a sentence a specified number of times; protected boundary of an area occupied by an army. ◆ v mark with lines; bring into line; be or form a border or edge; give a lining to; cover the inside of. **in line for** candidate for. **in line with** in accordance with. **line dancing** form of dancing performed by rows of people to country and western music. **line-up** n people or things assembled for a particular purpose.

lineage [lin-ee-ij] n descent from or descendants of an ancestor. **lineal** adj in direct line of descent.

lineament n facial feature.

linear [lin-ee-er] adj of or in lines.

linen n cloth or thread made from flax; sheets, tablecloths, etc.

liner n large passenger ship; something used as a lining.

linesman n (in some sports) an official who helps the referee or umpire; person who maintains railway, electricity, or telephone lines.

ling n slender food fish.

linger v delay or prolong departure; continue in a weakened state for a long time before dying or disappearing; spend a long time doing something. **lingering** adj

lingerie [lan-zher-ee] n women's underwear or nightwear.

lingo n, pl **-goes** Informal foreign or unfamiliar language or jargon.

lingua franca n, pl **lingua francas**, **linguae francae** language used for communication between people with different mother tongues.

lingual adj of the tongue; made by the tongue.

linguist n person skilled in foreign languages; person who studies linguistics. **linguistic** adj of languages; of linguistics. **linguistics** pl n scientific study of language.

liniment n medicated liquid rubbed on the skin to relieve pain.

lining n layer of cloth attached to the inside of a garment etc.; inner covering of anything.

link n any of the rings forming a chain; person or thing forming a connection. ◆ v connect with or as if with links; connect by association. **linkage** n **link-up** n joining together of two systems or groups.

links pl n golf course, esp. one by the sea.

linnet n songbird of the finch family.

lino n short for LINOLEUM.

linocut n design cut in relief on a block of linoleum; print from such a block.

linoleum n floor covering of hessian or jute with a smooth decorative coating of powdered cork.

Linotype n ® typesetting machine which casts lines of words in one piece.

linseed n seed of the flax plant.

lint n soft material for dressing a wound.

lintel n horizontal beam at the top of a door or window.

lion n large animal of the cat family, the male of which has a shaggy mane. **lioness** n fem **the lion's share** the biggest part. **lionize** v treat as a celebrity. **lion-hearted** adj brave.

lip n either of the fleshy edges of the mouth; rim of a jug etc.; Slang impudence. **lip-reading** n method of understanding speech by interpreting lip movements. **lip service** insincere tribute or respect. **lipstick** n cosmetic in stick form, for colouring the lips.

liquefy v **-fying, -fied** make or become liquid. **liquefaction** n

liqueur [lik-**cure**] n flavoured and sweetened alcoholic spirit.

liquid n substance in a physical state which can change shape but not size. ◆ adj of or being a liquid; flowing smoothly; (of assets) in the form of money or easily converted into money. **liquidize** v make or become liquid. **liquidity** n state of being able to meet financial obligations.

liquidate v pay (a debt); dissolve a company and share its assets between creditors; wipe out or kill. **liquidation** n **liquidator** n official appointed to liquidate a business.

liquor n alcoholic drink, esp. spirits; liquid in which food has been cooked.

liquorice [lik-ker-iss] n black substance used in medicine and as candy.

lira n, pl **-re, -ras** monetary unit of Turkey.

lisle [rhymes with **mile**] n strong fine cotton thread or fabric.

lisp n speech defect in which 's' and 'z' are pronounced 'th'. ◆ v speak or utter with a lisp.

lissom, lissome adj supple, agile.

list[1] n item-by-item record of names or things, usu. written one below another. ◆ v make a list of; include in a list.

list[2] v (of a ship) lean to one side. ◆ n leaning to one side.

listen v concentrate on hearing something; heed or pay attention to. **listener** n **listen in** v listen secretly, eavesdrop.

listeriosis n dangerous form of food poisoning.

listless adj lacking interest or energy. **listlessly** adv

lit v a past of LIGHT[1], LIGHT[2].

litany n, pl **-nies** prayer with responses from the congregation; any tedious recital.

literacy n ability to read and write.

literal adj according to the explicit meaning of a word or text, not figurative; (of a translation) word for word; actual, true. **literally** adv

literary adj of or learned in literature;

(of a word) formal.

literate adj able to read and write; educated. **literati** pl n literary people.

literature n written works such as novels, plays, and poetry; books and writings of a country, period, or subject.

lithe adj flexible or supple, pliant.

lithium n chemical element, the lightest known metal.

litho n, pl **-thos** short for LITHOGRAPH. ◆ adj short for LITHOGRAPHIC.

lithography [lith-**og**-ra-fee] n method of printing from a metal or stone surface in which the printing areas are made receptive to ink. **lithograph** n print made by lithography. ◆ v reproduce by lithography. **lithographer** n **lithographic** adj

litigate v bring or contest a law suit; engage in legal action. **litigant** n person involved in a lawsuit. **litigation** n lawsuit. **litigious** [lit-ij-uss] adj frequently going to law.

litmus n blue dye turned red by acids and restored to blue by alkali. **litmus paper** paper impregnated with litmus. **litmus test** something which is regarded as a simple and accurate test of a particular thing.

litotes n ironical understatement for rhetorical effect.

litre n unit of liquid measure equal to 1.76 pints.

litter n untidy rubbish dropped in public places; group of young animals produced at one birth; straw etc. as bedding for an animal; dry material to absorb a cat's excrement. ◆ v strew with litter; scatter or be scattered about untidily; give birth to young.

little adj small or smaller than average; young. ◆ n small amount, extent, or duration. ◆ adv not a lot; hardly; not much or often.

littoral adj of or by the seashore. ◆ n coastal district.

liturgy n, pl **-gies** prescribed form of public worship. **liturgical** adj

live[1] v be alive; remain in life or existence; exist in a specified way, e.g. we live well; reside; continue or last; subsist; enjoy life to the full. **live down** v wait till people forget a past mistake or misdeed. **live-in** adj sharing a house with one's sexual partner. **live**

together v (of an unmarried couple) share a house and have a sexual relationship. **live up to** v meet (expectations). **live with** v tolerate.

live² adj living, alive; (of a broadcast) transmitted during the actual performance; (of a performance) done in front of an audience; (of a wire, circuit, etc.) carrying an electric current; current; glowing or burning; capable of exploding. ♦ adv in the form of a live performance. **lively** adj full of life or vigour; animated; vivid. **liveliness** n **liven up** v make (more) lively.

livelihood n occupation.

livelong [liv-long] adj Lit long.

liver n organ secreting bile; animal liver as food. **liverish** adj unwell; touchy or irritable.

livery n, pl **-eries** distinctive dress, esp. of a servant or servants. **liveried** adj **livery stable** stable where horses are kept at a charge or hired out.

livestock n farm animals.

livid adj Informal angry or furious; bluish-grey.

living adj possessing life, not dead or inanimate; currently in use or existing; of everyday life, e.g. living conditions. ♦ n condition of being alive; manner of life; financial means; church benefice. **living room** room in a house used for relaxation and entertainment.

lizard n four-footed reptile with a long body and tail.

llama n woolly animal of the camel family used as a beast of burden in S America.

LLB Bachelor of Laws.

loach n carplike freshwater fish.

load n burden or weight; amount carried; amount of electrical energy drawn from a source; source of worry. ♦ pl Informal lots. ♦ v put a load on or into; burden or oppress; cause to be biased; put ammunition into a weapon; put film into a camera; transfer (a program) into computer memory. **loaded** adj (of a question) containing a hidden trap or implication; Slang wealthy; (of dice) dishonestly weighted.

loadstar n same as LODESTAR.

loaf¹ n, pl **loaves** shaped mass of baked bread; shaped mass of food;

Slang common sense, e.g. use your loaf.

loaf² v idle, loiter. **loafer** n

loam n fertile soil.

loan n money borrowed at interest; lending; thing lent. ♦ v lend, grant a loan of. **loan shark** person who lends money at an extremely high interest rate.

loath, loth [rhymes with **both**] adj unwilling or reluctant (to).

loathe v hate, be disgusted by. **loathing** n **loathsome** adj

lob Sport n ball struck or thrown high in the air. ♦ v **lobbing, lobbed** strike or throw (a ball) high in the air.

lobby n, pl **-bies** corridor into which rooms open; group which tries to influence legislators; hall in a legislative building to which the public has access. ♦ v **-bying, -bied** try to influence (legislators) in the formulation of policy. **lobbyist** n

lobe n rounded projection; soft hanging part of the ear; subdivision of a body organ. **lobed** adj **lobar** [loh-ber] adj of or affecting a lobe.

lobelia n garden plant with blue, red, or white lobed flowers.

lobotomy n, pl **-mies** surgical incision into a lobe of the brain.

lobster n shellfish with a long tail and claws, which turns red when boiled. **lobster pot** basket-like trap for catching lobsters.

local adj of or existing in a particular place; confined to a particular place. ♦ n person belonging to a particular district; Brit informal nearby pub. **locally** adv **locality** n neighbourhood or area. **localize** v restrict to a definite place. **locale** [loh-kahl] n scene of an event. **local anesthetic** anesthetic which produces insensibility in one part of the body. **local authority** governing body of a county or district. **local government** government of towns, counties, and districts by locally elected political bodies.

locate v discover the whereabouts of; situate or place. **location** n site or position; site of a film production away from the studio.

loch n Scot lake; long narrow bay.

lock¹ n appliance for fastening a door, case, etc.; section of a canal shut off by gates between which the water level can be altered to aid boats moving from one level to another; extent to which a vehicle's front wheels will turn; interlocking of parts; mechanism for firing a gun; wrestling hold. ◆ v fasten or become fastened securely; become or cause to become immovable; become or cause to become fixed or united; embrace closely. **lockout** n exclusion of workers by an employer as a means of coercion. **locksmith** n person who makes and mends locks. **lockup** n prison; garage or storage place away from the main premises.

lock² n tress of hair.

locker n small cupboard with a lock.

locket n small hinged pendant for a portrait etc.

lockjaw n tetanus.

locomotive n self-propelled engine for pulling trains. ◆ adj of locomotion. **locomotion** n action or power of moving.

locum n temporary stand-in for a doctor or clergyman.

locus n, pl **loci** area or place where something happens; Math set of points or lines satisfying one or more specified conditions.

locust n destructive African insect that flies in swarms and eats crops.

locution n word or phrase.

lode n vein of ore. **lodestar** n Pole Star. **lodestone** n magnetic iron ore.

lodge n house or cabin used occasionally by hunters, skiers, etc.; gatekeeper's house; porters' room in a university or college; local branch of some societies. ◆ v live in another's house at a fixed charge; stick or become stuck (in a place); deposit for safety or storage; make (a complaint etc.) formally. **lodger** n **lodgings** pl n rented room or rooms in another person's house.

loft n space between the top storey and roof of a building; gallery in a church etc. ◆ v Sport strike, throw, or kick (a ball) high into the air.

lofty adj **loftier, loftiest** of great height; exalted or noble; haughty. **loftily** adv haughtily. **loftiness** n

log¹ n portion of a felled tree stripped of branches; detailed record of a

journey of a ship, aircraft, etc. ◆ v **logging, logged** record in a log; saw logs from a tree. **logging** n work of cutting and transporting logs. **logbook** n **log in, out** v gain entrance to or leave a computer system by keying in a special command.

log² n short for LOGARITHM.

loganberry n purplish-red fruit, a cross between a raspberry and a blackberry.

logarithm n one of a series of arithmetical functions used to make certain calculations easier. **logarithmic** adj

loggerheads pl n **at loggerheads** quarrelling, disputing.

loggia [loj-ya] n covered gallery at the side of a building.

logic n philosophy of reasoning; reasoned thought or argument. **logical** adj of logic; reasonable; capable of or using clear valid reasoning. **logically** adv **logician** n

logistics pl n detailed planning and organization of a large, esp. military, operation. **logistical** adj

logo [loh-go] n, pl **-os** company emblem or similar device.

loin n part of the body between the ribs and the hips; cut of meat from this part of an animal. ◆ pl hips and inner thighs. **loincloth** n piece of cloth covering the loins only.

loiter v stand or wait aimlessly or idly. **loiterer** n

loll v lounge lazily; (esp. of the tongue) hang out.

lollipop n boiled candy on a small wooden stick.

lolly n, pl **-ies** Brit informal lollipop or ice lolly; Brit slang money.

lone adj solitary. **lonely** adj sad because alone; unfrequented; resulting from being alone. **loneliness** n **loner** n Informal person who prefers to be alone. **lonesome** adj lonely.

long¹ adj having length, esp. great length, in space or time. ◆ adv for a long time. **long-distance** adj going between places far apart. **long-drawn-out** adj lasting too long. **long face** glum expression. **longhand** n ordinary writing, not shorthand or typing. **long johns** Informal long underpants. **long-life** adj (of milk, batteries, etc.) lasting longer than the regular kind. **long-lived** *adj* living or lasting for a long time. **long-range** *adj* (of weapons) designed to hit a distant target; into the future. **long shot** competitor, undertaking, or bet with little chance of success. **long-standing** *adj* existing for a long time. **long-suffering** *adj* enduring trouble or unhappiness without complaint. **long-term** *adj* lasting or effective for a long time. **long wave** radio wave with a wavelength of over 1000 metres. **long-winded** *adj* speaking or writing at tedious length.

long² *v* (foll. by *for*) have a strong desire for. **longing** *n* yearning. **longingly** *adv*

longevity [lon-**jev**-it-ee] *n* long existence or life.

longitude *n* distance east or west from a standard meridian. **longitudinal** *adj* of length or longitude; lengthwise.

longshoreman *n* docker.

loo *n* Brit informal lavatory.

loofah *n* dried pod of a gourd, used as a sponge.

look *v* direct the eyes or attention (towards); seem; face in a particular direction; search (for); hope (for). ◆ *n* looking; search; (often pl.) appearance. **look after** *v* take care of. **lookalike** *n* person who is the double of another. **look down on** *v* treat as inferior or unimportant. **look forward to** *v* anticipate with pleasure. **look on** *v* be an onlooker; consider or regard. **lookout** *n* guard; place for watching; chances or prospect; Informal worry or concern. **look out** *v* be careful. **look up** *v* confirm by checking in a book; visit; improve. **look up to** *v* respect.

loom¹ *n* machine for weaving cloth.

loom² *v* appear dimly; seem ominously close; assume great importance.

loon *n* N American diving bird. **loonie, loony** *n* Informal Canadian dollar coin.

loony Slang ◆ *n, pl* **loonies** foolish or insane person. ◆ *adj* **loonier, looniest** foolish or insane. **loony bin** Slang mental hospital.

loop *n* rounded shape made by a curved line or rope crossing itself. ◆ *v* form a loop. **loop the loop** fly or be flown in a complete vertical circle. **loophole** *n* means of evading a rule

without breaking it.

loose *adj* not tight, fastened, fixed, or tense; slack; vague; dissolute or promiscuous. ◆ *adv* in a loose manner. ◆ *v* free; unfasten; slacken; let fly (an arrow, bullet, etc.). **at a loose end** bored, with nothing to do. **loosely** *adv* **looseness** *n* **loosen** *v* make loose. **loosen up** *v* relax, stop worrying. **loose-leaf** *adj* allowing the addition or removal of pages, e.g. *loose-leaf folder*.

loot *n, v* plunder. **looter** *n* **looting** *n*

lop *v* lopping, **lopped** cut away twigs and branches; chop off.

lope *v* run with long easy strides.

lop-eared *adj* having drooping ears.

lopsided *adj* greater in height, weight, or size on one side.

loquacious *adj* talkative. **loquacity** *n*

lord *n* person with power over others, such as a monarch or master; male member of the nobility; Hist feudal superior; (L-) God; (L-) title given to certain male officials and peers. **House of Lords** unelected upper chamber of the British parliament. **lord it over** act in a superior manner towards. **the Lord's Prayer** prayer taught by Christ to his disciples. **lordly** *adj* imperious, proud. **Lordship** *n* title of some male officials and peers.

lore *n* body of traditions on a subject.

lorgnette [lor-**nyet**] *n* pair of spectacles mounted on a long handle.

lorry *n* Brit truck.

lose *v* losing, **lost** come to be without, as by accident or carelessness; fail to keep or maintain; be deprived of; fail to get or make use of; have an income less than one's expenditure; fail to perceive or understand; be defeated in a competition etc.; be or become engrossed, e.g. *lost in thought*; go astray or allow to go astray; die or be destroyed; (of a clock etc.) run slow (by a specified amount). **loser** *n*

loss *n* losing; that which is lost; damage resulting from losing. **at a loss** confused or bewildered; not earning enough to cover costs. **loss leader** item sold at a loss to attract customers.

lot *pron* great number. ◆ *n* collection of people or things; large quantity; fate or destiny; item at auction; one of a set of objects drawn at random to make a selection or choice. ◆ *pl Informal* great numbers or quantities. **a lot** *adv Informal* a great deal.

loth *adj* same as LOATH.

lotion *n* medical or cosmetic liquid for use on the skin.

lottery *n, pl* **-teries** method of raising funds by selling tickets that win prizes by chance; gamble.

lotto *n* game of chance like bingo.

lotus *n* legendary plant whose fruit induces forgetfulness; Egyptian water lily.

loud *adj* relatively great in volume; capable of making much noise; insistent and emphatic; unpleasantly patterned or colourful. **loudly** *adv* **loudness** *n* **loudspeaker** *n* instrument for converting electrical signals into sound.

lough *n Irish* loch.

lounge *n* living room in a private house; area for waiting in an airport; more comfortable bar in a pub. ◆ *v* sit, lie, or stand in a relaxed manner; pass time idly. **lounge suit** man's suit for daytime wear.

lour *v* same as LOWER[2].

louse *n* (*pl* **lice**) wingless parasitic insect; (*pl* **louses**) unpleasant person. **lousy** *adj Slang* very bad or unpleasant; bad, inferior; unwell.

lout *n* crude, oafish, or aggressive person. **loutish** *adj*

louvre [loo-ver] *n* one of a set of parallel slats slanted to admit air but not rain. **louvred** *adj*

love *n* warm affection; sexual passion; wholehearted liking for something; beloved person; *Tennis, squash, etc.* score of nothing. ◆ *v* have a great affection for; feel sexual passion for; enjoy (something) very much. **fall in love** become in love. **in love (with)** feeling a strong emotional (and sexual) attraction (for). **make love (to)** have sexual intercourse (with). **lovable** *adj* **loveless** *adj* **lovely** *adj* very attractive; highly enjoyable. **lover** *n* **loving** *adj* affectionate, tender. **lovingly** *adv* **love affair** romantic or sexual relationship between two people who are not married to each other. **lovebird** *n* small parrot. **love life** person's romantic or sexual relationships. **lovelorn** *adj* forsaken by or pining for a lover. **lovemaking** *n*

low[1] *adj* not tall, high, or elevated; of little or less than the usual amount, degree, quality, or cost; coarse or vulgar; dejected; ill; not loud; deep in pitch; (of a gear) providing a relatively low speed. ◆ *n* low position, level, or degree; area of low atmospheric pressure, depression. ◆ *adv* in or to a low position, level, or degree. **lowly** *adj* modest, humble. **lowliness** *n* **lowbrow** *n, adj* (person) with nonintellectual tastes and interests. **Low Church** section of the Anglican Church stressing evangelical beliefs and practices. **lowdown** *n Informal* inside information. **low-down** *adj Informal* mean, shabby, or dishonest. **low-key** *adj* subdued, restrained, not intense. **lowland** *n* low-lying country. ◆ *pl* (**L-**) less mountainous parts of Scotland. **low profile** position or attitude avoiding prominence or publicity. **low-spirited** *adj* depressed.

low[2] *n* cry of cattle, moo. ◆ *v* moo.

lower[1] *v* cause or allow to move down; diminish or degrade; lessen. ◆ *adj* below one or more other things; smaller or reduced in amount or value. **lower case** small, as distinct from capital, letters.

lower[2], **lour** *v* (of the sky or weather) look gloomy or threatening. **lowering** *adj*

loyal *adj* faithful to one's friends, country, or government. **loyalty card** swipe card issued by a supermarket or chain store to a customer, used to record credit points awarded for money spent in the store. **loyally** *adv* **loyalty** *n* **loyalist** *n*

lozenge *n* medicated tablet held in the mouth until it dissolves; four-sided diamond-shaped figure.

LP *n* record playing approximately 20–25 minutes each side.

LSD lysergic acid diethylamide, a hallucinogenic drug.

Lt Lieutenant.

Ltd Limited (Liability).

lubricate [loo-brik-ate] *v* oil to lessen friction. **lubricant** *n* lubricating substance such as oil. **lubrication** *n*

lubricious [loo-**brish**-uss] *adj Lit* lewd.

lucerne *n* fodder plant like clover, alfalfa.

lucid *adj* clear and easily understood;

able to think clearly; bright and clear. **lucidly** *adv* **lucidity** *n*

Lucifer *n* Satan.

luck *n* fortune, good or bad; good fortune; chance. **lucky** *adj* having good luck. **luckily** *adv* fortunately. **luckless** *adj* having bad luck.

lucrative *adj* very profitable.

lucre [loo-ker] *n* **filthy lucre** *Informal usu facetious* money.

Luddite *n* person opposed to change in industrial methods.

ludicrous *adj* absurd or ridiculous. **ludicrously** *adv*

lug[1] *v* **lugging, lugged** carry or drag with great effort.

lug[2] *n* projection serving as a handle; *Informal* ear.

luggage *n* traveller's cases, bags, etc.

lugger *n* working boat rigged with an oblong sail.

lugubrious [loo-**goo**-bree-uss] *adj* mournful. **lugubriously** *adv*

lugworm *n* large worm used as bait.

lukewarm *adj* moderately warm, tepid; indifferent or half-hearted.

lull *n* brief time of quiet in a storm etc. ◆ *v* soothe (someone) by soft sounds or motions; calm (fears or suspicions) by deception.

lullaby *n, pl* **-bies** quiet song to send a child to sleep.

lumbago [lum-**bay**-go] *n* pain in the lower back. **lumbar** *adj* relating to the lower back.

lumber[1] *n* useless disused articles, such as old furniture; sawn timber. ◆ *v Informal* burden with something unpleasant. **lumberjack** *n* man who fells trees and prepares logs for transport.

lumber[2] *v* move heavily and awkwardly. **lumbering** *adj*

luminous *adj* reflecting or giving off light. **luminosity** *n* **luminary** *n* famous person; *Lit* heavenly body giving off light. **luminescence** *n* emission of light at low temperatures by any process other than burning. **luminescent** *adj*

lump[1] *n* shapeless piece or mass; swelling; *Informal* awkward or stupid person. ◆ *v* consider as a single group. **lump in one's throat** tight dry feeling in one's throat, usu. caused by great emotion. **lumpy** *adj* **lump sum** relatively large sum of money paid at one time.

lump[2] *v* **lump it** *Informal* tolerate it.

lunar *adj* relating to the moon. **lunar month, lunation** *n* time taken for the moon to go once round the earth, approx. 29½ days.

lunatic *adj* foolish and irresponsible. ◆ *n* foolish or annoying person; *Old-fashioned* insane person. **lunacy** *n*

lunch *n* meal taken in the middle of the day. ◆ *v* eat lunch. **luncheon** *n* formal lunch. **luncheon meat** canned ground mixture of meat and cereal. **luncheon voucher** voucher for a certain amount, given to an employee and accepted by some restaurants as payment for a meal.

lung *n* organ that allows an animal or bird to breathe air: humans have two lungs in the chest.

lunge *n* sudden forward motion; thrust with a sword. ◆ *v* move with or make a lunge.

lupin *n* garden plant with tall spikes of flowers.

lupine *adj* like a wolf.

lupus *n* ulcerous skin disease.

lurch[1] *v* tilt suddenly to one side; stagger. ◆ *n* lurching movement.

lurch[2] *n* **leave someone in the lurch** abandon someone in difficulties.

lurcher *n* crossbred dog trained to hunt silently.

lure *v* tempt or attract by the promise of reward. ◆ *n* person or thing that lures; brightly coloured artificial angling bait.

lurid *adj* vivid in shocking detail, sensational; glaring in colour. **luridly** *adv*

lurk *v* lie hidden or move stealthily, esp. for sinister purposes; be latent.

luscious [**lush**-uss] *adj* extremely pleasurable to taste or smell; very attractive.

lush[1] *adj* (of grass etc.) growing thickly and healthily; opulent. **lushly** *adv* **lushness** *n*

lush[2] *n Slang* alcoholic.

lust *n* strong sexual desire; any strong desire. ◆ *v* have passionate desire (for). **lustful** *adj* **lusty** *adj* vigorous, healthy. **lustily** *adv*

lustre *n* gloss, sheen; splendour or glory; metallic pottery glaze. **lustrous** *adj* shining, luminous.

lute n ancient guitar-like musical instrument with a body shaped like a half pear. **lutenist** n person who plays a lute.

Lutheran adj of Martin Luther (1483–1546), German Reformation leader, his doctrines, or a Church following these doctrines.

lux n, pl **lux** unit of illumination.

luxuriant adj rich and abundant; very elaborate. **luxuriantly** adv **luxuriance** n

luxuriate v take self-indulgent pleasure (in); flourish.

luxury n, pl **-ries** enjoyment of rich, very comfortable living; enjoyable but not essential thing. ◆ adj of or providing luxury. **luxurious** adj sumptuous. **luxuriously** adv

lychee [lie-**chee**] n Chinese fruit with a whitish juicy pulp.

Lycra n ® elastic fabric used for tight-fitting garments, such as swimming costumes.

lye n water made alkaline with wood ashes etc., esp. as formerly used for washing.

lying v present participle of LIE[1], LIE[2]. **lying-in** n Old-fashioned period of confinement during childbirth.

lymph n colourless bodily fluid consisting mainly of white blood cells. **lymphatic** adj

lymphocyte n type of white blood cell.

lynch v put to death without a trial.

lynx n animal of the cat family with tufted ears and a short tail.

lyre n ancient musical instrument like a U-shaped harp.

lyric n short poem expressing personal emotion in a songlike style. ◆ pl words of a popular song. ◆ adj of such poems; in the style of a song. **lyrical** adj lyric; enthusiastic. **lyricist** n person who writes the words of songs or musicals.

M m

m metre(s); mile(s); minute(s).

M Monsieur; Motorway.

m. male; married; masculine; meridian; month.

ma n Informal mother.

MA Master of Arts.

ma'am n madam.

mac n Informal mackintosh.

macabre [mak-**kahb**-ra] adj strange and horrible, gruesome.

macadam n road surface of pressed layers of small broken stones.

macaroni n pasta in short tubes.

macaroon n small cookie or cake made with ground almonds.

macaw n large tropical American parrot.

mace[1] n ceremonial staff of office; medieval weapon with a spiked metal head.

mace[2] n spice made from the dried husk of the nutmeg.

macerate [**mass**-a-rate] v soften by soaking. **maceration** n

machete [mash-**ett**-ee] n broad heavy knife used for cutting or as a weapon.

Machiavellian [mak-ee-a-**vel**-yan] adj unprincipled, crafty, and opportunist.

machinations [mak-in-**nay**-shunz] pl n cunning plots and ploys.

machine n apparatus, usu. powered by electricity, designed to perform a particular task; vehicle, such as an automobile or aircraft; controlling system of an organization. ◆ v make or produce by machine. **machinery** n machines or machine parts collectively. **machinist** n person who operates a machine. **machine gun** automatic gun that fires rapidly and continuously. **machine-gun** v fire at with such a gun. **machine-readable** adj (of data) in a form suitable for processing by a computer.

machismo [mak-**izz**-mow] n strong or exaggerated masculinity.

Mach number [mak] n ratio of the speed of a body in a particular medium to the speed of sound in that medium.

macho [**match**-oh] adj strongly or exaggeratedly masculine.

mackerel n edible sea fish with blue and silver stripes.

mackinaw coat n thick, short plaid coat.

mackintosh n waterproof raincoat of rubberized cloth; any raincoat.

macramé [mak-**rah**-mee] n ornamental work of knotted cord.

macrobiotics n dietary system

advocating whole grains and vegetables grown without chemical additives. **macrobiotic** adj

macrocosm n the universe; any large complete system.

mad adj **madder, maddest** mentally deranged, insane; very foolish; (foll. by about or on) very enthusiastic (about); frantic; Informal angry. **like mad** Informal with great energy, enthusiasm, or haste. **madly** adv **madness** n **madden** v infuriate or irritate. **maddening** adj **madman, madwoman** n

madam n polite form of address to a woman; Informal spoilt girl.

madame [mad-**dam**] n, pl **mesdames** [may-**dam**] French title equivalent to Mrs.

madcap adj, n reckless (person).

madder n climbing plant; red dye made from its root.

made v past of MAKE.

Madeira [mad-**deer**-a] n fortified white wine. **Madeira cake** rich sponge cake.

mademoiselle [mad-mwah-**zel**] n, pl **mesdemoiselles** [maid-mwah-**zel**] French title equivalent to Miss.

Madonna n the Virgin Mary; picture or statue of her.

madrigal n 16th–17th century part song for unaccompanied voices.

maelstrom [**male**-strom] n great whirlpool; turmoil.

maestro [**my**-stroh] n, pl **-tri, -tros** outstanding musician or conductor; any master of an art.

Mafia n international secret criminal organization founded in Sicily. **mafioso** n member of the Mafia.

magazine n periodical publication with articles by different writers; television or radio programme made up of short nonfictional items; appliance for automatically supplying cartridges to a gun or slides to a projector; storehouse for explosives or arms.

magenta [maj-**jen**-ta] adj deep purplish-red.

maggot n larva of an insect, esp. the blowfly. **maggoty** adj

Magi [**maje**-eye] pl n wise men from the East at the Nativity.

magic n supposed art of invoking supernatural powers to influence events; mysterious quality or power. ◆ adj (also **magical**) of, using, or like magic. **magically** adv **magician** n conjurer; person with magic powers.

magistrate n public officer administering the law; justice of the peace. **magisterial** adj authoritative; of a magistrate.

magma n molten rock inside the earth's crust.

magnanimous adj noble and generous. **magnanimously** adv **magnanimity** n

magnate n influential or wealthy person, esp. in industry.

magnesium n silvery-white metallic element. **magnesia** n compound of magnesium used in medicine.

magnet n piece of iron or steel capable of attracting iron and pointing north when suspended. **magnetic** adj having the properties of a magnet; powerfully attractive. **magnetic tape** plastic strip coated with a magnetic substance for recording sound or video signals. **magnetically** adv **magnetism** n magnetic property; science of this; powerful personal charm. **magnetize** v make into a magnet; attract strongly. **magnetization** n

magneto [mag-**nee**-toe] n, pl **-tos** apparatus for ignition in an internal-combustion engine.

magnificent adj splendid or impressive; excellent. **magnificently** adv **magnificence** n

magnify v **-fying, -fied** increase in apparent size, as with a lens; exaggerate. **magnification** n

magniloquent adj speaking pompously. **magniloquence** n

magnitude n relative importance; relative size or extent.

magnolia n shrub or tree with showy white or pink flowers.

magnum n large wine bottle holding about 1.5 litres.

magpie n black-and-white bird.

Magyar n member of the main ethnic group in Hungary; Hungarian language. ◆ adj of the Magyars or their language.

maharajah n former title of some Indian princes. **maharanee** n fem

maharishi *n* Hindu religious teacher.

mahatma *n Hinduism* person revered for holiness and wisdom.

mahjong, mahjongg *n* Chinese table game for four, played with tiles bearing different designs.

mahogany *n, pl* **-nies** hard reddish-brown wood of several tropical trees.

mahout [ma-**howt**] *n* elephant driver or keeper.

maid *n* (also **maidservant**) female servant; *Lit* young unmarried woman.

maiden *n Lit* young unmarried woman. ♦ *adj* unmarried; first, e.g. *maiden voyage*. **maidenly** *adj* modest. **maidenhood** *n* **maidenhair** *n* fern with delicate fronds. **maidenhead** *n* virginity. **maiden name** woman's surname before marriage.

mail[1] *n* letters and packages transported and delivered by the post office; postal system; single collection or delivery of mail; train, ship, or aircraft carrying mail. ♦ *v* send by post. **mailbox** *n* public box into which letters are put for collection and delivery; private box outside house where occupant's mail is delivered. **mail drop** receptacle or chute for mail. **mailman** *n* person who collects or delivers mail. **mail order** system of buying goods by post.

mail[2] *n* flexible armour of interlaced rings or links. **mailed** *adj*

maim *v* cripple or mutilate.

main *adj* chief or principal. ♦ *n* principal pipe or line carrying water, gas, or electricity. **in the main** on the whole. **mainly** *adv* for the most part, chiefly. **mainframe** *n, adj Computers* (denoting) a high-speed general-purpose computer. **mainland** *n* stretch of land which forms the main part of a country. **mainmast** *n* chief mast in a ship. **mainsail** *n* largest sail on a mainmast. **mainspring** *n* chief spring of a watch or clock; chief cause or motive. **mainstay** *n* chief support; rope securing a mainmast. **mainstream** *n* prevailing cultural trend.

maintain *v* continue or keep in existence; keep up or preserve; support financially; assert. **maintenance** *n* maintaining; upkeep of a building, automobile, etc.; provision of money for a separated or divorced spouse.

maître d'hôtel [met-ra dote-**tell**] *n French* head waiter.

maize *n* type of corn with spikes of yellow grains.

majesty *n, pl* **-ties** stateliness or grandeur; supreme power. **majestic** *adj* **majestically** *adv*

major *adj* greater in number, quality, or extent; significant or serious. ♦ *n* middle-ranking army officer; scale in music; principal field of study at a university etc. ♦ *v* (foll. by *in*) do one's principal study in (a particular subject). **major-domo** *n* chief steward of a great household.

majority *n, pl* **-ties** greater number; largest party voting together; number by which the votes on one side exceed those on the other; full legal age.

make *v* **making, made** create, construct, or establish; cause to do or be; bring about or produce; perform (an action); amount to; earn; serve as or become. ♦ *n* brand, type, or style. **make do** manage with an inferior alternative. **make it** *Informal* be successful. **on the make** *Informal* intent on gain. **maker** *n* **making** *n* creation or production. ♦ *pl* necessary requirements or qualities. **make-believe** *n* fantasy or pretence. **make for** *v* head towards. **make off with** *v* steal or abduct. **makeshift** *adj* serving as a temporary substitute. **make up** *v* form or constitute; prepare; invent; supply what is lacking, complete; (foll. by *for*) compensate (for); settle a quarrel; apply cosmetics. **make-up** *n* cosmetics; mental or physical constitution; way something is made. **makeweight** *n* something unimportant added to make up a lack.

mal- *combining form* bad or badly, e.g. *malformation, malfunction.*

malachite [mal-a-kite] *n* green mineral.

maladjusted *adj Psychol* unable to meet the demands of society. **maladjustment** *n*

maladministration *n* inefficient or dishonest administration.

maladroit [mal-a-**droyt**] *adj* clumsy or awkward.

malady [mal-a-dee] *n, pl* **-dies** disease or illness.

malaise [mal-**laze**] *n* vague feeling of

illness or unease.

malapropism *n* comical misuse of a word by confusion with one which sounds similar.

malaria *n* infectious disease caused by the bite of some mosquitoes. **malarial** *adj*

Malay *n* member of a people of Malaysia or Indonesia; language of this people. **Malayan** *adj, n*

malcontent *n* discontented person.

male *adj* of the sex which can fertilize female reproductive cells. ◆ *n* male person or animal.

malediction [mal-lid-**dik**-shun] *n* curse.

malefactor [**mal**-if-act-or] *n* criminal.

malevolent [mal-**lev**-a-lent] *adj* wishing evil to others. **malevolently** *adv* **malevolence** *n*

malfeasance [mal-**fee**-zanss] *n* misconduct, esp. by a public official.

malformed *adj* misshapen or deformed. **malformation** *n*

malfunction *v* function imperfectly or fail to function. ◆ *n* defective functioning or failure to function.

malice [**mal**-iss] *n* desire to cause harm to others. **malicious** *adj* **maliciously** *adv*

malign [mal-**line**] *v* slander or defame. ◆ *adj* evil in influence or effect. **malignity** *n* evil disposition.

malignant [mal-**lig**-nant] *adj* seeking to harm others; (of a tumour) harmful and uncontrollable. **malignancy** *n*

malinger [mal-**ling**-ger] *v* feign illness to avoid work. **malingerer** *n*

mall *n* street or shopping centre closed to vehicles.

mallard *n* wild duck.

malleable [**mal**-lee-a-bl] *adj* capable of being hammered or pressed into shape; easily influenced. **malleability** *n*

mallet *n* (wooden) hammer; stick with a head like a hammer, used in croquet or polo.

mallow *n* plant with pink or purple flowers.

malmsey *n* kind of strong sweet wine.

malnutrition *n* inadequate nutrition.

malodorous [mal-**lode**-or-uss] *adj* bad-smelling.

malpractice *n* immoral, illegal, or unethical professional conduct.

malt *n* grain, such as barley, prepared for use in making beer or whisky.

maltreat *v* treat badly. **maltreatment** *n*

mama, mamma [mam-ma] *n* Old-fashioned mother.

mamba *n* deadly S African snake.

mammal *n* animal of the type that suckles its young. **mammalian** *adj*

mammary *adj* of the breasts or milk-producing glands.

mammon *n* wealth regarded as a source of evil; (M-) wealth personified in the New Testament as a false god.

mammoth *n* extinct animal like an elephant. ◆ *adj* colossal.

man *n, pl* **men** adult male; human being or person; mankind; manservant; piece used in chess etc. ◆ *v* **manning, manned** supply with sufficient people for operation or defence **manful** *adj* determined and brave. **manfully** *adv* **manhood** *n* **mankind** *n* human beings collectively. **manly** *adj* (possessing qualities) appropriate to a man. **manliness** *n* **mannish** *adj* like a man. **manhandle** *v* treat roughly. **manhole** *n* hole with a cover, through which a person can enter a drain or sewer. **man-hour** *n* work done by one person in one hour. **man-made** *adj* synthetic. **manpower** *n* available number of workers. **manservant** *n* male servant, esp. a valet. **manslaughter** *n* unlawful but unintentional killing of a person.

Man. Manitoba.

manacle [**man**-a-kl] *n, v* fetter.

manage *v* succeed in doing; be in charge of, administer; handle or control; cope with (financial) difficulties. **manageable** *adj* **management** *n* managers collectively; administration or organization. **manager, manageress** *n* person in charge of a business, institution, actor, sports team, etc. **managerial** *adj*

manatee *n* large tropical plant-eating aquatic mammal.

mandarin *n* high-ranking government official; kind of small orange.

mandate *n* official or authoritative command; authorization or instruction from an electorate to its representative or government. ◆ *v* give authority to. **mandatory** *adj* compulsory.

mandible n lower jawbone or jawlike part.

mandolin n musical instrument with four pairs of strings.

mandrake n plant with a forked root, formerly used as a narcotic.

mandrel n shaft on which work is held in a lathe.

mandrill n large blue-faced baboon.

mane n long hair on the neck of a horse, lion, etc.

manganese n brittle greyish-white metallic element.

mange n skin disease of domestic animals. **mangy** adj having mange; scruffy or shabby.

mangelwurzel n Brit variety of beet used as cattle food.

manger n eating trough in a stable or barn.

mangetout [mawnzh-too] n Brit snow pea.

mangle¹ v destroy by crushing and twisting; spoil.

mangle² n machine with rollers for squeezing water from washed clothes. ◆ v put through a mangle.

mango n, pl **-goes, -gos** tropical fruit with sweet juicy yellow flesh.

mangrove n tropical tree with exposed roots, which grows beside water.

mania n madness; extreme enthusiasm. **maniac** n mad person; Informal person who has an extreme enthusiasm for something. **maniacal** [man-eye-a-kl], **manic** adj affected by mania.

manicure n cosmetic care of the fingernails and hands. ◆ v care for (the hands and fingernails) in this way. **manicurist** n

manifest adj easily noticed, obvious. ◆ v show plainly; be evidence of. ◆ n list of cargo or passengers for customs. **manifestation** n

manifesto n, pl **-toes, -tos** declaration of policy as issued by a political party.

manifold adj numerous and varied. ◆ n pipe with several outlets, esp. in an internal-combustion engine.

manikin n little man or dwarf; model of the human body.

manila, manilla n strong brown paper used for envelopes.

manipulate v handle skilfully; control cleverly or deviously. **manipulation** n **manipulative** adj **manipulator** n

Manitoba see Canadian Provincial Facts p 630.

manitou, manito n spirit of good or evil among N American Indians.

manna n Bible miraculous food which sustained the Israelites in the wilderness; windfall.

mannequin n woman who models clothes at a fashion show; life-size dummy of the human body used to fit or display clothes.

manner n way a thing happens or is done; person's bearing or behaviour; type or kind; custom or style. ◆ pl (polite) social behaviour. **mannered** adj affected. **mannerism** n person's distinctive habit or trait.

mannikin n same as MANIKIN.

manoeuvre [man-noo-ver] v move or do something with skill; manipulate a situation to gain some advantage; perform manoeuvres. ◆ n skilful movement; contrived, complicated, and possibly deceptive plan or action. ◆ pl military or naval exercises. **manoeuvrable** adj

manor n large country house and its lands. **manorial** adj

manqué [mong-kay] adj would-be, e.g. an actor manqué.

mansard roof n roof with a break in its slope, the lower part being steeper than the upper.

manse n minister's house in some religious denominations.

mansion n large house.

mantel n structure round a fireplace. **mantelpiece, mantel shelf** n shelf above a fireplace.

mantilla n (in Spain) a lace scarf covering a woman's head and shoulders.

mantis n, pl **-tises, -tes** carnivorous insect like a grasshopper.

mantle n loose cloak; covering; responsibilities that go with a particular job or position; incandescent gauze round a gas jet.

mantra n Hinduism, Buddhism any sacred word or syllable used as an object of concentration.

manual adj of or done with the hands; by human labour rather than automatic means. ◆ n handbook;

organ keyboard. **manually** *adv*

manufacture *v* process or make (goods) on a large scale using machinery; invent (an excuse etc.). ◆ *n* process of manufacturing goods. **manufacturer** *n*

manure *n* animal excrement used as a fertilizer. ◆ *v* fertilize (land) with this.

manuscript *n* book or document, orig. one written by hand; copy for printing.

Manx *adj* of the Isle of Man or its inhabitants. ◆ *n* Manx language. **Manx cat** tailless breed of cat.

many *adj* **more, most** numerous. ◆ *n* large number.

Maoism *n* form of Marxism advanced by Mao Tse-tung in China. **Maoist** *n, adj*

Maori *n* member of the indigenous race of New Zealand; Maori language. ◆ *adj* of the Maoris or their language.

map *n* representation of the earth's surface or some part of it, showing geographical features. ◆ *v* **mapping, mapped** make a map of. **map out** *v* plan.

maple *n* tree with broad leaves, a variety of which yields sugar. **maple syrup** very sweet syrup made from the sap of the sugar maple.

mar *v* **marring, marred** spoil.

Mar. March.

marabou *n* kind of African stork; its soft white down, used to trim hats etc.

maraca [mar-rak-a] *n* shaken percussion instrument made from a gourd containing dried seeds etc.

maraschino cherry [mar-rass-kee-no] *n* cherry preserved in a cherry liqueur with a taste like bitter almonds.

marathon *n* long-distance race of just over 26 miles; arduous task.

marauding *adj* hunting for plunder; pillaging. **marauder** *n*

marble *n* kind of limestone with a mottled appearance, which can be highly polished; slab of or sculpture in this; small glass ball used in playing marbles. ◆ *pl* game of rolling these. **marbled** *adj* having a mottled appearance like marble.

march¹ *v* walk with a military step; make (a person or group) proceed; progress steadily. ◆ *n* action of marching; distance covered by

marching; steady progress; piece of music, as for a march. **marcher** *n*

march² *n* border or frontier.

March *n* third month of the year.

marchioness [marsh-on-**ness**] *n* woman holding the rank of marquis; wife or widow of a marquis.

mare *n* female horse. **mare's nest** discovery which proves worthless; badly disordered situation or thing.

margarine *n* butter substitute made from animal or vegetable fats.

marge *n* Informal margarine.

margin *n* edge or border; blank space round a printed page; additional amount or one greater than necessary; limit. **marginal** *adj* insignificant, unimportant; near a limit; (of a constituency) won by only a small margin. ◆ *n* marginal constituency. **marginally** *adv*

marguerite *n* large daisy.

marigold *n* plant with yellow flowers.

marijuana [mar-ree-wah-na] *n* dried flowers and leaves of the hemp plant, used as a drug, esp. in cigarettes.

marina *n* harbour for yachts and other pleasure boats.

marine *adj* of the sea or shipping; used at or found in the sea. ◆ *n* soldier trained for land or sea combat; country's shipping or fleet. **mariner** *n* sailor.

marionette *n* puppet worked with strings.

marital *adj* relating to marriage.

maritime *adj* relating to shipping; of, near, or living in the sea.

marjoram *n* aromatic herb.

mark¹ *n* line, dot, scar, etc. visible on a surface; distinguishing sign or symbol; written or printed symbol; letter or number used to grade academic work; indication of position; indication of some quality; target or goal. ◆ *v* make a mark on; be a distinguishing mark of; indicate; pay attention to; notice or watch; grade (academic work); stay close to (a sporting opponent) to hamper his play. **marked** *adj* noticeable. **markedly** [mark-id-lee] *adv* **marker** *n*

mark² *n* same as DEUTSCHMARK.

market *n* assembly or place for buying and selling; demand for goods. ◆ *v* **-keting, -keted** offer or produce for

sale. **on the market** for sale.
marketable *adj* **marketing** *n* part of a business that controls the way that goods or services are sold. **market garden** place where fruit and vegetables are grown for sale.
marketing board board that regulates the price of agricultural commodities.
market maker *Stock Exchange* person who uses a firm's money to create a market for a stock. **marketplace** *n* market; commercial world. **market research** research into consumers' needs and purchases.

marksman *n* person skilled at shooting. **marksmanship** *n*

marl *n* soil formed of clay and lime, used as fertilizer.

marlinespike, marlinspike *n* pointed hook used to separate strands of rope.

marmalade *n* jam made from citrus fruits.

marmoreal [mar-more-ee-al] *adj* of or like marble.

marmoset *n* small bushy-tailed monkey.

marmot *n* burrowing rodent.

maroon[1] *adj* reddish-purple.

maroon[2] *v* abandon ashore, esp. on an island; isolate without resources.

marquee *n* large tent used for a party or exhibition.

marquess [mar-kwiss] *n* nobleman of the rank below a duke.

marquetry *n, pl* **-quetries** ornamental inlaid work of wood.

marquis *n, pl* **-quises, -quis** (in various countries) nobleman of the rank above a count.

marram grass *n* grass that grows on sandy shores.

marrow *n* fatty substance inside bones; oblong green striped vegetable.

marry *v* **-rying, -ried** take as a husband or wife; join or give in marriage; unite closely. **marriage** *n* state of being married; wedding. **marriageable** *adj*

Mars *n* Roman god of war; fourth planet from the sun **Martian** *adj* of Mars. ◆ *n* supposed inhabitant of Mars.

Marsala [mar-sah-la] *n* dark sweet wine.

marsh *n* low-lying wet land. **marshy** *adj*

marshal *n* officer of the highest rank; official who organizes ceremonies or events; *US* law officer. ◆ *v* **-shalling, -shalled** arrange in order; assemble; conduct with ceremony. **marshalling yard** railway depot for goods trains.

marshmallow *n* spongy pink or white candy.

marsupial [mar-soop-yal] *n* animal that carries its young in a pouch, such as a kangaroo.

mart *n* market.

Martello tower *n* round tower for coastal defence.

marten *n* weasel-like animal; its fur.

martial *adj* of war, warlike. **martial art** any of various philosophies and techniques of self-defence, orig. Eastern, such as karate. **martial law** law enforced by military authorities in times of danger or emergency.

martin *n* bird with a slightly forked tail.

martinet *n* strict disciplinarian.

martini *n* cocktail of vermouth and gin.

martyr *n* person who dies or suffers for his or her beliefs. ◆ *v* make a martyr of. **be a martyr to** be constantly suffering from. **martyrdom** *n*

marvel *v* **-velling, -velled** be filled with wonder. ◆ *n* wonderful thing. **marvellous** *adj* excellent; causing great surprise.

Marxism *n* socialism as conceived by Karl Marx. **Marxist** *n, adj*

marzipan *n* paste of ground almonds, sugar, and egg whites.

masc. masculine.

mascara *n* cosmetic for darkening the eyelashes.

mascot *n* thing supposed to bring good luck.

masculine *adj* relating to males; manly; *Grammar* of the gender of nouns that includes some male animate things. **masculinity** *n*

mash *n* bran or meal mixed with warm water as food for horses etc.; *Informal* mashed potatoes. ◆ *v* crush into a soft mass.

mask *n* covering for the face, as a disguise or protection; behaviour that hides one's true feelings. ◆ v cover with a mask; disguise.

masochism [mass-oh-kiz-zum] n form of (sexual) perversion marked by love of pain or of being humiliated. **masochist** n **masochistic** adj

mason n person who works with stone; (M-) Freemason. **Masonic** adj of Freemasonry. **masonry** n stonework; (M-) Freemasonry.

masque [mask] n Hist 16th–17th-century form of dramatic entertainment.

masquerade [mask-a-raid] n deceptive show or pretence; party at which masks and costumes are worn. ◆ v pretend to be someone or something else.

mass n coherent body of matter; large quantity or number; Physics amount of matter in a body. ◆ adj large-scale; involving many people. ◆ v form into a mass. **the masses** ordinary people. **massive** adj large and heavy. **mass-market** adj for or appealing to a large number of people. **mass media** means of communication to many people, such as television and newspapers. **mass-produce** v manufacture standardized goods in large quantities.

Mass n service of the Eucharist, esp. in the RC Church.

massacre [mass-a-ker] n indiscriminate killing of large numbers of people. ◆ v kill in large numbers.

massage [mass-ahzh] n rubbing and kneading of parts of the body to reduce pain or stiffness. ◆ v give a massage to. **masseur** [mass-ur], **masseuse** [mass-urz] n person who gives massages.

massif [mass-seef] n connected group of mountains.

mast[1] n tall pole for supporting something, esp. a ship's sails.

mast[2] n fruit of the beech, oak, etc., used as pig fodder.

mastectomy [mass-tek-tom-ee] n, pl -mies surgical removal of a breast.

master n person in control, such as an employer or an owner of slaves or animals; expert; great artist; original thing from which copies are made; male teacher. ◆ adj overall or controlling; main or principal. ◆ v overcome; acquire knowledge of or skill in. **masterful** adj domineering;

showing great skill. **masterly** adj showing great skill. **mastery** n expertise; control or command. **master key** key that opens all the locks of a set. **mastermind** v plan and direct (a complex task). ◆ n person who plans and directs a complex task. **masterpiece** n outstanding work of art.

mastic n gum obtained from certain trees; putty-like substance used as a filler, adhesive, or seal.

masticate v chew. **mastication** n

mastiff n large dog.

mastitis n inflammation of a breast or udder.

mastodon n extinct elephant-like mammal.

mastoid n projection of the bone behind the ear. **mastoiditis** n inflammation of this area.

masturbate v caress the genitals (of). **masturbation** n

mat n piece of fabric used as a floor covering or to protect a surface. ◆ v **matting, matted** become tangled. **on the mat** Informal summoned for a reprimand.

matador n man who kills the bull in bullfights.

match[1] n contest in a game or sport; person or thing exactly like, equal to, or in harmony with another; marriage. ◆ v be exactly like, equal to, or in harmony with; put in competition (with); find a match for; join (in marriage). **matchless** adj unequalled. **matchmaker** n person who schemes to bring about a marriage. **matchmaking** n

match[2] n small stick with a tip which ignites when scraped on a rough surface. **matchbox** n **matchstick** n wooden part of a match. ◆ adj (of drawn figures) thin and straight. **matchwood** n small splinters.

mate[1] n sexual partner of an animal; officer in a merchant ship; tradesman's assistant; Brit informal friend or associate; Informal common Brit. and Aust. term of address between males. ◆ v pair (animals) or (of animals) be paired for reproduction. **matey** adj Informal friendly or intimate.

mate[2] n, v Chess checkmate.

material n substance of which a thing

is made; cloth; information on which a piece of work may be based. ◆ *pl* things needed for an activity. ◆ *adj* of matter or substance; affecting physical wellbeing; unspiritual; relevant. **materially** *adv* considerably.

materialism *n* excessive interest in or desire for money and possessions; belief that only the material world exists. **materialist** *adj*, *n* **materialistic** *adj* **materialize** *v* come into existence or view; actually happen. **materialization** *n*

maternal *adj* of a mother; related through one's mother. **maternity** *n* motherhood. ◆ *adj* of or for pregnant women.

math *n Informal* mathematics.

mathematics *n* science of number, quantity, shape, and space. **mathematical** *adj* **mathematically** *adv* **mathematician** *n*

maths *n Brit informal* mathematics.

matinée [mat-in-nay] *n* afternoon performance in a theatre.

matins *pl n* early morning service in various Christian Churches.

matriarch [mate-ree-ark] *n* female head of a tribe or family. **matriarchal** *adj* **matriarchy** *n* society with matriarchal government and descent traced through the female line.

matricide *n* crime of killing one's mother; person who does this.

matriculate *v* enrol or be enrolled in a college or university. **matriculation** *n*

matrimony *n* marriage. **matrimonial** *adj*

matrix [may-trix] *n*, *pl* **matrices** [may-triss-eez] substance or situation in which something originates, takes form, or is enclosed; mould for casting; *Math* rectangular array of numbers or elements.

matron *n* staid or dignified married woman; woman who supervises the domestic or medical arrangements of an institution. **matronly** *adj*

matt *adj* dull, not shiny.

matter *n* substance of which something is made; physical substance; event, situation, or subject; written material in general; pus. ◆ *v* be of importance. **what's the matter? what is wrong?**

mattock *n* large pick with one of its blade ends flattened for loosening soil.

mattress *n* large stuffed flat case, often with springs, used on or as a bed.

mature *adj* fully developed or grown-up; ripe. ◆ *v* make or become mature; (of a bill or bond) become due for payment. **maturity** *n* **maturation** *n*

maudlin *adj* foolishly sentimental.

maul *v* handle roughly; beat or tear.

maunder *v* talk or act idly.

mausoleum [maw-so-lee-um] *n* stately tomb.

mauve *adj* pale purple.

maverick *n* independent unorthodox person.

maw *n* animal's mouth, throat, or stomach.

mawkish *adj* foolishly sentimental.

maxim *n* general truth or principle.

maximum *n*, *pl* **-mums**, **-ma** greatest possible amount or number. ◆ *adj* greatest. **maximal** *adj* **maximize** *v* increase to a maximum.

may *v*, *past tense* **might** used as an auxiliary to express possibility, permission, opportunity, etc.

May *n* fifth month of the year; (m-) same as HAWTHORN. **mayfly** *n* short-lived aquatic insect. **maypole** *n* pole set up for dancing round on the first day of May (**May Day**).

maybe *adv* perhaps; possibly.

Mayday *n* international radiotelephone distress signal.

mayhem *n* violent destruction or confusion.

mayonnaise *n* creamy sauce of egg yolks, oil, and vinegar.

mayor *n* head of a municipality. **mayoress** *n* mayor's wife; lady mayor. **mayoral** *adj* **mayoralty** *n* (term of) office of a mayor.

maze *n* complex network of paths or lines designed to puzzle; confusing network or system.

mazurka *n* lively Polish dance; music for this.

MB Bachelor of Medicine; Manitoba.

MBE Member of the Order of the British Empire.

MC Master of Ceremonies.

MD Doctor of Medicine.

MDT Mountain Daylight Time.

me *pron* the objective form of I.

ME myalgic encephalomyelitis, postviral syndrome.

mead n alcoholic drink made from honey.

meadow n piece of grassland. **meadowsweet** n plant with dense heads of small fragrant flowers.

meagre adj scanty or insufficient.

meal[1] n occasion when food is served and eaten; the food itself.

meal[2] n grain ground to powder. **mealy** adj **mealy-mouthed** adj not outspoken enough.

mean[1] v **meaning, meant** intend to convey or express; signify, denote, or portend; intend; have importance as specified. **meaning** n sense, significance. ◆ adj expressive. **meaningful** adj **meaningless** adj

mean[2] adj miserly, ungenerous, or petty; despicable or callous; Informal bad-tempered. **meanly** adv **meanness** n **meanie, meany** n miserly person.

mean[3] n middle point between two extremes; average. ◆ pl that by which something is done; money. ◆ adj intermediate in size or quantity; average. **by all means** certainly. **by no means** not at all. **means test** enquiry into a person's means to decide eligibility for financial aid. **meantime** n intervening period. ◆ adv meanwhile. **meanwhile** adv during the intervening period; at the same time.

meander [mee-**and**-er] v follow a winding course; wander aimlessly. ◆ n winding course.

measles n infectious disease producing red spots. **measly** adj Informal meagre.

measure n size or quantity; graduated scale etc. for measuring size or quantity; unit of size or quantity; extent; action taken; law; poetical rhythm. ◆ v determine the size or quantity of; be (a specified amount) in size or quantity. **measurable** adj **measured** adj slow and steady; carefully considered. **measurement** n measuring; size. **measure up to** v fulfil (expectations or requirements).

meat n animal flesh as food. **meaty** adj (tasting) of or like meat; brawny; full of significance.

Mecca n holy city of Islam; place that attracts visitors.

mechanic n person skilled in repairing or operating machinery ◆ pl scientific study of motion and force. **mechanical** adj of or done by machines; (of an action) without thought or feeling. **mechanically** adv

mechanism n way a machine works; piece of machinery; process or technique, e.g. defence mechanism. **mechanize** v equip with machinery; make mechanical or automatic; Mil equip (an army) with armoured vehicles. **mechanization** n

med. medical; medicine; medieval; medium.

medal n piece of metal with an inscription etc., given as a reward or memento. **medallion** n disc-shaped ornament worn on a chain round the neck; large medal; circular decorative device in architecture. **medallist** n winner of a medal.

meddle v interfere annoyingly. **meddler** n **meddlesome** adj

media n a plural of MEDIUM; the mass media collectively.

mediaeval [med-ee-**eve**-al] adj same as MEDIEVAL.

medial [mee-dee-al] adj of or in the middle. **median** adj, n middle (point or line).

mediate [mee-dee-ate] v intervene to bring about agreement; resolve (a dispute) by mediation. **mediation** n **mediator** n

medic n Informal doctor or medical student.

Medicare n system of national medical services financed mainly by taxation.

medicine n substance used to treat disease; science of preventing, diagnosing, or curing disease **medical** adj of the science of medicine. ◆ n Informal medical examination. **medically** adv **medicament** n a medicine. **medicate** v treat with a medicinal substance. **medication** n (treatment with) a medicinal substance. **medicinal** [med-**diss**-in-al] adj having therapeutic properties. **medicine man** witch doctor.

medieval, mediaeval [med-ee-**eve**-al] adj of the Middle Ages.

mediocre [mee-dee-**oak**-er] adj average in quality; second-rate.

mediocrity [mee-dee-ok-rit-ee] *n*

meditate *v* reflect deeply, esp. on spiritual matters; think about or plan. **meditation** *n* meditating. **meditative** *adj* **meditatively** *adv* **meditator** *n*

medium *adj* midway between extremes, average. ◆ *n, pl* **-dia, -diums** middle state, degree, or condition; intervening substance producing an effect; means of communicating news or information to the public, such as radio or newspapers; person who can supposedly communicate with the dead; surroundings or environment; category of art according to the material used. **medium wave** radio wave with a wavelength between 100 and 1000 metres.

medlar *n* apple-like fruit of a small tree, eaten when it begins to decay.

medley *n* miscellaneous mixture; musical sequence of different tunes.

medulla [mid-dull-la] *n, pl* **-las, -lae** marrow, pith, or inner tissue. **medullary** *adj*

meek *adj* submissive or humble. **meekly** *adv* **meekness** *n*

meerschaum [meer-shum] *n* white substance like clay; tobacco pipe with a bowl made of this.

meet[1] *v* **meeting, met** come together (with); come into contact (with); be at the place of arrival of; make the acquaintance of; satisfy (a need etc.); experience. ◆ *n* sports meeting; assembly of a hunt. **meeting** *n* coming together.

meet[2] *adj Obs* fit or suitable.

mega- *combining form* denoting one million, e.g. *megawatt*; very great, e.g. *megastar*.

megabyte *n Computers* 2^{20} or 1 048 576 bytes.

megalith *n* great stone, esp. as part of a prehistoric monument. **megalithic** *adj*

megalomania *n* craving for or mental delusions of power. **megalomaniac** *adj, n*

megaphone *n* cone-shaped instrument used to amplify the voice.

megaton *n* explosive power equal to that of one million tons of TNT.

melancholy [mel-an-kol-lee] *n* sadness or gloom. ◆ *adj* sad or gloomy. **melancholia** [mel-an-kole-ya]

n old name for depression. **melancholic** *adj, n*

melange [may-lahnzh] *n* mixture.

melanin *n* dark pigment found in the hair, skin, and eyes of man and animals.

mêlée [mel-lay] *n* noisy confused fight or crowd.

mellifluous [mel-lif-flew-uss] *adj* (of sound) smooth and sweet.

mellow *adj* soft; kind-hearted, esp. through maturity; (of fruit) ripe. ◆ *v* make or become mellow.

melodrama *n* play full of extravagant action and emotion; overdramatic behaviour or emotion. **melodramatic** *adj*

melody *n, pl* **-dies** series of musical notes which make a tune; sweet sound. **melodic** [mel-lod-ik] *adj* of melody; melodious. **melodious** [mellode-ee-uss] *adj* pleasing to the ear; tuneful.

melon *n* large round juicy fruit with a hard rind.

melt *v* (cause to) become liquid by heat; dissolve; soften through emotion; blend (into); disappear. **meltdown** *n* (in a nuclear reactor) melting of the fuel rods, with the possible release of radiation.

member *n* individual making up a body or society; limb. **membership** *n* **Member of Parliament** person elected to parliament.

membrane *n* thin flexible tissue in a plant or animal body. **membranous** *adj*

memento *n, pl* **-tos, -toes** thing serving to remind, souvenir.

memo *n, pl* **memos** short for MEMORANDUM.

memoir [mem-wahr] *n* biography or historical account based on personal knowledge. ◆ *pl* collection of these; autobiography.

memory *n, pl* **-ries** ability to remember; sum of things remembered; particular recollection; length of time one can remember; commemoration; part of a computer which stores information. **memorial** *n* something serving to commemorate a person or thing. ◆ *adj* serving as a memorial. **memorable** *adj* worth remembering, noteworthy.

memorably adv **memorandum** n written record or communication within a business; note of things to be remembered. **memorize** v commit to memory.

men n plural of MAN.

menace n threat; Informal nuisance. ◆ v threaten. **menacing** adj

ménage [may-nahzh] n household.

menagerie [min-**naj**-er-ee] n collection of wild animals for exhibition.

mend v repair or patch; make or become better; recover or heal. ◆ n mended area. **on the mend** regaining health.

mendacity n (tendency to) untruthfulness. **mendacious** adj

mendicant adj begging. ◆ n beggar.

menhir [**men**-hear] n single upright prehistoric stone.

menial [**mean**-yal] adj involving boring work of low status. ◆ n domestic servant.

meningitis [men-in-**jite**-iss] n inflammation of the membranes of the brain.

meniscus n, pl **-nisci, -niscuses** curved surface of a liquid; crescent-shaped lens.

menopause n time when a woman's menstrual cycle ceases. **menopausal** adj

menstruation n approximately monthly discharge of blood and cellular debris from the womb of a nonpregnant woman. **menstruate** v **menstrual** adj

mensuration n measuring, esp. in geometry.

mental adj of, in, or done by the mind; of or for mental illness; Informal insane. **mentally** adv **mentality** n way of thinking.

menthol n organic compound found in peppermint, used medicinally.

mention v refer to briefly; acknowledge. ◆ n acknowledgment; brief reference to a person or thing.

mentor n adviser or guide.

menu n list of dishes to be served, or from which to order; Computers list of options displayed on a screen.

mercantile adj of trade or traders.

Mercator projection [mer-**kate**-er] n method of map-making in which latitude and longitude form a rectangular grid.

mercenary adj influenced by greed; working merely for reward. ◆ n, pl **-aries** hired soldier.

mercerized adj (of cotton) given lustre by treating with chemicals.

merchant n person engaged in trade, wholesale trader **merchandise** n commodities. **merchant bank** bank dealing mainly with businesses and investment. **merchantman** n trading ship. **merchant navy** ships or crew engaged in a nation's commercial shipping.

mercury n silvery liquid metal; (M-) Roman myth messenger of the gods; (M-) planet nearest the sun. **mercurial** [mer-**cure**-ee-al] adj lively, changeable.

mercy n, pl **-cies** compassionate treatment of an offender or enemy who is in one's power; merciful act. **merciful** adj compassionate; giving relief. **merciless** adj

mere[1] adj nothing more than, e.g. mere chance. **merely** adv

mere[2] n Obs lake.

meretricious adj superficially or garishly attractive but of no real value.

merganser [mer-**gan**-ser] n large crested diving duck.

merge v (cause to) combine or blend. **merger** n combination of business firms into one.

meridian n imaginary circle of the earth passing through both poles; peak or zenith.

meringue [mer-**rang**] n baked mixture of egg whites and sugar; small cake of this.

merino n, pl **-nos** breed of sheep with fine soft wool; this wool.

merit n excellence or worth. ◆ pl admirable qualities. ◆ v **-iting, -ited** deserve. **meritorious** adj deserving praise. **meritocracy** [mer-it-**tok**-rass-ee] n rule by people of superior talent or intellect.

merlin n small falcon.

mermaid n imaginary sea creature with the upper part of a woman and the lower part of a fish.

merry adj **-rier, -riest** jolly; Informal slightly drunk. **merrily** adv **merriment** n **merry-go-round** n revolving circular platform on which people ride for amusement. **merrymaking** n revelry.

mesdames n plural of MADAME.

mesdemoiselles n plural of MADEMOISELLE.

mesh n network or net; (open space between) strands forming a network. ◆ v (of gear teeth) engage.

mesmerize v hold spellbound; *Obs* hypnotize.

meson [mee-zon] n elementary atomic particle.

mess n untidy or dirty confusion; trouble or difficulty; group of servicemen who regularly eat together; place where they eat. ◆ v muddle or dirty; (foll. by *about*) potter about; (foll. by *with*) interfere with; (of servicemen) eat in a group.

message n communication sent; meaning or moral. **messenger** n bearer of a message.

Messiah n Jews' promised deliverer; Christ. **Messianic** adj

messieurs n plural of MONSIEUR.

Messrs [mess-erz] n plural of MR.

messy adj **messier, messiest** dirty or untidy. **messily** adv **messiness** n

met v past of MEET¹.

metabolism [met-**tab**-oh-liz-zum] n chemical processes of a living body. **metabolic** adj **metabolize** v produce or be produced by metabolism.

metal n mineral substance, such as iron or copper, that is malleable and capable of conducting heat and electricity; short for ROAD METAL. **metallic** adj **metallurgy** n scientific study of the structure, properties, extraction, and refining of metals. **metallurgical** adj **metallurgist** n

metamorphosis [met-a-**more**-foss-is] n, pl **-phoses** [-foss-eez] change of form or character. **metamorphic** adj (of rocks) changed in texture or structure by heat and pressure. **metamorphose** v transform.

metaphor n figure of speech in which a term is applied to something it does not literally denote in order to imply a resemblance, such as *he is a lion in battle*. **metaphorical** adj **metaphorically** adv

metaphysics n branch of philosophy concerned with being and knowing. **metaphysical** adj

mete v (usu. with *out*) deal out as punishment.

meteor n small fast-moving heavenly body, visible as a streak of incandescence if it enters the earth's atmosphere. **meteoric** [meet-ee-or-rik] adj of a meteor; brilliant but short-lived. **meteorite** n meteor that has fallen to earth.

meteorology n study of the earth's atmosphere, esp. for weather forecasting. **meteorological** adj **meteorologist** n

meter n instrument for measuring and recording something, such as the consumption of gas or electricity. ◆ v measure by meter.

methane n colourless inflammable gas.

methanol n colourless poisonous liquid used as a solvent and fuel (also **methyl alcohol**).

methinks v, past tense **methought** *Obs* it seems to me.

method n way or manner; technique; orderliness. **methodical** adj orderly. **methodically** adv **methodology** n particular method or procedure.

Methodist n member of any of the Protestant churches originated by Wesley and his followers. ◆ adj of Methodists or their Church. **Methodism** n

methyl n (compound containing) a saturated hydrocarbon group of atoms. **methylated spirits** alcohol with methanol added, used as a solvent and for heating.

meticulous adj very careful about details. **meticulously** adv

métier [met-ee-ay] n profession or trade; one's strong point.

metonymy [mit-on-im-ee] n figure of speech in which one thing is replaced by another associated with it, such as 'the Crown' for 'the king'.

metre n basic unit of length equal to about 1.094 yards; rhythm of poetry. **metric** adj of the decimal system of weights and measures based on the metre. **metrical** adj of measurement; of poetic metre. **metrication** n conversion to the metric system.

Metro n metropolitan city administration.

metronome n instrument which marks musical time by means of a ticking pendulum.

metropolis [mit-**trop**-oh-liss] *n* chief city of a country or region.
metropolitan *adj* of a metropolis.

mettle *n* courage or spirit.

mew *n* cry of a cat. ◆ *v* utter this cry.

mews *n Brit* yard or street orig. of stables, now often converted to houses.

mezzanine [**mez**-zan-een] *n* intermediate storey, esp. between the ground and first floor.

mezzo-soprano [**met**-so-] *n* voice or singer between a soprano and contralto.

mezzotint [**met**-so-tint] *n* method of engraving by scraping the roughened surface of a metal plate; print so made.

mg milligram(s).

Mg *Chem* magnesium.

MHz megahertz.

miaow [mee-**ow**] *n, v* same as MEW.

miasma [mee-**azz**-ma] *n* foreboding atmosphere.

mica [**my**-ka] *n* glasslike mineral used as an electrical insulator.

mice *n* plural of MOUSE.

Michaelmas [**mik**-kl-mass] *n* Sept. 29th, feast of St Michael the archangel.

mickey[1] *n* half bottle of alcoholic liquor.

mickey[2] *n* **take the mickey (out of)** *Informal* tease.

micro *n, pl* **-cros** short for MICROCOMPUTER or MICROPROCESSOR.

microbe *n* minute organism, esp. one causing disease. **microbial** *adj*

microchip *n* small wafer of silicon containing electronic circuits.

microcomputer *n* computer having a central processing unit contained in one or more silicon chips.

microcosm *n* miniature representation of something; man regarded as epitomizing the universe.

microfiche [**my**-crow-feesh] *n* microfilm in sheet form.

microfilm *n* miniaturized recording of books or documents on a roll of film.

microlight *n* very small light private aircraft with large wings.

micrometer [my-**krom**-it-er] *n* instrument for measuring very small distances or angles.

micron [**my**-kron] *n* one millionth of a metre.

microorganism *n* organism of microscopic size.

microphone *n* instrument for amplifying or transmitting sounds.

microprocessor *n* integrated circuit acting as the central processing unit in a small computer.

microscope *n* instrument with lens (es) which produces a magnified image of a very small body.
microscopic *adj* too small to be seen except with a microscope; very small; of a microscope. **microscopically** *adv*
microscopy *n* use of a microscope.

microsurgery *n* intricate surgery using a special microscope and miniature precision instruments.

microwave *n* electromagnetic wave with a wavelength of a few centimetres, used in radar and cooking; microwave oven. ◆ *v* cook in a microwave oven. **microwave oven** oven using microwaves to cook food quickly.

mid *adj* intermediate, middle. **midday** *n* noon. **midland** *n* middle part of a country. **midnight** *n* twelve o'clock at night. **midshipman** *n* naval officer of the lowest commissioned rank.
midsummer *n* middle of summer; summer solstice. **Midsummer Day** June 24th. **midtown** *n* the centre of a town. **midway** *adj, adv* halfway. ◆ *n* place for games, rides, etc. at a fair.
midwinter *n* middle or depth of winter; winter solstice.

midden *n* dunghill or rubbish heap.

middle *n* point or part equidistant from two extremes. ◆ *adj* equidistant from two extremes; medium, intermediate. **middle age** period of life between youth and old age.
middle-aged *adj* **Middle Ages** period from about 1000 AD to the 15th century. **middle class** social class of businessmen and professional people.
middle-class *adj* **Middle East** area around the eastern Mediterranean up to and including Iran. **middleman** *n* trader who buys from the producer and sells to the consumer. **middle-of-the-road** *adj* politically moderate; (of music) generally popular.
middleweight *n* boxer weighing up to

160lb (professional) or 75kg (amateur).

middling *adj* mediocre; moderate. ◆ *adv* moderately.

midge *n* small mosquito-like insect.

midget *n* very small person or thing.

midriff *n* middle part of the body.

midst *n* **in the midst of** surrounded by; at a point during.

midwife *n* trained person who assists at childbirth. **midwifery** *n*

mien [mean] *n Lit* person's bearing, demeanour, or appearance.

miffed *adj Informal* offended.

might[1] *v* past tense of MAY.

might[2] *n* power or strength. **with might and main** forcefully. **mighty** *adj* powerful; important. ◆ *adv Informal* very. **mightily** *adv*

mignonette [min-yon-net] *n* grey-green plant with sweet-smelling flowers.

migraine [mee-grain] *n* severe headache, often with nausea and other symptoms.

migrate *v* move from one place to settle in another; (of animals) journey between different habitats at specific seasons. **migration** *n* **migrant** *n, adj* (person or animal) that migrates. **migratory** *adj*

mike *n Informal* microphone.

milch [miltch] *adj* (of a cow) giving milk.

mild *adj* not strongly flavoured; gentle; calm or temperate. **mildly** *adv* **mildness** *n*

mildew *n* destructive fungus on plants or things exposed to damp. **mildewed** *adj*

mile *n* unit of length equal to 1760 yards or 1.609 km. **mileage** *n* distance travelled in miles; miles travelled by a motor vehicle per gallon of gasoline; *Informal* usefulness of something. **milestone** *n* stone marker showing the distance to a certain place; significant event.

milieu [meal-yer] *n, pl* **milieus, milieux** [meal-yerz] environment or surroundings.

militant *adj* aggressive or vigorous in support of a cause. **militancy** *n*

military *adj* of or for soldiers, armies, or war. ◆ *n* armed services. **militarism** *n* belief in the use of military force and methods. **militarist** *n* **militarized** *adj*

militia [mill-ish-a] *n* military force of trained citizens for use in emergency only.

militate *v* (usu. with *against* or *for*) have a strong influence or effect.

milk *n* white fluid produced by female mammals to feed their young; milk of cows, goats, etc. used by man as food; fluid in some plants. ◆ *v* draw milk from; exploit (a person or situation). **milky** *adj* **Milky Way** luminous band of stars stretching across the night sky. **milkmaid** *n* (esp. formerly) woman who milks cows. **milkman** *n* man who delivers milk to people's houses. **milkshake** *n* frothy flavoured cold milk drink. **milksop** *n* feeble man. **milk teeth** first set of teeth in young mammals.

mill[1] *n* factory; machine for grinding, processing, or rolling. ◆ *v* put through a mill; move in a confused manner; cut fine grooves across the edges of (coins). **miller** *n* person who works in a mill. **millstone** *n* flat circular stone for grinding corn. **mill wheel** water wheel that drives a mill.

mill[2] *n* one thousandth of a dollar.

millennium [mill-en-yum] *n, pl* **-niums, -nia** period of a thousand years; future period of peace and happiness.

millet *n* a cereal grass.

milli- *combining form* denoting a thousandth part, e.g. *millisecond*.

millibar *n* unit of atmospheric pressure.

milliner *n* maker or seller of women's hats. **millinery** *n*

million *n* one thousand thousands. **millionth** *adj, n* **millionaire** *n* person who owns at least a million pounds, dollars, etc.

millipede, millepede [mill-lip-peed] *n* small animal with a jointed body and many pairs of legs.

milt *n* sperm of fish.

mime *n* acting without the use of words; performer who does this. ◆ *v* act in mime.

mimic *v* **-icking, -icked** imitate (a person or manner), esp. for satirical effect. ◆ *n* person or animal clever at mimicking. **mimicry** *n*

mimosa *n* shrub with fluffy yellow

flowers and sensitive leaves.
min. minimum; minute(s).
minaret *n* tall slender tower of a mosque.
mince *Brit* ◆ *v* cut or grind into very small pieces; soften or moderate (one's words); walk or speak in an affected manner. ◆ *n* minced meat. **mincer** *n* machine for mincing meat. **mincing** *adj* affected in manner. **mincemeat** *n* sweet mixture of dried fruit and spices. **mince pie** pie containing mincemeat.
mind *n* thinking faculties; memory or attention; intention; sanity. ◆ *v* take offence at; take care of; pay attention to; be cautious or careful about (something). **minded** *adj* having an inclination as specified, e.g. *politically minded*. **minder** *n* *Brit slang* aide or bodyguard. **mindful** *adj* keeping aware; heedful. **mindless** *adj* stupid; requiring no thought; careless.
mine[1] *pron* belonging to me.
mine[2] *n* deep hole for digging out coal, ores, etc.; bomb placed under the ground or in water; profitable source. ◆ *v* dig for minerals; dig (minerals) from a mine; place explosive mines in or on. **miner** *n* person who works in a mine. **minefield** *n* area of land or water containing mines. **minesweeper** *n* ship for clearing away mines.
mineral *n* naturally occurring inorganic substance, such as metal or coal. ◆ *adj* of, containing, or like minerals. **mineralogy** [min-er-**al**-a-jee] *n* study of minerals. **mineralogist** *n* **mineral water** water containing dissolved mineral salts or gases.
minestrone [min-ness-**strone**-ee] *n* soup containing vegetables and pasta.
mingle *v* mix or blend; come into association (with).
mingy *adj* **-gier, -giest** *Informal* miserly.
mini *n, adj* (something) small or miniature; short (skirt).
miniature *n* small portrait, model, or copy. ◆ *adj* small-scale. **miniaturist** *n* **miniaturize** *v* make to a very small scale.
minibus *n* small bus.
minicab *n* *Brit* ordinary automobile used as a taxi.
minicomputer *n* computer smaller

than a mainframe but more powerful than a microcomputer.
minidisc *n* small recordable compact disc.
minim *n* *Brit* half note.
minimum *adj, n* least possible (amount or quantity). **minimal** *adj* minimum. **minimize** *v* reduce to a minimum; belittle.
minion *n* servile assistant.
miniseries *n* TV programme shown in several parts, often on consecutive days.
minister *n* head of a government department; diplomatic representative; clergyman. ◆ *v* (foll. by *to*) attend to the needs of. **ministerial** *adj* **ministration** *n* giving of help. **ministry** *n* profession or duties of a clergyman; ministers collectively; government department.
mink *n* stoatlike animal; its highly valued fur.
minnow *n* small freshwater fish.
minor *adj* lesser; under age; *Music* (of a scale) having a semitone above the second note. ◆ *n* person below the age of legal majority; *Music* minor scale. **minority** *n* lesser number; smaller party voting together; group in a minority in any state; state of being a minor.
minster *n* cathedral or large church.
minstrel *n* medieval singer or musician.
mint[1] *n* place where money is coined. ◆ *v* make (coins).
mint[2] *n* aromatic herb; peppermint; candy flavoured with this.
minuet [min-new-**wet**] *n* stately dance; music for this.
minus *prep, adj* reduced by the subtraction of; *Informal* without; less than zero. ◆ *n* sign (-) denoting subtraction or a number less than zero.
minuscule [min-niss-**skyool**] *adj* very small.
minute[1] [**min**-it] *n* 60th part of an hour or degree; moment. ◆ *pl* record of the proceedings of a meeting. ◆ *v* record in the minutes.
minute[2] [my-**newt**] *adj* very small; precise. **minutely** *adv* **minutiae** [my-**new**-shee-eye] *pl n* trifling or precise details.

minx n bold or flirtatious girl.

miracle n wonderful supernatural event; marvel. **miraculous** adj **miraculously** adv **miracle play** medieval play based on a sacred subject.

mirage [mir-**rahzh**] n optical illusion, esp. one caused by hot air.

mire n swampy ground; mud.

mirror n coated glass surface for reflecting images. ♦ v reflect in or as if in a mirror.

mirth n laughter, merriment, or gaiety. **mirthful** adj **mirthless** adj

mis- prefix wrong(ly), bad(ly).

misadventure n unlucky chance.

misanthrope [**miz**-zan-thrope], **misanthropist** [miz-**zan**-thrope-ist] n person who dislikes people in general. **misanthropic** [miz-zan-**throp**-ik] adj **misanthropy** [miz-**zan**-throp-ee] n

misapprehend v misunderstand. **misapprehension** n

misappropriate v take and use (money) dishonestly. **misappropriation** n

miscarriage n spontaneous premature expulsion of a fetus from the womb; failure, e.g. a miscarriage of justice. **miscarry** v have a miscarriage; fail.

miscast v **-casting, -cast** cast (a role or actor) in (a play or film) inappropriately.

miscegenation [miss-ij-in-**nay**-shun] n interbreeding of races.

miscellaneous [miss-sell-**lane**-ee-uss] adj mixed or assorted. **miscellany** [miss-**sell**-a-nee] n mixed assortment.

mischance n unlucky event.

mischief n annoying but not malicious behaviour; inclination to tease; harm. **mischievous** [**miss**-chiv-uss] adj full of mischief; intended to cause harm. **mischievously** adv

miscible [**miss**-sib-bl] adj able to be mixed.

misconception n wrong idea or belief.

misconduct n immoral behaviour.

miscreant [**miss**-kree-ant] n wrongdoer.

misdeed n wrongful act.

misdemeanour n minor wrongdoing.

miser n person who hoards money and hates spending it. **miserly** adj

miserable adj very unhappy, wretched; causing misery; squalid; mean. **misery** n great unhappiness; Informal complaining person.

misfire v (of a firearm or engine) fail to fire correctly; (of a plan) fail to turn out as intended.

misfit n person not suited to his or her environment.

misfortune n (piece of) bad luck.

misgiving n feeling of doubt.

misguided adj mistaken or unwise.

mishandle v handle or treat badly or inefficiently.

mishap n minor accident.

misinform v give incorrect information to. **misinformation** n

misjudge v judge wrongly or unfairly. **misjudgment, misjudgement** n

mislay v lose (something) temporarily.

mislead v give false or confusing information to. **misleading** adj

mismanage v organize or run (something) badly. **mismanagement** n

misnomer [miss-**no**-mer] n wrongly applied name; use of this.

misogyny [miss-**oj**-in-ee] n hatred of women. **misogynist** n

misplace v put in the wrong place; mislay; give (trust or affection) inappropriately.

misprint n printing error.

misrepresent v represent wrongly or inaccurately.

miss v fail to hit, reach, find, catch, or notice; not be in time for; notice or regret the absence of; avoid; fail to take advantage of. ♦ n fact or instance of missing. **missing** adj lost or absent.

Miss n title of a girl or unmarried woman.

missal n book containing the prayers and rites of the Mass.

misshapen adj badly shaped, deformed.

missile n object or weapon thrown, shot, or launched at a target.

mission n specific task or duty; group of people sent on a mission; building in which missionaries work. **missionary** n, pl **-aries** person sent abroad to spread religion.

missive n letter.

misspent adj wasted or misused.

mist n thin fog; fine spray of liquid.

misty *adj* full of mist; dim or obscure. **mistiness** *n*

mistake *n* error or blunder. ◆ *v* **-taking, -took, -taken** misunderstand; confuse (a person or thing) with another.

Mister *n* polite form of address to a man.

mistletoe *n* evergreen plant with white berries growing as a parasite on trees.

mistral *n* strong dry northerly wind of S France.

mistress *n* woman who is the illicit lover of a married man; woman in control of people or things; female teacher.

mistrial *n Law* trial which is invalid because of some error.

mistrust *v* not trust. ◆ *n* lack of trust. **mistrustful** *adj*

misunderstand *v* fail to understand properly. **misunderstanding** *n*

misuse *n* incorrect, or careless use. ◆ *v* use wrongly; treat badly.

mite *n* very small spider-like animal; very small thing or amount.

mitigate *v* make less severe. **mitigation** *n*

mitre [my-ter] *n* bishop's pointed headdress; joint between two pieces of wood bevelled to meet at right angles. ◆ *v* join with a mitre joint.

mitt *n* short for MITTEN; baseball catcher's glove.

mitten *n* glove with one section for the thumb and one for the four fingers together.

mix *v* combine or blend into one mass; form (something) by mixing; be sociable. ◆ *n* mixture. **mixed** *adj* **mix up** *v* confuse; make into a mixture. **mixer** *n* **mixture** *n* something mixed; combination. **mix-up** *n* confused situation. **mixed-up** *adj Informal* confused.

mizzenmast *n* mast nearest the stern of a full-rigged ship.

mks units *pl n* metric system of units based on the metre, kilogram, and second.

ml millilitre(s).

MLA Member of the Legislative Assembly.

mm millimetre(s).

Mn *Chem* manganese.

MNA Member of the National Assembly (of Quebec).

mnemonic [nim-on-ik] *n, adj* (rhyme etc.) intended to help the memory.

mo *n Brit informal* short for MOMENT.

MO Medical Officer.

moan *n* low cry of pain; *Informal* grumble. ◆ *v* make or utter with a moan; *Informal* grumble.

moat *n* deep wide ditch, esp. round a castle.

mob *n* disorderly crowd; *Slang* gang. ◆ *v* **mobbing, mobbed** surround in a mob to acclaim or attack.

mobile *adj* able to move. ◆ *n* hanging structure designed to move in air currents. **mobile phone** cordless phone powered by batteries. **mobility** *n*

mobilize *v* (of the armed services) prepare for active service; organize for a purpose. **mobilization** *n*

moccasin *n* soft leather shoe.

mocha [mock-a] *n* kind of strong dark coffee; flavouring made from coffee and chocolate.

mock *v* make fun of; mimic. ◆ *n* imitation. ◆ *pl Informal* practice exams taken before public exams. ◆ *adj* sham or imitation. **put the mockers on** *Informal* ruin the chances of success of. **mockery** *n* derision; inadequate attempt. **mocking bird** N American bird which imitates other birds' songs. **mock orange** shrub with white fragrant flowers. **mock-up** *n* full-scale model for test or study.

mod. moderate; modern.

mode *n* method or manner; particular fashion. **modish** [mow-dish] *adj* in fashion.

model *n* (miniature) representation; pattern; person or thing worthy of imitation; person who poses for an artist or photographer; person who wears clothes to display them to prospective buyers. ◆ *v* **-elling, -elled** make a model of; mould; display (clothing) as a model.

modem [mow-dem] *n* device for connecting two computers by a telephone line.

moderate *adj* not extreme; temperate; average. ◆ *n* person of moderate views. ◆ *v* make or become less violent or extreme; preside over a

meeting etc. **moderately** adv
moderation n **moderator** n president of a Presbyterian body; arbitrator.

modern adj of present or recent times; in current fashion. **modernity** n **modernism** n (support of) modern tendencies, thoughts, or styles. **modernist** n **modernize** v bring up to date. **modernization** n

modest adj not vain or boastful; shy; not excessive; not showy. **modestly** adv **modesty** n

modicum n small quantity.

modify v **-fying, -fied** change slightly; tone down; (of a word) qualify (another word). **modifier** n word that qualifies another. **modification** n

modulate v vary in tone; adjust; change the key of (music). **modulation** n modulating; Electronics superimposing of a wave or signal on to another wave or signal. **modulator** n

module n self-contained unit, section, or component with a specific function.

modus operandi [mow-duss op-er-an-die] n Latin method of operating.

mogul [mow-gl] n important or powerful person.

mohair n fine hair of the Angora goat; yarn or fabric made from this.

Mohammedan adj, n Not in Muslim use same as MUSLIM.

mohican n punk hairstyle with shaved sides and a stiff central strip of hair, often brightly coloured.

moiety [moy-it-ee] n, pl **-ties** half.

moist adj slightly wet. **moisten** v make or become moist. **moisture** n liquid diffused as vapour or condensed in drops. **moisturize** v add moisture to (the skin etc.).

molar n large back tooth used for grinding.

molasses n dark syrup, a by-product of sugar refining.

mold n same as MOULD.

mole[1] n small dark raised spot on the skin.

mole[2] n small burrowing mammal; Informal spy who has infiltrated and become a trusted member of an organization.

mole[3] n breakwater; harbour protected by this.

mole[4] n unit of amount of substance.

molecule [mol-lik-kyool] n simplest freely existing chemical unit, composed of two or more atoms; very small particle. **molecular** [mol-lek-yew-lar] adj

molest v interfere with sexually; annoy or injure. **molester** n **molestation** n

moll n Slang gangster's female accomplice; prostitute.

mollify v **-fying, -fied** pacify.

mollusc n soft-bodied, usu. hard-shelled animal such as a snail.

mollycoddle v pamper.

Molotov cocktail n gasoline bomb.

molten adj liquefied or melted.

molybdenum [mol-lib-din-um] n silver-white metallic element.

mom n an informal word for MOTHER

moment n short space of time; (present) point in time. **momentary** adj lasting only a moment. **momentarily** adv

momentous [mow-men-tuss] adj of great significance.

momentum [mow-men-tum] n, pl **-ta, -tums** product of a body's mass and velocity; impetus of a moving body.

monarch n sovereign ruler of a state. **monarchical** adj **monarchist** n supporter of monarchy. **monarchy** n government by or a state ruled by a sovereign.

monastery n, pl **-teries** residence of a religious order. **monastic** adj of monks, nuns, or monasteries; ascetic. **monasticism** n

Monday n second day of the week.

money n medium of exchange, coins or banknotes. **moneyed, monied** adj rich **monetary** adj of money or currency. **monetarism** n theory that inflation is caused by an increase in the money supply. **monetarist** n, adj

mongolism n Offens Down's syndrome. **mongol** n, adj Offens (person) affected by this.

mongoose n, pl **-gooses** stoatlike mammal of Asia and Africa that kills snakes.

mongrel n animal, esp. a dog, of mixed breed; hybrid. ◆ adj of mixed breed.

monitor n person or device that checks, controls, warns, or keeps a record of something; pupil assisting a teacher with duties; television set used in a studio to check what is being transmitted; type of large lizard. ◆ v watch and check on.

monk n member of an all-male religious community bound by vows. **monkish** adj **monkshood** n poisonous plant with hooded flowers.

monkey n long-tailed primate; mischievous child. ◆ v (usu. foll. by about or around) meddle. **monkey puzzle** coniferous tree with sharp stiff leaves. **monkey wrench** wrench with adjustable jaws.

mono- combining form single, e.g. monolingual.

monochrome adj in only one colour; black-and-white.

monocle [mon-a-kl] n eyeglass for one eye only.

monocular adj having or for one eye only.

monogamy n custom of being married to one person at a time.

monogram n design of combined letters, esp. a person's initials.

monograph n book or paper on a single subject.

monolith n large upright block of stone. **monolithic** adj

monologue n dramatic piece for one performer; long speech by one person.

monomania n obsession with one thing. **monomaniac** n, adj

monoplane n airplane with one pair of wings.

monopoly n, pl -lies exclusive possession of or right to do something. **monopolist** n **monopolize** v have or take exclusive possession of.

monorail n single-rail railway.

monotheism n belief in only one God. **monotheist** n **monotheistic** adj

monotone n unvaried pitch in speech or sound. **monotonous** adj tedious due to lack of variety. **monotonously** adv **monotony** n

Monseigneur [mon-sen-**nyur**] n, pl **Messeigneurs** [may-sen-**nyur**] title of French prelates.

monsieur [muss-**syur**] n, pl **messieurs** [may-**syur**] French title of address equivalent to sir or Mr.

Monsignor n RC Church title attached to certain offices.

monsoon n seasonal wind of SE Asia;

rainy season accompanying this.

monster n imaginary, usu. frightening beast; very wicked person; huge person, animal, or thing. ◆ adj huge. **monstrosity** n large ugly thing. **monstrous** adj unnatural or ugly; shocking or unjust; huge. **monstrously** adv

monstrance n RC Church container in which the consecrated Host is exposed for adoration.

montage [mon-**tahzh**] n (making of) a picture composed from pieces of others; method of film editing incorporating several shots to form a single image.

month n one of the twelve divisions of the calendar year; period of four weeks. **monthly** adj happening or payable once a month. ◆ adv once a month. ◆ n monthly periodical.

monument n something that commemorates, esp. a building or statue. **monumental** adj large, impressive, or lasting; of or being a monument; Informal extreme. **monumentally** adv

moo n long deep cry of a cow. ◆ v make this noise.

mooch v Slang loiter about aimlessly.

mood[1] n temporary (gloomy) state of mind. **moody** adj gloomy or sullen; changeable in mood. **moodily** adv

mood[2] n Grammar form of a verb indicating whether it expresses a fact, wish, supposition, or command.

moon n natural satellite of the earth; natural satellite of any planet. ◆ v (foll. by about or around) be idle in a listless or dreamy way. **moonlight** n light from the moon. ◆ v Informal work at a secondary job, esp. illegally. **moonshine** n illicitly distilled whisky; nonsense. **moonstone** n translucent semiprecious stone. **moonstruck** adj deranged.

moor[1] n tract of open uncultivated ground covered with grass and heather. **moorhen** n small black water bird.

moor[2] v secure (a ship) with ropes etc. **mooring** n place for mooring a ship. ◆ pl ropes etc. used in mooring a ship.

Moor n member of a Muslim people of NW Africa who ruled Spain between the 8th and 15th centuries. **Moorish** adj

moose n large N American deer.
moose pasture Slang worthless mining claim.

moot adj debatable, e.g. a moot point. ◆ v bring up for discussion.

mop n long stick with twists of cotton or a sponge on the end, used for cleaning; thick mass of hair. ◆ v **mopping, mopped** clean or soak up with or as if with a mop.

mope v be gloomy and apathetic.

moped [mow-ped] n light motorcycle not over 50cc.

moraine n accumulated mass of debris deposited by a glacier.

moral adj concerned with right and wrong conduct; based on a sense of right and wrong; (of support or a victory) psychological rather than practical. ◆ n lesson to be obtained from a story or event. ◆ pl behaviour with respect to right and wrong. **morally** adv **moralist** n person who lives by or expresses moral principles. **morality** n good moral conduct; moral goodness or badness. **morality play** medieval play with a moral lesson. **moralize** v make moral pronouncements.

morale [mor-rahl] n degree of confidence or hope of a person or group.

morass n marsh; mess.

moratorium n, pl **-ria, -riums** legally authorized ban or delay.

moray n large voracious eel.

morbid adj unduly interested in death or unpleasant events; gruesome.

mordant adj sarcastic or scathing. ◆ n substance used to fix dyes.

more adj greater in amount or degree; comparative of MUCH or MANY; additional or further. ◆ adv to a greater extent; in addition. ◆ pron greater or additional amount or number. **moreover** adv besides.

mores [more-rayz] pl n customs and conventions embodying the fundamental values of a community.

morganatic marriage n marriage of a person of high rank to a lower-ranking person whose status remains unchanged.

morgue n mortuary.

moribund adj without vitality.

Mormon n member of a religious sect founded in the USA. **Mormonism** n

morn n Poetic morning.

morning n part of the day before noon. **morning-glory** n plant with trumpet-shaped flowers which close in the late afternoon.

morocco n goatskin leather.

moron n mentally deficient person; Informal fool. **moronic** adj

morose [mor-rohss] adj sullen.

morphine, morphia n drug extracted from opium, used as an anesthetic and sedative.

morphology n science of forms and structures of organisms or words. **morphological** adj

morris dance n traditional English folk dance performed by men.

morrow n Poetic next day.

Morse n system of signalling in which letters of the alphabet are represented by combinations of short and long signals.

morsel n small piece, esp. of food.

mortal adj subject to death; causing death. ◆ n mortal creature. **mortally** adv **mortality** n state of being mortal; great loss of life; death rate. **mortal sin** RC Church sin meriting damnation.

mortar n mixture of lime, sand, and water for holding bricks and stones together; small cannon with a short range; bowl in which substances are pounded. **mortarboard** n square academic cap.

mortgage n conditional pledging of property, esp. a house, as security for the repayment of a loan; the loan itself. ◆ v pledge (property) as security thus. **mortgagee** n creditor in a mortgage. **mortgagor, mortgager** n debtor in a mortgage.

mortify v **-fying, -fied** humiliate; subdue by self-denial; (of flesh) become gangrenous. **mortification** n

mortise, mortice [more-tiss] n hole in a piece of wood or stone shaped to receive a matching projection on another piece. **mortise lock** lock set into a door.

mortuary n, pl **-aries** building where corpses are kept before burial or cremation.

mosaic [mow-zay-ik] n design or decoration using small bits of coloured stone or glass.

Mosaic adj of Moses.

Moselle n light white wine.

Moslem n, adj same as MUSLIM.

mosque n Muslim temple.

mosquito n, pl -toes, -tos blood-sucking flying insect.

moss n small flowerless plant growing in masses on moist surfaces. **mossy** adj

most adj greatest in number or degree; superlative of MUCH or MANY ◆ n greatest number or degree. ◆ adv in the greatest degree. **mostly** adv for the most part, generally.

motel n roadside hotel for motorists.

motet [mow-tet] n short sacred choral song.

moth n nocturnal insect like a butterfly. **mothball** n small ball of camphor or naphthalene used to repel moths from stored clothes. ◆ v store (something operational) for future use; postpone (a project etc.). **moth-eaten** adj eaten or damaged by moth larvae; scruffy.

mother n female parent; head of a female religious community. ◆ adj native or inborn, e.g. mother wit. ◆ v look after as a mother. **motherhood** n **motherly** adj **motherless** adj **mother-in-law** n mother of one's husband or wife. **mother of pearl** iridescent lining of certain shells. **mother tongue** one's native language.

motif [mow-teef] n (recurring) theme or design.

motion n process, action, or way of moving; proposal in a meeting; Brit evacuation of the bowels. ◆ v direct (someone) by gesture. **motionless** adj not moving. **motion picture** film.

motive n reason for a course of action. ◆ adj causing motion. **motivate** v give incentive to. **motivation** n

motley adj miscellaneous; multicoloured. ◆ n Hist jester's costume.

motocross n motorcycle race over a rough course.

motor n engine, esp. of a vehicle; machine that converts electrical energy into mechanical energy; automobile. ◆ v travel by automobile. **motorist** n driver of an automobile. **motorize** v equip with a motor or motor transport. **motorbike** n **motorboat** n **motorcar** n **motorcycle**

n **motorcyclist** n **motor scooter** a light motorcycle with small wheels and an enclosed engine. **motorway** n Brit highway.

mottled adj marked with blotches.

motto n, pl -toes, -tos saying expressing an ideal or rule of conduct; verse or maxim in a paper cracker.

mould¹, **mold** n hollow container in which metal etc. is cast; shape, form, or pattern; nature or character. ◆ v shape; influence or direct. **moulding** n moulded ornamental edging.

mould², **mold** n fungal growth caused by dampness. **mouldy** adj stale or musty; dull or boring.

mould³, **mold** n loose soil. **moulder** v decay into dust.

moult v shed feathers, hair, or skin to make way for new growth. ◆ n process of moulting.

mound n heap, esp. of earth or stones; small hill.

mount v climb or ascend; get up on (a horse etc.); organize, e.g. mount a campaign; increase; fix on a support or backing. ◆ n backing or support on which something is fixed; horse for riding; hill.

mountain n hill of great size; large heap. **mountainous** adj full of mountains; huge. **mountaineer** n person who climbs mountains. **mountaineering** n **mountain bike** bicycle with straight handlebars and heavy-duty tires.

mountebank n charlatan or fake.

Mountie n Informal member of the Royal Canadian Mounted Police.

mourn v feel or express sorrow for (a dead person or lost thing). **mourner** n **mournful** adj sad or dismal. **mournfully** adv **mourning** n grieving; conventional symbols of grief for death, such as the wearing of black.

mouse n, pl mice small long-tailed rodent; timid person; Computers hand-held device for moving the cursor without keying. **mouser** n cat used to catch mice. **mousy** adj like a mouse, esp. in hair colour; meek and shy.

mousse n dish of flavoured cream whipped and set.

moustache n hair on the upper lip.

mouth n opening in the head for eating and issuing sounds; opening;

entrance; point where a river enters the sea. ◆ v speak or utter insincerely, esp. in public; form (words) with the lips without speaking. **mouth organ** small musical instrument played by sucking and blowing. **mouthpiece** n part of a telephone into which a person speaks; part of a wind instrument into which the player blows; spokesman.

move v change in place or position; change (one's house etc.); take action; stir the emotions of; incite; suggest (a proposal) formally. ◆ n moving towards some goal. **movable, moveable** adj, n **movement** n action or process of moving; moving parts of a machine; group with a common aim; division of a piece of music.

movie n Informal film.

mow v mowing, mowed, mowed or mown. cut (grass or crops). **mower** n **mow down** v kill in large numbers.

mozzarella [mot-sa-rel-la] n moist white cheese originally made in Italy from buffalo milk.

MP Member of Parliament; Military Police.

MP3 Computing Motion Picture Expert Group-1, Audio Layer-3: a digital compression format used to compress audio files to a fraction of their original size without loss of sound quality.

MPEG (em-peg) Computing Motion Picture Expert Group: standard compressed file format used for audio and video files.

mpg miles per gallon.

mph miles per hour.

MPP Member of the Provincial Parliament.

Mr Mister.

Mrs n title of a married woman.

Ms [mizz] n title used instead of Miss or Mrs.

MS manuscript; multiple sclerosis.

MSc Master of Science.

MSS manuscripts.

Mt Mount.

much adj more, most existing in quantity. ◆ n large amount or degree. ◆ adv more, most to a great degree; nearly.

mucilage [mew-sill-ij] n gum or glue.

muck n dirt, filth; manure. **mucky** adj

muckamuck n high muckamuck Informal important person.

mucus [mew-kuss] n slimy secretion of the mucous membranes. **mucous membrane** membrane lining body cavities or passages.

mud n wet soft earth. **muddy** adj **mudguard** n cover over a wheel to prevent mud or water being thrown up by it. **mudpack** n cosmetic paste to improve the complexion.

muddle n state of confusion. ◆ v (often with up) confuse; mix up.

muesli [mewz-lee] n mixture of grain, nuts, and dried fruit eaten with milk.

muezzin [moo-ezz-in] n official who summons Muslims to prayer.

muff[1] n tube-shaped covering to keep the hands warm.

muff[2] v bungle (an action).

muffin n small cup-shaped sweet bread roll.; see ENGLISH MUFFIN.

muffle v wrap up for warmth or to deaden sound. **muffler** n scarf.

mufti n civilian clothes worn by a person who usually wears a uniform.

mug[1] n large drinking cup.

mug[2] n Slang face; Brit slang person who is easily swindled. ◆ v **mugging, mugged** Informal rob violently. **mugger** n

mug[3] v mugging, mugged (esp. with up) Brit informal study hard.

muggy adj -gier, -giest (of weather) damp and stifling.

mukluk n Inuit's soft (sealskin) boot.

mulatto [mew-lat-toe] n, pl -tos, -toes child of one Black and one White parent.

mulberry n tree whose leaves are used to feed silkworms; purple fruit of this tree.

mulch n mixture of wet straw, leaves, etc., used to protect the roots of plants. ◆ v cover (land) with mulch.

mulct v fine (a person).

mule[1] n offspring of a horse and a donkey. **mulish** adj obstinate. **muleteer** n mule driver.

mule[2] n backless shoe or slipper.

mull v heat (wine) with sugar and spices; think (over) or ponder.

mullah n Muslim theologian.

mullet n edible sea fish.

mulligatawny n soup made with curry powder.

mullion n upright dividing bar in a window. **mullioned** adj

multi- combining form many, e.g. multicultural.

multifarious [mull-tiff-**fare**-ee-uss] adj having many various parts.

multiple adj having many parts. ◆ n quantity which contains another an exact number of times.

multiplex adj having many elements, complex.

multiplicity n, pl -ties large number or great variety.

multiply v -plying, -plied (cause to) increase in number, quantity, or degree; add (a number or quantity) to itself a given number of times; increase in number by reproduction. **multiplication** n **multiplicand** n Math number to be multiplied.

multitude n great number; great crowd. **multitudinous** adj very numerous.

mum[1] n Informal mother.

mum[2] adj silent, e.g. keep mum.

mumble v speak indistinctly, mutter.

mumbo jumbo n meaningless religious ritual; deliberately complicated language.

mummer n actor in a folk play or mime.

mummy[1] n, pl -mies body embalmed and wrapped for burial in ancient Egypt. **mummify** v -fying, -fied preserve (a body) as a mummy.

mummy[2] n, pl -mies child's word for MOTHER.

mumps n infectious disease with swelling in the glands of the neck.

munch v chew noisily and steadily.

mundane adj everyday; earthly.

municipal adj relating to a city or town. **municipality** n city or town with local self-government; governing body of this.

munificent [mew-**niff**-fiss-sent] adj very generous. **munificence** n

muniments [mew-**nim**-ments] pl n title deeds or similar documents.

munitions [mew-**nish**-unz] pl n military stores.

mural [**myoor**-al] n painting on a wall. ◆ adj of or on a wall.

murder n unlawful intentional killing of a human being. ◆ v kill thus. **murderer, murderess** n

murderous adj

murk n thick darkness. **murky** adj dark or gloomy.

murmur v -muring, -mured speak in a quiet indistinct way; complain. ◆ n continuous low indistinct sound.

murrain [**murr**-rin] n cattle plague.

muscat n sweet white grape. **muscatel** [musk-a-**tell**] n wine from muscat grapes; muscat grape or raisin.

muscle n tissue in the body which produces movement by contracting; strength or power. **muscular** adj with well-developed muscles; of muscles. **muscular dystrophy** disease with wasting of the muscles. **muscle in** v Informal force one's way in.

muse v ponder.

Muse n Greek myth one of nine goddesses, each of whom inspired an art or science; (m-) force that inspires a creative artist.

museum n building where natural, artistic, historical, or scientific objects are exhibited and preserved.

mush[1] n soft pulpy mass; Informal cloying sentimentality. **mushy** adj

mush[2] interj order to dogs in sled team to advance. ◆ v travel by or drive dogsled. ◆ n journey with dogsled.

mushroom n edible fungus with a stem and cap. ◆ v grow rapidly.

music n art form using a melodious and harmonious combination of notes; written or printed form of this. **musical** adj of or like music; talented in or fond of music; pleasant-sounding. ◆ n play or film with songs and dancing. **musically** adv **musician** n **musicology** n scientific study of music. **musicologist** n **music hall** variety theatre.

musk n scent obtained from a gland of the musk deer or produced synthetically. **musky** adj **muskrat** n N American beaver-like rodent; its fur.

muskeg n bog or swamp.

muskellunge n N American freshwater game fish.

musket n Hist long-barrelled gun. **musketeer** n **musketry** n (use of) muskets.

Muslim n follower of the religion of Islam. ◆ adj of or relating to Islam.

muslin n fine cotton fabric.

muss v inf to make untidy.

mussel n kind of bivalve mollusc.

must¹ v used as an auxiliary to express obligation, certainty, or resolution. ◆ n something one must do.

must² n newly pressed grape juice.

mustang n wild horse of SW America.

mustard n paste made from the powdered seeds of a plant, used as a condiment; the plant. **mustard gas** poisonous gas causing blistering.

muster v assemble. ◆ n assembly.

musty adj **-tier, -tiest** smelling mouldy and stale. **mustiness** n

mutable [mew-tab-bl] adj liable to change. **mutability** n

mutation [mew-**tay**-shun] n (genetic) change. **mutate** [mew-**tate**] v (cause to) undergo mutation. **mutant** [mew-tant] n mutated animal, plant, etc.

mute adj unable to speak; silent. ◆ n person unable to speak; Music device to soften the tone of an instrument. **muted** adj (of a reaction) subdued; (of sound or colour) softened. **mutely** adv

mutilate [mew-till-ate] v deprive of a limb or other part; damage (a book or text). **mutilation** n

mutiny [mew-tin-ee] n, pl **-nies** rebellion against authority, esp. by soldiers or sailors. ◆ v **-nying, -nied** commit mutiny. **mutineer** n **mutinous** adj

mutt n Slang stupid person; mongrel dog.

mutter v speak indistinctly; grumble. ◆ n muttered sound or grumble.

mutton n flesh of sheep, used as food.

mutual [mew-chew-al] adj felt or expressed by each of two people about the other; Informal common to both or all. **mutually** adv

Muzak n ® recorded light music played in shops etc.

muzzle n animal's mouth and nose; cover for these to prevent biting; open end of a gun. ◆ v put a muzzle on; force to keep silent.

muzzy adj **-zier, -ziest** confused or muddled; blurred. **muzziness** n

mW milliwatt(s).

MW megawatt(s).

my adj belonging to me.

mycology n study of fungi.

myna, mynah n Indian bird which can mimic human speech.

myocardium n, pl **-dia** the muscular tissue of the heart. **myocardial** adj

myopia [my-oh-pee-a] n short-sightedness. **myopic** [my-op-ic] adj

myriad [mir-ree-ad] adj innumerable. ◆ n large indefinite number.

myriapod n invertebrate with a long segmented body and many legs, such as a centipede.

myrrh [mur] n aromatic gum, formerly used in incense.

myrtle [mur-tl] n flowering evergreen shrub.

myself pron emphatic or reflexive form of I or ME.

mystery n, pl **-teries** strange or inexplicable event or phenomenon; obscure or secret thing; story or film that arouses suspense. **mysterious** adj **mysteriously** adv

mystic n person who seeks spiritual knowledge. ◆ adj having a spiritual or religious significance beyond human understanding. **mystical** adj mystic. **mysticism** n

mystify v **-fying, -fied** bewilder or puzzle. **mystification** n

mystique [miss-steek] n aura of mystery or power.

myth n tale with supernatural characters, usu. of how the world and mankind began; untrue idea or explanation; imaginary person or object. **mythical** adj **mythology** n myths collectively; study of myths. **mythological** adj

myxomatosis [mix-a-mat-oh-siss] n contagious fatal viral disease of rabbits.

N n

N Chess knight; Chem nitrogen; Physics newton(s); north(ern).

n. neuter; noun; number.

Na Chem sodium.

naan n same as NAN BREAD.

nab v **nabbing, nabbed** Informal arrest (someone); catch (someone) in wrongdoing.

nadir n point in the sky opposite the zenith; lowest point.

naevus [nee-vuss] n, pl **-vi** birthmark or mole.

naff *adj Slang* inferior or useless.

nag¹ *v* **nagging, nagged** scold or find fault (with) constantly; be a constant source of discomfort, pain, or worry (to). ◆ *n* person who nags. **nagging** *adj, n*

nag² *n Informal* (old) horse.

naiad [nye-ad] *n Greek myth* water nymph.

nail *n* hard covering of the upper tips of the fingers and toes; pointed piece of metal with a head, hit with a hammer to join two objects together. ◆ *v* attach (something) with nails; *Informal* catch or arrest. **hit the nail on the head** say something exactly correct. **nailfile** *n* small metal file used to smooth or shape the finger or toe nails. **nail polish, varnish** cosmetic lacquer applied to the finger or toe nails.

naive [nye-eev] *adj* innocent and credulous; lacking developed powers of reasoning and criticism. **naively** *adv* **naivety, naiveté** [nye-eev-tee] *n*

naked *adj* without clothes or covering. **the naked eye** the eye unassisted by any optical instrument. **nakedness** *n*

namby-pamby *adj* insipid.

name *n* word by which a person or thing is known; reputation, esp. a good one; abusive word or description. ◆ *v* give a name to; refer to by name; specify. **nameless** *adj* without a name; unspecified; too horrible to be mentioned. **namely** *adv* that is to say. **namesake** *n* person with the same name as another.

nan bread *n* slightly leavened Indian bread in a large flat leaf shape.

nanny *n, pl* **-nies** woman whose job is looking after young children. **nanny goat** female goat.

nap¹ *n* short sleep. ◆ *v* **napping, napped** have a short sleep.

nap² *n* raised fibres of velvet or similar cloth.

nap³ *n* card game similar to whist.

napalm *n* highly inflammable gasoline, used in bombs.

nape *n* back of the neck.

naphtha *n* liquid mixture distilled from coal tar or petroleum, used as a solvent and in petrol. **naphthalene** *n* white crystalline product distilled from coal tar or petroleum, used in disinfectants, mothballs, and explosives.

napkin *n* piece of cloth or paper for wiping the mouth or protecting the clothes while eating.

nappy *n, pl* **-pies** *Brit* diaper.

narcissism *n* abnormal love and admiration for oneself. **narcissistic** *adj*

narcissus *n, pl* **-cissi** yellow, orange, or white flower related to the daffodil.

narcotic *n, adj* (of) a drug, such as morphine or opium, which produces numbness and drowsiness, used medicinally but addictive. **narcosis** *n* effect of a narcotic.

nark *Brit slang* ◆ *v* annoy. ◆ *n* someone who complains in an irritating manner; informer. **narky** *adj Slang* irritable or complaining.

narrate *v* tell (a story); speak the words accompanying and telling what is happening in a film or TV programme. **narration** *n* **narrator** *n* **narrative** *n* account, story.

narrow *adj* of little breadth in comparison to length; limited in range, extent, or outlook; with little margin, e.g. *a narrow escape*. ◆ *v* make or become narrow; (often foll. by *down*) limit or restrict. **narrows** *pl n* narrow part of a strait, river, or current. **narrowly** *adv* **narrowness** *n* **narrow-minded** *adj* intolerant.

narwhal *n* arctic porpoise with a long spiral tusk.

NASA *US* National Aeronautics and Space Administration.

nasal *adj* of the nose; pronounced with air passing through the nose. **nasally** *adv*

nascent *adj* starting to grow or develop.

nasturtium *n* plant with yellow, red, or orange trumpet-shaped flowers.

nasty *adj* **-tier, -tiest** unpleasant; (of an injury) dangerous or painful; spiteful or unkind. **nastily** *adv* **nastiness** *n*

natal [nay-tal] *adj* of or relating to birth.

nation *n* people of one or more cultures or races organized as a single state. **national** *adj* of or characteristic of a nation. ◆ *n* citizen of a nation. **nationally** *adv* **nationalism** *n* policy of national independence; patriotism.

nationalist *n, adj* **nationality** *n* fact of being a citizen of a particular nation; nation. **nationalize** *v* put (an industry or a company) under state control. **nationalization** *n* **national insurance** state insurance scheme providing payments to the unemployed, sick, and retired. **national park** area of countryside protected by a government for its natural or environmental importance.

native *adj* relating to a place where a person was born; born in a specified place; (foll. by *to*) originating (in); inborn. ◆ *n* person born in a specified place; member of the original race of a country; indigenous animal or plant.

Nativity *n Christianity* birth of Jesus Christ.

NATO North Atlantic Treaty Organization.

natter *Informal* ◆ *v* talk idly or chatter. ◆ *n* long idle chat.

natty *adj* **-tier, -tiest** *Informal* smart and spruce.

natural *adj* normal; genuine, not affected; of, according to, existing in, or produced by nature; not created by human beings; not synthetic; (of a parent) not adoptive; (of a child) illegitimate; *Music* not sharp or flat. ◆ *n* person with an inborn talent or skill. **naturally** *adv* of course; in a natural or normal way; instinctively. **naturalist** *n* student of natural history. **naturalism** *n* movement in art and literature advocating detailed realism. **naturalistic** *adj* **naturalize** *v* give citizenship to (a person born in another country). **naturalization** *n* **natural gas** gas found below the ground, used mainly as a fuel. **natural history** study of animals and plants. **natural selection** process by which only creatures and plants well adapted to their environment survive.

nature *n* whole system of the existence, forces, and events of the physical world that are not controlled by human beings; fundamental or essential qualities of a person or thing; kind or sort.

naturism *n* nudism. **naturist** *n*

naught *n Obs* nothing; figure 0.

naughty *adj* **-tier, -tiest** disobedient or mischievous; mildly indecent. **naughtily** *adv* **naughtiness** *n*

nausea [naw-zee-a] *n* feeling of being about to vomit. **nauseate** *v* make (someone) feel sick; disgust. **nauseous** *adj* as if about to vomit; sickening.

nautical *adj* of the sea or ships. **nautical mile** 1852 metres.

nautilus *n, pl* **-luses, -li** shellfish with many tentacles.

naval *adj* see NAVY.

nave *n* main part of a church.

navel *n* hollow in the middle of the abdomen where the umbilical cord was attached.

navigate *v* direct or plot the path or position of a ship, aircraft, or automobile; travel over or through. **navigation** *n* **navigator** *n* **navigable** *adj* wide, deep, or safe enough to be sailed through; able to be steered.

navvy *n, pl* **-vies** *Brit* labourer employed on a road or a building site.

navy *n, pl* **-vies** branch of a country's armed services comprising warships with their crews and organization; warships of a nation. ◆ *adj* navy-blue. **naval** *adj* of or relating to a navy or ships. **navy-blue** *adj* very dark blue.

nay *interj Obs* no.

Nazi *n* member of the National Socialist Party, which seized political control in Germany in 1933 under Adolf Hitler. ◆ *adj* of or relating to the Nazis. **Nazism** *n*

NB note well; (also **N.B.**) New Brunswick.

NCO noncommissioned officer.

NDP New Democratic Party.

NDT Newfoundland Daylight Time.

Ne *Chem* neon.

NE northeast(ern).

Neanderthal [nee-ann-der-tahl] *adj* of a type of primitive man that lived in Europe before 12 000 BC.

neap tide *n* tide at the first and last quarters of the moon when there is the smallest rise and fall in tidal level.

near *prep* close to, not far from. ◆ *adv* at or to a place or time not far away. ◆ *adj* (situated) at or in a place or time not far away; (of people) closely related; almost being the thing specified, e.g. *a near tragedy.* ◆ *v* approach and be about to reach. **nearly** *adv* almost. **nearness** *n* **nearby** *adj* not far away. **nearside** *n* side of a vehicle that is nearer the curb.

neat *adj* tidy and clean; smoothly or competently done; undiluted. **neatly** *adv* **neatness** *n*

nebula [neb-yew-la] *n Astronomy* hazy cloud of particles and gases. **nebulous** *adj* vague, indistinct.

necessary *adj* indispensable or required, e.g. *the necessary skills*; certain or unavoidable, e.g. *the necessary consequences*. **necessarily** *adv* **necessitate** *v* compel or require. **necessity** *n* something needed; compulsion.

neck *n* part of the body joining the head to the shoulders; part of a garment round the neck; narrow part of a bottle or violin. ◆ *v Slang* kiss and cuddle. **neck and neck** absolutely level in a race or competition. **neckerchief** *n* piece of cloth worn tied round the neck. **necklace** *n* decorative piece of jewellery worn around the neck.

necromancy [neck-rome-man-see] *n* communication with the dead; sorcery.

necropolis [neck-rop-pol-liss] *n* cemetery.

nectar *n* sweet liquid collected from flowers by bees; drink of the gods.

nectarine *n* smooth-skinned peach.

née [nay] *prep* indicating the maiden name of a married woman.

need *v* want or require; be obliged (to do something). ◆ *n* condition of lacking something; requirement, necessity; poverty. **needs** *adv* (preceded or foll. by *must*) necessarily. **needy** *adj* poor, in need of financial support. **needful** *adj* necessary or required. **needless** *adj* unnecessary.

needle *n* thin pointed piece of metal with an eye through which thread is passed for sewing; long pointed rod used in knitting; pointed part of a hypodermic syringe; small pointed part in a record player that touches the record and picks up the sound signals; pointer on a measuring instrument or compass; long narrow stiff leaf. ◆ *v Informal* goad or provoke. **needlework** *n* sewing and embroidery.

ne'er *adv Lit* never. **ne'er-do-well** *n* useless or lazy person.

nefarious [nif-fair-ee-uss] *adj* wicked.

negate *v* invalidate; deny. **negation** *n*

negative *adj* expressing a denial or refusal; lacking positive qualities; (of an electrical charge) having the same electrical charge as an electron. ◆ *n* negative word or statement; *Photog* image with a reversal of tones or colours from which positive prints are made.

neglect *v* take no care of; disregard; fail (to do something) through carelessness. ◆ *n* neglecting or being neglected. **neglectful** *adj*

negligee [neg-lee-zhay] *n* woman's lightweight usu. lace-trimmed dressing gown.

negligence *n* neglect or carelessness. **negligent** *adj* **negligently** *adv*

negligible *adj* so small or unimportant as to be not worth considering.

negotiate *v* discuss in order to reach (an agreement); succeed in passing round or over (a place or problem). **negotiation** *n* **negotiator** *n* **negotiable** *adj*

Negro *n, pl* **-groes** *Old-fashioned* member of any of the Black peoples originating in Africa. **Negroid** *adj* of or relating to a Black people.

neigh *n* loud high-pitched sound made by a horse. ◆ *v* make this sound.

neighbour, neighbor *n* one who lives or is situated near another. **neighbouring, neighboring** *adj* situated nearby. **neighbourhood, neighborhood** *n* district where people live; surroundings. **neighbourly, neighborly** *adj* kind, friendly, and helpful.

neither *adj, pron* not one nor the other. ◆ *conj* not.

nemesis [nem-miss-iss] *n, pl* **-ses** retribution or vengeance.

neo- *combining form* new, recent, or a modern form of, e.g. *neoclassicism*.

neolithic *adj* of the later Stone Age.

neologism [nee-ol-a-jiz-zum] *n* new-coined word or an established word used in a new sense.

neon *n* colourless odourless gaseous element used in illuminated signs and lights.

neophyte *n* beginner; new convert.

nephew *n* son of one's sister or brother.

nephritis [nif-**frite**-tiss] *n*

inflammation of a kidney.

nepotism [nep-a-tiz-zum] *n* favouritism in business shown to relatives and friends.

Neptune *n* Roman god of the sea; eighth planet from the sun.

neptunium *n* synthetic metallic element.

nerd, nurd *n Slang* boring person obsessed with a particular subject; stupid and feeble person.

nerve *n* cordlike bundle of fibres that conducts impulses between the brain and other parts of the body; bravery and determination; impudence. ♦ *pl* anxiety or tension; ability or inability to remain calm in a difficult situation. **get on someone's nerves** irritate someone. **nerve oneself** prepare oneself (to do something difficult or unpleasant). **nerveless** *adj* fearless; numb, without feeling. **nervy** *adj Informal* brash or cheeky. **nerve centre** place from which a system or organization is controlled. **nerve-racking** *adj* very distressing or harrowing.

nervous *adj* apprehensive or worried; of or relating to the nerves. **nervously** *adv* **nervousness** *n* **nervous breakdown** mental illness in which the sufferer ceases to function properly.

nest *n* place or structure in which birds or certain animals lay eggs or give birth to young; snug retreat; set of things of graduated sizes designed to fit together. ♦ *v* make or inhabit a nest. **nest egg** fund of money kept in reserve.

nestle *v* snuggle; be in a sheltered position.

nestling *n* bird too young to leave the nest.

net[1] *n* openwork fabric of meshes of string, thread, or wire; piece of net used to protect or hold things or to trap animals. ♦ *v* **netting, netted** cover with or catch in a net. **netting** *n* material made of net.

net[2], **nett** *adj* left after all deductions; (of weight) excluding the wrapping or container. ♦ *v* **netting, netted** yield or earn as a clear profit.

nether *adj* lower.

nettle *n* plant with stinging hairs on the leaves. ♦ *v* irritate.

network *n* system of intersecting lines, roads, etc.; interconnecting group or system; (in broadcasting) group of stations that all transmit the same programmes simultaneously.

neural *adj* of a nerve or the nervous system.

neuralgia *n* severe pain along a nerve.

neuritis [nyoor-rite-tiss] *n* inflammation of a nerve or nerves.

neurology *n* scientific study of the nervous system. **neurologist** *n*

neurosis *n, pl* **-ses** mental disorder producing hysteria, anxiety, depression, or obsessive behaviour. **neurotic** *adj* abnormally sensitive; suffering from neurosis. ♦ *n* neurotic person.

neuter *adj* belonging to a particular class of grammatical inflections in some languages. ♦ *v* castrate (an animal).

neutral *adj* taking neither side in a war or dispute; of or belonging to a neutral party or country; (of a colour) not definite or striking; of no distinctive quality or type. ♦ *n* neutral person or nation; neutral gear. **neutrality** *n* **neutralize** *v* make ineffective or neutral. **neutral gear** position of the controls of a gearbox that leaves the gears unconnected to the engine.

neutrino [new-tree-no] *n, pl* **-nos** elementary particle with no mass or electrical charge.

neutron *n* electrically neutral elementary particle of about the same mass as a proton. **neutron bomb** nuclear bomb designed to kill people and animals while leaving buildings virtually undamaged.

never *adv* at no time. **nevertheless** *adv* in spite of that.

new *adj* not existing before; having lately come into some state; additional; (foll. by *to*) unfamiliar. ♦ *adv* recently. **newness** *n* **New Age** philosophy characterized by a belief in alternative medicine and spiritualism. **newbie** *Informal* ♦ *n* person new to a job, club, etc. **newborn** *adj* recently or just born. **newcomer** *n* recent arrival or participant. **New Democratic Party** major political party with policies to the left of Liberal and Progressive-Conservative Parties. **new-fangled** *adj* objectionably or unnecessarily modern. **new moon** moon when it appears as a narrow crescent at the beginning of its cycle.

New Brunswick see Canadian Provincial Facts p630.

newel n post at the top or bottom of a flight of stairs that supports the handrail.

Newfie n Informal person from Newfoundland.

Newfoundland see Canadian Provincial Facts p630.

news n important or interesting recent happenings; information about such events reported in the mass media. **newsy** adj full of news. **newsagent** n shopkeeper who sells newspapers and magazines. **newscaster** n person who reads the news on the television or radio. **newsflash** n brief important news item, which interrupts a radio or television programme. **newsletter** n bulletin issued periodically to members of a group. **newspaper** n weekly or daily publication containing news. **newsprint** n inexpensive paper used for newspapers. **newsroom** n room where news is received and prepared for publication or broadcasting. **newsworthy** adj sufficiently interesting to be reported as news.

newt n small amphibious creature with a long slender body and tail.

newton n unit of force.

next adj, adv immediately following; nearest. **next-of-kin** n closest relative.

nexus n, pl **nexus** connection or link.

NF, N.F. Newfoundland.

Nfld. Newfoundland.

Ni Chem nickel.

nib n writing point of a pen.

nibble v take little bites (of). ◆ n little bite; light meal.

nibs n **his, her nibs** Slang mock title of respect.

nice adj pleasant; kind, e.g. a nice gesture; good or satisfactory, e.g. they made a nice job of it; subtle, e.g. a nice distinction. **nicely** adv **niceness** n **nicety** n subtle point; refinement or delicacy.

niche [neesh] n hollow area in a wall; exactly suitable position for a particular person.

nick v make a small cut in; Slang steal; Brit slang arrest. ◆ n small cut; Brit slang prison or police station. **in good nick** Informal in good condition. **in the nick of time** just in time.

nickel n silvery-white metal often used in alloys; Canadian and US coin worth five cents.

nickelodeon n US early type of jukebox.

nickname n familiar name given to a person or place. ◆ v call by a nickname.

nicotine n poisonous substance found in tobacco.

niece n daughter of one's sister or brother.

nifty adj -tier, -tiest Informal smart.

niggard n stingy person. **niggardly** adj

nigger n Offens Black person.

niggle v worry slightly; continually find fault (with). ◆ n small worry.

nigh adv, prep Lit near.

night n time of darkness between sunset and sunrise. **nightly** adj, adv (happening) each night. **nightcap** n drink taken just before bedtime; soft cap formerly worn in bed. **nightclub** n establishment for dancing, music, etc., open late at night. **nightdress** n woman's loose dress worn in bed. **nightfall** n approach of darkness. **nightie** n Informal nightdress. **nightingale** n small bird with a musical song usually heard at night. **nightjar** n nocturnal bird with a harsh cry. **nightlife** n entertainment and social activities available at night in a town or city. **nightmare** n very bad dream; very unpleasant experience. **night school** place where adults can attend educational courses in the evenings. **nightshade** n plant with bell-shaped flowers which are often poisonous. **nightshirt** n man's long loose shirt worn in bed. **night-time** n time from sunset to sunrise.

nihilism [nye-ill-liz-zum] n rejection of all established authority and institutions. **nihilist** n **nihilistic** adj

nil n nothing, zero.

nimble adj agile and quick; mentally alert or acute. **nimbly** adv

nimbus n, pl **-bi, -buses** dark grey rain cloud; halo.

nincompoop n Informal stupid

person.

nine *adj, n* one more than eight. **ninth** *adj, n* (of) number nine in a series. **nineteen** *adj, n* ten and nine. **nineteenth** *adj, n* **ninety** *adj, n* ten times nine. **ninetieth** *adj, n* **ninepins** *n* game of skittles.

nip *v* **nipping, nipped** *Informal* hurry; pinch or squeeze; bite lightly. ◆ *n* pinch; light bite; small alcoholic drink; sharp coldness, e.g. *a nip in the air.* **nippy** *adj* frosty or chilly; *Brit informal* quick or nimble. **nipper** *n Informal* small child.

nipple *n* projection in the centre of a breast.

nirvana [near-vah-na] *n Buddhism, Hinduism* absolute spiritual enlightenment and bliss.

nit *n* egg or larva of a louse; *Informal* short for NITWIT. **nit-picking** *adj Informal* overconcerned with insignificant detail, esp. to find fault. **nitwit** *n Informal* stupid person.

nitrogen [nite-roj-jen] *n* colourless odourless gas that forms four fifths of the air. **nitric, nitrous, nitrogenous** *adj* of or containing nitrogen. **nitrate** *n* compound of nitric acid, used as a fertilizer. **nitroglycerin, nitroglycerine** *n* explosive liquid.

nitty-gritty *n Informal* basic facts.

no *interj* expresses denial, disagreement, or refusal. ◆ *adj* not any, not a. ◆ *adv* not at all. ◆ *n, pl* **noes, nos** answer or vote of 'no'; person who answers or votes 'no'. **no-go area** district barricaded off so that the police or army can enter only by force. **no-man's-land** *n* land between boundaries, esp. contested land between two opposing forces. **no-one, no one** *pron* nobody.

no. number.

nob *n Slang* person of wealth or social distinction.

nobble *v Slang* attract the attention of (someone) in order to talk to him or her; bribe or threaten.

Nobel Prize [no-bell] *n* prize awarded annually for outstanding achievement in various fields.

noble *adj* showing or having high moral qualities; of the nobility; impressive and magnificent. ◆ *n* member of the nobility. **nobility** *n* quality of being noble; class of people holding titles and high social rank. **nobly** *adv* **nobleman, noblewoman** *n*

nobody *pron* no person. ◆ *n, pl* **-bodies** person of no importance.

nocturnal *adj* of the night; active at night.

nocturne *n* short dreamy piece of music.

nod *v* **nodding, nodded** lower and raise (one's head) briefly in agreement or greeting; let one's head fall forward with sleep. ◆ *n* act of nodding. **nod off** *v Informal* fall asleep.

node *n* point on a plant stem from which leaves grow; point at which a curve crosses itself.

nodule *n* small knot or lump; rounded mineral growth on the root of a plant.

Noel *n* Christmas.

noggin *n* small quantity of an alcoholic drink; *Informal* head.

noise *n* sound, usually a loud or disturbing one. **be noised abroad** be rumoured. **noisy** *adj* making a lot of noise; full of noise. **noisily** *adv* **noiseless** *adj*

noisome *adj* (of smells) offensive; harmful or poisonous.

nomad *n* member of a tribe with no fixed dwelling place, wanderer. **nomadic** *adj*

nom de plume *n, pl* **noms de plume** pen name.

nomenclature [no-men-klatch-er] *n* system of names used in a particular subject.

nominal *adj* in name only; very small in comparison with real worth. **nominally** *adv*

nominate *v* suggest as a candidate; appoint to an office or position. **nomination** *n* **nominee** *n* candidate. **nominative** *n* form of a noun indicating subject of a verb.

non- *prefix* indicating: negation, e.g. *nonexistent;* refusal or failure, e.g. *noncooperation;* exclusion from a specified class, e.g. *nonfiction;* lack or absence, e.g. *nonevent.*

nonagenarian *n* person aged between ninety and ninety-nine.

nonaggression *n* (of countries) not attacking.

nonagon *n* geometric figure with nine sides.

nonalcoholic *adj* containing no

alcohol.

nonaligned *adj* (of a country) not part of a major alliance.

nonce *n* **for the nonce** for the present.

nonchalant [non-shall-ant] *adj* casually unconcerned or indifferent. **nonchalantly** *adv* **nonchalance** *n*

noncombatant *n* member of the armed forces whose duties do not include fighting.

noncommissioned officer *n* (in the armed forces) a subordinate officer, risen from the ranks.

noncommittal *adj* not committing oneself to any particular opinion.

non compos mentis *adj* of unsound mind.

nonconductor *n* substance that is a poor conductor of heat, electricity, or sound.

nonconformist *n* person who does not conform to generally accepted patterns of behaviour or thought; (**N-**) member of a Protestant group separated from the Church of England. ◆ *adj* (of behaviour or ideas) not conforming to accepted patterns. **nonconformity** *n*

noncontributory *adj* denoting a pension scheme for employees, the premiums of which are paid entirely by the employer.

nondescript *adj* lacking outstanding features.

none *pron* not any; no-one. **nonetheless** *adv* however.

nonentity [non-**enn**-tit-tee] *n, pl* **-ties** insignificant person or thing.

nonevent *n* disappointing or insignificant occurrence.

nonflammable *adj* not easily set on fire.

nonintervention *n* refusal to intervene in the affairs of others.

nonpareil [non-par-**rail**] *n* person or thing that is unsurpassed.

nonpayment *n* failure to pay money owed.

nonplussed *adj* perplexed.

nonsense *n* something that has or makes no sense; absurd language; foolish behaviour. **nonsensical** *adj*

non sequitur [sek-wit-tur] *n* statement with little or no relation to what preceded it.

nonstandard *adj* denoting language that is not regarded as correct by educated native speakers.

nonstarter *n* person or idea that has little chance of success.

nonstick *adj* coated with a substance that food will not stick to when cooked.

nonstop *adj, adv* without a stop.

nontoxic *adj* not poisonous.

noodle *n* strip of pasta.

nook *n* sheltered place.

noon *n* twelve o'clock midday. **noonday** *n Lit* noon.

noose *n* loop in the end of a rope, tied with a slipknot.

nor *conj* and not.

Nordic *adj* of Scandinavia.

norm *n* standard that is regarded as normal.

normal *adj* usual, regular, or typical; free from mental or physical disorder. **normally** *adv* **normality** *n* **normalize** *v*

Norse *n, adj* (language) of ancient and medieval Norway.

north *n* direction towards the North Pole, opposite south; area lying in or towards the north. ◆ *adv* in, to, or towards the north. ◆ *adj* to or in the north; (of a wind) from the north. **northerly** *adj* **northern** *adj* **northerner** *n* person from the north of a country or area. **northwards** *adv* **northeast** *n, adj, adv* (in or to) direction between north and east. **northwest** *n, adj, adv* (in or to) direction between north and west. **North Pole** northernmost point on the earth's axis.

Northwest Territories *see* Canadian Provincial Facts p630.

nos. numbers.

nose *n* organ of smell, used also in breathing; front part of a vehicle. ◆ *v* move forward slowly and carefully; pry or snoop. **nosy, nosey** *adj Informal* prying or inquisitive. **nosiness** *n* **nose dive** (of an aircraft) sudden drop. **nosegay** *n* small bunch of flowers.

nosh *Slang* ◆ *n* food. ◆ *v* eat.

nostalgia *n* sentimental longing for the past. **nostalgic** *adj*

nostril *n* one of the two openings at the end of the nose.

nostrum *n* quack medicine; favourite remedy.

not *adv* expressing negation, refusal,

or denial.

notable [note-a-bl] *adj* worthy of being noted, remarkable. ◆ *n* person of distinction. **notably** *adv* **notability** [note-a-**bill**-lit-tee] *n*

notary [note-a-ree] *n, pl* -ries person authorized to witness the signing of legal documents.

notation [no-**tay**-shun] *n* representation of numbers or quantities in a system by a series of symbols; set of such symbols.

notch *n* V-shaped cut; *Informal* step or level. ◆ *v* make a notch in.

note *n* short letter; brief comment or record; banknote; (symbol for) a musical sound; hint or mood. ◆ *v* notice, pay attention to; record in writing; remark upon. **noted** *adj* well-known. **notebook** *n* book for writing in. **noteworthy** *adj* worth noting, remarkable.

nothing *pron* not anything; matter of no importance; figure 0. ◆ *adv* not at all. **nothingness** *n* nonexistence; insignificance.

notice *n* observation or attention; sign giving warning or an announcement; advance notification of intention to end a contract of employment. ◆ *v* observe, become aware of; point out or remark upon. **noticeable** *adj* easily seen or detected.

notify *v* -fying, -fied inform. **notification** *n* **notifiable** *adj* having to be reported to the authorities.

notion *n* idea or opinion; whim. **notional** *adj* speculative, imaginary, or unreal.

notorious *adj* well known for something bad. **notoriously** *adv* **notoriety** *n*

notwithstanding *prep* in spite of.

nougat *n* chewy candy containing nuts and fruit.

nought *n* nothing; figure 0. **noughties** *Informal* ◆ *pl n* decade from 2000 to 2009.

noun *n* word that refers to a person, place, or thing.

nourish *v* feed; encourage or foster (an idea or feeling). **nourishment** *n* **nourishing** *adj* providing the food necessary for life and growth.

nouvelle cuisine [noo-vell kwee-zeen] *n* style of preparing and presenting food with light sauces and unusual combinations of flavours.

Nov. November.

nova *n, pl* -vae, -vas star that suddenly becomes brighter and then gradually decreases to its original brightness.

Nova Scotia *see* Canadian Provincial Facts p631.

novel[1] *n* long fictitious story in book form. **novelist** *n* writer of novels. **novella** *n, pl* -las, -lae short novel.

novel[2] *adj* fresh, new, or original. **novelty** *n* newness; something new or unusual; cheap toy or trinket.

November *n* eleventh month of the year.

novena [no-**vee**-na] *n, pl* -nae *RC Church* set of prayers or services on nine consecutive days.

novice [**nov**-viss] *n* beginner; person who has entered a religious order but has not yet taken vows.

now *adv* at or for the present time; immediately. ◆ *conj* seeing that, since. **just now** very recently. **now and again, then** occasionally. **nowadays** *adv* in these times.

nowhere *adv* not anywhere.

noxious *adj* poisonous or harmful; extremely unpleasant.

nozzle *n* projecting spout through which fluid is discharged.

NS, N.S. Nova Scotia.

NST Newfoundland Standard Time.

NT New Testament.

nuance [**new**-ahnss] *n* subtle difference in colour, meaning, or tone.

nub *n* point or gist (of a story etc.).

nubile [**new**-bile] *adj* (of a young woman) sexually attractive; old enough to get married.

nuclear *adj* of nuclear weapons or energy; of a nucleus, esp. the nucleus of an atom. **nuclear bomb** bomb whose force is due to uncontrolled nuclear fusion or fission. **nuclear energy** energy released as a result of nuclear fission or fusion. **nuclear fission** splitting of an atomic nucleus. **nuclear fusion** combination of two nuclei to form a heavier nucleus with the release of energy. **nuclear power** power produced by a nuclear reactor. **nuclear reaction** change in structure and energy content of an atomic nucleus by interaction with another nucleus or particle. **nuclear reactor** device in which a nuclear reaction is maintained and controlled to produce nuclear energy. **nuclear winter** theoretical period of low temperatures and little light after a nuclear war.

nucleic acid n complex compound, such as DNA or RNA, found in all living cells.

nucleonics n branch of physics dealing with the applications of nuclear energy.

nucleus n, pl **-clei** centre, esp. of an atom or cell; central thing around which others are grouped.

nude adj naked. ◆ n naked figure in painting, sculpture, or photography. **nudity** n **nudism** n practice of not wearing clothes. **nudist** n

nudge v push gently, esp. with the elbow. ◆ n gentle push or touch.

nugatory [new-gat-tree] adj trifling; not valid.

nugget n small lump of gold in its natural state; something small but valuable.

nuisance n something or someone that causes annoyance or bother.

nuke Slang ◆ v attack with nuclear weapons. ◆ n nuclear bomb.

null adj **null and void** not legally valid. **nullity** n **nullify** v make ineffective; cancel.

numb adj without feeling, as through cold, shock, or fear. ◆ v make numb. **numbly** adv **numbness** n **numbskull** n same as NUMSKULL.

number n sum or quantity; word or symbol used to express a sum or quantity, numeral; one of a series, such as a copy of a magazine; Grammar classification of words depending on how many persons or things are referred to; song or piece of music; group of people; numeral or string of numerals used to identify a person or thing. ◆ v count; give a number to; amount to; include in a group. **numberless** adj too many to be counted. **number crunching** Computers large-scale processing of numerical data. **number one** Informal oneself; first in importance or quality.

numeral n word or symbol used to express a sum or quantity.

numerate adj able to do basic

arithmetic. **numeracy** n

numeration n act or process of numbering or counting.

numerator n Math number above the line in a fraction.

numerical adj measured or expressed in numbers. **numerically** adv

numerous adj existing or happening in large numbers.

numismatist n coin collector.

numskull n stupid person.

nun n female member of a religious order. **nunnery** n convent.

Nunavut see Canadian Provincial Facts p631.

nuncio n RC Church pope's ambassador.

nuptial adj relating to marriage. **nuptials** pl n wedding.

nurse n person employed to look after sick people, usu. in hospital; woman employed to look after children. ◆ v look after (a sick person); breast-feed (a baby); try to cure (an ailment); harbour or foster (a feeling). **nursery** n room where children sleep or play; place where children are taken care of while their parents are at work; place where plants are grown for sale. **nurseryman** n person who raises plants for sale. **nursery school** school for children from 3 to 5 years old. **nursery slope** gentle ski slope for beginners. **nursing home** private hospital or home for old people.

nurture n act or process of promoting the development of a child or young plant. ◆ v promote or encourage the development of.

nut n fruit consisting of a hard shell and a kernel; small piece of metal that screws onto a bolt; Slang head; Slang eccentric person. **nutty** adj containing or resembling nuts; Slang insane or eccentric. **nutter** n Slang insane or violent person. **nutcracker** n device for cracking the shells of nuts. **nuthatch** n small songbird. **nutmeg** n spice made from the seed of a tropical tree.

nutria [new-tree-a] n fur of the coypu.

nutrient [new-tree-ent] n substance that provides nourishment.

nutriment [new-tree-ment] n food or nourishment required by all living things to grow and stay healthy.

nutrition [new-trish-shun] n process

of taking in and absorbing nutrients; process of being nourished. **nutritious, nutritive** adj nourishing.

nuzzle v push or rub gently with the nose or snout.

NW northwest(ern).

NWT, N.W.T. Northwest Territories.

nylon n synthetic material used for clothing etc. ◆ pl stockings made of nylon.

nymph n mythical spirit of nature, represented as a beautiful young woman.

nymphet n sexually precocious young girl.

nymphomaniac n woman with an abnormally intense sexual desire.

NZ New Zealand.

O o

oaf n stupid or clumsy person. **oafish** adj

oak n deciduous forest tree; its wood, used for furniture. **oaken** adj **oak apple** brownish lump found on oak trees.

oakum n fibre obtained by unravelling old rope.

oar n pole with a broad blade, used for rowing a boat.

oasis n, pl **-ses** fertile area in a desert.

oast n kiln for drying hops.

oath n solemn promise, esp. to be truthful in court; swearword.

oats pl n grain of a cereal plant, used for food. **sow one's wild oats** have many sexual relationships when young. **oaten** adj **oatmeal** adj pale brownish-cream.

obbligato [ob-lig-gah-toe] n Music essential part or accompaniment.

obdurate adj hardhearted; stubborn. **obduracy** n

OBE Officer of the Order of the British Empire.

obedient adj obeying or willing to obey. **obediently** adv **obedience** n

obeisance [oh-bay-sanss] n attitude of respect; bow or curtsy.

obelisk [ob-bill-isk] n four-sided stone column tapering to a pyramid at the top.

obese [oh-**beess**] adj very fat. **obesity** n

obey v carry out the instructions of (someone); comply with (instructions).

obfuscate v darken; make (something) confusing.

obituary n, pl **-aries** announcement of someone's death, esp. in a newspaper. **obituarist** n

object[1] n physical thing; focus of thoughts or action; aim or purpose; Grammar word that a verb or preposition affects. **no object** not a hindrance.

object[2] v (foll. by to) oppose. **objection** n **objectionable** adj unpleasant. **objector** n

objective adj existing in the real world outside the human mind; not biased. ◆ n aim or purpose. **objectively** adv **objectivity** n

objet d'art [ob-zhay **dahr**] n, pl **objets d'art** small object of artistic value.

oblate adj (of a sphere) flattened at the poles.

oblation n religious offering.

oblige v compel (someone) morally or by law to do (something); do a favour for (someone). **obliging** adj ready to help other people. **obligingly** adv

obligate v cause (someone) to be obliged to do (something). **obligation** n duty. **obligatory** adj required by a rule or law.

oblique [oh-**bleak**] adj slanting; indirect. ◆ n the symbol (/). **obliquely** adv **obliqueness** n **oblique angle** angle that is not a right angle.

obliterate v wipe out, destroy. **obliteration** n

oblivious adj (foll. by to or of) unaware (of). **oblivion** n state of being forgotten; state of being unaware or unconscious.

oblong adj having two long sides, two short sides, and four right angles. ◆ n oblong figure.

obloquy [ob-lock-wee] n, pl **-quies** verbal abuse; discredit.

obnoxious adj offensive. **obnoxiousness** n

oboe n double-reeded woodwind instrument. **oboist** n

obscene adj portraying sex offensively; disgusting. **obscenity** n

obscure adj not well known; hard to understand; indistinct. ◆ v make (something) obscure. **obscurity** n

obsequies [ob-**sick**-weez] pl n funeral rites.

obsequious [ob-**seek**-wee-uss] adj too eager to please in order to be liked. **obsequiousness** n

observe v watch (someone or something) carefully; perceive visually; remark; act according to (a law or custom). **observation** n action or habit of observing; something observed; remark. **observer** n **observable** adj **observably** adv **observance** n observing of a custom. **observant** adj quick to notice things. **observatory** n building equipped for astronomical or meteorological observations.

obsess v preoccupy (someone) compulsively. **obsessed** adj **obsessive** adj **obsession** n

obsidian n dark glassy volcanic rock.

obsolete adj no longer in use. **obsolescent** adj becoming obsolete. **obsolescence** n

obstacle n something that makes progress difficult.

obstetrics n branch of medicine concerned with pregnancy and childbirth. **obstetric** adj **obstetrician** n

obstinate adj stubborn; (of a stain) difficult to remove. **obstinately** adv **obstinacy** n

obstreperous adj unruly, noisy.

obstruct v block with an obstacle. **obstruction** n **obstructionist** n person who deliberately obstructs formal proceedings. **obstructive** adj

obtain v acquire intentionally; be customary. **obtainable** adj

obtrude v push oneself or one's ideas on others. **obtrusion** n **obtrusive** adj **obtrusively** adv

obtuse adj mentally slow; Math (of an angle) between 90° and 180°; not pointed. **obtusely** adv **obtuseness** n

obverse n opposite way of looking at an idea; main side of a coin or medal.

obviate v make unnecessary.

obvious adj easy to see or understand, evident. **obviously** adv

ocarina n small oval wind instrument made of clay.

occasion n time at which a particular thing happens; special event; reason, e.g. no occasion for complaint. ◆ v cause. **occasional** adj happening sometimes; for a special event. **occasionally** adv

Occident n Lit the West. **Occidental** adj

occiput [ox-sip-put] n back of the head.

occlude v obstruct; close off. **occlusion** n **occlusive** adj **occluded front** Meteorol front formed when a cold front overtakes a warm front and warm air rises.

occult n the occult knowledge or study of the supernatural. ◆ adj relating to the supernatural.

occupant n person occupying a specified place. **occupancy** n (length of a) person's stay in a specified place.

occupation n profession; activity that occupies one's time; control of a country by a foreign military power; being occupied. **occupational** adj **occupational therapy** treatment of physical, emotional, or social problems by means of purposeful activity.

occupy v -pying, -pied live or work in (a building); take up the attention of (someone); take up (space or time); take possession of (a place) by force. **occupier** n

occur v -curring, -curred take place; exist; (foll. by to) come to the mind (of). **occurrence** n something that occurs; occurring.

ocean n vast area of sea between continents. **oceanic** adj **oceanography** n scientific study of the oceans. **oceangoing** adj able to sail on the open sea.

ocelot [oss-ill-lot] n American wild cat with a spotted coat.

oche [ok-kee] n Darts mark on the floor behind which a player must stand.

ochre [oak-er] adj brownish-yellow.

o'clock adv used after a number to specify an hour.

Oct. October.

octagon n geometric figure with eight sides. **octagonal** adj

octahedron [ok-ta-heed-ron] n, pl -drons, -dra three-dimensional geometric figure with eight faces.

octane n hydrocarbon found in gasoline. **octane rating** measure of gasoline quality.

octave n Music (interval between the first and) eighth note of a scale.

octet n group of eight performers; music for such a group.

October n tenth month of the year.

octogenarian n person aged between eighty and eighty-nine.

octopus n, pl **-puses** sea creature with a soft body and eight tentacles.

ocular adj relating to the eyes or sight.

OD n Med overdose. ◆ v **OD'ing, OD'd** Informal take an overdose.

odd adj unusual; occasional; not divisible by two; not part of a set. **odds** pl n (ratio showing) the probability of something happening. **at odds** in conflict. **odds and ends** small miscellaneous items. **oddness** n quality of being odd. **oddity** n odd person or thing. **oddments** pl n things left over.

ode n lyric poem, usu. addressed to a particular subject.

odium [oh-dee-um] n widespread dislike. **odious** adj offensive.

odometer n device that records the distance a vehicle has travelled.

odour, odor n particular smell. **odorous** adj **odourless, odorless** adj **odoriferous** adj giving off a pleasant smell. **odorize** v fill (something) with scent.

odyssey [odd-iss-ee] n long eventful journey.

OECD Organization for Economic Cooperation and Development.

oedema [id-deem-a] n, pl **-mata** abnormal swelling.

oesophagus [ee-soff-a-guss] n, pl **-gi** passage between the mouth and stomach.

oestrogen [ee-stra-jen] n female hormone that controls the reproductive cycle.

of prep belonging to; consisting of; connected with; characteristic of.

off prep away from. ◆ adv away. ◆ adj not operating; cancelled or postponed; (of food) gone bad; not up to the usual standard, e.g. an off day. **off colour** slightly ill. **off-line** adj (of a computer) not directly controlled by a central processor. **off-message** adj (esp. of a politician) not following the official Party line.

offal n edible organs of an animal, such as liver or kidneys.

offcut n piece remaining after the required parts have been cut out.

offend v hurt the feelings of, insult; commit a crime. **offender** n **offence** n (cause of) hurt feelings or annoyance; illegal act. **offensive** adj insulting; aggressive; disagreeable. ◆ n position or action of attack.

offer v present (something) for acceptance or rejection; provide; be willing (to do something); propose (a sum of money) as payment. ◆ n instance of offering something. **offering** n thing offered. **offertory** n Christianity offering of the bread and wine for Communion.

offhand adj (also **offhanded**) curt. ◆ adv without preparation.

office n room or building where people work at desks; department of a commercial organization; formal position of responsibility; duty, function; (esp. pl.) something done for another. **officer** n person in authority in the armed services; a member of the police force; person with special responsibility in an organization.

official adj approved or arranged by someone in authority; of a position of authority. ◆ n person who holds a position of authority. **officialdom** n Offens officials collectively.

officiate v conduct a ceremony in an official role.

officious adj giving unnecessary instructions; interfering.

offing n area of the sea visible from the shore. **in the offing** likely to happen soon.

off-licence n shop licensed to sell alcohol.

offset v cancel out, compensate for.

offside adj, adv Sport (positioned) illegally ahead of the ball or puck.

offspring n, pl **offspring** one's child.

often adv frequently, much of the time. **oft** adv Poetic often.

ogee arch [oh-jee] n pointed arch with an S-shaped curve on both sides.

ogle v stare at (someone) lustfully.

ogre n giant that eats human flesh.

oh interj exclamation of surprise, pain, etc.

ohm n unit of electrical resistance.

oil *n* viscous liquid, insoluble in water and usu. flammable; same as PETROLEUM; petroleum derivative, used as a fuel or lubricant. ◆ *pl* oil-based paints used in art. ◆ *v* lubricate (a machine) with oil. **oily** *adj* **oilfield** *n* area containing oil reserves. **oil rig** platform constructed for boring oil wells. **oilskins** *pl n* waterproof clothing.

ointment *n* greasy substance used for healing skin or as a cosmetic.

O.K., okay *Informal* ◆ *interj* all right. ◆ *n* approval. ◆ *v* approve (something).

okapi [ok-kah-pee] *n* African animal related to the giraffe but with a shorter neck.

okra *n* tropical plant with edible green pods.

old *adj* having lived or existed for a long time; of a specified age, e.g. *two years old*; former. **olden** *adj* old, e.g. *in the olden days*. **oldie** *n Informal* old but popular song or film. **old-fashioned** *adj* no longer commonly used or valued. **old guard** group of people in an organization who have traditional values. **old hat** boring because so familiar. **old maid** elderly unmarried woman. **old master** European painter or painting from the period 1500–1800. **Old Nick** *Informal* the Devil. **old school tie** system of mutual help between former pupils of a British public school. **Old Testament** part of the Bible recording Hebrew history. **Old World** world as it was known before the discovery of the Americas.

oleaginous [ol-lee-aj-in-uss] *adj* oily, producing oil.

oleander [ol-lee-ann-der] *n* Mediterranean evergreen shrub with fragrant flowers.

olfactory *adj* relating to the sense of smell.

oligarchy [ol-lee-gark-ee] *n, pl* **-chies** government by a small group of people; state governed this way. **oligarch** *n* member of an oligarchy. **oligarchic, oligarchical** *adj*

olive *n* small green or black fruit used as food or pressed for its oil; tree on which this fruit grows. ◆ *adj* greyish-green. **olive branch** conciliatory gesture.

Olympic Games *pl n* four-yearly

international sports competition.

ombudsman *n* official who investigates complaints against government organizations.

omelet *n* dish of eggs beaten and fried.

omen *n* happening or object thought to foretell success or misfortune. **ominous** *adj* worrying, seeming to foretell of misfortune.

omit *v* **omitting, omitted** leave out; neglect (to do something). **omission** *n*

omni- *combining form* all, everywhere, e.g. *omnidirectional*.

omnibus *n Old-fashioned* bus; several books or TV or radio programmes made into one.

omnipotent [om-nip-a-tent] *adj* having unlimited power. **omnipotence** *n*

omnipresent *adj* present everywhere. **omnipresence** *n*

omniscient [om-niss-ee-ent] *adj* knowing everything. **omniscience** *n*

omnivorous [om-niv-vor-uss] *adj* eating food obtained from both animals and plants. **omnivore** *n* omnivorous animal.

on *prep* above and touching; attached to; concerning, e.g. *an article on slimming*; during, e.g. *on Monday*; through the medium of, e.g. *on television*. ◆ *adv* in operation; forwards; continuing. ◆ *adj* operating; taking place, e.g. *the party's on*. **on-message** *adj* (esp. of a politician) following the official Party line.

ON, O.N. Ontario.

once *adv* on one occasion; formerly. ◆ *conj* as soon as. **at once** immediately; simultaneously. **once-over** *n Informal* quick examination.

oncogene [on-koh-jean] *n* gene that can cause cancer when abnormally activated.

oncoming *adj* approaching from the front.

one *adj* single, lone. ◆ *n* number or figure 1; single unit. ◆ *pron* any person. **oneness** *n* unity. **oneself** *pron* reflexive form of ONE. **one-armed bandit** fruit machine operated by a lever on one side. **one-liner** *n* witty remark. **one-night stand** sexual encounter lasting one night. **one-sided** *adj* considering only one point of view. **one-way** adj allowing movement in one direction only.

onerous [**own**-er-uss] adj (of a task) difficult to carry out.

ongoing adj continuing.

onion n strongly flavoured edible bulb.

on-line adj Computers (of equipment) directly connected to and controlled by the computer.

onlooker n person who watches something happening without taking part.

only adj alone of its kind. ◆ adv exclusively; merely; no more than. ◆ conj but.

onomatopoeia [on-a-mat-a-**pee**-a] n formation of a word which imitates the sound it represents, such as hiss. **onomatopoeic** adj

onset n beginning.

onslaught n violent attack.

Ont. Ontario.

Ontario see Canadian Provincial Facts p631.

onto prep to a position on; aware of, e.g. she's onto us.

ontology n Philosophy study of existence. **ontological** adj

onus [**own**-uss] n, pl **onuses** responsibility or burden.

onward adj directed or moving forward. ◆ adv (also **onwards**) ahead, forward.

onyx n type of quartz with coloured layers.

oodles pl n Informal great quantities.

ooze v flow slowly. ◆ n sluggish flow; soft mud at the bottom of a lake or river. **oozy** adj

opacity [oh-**pass**-it-tee] n state of being opaque.

opal n iridescent precious stone. **opalescent** adj iridescent like an opal.

opaque adj not able to be seen through, not transparent.

op. cit. [op sit] in the work cited.

OPEC Organization of Petroleum Exporting Countries.

open adj not closed; uncovered; unfolded; ready for business; free from obstruction, accessible; unrestricted; not finalized; frank. ◆ v (cause to) become open; begin. ◆ n Sport competition open to everyone. **in the open** outdoors. **openly** adv without concealment. **opening** n hole;

opportunity. ◆ adj first. **open-and-shut case** problem that is easily solved. **open day** day on which a school or college is open to the public. **open-handed** adj generous. **open-hearted** adj generous; frank. **open-heart surgery** surgery on the heart during which the blood circulation is maintained by machine. **open house** hospitality to visitors at any time. **open letter** letter to an individual that the writer makes public in a newspaper or magazine. **open-minded** adj receptive to new ideas. **open-pit mining** mining at the surface and not underground. **open-plan** adj (of a house or office) having few interior walls. **openwork** n patterns made by leaving spaces in a design.

opera[1] n drama in which the text is sung to an orchestral accompaniment. **operatic** adj **operetta** n light-hearted comic opera.

opera[2] n a plural of OPUS.

operate v (cause to) function; direct; perform an operation. **operator** n **operation** n method or procedure of working; medical procedure in which the body is worked on to repair a damaged part. **operational** adj in working order; relating to a working procedure, e.g. operational difficulties. **operative** [**op**-rat-tiv] adj working. ◆ n worker with a special skill.

ophidian adj, n (reptile) of the snake family.

ophthalmic adj relating to the eyes. **ophthalmic optician** see OPTICIAN. **ophthalmology** n study of the eye and its diseases. **ophthalmologist** n

opiate [oh-**pee**-ate] n narcotic drug containing opium.

opinion n personal belief or judgment. **opinion poll** see POLL. **opinionated** adj having strong opinions. **opine** v Old-fashioned express an opinion.

opium [oh-**pee**-um] n addictive narcotic drug made from poppy seeds.

opossum n small marsupial of N America or Australia.

opponent n person one is working against in a contest, battle, or argument.

opportunity n, pl **-ties** favourable time or condition; good chance. **opportune** adj happening at a suitable time. **opportunist** n person who does whatever is advantageous without regard for principles. **opportunism** n

oppose v work against. **be opposed to** disagree with or disapprove of. **opposition** n obstruction or hostility; largest political party not in power; group opposing another.

opposite adj situated on the other side; facing; diametrically different. ◆ n person or thing that is opposite. ◆ prep, adv facing; on the other side (from).

oppress v subjugate by cruelty or force; depress. **oppression** n **oppressor** n **oppressive** adj tyrannical; (of weather) hot and humid. **oppressively** adv

opprobrium [op-**probe**-ree-um] n state of being criticized severely for wrong one has done. **opprobrious** adj

oppugn [op-**pewn**] v dispute; question.

opt v (foll. by for) show a preference (for), choose.

optic adj relating to the eyes or sight. **optics** n science of sight and light. **optical** adj **optical character reader** device that electronically reads and stores text. **optical fibre** fine glass-fibre tube used to transmit information.

optician n person who makes or sells glasses. **dispensing optician** person who supplies and fits glasses. **ophthalmic optician** person qualified to prescribe glasses.

optimism n tendency to always take the most hopeful view. **optimist** n **optimistic** adj **optimistically** adv

optimum n, pl **-ma**, **-mums** best possible conditions. ◆ adj most favourable. **optimal** adj **optimize** v make the most of.

option n choice; thing chosen; right to buy or sell something at a specified price within a given time. **optional** adj possible but not compulsory.

optometrist [op-**tom**-met-trist] n person qualified to prescribe glasses. **optometry** n

opulent [op-**pew**-lent] adj having or indicating wealth. **opulence** n

opus [**oh**-puss] n, pl **opuses**, **opera** artistic creation, esp. a musical work.

or conj used to join alternatives, e.g. tea or coffee.

oracle n shrine of an ancient god; prophecy, often obscure, revealed at a shrine; person believed to make infallible predictions. **oracular** adj

oral adj spoken; (of a drug) to be taken by mouth. ◆ n spoken examination. **orally** adv

orange adj reddish-yellow. ◆ n reddish-yellow citrus fruit. **orangeade** n orange-flavoured, usu. fizzy drink. **orangery** n greenhouse for growing orange trees.

orang-utan, orang-outang n large reddish-brown ape with long arms.

orator [or-**rat**-tor] n skilful public speaker. **oration** n formal speech. **oratorical** adj **oratory** [or-**rat**-tree] n art of making speeches; small private chapel.

oratorio [or-rat-**tor**-ee-oh] n, pl **-rios** musical composition for choir and orchestra, usu. with a religious theme.

orb n ceremonial decorated sphere with a cross on top, carried by a monarch.

orbit n curved path of a planet, satellite, or spacecraft around another heavenly body; sphere of influence. ◆ v **orbiting**, **orbited** move in an orbit around; put (a satellite or spacecraft) into orbit. **orbital** adj

orchard n area where fruit trees are grown.

orchestra n large group of musicians, esp. playing a variety of instruments. **orchestral** adj **orchestrate** v arrange (music) for orchestra; organize (something) to particular effect. **orchestration** n **orchestra pit** area of a theatre in front of the stage, for the orchestra.

orchid n plant with flowers that have unusual lip-shaped petals.

ordain v make (someone) a member of the clergy; order or establish with authority.

ordeal n painful or difficult experience.

order n instruction to be carried out; request for goods to be supplied; methodical arrangement or sequence; established social system; condition of a law-abiding society; social class; group of similar plants or animals; kind, sort; religious society, usu. of monks or nuns. ◆ v give an instruction to; request (something) to be supplied; arrange methodically. **in order** so that it is possible. **orderly** *adj* well organized; well behaved. ◆ *n, pl* **-lies** male hospital attendant. **orderliness** *n* **Order of Canada** order awarded to Canadians for outstanding achievement.

ordinal number *n* number showing a position in a series, e.g. *first, second.*

ordinance *n* official rule or order.

ordinary *adj* usual or normal; dull or commonplace. **ordinarily** *adv*

ordination *n* ordaining.

ordnance *n* weapons and military supplies.

ordure *n* excrement.

ore *n* (rock containing) a mineral which yields metal.

oregano [or-rig-**gah**-no] *n* aromatic herb used in cooking.

organ *n* part of an animal or plant that has a particular function, such as the heart or lungs; musical keyboard instrument in which notes are produced by forcing air through pipes; means of conveying information, esp. a newspaper. **organic** *adj* of or produced from animals or plants; *Chem* relating to compounds of carbon; grown without artificial fertilizers or pesticides; organized systematically. **organically** *adv* **organism** *n* any living animal or plant. **organist** *n* organ player.

organdie *n* fine cotton fabric.

organize *v* make arrangements for; arrange systematically; unite (people) for a shared purpose. **organization** *n* group of people working together; act of organizing. **organizational** *adj* **organizer** *n*

orgasm *n* most intense point of sexual pleasure. **orgasmic** *adj*

orgy *n, pl* **-gies** party involving promiscuous sexual activity; unrestrained indulgence, e.g. *an orgy of destruction.*

oriel *n* upper window built out from a wall.

Orient *n* **the Orient** *Lit* East Asia. **Oriental** *adj* **Orientalist** *n* specialist in the languages and history of the Far East. **orient, orientate** *v* position (oneself) according to one's surroundings; position (a map) in

relation to the points of the compass. **orientation** *n* **orienteering** *n* sport in which competitors hike over a course using a compass and map.

orifice [**or**-rif-fiss] *n* opening.

origami [or-rig-**gah**-mee] *n* Japanese decorative art of paper folding.

origin *n* point from which something develops. **original** *adj* earliest; new, not copied or based on something else; able to think up new ideas. ◆ *n* first version, from which others are copied. **original sin** human imperfection and mortality as a result of Adam's disobedience. **originally** *adv* **originality** *n* **originate** *v* come or bring into existence. **origination** *n* **originator** *n*

oriole *n* tropical or N American songbird.

ormolu *n* gold-coloured alloy used for decoration.

ornament *n* decorative object. ◆ *v* decorate. **ornamental** *adj* **ornamentation** *n*

ornate *adj* elaborate.

ornithology *n* study of birds. **ornithological** *adj* **ornithologist** *n*

orotund *adj* (of a voice) resonant; (of language) pompous.

orphan *n* child whose parents are dead. **orphanage** *n* children's home for orphans. **orphaned** *adj* having no living parents.

orrery *n, pl* **-ries** mechanical model of the solar system.

orris *n* kind of iris; (also **orrisroot**) fragrant root used for perfume.

orthodontics *n* branch of dentistry concerned with correcting irregular teeth. **orthodontist** *n*

orthodox *adj* conforming to established views. **orthodoxy** *n* **Orthodox Church** dominant Christian Church in Eastern Europe.

orthography *n* correct spelling.

orthopedics, orthopaedics *n* branch of medicine concerned with disorders of the muscles or joints. **orthopedic, orthopaedic** *adj* **orthopedist, orthopaedist** *n*

ortolan *n* small European bird eaten as a delicacy.

oryx *n* large African antelope.

Oscar *n* award in the form of a statuette given for achievements in films.

oscillate [oss-ill-late] v swing back and forth. **oscillation** n **oscillator** n **oscillatory** adj **oscilloscope** [oss-sill-oh-scope] n instrument that shows the shape of a wave on a cathode-ray tube.

osier [oh-zee-er] n willow tree; willow branch used in basketwork.

osmium n heaviest known metallic element.

osmosis n movement of a liquid through a membrane from a lower to a higher concentration; process of subtle influence. **osmotic** adj

osprey n large fish-eating bird of prey.

osseous adj made of or like bone.

ossify v **-fying, -fied** (cause to) become bone, harden; become inflexible. **ossification** n

ostensible adj apparent, seeming. **ostensibly** adv

ostentation n pretentious display. **ostentatious** adj **ostentatiously** adv

osteopathy n medical treatment involving manipulation of the joints. **osteopath** n

osteoporosis n brittleness of the bones, caused by lack of calcium.

ostracize v exclude (a person) from a group. **ostracism** n

ostrich n large African bird that runs fast but cannot fly.

OT Old Testament.

other adj remaining in a group of which one or some have been specified; different from the ones specified or understood; additional. ♦ n other person or thing. **otherwise** adv differently. ♦ conj or else, if not. **otherworldly** adj concerned with spiritual rather than practical matters.

otiose [oh-tee-oze] adj not useful, e.g. otiose language.

otter n small brown freshwater mammal that eats fish.

ottoman n, pl **-mans** storage chest with a padded lid for use as a seat. **Ottoman** n, adj Hist (member) of the former Turkish empire.

ouananiche [wah-ni-neesh] n variety of Atlantic salmon found only in lakes.

oubliette [oo-blee-ett] n dungeon entered only by a trapdoor.

ouch interj exclamation of sudden pain.

ought v (foll. by to) used to express: obligation, e.g. you ought to pay; advisability, e.g. you ought to diet; probability, e.g. you ought to know by then.

Ouija n ® lettered board on which supposed messages from the dead are spelt out.

ounce n unit of weight equal to one sixteenth of a pound (28.4 grams).

our adj belonging to us. **ours** pron thing(s) belonging to us. **ourselves** pron emphatic and reflexive form of WE or US.

oust v force (someone) out, expel.

out adv, adj away from inside; not at home; revealed or made public; used up; no longer burning or shining; not correct, e.g. the calculations were out; not fashionable; on strike; openly homosexual; Sport dismissed. ♦ v Informal name (a public figure) as being homosexual. **out of** at or to a point outside. **outer** adj on the outside. **outermost** adj furthest out. **outing** n leisure trip. **outward** adj apparent. ♦ adv (also **outwards**) away from somewhere. **outwardly** adv

out- prefix surpassing, e.g. outlive, outdistance.

outback n remote bush country of Australia.

outbid v offer a higher price than.

outboard motor n engine externally attached to the stern of a boat.

outbreak n sudden occurrence (of something unpleasant).

outburst n sudden expression of emotion.

outcast n person rejected by a particular group.

outclass v surpass in quality.

outcome n result.

outcrop n Geology area where bedrock is covered by little or no soil.

outcry n, pl **-cries** expression of vehement or widespread protest.

outdo v surpass in performance.

outdoors adv in(to) the open air. ♦ n the open air. **outdoor** adj

outface v subdue or disconcert (someone) by staring.

outfall n mouth of a river or pipe.

outfield n Baseball area beyond home plate and the three bases.

outfit n matching set of clothes;

Informal group of people working together. **outfitter** *n Old-fashioned* supplier of men's clothes.

outflank *v* get round the side of (an enemy army); outdo (someone).

outgoing *adj* leaving; sociable. **outgoings** *pl n* expenses.

outgrow *v* become too large or too old for. **outgrowth** *n* thing growing out from a main body; natural development.

outhouse *n* building near a main building.

outlandish *adj* extravagantly eccentric.

outlaw *n Hist* criminal deprived of legal protection, bandit. ◆ *v* make illegal; *Hist* make (someone) an outlaw.

outlay *n* expenditure.

outlet *n* means of expressing emotion; market for a product; place where a product is sold; opening or way out.

outline *n* line defining the shape of something; short general explanation. ◆ *v* draw the outline of; summarize.

outlook *n* attitude; probable outcome.

outlying *adj* distant from the main area.

outmanoeuvre *v* get an advantage over.

outmoded *adj* no longer fashionable or accepted.

outnumber *v* exceed in number.

outpatient *n* patient who does not stay in hospital overnight.

outport *n* isolated fishing village, esp. in Newfoundland.

outpost *n* outlying settlement.

output *n* amount produced; power, voltage, or current delivered by an electrical circuit; *Computers* data produced. ◆ *v Computers* produce (data) at the end of a process.

outrage *n* great moral indignation; gross violation of morality. ◆ *v* offend morally. **outrageous** *adj* shocking; offensive. **outrageously** *adv*

outré [oo-tray] *adj* shockingly eccentric.

outrider *n* motorcyclist acting as an escort.

outrigger *n* stabilizing frame projecting from a boat.

outright *adj, adv* absolute(ly); open (ly) and direct(ly).

outrun *v* run faster than; exceed.

outset *n* beginning.

outshine *v* surpass (someone) in excellence.

outside *prep* to the exterior of; beyond the limits of. ◆ *adj* exterior; unlikely, e.g. *an outside chance*; coming from outside. ◆ *adv* on or to the exterior; in(to) the open air. ◆ *n* external area or surface. **outsider** *n* person outside a specific group; contestant thought unlikely to win.

outsize, outsized *adj* larger than normal.

outskirts *pl n* outer areas, esp. of a town.

outsmart *v Informal* outwit.

outspoken *adj* tending to say what one thinks; said openly.

outstanding *adj* excellent; still to be dealt with or paid.

outstrip *v* go faster than; surpass.

outtake *n* unreleased take from a recording session or film.

outweigh *v* be more important, significant or influential than.

outwit *v* get the better of (someone) by cunning.

outworks *pl n* secondary external defences of a fort.

ouzel, ousel [ooze-el] *n* same as DIPPER (the bird).

ova *n* plural of OVUM.

oval *adj* egg-shaped. ◆ *n* anything that is oval in shape.

ovary *n, pl* **-ries** female egg-producing organ. **ovarian** *adj*

ovation *n* enthusiastic round of applause.

oven *n* heated compartment or container for cooking or for drying or firing ceramics.

over *prep* higher than; on or across the top of; on or to the other side of; during; more than; recovered from. ◆ *adv* above or across something; onto its side, e.g. *the jug toppled over*; in excess. ◆ *adj* finished. ◆ *n Cricket* series of six balls bowled from one end. **overly** *adv* excessively.

over- *prefix* too much, e.g. *overeat*; above, e.g. *overlord*; on top, e.g. *overshoe*.

overall *n* coat-shaped protective garment. ◆ *pl* protective garment consisting of trousers with a jacket or bib and braces attached. ◆ *adj, adv* in total.

overarm *adv, adj* (thrown) with the arm above the shoulder.

overawe *v* affect (someone) with an overpowering sense of awe.

overbalance *v* lose balance.

overbearing *adj* domineering.

overblown *adj* inflated or excessive, e.g. *overblown pride.*

overboard *adv* from a boat into the water. **go overboard** go to extremes, esp. in enthusiasm.

overcast *adj* (of the sky) covered by clouds.

overcoat *n* heavy coat.

overcome *v* gain control over after an effort; (of an emotion) affect strongly.

overdo *v* do to excess; exaggerate (something). **overdo it** do something to a greater degree than is advisable.

overdose *n* excessive dose of a drug. ◆ *v* take an overdose.

overdraft *n* overdrawing; amount overdrawn.

overdraw *v* withdraw more money than is in (one's bank account). **overdrawn** *adj* having overdrawn one's account; (of an account) in debit.

overdrive *n* very high gear in a motor vehicle.

overdue *adj* still due after the time allowed.

overgrown *adj* thickly covered with plants and weeds.

overhaul *v* examine and repair. ◆ *n* examination and repair.

overhead *adv* over the sky. ◆ *adj* over one's head. **overheads** *pl n* general cost of maintaining a business.

overhear *v* hear (a speaker or remark) unintentionally or without the speaker's knowledge.

overjoyed *adj* very pleased.

overkill *n* treatment that is greater than required.

overland *adj, adv* by land.

overlap *v* share part of the same space or period of time (as). ◆ *n* area overlapping.

overleaf *adv* on the back of the current page.

overlook *v* fail to notice; ignore; look at from above.

overnight *adj, adv* (taking place) during one night; (happening) very quickly.

overpower *v* subdue or overcome (someone).

overreach *v* **overreach oneself** fail by trying to be too clever.

override *v* overrule; replace.

overrule *v* reverse the decision of (a person with less power); reverse (someone else's decision).

overrun *v* spread over (a place) rapidly; extend beyond a set limit.

overseas *adj, adv* to, of, or from a distant country.

oversee *v* watch over from a position of authority. **overseer** *n*

overshadow *v* reduce the significance of (a person or thing) by comparison; sadden the atmosphere of.

oversight *n* mistake caused by not noticing something.

overspill *n* rehousing of people from crowded cities to smaller towns.

overstay *v* **overstay one's welcome** stay longer than one's host or hostess would like.

overt *adj* open. **overtly** *adv*

overtake *v* move past (a vehicle or person) while travelling in the same direction.

overthrow *v* defeat and replace. ◆ *n* downfall, destruction.

overtime *n, adv* (paid work done) in addition to one's normal working hours.

overtone *n* additional meaning.

overture *n Music* orchestral introduction. ◆ *pl* opening moves in a new relationship.

overturn *v* turn upside down; overrule (a legal decision); overthrow (a government).

overweight *adj* weighing more than is healthy.

overwhelm *v* overpower, esp. emotionally; defeat by force. **overwhelming** *adj* **overwhelmingly** *adv*

overwrought *adj* nervous and agitated.

oviparous [oh-**vip**-par-uss] *adj* producing young by laying eggs.

ovoid [oh-void] *adj* egg-shaped.

ovulate [ov-yew-late] *v* release an egg

cell from an ovary. **ovulation** n

ovum [oh-vum] n, pl **ova** unfertilized egg cell.

owe v be obliged to pay (a sum of money) to (a person). **owing to** as result of.

owl n night bird of prey. **owlish** adj **owlet** n young owl.

own adj used to emphasize possession, e.g. my own idea. ♦ v possess. **owner** n **ownership** n **own up** v confess.

ox n, pl **oxen** castrated bull.

oxeye n plant with daisy-like flowers.

oxide n compound of oxygen and one other element. **oxidize** v combine chemically with oxygen, as in burning or rusting.

oxygen n gaseous element essential to life and combustion. **oxygenate** v add oxygen to. **oxyacetylene** n mixture of oxygen and acetylene used in high-temperature welding.

oxymoron [ox-see-more-on] n figure of speech that combines two apparently contradictory ideas, such as cruel kindness.

oyez interj Hist (shouted three times by a public crier) listen.

oyster n edible shellfish. **oystercatcher** n wading bird with black-and-white feathers.

oz. ounce.

ozone n highly reactive strong-smelling form of oxygen. **ozone layer** layer of ozone in the upper atmosphere that filters out ultraviolet radiation.

P p

p page; Music piano.

P Chem phosphorus.

PA personal assistant; public-address system.

p.a. per annum.

pace n single step in walking; length of a step; rate of progress. ♦ v walk with regular steps; set the speed for (competitors in a race); cross or measure with steps. **put someone through his** or **her paces** test someone's ability. **pacemaker** n person who sets the speed of a race; electronic device surgically implanted

in a person with heart disease to regulate the heartbeat.

pachyderm [pak-ee-durm] n thick-skinned animal such as an elephant.

pacifist n person who refuses on principle to take part in war. **pacifism** n

pacify v **-fying, -fied** soothe, calm; establish peace in. **pacification** n **pacifier** n rubber or plastic teat for a baby to suck.

pack n load carried on the back; set of things sold together; container for things sold; same as PACKET; set of playing cards; group of hunting animals. ♦ v put (clothes etc.) together in a suitcase or bag; put (goods) into containers or parcels; press tightly together, cram; fill with things. **packhorse** n horse for carrying goods. **pack ice** mass of floating ice in the sea. **pack in** v Informal stop doing. **pack off** v send away.

package n parcel; set of things offered together. ♦ v put into packages. **packaging** n **package holiday** holiday in which everything is arranged by one company for a fixed price.

packet n small parcel; small container (and contents); Brit slang large sum of money. **packet boat** Hist boat that carried mail, goods, or passengers on a fixed short route.

packsack n canvas bag carried on the back or shoulder.

pact n formal agreement.

pad n piece of soft material used for protection, support, absorption of liquid, etc.; block of sheets of paper fastened at the edge; fleshy underpart of an animal's paw; place for launching rockets; Slang home. ♦ v **padding, padded** protect or fill in with soft material; walk with soft or muffled steps. **padding** n material used to pad; words put in simply to increase length.

paddle¹ n short oar with a broad blade at one or each end. ♦ v move (a canoe etc.) with a paddle. **paddle steamer** ship propelled by paddle wheels. **paddle wheel** wheel with crosswise blades that strike the water successively to propel a ship.

paddle² v walk with bare feet in shallow water.

paddock *n* small field or enclosure for horses.

paddy field *n* field where rice is grown.

padlock *n* detachable lock with a hinged hoop fastened over a ring on the object to be secured.

padre [**pah**-dray] *n* chaplain in the armed forces.

paean [**pee**-an] *n* song of triumph or thanksgiving.

paediatrics *n* same as PEDIATRICS.

paedophilia *n* same as PEDOPHILIA.

paella [pie-**ell**-a] *n* Spanish dish made of rice, chicken, shellfish, and vegetables.

pagan *adj* not belonging to one of the world's main religions. ◆ *n* pagan person.

page¹ *n* (one side of) a sheet of paper forming a book etc.

page² *n* Hist boy in training for knighthood; attendant. ◆ *v* summon (a person whose whereabouts are unknown), for example by electronic bleeper or loudspeaker announcement.

pageant *n* parade or display of people in costume, usu. illustrating a scene from history. **pageantry** *n*

paginate *v* number the pages of (a book etc.). **pagination** *n*

pagoda *n* pyramid-shaped Asian temple or tower.

paid *v* past of PAY. **put paid to** *Informal* end, destroy.

pail *n* bucket. **pailful** *n*

pain *n* bodily or mental suffering. ◆ *pl* trouble, effort. **on pain of** subject to the penalty of. **painful** *adj* **painfully** *adv* **painless** *adj* **painlessly** *adv* **painkiller** *n* drug that reduces pain.

painstaking *adj* thorough and careful.

paint *n* colouring spread on a surface with a brush or roller. ◆ *v* colour or coat with paint; make a picture of. **painter** *n* **painting** *n*

painter *n* rope at the bow of a boat for tying it up.

pair *n* set of two things. ◆ *v* group or be grouped in twos.

paisley pattern *n* pattern of small curving shapes.

pajamas *pl n* same as PYJAMAS.

pal *n* Informal friend.

palace *n* residence of a king, bishop, etc.; large grand building.

palatable *adj* pleasant to eat.

palate *n* roof of the mouth; sense of taste.

palatial *adj* like a palace; magnificent.

palaver [pal-**lah**-ver] *n* time-wasting fuss.

pale¹ *adj* light; having less colour than normal. ◆ *v* become pale.

pale² *n* Hist fence; boundary. **beyond the pale** outside the limits of social convention.

paleography, palaeography [pal-ee-**og**-ra-fee] *n* study of ancient writings.

paleolithic, palaeolithic [pal-ee-oh-**lith**-ik] *adj* of the Old Stone Age.

paleontology, palaeontology [pal-ee-on-**tol**-a-jee] *n* study of past geological periods and fossils. **paleontological, palaeontological** *adj*

palette *n* artist's flat board for mixing colours on.

palindrome *n* word, phrase, or sentence that reads the same backwards as forwards.

paling *n* any of the upright planks in a fence.

palisade *n* fence made of stakes.

pall¹ *n* cloth spread over a coffin; depressing oppressive atmosphere; dark cloud (of smoke). **pallbearer** *n* person carrying a coffin at a funeral.

pall² *v* become boring.

pallet¹ *n* portable platform for storing and moving goods.

pallet² *n* straw mattress; small bed.

palliasse *n* straw mattress.

palliate *v* lessen the severity of (something) without curing it. **palliative** *adj* giving temporary or partial relief. ◆ *n* something, for example a drug, that palliates.

pallid *adj* pale, esp. because ill or weak. **pallor** *n*

pally *adj* **-lier, -liest** Informal on friendly terms.

palm *n* inner surface of the hand; tropical tree with a straight trunk crowned with long pointed leaves. **palm off** *v* get rid of (an unwanted thing or person), esp. by deceit. **Palm Sunday** the Sunday before Easter. **palmtop** *n* computer small enough to be held in the hand.

palmistry n fortune-telling from lines on the palm of the hand. **palmist** n

palomino n, pl **-nos** gold-coloured horse with a white mane and tail.

palpable adj obvious; able to be touched or felt. **palpably** adv

palpate v Med examine (an area of the body) by touching.

palpitate v (of the heart) beat rapidly; flutter. **palpitation** n

palsy [pawl-zee] n paralysis. **palsied** adj affected with palsy.

paltry adj **-trier, -triest** worthless, insignificant.

pampas pl n vast grassy treeless plains in S America. **pampas grass** tall grass with feathery ornamental flower branches.

pamper v treat (someone) with great indulgence, spoil.

pamphlet n thin paper-covered booklet. **pamphleteer** n writer of pamphlets.

pan¹ n wide long-handled metal container used in cooking; Brit bowl of a lavatory. ♦ v **panning, panned** sift gravel (in a riverbed) in a pan to search for gold; Informal criticize harshly. **pan out** v result.

pan² v **panning, panned** move a film camera slowly so as to cover a whole scene or follow a moving object.

pan- combining form all, e.g. pan-African.

panacea [pan-a-see-a] n remedy for all diseases or problems.

panache [pan-ash] n confident elegant style.

panama n straw hat.

panatella n long slender cigar.

pancake n thin flat circle of fried batter.

panchromatic adj Photog sensitive to light of all colours.

pancreas [pang-kree-ass] n large gland behind the stomach that produces insulin and helps digestion. **pancreatic** adj

panda n large black-and-white bearlike mammal from China.

pandemic adj (of a disease) occurring over a wide area.

pandemonium n wild confusion; uproar.

pander n person who procures a sexual partner for someone. **pander to** v indulge (a person or his or her desires).

pane n single piece of glass in a window or door.

panegyric [pan-ee-jire-ik] n formal speech or piece of writing in praise of someone or something.

panel n flat distinct section of a larger surface, such as that in a door; group of people as a team in a quiz etc.; list of jurors, doctors, etc. ♦ v **-elling, -elled** decorate or cover with panels. **panelling** n panels collectively, such as those on a wall. **panellist** n member of a panel. **panel beater** person who repairs damage to car bodies.

pang n sudden sharp feeling of pain or sadness.

pangolin n scaly anteater.

panic n sudden overwhelming fear, often infectious. ♦ v **-icking, -icked** feel or cause to feel panic. **panicky** adj **panic-stricken, -struck** adj

pannier n bag fixed on the back of a bike or motorbike; basket carried by a beast of burden.

panoply [pan-a-plee] n magnificent array.

panorama n wide or complete view. **panoramic** adj

pansy n, pl **-sies** garden flower with velvety petals; Offens effeminate or homosexual man.

pant v breathe quickly and noisily after exertion.

pantaloons pl n baggy trousers gathered at the ankles.

pantechnicon n large van for furniture removals.

pantheism n belief that God is present in everything. **pantheist** n **pantheistic** adj

pantheon n (in ancient Greece and Rome) temple to all the gods.

panther n leopard, esp. a black one.

panties pl n women's underpants.

pantile n roofing tile with an S-shaped cross section.

pantograph n instrument for copying maps etc. to any scale; device on the roof of an electric train for picking up the electric current.

pantomime n play based on a fairy tale, performed in Britain at Christmas time.

pantry n, pl **-tries** room or cupboard

for storing food or cooking utensils.

pants pl n undergarment for the lower part of the body; trousers.

pap[1] n soft food for babies or invalids; worthless ideas.

pap[2] n Obs nipple.

papacy [pay-pa-see] n, pl -cies the position or term of office of a pope. **papal** adj of the pope or papacy.

paparazzo [pap-a-rat-so] n, pl -razzi photographer specializing in unposed shots of famous people.

papaya [pa-pie-ya], **papaw** [pa-paw] n large sweet West Indian fruit.

paper n material made in sheets from wood pulp or other fibres; printed sheet of this; newspaper; set of examination questions; article or essay. ◆ pl personal documents. ◆ v cover (walls) with wallpaper. **paperback** n book with flexible paper covers. **paperweight** n heavy decorative object placed on top of loose papers. **paperwork** n the part of a job that consists of dealing with routine letters, forms, etc.

papier-mâché [pap-yay mash-ay] n material made from paper mixed with paste, shaped by moulding and dried hard.

papist n, adj Offens Roman Catholic.

papoose n N American Indian baby or toddler.

paprika n (powdered seasoning made from) a type of red pepper.

papyrus [pap-ire-uss] n, pl -ri, -ruses tall water plant; (manuscript written on) a kind of paper made from this plant.

par n usual or average condition; face value of stocks and shares; Golf expected standard score. **on a par with** equal to.

parable n story that illustrates a religious teaching.

parabola [par-ab-bol-a] n regular curve resembling the course of an object thrown forward and up. **parabolic** adj

paracetamol n mild pain-relieving drug.

parachute n large fabric canopy that slows the descent of a person or object from an aircraft. ◆ v land or drop by parachute. **parachutist** n

parade n ordered march or

procession; public promenade or street of shops; blatant display, e.g. parade of one's grief. ◆ v display or flaunt; march in procession.

paradigm [par-a-dime] n example or model.

paradise n heaven; state of bliss; Garden of Eden.

paradox n statement that seems self-contradictory but may be true. **paradoxical** adj **paradoxically** adv

paraffin n waxy substance derived from petroleum and used as a solvent, etc.

paragliding n cross-country gliding using a parachute.

paragon n model of perfection.

paragraph n section of a piece of writing starting on a new line.

parakeet n small long-tailed parrot.

parallax n apparent difference in an object's position or direction as viewed from different points.

parallel adj separated by equal distance at every point; precisely corresponding. ◆ n line equidistant from another at all points; thing with similar features to another; line of latitude. ◆ v be parallel to; correspond to. **parallelism** n

parallelogram n four-sided geometric figure with opposite sides parallel.

paralysis n inability to move or feel, because of damage to the nervous system. **paralyse** v affect with paralysis; make immobile. **paralytic** n, adj (person) affected with paralysis.

paramedic n person working in support of the medical profession. **paramedical** adj

parameter [par-am-it-er] n limiting factor, boundary.

paramilitary adj organized on military lines.

paramount adj of the greatest importance or significance.

paramour n Obs mistress.

paranoia n mental illness causing delusions of fame or persecution; Informal intense fear or suspicion. **paranoiac, paranoid** adj, n

paranormal adj beyond scientific explanation.

parapet n low wall or railing along the edge of a balcony, bridge, etc.

paraphernalia *n* personal belongings or bits of equipment.

paraphrase *v* express (meaning) in different words.

paraplegia [par-a-**pleej**-ya] *n* paralysis of the lower half of the body. **paraplegic** *n, adj*

parapsychology *n* study of phenomena outside normal human ability, such as telepathy.

parasite *n* animal or plant living in or on another; person who lives at the expense of others, sponger. **parasitic** *adj*

parasol *n* umbrella-like sunshade.

paratroops, -troopers *pl n* troops trained to attack by descending by parachute.

parboil *v* boil until partly cooked.

parcel *n* something wrapped up, a package. ◆ *v* **-celling, -celled** wrap up. **parcel out** *v* divide into parts.

parch *v* make very hot and dry; make thirsty.

parchment *n* thick smooth writing material made from animal skin.

pardon *v* forgive or excuse. ◆ *n* forgiveness; official release from punishment. **pardonable** *adj* **pardonably** *adv*

pare *v* trim or cut the edge of. **paring** *n* piece pared off.

parent *n* father or mother. **parental** *adj* **parenthood** *n* **parentage** *n* ancestry or family. **parenting** *n* activity of bringing up children.

parenthesis [par-en-**thiss**-iss] *n, pl* **-ses** word or sentence inserted in a passage, usu. marked off by brackets, dashes, or commas. ◆ *pl* round brackets, ( ). **parenthetical** *adj*

pargeting *n* ornamental plasterwork on the outside of a house.

pariah [par-**rye**-a] *n* social outcast.

parietal [par-**rye**-it-al] *adj* of the walls of body cavities such as the skull.

parish *n* area that has its own church and clergyman. **parishioner** *n* inhabitant of a parish.

parity *n* equality or equivalence.

park *n* area of open land for recreational use by the public; area containing a number of related businesses; large enclosed piece of ground attached to a country house. ◆ *v* stop and leave (a vehicle) temporarily. **parking lot** area or building where vehicles may be left for a time.

parka *n* warm waterproof hooded jacket.

parkade *n* a building used as a car park.

parkette *n* a small public park.

parlance *n* particular way of speaking, idiom.

parley *n* meeting between leaders or representatives of opposing forces to discuss terms. ◆ *v* have a parley.

parliament *n* law-making assembly of a country. **parliamentary** *adj*

parlour, parlor *n* Old-fashioned living room for receiving visitors.

parlous *adj Obs* dangerous.

Parmesan *n* hard strong-flavoured Italian cheese.

parochial *adj* narrow in outlook; of a parish. **parochialism** *n*

parody *n, pl* **-dies** exaggerated and amusing imitation of someone else's style. ◆ *v* **-dying, -died** make a parody of.

parole *n* early freeing of a prisoner on condition that he or she behaves well. ◆ *v* place on parole. **on parole** (of a prisoner) released on condition that he or she behaves well.

paroxysm *n* uncontrollable outburst, as of laughter; spasm or convulsion, as of pain.

parquet [par-**kay**] *n* wooden blocks arranged in a pattern and forming a floor. **parquetry** *n*

parricide *n* person who kills one of his or her parents; act of killing either of one's parents.

parrot *n* tropical bird with a short hooked beak, some varieties of which can imitate speaking. ◆ *v* **-roting, -roted** repeat (words) without thinking.

parry *v* **-rying, -ried** ward off (an attack); cleverly avoid (an awkward question).

parse [parz] *v* analyse (a sentence) in terms of grammar.

parsec *n* unit of length used in expressing the distance of stars.

parsimony *n* stinginess. **parsimonious** *adj*

parsley *n* herb used for seasoning and decorating food.

parsnip n long tapering cream-coloured root vegetable.

parson n parish priest in the Anglican Church. **parsonage** n parson's house. **parson's nose** rump of a cooked fowl.

part n piece or portion; one of several equal divisions; actor's role; region, area; component of a vehicle or machine; division between sections of hair on the head. ♦ v divide; (of people) leave each other. **take someone's part** support someone in an argument etc. **take something in good part** respond (to criticism etc.) with good humour. **parting** n separation; leave-taking. **partly** adv not completely. **part of speech** particular grammatical class of words, such as noun or verb. **part song** song for several voices singing in harmony. **part-time** adj occupying or working less than the full working week. **part with** v give up ownership of.

partake v -taking, -took, -taken (foll. by of) take food or drink; (foll. by in) take part in.

parterre n formally patterned flower garden.

partial adj not general or complete; prejudiced. **partial to** very fond of. **partiality** n favouritism; fondness for. **partially** adv

participate v become actively involved in. **participant** n **participation** n **participator** n

participle n form of a verb used in compound tenses or as an adjective, e.g. worried, worrying. **participial** adj

particle n extremely small piece or amount; Physics minute piece of matter, such as a proton or electron.

parti-coloured adj differently coloured in different parts.

particular adj relating to one person or thing, not general; exceptional or special; very exact; not easily satisfied, fastidious. ♦ n detail; item of information. **particularly** adv **particularize** v give details about. **particularity** n

Parti Quebecois [par-tee kay-beck-wah] n political party in Quebec originally advocating separation of Quebec from rest of country.

partisan n strong supporter of a party or group; guerrilla, member of a resistance movement. ♦ adj prejudiced or one-sided.

partition n screen or thin wall that divides a room; division of a country into independent parts. ♦ v divide with a partition.

partner n either member of a couple in a relationship or activity; member of a business partnership. ♦ v be the partner of (someone). **partnership** n joint business venture between two or more people.

partridge n game bird of the grouse family.

parturition n act of giving birth.

party n, pl -ties social gathering for pleasure; group of people travelling or working together; group of people with a common political aim; person or people forming one side in a lawsuit etc. **party line** official view of a political party. **party wall** common wall separating adjoining buildings.

parvenu [par-ven-new] n person newly risen to a position of power or wealth, upstart.

pascal n unit of pressure.

paschal [pass-kal] adj of the Passover or Easter.

pass v go by, beyond, through, etc.; be successful in a test etc.; spend (time) or (of time) elapse; exchange; be inherited by; bring (a law) into force; move onwards or over; exceed; choose not to take one's turn in a game or quiz; discharge (urine etc.) from the body; come to an end; Sport transfer (the ball) to another player. ♦ n successful result in a test; Sport transfer of a ball; permit or licence; narrow gap through mountains. **make a pass at** Informal try to start a sexual relationship. **passable** adj (just) acceptable; (of a road) capable of being travelled along. **passing** adj brief or transitory; cursory or casual. **pass away** v die. **pass out** v Informal faint. **pass up** v Informal ignore or reject.

passage n channel or opening providing a way through; hall or corridor; section of a book etc.; journey by sea; right or freedom to pass. **passageway** n corridor.

passé [pas-say] adj out-of-date.

passenger n person travelling in a vehicle driven by someone else; one of a team who does not pull his or her weight.

passer-by n, pl **passers-by** person who is walking past something or someone.

passerine adj belonging to the order of perching birds.

passim adv Latin everywhere.

passion n intense sexual love; any strong emotion; great enthusiasm; (P-) Christianity the suffering of Christ. **passionate** adj **passionflower** n tropical American plant. **passion fruit** edible fruit of the passionflower. **Passion play** play about Christ's suffering.

passive adj not playing an active part; submissive and receptive to outside forces; Grammar denoting a form of verbs indicating that the subject receives the action, such as was jeered in He was jeered by the crowd. **passive resistance** resistance to a government, law, etc. by nonviolent acts. **passive smoking** inhalation of smoke from others' cigarettes by a nonsmoker.

Passover n Jewish festival commemorating the sparing of the Jews in Egypt.

passport n official document granting permission to travel abroad.

password n secret word or phrase that ensures admission.

past adj of the time before the present; ended, gone by; (of a verb tense) indicating that the action specified took place earlier. ◆ n bygone times; person's past life, esp. an earlier, disreputable period; past tense. ◆ adv by; along. ◆ prep beyond. **past it** Informal unable to do the things one could do when younger. **past master** person with great talent or experience in a particular subject.

pasta n type of food, such as spaghetti, that is made in different shapes from flour and water.

paste n moist soft mixture, such as toothpaste; adhesive, esp. for paper; pastry dough; shiny glass used to make imitation jewellery. ◆ v fasten with paste. **pasting** n Slang defeat; strong criticism. **pasteboard** n stiff thick paper.

pastel n coloured chalk crayon for drawing; picture drawn in pastels; pale delicate colour. ◆ adj pale and delicate in colour.

pasteurize v sterilize by heat. **pasteurization** n

pastiche [pass-teesh] n work of art that mixes styles or copies the style of another artist.

pastille n small fruit-flavoured and sometimes medicated candy.

pastime n activity that makes time pass pleasantly.

pastor n clergyman in charge of a congregation. **pastoral** adj of or depicting country life; of a clergyman or his duties.

pastrami n highly seasoned smoked beef.

pastry n, pl **-ries** baking dough made of flour, fat, and water; cake or pie.

pasture n grassy land for farm animals to graze on. **pasturage** n (right to) pasture.

pasty[1] [pay-stee] adj **pastier, pastiest** (of a complexion) pale and unhealthy.

pasty[2] [pass-tee] n, pl **pasties** round of pastry folded over a savoury filling.

pat v **patting, patted** tap lightly. ◆ n gentle tap or stroke; small shaped mass of butter etc. ◆ adj quick, ready, or glib. **off pat** learned thoroughly.

patch n piece of material sewn on a garment; small contrasting section; plot of ground; protecting pad for the eye. ◆ v mend with a patch; repair clumsily. **patchy** adj of uneven quality or intensity. **patch up** v make up (a quarrel). **patchwork** n needlework made of pieces of different materials sewn together.

pate n Old-fashioned head.

pâté [pat-ay] n spread of finely minced liver etc.

patella n, pl **-lae** kneecap.

paten [pat-in] n plate for bread in Communion.

patent n document giving the exclusive right to make or sell an invention. ◆ adj open to public inspection, e.g. letters patent; obvious; protected by a patent. ◆ v obtain a patent for. **patently** adv obviously. **patent leather** leather processed to give a hard glossy surface.

paternal adj fatherly; related through one's father. **paternity** n relation of a father to his offspring; fatherhood. **paternalism** n authority exercised in a way that limits individual responsibility. **paternalistic** *adj*

Paternoster *n RC Church* the Lord's Prayer.

path *n* surfaced walk or track; course of action.

pathetic *adj* causing feelings of pity or sadness; distressingly inadequate. **pathetically** *adv*

pathogen *n* thing that causes disease. **pathogenic** *adj*

pathology *n* scientific study of diseases. **pathological** *adj* of pathology; *Informal* compulsively motivated. **pathologist** *n*

pathos *n* power of arousing pity or sadness.

patient *adj* enduring difficulties calmly. ◆ *n* person receiving medical treatment. **patience** *n* quality of being patient; card game for one.

patina *n* fine layer on a surface; sheen of age on woodwork.

patio *n, pl* **-tios** paved area adjoining a house.

patois [pat-wah] *n, pl* **patois** [pat-wahz] regional dialect.

patriarch *n* male head of a family or tribe; highest-ranking bishop in Orthodox Churches. **patriarchal** *adj* **patriarchy** *n* society in which men have most of the power.

patriate *v* pass (powers) from the control of a colonial government to that of the region to which they apply.

patrician *n* member of the nobility, esp. of ancient Rome. ◆ *adj* of noble birth.

patricide *n* crime of killing one's father; person who does this.

patrimony *n, pl* **-nies** property inherited from ancestors.

patriot *n* person who loves his or her country and supports its interests. **patriotic** *adj* **patriotism** *n*

patrol *n* regular circuit by a guard; person or small group patrolling; unit of Scouts or Guides. ◆ *v* **-trolling, -trolled** go round on guard, or reconnoitring.

patron *n* person who gives (financial) support to charities, artists, etc.; regular customer of a shop, pub, etc. **patronage** *n* support given by a patron. **patronize** *v* treat in a condescending way; be a patron of. **patron saint** saint regarded as the

guardian of a country or group.

patronymic *n* name derived from one's father or a male ancestor.

patten *n Hist* type of clog.

patter *v* make repeated soft tapping sounds. ◆ *n* quick succession of taps; glib rapid speech.

pattern *n* arrangement of repeated parts or decorative designs; regular way something is done; diagram or shape used as a guide to make something. ◆ *v* (foll. by *on*) make or do on the model of. **patterned** *adj* decorated with a pattern.

patty *n, pl* **-ties** small pie; minced meat formed into a small disc.

paucity *n* scarcity; smallness of amount or number.

paunch *n* belly.

pauper *n* very poor person.

pause *v* stop for a time. ◆ *n* stop or rest.

pave *v* form (a surface) with stone or brick. **pavement** *n* paved surface of road or street; *Brit* sidewalk.

pavilion *n* clubhouse on a playing field etc.; building for housing an exhibition etc.

paw *n* animal's foot with claws and pads. ◆ *v* scrape with the paw or hoof; handle roughly; stroke in an overfamiliar way.

pawn[1] *v* deposit (an article) as security for money borrowed. **in pawn** deposited as security with a pawnbroker. **pawnbroker** *n* lender of money on goods deposited.

pawn[2] *n* chessman of the lowest value; person manipulated by someone else.

pay *v* **paying, paid** give (money) in return for goods or services; settle (a debt or obligation); compensate (for); give, bestow; be profitable to. ◆ *n* wages or salary. **payment** *n* act of paying; money paid. **payable** *adj* due to be paid. **payee** *n* person to whom money is paid or due. **paying guest** lodger. **pay off** *v* pay (debt) in full; turn out successfully. **pay out** *v* spend; release (a rope) bit by bit.

payload *n* passengers or cargo of an aircraft; explosive power of a missile etc.

payola *n Informal* bribe to get special treatment, esp. to promote a commercial product.

Pb *Chem* lead.

pc per cent; postcard.

PC personal computer; Police Constable; politically correct; Privy Councillor.

PDA personal digital assistant.

PDT Pacific Daylight Time.

PE physical education; Prince Edward Island.

pea *n* climbing plant with seeds growing in pods; its seed, eaten as a vegetable. **pea-green** *adj* yellowish-green. **peasouper** *n Informal* thick fog.

peace *n* stillness or silence; absence of anxiety; freedom from war; harmony between people. **peaceable** *adj* inclined towards peace. **peaceably** *adv* **peaceful** *adj* **peacefully** *adv*

peach *n* soft juicy fruit with a stone and a downy skin; *Informal* very pleasing person or thing. ♦ *adj* pinkish-orange.

peacock *n* large male bird with a brilliantly coloured fanlike tail. **peahen** *n fem* **peafowl** *n* peacock or peahen.

peak *n* pointed top, esp. of a mountain; point of greatest development etc.; projecting piece on the front of a cap. ♦ *adj* of or at the point of greatest demand. ♦ *v* (cause to) form or reach peaks. **peaked** *adj* **peaky** *adj Informal* looking pale and sickly.

peal *n* long loud echoing sound, esp. of bells or thunder. ♦ *v* sound with a peal or peals.

peanut *n* pea-shaped nut that ripens underground. ♦ *pl Informal* trifling amount of money.

pear *n* sweet juicy fruit with a narrow top and rounded base.

pearl *n* hard round lustrous object found inside some oyster shells and used as a jewel. **pearly** *adj*

peasant *n* (in some countries) farmer or farmworker of a low social class. **peasantry** *n* peasants collectively.

peat *n* decayed vegetable material found in bogs, used as fertilizer or fuel.

pebble *n* small roundish stone. **pebbly** *adj*

pecan [pee-kan] *n* edible nut of a N American tree.

peccadillo *n, pl* **-los, -loes** trivial misdeed.

peccary *n, pl* **-ries** wild pig of American forests.

peck *v* strike or pick up with the beak; *Informal* kiss quickly. ♦ *n* pecking movement. **peckish** *adj Informal* hungry. **peck at** *v* nibble, eat reluctantly.

pectin *n* substance in fruit that makes jam set.

pectoral *adj* of the chest or thorax. ♦ *n* pectoral muscle or fin.

peculation *n* embezzlement, theft.

peculiar *adj* strange; distinct, special; belonging exclusively to. **peculiarity** *n* oddity, eccentricity; characteristic.

pecuniary *adj* relating to, or consisting of, money.

pedagogue *n* schoolteacher, esp. a pedantic one.

pedal *n* foot-operated lever used to control a vehicle or machine, or to modify the tone of a musical instrument. ♦ *v* **-alling, -alled** propel (a bicycle) by using its pedals.

pedant *n* person who is overconcerned with details and rules, esp. in academic work. **pedantic** *adj* **pedantry** *n*

peddle *v* sell (goods) from door to door. **peddler** *n* person who sells illegal drugs.

pederast *n* man who has homosexual relations with boys. **pederasty** *n*

pedestal *n* base supporting a column, statue, etc.

pedestrian *n* person who is walking, esp. in a street. ♦ *adj* dull. **pedestrian crossing** crosswalk. **pedestrian precinct** (shopping) area for pedestrians only.

pediatrics, paediatrics *n* branch of medicine concerned with diseases of children. **pediatrician, paediatrician** *n*

pedicel *n* small short stalk of a leaf, flower, or fruit.

pedicure *n* medical or cosmetic treatment of the feet.

pedigree *n* register of ancestors, esp. of a purebred animal.

pediment *n* triangular part over a door etc.

pedlar *n* person who sells goods from door to door.

pedometer [pid-dom-it-er] *n* instrument which measures the distance walked.

pedophilia, paedophilia *n*

condition of being sexually attracted to children. **pedophile, paedophile** n person who is sexually attracted to children.

peduncle n flower stalk; Anat stalklike structure.

pee Informal ◆ v **peeing, peed** urinate. ◆ n urinating.

peek v, n peep or glance.

peel v remove the skin or rind of (a vegetable or fruit); (of skin or a surface) come off in flakes. ◆ n rind or skin. **peelings** pl n

peep¹ v look slyly or quickly. ◆ n peeping look. **Peeping Tom** man who furtively watches women undressing.

peep² v make a small shrill noise. ◆ n small shrill noise.

peer¹ n (fem **peeress**) nobleman; person of the same status, age, etc. **peerage** n whole body of peers; rank of a peer. **peerless** adj unequalled, unsurpassed. **peer group** group of people of similar age, status, etc.

peer² v look closely and intently.

peeved adj Informal annoyed.

peevish adj fretful; irritable. **peevishly** adv **peevishness** n

peewit n same as LAPWING.

peg n pin or clip for joining, fastening, marking, etc.; hook or knob for hanging things on. ◆ v **pegging, pegged** fasten with pegs; stabilize (prices). **off the peg** (of clothes) ready-to-wear.

P.E.I. Prince Edward Island.

peignoir [pay-nwahr] n woman's light dressing gown.

pejorative [pij-jor-a-tiv] adj (of words etc.) with an insulting or critical connotation.

Pekingese, Pekinese n, pl **-ese** small dog with a short wrinkled muzzle.

pelargonium n plant with red, white, or pink flowers.

pelican n large water bird with a pouch beneath its bill for storing fish.

pellagra n disease caused by lack of vitamin B.

pellet n small ball of something.

pell-mell adv in utter confusion, headlong.

pellucid adj very clear.

pelmet n ornamental drapery or board, concealing a curtain rail.

pelt¹ v throw missiles at; run fast, rush; rain heavily. **at full pelt** at top speed.

pelt² n skin of a fur-bearing animal.

pelvis n framework of bones at the base of the spine, to which the hips are attached. **pelvic** adj

pemmican n dried lean meat and melted fat pounded into paste and used as food for a long journey.

pen¹ n instrument for writing in ink. ◆ v **penning, penned** write or compose. **pen friend** friend with whom a person corresponds without meeting. **penknife** n small knife with blade(s) that fold into the handle. **pen name** name used by an author instead of his or her real name.

pen² n small enclosure for domestic animals. ◆ v **penning, penned** put or keep in a pen.

pen³ n female swan.

penal [pee-nal] adj of or used in punishment. **penalize** v impose a penalty on; handicap, hinder. **penalty** n punishment for a crime or offence; Sport handicap or disadvantage imposed for an infringement of a rule.

penance n voluntary self-punishment to make amends for wrongdoing.

pence n a plural of PENNY.

penchant [pon-shon] n liking.

pencil n thin cylindrical instrument containing graphite, for writing or drawing. ◆ v **-cilling, -cilled** draw, write, or mark with a pencil.

pendant n ornament worn on a chain round the neck.

pendent adj hanging.

pending prep while waiting for. ◆ adj not yet decided or settled.

pendulous adj hanging, swinging.

pendulum n suspended weight swinging to and fro, esp. as a regulator for a clock.

penetrate v find or force a way into or through; arrive at the meaning of. **penetrable** adj capable of being penetrated. **penetrating** adj quick to understand; (of a sound) loud and unpleasant. **penetration** n

penguin n flightless black-and-white Antarctic sea bird.

penicillin n antibiotic drug effective against a wide range of diseases and infections.

peninsula n strip of land nearly

surrounded by water. **peninsular** adj

penis n organ of copulation and urination in male mammals.

penitent adj feeling sorry for having done wrong. ♦ n someone who is penitent. **penitence** n **penitentiary** n prison. ♦ adj (also **penitential**) relating to penance.

pennant n long narrow flag.

pennon n small triangular or swallow-tailed flag.

penny n, pl **pence, pennies** one cent; Brit bronze coin now worth one hundredth of a pound. **penniless** adj having no money; poor.

penology [pee-**nol**-a-jee] n study of punishment and prison management.

pension[1] n regular payment to people above a certain age, retired employees, widows, etc. **pensionable** adj **pensioner** n person receiving a pension. **pension off** v force (someone) to retire from a job and pay him or her a pension.

pension[2] [**pon**-syon] n boarding house in Europe.

pensive adj deeply thoughtful, often with a tinge of sadness.

pentacle, pentagram n five-pointed star.

pentagon n geometric figure with five sides; (P-) headquarters of the US military. **pentagonal** adj

pentameter [pen-**tam**-it-er] n line of poetry with five metrical feet.

Pentateuch [**pent**-a-tyuke] n first five books of the Old Testament.

pentathlon n athletic event consisting of five sports.

Pentecost n Christian festival celebrating the descent of the Holy Spirit to the apostles, Whitsuntide; Jewish harvest festival fifty days after Passover.

penthouse n apartment built on the roof or top floor of a building.

pent-up adj (of an emotion) not released, repressed.

penultimate adj second last.

penumbra n, pl **-brae, -bras** partial shadow; (in an eclipse) the partially shadowed region which surrounds the full shadow. **penumbral** adj

penury n extreme poverty. **penurious** adj

peony n, pl **-nies** garden plant with showy red, pink, or white flowers.

people pl n persons generally; the community; one's family or ancestors. ♦ sing race or nation. ♦ v stock with inhabitants; populate.

pep n Informal high spirits, energy or enthusiasm. **pep talk** Informal talk designed to increase confidence, enthusiasm, etc. **pep up** v stimulate, invigorate.

pepper n sharp hot condiment made from the fruit of an East Indian climbing plant; colourful tropical fruit used as a vegetable, capsicum. ♦ v season with pepper; sprinkle, dot; pelt with missiles. **peppery** adj tasting of pepper; irritable. **peppercorn** n dried berry of the pepper plant. **peppercorn rent** low or nominal rent.

peppermint n plant that yields an oil with a strong sharp flavour; candy flavoured with this.

peptic adj relating to digestion or the digestive juices.

Péquiste [pay-**keest**] n member or supporter of Parti Quebecois.

per prep for each; in the manner of.

perambulate v walk through or about (a place). **perambulation** n **perambulator** n Brit baby carriage.

per annum adv Latin in each year.

percale n woven cotton used esp. for sheets.

per capita adj, adv Latin of or for each person.

perceive v become aware of (something) through the senses; understand.

percentage n proportion or rate per hundred. **per cent** in each hundred.

perceptible adj discernible, recognizable.

perception n act of perceiving; intuitive judgment. **perceptive** adj

perch[1] n resting place for a bird. ♦ v alight, rest, or place on or as if on a perch.

perch[2] n edible freshwater fish.

perchance adv Old-fashioned perhaps.

percipient adj quick to notice things, observant. **percipience** n

percolate v pass or filter through small holes; permeate; make (coffee) or (of coffee) be made in a percolator. **percolation** n **percolator** n coffeepot in which boiling water is forced through a tube and filters down through coffee.

percussion *n* striking of one thing against another. **percussion instrument** musical instrument played by being struck, such as drums or cymbals.

perdition *n* spiritual ruin.

peregrination *n* travels, roaming.

peregrine *n* falcon with dark upper parts and a light underside.

peremptory *adj* authoritative.

perennial *adj* lasting through the years; recurring perpetually. ♦ *n* plant lasting more than two years. **perennially** *adv*

perestroika *n* formerly, policy of restructuring the Soviet economy and political system.

perfect *adj* having all the essential elements, complete; unspoilt; faultless; correct, precise; excellent. ♦ *n* *Grammar* tense of verb describing an action that has been completed. ♦ *v* improve; make fully correct. **perfectly** *adv* **perfection** *n* state of being perfect. **perfectionist** *n* person who demands the highest standards of excellence. **perfectionism** *n*

perfidy *n*, *pl* **-dies** treachery, disloyalty. **perfidious** *adj*

perforate *v* make holes in. **perforation** *n*

perforce *adv* of necessity.

perform *v* carry out (an action); fulfil (a request etc.); act, sing, or present a play before an audience; work or function. **performance** *n* **performer** *n*

perfume *n* liquid cosmetic worn for its pleasant smell; fragrance. ♦ *v* give a pleasant smell to. **perfumery** *n* perfumes in general.

perfunctory *adj* done only as a matter of routine, superficial. **perfunctorily** *adv*

pergola *n* arch or framework of trellis supporting climbing plants.

perhaps *adv* it may be (so), possibly.

pericardium *n*, *pl* **-dia** membrane enclosing the heart.

perihelion *n*, *pl* **-lia** point in the orbit of a planet or comet nearest to the sun.

peril *n* great danger. **perilous** *adj* **perilously** *adv*

perimeter [per-**rim**-it-er] *n* (length

of) the outer edge of an area.

perinatal *adj* of or in the weeks shortly before or after birth.

period *n* particular portion of time; series of years; single occurrence of menstruation; division of time at school etc. when a particular subject is taught; same as FULL STOP. ♦ *adj* (of furniture, dress, a play, etc.) dating from or in the style of an earlier time in history. **periodic** *adj* recurring at intervals. **periodic table** chart of the elements, arranged to show their relationship to each other. **periodical** *n* magazine issued at regular intervals. ♦ *adj* periodic.

peripatetic [per-rip-a-**tet**-ik] *adj* travelling about from place to place.

periphery [per-**if**-er-ee] *n*, *pl* **-eries** circumference; fringes of a field of activity. **peripheral** [per-**if**-er-al] *adj* unimportant, not central; of or on the periphery.

periphrasis [per-**if**-ra-siss] *n*, *pl* **-rases** [-ra-seez] roundabout speech or expression. **periphrastic** *adj*

periscope *n* instrument used, esp. in submarines, for giving a view of objects on a different level.

perish *v* be destroyed or die; decay, rot. **perishable** *adj* liable to rot quickly. **perishing** *adj* *Informal* very cold.

peritoneum [per-rit-toe-**nee**-um] *n*, *pl* **-nea, -neums** membrane lining the internal surface of the abdomen. **peritonitis** [per-rit-tone-**ite**-iss] *n* inflammation of the peritoneum.

periwig *n* *Hist* wig.

periwinkle[1] *n* small edible shellfish, the winkle.

periwinkle[2] *n* plant with trailing stems and blue flowers.

perjury [per-**jer**-ee] *n*, *pl* **-juries** act or crime of lying while under oath in a court. **perjure** *v* **perjure oneself** commit perjury.

perk *n* *Informal* incidental benefit gained from a job, such as a company car.

perk up *v* cheer up. **perky** *adj* lively or cheerful.

perm *n* long-lasting curly hairstyle produced by treating the hair with chemicals. ♦ *v* give (hair) a perm.

permafrost *n* permanently frozen

ground.

permanent *adj* lasting forever. **permanently** *adv* **permanence** *n* **permanent resident** immigrant allowed to live and work in Canada but who is not yet a citizen.

permanganate *n* a salt of an acid of manganese.

permeate *v* pervade or pass through the whole of (something). **permeable** *adj* able to be permeated, esp. by liquid.

permit *v* -mitting, -mitted give permission; allow. ♦ *n* document giving permission to do something. **permission** *n* authorization to do something. **permissible** *adj* **permissive** *adj* (excessively) tolerant, esp. in sexual matters.

permutation *n* any of the ways a number of things can be arranged or combined.

pernicious *adj* wicked; extremely harmful, deadly.

pernickety *adj* Informal (excessively) fussy about details.

peroration *n* concluding part of a speech, usu. summing up the main points.

peroxide *n* oxide of a given base with a high proportion of oxygen; short for HYDROGEN PEROXIDE.

perpendicular *adj* at right angles to a line or surface; upright or vertical. ♦ *n* line at right angles to another line or plane.

perpetrate *v* commit or be responsible for (a wrongdoing). **perpetration** *n* **perpetrator** *n*

perpetual *adj* lasting forever; continually repeated. **perpetually** *adv* **perpetuate** *v* cause to continue or be remembered. **perpetuation** *n* **in perpetuity** forever.

perplex *v* puzzle, bewilder. **perplexity** *n*

perquisite *n* same as PERK.

perry *n, pl* -ries alcoholic drink made from fermented pears.

per se [per **say**] *adv* Latin in itself.

persecute *v* treat cruelly because of race, religion, etc.; subject to persistent harassment. **persecution** *n* **persecutor** *n*

persevere *v* keep making an effort despite difficulties. **perseverance** *n*

persiflage [per-sif-flahzh] *n* light frivolous talk or writing.

persimmon *n* sweet red tropical fruit.

persist *v* continue without interruption; continue obstinately despite opposition. **persistent** *adj* **persistently** *adv* **persistence** *n*

person *n* human being; body of a human being; Grammar form of pronouns and verbs that shows if a person is speaking, spoken to, or spoken of. **in person** actually present.

persona [per-soh-na] *n, pl* -nae someone's personality as presented to others.

personable *adj* pleasant in appearance and personality.

personage *n* important person.

personal *adj* individual or private; of the body, e.g. *personal hygiene*; (of a remark etc.) offensive. **personally** *adv* in one's own opinion; directly, not by delegation to others. **personal computer** small computer used for word processing or computer games. **personal pronoun** pronoun like *I* or *she* that stands for a definite person. **personal stereo** very small portable cassette player with headphones.

personality *n, pl* -ties person's whole character; celebrity. ♦ *pl* personal remarks.

personify *v* -fying, -fied give human characteristics to; be an example of, typify. **personification** *n*

personnel *n* people employed in an organization.

perspective *n* mental view; method of drawing that gives the effect of solidity and relative distances and sizes.

perspicacious *adj* having quick mental insight. **perspicacity** *n*

perspire *v* sweat. **perspiration** *n* sweat.

persuade *v* make (someone) do something by argument, charm, etc.; convince. **persuasion** *n* act of persuading; way of thinking or belief. **persuasive** *adj*

pert *adj* bright and cheeky.

pertain *v* belong or be relevant (to).

pertinacious *adj* very persistent and determined. **pertinacity** *n*

pertinent *adj* relevant. **pertinence** *n*

perturb *v* disturb greatly; alarm.

perturbation n

peruke n Hist wig.

peruse v read in a careful or leisurely manner. **perusal** n

pervade v spread right through (something). **pervasive** adj

perverse adj deliberately doing something different from what is thought normal or proper. **perversely** adv **perversity** n

pervert v use or alter for a wrong purpose; lead into abnormal (sexual) behaviour. ◆ n person who practises sexual perversion. **perversion** n sexual act or desire considered abnormal; act of perverting.

pervious adj able to be penetrated, permeable.

peseta [pa-say-ta] n a former monetary unit of Spain.

pessary n, pl -ries appliance worn in the vagina, either to prevent conception or to support the womb; medicated suppository.

pessimism n tendency to expect the worst in all things. **pessimist** n **pessimistic** adj **pessimistically** adv

pest n annoying person; insect or animal that damages crops. **pesticide** n chemical for killing insect pests.

pester v annoy or nag continually.

pestilence n deadly epidemic disease. **pestilential** adj annoying, troublesome; deadly.

pestle n club-shaped implement for grinding things to powder in a mortar.

pet n animal kept for pleasure and companionship; person favoured or indulged. ◆ adj kept as a pet; particularly cherished. ◆ v **petting**, **petted** treat as a pet; pat or stroke affectionately; Informal kiss and caress erotically.

petal n one of the white or coloured outer parts of a flower.

petard n Hist explosive device. **hoist with one's own petard** being the victim of one's own schemes.

peter out v gradually come to an end.

petite adj (of a woman) small and dainty.

petition n formal request, esp. one signed by many people and presented to parliament. ◆ v present a petition to. **petitioner** n

petrel n long-winged dark-coloured sea bird.

petrify v -fying, -fied frighten severely; turn to stone. **petrification** n

petrochemical n a substance, such as acetone, obtained from petroleum.

petrol n Brit gasoline.

petroleum n thick dark crude oil found underground.

petticoat n woman's skirt-shaped undergarment.

pettifogging adj overconcerned with unimportant detail.

pettish adj fretful, irritable.

petty adj -tier, -tiest unimportant, trivial; small-minded; on a small scale, e.g. petty crime. **pettiness** n **petty cash** cash kept by a firm to pay minor expenses. **petty officer** noncommissioned officer in the navy.

petulant adj childishly irritable or peevish. **petulantly** adv **petulance** n

petunia n garden plant with funnel-shaped flowers.

pew n fixed benchlike seat in a church; Brit informal chair, seat.

pewter n greyish metal made of tin and lead.

pH Chem measure of the acidity of a solution.

phalanger n long-tailed Aust. tree-dwelling marsupial.

phalanx n, pl **phalanxes**, **phalanges** closely grouped mass of people.

phalarope n small wading bird.

phallus n, pl -li, -luses penis, esp. as a symbol of reproductive power in primitive rites. **phallic** adj

phantasm n unreal vision, illusion. **phantasmal** adj

phantasmagoria n shifting medley of dreamlike figures.

phantasy n, pl -sies same as FANTASY.

phantom n ghost; unreal vision.

Pharaoh [fare-oh] n title of the ancient Egyptian kings.

pharisee n self-righteous hypocrite. **pharisaic, pharisaical** adj

pharmaceutical adj of pharmacy.

pharmacology n study of drugs. **pharmacological** adj **pharmacologist** n

pharmacopoeia [far-ma-koh-pee-a] n book with a list of and directions for the use of drugs.

pharmacy *n, pl* **-cies** preparation and dispensing of drugs and medicines; pharmacist's shop. **pharmacist** *n* person qualified to prepare and sell drugs and medicines.

pharynx [far-rinks] *n, pl* **pharynges, pharynxes** cavity forming the back part of the mouth. **pharyngeal** *adj* **pharyngitis** [far-rin-jite-iss] *n* inflammation of the pharynx.

phase *n* any distinct or characteristic stage in a development or chain of events. ◆ *v* arrange or carry out in stages or to coincide with something else. **phase in, out** *v* introduce or discontinue gradually.

PhD Doctor of Philosophy.

pheasant *n* game bird with bright plumage.

phenobarbitone *n* drug inducing sleep or relaxation.

phenol *n* chemical used in disinfectants and antiseptics.

phenomenon *n, pl* **-ena** anything appearing or observed; remarkable person or thing. **phenomenal** *adj* extraordinary, outstanding. **phenomenally** *adv*

phial *n* small bottle for medicine etc.

philadelphus *n* shrub with sweet-scented flowers.

philanderer *n* man who flirts or has many casual love affairs. **philandering** *n*

philanthropy *n* practice of helping people less well-off than oneself. **philanthropic** *adj* **philanthropist** *n*

philately [fill-lat-a-lee] *n* stamp collecting. **philatelic** *adj* **philatelist** *n*

philharmonic *adj* (in names of orchestras etc.) music-loving.

philistine *adj, n* boorishly uncultivated (person). **philistinism** *n*

philology *n* science of the structure and development of languages. **philological** *adj* **philologist** *n*

philosophy *n, pl* **-phies** study of the meaning of life, knowledge, thought, etc.; theory or set of ideas held by a particular philosopher; person's outlook on life. **philosopher** *n* person who studies philosophy. **philosophical** *adj* of philosophy; calm in the face of difficulties or disappointments. **philosophically** *adv* **philosophize** *v* talk in a boring and pretentious

manner about basic things.

philtre *n* magic drink supposed to arouse love in the person who drinks it.

phlebitis [fleb-bite-iss] *n* inflammation of a vein.

phlegm [flem] *n* thick yellowish substance formed in the nose and throat during a cold.

phlegmatic [fleg-mat-ik] *adj* not easily excited, unemotional. **phlegmatically** *adv*

phlox *n, pl* **phlox, phloxes** flowering garden plant.

phobia *n* intense and unreasoning fear or dislike.

phoenix *n* legendary bird said to set fire to itself and rise anew from its ashes.

phone *n, v* *Informal* telephone. **phonecard** *n* card used to operate certain public telephones. **phone-in** *n* broadcast in which telephone comments or questions from the public are transmitted live.

phonetic *adj* of speech sounds; (of spelling) written as sounded. **phonetics** *pl n* science of speech sounds. **phonetically** *adv*

phonograph *n* *Old-fashioned* record player.

phonology *n, pl* **-gies** study of the speech sounds in a language. **phonological** *adj*

phony, phoney *Informal* ◆ *adj* **phonier, phoniest** not genuine; false; insincere. ◆ *n, pl* **phonies** phony person or thing.

phosgene [foz-jean] *n* poisonous gas used in warfare.

phosphorescence *n* faint glow in the dark. **phosphorescent** *adj*

phosphorus *n* toxic flammable nonmetallic element which appears luminous in the dark. **phosphate** *n* compound of phosphorus; fertilizer containing phosphorus.

photo *n, pl* **photos** short for PHOTOGRAPH. **photo finish** finish of a race in which the contestants are so close that a photo is needed to decide the result.

photocopy *n, pl* **-copies** photographic reproduction. ◆ *v* make a photocopy of.

photoelectric *adj* using or worked by

electricity produced by the action of light.

photogenic *adj* always looking attractive in photographs.

photograph *n* picture made by the chemical action of light on sensitive film. ◆ *v* take a photograph of. **photographer** *n* **photographic** *adj* **photography** *n* art of taking photographs.

photogravure *n* process in which an etched metal plate for printing is produced by photography.

photolithography *n* lithographic printing process using photographically made plates.

photometer [foe-**tom**-it-er] *n* instrument for measuring the intensity of light.

Photostat *n* ® type of photocopying machine; copy made by it.

photosynthesis *n* process by which a green plant uses sunlight to build up carbohydrate reserves.

phrase *n* group of words forming a unit of meaning, esp. within a sentence; short effective expression. ◆ *v* express in words. **phrasal verb** phrase consisting of a verb and an adverb or preposition, with a meaning different from the parts, such as *take in* meaning *deceive*.

phraseology *n, pl* **-gies** way in which words are used.

phut *adv* **go phut** *Informal* (of a machine) break down.

phylactery *n, pl* **-teries** leather case containing religious texts, worn by Jewish men.

physical *adj* of the body, as contrasted with the mind or spirit; of material things or nature; of physics. **physically** *adv* **physical geography** branch of geography dealing with the features of the earth's surface. **physical education** training and practice in sports and gymnastics.

physician *n* doctor of medicine.

physics *n* science of the properties of matter and energy. **physicist** *n* person skilled in, or studying, physics.

physiognomy [fiz-ee-**on**-om-ee] *n, pl* **-mies** face.

physiology *n* science of the normal function of living things. **physiological** *adj* **physiologist** *n*

physiotherapy *n* treatment of disease or injury by physical means such as massage, rather than by drugs. **physiotherapist** *n*

physique *n* person's bodily build and muscular development.

pi *n, pl* **pis** *Math* ratio of the circumference of a circle to its diameter.

pianissimo *adv Music* very quietly.

piano¹ *n, pl* **pianos** (also **pianoforte**) musical instrument with strings which are struck by hammers worked by a keyboard. **pianist** *n* **Pianola** *n* ® mechanically played piano.

piano² *adv Music* quietly.

piazza *n* large open square or marketplace, esp. in Italy.

pibroch [**pee**-brok] *n* form of bagpipe music.

pic *n, pl* **pics, pix** *Informal* photograph or illustration.

pica [**pie**-ka] *n* printing type of 6 lines to the inch; typewriter typesize of 10 letters to the inch.

picador *n* mounted bullfighter with a lance.

picaresque *adj* denoting a type of fiction in which the hero, a rogue, has a series of adventures.

piccalilli *n* pickle of vegetables in mustard sauce.

piccaninny *n, pl* **-nies** *Offens* Black child.

piccolo *n, pl* **-los** small flute.

pick¹ *v* choose; remove (flowers or fruit) from a plant; remove loose particles from; (foll. by *at*) nibble (at) without appetite; provoke (a fight etc.) deliberately; open (a lock) by means other than a key. ◆ *n* choice, e.g. *take your pick*; best part. **pick-me-up** *n Informal* tonic; stimulating drink. **pick on** *v* find fault with. **pick out** *v* recognize, distinguish. **pickpocket** *n* thief who steals from someone's pocket. **pick up** *v* raise, lift; obtain or purchase; improve, get better; collect; *Informal* become acquainted with for a sexual purpose; accelerate. **pick-up** *n* small truck; *Informal* casual acquaintance made for a sexual purpose; device for conversion of mechanical energy into electric signals, as in a record player.

pick² *n* tool with a curved iron

crossbar and wooden shaft, for breaking up hard ground or masonry.

pickaback n same as PIGGYBACK.

pickaxe n large pick.

picket n person or group standing outside a workplace to deter would-be workers during a strike; sentry or sentries posted to give warning of an attack; pointed stick used as part of a fence. ◆ v form a picket outside (a workplace). **picket line** line of people acting as pickets.

pickings pl n money easily acquired.

pickle n food preserved in vinegar or salt water; Informal awkward situation. ◆ v preserve in vinegar or salt water. **pickled** adj Informal drunk.

picnic n informal meal out of doors. ◆ v -nicking, -nicked have a picnic.

Pict n member of an ancient race of N Britain. **Pictish** adj

pictorial adj of or in painting or pictures; illustrated. ◆ n newspaper etc. with many pictures. **pictorially** adv

picture n drawing or painting; photograph; mental image; beautiful or picturesque object; image on a TV screen. ◆ pl cinema. ◆ v visualize, imagine; represent in a picture. **picturesque** adj (of a place or view) pleasant to look at; (of language) forceful, vivid. **picture window** large window made of a single sheet of glass.

piddle v Informal urinate.

pidgin n language, not a mother tongue, made up of elements of two or more other languages.

pie n dish of meat, fruit, etc. baked in pastry. **pie chart** circular diagram with sectors representing quantities.

piebald n, adj (horse) with irregular black-and-white markings.

piece n separate bit or part; instance, e.g. a piece of luck; example, specimen; literary or musical composition; coin; small object used in checkers, chess, etc. **piece together** v make or assemble bit by bit.

pièce de résistance [pyess de ray-ziss-tonss] n French most impressive item.

piecemeal adv a bit at a time.

piecework n work paid for according to the quantity produced.

pied adj having markings of two or more colours.

pied-à-terre [pyay da tair] n, pl **pieds-à-terre** [pyay da tair] small apartment or house for occasional use.

pie-eyed adj Slang drunk.

pier n platform on stilts sticking out into the sea; pillar, esp. one supporting a bridge.

pierce v make a hole in or through with a sharp instrument; make a way through. **piercing** adj (of a sound) shrill and high-pitched; (of wind or cold) fierce, penetrating.

pierrot [pier-roe] n pantomime character, clown.

piety n, pl -ties deep devotion to God and religion.

piffle n Informal nonsense.

pig n animal kept and killed for pork, ham, and bacon; Informal greedy, dirty, or rude person. **piggish, piggy** adj Informal dirty; greedy; stubborn. **piggery** n place for keeping and breeding pigs. **pig-headed** adj obstinate. **pig iron** crude iron produced in a blast furnace.

pigeon n bird with a heavy body and short legs, sometimes trained to carry messages; Informal concern or responsibility. **pigeonhole** n compartment for papers in a desk etc. ◆ v classify; put aside and do nothing about. **pigeon-toed** adj with the feet or toes turned inwards.

piggyback n ride on someone's shoulders. ◆ adv carried on someone's shoulders.

pigment n colouring matter, paint or dye. **pigmentation** n

Pigmy adj, n, pl -mies same as PYGMY.

pigtail n plait of hair hanging from the back or either side of the head.

pike[1] n large predatory freshwater fish.

pike[2] n Hist long-handled spear.

pilaster n square column, usu. set in a wall.

pilau, pilaf, pilaff n Middle Eastern dish of meat or poultry boiled with rice, spices, etc.

pilchard n small edible sea fish of the herring family.

pile[1] n number of things lying on top of each other; Informal large amount; large building. ◆ v collect into a pile; (foll. by in, out, off etc.) move in a group. **pile-up** n Informal traffic accident involving several vehicles.

pile² n beam driven into the ground, esp. as a foundation for building in water or wet ground.

pile³ n fibres of a carpet or a fabric, esp. velvet, that stand up from the weave.

piles pl n swollen veins in the rectum, hemorrhoids.

pilfer v steal in small quantities.

pilgrim n person who journeys to a holy place. **pilgrimage** n

pill n small ball of medicine swallowed whole. **the pill** pill taken by a woman to prevent pregnancy. **pillbox** n small box for pills; small concrete fort.

pillage v steal property by violence in war. ◆ n violent seizure of goods, esp. in war.

pillar n slender upright post, usu. supporting a roof; strong supporter. **pillar box** red pillar-shaped letter box in the street.

pillion n seat for a passenger behind the rider of a motorcycle.

pillory n, pl **-ries** Hist frame with holes for the head and hands in which an offender was locked and exposed to public abuse. ◆ v **-rying, -ried** ridicule publicly.

pillow n stuffed cloth bag for supporting the head in bed. ◆ v rest as if on a pillow. **pillowcase** n removable cover for a pillow.

pilot n person qualified to fly an aircraft or spacecraft; person employed to steer a ship entering or leaving a harbour. ◆ adj experimental and preliminary. ◆ v act as the pilot of; guide, steer. **pilot light** small flame lighting the main one in a gas appliance.

pimento n, pl **-tos** mild-tasting red pepper.

pimp n man who gets customers for a prostitute in return for a share of his or her earnings. ◆ v act as a pimp.

pimpernel n wild plant with small flowers that close in dull weather.

pimple n small pus-filled spot on the skin. **pimply** adj

pin n short thin piece of stiff wire with a point and head, for fastening things; wooden or metal peg or stake. ◆ v **pinning, pinned** fasten with a pin;

seize and hold fast. **pin down** v force (someone) to make a decision, take action, etc.; define clearly. **pinball** n electrically operated table game, in which a small ball is shot through various hazards. **pin money** small amount earned to buy small luxuries. **pinpoint** v locate or identify exactly. **pinstripe** n very narrow stripe in fabric; the fabric itself. **pin-up** n picture of a sexually attractive person, esp. (partly) naked.

pinafore n apron; dress with a bib top.

pince-nez [panss-**nay**] n, pl **pince-nez** glasses kept in place only by a clip on the bridge of the nose.

pincers pl n tool consisting of two hinged arms, for gripping; claws of a lobster etc.

pinch v squeeze between finger and thumb; cause pain by being too tight; Informal steal; Informal arrest. ◆ n squeeze or sustained nip; as much as can be taken up between the finger and thumb. **at a pinch** if absolutely necessary. **feel the pinch** have to economize.

pinchbeck n alloy of zinc and copper, used as imitation gold.

pine¹ n evergreen coniferous tree; its wood. **pine cone** woody cone-shaped fruit of the pine tree.

pine² v (foll. by for) feel great longing (for); become thin and ill through grief etc.

pineal gland [pin-ee-al] n small cone-shaped gland at the base of the brain.

pineapple n large tropical fruit with juicy yellow flesh and a hard skin.

ping v, n (make) a short high-pitched sound. **pinger** n device, esp. a timer, that makes a pinging sound.

Ping-Pong n ® table tennis.

pinion¹ n bird's wing. ◆ v immobilize (someone) by tying or holding his or her arms.

pinion² n small cogwheel.

pink n pale reddish colour; fragrant garden plant. ◆ adj of the colour pink. ◆ v (of an engine) make a metallic noise because not working properly, knock. **in the pink** in good health.

pinking shears pl n scissors with a serrated edge that give a wavy edge to material to prevent fraying.

pinnacle n highest point of success etc.; mountain peak; small slender spire.

pint n liquid measure, half a quart, ⅛ gallon (.568 litre).

Pinyin n system for representing Chinese in Roman letters.

pioneer n explorer or early settler of a new country; originator or developer of something new. ◆ v be the pioneer or leader of.

pious adj deeply religious, devout.

pip¹ n small seed in a fruit.

pip² n high-pitched sound used as a time signal on radio; Informal star on a junior army officer's shoulder showing rank.

pip³ n give someone the pip Slang annoy someone.

pipe n tube for conveying liquid or gas; tube with a small bowl at the end for smoking tobacco; tubular musical instrument. ◆ pl bagpipes. ◆ v play on a pipe; utter in a shrill tone; convey by pipe; decorate with piping. **piper** n player on a pipe or bagpipes. **piping** n system of pipes; decoration of icing on a cake etc.; fancy edging on clothes. **piped music** recorded music played as background music in public places. **pipe down** v Informal stop talking. **pipe dream** fanciful impossible plan etc. **pipeline** n long pipe for transporting oil, water, etc.; means of communication. **in the pipeline** in preparation. **pipe up** v speak suddenly or shrilly.

pipette n slender glass tube used to transfer or measure fluids.

pipit n small brownish bird.

pippin n type of eating apple.

piquant [pee-kant] adj having a pleasant spicy taste; mentally stimulating. **piquancy** n

pique [peek] n feeling of hurt pride, baffled curiosity, or resentment. ◆ v hurt the pride of; arouse (curiosity).

piqué [pee-kay] n stiff ribbed cotton fabric.

piquet [pik-ket] n card game for two.

piranha n small fierce freshwater fish of tropical America.

pirate n sea robber; person who illegally publishes or sells work owned by someone else; person or company that broadcasts illegally. ◆ v sell or

reproduce (artistic work etc.) illegally. **piracy** n **piratical** adj

pirouette v, n (make) a spinning turn balanced on the toes of one foot.

piscatorial adj of fishing or fishes.

piss Taboo ◆ v urinate. ◆ n act of urinating; urine.

pistachio n, pl -os edible nut of a Mediterranean tree.

piste [peest] n ski slope.

pistil n seed-bearing part of a flower.

pistol n short-barrelled handgun.

piston n cylindrical part in an engine that slides to and fro in a cylinder.

pit n deep hole in the ground; coal mine; dent or depression; servicing and refuelling area on a motor-racing track; same as ORCHESTRA PIT. ◆ v **pitting, pitted** mark with small dents or scars. **pit one's wits against** compete against in a test or contest. **pit bull terrier** strong muscular terrier with a short coat.

pitch¹ v throw, hurl; set up (a tent); fall headlong; (of a ship or plane) move with the front and back going up and down alternately; set the level or tone of. ◆ n area marked out for playing sport; degree or angle of slope; degree of highness or lowness of a (musical) sound; place where a street or market trader regularly sells; Informal persuasive sales talk. **pitcher** n **pitch in** v join in enthusiastically. **pitch into** v Informal attack.

pitch² n dark sticky substance obtained from tar. **pitch-black, -dark** adj very dark.

pitchblende n mineral composed largely of uranium oxide, yielding radium.

pitcher n large jug with a narrow neck.

pitchfork n large long-handled fork for lifting hay. ◆ v thrust abruptly or violently.

pitfall n hidden difficulty or danger.

pith n soft white lining of the rind of oranges etc.; soft tissue in the stems of certain plants; essential part. **pithy** adj short and full of meaning.

piton [peet-on] n metal spike used in climbing to secure a rope.

pittance n very small allowance of money.

pituitary n, pl -taries gland at the

base of the brain, that helps to control growth (also **pituitary gland**).

pity *n, pl* -**ties** sympathy or sorrow for others' suffering; regrettable fact. ◆ *v* **pitying, pitied** feel pity for. **piteous, pitiable** *adj* arousing pity. **pitiful** *adj* arousing pity; woeful, contemptible. **pitifully** *adv* **pitiless** *adj* feeling no pity, hard.

pivot *n* central shaft on which something turns. ◆ *v* provide with or turn on a pivot. **pivotal** *adj* of crucial importance.

pix *n Informal* a plural of PIC.

pixie *n* (in folklore) fairy.

pizza *n* flat disc of dough covered with a wide variety of savoury toppings and baked.

pizzazz *n Informal* attractive combination of energy and style.

pizzicato [pit-see-kah-toe] *adv Music* played by plucking the string of a violin etc. with the finger.

placard *n* large board with a slogan on it that is carried or displayed in public.

placate *v* make (someone) stop feeling angry. **placatory** *adj*

place *n* particular part of an area or space; particular town, building, etc.; position or point reached; usual position; duty or right; position of employment; seat or space. ◆ *v* put in a particular place; identify, put in context; make (an order, bet, etc.). **be placed** (of a competitor in a race) be among the first three. **take place** happen.

placebo [plas-see-bo] *n, pl* -**bos, -boes** sugar pill etc. given to an unsuspecting patient as an active drug.

placenta [plass-ent-a] *n, pl* -**tas, -tae** organ formed in the womb during pregnancy, providing nutrients for the fetus. **placental** *adj*

placid *adj* calm, not easily excited or upset. **placidity** *n*

placket *n* opening at the top of a skirt etc. fastened with buttons or a zip.

plagiarize [play-jer-ize] *v* steal ideas, passages, etc. from (someone else's work) and present them as one's own. **plagiarism** *n*

plague *n* fast-spreading fatal disease; *Hist* bubonic plague; widespread infestation. ◆ *v* **plaguing, plagued** trouble or annoy continually.

plaice *n* edible European flatfish.

plaid *n* long piece of tartan cloth worn as part of Highland dress; tartan cloth or pattern.

plain *adj* easy to see or understand; expressed honestly and clearly; without decoration or pattern; simple, ordinary. ◆ *n* large stretch of level country. **plainly** *adv* **plainness** *n* **plain clothes** ordinary clothes, as opposed to uniform. **plain sailing** easy progress. **plain speaking** saying exactly what one thinks.

plainsong *n* unaccompanied singing, esp. in a medieval church.

plaintiff *n* person who sues in a court of law.

plaintive *adj* sad, mournful. **plaintively** *adv*

plait [platt] *v* intertwine separate strands to form one ropelike length. ◆ *n* length of hair that has been plaited.

plan *n* way thought out to do or achieve something; diagram showing the layout or design of something. ◆ *v* **planning, planned** arrange beforehand; make a diagram of.

plane[1] *n* an aircraft. ◆ *v* (of a boat) rise and partly skim over water.

plane[2] *n Math* flat surface; level of attainment etc.; tool for smoothing wood. ◆ *v* smooth (wood) with a plane. ◆ *adj* perfectly flat or level.

plane[3] *n* tree with broad leaves.

planet *n* large body in space that revolves round the sun or another star. **planetary** *adj*

planetarium *n, pl* -**iums, -ia** building where the movements of the stars, planets, etc. are shown by projecting lights on the inside of a dome.

plangent [plan-jent] *adj* (of sounds) mournful and resounding.

plank *n* long flat piece of sawn timber.

plankton *n* minute animals and plants floating in the surface water of a sea or lake.

plant *n* living organism that grows in the ground and has no power to move; equipment or machinery used in industrial processes; factory or other industrial premises. ◆ *v* put in the ground to grow; place firmly in position; *Informal* hide (stolen goods etc.) on a person to make him or her seem guilty; *Informal* put (a person) secretly in an organization to spy.

planter *n* ornamental pot for house plants; owner of a plantation.

plantain[1] *n* low-growing wild plant with broad leaves.

plantain[2] *n* tropical fruit like a green banana.

plantation *n* estate for the cultivation of tea, tobacco, etc.; wood of cultivated trees.

plaque *n* inscribed commemorative stone or metal plate fixed to a wall; filmy deposit on teeth that causes decay.

plasma *n* clear liquid part of blood.

plaster *n* mixture of lime, sand, etc. for coating walls; adhesive strip of material for dressing cuts etc. ◆ *v* cover with plaster; coat thickly. **plastered** *adj Slang* drunk. **plaster of Paris** white powder which dries to form a hard solid when mixed with water, used for sculptures and casts for broken limbs.

plastic *n* synthetic material that can be moulded when soft but sets in a hard long-lasting shape. ◆ *adj* made of plastic; easily moulded, pliant. **plasticity** *n* ability to be moulded. **plastic bullet** solid PVC cylinder fired by police in riot control. **plastic surgery** repair or reconstruction of missing or malformed parts of the body for medical or cosmetic reasons.

Plasticine *n* ® soft coloured modelling material used esp. by children.

plate *n* shallow round dish for holding food; flat thin sheet of metal, glass, etc.; thin coating of metal on another metal; dishes or cutlery made of gold or silver; illustration, usu. on fine quality paper, in a book; *Informal* set of false teeth. ◆ *v* cover with a thin coating of gold, silver, or other metal. **plateful** *n* **plate glass** kind of thick glass used for mirrors and windows. **plate tectonics** study of the structure of the earth's crust, esp. the movement of layers of rocks.

plateau *n, pl* **-teaus, -teaux** area of level high land; stage when there is no change or development.

platen *n* roller of a typewriter, against which the paper is held; plate in a printing press by which the paper is pressed against the type.

platform *n* raised floor for speakers; raised area in a station from which passengers board trains; programme of a political party; structure in the sea which holds machinery, stores, etc. for drilling an oil well.

platinum *n* very valuable silvery-white metal. **platinum blonde** woman with silvery-blonde hair.

platitude *n* remark that is true but not interesting or original. **platitudinous** *adj*

platonic *adj* friendly or affectionate but not sexual.

platoon *n* subunit of a company of soldiers.

platteland *n S Afr* rural district.

platter *n* large dish.

platypus *n Aust.* egg-laying amphibious mammal, with dense fur, webbed feet, and a ducklike bill (also **duck-billed platypus**).

plaudit *n* expression of approval.

plausible *adj* apparently true or reasonable; persuasive but insincere. **plausibly** *adv* **plausibility** *n*

play *v* occupy oneself in (a game or recreation); compete against in a game or sport; fulfil (a particular role) in a team game, e.g. *he plays in the defence*; behave carelessly; act (a part) on the stage; perform (music) on an instrument; cause (a radio, record player, etc.) to give out sound; move lightly or irregularly, flicker. ◆ *n* story performed on stage or broadcast; activities children take part in for amusement; playing of a game; conduct, e.g. *fair play*; (scope for) freedom of movement. **player** *n* **playful** *adj* lively. **play back** *v* listen to or watch (something recorded). **playboy** *n* rich man who lives only for pleasure. **play down** *v* minimize the importance of. **playgroup** *n* regular meeting of very young children for supervised play. **playhouse** *n* theatre. **playing card** one of a set of 52 cards used in card games. **playing fields** extensive piece of ground for open-air games. **play off** *v* set (two people) against each other for one's own ends. **play on** *v* exploit or encourage (someone's sympathy or weakness).

playschool n nursery group for young children. **plaything** n toy. **play up** v cause trouble; give prominence to. **playwright** n author of plays.

plaza n modern shopping complex; open space or square.

PLC, plc Public Limited Company.

plea n serious or urgent request, entreaty; statement of a prisoner or defendant; excuse.

plead v ask urgently or with deep feeling; give as an excuse; *Law* declare oneself to be guilty or innocent of a charge made against one.

pleasant adj pleasing, enjoyable. **pleasantly** adv **pleasantry** n polite or joking remark.

please adv polite word of request. ♦ v give pleasure or satisfaction to. **please oneself** do as one likes. **pleased** adj **pleasing** adj giving pleasure or satisfaction.

pleasure n feeling of happiness and satisfaction; something that causes this. **pleasurable** adj giving pleasure. **pleasurably** adv

pleat n fold made by doubling material back on itself. ♦ v arrange (material) in pleats.

plebeian [pleb-ee-an] adj of the lower social classes; vulgar or rough. ♦ n (also **pleb**) member of the lower social classes.

plebiscite [pleb-iss-ite] n decision by direct voting of the people of a country.

plectrum n, pl **-trums, -tra** small implement for plucking the strings of a guitar etc.

pledge n solemn promise; something valuable given as a guarantee that a promise will be kept or a debt paid. ♦ v promise solemnly; bind by or as if by a pledge, e.g. *pledge to secrecy.*

plenary adj (of a meeting) attended by all members.

plenipotentiary n, pl **-aries** diplomat or representative having full powers. ♦ adj having full powers.

plenitude n abundance.

plenteous adj plentiful.

plentiful adj existing in large amounts or numbers. **plentifully** adv

plenty n large amount or number; quite enough.

pleonasm n use of more words than

necessary. **pleonastic** adj

plethora n oversupply.

pleurisy n inflammation of the membrane lining the chest and covering the lungs.

pliable adj easily bent; easily influenced. **pliability** n

pliant adj pliable. **pliancy** n

pliers pl n tool with hinged arms and jaws for gripping.

plight[1] n difficult or dangerous situation.

plight[2] v **plight one's troth** *Old-fashioned* promise to marry.

Plimsoll line n mark on a ship showing the level water should reach when the ship is fully loaded.

plinth n slab forming the base of a column etc.

PLO Palestine Liberation Organization.

plod v **plodding, plodded** walk with slow heavy steps; work slowly but determinedly. **plodder** n

plonk[1] v put (something) down heavily and carelessly.

plonk[2] n *Informal* cheap inferior wine.

plop n sound of an object falling into water without a splash. ♦ v **plopping, plopped** make this sound.

plot[1] n secret plan to do something illegal or wrong; sequence of events on which a film, novel, etc. is based. ♦ v **plotting, plotted** plan secretly, conspire; mark the position or course of (a ship or aircraft) on a map; mark and join up (points on a graph).

plot[2] n small piece of land.

plow, plough n agricultural tool for turning over soil. ♦ v turn over (earth) with a plow; move or work through slowly and laboriously. **plowman, ploughman** n **plowshare, ploughshare** n blade of a plow. **plow back** reinvest (money).

plover n shore bird with a straight bill and long pointed wings.

ploy n manoeuvre designed to gain an advantage.

pluck v pull or pick off; pull out the feathers of (a bird for cooking); sound the strings of (a guitar etc.) with the fingers or a plectrum. ♦ n courage. **plucky** adj brave. **pluckily** adv **pluck up** v summon up (courage).

plug n thing fitting into and filling a hole; device connecting an appliance to an electricity supply; *Informal* favourable mention of a product etc., designed to encourage people to buy it. ◆ *v* **plugging, plugged** block or seal (a hole or gap) with a plug; *Informal* advertise (a product etc.) by constant repetition. **plug away** *v* *Informal* work steadily. **plug in** *v* connect (an electrical appliance) to a power source by pushing a plug into a socket.

plum *n* oval usu. dark red fruit with a stone in the middle. ◆ *adj* dark purplish-red; very desirable.

plumage *n* bird's feathers.

plumb *v* understand (something obscure); test with a plumb line. ◆ *adv* exactly. **plumb the depths of** experience the worst extremes of (an unpleasant quality or emotion). **plumber** *n* person who fits and repairs pipes and fixtures for water and drainage systems. **plumbing** *n* pipes and fixtures used in water and drainage systems. **plumb in** *v* connect (an appliance such as a washing machine) to a water supply. **plumb line** string with a weight at the end, used to test the depth of water or to test whether something is vertical.

plume *n* feather, esp. one worn as an ornament. **plume oneself on** be proud of oneself because of.

plummet *v* **-meting, -meted** plunge downward.

plump[1] *adj* moderately or attractively fat. **plumpness** *n* **plump up** *v* make (a pillow) fuller or rounded.

plump[2] *v* sit or fall heavily and suddenly. ◆ *adv* suddenly and heavily; directly. **plump for** *v* choose, vote only for.

plunder *v* take by force, esp. in time of war. ◆ *n* things plundered.

plunge *v* put or throw forcibly or suddenly (into). ◆ *n* plunging, dive. **take the plunge** *Informal* embark on a risky enterprise; get married. **plunger** *n* rubber suction cup used to clear blocked pipes. **plunging** *adj* (of the neckline of a dress) cut low so as to show the top of the breasts. **plunge into** *v* become deeply involved in.

plunk *v* pluck the strings of (a banjo etc.) to produce a twanging sound.

pluperfect *adj, n Grammar* (tense) expressing action completed before a past time, such as *had gone* in *his wife had gone already*.

plural *adj* of or consisting of more than one. ◆ *n* a word in its plural form.

pluralism *n* existence and toleration of a variety of peoples, opinions, etc. in a society. **pluralist** *n* **pluralistic** *adj*

plus *prep* with the addition of: usu. indicated by the sign (+). ◆ *adj* more than zero or the number already mentioned; positive; advantageous. ◆ *n* plus sign; advantage.

plus fours *pl n* trousers gathered in at the knee.

plush *n* fabric with long velvety pile. ◆ *adj* (also **plushy**) luxurious.

Pluto *n* Greek god of the underworld; farthest planet from the sun.

plutocrat *n* person who is powerful because of being very rich. **plutocratic** *adj*

plutonium *n* radioactive metallic element used esp. in nuclear reactors and weapons.

pluvial *adj* of or caused by the action of rain.

ply[1] *v* **plying, plied** work at (a job or trade); use (a tool); (of a ship) travel regularly along or between. **ply with** *v* supply with or subject to persistently.

ply[2] *n* thickness of wool, fabric, etc.

plywood *n* board made of thin layers of wood glued together.

pm, PM after noon; postmortem.

PM prime minister.

PMT premenstrual tension.

pneumatic *adj* worked by or inflated with wind or air.

pneumonia *n* inflammation of the lungs.

PO postal order; Post Office.

poach[1] *v* catch (animals) illegally on someone else's land; encroach on or steal something belonging to someone else. **poacher** *n*

poach[2] *v* simmer (food) gently in liquid.

pocket *n* small bag sewn into clothing for carrying things; pouchlike container, esp. for catching balls at the edge of a snooker table; isolated or distinct group or area. ◆ *v* **pocketing, pocketed** put into one's pocket; take secretly or dishonestly. ◆ *adj* small. **in, out of pocket** having made a profit or loss. **pocket money** small regular allowance given to children by parents; allowance for small personal expenses.

pockmarked adj (of the skin) marked with hollow scars where diseased spots have been.

pod n long narrow seed case of peas, beans, etc.

podgy adj **podgier, podgiest** short and fat.

podium n, pl **-diums, -dia** small raised platform for a conductor or speaker.

poem n imaginative piece of writing in rhythmic lines.

poesy n Obs poetry.

poet n writer of poems. **poet laureate** see LAUREATE. **poetaster** n would-be or inferior poet. **poetry** n poems; art of writing poems; beautiful or pleasing quality. **poetic** adj (also **poetical**) of or like poetry. **poetically** adv **poetic justice** suitable reward or punishment for someone's past actions.

pogey n Slang unemployment insurance; dole.

pogrom n organized persecution and massacre.

poignant adj sharply painful to the feelings. **poignancy** n

poinsettia n Central American shrub widely cultivated for its clusters of scarlet leaves, which resemble petals.

point n single idea in a discussion, argument, etc.; aim or purpose; detail or item; main or essential aspect; characteristic; particular position, stage, or time; dot indicating decimals; full stop; sharp end; headland; unit for recording a value or score; one of the direction marks of a compass; electrical socket. ♦ pl electrical contacts in the distributor of an engine. ♦ v show the direction or position of something or draw attention to it by extending a finger or other pointed object towards it; direct (a gun etc.) towards; finish or repair the joints in brickwork with mortar; (of a gun dog) show where game is by standing rigidly with the muzzle towards it. **on the point of** very shortly going to. **pointed** adj having a sharp end; (of a remark) obviously directed at a particular person. **pointedly** adv **pointer** n helpful hint; indicator on a measuring instrument;

breed of gun dog. **pointless** adj meaningless, irrelevant. **point-blank** adj, adv fired at a very close target; (of a remark or question) direct, blunt. **point duty** policeman's position at a road junction to control traffic. **point of view** way of considering something. **point-to-point** n horse race across open country.

poise n calm dignified manner. **poised** adj absolutely ready; behaving with or showing poise.

poison n substance that kills or injures when swallowed or absorbed. ♦ v give poison to; have a harmful or evil effect on, spoil. **poisoner** n **poisonous** adj **poison-pen letter** malicious anonymous letter.

poke v jab or prod with one's finger, a stick, etc.; thrust forward or out. ♦ n poking. **poky** adj Informal small and cramped.

poker[1] n metal rod for stirring a fire to make it burn more brightly.

poker[2] n card game involving bluff. **poker-faced** adj expressionless.

polar adj of or near either of the earth's poles. **polar bear** white bear that lives in the regions around the North Pole.

polarize v form or cause to form into groups with directly opposite views; Physics restrict (light waves) to certain directions of vibration. **polarization** n

Polaroid n ® plastic which polarizes light and so reduces glare; camera that develops a print very quickly inside itself.

polder n land reclaimed from the sea.

pole[1] n long rounded piece of wood, metal, or other material.

pole[2] n point furthest north (**South Pole**) or furthest south (**North Pole**) on the earth's axis of rotation either of the opposite ends of a magnet or electric cell. **Pole Star** star nearest to the North Pole in the northern hemisphere.

poleaxe v hit with a heavy blow.

polecat n small animal of the weasel family.

polemic [pol-em-ik] n fierce attack on or defence of a particular opinion, belief, etc. **polemical** adj

police n organized force in a state which keeps law and order. ♦ v control or watch over with police or a similar body. **policeman, policewoman** n member of a police force.

policy[1] n, pl -**cies** plan of action adopted by a person, group, or state.

policy[2] n, pl -**cies** document containing an insurance contract.

polio n disease affecting the spinal cord, which often causes paralysis (also **poliomyelitis**).

polish v make smooth and shiny by rubbing; make more nearly perfect. ♦ n liquid, aerosol, etc. for polishing; pleasing elegant style. **polished** adj (of a person) socially sophisticated in manner; done or performed well or professionally. **polish off** v finish completely.

Politburo n decision-making committee in a Communist country.

polite adj showing consideration for others in one's manners, speech, etc.; socially correct or refined. **politely** adv **politeness** n

politic adj wise and likely to prove advantageous.

politics n (study of) the art of government; person's beliefs about how a country should be governed; winning and using of power to govern society. **political** adj of the state, government, or public administration. **politically** adv **politically correct** (of language) intended to avoid any implied prejudice. **political prisoner** person imprisoned because of his or her political beliefs. **politician** n person actively engaged in politics, esp. a member of parliament.

polka n lively 19th-century dance; music for this. **polka dots** pattern of bold spots on fabric.

poll n (also **opinion poll**) questioning of a random sample of people to find out general opinion; voting; number of votes recorded. ♦ v receive (votes); question as part of an opinion poll. **pollster** n person who conducts opinion polls. **polling station** building where people vote in an election.

pollarded adj (of a tree) growing very bushy because its top branches have been cut short.

pollen n fine dust produced by flowers that fertilizes other flowers. **pollinate** v fertilize with pollen. **pollen count** measure of the amount of pollen in

the air, esp. as a warning to people with hay fever.

pollute v contaminate with something poisonous or harmful. **pollution** n **pollutant** n something that pollutes.

polo n game like hockey played by teams of players on horseback. **polo neck** sweater with tight turned-over collar.

polonaise n old stately dance; music for this.

poltergeist n spirit believed to move furniture and throw objects around.

poltroon n Obs utter coward.

poly- combining form many, much.

polyandry n practice of having more than one husband at the same time.

polyanthus n garden primrose.

polychromatic adj many-coloured.

polyester n synthetic material used to make plastics and textile fibres.

polygamy [pol-ig-a-mee] n practice of having more than one husband or wife at the same time. **polygamous** adj **polygamist** n

polyglot adj, n (person) able to speak or write several languages.

polygon n geometrical figure with three or more angles and sides. **polygonal** adj

polygyny n practice of having more than one wife at the same time.

polyhedron n, pl -**drons**, -**dra** solid figure with four or more sides.

polymer n chemical compound with large molecules made of simple molecules of the same kind. **polymerize** v form into polymers. **polymerization** n

polyp n small simple sea creature with a hollow cylindrical body; small growth on a mucous membrane.

polyphonic adj Music consisting of several melodies played simultaneously.

polystyrene n synthetic material used esp. as white rigid foam for packing and insulation.

polytheism n belief in many gods. **polytheist** n **polytheistic** adj

polythene n light plastic used for many everyday articles.

polyunsaturated adj of a group of fats that do not form cholesterol in the blood.

polyurethane n synthetic material

used esp. in paints.

polyvinyl chloride *n* see PVC.

pomander *n* (container for) a mixture of sweet-smelling petals, herbs, etc.

pomegranate *n* round tropical fruit with a thick rind containing many seeds in a red pulp.

Pomeranian *n* small dog with long straight hair.

pommel *n* raised part on the front of a saddle; knob at the top of a sword hilt.

pommy *n, pl* **-ies** *Aust NZ slang* person from Britain (also **pom**).

pomp *n* stately display or ceremony.

pompom *n* decorative ball of tufted wool, silk, etc.

pompous *adj* foolishly serious and grand, self-important. **pompously** *adv* **pomposity** *n*

ponce *n Offens* effeminate man; pimp. **ponce around** *v Offens* act stupidly, waste time.

poncho *n, pl* **-chos** loose circular cloak with a hole for the head.

pond *n* small area of still water. **pondweed** *n* plant that grows in ponds.

ponder *v* think thoroughly or deeply (about).

ponderous *adj* serious and dull; heavy or huge; (of movement) slow and clumsy. **ponderously** *adv*

pong *n, v Informal* (give off a) strong unpleasant smell.

pontiff *n* the Pope. **pontifical** *adj* pompous and dogmatic. **pontificate** *v* state one's opinions as if they were the only possible correct ones. ♦ *n* period of office of a Pope.

pontoon[1] *n* floating platform supporting a temporary bridge.

pontoon[2] *n* gambling card game.

pony *n* small horse. **ponytail** *n* long hair tied in one bunch at the back of the head.

poodle *n* dog with curly hair often clipped fancifully.

poof *n Offens* homosexual man.

pool[1] *n* small body of still water; puddle of spilt liquid; swimming pool.

pool[2] *n* shared fund or group of workers or resources; game like snooker. ♦ *pl* see FOOTBALL POOLS. ♦ *v* put in a common fund.

poop *n* raised part at the back of a sailing ship.

poor *adj* having little money and few possessions; less, smaller, or weaker than is needed or expected; unproductive; unlucky; pitiable. **poorly** *adv* in a poor manner. ♦ *adj* not in good health. **poorness** *n*

pop[1] *v* **popping, popped** make or cause to make a small explosive sound; *Informal* go, put, or come unexpectedly or suddenly. ♦ *n* small explosive sound; nonalcoholic fizzy drink. **popcorn** *n* corn kernels heated until they puff up and burst.

pop[2] *n* music of general appeal, esp. to young people. ♦ *adj* popular.

pop[3] *n Informal* father.

Pope *n* head of the Roman Catholic Church. **popish** *adj Offens* Roman Catholic.

poplar *n* tall slender tree.

poplin *n* ribbed cotton material.

poppadom *n* thin round crisp Indian bread.

poppy *n, pl* **-ies** plant with a large delicate red flower.

Popsicle *n* flavoured ice on a stick.

populace *n* the ordinary people; the masses.

popular *adj* widely liked and admired; of or for the public in general. **popularly** *adv* **popularity** *n* **popularize** *v* make popular; make (something technical or specialist) easily understood.

populate *v* live in, inhabit; fill with inhabitants. **population** *n* all the people who live in a particular place; the number of people living in a particular place. **populous** *adj* thickly populated.

porbeagle *n* kind of shark.

porcelain *n* fine china; objects made of it.

porch *n* covered approach to the entrance of a building.

porcine *adj* of or like a pig.

porcupine *n* animal covered with long pointed quills.

pore *n* tiny opening in the skin or in the surface of a plant.

pork *n* pig meat. **porker** *n* pig raised for food.

porn, porno *n, adj Informal* short for PORNOGRAPHY or PORNOGRAPHIC.

pornography *n* writing, films, or

pictures designed to be sexually exciting. **pornographer** n producer of pornography. **pornographic** adj

porous adj allowing liquid to pass through gradually. **porosity** n

porphyry [por-fir-ee] n reddish rock with large crystals in it.

porpoise n fishlike sea mammal.

porridge n breakfast food made of oatmeal cooked in water or milk; Brit slang prison term.

port[1] n harbour; town with a harbour.

port[2] n left side of a ship or aircraft when facing the front of it.

port[3] n strong sweet wine, usu. red.

port[4] n opening in the side of a ship; porthole.

portable adj easily carried.

portage n (place for) transporting boats and supplies overland between navigable waterways.

portal n large imposing doorway.

portcullis n grating suspended above a castle gateway, that can be lowered to block the entrance.

portend v be a sign of.

portent n sign of a future event. **portentous** adj of great or ominous significance; pompous, self-important.

porter n man on duty at the entrance to a hotel etc.; man who carries luggage; hospital worker who transfers patients between rooms etc.

portfolio n, pl -os (flat case for carrying) examples of an artist's work; area of responsibility of a minister of state; list of investments held by an investor.

porthole n small round window in a ship or aircraft.

portico n, pl -cos, -coes porch or covered walkway with columns supporting the roof.

portion n part or share; helping of food for one person; fate. **portion out** v divide into shares.

portly adj -lier, -liest rather fat.

portmanteau n, pl -teaus, -teaux Old-fashioned large suitcase that opens into two compartments. ◆ adj combining aspects of different things.

portrait n picture of a person; lifelike description.

portray v describe or represent by artistic means, as in writing or film. **portrayal** n

Portuguese adj of Portugal or its inhabitants. ◆ n person from Portugal; language of Portugal and Brazil. **Portuguese man-of-war** sea creature resembling a jellyfish, with stinging tentacles.

pose v place in or take up a particular position to be photographed or drawn; behave in an affected way in order to impress others; ask (a question); raise (a problem). ◆ n position while posing; behaviour adopted for effect. **pose as** pretend to be. **poser** n Informal person who wears trendy clothes and frequents fashionable places; person who poses; puzzling question. **poseur** n person who behaves in an affected way to impress others.

posh adj Informal smart, luxurious; affectedly upper-class.

posit [pozz-it] v lay down as a basis for argument.

position n place; usual or expected place; way in which something is placed or arranged; attitude, point of view; social standing; state of affairs; job. ◆ v place.

positive adj feeling no doubts, certain; helpful, providing encouragement; confident, hopeful; absolute, downright; Math greater than zero; Electricity having a deficiency of electrons. **positively** adv **positive discrimination** provision of special opportunities for a disadvantaged group.

positron n positive electron.

posse [poss-ee] n US group of men organized to maintain law and order; Informal group or gang.

possess v have as one's property; (of a feeling, belief, etc.) have complete control of, dominate. **possessor** n **possession** n state of possessing, ownership. ◆ pl things a person possesses. **possessive** adj wanting all the attention or love of another person; (of a word) indicating the person or thing that something belongs to. **possessiveness** n

possible adj able to exist, happen, or be done; worthy of consideration. ◆ n person or thing that might be suitable or chosen. **possibility** n **possibly** adv perhaps.

possum n same as OPOSSUM. **play**

possum pretend to be dead or asleep to deceive an opponent.

post¹ n official system of carrying and delivering letters and parcels; (single collection or delivery of) letters and parcels sent by this system. ◆ v send by post. **keep someone posted** inform someone regularly of the latest news. **postage** n charge for sending a letter or parcel by post. **postal** adj **postal code** n system of letters and numbers used to aid the sorting of mail. **postal order** written money order sent by post and cashed at a post office by the person who receives it. **postcard** n card for sending a message by post without an envelope. **postman** n man who collects and delivers post. **postmark** n official mark stamped on letters showing place and date of posting. **postmaster, postmistress** n official in charge of a post office. **post office** place where postal business is conducted.

post² n length of wood, concrete, etc. fixed upright to support or mark something. ◆ v put up (a notice) in a public place.

post³ n job; position to which someone, esp. a soldier, is assigned for duty; military establishment. ◆ v send (a person) to a new place to work; put (a guard etc.) on duty.

post- prefix after, later than, e.g. postwar.

postdate v write a date on (a cheque) that is later than the actual date.

poster n large picture or notice stuck on a wall.

poste restante n Brit general delivery.

posterior n buttocks. ◆ adj behind, at the back of.

posterity n future generations.

postern n small back door or gate.

postgraduate n person with a degree who is studying for a more advanced qualification.

posthaste adv with great speed.

posthumous [poss-tume-uss] adj occurring after one's death; born after one's father's death; published after the author's death. **posthumously** adv

postilion, postillion n Hist person riding one of a pair of horses drawing a carriage.

postmortem n medical examination of a body to establish the cause of death.

postnatal adj occurring after childbirth.

postpone v put off to a later time. **postponement** n

postprandial adj after dinner.

postscript n passage added at the end of a letter.

postulant n candidate for admission to a religious order.

postulate v assume to be true as the basis of an argument or theory. **postulation** n

posture n position or way in which someone stands, walks, etc. ◆ v behave in an exaggerated way to get attention.

posy n, pl -sies small bunch of flowers.

pot n round deep container; teapot; Slang cannabis. ◆ pl Informal a lot. ◆ v potting, potted plant in a pot; Snooker hit (a ball) into a pocket. **potted** adj grown in a pot; (of meat or fish) preserved in a pot; Informal abridged. **potluck** n whatever is available. **potsherd** n broken fragment of pottery. **pot shot** shot taken without aiming carefully. **potting shed** shed where plants are potted.

potable [pote-a-bl] adj drinkable.

potash n white powdery substance obtained from ashes and used as fertilizer.

potassium n white metallic element.

potato n, pl -toes roundish starchy vegetable that grows underground. **potato chip** n very thin slice of potato fried till crunchy.

poteen n (in Ireland) illicitly distilled alcoholic drink.

potent adj having great power or influence; (of a male) capable of having sexual intercourse. **potency** n

potentate n ruler or monarch.

potential adj possible but not yet actual. ◆ n ability or talent not yet fully used; Electricity level of electric pressure. **potentially** adv **potentiality** n

pothole n hole in the surface of a road; deep hole in a limestone area. **potholing** n sport of exploring underground caves. **potholer** n

potion n dose of medicine or poison.

potpourri [po-poor-ee] *n* fragrant mixture of dried flower petals; musical or literary medley.

pottage *n* thick soup or stew.

potter[1] *n* person who makes pottery.

potter[2], **putter** *v* be busy in a pleasant but aimless way. **potterer, putterer** *n*

pottery *n, pl* **-ries** articles made from baked clay; place where they are made.

potty[1] *n, pl* **-ties** bowl used by a small child as a toilet.

potty[2] *adj* **-tier, -tiest** *Brit informal* crazy or silly.

pouch *n* small bag; baglike pocket of skin on an animal.

pouf, pouffe [poof] *n* large solid cushion used as a seat.

poulterer *n* person who sells poultry.

poultice [**pole**-tiss] *n* moist dressing, often heated, applied to inflamed skin.

poultry *n* domestic fowls.

pounce *v* spring upon suddenly to attack or capture. ♦ *n* pouncing.

pound[1] *n* monetary unit of Britain and some other countries; unit of weight equal to 0.454 kg.

pound[2] *v* hit heavily and repeatedly; crush to pieces or powder; (of the heart) throb heavily; run with heavy steps.

pound[3] *n* enclosure for stray animals or officially removed vehicles.

pour *v* flow or cause to flow out in a stream; rain heavily; come or go in large numbers.

pout *v* thrust out one's lips, look sulky. ♦ *n* pouting look.

pouter *n* pigeon that can puff out its crop.

poverty *n* state of being without enough food or money; lack of.

POW prisoner of war.

powder *n* substance in the form of tiny loose particles; medicine or cosmetic in this form. ♦ *v* apply powder to. **powdered** *adj* in the form of a powder, e.g. *powdered milk.* **powdery** *adj* **powder room** ladies' lavatory.

power *n* ability to do or act; strength; position of authority or control; person or thing having authority; particular form of energy, e.g. *nuclear power;* electricity supply; *Physics* rate at which work is done; *Math* product from continuous multiplication of a number by itself. **powered** *adj* having or operated by mechanical or electrical power. **powerful** *adj* **powerless** *adj* **power cut** temporary interruption in the supply of electricity. **power station** installation for generating and distributing electric power.

powwow *n* talk, conference.

pox *n* disease in which skin pustules form; *Informal* syphilis.

pp pages.

PQ Parti Quebecois.

PR proportional representation; public relations.

practicable *adj* capable of being carried out successfully. **practicability** *n*

practical *adj* involving experience or actual use rather than theory; sensible; adapted for use; good at making or doing things; in effect though not in name. ♦ *n* an examination in which something has to be done or made. **practically** *adv* **practical joke** trick intended to make someone look foolish.

practice *n* something done regularly or habitually; repetition of something so as to gain skill; doctor's or lawyer's place of work. **in practice** what actually happens as distinct from what is supposed to happen. **put into practice** carry out, do.

practise *v* do repeatedly so as to gain skill; take part in, follow (a religion etc.); work at, e.g. *practise medicine;* do habitually.

practitioner *n* person who practises a profession.

pragmatic *adj* concerned with practical consequences rather than theory. **pragmatism** *n* **pragmatist** *n*

prairie *n* large treeless area of grassland, esp. in N America. **Prairies** *pl n* this grassland in Manitoba, Saskatchewan, and Alberta. **prairie dog** burrow-dwelling rodent of the N American prairies.

praise *v* express approval or admiration of (someone or something); express honour and thanks to (one's God). ♦ *n* something said or written to show approval or admiration. **sing someone's praises**

praise someone highly. **praiseworthy** *adj*

praline [prah-leen] *n* candy made of nuts and caramelized sugar.

pram *n Brit* baby carriage.

prance *v* walk with exaggerated bouncing steps.

prank *n* mischievous trick or escapade, frolic.

prattle *v* chatter in a childish or foolish way. ◆ *n* childish or foolish talk. **prattler** *n*

prawn *n* edible shellfish like a large shrimp.

praxis *n* practice as opposed to theory.

pray *v* say prayers; ask earnestly. **prayer** *n* thanks or appeal addressed to one's God; set form of words used in praying; earnest request.

pre- *prefix* before, beforehand, e.g. *prenatal, prerecord, preshrunk.*

preach *v* give a talk on a religious theme as part of a church service; speak in support of (an idea, principle, etc.). **preacher** *n*

preamble *n* introductory part to something said or written.

prearranged *adj* arranged beforehand.

prebendary *n, pl* **-daries** clergyman who is a member of the chapter of a cathedral.

precarious *adj* insecure, unsafe, likely to fall or collapse. **precariously** *adv*

precaution *n* action taken in advance to prevent something bad happening. **precautionary** *adj*

precede *v* go or be before. **precedence** [**press**-ee-denss] *n* formal order of rank or position. **take precedence over** be more important than. **precedent** *n* previous case or occurrence regarded as an example to be followed.

precentor *n* person who leads the singing in a church.

precept *n* rule of behaviour.

precession *n* **precession of the equinoxes** slightly earlier occurrence of the equinoxes each year.

precinct *n* area in a town closed to traffic; enclosed area round a building, e.g. *cathedral precinct; US* administrative area of a city. ◆ *pl* surrounding region.

precious *adj* of great value and importance; loved and treasured; (of behaviour) affected, unnatural. **precious metal** gold, silver, or platinum. **precious stone** rare mineral, such as a ruby, valued as a gem.

precipice *n* very steep cliff or rockface. **precipitous** *adj* sheer.

precipitant *adj* hasty or rash.

precipitate *v* cause to happen suddenly; throw headlong; *Chem* cause to be deposited in solid form from a solution. ◆ *adj* done rashly or hastily. ◆ *n Chem* substance precipitated from a solution. **precipitately** *adv* **precipitation** *n* precipitating; rain, snow, etc.

précis [**pray**-see] *n, pl* **précis** short written summary of the main points of a longer piece. ◆ *v* make a précis of.

precise *adj* exact, accurate in every detail; strict in observing rules or standards. **precisely** *adv* **precision** *n*

preclude *v* make impossible to happen.

precocious *adj* having developed or matured early or too soon. **precocity, precociousness** *n*

precognition *n* alleged ability to foretell the future.

preconceived *adj* (of an idea) formed without real experience or reliable information. **preconception** *n*

precondition *n* something that must happen or exist before something else can.

precursor *n* something that precedes and is a signal of something else, forerunner.

predate *v* occur at an earlier date than; write a date on (a document) that is earlier than the actual date.

predatory [**pred**-a-tree] *adj* habitually hunting and killing other animals for food. **predator** *n* predatory animal.

predecease *v* die before (someone else).

predecessor *n* person who precedes another in an office or position; ancestor.

predestination *n* belief that future events have already been decided by God. **predestined** *adj*

predetermined *adj* decided in advance.

predicament *n* embarrassing or

difficult situation.

predicate n part of a sentence in which something is said about the subject, e.g. *went home* in *I went home*. ◆ v declare or assert.

predict v tell about in advance, prophesy. **predictive** adj (of a word processer or cell phone) able to complete words after only part of a word has been keyed. **predictable** adj **prediction** n

predilection n preference or liking.

predispose v influence (someone) in favour of something; make (someone) susceptible to something. **predisposition** n

predominate v be the main or controlling element. **predominance** n **predominant** adj **predominantly** adv

pre-eminent adj excelling all others, outstanding. **pre-eminently** adv **pre-eminence** n

pre-empt v get or do in advance of or to the exclusion of others. **pre-emption** n **pre-emptive** adj

preen v (of a bird) clean or trim (its feathers) with its beak. **preen oneself** smarten oneself; show self-satisfaction.

prefab n prefabricated house.

prefabricated adj (of a building) manufactured in shaped sections for rapid assembly on site.

preface [pref-iss] n introduction to a book. ◆ v serve as an introduction to (a book, speech, etc.). **prefatory** adj

prefect n senior pupil in a school, with limited power over others; senior administrative officer in some countries. **prefecture** n office or area of authority of a prefect.

prefer v **-ferring, -ferred** like better; *Law* bring (charges) before a court. **preferable** adj more desirable. **preferably** adv **preference** n **preferential** adj showing preference. **preferment** n promotion or advancement.

prefigure v represent or suggest in advance.

prefix n letter or group of letters put at the beginning of a word to make a new word, such as *un-* in *unhappy*; title before a name. ◆ v put as an introduction or prefix (to).

pregnant adj carrying a fetus in the womb; full of meaning or significance.

pregnancy n

prehensile adj capable of grasping. **prehensility** n

prehistoric adj of the period before written history begins. **prehistory** n

prejudice n unreasonable or unfair dislike of someone or something. ◆ v cause (someone) to have a prejudice; harm, cause disadvantage to. **prejudicial** adj harmful, disadvantageous.

prelate [prel-it] n bishop or other churchman of high rank. **prelacy** n

preliminary adj happening before and in preparation, introductory. ◆ n, pl **-naries** something that happens before something else.

prelude [prel-yewd] n introductory movement in music; event preceding and introducing something else.

premarital adj occurring before marriage.

premature adj happening or done before the normal or expected time; (of a baby) born before the end of the normal period of pregnancy. **prematurely** adv

premedication n drugs given to prepare a patient for a general anesthetic.

premeditated adj planned in advance. **premeditation** n

premenstrual adj occurring or experienced before a menstrual period, e.g. *premenstrual tension*.

premier n prime minister. ◆ adj chief, leading. **premiership** n

première n first performance of a play, film, etc.

premise, premiss n statement assumed to be true and used as the basis of reasoning.

premises pl n house or other building and its land.

premium n additional sum of money, as on a wage or charge; (regular) sum paid for insurance. **at a premium** in great demand because scarce.

premonition n feeling that something unpleasant is going to happen. **premonitory** adj

prenatal adj before birth; during pregnancy.

preoccupy v **-pying, -pied** fill the thoughts or attention of (someone) to the exclusion of other things.

preoccupation n

preordained adj decreed or determined in advance.

prep. preparatory; preposition.

prepacked adj sold already wrapped.

prepaid adj paid for in advance.

prepare v make or get ready. **prepared** adj willing; ready. **preparation** n preparing; something done in readiness for something else; mixture prepared for use as a cosmetic, medicine, etc. **preparatory** [prip-par-a-tree] adj preparing for. **preparatory school** private school for children going on to public school.

preponderant adj greater in amount, force, or influence. **preponderantly** adv **preponderance** n

preposition n word used before a noun or pronoun to show its relationship with other words, such as by in go by bus. **prepositional** adj

prepossessing adj making a favourable impression, attractive.

preposterous adj utterly absurd.

prep school n short for PREPARATORY SCHOOL.

prepuce [pree-pyewss] n retractable fold of skin covering the tip of the penis, foreskin.

prerecorded adj recorded in advance to be played or broadcast later.

prerequisite n, adj (something) that must happen or exist before something else is possible.

prerogative n special power or privilege.

presage [press-ij] v be a sign or warning of.

presbyopia n inability of the eye to focus on nearby objects.

Presbyterian adj, n (member) of a Protestant church governed by lay elders. **Presbyterianism** n

presbytery n, pl -teries Presbyterian Church local church court; RC Church priest's house.

prescience [press-ee-enss] n knowledge of events before they happen. **prescient** adj

prescribe v recommend the use of (a medicine); lay down as a rule. **prescription** n written instructions from a doctor for the making up and use of a medicine. **prescriptive** adj laying down rules.

presence n fact of being in a specified place; impressive dignified appearance. **presence of mind** ability to act sensibly in a crisis.

present[1] adj being in a specified place; existing or happening now; (of a verb tense) indicating that the action specified is taking place now. ◆ n present time or tense. **presently** adv soon; now.

present[2] n something given to bring pleasure to another person. ◆ v introduce formally or publicly; introduce and compère (a TV or radio show); cause, e.g. present a difficulty; give, award. **presentation** n **presentable** adj attractive, neat, fit for people to see. **presenter** n person introducing a TV or radio show.

presentiment [pree-zen-tim-ent] n sense of something usu. unpleasant about to happen.

preserve v keep from being damaged, changed, or ended; treat (food) to prevent it decaying. ◆ n area of interest restricted to a particular person or group; fruit preserved by cooking in sugar; area where game is kept for private fishing or shooting. **preservation** n **preservative** n chemical that prevents decay.

preshrunk adj (of fabric or a garment) having been shrunk during manufacture so that further shrinkage will not occur when washed.

preside v be in charge, esp. of a meeting.

president n head of state in countries without a king or queen; head of a society, institution, etc. **presidential** adj **presidency** n

press[1] v apply force or weight to; squeeze; smooth by applying pressure or heat; crowd, push; urge insistently. ◆ n printing machine. **pressed for** short of. **pressing** adj urgent. **press box** room at a sports ground reserved for reporters. **press conference** interview for reporters given by a celebrity.

press[2] v **press into service** force to be involved or used. **press gang** Hist group of men who captured men and boys and forced them to join the navy.

pressure n force produced by pressing; urgent claims or demands, e.g. working under pressure; Physics force applied to a surface per unit of area. **bring pressure to bear on** use influence or authority to persuade. **pressure cooker** airtight pot which cooks food quickly by steam under pressure. **pressure group** group that tries to influence policies, public opinion, etc.

prestidigitation *n* skilful quickness with the hands, conjuring.

prestige *n* high status or respect resulting from success or achievements. **prestigious** *adj*

presto *adv Music* very quickly.

prestressed *adj* (of concrete) containing stretched steel wires to strengthen it.

presume *v* suppose to be the case; (foll. by *to*) dare (to), take the liberty (of). **presumably** *adv* one supposes (that). **presumption** *n* strong probability; bold insolent behaviour. **presumptuous** *adj* doing things one has no right or authority to do. **presumptuously** *adv* **presumptive** *adj* assumed to be true or valid until the contrary is proved. **heir presumptive** heir whose right may be defeated by the birth of a closer relative.

presuppose *v* need as a previous condition in order to be true. **presupposition** *n*

pretend *v* claim or give the appearance of (something untrue) to deceive or in play. **pretender** *n* person who makes a false or disputed claim to a position of power. **pretence** *n* behaviour intended to deceive, pretending. **pretentious** *adj* making (unjustified) claims to special merit or importance. **pretension** *n*

preterite [pret-er-it] *adj, n Grammar* (expressing) a past tense, such as *jumped, swam.*

preternatural *adj* beyond what is natural, supernatural.

pretext *n* false reason given to hide the real one.

pretty *adj* **-tier, -tiest** pleasing to look at. ◆ *adv* fairly, moderately. **prettily** *adv* **prettiness** *n*

pretzel *n* brittle salted biscuit.

prevail *v* gain mastery; be generally established. **prevailing** *adj* widespread; predominant. **prevalence** *n* **prevalent** *adj* widespread, common.

prevaricate *v* be evasive, avoid giving a direct or truthful answer. **prevarication** *n*

prevent *v* keep from happening or doing. **preventable** *adj* **prevention** *n* **preventive** *adj, n*

preview *n* advance showing of a film or exhibition before it is shown to the public.

previous *adj* coming or happening before. **previously** *adv*

prey *n* animal hunted and killed for food by another animal; victim. **bird of prey** bird that kills and eats other birds or animals. **prey on** *v* hunt and kill for food; worry.

price *n* amount of money for which a thing is bought or sold; unpleasant thing that must be endured to get something desirable. ◆ *v* fix or ask the price of. **priceless** *adj* very valuable; *Informal* very funny. **pricey, pricy** *adj Informal* expensive.

prick *v* pierce slightly with a sharp point; cause to feel mental pain; (of an animal) make (the ears) stand erect. ◆ *n* sudden sharp pain caused by pricking; mark made by pricking; remorse. **prick up one's ears** listen intently.

prickle *n* thorn or spike on a plant. ◆ *v* have a tingling or pricking sensation. **prickly** *adj* **prickly heat** itchy rash occurring in hot moist weather.

pride *n* feeling of pleasure and satisfaction when one has done well; too high an opinion of oneself; sense of dignity and self-respect; something that causes one to feel pride; group of lions. **pride of place** most important position. **pride oneself on** feel pride about.

priest *n* (in the Christian Church) a person who can administer the sacraments and preach; (in some other religions) an official who performs religious ceremonies. **priestess** *n* woman priest. **priesthood** *n* **priestly** *adj*

prig *n* self-righteous person who acts as if superior to others. **priggish** *adj* **priggishness** *n*

prim *adj* **primmer, primmest** formal, proper, and rather prudish. **primly** *adv* **primness** *n*

prima ballerina *n* leading female ballet dancer.

primacy *n, pl* **-cies** state of being first in rank, grade, etc.; office of an archbishop.

prima donna *n* leading female opera singer; *Informal* temperamental person.

primaeval *adj* same as PRIMEVAL.

prima facie [**prime**-a **fay**-shee] *Latin* as it seems at first.

primal *adj* of basic causes or origins.

primary *adj* chief, most important; being the first stage, elementary. **primarily** *adv* **primary colours** (in physics) red, green, and blue or (in art) red, yellow, and blue, from which all other colours can be produced by mixing. **primary school** school for children from five to eleven years.

primate[1] *n* archbishop.

primate[2] *n* member of an order of mammals including monkeys and humans.

prime *adj* main, most important; of the highest quality. ♦ *n* time when someone is at his or her best or most vigorous. ♦ *v* give (someone) information in advance to prepare them for something; prepare (a surface) for painting; prepare (a gun, pump, etc.) for use. **Prime Minister** leader of a government. **prime number** number that can be divided exactly only by itself and one.

primer *n* special paint applied to bare wood etc. before the main paint; beginners' school book.

primeval, primaeval [prime-**ee**-val] *adj* of the earliest age of the world.

primitive *adj* of an early simple stage of development; basic, crude, e.g. *a primitive hut.*

primogeniture *n* system under which the eldest son inherits all his parents' property.

primordial *adj* existing at or from the beginning.

primrose *n* pale yellow spring flower.

primula *n* type of primrose with brightly coloured flowers.

Primus *n* ® portable cooking stove used esp. by campers.

prince *n* male member of a royal family, esp. the son of the king or queen; male ruler of a small country. **princely** *adj* of or like a prince; generous, lavish, or magnificent.

prince consort husband of a reigning queen. **Prince of Wales** eldest son of the British sovereign. **princess** *n* female member of a royal family, esp. the daughter of the king or queen. **Princess Royal** title sometimes given to the eldest daughter of the British sovereign.

Prince Edward Island *see* Canadian Provincial Facts p631.

principal *adj* main, most important. ♦ *n* head of a school or college; person taking a leading part in something; sum of money lent on which interest is paid. **principally** *adv* **principal boy** leading male role in pantomime, played by a woman.

principality *n, pl* **-ties** territory ruled by a prince.

principle *n* moral rule guiding behaviour; general or basic truth, e.g. *the principle of equality*; scientific law concerning the working of something. **in principle** in theory but not always in practice. **on principle** because of one's beliefs.

print *v* reproduce (a newspaper, book, etc.) in large quantities by mechanical or electronic means; reproduce (text or pictures) by pressing ink onto paper etc.; write in letters that are not joined up; stamp (fabric) with a design; *Photog* produce (pictures) from negatives. ♦ *n* printed words etc.; printed lettering; photograph; printed copy of a painting; mark left on a surface by something that has pressed against it; printed fabric. **out of print** no longer available from a publisher. **printer** *n* person or company engaged in printing; machine that prints. **printed circuit** electronic circuit with wiring printed on an insulating base. **print-out** *n* printed information from a computer.

prior[1] *adj* earlier. **prior to** before.

prior[2] *n* head monk in a priory. **prioress** *n* deputy head nun in a convent. **priory** *n* place where certain orders of monks or nuns live.

priority *n, pl* **-ties** most important thing that must be dealt with first; right to be or go before others.

prise *v* force open by levering.

prism *n* transparent block usu. with triangular ends and rectangular sides, used to disperse light into a spectrum

or refract it in optical instruments.
prismatic *adj* of or shaped like a
prism; (of colour) as if produced by
refraction through a prism, rainbow-
like.

prison *n* building where criminals and
accused people are held. **prisoner** *n*
person held captive. **prisoner of war**
serviceman captured by an enemy in
wartime.

prissy *adj* **-sier, -siest** prim, correct,
and easily shocked. **prissily** *adv*

pristine *adj* completely new, clean,
and pure.

private *adj* for the use of one person
or group only; secret; owned or paid
for by individuals rather than by the
government; quiet, not likely to be
disturbed; personal, unconnected with
one's work. ◆ *n* soldier of the lowest
rank. **privately** *adv* **privacy** *n*

privateer *n Hist* privately owned
armed vessel authorized by the
government to take part in a war;
captain of such a ship.

privation *n* loss or lack of the
necessities of life.

privatize *v* sell (a publicly owned
company) to individuals or a private
company. **privatization** *n*

privet *n* bushy evergreen shrub used
for hedges.

privilege *n* advantage or favour that
only some people have. **privileged** *adj*
enjoying a special right or immunity.

privy *adj* sharing knowledge of
something secret. ◆ *n, pl* **privies** *Obs*
lavatory, esp. an outside one. **privy
council** council of state of a monarch.

prize[1] *n* reward given for success in a
competition etc. ◆ *adj* winning or
likely to win a prize. ◆ *v* value highly.
prizefighter *n* boxer who fights for
money. **prizefight** *n*

prize[2] *v* same as PRISE.

pro[1] *adj, adv* in favour of. **pros and
cons** arguments for and against.

pro[2] *n* professional; prostitute.

pro- *prefix* in favour of, e.g. *pro-
Russian*; instead of, e.g. *pronoun*.

proactive *adj* tending to initiate
change rather than reacting to events.

probable *adj* likely to happen or be
true. **probably** *adv* **probability** *n*

probate *n* process of proving the
authenticity of a will; certificate of this.

probation *n* system of dealing with
law-breakers, esp. juvenile ones, by
placing them under supervision;
period when someone is assessed for
suitability for a job etc. **probationer** *n*
person on probation.

probe *v* examine closely. ◆ *n* surgical
instrument used to examine a wound,
cavity, etc.

probiotic *n* bacterium that protects
the body from harmful bacteria. ◆ *adj*
relating to probiotics: *probiotic yogurts.*

probity *n* honesty, integrity.

problem *n* something difficult to deal
with or solve; question or puzzle set
for solution. **problematical** *adj*

proboscis [pro-**boss**-iss] *n* elephant's
trunk; long snout; elongated
mouthpart of some insects.

procedure *n* way of doing
something, esp. the correct or usual
one.

proceed *v* start or continue doing;
Formal walk, go; start a legal action;
arise from. **proceeds** *pl n* money
obtained from an event or activity.
proceedings *pl n* organized or related
series of events; minutes of a meeting;
legal action.

process *n* series of actions or changes;
method of doing or producing
something. ◆ *v* handle or prepare by a
special method of manufacture; treat
(food) to prevent it decaying.
processor *n*

procession *n* line of people or
vehicles moving forward together in
order.

proclaim *v* declare publicly.
proclamation *n*

proclivity *n, pl* **-ties** inclination,
tendency.

proconsul *n Hist* governor of a
province, esp. of the Roman Empire.

procrastinate *v* put off taking action,
delay. **procrastination** *n*
procrastinator *n*

procreate *v Formal* produce offspring.
procreation *n*

Procrustean *adj* ruthlessly enforcing
uniformity.

procure *v* get, provide; obtain
(people) to act as prostitutes.
procurement *n* **procurer, procuress** *n*
person who obtains people to act as
prostitutes.

prod v **prodding, prodded** poke with something pointed; goad (someone) to take action. ◆ n **prodding.**

prodigal adj recklessly extravagant, wasteful. **prodigality** n

prodigy n, pl **-gies** person with some marvellous talent; wonderful thing. **prodigious** adj very large; wonderful. **prodigiously** adv

produce v bring into existence; present to view, show; make, manufacture; present on stage, film, or television. ◆ n food grown for sale. **producer** n person with financial and administrative control of a film etc.; Brit person responsible for the artistic direction of a play; person or company that produces something.

product n something produced; number resulting from multiplication. **production** n producing; things produced; presentation of a play, opera, etc. **productive** adj producing large quantities; useful, profitable. **productivity** n

profane adj showing disrespect for religion or holy things; (of language) coarse, blasphemous. ◆ v treat (something sacred) irreverently, desecrate. **profanation** n act of profaning. **profanity** n profane talk or behaviour.

profess v state or claim (something as true), sometimes falsely; have as one's belief or religion. **professed** adj supposed.

profession n type of work, such as being a doctor, that needs special training; all the people employed in a profession, e.g. the legal profession; declaration of a belief or feeling. **professional** adj working in a profession; taking part in an activity, such as sport or music, for money; very competent. ◆ n person who works in a profession; person paid to take part in sport, music, etc. **professionally** adv **professionalism** n

professor n teacher in a university. **professorial** adj **professorship** n

proffer v offer.

proficient adj skilled, expert. **proficiency** n

profile n outline, esp. of the face, as seen from the side; brief biographical sketch.

profit n money gained; benefit obtained. ◆ v gain or benefit.

profitable adj making profit. **profitably** adv **profitability** n

profiteer n person who makes excessive profits at the expense of the public. **profiteering** n

profligate adj recklessly extravagant; shamelessly immoral. ◆ n dissolute person. **profligacy** n

pro forma Latin prescribing a set form.

profound adj showing or needing great knowledge; strongly felt, intense. **profundity** n

profuse adj plentiful. **profusion** n

progeny [proj-in-ee] n, pl **-nies** children. **progenitor** [pro-**jen**-it-er] n ancestor.

progesterone n hormone which prepares the womb for pregnancy and prevents further ovulation.

prognathous adj having a projecting lower jaw.

prognosis n, pl **-noses** doctor's forecast about the progress of an illness; any forecast.

prognostication n forecast or prediction.

program n sequence of coded instructions for a computer. ◆ v **-gramming, -grammed** arrange (data) so that it can be processed by a computer; feed a program into (a computer). **programmer** n **programmable** adj

programme n planned series of events; broadcast on radio or television; list of items or performers in an entertainment.

progress n improvement, development; movement forward. ◆ v become more advanced or skilful; move forward. **in progress** taking place. **progression** n act of progressing, advance; sequence of numbers in which each differs from the next by a fixed ratio. **progressive** adj favouring political or social reform; happening gradually. **progressively** adv

prohibit v forbid or prevent from happening. **prohibition** n act of forbidding; ban on the sale or drinking of alcohol. **prohibitive** adj (of prices) too high to be affordable. **prohibitively** adv

project n planned scheme to do or examine something over a period. ◆ v make a forecast based on known data; make (a film or slide) appear on a screen; communicate (an impression); stick out beyond a surface or edge.

projector n apparatus for projecting photographic images, films, or slides on a screen. **projection** n

projectionist n person who operates a projector.

projectile n object thrown as a weapon or fired from a gun.

prolapse n slipping down of an internal organ of the body from its normal position.

prole adj, n Informal proletarian.

proletariat [pro-lit-air-ee-at] n working class. **proletarian** adj, n

proliferate v increase rapidly in numbers; grow or reproduce (new parts, such as cells) rapidly. **proliferation** n

prolific adj very productive. **prolifically** adv

prolix adj (of speech or a piece of writing) overlong and boring.

prologue n introduction to a play or book.

prolong v make (something) last longer. **prolongation** n

prom n formal dance at a school; short for PROMENADE or PROMENADE CONCERT.

promenade n paved walkway along the seafront at a holiday resort. ◆ v, n Old-fashioned (take) a leisurely walk. **promenade concert** concert at which part of the audience stands rather than sits.

prominent adj famous, widely known; very noticeable. **prominently** adv **prominence** n

promiscuous adj having many casual sexual relationships. **promiscuity** n

promise v say that one will definitely do or not do something; show signs of, seem likely. ◆ n undertaking to do or not to do something; indication of future success. **show promise** seem likely to succeed. **promising** adj likely to succeed or turn out well.

promo n Informal short video film made to promote a pop record.

promontory n, pl -ries point of high land jutting out into the sea.

promote v help to make (something)

happen or increase; raise to a higher rank or position; encourage the sale of by advertising. **promoter** n person who organizes or finances an event etc. **promotion** n **promotional** adj

prompt v cause (an action); remind (an actor or speaker) of words that he or she has forgotten. ◆ adj done without delay. ◆ adv exactly, e.g. six o'clock prompt. **promptly** adv immediately, without delay. **promptness** n **prompter** n person offstage who prompts actors.

promulgate v put (a law etc.) into effect by announcing it officially; make widely known. **promulgation** n **promulgator** n

prone adj (foll. by to) likely to do or be affected by (something); lying face downwards.

prong n one spike of a fork or similar instrument. **pronged** adj

pronoun n word, such as she, it, used to replace a noun. **pronominal** adj

pronounce v form the sounds of (words or letters), esp. clearly or in a particular way; declare formally or officially. **pronounceable** adj **pronounced** adj very noticeable. **pronouncement** n formal announcement. **pronunciation** n way in which a word or language is pronounced.

pronto adv Informal at once.

proof n evidence that shows that something is true or has happened; copy of something printed, such as the pages of a book, for checking before final production. ◆ adj able to withstand, e.g. proof against criticism; denoting the strength of an alcoholic drink, e.g. seventy proof. **proofread** v read and correct (printer's proofs). **proofreader** n

prop¹ v propping, propped support (something) so that it stays upright or in place. ◆ n pole, beam, etc. used as a support.

prop² n movable object used on the set of a film or play.

prop³ n Informal propeller.

propaganda n (organized promotion of) information to assist or damage the cause of a government or movement. **propagandist** n

propagate v spread (information and ideas); reproduce, breed, or grow.

propagation n

propane n flammable gas found in petroleum and used as a fuel.

propel v **-pelling, -pelled** cause to move forward. **propellant** n something that provides or causes propulsion; gas used in an aerosol spray. **propeller** n revolving shaft with blades for driving a ship or aircraft. **propulsion** n propelling or being propelled; method by which something is propelled.

propensity n, pl **-ties** natural tendency.

proper adj real or genuine; appropriate; suited to a particular purpose; correct in behaviour; excessively moral; Informal complete. **properly** adv

property n, pl **-ties** something owned; possessions collectively; land or buildings owned by somebody; quality or attribute.

prophet n person supposedly chosen by God to spread His word; person who predicts the future. **prophetic** adj **prophetically** adv **prophecy** n prediction; message revealing God's will. **prophesy** v foretell.

prophylactic n, adj (drug) used to prevent disease.

propinquity n nearness in time, place, or relationship.

propitiate v appease, win the favour of. **propitiation** n **propitiatory** adj intended to appease someone. **propitious** adj favourable or auspicious.

proponent n person who argues in favour of something.

proportion n relative size or extent; correct relation between connected parts; part considered with respect to the whole. ◆ pl dimensions or size. ◆ v adjust in relative amount or size. **in proportion** comparable in size, rate of increase, etc.; without exaggerating. **proportional, proportionate** adj being in proportion. **proportionally** adv

propose v put forward for consideration; nominate; intend or plan (to do); make an offer of marriage. **proposal** n **proposition** n offer; statement or assertion; theorem; Informal thing to be dealt with. ◆ v Informal ask (someone) to have sexual intercourse with one.

propound v put forward for consideration.

proprietor n owner of a business establishment. **proprietress** n fem **proprietary** adj made and distributed under a trade name; denoting or suggesting ownership.

propriety n, pl **-ties** correct conduct.

propulsion n see PROPEL.

pro rata Latin in proportion.

prorogue v suspend (parliament) without dissolving it. **prorogation** n

prosaic [pro-zay-ik] adj lacking imagination, dull. **prosaically** adv

proscenium n, pl **-niums, -nia** arch in a theatre separating the stage from the auditorium.

proscribe v prohibit, outlaw. **proscription** n **proscriptive** adj

prose n ordinary speech or writing in contrast to poetry.

prosecute v bring a criminal charge against; continue to do. **prosecution** n **prosecutor** n

proselyte [pross-ill-ite] n recent convert. **proselytize** [pross-ill-it-ize] v attempt to convert.

prosody [pross-a-dee] n study of poetic metre and techniques. **prosodic** adj **prosodist** n

prospect n something anticipated, e.g. the prospect of defeat; Old-fashioned view from a place. ◆ pl probability of future success. ◆ v explore, esp. for gold. **prospective** adj expected; future. **prospector** n person who searches, esp. for gold. **prospectus** n booklet giving details of a university, company, etc.

prosper v be successful. **prosperity** n success and wealth. **prosperous** adj

prostate n gland in male mammals that surrounds the neck of the bladder.

prosthesis [pross-theess-iss] n, pl **-ses** [-seez] artificial body part, such as a limb or breast. **prosthetic** adj

prostitute n person who offers sexual intercourse in return for payment. ◆ v make a prostitute of; offer (oneself or one's talents) for unworthy purposes. **prostitution** n

prostrate adj lying face downwards; physically or emotionally exhausted. ◆ v lie face downwards; exhaust

physically or emotionally. **prostration**
n

protagonist *n* leading character in a
play or a story; supporter of a cause.

protea [pro-tee-a] *n* African shrub
with showy flowers.

protean [pro-tee-an] *adj* constantly
changing.

protect *v* defend from trouble, harm,
or loss. **protection** *n* **protectionism** *n*
policy of protecting industries by
taxing competing imports.
protectionist *n* **protective** *adj* giving
protection, e.g. *protective clothing*;
tending or wishing to protect
someone. **protector** *n* person or thing
that protects; regent. **protectorate** *n*
territory largely controlled by a
stronger state; (period of) rule of a
regent.

protégé [pro-ti-zhay] *n* person who is
protected and helped by another.
protégée *n fem*

protein *n* any of a group of complex
organic compounds that are essential
for life.

pro tempore *adv, adj* (also **pro tem**)
for the time being.

protest *n* declaration or
demonstration of objection. ◆ *v* object,
disagree; assert formally. **protestation**
n strong declaration.

Protestant *adj* of or relating to any of
the Christian churches that split from
the Roman Catholic Church in the
sixteenth century. ◆ *n* member of a
Protestant church. **Protestantism** *n*

proto-, prot- *combining form* first, e.g.
protohuman.

protocol *n* rules of behaviour for
formal occasions.

proton *n* positively charged particle in
the nucleus of an atom.

protoplasm *n* substance forming the
living contents of a cell.

prototype *n* original or model after
which something is copied.

protozoan [pro-toe-zoe-an] *n, pl* **-zoa**
microscopic one-celled creature.

protract *v* lengthen or extend.
protracted *adj* **protraction** *n*
protractor *n* instrument for measuring
angles.

protrude *v* stick out, project.
protrusion *n*

protuberant *adj* swelling out,

bulging. **protuberance** *n*

proud *adj* feeling pleasure and
satisfaction; feeling honoured; thinking
oneself superior to other people;
dignified. **proudly** *adv* **proud flesh**
flesh growing around a healing
wound.

prove *v* **proving, proved, proved** or
proven. establish the validity of;
demonstrate, test; be found to be.
proven *adj* known from experience to
work.

provenance [prov-in-anss] *n* place of
origin.

provender *n Old-fashioned* fodder.

proverb *n* short saying that expresses
a truth or gives a warning. **proverbial**
adj

provide *v* make available; (foll. by *for*)
take precautions (against); support
financially. **provider** *n* **provided that**
on condition that.

providence *n* God or nature seen as a
protective force that arranges people's
lives. **provident** *adj* thrifty; showing
foresight. **providential** *adj* lucky.
providentially *adv*

province *n* territory governed as a
unit of a country or empire; area of
learning, activity, etc. ◆ *pl* any part of
a country outside the capital.
provincial *adj* of a province or the
provinces; unsophisticated or narrow-
minded. ◆ *n* unsophisticated person;
person from a province or the
provinces. **provincialism** *n* narrow-
mindedness and lack of sophistication.

provision *n* act of supplying
something; something supplied. ◆ *pl*
food; *Law* condition incorporated in a
document. ◆ *v* supply with food.
provisional *adj* temporary;
conditional. **provisionally** *adv*

proviso [pro-vize-oh] *n, pl* **-sos, -soes**
condition, stipulation.

provoke *v* deliberately anger; cause
(an adverse reaction). **provocation** *n*
provocative *adj*

provost *n* head of certain university
colleges; chief councillor of a Scottish
town. **provost marshal** head of
military police.

prow *n* bow of a vessel.

prowess *n* superior skill or ability;
bravery, fearlessness.

prowl *v* move stealthily around a place

as if in search of prey or plunder. ♦ *n* prowling. **prowler** *n*

proximity *n* nearness in space or time; nearness or closeness in a series. **proximate** *adj*

proxy *n*, *pl* **proxies** person authorized to act on behalf of someone else; authority to act on behalf of someone else.

prude *n* person who is excessively modest, prim, or proper. **prudish** *adj* **prudery** *n*

prudent *adj* cautious, discreet, and sensible. **prudence** *n* **prudential** *adj* *Old-fashioned* prudent.

prune[1] *n* dried plum.

prune[2] *v* cut out dead parts or excessive branches from (a tree or plant); shorten, reduce.

prurient *adj* excessively interested in sexual matters. **prurience** *n*

pry *v* **prying, pried** make an impertinent or uninvited inquiry into a private matter.

PS postscript.

psalm *n* sacred song. **psalmist** *n* writer of psalms. **psalmody** *n* singing of sacred music.

Psalter *n* book containing (a version of) psalms from the Bible. **psaltery** *n* ancient instrument played by plucking strings.

psephology [sef-**fol**-a-jee] *n* statistical study of elections.

pseud *n* *Informal* pretentious person.

pseudo-, pseud- *combining form* false, pretending, or unauthentic, e.g. *pseudo-intellectual*.

pseudonym *n* fictitious name adopted, esp. by an author. **pseudonymous** *adj*

psittacosis *n* disease of parrots that can be transmitted to humans.

PST Pacific Standard Time.

psyche *n* human mind or soul.

psychedelic *adj* denoting a drug that causes hallucinations; having vivid colours and complex patterns similar to those experienced during hallucinations.

psychiatry *n* branch of medicine concerned with mental disorders. **psychiatric** *adj* **psychiatrist** *n*

psychic *adj* (also **psychical**) having mental powers which cannot be explained by natural laws; relating to the mind. ♦ *n* person with psychic powers.

psycho *n* *Informal* short for PSYCHOPATH.

psychoanalysis *n* method of treating mental and emotional disorders by discussion and analysis of one's thoughts and feelings. **psychoanalyse** *v* **psychoanalyst** *n*

psychology *n*, *pl* **-gies** study of human and animal behaviour; *Informal* person's mental make-up. **psychological** *adj* of or affecting the mind; of psychology. **psychologist** *n*

psychopath *n* person afflicted with a personality disorder causing him or her to commit antisocial or violent acts. **psychopathic** *adj*

psychosis *n*, *pl* **-choses** severe mental disorder in which the sufferer's contact with reality becomes distorted. **psychotic** *adj, n*

psychosomatic *adj* (of a physical disorder) thought to have psychological causes.

psychotherapy *n* treatment of nervous disorders by psychological methods. **psychotherapist** *n*

psych up *v* prepare (oneself) mentally for a contest or task.

pt part; point; port.

Pt *Chem* platinum.

PT *Old-fashioned* physical training.

pt. pint.

PTA Parent-Teacher Association.

ptarmigan [**tar**-mig-an] *n* bird of the grouse family which turns white in winter.

pterodactyl [terr-roe-**dak**-til] *n* extinct flying reptile with batlike wings.

ptomaine [**toe**-main] *n* any of a group of poisonous alkaloids found in decaying matter.

Pu *Chem* plutonium.

pub *n* building with a bar licensed to sell alcoholic drinks.

puberty [**pew**-ber-tee] *n* sexual maturity. **pubertal** *adj*

pubic [**pew**-bik] *adj* of the lower abdomen.

public *adj* of or concerning the people as a whole; for use by everyone; well-known; performed or made openly. ♦ *n* the community, people in general. **publicly** *adv* **publican** *n* *Brit* person who owns or runs a pub. **public house** pub. **public relations** promotion of a favourable opinion towards an organization among the public. **public school** private fee-paying school in Britain. **public servant** member of the public service. **public service** service responsible for the administration of the government. **public-spirited** *adj* showing an active interest in the good of the community.

publicity *n* process or information used to arouse public attention; public interest aroused. **publicize** *v* advertise. **publicist** *n* person who publicizes something, such as a press agent or journalist.

publish *v* produce and issue (printed matter) for sale; announce formally or in public. **publication** *n* **publisher** *n*

puce *adj* purplish-brown.

puck¹ *n* small rubber disc used in ice hockey.

puck² *n* mischievous or evil spirit. **puckish** *adj*

pucker *v* gather into wrinkles. ◆ *n* wrinkle or crease.

pudding *n* dessert, esp. a cooked one served hot; savoury dish with pastry or batter, e.g. *steak-and-kidney pudding*; sausage-like mass of meat, e.g. *black pudding*.

puddle *n* small pool of water, esp. of rain.

puerile *adj* silly and childish.

puerperium [pure-**peer**-ee-um] *n* period following childbirth. **puerperal** [pure-**per**-al] *adj*

puff *n* (sound of) a short blast of breath, wind, etc.; instance of breathing in and out; act of inhaling cigarette smoke. ◆ *v* blow or breathe in short quick drafts; take draws at (a cigarette); send out in small clouds; swell. **out of puff** out of breath. **puffy** *adj* **puffball** *n* ball-shaped fungus. **puff pastry** light flaky pastry.

puffin *n* black-and-white sea bird with a large brightly-coloured beak.

pug *n* small snub-nosed dog. **pug nose** short stubby upturned nose.

pugilism [**pew**-jil-iz-zum] *n* boxing. **pugilist** *n* **pugilistic** *adj*

pugnacious *adj* ready and eager to fight. **pugnacity** *n*

puissant [pew-**iss**-sant] *adj Poetic* powerful. **puissance** *n* showjumping competition that tests a horse's ability to jump large obstacles.

puke *Slang* ◆ *v* vomit. ◆ *n* act of vomiting; vomited matter.

pulchritude *n Lit* beauty.

pule *v* whine; whimper.

pull *v* exert force on (an object) to move it towards the source of the force; strain or stretch; remove or extract; attract. ◆ *n* pulling; force used in pulling; act of taking in drink or smoke; *Informal* power, influence. **pull in** *v* (of a vehicle or driver) draw in to the side of the road or stop; reach a destination; attract in large numbers; *Slang* arrest. **pull off** *v Informal* succeed in performing. **pull out** *v* (of a vehicle or driver) move away from the side of the road or move out to overtake; (of a train) depart; withdraw; remove by pulling. **pull up** *v* (of a vehicle or driver) stop; remove by the roots; reprimand.

pullet *n* young hen.

pulley *n* wheel with a grooved rim in which a belt, chain, or piece of rope runs in order to lift weights by a downward pull.

Pullman *n, pl* **-mans** luxurious railway coach.

pullover *n* sweater that is pulled on over the head.

pulmonary *adj* of the lungs.

pulp *n* soft moist plant tissue, such as the material used to make paper; flesh of a fruit or vegetable; any soft soggy mass; poor-quality books and magazines. ◆ *v* reduce to pulp.

pulpit *n* raised platform for a preacher.

pulsar *n* small dense star which emits regular bursts of radio waves.

pulse¹ *n* regular beating of blood through the arteries at each heartbeat which can be felt at the wrists and elsewhere; any regular beat or vibration. **pulsate** *v* throb, quiver. **pulsation** *n*

pulse² *n* edible seed of a pod-bearing plant, e.g. a bean or pea.

pulverize *v* reduce to fine pieces; destroy completely. **pulverization** *n*

puma *n* large American cat with a greyish-brown coat.

pumice [**pumm**-iss] *n* light porous stone used for scouring.

pummel v -melling, -melled strike repeatedly with or as if with the fists.

pump[1] n machine used to force a liquid or gas to move in a particular direction. ◆ v raise or drive with a pump; supply in large amounts; extract information from; operate or work in the manner of a pump.

pump[2] n light flat-soled shoe.

pumpkin n large round fruit with an orange rind, soft flesh, and many seeds.

pun n use of words to exploit double meanings for humorous effect. ◆ v **punning, punned** make puns. **punster** n person fond of making puns.

punch[1] v strike at with a clenched fist. ◆ n blow with a clenched fist; Informal effectiveness or vigour. **punchy** adj forceful. **punch-drunk** adj dazed by or as if by repeated blows to the head.

punch[2] n tool or machine for shaping, piercing, or engraving. ◆ v pierce, cut, stamp, shape, or drive with a punch.

punch[3] n drink made from a mixture of wine, spirits, fruit, sugar, and spices.

punctilious adj paying great attention to correctness in etiquette; careful about small details.

punctual adj arriving or taking place at the correct time. **punctuality** n **punctually** adv

punctuate v put punctuation marks in; interrupt at frequent intervals. **punctuation** n (use of) marks such as commas, colons, etc. in writing, to assist in making the sense clear.

puncture n small hole made by a sharp object, esp. in a tire. ◆ v pierce a hole in.

pundit n expert who speaks publicly on a subject.

pungent adj having a strong sharp bitter flavour. **pungency** n

punish v cause (someone) to suffer or undergo a penalty for some wrongdoing. **punishing** adj harsh or difficult. **punishment** n **punitive** [pew-nit-tiv] adj relating to punishment.

punk n worthless person; anti-Establishment youth movement and style of rock music of the late 1970s; follower of this music.

punnet n small basket for fruit.

punt[1] n open flat-bottomed boat propelled by a pole. ◆ v travel in a punt.

punt[2] Sport v kick (a ball) before it touches the ground when dropped from the hands. ◆ n such a kick.

punt[3] n a former monetary unit of the Irish Republic.

punter n person who bets; any member of the public.

puny adj -nier, -niest small and feeble.

pup n young of certain animals, such as dogs and seals.

pupa [pew-pa] n, pl -pae, -pas insect at the stage of development between a larva and an adult. **pupal** adj

pupil[1] n person who is taught by a teacher.

pupil[2] n round dark opening in the centre of the eye.

puppet n small doll or figure moved by strings or by the operator's hand; person or country controlled by another. **puppeteer** n

puppy n, pl -pies young dog.

purblind adj partly or nearly blind.

purchase v obtain by payment. ◆ n buying; what is bought; leverage, grip. **purchaser** n

purdah n Muslim and Hindu custom of keeping women in seclusion, with clothing that conceals them completely when they go out.

pure adj unmixed, untainted; faultless; innocent; complete, e.g. pure delight; concerned with theory only, e.g. pure mathematics. **purely** adv **purity** n **purify** v make or become pure. **purification** n **purist** n person obsessed with strict obedience to the traditions of a subject.

purée [pure-ray] n pulp of cooked food. ◆ v -réeing, -réed make into a purée.

purgatory n place or state of temporary suffering; (P-) RC Church place where souls of the dead undergo punishment for their sins before being admitted to Heaven. **purgatorial** adj

purge v rid (a thing or place) of (unwanted things or people). ◆ n purging. **purgation** n **purgative** adj, n (medicine) designed to cause defecation.

Puritan n Hist member of the English Protestant group who wanted simpler church ceremonies; (p-) person with strict moral and religious principles.

puritanical adj **puritanism** n

purl n stitch made by knitting a plain stitch backwards. ◆ v knit in purl.

purlieus [per-lyooz] pl n Lit outskirts.

purloin v steal.

purple adj of a colour between red and blue.

purport v claim (to be or do something). ◆ n apparent meaning, significance.

purpose n reason for which something is done or exists; determination; practical advantage or use, e.g. use the time to good purpose. ◆ v Old-fashioned intend. **purposely** adv (also **on purpose**) intentionally.

purr n low vibrant sound that a cat makes when pleased. ◆ v make this sound.

purse n small bag for money; small bag carried to contain personal articles; financial resources; prize money. ◆ v draw (one's lips) together into a small round shape. **purser** n ship's officer who keeps the accounts.

pursue v chase; follow (a goal); engage in; continue to discuss or ask about (something). **pursuer** n **pursuit** n pursuing; occupation. **pursuance** n carrying out.

purulent [pure-yoo-lent] adj of or containing pus. **purulence** n

purvey v supply (provisions). **purveyance** n **purveyor** n

purview n scope or range of activity or outlook.

pus n yellowish matter produced by infected tissue.

push v move or try to move by steady force; drive or spur (oneself or another person) to do something; Informal sell (drugs) illegally. ◆ n pushing; special effort. **the push** Slang dismissal from a job; ending of a relationship. **pusher** n person who sells illegal drugs. **pushy** adj too assertive or ambitious.

pushover n Informal something easily achieved; person or team easily taken advantage of or defeated.

pusillanimous adj cowardly. **pusillanimity** n

puss, pussy n, pl **pusses, pussies** cat.

pussyfoot v Informal behave too cautiously.

pustule n pimple containing pus. **pustular** adj

put v **putting, put** cause to be (in a position, state, or place); express; throw (the shot) in the shot put. ◆ n throw in putting the shot. **put across** v express successfully. **put off** v postpone; disconcert; repel. **put up** v erect; accommodate; nominate. **put-upon** adj taken advantage of.

putative [pew-tat-iv] adj supposed.

putrid adj rotten and foul-smelling. **putrefy** v rot and produce an offensive smell. **putrefaction** n **putrescent** adj becoming putrid; rotting.

putsch n sudden violent attempt to remove a government from power.

putt Golf n stroke on the green with a putter to roll the ball into or near the hole. ◆ v strike (the ball) in this way. **putter** n golf club with a short shaft for putting.

puttee n strip of cloth worn wound around the leg from the ankle to the knee.

putter v same as POTTER².

putty n paste used to fix glass into frames and fill cracks in woodwork.

puzzle v perplex and confuse or be perplexed or confused. ◆ n problem that cannot be easily solved; toy, game, or question that requires skill or ingenuity to solve. **puzzlement** n **puzzling** adj

PVC polyvinyl chloride: synthetic thermoplastic material.

pyemia, pyaemia n blood poisoning.

Pygmy n, pl **-mies** member of one of the dwarf peoples of Equatorial Africa. ◆ adj (p-) very small.

pyjamas, pajamas pl n loose trousers and top worn in bed.

pylon n steel tower-like structure supporting electrical cables.

pyorrhea, pyorrhoea [pire-ree-a] n disease of the gums and tooth sockets which causes bleeding of the gums and the formation of pus.

pyramid n solid figure with a flat base and triangular sides sloping upwards to a point; structure of this shape, esp. an ancient Egyptian one. **pyramidal** adj

pyre n pile of wood for burning a dead body on.

Pyrex n ® heat-resistant glassware.

pyrites [pie-rite-eez] n sulfide of a metal, esp. iron pyrites.

pyromania *n* uncontrollable urge to set things on fire. **pyromaniac** *n*

pyrotechnics *n* art of making fireworks; firework display. **pyrotechnic** *adj*

Pyrrhic victory [pir-ik] *n* victory in which the victor's losses are as great as those of the defeated.

python *n* large nonpoisonous snake that crushes its prey.

Q q

QC Quebec; Queen's Counsel.

QED which was to be shown or proved.

QM Quartermaster.

qr. quarter; quire.

qt. quart.

qua [kwah] *prep* in the capacity of.

quack[1] *v* (of a duck) utter a harsh guttural sound. ◆ *n* sound made by a duck.

quack[2] *n* unqualified person who claims medical knowledge; *Informal* doctor.

quad *n* short for QUADRANGLE; *Informal* quadruplet. ◆ *adj* short for QUADRAPHONIC. **quad bike** vehicle like a small motorcycle with four large wheels, designed for agricultural and sporting uses.

quadrangle *n* rectangular courtyard with buildings on all four sides; geometric figure consisting of four points connected by four lines. **quadrangular** *adj*

quadrant *n* quarter of a circle; quarter of a circle's circumference; instrument for measuring the altitude of the stars.

quadraphonic *adj* using four independent channels to reproduce or record sound.

quadratic *Math n* equation in which the variable is raised to the power of two, but nowhere raised to a higher power. ◆ *adj* of the second power.

quadrennial *adj* occurring every four years; lasting four years.

quadri- *combining form* four, e.g. *quadrilateral.*

quadrilateral *adj* having four sides. ◆ *n* polygon with four sides.

quadrille *n* square dance for four couples.

quadruped [kwod-roo-ped] *n* any animal with four legs.

quadruple *v* multiply by four. ◆ *adj* four times as much or as many; consisting of four parts.

quadruplet *n* one of four offspring born at one birth.

quaff [kwoff] *v* drink heartily or in one draft.

quagmire [kwog-mire] *n* soft wet area of land.

quail[1] *n* small game bird of the partridge family.

quail[2] *v* shrink back with fear.

quaint *adj* attractively unusual, esp. in an old-fashioned style. **quaintly** *adv* **quaintness** *n*

quake *v* tremble with or as if with fear. ◆ *n Informal* earthquake.

Quaker *n* member of a Christian sect, the Society of Friends. **Quakerism** *n*

qualify *v* -**fying**, -**fied** provide or be provided with the abilities necessary for a task, office, or duty; moderate or restrict (something, esp. a statement). **qualified** *adj* **qualification** *n* quality or skill needed for a particular activity; condition that modifies or limits; act of qualifying.

quality *n, pl* -**ties** degree or standard of excellence; distinguishing characteristic; basic character or nature of something. **qualitative** *adj* of or relating to quality.

qualm [kwahm] *n* pang of conscience; sudden sensation of misgiving.

quandary *n, pl* -**ries** difficult situation or dilemma.

quango *n, pl* -**gos** partly independent official body, set up by a government.

quanta *n* plural of QUANTUM.

quantify *v* -**fying**, -**fied** discover or express the quantity of. **quantifiable** *adj* **quantification** *n*

quantity *n, pl* -**ties** specified or definite amount or number; aspect of anything that can be measured, weighed, or counted. **quantitative** *adj* of or relating to quantity.

quantum *n, pl* -**ta** desired or required amount. ◆ *adj* designating a major breakthrough or sudden advance, e.g. *quantum leap.* **quantum theory** physics theory based on the idea that energy of electrons is discharged in discrete quanta.

quarantine *n* period of isolation of people or animals to prevent the spread of disease. ◆ *v* isolate in or as if in quarantine.

quark *n Physics* particle thought to be the fundamental unit of matter.

quarrel *n* angry disagreement; cause of dispute. ◆ *v* **-relling, -relled** have a disagreement or dispute. **quarrelsome** *adj*

quarry¹ *n, pl* **-ries** place where stone is dug from the surface of the earth. ◆ *v* **-rying, -ried** extract (stone) from a quarry.

quarry² *n, pl* **-ries** person or animal that is being hunted.

quart *n* unit of liquid measure equal to two pints.

quarter *n* one of four equal parts of something; fourth part of a year; region or district of a town or city; coin worth 25 cents; mercy or pity, as shown towards a defeated opponent. ◆ *pl* lodgings. ◆ *v* divide into four equal parts; billet or be billeted in lodgings. **quarterly** *adj* occurring, due, or issued every three months. ◆ *adv* once every three months. **quarterback** *n* player in football who directs attacking play. **quarterdeck** *n Naut* rear part of the upper deck of a ship. **quarterfinal** *n* round before the semifinal in a competition. **quarter horse** small powerful breed of horse. **quartermaster** *n* military officer responsible for accommodation, food, and equipment. **quarter note** musical note half the length of a half note.

quartet *n* group of four performers; music for such a group.

quarto *n, pl* **-tos** book size in which the sheets are folded into four leaves.

quartz *n* hard glossy mineral, used in making very accurate clocks and watches.

quasar [kway-zar] *n* extremely distant starlike object that emits powerful radio waves.

quash *v* annul or make void; subdue forcefully and completely.

quasi- [kway-zie] *combining form* almost but not really, e.g. *quasi-religious, quasi-scholar*.

quatrain *n* stanza or poem of four lines.

quaver *v* (of a voice) quiver or tremble. ◆ *n Music* note half the length of a crotchet; tremulous sound or note.

quay [kee] *n* wharf built parallel to the shore.

Que. Quebec.

queasy *adj* **-sier, -siest** having the feeling that one is about to vomit; feeling or causing uneasiness. **queasily** *adv* **queasiness** *n*

Quebec *see* Canadian Provincial Facts p631.

queen *n* female sovereign who is the official ruler or head of state; wife of a king; woman, place, or thing considered to be the best of her or its kind; *Slang* effeminate male homosexual; only fertile female in a colony of bees, wasps, or ants; the most powerful piece in chess. **queen it** *Informal* behave in an overbearing manner. **queenly** *adj* **Queen's Counsel** barrister or advocate appointed Counsel to the Crown.

queer *adj* not normal or usual; faint, giddy, or queasy; *Offens* homosexual. ◆ *n Offens* homosexual. **queer someone's pitch** *Informal* spoil someone's chances of something.

quell *v* suppress; overcome.

quench *v* satisfy (one's thirst); put out or extinguish.

quern *n* stone hand mill for grinding corn.

querulous [kwer-yoo-luss] *adj* complaining. **querulously** *adv*

query *n, pl* **-ries** question, esp. one raising doubt; question mark. ◆ *v* **-rying, -ried** express uncertainty, doubt, or an objection concerning (something).

quest *n* long and difficult search. ◆ *v* (foll. by *for* or *after*) go in search of.

question *n* form of words addressed to a person in order to obtain an answer; point at issue; difficulty or uncertainty. ◆ *v* put a question or questions to (a person); express uncertainty about. **in question** under discussion. **out of the question** impossible. **questionable** *adj* of disputable value or authority. **questionably** *adv* **questionnaire** *n* set of questions on a form, used to collect information from people. **question**

mark punctuation mark (?) written at the end of questions.

queue *n* line of people or vehicles waiting for something. ◆ *v* **queueing** *or* **queuing, queued** (often foll. by *up*) form or remain in a line while waiting.

quibble *v* make trivial objections. ◆ *n* trivial objection.

quiche [keesh] *n* savoury flan with an egg custard filling to which vegetables etc. are added.

quick *adj* speedy, fast; lasting or taking a short time; alert and responsive; easily excited or aroused. ◆ *n* area of sensitive flesh under a nail. ◆ *adv Informal* in a rapid manner. **cut someone to the quick** hurt someone's feelings deeply. **quickly** *adv* **quicken** *v* make or become faster or more lively. **quicklime** *n* white solid used in the manufacture of glass and steel. **quicksand** *n* deep mass of loose wet sand that sucks anything on top of it into it. **quicksilver** *n* mercury. **quickstep** *n* fast modern ballroom dance.

quid pro quo *n* one thing, esp. an advantage or object, given in exchange for another.

quiescent [kwee-**ess**-ent] *adj* quiet, inactive, or dormant. **quiescence** *n*

quiet *adj* with little noise; calm or tranquil; untroubled. ◆ *n* quietness. ◆ *v* make or become quiet. **on the quiet** without other people knowing, secretly. **quietly** *adv* **quietness** *n* **quieten** *v* (often foll. by *down*) make or become quiet. **quietude** *n* quietness, peace, or tranquillity.

quietism *n* passivity and calmness of mind towards external events. **quietist** *n, adj*

quiff *n* tuft of hair brushed up above the forehead.

quill *n* pen made from the feather of a bird's wing or tail; stiff hollow spine of a hedgehog or porcupine.

quilt *n* padded covering for a bed. **quilted** *adj* consisting of two layers of fabric with a layer of soft material between them.

quince *n* acid-tasting pear-shaped fruit.

quinine *n* bitter drug used as a tonic and formerly to treat malaria.

quinquennial *adj* occurring every five years; lasting five years.

quinsy *n* inflammation of the throat or tonsils.

quint *n Informal* quintuplet.

quintessence *n* most perfect representation of a quality or state. **quintessential** *adj*

quintet *n* group of five performers; music for such a group.

quintuplet *n* one of five offspring born at one birth.

quip *n* witty saying. ◆ *v* **quipping, quipped** make a quip.

quire *n* set of 24 or 25 sheets of paper.

quirk *n* peculiarity of character; unexpected twist or turn, e.g. *a quirk of fate*. **quirky** *adj*

quisling *n* traitor who aids an occupying enemy force.

quit *v* **quitting, quit** depart from; give up (a job); stop (doing something). **quitter** *n* person who lacks perseverance. **quits** *adj Informal* on an equal footing.

quite *adv* to a greater than average extent, e.g. *she's quite pretty*; absolutely, e.g. *you're quite right*; in actuality, truly. ◆ *interj* expression of agreement.

quiver¹ *v* shake with a tremulous movement. ◆ *n* trembling.

quiver² *n* case for arrows.

quixotic [kwik-**sot**-ik] *adj* romantic and unrealistic. **quixotically** *adv*

quiz *n, pl* **quizzes** entertainment in which the knowledge of the players is tested by a series of questions. ◆ *v* **quizzing, quizzed** investigate by close questioning. **quizzical** *adj* questioning and mocking, e.g. *a quizzical look*. **quizzically** *adv*

quoit *n* large ring used in the game of quoits. ◆ *pl* game in which quoits are tossed at a stake in the ground in attempts to encircle it.

quorum *n* minimum number of people required to be present at a meeting before any transactions can take place. **quorate** *adj* having or being a quorum.

quota *n* share that is due from, due to, or allocated to a group or person; prescribed number or quantity allowed, required, or admitted.

quote *v* repeat (words) exactly from (an earlier work, speech, or conversation); state (a price) for goods or a job of work. ♦ *n Informal* quotation. **quotable** *adj* **quotation** *n* written or spoken passage repeated exactly in a later work, speech, or conversation; act of quoting; estimate of costs submitted by a contractor to a prospective client.

quoth *v Obs* said.

quotidian *adj* daily; commonplace.

quotient *n* result of the division of one number or quantity by another.

q.v. which see: used to refer a reader to another item in the same book.

qwerty *n* standard English language typewriter or computer keyboard.

R r

r radius; ratio; right.

R Queen; King; River; *Chess* rook.

Ra *Chem* radium.

RA Royal Academy; Royal Artillery.

rabbi [rab-bye] *n, pl* -**bis** Jewish spiritual leader. **rabbinical** *adj*

rabbit *n* small burrowing mammal with long ears. **rabbit on** *v Informal* talk too much.

rabble *n* disorderly crowd of noisy people.

rabies [ray-beez] *n* acute infectious viral disease transmitted by dogs and certain other animals.

raccoon *n* small N American mammal with a long striped tail.

race¹ *n* contest of speed. ♦ *pl* meeting for horse racing. ♦ *v* compete with in a race; run swiftly; (of an engine) run faster than normal. **racer** *n* **racecourse** *n* **racehorse** *n* **racetrack** *n*

race² *n* group of people of common ancestry with distinguishing physical features, such as skin colour. **racial** *adj* **racism, racialism** *n* hostile attitude or behaviour to members of other races, based on a belief in the innate superiority of one's own race. **racist, racialist** *adj, n*

raceme [rass-eem] *n* cluster of flowers along a central stem, as in the foxglove.

rack¹ *n* framework for holding particular articles, such as coats or luggage; straight bar with teeth on its edge, to work with a cogwheel; *Hist* instrument of torture that stretched the victim's body. ♦ *v* cause great suffering to. **rack one's brains** try very hard to remember.

rack² *n* **go to rack and ruin** be destroyed.

racket¹ *n* noisy disturbance, din; occupation by which money is made illegally. **racketeer** *n* person making illegal profits.

racket², racquet *n* bat with strings stretched in an oval frame, used in tennis etc. **rackets** *n* ball game played in a paved walled court.

raconteur [rak-on-**tur**] *n* skilled storyteller.

racy *adj* **racier, raciest** slightly shocking; spirited or lively. **racily** *adv* **raciness** *n*

radar *n* device for tracking distant objects by bouncing high-frequency radio pulses off them.

radial *adj* emanating from a common central point; of a radius; (also **radial-ply**) (of a tire) having flexible sidewalls strengthened with radial cords.

radiate *v* emit or be emitted as radiation; spread out from a centre.

radiant *adj* looking happy; shining; emitting radiation. **radiance** *n* **radiation** *n* transmission of heat or light from one body to another; particles or rays emitted in nuclear decay; process of radiating. **radiator** *n* arrangement of pipes containing hot water or steam to heat a room; tubes containing water as cooling apparatus for an automobile engine.

radical *adj* advocating fundamental change; fundamental; thorough. ♦ *n* person advocating fundamental (political) change; number expressed as the root of another. **radically** *adv* **radicalism** *n*

radicle *n* small or developing root.

radii *n* a plural of RADIUS.

radio *n, pl* -**dios** use of electromagnetic waves for broadcasting, communication, etc.; device for receiving and amplifying radio signals; sound broadcasting. ♦ *v* transmit (a message) by radio.

radio- *combining form* of rays, radiation, or radium.

radioactive *adj* emitting radiation as

a result of nuclear decay. **radioactivity** *n*

radiography [ray-dee-**og**-ra-fee] *n* production of an image on a film or plate by radiation. **radiographer** *n*

radiology [ray-dee-**ol**-a-jee] *n* science of using x-rays in medicine. **radiologist** *n*

radiotherapy *n* treatment of disease, esp. cancer, by radiation. **radiotherapist** *n*

radish *n* small hot-flavoured root vegetable eaten raw in salads.

radium *n* radioactive metallic element.

radius *n, pl* **radii, radiuses** (length of) a straight line from the centre to the circumference of a circle; outer of two bones in the forearm.

radon [**ray**-don] *n* radioactive gaseous element.

raffia *n* prepared palm fibre for weaving mats etc.

raffish *adj* disreputable.

raffle *n* lottery with an article as a prize. ◆ *v* offer as a prize in a raffle.

raft *n* floating platform of logs, planks, etc.

rafter *n* one of the main beams of a roof.

rag[1] *n* fragment of cloth; torn piece; *Informal* newspaper. ◆ *pl* tattered clothing. **ragged** [**rag**-gid] *adj* dressed in shabby or torn clothes; torn; lacking smoothness. **ragtime** *n* style of jazz piano music.

rag[2] *v* **ragging, ragged** tease; play practical jokes on. ◆ *n* carnival with processions etc., organized by students to raise money for charities.

ragamuffin *n* ragged dirty child.

rage *n* violent anger or passion. ◆ *v* speak or act with fury; proceed violently and without check, e.g. *a storm was raging*. **all the rage** very popular.

raglan *adj* (of a sleeve) joined to a garment by diagonal seams from the neck to the underarm.

ragout [rag-**goo**] *n* richly seasoned stew of meat and vegetables.

raid *n* sudden surprise attack or search. ◆ *v* make a raid on. **raider** *n*

rail[1] *n* horizontal bar, esp. as part of a fence or track; railway. **railing** *n* fence made of rails supported by posts. **railway, railroad** *n* track of iron rails on which trains run; company operating a railway.

rail[2] *v* (foll. by *at* or *against*) complain bitterly or loudly. **raillery** *n* teasing or joking.

rail[3] *n* small marsh bird.

raiment *n Obs* clothing.

rain *n* water falling in drops from the clouds. ◆ *v* fall or pour down as rain. **rainy** *adj* **rainbow** *n* arch of colours in the sky. **raincoat** *n* water-resistant overcoat. **rainfall** *n* amount of rain. **rainforest** *n* dense forest in the tropics.

raise *v* lift up; set upright; increase in amount or intensity; bring up (a family); put forward for consideration; collect or levy; build; end, e.g. *raise a siege*. ◆ *n* increase, esp. of wages.

raisin *n* dried grape.

raison d'être [ray-zon **det**-ra] *n French* reason or justification for existence.

Raj *n* **the Raj** former British rule in India.

rajah *n* Indian prince or ruler.

rake[1] *n* tool with a long handle and a crosspiece with teeth, used for smoothing earth or gathering leaves, hay, etc. ◆ *v* gather or smooth with a rake; search (through); sweep (with gunfire). **rake it in** *Informal* make a large amount of money. **rake-off** *n Slang* share of profits, esp. illegal. **rake up** *v* revive memories of (a forgotten unpleasant event).

rake[2] *n* dissolute or immoral man. **rakish** *adj*

rakish [**ray**-kish] *adj* dashing or jaunty.

rally *n, pl* **-lies** large gathering of people for a (political) meeting; marked recovery of strength; *Tennis* lively exchange of strokes; automobile driving competition on public roads. ◆ *v* **rallying, rallied** bring or come together after dispersal or for a common cause; regain health or strength, revive.

ram *n* male sheep; hydraulic machine. ◆ *v* **ramming, rammed** strike against with force; force or drive; cram or stuff. **ram raid** *Informal* raid on a shop in which a stolen automobile is driven into the window. **ram raider** person who carries out a ram raid.

RAM *Computers* random access

memory.

Ramadan n 9th Muslim month; strict fasting observed during this time.

ramble v walk without a definite route; talk incoherently. ◆ n walk, esp. in the country. **rambler** n climbing rose; person who rambles.

ramekin [ram-ik-in] n small ovenproof dish for a single serving of food.

ramify v -**ifying, -ified** become complex; spread in branches, subdivide. **ramification** n consequence.

ramp n slope joining two level surfaces; small hump on a road to make traffic slow down.

rampage v dash about violently. **on the rampage** behaving violently or destructively.

rampant adj unrestrained in growth or spread, rife; (of a heraldic beast) on its hind legs.

rampart n mound or wall for defence.

ramshackle adj tumbledown, rickety, or makeshift.

ran v past tense of RUN.

ranch n large cattle farm in the N American West. **rancher** n

rancid adj (of butter, bacon, etc.) stale and having an offensive smell.

rancour n deep bitter hate. **rancorous** adj

rand n monetary unit of S Africa.

random adj made or done by chance or without plan. **at random** haphazard (ly).

randy adj **randier, randiest** Slang sexually aroused.

rang v past tense of RING[1].

range n limits of effectiveness or variation; distance that a missile or plane can travel; distance of a mark shot at; whole set of related things; place for shooting practice or rocket testing; chain of mountains; kitchen stove. ◆ v vary between one point and another; cover or extend over; roam. **ranger** n official in charge of a nature reserve etc.; (R-) member of the senior branch of Guides. **rangefinder** n instrument for finding how far away an object is.

rangy [rain-jee] adj **rangier, rangiest** having long slender limbs.

rank[1] n status; relative place or position; social class; order; row or line. ◆ v have a specific rank or position; arrange in rows or lines. **rank and file** ordinary people or members. **the ranks** common soldiers.

rank[2] adj complete or absolute, e.g. rank favouritism; smelling offensively strong; growing too thickly. **rankly** adv

rankle v continue to cause resentment or bitterness.

ransack v search thoroughly; pillage, plunder.

ransom n money demanded in return for the release of someone who has been kidnapped.

rant v talk in a loud and excited way. **ranter** n

ranunculus n, pl -**luses, -li** genus of plants including the buttercup.

rap v **rapping, rapped** hit with a sharp quick blow; utter (a command) abruptly; perform a rhythmic monologue with musical backing. ◆ n sharp quick blow; rhythmic monologue performed to music. **take the rap** Slang suffer punishment for something whether guilty or not. **rapper** n

rapacious adj greedy or grasping. **rapacity** n

rape[1] v force to submit to sexual intercourse. ◆ n act of raping; any violation or abuse. **rapist** n

rape[2] n plant with oil-yielding seeds, also used as fodder.

rapid adj quick, swift. **rapid eye movement** movement of the eyeballs while a person is dreaming. **rapids** pl n stretch of a river with a fast turbulent current. **rapidly** adv **rapidity** n

rapier [ray-pyer] n fine-bladed sword.

rapport [rap-pore] n harmony or agreement.

rapprochement [rap-prosh-mong] n re-establishment of friendly relations, esp. between nations.

rapt adj engrossed or spellbound. **rapture** n ecstasy. **rapturous** adj

raptorial adj predatory; of birds of prey.

rare[1] adj uncommon; infrequent; of uncommonly high quality; (of air at high altitudes) having low density, thin. **rarely** adv seldom. **rarity** n

rare[2] adj (of meat) lightly cooked.

rarebit n savoury cheese dish.

rarefied [rare-if-ide] adj highly specialized, exalted; (of air) thin.

raring adj **raring to go** enthusiastic, willing, or ready.

rascal n rogue; naughty (young) person. **rascally** adj

rash¹ adj hasty, reckless, or incautious. **rashly** adv

rash² n skin eruption; outbreak of (unpleasant) occurrences.

rasher n thin slice of bacon.

rasp n harsh grating noise; coarse file. ◆ v speak in a grating voice; make a scraping noise.

raspberry n red juicy edible berry; plant which bears it; Informal spluttering noise made with the tongue and lips, to show contempt.

Rastafarian n, adj (member) of a cult originating in Jamaica and regarding Haile Selassie as God (also **Rasta**).

rat n small rodent; Informal contemptible person, esp. a deserter or informer. ◆ v **ratting, ratted** Informal inform (on); hunt rats. **ratty** adj Slang bad-tempered, irritable. **rat race** continual hectic competitive activity.

ratafia [rat-a-fee-a] n liqueur made from fruit; almond-flavoured biscuit.

ratatouille [rat-a-twee] n vegetable casserole of tomatoes, eggplants, etc.

ratchet n set of teeth on a bar or wheel allowing motion in one direction only.

rate n degree of speed or progress; proportion between two things; charge. ◆ pl local tax on property. ◆ v consider or value; estimate the value of. **at any rate** in any case. **rateable, ratable** adj able to be rated; (of property) liable to payment of rates. **ratepayer** n

rather adv to some extent; preferably; more willingly.

ratify v -ifying, -ified give formal approval to. **ratification** n

rating n valuation or assessment; classification; noncommissioned sailor. ◆ pl size of the audience for a TV programme.

ratio n, pl -tios relationship between two numbers or amounts expressed as a proportion.

ratiocinate [rat-ee-oss-in-nate] v reason or think out. **ratiocination** n

ration n fixed allowance of food etc. ◆ v limit to a certain amount per person.

rational adj reasonable, sensible; capable of reasoning. **rationally** adv **rationality** n **rationale** [rash-a-nahl] n reason for an action or decision. **rationalism** n philosophy that regards reason as the only basis for beliefs or actions. **rationalist** n **rationalize** v justify by plausible reasoning; reorganize to improve efficiency or profitability. **rationalization** n

rattan n climbing palm with jointed stems; cane from this.

rattle v give out a succession of short sharp sounds; clatter; shake briskly causing sharp sounds; Informal confuse or fluster. ◆ n short sharp sound; instrument for making it. **rattlesnake** n poisonous snake with loose horny segments on the tail that make a rattling sound.

raucous adj hoarse or harsh.

raunchy adj **raunchier, raunchiest** Slang earthy, sexy.

ravage v Lit lay waste or plunder. **ravages** pl n destruction.

rave v talk wildly in delirium or with enthusiasm. ◆ n Informal enthusiastically good review. **raving** adj delirious; Informal exceptional, e.g. a raving beauty.

ravel v -elling, -elled tangle or become entangled.

raven n black bird like a crow. ◆ adj (of hair) shiny black.

ravenous adj very hungry.

ravine [rav-veen] n narrow steep-sided valley worn by a stream.

ravioli pl n small squares of pasta with a savoury filling.

ravish v enrapture; Lit rape. **ravishing** adj lovely or entrancing.

raw adj uncooked; not refined; inexperienced, e.g. raw recruits; chilly. **raw deal** unfair or dishonest treatment. **rawhide** n untanned hide.

ray¹ n single line or narrow beam of light; any of a set of radiating lines.

ray² n large sea fish with a whiplike tail.

rayon n (fabric made of) a synthetic fibre.

raze v destroy (buildings or a town) completely.

razor *n* sharp instrument for shaving. **razorbill** *n* N Atlantic auk.

razzle-dazzle, razzmatazz *n Slang* showy activity; spree.

RC Red Cross; Roman Catholic.

RCAF Royal Canadian Air Force.

RCMP Royal Canadian Mounted Police.

RCN Royal Canadian Navy.

Rd Road.

re *prep* with reference to, concerning.

re- *prefix* again, e.g. *re-enter, retrial*.

reach *v* arrive at; make a movement in order to grasp or touch; succeed in touching; make contact or communication with; extend to. ◆ *n* distance that one can reach; range of influence; stretch of a river between two bends. **reachable** *adj*

react *v* act in response or opposition (to). **reaction** *n* physical or emotional response to a stimulus; any action resisting another; opposition to change; chemical or nuclear change, combination, or decomposition. **reactionary** *n, adj* (person) opposed to change, esp. in politics. **reactance** *n Electricity* resistance in a coil due to the current reacting on itself. **reactive** *adj* chemically active. **reactor** *n* apparatus in which a nuclear reaction is maintained and controlled to produce nuclear energy.

read *v* **reading, read** look at and understand or take in (written or printed matter); look at and say aloud; understand (an indicating instrument); (of an instrument) register; study; matter suitable for reading, e.g. *a good read*. **reading** *n* **reader** *n* person who reads; senior university lecturer; textbook. **readership** *n* readers of a publication collectively. **readable** *adj* enjoyable to read; legible. **readability** *n*

readjust *v* adapt to a new situation. **readjustment** *n*

ready *adj* **readier, readiest** prepared for use or action; willing, prompt. **readily** *adv* **readiness** *n* **ready-made** *adj* for immediate use by any customer.

reagent [ree-**age**-ent] *n* chemical substance that reacts with another, used to detect the presence of the other.

real *adj* existing in fact; happening; actual; genuine; (of property) consisting of land and houses. **really** *adv* very; truly. ◆ *interj* indeed! **reality** *n* real existence. **reality TV** television programmes focusing on members of the public living in conditions created especially by the programme makers. **realtor** *n* agent, esp. accredited one who sells houses etc. for others. **realty** *n* real estate. **real ale** *Brit* beer allowed to ferment in the barrel. **real estate** landed property.

realistic *adj* seeing and accepting things as they really are, practical. **realistically** *adv* **realism** *n* **realist** *n*

realize *v* become aware or grasp the significance of; achieve (a plan, hopes, etc.); convert into money. **realization** *n*

realm *n* kingdom; sphere of interest.

ream *n* twenty quires of paper, generally 500 sheets. ◆ *pl Informal* large quantity (of written matter).

reap *v* cut and gather (harvest); receive as the result of a previous activity. **reaper** *n*

reappear *v* appear again. **reappearance** *n*

rear¹ *n* back part; part of an army, procession, etc. behind the others. **bring up the rear** come last. **rearmost** *adj* **rear admiral** high-ranking naval officer. **rearguard** *n* troops protecting the rear of an army.

rear² *v* care for and educate (children); breed (animals); (of a horse) rise on its hind feet.

rearrange *v* organize differently, alter. **rearrangement** *n*

reason *n* ground or motive; faculty of rational thought; sanity. ◆ *v* think logically in forming conclusions; (usu. foll. by *with*) persuade by logical argument into doing something. **reasonable** *adj* sensible; not excessive; suitable; logical. **reasonably** *adv*

reassess *v* reconsider the value or importance of.

reassure *v* restore confidence to. **reassurance** *n*

rebate *n* discount or refund.

rebel *v* **-belling, -belled** revolt against the ruling power; reject accepted conventions. ◆ *n* person who rebels. **rebellion** *n* organized open resistance to authority; rejection of conventions. **rebellious** *adj*

rebore, reboring *n* boring of a cylinder to restore its true shape.

rebound *v* spring back; misfire so as to hurt the perpetrator of a plan or deed. **on the rebound** *Informal* while recovering from rejection.

rebuff *v* reject or snub. ◆ *n* blunt refusal, snub.

rebuke *v* scold sternly. ◆ *n* stern scolding.

rebus [ree-buss] *n, pl* **-buses** puzzle consisting of pictures and symbols representing words or syllables.

rebut *v* **-butting, -butted** refute or disprove. **rebuttal** *n*

recalcitrant *adj* wilfully disobedient. **recalcitrance** *n*

recall *v* recollect or remember; order to return; annul or cancel. ◆ *n* order to return; ability to remember.

recant *v* withdraw (a statement or belief) publicly. **recantation** *n*

recap *Informal* ◆ *v* **-capping, -capped** recapitulate. ◆ *n* recapitulation.

recapitulate *v* state again briefly, repeat. **recapitulation** *n*

recapture *v* experience again; capture again.

recce *Slang* ◆ *v* **-ceing, -ced** *or* **-ceed** reconnoitre. ◆ *n* reconnaissance.

recede *v* become distant; (of the hair) stop growing at the front.

receipt *n* written acknowledgment of money or goods received; receiving or being received.

receive *v* take, accept, or get; experience; greet (guests). **received** *adj* generally accepted. **receiver** *n* detachable part of a telephone that is held to the ear; equipment in a telephone, radio, or television that converts electrical signals into sound; person appointed by court to manage property of a bankrupt; person who handles stolen goods knowing they have been stolen. **receivership** *n*

recent *adj* having happened lately; new. **recently** *adv*

receptacle *n* object used to contain something.

reception *n* area for receiving guests, clients, etc.; formal party; manner of receiving; welcome; (in broadcasting) quality of signals received.

receptionist *n* person who receives guests, clients, etc.

receptive *adj* willing to receive new ideas, suggestions, etc. **receptivity** *n*

recess *n* niche or alcove; holiday between sessions of work; secret hidden place. **recessed** *adj* hidden or placed in a recess.

recession *n* period of reduction in trade. **recessive** *adj* receding.

recherché [rish-**air**-shay] *adj* of studied elegance; choice or rare.

recidivist *n* person who relapses into crime.

recipe *n* directions for cooking a dish; method for achieving something.

recipient *n* person who receives something.

reciprocal [ris-**sip**-pro-kal] *adj* mutual; given or done in return. **reciprocally** *adv* **reciprocity** *n*

reciprocate *v* give or feel in return; (of a machine part) move backwards and forwards. **reciprocation** *n*

recite *v* repeat aloud, esp. to an audience. **recital** [ris-**site**-al] *n* musical performance; act of reciting. **recitation** *n* recital, usu. from memory, of poetry or prose. **recitative** [ress-it-a-**teev**] *n* musical narration.

reckless *adj* heedless of danger. **recklessly** *adv* **recklessness** *n*

reckon *v* expect; consider or think; make calculations, count. **reckoner** *n* **reckoning** *n*

reclaim *v* regain possession of; make fit for cultivation. **reclamation** *n*

recline *v* rest in a leaning position. **reclining** *adj*

recluse *n* person avoiding society; hermit. **reclusive** *adj*

recognize *v* identify as (a person or thing) already known; accept as true or existing; treat as valid; notice, show appreciation of. **recognition** *n* **recognizable** *adj* **recognizance** [rik-**og**-nizz-anss] *n* undertaking before a court to observe some condition.

recoil *v* jerk or spring back; draw back in horror; (of an action) go wrong so as to hurt the perpetrator. ◆ *n* backward jerk; recoiling.

recollect *v* call back to mind, remember. **recollection** *n*

recommend *v* advise or counsel; praise or commend; make acceptable.

recommendation n

recompense v pay or reward; compensate or make up for. ◆ n compensation; reward.

reconcile v harmonize (conflicting beliefs etc.); bring back into friendship; accept or cause to accept (an unpleasant situation). **reconcilable** adj **reconciliation** n

recondite adj difficult to understand, abstruse.

recondition v restore to good condition or working order.

reconnaissance [rik-kon-iss-anss] n survey for military or engineering purposes.

reconnoitre [rek-a-noy-ter] v make a reconnaissance of.

reconsider v think about again, consider changing.

reconstitute v reorganize in a slightly different form; restore (food) to its former state, esp. by the addition of water to a concentrate. **reconstitution** n

reconstruct v use evidence to re-create; rebuild. **reconstruction** n

record n document or other thing that preserves information; disc with indentations which a record player transforms into sound; best recorded achievement; known facts about a person's past. ◆ v put in writing; preserve (sound, TV programmes, etc.) on plastic disc, magnetic tape, etc., for reproduction on a playback device; show or register. **off the record** not for publication. **recorder** n person or machine that records, esp. a video, cassette, or tape recorder; type of flute, blown at one end; judge in certain courts. **recording** n **record player** instrument for reproducing sound on records.

recount v tell in detail.

re-count v count again. ◆ n second or subsequent count, esp. of votes.

recoup [rik-**koop**] v regain or make good (a loss); recompense or compensate.

recourse n (resorting to) a source of help; Law right of action or appeal.

recover v become healthy again; get back (a loss or expense). **recovery** n **recoverable** adj

recreant n Old-fashioned cowardly or disloyal person.

re-create v make happen or exist again.

recreation n agreeable or refreshing occupation, relaxation or amusement. **recreational** adj **recreational vehicle** n a large vanlike vehicle equipped to be lived in Abbrev: **RV**.

recrimination n mutual blame. **recriminatory** adj

recruit n newly enlisted soldier; new member or supporter. ◆ v enlist (new soldiers, members, etc.). **recruitment** n

rectangle n oblong four-sided figure with four right angles. **rectangular** adj

rectify v **-fying, -fied** put right, correct; purify by distillation; Electricity convert (alternating current) into direct current. **rectification** n **rectifier** n

rectilinear [rek-tee-**lin**-ee-er] adj in a straight line; characterized by straight lines.

rectitude n moral correctness.

recto n, pl **-tos** right-hand page of a book; front of a sheet of paper.

rector n clergyman in charge of a parish; head of certain academic institutions. **rectory** n rector's house.

rectum n, pl **-ta** final section of the large intestine. **rectal** adj

recumbent adj lying down.

recuperate v recover from illness. **recuperation** n **recuperative** adj

recur v **-curring, -curred** happen again. **recurrence** n repetition. **recurrent** adj

recusant [rek-yew-zant] n Hist person who refused to obey the Church of England; person refusing to obey authority.

recycle v reprocess (used materials) for further use.

red adj **redder, reddest** of a colour varying from crimson to orange and seen in blood, fire, etc.; flushed in the face from anger, shame, etc. ◆ n red colour; (R-) Informal communist. **in the red** Informal in debt. **see red** Informal be angry. **redness** n **redden** v make or become red. **reddish** adj **red-blooded** adj Informal vigorous; virile. **redbrick** adj (of a British university) founded in the late 19th or early 20th century. **red carpet** very special

welcome for an important guest.
redcoat n Hist British soldier. **Red Cross** international organization providing help for victims of war or natural disasters. **red-handed** adj Informal (caught) in the act of doing something wrong or illegal. **red herring** something which diverts attention from the main issue. **red-hot** adj glowing red; extremely hot; very keen. **red light** traffic signal to stop; danger signal. **red meat** dark meat, esp. beef or lamb. **red tape** excessive adherence to official rules.

redeem v make up for; reinstate (oneself) in someone's good opinion; free from sin; buy back; pay off (a loan or debt). **the Redeemer** Jesus Christ. **redeemable** adj **redemption** n **redemptive** adj

redeploy v assign to a new position or task.

redevelop v rebuild or renovate (an area or building). **redevelopment** n

redolent adj smelling strongly (of); reminiscent (of). **redolence** n

redouble v increase, multiply, or intensify.

redoubt n small fort defending a hilltop or pass.

redoubtable adj formidable.

redound v cause advantage or disadvantage (to).

redox n chemical reaction in which one substance is reduced and the other is oxidized.

redress v make amends for. ◆ n compensation or amends.

reduce v bring down, lower; lessen, weaken; bring by force or necessity to some state or action; slim; simplify; make (sauce) more concentrated; Chem separate (a substance) from others with which it is combined. **reducible** adj **reduction** n

redundant adj (of a worker) no longer needed; superfluous. **redundancy** n

reed n tall grass that grows in swamps and shallow water; tall straight stem of this plant; Music vibrating cane or metal strip in certain wind instruments. **reedy** adj full of reeds; harsh and thin in tone.

reef¹ n ridge of rock or coral near the surface of the sea; vein of ore.

reef² n part of a sail which can be rolled up to reduce its area. ◆ v take in a reef of. **reefer** n short thick jacket worn esp. by sailors; Old-fashioned slang hand-rolled cigarette containing cannabis. **reef knot** two overhand knots turned opposite ways.

reek n strong (unpleasant) smell. ◆ v smell strongly; (foll. by of) be full (of).

reel¹ n cylindrical object on which film, tape, thread, or wire is wound; winding apparatus, as of a fishing rod. ◆ v wind on a reel; draw in by means of a reel. **reel off** v recite or write fluently.

reel² v stagger, sway, or whirl.

reel³ n lively Scottish dance.

reeve n president of local (esp. rural) council; Hist manorial steward or official.

ref n Informal referee in sport.

refectory n, pl -tories room for meals in a college etc.

refer v -ferring, -ferred (foll. by to) mention or allude (to); be relevant (to); send (to) for information; submit (to) for decision. **referral** n **reference** n act of referring; citation or direction in a book; appeal to the judgment of another; testimonial; person to whom inquiries as to character etc. may be made. **with reference to** concerning.

referee n umpire in sports, esp. football or boxing; person willing to testify to someone's character etc.; arbitrator. ◆ v -eeing, -eed act as referee of.

referendum n, pl -dums, -da submitting of a question to the electorate.

refill v fill again. ◆ n subsequent filling; replacement supply of something in a permanent container.

refine v purify; improve. **refined** adj cultured or polite; purified. **refinement** n improvement or elaboration; fineness of taste or manners; subtle point or distinction. **refinery** n place where sugar, oil, etc. is refined. **refiner** n

reflation n (steps taken to produce) an increase in the economic activity of a country etc. **reflate** v **reflationary** adj

reflect v throw back, esp. rays of light, heat, etc.; form an image of; show;

bring credit or discredit upon; consider at length. **reflection** n act of reflecting; return of rays of heat, light, etc. from a surface; image of an object given back by a mirror etc.; conscious thought or meditation; attribution of discredit or blame. **reflective** adj quiet, contemplative; capable of reflecting images. **reflector** n polished surface for reflecting light etc.

reflex n involuntary response to a stimulus or situation. ◆ adj (of a muscular action) involuntary; reflected; (of an angle) more than 180°. **reflexive** adj Grammar denoting a verb whose subject is the same as its object, e.g. to dress oneself.

reflexology n foot massage as a therapy in alternative medicine.

reform v improve; abandon evil practices. ◆ n improvement. **reformer** n **reformation** [ref-fer-may-shun] n a reforming; (R-) religious movement in 16th-century Europe that resulted in the establishment of the Protestant Churches. **reformatory** n (formerly) institution for reforming juvenile offenders. **Reform Party** major political party with policy of low taxation.

refract v change the course of (light etc.) passing from one medium to another. **refraction** n **refractive** adj **refractor** n

refractory adj unmanageable or rebellious; Med resistant to treatment; resistant to heat.

refrain¹ v (foll. by from) keep oneself from doing.

refrain² n frequently repeated part of a song.

refrangible adj that can be refracted. **refrangibility** n

refresh v revive or reinvigorate, as through food, drink, or rest; stimulate (the memory). **refresher** n **refreshing** adj having a reviving effect; pleasantly different or new. **refreshment** n something that refreshes, esp. food or drink.

refrigerate v freeze; cool. **refrigeration** n **refrigerator** n apparatus in which food and drinks are kept cool.

refuge n (source of) protection. **refugee** n person who seeks refuge, esp. in a foreign country.

refulgent adj shining, radiant. **refulgence** n

refund v pay back. ◆ n return of money; amount returned.

refurbish v renovate and brighten up.

refuse¹ v decline, deny, or reject. **refusal** n denial of anything demanded or offered.

refuse² n garbage or useless matter.

refute v disprove. **refutable** adj **refutation** n

regain v get back or recover; reach again.

regal adj of or like a king or queen. **regally** adv **regality** n **regalia** pl n ceremonial emblems of royalty, an order, etc.

regale v (foll. by with) attempt to entertain (someone) with (stories).

regard v look at; relate to; consider; heed. ◆ n particular respect; attention; look; esteem. ◆ pl expression of goodwill. **as regards, regarding** in respect of, concerning. **regardless** adj heedless. ◆ adv in spite of everything.

regatta n meeting for yacht or boat races.

regenerate v (cause to) undergo spiritual, moral, or physical renewal; reproduce or re-create. **regeneration** n **regenerative** adj

regent n ruler of a kingdom during the absence, childhood, or illness of its monarch. ◆ adj ruling as a regent, e.g. prince regent. **regency** n status or period of office of a regent.

reggae n style of Jamaican popular music with a strong beat.

regicide n person who kills a king; killing of a king.

regime [ray-zheem] n system of government; particular administration.

regimen n prescribed system of diet etc.; rule.

regiment n organized body of troops as a unit of the army. ◆ v discipline, organize (too) rigidly. **regimental** adj **regimentation** n

region n administrative division of a country; an area considered as a unit but with no definite boundaries; part of the body. **regional** adj

register n (book containing) an official list or record of things; range of a voice or instrument. ◆ v enter in a register, record, or set down in writing; show or be shown on a scale or other measuring instrument. **registration** n **registrar** n keeper of official records. **register office, registry office** place where births, marriages, and deaths are recorded.

regress v revert to a former worse condition. **regression** n act of regressing; *Psychol* using an earlier (inappropriate) mode of behaviour. **regressive** adj

regret v **-gretting, -gretted** feel sorry about; express apology or distress. ◆ n feeling of repentance, guilt, or sorrow. **regretful** adj **regrettable** adj

regular adj normal; symmetrical or even; habitual; done or occurring according to a rule; periodical; employed continuously in the armed forces; straight or level. ◆ n regular soldier; *Informal* regular customer. **regularity** n **regularize** v

regulate v control, esp. by rules; adjust slightly. **regulation** n rule; regulating. **regulator** n device that automatically controls pressure, temperature, etc.

regurgitate v vomit; (of some birds and animals) bring back (partly digested food) into the mouth; reproduce (ideas, facts, etc.) without understanding them. **regurgitation** n

rehabilitate v help (a person) to readjust to society after illness, imprisonment, etc.; restore to a former position or rank; restore the good reputation of. **rehabilitation** n

rehash v rework or reuse. ◆ n old materials presented in a new form.

rehearse v practise (a play, concert, etc.); repeat aloud. **rehearsal** n

rehouse v provide with a new (and better) home.

reign n period of a sovereign's rule. ◆ v rule (a country); be supreme.

reimburse v refund, pay back. **reimbursement** n

rein n (usu. pl.) narrow strap attached to a bit to guide a horse; means of control. ◆ v check or manage with reins; control.

reincarnation n rebirth of a soul in successive bodies; one of a series of such transmigrations. **reincarnate** v

reindeer n deer of arctic regions with large branched antlers.

reinforce v strengthen with new support, material, or force; strengthen with additional troops, ships, etc. **reinforcement** n

reinstate v restore or re-establish. **reinstatement** n

reiterate v repeat again and again. **reiteration** n

reject v refuse to accept or believe; discard as useless; rebuff (a person). ◆ n person or thing rejected as not up to standard. **rejection** n

rejig v **-jigging, -jigged** re-equip (a factory or plant); rearrange.

rejoice v feel or express great happiness.

rejoin v reply; join again.

rejoinder n answer, retort.

rejuvenate v restore youth or vitality to. **rejuvenation** n

relapse v fall back into bad habits, illness, etc. ◆ n return of bad habits, illness, etc.

relate v establish a relation between; have reference or relation to; (foll. by *to*) have an understanding (of people or ideas), e.g. *inability to relate to others*; tell (a story) or describe (an event). **related** adj

relation n connection between things; relative; connection by blood or marriage; act of relating (a story). ◆ pl social or political dealings; family; *Euphemistic* sexual intercourse. **relationship** n dealings and feelings between people or countries; emotional or sexual affair; connection between two things; association by blood or marriage, kinship.

relative adj dependent on relation to something else, not absolute; having reference or relation (to); *Grammar* referring to a word or clause earlier in the sentence. ◆ n person connected by blood or marriage; *Grammar* relative pronoun or clause. **relatively** adv **relativity** n state of being relative; subject of two theories of Albert Einstein, dealing with relationships of space, time, and motion, and acceleration and gravity.

relax v make or become looser, less tense, or less rigid; ease up from effort or attention, rest; become more friendly; be less strict about. **relaxing** adj **relaxation** n

relay n fresh set of people or animals relieving others; *Electricity* device for making or breaking a local circuit; broadcasting station receiving and retransmitting programmes. ◆ v -laying, -layed pass on (a message). **relay race** race between teams of which each runner races part of the distance.

release v set free; let go or fall; permit public showing of (a film etc.); emit heat, energy, etc. ◆ n setting free; written discharge; statement to the press; act of issuing for sale or publication; catch or handle; newly issued film, record, etc.

relegate v put in a less important position, demote. **relegation** n

relent v give up a harsh intention, become less severe. **relentless** adj merciless; unremitting.

relevant adj to do with the matter in hand. **relevance** n

reliable adj see RELY.

reliance n see RELY.

relic n something that has survived from the past; body or possession of a saint, regarded as holy. ◆ pl remains or traces. **relict** n Obs widow.

relief n gladness at the end or removal of pain, distress, etc.; money or food given to victims of disaster, poverty, etc.; release from monotony or duty; person who replaces another at a duty etc.; freeing of a besieged city etc.; projection of a carved design from the surface; distinctness or prominence, e.g. *stand out in bold relief*. **relieve** v bring relief to. **relieve oneself** urinate or defecate. **relief map** map showing the shape and height of land by shading.

religion n system of belief in and worship of a supernatural power or god. **religious** adj of religion; pious or devout; scrupulous or conscientious. **religiously** adv

relinquish v give up or abandon. **relinquishment** n

reliquary [rel-lik-wer-ee] n, pl -ries case or shrine for holy relics.

relish v enjoy, like very much. ◆ n liking or gusto; appetizing savoury food, such as pickle; zestful quality or flavour.

relocate v move to a new place to live or work. **relocation** n

reluctant adj unwilling. **reluctantly** adv **reluctance** n

rely v -lying, -lied depend (on); trust. **reliable** adj able to be trusted, dependable. **reliably** adv **reliability** n **reliance** n dependence, confidence, or trust. **reliant** adj

REM rapid eye movement.

remain v continue to be; stay, be left behind; be left (over); be left to be done, said, etc. **remains** pl n relics, esp. of ancient buildings; dead body. **remainder** n part which is left; amount left over after subtraction or division. ◆ v offer (copies of a poorly selling book) at reduced prices.

remand v send back into custody. **on remand** in custody. **remand centre** place where accused people are detained awaiting trial.

remark v make casual comment (on); say; observe or notice. ◆ n observation or comment. **remarkable** adj worthy of note or attention; striking or unusual. **remarkably** adv

remedy n, pl -dies means of curing pain or disease; means of solving a problem. ◆ v -edying, -edied put right. **remedial** adj intended to correct a specific disability, handicap, etc.

remember v retain in or recall to one's memory; have in mind. **remembrance** n memory; token or souvenir; honouring of the memory of a person or event.

remind v cause to remember; put in mind (of). **reminder** n something that recalls the past; note to remind a person of something not done.

reminisce v talk or write of past times, experiences, etc. **reminiscence** n remembering; thing recollected. ◆ pl memoirs. **reminiscent** adj reminding or suggestive (of).

remiss adj negligent or careless.

remission n reduction in the length of a prison term; pardon or forgiveness; easing of intensity, as of an illness.

remit v -mitting, -mitted send (money) for goods, services, etc., esp. by post; cancel (a punishment or debt); refer (a decision) to a higher authority or later date. ◆ n area of competence or authority. **remittance** n sending of money; money sent.

remnant *n* small piece, esp. of fabric, left over; surviving trace.

remonstrate *v* argue in protest. **remonstrance** *n*

remorse *n* feeling of sorrow and regret for something one did. **remorseful** *adj* **remorsefully** *adv* **remorseless** *adj* pitiless; persistent. **remorselessly** *adv*

remote *adj* far away, distant; aloof; slight or faint. **remotely** *adv* **remote control** control of an apparatus from a distance by an electrical device.

remould *v* renovate (a worn tire). ◆ *n* renovated tire.

remove *v* take away or off; dismiss from office; get rid of. ◆ *n* degree of difference. **removable** *adj* **removal** *n* removing, esp. changing residence.

remunerate *v* reward or pay. **remuneration** *n* **remunerative** *adj*

renaissance *n* revival or rebirth, esp. (R-) the revival of learning in the 14th–16th centuries.

renal [ree-nal] *adj* of the kidneys.

renascent *adj* becoming active or vigorous again. **renascence** *n*

rend *v* **rending, rent** tear or wrench apart; (of a sound) break (the silence) violently.

render *v* cause to become; give or provide (aid, a service, etc.); submit or present (a bill); portray or represent; cover with plaster; melt down (fat).

rendezvous [ron-day-voo] *n, pl* **-vous** appointment; meeting place. ◆ *v* meet as arranged.

rendition *n* performance; translation.

renegade *n* person who deserts a cause.

renege [rin-nayg] *v* (usu. foll. by *on*) go back on (a promise etc.).

renew *v* begin again; reaffirm; make valid again; grow again; restore to a former state; replace (a worn part). **renewable** *adj* **renewal** *n*

rennet *n* substance for curdling milk to make cheese.

renounce *v* give up (a belief, habit, etc.) voluntarily; give up (a title or claim) formally. **renunciation** *n*

renovate *v* restore to good condition. **renovation** *n*

renown *n* widespread good reputation. **renowned** *adj* famous.

rent[1] *n* regular payment for use of

land, a building, machine, etc. ◆ *v* give or have use of in return for rent. **rental** *n* sum payable as rent.

rent[2] *n* tear or fissure. ◆ *v* past of REND.

renunciation *n* see RENOUNCE.

reorganize *v* organize in a new and more efficient way. **reorganization** *n*

rep[1] *n* short for REPERTORY COMPANY.

rep[2] *n* short for REPRESENTATIVE.

repair[1] *v* restore to good condition, mend. ◆ *n* act of repairing; repaired part; state or condition, e.g. *in good repair*. **repairable** *adj* **reparation** *n* something done or given as compensation.

repair[2] *v* go (to).

repartee *n* interchange of witty retorts; witty retort.

repast *n* meal.

repatriate *v* send (someone) back to his or her own country. **repatriation** *n*

repay *v* pay back, refund; make a return for. **repayable** *adj* **repayment** *n*

repeal *v* cancel (a law) officially. ◆ *n* act of repealing.

repeat *v* say, write, or do again; disclose; happen again, recur. ◆ *n* act or instance of repeating; programme broadcast again. **repeatedly** *adv* **repeater** *n* firearm that may be discharged many times without reloading.

repel *v* **-pelling, -pelled** be disgusting to; drive back, ward off; resist. **repellent** *adj* distasteful; resisting water etc. ◆ *n* something that repels, esp. a chemical to repel insects.

repent *v* feel regret for (a deed or omission). **repentance** *n* **repentant** *adj*

repercussion *n* indirect effect, often unpleasant.

repertoire *n* stock of plays, songs, etc. that a player or company can give.

repertory *n, pl* **-ries** repertoire. **repertory company** permanent theatre company producing a succession of plays.

repetition *n* act of repeating; thing repeated. **repetitive, repetitious** *adj* full of repetition.

rephrase *v* express in different words.

repine *v* fret or complain.

replace *v* substitute for; put back. **replacement** *n*

replay n (also **action replay**) immediate reshowing on TV of an incident in sport, esp. in slow motion; second sports match, esp. one following an earlier draw. ◆ v play (a match, recording, etc.) again.

replenish v fill up again, resupply. **replenishment** n

replete adj filled or gorged.

replica n exact copy. **replicate** v make or be a copy of.

reply v -plying, -plied answer or respond. ◆ n, pl -plies answer or response.

report v give an account of; make a report (on); announce or relate; make a formal complaint about; present oneself (to); be responsible (to). ◆ n account or statement; rumour; written statement of a child's progress at school; bang. **reportedly** adv according to rumour. **reporter** n person who gathers news for a newspaper, TV, etc.

repose n peace; composure; sleep. ◆ v lie or lay at rest.

repository n, pl -ries place where valuables are deposited for safekeeping, store.

repossess v (of a lender) take back property from a customer who is behind with payments. **repossession** n

reprehend v find fault with. **reprehensible** adj open to criticism, unworthy.

represent v stand for; act as a delegate for; symbolize; make out to be; portray, as in art. **representation** n **representative** n person chosen to act for or represent a group; (travelling) salesperson. ◆ adj typical of a class or kind.

repress v keep (feelings) under control; subjugate. **repression** n **repressive** adj

reprieve v postpone the execution of (a condemned person); give temporary relief to. ◆ n postponement or cancellation of a punishment; temporary relief.

reprimand v blame (someone) officially for a fault. ◆ n official blame.

reprint v print further copies of (a book). ◆ n reprinted copy.

reprisal n retaliation.

reproach v blame or rebuke. ◆ n scolding or blame. **reproachful** adj **reproachfully** adv

reprobate [rep-roh-bate] adj, n depraved or disreputable (person). **reprobation** n disapproval or blame.

reproduce v produce a copy of; bring new individuals into existence; re-create. **reproducible** adj **reproduction** n process of reproducing; thing that is reproduced; facsimile, as of a painting etc.; quality of sound from an audio system. **reproductive** adj

reprove v speak severely to (someone) about a fault. **reproof** n severe blaming of someone for a fault.

reptile n cold-blooded air-breathing vertebrate with horny scales or plates, such as a snake or tortoise. **reptilian** adj

republic n form of government in which the people or their elected representatives possess the supreme power; country in which a president is the head of state. **Republican** n, adj (member or supporter) of the Republican Party, the more conservative of the two main political parties in the US. **Republicanism** n

repudiate [rip-pew-dee-ate] v reject the authority or validity of; disown. **repudiation** n

repugnant adj offensive or distasteful. **repugnance** n

repulse v be disgusting to; drive (an army) back; rebuff or reject. ◆ n driving back; rejection; rebuff. **repulsion** n distaste or aversion; Physics force separating two objects. **repulsive** adj disgusting.

reputation n estimation in which a person or thing is held. **reputable** [rep-yoo-tab-bl] adj of good reputation, respectable. **repute** n reputation. **reputed** adj supposed. **reputedly** adv

request n asking; thing asked for. ◆ v ask or politely demand.

Requiem [rek-wee-em] n Mass for the dead; music for this.

require v want or need; demand. **requirement** n essential condition; specific need or want.

requisite [rek-wizz-it] adj necessary, essential. ◆ n an essential.

requisition n formal demand, such as

for materials or supplies. ◆ v demand (supplies).

requite v return to someone (the same treatment or feeling as received). **requital** n

reredos [rear-doss] n ornamental screen behind an altar.

rescind v annul or repeal.

rescue v -cuing, -cued deliver from danger or trouble, save. ◆ n rescuing. **rescuer** n

research n systematic investigation to discover facts or collect information. ◆ v carry out investigations. **researcher** n

resemble v be or look like. **resemblance** n

resent v feel indignant or bitter about. **resentful** adj **resentment** n

reservation n doubt; exception or limitation; seat etc. that has been reserved; area of land reserved for use by a particular group, esp. as a home for Native Americans.

reserve v set aside, keep for future use; obtain by arranging beforehand, book; retain. ◆ n something, esp. money or troops, kept for emergencies; Sport substitute; area of land reserved for a particular purpose, esp. as a home for Canadian Indians; concealment of feelings or friendliness. **reserved** adj not showing one's feelings, lacking friendliness; set aside for use by a particular person. **reservist** n member of a military reserve.

reservoir n natural or artificial lake storing water for community supplies; store of something.

reshuffle n reorganization. ◆ v reorganize.

reside v dwell permanently. **residence** n home or house. **resident** adj, n **residential** adj (of part of a town) consisting mainly of houses; providing living accommodation.

residue n what is left, remainder. **residual** adj

resign v give up office, a job, etc.; reconcile (oneself) to. **resigned** adj content to endure. **resignation** n resigning; passive endurance of difficulties.

resilient adj (of a person) recovering quickly from a shock etc.; (of an

object) able to return to normal shape after stretching etc. **resilience** n

resin [rezz-in] n sticky substance from plants, esp. pines; similar synthetic substance. **resinous** adj

resist v withstand or oppose; refrain from despite temptation; be proof against. **resistance** n act of resisting; opposition; Electricity opposition offered by a circuit to the passage of a current through it. **resistant** adj **resistible** adj **resistivity** n measure of electrical resistance. **resistor** n component of an electrical circuit producing resistance.

resit v retake (an exam). ◆ n exam that has to be retaken.

resolute adj firm in purpose. **resolutely** adv **resolution** n resolving; firmness; thing resolved upon; decision of a court or vote of an assembly.

resolve v make up one's mind; decide with an effort of will; form (a resolution) by a vote; separate the component parts of; make clear, settle. **resolved** adj determined.

resonance n echoing, esp. with a deep sound; sound produced in one object by sound waves coming from another object. **resonant** adj **resonate** v **resonator** n

resort v have recourse (to) for help etc. ◆ n place for holidays; recourse.

resound [riz-zownd] v echo or ring with sound. **resounding** adj echoing; clear and emphatic.

resource n thing resorted to for support; expedient; ingenuity. ◆ pl sources of economic wealth; stock that can be drawn on, funds. **resourceful** adj **resourcefully** adv **resourcefulness** n

respect n consideration; deference or esteem; point or aspect; reference or relation, e.g. with respect to. ◆ v treat with esteem; show consideration for. **respecter** n **respectful** adj **respecting** prep concerning.

respectable adj worthy of respect; fairly good. **respectably** adv **respectability** n

respective adj relating separately to each of those in question. **respectively** adv

respiration [ress-per-ray-shun] n breathing. **respirator** n apparatus worn over the mouth and breathed through as protection against dust, poison gas, etc., or to provide artificial respiration. **respiratory** adj **respire** v breathe.

respite n interval of rest; delay.

resplendent adj brilliant or splendid; shining. **resplendence** n

respond v answer; act in answer to any stimulus; react favourably. **respondent** n Law defendant. **response** n answer; reaction to a stimulus. **responsive** adj readily reacting to some influence. **responsiveness** n

responsible adj having control and authority; reporting or accountable (to); sensible and dependable; involving responsibility. **responsibly** adv **responsibility** n, pl **-ties** state of being responsible; person or thing for which one is responsible.

rest[1] n repose; freedom from exertion etc.; an object used for support; pause, esp. in music. ◆ v take a rest; give a rest (to); be supported; place on a support. **restful** adj **restless** adj

rest[2] n what is left; others. ◆ v remain, continue to be.

restaurant n commercial establishment serving meals. **restaurateur** [rest-er-a-**tur**] n person who owns or runs a restaurant.

restitution n giving back; reparation or compensation.

restive adj restless or impatient.

restore v return (a building, painting, etc.) to its original condition; re-establish; give back, return; cause to recover health or spirits. **restoration** n **restorative** [rest-or-a-tiv] adj restoring. ◆ n food or medicine to strengthen etc. **restorer** n

restrain v hold (someone) back from action; control or restrict. **restraint** n restraining; control, esp. self-control. **restrained** adj not displaying emotion.

restrict v confine to certain limits. **restriction** n **restrictive** adj

restructure v reorganize.

result n outcome or consequence; number obtained from a calculation; score; exam mark or grade. ◆ v (foll. by from) be the outcome or consequence (of); (foll. by in) end (in). **resultant** adj arising as a result.

resume v begin again; occupy or take again. **resumption** n

résumé [**rez**-yoo-may] n summary.

resurgence n rising again to vigour. **resurgent** adj

resurrect v restore to life; use once more (something discarded etc.), revive. **resurrection** n rising again (esp. from the dead); revival.

resuscitate [ris-**suss**-it-tate] v restore to consciousness. **resuscitation** n

retail n selling of goods to the public. ◆ adv by retail. ◆ v sell or be sold retail; recount in detail. **retailer** n

retain v keep; engage the services of. **retainer** n fee to retain someone's services; old-established servant of a family.

retaliate v repay (an injury or wrong) in kind. **retaliation** n **retaliatory** adj

retard v delay or slow (progress or development). **retarded** adj underdeveloped, esp. mentally. **retardation** n

retch v try to vomit.

rethink v consider again, esp. with a view to changing one's tactics.

reticent adj reserved. **reticence** n

reticulate adj made or arranged like a net. **reticulation** n

retina n, pl **-nas, -nae** light-sensitive membrane at the back of the eye.

retinue n band of attendants.

retire v (cause to) give up office or work, esp. through age; go away or withdraw; go to bed. **retired** adj having given up work etc. **retirement** n **retiring** adj shy.

retort[1] v reply quickly, wittily, or angrily. ◆ n quick, witty, or angry reply.

retort[2] n glass container with a bent neck used for distilling.

retouch v restore or improve by new touches, esp. of paint.

retrace v go back over (a route etc.) again.

retract v withdraw (a statement etc.); draw in or back. **retractable, retractile** adj able to be retracted. **retraction** n

retread v, n same as REMOULD.

retreat v move back from a position, withdraw. ◆ n act of or military signal for retiring or withdrawal; place to which anyone retires, refuge.

retrench v reduce expenditure, cut back. **retrenchment** n

retrial n second trial of a case or defendant in a court of law.

retribution n punishment or vengeance for evil deeds. **retributive** adj

retrieve v fetch back again; restore to a better state; recover (information) from a computer. **retrievable** adj **retrieval** n **retriever** n dog trained to retrieve shot game.

retroactive adj effective from a date in the past.

retroflex adj bent backwards.

retrograde adj tending towards an earlier worse condition. **retrogression** n **retrogressive** adj

retrorocket n small rocket engine used to slow a spacecraft.

retrospect n **in retrospect** when looking back on the past. **retrospective** adj looking back in time; applying from a date in the past. ◆ n exhibition of an artist's life's work.

retroussé [rit-troo-say] adj (of a nose) turned upwards.

retsina n resinous Greek wine.

return v go or come back; give, put, or send back; reply; elect. ◆ n returning; being returned; profit; official report, as of taxable income; return ticket. **returnable** adj **returning officer** person in charge of an election. **return ticket** ticket allowing a passenger to travel to a place and back.

reunion n gathering of people who have been apart. **reunite** v bring or come together again after a separation.

reuse v use again. **reusable** adj

rev Informal ◆ n revolution (of an engine). ◆ v **revving, revved** (foll. by up) increase the speed of revolution of (an engine).

Rev., Revd. Reverend.

revalue v adjust the exchange value of (a currency) upwards. **revaluation** n

revamp v renovate or restore.

reveal v make known; expose or show. **revelation** n

reveille [riv-val-ee] n morning bugle call to waken soldiers.

revel v **-elling, -elled** take pleasure (in); make merry. ◆ n (usu. pl.) merrymaking. **reveller** n **revelry** n festivity.

revenge n retaliation for wrong done. ◆ v avenge (oneself or another); make retaliation for. **revengeful** adj

revenue n income, esp. of a state, as taxes.

reverberate v echo or resound. **reverberation** n

revere v be in awe of and respect greatly. **reverence** n awe mingled with respect and esteem. **Reverend** adj (as a prefix to a clergyman's name) worthy of reverence. **reverent** adj showing reverence. **reverently** adv **reverential** adj marked by reverence.

reverie n absent-minded daydream.

reverse v turn upside down or the other way round; change completely; move (a vehicle) backwards. ◆ n opposite or contrary; back side, obverse; defeat; reverse gear. ◆ adj opposite or contrary. **reversal** n **reversible** adj **reverse gear** mechanism enabling a vehicle to move backwards.

revert v return to a former state; come back to a subject; (of property) return to its former owner. **reversion** n (of property) rightful passing to the owner, designated heir, etc.

revetment n facing of stone, sandbags, etc. for a wall.

review v hold or write a review of; examine, reconsider, or look back on; inspect formally. ◆ n critical assessment of a book, concert, etc.; periodical with critical articles; general survey; inspection of troops. **reviewer** n writer of reviews.

revile v be abusively scornful of.

revise v change or alter; look over and correct; restudy (work) in preparation for an examination. **revision** n

revive v bring or come back to life, vigour, use, etc. **revival** n reviving or renewal; movement seeking to restore religious faith. **revivalism** n **revivalist** n

revoke v cancel (a will, agreement, etc.). **revocation** n

revolt n uprising against authority. ◆ v rise in rebellion; cause to feel disgust. **revolting** adj disgusting.

revolution n overthrow of a government by the governed; great change; complete rotation; spinning

round. **revolutionary** adj, n
revolutionize v change considerably.
revolve v turn round, rotate; (foll. by around) be centred (on). **revolver** n repeating pistol.
revue n theatrical entertainment with topical sketches and songs.
revulsion n strong disgust.
reward n something given in return for a service; sum of money offered for finding a criminal or missing property. ◆ v pay or give something to (someone) for a service, information, etc. **rewarding** adj giving personal satisfaction, worthwhile.
rewind v run (a tape or film) back to an earlier point in order to replay.
rewire v provide (a house, engine, etc.) with new wiring.
rewrite v write again in a different way. ◆ n something rewritten.
rhapsody n, pl **-dies.** freely structured emotional piece of music; expression of ecstatic enthusiasm. **rhapsodic** adj **rhapsodize** v speak or write with extravagant enthusiasm.
rhea [ree-a] n S American three-toed ostrich.
rheostat n instrument for varying the resistance of an electric circuit.
rhesus [ree-suss] n small long-tailed monkey of S Asia. **rhesus factor, Rh factor** feature distinguishing different types of human blood.
rhetoric [ret-a-rik] n art of effective speaking or writing; artificial or exaggerated language. **rhetorical** [rit-tor-ik-kal] adj (of a question) not requiring an answer. **rhetorically** adv
rheumatism n painful inflammation of joints or muscles. **rheumatic** n, adj (person) affected by rheumatism. **rheumatoid** adj of or like rheumatism.
Rh factor n see RHESUS.
rhinestone n imitation diamond.
rhino n short for RHINOCEROS.
rhinoceros n, pl **-oses, -os.** large thick-skinned animal with one or two horns on its nose.
rhizome n thick underground stem producing new plants.
rhodium n hard metal like platinum.
rhododendron n evergreen flowering shrub.
rhombus n, pl **-buses, -bi.** parallelogram with sides of equal

length but no right angles, diamond-shaped figure. **rhomboid** n parallelogram with adjacent sides of unequal length.
rhubarb n garden plant of which the fleshy stalks are cooked as fruit.
rhyme n sameness of the final sounds at the ends of lines of verse, or in words; word or syllable identical in sound to another; verse marked by rhyme. ◆ v make a rhyme.
rhythm n measured beat esp. of words, music, etc. **rhythmic, rhythmical** adj **rhythmically** adv **rhythm and blues** popular music, orig. Black American, influenced by the blues.
rib¹ n one of the curved bones forming the framework of the upper part of the body; cut of meat including the rib(s); curved supporting part, as in the hull of a boat; raised series of rows in knitting. ◆ v **ribbing, ribbed.** provide or mark with ribs; knit to form a rib pattern. **ribbed** adj **ribbing** n **ribcage** n bony structure of ribs enclosing the lungs.
rib² v **ribbing, ribbed** Informal tease or ridicule. **ribbing** n
ribald adj humorously or mockingly rude or obscene. **ribaldry** n
ribbon n narrow band of fabric used for trimming, tying, etc.; any long strip, for example of inked tape in a typewriter.
riboflavin [rye-boe-flay-vin] n form of vitamin B.
rice n cereal plant grown on wet ground in warm countries; its seeds as food.
rich adj owning a lot of money or property, wealthy; fertile; abounding; valuable; (of food) containing much fat or sugar; mellow; amusing. **riches** pl n wealth. **richly** adv elaborately; fully. **richness** n
rick¹ n stack of hay etc.
rick² v, n sprain or wrench.
rickets n disease of children marked by softening of the bones, bow legs, etc., caused by vitamin D deficiency.
rickety adj shaky or unstable.
rickshaw n light two-wheeled man-drawn Asian vehicle.
ricochet [rik-osh-ay] v (of a bullet) rebound from a solid surface. ◆ n such a rebound.

rid v **ridding, rid**. clear or relieve (of). **get rid of** free oneself of (something undesirable). **good riddance** relief at getting rid of something or someone.

ridden v past participle of RIDE ◆ adj afflicted or affected by the thing specified, e.g. disease-ridden.

riddle¹ n question made puzzling to test one's ingenuity; puzzling person or thing.

riddle² v pierce with many holes. ◆ n coarse sieve for gravel etc. **riddled with** full of.

ride v **riding, rode, ridden**. sit on and control or propel (a horse, bicycle, etc.); go on horseback or in a vehicle; be carried on or across; travel over; lie at anchor. ◆ n journey on a horse etc., or in a vehicle; type of movement experienced in a vehicle. **rider** n person who rides; supplementary clause added to a document. **ride up** v (of a garment) move up from the proper position.

ridge n long narrow hill; long narrow raised part on a surface; line where two sloping surfaces meet; elongated area of high pressure. **ridged** adj

ridiculous adj deserving to be laughed at, absurd. **ridicule** n treatment of a person or thing as ridiculous. ◆ v make fun of.

riding n electoral constituency.

riesling n type of white wine.

rife adj widespread or common. **rife with** full of.

riff n Jazz rock short repeated melodic figure.

riffle v flick through (pages etc.) quickly.

riffraff n rabble, disreputable people.

rifle¹ n firearm with a long barrel.

rifle² v search and rob; ransack.

rift n break in friendly relations; crack, split, or cleft. **rift valley** long narrow valley resulting from subsidence between faults.

rig v **rigging, rigged**. arrange in a dishonest way; (often foll. by up) set up, esp. as a makeshift; equip; provide (a ship) with spars, ropes, etc. ◆ n apparatus for drilling for oil and gas; way a ship's masts and sails are arranged ; (also **rigout**) Informal outfit of clothes. **rigging** n ship's spars and ropes.

right adj just; in accordance with truth and duty; true; correct; proper; of the side that faces east when the front is turned to the north ; (also **right-wing**) Politics conservative or reactionary; straight; upright; of the outer side of a fabric. ◆ v bring or come back to a vertical position; do justice to. ◆ n claim, title, etc. allowed or due; what is just or due; conservative political party. ◆ adv straight; properly; very; on or to the right side. **in the right** morally or legally correct. **right away** immediately. **rightly** adv **rightful** adj **rightist** n, adj (person) on the political right. **right angle** angle of 90°. **right-handed** adj using or for the right hand. **right-hand man** person's most valuable assistant. **right of way** Law right of one vehicle to go before another; legal right to pass over someone's land.

righteous [rye-chuss] adj upright, godly, or virtuous; morally justified. **righteousness** n

rigid adj inflexible or strict; stiff. **rigidly** adv **rigidity** n

rigmarole n meaningless string of words; long complicated procedure.

rigor mortis n stiffening of the body after death.

rigour, rigor n harshness, severity, or strictness; hardship. **rigorous** adj harsh, severe, or stern.

rile v anger or annoy.

rill n small stream.

rim n edge or border; outer ring of a wheel. **rimmed** adj

rime n Lit hoarfrost.

rind n outer coating of fruits, cheese, or bacon.

ring¹ v **ringing, rang, rung**. give out a clear resonant sound, as a bell; resound; cause (a bell) to sound ; (also **ring up**) telephone. ◆ n ringing; telephone call. **ringtone** n tune played by a cell phone when it receives a call.

ring² n circle of gold etc., esp. for a finger; any circular band, coil, or rim; circle of people; enclosed area, esp. a circle for a circus or a roped-in square for boxing; group operating (illegal) control of a market. ◆ v put a ring round; mark (a bird) with a ring; kill (a tree) by cutting the bark round the trunk. **ringer** n Slang person or thing apparently identical to another ; (also **dead ringer**). **ringlet** n curly lock of hair. **ringleader** n instigator of a mutiny, riot, etc. **ring road** Brit main road that bypasses a town (centre). **ringside** n row of seats nearest a boxing or circus ring. **ringworm** n fungal skin disease in circular patches.

rink n sheet of ice for skating or ice hockey; floor for roller skating. **rink rat** Slang youth who helps with chores at an ice-hockey rink in return for free admission to games.

rinse v remove soap from (washed clothes, hair, etc.) by applying clean water; wash lightly. ◆ n rinsing; liquid to tint hair.

riot n disorderly unruly disturbance; loud revelry; Slang very amusing person or thing; profusion. ◆ v take part in a riot. **read the riot act** reprimand severely. **run riot** behave without restraint; grow profusely. **riotous** adj unrestrained; unruly or rebellious.

rip v **ripping, ripped.** tear violently; tear away; Informal rush. ◆ n split or tear. **let rip** act or speak without restraint. **ripcord** n cord pulled to open a parachute. **rip off** v Slang cheat by overcharging. **rip-off** n Slang cheat or swindle. **rip-roaring** adj Informal boisterous.

RIP rest in peace.

riparian [rip-**pair**-ee-an] adj of or on the banks of a river.

ripe adj mature enough to be eaten or used; fully developed in mind or body; suitable, e.g. wait until the time is ripe. **ripen** v grow ripe; mature.

riposte [rip-**posst**] n verbal retort; counterattack. ◆ v make a riposte.

ripple n slight wave, ruffling of a surface; sound like ripples of water. ◆ v flow or form into little waves (on); (of sounds) rise and fall gently.

rise v **rising, rose, risen.** get up; move upwards; (of the sun or moon) appear above the horizon; reach a higher level; (of an amount or price) increase; rebel; (of a court) adjourn; have its source. ◆ n rising; upward slope; Brit raise. **get a rise out of** Slang provoke an angry reaction from. **give rise to** cause. **riser** n person who rises, esp. from bed; vertical part of a step. **rising** n revolt. ◆ adj increasing in rank or maturity.

risible [**riz**-zib-bl] adj causing laughter, ridiculous.

risk n chance of disaster or loss; person or thing considered as a potential hazard. ◆ v act in spite of the possibility of (injury or loss); expose to danger or loss. **risky** adj full of risk, dangerous. **riskily** adv

risotto n, pl **-tos.** dish of rice cooked in stock with vegetables, meat, etc.

risqué [**risk**-ay] adj making slightly rude references to sex.

rissole n cake of minced meat, coated with breadcrumbs and fried.

rite n formal practice or custom, esp. religious. **ritual** n prescribed order of rites; regular repeated action or behaviour. ◆ adj concerning rites. **ritually** adv **ritualistic** adj like a ritual.

ritzy adj **ritzier, ritziest** Slang luxurious or elegant.

rival n person or thing that competes with or equals another for favour, success, etc. ◆ adj in the position of a rival. ◆ v **-valling, -valled.** (try to) equal. **rivalry** n keen competition.

riven adj split.

river n large natural stream of water; copious flow.

rivet [**riv**-vit] n bolt for fastening metal plates, the end being put through holes and then beaten flat. ◆ v **riveting, riveted.** cause to be fixed, as in fascination; fasten with rivets. **riveter** n **riveting** adj very interesting and exciting.

rivulet n small stream.

RN Royal Navy.

RNA ribonucleic acid: substance in living cells essential for the synthesis of protein.

roach n freshwater fish.

road n way prepared for passengers, vehicles, etc.; way or course, e.g. the road to fame; street. **on the road** travelling. **roadie** n Informal person who transports and sets up equipment for a band. **roadblock** n barricade across a road to stop traffic for inspection etc. **road hog** Informal selfish aggressive driver. **roadhouse** n pub or restaurant on a country road. **road metal** broken stones used in building roads. **roadside** n, adj **road test** test of a vehicle etc. in actual use. **roadway** n the part of a road used by vehicles. **roadworks** pl n repairs to a road, esp. blocking part of the road. **roadworthy** adj (of a vehicle) mechanically sound.

roam v wander about.

roan adj (of a horse) having a brown or black coat sprinkled with white hairs. ◆ n roan horse.

roar v make or utter a loud deep hoarse sound like that of a lion; shout (something) as in anger; laugh loudly. ◆ n such a sound. **roaring** adj boisterous; Informal brisk and profitable. ◆ adv noisily.

roast v cook by dry heat, as in an oven; make or be very hot. ◆ n roasted joint of meat. ◆ adj roasted. **roasting** Informal ◆ adj extremely hot. ◆ n severe criticism or scolding.

rob v **robbing, robbed** steal from; deprive. **robber** n **robbery** n

robe n long loose outer garment. ◆ v put a robe on.

robin n large thrush with a red breast.

robot n automated machine, esp. one performing functions in a human manner; person of machine-like efficiency. **robotic** adj **robotics** n science of designing and using robots.

robust adj very strong and healthy. **robustly** adv **robustness** n

roc n monstrous bird of Arabian mythology.

rock¹ n hard mineral substance that makes up part of the earth's crust, stone; large rugged mass of stone; hard candy in sticks. **on the rocks** (of a marriage) about to end; (of an alcoholic drink) served with ice. **rocky** adj having many rocks. **rockery** n mound of stones in a garden for (alpine) plants. **rock bottom** lowest possible level. **rock tripe** any of various edible lichens that grow on rocks.

rock² v (cause to) sway to and fro. ◆ n style of pop music with a heavy beat. **rocky** adj shaky or unstable. **rock and roll** style of pop music blending rhythm and blues and country music. **rocking chair** chair allowing the sitter to rock backwards and forwards.

rocker n curved piece of wood etc. on which something may rock; rocking chair. **off one's rocker** Informal insane.

rocket n self-propelling device powered by the burning of explosive contents (used as a firework, weapon, etc.); vehicle propelled by a rocket engine, as a weapon or carrying a spacecraft. ◆ v **rocketing, rocketed** move fast, esp. upwards, as a rocket. **rocketry** n

rococo [rok-koe-koe] adj (of furniture, architecture, etc.) having much elaborate decoration in an early 18th-century French style.

rod n slender straight bar, stick; cane.

rode v past tense of RIDE.

rodent n animal with teeth specialized for gnawing, such as a rat.

rodeo n, pl **-deos** display of skill by cowboys, such as bareback riding.

roe¹ n small species of deer.

roe² n mass of eggs in a fish.

roentgen [ront-gan] n unit measuring a radiation dose.

rogue n dishonest or unprincipled person; mischief-loving person. ◆ adj (of a wild beast) having a savage temper and living apart from the herd. **roguery** n **roguish** adj

roister v make merry noisily or boisterously. **roisterer** n

role, rôle n actor's part; task or function.

roll v move by turning over and over; wind round; smooth out with a roller; move or sweep along; undulate; (of a ship or aircraft) turn from side to side about a line from nose to tail. ◆ n act of rolling over or from side to side; piece of paper etc. rolled up; list or register; small rounded individually baked piece of bread; swaying unsteady movement or gait; continuous sound, as of drums, thunder, etc. **rolling pin** cylindrical roller for pastry. **rolling stock** locomotives, carriages, etc. of a railway. **rolling stone** restless, wandering person. **roll call** calling out of a list of names, as in a school or the army, to check who is present. **rolled gold** metal coated with a thin layer of gold. **roll-on/roll-off** adj denoting a ship which vehicles can be driven straight onto or off. **roll-top** adj (of a desk) having a flexible lid sliding in grooves. **roll up** v Informal appear or arrive.

roller n rotating cylinder used for smoothing or supporting a thing to be moved, spreading paint, etc.; long wave of the sea. **Rollerblade** n ® roller skate with the wheels set in one straight line. **roller coaster** (at a funfair) narrow railway with steep slopes. **roller skate** skate with wheels.

rollicking *adj* boisterously carefree.

roly-poly *adj* round or plump.

ROM *Computers* read only memory.

Roman *adj* of Rome or the Church of Rome. **Roman Catholic** member of that section of the Christian Church that acknowledges the supremacy of the Pope. **Roman numerals** the letters I, V, X, L, C, D, M, used to represent numbers. **roman type** plain upright letters in printing.

romance *n* love affair; mysterious or exciting quality; novel or film dealing with love, esp. sentimentally; story with scenes remote from ordinary life. ◆ *v* exaggerate or fantasize. **romancer** *n*

Romance *adj* (of a language) developed from Latin, such as French, Spanish, or Italian.

Romanesque *adj, n* (in) a style of architecture of 9th–12th centuries characterized by round arches.

romantic *adj* of or dealing with love; idealistic but impractical; (of literature, music, etc.) displaying passion and imagination rather than order and form. ◆ *n* romantic person or artist. **romantically** *adv* **romanticism** *n* **romanticist** *n* **romanticize** *v*

Romany *n, pl* **-nies**, *adj* Gypsy.

romp *v* play wildly and joyfully. ◆ *n* spell of romping. **romp home** win easily. **rompers** *pl n* child's overalls.

rondeau *n, pl* **-deaux** short poem with the opening words used as a refrain.

rondo *n, pl* **-dos** piece of music with a leading theme continually returned to.

rood *n Christianity* the Cross; crucifix. **rood screen** (in a church) screen separating the nave from the choir.

roof *n, pl* **roofs** outside upper covering of a building, automobile, etc. ◆ *v* put a roof on.

rook[1] *n* bird of the crow family. ◆ *v* *Old-fashioned slang* swindle. **rookery** *n* colony of rooks.

rook[2] *n* piece in chess.

rookie *n Informal* recruit, esp. in the army.

room *n* space; space enough; division of a house; scope or opportunity. ◆ *pl* lodgings. **roomy** *adj* spacious.

roost *n* perch for fowls. ◆ *v* perch. **rooster** *n* domestic cock.

root *n* part of a plant that grows down into the earth obtaining nourishment; plant with an edible root, such as a carrot; part of a tooth, hair, etc. below the skin; source or origin; form of a word from which other words and forms are derived; *Math* factor of a quantity which, when multiplied by itself the number of times indicated, gives the quantity. ◆ *pl* person's sense of belonging. ◆ *v* establish a root and start to grow; dig or burrow. **rootless** *adj* having no sense of belonging. **root for** *v Informal* cheer on. **root out** *v* get rid of completely. **root up** *v* pull up by the roots.

rope *n* thick cord. **know the ropes** be thoroughly familiar with an activity. **rope in** *v* persuade to join in.

ropy *adj* **ropier, ropiest** *Informal* inferior or inadequate; not well. **ropiness** *n*

rorqual *n* whalebone whale with a dorsal fin.

rosary *n, pl* **-saries** series of prayers; string of beads for counting these prayers.

rose[1] *n* shrub or climbing plant with prickly stems and fragrant flowers; the flower; perforated flat nozzle for a hose; pink colour. ◆ *adj* reddish-pink. **roseate** [roe-zee-ate] *adj* rose-coloured. **rosy** *adj* flushed; hopeful or promising. **rose-coloured** *adj* unjustifiably optimistic. **rose window** circular window with spokes branching from the centre. **rosewood** *n* fragrant wood.

rose[2] *v* past tense of RISE.

rosé [roe-zay] *n* pink wine.

rosehip *n* berry-like fruit of a rose plant.

rosemary *n* fragrant flowering shrub; its leaves as a herb.

rosette *n* rose-shaped ornament, esp. a circular bunch of ribbons.

rosin [rozz-in] *n* resin.

roster *n* list of people and their turns of duty.

rostrum *n, pl* **-trums, -tra** stage.

rot *v* **rotting, rotted** decompose or decay; slowly deteriorate physically or mentally. ◆ *n* decay; *Informal* nonsense.

rota *n* list of people who take it in turn to do a particular task.

rotary *n* traffic circle. ◆ *adj* revolving;

operated by rotation.

rotate v (cause to) move round a centre or on a pivot; (cause to) follow a set sequence. **rotation** n

rote n mechanical repetition. **by rote** by memory.

rotisserie n (electrically driven) rotating spit for cooking meat.

rotor n revolving portion of a dynamo, motor, or turbine; rotating device with long blades that provides thrust to lift a helicopter.

rotten adj decomposed; Informal very bad; corrupt.

rotter n Slang despicable person.

Rottweiler [rawt-vile-er] n large sturdy dog with a smooth black and tan coat and usu. a docked tail.

rotund [roe-tund] adj round and plump; sonorous. **rotundity** n

rotunda n circular building or room, esp. with a dome.

rouble [roo-bl] n monetary unit of Russia.

roué [roo-ay] n man given to immoral living.

rouge n red cosmetic used to colour the cheeks.

rough adj not smooth, uneven or irregular; violent, stormy, or boisterous; approximate; incomplete or rudimentary; lacking refinement. ◆ v make rough; plan out approximately. ◆ n rough state or area. **rough it** live without the usual comforts etc. **roughen** v **roughly** adv **roughness** n **roughage** n indigestible constituents of food which aid digestion. **rough-and-ready** adj hastily prepared but adequate. **rough-and-tumble** n playful fight. **rough-hewn** adj roughly shaped.

roughcast n mixture of plaster and small stones for outside walls. ◆ v coat with this.

roughshod adv **ride roughshod over** act with total disregard for.

roulette n gambling game played with a revolving wheel and a ball.

round adj spherical, cylindrical, circular, or curved; complete or whole, e.g. round numbers; plump. ◆ adv with a circular or circuitous course; on all sides, e.g. books scattered round the room. ◆ n thing round in shape; recurrent duties; customary course, as of a milkman; stage in a competition;

game (of golf); one of several periods in a boxing match etc.; number of drinks bought at one time; bullet or shell for a gun; part song in which singers join at equal intervals; circular movement; set of sandwiches. ◆ prep surrounding or encircling; on or outside the perimeter of; on all sides of. ◆ v make or become round; move round. **roundly** adv thoroughly. **round robin** petition signed with names in a circle to conceal the order. **round-the-clock** adj throughout the day and night. **round trip** journey out and back again, esp. by a different route. **round up** v gather (people or animals) together. **roundup** n

roundabout n Brit traffic circle; merry-go-round. ◆ adj not straightforward, e.g. a roundabout route.

roundel n small disc; rondeau. **roundelay** n simple song with a refrain.

Roundhead n supporter of Parliament against Charles I in the English Civil War.

rouse v wake up; provoke or excite. **rousing** adj lively, vigorous.

roustabout n labourer on an oil rig.

rout n overwhelming defeat; disorderly retreat. ◆ v defeat and put to flight. **rout out** v search for; drive out.

route n choice of roads taken to reach a destination; fixed path followed by buses, etc. between two places; chosen way or method. **routemarch** n long training march.

routine n usual or regular method of procedure; boring repetition of tasks, e.g. mindless routine; set sequence. ◆ adj ordinary; regular.

roux [roo] n fat and flour cooked together as a basis for sauces.

rove v wander. **rover** n person who roves; pirate.

row[1] n straight line of people or things. **in a row** in succession.

row[2] v propel (a boat) by oars. ◆ n spell of rowing.

row[3] Informal ◆ n dispute; disturbance; reprimand. ◆ v quarrel noisily.

rowan n tree producing bright red berries, mountain ash.

rowdy adj -dier, -diest disorderly, noisy, and rough. ◆ n, pl -dies person like this.

rowel [rhymes with **towel**] n small

spiked wheel on a spur.

rowlock *n* device on the gunwale of a boat that holds an oar in place.

royal *adj* of, befitting, or supported by a king or queen; splendid. ◆ *n Informal* member of a royal family. **royally** *adv* **royalist** *n* supporter of monarchy. **royalty** *n* royal people; rank; payment to author, musician, inventor, etc. **royal blue** bright blue.

rpm revolutions per minute.

RSI repetitive strain injury.

RSVP please reply.

rub *v* **rubbing, rubbed** apply pressure and friction to (something) with a circular or backwards-and-forwards movement; clean, polish, or dry by rubbing; remove by rubbing; chafe or fray through rubbing. ◆ *n* act of rubbing. **rub it in** emphasize an unpleasant fact. **rub out** *v* remove with a rubber.

rubato *adv Music* with expressive flexibility of tempo.

rubber¹ *n* strong waterproof elastic material, orig. made from the dried sap of a tropical tree, now usually synthetic; piece of rubber used for erasing mistakes. ◆ *adj* made of or producing rubber. **rubberize** *v* coat or treat with rubber. **rubbery** *adj* like rubber, soft or elastic. **rubberneck** *v* stare with unthinking curiosity. **rubber stamp** device for imprinting the date, a name, etc.; automatic authorization.

rubber² *n* match consisting of three games of bridge, whist, etc.

rubbish *n* waste matter; anything worthless; nonsense. **rubbishy** *adj*

rubble *n* fragments of broken stone, brick, etc.

rubella [roo-**bell**-a] *n* same as GERMAN MEASLES.

rubicund [roo-bik-kund] *adj* ruddy.

rubric [roo-brik] *n* heading or explanation inserted in a text.

ruby *n*, *pl* **-bies** red precious gemstone. ◆ *adj* deep red.

ruck¹ *n* rough crowd of common people.

ruck² *n*, *v* wrinkle or crease.

rucksack *n* large pack carried on the back.

ructions *pl n Informal* noisy uproar.

rudder *n* vertical hinged piece at the stern of a boat or at the rear of an aircraft, for steering.

ruddy *adj* **-dier, -diest** of a fresh healthy red colour.

rude *adj* impolite or insulting; coarse, vulgar, or obscene; roughly made; robust; unexpected and unpleasant. **rudely** *adv* **rudeness** *n*

rudiments *pl n* simplest and most basic stages of a subject. **rudimentary** *adj* basic, elementary.

rue¹ *v* **ruing, rued** feel regret for. **rueful** *adj* regretful or sorry. **ruefully** *adv*

rue² *n* plant with evergreen bitter leaves.

ruff *n* starched and frilled collar; natural collar of feathers, fur, etc. on certain birds and animals.

ruffian *n* violent lawless person.

ruffle *v* disturb the calm of; annoy, irritate. ◆ *n* frill or pleat.

rug *n* small carpet; thick woollen blanket.

rugby *n* form of football played with an oval ball which may be handled by the players.

rugged [rug-gid] *adj* rough; uneven and jagged; strong-featured; tough and sturdy.

rugger *n Informal* rugby.

ruin *v* destroy or spoil completely; impoverish. ◆ *n* destruction or decay; loss of wealth, position, etc.; broken-down unused building(s). **ruination** *n* act of ruining; state of being ruined; cause of ruin. **ruinous** *adj* causing ruin; more expensive than is reasonable. **ruinously** *adv*

rule *n* statement of what is allowed, for example in a game or procedure; what is usual; government, authority, or control; measuring device with a straight edge. ◆ *v* govern; restrain; give a formal decision; be pre-eminent; mark with straight line(s). **as a rule** usually. **ruler** *n* person who governs; measuring device with a straight edge. **ruling** *n* formal decision. **rule of thumb** practical but imprecise approach. **rule out** *v* exclude.

rum *n* alcoholic drink distilled from sugar cane.

rumba *n* lively ballroom dance of Cuban origin.

rumble¹ *v* (of traffic etc.) make a low continuous noise. ◆ *n* such a noise.

rumble² *v Informal* discover the (disreputable) truth about.

rumbustious *adj* boisterous.

ruminate *v* ponder or meditate; chew the cud. **ruminant** *adj, n* cud-chewing (animal, such as a cow, sheep, or deer). **rumination** *n* quiet meditation and reflection. **ruminative** *adj*

rummage *v* search untidily and at length. ◆ *n* untidy search through a collection of things.

rummy *n* card game in which players try to collect sets or sequences.

rumour *n* gossip or common talk; unproved statement. **be rumoured be** circulated as a rumour.

rump *n* buttocks; rear of an animal.

rumple *v* make untidy or crumpled.

rumpus *n, pl* **-puses** noisy or confused commotion.

run *v* **running, ran, run** move with a more rapid gait than walking; go quickly (across); flow; compete in a race, election, etc.; continue (for a specified period); function; travel according to schedule; melt; spread; (of stitches) unravel; expose oneself to (a risk); (of a newspaper) publish (a story); smuggle (goods, esp. arms); manage or be in charge of. ◆ *n* act or spell of running; ride in an automobile; unrestricted access; tendency or trend, e.g. *the run of the market*; continuous period, e.g. *a run of good luck*; sequence; heavy demand; enclosure for domestic fowls; series of unravelled stitches, ladder; score of one at baseball; steep snow-covered course for skiing. **run away** *v* make one's escape, flee. **run down** *v* be rude about; stop working; reduce in number or size. **rundown** *n* **run-down** *adj* exhausted. **run into** *v* meet. **run-of-the-mill** *adj* ordinary. **run out** *v* be completely used up. **run over** *v* knock down (a person) with a moving vehicle. **run up** *v* incur (a debt).

rune *n* any character of the earliest Germanic alphabet. **runic** *adj*

rung[1] *n* crossbar on a ladder.

rung[2] *v* past participle of RING[1].

runnel *n* small brook or rivulet.

runner *n* competitor in a race; messenger; part underneath an ice skate etc., on which it slides; slender horizontal stem of a plant, such as a strawberry, running along the ground and forming new roots at intervals; long strip of carpet or decorative cloth. **runner-up** *n* person who comes second in a competition.

running *adj* continuous; consecutive; (of water) flowing. ◆ *n* act of moving or flowing quickly; management of a business etc. **in, out of the running** having or not having a good chance in a competition.

runny *adj* **-nier, -niest** tending to flow; exuding moisture.

runt *n* smallest animal in a litter; *Offens* undersized person.

runway *n* hard level roadway where aircraft take off and land.

rupee *n* monetary unit of India and Pakistan.

rupture *n* breaking, breach; hernia. ◆ *v* break, burst, or sever.

rural *adj* in or of the countryside.

ruse [rooz] *n* stratagem or trick.

rush[1] *v* move or do very quickly; force (someone) to act hastily; make a sudden attack upon (a person or place). ◆ *n* sudden quick or violent movement. ◆ *pl* first unedited prints of a scene for a film. ◆ *adj* done with speed, hasty. **rush hour** period at the beginning and end of the working day, when many people are travelling to or from work.

rush[2] *n* marsh plant with a slender pithy stem. **rushy** *adj* full of rushes.

rusk *n* hard brown crisp biscuit, used esp. for feeding babies.

russet *adj* reddish-brown. ◆ *n* the colour; apple with rough reddish-brown skin.

rust *n* reddish-brown coating formed on iron etc. that has been exposed to moisture; disease of plants with rust-coloured spots. ◆ *adj* reddish-brown. ◆ *v* become coated with rust. **rusty** *adj* coated with rust; of a rust colour; out of practice. **rustproof** *adj*

rustic *adj* of or resembling country people; rural; crude, awkward, or uncouth; (of furniture) made of untrimmed branches. ◆ *n* person from the country. **rusticity** *n*

rusticate *v* banish temporarily from university as a punishment. **rustication** *n*

rustle[1] *v* make a low whispering sound, as of dry leaves. ◆ *n* this sound.

rustle[2] *v* steal (cattle). **rustler** *n* cattle thief. **rustle up** *v* prepare at short notice.

rut¹ n furrow made by wheels; dull settled habits or way of living.

rut² n recurrent period of sexual excitability in male deer. ◆ v **rutting, rutted** be in a period of sexual excitability.

rutabaga n kind of turnip.

ruthless adj pitiless, merciless. **ruthlessly** adv **ruthlessness** n

rye n kind of grain used for fodder and bread; whiskey made from rye.

rye-grass n any of several kinds of grass cultivated for fodder.

S s

s second(s); singular.

S Saint; South(ern); *Chem* sulfur.

SA Salvation Army; South Africa.

Sabbath n day of worship and rest: Saturday for Jews, Sunday for Christians. **sabbatical** adj, n (denoting) leave for study.

sable n dark fur from a small weasel-like Arctic animal. ◆ adj black.

sabot [sab-oh] n wooden shoe, clog.

sabotage n intentional damage done to machinery, systems, etc. ◆ v damage intentionally. **saboteur** n person who commits sabotage.

sabre n curved cavalry sword.

sac n pouchlike structure in an animal or plant.

saccharin, saccharine n artificial sweetener. **saccharine** adj excessively sweet.

sacerdotal adj of priests.

sachet n small envelope or bag containing a single portion.

sack n large bag made of coarse material; plundering of a captured town; *Informal* dismissal; *Slang* bed. ◆ v plunder (a captured town); *Informal* dismiss. **sackcloth** n coarse fabric used for sacks, formerly worn as a penance.

sacrament n ceremony of the Christian Church, esp. Communion. **sacramental** adj

sacred adj holy; set apart, reserved; connected with religion.

sacrifice n giving something up; thing given up; making of an offering to a god; thing offered. ◆ v offer as a sacrifice; give (something) up. **sacrificial** adj

sacrilege n misuse or desecration of something sacred. **sacrilegious** adj

sacristan n person in charge of the contents of a church. **sacristy** n room in a church where sacred objects are kept.

sacrosanct adj regarded as sacred, inviolable.

sacrum [say-krum] n, pl -cra compound bone at the base of the spine.

sad adj **sadder, saddest** sorrowful, unhappy; deplorably bad; regrettable. **sadden** v make (someone) sad. **sadly** adv **sadness** n

saddle n rider's seat on a horse or bicycle; joint of meat. ◆ v put a saddle on (a horse); burden (with a responsibility). **saddler** n maker or seller of saddles.

sadism [say-dizz-um] n gaining of (sexual) pleasure from inflicting pain. **sadist** n **sadistic** adj **sadistically** adv

sadomasochism n combination of sadism and masochism. **sadomasochist** n

s.a.e. stamped addressed envelope.

safari n, pl -ris expedition to hunt or observe wild animals, esp. in Africa. **safari park** park where lions, elephants, etc. are kept uncaged so that people can see them from automobiles.

safe adj secure, protected; uninjured, out of danger; not involving risk. ◆ n strong lockable container. **safely** adv **safe-conduct** n permit allowing travel through a dangerous area. **safe deposit** place where valuables can be stored safely. **safekeeping** n protection.

safeguard n protection. ◆ v protect.

safety n, pl -ties state of being safe. **safety net** net to catch performers on a trapeze or high wire if they fall. **safety pin** pin with a spring fastening and a guard over the point when closed. **safety valve** that allows steam etc. to escape if pressure becomes excessive.

saffron n orange-coloured flavouring obtained from a crocus. ◆ adj orange.

sag v **sagging, sagged** sink in the middle; tire; (of clothes) hang loosely. ◆ n droop.

saga [sah-ga] *n* legend of Norse heroes; any long story.

sagacious *adj* wise. **sagaciously** *adv* **sagacity** *n*

sage[1] *n* aromatic herb with grey-green leaves.

sage[2] *n* very wise man. ◆ *adj Lit* wise. **sagely** *adv*

sago *n* starchy cereal from the powdered pith of the sago palm tree.

said *v* past of SAY.

sail *n* sheet of fabric stretched to catch the wind for propelling a sailing boat; journey by boat; arm of a windmill. ◆ *v* travel by water; move smoothly; begin a voyage. **sailor** *n* member of a ship's crew. **sailboard** *n* board with a mast and single sail, used for windsurfing.

saint *n Christianity* person venerated after death as specially holy; exceptionally good person. **saintly** *adj* **saintliness** *n*

saithe *n* dark-coloured edible sea fish.

sake[1] *n* benefit; purpose. **for the sake of** for the purpose of; to please or benefit (someone).

sake[2], **saki** [sah-kee] *n* Japanese alcoholic drink made from fermented rice.

salaam [sal-ahm] *n* low bow of greeting among Muslims.

salacious *adj* excessively concerned with sex.

salad *n* dish of raw vegetables, eaten as a meal or part of a meal.

salamander *n* type of lizard; mythical reptile supposed to live in fire.

salami *n* highly spiced sausage.

salary *n*, *pl* **-ries** fixed regular payment, usu. monthly, to an employee. **salaried** *adj*

sale *n* exchange of goods for money; selling of goods at unusually low prices; auction. **saleable** *adj* fit or likely to be sold. **salesman, saleswoman** *n* person who sells goods. **salesmanship** *n* skill in selling.

salient [say-lee-ent] *adj* prominent, noticeable. ◆ *n Mil* projecting part of a front line.

saline [say-line] *adj* containing salt. **salinity** *n*

saliva [sal-lie-va] *n* liquid that forms in the mouth, spittle. **salivary** *adj* **salivate** *v* produce saliva.

sallow[1] *adj* of an unhealthy pale or yellowish colour.

sallow[2] *n* tree or shrub related to the willow.

sally *n*, *pl* **-lies** sudden brief attack by troops; witty remark. ◆ *v* **-lying, -lied** (foll. by *forth*) rush out; go out.

salmon *n* large fish with orange-pink flesh valued as food. ◆ *adj* orange-pink.

salmonella *n*, *pl* **-lae** bacterium causing food poisoning.

salon *n* commercial premises of a hairdresser, beautician, etc.; elegant reception room for guests.

saloon *n* large public room, as on a ship; bar serving alcoholic drinks; *Brit* sedan.

salsify *n* plant with a long white edible root.

salt *n* white crystalline substance used to season food; chemical compound of acid and metal. ◆ *v* season with salt. **old salt** experienced sailor. **with a pinch, grain of salt** allowing for exaggeration. **worth one's salt** efficient. **salty** *adj* **saltcellar** *n* small container for salt at table.

saltpetre *n* compound used in gunpowder and as a preservative.

salubrious *adj* favourable to health.

Saluki *n* tall hound with a silky coat.

salutary *adj* producing a beneficial result.

salute *n* motion of the arm as a formal military sign of respect; firing of guns as a military greeting of honour. ◆ *v* greet with a salute; make a salute; acknowledge with praise. **salutation** *n* greeting by words or actions.

salvage *n* saving of a ship or other property from destruction; property so saved. ◆ *v* save from destruction or waste.

salvation *n* fact or state of being saved from harm or the consequences of sin.

salve *n* healing or soothing ointment. ◆ *v* soothe or appease, e.g. *salve one's conscience.*

salver *n* (silver) tray on which something is presented.

salvia *n* plant with blue or red flowers.

salvo *n*, *pl* **-vos, -voes** simultaneous discharge of guns etc.; burst of applause or questions.

sal volatile [sal vol-at-ill-ee] *n*

preparation of ammonia, used to revive a person who feels faint.

SAM surface-to-air missile.

Samaritan n person who helps people in distress.

samba n, pl **-bas** lively Brazilian dance.

same adj identical, not different, unchanged; just mentioned. **sameness** n

samovar n Russian tea urn.

Samoyed n dog with a thick white coat and tightly curled tail.

sampan n small boat with oars used in China.

samphire n plant found on rocks by the seashore.

sample n part taken as representative of a whole. n Music short extract from an existing recording mixed into a backing track to produce a new recording. ♦ v take and test a sample of. **sampler** n piece of embroidery showing the embroiderer's skill. **sampling** n

samurai n, pl **-rai** member of an ancient Japanese warrior caste.

sanatorium n, pl **-riums, -ria** institution for invalids or convalescents; room for sick pupils at a boarding school.

sanctify v **-fying, -fied** make holy.

sanctimonious adj making a show of piety.

sanction n permission, authorization; (usu. pl.) coercive measure or penalty. ♦ v allow, authorize.

sanctity n sacredness, inviolability.

sanctuary n, pl **-aries** place of safety for a fugitive; place where animals or birds can live undisturbed; holy place; part of a church nearest the altar.

sanctum n, pl **-tums, -ta** sacred place; person's private room.

sand n substance consisting of small grains of rock, esp. on a beach or in a desert. ♦ pl stretches of sand forming a beach or desert. ♦ v smooth with sandpaper. **sander** n power tool for smoothing surfaces. **sandy** adj covered with sand; (of hair) reddish-fair. **sandbag** n bag filled with sand, used as protection against gunfire, floodwater, etc. **sandblast** v, n (clean with) a jet of sand blown from a nozzle under pressure. **sandpaper** n paper coated with sand for smoothing a surface. **sandpiper** n shore bird with

a long bill and slender legs. **sandstone** n rock composed of sand. **sandstorm** n desert wind that whips up clouds of sand.

sandal n light shoe consisting of a sole attached by straps.

sandalwood n sweet-scented wood.

sandwich n two slices of bread with a layer of food between. ♦ v insert between two other things. **sandwich board** pair of boards hung over a person's shoulders to display advertisements in front and behind.

sane adj of sound mind; sensible, rational. **sanity** n

sang v past tense of SING.

sang-froid [sahng frwah] n composure, self-possession.

sanguinary adj accompanied by bloodshed; bloodthirsty.

sanguine adj cheerful, optimistic.

sanitary adj promoting health by getting rid of dirt and germs. **sanitation** n sanitary measures, esp. drainage or sewerage.

sank v past tense of SINK.

Sanskrit n ancient language of India.

sap[1] n moisture that circulates in plants; energy; Informal gullible person.

sap[2] v **sapping, sapped** undermine; weaken. ♦ n trench dug to undermine an enemy position. **sapper** n soldier in an engineering unit.

sapient [say-pee-ent] adj Lit wise.

sapling n young tree.

sapphire n blue precious stone. ♦ adj deep blue.

saraband, sarabande n slow stately Spanish dance.

Saracen n Hist Arab or Muslim who opposed the Crusades.

sarcasm n (use of) bitter or wounding ironic language. **sarcastic** adj **sarcastically** adv

sarcophagus n, pl **-gi, -guses** stone coffin.

sardine n small fish of the herring family, usu. preserved in tightly packed cans.

sardonic adj mocking or scornful. **sardonically** adv

sargassum, sargasso n type of floating seaweed.

sari, saree n long piece of cloth draped around the body and over one shoulder, worn by Hindu women.

sarong n long piece of cloth tucked around the waist or under the armpits, worn esp. in Malaysia.

sarsaparilla n soft drink, orig. made from the root of a tropical American plant.

sartorial adj of men's clothes or tailoring.

sash[1] n decorative strip of cloth worn round the waist or over one shoulder.

sash[2] n wooden frame containing the panes of a window. **sash window** window consisting of two sashes that can be opened by sliding one over the other.

Sask. Saskatchewan.

Saskatchewan see Canadian Provincial Facts p631.

saskatoon n N American shrub with purplish berries.

Sasquatch n same as BIGFOOT.

sassafras n American tree with aromatic bark used medicinally.

Sassenach n Scot English person.

sat v past of SIT.

Satan n the Devil. **satanic** adj of Satan; supremely evil. **Satanism** n worship of Satan.

satay, saté (sat-ay) n Indonesian and Malaysian dish consisting of pieces of chicken, pork, etc., grilled on skewers and served with peanut sauce.

satchel n bag, usu. with a shoulder strap, for carrying school books.

sate v satisfy (a desire or appetite) fully.

satellite n man-made device orbiting in space; heavenly body that orbits another; country that is dependent on a more powerful one; of or used in the transmission of television signals from a satellite to the home.

satiate [say-she-ate] v satisfy fully; surfeit. **satiety** [sat-tie-a-tee] n feeling of having had too much.

satin n silky fabric with a glossy surface on one side. **satiny** adj of or like satin. **satinwood** n tropical tree yielding hard wood.

satire n use of ridicule to expose vice or folly; poem or other work that does this. **satirical** adj **satirist** n **satirize** v ridicule by means of satire.

satisfy v **-fying, -fied** please, content; provide amply for (a need or desire); convince, persuade. **satisfaction** n

satisfactory adj

satnav n Motoring Informal satellite navigation.

satsuma n kind of small orange.

saturate v soak thoroughly; cause to absorb the maximum amount of something. **saturation** n

Saturday n seventh day of the week.

Saturn n Roman god; one of the planets. **saturnine** adj gloomy in temperament or appearance. **saturnalia** n wild revelry.

satyr n woodland god, part man, part goat; lustful man.

sauce n liquid added to food to enhance flavour; Informal impudence. **saucy** adj impudent; pert, jaunty. **saucily** adv **saucepan** n cooking pot with a long handle.

saucer n small round dish put under a cup.

sauerkraut n shredded cabbage fermented in brine.

sauna n Finnish-style steam bath.

saunter v walk in a leisurely manner, stroll. ◆ n leisurely walk.

saurian adj of or like a lizard.

sausage n minced meat in an edible tube-shaped skin. **sausage roll** skinless sausage covered in pastry.

sauté [so-tay] v fry quickly in a little fat.

savage adj wild, untamed; cruel and violent; uncivilized, primitive. ◆ n uncivilized person. ◆ v attack ferociously. **savagely** adv **savagery** n

savanna, savannah n extensive open grassy plain in Africa.

savant n learned person.

save v rescue or preserve from harm, protect; keep for the future; set aside (money); Sport prevent the scoring of (a goal). ◆ n Sport act of preventing a goal. **saver** n **saving** n economy. **savings** pl n money put by for future use.

saveloy n spicy smoked sausage.

saviour n person who rescues another; (S-) Christ.

savoir-faire [sav-wahr fair] n French ability to do and say the right thing in any situation.

savory n aromatic herb used in cooking.

savour n characteristic taste or odour; slight but distinctive quality. ◆ v (foll.

by *of*) have a flavour or suggestion of; enjoy, relish. **savoury** *adj* salty or spicy; not sweet. ◆ *n Brit* savoury dish served before or after a meal.

savoy *n* variety of cabbage.

savvy *Slang* ◆ *v* **-vying, -vied** understand. ◆ *n* intelligence.

saw¹ *n* cutting tool with a toothed metal blade. ◆ *v* **sawing, sawed, sawed** *or* **sawn.** cut with a saw; move (something) back and forth. **sawyer** *n* person who saws timber for a living. **sawdust** *n* fine wood fragments made in sawing. **sawfish** *n* fish with a long toothed snout. **sawmill** *n* mill where timber is sawn into planks. **saw-off** *n Slang* compromise or settlement.

saw² *v* past tense of SEE¹.

saw³ *n* wise saying, proverb.

sax *n Informal* short for SAXOPHONE.

saxifrage *n* alpine rock plant with small flowers.

Saxon *n* member of the W Germanic people who settled widely in Europe in the early Middle Ages. ◆ *adj* of the Saxons.

saxophone *n* brass wind instrument with keys and a curved body. **saxophonist** *n*

say *v* **saying, said** speak or utter; express (an idea) in words; suppose as an example or possibility; give as one's opinion. ◆ *n* right or chance to speak; share in a decision. **saying** *n* proverb.

SC Star of Courage.

scab *n* crust formed over a wound; *Offens* blackleg. **scabby** *adj* covered with scabs; *Informal* despicable.

scabbard *n* sheath for a sword or dagger.

scabies [skay-beez] *n* itchy skin disease.

scabious [skay-bee-uss] *n* plant with globular blue flower heads.

scabrous [skay-bruss] *adj* indecent; rough and scaly.

scaffold *n* temporary platform for workmen; gallows. **scaffolding** *n* (materials for building) scaffolds.

scalar *n, adj* (variable quantity) having magnitude but no direction.

scald *v* burn with hot liquid or steam; sterilize with boiling water; heat (liquid) almost to boiling point. ◆ *n* injury by scalding.

scale¹ *n* one of the thin overlapping plates covering fishes and reptiles; thin flake; coating which forms in kettles etc. due to hard water; tartar formed on the teeth. ◆ *v* remove scales from; come off in scales. **scaly** *adj*

scale² *n* (often *pl.*) weighing instrument.

scale³ *n* graduated table or sequence of marks at regular intervals, used as a reference in making measurements; fixed series of notes in music; ratio of size between a thing and a representation of it; relative degree or extent. ◆ *v* climb. **scale up, down** *v* increase *or* decrease proportionally in size.

scalene *adj* (of a triangle) with three unequal sides.

scallop *n* edible shellfish; one of a series of small curves along an edge. **scalloped** *adj* decorated with small curves along the edge.

scallywag *n Informal* scamp, rascal.

scalp *n* skin and hair on top of the head. ◆ *v* cut off the scalp of.

scalpel *n* small surgical knife.

scamp *n* mischievous child. ◆ *v* do carelessly.

scamper *v* run about hurriedly or in play. ◆ *n* scampering.

scampi *pl n* large prawns.

scan *v* **scanning, scanned** scrutinize carefully; glance over quickly; examine or search (an area) by passing a radar or sonar beam over it; (of verse) conform to metrical rules. ◆ *n* scanning. **scanner** *n* electronic device used for scanning. **scansion** *n* metrical scanning of verse.

scandal *n* disgraceful action or event; malicious gossip. **scandalize** *v* shock by scandal. **scandalous** *adj*

scant *adj* barely sufficient, meagre.

scanty *adj* **scantier, scantiest** barely sufficient or not sufficient. **scantily** *adv* **scantiness** *n*

scapegoat *n* person made to bear the blame for others.

scapula *n, pl* **-lae, -las** shoulder blade. **scapular** *adj* of the scapula.

scar *n* mark left by a healed wound; permanent emotional damage left by an unpleasant experience. ◆ *v* **scarring, scarred** mark or become marked with a scar.

scarab *n* sacred beetle of ancient Egypt.

scarce *adj* not common, rarely found;

insufficient to meet demand. **make oneself scarce** *Informal* go away. **scarcely** *adv* only just; not quite; definitely or probably not. **scarcity** *n*

scare *v* frighten or be frightened. ◆ *n* fright, sudden panic. **scary** *adj* *Informal* frightening. **scarecrow** *n* figure dressed in old clothes, set up to scare birds away from crops; raggedly dressed person. **scaremonger** *n* person who spreads alarming rumours.

scarf[1] *n* piece of material worn round the neck, head, or shoulders.

scarf[2] *n* joint between two pieces of timber made by notching the ends and fastening them together. ◆ *v* join in this way.

scarify *v* **-fying, -fied** scratch or cut slightly all over; break up and loosen (topsoil); criticize mercilessly. **scarification** *n*

scarlet *adj, n* brilliant red. **scarlet fever** infectious fever with a scarlet rash.

scarp *n* steep slope.

scarper *v* *Slang* run away.

scat[1] *v* **scatting, scatted** *Informal* go away.

scat[2] *n* jazz singing using improvised vocal sounds instead of words.

scathing *adj* harshly critical.

scatter *v* throw about in various directions; put here and there; disperse. **scatterbrain** *n* empty-headed person.

scatty *adj* **-tier, -tiest** *Informal* empty-headed.

scavenge *v* search for (anything usable) among discarded material. **scavenger** *n* person who scavenges; animal that feeds on decaying matter.

scenario *n, pl* **-rios** summary of the plot of a play or film; imagined sequence of future events.

scene *n* place of action of a real or imaginary event; subdivision of a play or film in which the action is continuous; view of a place; display of emotion; *Informal* specific activity or interest, e.g. *the fashion scene*. **behind the scenes** backstage; in secret. **scenery** *n* natural features of a landscape; painted backcloths or screens used on stage to represent the scene of action. **scenic** *adj* picturesque.

scent *n* pleasant smell; smell left in

passing, by which an animal can be traced; series of clues; perfume. ◆ *v* detect by smell; suspect; fill with fragrance.

sceptic [skep-tik] *n* person who habitually doubts generally accepted beliefs. **sceptical** *adj* **sceptically** *adv* **scepticism** *n*

sceptre *n* ornamental rod symbolizing royal power.

schedule *n* plan of procedure for a project; timetable; list. ◆ *v* plan to occur at a certain time.

schema *n, pl* **-mata** overall plan or diagram. **schematic** *adj* presented as a plan or diagram.

scheme *n* systematic plan; secret plot. ◆ *v* plan in an underhand manner. **scheming** *adj, n*

scherzo [skairt-so] *n, pl* **-zos, -zi** brisk lively piece of music.

schism [skizz-um] *n* (group resulting from) division in an organization. **schismatic** *adj, n*

schist [skist] *n* crystalline rock which splits into layers.

schizoid *adj* abnormally introverted; *Informal* contradictory. ◆ *n* schizoid person.

schizophrenia *n* mental disorder involving deterioration of or confusion about the personality; *Informal* contradictory behaviour or attitudes. **schizophrenic** *adj, n*

schmaltz *n* excessive sentimentality. **schmaltzy** *adj*

schnapps *n* strong alcoholic spirit.

schnitzel *n* thin slice of meat, esp. veal.

scholar *n* learned person; pupil; student receiving a scholarship. **scholarly** *adj* learned. **scholarship** *n* learning; financial aid given to a student because of academic merit. **scholastic** *adj* of schools.

school[1] *n* place where children are taught or instruction is given in a subject; group of artists, thinkers, etc. with shared principles or methods. ◆ *v* educate; train.

school[2] *n* shoal of fish, whales, etc.

schooner *n* sailing ship rigged fore-and-aft; large glass.

sciatica *n* severe pain in the large nerve in the back of the leg. **sciatic** *adj* of the hip; of or afflicted with sciatica.

science *n* systematic study and

knowledge of natural or physical phenomena. **scientific** *adj* of science; systematic. **scientifically** *adv* **scientist** *n* person who studies or practises a science. **science fiction** stories making imaginative use of scientific knowledge.

sci-fi *n* short for SCIENCE FICTION.

scimitar *n* curved oriental sword.

scintillating *adj* animated or witty.

scion [sy-on] *n* descendant or heir; shoot of a plant for grafting.

scissors *pl n* cutting instrument with two crossed pivoted blades.

sclerosis *n*, *pl* **-ses** abnormal hardening of body tissues.

scoff[1] *v* express derision.

scoff[2] *v Slang* eat rapidly.

scold *v* find fault with, reprimand. ◆ *n* person who scolds. **scolding** *n*

sconce *n* bracket on a wall for holding candles or lights.

scone *n* small plain cake baked in an oven or on a griddle.

scoop *n* shovel-like tool for ladling or hollowing out; news story reported in one newspaper before all its rivals. ◆ *v* take up or hollow out with or as if with a scoop; beat (rival newspapers) in reporting a news item.

scoot *v Slang* leave or move quickly. **scooter** *n* child's vehicle propelled by pushing on the ground with one foot; light motorcycle.

scope *n* range of activity; opportunity for using abilities.

scorch *v* burn on the surface; parch or shrivel from heat. ◆ *n* slight burn. **scorcher** *n Informal* very hot day.

score *n* points gained in a game or competition; twenty; written version of a piece of music showing parts for each musician; mark or cut; grievance, e.g. *settle old scores.* ◆ *pl* lots. ◆ *v* gain points in a game; mark or cut; (foll. by *out*) cross out; arrange music (for); keep a record of points; achieve a success.

scorn *n* contempt, derision. ◆ *v* despise; reject with contempt. **scornful** *adj* **scornfully** *adv*

scorpion *n* small lobster-shaped animal with a sting at the end of a jointed tail.

Scot *n* person from Scotland. **Scottish** *adj* of Scotland, its people, or their languages (also **Scots**). **Scotch** *n*

whisky distilled in Scotland. **Scotch tape** *n* ® type of adhesive tape. ◆ *v* stick with Scotch tape. **Scotsman, Scotswoman** *n*

scotch *v* put an end to.

scot-free *adj* without harm or punishment.

scoundrel *n Old-fashioned* villainous person.

scour[1] *v* clean or polish by rubbing with something rough; clear or flush out. **scourer** *n* small rough nylon pad used for cleaning pots and pans.

scour[2] *v* search thoroughly and energetically.

scourge *n* person or thing causing severe suffering; whip. ◆ *v* cause severe suffering to; whip.

scout *n* person sent out to reconnoitre; (S-) member of the Scout Association, an organization for boys which aims to develop character and promotes outdoor activities. ◆ *v* act as a scout; reconnoitre. **Scouter** *n* leader of a troop of Scouts.

scow *n* unpowered barge.

scowl *v, n* (have) an angry or sullen expression.

scrabble *v* scrape at with the hands, feet, or claws.

scrag *n* lean end of a neck of mutton. **scraggy** *adj* thin, bony.

scram *v* **scramming, scrammed** (of a nuclear reactor) shut or be shut down in an emergency; *Informal* go away hastily. ◆ *n* emergency shutdown of a nuclear reactor.

scramble *v* climb or crawl hastily or awkwardly; struggle with others (for); mix up; cook (eggs beaten up with milk); render (transmitted speech) unintelligible by an electronic device; (of an aircraft or aircrew) take off hurriedly in an emergency. ◆ *n* scrambling; rough climb; disorderly struggle; motorcycle race over rough ground. **scrambler** *n* electronic device that renders transmitted speech unintelligible.

scrap *n* small piece; waste metal collected for reprocessing; *Informal* fight or quarrel. ◆ *pl* leftover food. ◆ *v* **scrapping, scrapped** discard as useless; *Informal* fight or quarrel. **scrappy** *adj* badly organized or done. **scrapbook** *n* book with blank pages in which newspaper cuttings or pictures are stuck.

scrape v rub with something rough or sharp; clean or smooth thus; rub with a harsh noise; economize. ◆ n act or sound of scraping; mark or wound caused by scraping; *Informal* awkward situation. **scraper** n **scrape through** v succeed in or obtain with difficulty.

scratch v mark or cut with claws, nails, or anything rough or sharp; scrape (skin) with nails or claws to relieve itching; withdraw from a race or competition. ◆ n wound, mark, or sound made by scratching. ◆ adj put together at short notice. **from scratch** from the very beginning. **up to scratch** up to standard. **scratchy** adj

scrawl v write carelessly or hastily. ◆ n scribbled writing.

scrawny adj **scrawnier, scrawniest** thin and bony.

scream v utter a piercing cry, esp. of fear or pain; utter with a scream. ◆ n shrill piercing cry; *Informal* very funny person or thing.

scree n slope of loose shifting stones.

screech¹ v, n (utter) a shrill cry.

screech² n *Slang* (esp. in Newfoundland) a type of cheap dark rum.

screed n long tedious piece of writing.

screen n movable structure used to shelter, divide, or conceal something; surface of a television set, VDU, etc., on which an image is formed; white surface on which photographs are projected. ◆ v shelter or conceal with or as if with a screen; show (a film); examine (a person or group) to determine suitability for a task or to detect the presence of disease or weapons. **screen saver** *Computers* a changing image on a monitor when the computer is operative but idle. **the screen** cinema generally.

screw n metal pin with a spiral ridge along its length, twisted into materials to fasten them together; *Slang* a prison guard. ◆ v turn (a screw); fasten with screw(s); twist; *Informal* extort. **screwy** adj *Informal* crazy or eccentric. **screwdriver** n tool for turning screws. **screw up** v *Informal* bungle; distort.

scribble v write hastily or illegibly; make meaningless or illegible marks. ◆ n something scribbled.

scribe n person who copied

manuscripts before the invention of printing; *Bible* scholar of the Jewish Law. **scribal** adj

scrimmage n disorderly struggle.

scrimp v be very economical.

scrip n certificate representing a claim to stocks or shares.

script n text of a film, play, or TV programme; particular system of writing, e.g. *Arabic script*; handwriting.

scripture n sacred writings of a religion. **scriptural** adj

scrofula n tuberculosis of the lymphatic glands. **scrofulous** adj

scroll n roll of parchment or paper; ornamental carving shaped like this. ◆ v move (text) up or down on a VDU screen.

scrotum n, pl **-ta, -tums** pouch of skin containing the testicles.

scrounge v *Informal* get by cadging or begging. **scrounger** n

scrub¹ v **scrubbing, scrubbed** clean by rubbing, often with a hard brush and water; *Informal* delete or cancel. ◆ n scrubbing.

scrub² n stunted trees; area of land covered with scrub. **scrubby** adj covered with scrub; stunted; *Informal* shabby.

scruff n nape (of the neck).

scruffy adj **scruffier, scruffiest** unkempt or shabby.

scrum, scrummage n *Rugby* restarting of play in which opposing packs of forwards push against each other to gain possession of the ball; disorderly struggle.

scrumptious adj *Informal* delicious.

scrunch v crumple or crunch or be crumpled or crunched. ◆ n act or sound of scrunching. **scrunchie** n loop of elastic covered loosely with fabric, used to hold the hair in a ponytail.

scruple n doubt produced by one's conscience or morals. ◆ v have doubts on moral grounds. **scrupulous** adj very conscientious; very careful. **scrupulously** adv

scrutiny n, pl **-nies** close examination. **scrutinize** v examine closely.

scuba diving n sport of swimming under water using cylinders containing compressed air attached to breathing apparatus.

scud v **scudding, scudded** move along swiftly.

scuff v drag (the feet) while walking; scrape (one's shoes) by doing so. ◆ n mark caused by scuffing.

scuffle v fight in a disorderly manner; move by shuffling. ◆ n disorderly struggle; scuffling sound.

scull n small oar. ◆ v row (a boat) using a scull.

scullery n, pl **-leries** small room where washing-up and other kitchen work is done.

sculpture n art of making figures or designs in wood, stone, etc.; product of this art. ◆ v (also **sculpt**) represent in sculpture. **sculptor, sculptress** n **sculptural** adj

scum n impure or waste matter on the surface of a liquid; worthless people. **scummy** adj

scupper v Informal defeat or ruin.

scurf n flaky skin on the scalp.

scurrilous adj untrue and defamatory. **scurrility** n

scurry v **-rying, -ried** move hastily. ◆ n act or sound of scurrying.

scurvy n disease caused by lack of vitamin C.

scut n short tail of the hare, rabbit, or deer.

scuttle¹ n fireside container for coal.

scuttle² v run with short quick steps. ◆ n hurried run.

scuttle³ v make a hole in (a ship) to sink it.

scythe n long-handled tool with a curved blade for cutting grass. ◆ v cut with a scythe.

SE southeast(ern).

sea n mass of salt water covering three quarters of the earth's surface; particular area of this; turbulence or swell; vast expanse. **at sea** in a ship on the ocean; confused or bewildered. **sea anemone** sea animal with suckers like petals. **seaboard** n coast. **sea dog** experienced sailor. **seafaring** adj working or travelling by sea. **seafood** n edible saltwater fish or shellfish. **sea gull** gull. **sea horse** small sea fish with a plated body and horselike head. **sea level** average level of the sea's surface in relation to the land. **sea lion** kind of large seal. **seaman** n sailor. **seaplane** n aircraft designed to take off from and land on water. **seasick** adj suffering from nausea caused by the motion of a ship. **seasickness** n **seaside** n area,

esp. a holiday resort, on the coast. **sea urchin** sea animal with a round spiky shell. **seaweed** n plant growing in the sea. **seaworthy** adj (of a ship) in fit condition for a sea voyage.

seal¹ n piece of wax, lead, etc. with a special design impressed upon it, attached to a letter or document as a mark of authentication; device or material used to close an opening tightly. ◆ v make airtight or watertight; close with or as if with a seal; affix a seal to or stamp with a seal; decide (one's fate) irrevocably. **sealant** n any substance used for sealing. **seal off** v enclose (a place) completely.

seal² n amphibious mammal with flippers as limbs. **sealskin** n

seam n line where two edges are joined, as by stitching; thin layer of coal or ore. ◆ v mark with furrows or wrinkles. **seamless** adj **seamy** adj sordid.

seamstress n woman who sews.

seance [say-anss] n meeting at which spiritualists attempt to communicate with the dead.

sear v scorch, burn the surface of; cause to wither.

search v examine closely in order to find something. ◆ n searching. **searching** adj keen or thorough, e.g. a searching look. **search engine** Computers Internet service enabling users to search for items of interest. **searchlight** n powerful light with a beam that can be shone in any direction.

season n one of four divisions of the year, each of which has characteristic weather conditions; period during which a thing happens or is plentiful; fitting or proper time. ◆ v flavour with salt, herbs, etc.; dry (timber) till ready for use. **seasonable** adj appropriate for the season; timely or opportune. **seasonal** adj depending on or varying with the seasons. **seasoned** adj experienced. **seasoning** n salt, herbs, etc. added to food to enhance flavour. **season ticket** ticket for a series of journeys or events within a specified period.

seat n thing designed or used for sitting on; place to sit in a theatre, esp. one that requires a ticket; buttocks; membership of a legislative or administrative body; country house.

◆ v cause to sit; provide seating for.
seat belt belt worn in an automobile
or aircraft to prevent a person being
thrown forward in a crash.

sebaceous adj of, like, or secreting fat
or oil.

secateurs pl n small pruning shears.

secede v withdraw formally from a
political alliance or federation.
secession n

seclude v keep (a person) from
contact with others. **secluded** adj
private, sheltered. **seclusion** n

second[1] adj coming directly after the
first; alternate, additional; inferior. ◆ n
person or thing coming second;
sixtieth part of a minute; moment;
attendant in a duel or boxing match.
◆ pl inferior goods. ◆ v express formal
support for (a motion proposed in a
meeting). **secondly** adv **second-class**
adj inferior; cheaper, slower, or less
comfortable than first-class. **second-
hand** adj bought after use by another.
second nature something so habitual
that it seems part of one's character.
second sight supposed ability to
predict events. **second thoughts**
revised opinion on a matter already
considered. **second wind** renewed
ability to continue effort.

second[2] [si-kawnd] v transfer (a
person) temporarily to another job.
secondment n

secondary adj coming after or
derived from what is primary or first;
of less importance; relating to the
education of people between the ages
of 11 and 18.

secret adj kept from the knowledge of
others. ◆ n something kept secret;
mystery; underlying explanation, e.g.
the secret of my success. **in secret**
without other people knowing.
secretly adv **secrecy** n **secretive** adj
inclined to keep things secret.
secretiveness n

secretariat n administrative office or
staff of a legislative body.

secretary n, pl **-ries** person who deals
with correspondence and general
clerical work; head of a state
department, e.g. Home Secretary.
secretarial adj **Secretary of State**
head of a major government
department.

secrete v hide or conceal; (of an
organ, gland, etc.) produce and

release (a substance). **secretion** n
secretory [sek-reet-or-ee] adj

sect n subdivision of a religious or
political group, esp. one with extreme
beliefs. **sectarian** adj of a sect; narrow-
minded.

section n part cut off; part or
subdivision of something; distinct part
of a country or community; cutting;
drawing of something as if cut
through. ◆ v cut or divide into
sections. **sectional** adj

sector n part or subdivision; part of a
circle enclosed by two radii and the
arc which they cut off.

secular adj worldly, as opposed to
sacred; not connected with religion or
the church.

secure adj free from danger; free from
anxiety; firmly fixed; reliable. ◆ v
obtain; make safe; make firm;
guarantee payment of (a loan) by
giving something as security. **securely**
adv **security** n state of being secure;
precautions against theft, espionage,
or other danger; something given or
pledged to guarantee payment of a
loan; certificate of ownership of a
share, stock, or bond.

sedan n automobile with a fixed roof.
sedan chair Hist enclosed chair for
one person, carried on poles by two
bearers.

sedate[1] adj calm and dignified; sober
or decorous. **sedately** adv

sedate[2] v give a sedative drug to.
sedation n **sedative** adj having a
soothing or calming effect. ◆ n
sedative drug.

sedentary [sed-en-tree] adj done
sitting down.

sedge n coarse grasslike plant
growing on wet ground.

sediment n matter which settles to
the bottom of a liquid; material
deposited by water, ice, or wind.
sedimentary adj

sedition n speech or action
encouraging rebellion against the
government. **seditious** adj

seduce v persuade into sexual
intercourse; tempt into wrongdoing.
seducer, **seductress** n **seduction** n
seductive adj

sedulous adj diligent or persevering.
sedulously adv

see[1] v **seeing**, **saw**, **seen** perceive with

the eyes or mind; watch; find out; make sure (of something); consider or decide; have experience of; meet or visit; interview; frequent the company of; accompany. **seeing** conj in view of the fact that.

see² n diocese of a bishop.

seed n mature fertilized grain of a plant; such grains used for sowing; origin; Obs offspring; Sport seeded player. ◆ v sow with seed; remove seeds from; arrange (the draw of a sports tournament) so that the outstanding competitors will not meet in the early rounds. **go, run to seed** (of plants) produce or shed seeds after flowering; lose vigour or usefulness. **seedling** n young plant raised from a seed. **seedy** adj shabby; Informal unwell.

seek v **seeking, sought** try to find or obtain; try (to do something).

seem v appear to be. **seeming** adj apparent but not real. **seemingly** adv

seemly adj **-lier, -liest** proper or fitting. **seemliness** n

seen v past participle of SEE.

seep v ooze. **seepage** n

seer n prophet.

seersucker n light cotton fabric with a slightly crinkled surface.

seesaw n plank balanced in the middle so that two people seated on either end ride up and down alternately. ◆ v move up and down.

seethe v **seething, seethed** be very agitated; (of a liquid) boil or foam.

segment n one of several sections into which something may be divided. ◆ v divide into segments. **segmentation** n

segregate v set apart. **segregation** n

seine [sane] n large fishing net that hangs vertically from floats.

seismic adj relating to earthquakes. **seismology** n study of earthquakes. **seismologic, seismological** adj **seismologist** n **seismograph, seismometer** n instrument that records the strength of earthquakes.

seize v take hold of forcibly or quickly; take immediate advantage of; (usu. foll. by up) (of mechanical parts) stick tightly through overheating. **seizure** n seizing or being seized; sudden violent attack of an illness.

seldom adv not often, rarely.

select v pick out or choose. ◆ adj chosen in preference to others; restricted to a particular group, exclusive. **selection** n selecting; things that have been selected; range from which something may be selected. **selective** adj chosen or choosing carefully. **selectively** adv **selectivity** n **selector** n

selenium n nonmetallic element with photoelectric properties.

self n, pl **selves** distinct individuality or identity of a person or thing; one's basic nature; one's own welfare or interests. **selfish** adj caring too much about oneself and not enough about others. **selfishly** adv **selfishness** n **selfless** adj unselfish.

self- combining form used with many main words to mean: of oneself or itself; by, to, in, due to, for, or from the self; automatic(ally). **self-assured** adj confident. **self-catering** adj (of accommodation) for people who provide their own food. **self-coloured** adj having only a single colour. **self-conscious** adj embarrassed at being the object of others' attention. **self-contained** adj containing everything needed, complete; (of an apartment) having its own facilities. **self-determination** n the right of a nation to decide its own form of government. **self-evident** adj obvious without proof. **self-help** n use of one's own abilities to solve problems; practice of solving one's problems within a group of people with similar problems. **self-interest** n one's own advantage. **self-made** adj having achieved wealth or status by one's own efforts. **self-possessed** adj having control of one's emotions, calm. **self-righteous** adj thinking oneself more virtuous than others. **self-rising** adj (of flour) containing a raising agent. **selfsame** adj the very same. **self-seeking** adj, n seeking to promote only one's own interests. **self-service** adj denoting a shop, café, or garage where customers serve themselves and then pay a cashier. **self-styled** adj using a title or name that one has taken without right. **self-sufficient** adj able to provide for oneself without help. **self-willed** adj stubbornly determined to get one's own way.

sell v **selling, sold** exchange

(something) for money; stock, deal in; (of goods) be sold; (foll. by *for*) have a specified price; *Informal* persuade (someone) to accept (something). ◆ *n* manner of selling. **seller** *n* **sell out** *v* dispose of (something) completely by selling; *Informal* betray. **sellout** *n* performance of a show etc. for which all the tickets are sold; *Informal* betrayal.

selvage, selvedge *n* edge of cloth, woven so as to prevent unravelling.

selves *n* plural of SELF.

semantic *adj* relating to the meaning of words. **semantics** *pl n* study of linguistic meaning.

semaphore *n* system of signalling by holding two flags in different positions to represent letters of the alphabet.

semblance *n* outward or superficial appearance.

semen *n* sperm-carrying fluid produced by male animals.

semester *n* either of two divisions of the academic year.

semi *n Informal* semidetached house.

semi- *prefix* used with many main words to mean: half, e.g. *semidome*; partly or almost, e.g. *semiprofessional*.

semibreve *n Brit* whole note.

semicolon *n* the punctuation mark (;).

semiconductor *n* substance with an electrical conductivity that increases with temperature.

semidetached *adj* (of a house) joined to another on one side.

semifinal *n* match or round before the final. **semifinalist** *n*

seminal *adj* capable of developing; original and influential; of semen or seed.

seminar *n* meeting of a group of students for discussion.

seminary *n, pl* **-ries** college for priests.

semiprecious *adj* (of gemstones) having less value than precious stones.

semiquaver *n* musical note half the length of a quaver.

Semite *n* member of the group of peoples including Jews and Arabs. **Semitic** *adj*

semitone *n* smallest interval between two notes in Western music.

semolina *n* hard grains of wheat left after the milling of flour, used to make puddings and pasta.

Senate *n* upper house of some parliaments; governing body of some universities. **senator** *n* member of a Senate. **senatorial** *adj*

send *v* **sending, sent** cause (a person or thing) to go to or be taken or transmitted to a place; bring into a specified state or condition. **sendoff** *n* demonstration of good wishes at a person's departure. **send up** *v Informal* make fun of by imitating. **send-up** *n Informal* imitation.

senile *adj* mentally or physically weak because of old age. **senility** *n*

senior *adj* superior in rank or standing; older; of or for older pupils. ◆ *n* senior person. **seniority** *n*

senna *n* tropical plant; its dried leaves or pods used as a laxative.

señor [sen-**nyor**] *n, pl* **-ores** Spanish term of address equivalent to *sir* or *Mr*. **señora** [sen-**nyor**-a] *n* Spanish term of address equivalent to *madam* or *Mrs*. **señorita** [sen-nyor-**ee**-ta] *n* Spanish term of address equivalent to *madam* or *Miss*.

sensation *n* ability to feel things physically; physical feeling; general feeling or awareness; state of excitement; exciting person or thing. **sensational** *adj* causing intense shock, anger, or excitement; *Informal* very good. **sensationalism** *n* deliberate use of sensational language or subject matter. **sensationalist** *adj, n*

sense *n* any of the faculties of perception or feeling (sight, hearing, touch, taste, or smell); ability to perceive; feeling perceived through one of the senses; awareness; (sometimes pl.) sound practical judgment or intelligence; specific meaning. ◆ *v* perceive. **senseless** *adj*

sensible *adj* having or showing good sense; (foll. by *of*) aware; practical, e.g. *sensible shoes*. **sensibly** *adv* **sensibility** *n* ability to experience deep feelings.

sensitive *adj* responsive to external stimuli; easily hurt or offended; (of an instrument) responsive to slight changes; (of a subject) liable to arouse controversy or strong feelings. **sensitively** *adv* **sensitivity** *n* **sensitize** *v* make sensitive.

sensor *n* device that detects or measures the presence of something, such as radiation.

sensory *adj* of the senses or sensation.

sensual *adj* giving pleasure to the body and senses rather than the mind; having a strong liking for physical pleasures. **sensually** *adv* **sensuality** *n* **sensualism** *n* **sensualist** *n*

sensuous *adj* pleasing to the senses. **sensuously** *adv*

sent *v* past of SEND.

sentence *n* sequence of words capable of standing alone as a statement, question, or command; punishment passed on a criminal. ◆ *v* pass sentence on (a convicted person).

sententious *adj* trying to sound wise; pompously moralizing. **sententiously** *adv* **sententiousness** *n*

sentient [sen-tee-ent] *adj* capable of feeling. **sentience** *n*

sentiment *n* thought, opinion, or attitude; feeling expressed in words; exaggerated or mawkish emotion. **sentimental** *adj* excessively romantic or nostalgic. **sentimentalism** *n* **sentimentality** *n* **sentimentalize** *v* make sentimental.

sentinel *n* sentry.

sentry *n*, *pl* **-tries** soldier on watch.

sepal *n* leaflike division of the calyx of a flower.

separate *v* act as a barrier between; divide up into parts; distinguish between; (of a married couple) stop living together. ◆ *adj* set apart; not the same, different; not shared, individual. **separately** *adv* **separation** *n* separating or being separated; *Law* living apart of a married couple without divorce. **separable** *adj* **separatist** *n* person who advocates the separation of a group or province from an organization or country, such as Quebec from Canada. **separatism** *n* **separate school** school for a large religious minority.

sepia *adj*, *n* reddish-brown (pigment).

sepsis *n* poisoning caused by pus-forming bacteria.

Sept. September.

September *n* ninth month of the year.

septet *n* group of seven performers; music for such a group.

septic *adj* (of a wound) infected; of or caused by harmful bacteria. **septic tank** tank in which sewage is decomposed by the action of bacteria.

septicemia, septicaemia [sep-tis-see-mee-a] *n* blood poisoning.

septuagenarian *n*, *adj* (person) between seventy and seventy-nine years old.

sepulchre [sep-pull-ker] *n* tomb or burial vault. **sepulchral** [sip-pulk-ral] *adj* gloomy.

sequel *n* novel, play, or film that continues the story of an earlier one; consequence.

sequence *n* arrangement of two or more things in successive order; the successive order of two or more things; section of a film showing a single uninterrupted episode. **sequential** *adj*

sequester *v* separate; seclude.

sequestrate *v* confiscate (property) until its owner's debts are paid or a court order is complied with. **sequestration** *n*

sequin *n* small ornamental metal disc on a garment. **sequined** *adj*

sequoia *n* giant Californian coniferous tree.

seraglio [sir-ah-lee-oh] *n*, *pl* **-raglios** harem of a Muslim palace; Turkish sultan's palace.

seraph *n* member of the highest order of angels. **seraphic** *adj*

Serbian, Serb *adj* of Serbia. ◆ *n* person from Serbia. **Serbo-Croat, Serbo-Croatian** *adj*, *n* (of) the chief official language of Serbia and Croatia.

serenade *n* music played or sung to a woman by a lover. ◆ *v* sing or play a serenade to (someone).

serendipity *n* gift of making fortunate discoveries by accident.

serene *adj* calm, peaceful. **serenely** *adv* **serenity** *n*

serf *n* medieval farm labourer who could not leave the land he worked on. **serfdom** *n*

serge *n* strong woollen fabric.

sergeant *n* noncommissioned officer in the army; police officer ranking between constable and inspector. **sergeant at arms** parliamentary or court officer with ceremonial duties. **sergeant major** highest rank of noncommissioned officer in the army.

serial *n* story or play produced in successive instalments. ◆ *adj* of or forming a series; published or presented as a serial. **serialize** *v* publish or present as a serial. **serial killer** person who commits a series of murders.

seriatim [seer-ree-ah-tim] *adv* one after another.

series *n, pl* **-ries** group or succession of related things, usu. arranged in order; set of radio or TV programmes about the same subject or characters.

serious *adj* giving cause for concern; concerned with important matters; not cheerful, grave; sincere, not joking; *Informal* extreme or remarkable. **seriously** *adv* **seriousness** *n*

sermon *n* speech on a religious or moral subject by a clergyman in a church service; long moralizing speech. **sermonize** *v* make a long moralizing speech.

serpent *n* snake. **serpentine** *adj* twisting like a snake.

serrated *adj* having a notched or sawlike edge. **serration** *n*

serried *adj* in close formation.

serum [seer-um] *n* yellowish watery fluid left after blood has clotted; this fluid from the blood of immunized animals used for inoculation or vaccination.

servant *n* person employed to do household work for another.

serve *v* work for (a person, community, or cause); perform official duties; attend to (customers); provide with food or drink; present (food or drink); provide with a service; be a member of the armed forces; spend (time) in prison; be useful or suitable; *Tennis, etc* put (the ball) into play; deliver (a legal document) to (a person). ♦ *n Tennis, etc* act of serving the ball.

service *n* serving; system that provides something needed by the public; overhaul of a machine or vehicle; availability for use; department of public employment and its employees; set of dishes etc. for serving a meal; formal religious ceremony; *Tennis, etc* act, manner, or right of serving the ball. ♦ *pl* armed forces. ♦ *v* provide a service or services to; overhaul (a machine or vehicle). **serviceable** *adj* useful or helpful; able or ready to be used. **service apartment** apartment where domestic services are provided.

serviceberry *n* same as SASKATOON.

serviceman *n* member of the armed forces. **service road** narrow road giving access to houses and shops. **service station** garage selling fuel for motor vehicles.

serviette *n* table napkin.

servile *adj* too eager to obey people, fawning; suitable for a slave. **servility** *n*

servitude *n* bondage or slavery.

servomechanism *n* device which converts a small force into a larger force, used esp. in steering mechanisms.

sesame [sess-am-ee] *n* plant cultivated for its seeds and oil, which are used in cooking.

session *n* meeting of a court, parliament, or council; series or period of such meetings; period spent in an activity; academic year.

set *v* **setting, set** put in a specified position or state; make ready; make or become firm or rigid; put (a broken bone) or (of a broken bone) be put into a normal position for healing; establish, arrange; prescribe, assign; put to music; arrange (hair) while wet, so that it dries in position; (of the sun) go down. ♦ *adj* fixed or established beforehand; rigid or inflexible; conventional or stereotyped; determined (to do something); ready. ♦ *n* number of things or people grouped or belonging together; *Math* group of numbers or objects that satisfy a given condition or share a property; television or radio receiver; scenery used in a play or film; *Tennis, etc* group of games in a match. **setback** *n* anything that delays progress. **set square** flat right-angled triangular instrument used for drawing angles. **set theory** branch of mathematics concerned with the properties of sets. **set up** *v* arrange or establish. **setup** *n* way in which anything is organized or arranged.

sett, set *n* badger's burrow.

settee *n* couch.

setter *n* long-haired gun dog.

setting *n* background or surroundings; time and place where a film, book, etc. is supposed to have taken place; music written for the words of a text; decorative metalwork in which a gem is set; plates and cutlery for a single place at table; descending below the horizon of the sun; position to which the controls of a machine can be adjusted.

settle[1] v arrange or put in order; establish or become established as a resident; colonize; make quiet, calm, or stable; come to rest; dispose of, conclude; end (a dispute); pay (a bill); bestow (property) legally. **settlement** n act of settling; place newly colonized; property bestowed legally; subsidence (of a building). **settler** n colonist.

settle[2] n long wooden bench with high back and arms.

seven adj, n one more than six. **seventh** adj, n (of) number seven in a series. **seventeen** adj, n ten and seven. **seventeenth** adj, n **seventy** adj, n ten times seven. **seventieth** adj, n

sever v separate, divide; cut off. **severance** n **severance pay** compensation paid by a firm to an employee for loss of employment.

several adj some, a few; various, separate. ◆ pron indefinite small number. **severally** adv separately.

severe adj strict or harsh; very intense or unpleasant; strictly restrained in appearance. **severely** adv **severity** n

sew v sewing, sewed, sewn or sewed. join with thread repeatedly passed through with a needle; make or fasten by sewing.

sewage n waste matter or excrement carried away in sewers. **sewer** n drain to remove waste water and sewage. **sewerage** n system of sewers.

sewn v a past participle of SEW.

sex n state of being male or female; male or female category; sexual intercourse; sexual feelings or behaviour. ◆ v ascertain the sex of. **sexy** adj sexually exciting or attractive; Informal exciting or trendy. **sexism** n discrimination on the basis of a person's sex. **sexist** adj, n **sexual** adj **sexually** adv **sexuality** n **sexual intercourse** genital sexual activity between two people. **sex up** vb Informal make (something) more exciting.

sexagenarian n, adj (person) between sixty and sixty-nine years old.

sextant n navigator's instrument for measuring angles, as between the sun and horizon, to calculate one's position.

sextet n group of six performers; music for such a group.

sexton n official in charge of a church and churchyard.

SF science fiction.

shabby adj -bier, -biest worn or dilapidated in appearance; mean or unworthy, e.g. shabby treatment. **shabbily** adv **shabbiness** n

shack n rough hut. **shack up with** v Slang live with (one's lover).

shackle n one of a pair of metal rings joined by a chain, for securing a person's wrists or ankles. ◆ v fasten with shackles; hamper.

shad n herring-like fish.

shade n relative darkness; place sheltered from sun; depth of colour; slight amount; Lit ghost; screen or cover used to protect from a direct source of light. ◆ pl Slang sunglasses. ◆ v screen from light; darken; represent (darker areas) in drawing; change slightly or by degrees. **shady** adj situated in or giving shade; of doubtful honesty or legality.

shadow n dark shape cast on a surface when something stands between a light and the surface; patch of shade; slight trace; threatening influence; inseparable companion. ◆ v cast a shadow over; follow secretly. **shadowy** adj **shadow-boxing** n boxing against an imaginary opponent for practice. **Shadow Cabinet** members of the main opposition party in Parliament who would be ministers if their party were in power.

shaft n long narrow straight handle of a tool or weapon; ray of light; revolving rod that transmits power in a machine; vertical passageway, as for an elevator; one of the bars between which an animal is harnessed to a vehicle.

shag[1] n coarse shredded tobacco. ◆ adj (of a carpet) having a long pile. **shaggy** adj covered with rough hair or wool; tousled, unkempt. **shagginess** n **shaggy-dog story** long anecdote with a humorous twist at the end.

shag[2] n kind of cormorant.

shagreen n rough grainy untanned leather; sharkskin.

shah n formerly, ruler of Iran.

shake v **shaking, shook, shaken** move quickly up and down or back and forth; make unsteady; tremble; grasp (someone's hand) in greeting or agreement; shock or upset. ◆ n shaking; vibration; *Informal* short period of time. **shaky** adj unsteady; uncertain or questionable. **shakily** adv

shale n flaky sedimentary rock.

shall v, *past tense* **should** used as an auxiliary to make the future tense or to indicate intention, obligation, or inevitability.

shallot [shal-**lot**] n kind of small onion.

shallow adj not deep; lacking depth of character or intellect. **shallows** pl n area of shallow water. **shallowness** n

sham n thing or person that is not genuine. ◆ adj not real or genuine. ◆ v **shamming, shammed** fake.

shamble v walk in a shuffling awkward way.

shambles n disorderly event or place.

shame n painful emotion caused by awareness of having done something dishonourable or foolish; capacity to feel shame; cause of shame; cause for regret. ◆ v cause to feel shame; disgrace; compel by shame, e.g. *she was shamed into helping.* **shameful** adj causing or deserving shame. **shamefully** adv **shameless** adj with no sense of shame. **shamefaced** adj looking ashamed.

shampoo n liquid soap for washing hair, carpets, or upholstery; process of shampooing. ◆ v wash with shampoo.

shamrock n clover leaf, esp. as the Irish emblem.

shandy n, pl **-dies** drink made of beer and lemonade.

shanghai v force or trick (someone) into doing something.

shank n lower leg; shaft or stem.

shan't shall not.

shantung n soft Chinese silk with a knobbly surface.

shanty[1] n, pl **-ties** shack or crude dwelling. **shantytown** n slum consisting of shanties.

shanty[2] n, pl **-ties** sailor's traditional song.

shape n outward form of an object; way in which something is organized; pattern or mould; condition or state.

◆ v form or mould; devise or develop. **shapeless** adj **shapely** adj having an attractive shape.

shard n broken piece of pottery.

share[1] n part of something that belongs to or is contributed by a person; one of the equal parts into which the capital stock of a public company is divided. ◆ v give or take a share of (something); join with others in doing or using (something). **shareholder** n

share[2] n blade of a plough.

shark n large usu. predatory sea fish; person who cheats others.

sharkskin n stiff glossy fabric.

sharp adj having a keen cutting edge or fine point; not gradual; clearly defined; mentally acute; clever but underhand; shrill; bitter or sour in taste; (of a note) being one semitone above natural pitch; (of an instrument or voice) out of tune by being too high in pitch. ◆ adv promptly. ◆ n *Music* symbol raising a note one semitone above natural pitch; note raised in this way. **sharply** adv **sharpness** n **sharpen** v make or become sharp or sharper. **sharpener** n **sharpshooter** n marksman.

shatter v break into pieces; destroy completely; upset (someone) greatly. **shattered** adj *Informal* completely exhausted.

shave v **shaving, shaved, shaved** or **shaven.** remove (hair) from (the face, head, or body) with a razor or shaver; pare away; touch lightly in passing; reduce. ◆ n shaving. **close shave** see CLOSE. **shaver** n electric razor. **shavings** pl n parings.

shawl n piece of cloth worn over a woman's head or shoulders or wrapped around a baby.

she pron female person or animal previously mentioned; something regarded as female, such as an automobile, ship, or nation.

sheaf n, pl **sheaves** bundle of papers; tied bundle of reaped corn.

shear v **shearing, sheared, sheared** or **shorn.** clip hair or wool from; cut through. **shears** pl n large scissors or a cutting tool shaped like these. **shearer** n

sheath n close-fitting cover, esp. for a knife or sword; condom. **sheathe** v put into a sheath.

shed[1] n building used for storage or shelter or as a workshop.

shed[2] v **shedding, shed** pour forth (tears); cast off (skin); lose (hair).

sheen n glistening brightness on the surface of something.

sheep n, pl **sheep** ruminant animal bred for wool and meat. **sheep-dip** n liquid disinfectant in which sheep are immersed. **sheepdog** n dog used for herding sheep. **sheepskin** n skin of a sheep with the fleece still on, used for clothing or rugs.

sheepish adj embarrassed because of feeling foolish. **sheepishly** adv

sheer[1] adj absolute, complete, e.g. sheer folly; (of material) so fine as to be transparent; steep.

sheer[2] v change course suddenly.

sheet[1] n large piece of cloth used as an inner bedcover; broad thin piece of any material; large expanse.

sheet[2] n rope for controlling the position of a sail. **sheet anchor** strong anchor for use in an emergency; person or thing relied on.

sheikh, sheik [shake] n Arab chief. **sheikhdom, sheikdom** n

sheila n Aust slang girl or woman.

shekel n monetary unit of Israel. ◆ pl Informal money.

shelf n, pl **shelves** board fixed horizontally for holding things; ledge. **shelf life** time a packaged product will remain fresh.

shell n hard outer covering of an egg, nut, or certain animals; explosive projectile fired from a large gun; external frame of something. ◆ v take the shell from; fire at with artillery shells. **shellfish** n aquatic mollusc or crustacean. **shell out** v Informal pay out or hand over (money). **shell shock** nervous disorder caused by exposure to battle conditions.

shellac n resin used in varnishes. ◆ v -lacking, -lacked coat with shellac.

shelter n structure providing protection from danger or the weather; protection. ◆ v give shelter to; take shelter.

shelve v postpone; slope. **shelving** n (material for) shelves.

shenanigans pl n Informal mischief or nonsense; trickery.

shepherd n person who tends sheep.

◆ v guide or watch over (people). **shepherdess** n fem **shepherd's pie** baked dish of mince covered with mashed potato.

sherbet n fruit-flavoured fizzy powder.

sheriff n municipal officer who enforces court orders etc.; (in the US) law enforcement officer; (in England and Wales) chief executive officer of the Crown in a county; (in Scotland) chief judge of a district. **sheriffdom** n

Sherpa n member of a people of Tibet and Nepal.

sherry n, pl **-ries** pale or dark brown fortified wine.

shibboleth n slogan or principle, usu. considered outworn, characteristic of a particular group.

shield n piece of armour carried on the arm to protect the body from blows or missiles; anything that protects; sports trophy in the shape of a shield. ◆ v protect.

shift v move; transfer (blame or responsibility); remove or be removed. ◆ n shifting; group of workers who work during a specified period; period of time during which they work; loose-fitting straight underskirt or dress. **shiftless** adj lacking in ambition or initiative. **shifty** adj evasive or untrustworthy. **shiftiness** n

shillelagh [shil-lay-lee] n (in Ireland) a cudgel.

shilling n former British coin, replaced by the 5p piece.

shillyshally v -lying, -lied Informal be indecisive.

shimmer v, n (shine with) a faint unsteady light.

shin n front of the lower leg. ◆ v **shinning, shinned** climb by using the hands or arms and legs. **shinbone** n tibia.

shindig n Informal noisy party; brawl.

shine v **shining, shone** give out or reflect light; aim (a light); polish; excel. ◆ n brightness or lustre. **take a shine to** Informal take a liking to (someone). **shiny** adj **shiner** n Informal black eye.

shingle[1] n wooden roof tile. ◆ v cover (a roof) with shingles.

shingle[2] n coarse gravel found on beaches.

shingles n disease causing a rash of small blisters along a nerve.

Shinto n Japanese religion in which ancestors and nature spirits are worshipped. **Shintoism** n

shinty n game like hockey.

ship n large seagoing vessel. ◆ v **shipping, shipped** send or transport by carrier, esp. a ship; bring or go aboard a ship. **shipment** n act of shipping cargo; consignment of goods shipped. **shipping** n freight transport business; ships collectively. **shipshape** adj orderly or neat. **shipwreck** n destruction of a ship through storm or collision. ◆ v cause to undergo shipwreck. **shipyard** n place where ships are built.

shire n county.

shire horse n large powerful breed of horse.

shirk v avoid (duty or work). **shirker** n

shirt n garment for the upper part of the body.

shirty adj **-tier, -tiest** Slang annoyed.

shish kebab n meat and vegetable dish cooked on a skewer.

shiver¹ v tremble, as from cold or fear. ◆ n shivering.

shiver² v splinter into pieces.

shoal¹ n large number of fish swimming together.

shoal² n stretch of shallow water; sandbank.

shock¹ v horrify, disgust, or astonish. ◆ n sudden violent emotional disturbance; sudden violent blow or impact; something causing this; state of bodily collapse caused by physical or mental shock; pain and muscular spasm caused by an electric current passing through the body. **shocker** n **shocking** adj causing horror, disgust, or astonishment; Informal very bad.

shock² n bushy mass (of hair).

shod v past of SHOE.

shoddy adj **-dier, -diest** of poor quality.

shoe n outer covering for the foot, ending below the ankle; horseshoe. ◆ v shoeing, shod fit with a shoe or shoes. **shoehorn** n smooth curved implement inserted at the heel of a shoe to ease the foot into it. **shoestring** n on a shoestring using a very small amount of money.

shone v past of SHINE.

shoo interj go away! ◆ v drive away as by saying 'shoo'.

shook v past tense of SHAKE.

shoot v shooting, shot hit, wound, or kill with a missile fired from a weapon; fire (a missile from) a weapon; send out or move rapidly; hunt; (of a plant) sprout; photograph or film; Sport take a shot at goal. ◆ n new branch or sprout of a plant; hunting expedition. **shooting star** meteor. **shooting stick** stick with a spike at one end and a folding seat at the other.

shop n place for sale of goods and services; workshop. ◆ v shopping, shopped visit a shop or shops to buy goods; Slang inform against (someone). **talk shop** discuss one's work, esp. on a social occasion. **shop around** v visit various shops to compare goods and prices. **shop floor** production area of a factory; workers in a factory. **shoplifter** n person who steals from a shop. **shopsoiled** adj soiled or faded from being displayed in a shop. **shop steward** trade-union official elected to represent his or her fellow workers.

shore¹ n edge of a sea or lake.

shore² v (foll. by up) support.

shorn v a past participle of SHEAR.

short adj not long; not tall; not lasting long, brief; deficient, e.g. short of cash; abrupt, rude; (of a drink) consisting chiefly of a spirit; (of pastry) crumbly. ◆ adv abruptly. ◆ n drink of spirits; short film; Informal short circuit. ◆ pl short trousers. **shortage** n deficiency. **shorten** v make or become shorter. **shortly** adv soon; rudely. **shortbread, shortcake** n crumbly cookie made with butter. **short-change** v give (someone) less than the correct amount of change; Slang swindle. **short circuit** faulty or accidental connection in a circuit, which deflects current through a path of low resistance. **shortcoming** n failing or defect. **short cut** quicker route or method. **shortfall** n deficit. **shorthand** n system of rapid writing using symbols to represent words. **short-handed** adj not having enough workers. **short list** selected list of candidates for a job or prize, from which the final choice will be made. **short-list** v put on a short list. **short shrift** brief and unsympathetic treatment. **short-sighted** adj unable to see faraway things clearly; lacking in foresight. **short wave** radio wave with a wavelength of less than 60 metres.

shot n shooting; small lead pellets used in a shotgun; person with specified skill in shooting; Slang attempt; Sport act or instance of hitting, kicking, or throwing the ball; photograph; uninterrupted film sequence; Informal injection; Informal drink of spirits. ♦ adj woven so that the colour varies according to the angle of light. ♦ v past of SHOOT.

shotgun n gun for firing a charge of shot at short range.

shot put n athletic event in which contestants hurl a heavy metal ball as far as possible. **shot-putter** n

should v past tense of SHALL: used as an auxiliary to make the subjunctive mood or to indicate obligation or possibility.

shoulder n part of the body to which an arm, foreleg, or wing is attached; cut of meat including the upper foreleg; part of a garment which covers the shoulder; side of a road. ♦ v bear (a burden or responsibility); put on one's shoulder; push with one's shoulder. **shoulder blade** large flat triangular bone at the shoulder.

shouldn't should not.

shout n loud cry. ♦ v cry out loudly. **shout down** v silence (someone) by shouting.

shove v push roughly; Informal put. ♦ n rough push. **shove off** v Informal go away.

shovel n tool for lifting or moving loose material. ♦ v -elling, -elled lift or move as with a shovel.

show v showing, showed, shown or showed. make, be, or become noticeable or visible; exhibit or display; indicate; instruct by demonstration; prove; guide; reveal or display (an emotion). ♦ n public exhibition; theatrical or other entertainment; mere display or pretence. **showy** adj gaudy; ostentatious. **showily** adv **show business** the entertainment industry. **showcase** n glass case used to display objects; situation in which something is displayed to best advantage. **showdown** n confrontation that settles a dispute. **showjumping** n competitive sport of riding horses to demonstrate skill in jumping. **showman** n man skilled at presenting anything

spectacularly. **showmanship** n **show off** v exhibit to invite admiration; Informal behave flamboyantly in order to attract attention. **show-off** n Informal person who shows off.

showpiece n excellent specimen shown for display or as an example.

showroom n room in which goods for sale are on display. **show up** v reveal or be revealed clearly; expose the faults or defects of; Informal embarrass; Informal arrive.

shower n kind of bath in which a person stands while being sprayed with water; wash in this; short period of rain, hail, or snow; sudden abundant fall of objects, e.g. shower of sparks. ♦ v wash in a shower; bestow (things) or present (someone) with things liberally. **showery** adj

shown v a past participle of SHOW.

shrank v a past tense of SHRINK.

shrapnel n artillery shell filled with pellets which scatter on explosion; fragments from this.

shred n long narrow strip torn from something; small amount. ♦ v shredding, shredded or shred. tear to shreds.

shrew n small mouselike animal; bad-tempered nagging woman. **shrewish** adj

shrewd adj clever and perceptive. **shrewdly** adv **shrewdness** n

shriek n shrill cry. ♦ v utter (with) a shriek.

shrike n songbird with a heavy hooked bill.

shrill adj (of a sound) sharp and high-pitched. **shrillness** n **shrilly** adv

shrimp n small edible shellfish; Informal small person. **shrimping** n fishing for shrimps.

shrine n place of worship associated with a sacred person or object.

shrink v shrinking, shrank or shrunk, shrunk or shrunken. become or make smaller; recoil. ♦ n Slang psychiatrist. **shrinkage** n decrease in size, value, or weight.

shrive v shriving, shrived or shrove, shriven Old-fashioned give absolution to after hearing confession.

shrivel v -elling, -elled shrink and wither.

shroud n piece of cloth used to wrap a dead body; anything which conceals. ◆ v conceal.

Shrovetide n the three days preceding Lent. **Shrove Tuesday** day before Ash Wednesday.

shrub n woody plant smaller than a tree. **shrubbery** n area planted with shrubs.

shrug v **shrugging, shrugged** raise and then drop (the shoulders) as a sign of indifference, ignorance, or doubt. ◆ n shrugging. **shrug off** v dismiss as unimportant.

shrunk v a past of SHRINK.

shrunken v a past participle of SHRINK.

shudder v shake or tremble violently, esp. with horror. ◆ n shaking or trembling.

shuffle v walk without lifting the feet; rearrange; jumble together. ◆ n shuffling; rearrangement.

shun v **shunning, shunned** avoid.

shunt v move (objects or people) to a different position; move (a train) from one track to another.

shush interj be quiet!

shut v **shutting, shut** bring together or fold, close; prevent access to; (of a shop etc.) stop operating for the day. **shutter** n hinged doorlike cover for closing off a window; device in a camera letting in the light required to expose a film. **shut down** v close or stop (a factory, machine, or business). **shutdown** n

shuttle n vehicle going to and fro over a short distance; instrument which passes the weft thread between the warp threads in weaving. ◆ v travel by or as if by shuttle.

shuttlecock n small light cone with feathers stuck in one end, struck to and fro in badminton.

shy[1] adj not at ease in company; timid; (foll. by of) cautious or wary. ◆ v **shying, shied** start back in fear; (foll. by away from) avoid (doing something) through fear or lack of confidence. **shyly** adv **shyness** n

shy[2] v **shying, shied** throw. ◆ n, pl **shies** throw.

Si Chem silicon.

SI French Système International (d'Unités), international metric system of units of measurement.

Siamese adj of Siam, former name of Thailand. **Siamese cat** breed of cat with cream fur, dark ears and face, and blue eyes. **Siamese twins** twins born joined to each other at some part of the body.

sibilant adj hissing. ◆ n consonant pronounced with a hissing sound.

sibling n brother or sister.

sibyl n (in ancient Greece and Rome) prophetess. **sibylline** adj

sic Latin thus: used to indicate that an odd spelling or reading is in fact accurate.

sick adj vomiting or likely to vomit; physically or mentally unwell; Informal amused by something sadistic or morbid; (foll. by of) Informal disgusted (by) or weary (of). **sickness** n **sicken** v make nauseated or disgusted; become ill. **sickly** adj unhealthy, weak; causing revulsion or nausea. **sickbay** n place for sick people, such as that on a ship.

sickle n tool with a curved blade for cutting grass or grain.

side n line or surface that borders anything; either surface of a flat object; either of two halves into which something can be divided; area immediately next to a person or thing; region; aspect or part; one of two opposing groups or teams; line of descent through one parent; Slang conceit. ◆ adj at or on the side; subordinate. **on the side** as an extra; unofficially. **siding** n short stretch of railway track on which trains or cars are shunted from the main line. **sideboard** n piece of furniture for holding plates, cutlery, etc. in a dining room. ◆ pl (also **sideburns**) man's side whiskers. **side-effect** n additional undesirable effect. **sidekick** n Informal close friend or associate. **sidelight** n either of two small lights on the front of a vehicle. **sideline** n subsidiary interest or source of income; Sport line marking the boundary of a playing area. **sidelong** adj sideways; oblique. ◆ adv obliquely. **side-saddle** n saddle designed to allow a woman rider to sit with both legs on the same side of the horse. **sidestep** v dodge (an issue); avoid by stepping sideways. **sidetrack** v divert from the main topic. **sidewalk** n paved path for pedestrians. **sideways** adv to or from the side; obliquely. **side with** v support (one side in a dispute).

sidereal [side-eer-ee-al] adj of or determined with reference to the stars.

sidle v move in a furtive manner.

SIDS sudden infant death syndrome, crib death.

siege n surrounding and blockading of a place.

sienna n reddish- or yellowish-brown pigment made from natural earth.

sierra n range of mountains in Spain or America with jagged peaks.

siesta n afternoon nap, taken in hot countries.

sieve [siv] n utensil with mesh through which a substance is sifted or strained. ◆ v sift or strain through a sieve.

sift v remove the coarser particles from a substance with a sieve; examine (information or evidence) to select what is important.

sigh n long audible breath expressing sadness, tiredness, relief, or longing. ◆ v utter a sigh.

sight n ability to see; instance of seeing; range of vision; thing seen; thing worth seeing; *Informal* unsightly thing; device for guiding the eye while using a gun or optical instrument; *Informal* a lot. ◆ v catch sight of. **sightless** adj blind. **sight-read** v play or sing printed music without previous preparation. **sightseeing** n visiting places of interest. **sightseer** n

sign n indication of something not immediately or outwardly observable; notice displayed to advertise, inform, or warn; gesture, mark, or symbol conveying a meaning; omen. ◆ v write (one's name) on (a document or letter) to show its authenticity or one's agreement; communicate using sign language; make a sign or gesture. **signing** n (also **sign language**) system of manual signs used to communicate with deaf people. **sign on** v register as unemployed; sign a document committing oneself to a job, course, etc. **signpost** n post bearing a sign that shows the way.

signal n sign or gesture to convey information; sequence of electrical impulses or radio waves transmitted or received. ◆ adj remarkable or striking. ◆ v **-nalling, -nalled** make a signal; convey (information) by signal. **signally** adv **signal box** building from which railway signals are operated. **signalman** n railwayman in charge of signals and points.

signatory [sig-na-tree] n, pl **-ries** one of the parties who sign a document.

signature n person's name written by himself or herself in signing something; sign at the start of a piece of music to show the key or tempo. **signature tune** tune used to introduce a particular television or radio programme.

signet n small seal used to authenticate documents. **signet ring** finger ring bearing a signet.

significant adj important; having or expressing a meaning. **significantly** adv **significance** n

signify v **-fying, -fied** indicate; be a symbol or sign for; be important. **signification** n meaning.

signor [see-nyor] n Italian term of address equivalent to *Sir* or *Mr*. **signora** [see-nyor-a] n Italian term of address equivalent to *madam* or *Mrs*. **signorina** [see-nyor-ee-na] n Italian term of address equivalent to *madam* or *Miss*.

Sikh [seek] n member of an Indian religion having only one God.

silage [sile-ij] n fodder crop harvested while green and partially fermented in a silo.

silence n absence of noise or speech. ◆ v make silent; put a stop to. **silent** adj **silently** adv **silencer** n device to reduce the noise of an engine exhaust or gun.

silhouette n outline of a dark shape seen against a light background. ◆ v show in silhouette.

silica n hard glossy mineral found as quartz and in sandstone **silicosis** n lung disease caused by inhaling silica dust.

silicon n brittle nonmetallic element widely used in chemistry and industry. **silicone** n tough synthetic substance made from silicon and used in lubricants, paints, and resins. **silicon chip** tiny wafer of silicon processed to form an integrated circuit.

silk n fibre made by the larva of a moth called the silkworm; thread or fabric made from this. **silky, silken** adj of or like silk.

sill n ledge at the bottom of a window.

silly adj **-lier, -liest** foolish. **silliness** n

silo n, pl **-los** pit or airtight tower for

storing silage; underground structure in which nuclear missiles are kept ready for launching.

silt n mud deposited by moving water. ◆ v (foll. by *up*) fill or be choked with silt.

silvan adj same as SYLVAN.

silver n white precious metal; coins or articles made of silver. ◆ adj made of or of the colour of silver. **silver birch** tree with silvery-white bark. **silverfish** n small wingless silver-coloured insect. **silverside** n Brit cut of beef from below the rump and above the leg. **silver thaw** quick-freezing rain that encrusts trees, rocks, etc. **silver wedding** twenty-fifth wedding anniversary.

sim n computer game that simulates an activity such as flying or playing a sport.

simian adj, n (of or like) a monkey or ape.

similar adj alike but not identical. **similarity** n **similarly** adv

simile [sim-ill-ee] n figure of speech comparing one thing to another, using 'as' or 'like'.

similitude n similarity, likeness.

simmer v cook gently at just below boiling point; be in a state of suppressed rage. **simmer down** v calm down.

simnel cake n fruit cake covered with marzipan.

simper v smile in a silly or affected way; utter (something) with a simper. ◆ n simpering smile.

simple adj easy to understand or do; plain or unpretentious; not combined or complex; sincere or frank; feeble-minded. **simply** adv **simplicity** n **simplify** v -fying, -fied make less complicated. **simplification** n **simplistic** adj oversimplified or oversimplifying. **simpleton** n half-witted person.

simulate v make a pretence of; have the appearance of; imitate the conditions of (a particular situation). **simulation** n **simulator** n

simultaneous adj occurring at the same time. **simultaneity** n **simultaneously** adv

SIN Social Insurance Number.

sin¹ n breaking of a religious or moral law; offence against a principle or standard. ◆ v **sinning, sinned** commit a sin. **sinful** adj being a sin; guilty of sin. **sinfully** adv **sinner** n

sin² Math sine.

since prep during the period of time after. ◆ conj from the time when; for the reason that. ◆ adv from that time.

sincere adj without pretence or deceit. **sincerely** adv **sincerity** n

sine n (in trigonometry) ratio of the length of the opposite side to that of the hypotenuse in a right-angled triangle.

sinecure [sin-ee-cure] n paid job with minimal duties.

sine die [sin-ay dee-ay] adv Latin with no date fixed for future action.

sine qua non [sin-ay kwah non] n Latin essential requirement.

sinew n tough fibrous tissue joining muscle to bone; muscles or strength. **sinewy** adj

sing v **singing, sang, sung** make musical sounds with the voice; perform (a song); make a humming or whistling sound. **singer** n **singsong** n informal singing session. ◆ adj (of the voice) repeatedly rising and falling in pitch.

singe v **singeing, singed** burn the surface of. ◆ n superficial burn.

single adj one only; distinct from others of the same kind; unmarried; designed for one user; formed of only one part; (of a ticket) valid for an outward journey only. ◆ n single thing; thing intended for one person; record with one short song or tune on each side; single ticket. ◆ pl game between two players. ◆ v (foll. by *out*) pick out from others. **singly** adv **single file** (of people or things) arranged in one line. **single-handed** adj without assistance. **single-minded** adj having one aim only.

singlet n sleeveless vest.

singular adj (of a word or form) denoting one person or thing; remarkable, unusual. ◆ n singular form of a word. **singularity** n **singularly** adv

sinister adj threatening evil.

sink v **sinking, sank** or **sunk, sunk** or **sunken** submerge (in liquid); cause (a ship) to submerge by attacking it with bombs, etc.; descend or cause to descend; decline in value or amount; become weaker in health; dig or drill (a hole or shaft); invest (money); *Golf, snooker* hit (a ball) into a hole or pocket. ◆ *n* fixed basin with a water supply and drainage pipe. **sinker** *n* weight for a fishing line. **sink in** *v* penetrate the mind. **sinking fund** money set aside regularly to repay a long-term debt.

Sino- *combining form* Chinese.

sinuous *adj* curving; lithe. **sinuously** *adv*

sinus [sine-uss] *n* hollow space in a bone, esp. an air passage opening into the nose.

sip *v* **sipping, sipped** drink in small mouthfuls. ◆ *n* amount sipped.

siphon *n* bent tube which uses air pressure to draw liquid from a container. ◆ *v* draw off thus; redirect (resources).

sir *n* polite term of address for a man; (S-) title of a knight or baronet.

sire *n* male parent of a horse or other domestic animal; respectful term of address to a king. ◆ *v* father.

siren *n* device making a loud wailing noise as a warning; dangerously alluring woman.

sirloin *n* prime cut of loin of beef.

sirocco *n, pl* **-cos** hot wind blowing from N Africa into S Europe.

sisal [size-al] *n* (fibre of) plant used in making ropes.

siskin *n* yellow-and-black finch.

sissy *n, pl* **-sies** weak or cowardly person.

sister *n* girl or woman with the same parents as another person; senior nurse; nun; female fellow-member of a group. ◆ *adj* closely related, similar. **sisterhood** *n* state of being a sister; group of women united by common aims or beliefs. **sisterly** *adj* **sister-in-law** *n, pl* **sisters-in-law** sister of one's husband or wife; one's brother's wife.

sit *v* **sitting, sat** rest one's body upright on the buttocks; cause to sit; perch; (of a bird) incubate (eggs) by sitting on them; be situated; pose for a portrait; occupy an official position; (of an official body) hold a session; take (an examination). **sitting room** room in a house where people sit and relax. **sit-in** *n* protest in which demonstrators occupy a place and refuse to move.

sitar *n* Indian stringed musical instrument.

sitcom *n Informal* situation comedy.

site *n* **1** same as WEBSITE **2** place where something is, was, or is intended to be located. ◆ *v* provide with a site.

situate *v* place. **situation** *n* location and surroundings; state of affairs; position of employment. **situation comedy** radio or television series involving the same characters in various situations.

six *adj, n* one more than five. **sixth** *adj, n* (of) number six in a series. **sixteen** *adj, n* six and ten. **sixteenth** *adj, n* **sixty** *adj, n* six times ten. **sixtieth** *adj, n*

size[1] *n* dimensions, bigness; one of a series of standard measurements of goods. ◆ *v* arrange according to size. **sizeable, sizable** *adj* quite large. **size up** *Informal* assess.

size[2] *n* gluey substance used as a sealer.

sizzle *v* make a hissing sound like frying fat.

SK Saskatchewan.

skanky *adj Slang* dirty.

skate[1] *n* boot with a steel blade or sets of wheels attached to the sole for gliding over ice or a hard surface. ◆ *v* glide on or as if on skates. **skateboard** *n* board mounted on small wheels for riding on while standing up. **skate over, round** *v* avoid discussing or dealing with (a matter) fully.

skate[2] *n* large marine flatfish.

skedaddle *v Informal* run off.

skein *n* yarn wound in a loose coil; flock of geese in flight.

skeleton *n* framework of bones inside a person's or animal's body; essential framework of a structure. ◆ *adj* reduced to a minimum. **skeletal** *adj* **skeleton key** key which can open many different locks.

skerry *n, pl* **-ries** rocky island or reef.

sketch *n* rough drawing; brief description; short humorous play. ◆ *v* make a sketch (of). **sketchy** *adj* incomplete or inadequate.

skew *adj* slanting or crooked. ◆ *v* make slanting or crooked. **skewed** *adj* (of an opinion or analysis) distorted or biased because of prejudice or lack of information.

skewbald *adj* (of a horse) marked with patches of white and another colour.

skewer n pin to hold meat together during cooking. ◆ v fasten with a skewer.

ski n one of a pair of long runners fastened to boots for gliding over snow or water. ◆ v **skiing, skied** or **ski'd.** travel on skis. **skier** n

skid v **skidding, skidded** (of a moving vehicle) slide sideways uncontrollably. ◆ n skidding. **skid row** Slang dilapidated part of a city frequented by vagrants.

skidoo n snowmobile.

skiff n small boat.

skill n special ability or expertise; something requiring special training or expertise. **skilful** adj having or showing skill. **skilfully** adv **skilled** adj

skillet n small frying pan.

skim v **skimming, skimmed** remove floating matter from the surface of (a liquid); glide smoothly over; read quickly. **skimmed, skim milk** milk from which the cream has been removed.

skimp v not invest enough time, money, material, etc. **skimpy** adj scanty or insufficient.

skin n outer covering of the body; complexion; outer layer or covering; film on a liquid; animal skin used as a material or container. ◆ v **skinning, skinned** remove the skin of. **skinless** adj **skinny** adj thin. **skin-deep** adj superficial. **skin diving** underwater swimming using flippers and light breathing apparatus. **skin-diver** n **skinflint** n miser. **skinhead** n youth with very short hair.

skint adj Slang having no money.

skip¹ v **skipping, skipped** leap lightly from one foot to the other; jump over a rope as it is swung under one; Informal pass over, omit. ◆ n skipping.

skip² n large open container for builders' rubbish.

skipper n, v captain.

skirl n sound of bagpipes.

skirmish n brief fight or argument. ◆ v take part in a skirmish.

skirt n woman's garment hanging from the waist; part of a dress or coat below the waist; cut of beef from the flank. ◆ v border; go round; avoid dealing with (an issue). **skirting board** narrow board round the bottom of an interior wall.

skit n brief satirical sketch.

skittish adj playful or lively.

skittle n bottle-shaped object used as a target in some games. ◆ pl game in which players try to knock over skittles by rolling a ball at them.

skookum adj powerful or big.

skua n large predatory gull.

skulduggery n Informal trickery.

skulk v move stealthily; lurk.

skull n bony framework of the head. **skullcap** n close-fitting brimless cap.

skunk n small black-and-white N American mammal which emits an evil-smelling fluid when attacked; Slang despicable person.

sky n, pl **skies** upper atmosphere as seen from the earth. **skydiving** n sport of jumping from an aircraft and performing manoeuvres before opening one's parachute. **skylark** n lark that sings while soaring at a great height. **skylight** n window in a roof or ceiling. **skyscraper** n very tall building.

slab n broad flat piece.

slack¹ adj not tight; negligent; not busy. ◆ n slack part. ◆ pl informal trousers. ◆ v neglect one's work or duty. **slackness** n **slacken** v make or become slack. **slacker** n

slack² n coal dust or small pieces of coal.

slag n waste left after metal is smelted. ◆ v **slagging, slagged** Slang criticize.

slain v past participle of SLAY.

slake v satisfy (thirst or desire); combine (quicklime) with water.

slalom n skiing or canoeing race over a winding course.

slam v **slamming, slammed** shut, put down, or hit violently and noisily; Informal criticize harshly. ◆ n act or sound of slamming. **grand slam** winning of all the games or major tournaments in a sport in one season.

slander n false and malicious statement about a person; crime of making such a statement. ◆ v utter slander about. **slanderous** adj

slang n very informal language. **slangy** adj **slanging match** abusive argument.

slant v lean at an angle, slope; present (information) in a biased way. ◆ n slope; point of view, esp. a biased one. **slanting** adj

slap n blow with the open hand or a flat object. ◆ v **slapping, slapped** strike with the open hand or a flat object; *Informal* place forcefully or carelessly. **slapdash** *adj* careless and hasty. **slap-happy** *adj Informal* cheerfully careless. **slapstick** *n* boisterous knockabout comedy. **slap-up** *adj Brit* (of a meal) large and luxurious.

slash *v* gash; cut with a sweeping stroke; reduce drastically. ♦ *n* gash; sweeping stroke.

slat *n* narrow strip of wood or metal.

slate *n* rock which splits easily into thin layers; piece of this for covering a roof or, formerly, for writing on. ♦ *v* criticize severely.

slattern *n Old-fashioned* slovenly woman. **slatternly** *adj*

slaughter *v* kill (animals) for food; kill (people) savagely or indiscriminately. ♦ *n* slaughtering. **slaughterhouse** *n* place where animals are killed for food.

Slav *n* member of any of the peoples of E Europe or the former Soviet Union who speak a Slavonic language. **Slavonic** *n* language group including Russian, Polish, and Czech. ♦ *adj* of this language group.

slave *n* person owned by another for whom he or she has to work; person dominated by another or by a habit; drudge. ♦ *v* work like a slave. **slaver** *n* person or ship engaged in the slave trade. **slavery** *n* state or condition of being a slave; practice of owning slaves. **slavish** *adj* of or like a slave; imitative. **slave-driver** *n* person who makes others work very hard.

slaver *v* dribble saliva from the mouth.

slay *v* **slaying, slew, slain** kill.

sleazy *adj* **-zier, -ziest** sordid. **sleaziness** *n*

sled, sledge *n* carriage on runners for sliding on snow; light wooden frame for sliding over snow. ♦ *v* travel by sled.

sledge, sledgehammer *n* heavy hammer with a long handle.

sleek *adj* glossy, smooth, and shiny.

sleep *n* state of rest characterized by unconsciousness; period of this. ♦ *v* **sleeping, slept** be in or as if in a state of sleep; have sleeping accommodation for (a specified number). **sleeper** *n* person who sleeps; beam supporting the rails of a railway; railway car fitted for sleeping in; ring worn in a pierced ear to stop the hole from closing up. **sleepy** *adj* **sleepily** *adv* **sleepiness** *n* **sleepless** *adj* **sleeping bag** padded bag for sleeping in. **sleeping sickness** African disease spread by the tsetse fly. **sleepover** *n* occasion when a person stays overnight at a friend's house. **sleep with, together** *v* have sexual intercourse (with).

sleet *n* rain and snow or hail falling together.

sleeve *n* part of a garment which covers the arm; tubelike cover; gramophone record cover. **up one's sleeve** secretly ready. **sleeveless** *adj*

sleigh *n* sled.

sleight of hand [slite] *n* skilful use of the hands when performing conjuring tricks.

slender *adj* slim; small in amount.

slept *v* past of SLEEP.

sleuth [slooth] *n* detective.

slew[1] *v* past tense of SLAY.

slew[2] *v* twist or swing round.

slice *n* thin flat piece cut from something; share; kitchen tool with a broad flat blade; *Sport* hitting of a ball so that it travels obliquely. ♦ *v* cut into slices; *Sport* hit (a ball) with a slice.

slick *adj* persuasive and glib; skilfully devised or carried out; well-made and attractive, but superficial. ♦ *v* make smooth or sleek. ♦ *n* patch of oil on water.

slide *v* **sliding, slid** slip smoothly along (a surface); pass unobtrusively. ♦ *n* sliding; surface or structure for sliding on or down; piece of glass holding an object to be viewed under a microscope; photographic transparency; ornamental hair clip. **sliding scale** variable scale according to which things such as wages fluctuate in response to changes in other factors.

slight *adj* small in quantity or extent; not important; slim and delicate. ♦ *v, n* snub. **slightly** *adv*

slim *adj* **slimmer, slimmest** not heavy or stout, thin; slight. ♦ *v* **slimming, slimmed** make or become slim by diet and exercise. **slimmer** *n*

slime *n* unpleasant thick slippery substance. **slimy** *adj* of, like, or covered with slime; ingratiating.

sling[1] *n* bandage hung from the neck

to support an injured hand or arm; strap with a string at each end for throwing a stone; rope or strap for lifting something. ◆ v **slinging, slung** throw; carry, hang, or throw with or as if with a sling.

sling² n sweetened drink with a spirit base, e.g. *gin sling*.

slink v **slinking, slunk** move furtively or guiltily. **slinky** adj (of clothes) figure-hugging; sinuously graceful.

slip¹ v **slipping, slipped** lose balance by sliding; move smoothly, easily, or quietly; (foll. by on or off) put on or take off easily or quickly; pass out of (the mind). ◆ n slipping; mistake; petticoat; small piece (of paper). **give someone the slip** escape from someone. **slippy** adj Informal slippery. **slipknot** n knot tied so that it will slip along the rope round which it is made. **slipped disc** painful condition in which one of the discs connecting the bones of the spine becomes displaced. **slipshod** adj (of an action) careless. **slipstream** n stream of air forced backwards by a fast-moving object. **slip up** v make a mistake. **slipway** n launching slope on which ships are built or repaired.

slip² n clay mixed with water used for decorating pottery.

slipper n light shoe for indoor wear.

slippery adj so smooth or wet as to cause slipping or be difficult to hold; (of a person) untrustworthy.

slit v **slitting, slit** make a long straight cut in. ◆ n long narrow cut.

slither v slide unsteadily.

sliver [sliv-ver] n small thin piece.

slob n Informal lazy and untidy person. **slobbish** adj

slobber v dribble or drool. **slobbery** adj

sloe n sour blue-black fruit.

slog v **slogging, slogged** work hard and steadily; make one's way with difficulty; hit hard. ◆ n long and exhausting work or walk.

slogan n catchword or phrase used in politics or advertising.

sloop n small single-masted ship.

slop v **slopping, slopped** splash or spill. ◆ n spilt liquid; liquid food. ◆ pl liquid refuse and waste food used to feed animals. **sloppy** adj untidy; gushingly sentimental.

slope v slant. ◆ n sloping surface; degree of inclination. ◆ pl hills. **slope off** v Informal go furtively.

slosh n splashing sound. ◆ v splash carelessly; Slang hit hard. **sloshed** adj Slang drunk.

slot n narrow opening for inserting something; Informal place in a series or scheme. ◆ v **slotting, slotted** make a slot or slots in; fit into a slot. **slot machine** automatic machine worked by placing a coin in a slot.

sloth [rhymes with **both**] n slow-moving animal of tropical America; laziness. **slothful** adj lazy or idle.

slouch v sit, stand, or move with a drooping posture. ◆ n drooping posture; Informal incompetent or lazy person.

slough¹ [rhymes with **now**] n bog.

slough² [sluff] v (of a snake) shed (its skin) or (of a skin) be shed. **slough off** v get rid of (something unwanted or unnecessary).

sloven n habitually dirty or untidy person. **slovenly** adj dirty or untidy; careless.

slow adj taking a longer time than is usual or expected; not fast; (of a clock or watch) showing a time earlier than the correct one; stupid. ◆ v reduce the speed (of). **slowly** adv **slowness** n **slowcoach** n Informal person who moves or works slowly.

sludge n thick mud; sewage.

slug¹ n land snail with no shell; bullet. **sluggish** adj slow-moving, lacking energy. **sluggishly** adv **sluggishness** n **sluggard** n lazy person.

slug² v **slugging, slugged** hit hard. ◆ n heavy blow; Informal mouthful of an alcoholic drink.

sluice n channel carrying off water; sliding gate used to control the flow of water in this; water controlled by a sluice. ◆ v pour a stream of water over or through.

slum n squalid overcrowded house or area. ◆ v **slumming** temporarily and deliberately experience poorer places or conditions than usual.

slumber v, n Lit sleep.

slump v sink or fall heavily; (of prices or demand) decline suddenly. ◆ n sudden decline in prices or demand; time of substantial unemployment.

slung v past of SLING[1].

slunk v past of SLINK.

slur v **slurring, slurred** pronounce or utter (words) indistinctly; *Music* sing or play (notes) smoothly without a break. ◆ n slurring of words; remark intended to discredit someone; *Music* slurring of notes; curved line indicating notes to be slurred.

slurp *Informal* ◆ v eat or drink noisily. ◆ n slurping sound.

slurry n, pl **-ries** muddy liquid mixture.

slush n watery muddy substance; sloppy sentimental talk or writing. **slushy** adj **slush fund** fund for financing bribery or corruption.

slut n dirty or immoral woman. **sluttish** adj

sly adj **slyer, slyest** or **slier, sliest** crafty; secretive and cunning; roguish. ◆ n **on the sly** secretly. **slyly** adv **slyness** n

smack[1] v slap sharply; open and close (the lips) loudly in enjoyment or anticipation. ◆ n sharp slap; slapping sound; loud kiss. ◆ adv *Informal* squarely or directly, e.g. *smack in the middle.* **smacker** n *Slang* loud kiss.

smack[2] n slight flavour or trace; *Slang* heroin. ◆ v have a slight flavour or trace (of).

smack[3] n small single-masted fishing boat.

small adj not large in size, number, or amount; unimportant; mean or petty. ◆ n narrow part of the lower back. ◆ pl *Informal* underwear. **smallness** n **smallholding** n *Brit* small area of farming land. **small hours** hours just after midnight. **small-minded** adj intolerant, petty. **smallpox** n contagious disease with blisters that leave scars. **small talk** light social conversation. **small-time** adj insignificant or minor.

smarmy adj **smarmier, smarmiest** *Informal* unpleasantly suave.

smart adj well-kept and neat; astute; witty; impertinent; fashionable; brisk. ◆ v feel or cause stinging pain. ◆ n stinging pain. **smart aleck** *Informal* irritatingly clever person. **smarten** v make or become smart. **smartly** adv **smartness** n

smash v break violently and noisily; throw (against) violently; collide forcefully; destroy. ◆ n act or sound of smashing; violent collision of vehicles; *Informal* popular success; *Sport* powerful overhead shot. **smasher** n *Informal* attractive person or thing. **smashing** adj *Informal* excellent.

smattering n slight knowledge.

smear v spread with a greasy or sticky substance; rub so as to produce a dirty mark or smudge; slander. ◆ n dirty mark or smudge; slander; *Med* sample of a secretion smeared on to a slide for examination under a microscope.

smell v **smelling, smelt** or **smelled**. perceive (a scent or odour) by means of the nose; have or give off a smell; have an unpleasant smell; detect by instinct. ◆ n odour or scent; smelling; ability to perceive odours by the nose. **smelly** adj having a nasty smell. **smelling salts** preparation of ammonia used to revive a person who feels faint.

smelt[1] v extract (a metal) from (an ore) by heating. **smelter** n

smelt[2] n small fish of the salmon family.

smelt[3] v a past of SMELL.

smile n turning up of the corners of the mouth to show pleasure, amusement, or friendliness. ◆ v give a smile. **smile on, upon** v regard favourably.

smirch v, n disgrace.

smirk n smug smile. ◆ v give a smirk.

smite v **smiting, smote, smitten** *Old-fashioned* strike hard; affect severely.

smith n worker in metal. **smithy** n blacksmith's workshop.

smithereens pl n shattered fragments.

smitten v past participle of SMITE.

smock n loose overall; woman's loose blouselike garment. ◆ v gather (material) by sewing in a honeycomb pattern. **smocking** n

smog n mixture of smoke and fog.

smoke n cloudy mass that rises from something burning; spell of smoking tobacco. ◆ v give off smoke; inhale and expel smoke of (a cigar, cigarette, or pipe); do this habitually; cure (meat, fish, or cheese) by treating with smoke. **smokeless** adj **smoker** n **smoky** adj **smoke screen** something said or done to hide the truth.

smooch *Informal* ◆ v kiss and cuddle. ◆ n smooching.

smooth adj even in surface, texture, or consistency; without obstructions; charming and polite but possibly insincere; free from jolts; not harsh in taste. ◆ v make smooth; calm. **smoothly** adv

smorgasbord n buffet meal of assorted dishes.

smote v past tense of SMITE.

smother v suffocate or stifle; cover thickly; suppress.

smoulder v burn slowly with smoke but no flame; (of feelings) exist in a suppressed state.

SMS short message system: used for sending data to mobile phones.

smudge v make or become smeared or soiled. ◆ n dirty mark; blurred form. **smudgy** adj

smug adj **smugger**, **smuggest** self-satisfied. **smugly** adv **smugness** n

smuggle v import or export (goods) secretly and illegally; take somewhere secretly. **smuggler** n

smut n speck of soot; mark left by this; obscene jokes, pictures, etc. **smutty** adj

Sn Chem tin.

snack n light quick meal. **snack bar** place where snacks are sold.

snaffle n jointed bit for a horse. ◆ v Slang steal.

snag n difficulty or disadvantage; sharp projecting point; hole in fabric caused by a sharp object. ◆ v **snagging**, **snagged** catch or tear on a point.

snail n slow-moving mollusc with a spiral shell. **snail mail** Informal conventional post, as opposed to e-mail. **snail's pace** very slow speed.

snake n long thin scaly limbless reptile. ◆ v move in a winding course like a snake. **snake in the grass** treacherous person. **snaky** adj twisted or winding.

snap v **snapping**, **snapped** break suddenly; (cause to) make a sharp cracking sound; (of animals) bite (at) suddenly; move suddenly; speak sharply and angrily; take a snapshot of. ◆ n act or sound of snapping; fastener that closes with a snapping sound; Informal snapshot; sudden brief spell of cold weather; card game in which the word 'snap' is called when two similar cards are put down. ◆ adj

made on the spur of the moment. **snapper** n fish of the perch family. **snappy** adj irritable; Slang quick; Slang smart and fashionable. **snapdragon** n plant with flowers that can open and shut like a mouth. **snapshot** n informal photograph. **snap up** v take eagerly and quickly.

snare n trap with a noose. ◆ v catch in or as if in a snare.

snarl v (of an animal) growl with bared teeth; speak or utter fiercely; make tangled. ◆ n act or sound of snarling; tangled mass. **snarl-up** n Informal confused situation such as a traffic jam.

snatch v seize or try to seize suddenly; take (food, rest, etc.) hurriedly. ◆ n snatching; fragment.

snazzy adj **-zier**, **-ziest** Informal stylish and flashy.

sneak v move furtively; bring, take, or put furtively; Informal tell tales. ◆ n underhand person; Informal telltale. **sneaking** adj secret; slight but persistent. **sneaky** adj

sneakers pl n canvas shoes with rubber soles.

sneer n contemptuous expression or remark. ◆ v show contempt by a sneer.

sneeze v expel air from the nose suddenly, involuntarily, and noisily. ◆ n act or sound of sneezing.

snib n catch of a door or window.

snicker n, v same as SNIGGER.

snide adj maliciously derogatory.

sniff v inhale through the nose in short audible breaths; smell by sniffing. ◆ n act or sound of sniffing. **sniffle** v sniff repeatedly, as when suffering from a cold. ◆ n slight cold. **sniff at** v express contempt for. **sniffer dog** Brit police dog trained to detect drugs or explosives by smell.

snifter n Informal small quantity of alcoholic drink.

snigger n sly disrespectful laugh, esp. one partly stifled. ◆ v utter a snigger.

snip v **snipping**, **snipped** cut in small quick strokes with scissors or shears. ◆ n act or sound of snipping; Informal bargain. **snippet** n small piece.

snipe n wading bird with a long straight bill. ◆ v (foll. by at) shoot at (a person) from cover; make critical remarks about. **sniper** n

snitch Informal ◆ v act as an informer;

steal. ◆ *n* informer.

snivel *v* **-elling, -elled** cry in a whining way.

snob *n* person who judges others by social rank; person who feels smugly superior in his or her tastes or interests. **snobbery** *n* **snobbish** *adj*

snood *n* pouch, often of net, loosely holding a woman's hair at the back.

snook *n* **cock a snook at** show contempt for.

snooker *n* game played on a billiard table. ◆ *v* leave (a snooker opponent) in a position such that another ball blocks the target ball; *Informal* put (someone) in a position where he or she can do nothing.

snoop *Informal* ◆ *v* pry. ◆ *n* snooping. **snooper** *n*

snooty *adj* **snootier, snootiest** *Informal* haughty.

snooze *Informal* ◆ *v* take a brief light sleep. ◆ *n* brief light sleep.

snore *v* make snorting sounds while sleeping. ◆ *n* sound of snoring.

snorkel *n* tube allowing a swimmer to breathe while face down on the surface of the water. ◆ *v* **-kelling, -kelled** swim using a snorkel.

snort *v* exhale noisily through the nostrils; express contempt or anger by snorting. ◆ *n* act or sound of snorting.

snot *n Taboo* mucus from the nose.

snout *n* animal's projecting nose and jaws.

snow *n* frozen vapour falling from the sky in flakes; *Slang* cocaine. ◆ *v* fall as or like snow. **be snowed under** be overwhelmed, esp. with paperwork. **snowy** *adj* **snowball** *n* snow pressed into a ball for throwing. ◆ *v* increase rapidly. **snowbird** *n* small N American songbird that breeds in the Arctic. **snowblindness** *n* temporary blindness caused by the reflection of sunlight on snow. **snowdrift** *n* bank of deep snow. **snowdrop** *n* small white bell-shaped spring flower. **snow fence** fence erected in winter to prevent snow drifting across a road. **snowflake** *n* single crystal of snow. **snow line** (on a mountain) height above which there is permanent snow. **snowboard** *n* board on which a person stands to slide across the snow. **snowboarding** *n* **snowman** *n* figure shaped out of snow. **snowmobile** *n* motor vehicle

with caterpillar tracks and front skis. **snow pea** variety of pea with an edible pod. **snowplow, snowplough** *n* vehicle for clearing away snow. **snowshoes** *pl n* racket-shaped shoes for travelling on snow.

snub *v* **snubbing, snubbed** insult deliberately. ◆ *n* deliberate insult. ◆ *adj* (of a nose) short and blunt. **snub-nosed** *adj*

snuff¹ *n* powdered tobacco for sniffing up the nostrils.

snuff² *v* extinguish (a candle). **snuff it** *Informal* die.

snuffle *v* breathe noisily.

snug *adj* **snugger, snuggest** warm and comfortable; comfortably close-fitting. **snugly** *adv*

snuggle *v* nestle into a person or thing for warmth or from affection.

so *adv* to such an extent; in such a manner; very; also; thereupon. ◆ *conj* in order that; with the result that; therefore. ◆ *interj* exclamation of surprise, triumph, or realization. **so-and-so** *n Informal* person whose name is not specified; unpleasant person or thing. **so-called** *adj* called (in the speaker's opinion, wrongly) by that name. **so long** goodbye. **so that** in order that.

soak *v* make wet; put or lie in liquid so as to become thoroughly wet; (of liquid) penetrate. ◆ *n* soaking; *Slang* drunkard. **soaking** *n, adj* **soak up** *v* absorb.

soap *n* compound of alkali and fat, used with water as a cleaning agent; *Informal* soap opera. ◆ *v* apply soap to. **soapy** *adj* **soap opera** television or radio serial dealing with domestic themes.

soapstone *n* soft mineral used for making table tops and ornaments.

soar *v* rise or fly upwards; increase suddenly.

sob *v* **sobbing, sobbed** weep with convulsive gasps; utter with sobs. ◆ *n* act or sound of sobbing. **sob story** tale of personal distress told to arouse sympathy.

sober *adj* not drunk; serious; (of colours) plain and dull. ◆ *v* make or become sober. **soberly** *adv* **sobriety** *n* state of being sober.

sobriquet [so-brik-ay] *n* nickname.

soccer *n* football played by two teams

of eleven kicking or heading a spherical ball.

sociable *adj* friendly or companionable; (of an occasion) providing companionship. **sociability** *n* **sociably** *adv*

social *adj* living in a community; of society or its organization; sociable. ◆ *n* convivial gathering. **socially** *adv* **socialize** *v* meet others socially. **socialite** *n* member of fashionable society. **social security** state provision for the unemployed, aged, or sick. **social services** welfare services provided by the local authorities. **social work** work which involves helping people with serious financial or family problems.

socialism *n* political system which advocates public ownership of industries, resources, and transport. **socialist** *n, adj* **socialistic** *adj*

society *n, pl* **-ties** human beings considered as a group; organized community; structure and institutions of such a community; organized group with common aims and interests; upper-class or fashionable people collectively; companionship.

sociology *n* study of human societies. **sociological** *adj* **sociologist** *n*

sock¹ *n* cloth covering for the foot.

sock² *Slang* ◆ *v* hit hard. ◆ *n* hard blow.

socket *n* hole or recess into which something fits.

sod *n* (piece of) turf; *Slang* obnoxious person.

soda *n* compound of sodium; soda water. **soda water** fizzy drink made from water charged with carbon dioxide.

sodden *adj* soaked.

sodium *n* silver-white metallic element. **sodium bicarbonate** white soluble compound used in baking powder.

sodomy *n* anal intercourse. **sodomite** *n* person who practises sodomy.

sofa *n* couch.

soft *adj* not hard, rough, or harsh; (of a breeze or climate) mild; (too) lenient; easily influenced or imposed upon; feeble or silly; not robust; *Informal* easy; (of water) containing few mineral salts; (of drugs) not liable to cause addiction. **softly** *adv* **soften** *v*

make or become soft or softer. **soft drink** nonalcoholic drink. **soft option** easiest alternative. **soft-pedal** *v* deliberately avoid emphasizing something. **soft-soap** *v Informal* flatter. **software** *n* computer programs. **softwood** *n* wood of a coniferous tree.

soggy *adj* **-gier, -giest** soaked; moist and heavy. **sogginess** *n*

soigné (*fem*) **soignée** [swah-nyay] *adj* well-groomed, elegant.

soil¹ *n* top layer of earth; country or territory.

soil² *v* make or become dirty; disgrace.

soiree [swah-ray] *n* evening party.

sojourn [soj-urn] *v* stay temporarily. ◆ *n* temporary stay.

solace [sol-iss] *n, v* comfort in distress.

solar *adj* of the sun; using the energy of the sun. **solar plexus** network of nerves at the pit of the stomach; this part of the stomach. **solar system** the sun and the heavenly bodies that go round it.

solarium *n, pl* **-laria, -lariums** place with beds and ultraviolet lights used for acquiring an artificial suntan.

sold *v* past of SELL.

solder *n* soft alloy used to join two metal surfaces. ◆ *v* join with solder. **soldering iron** tool for melting and applying solder.

soldier *n* member of an army. ◆ *v* serve in an army. **soldierly** *adj* **soldier on** *v* persist doggedly.

sole¹ *adj* one and only; not shared, exclusive. **solely** *adv* only, completely; entirely; alone.

sole² *n* underside of the foot; underside of a shoe. ◆ *v* provide (a shoe) with a sole.

sole³ *n* small edible flatfish.

solecism [sol-iss-izz-um] *n* minor grammatical mistake; breach of etiquette.

solemn *adj* serious, deeply sincere; formal. **solemnly** *adv* **solemnity** *n* **solemnize** *v* celebrate or perform (a ceremony); make solemn.

solenoid [sole-in-oid] *n* coil of wire magnetized by passing a current through it.

sol-fa *n* system of syllables used as names for the notes of a scale.

solicit *v* **-iting, -ited** request; (of a prostitute) offer (a person) sex for money. **solicitation** *n*

solicitor n lawyer who advises clients and prepares documents and cases.

solicitous adj anxious about someone's welfare. **solicitude** n

solid adj (of a substance) keeping its shape; strong or substantial; not liquid or gas; not hollow; of the same substance throughout; sound or reliable; having three dimensions. ◆ n three-dimensional shape; solid substance. **solidly** adv **solidify** v make or become solid or firm. **solidity** n

solidarity n agreement in aims or interests, total unity.

soliloquy n, pl **-quies** speech made by a person while alone, esp. in a play. **soliloquize** v utter a soliloquy.

solipsism n doctrine that the self is the only thing known to exist. **solipsist** n

solitaire n game for one person played with pegs set in a board; gem set by itself.

solitary adj alone, single; (of a place) lonely. **solitude** n state of being solitary.

solo n, pl **-los** music for one performer; any act done without assistance. ◆ adj done alone. ◆ adv by oneself, alone. **soloist** n

solstice n either the shortest (in winter) or longest (in summer) day of the year.

soluble adj able to be dissolved; able to be solved. **solubility** n

solution n answer to a problem; act of solving a problem; liquid with something dissolved in it; process of dissolving.

solve v find the answer to (a problem). **solvable** adj

solvent adj able to meet financial obligations. ◆ n liquid capable of dissolving other substances. **solvency** n **solvent abuse** deliberate inhaling of intoxicating fumes from certain solvents.

sombre adj dark, gloomy.

sombrero n, pl **-ros** wide-brimmed Mexican hat.

some adj unknown or unspecified; unknown or unspecified quantity or number of; considerable number or amount of; Informal remarkable. ◆ pron certain unknown or unspecified people or things; unknown or unspecified number or quantity.

somebody pron some person. ◆ n important person. **somehow** adv in some unspecified way. **someone** pron somebody. **something** pron unknown or unspecified thing or amount; impressive or important thing. **sometime** adv at some unspecified time. ◆ adj former. **sometimes** adv from time to time, now and then. **somewhat** adv to some extent, rather. **somewhere** adv in, to, or at some unspecified or unknown place.

somersault n leap or roll in which the trunk and legs are turned over the head. ◆ v perform a somersault.

somnambulist n person who walks in his or her sleep. **somnambulism** n

somnolent adj drowsy. **somnolence** n

son n male offspring. **son-in-law** n, pl **sons-in-law** daughter's husband.

sonar n device for detecting underwater objects by the reflection of sound waves.

sonata n piece of music in several movements for one instrument with or without piano. **sonatina** n short sonata.

son et lumière [sawn eh loo-mee-er] n French night-time entertainment with lighting and sound effects, telling the story of the place where it is staged.

song n music for the voice; tuneful sound made by certain birds; singing. **for a song** very cheaply. **songster**, **songstress** n singer. **songbird** n any bird with a musical call.

sonic adj of or producing sound. **sonic boom** loud bang caused by an aircraft flying faster than sound.

sonnet n fourteen-line poem with a fixed rhyme scheme.

sonorous adj (of sound) deep or resonant. **sonorously** adv **sonority** n

soon adv in a short time. **sooner** adv rather, e.g. I'd sooner go alone. **sooner or later** eventually.

soot n black powder formed by the incomplete burning of an organic substance. **sooty** adj

soothe v make calm; relieve (pain etc.).

soothsayer n seer or prophet.

sop n concession to pacify someone. ◆ v **sopping**, **sopped** mop up or absorb (liquid). **sopping** adj completely soaked. **soppy** adj Informal oversentimental.

sophist n person who uses clever but invalid arguments. **sophism, sophistry** n clever but invalid argument.

sophisticate v make less natural or innocent; make more complex or refined. ♦ n sophisticated person. **sophisticated** adj having or appealing to refined or cultured tastes and habits; complex and refined. **sophistication** n

sophomore n student in second year at college.

soporific adj causing sleep. ♦ n drug that causes sleep.

soprano n, pl **-pranos** (singer with) the highest female or boy's voice; highest pitched of a family of instruments.

sorbet n flavoured water ice.

sorcerer n magician. **sorceress** n fem **sorcery** n witchcraft or magic.

sordid adj dirty, squalid; base, vile; selfish and grasping. **sordidly** adv **sordidness** n

sore adj painful; causing annoyance; resentful; (of need) urgent. ♦ adv Obs greatly. ♦ n painful area on the body. **sorely** adv greatly; grievously. **soreness** n

sorghum n kind of grass cultivated for grain.

sorrel n bitter-tasting plant; reddish-brown colour; horse of this colour.

sorrow n grief or sadness; cause of sorrow. ♦ v grieve. **sorrowful** adj **sorrowfully** adv

sorry adj **-rier, -riest** feeling pity or regret; pitiful or wretched.

sort n group all sharing certain qualities or characteristics; Informal type of character. ♦ v arrange according to kind; mend or fix. **out of sorts** slightly unwell or bad-tempered.

sortie n relatively short return trip; operational flight made by military aircraft; raid into enemy territory.

SOS n international code signal of distress; call for help.

so-so adj Informal mediocre.

sot n habitual drunkard.

sotto voce [sot-toe **voe**-chay] adv in an undertone.

soubriquet n same as SOBRIQUET.

soufflé [**soo**-flay] n light fluffy dish made with beaten egg whites and other ingredients.

sough [rhymes with **now**] v (of the wind) make a sighing sound.

sought [**sawt**] v past of SEEK.

souk [**sook**] n open-air marketplace in Muslim countries.

soul n spiritual and immortal part of a human being; essential part or fundamental nature; deep and sincere feelings; person regarded as typifying some quality; person; (also **soul music**) type of Black music combining blues, pop, and gospel. **soulful** adj full of emotion. **soulless** adj lacking human qualities, mechanical; (of a person) lacking sensitivity.

sound[1] n something heard, noise. ♦ v make or cause to make a sound; seem to be as specified; pronounce. **sound barrier** Informal sudden increase in air resistance against an object as it approaches the speed of sound. **soundproof** adj not penetrable by sound. ♦ v make soundproof. **sound track** recorded sound accompaniment to a film.

sound[2] adj in good condition; firm, substantial; showing good judgment; ethically correct; financially reliable; thorough; (of sleep) deep. **soundly** adv

sound[3] v find the depth of (water etc.); ascertain the views of; examine with a probe. **soundings** pl n measurements of depth taken by sounding; questions asked of someone to find out his or her opinion. **sounding board** person or group used to test a new idea.

sound[4] n channel or strait.

soup n liquid food made from meat, vegetables, etc. **soupy** adj **soup kitchen** place where food and drink is served to needy people. **soup up** v modify (an engine) to increase its power.

soupçon [**soop**-sonn] n small amount.

sour adj sharp-tasting; (of milk) gone bad; (of a person's temperament) sullen. ♦ v make or become sour. **sourly** adv **sourness** n **sourpuss** n Informal sullen person.

source n origin or starting point; spring where a river or stream begins; person, book, etc. providing information.

souse v plunge (something) into liquid; drench; pickle.

soutane [soo-tan] n Roman Catholic priest's cassock.

south n direction towards the South Pole, opposite north; area lying in or towards the south. ◆ adj to or in the south; (of a wind) from the south. ◆ adv in, to, or towards the south. **southerly** adj **southern** adj **southerner** n person from the south of a country or area. **southward** adj, adv **southwards** adv **southeast** n, adj, adv (in or to) direction between south and east. **southwest** n, adj, adv (in or to) direction between south and west. **southpaw** n Informal left-handed person, esp. a boxer. **South Pole** southernmost point on the earth's axis.

souvenir n keepsake, memento.

sou'wester n seaman's waterproof hat covering the head and back of the neck.

sovereign n king or queen; former British gold coin worth one pound. ◆ adj supreme in rank or authority; excellent; (of a state) independent. **sovereigntist** n, adj promoter of, or promoting, sovereignty for Quebec. **sovereignty** n **sovereignty-association** n proposal for political sovereignty for Quebec with economic association with the rest of Canada.

soviet n formerly, elected council at various levels of government in the USSR. ◆ adj (S-) of the former USSR.

sow[1] v sowing, sowed, sown or sowed. scatter or plant (seed) in or on (the ground); implant.

sow[2] n female adult pig.

soya n plant whose edible bean (**soya bean**) is used for food and as a source of oil. **soy sauce** sauce made from fermented soya beans, used in Chinese and Japanese cookery.

sozzled adj Slang drunk.

spa n resort with a mineral-water spring.

space n unlimited expanse in which all objects exist and move; interval; blank portion; unoccupied area; the universe beyond the earth's atmosphere. ◆ v place at intervals. **spacious** adj having a large capacity or area. **spacecraft**, **spaceship** n vehicle for travel beyond the earth's atmosphere. **space shuttle** manned reusable vehicle for repeated space flights. **spacesuit** n sealed pressurized suit worn by an astronaut.

spade[1] n tool for digging. **spadework** n hard preparatory work.

spade[2] n playing card of the suit marked with black leaf-shaped symbols.

spaghetti n pasta in the form of long strings.

span n space between two points; complete extent; distance from thumb to little finger of the expanded hand. ◆ v **spanning, spanned** stretch or extend across.

spangle n small shiny metallic ornament. ◆ v decorate with spangles.

spaniel n dog with long ears and silky hair.

spank v slap with the open hand, esp. on the buttocks. ◆ n such a slap. **spanking** n series of spanks. ◆ adj Informal quick; outstandingly fine or smart.

spanner n tool for gripping and turning a nut or bolt.

spar[1] n pole used as a ship's mast, boom, or yard.

spar[2] v **sparring, sparred** Boxing, martial arts fight using light blows for practice; argue (with someone).

spare v refrain from punishing or harming; protect (someone) from (something unpleasant); afford to give. ◆ adj extra; in reserve; (of a person) thin. ◆ n duplicate kept in case of damage or loss. **to spare** in addition to what is needed. **sparing** adj economical. **spare ribs** pork ribs with most of the meat trimmed off.

spark n fiery particle thrown out from a fire or caused by friction; flash of light produced by an electrical discharge; trace or hint (of a particular quality). ◆ v give off sparks; initiate. **spark plug, sparking plug** device in an engine that ignites the fuel by producing an electric spark.

sparkle v glitter with many points of light; be vivacious or witty. ◆ n sparkling points of light; vivacity or wit. **sparkler** n hand-held firework that emits sparks. **sparkling** adj (of wine or mineral water) slightly fizzy.

sparrow n small brownish bird. **sparrowhawk** n small hawk.

sparse adj thinly scattered. **sparsely** adv **sparseness** n

spartan adj strict and austere.

spasm n involuntary muscular contraction; sudden burst of activity or feeling. **spasmodic** adj occurring in spasms. **spasmodically** adv

spastic n person with cerebral palsy. ◆ adj suffering from cerebral palsy; affected by spasms.

spat[1] v past of SPIT[1].

spat[2] n slight quarrel.

spat[3] n old-fashioned short gaiter.

spate n large number of things happening within a period of time; sudden outpouring or flood.

spathe n large sheathlike leaf enclosing a flower cluster.

spatial adj of or in space.

spatter v scatter or be scattered in drops over (something). ◆ n spattering sound; something spattered.

spatula n utensil with a broad flat blade for spreading or stirring.

spawn n jelly-like mass of eggs of fish, frogs, or molluscs. ◆ v (of fish, frogs, or molluscs) lay eggs; generate.

spay v remove the ovaries from (a female animal).

speak v **speaking, spoke, spoken** say words, talk; communicate or express in words; give a speech or lecture; know how to talk in (a specified language). **speaker** n person who speaks, esp. at a formal occasion; loudspeaker; (**S-**) official chairman of a body.

spear n weapon consisting of a long shaft with a sharp point; slender shoot; single stalk of broccoli or asparagus. ◆ v pierce with or as if with a spear. **spearhead** n leading force in an attack or campaign. ◆ v lead (an attack or campaign).

spearmint n type of mint.

spec n **on spec** Informal as a risk or gamble.

special adj distinguished from others of its kind; for a specific purpose; exceptional; particular. **specially** adv **specialist** n expert in a particular activity or subject. **speciality** n special interest or skill; product specialized in. **specialize** v be a specialist. **specialization** n

specie n coins as distinct from paper money.

species n, pl **-cies** group of plants or animals that are related closely enough to interbreed naturally.

specific adj particular, definite. ◆ n drug used to treat a particular disease. ◆ pl particular details. **specifically** adv **specification** n detailed description of something to be made or done. **specify** v refer to or state specifically. **specific gravity** ratio of the density of a substance to that of water.

specimen n individual or part typifying a whole; sample of blood etc. taken for analysis.

specious [spee-shuss] adj apparently true, but actually false.

speck n small spot or particle. **speckle** n small spot. ◆ v mark with speckles.

specs pl n Informal short for SPECTACLES.

spectacle n strange, interesting, or ridiculous sight; impressive public show. ◆ pl pair of glasses for correcting faulty vision. **spectacular** adj impressive. ◆ n spectacular public show. **spectacularly** adv

spectate v watch. **spectator** n person viewing anything, onlooker.

spectre n ghost; menacing mental image. **spectral** adj

spectrum n, pl **-tra** range of different colours, radio waves, etc. in order of their wavelengths; entire range of anything. **spectroscope** n instrument for producing or examining spectra.

speculate v guess, conjecture; buy property, shares, etc. in the hope of selling them at a profit. **speculation** n **speculative** adj **speculator** n

speculum n, pl **-la, -lums** medical instrument for examining body cavities.

sped v a past of SPEED.

speech n act, power, or manner of speaking; talk given to an audience; language or dialect. **speechify** v make speeches, esp. boringly. **speechless** adj unable to speak because of great emotion.

speed n swiftness; rate at which something moves or acts; Slang amphetamine. ◆ v **speeding, sped** or **speeded**. go quickly; drive faster than the legal limit. **speedy** adj rapid; prompt. **speedily** adv **speedboat** n light fast motorboat. **speedometer** n instrument to show the speed of a vehicle. **speed up** v accelerate. **speedway** n track for motorcycle racing. **speedwell** n plant with small blue flowers.

speleology n study and exploration of caves.

spell¹ v **spelling, spelt** or **spelled**. give in correct order the letters that form (a word); (of letters) make up (a word); indicate. **spelling** n way a word is spelt; person's ability to spell. **spell out** v make explicit.

spell² n formula of words supposed to have magic power; effect of a spell; fascination. **spellbound** adj entranced.

spell³ n period of time of weather or activity.

spelt v a past of SPELL¹.

spend v **spending, spent** pay out (money); use or pass (time); use up completely. **spendthrift** n person who spends money wastefully.

sperm n male reproductive cell; semen. **spermicide** n substance that kills sperm. **sperm whale** large toothed whale.

spermaceti [sper-ma-set-ee] n waxy solid obtained from the sperm whale.

spermatozoon [sper-ma-toe-zoe-on] n, pl **-zoa** sperm.

spew v vomit; send out in a stream.

sphagnum n moss found in bogs.

sphere n perfectly round solid object; field of activity. **spherical** adj

sphincter n ring of muscle which controls the opening and closing of a hollow organ.

Sphinx n statue in Egypt with a lion's body and human head; (s-) enigmatic person.

spice n aromatic substance used as flavouring; something that adds zest or interest. ◆ v flavour with spices. **spicy** adj flavoured with spices; Informal slightly scandalous.

spick-and-span adj neat and clean.

spider n small eight-legged creature which spins a web to catch insects for food. **spidery** adj

spiel n glib plausible talk.

spigot n stopper for, or tap fitted to, a cask.

spike n sharp point; sharp pointed metal object. ◆ v put spikes on; pierce or fasten with a spike; add alcohol to (a drink). **spike someone's guns** thwart someone. **spiky** adj

spill¹ v **spilling, spilt** or **spilled**. pour from or as if from a container. ◆ n fall; amount spilt. **spill the beans** Informal

give away a secret. **spillage** n

spill² n thin strip of wood or paper for lighting pipes or fires.

spin v **spinning, spun** revolve or cause to revolve rapidly; draw out and twist (fibres) into thread. ◆ n revolving motion; continuous spiral descent of an aircraft; Informal short drive for pleasure; Informal presenting of information in a way that creates a favourable impression. **spin doctor** Informal person who provides a favourable slant to a news item or policy on behalf of a politician or a political party. **spin a yarn** SEE YARN. **spinner** n **spin-dry** v dry (clothes) in a spin-dryer. **spin-dryer** n machine in which washed clothes are spun in a perforated drum to remove excess water. **spin-off** n incidental benefit. **spin out** v prolong.

spina bifida n condition in which part of the spinal cord protrudes through a gap in the backbone, often causing paralysis.

spinach n dark green leafy vegetable.

spindle n rotating rod that acts as an axle; weighted rod rotated for spinning thread by hand. **spindly** adj long, slender, and frail.

spindrift n spray blown along the surface of the sea.

spine n backbone; sharp point on an animal or plant; edge of a book, record sleeve, etc. on which the title is printed. **spinal** adj of the spine. **spineless** adj lacking courage. **spiny** adj covered with spines.

spinet n small harpsichord.

spinnaker n large sail on a racing yacht.

spinney n small wood.

spinster n unmarried woman.

spiral n continuous curve formed by a point winding about a central axis at an ever-increasing distance from it; steadily accelerating increase or decrease. ◆ v **-ralling, -ralled** move in a spiral; increase or decrease with steady acceleration. ◆ adj having the form of a spiral.

spire n pointed part of a steeple.

spirit n nonphysical aspect of a person concerned with profound thoughts; nonphysical part of a person believed to live on after death; prevailing feeling; temperament or disposition;

liveliness; courage; essential meaning as opposed to literal interpretation; ghost. ◆ *pl* emotional state; strong alcoholic drink. ◆ *v* **-iting, -ited** carry away mysteriously. **spirited** *adj* lively. **spirituous** *adj* alcoholic. **spirit level** glass tube containing a bubble in liquid, used to check whether a surface is level.

spiritual *adj* relating to the spirit; relating to sacred things. ◆ *n* type of religious folk song originating among Black slaves in N America. **spiritually** *adv* **spirituality** *n* **spiritualism** *n* belief that the spirits of the dead can communicate with the living. **spiritualist** *n*

spit[1] *v* **spitting, spat** eject (saliva or food) from the mouth; throw out particles explosively; rain slightly; utter (words) in a violent manner. ◆ *n* saliva. **spitting image** *Informal* person who looks very like another. **spittle** *n* saliva. **spittoon** *n* bowl to spit into.

spit[2] *n* sharp rod on which meat is skewered for roasting; long strip of land projecting into the sea.

spite *n* deliberate nastiness. ◆ *v* annoy or hurt from spite. **in spite of** in defiance of. **spiteful** *adj* **spitefully** *adv*

spitfire *n* person with a fiery temper.

splake *n* hybrid trout.

splash *v* scatter (liquid) or (of liquid) be scattered in drops; scatter liquid on (something); print (a story or photograph) prominently in a newspaper. ◆ *n* splashing sound; patch (of colour or light); extravagant display; small amount of liquid added to a drink. **splash out** *v Informal* spend extravagantly.

splatter *v, n* splash.

splay *v* spread out; slant outwards. ◆ *adj* splayed.

spleen *n* abdominal organ which filters bacteria from the blood; bad temper. **splenetic** *adj* irritable.

splendid *adj* excellent; brilliant in appearance. **splendidly** *adv* **splendour** *n*

splice *v* join by interweaving or overlapping ends. **get spliced** *Slang* get married.

splint *n* rigid support for a broken bone.

splinter *n* thin sharp piece broken off, esp. from wood. ◆ *v* break into

fragments. **splinter group** group that has broken away from an organization.

split *v* **splitting, split** break into separate pieces; separate; share. ◆ *n* crack or division caused by splitting. ◆ *pl* act of sitting with the legs outstretched in opposite directions. **split second** very short period of time. **split up** *v* separate (something) into parts; (of a couple) end a relationship or marriage.

splotch, splodge *n, v* splash, daub.

splurge *v* spend money extravagantly. ◆ *n* bout of extravagance.

splutter *v* make hissing spitting sounds; utter with spitting sounds. ◆ *n* spluttering.

spoil *v* **spoiling, spoilt** or **spoiled**. damage; harm the character of (a child) by giving it all it wants; rot. **spoiling for** eager for. **spoils** *pl n* booty. **spoilsport** *n* person who spoils the enjoyment of others.

spoke[1] *v* past tense of SPEAK.

spoke[2] *n* bar joining the hub of a wheel to the rim.

spoken *v* past participle of SPEAK.

spokesman, spokeswoman, spokesperson *n* person chosen to speak on behalf of a group.

spoliation *n* plundering.

sponge *n* sea animal with a porous absorbent skeleton; skeleton of a sponge, or a substance like it, used for cleaning; type of light cake. ◆ *v* wipe with a sponge; live at the expense of others. **sponger** *n Slang* person who sponges on others. **spongy** *adj*

sponsor *n* person who promotes something; person who agrees to give money to a charity on completion of a specified activity by another; godparent. ◆ *v* act as a sponsor for. **sponsorship** *n*

spontaneous *adj* voluntary and unpremeditated; occurring through natural processes without outside influence. **spontaneously** *adv* **spontaneity** *n*

spoof *n* mildly satirical parody.

spook *n Informal* ghost. **spooky** *adj*

spool *n* cylinder round which something can be wound.

spoon *n* shallow bowl attached to a handle for eating, stirring, or serving food. ◆ *v* lift with a spoon. **spoonful** *n*

spoon-feed v feed with a spoon; give (someone) too much help.

spoonerism n accidental changing over of the initial sounds of a pair of words, such as *half-warmed fish* for *half-formed wish*.

spoor n trail of an animal.

sporadic adj intermittent, scattered. **sporadically** adv

spore n minute reproductive body of some plants.

sporran n pouch worn in front of a kilt.

sport n activity for pleasure, competition, or exercise; such activities collectively; enjoyment; playful joking; person who reacts cheerfully. ◆ v wear proudly. **sporting** adj of sport; having a sportsmanlike attitude. **sporting chance** reasonable chance of success. **sporty** adj **sportive** adj playful. **sports car** fast low-built car, usu. open-topped. **sports jacket** man's casual jacket. **sportsman, sportswoman** n person who plays sports; person who plays fair and is good-humoured when losing. **sportsmanlike** adj **sportsmanship** n **sport utility vehicle** powerful four-wheel drive vehicle for rough terrain.

spot n small mark on a surface; pimple; location; *Informal* awkward situation; *Informal* small quantity. ◆ v **spotting, spotted** notice; watch for and take note of; mark with spots. **on the spot** at the place in question; immediately; in an awkward predicament. **spotless** adj absolutely clean. **spotlessly** adv **spotty** adj with spots. **spot check** random examination. **spotlight** n powerful light illuminating a small area; centre of attention. **spot-on** adj *Informal* absolutely accurate.

spouse n husband or wife.

spout n projecting tube or lip for pouring liquids; stream or jet of liquid. ◆ v pour out in a stream or jet; *Slang* utter (a stream of words) lengthily.

sprain v injure (a joint) by a sudden twist. ◆ n such an injury.

sprang v a past tense of SPRING.

sprat n small sea fish.

sprawl v lie or sit with the limbs spread out; spread out in a straggling manner. ◆ n anything that spreads out in an untidy and uncontrolled way, e.g. *urban sprawl*.

spray[1] n (device for producing) fine drops of liquid. ◆ v scatter in fine drops; cover with a spray. **spray gun** device for spraying paint etc.

spray[2] n branch with buds, leaves, flowers, or berries; ornament like this.

spread v **spreading, spread** open out or be displayed to the fullest extent; extend over a larger expanse; apply as a coating; send or be sent in all directions; distribute or be distributed over a period of time. ◆ n spreading; extent; *Informal* ample meal; soft food which can be spread. **spread-eagled** adj with arms and legs outstretched.

spree n session of overindulgence, usu. in drinking or spending money.

sprig n twig or shoot.

sprightly adj **-lier, -liest** lively and brisk. **sprightliness** n

spring v **springing, sprang** or **sprung, sprung** move suddenly upwards or forwards in a single motion, jump; develop unexpectedly; originate (from); *Informal* arrange the escape of (someone) from prison. ◆ n season between winter and summer; coil which can be compressed, stretched, or bent and returns to its original shape when released; natural pool forming the source of a stream; jump; elasticity. **springy** adj elastic. **springboard** n flexible board used to gain height or momentum in diving or gymnastics. **spring-clean** v clean (a house) thoroughly. **spring tide** high tide at new or full moon.

springbok n S African antelope.

springer n small spaniel.

sprinkle v scatter (liquid or powder) in tiny drops or particles over (something). **sprinkler** n **sprinkling** n small quantity or number.

sprint v run a short distance at top speed. ◆ n short race run at top speed; fast run. **sprinter** n

sprit n small spar set diagonally across a sail to extend it. **spritsail** n sail extended by a sprit.

sprite n elf.

sprocket n wheel with teeth on the rim, that drives or is driven by a chain.

sprout v put forth shoots; begin to grow or develop. ◆ n shoot; short for BRUSSELS SPROUT.

spruce¹ n kind of fir.

spruce² adj neat and smart. **spruce up** v make neat and smart.

sprung v a past tense of SPRING.

spry adj **spryer, spryest** or **sprier, spriest** active or nimble.

spud n Informal potato.

spume n, v froth.

spun v past of SPIN.

spunk n Informal courage, spirit. **spunky** adj

spur n spiked wheel on the heel of a rider's boot used to urge on a horse; stimulus or incentive; projection. ◆ v **spurring, spurred** urge on, incite (someone). **on the spur of the moment** on impulse.

spurge n plant with milky sap.

spurious adj not genuine.

spurn v reject with scorn.

spurt v gush or cause to gush out in a jet. ◆ n short sudden burst of activity or speed; sudden gush.

sputnik n early Soviet artificial satellite.

sputter v, n splutter.

sputum n, pl **-ta** spittle, usu. mixed with mucus.

spy n, pl **spies** person employed to obtain secret information; person who secretly watches others. ◆ v **spying, spied** act as a spy; catch sight of.

Sq. Square.

squabble v, n (engage in) a petty or noisy quarrel.

squad n small group of people working or training together.

squadron n division of an air force, fleet, or cavalry regiment.

squalid adj dirty and unpleasant; morally sordid. **squalor** n disgusting dirt and filth.

squall n sudden strong wind; harsh cry. ◆ v cry noisily, yell.

squander v waste (money or resources).

square n geometric figure with four equal sides and four right angles; open area in a town in this shape; product of a number multiplied by itself. ◆ adj square in shape; denoting a measure of area; straight or level; fair and honest; with all accounts or debts settled. ◆ v make square; multiply (a number) by itself; be or cause to be consistent. ◆ adv squarely, directly.

squarely adv in a direct way; in an honest and frank manner. **square dance** formation dance in which the couples form squares. **square meal** substantial meal. **square root** number of which a given number is the square. **square up to** v prepare to confront (a person or problem).

squash v crush flat; suppress; humiliate with a crushing retort; push into a confined space. ◆ n sweet fruit drink diluted with water; crowd of people in a confined space; (also **squash rackets**) game played in an enclosed court with a rubber ball and long-handled rackets; marrow-like vegetable. **squashy** adj

squat v **squatting, squatted** crouch with the knees bent and the weight on the feet; occupy unused premises to which one has no legal right. ◆ n place where squatters live. ◆ adj short and broad. **squatter** n illegal occupier of unused premises.

squaw n Offens native American or Canadian Indian woman.

squawk n loud harsh cry. ◆ v utter a squawk.

squeak n short shrill cry or sound. ◆ v make or utter a squeak. **narrow squeak** Informal narrow escape. **squeaky** adj

squeal n long shrill cry or sound. ◆ v make or utter a squeal; Slang inform on someone to the police.

squeamish adj easily sickened.

squeegee n tool with a rubber blade for clearing water from a surface.

squeeze v grip or press firmly; crush or press to extract liquid; push into a confined space; hug; obtain (something) by force or great effort. ◆ n squeezing; amount extracted by squeezing; hug; crush of people in a confined space; restriction on borrowing.

squelch v make a wet sucking sound, as by walking through mud. ◆ n squelching sound.

squib n small firework that hisses before exploding.

squid n sea creature with a torpedo-shaped body and ten tentacles.

squiggle n wavy line. **squiggly** adj

squint v have eyes which face in different directions; glance sideways. ◆ n squinting condition of the eye; Informal glance. ◆ adj crooked.

squire n country gentleman, usu. the main landowner in a community; *Hist* knight's apprentice.

squirm v wriggle, writhe; feel embarrassed. ◆ n wriggling movement.

squirrel n small bushy-tailed tree-living animal.

squirt v force (a liquid) or (of a liquid) be forced out of a narrow opening; squirt liquid at. ◆ n jet of liquid; *Informal* small or insignificant person.

squish v, n (make) a soft squelching sound. **squishy** adj

Sr *Chem* strontium.

Sr. Senior; Señor.

SS Schutzstaffel: Nazi paramilitary security force; steamship.

st. stone (weight).

St. Saint; Street.

stab v **stabbing, stabbed** pierce with something pointed; jab (at). ◆ n stabbing; sudden unpleasant sensation; *Informal* attempt.

stabilize v make or become stable. **stabilization** n **stabilizer** n device for stabilizing a child's bicycle, an aircraft, or a ship.

stable¹ n building in which horses are kept; establishment that breeds and trains racehorses; establishment that manages or trains several entertainers or athletes. ◆ v put or keep (a horse) in a stable.

stable² adj firmly fixed or established; firm in character; *Science* not subject to decay or decomposition. **stability** n

staccato [stak-ah-toe] adj, adv *Music* with the notes sharply separated. ◆ adj consisting of short abrupt sounds.

stack n ordered pile; large amount; chimney. ◆ v pile in a stack; control (aircraft waiting to land) so that they fly at different altitudes.

stadium n, pl **-diums, -dia** sports arena with tiered seats for spectators.

staff¹ n people employed in an organization; stick used as a weapon, support, etc. ◆ v supply with personnel.

staff² n, pl **staves** set of five horizontal lines on which music is written.

stag n adult male deer. **stag beetle** beetle with large branched jaws. **stag party, night** party for men only.

stage n step or period of development; platform in a theatre where actors perform; portion of a journey; separate unit of a rocket that can be jettisoned. ◆ v put (a play) on stage; organize and carry out (an event). **the stage** theatre as a profession. **stagy** adj overtheatrical.

stagecoach n large horse-drawn vehicle formerly used to carry passengers and mail. **stage fright** nervousness felt by a person about to face an audience. **stage whisper** loud whisper intended to be heard by an audience.

stagger v walk unsteadily; astound; arrange in alternating positions or periods. ◆ n staggering. **staggering** adj

stagnant adj (of water or air) stale from not moving; not growing or developing. **stagnate** v be stagnant. **stagnation** n

staid adj sedate, serious, and dull.

stain v discolour, mark; colour with a penetrating pigment. ◆ n discoloration or mark; moral blemish; penetrating liquid used to colour things. **stainless** adj **stainless steel** steel alloy that does not rust.

stairs pl n flight of steps between floors, usu. indoors. **staircase, stairway** n flight of stairs with a handrail or banisters.

stake n pointed stick or post driven into the ground as a support or marker; money wagered; an interest, usu. financial, held in something. **stakeholder** n person who has a concern or interest in something, esp. a business. ◆ v support or mark out with stakes; wager, risk. **at stake** being risked. **stake a claim to** claim a right to. **stake out** v *Slang* (of police) keep (a place) under surveillance.

stalactite n lime deposit hanging from the roof of a cave.

stalagmite n lime deposit sticking up from the floor of a cave.

stale adj not fresh; uninteresting from overuse; lacking energy or ideas through overwork or monotony. **staleness** n

stalemate n *Chess* position in which any of a player's moves would put his king in check, resulting in a draw; deadlock, impasse.

stalk¹ n plant's stem.

stalk² v follow or approach stealthily;

pursue persistently and, sometimes, attack (a person with whom one is obsessed); walk in a stiff or haughty manner. **stalking-horse** n pretext.

stall n small stand for the display and sale of goods; ground-floor seat in a theatre or cinema; one of a row of seats in a church for the choir or clergy; compartment in a stable; small room or compartment. ◆ v stop (a motor vehicle or engine) or (of a motor vehicle or engine) stop accidentally; (of an aircraft) begin to drop because the speed is too low; employ delaying tactics.

stallion n uncastrated male horse.

stalwart [stawl-wart] adj strong and sturdy; dependable. ◆ n stalwart person.

stamen n pollen-producing part of a flower.

stamina n enduring energy and strength.

stammer v speak or say with involuntary pauses or repetition of syllables. ◆ n tendency to stammer.

stamp v stick a postage stamp on; impress (a pattern or mark) on; bring (one's foot) down forcefully; walk with heavy footsteps; characterize. ◆ n (also **postage stamp**) piece of gummed paper stuck to an envelope or parcel to show that the postage has been paid; instrument for stamping a pattern or mark; pattern or mark stamped; act of stamping the foot; characteristic feature. **stamping ground** favourite meeting place. **stamp out** v suppress by force.

stampede n sudden rush of frightened animals or of a crowd. ◆ v (cause to) take part in a stampede.

stance n manner of standing; attitude.

stanch [stahnch] v same as STAUNCH[2].

stanchion n upright bar used as a support.

stand v **standing, stood** be in, rise to, or place in an upright position; be situated; be in a specified state or position; remain unchanged or valid; tolerate; offer oneself as a candidate; Informal treat to. ◆ n stall for the sale of goods; structure for spectators at a sports ground; firmly held opinion; US witness box; rack or piece of furniture on which things may be placed. **standing** n reputation or status;

duration. ◆ adj permanent, lasting. **stand for** v represent or mean; Informal tolerate. **stand in** v act as a substitute. **stand-in** n substitute. **stand-offish** adj reserved or haughty. **stand up for** v defend.

standard n level of quality; example against which others are judged or measured; moral principle; distinctive flag; upright pole. ◆ adj usual, regular, or average; accepted as correct; of recognized authority. **standardize** v cause to conform to a standard. **standardization** n **standard lamp** lamp attached to an upright pole on a base.

standpipe n tap attached to a water main to provide a public water supply.

standpoint n point of view.

standstill n complete halt.

stank v a past tense of STINK.

stanza n verse of a poem.

staple[1] n U-shaped piece of metal used to fasten papers or secure things. ◆ v fasten with staples. **stapler** n small device for fastening papers together.

staple[2] adj of prime importance. ◆ n main constituent of anything.

star n hot gaseous mass in space, visible in the night sky as a point of light; star-shaped mark used to indicate excellence; asterisk; celebrity in the entertainment or sports world. ◆ pl astrological forecast, horoscope. ◆ v **starring, starred** mark with a star or stars; feature or be featured as a star. ◆ adj leading, famous. **stardom** n status of a star in the entertainment or sports world. **starry** adj full of or like stars. **starry-eyed** adj full of naive optimism. **starfish** n star-shaped sea creature.

starboard n right-hand side of a ship, when facing forward. ◆ adj of or on this side.

starch n carbohydrate forming the main food element in bread, potatoes, etc., and used mixed with water for stiffening fabric. ◆ v stiffen (fabric) with starch. **starchy** adj containing starch; stiff and formal.

stare v look or gaze fixedly (at). ◆ n fixed gaze.

stark adj desolate, bare; without elaboration; absolute. ◆ adv completely.

starling n songbird with glossy black

speckled feathers.

start v take the first step, begin; set or be set in motion; establish or set up; make a sudden involuntary movement from fright. ◆ n first part of something; place or time of starting; advantage or lead in a competitive activity; starting movement from fright. **starter** n first course of a meal; device for starting an automobile's engine; person who signals the start of a race. **start-up** n recently launched project or business enterprise.

startle v slightly surprise or frighten.

starve v die or suffer or cause to die or suffer from hunger; deprive of something needed. **starvation** n

stash v Informal store in a secret place.

state n condition of a person or thing; Informal excited or agitated condition; pomp; (S-) sovereign political power or its territory; (S-) the government. ◆ adj of or concerning the State; involving ceremony. ◆ v express in words. **stately** adj dignified or grand. **statement** n something stated; printed financial account. **stateroom** n private cabin on a ship; large room in a palace, used for ceremonial occasions. **statesman, stateswoman** n experienced and respected political leader. **statesmanship** n

static adj stationary or inactive; (of a force) acting but producing no movement. ◆ n crackling sound or speckled picture caused by interference in radio or television reception; (also **static electricity**) electric sparks produced by friction. **statics** n branch of mechanics dealing with the forces producing a state of equilibrium.

station n place where trains stop for passengers; headquarters of the police; building with special equipment for a particular purpose, e.g. power station; television or radio channel; position in society. ◆ v assign (someone) to a particular place. **station wagon** automobile with a rear door and luggage space behind the rear seats.

stationary adj not moving.

stationery n writing materials such as paper and pens. **stationer** n dealer in stationery.

statistic n numerical fact collected and classified systematically. **statistics** n science of classifying and interpreting numerical information. **statistical** adj **statistically** adv

statistician n person who compiles and studies statistics.

statue n large sculpture of a human or animal figure. **statuary** n statues collectively. **statuesque** [stat-yoo-**esk**] adj (of a woman) tall and well-proportioned. **statuette** n small statue.

stature n person's height; intellectual or moral greatness.

status n social position; prestige; person's legal standing. **status quo** existing state of affairs.

statute n written law. **statutory** adj required or authorized by law.

staunch[1] adj loyal, firm.

staunch[2], **stanch** v stop (a flow of blood).

stave n one of the strips of wood forming a barrel; Music same as STAFF. ◆ v **staving, staved** or **stove**. burst a hole in. **stave off** v ward off.

stay[1] v remain in a place or condition; reside temporarily; endure. ◆ n period of staying in a place; postponement. **staying power** stamina.

stay[2] n prop or buttress. ◆ pl corset.

STD sexually transmitted disease.

stead n **in someone's stead** in someone's place. **stand someone in good stead** be useful to someone.

steadfast adj firm, determined. **steadfastly** adv

steady adj **steadier, steadiest** not shaky or wavering; sensible and dependable; regular or continuous. ◆ v **steadying, steadied** make steady. ◆ adv in a steady manner. **steadily** adv **steadiness** n

steak n thick slice of meat, esp. beef; slice of fish.

steal v **stealing, stole, stolen** take unlawfully or without permission; move stealthily.

stealth n 1 secret or underhand behaviour. 2 (of technology) able to render an aircraft almost invisible to radar. 3 disguised or hidden, e.g. stealth taxes. **stealthy** adj **stealthily** adv

steam n vapour into which water changes when boiled; power, energy, or speed. ◆ v give off steam; (of a vehicle) move by steam power; cook or treat with steam. **steamer** n steam-propelled ship; container used to cook food in steam. **steam engine** engine worked by steam. **steamroller** n steam-powered vehicle with heavy rollers, used to level road surfaces. ◆ v use overpowering force to make (someone) do what one wants.

steatite [stee-a-tite] n same as SOAPSTONE.

steed n Lit horse.

steel n hard malleable alloy of iron and carbon; steel rod used for sharpening knives; hardness of character or attitude. ◆ v make (oneself) hard and unfeeling. **steely** adj

steep¹ adj sloping sharply; Informal (of a price) unreasonably high. **steeply** adv **steepness** n

steep² v soak or be soaked in liquid. **steeped in** filled with, e.g. Scotland is steeped in history.

steeple n church tower with a spire. **steeplejack** n person who repairs steeples and chimneys.

steeplechase n horse race with obstacles to jump; track race with hurdles and a water jump.

steer¹ v direct the course of (a vehicle or ship); direct (one's course). **steerage** n cheapest accommodation on a passenger ship. **steering wheel** wheel turned by the driver of a vehicle in order to steer it.

steer² n castrated male ox.

stein [stine] n earthenware beer mug.

stellar adj of stars.

stem¹ n long thin central part of a plant; long slender part, as of a wineglass; part of a word to which inflections are added. ◆ v **stemming**, **stemmed**. **stem from** originate from.

stem² v **stemming**, **stemmed** stop (the flow of something).

stench n foul smell.

stencil n thin sheet with cut-out pattern through which ink or paint passes to form the pattern on the surface below; pattern made thus. ◆ v -cilling, -cilled make (a pattern) with a stencil.

stenography n shorthand. **stenographer** n shorthand typist.

stentorian adj (of a voice) very loud.

step v **stepping**, **stepped** move and set down the foot, as when walking; walk a short distance. ◆ n stepping; distance covered by a step; sound made by stepping; foot movement in a dance; one of a sequence of actions taken in order to achieve a goal; degree in a series or scale; flat surface for placing the foot on when going up or down. ◆ pl stepladder. **step in** v intervene. **stepladder** n folding portable ladder with supporting frame. **stepping stone** one of a series of stones for stepping on in crossing a stream; means of progress towards a goal. **step up** v increase (something) by steps.

step- combining form denoting a relationship created by the remarriage of a parent, e.g. stepmother.

steppe n wide grassy treeless plain.

stereo adj short for STEREOPHONIC. ◆ n stereophonic record player; stereophonic sound.

stereophonic adj using two separate loudspeakers to give the effect of naturally distributed sound.

stereoscopic adj having a three-dimensional effect.

stereotype n standardized idea of a type of person or thing. ◆ v form a stereotype of.

sterile adj free from germs; unable to produce offspring; lacking inspiration or vitality. **sterility** n **sterilize** v make sterile. **sterilization** n

sterling n British money system. ◆ adj genuine; reliable.

stern¹ adj severe, strict. **sternly** adv **sternness** n

stern² n rear part of a ship.

sternum n, pl -na, -nums breast bone.

steroid n organic compound containing a carbon ring system, such as many hormones.

stertorous adj (of breathing) laboured and noisy.

stethoscope n medical instrument for listening to sounds made inside the body.

Stetson n ® tall broad-brimmed hat, worn mainly by cowboys.

stevedore n person who loads and unloads ships.

stew n food cooked slowly in a closed pot; Informal troubled or worried state. ◆ v cook slowly in a closed pot.

steward n person who looks after passengers on a ship or aircraft; official who helps at a public event such as a race; person who administers another's property. **stewardess** n fem

stick[1] n long thin piece of wood; such a piece of wood shaped for a special purpose, e.g. *hockey stick*; something like a stick, e.g. *stick of celery*; *Slang* verbal abuse, criticism. **stickhandle** v control a puck or ball in hockey, lacrosse, etc.

stick[2] v **sticking, stuck** push (a pointed object) into (something); fasten or be fastened by or as if by pins or glue; (foll. by *out*) extend beyond something else, protrude; *Informal* put; come to a standstill; jam; remain for a long time; *Slang* tolerate, abide. **sticker** n adhesive label or sign. **sticky** adj covered with an adhesive substance; (of weather) warm and humid; *Informal* difficult, unpleasant. **stick-in-the-mud** n person who does not like anything new. **stick-up** n *Slang* robbery at gunpoint. **stick up for** v *Informal* support or defend.

stickleback n small fish with sharp spines in its back.

stickler n person who insists on something, e.g. *stickler for accuracy*.

stiff adj not easily bent or moved; firm in consistency; unrelaxed or awkward; severe, e.g. *stiff punishment*; strong, e.g. *a stiff drink*. ◆ n *Slang* corpse. **stiffly** adv **stiffness** n **stiffen** v make or become stiff. **stiff-necked** adj haughtily stubborn.

stifle v suffocate; suppress.

stigma n mark of social disgrace; part of a plant that receives pollen. **stigmata** pl n marks resembling the wounds of the crucified Christ. **stigmatize** v mark as being shameful.

stile n set of steps allowing people to climb a fence.

stiletto n, pl **-tos** small slender dagger; (also **stiletto heel**) high narrow heel on a woman's shoe.

still[1] adv now or in the future as before; up to this or that time; even or yet, e.g. *still more insults*; quietly or without movement. ◆ adj motionless; silent and calm, undisturbed; (of a drink) not fizzy. ◆ v make still. ◆ n photograph from a film scene. **stillness** n **stillborn** adj born dead. **still life** painting of inanimate objects.

still[2] n apparatus for distilling alcoholic drinks.

stilted adj stiff and formal in manner.

stilts pl n pair of poles with footrests for walking raised from the ground; long posts supporting a building above ground level.

stimulus n, pl **-li** something that acts as an incentive to (someone); something, such as a drug, capable of causing a response in a person or animal. **stimulant** n drug, food, etc. that makes the body work faster, increases heart rate, etc. **stimulate** v encourage to start or progress further, e.g. *methods to stimulate job creation*; fill (a person) with ideas or enthusiasm; act as a stimulus on. **stimulation** n

sting v **stinging, stung** (of certain animals or plants) wound by injecting with poison; feel or cause to feel sharp physical or mental pain; *Slang* cheat (someone) by overcharging. ◆ n wound or pain caused by or as if by stinging; mental pain; sharp pointed organ of certain animals or plants by which poison can be injected.

stingy adj **-gier, -giest** mean or miserly. **stinginess** n

stink v **stinking, stank** or **stunk, stunk** give off a strong unpleasant smell; *Slang* be very unpleasant. ◆ n strong unpleasant smell; *Slang* unpleasant fuss.

stint v (foll. by *on*) be miserly with (something). ◆ n allotted amount of work.

stipend [sty-pend] n regular allowance or salary, esp. that paid to a clergyman.

stipple v paint, draw, or engrave using dots. **stippling** n

stipulate v specify as a condition of an agreement. **stipulation** n

stir v **stirring, stirred** mix up (a liquid) by moving a spoon etc. around in it; move; excite or stimulate (a person) emotionally. ◆ n a stirring; strong reaction, usu. of excitement.

stirrup n metal loop attached to a saddle for supporting a rider's foot.

stitch n link made by drawing thread through material with a needle; loop of yarn formed round a needle or hook in knitting or crochet; sharp pain in the side. ◆ v sew. **in stitches** *Informal* laughing uncontrollably. **not a stitch** *Informal* no clothes at all.

stoat *n* small mammal of the weasel family, with brown fur that turns white in winter.

stock *n* total amount of goods available for sale in a shop; supply stored for future use; financial shares in, or capital of, a company; lineage; livestock; handle of a rifle; liquid produced by boiling meat, fish, bones, or vegetables; fragrant flowering plant; standing or status. ◆ *pl Hist* instrument of punishment consisting of a wooden frame with holes into which the hands and feet of the victim were locked. ◆ *adj* kept in stock, standard; hackneyed. ◆ *v* keep for sale or future use; supply (a farm) with livestock or (a lake etc.) with fish. **stockist** *n* dealer who stocks a particular product. **stocky** *adj* (of a person) broad and sturdy. **stockbroker** *n* person who buys and sells stocks and shares for customers. **stock car** standard car modified for racing. **stock exchange, market** institution for the buying and selling of shares. **stockpile** *v* acquire and store a large quantity of (something) for future use. ◆ *n* accumulated store. **stock-still** *adj* motionless. **stocktaking** *n* counting and valuing of the goods in a shop.

stockade *n* enclosure or barrier made of stakes.

stockinet *n* machine-knitted elastic fabric.

stocking *n* close-fitting covering for the foot and leg. **stocking stitch** alternate rows of plain and purl in knitting.

stodgy *adj* **stodgier, stodgiest** (of food) heavy and starchy; (of a person) serious and boring. **stodge** *n* heavy starchy food.

stoic [**stow-ik**] *n* person who suffers hardship without showing his or her feelings. ◆ *adj* (also **stoical**) suffering hardship without showing one's feelings. **stoically** *adv* **stoicism** [**stow-iss-izz-um**] *n*

stoke *v* feed and tend a (fire or furnace). **stoker** *n*

stole[1] *v* past tense of STEAL.

stole[2] *n* long scarf or shawl.

stolen *v* past participle of STEAL.

stolid *adj* showing little emotion or interest. **stolidity** *n* **stolidly** *adv*

stomach *n* organ in the body which digests food; front of the body around the waist; desire or inclination. ◆ *v* put up with.

stomp *v* tread heavily.

stone *n* material of which rocks are made; piece of this; gem; hard central part of a fruit; hard deposit formed in the kidney or bladder; *Brit* unit of weight equal to 14 pounds. ◆ *v* throw stones at; remove stones from (a fruit). **stoned** *adj Slang* under the influence of alcohol or drugs. **stony** *adj* of or like stone; unfeeling or hard. **stony-broke** *adj Slang* completely penniless. **stonily** *adv* **Stone Age** prehistoric period when tools were made of stone. **stone-cold** *adj* completely cold. **stone-deaf** *adj* completely deaf. **stonewall** *v* obstruct or hinder discussion. **stoneware** *n* hard kind of pottery fired at a very high temperature.

stood *v* past of STAND.

stooge *n* actor who feeds lines to a comedian or acts as the butt of his jokes; *Slang* person taken advantage of by a superior.

stool *n* chair without arms or back; piece of excrement.

stool pigeon *n* informer for the police.

stoop *v* bend (the body) forward and downward; carry oneself habitually in this way; degrade oneself. ◆ *n* stooping posture.

stop *v* **stopping, stopped** bring to or come to a halt; cease or cause to cease from doing (something); prevent or restrain; withhold; block or plug; stay or rest. ◆ *n* place where something stops; stopping or being stopped; full stop; knob on an organ that is pulled out to allow a set of pipes to sound. **stoppage** *n* **stoppage time** same as INJURY TIME. **stopper** *n* plug for closing a bottle etc. **stopcock** *n* valve to control or stop the flow of fluid in a pipe. **stopgap** *n* temporary substitute. **stopover** *n* short break in a journey. **stop press** news item put into a newspaper after printing has been started. **stopwatch** *n* watch which can be stopped instantly for exact timing of a sporting event.

store *v* collect and keep (things) for future use; put (furniture etc.) in a warehouse for safekeeping; stock (goods); *Computers* enter or retain (data). ◆ *n* shop; supply kept for future use; storage place, such as a warehouse. ◆ *pl* stock of provisions. **in store** forthcoming or imminent. **set great store by** value greatly. **storage** *n* storing; space for storing. **storage heater** electric device that can accumulate and radiate heat generated by off-peak electricity.

storey *n* floor or level of a building.

stork *n* large wading bird.

storm *n* violent weather with wind, rain, or snow; strongly expressed reaction. ◆ *v* rush violently or angrily; rage; attack or capture (a place) suddenly. **stormy** *adj* characterized by storms; involving violent emotions. **stormstayed** *adj* unable to leave a place because of stormy conditions.

story *n, pl* **-ries** description of a series of events told or written for entertainment; plot of a book or film; newspaper report; *Informal* lie.

stoup [stoop] *n* small basin for holy water.

stout *adj* fat; thick and strong; brave and resolute. ◆ *n* strong dark beer. **stoutly** *adv* **stoutness** *n*

stove¹ *n* apparatus for cooking or heating.

stove² *v* a past of STAVE.

stow *v* pack or store. **stow away** *v* hide as a stowaway. **stowaway** *n* person who hides on a ship or aircraft in order to travel free.

straddle *v* have one leg or part on each side of (something).

strafe *v* attack (an enemy) with machine guns from the air.

straggle *v* go or spread in a rambling or irregular way. **straggler** *n* **straggly** *adj*

straight *adj* not curved or crooked; level or upright; orderly; honest or frank; in continuous succession; (of spirits) undiluted; *Theatre* serious; *Slang* heterosexual; *Slang* conventional. ◆ *n* straight part. ◆ *adv* in a straight line; immediately; in a level or upright position. **go straight** *Informal* reform after being a criminal. **straighten** *v* **straightaway** *adv* immediately. **straight face** serious facial expression concealing a desire to laugh. **straightforward** *adj* (of a task) easy; honest, frank.

strain¹ *n* great demand on strength or resources; force exerted by straining; injury from overexertion; tension or tiredness; melody or theme. ◆ *v* cause (something) to be used or tested beyond its limits; make an intense effort; injure by overexertion; sieve. **strained** *adj* not relaxed, tense; not natural, forced. **strainer** *n* sieve.

strain² *n* breed or race; streak.

strait *n* narrow channel connecting two areas of sea. ◆ *pl* position of acute difficulty. **straitjacket** *n* strong jacket with long sleeves used to bind the arms of a violent person. **strait-laced** *adj* prudish.

straitened *adj* **in straitened circumstances** not having much money.

strand¹ *v* run aground; leave in difficulties. ◆ *n Poetic* shore.

strand² *n* single thread of string, wire, etc.

strange *adj* odd or unusual; not familiar. **strange to** inexperienced (in) or unaccustomed (to). **strangely** *adv* **strangeness** *n* **stranger** *n* person who is not known or is new to a place or experience.

strangle *v* kill by squeezing the throat; prevent the development of. **strangler** *n* **strangulation** *n* strangling. **stranglehold** *n* strangling grip in wrestling; powerful control.

strap *n* strip of flexible material for lifting, fastening, or holding in place. ◆ *v* **strapping**, **strapped** fasten with a strap or straps. **strapping** *adj* tall and sturdy.

strata *n* plural of STRATUM.

stratagem *n* clever plan, trick.

strategy *n, pl* **-gies** overall plan; art of planning in war. **strategic** [strat-ee-jik] *adj* advantageous; (of weapons) aimed at an enemy's homeland. **strategically** *adv* **strategist** *n*

strathspey *n* Scottish dance with gliding steps.

stratosphere *n* atmospheric layer between about 15 and 50 km above the earth.

stratum [strah-tum] *n, pl* **strata** layer, esp. of rock; social class. **stratify** *v* divide into strata. **stratification** *n*

straw *n* dried stalks of grain; single stalk of straw; long thin tube used to suck up liquid into the mouth. **straw poll** unofficial poll taken to determine general opinion.

strawberry n sweet fleshy red fruit with small seeds on the outside. **strawberry mark** red birthmark.

stray v wander; digress; deviate from certain moral standards. ♦ adj having strayed; scattered, random. ♦ n stray animal.

streak n long band of contrasting colour or substance; quality or characteristic; short stretch (of good or bad luck). ♦ v mark with streaks; move rapidly; Informal run naked in public. **streaker** n **streaky** adj

stream n small river; steady flow, as of liquid, speech, or people; schoolchildren grouped together because of similar ability. ♦ v flow steadily; move in unbroken succession; float in the air; group (pupils) in streams. **streamer** n strip of coloured paper that unrolls when tossed; long narrow flag.

streamline v make more efficient by removing the parts that are least useful or profitable; give (an automobile, plane, etc.) a smooth even shape to offer least resistance to the flow of air or water.

street n public road, usu. lined with buildings. **streetcar** n public transport vehicle powered by an overhead wire and running on rails laid in the road. **streetwalker** n prostitute. **streetwise** adj knowing how to survive in big cities.

strength n quality of being strong; quality or ability considered an advantage; degree of intensity; total number of people in a group. **on the strength of** on the basis of. **strengthen** v

strenuous adj requiring great energy or effort. **strenuously** adv

streptococcus [strep-toe-kok-uss] n, pl -**cocci** bacterium occurring in chains, many species of which cause disease.

streptomycin n antibiotic drug.

stress n emphasis; tension or strain; stronger sound in saying a word or syllable; Physics force producing strain. ♦ v emphasize; subject to stress; put stress on (a word or syllable).

stretch v extend or be extended; be able to be stretched; extend the limbs or body; strain (resources or abilities)

to the utmost. ♦ n stretching; continuous expanse; period; ability to be stretched; Informal term of imprisonment. **stretchy** adj **stretcher** n frame covered with canvas, on which an injured person is carried.

strew v strewing, strewed, strewed or strewn. scatter (things) over a surface.

striation n scratch or groove; pattern of scratches or grooves.

stricken adj seriously affected by disease, grief, pain, etc.

strict adj stern or severe; adhering closely to specified rules; complete, absolute. **strictly** adv **strictness** n

stricture n severe criticism.

stride v striding, strode, stridden walk with long steps. ♦ n long step; regular pace. ♦ pl progress.

strident adj loud and harsh. **stridently** adv **stridency** n

strife n conflict, quarrelling.

strike v striking, struck cease work as a protest; hit; attack suddenly; afflict; enter the mind of; agree (a bargain); ignite (a match) by friction; (of a clock) indicate (a time) by sounding a bell; discover (gold, oil, etc.); make (a coin) by stamping it; take up (a posture). ♦ n stoppage of work as a protest; striking. **strike camp** dismantle and pack up tents. **strike home** have the desired effect. **striker** n striking worker; attacking footballer. **striking** adj noteworthy; impressive. **strike off, out** v cross out. **strike up** v begin (a conversation or friendship); begin to play music.

string n thin cord used for tying; set of objects threaded on a string; series of things or events; stretched wire or cord on a musical instrument that produces sound when vibrated. ♦ pl restrictions or conditions; section of an orchestra consisting of stringed instruments. ♦ v stringing, strung provide with a string or strings; thread on a string. **pull strings** use one's influence. **stringed** adj (of a musical instrument) having strings that are plucked or played with a bow. **stringy** adj like string; (of meat) fibrous. **string along** v Informal accompany; deceive over a period of time. **string up** v Informal kill by hanging.

stringent [strin-jent] adj strictly controlled or enforced. **stringently** adv stringency n

strip v **stripping, stripped** take (the covering or clothes) off; take a title or possession away from (someone); dismantle (an engine). ◆ n long narrow piece; clothes a football team plays in. **stripper** n person who performs a striptease. **strip cartoon** sequence of drawings telling a story. **striptease** n entertainment in which a performer undresses to music.

stripe n long narrow band of contrasting colour or substance; chevron on a uniform to indicate rank. **striped, stripy** adj

stripling n youth.

strive v **striving, strove, striven** make a great effort.

strobe n short for STROBOSCOPE.

stroboscope n instrument producing a very bright flashing light.

strode v past tense of STRIDE.

stroke v touch or caress lightly with the hand. ◆ n light touch or caress with the hand; rupture of a blood vessel in the brain; mark made by a pen or paintbrush; style or method of swimming; blow; action or occurrence of the kind specified, e.g. a stroke of luck; chime of a clock.

stroll v walk in a leisurely manner. ◆ n leisurely walk. **stroller** n chair-shaped carriage for a baby.

strong adj having physical power; not easily broken; having an extreme or drastic effect, e.g. strong discipline; great in degree or intensity; having moral force; (of a drink) containing a lot of alcohol; having a specified number, e.g. twenty strong. **strongly** adv **stronghold** n fortress; area of predominance of a particular belief. **strongroom** n room designed for the safekeeping of valuables.

strontium n silvery-white metallic element. **strontium-90** n radioactive isotope present in the fallout of nuclear explosions.

strop n leather strap for sharpening razors.

stroppy adj **-pier, -piest** Slang angry or awkward.

strove v past tense of STRIVE.

struck v past of STRIKE.

structure n complex construction; manner or basis of construction or organization. ◆ v give a structure to.

structural adj **structuralism** n approach to literature, social sciences, etc., which sees changes in the subject as caused and organized by a hidden set of universal rules. **structuralist** n, adj

strudel n thin sheet of filled dough rolled up and baked, usu. with an apple filling.

struggle v work, strive, or make one's way with difficulty; move about violently in an attempt to get free; fight (with someone). ◆ n striving; fight.

strum v **strumming, strummed** play (a guitar or banjo) by sweeping the thumb or a plectrum across the strings.

strumpet n Old-fashioned prostitute.

strung v past of STRING.

strut v **strutting, strutted** swagger. ◆ n bar supporting a structure; strutting walk.

strychnine [strik-neen] n very poisonous drug used in small quantities as a stimulant.

stub n short piece left after use; counterfoil of a cheque or ticket. ◆ v **stubbing, stubbed** strike (the toe) painfully against an object; put out (a cigarette) by pressing the end against a surface. **stubby** adj short and broad.

stubble n short stalks of grain left in a field after reaping; short growth of hair on the chin of a man who has not shaved recently. **stubbly** adj **stubble-jumper** n Slang prairie grain farmer.

stubborn adj refusing to agree or give in; difficult to deal with. **stubbornly** adv **stubbornness** n

stucco n plaster used for coating or decorating walls. **stuccoed** adj

stuck v past of STICK[2]. **stuck-up** adj Informal conceited or snobbish.

stud[1] n small piece of metal attached to a surface for decoration; dislike removable fastener for clothes; one of several small round objects fixed to the sole of a football boot to give better grip. ◆ v **studding, studded** set with studs.

stud[2] n male animal, esp. a stallion, kept for breeding; (also **stud farm**) place where horses are bred; Slang virile or sexually active man.

student n person who studies a subject, esp. at university.

studio n, pl **-dios** workroom of an artist or photographer; room or building in which television or radio programmes, records, or films are made. **studio apartment** one-room apartment with a small kitchen and bathroom.

study v **studying, studied** be engaged in learning (a subject); investigate by observation and research; scrutinize. ◆ n, pl **studies** act or process of studying; room for studying in; book or paper produced as a result of study; sketch done as practice or preparation; musical composition designed to improve playing technique. **studied** adj carefully practised or planned. **studious** [styoo-dee-uss] adj fond of study; careful and deliberate. **studiously** adv

stuff v pack, cram, or fill completely; fill (food) with a seasoned mixture; fill (an animal's skin) with material to restore the shape of the live animal; fill with padding. ◆ n substance or material; collection of unnamed things. **stuff oneself** Informal eat large quantities. **stuffing** n seasoned mixture with which food is stuffed; padding.

stuffy adj **stuffier, stuffiest** lacking fresh air; Informal dull or conventional.

stultify v **-fying, -fied** dull the mind of (someone) by boring routine.

stumble v trip and nearly fall; walk with frequent stumbling; make frequent mistakes in speech. ◆ n stumbling. **stumble across** v discover accidentally. **stumbling block** obstacle or difficulty.

stump n base of a tree left when the main trunk has been cut away; part of a thing left after a larger part has been removed. ◆ v baffle; walk with heavy steps. **stumpy** adj short and stubby.

stun v **stunning, stunned** knock senseless; shock or overwhelm. **stunning** adj very attractive or impressive.

stung v past of STING.

stunk v a past of STINK.

stunt¹ v prevent or impede the growth of. **stunted** adj

stunt² n acrobatic or dangerous action; anything spectacular done to gain publicity.

stupefy v **-fying, -fied** make

insensitive or lethargic; astound. **stupefaction** n

stupendous adj astonishing; huge. **stupendously** adv

stupid adj lacking intelligence; silly; in a stupor. **stupidity** n **stupidly** adv

stupor n dazed or unconscious state.

sturdy adj **-dier, -diest** healthy and robust; strongly built. **sturdily** adv **sturdiness** n

sturgeon n fish from which caviar is obtained.

stutter v speak with repetition of initial consonants. ◆ n tendency to stutter.

sty¹ n, pl **sties** pen for pigs.

sty², **stye** n, pl **sties, styes** inflammation at the base of an eyelash.

style n manner of writing, speaking, or doing something; shape or design; elegance, refinement; prevailing fashion. ◆ v shape or design; name or call. **stylish** adj smart, elegant, and fashionable. **stylishly** adv **stylist** n hairdresser; designer; person who writes with great attention to style. **stylistic** adj of literary or artistic style. **stylize** v cause to conform to an established stylistic form. **styling mousse** foamy substance applied to hair before styling to hold the style.

stylus n needle-like device on a record player that rests in the groove of the record and picks up the sound signals.

stymie v **-mieing, -mied** thwart.

styptic n, adj (drug) used to stop bleeding.

suave [swahv] adj smooth and sophisticated in manner. **suavely** adv **suavity** n

sub n submarine; subscription; substitute; Informal advance payment of wages or salary. ◆ v **subbing, subbed** act as a substitute; grant advance payment to.

sub- prefix used with many main words to mean: under or beneath, e.g. submarine; subordinate, e.g. sublieutenant; falling short of, e.g. subnormal; forming a subdivision, e.g. subheading.

subaltern n army officer below the rank of captain.

subatomic adj of or being one of the particles which make up an atom.

subcommittee n small committee

formed from some members of a larger committee.

subconscious adj happening or existing without one's awareness. ◆ n Psychoanalysis that part of the mind of which one is not aware but which can influence one's behaviour. **subconsciously** adv

subcontinent n large land mass that is a distinct part of a continent.

subcontract n secondary contract by which the main contractor for a job puts work out to others. ◆ v put out (work) on a subcontract. **subcontractor** n

subcutaneous [sub-cute-**ayn**-ee-uss] adj under the skin.

subdivide v divide (a part of something) into smaller parts. **subdivision** n

subdue v -duing, -dued overcome; make less intense.

subeditor n Brit person who checks and edits text for a newspaper or magazine.

subject n person or thing being dealt with or studied; Grammar word or phrase that represents the person or thing performing the action of the verb in a sentence; person under the rule of a monarch or government. ◆ adj being under the rule of a monarch or government. ◆ v (foll. by to) cause to undergo. **subject to** liable to; conditional upon. **subjection** n **subjective** adj based on personal feelings or prejudices. **subjectively** adv

sub judice [sub joo-**diss**-ee] adj Latin under judicial consideration.

subjugate v bring (a group of people) under one's control. **subjugation** n

subjunctive Grammar n mood of verbs used when the content of the clause is doubted, supposed, or wished. ◆ adj in or of that mood.

sublet v -letting, -let rent out (property rented from someone else).

sublimate v Psychol direct the energy of (a primitive impulse) into socially acceptable activities. **sublimation** n

sublime adj of high moral, intellectual, or spiritual value; supreme. ◆ v Chem change from a solid to a vapour without first melting. **sublimely** adv

subliminal adj relating to mental processes of which the individual is not aware.

sub-machine-gun n portable machine-gun with a short barrel.

submarine n vessel which can operate below the surface of the sea. ◆ adj below the surface of the sea.

submerge v put or go below the surface of water or other liquid. **submersion** n

submit v -mitting, -mitted surrender; be (voluntarily) subjected to a process or treatment; put forward for consideration. **submission** n submitting; something submitted for consideration; state of being submissive. **submissive** adj meek and obedient.

subordinate adj of lesser rank or importance. ◆ n subordinate person or thing. ◆ v make or treat as subordinate. **subordination** n

suborn v bribe or incite (a person) to commit a wrongful act.

subpoena [sub-**pee**-na] n writ requiring a person to appear before a lawcourt. ◆ v summon (someone) with a subpoena.

subscribe v pay (a subscription); give support or approval (to). **subscriber** n **subscription** n payment for issues of a publication over a period; money contributed to a charity etc.; membership fees paid to a society.

subsection n division of a section.

subsequent adj occurring after, succeeding. **subsequently** adv

subservient adj submissive, servile. **subservience** n

subside v become less intense; sink to a lower level. **subsidence** n act or process of subsiding.

subsidiary adj of lesser importance; subordinate. ◆ n, pl -aries subsidiary person or thing.

subsidize v help financially. **subsidy** n financial aid.

subsist v manage to live. **subsistence** n

subsonic adj moving at a speed less than that of sound.

substance n solid, powder, liquid, or paste; physical composition of something; essential meaning of something; solid or meaningful quality; wealth. **substantial** adj of considerable size or value; (of food or a meal) sufficient and nourishing; solid or strong; real. **substantially** adv

substantiate v support (a story) with evidence. **substantiation** n

substantive adj of or being the essential element of a thing. ◆ n noun.

substitute v take the place of or put in place of another. ◆ n person or thing taking the place of another. **substitution** n

subsume v incorporate (an idea, case, etc.) under a comprehensive classification.

subterfuge n trick used to achieve an objective.

subterranean adj underground.

subtitle n secondary title of a book. ◆ pl printed translation at the bottom of the picture in a film with foreign dialogue. ◆ v provide with a subtitle or subtitles.

subtle adj not immediately obvious; having or requiring ingenuity. **subtly** adv **subtlety** n

subtract v take (one number or quantity) from another. **subtraction** n

subtropical adj of the regions bordering on the tropics.

suburb n residential area on the outskirts of a city. **suburban** adj of or inhabiting a suburb; narrow or unadventurous in outlook. **suburbia** n suburbs and their inhabitants.

subvention n subsidy.

subvert v overthrow the authority of. **subversion** n **subversive** adj

subway n passage under a road or railway; electric passenger railway operated in underground tunnels.

succeed v accomplish an aim; turn out satisfactorily; come next in order after (something); take over a position from (someone). **success** n favourable outcome of an attempt; attainment of wealth, fame, or position; successful person or thing. **successful** adj having success. **successfully** adv **succession** n series of people or things following one another in order; act or right by which one person succeeds another in a position. **successive** adj consecutive. **successively** adv **successor** n person who succeeds someone in a position.

succinct adj brief and clear. **succinctly** adv

succour v, n help in distress.

succulent adj juicy and delicious; (of a plant) having thick fleshy leaves. ◆ n succulent plant. **succulence** n

succumb v (foll. by to) give way (to something overpowering); die of (an illness).

such adj of the kind specified; so great, so much. ◆ pron such things. **such-and-such** adj specific, but not known or named. **suchlike** adj Informal of the kind specified.

suck v draw (liquid or air) into the mouth; take (something) into the mouth and moisten, dissolve, or roll it around with the tongue; (foll. by in) draw in by irresistible force. ◆ n sucking. **sucker** n Slang person who is easily deceived or swindled; organ or device which adheres by suction; shoot coming from a plant's root or the base of its main stem. **suck up to** v Informal flatter (someone) for one's own profit.

suckle v feed at the breast. **suckling** n unweaned baby or young animal.

sucrose [soo-kroze] n chemical name for sugar.

suction n sucking; force produced by drawing air out of a space to make a vacuum that will suck in a substance from another space.

sudden adj done or occurring quickly and unexpectedly. ◆ n all of a sudden quickly and unexpectedly. **suddenly** adv **suddenness** n **sudden death** Sport period of extra time in which the first competitor to score wins.

sudorific [syoo-dor-if-ik] n, adj (drug) causing sweating.

suds pl n froth of soap and water.

sue v **suing, sued** start legal proceedings against.

suede n leather with a velvety finish on one side.

suet n hard fat obtained from sheep and cattle, used in cooking.

suffer v undergo or be subjected to; tolerate. **sufferer** n **suffering** n **sufferance** n **on sufferance** tolerated with reluctance.

suffice [suf-fice] v be enough for a purpose. **sufficiency** n adequate amount. **sufficient** adj enough, adequate. **sufficiently** adv

suffix n letter or letters added to the end of a word to form another word.

suffocate v kill or be killed by deprivation of oxygen; feel or cause to feel discomfort from heat and lack of air. **suffocation** n

suffragan n bishop appointed to assist an archbishop or another bishop.

suffrage n vote or right of voting. **suffragist** (fem **suffragette**) n one claiming a right of voting.

suffuse v spread through or over (something). **suffusion** n

sugar n sweet crystalline carbohydrate found in many plants and used to sweeten food and drinks. ◆ v sweeten or cover with sugar. **sugary** adj **sugar beet** beet cultivated for the sugar obtained from its roots. **sugar bush** plantation of sugar maples. **sugar cane** tropical grass cultivated for the sugar obtained from its canes. **sugar daddy** Slang elderly man who gives a young woman money and gifts in return for sexual favours. **sugar maple** large N American maple tree yielding sweet sap from which sugar and syrup are made. **sugar off** v reduce maple sap to syrup by boiling.

suggest v put forward (an idea) for consideration; bring to mind by the association of ideas; give a hint of. **suggestible** adj easily influenced. **suggestion** n suggesting; thing suggested; hint or indication. **suggestive** adj suggesting something indecent; conveying a hint (of). **suggestively** adv

suicide n killing oneself intentionally; person who kills himself intentionally; self-inflicted ruin of one's own prospects or interests. **suicidal** adj liable to commit suicide. **suicidally** adv

suit n set of clothes designed to be worn together; outfit worn for a specific purpose; one of the four sets into which a pack of cards is divided; lawsuit. ◆ v be appropriate for; be acceptable to. **suitable** adj appropriate or proper. **suitably** adv **suitability** n **suitcase** n portable travelling case for clothing.

suite n set of connected rooms in a hotel; matching set of furniture; set of musical pieces in the same key.

suitor n Old-fashioned man who is courting a woman.

sulfate n salt or ester of sulfuric acid.

sulfide n compound of sulfur with another element.

sulfite n salt or ester of sulfurous acid.

sulfonamide [sulf-on-a-mide] n any of a class of drugs that prevent the growth of bacteria.

sulfur n pale yellow nonmetallic element. **sulfuric, sulfurous** adj of or containing sulfur.

sulk v be silent and sullen because of resentment or bad temper. ◆ n resentful or sullen mood. **sulky** adj **sulkily** adv **sulkiness** n

sullen adj unwilling to talk or be sociable; dark and dismal. **sullenly** adv **sullenness** n

sully v -lying, -lied make dirty; ruin (someone's reputation).

sultan n sovereign of a Muslim country. **sultana** n kind of raisin; sultan's wife, mother, or daughter. **sultanate** n territory of a sultan.

sultry adj -trier, -triest (of weather or climate) hot and humid; passionate, sensual.

sum n result of addition, total; problem in arithmetic; quantity of money. **sum total** complete or final total. **sum up** v summing, summed summarize; form a quick opinion of.

summary n, pl -ries brief account giving the main points of something. ◆ adj done quickly. **summarily** adv **summarize** v make or be a summary of (something). **summation** n summary; adding up.

summer n warmest season of the year, between spring and fall. **summery** adj **summertime** n period or season of summer.

summit n highest point; top of a mountain or hill; conference between heads of state.

summon v order (someone) to come; send for (someone) to appear in court; call upon (someone) to do something; gather (one's courage, strength, etc.). **summons** n command summoning someone; order requiring someone to appear in court. ◆ v order (someone) to appear in court.

sumo n Japanese style of wrestling.

sump n receptacle in an internal-combustion engine into which oil can drain; hollow into which liquid drains.

sumptuous adj lavish, magnificent. **sumptuously** adv **sumptuousness** n

sun n star around which the earth and other planets revolve; any star around which planets revolve; heat and light from the sun. ◆ v sunning, sunned expose (oneself) to the sun's rays.

sunless adj **sunny** adj full of or exposed to sunlight; cheerful.
sunbathe v lie in the sunshine in order to get a suntan. **sunbeam** n ray of sun. **sunburn** n painful reddening of the skin caused by overexposure to the sun. **sunburnt, sunburned** adj **sundial** n device showing the time by means of a pointer that casts a shadow on a marked dial. **sundown** n sunset. **sunflower** n tall plant with large golden flowers. **sunrise** n daily appearance of the sun above the horizon; time of this. **sunset** n daily disappearance of the sun below the horizon; time of this. **sunshine** n light and warmth from the sun. **sunspot** n dark patch appearing temporarily on the sun's surface. **sunstroke** n illness caused by prolonged exposure to intensely hot sunlight. **suntan** n browning of the skin caused by exposure to the sun. **sun-up** n sunrise.

sundae n ice cream topped with fruit etc.

Sunday n first day of the week and the Christian day of worship. **Sunday school** school for teaching children about Christianity.

sunder v break or tear apart.

sundry adj several, various. **sundries** pl n miscellaneous unspecified items. **all and sundry** everybody.

sung v past participle of SING.

sunk, sunken v past participle of SINK.

sup v **supping, supped** take (liquid) by sips; Obs take supper.

super adj Informal excellent.

super- prefix used with many main words to mean: above or over, e.g. superimpose; outstanding, e.g. supergroup; of greater size or extent, e.g. supermarket.

superbug n Informal bacterium resistant to antibiotics.

superannuation n regular payment by an employee into a pension fund; pension paid from this. **superannuated** adj discharged with a pension, owing to old age or illness.

superb adj excellent. **superbly** adv

supercharged adj (of an engine) having a supercharger. **supercharger** n device that increases the power of an internal-combustion engine by forcing extra air into it.

supercilious adj showing arrogant pride or scorn. **superciliousness** n

superconductor n substance which has almost no electrical resistance at very low temperatures. **superconductivity** n

superficial adj of or on the surface; not careful or thorough; (of a person) without depth of character, shallow. **superficially** adv **superficiality** n

superfluous [soo-per-flew-uss] adj more than is needed. **superfluity** n

superhuman adj beyond normal human ability or experience.

superimpose v place (something) on or over something else.

superintend v supervise (a person or activity). **superintendence** n **superintendent** n senior police officer; supervisor.

superior adj greater in quality, quantity, or merit; higher in position or rank; believing oneself to be better than others. ◆ n person of greater rank or status. **superiority** n

superlative [soo-per-lat-iv] adj of outstanding quality; Grammar denoting the form of an adjective or adverb indicating most. ◆ n Grammar superlative form of a word.

superman n man of apparently superhuman powers.

supermarket n large self-service store selling food and household goods.

supermodel n famous and highly-paid fashion model.

supernatural adj of or relating to things beyond the laws of nature. ◆ n **the supernatural** supernatural forces, occurrences, and beings collectively.

supernova n, pl -vae, -vas star that explodes and briefly becomes exceptionally bright.

supernumerary adj exceeding the required or regular number. ◆ n, pl -ries supernumerary person or thing.

superphosphate n chemical fertilizer containing phosphates.

superpower n extremely powerful nation.

superscript adj (of a character) printed or written above the line. ◆ n superscript character.

supersede v replace, supplant.

supersonic adj of or travelling at a speed greater than the speed of sound.

superstition n belief in omens,

ghosts, etc.; idea or practice based on this. **superstitious** adj

superstore n large supermarket.

superstructure n structure erected on something else; part of a ship above the main deck.

supervene v occur as an unexpected development.

supervise v watch over to direct or check. **supervision** n **supervisor** n **supervisory** adj

supine [soo-pine] adj lying flat on one's back.

supper n light evening meal.

supplant v take the place of, oust.

supple adj (of a person) moving and bending easily and gracefully; bending easily without damage. **suppleness** n **supply** adv

supplement n thing added to complete something or make up for a lack; magazine inserted into a newspaper; section added to a publication to supply further information. ◆ v provide or be a supplement to (something). **supplementary** adj

supplication n humble request. **supplicant** n person who makes a humble request.

supply v **-plying, -plied** provide with something required; make available. ◆ n, pl **-plies** supplying; amount available; Economics willingness and ability to provide goods and services. ◆ pl food or equipment. **supplier** n

support v bear the weight of; provide the necessities of life for; give practical or emotional help to; take an active interest in (a sports team, political principle, etc.); help to prove (a theory etc.); speak in favour of. ◆ n supporting; means of support. **supporter** n person who supports a team, principle, etc. **supportive** adj

suppose v presume to be true; consider as a proposal for the sake of discussion. **supposed** adj presumed to be true without proof; doubtful. **supposed to** expected or required to, e.g. you were supposed to phone me; permitted to, e.g. we're not supposed to swim here. **supposedly** adv **supposition** n supposing; something supposed.

suppository n, pl **-ries** solid medication inserted into the rectum or vagina and left to melt.

suppress v put an end to; restrain (an emotion or response); prevent publication of (information). **suppression** n

suppurate v (of a wound etc.) produce pus. **suppuration** n

supreme adj highest in authority, rank, or degree. **supremely** adv extremely. **supremacy** n supreme power; state of being supreme. **supremo** n Informal person in overall authority.

surcharge n additional charge.

surd n Math number that cannot be expressed in whole numbers.

sure adj free from uncertainty or doubt; reliable; inevitable. ◆ adv, interj Informal certainly. **surely** adv it must be true that. **sure-footed** adj unlikely to slip or stumble.

surety n, pl **-ties** person who takes responsibility, or thing given as a guarantee, for the fulfilment of another's obligation.

surf n foam caused by waves breaking on the shore. ◆ v take part in surfing; move quickly through a medium such as the Internet. **surfing** n sport of riding towards the shore on a surfboard on the crest of a wave. **surfer** n **surfboard** n board used in surfing.

surface n outside or top of an object; material covering the surface of an object; superficial appearance. ◆ v rise to the surface; put a surface on.

surfeit n excessive amount.

surge n sudden powerful increase; strong rolling movement of the sea. ◆ v increase suddenly; move forward strongly.

surgeon n doctor who specializes in surgery. **surgery** n treatment in which the patient's body is cut open in order to treat the affected part; Brit place where, or time when, a doctor, dentist, MP, etc. can be consulted. **surgical** adj **surgically** adv

surly adj **-lier, -liest** ill-tempered and rude. **surliness** n

surmise v, n guess, conjecture.

surmount v overcome (a problem); be on top of (something).

surname n family name.

surpass v be greater than or superior to.

surplice n loose white robe worn by clergymen and choristers.

surplus n amount left over in excess of what is required.

surprise n unexpected event; amazement and wonder. ◆ v cause to feel amazement or wonder; come upon, attack, or catch suddenly and unexpectedly. **take someone by surprise** catch someone unprepared.

surrealism n movement in art and literature involving the combination of incongruous images, as in a dream. **surreal** adj **surrealist** n, adj **surrealistic** adj

surrender v give oneself up; give (something) up to another; yield (to a temptation or influence). ◆ n surrendering.

surreptitious adj done secretly or stealthily. **surreptitiously** adv

surrogate n substitute. **surrogate mother** woman who gives birth to a child on behalf of a couple who cannot have children.

surround v be, come, or place all around (a person or thing). ◆ n border or edging. **surroundings** pl n conditions, scenery, etc. around a person, place, or thing.

surtax n extra tax on incomes above a certain level.

surveillance n close observation.

survey v view or consider in a general way; make a map of (an area); inspect (a building) to assess its condition and value; find out the incomes, opinions, etc. of (a group of people). ◆ n surveying; report produced by a survey. **surveyor** n

survive v continue to live or exist after (a difficult experience); live after the death of (another). **survival** n condition of having survived; thing that has survived from an earlier time. **survivor** n

susceptible adj liable to be influenced or affected by. **susceptibility** n

suspect v believe (someone) to be guilty without having any proof; think (something) to be false or questionable; believe (something) to be the case. ◆ adj not to be trusted. ◆ n person who is suspected.

suspend v hang from a high place; cause to remain floating or hanging;

cause to cease temporarily; remove (someone) temporarily from a job or team. **suspenders** pl n straps worn over the shoulders to hold up trousers; Brit straps for holding up stockings.

suspense n state of uncertainty while awaiting news, an event, etc.

suspension n suspending or being suspended; system of springs and shock absorbers supporting the body of a vehicle; mixture of fine particles of a solid in a fluid. **suspension bridge** bridge hanging from cables attached to towers at each end.

suspicion n feeling of not trusting a person or thing; belief that something is true without definite proof; slight trace. **suspicious** adj feeling or causing suspicion. **suspiciously** adv

suss out v Slang work out using one's intuition.

sustain v maintain or prolong; suffer (an injury or loss); keep up the vitality or strength of; support. **sustenance** n food.

suture [soo-cher] n stitch joining the edges of a wound.

SUV sport utility vehicle.

suzerain n state or sovereign with limited authority over another self-governing state. **suzerainty** n

svelte adj attractively slim.

SW southwest(ern).

swab n small piece of cotton batting used to apply medication, clean a wound, etc. ◆ v **swabbing, swabbed** clean (a wound) with a swab; clean (the deck of a ship) with a mop.

swaddle v wrap (a baby) in swaddling clothes. **swaddling clothes** long strips of cloth formerly wrapped round a newborn baby.

swag n Slang stolen property; Aust informal bundle of belongings carried by a swagman. **swagman** n Aust tramp who carries his belongings in a bundle on his back.

swagger v walk or behave arrogantly. ◆ n arrogant walk or manner.

swain n Poetic suitor; country youth.

swallow[1] v cause to pass down one's throat; make a gulping movement in the throat, as when nervous; Informal believe (something) gullibly; refrain from showing (a feeling); engulf or absorb. ◆ n swallowing; amount swallowed.

swallow² n small migratory bird with long pointed wings and a forked tail.

swam v past tense of SWIM.

swamp n watery area of land, bog. ◆ v cause (a boat) to fill with water and sink; overwhelm. **swampy** adj

swan n large usu. white water bird with a long graceful neck. **swan song** person's last performance before retirement or death.

swank Slang ◆ v show off or boast. ◆ n showing off or boasting. **swanky** adj Slang expensive and showy, stylish.

swap v swapping, swapped exchange (something) for something else. ◆ n exchange.

sward n stretch of short grass.

swarm¹ n large group of bees or other insects; large crowd. ◆ v move in a swarm; (of a place) be crowded or overrun.

swarm² v (foll. by up) climb (a ladder or rope) by gripping with the hands and feet.

swarthy adj -thier, -thiest dark-complexioned.

swashbuckler n daredevil adventurer. **swashbuckling** adj

swastika n symbol in the shape of a cross with the arms bent at right angles, used as the emblem of Nazi Germany.

swat v swatting, swatted hit sharply. ◆ n sharp blow.

swatch n sample of cloth.

swath [swawth] n the width of one sweep of a scythe or mower.

swathe v wrap in bandages or layers of cloth. ◆ n same as SWATH.

sway v swing to and fro or from side to side; waver or cause to waver in opinion. ◆ n power or influence; swaying motion.

swear v swearing, swore, sworn use obscene or blasphemous language; state earnestly; state or promise on oath. **swear by** v have complete confidence in. **swear in** v cause to take an oath. **swearword** n word considered obscene or blasphemous.

sweat n salty liquid given off through the pores of the skin; Slang drudgery or hard labour. ◆ v have sweat coming through the pores; be anxious; toil. **sweaty** adj **sweatband** n strip of cloth tied around the forehead or wrist to absorb sweat. **sweatshirt** n long-sleeved cotton jersey. **sweatshop** n place where employees work long hours in poor conditions for low pay.

sweater n (woollen) garment for the upper part of the body.

swede n kind of turnip.

sweep v sweeping, swept remove dirt from (a floor) with a broom; move smoothly and quickly; spread rapidly; move majestically; carry away suddenly or forcefully; stretch in a long wide curve. ◆ n sweeping; sweeping motion; wide expanse; person who cleans chimneys; sweepstake. **sweeping** adj indiscriminate; wide-ranging. **sweepstake** n lottery in which the stakes of the participants make up the prize.

sweet adj tasting of or like sugar; kind and charming; agreeable to the senses or mind; (of wine) with a high sugar content. ◆ n Brit shaped piece of food consisting mainly of sugar; dessert. **sweetly** adv **sweetness** n **sweeten** v **sweetener** n sweetening agent that does not contain sugar; Slang bribe. **sweetbread** n animal's pancreas used as food. **sweetbrier** n wild rose. **sweet corn** type of corn with sweet yellow kernels, eaten as a vegetable. **sweetheart** n lover. **sweetmeat** n Old-fashioned a sweet delicacy such as a small cake. **sweet pea** climbing plant with bright fragrant flowers. **sweet potato** tropical root vegetable with yellow flesh. **sweet-talk** v Informal coax or flatter. **sweet tooth** strong liking for sweet foods. **sweet william** garden plant with flat clusters of scented flowers.

swell v swelling, swelled, swollen or swelled. expand or increase; be puffed up with pride or other emotion; (of a sound) become gradually louder. ◆ n swelling or being swollen; movement of waves in the sea; Old-fashioned slang fashionable person. ◆ adj Slang excellent or fine. **swelling** n enlargement of part of the body, caused by injury or infection.

swelter v be oppressed by heat.

swept v past of SWEEP.

swerve v turn aside from a course sharply or suddenly. ◆ n swerving.

swift adj moving or able to move quickly. ◆ n fast-flying bird with pointed wings. **swiftly** adv **swiftness** n

swig n large mouthful of drink. ◆ v **swigging**, **swigged** drink in large mouthfuls.

swill v drink greedily; rinse (something) in large amounts of water. ◆ n sloppy mixture containing waste food, fed to pigs; deep drink; rinsing.

swim v **swimming**, **swam**, **swum** move along in water by movements of the limbs; be covered or flooded with liquid; reel, e.g. *her head was swimming*. ◆ n act or period of swimming. **swimmer** n **swimmingly** adv successfully and effortlessly. **swimming pool** (building containing an) artificial pond for swimming in.

swindle v cheat (someone) out of money. ◆ n instance of swindling. **swindler** n

swine n contemptible person; pig. **swinish** adj

swing v **swinging**, **swung** move to and fro, sway; move in a curve; hit out with a sweeping motion; (of an opinion or mood) change sharply; *Slang* be hanged. ◆ n swinging; suspended seat on which a child can swing to and fro; style of popular dance music played by big bands in the 1930s.

swipe v strike (at) with a sweeping blow; *Slang* steal; pass (a credit card or debit card) through a machine that electronically reads information stored in the card. ◆ n sweeping blow.

swirl v turn with a whirling motion. ◆ n whirling motion; twisting shape.

swish v move with a whistling or hissing sound. ◆ n whistling or hissing sound. ◆ adj *Informal* fashionable, smart.

Swiss adj of Switzerland or its people. ◆ n, pl **Swiss** person from Switzerland. **swiss roll** sponge cake spread with jam or cream and rolled up.

switch n device for opening and closing an electric circuit; abrupt change; exchange or swap; movable rail used to change a train to other rails; flexible rod or twig. ◆ v change abruptly; exchange or swap. **switchback** n road or railway with many sharp hills or bends. **switchboard** n installation in a telephone exchange or office where telephone calls are connected. **switch on, off** v turn (a device) on or off by

means of a switch.

swivel n coupling device that allows an attached object to turn freely. ◆ v **-elling**, **-elled** turn on or as if on a swivel.

swizzle stick n small ornamental stick used to stir a cocktail.

swollen v a past participle of SWELL.

swoon v, n faint.

swoop v sweep down or pounce on suddenly. ◆ n swooping.

swop v **swopping**, **swopped** same as SWAP ◆ n same as SWAP.

sword n weapon with a long sharp blade. **swordfish** n large fish with a very long upper jaw. **swordsman** n person skilled in the use of a sword.

swore v past tense of SWEAR.

sworn v past participle of SWEAR ◆ adj bound by or as if by an oath, e.g. *sworn enemies*.

swot *Informal* ◆ v **swotting**, **swotted** study hard. ◆ n person who studies hard.

swum v past participle of SWIM.

swung v past of SWING.

sybarite [sib-bar-ite] n lover of luxury. **sybaritic** adj

sycamore n tree with five-pointed leaves and two-winged fruits.

sycophant n person who uses flattery to win favour from people with power or influence. **sycophantic** adj **sycophancy** n

syllable n part of a word pronounced as a unit. **syllabic** adj

syllabub n dessert of beaten cream, sugar, and wine.

syllabus n list of subjects for a course of study.

syllogism n form of logical reasoning consisting of two premises and a conclusion. **syllogistic** adj

sylph n imaginary being supposed to inhabit the air; slender graceful girl or woman. **sylphlike** adj

sylvan adj *Lit* relating to woods and trees.

symbiosis n close association of two species living together to their mutual benefit. **symbiotic** adj

symbol n sign or thing that stands for something else. **symbolic** adj **symbolically** adv **symbolism** n representation of something by symbols; movement in art and literature using symbols to express abstract and mystical ideas. **symbolist** *n, adj* **symbolize** *v* be a symbol of; represent with a symbol.

symmetry *n* state of having two halves that are mirror images of each other. **symmetrical** *adj* **symmetrically** *adv*

sympathy *n, pl* **-thies** compassion for someone's pain or distress; agreement with someone's feelings or interests. **sympathetic** *adj* feeling or showing sympathy; likeable or appealing. **sympathetically** *adv* **sympathize** *v* feel or express sympathy. **sympathizer** *n*

symphony *n, pl* **-nies** composition for orchestra, with several movements. **symphonic** *adj*

symposium *n, pl* **-siums, -sia** conference for discussion of a particular topic.

symptom *n* sign indicating the presence of an illness; sign that something is wrong. **symptomatic** *adj*

synagogue *n* Jewish place of worship and religious instruction.

sync, synch *n Informal* synchronization.

synchromesh *adj* (of a gearbox) having a device that synchronizes the speeds of gears before they engage.

synchronize *v* (of two or more people) perform (an action) at the same time; match (the soundtrack and action of a film) precisely; set (watches) to show the same time. **synchronization** *n* **synchronous, synchronic** *adj* happening or existing at the same time.

syncline *n* downward fold of rock strata in the earth's surface.

syncopate *v Music* stress the weak beats in (a rhythm) instead of the strong ones. **syncopation** *n*

syncope [sing-kop-ee] *n Med* a faint.

syndicate *n* group of people or firms undertaking a joint business project; agency that sells material to several newspapers. ◆ *v* form a syndicate; publish (material) in several newspapers. **syndication** *n*

syndrome *n* combination of symptoms indicating a particular disease; set of characteristics indicating a particular problem.

synod *n* church council.

synonym *n* word with the same

meaning as another. **synonymous** *adj*

synopsis *n, pl* **-ses** summary.

syntax *n Grammar* way in which words are arranged to form phrases and sentences. **syntactic** *adj* **syntactically** *adv*

synthesis *n, pl* **-ses** combination of objects or ideas into a whole; artificial production of a substance. **synthesize** *v* produce by synthesis. **synthesizer** *n* electronic musical instrument producing a range of sounds. **synthetic** *adj* (of a substance) made artificially. **synthetically** *adv*

syphilis *n* serious sexually transmitted disease. **syphilitic** *adj*

syphon *n, v* same as SIPHON.

syringa *n* same as MOCK ORANGE or LILAC.

syringe *n* device for withdrawing or injecting fluids, consisting of a hollow cylinder, a piston, and a hollow needle. ◆ *v* wash out or inject with a syringe.

syrup *n* solution of sugar in water; thick sweet liquid; excessive sentimentality. **syrupy** *adj*

system *n* method or set of methods; scheme of classification or arrangement; network or assembly of parts that form a whole. **systematic** *adj* **systematically** *adv* **systematize** *v* organize using a system. **systematization** *n* **systemic** *adj* affecting the entire animal or body.

systole [siss-tol-ee] *n* regular contraction of the heart as it pumps blood. **systolic** *adj*

T t

t tonne.

T *n* **to a T** in every detail; perfectly.

t. ton.

ta *interj Informal* thank you.

tab *n* small flap or projecting label. **keep tabs on** *Informal* watch closely.

tabard *n* short sleeveless tunic.

Tabasco *n* ® very hot red pepper sauce.

tabby *n, pl* **-bies,** *adj* (cat) with dark stripes on a lighter background.

tabernacle *n* portable shrine of the Israelites; *RC Church* receptacle for the consecrated Host; Christian place of worship not called a church.

tabla *n, pl* **-blas, -bla** one of a pair of Indian drums played with the hands.

table *n* piece of furniture with a flat top supported by legs; arrangement of information in columns. ◆ *v* submit (a motion) for discussion by a meeting; *US* suspend discussion of (a proposal). **tableland** *n* high plateau. **tablespoon** *n* large spoon for serving food. **table tennis** game like tennis played on a table with small bats and a light ball.

tableau [tab-loh] *n, pl* **-leaux, -leaus** silent motionless group arranged to represent some scene.

table d'hôte [tah-bla **dote**] *n, pl* **tables d'hôte,** *adj* (meal) having a set number of dishes at a fixed price.

tablet *n* pill of compressed medicinal substance; flattish cake of soap etc.; inscribed slab of stone etc.

tabloid *n* small-sized newspaper with many photographs and a concise, usu. sensational style.

taboo *n, pl* **-boos** prohibition resulting from religious or social conventions. ◆ *adj* forbidden by a taboo.

tabular *adj* arranged in a table. **tabulate** *v* arrange (information) in a table. **tabulation** *n*

tachograph *n* device for recording the speed and distance travelled by a motor vehicle.

tachometer *n* device for measuring speed, esp. that of a revolving shaft, often fitted to automobiles.

tacit [tass-it] *adj* implied but not spoken. **tacitly** *adv*

taciturn [tass-it-turn] *adj* habitually uncommunicative. **taciturnity** *n*

tack¹ *n* short nail with a large head; long loose stitch. ◆ *v* fasten with tacks; stitch with tacks; append.

tack² *n* course of a ship sailing obliquely into the wind; course of action. ◆ *v* sail into the wind on a zigzag course.

tack³ *n* riding harness for horses.

tackle *n* set of ropes and pulleys for lifting heavy weights; equipment for a particular activity; *Sport* act of tackling an opposing player. ◆ *v* undertake (a task); confront (an opponent); *Sport* attempt to get the ball from (an opposing player).

tacky¹ *adj* **tackier, tackiest** slightly sticky. **tackiness** *n*

tacky² *adj* **tackier, tackiest** *Informal* vulgar and tasteless; shabby.

taco (**tah**-koh) *n, pl* **tacos** *Mexican cookery* tortilla fried until crisp, served with a filling.

tact *n* skill in avoiding giving offence. **tactful** *adj* **tactfully** *adv* **tactless** *adj* **tactlessly** *adv*

tactics *pl n* art of directing military forces in battle; methods or plans to achieve an end. **tactical** *adj* **tactician** *n*

tactile *adj* of or having the sense of touch.

tadpole *n* limbless tailed larva of a frog or toad.

taffeta *n* shiny silk or rayon fabric.

taffrail *n* rail at the stern of a ship.

tag¹ *n* label bearing information; pointed end of a cord or lace; trite quotation. ◆ *v* **tagging, tagged** attach a tag to. **tag along** *v* accompany someone, esp. if uninvited.

tag² *n* children's game where the person being chased becomes the chaser upon being touched. ◆ *v* **tagging, tagged** touch and catch in this game.

tagliatelle *n* pasta in long narrow strips.

tail *n* rear part of an animal's body, usu. forming a flexible appendage; rear or last part or parts of something; *Informal* person employed to follow and spy on another. ◆ *pl* side of a coin without a portrait of a head on it; *Informal* tail coat. ◆ *v* *Informal* follow (someone) secretly. ◆ *adj* at the rear. **turn tail** run away. **tailless** *adj* **tailback** *n* queue of traffic stretching back from an obstruction. **tailboard** *n* removable or hinged rear board on a truck etc. **tail coat** man's coat with a long back split into two below the waist. **tail off, away** *v* diminish gradually. **tailspin** *n* uncontrolled spinning dive of an aircraft. **tailwind** *n* wind coming from the rear.

tailor *n* person who makes men's clothes. ◆ *v* adapt to suit a purpose. **tailor-made** *adj* made by a tailor; perfect for a purpose.

taint *v* spoil with a small amount of decay, contamination, or other bad quality. ◆ *n* something that taints.

take *v* **taking, took, taken** remove from a place; get possession of, esp. dishonestly; carry or accompany;

capture; require (time, resources, or ability); use; assume; write down; accept; subtract or deduct. ◆ *n* one of a series of recordings from which the best will be used. **take place** see PLACE. **taking** *adj* charming. **takings** *pl n* money received by a shop. **take after** *v* look or behave like (a parent etc.). **take against** *v* start to dislike. **take away** *v* subtract. **takeaway** *n Brit* shop or restaurant selling meals for eating elsewhere; meal bought at a takeaway. **take in** *v* understand; make (clothing) smaller; deceive or swindle. **take off** *v* (of an aircraft) leave the ground; *Informal* depart; *Informal* parody. **take-off** *n* act of taking control of a company by buying a large number of its shares. **take up** *v* occupy or fill (space or time); adopt the study or activity of; accept (an offer); shorten (a garment).

talc *n* soft mineral of magnesium silicate; talcum powder. **talcum powder** powder, usu. scented, used to dry or perfume the body.

tale *n* story; malicious piece of gossip.

talent *n* natural ability; ancient unit of weight or money. **talented** *adj*

talisman *n, pl* **-mans** object believed to have magic power. **talismanic** *adj*

talk *v* express ideas or feelings by means of speech; utter; discuss, e.g. *let's talk business*; reveal information; (be able to) speak in a specified language. ◆ *n* speech or lecture. **talker** *n* **talkative** *adj* fond of talking. **talk back** *v* answer impudently. **talking point** something which provokes discussion. **talking-to** *n Informal* reproof.

tall *adj* higher than average; of a specified height. **tall order** difficult task. **tall story** unlikely and probably untrue tale.

tallboy *n* high chest of drawers.

tallow *n* hard animal fat used to make candles.

tally *v* **-lying, -lied** (of two things) correspond. ◆ *n, pl* **-lies** record of a debt or score.

tally-ho *interj* huntsman's cry when the quarry is sighted.

Talmud *n* body of Jewish law. **Talmudic** *adj*

talon *n* bird's hooked claw.

tamarind *n* tropical tree; its acid fruit.

tamarisk *n* evergreen shrub with slender branches and feathery flower clusters.

tambourine *n* percussion instrument like a small drum with jingling metal discs attached.

tame *adj* (of animals) brought under human control; (of animals) not afraid of people; meek or submissive; uninteresting. ◆ *v* make tame. **tamely** *adv* **tamer** *n*

Tamil *n* member of a people of Sri Lanka and S India; their language.

tam-o'-shanter *n* brimless wool cap with a bobble in the centre.

tamp *v* pack down by repeated blows.

tamper *v* (foll. by *with*) interfere.

tampon *n* absorbent plug of cotton batting inserted into the vagina during menstruation.

tan *v* **tanning, tanned** (of skin) go brown from exposure to sunlight; convert (a hide) into leather. ◆ *n* brown colour of tanned skin. ◆ *adj* yellowish-brown. **tannery** *n* place where hides are tanned. **tanner** *n*

tandem *n* bicycle for two riders, one behind the other. **in tandem** together.

tandoor *n* Indian clay oven. **tandoori** *adj* cooked in a tandoor.

tang *n* strong taste or smell; trace or hint. **tangy** *adj*

tangent *n* line that touches a curve without intersecting it; (in trigonometry) ratio of the length of the opposite side to that of the adjacent side of a right-angled triangle. **go off at a tangent** suddenly take a completely different line of thought or action. **tangential** *adj* of a tangent; of superficial relevance only.

tangerine *n* small orange-like fruit of an Asian citrus tree.

tangible *adj* able to be touched; clear and definite. **tangibly** *adv*

tangle *n* confused mass or situation. ◆ *v* twist together in a tangle; (often foll. by *with*) come into conflict.

tango *n, pl* **-gos** S American dance. ◆ *v* dance a tango.

tank *n* container for liquids or gases; armoured fighting vehicle moving on tracks. **tanker** *n* ship or truck for carrying liquid in bulk.

tankard *n* large beer-mug, often with a hinged lid.

tannic acid, tannin *n* vegetable

substance used in tanning.

tansy n, pl **-sies** yellow-flowered plant.

tantalize v torment by showing but withholding something desired. **tantalizing** adj **tantalizingly** adv

tantalus n case in which bottles can be locked with their contents visible.

tantamount adj (foll. by to) equivalent in effect to.

tantrum n childish outburst of temper.

tap¹ v **tapping, tapped** knock lightly and usu. repeatedly. ◆ n light knock. **tap dance** dance in which the feet beat out an elaborate rhythm.

tap² n valve to control the flow of liquid from a pipe or cask. ◆ v **tapping, tapped** listen in on (a telephone) secretly by making an illegal connection; fit a tap to (a pipe etc.); draw off with or as if with a tap. **on tap** Informal readily available; (of beer etc.) drawn from a cask.

tape n narrow long strip of material; string stretched across a race track to mark the finish; recording made on magnetized tape. ◆ v bind or fasten with tape; record on magnetized tape. **have a person, situation taped** Informal have full understanding and control of a person or situation. **tape measure** tape marked off in centimetres or inches for measuring. **tape recorder** device for recording and reproducing sound on magnetized tape. **tapeworm** n long flat parasitic worm living in the intestines of vertebrates.

taper v become narrower towards one end. ◆ n long thin candle; narrowing. **taper off** v become gradually less.

tapestry n, pl **-tries** fabric decorated with coloured woven designs.

tapioca n beadlike starch made from cassava root, used in puddings.

tapir [tape-er] n piglike mammal of tropical America and SE Asia, with a long snout.

tappet n short steel rod in an engine, transferring motion from one part to another.

taproot n main root of a plant, growing straight down.

tar n thick black liquid distilled from coal etc. ◆ v **tarring, tarred** coat with tar.

taramasalata n creamy pink pâté made from fish roe.

tarantella n lively Italian dance; music for this.

tarantula n, pl **-las, -lae** large poisonous hairy spider.

tardy adj **-dier, -diest** slow or late. **tardily** adv **tardiness** n

tare¹ n weight of the wrapping or container of goods; unladen weight of a vehicle.

tare² n type of vetch; Bible weed.

target n object or person a missile is aimed at; goal or objective; object of criticism. ◆ v **-geting, -geted** aim or direct.

tariff n tax levied on imports; list of fixed prices.

Tarmac n ® mixture of tar, bitumen, and crushed stones used for roads etc.; (**t-**) airport runway.

tarn n small mountain lake.

tarnish v make or become stained or less bright; damage or taint. ◆ n discoloration or blemish.

tarot [tarr-oh] n special pack of cards used mainly in fortune-telling. **tarot card**

tarpaulin n (sheet of) heavy waterproof fabric.

tarragon n aromatic herb.

tarry v **-rying, -ried** Old-fashioned linger or delay; stay briefly.

tarsier n monkey-like mammal of the E Indies.

tarsus n, pl **-si** bones of the heel and ankle collectively.

tart¹ n pie or flan with a sweet filling.

tart² adj sharp or bitter. **tartly** adv **tartness** n

tart³ n Informal sexually provocative or promiscuous woman. **tart up** v Informal dress or decorate in a smart or flashy way.

tartan n design of straight lines crossing at right angles, esp. one associated with a Scottish clan; cloth with such a pattern.

tartar¹ n hard deposit on the teeth; brownish-red deposit formed during the fermentation of wine.

tartar² n formidable person.

tartrazine [tar-traz-zeen] n artificial yellow dye used in food etc.

task n (difficult or unpleasant) piece of work to be done. **take to task** criticize or scold. **task force** (military) group formed to carry out a specific task.

taskmaster n person who enforces hard work.

tassel n decorative fringed knot of threads. **tasselled** adj

taste n sense by which the flavour of a substance is distinguished in the mouth; distinctive flavour; brief experience of something; small amount tasted; liking; ability to appreciate what is beautiful or excellent. ◆ v distinguish the taste of (a substance); take a small amount of (something) into the mouth; have a specific taste; experience briefly. **tasteful** adj having or showing good taste. **tastefully** adv **tasteless** adj bland or insipid; showing bad taste. **tastelessly** adv **tasty** adj pleasantly flavoured. **taste bud** small organ on the tongue which perceives flavours.

tat n tatty or tasteless article(s).

tattered adj ragged or torn. **tatters** pl n ragged pieces.

tattle n, v gossip or chatter. **tattletale** n a scandalmonger.

tattoo[1] v **-tooing, -tooed** make (a pattern) on the skin by pricking and staining it with indelible inks. ◆ n pattern so made. **tattooist** n

tattoo[2] n military display or pageant; drumming or tapping.

tatty adj **-tier, -tiest** shabby or worn out. **tattiness** n

taught v past of TEACH.

taunt v tease with jeers. ◆ n jeering remark.

taupe adj brownish-grey.

taut adj drawn tight, tense; showing nervous strain, stressed. **tauten** v make or become taut.

tautology n, pl **-gies** use of words which merely repeat something already stated. **tautological** adj

tavern n Old-fashioned pub.

tawdry adj **-drier, -driest** cheap, showy, and of poor quality. **tawdriness** n

tawny adj yellowish-brown.

tax n compulsory payment levied by a government on income, property, etc. to raise revenue; heavy demand on something. ◆ v levy a tax on; make heavy demands on. **taxable** adj **taxation** n levying of taxes. **taxpayer** n **tax return** statement of personal income for tax purposes.

taxi n (also **taxicab**) automobile with a driver that may be hired to take people to any specified destination. ◆ v **taxiing, taxied** (of an aircraft) run along the ground before taking off or after landing. **taxi rank** place where taxis wait to be hired.

taxidermy n art of stuffing and mounting animal skins to give them a lifelike appearance. **taxidermist** n

taxonomy n classification of plants and animals into groups. **taxonomic** adj **taxonomist** n

TB tuberculosis.

tbs., tbsp. tablespoon(ful).

tea n dried leaves of an Asian bush; drink made by infusing these leaves in boiling water; drink made like tea from other plants; main evening meal; light afternoon meal of tea, cakes, etc. **tea bag** small porous bag of tea leaves. **tea cosy** covering for a teapot to keep the tea warm. **teapot** n container with a lid, spout, and handle for making and serving tea. **teaspoon** n small spoon for stirring tea. **tea towel** towel for drying dishes.

teach v **teaching, taught** tell or show (someone) how to do something; cause to learn or understand; give lessons in (a subject). **teacher** n **teaching** n

teak n very hard wood of an E Indian tree.

teal n kind of small duck.

team n group of people forming one side in a game; group of people or animals working together. **teamster** n driver of team of draft animals; truck driver. **team up** v make or join a team. **teamwork** n cooperative work by a team.

tear[1], **teardrop** n drop of fluid appearing in and falling from the eye. **in tears** weeping. **tearful** adj weeping or about to weep. **tear gas** gas that stings the eyes and causes temporary blindness. **tear-jerker** n Informal excessively sentimental film or book.

tear[2] v **tearing, tore, torn** rip a hole in; rip apart; become ripped; rush. ◆ n hole or split. **tearaway** n wild or unruly person.

tease v make fun of (someone) in a provoking or playful way; separate the fibres of. ◆ n person who teases. **teasing** adj, n

teasel, teazel, teazle n plant with

prickly leaves and flowers.

teat *n* rubber nipple of a feeding bottle; nipple of a breast or udder.

tech *n* Informal technical college.

techie *Informal* ♦ *n* person who is skilled in the use of technology. ♦ *adj* relating to or skilled in the use of technology.

technical *adj* of or specializing in industrial, practical, or mechanical arts and applied sciences; skilled in technical subjects; relating to a particular field; according to the letter of the law; showing technique, e.g. *technical brilliance*. **technically** *adv* **technicality** *n* petty point based on a strict application of rules. **technician** *n* person skilled in a particular technical field. **technical college** higher educational institution with courses in art and technical subjects.

Technicolor *n* ® system of colour photography used for the cinema.

technique *n* method or skill used for a particular task; technical proficiency.

technocracy *n, pl* **-cies** government by technical experts. **technocrat** *n*

technology *n, pl* **-gies** application of practical or mechanical sciences to industry or commerce; sciences applied thus. **technological** *adj* **technologist** *n*

tectonics *pl n* study of the earth's crust and the forces affecting it.

teddy *n, pl* **-dies** teddy bear; combined camisole and knickers. **teddy bear** soft toy bear.

tedious *adj* causing fatigue or boredom. **tediously** *adv* **tedium** *n* monotony.

tee *n* small peg supporting a golf ball when teeing off; area of a golf course from which the first stroke of a hole is made. **tee off** *v* make the first stroke of a hole in golf.

teem *v* abound in; rain heavily.

teenage *adj* of the period of life between the ages of 13 and 19. **teenager** *n* person aged between 13 and 19.

teens *pl n* period of being a teenager.

teepee *n* same as TEPEE.

tee-shirt *n* same as T-SHIRT.

teeter *v* wobble or cause to move unsteadily.

teeth *n* plural of TOOTH.

teethe *v* (of a baby) grow his or her

first teeth. **teething troubles** problems during the early stages of something.

teetotal *adj* drinking no alcohol. **teetotaller** *n*

TEFL Teaching of English as a Foreign Language.

Teflon *n* ® substance used for nonstick coatings on saucepans etc.

tele- *prefix* at or over a distance, e.g. *telescope*; involving television or telephone, e.g. *telesales*.

telecommunications *pl n* communications using telephone, radio, television, etc.

telegram *n* (formerly) message sent by telegraph.

telegraph *n* (formerly) system for sending messages over a distance along a cable. ♦ *v* communicate by telegraph. **telegraphic** *adj* **telegraphist** *n* person who works a telegraph. **telegraphy** *n* science or use of a telegraph.

telekinesis *n* movement of objects by thought or willpower.

telemeter *n* device for recording or measuring a distant event and transmitting the data to a receiver. **telemetry** *n* **telemetric** *adj*

teleology *n* belief that all things have a predetermined purpose. **teleological** *adj*

telepathy *n* direct communication between minds. **telepathic** *adj*

telephone *n* device for transmitting sound over a distance along wires. ♦ *v* call or talk to (a person) by telephone. **telephony** *n* **telephonic** *adj* **telephonist** *n* person operating a telephone switchboard. **telephone booth** kiosk for a public telephone.

telephoto lens *n* camera lens producing a magnified image of a distant object.

teleprinter *n* apparatus like a typewriter for sending and receiving typed messages by wire.

Teleprompter *n* ® device under a television camera enabling a speaker to read the script while appearing to look at the camera.

telesales *pl n* selling of a product or service by telephone.

telescope *n* optical instrument for magnifying distant objects. ♦ *v* shorten by the sliding of each part over the next; shorten by crushing. **telescopic** *adj*

teletext *n* system which shows information and news on subscribers' television screens.

television *n* system of producing a moving image and accompanying sound on a distant screen; device for receiving broadcast signals and converting them into sound and pictures; content of television programmes. **televise** *v* broadcast on television. **televisual** *adj*

teleworking *n* use of home computers, telephones, etc., to enable a person to work from home while maintaining contact with colleagues or customers. **teleworker** *n*

telex *n* international communication service using teleprinters; message sent by telex. ◆ *v* transmit by telex.

tell *v* **telling, told** make known in words; order or instruct; give an account of; discern or distinguish; have an effect; *Informal* reveal secrets. **teller** *n* narrator; bank cashier; person who counts votes. **telling** *adj* having a marked effect. **tell off** *v* reprimand. **telling-off** *n* **telltale** *n* person who reveals secrets. ◆ *adj* revealing.

tellurian *adj* of the earth.

telly *n, pl* **-lies** *Informal* television.

temerity [tim-**merr**-it-tee] *n* boldness or audacity.

temp *Informal* ◆ *n* temporary employee, esp. a secretary. ◆ *v* work as a temp.

temp. temperature; temporary.

temper *n* outburst of anger; tendency to become angry; calm mental condition, e.g. *I lost my temper*; frame of mind. ◆ *v* make less extreme; strengthen or toughen (metal).

tempera *n* painting medium of pigment and egg yolk.

temperament *n* person's character or disposition. **temperamental** *adj* having changeable moods; of temperament; *Informal* erratic and unreliable. **temperamentally** *adv*

temperate *adj* (of climate) not extreme; self-restrained or moderate. **temperance** *n* moderation; abstinence from alcohol.

temperature *n* degree of heat or cold; *Informal* abnormally high body temperature.

tempest *n* violent storm. **tempestuous** *adj* violent or stormy. **tempestuously** *adv*

template *n* pattern used to cut out shapes accurately.

temple[1] *n* building for worship.

temple[2] *n* region on either side of the forehead.

tempo *n, pl* **-pos, -pi** speed of a piece of music; rate or pace.

temporal *adj* of time; secular rather than spiritual; of the temple(s) of the head.

temporary *adj* lasting only for a short time. **temporarily** *adv*

temporize *v* gain time by negotiation or evasiveness; adapt to circumstances. **temporization** *n*

tempt *v* (try to) entice (a person) to do something wrong; risk provoking, e.g. *you're tempting fate*. **tempter, temptress** *n* **temptation** *n* tempting; tempting thing. **tempting** *adj* attractive or inviting.

ten *adj, n* one more than nine. **tenth** *adj, n* (of) number ten in a series.

tenable *adj* able to be held or maintained.

tenacious *adj* holding fast; stubborn. **tenacity** *n*

tenant *n* person who rents land or a building. **tenancy** *n*

tench *n, pl* **tench** freshwater game fish.

tend[1] *v* be inclined; go in the direction of. **tendency** *n* inclination to act in a certain way. **tendentious** *adj* biased.

tend[2] *v* take care of.

tender[1] *adj* not tough; gentle and affectionate; vulnerable or sensitive. **tenderly** *adv* **tenderness** *n* **tenderize** *v* soften (meat) by pounding or treatment with a special substance. **tenderizer** *n*

tender[2] *v* offer; make a tender. ◆ *n* formal offer to supply goods or services at a stated cost. **legal tender** currency that must, by law, be accepted as payment.

tender[3] *n* small boat that brings supplies to a larger ship in a port; carriage for fuel and water attached to a steam locomotive.

tendon *n* sinew attaching a muscle to a bone.

tendril *n* slender stem by which a climbing plant clings.

tenement *n* building divided into several apartments.

tenet [ten-nit] *n* doctrine or belief.

tennis *n* game in which players use rackets to hit a ball back and forth over a net.

tenon *n* projecting end on a piece of wood fitting into a slot in another.

tenor *n* (singer with) the second highest male voice; general meaning. ◆ *adj* (of a voice or instrument) between alto and baritone.

tenpin bowling *n* game in which players try to knock over ten skittles by rolling a ball at them.

tense[1] *n* form of a verb showing the time of action.

tense[2] *adj* stretched tight; emotionally strained. ◆ *v* make or become tense. **tensile** *adj* of tension. **tension** *n* degree of stretching; emotional strain; suspense; *Electricity* voltage.

tent *n* portable canvas shelter.

tentacle *n* flexible organ of many invertebrates, used for grasping, feeding, etc.

tentative *adj* provisional or experimental; cautious or hesitant. **tentatively** *adv*

tenterhooks *pl n* **on tenterhooks** in anxious suspense.

tenuous *adj* slight or flimsy. **tenuously** *adv* **tenuousness** *n*

tenure *n* (period of) the holding of an office or position.

tepee [tee-pee] *n* N American Indian cone-shaped tent.

tepid *adj* slightly warm; half-hearted.

tequila *n* Mexican alcoholic drink.

tercentenary *adj, n, pl* **-naries** (of) a three hundredth anniversary.

term *n* word or expression; fixed period; period of the year when a school etc. is open or a lawcourt holds sessions. ◆ *pl* conditions; mutual relationship. ◆ *v* name or designate.

terminal *adj* at or being an end; (of an illness) ending in death. ◆ *n* terminating point or place; point where current enters or leaves an electrical device; keyboard and VDU having input and output links with a computer; place where people or vehicles begin or end a journey. **terminally** *adv*

terminate *v* bring or come to an end. **termination** *n*

terminology *n, pl* **-gies** technical terms relating to a subject. **terminological** *adj*

terminus *n, pl* **-ni, -nuses** final point; railway or bus station at the end of a line.

termite *n* white antlike insect destructive to timber.

tern *n* gull-like sea bird.

ternary *adj* consisting of three parts.

Terpsichorean *adj* of dancing.

terrace *n* row of houses built as one block; paved area next to a building; level tier cut out of a hill. ◆ *pl* (also **terracing**) tiered area in a stadium where spectators stand. ◆ *v* form into or provide with a terrace.

terracotta *adj, n* (made of) brownish-red unglazed pottery. ◆ *adj* brownish-red.

terra firma *n* dry land or solid ground.

terrain *n* area of ground, esp. with reference to its physical character.

terrapin *n* kind of aquatic tortoise.

terrarium *n, pl* **-rariums, -raria** enclosed container for small plants or animals.

terrazzo *n, pl* **-zos** floor of marble chips set in mortar and polished.

terrestrial *adj* of the earth; of or living on land.

terrible *adj* very serious; *Informal* very bad; causing fear. **terribly** *adv*

terrier *n* any of various breeds of small active dog.

terrific *adj* great or intense; *Informal* excellent.

terrify *v* **-fying, -fied** fill with fear. **terrifying** *adj*

terrine [terr-reen] *n* pâté or similar food; earthenware dish with a lid.

territory *n, pl* **-ries** district; area under the control of a particular government; area inhabited and defended by an animal; area of knowledge or experience. **territorial** *adj*

terror *n* great fear; terrifying person or thing; *Informal* troublesome person or thing. **terrorism** *n* use of violence and intimidation to achieve political ends. **terrorist** *n, adj* **terrorize** *v* force or oppress by fear or violence.

terry *n* fabric with the loops in its pile uncut.

terse adj concise; curt. **tersely** adv

tertiary [tur-shar-ee] adj third in degree, order, etc.

Terylene n ® synthetic polyester yarn or fabric.

tessellated adj paved or inlaid with a mosaic of small tiles.

test v try out to ascertain the worth, capability, or endurance of; carry out an examination on. ◆ n critical examination; method or standard of judgment; test match. **testing** adj test **case** lawsuit that establishes a precedent. **test match** one of a series of international cricket or rugby matches. **test tube** narrow cylindrical glass vessel used in scientific experiments. **test-tube baby** baby that is conceived outside the mother's body.

testament n Law will; proof or tribute; (T-) one of the two main divisions of the Bible. **testamentary** adj

testate adj having left a valid will. **testacy** n **testator** [test-tay-tor], (fem) **testatrix** [test-tay-triks] n maker of a will.

testicle n either of the two male reproductive glands.

testify v **-fying, -fied** give evidence under oath; (foll. by to) be evidence (of).

testimony n, pl **-nies** declaration of truth or fact; evidence given under oath. **testimonial** n recommendation of the worth of a person or thing; tribute for services or achievement.

testis n, pl **-tes** testicle.

testosterone n male sex hormone secreted by the testes.

testy adj **-tier, -tiest** irritable or touchy. **testily** adv **testiness** n

tetanus n acute infectious disease producing muscular spasms and convulsions.

tête-à-tête n, pl **-têtes, -tête** private conversation.

tether n rope or chain for tying an animal to a spot. ◆ v tie up with rope. **at the end of one's tether** at the limit of one's endurance.

tetrahedron [tet-ra-heed-ron] n, pl **-drons, -dra** Geom solid figure with four faces.

tetralogy n, pl **-gies** series of four related works.

Teutonic [tew-tonn-ik] adj of or like the (ancient) Germans.

text n main body of a book as distinct from illustrations etc.; passage of the Bible as the subject of a sermon; novel or play needed for a course. **textual** adj **textbook** n standard book on a particular subject. ◆ adj perfect, e.g. a textbook landing.

text n 1 text message. ◆ v 2 send a text message to (someone). **text message** message sent in text form, esp. by means of a cell phone.

textile n fabric or cloth, esp. woven.

texture n structure, feel, or consistency. **textured** adj **textural** adj

thalidomide [thal-lid-oh-mide] n drug formerly used as a sedative, but found to cause abnormalities in developing fetuses.

thallium n highly toxic metallic element.

than conj used to introduce the second element of a comparison.

thane n Hist Anglo-Saxon or medieval Scottish nobleman.

thank v express gratitude to; hold responsible. **thanks** pl n words of gratitude. ◆ interj (also **thank you**) polite expression of gratitude. **thanks to** because of. **thankful** adj grateful. **thankless** adj unrewarding or unappreciated. **Thanksgiving Day** public holiday on second Monday of October in Canada and fourth Thursday in November in the US.

that adj, pron used to refer to something already mentioned or familiar, or further away. ◆ conj used to introduce a noun clause. ◆ pron used to introduce a relative clause.

thatch n roofing material of reeds or straw. ◆ v roof (a house) with reeds or straw. **thatcher** n

thaw v make or become unfrozen; become more relaxed or friendly. ◆ n thawing; weather causing snow or ice to melt.

the adj the definite article.

theatre n place where plays etc. are performed; drama and acting in general; hospital operating room. **theatrical** adj of the theatre; exaggerated or affected. **theatricals** pl n (amateur) dramatic performances. **theatrically** adv **theatricality** n

thee pron Obs objective form of THOU.

theft n stealing.

their adj of or associated with them. **theirs** pron (thing or person) belonging to them.

theism [**thee**-iz-zum] n belief in the creation of the universe by one God. **theist** n, adj **theistic** adj

them pron refers to people or things other than the speaker or those addressed. **themselves** pron emphatic and reflexive form of THEY or THEM.

theme n main idea or subject being discussed; recurring melodic figure in music. **thematic** adj **theme park** leisure area based on a single theme.

then adv at that time; after that; that being so.

thence adv from that place or time; therefore.

theocracy n, pl -cies government by a god or priests. **theocratic** adj

theodolite [thee-**odd**-oh-lite] n surveying instrument for measuring angles.

theology n, pl -gies study of religions and religious beliefs. **theologian** n **theological** adj **theologically** adv

theorem n proposition that can be proved by reasoning.

theory n, pl -ries set of ideas to explain something; abstract knowledge or reasoning; idea or opinion; ideal or hypothetical situation. **theoretical** adj based on theory rather than practice or fact. **theoretically** adv **theorist** n **theorize** v form theories, speculate.

theosophy n religious or philosophical system claiming to be based on intuitive insight into the divine nature. **theosophical** adj

therapy n, pl -pies curing treatment. **therapist** n **therapeutic** [ther-rap-**pew**-tik] adj curing. **therapeutics** n art of curing.

there adv in or to that place; in that respect. **thereby** adv by that means. **therefore** adv consequently, that being so. **thereupon** adv immediately after that.

therm n unit of heat. **thermal** adj of heat; hot or warm; (of clothing) retaining heat. ♦ n rising current of warm air.

thermionic valve n electronic valve in which electrons are emitted from a heated rather than a cold cathode.

thermocouple n device for measuring heat, consisting of two wires of different metals joined at both ends.

thermodynamics pl n scientific study of the relationship between heat and other forms of energy.

thermometer n instrument for measuring temperature.

thermonuclear adj involving nuclear fusion.

thermoplastic adj (of a plastic) softening when heated and resetting on cooling.

thermos n double-walled flask with a vacuum between the walls that keeps drinks hot or cold.

thermosetting adj (of a plastic) remaining hard when heated.

thermostat n device for automatically regulating temperature. **thermostatic** adj **thermostatically** adv

thesaurus [thiss-**sore**-uss] n, pl -ri, -ruses book containing lists of synonyms and related words.

these adj, pron plural of THIS.

thesis n, pl **theses** written work submitted for a degree; doctrine maintained in argument.

Thespian adj of the theatre. ♦ n actor or actress.

they pron refers to: people or things other than the speaker or people addressed; people in general; Informal he or she.

thiamine n vitamin found in the outer coat of rice and other grains.

thick adj of great or specified extent from one side to the other; having a dense consistency; full of; Informal stupid or insensitive; (of a voice) throaty; Informal friendly. **a bit thick** Informal unfair or unreasonable. **the thick** busiest or most intense part. **thickly** adv **thickness** n state of being thick; dimension through an object; layer. **thicken** v make or become thick or thicker. **thickset** adj stocky in build; set closely together.

thicket n dense growth of small trees.

thief n, pl **thieves** person who steals. **thieve** v steal. **thieving** adj, n

thigh n upper part of the human leg.

thimble n cap protecting the end of the finger when sewing.

thin adj thinner, thinnest not thick; slim or lean; sparse or meagre; of low

density; poor or unconvincing. ◆ v
thinning, thinned make or become
thin. **thinly** adv **thinness** n

thine pron Obs (something) of or
associated with you (thou).

thing n material object; object, fact, or
idea considered as a separate entity;
Informal obsession. ◆ pl possessions,
clothes, etc.

think v **thinking, thought** consider,
judge, or believe; make use of the
mind; be considerate enough or
remember to do something. **thinker** n
thinking adj, n **think-tank** n group of
experts studying specific problems.
think up v invent or devise.

third adj of number three in a series;
rated or graded below the second
level. ◆ n one of three equal parts.
third degree violent interrogation.
third party (applying to) a person
involved by chance or only incidentally
in legal proceedings, an accident, etc.
Third World developing countries of
Africa, Asia, and Latin America.

thirst n desire to drink; craving or
yearning. ◆ v feel thirst. **thirsty** adj
thirstily adv

thirteen adj, n three plus ten.
thirteenth adj, n

thirty adj, n three times ten. **thirtieth**
adj, n

this adj, pron used to refer to a thing
or person nearby or just mentioned.
◆ adj used to refer to the present time,
e.g. this morning.

thistle n prickly plant with dense
flower heads.

thither adv Obs to or towards that
place.

thong n thin strip of leather etc;
skimpy article of underwear that leaves
the buttocks bare.

thorax n, pl **thoraxes, thoraces** part
of the body between the neck and the
abdomen. **thoracic** adj

thorium n radioactive metallic
element.

thorn n prickle on a plant; bush with
thorns. **thorn in one's side**, flesh
source of irritation. **thorny** adj

thorough adj careful or methodical;
complete. **thoroughly** adv
thoroughness n **thoroughbred** n, adj
(animal) of pure breed. **thoroughfare**
n way through from one place to
another.

those adj, pron plural of THAT.

thou pron Obs singular form of YOU.

though conj despite the fact that.
◆ adv nevertheless.

thought v past of THINK. ◆ n thinking;
concept or idea; ideas typical of a time
or place; consideration; intention or
expectation. **thoughtful** adj
considerate; showing careful thought;
pensive or reflective. **thoughtless** adj
inconsiderate.

thousand adj, n ten hundred; large
but unspecified number. **thousandth**
adj, n (of) number one thousand in a
series.

thrall, thraldom n state of being in
the power of another person.

thrash v beat, esp. with a stick or
whip; defeat soundly; move about
wildly; thresh. **thrashing** n severe
beating. **thrash out** v solve by
thorough argument.

thread n fine strand or yarn; spiral
ridge on a screw, nut, or bolt; unifying
theme. ◆ v pass thread through; fit (a
film, tape, etc.) into a machine; pick
(one's way etc.). **threadbare** adj (of
fabric) with the nap worn off;
hackneyed; shabby.

threat n declaration of intent to harm;
dangerous person or thing. **threaten** v
make or be a threat to; be a menacing
indication of.

three adj, n one more than two.
threefold adj, adv (having) three
times as many or as much. **threesome**
n group of three. **three-dimensional,
3-D** adj having three dimensions.
three-ply adj (of wood) having three
layers; (of wool) having three strands.

threnody n, pl **-dies** lament or speech
for the dead.

thresh v beat (wheat etc.) to separate
the grain from the husks and straw;
move about wildly.

threshold n bar forming the bottom
of a doorway; entrance; starting point;
point at which a stimulus produces a
response.

threw v past tense of THROW.

thrice adv Lit three times.

thrift n wisdom and caution with
money; low-growing plant with pink
flowers. **thrifty** adj **thriftily** adv
thriftiness n **thriftless** adj

thrill n sudden feeling of excitement.
◆ v (cause to) feel a thrill. **thrilling** adj

thriller n book, film, etc. with an atmosphere of mystery or suspense.

thrive v **thriving, thrived** or **throve, thrived** or **thriven.** grow well; flourish or prosper.

throat n front of the neck; passage from the mouth and nose to the stomach and lungs. **throaty** adj (of the voice) hoarse.

throb v **throbbing, throbbed** pulsate repeatedly; vibrate rhythmically. ◆ n throbbing.

throes pl n violent pangs or pains. **in the throes of** Informal struggling with difficulty with.

thrombosis n, pl **-ses** forming of a clot in a blood vessel or the heart.

throne n ceremonial seat of a monarch or bishop; sovereign power.

throng n, v crowd.

throstle n song-thrush.

throttle n device controlling the amount of fuel entering an engine. ◆ v strangle.

through prep from end to end or side to side of; because of; during. ◆ adj finished; (of transport) going directly to a place; (on a telephone line) connected. **through and through** completely. **throughout** adv, prep in every part (of). **throughput** n amount of material processed.

throve v past tense of THRIVE.

throw v **throwing, threw, thrown** hurl through the air; move or put suddenly or carelessly; bring into a specified state, esp. suddenly; direct (a look, light, etc.); give (a party); project (the voice) so that it seems to come from elsewhere; shape (pottery) on a wheel; move (a switch, lever, etc.); Informal baffle or disconcert. ◆ n throwing; distance thrown. **throwaway** adj designed to be discarded after use; done or said casually. **throwback** n person or thing that reverts to an earlier type. **throw up** v vomit.

thrush[1] n brown songbird.

thrush[2] n fungal disease of the mouth or vagina.

thrust v **thrusting, thrust** push forcefully; stab. ◆ n lunge or stab; force or power; intellectual or emotional drive.

thud n dull heavy sound. ◆ v **thudding, thudded** make such a sound.

thug n violent criminal. **thuggery** n **thuggish** adj

thumb n short thick finger set apart from the others. ◆ v touch or handle with the thumb; flick through (a book or magazine); signal with the thumb for (a lift in a vehicle). **thumbtack** n short tack with a smooth broad head.

thump n (sound of) a dull heavy blow. ◆ v strike heavily.

thunder n loud noise accompanying lightning. ◆ v rumble with thunder; shout; move fast, heavily, and noisily. **thunderous** adj **thundery** adj **thunderbolt** n lightning flash; something sudden and unexpected. **thunderclap** n peal of thunder. **thunderstruck** adj amazed.

Thursday n fifth day of the week.

thus adv in this way; therefore.

thwack v, n whack.

thwart v foil or frustrate. ◆ n seat across a boat.

thy adj Obs of or associated with you (thou). **thyself** pron Obs emphatic form of THOU.

thyme [time] n aromatic herb.

thymus n, pl **-muses, -mi** small gland at the base of the neck.

thyroid adj, n (of) a gland in the neck controlling body growth.

Ti Chem titanium.

tiara n semicircular jewelled headdress.

tibia n, pl **tibiae, tibias** inner bone of the lower leg. **tibial** adj

tic n spasmodic muscular twitch.

tick[1] n mark (✓) used to check off or indicate the correctness of something; recurrent tapping sound, as of a clock; Informal moment. ◆ v mark with a tick; make a ticking sound. **tick off** v mark off; reprimand. **tick over** v (of an engine) idle; function smoothly. **ticktack** n bookmakers' sign language.

tick[2] n tiny bloodsucking parasitic animal.

tick[3] n Informal credit or account.

ticket n card or paper entitling the holder to admission, travel, etc.; label; official notification of a parking or traffic offence; declared policy of a political party. ◆ v **-eting, -eted** attach or issue a ticket to.

ticking n strong cotton fabric used for mattress covers.

tickle v touch or stroke (a person) to

produce laughter; please or amuse; itch or tingle. ◆ n tickling. **ticklish** adj sensitive to tickling; requiring care or tact.

tiddler n Informal very small fish.

tiddly adj tiny; Informal slightly drunk.

tiddlywinks pl n game in which players try to flip small plastic discs into a cup.

tide n rise and fall of the sea caused by the gravitational pull of the sun and moon; current caused by this; widespread feeling or tendency. **tidal** adj **tidal wave** huge wave produced by an earthquake. **tide over** v help (someone) temporarily.

tidings pl n news.

tidy adj -dier, -diest neat and orderly; Informal considerable. ◆ v -dying, -died put in order. **tidily** adv **tidiness** n

tie v tying, tied fasten or be fastened with string, rope, etc.; make (a knot or bow) in (something); restrict or limit; score the same as another competitor. ◆ n bond or fastening; long narrow piece of material worn knotted round the neck; drawn game or contest.

tier n row, layer, or level.

tiff n petty quarrel.

tiger n large yellow-and-black striped Asian cat. **tigress** n female tiger; fierce woman.

tight adj stretched or drawn taut; closely fitting; secure or firm; cramped; Informal mean; Informal drunk; (of a match or game) very close. **tights** pl n one-piece clinging garment covering the body from the waist to the feet. **tightly** adv **tighten** v make or become tight or tighter. **tightrope** n rope stretched taut on which acrobats perform.

tike n Informal same as TYKE.

tikka adj Indian cookery marinated in spices and dry-roasted, e.g. chicken tikka.

tilde n accent (~) used in Spanish to indicate that the letter 'n' is to be pronounced in a particular way.

tile n flat piece of ceramic, plastic, etc. used to cover a roof, floor, or wall. ◆ v cover with tiles. **tiled** adj **tiling** n tiles collectively.

till[1] prep, conj until.

till[2] v cultivate (land). **tillage** n **tiller** n

till[3] n drawer for money, usu. in a cash register.

tiller n lever used to move the a rudder of a boat when steering.

tilt v slant at an angle; compete against in a jousting contest; aim or thrust with a lance. ◆ n slope; Hist jousting contest. **at full tilt** at full speed or force.

timber n wood as a building material; trees collectively; wooden beam in the frame of a house, boat, etc. **timbered** adj **timber line** geographical limit beyond which trees will not grow.

timbre [tam-bra] n distinctive quality of sound of a voice or instrument.

time n past, present, and future as a continuous whole; specific point in time; unspecified interval; period with specific features; instance; occasion; tempo; Slang imprisonment. ◆ v note the time taken by; choose a time for. **timeless** adj unaffected by time; eternal. **timely** adj at the appropriate time. **time-honoured** adj sanctioned by custom. **time-lag** n period between cause and effect. **timepiece** n watch or clock. **timeserver** n person who changes his or her views to gain support or favour. **time sharing** system of part ownership of a holiday property for a specified period each year; system enabling users at different terminals of a computer to use it at the same time. **timetable** n plan showing the times when something takes place, the departure and arrival times of trains or buses, etc.

timid adj easily frightened; shy, not bold. **timidly** adv **timidity** n **timorous** [tim-mor-uss] adj timid.

timpani [tim-pan-ee] pl n set of kettledrums. **timpanist** n

tin n soft metallic element; Brit airtight metal container. **tinned** adj Brit (of food) preserved by being sealed in a tin. **tinny** adj (of sound) thin and metallic. **tinpot** adj Informal worthless or unimportant.

tincture n medicinal extract in a solution of alcohol.

tinder n dry easily-burning material used to start a fire. **tinderbox** n

tine n prong of a fork or antler.

ting n high metallic sound, as of a small bell.

tinge n slight tint; trace. ◆ v **tingeing**, **tinged** give a slight tint or trace to.

tingle *v, n* (feel) a prickling or stinging sensation.

tinker *n* travelling mender of pots and pans; *Scot & Irish* Gypsy; tinkering. ◆ *v* fiddle with (an engine etc.) in an attempt to repair it.

tinkle *v* ring with a high tinny sound like a small bell. ◆ *n* tinkling.

tinsel *n* decorative metallic strips or threads; anything cheap and gaudy.

tint *n* (pale) shade of a colour; dye for the hair; trace. ◆ *v* give a tint to.

tiny *adj* **tinier, tiniest** very small.

tip¹ *n* narrow or pointed end of anything; small piece forming an end. ◆ *v* **tipping, tipped** put a tip on.

tip² *n* money given in return for service; helpful hint or warning; piece of inside information. ◆ *v* **tipping, tipped** give a tip to. **tipster** *n* person who sells tips about races.

tip³ *Brit* ◆ *v* **tipping, tipped** tilt or overturn; dump (garbage). ◆ *n* garbage dump.

tippet *n* piece of fur worn as a scarf.

tipple *v* drink (alcohol) habitually, esp. in small quantities. ◆ *n* drink. **tippler** *n*

tipsy *adj* **-sier, -siest** slightly drunk.

tiptoe *v* **-toeing, -toed** walk quietly with the heels off the ground.

tiptop *adj* of the highest quality.

tirade *n* long angry speech.

tire¹ *v* reduce the energy of, as by exertion; weary or bore. **tired** *adj* weary; hackneyed or stale. **tiring** *adj* **tireless** *adj* not tiring easily. **tiresome** *adj* boring and irritating.

tire² *n* rubber ring, usu. inflated, over the rim of a vehicle's wheel to grip the road.

tissue *n* substance of an animal body or plant; piece of thin soft paper used as a handkerchief etc.; interwoven series, e.g. *a tissue of lies.*

tit¹ *n* any of various small songbirds.

tit² *n* *Slang* female breast.

titanic *adj* huge.

titanium *n* strong light metallic element used to make alloys.

titbit *n* tasty piece of food; pleasing scrap of scandal.

tit for tat *n* equivalent given in retaliation.

tithe *n* esp. formerly, one tenth of one's income or produce paid to the church as a tax. ◆ *v* charge or pay a tithe.

titillate *v* excite or stimulate pleasurably. **titillating** *adj* **titillation** *n*

titivate *v* smarten up. **titivation** *n*

title *n* name of a book, film, etc.; name signifying rank or position; formal designation, such as *Mrs*; *Sport* championship; *Law* legal right of possession. **titled** *adj* aristocratic. **title deed** legal document of ownership.

titter *v* laugh in a suppressed way. ◆ *n* suppressed laugh.

tittle-tattle *n, v* gossip.

titular *adj* of a title; in name only.

tizzy *n, pl* **-zies** *Informal* confused or agitated state.

TNT *n* trinitrotoluene, a powerful explosive.

to *prep* towards; as far as; used to mark the indirect object or infinitive of a verb; used to indicate equality or comparison; before the hour of. ◆ *adv* to a closed position, e.g. *pull the door to.* **to and fro** back and forth.

toad *n* animal like a large frog. **toady** *n, pl* **toadies** ingratiating person. ◆ *v* **toadying, toadied** be ingratiating. **toadstool** *n* poisonous fungus like a mushroom.

toast *n* slice of bread browned by heat; tribute or proposal of health or success marked by people raising glasses and drinking together; person or thing so honoured. ◆ *v* brown bread by heat; drink a toast to; warm or be warmed. **toaster** *n* electrical device for toasting bread.

tobacco *n, pl* **-cos, -coes** plant with large leaves dried for smoking. **tobacconist** *n* person or shop selling tobacco, cigarettes, etc.

toboggan *n* narrow sledge for sliding over snow. ◆ *v* **-ganing, -ganed** ride a toboggan.

toby jug *n* mug in the form of a stout seated man.

toccata [tok-kah-ta] *n* rapid piece of music for a keyboard instrument.

tocsin *n* alarm signal or bell.

today *n* this day; the present age. ◆ *adv* on this day; nowadays.

toddle *v* walk with short unsteady steps. **toddler** *n* child beginning to walk.

toddy *n, pl* **-dies** sweetened drink of spirits and hot water.

to-do *n, pl* **-dos** *Informal* fuss or

commotion.

toe n digit of the foot; part of a shoe or sock covering the toes. ◆ v **toeing, toed** touch or kick with the toe. **toe the line** conform. **toerag** n Slang contemptible person.

toff n Brit slang well-dressed or upper-class person.

toffee n chewy candy made of boiled sugar.

tofu n soft food made from soya-bean curd.

tog n unit for measuring the insulating power of duvets. ◆ pl Informal clothes.

toga [toe-ga] n garment worn by citizens of ancient Rome.

together adv in company; simultaneously. ◆ adj Informal organized.

toggle n small bar-shaped button inserted through a loop for fastening; switch used to turn a machine or computer function on or off.

toil n hard work. ◆ v work hard; progress with difficulty. **toilsome** adj requiring hard work.

toilet n (room with) a bowl connected to a drain for receiving and disposing of urine and feces; washing and dressing. **toiletry** n, pl **-ries** object or cosmetic used to clean or groom oneself. **toilet water** light perfume.

token n sign or symbol; memento; disc used as money in a slot machine; voucher exchangeable for goods of a specified value. ◆ adj nominal or slight. **tokenism** n policy of making only a token effort, esp. to comply with a law.

told v past of TELL.

tolerate v put up with; permit. **toleration** n **tolerable** adj bearable; Informal quite good. **tolerably** adv **tolerance** n acceptance of other people's rights to their own opinions or actions; ability to endure something. **tolerant** adj **tolerantly** adv **toleration** n

toll[1] v ring (a bell) slowly and regularly, esp. to announce a death. ◆ n tolling.

toll[2] n charge for the use of a bridge or road; total loss or damage from a disaster.

tom n male cat.

tomahawk n fighting axe of the N American Indians.

tomato n, pl **-toes** red fruit used in salads and as a vegetable.

tomb n grave; monument over a grave. **tombstone** n gravestone.

tombola n lottery with tickets drawn from a revolving drum.

tomboy n girl who acts or dresses like a boy.

tome n large heavy book.

tomfoolery n foolish behaviour.

Tommy gun n light sub-machine-gun.

tomorrow adv, n (on) the day after today; (in) the future.

tom-tom n drum beaten with the hands.

ton n unit of weight equal to 2000 lbs or 907 kg (**long ton**) or, in Britain, 2240 lbs or 1016 kg (**short ton**). **metric ton** same as TONNE. **tonnage** n weight capacity of a ship.

tone n sound with reference to its pitch, volume, etc.; Music (also **whole tone**) interval of two semitones; quality of a colour; general character; healthy bodily condition. ◆ v give tone to; harmonize (with). **tonal** adj Music written in a key. **tonality** n **toneless** adj **tone-deaf** adj unable to perceive subtle differences in pitch. **tone down** v make or become more moderate.

tongs pl n large pincers for grasping and lifting.

tongue n muscular organ in the mouth, used in speaking and tasting; animal tongue as food; language; flap of leather on a shoe; thin projecting strip.

tonic n medicine to improve body tone; Music first note of a scale. ◆ adj invigorating. **tonic water** mineral water containing quinine.

tonight adv, n (in or during) the night or evening of this day.

tonne [tunn] n unit of weight equal to 1000 kg.

tonsil n small gland in the throat. **tonsillectomy** n surgical removal of the tonsils. **tonsillitis** n inflammation of the tonsils.

tonsure n shaving of all or the top of the head as a religious or monastic practice; part shaved.

too adv also; to excess; extremely.

took v past tense of TAKE.

tool n implement used by hand; person used by another to perform unpleasant or dishonourable tasks. ◆ v work on with a tool; equip with tools.

toonie, twonie n *Informal* Canadian two-dollar coin.

toot n short hooting sound. ◆ v (cause to) make such a sound.

tooth n, pl **teeth** bonelike projection in the jaws of most vertebrates for biting and chewing; toothlike prong or point. **sweet tooth** see SWEET. **toothless** adj **toothpaste** n paste used to clean the teeth. **toothpick** n small stick for removing scraps of food from between the teeth.

top[1] n highest point or part; lid or cap; highest rank; garment for the upper part of the body. ◆ adj at or of the top. ◆ v **topping, topped** form a top on; be at the top of; exceed or surpass. **topping** n sauce or garnish for food. **topless** adj (of a costume or woman) with no covering for the breasts. **topmost** adj highest or best. **top brass** most important officers or leaders. **top-dress** v spread fertilizer on the surface of the land. **top-dressing** n **top hat** man's tall cylindrical hat. **top-heavy** adj unstable through being overloaded at the top. **top-notch** adj excellent, first-class. **topsoil** n surface layer of soil.

top[2] n toy which spins on a pointed base.

topaz [toe-pazz] n semiprecious stone in various colours.

tope[1] v drink (alcohol) regularly.

tope[2] n small European shark.

topee, topi [toe-pee] n lightweight pith hat.

topiary [tope-yar-ee] n art of trimming trees and bushes into decorative shapes. **topiarist** n

topic n subject of a conversation, book, etc. **topical** adj relating to current events. **topicality** n

topography n, pl **-phies** (science of describing) the surface features of a place. **topographer** n **topographic** adj

topology n geometry of the properties of a shape which are unaffected by continuous distortion. **topological** adj

topple v (cause to) fall over; overthrow (a government etc.).

topsy-turvy adj upside down; in confusion.

toque [toke] n small round hat.

tor n high rocky hill.

Torah n body of traditional Jewish teaching.

torch n burning brand carried as a light; *Brit* flashlight. ◆ v *Slang* set fire to deliberately.

tore v past tense of TEAR[2].

toreador [torr-ee-a-dor] n bullfighter.

torment v cause (someone) great suffering; tease cruelly. ◆ n great suffering; source of suffering. **tormentor** n

torn v past participle of TEAR[2].

tornado n, pl **-does, -dos** violent whirlwind.

torpedo n, pl **-does** self-propelled underwater missile. ◆ v **-doing, -doed** attack or destroy with or as if with torpedoes.

torpid adj sluggish and inactive. **torpidity** n **torpor** n torpid state.

torque [tork] n force causing rotation; Celtic necklace or armband of twisted metal.

torrent n rushing stream; downpour. **torrential** adj (of rain) very heavy.

torrid adj very hot and dry; highly emotional.

torsion n twisting.

torso n, pl **-sos** trunk of the human body; statue of a nude human trunk.

tort n *Law* civil wrong or injury for which damages may be claimed.

tortilla n thin Mexican pancake.

tortoise n slow-moving land reptile with a dome-shaped shell. **tortoiseshell** n mottled brown shell of a turtle, used for making ornaments. ◆ adj having brown, orange, and black markings.

tortuous adj winding or twisting; not straightforward.

torture v cause (someone) severe pain or mental anguish. ◆ n severe physical or mental pain; torturing. **torturer** n

Tory n, pl **Tories** member or supporter of the Progressive Conservative Party. ◆ adj of Tories. **Toryism** n

toss v throw lightly; fling or be flung about; (of a horse) throw (its rider); coat (food) by gentle stirring or mixing; throw up (a coin) to decide between alternatives by guessing which side will land uppermost. ◆ n tossing. **toss up** v toss a coin. **toss-up** n even chance or risk.

tot[1] *n* small child; small drink of spirits.

tot[2] *v* **totting, totted. tot up** add (numbers) together.

total *n* whole, esp. a sum of parts. ◆ *adj* complete; of or being a total. ◆ *v* **totalling, totalled** amount to; add up. **totally** *adv* **totality** *n* **totalizator** *n* machine operating a betting system in which money is paid out to the winners in proportion to their stakes.

totalitarian *adj* of a dictatorial one-party government. **totalitarianism** *n*

tote[1] *n* short for TOTALIZATOR.

tote[2] *v* haul or carry.

totem *n* tribal badge or emblem. **totem pole** post carved or painted with totems by N American Indians on the Pacific coast.

totter *v* move unsteadily; be about to fall.

toucan *n* large-billed tropical American bird.

touch *n* sense by which an object's qualities are perceived when they come into contact with part of the body; gentle tap, push, or caress; small amount; characteristic style; detail. ◆ *v* come into contact with; tap, feel, or stroke; affect; move emotionally; eat or drink; refer to in passing; equal or match; *Slang* ask for money. **touch and go** risky or critical. **touched** *adj* emotionally moved; slightly mad. **touching** *adj* emotionally moving. **touchy** *adj* easily offended. **touch base** make contact, renew communication. **touch down** *v* (of an aircraft) land. **touchdown** *n* Football score gained by being in possession of the ball before crossing the opponents' goal line. **touchline** *n* side line of the field in some games. **touchstone** *n* criterion. **touch-type** *v* type without looking at the keyboard.

touché [too-**shay**] *interj* acknowledgment of the striking home of a remark or witty reply.

tough *adj* strong or resilient; difficult to chew or cut; hardy and fit; rough and violent; difficult; firm and determined; *Informal* unlucky or unfair. ◆ *n* *Informal* rough violent person. **toughness** *n* **toughen** *v* make or become tough or tougher.

toupee [too-**pay**] *n* wig.

tour *n* journey visiting places of interest along the way; trip to perform or play in different places. ◆ *v* make a tour (of). **tourism** *n* tourist travel as an industry. **tourist** *n* person travelling for pleasure. **touristy** *adj* full of tourists or tourist attractions.

tour de force *n, pl* **tours de force** *French* brilliant achievement.

tournament *n* sporting competition with several stages to decide the overall winner; *Hist* (also **tourney**) contest between knights on horseback.

tourniquet [**tour**-nick-kay] *n* something twisted round a limb to stop bleeding.

tousled *adj* ruffled and untidy.

tout [rhymes with **shout**] *v* solicit custom in a persistent manner; obtain and sell information about racehorses. ◆ *n* person who sells tickets for a popular event at inflated prices.

tow[1] *v* drag, esp. by means of a rope. ◆ *n* towing. **in tow** following closely behind. **on tow** being towed. **towbar** *n* metal bar on an automobile for towing vehicles. **towpath** *n* path beside a canal or river, originally for horses towing boats.

tow[2] *n* fibre of hemp or flax. **tow-headed** *adj* with blond hair.

towards, toward *prep* in the direction of; with regard to; as a contribution to.

towel *n* cloth for drying things. **towelling** *n* material used for making towels.

tower *n* tall structure, often forming part of a larger building. ◆ *v* be very tall; loom (over). **tower of strength** person who supports or comforts.

town *n* group of buildings larger than a village; central part of this; people of a town. **township** *n* small town. **town hall** large building used for council meetings, concerts, etc.

toxemia, toxaemia [tox-**seem**-ya] *n* blood poisoning; high blood pressure in pregnancy.

toxic *adj* poisonous; caused by poison. **toxicity** *n* **toxicology** *n* study of poisons. **toxin** *n* poison of bacterial origin.

toy *n* something designed to be played with. ◆ *adj* (of a dog) of a variety much smaller than is normal for that breed. **toy with** *v* play or fiddle with.

trace[1] *n* track left by something; indication; minute quantity. ◆ *v* follow the course of; track down and find; copy exactly by drawing on a thin sheet of transparent paper set on top of the original. **traceable** *adj* **tracer** *n* projectile which leaves a visible trail. **tracing** *n* traced copy. **tracery** *n* pattern of interlacing lines. **trace element** chemical element occurring in very small amounts in soil etc.

trace[2] *n* strap by which a horse pulls a vehicle. **kick over the traces** escape or defy control.

trachea [track-kee-a] *n, pl* **tracheae** windpipe. **tracheotomy** [track-ee-ot-a-mee] *n* surgical incision into the trachea.

track *n* mark or trail left by the passage of anything; rough road or path; railway line; course of action or thought; endless band round the wheels of a tank, bulldozer, etc.; course for racing; separate section on a record, tape, or CD. ◆ *v* follow the trail or path of. **track down** *v* hunt for and find. **track event** athletic sport held on a track. **track record** past accomplishments of a person or organization. **tracksuit** *n* warm loose-fitting suit worn by athletes etc., esp. during training.

tract[1] *n* wide area; *Anat* system of organs with a particular function.

tract[2] *n* pamphlet, esp. a religious one.

tractable *adj* easy to control.

traction *n* pulling, esp. by engine power; *Med* application of a steady pull on an injured limb by weights and pulleys; grip of the wheels of a vehicle on the ground.

tractor *n* motor vehicle with large rear wheels for pulling farm machinery. **tractor-trailer** *n* freight vehicle consisting of a truck with engine and cab pulling an open or closed trailer.

trade *n* buying, selling, or exchange of goods; person's job or craft; (people engaged in) a particular industry or business. ◆ *v* buy and sell; exchange; engage in trade. **trader** *n* **trading** *n* **trade-in** *n* used article given in part payment for a new one. **trademark, tradename** *n* (legally registered) name or symbol used by a firm to distinguish its goods. **trade-off** *n* exchange made as a compromise.

tradesman *n* skilled worker; shopkeeper. **trade union** society of workers for the protection of their interests. **trade wind** wind blowing steadily towards the equator.

tradition *n* unwritten body of beliefs, customs, etc. handed down from generation to generation; custom or practice of long standing. **traditional** *adj* **traditionally** *adv*

traduce *v* slander.

traffic *n* vehicles coming and going on a road; (illicit) trade. ◆ *v* **-ficking, -ficked** trade, usu. illicitly. **trafficker** *n* **traffic circle** road junction at which traffic passes around a central island. **traffic cop** *Informal* police officer who directs the movement of traffic. **traffic lights** set of coloured lights at a junction to control the traffic flow.

tragedy *n, pl* **-dies** shocking or sad event; serious play, film, etc. in which the hero is destroyed by a personal failing in adverse circumstances. **tragedian** [traj-**jee**-dee-an] *n* actor in or writer of tragedies. **tragedienne** [traj-jee-dee-**enn**] *n* actress in tragedies. **tragic** *adj* of or like a tragedy. **tragically** *adv* **tragicomedy** *n* play with both tragic and comic elements.

trail *v* drag along the ground; follow the tracks of; lag behind; (of plants) grow along the ground or hang loosely. ◆ *n* track or trace; path, track, or road. **trailer** *n* vehicle designed to be towed by another vehicle; extract from a film or programme used to advertise it. **trailer park** site for parking mobile homes.

train *v* instruct in a skill; learn the skills needed to do a particular job or activity; cause (an animal) to perform or (a plant) to grow in a particular way; aim (a gun etc.); exercise in preparation for a sports event. ◆ *n* line of railway coaches or wagons drawn by an engine; sequence or series; long trailing back section of a dress; body of attendants. **trainee** *n* person being trained. **trainer** *n* person who trains an athlete or sportsman; sports shoe.

traipse *v Informal* walk wearily.

trait *n* characteristic feature.

traitor *n* person guilty of treason or treachery. **traitorous** *adj*

trajectory *n, pl* **-ries** line of flight, esp. of a projectile.

tram n Brit streetcar. **tramlines** pl n track for trams.

trammel v **-elling, -elled** restrain.

tramp v travel on foot, hike; walk heavily. ◆ n homeless person who travels on foot; hike; sound of tramping; cargo ship available for hire; Slang promiscuous woman.

trample v tread on and crush.

trampoline n tough canvas sheet attached to a frame by springs, used by acrobats etc. ◆ v bounce on a trampoline.

trance n unconscious or dazed state; state of ecstasy or total absorption.

tranche n portion of something large, esp. a sum of money.

tranquil adj calm and quiet. **tranquilly** adv **tranquillity** n **tranquillize** v make calm. **tranquillizer** n drug which reduces anxiety or tension.

trans- prefix across, through, or beyond.

transact v conduct or negotiate (a business deal). **transaction** n transacting; business deal transacted.

transatlantic adj on, from, or to the other side of the Atlantic.

transceiver n combined radio transmitter and receiver.

transcend v rise above; be superior to. **transcendence** n **transcendent** adj **transcendental** adj based on intuition rather than experience; supernatural or mystical. **transcendentalism** n

transcribe v copy out; write down (something said); record for a later broadcast; arrange (music) for a different instrument. **transcript** n written or printed copy.

transducer n device that converts one form of energy to another.

transept n either of the two shorter wings of a cross-shaped church.

transfer v **-ferring, -ferred** move or send from one person or place to another. ◆ n transferring; design which can be transferred from one surface to another. **transferable** adj **transference** n transferring.

transfigure v change in appearance. **transfiguration** n

transfix v astound or stun; pierce through.

transform v change the shape or character of. **transformation** n **transformer** n device for changing the

voltage of an alternating current.

transfusion n injection of blood into the blood vessels of a patient. **transfuse** v give a transfusion to; permeate or infuse.

transgress v break (a moral law). **transgression** n **transgressor** n

transient adj lasting only for a short time. **transience** n

transistor n semiconducting device used to amplify electric currents; portable radio using transistors.

transit n going from one place to another. **transition** n change from one state to another. **transitional** adj **transitive** adj (of a verb) requiring a direct object. **transitory** adj not lasting long.

translate v turn from one language into another. **translation** n **translator** n

transliterate v convert to the letters of a different alphabet. **transliteration** n

translucent adj letting light pass through, but not transparent. **translucence** n

transmigrate v (of a soul) pass into another body. **transmigration** n

transmit v **-mitting, -mitted** pass (something) from one person or place to another; send out (signals) by radio waves; broadcast (a radio or television programme). **transmission** n transmitting; shafts and gears through which power passes from a vehicle's engine to its wheels. **transmittable** adj **transmitter** n

transmogrify v **-fying, -fied** Informal change completely.

transmute v change the form or nature of. **transmutation** n

transom n horizontal bar across a window; bar separating a door from the window over it.

transparent adj able to be seen through, clear; easily understood or recognized. **transparently** adv **transparency** n transparent quality; colour photograph on transparent film, viewed by means of a projector.

transpire v become known; Informal happen; give off water vapour through pores. **transpiration** n

transplant v remove and transfer (a plant) to another place; transfer (an organ or tissue) surgically from one part or body to another. ◆ *n* surgical transplanting; thing transplanted. **transplantation** *n*

transport *v* convey from one place to another; *Hist* exile (a criminal) to a penal colony; enrapture. ◆ *n* business or system of transporting; vehicle used in transport; ecstasy or rapture. **transportation** *n* **transporter** *n* large goods vehicle.

transpose *v* interchange two things; put (music) into a different key. **transposition** *n*

transsexual *n* person of one sex who believes their true identity is of the opposite sex; person who has had a sex-change operation.

transubstantiation *n* *Christianity* doctrine that the bread and wine consecrated in the Eucharist changes into the substance of Christ's body.

transuranic [tranz-yoor-**ran**-ik] *adj* (of an element) having an atomic number greater than that of uranium.

transverse *adj* crossing from side to side.

transvestite *n* person who seeks sexual pleasure by wearing the clothes of the opposite sex. **transvestism** *n*

trap *n* device for catching animals; plan for tricking or catching a person; bend in a pipe containing liquid to prevent the escape of gas; *Hist* two-wheeled carriage; *Slang* mouth. ◆ *v* **trapping, trapped** catch; trick. **trapper** *n* person who traps animals for their fur. **trapdoor** *n* door in a floor or roof.

trapeze *n* horizontal bar suspended from two ropes, used by circus acrobats.

trapezium *n*, *pl* **-ziums, -zia** quadrilateral with no sides parallel; *Brit* trapezoid. **trapezoid** [**trap**-piz-zoid] *n* quadrilateral with two parallel sides of unequal length; *Brit* trapezium.

trappings *pl n* equipment.

Trappist *n* member of an order of Christian monks who observe strict silence.

trash *n* anything worthless; rubbish. **trashy** *adj*

trauma [**traw**-ma] *n* emotional shock; injury or wound. **traumatic** *adj* **traumatize** *v*

travail *v*, *n* *Lit* labour or toil.

travel *v* **-elling, -elled** go from one

place to another, through an area, or for a specified distance. ◆ *n* travelling, esp. as a tourist. ◆ *pl* (account of) travelling. **traveller** *n* **travelogue** *n* film or talk about someone's travels.

traverse *v* move over or back and forth over; move sideways. ◆ *n* traversing; path or road across.

travesty *n*, *pl* **-ties** grotesque imitation or mockery. ◆ *v* **-tying, -tied** make or be a travesty of.

trawl *n* net dragged at deep levels behind a fishing boat. ◆ *v* fish with such a net. **trawler** *n* trawling boat.

tray *n* flat board, usu. with a rim, for carrying things; open receptacle for office correspondence.

treachery *n*, *pl* **-eries** wilful betrayal. **treacherous** *adj* disloyal; unreliable or dangerous. **treacherously** *adv*

treacle *n* thick dark syrup produced when sugar is refined. **treacly** *adj*

tread *v* **treading, trod, trodden** or **trod.** set one's foot on; crush by walking on. ◆ *n* way of walking or dancing; treading; upper surface of a step; part of a tire that touches the ground. **treadmill** *n* *Hist* cylinder turned by treading on steps projecting from it; dreary routine.

treadle [**tred**-dl] *n* lever worked by the foot to turn a wheel.

treason *n* betrayal of one's sovereign or country; treachery. **treasonable, treasonous** *adj*

treasure *n* collection of wealth, esp. gold or jewels; valued person or thing. ◆ *v* prize or cherish. **treasurer** *n* official in charge of funds. **treasury** *n* storage place for treasure; government department in charge of finance. **treasure-trove** *n* treasure found with no evidence of ownership.

treat *n* pleasure, entertainment, etc. given or paid for by someone else. ◆ *v* deal with or regard in a certain manner; give medical treatment to; subject to a chemical or industrial process; provide (someone) with (something) as a treat. **treatment** *n* way of treating a person or thing; medical care.

treatise [**treat**-izz] *n* formal piece of writing on a particular subject.

treaty *n*, *pl* **-ties** signed contract between states.

treble *adj* threefold, triple; *Music* high-pitched. ◆ n (singer with or part for) a soprano voice. ◆ v increase threefold. **trebly** adv

tree n large perennial plant with a woody trunk. **treeless** adj **tree surgery** repair of damaged trees. **tree surgeon**

trefoil [tref-foil] n plant, such as clover, with a three-lobed leaf; carved ornament like this.

trek n long difficult journey, esp. on foot. ◆ v **trekking, trekked** make such a journey.

trellis n framework of horizontal and vertical strips of wood.

tremble v shake or quiver; feel fear or anxiety. ◆ n **trembling** adj

tremendous adj huge; Informal great in quality or amount. **tremendously** adv

tremolo n, pl **-los** Music quivering effect in singing or playing.

tremor n involuntary shaking; minor earthquake.

tremulous adj trembling, as from fear or excitement.

trench n long narrow ditch, esp. one used as a shelter in war. **trench coat** double-breasted waterproof coat.

trenchant adj incisive; effective.

trencher n Hist wooden plate for serving food. **trencherman** n hearty eater.

trend n general tendency or direction; fashion. **trendy** adj, n Informal consciously fashionable (person). **trendiness** n

trepidation n fear or anxiety.

trespass v go onto another's property without permission. ◆ n trespassing; Old-fashioned sin or wrongdoing. **trespasser** n **trespass on** v take unfair advantage of (someone's friendship, patience, etc.).

tress n long lock of hair.

trestle n board fixed on pairs of spreading legs, used as a support.

trews pl n close-fitting tartan trousers.

tri- prefix three.

triad n group of three; (T-) Chinese criminal secret society.

trial n trying or testing; Law investigation of a case before a judge; thing or person straining endurance or patience. ◆ pl sporting competition for individuals.

triangle n geometric figure with three sides; triangular percussion instrument; situation involving three people. **triangular** adj

tribe n group of clans or families believed to have a common ancestor. **tribal** adj **tribalism** n loyalty to a tribe.

tribulation n great distress.

tribune n person who upholds public rights; people's representative in ancient Rome. **tribunal** n lawcourt; board appointed to inquire into a specific matter.

tributary n, pl **-taries** stream or river flowing into a larger one. ◆ adj (of a stream or river) flowing into a larger one.

tribute n sign of respect or admiration; tax paid by one state to another.

trice n in a trice instantly.

triceps n muscle at the back of the upper arm.

trichology [trick-ol-a-jee] n study and treatment of hair and its diseases. **trichologist** n

trick n deceitful or cunning action or plan; joke or prank; feat of skill or cunning; knack; mannerism; cards played in one round. ◆ v cheat or deceive. **trickery** n **trickster** n **tricky** adj difficult, needing careful handling; crafty.

trickle v (cause to) move in a thin stream or drops; move gradually. ◆ n gradual flow.

tricolour [trick-kol-lor] n three-coloured striped flag.

tricycle n three-wheeled cycle.

trident n three-pronged spear.

triennial adj happening every three years.

trifle n insignificant thing; small amount; dessert of sponge cake, custard, etc. ◆ v (usu. foll. by with) toy with. **trifling** adj insignificant.

trigger n small lever releasing a catch on a gun or machine; action that sets off a course of events. ◆ v (usu. foll. by off) set (an action or process) in motion. **trigger-happy** adj too quick to use guns.

trigonometry n branch of mathematics dealing with relations of the sides and angles of triangles. **trigonometrical** adj

trike n Informal tricycle.

trilateral *adj* having three sides.

trilby *n, pl* **-bies** man's soft felt hat.

trill *n* rapid alternation between two notes; shrill warbling sound made by some birds. ◆ *v* play or sing a trill.

trillion *n* one million million, 10^{12}; *Brit (formerly)* one million million million, 10^{18}.

trilobite [**trile**-oh-bite] *n* small prehistoric sea animal.

trilogy [**trill**-a-jee] *n, pl* **-gies** series of three related books, plays, etc.

trim *adj* **trimmer, trimmest** neat and smart; slender; in good condition. ◆ *v* **trimming, trimmed** cut or prune into good shape; decorate with lace, ribbons, etc.; adjust the balance of (a ship or aircraft) by shifting the cargo etc. ◆ *n* decoration; upholstery and decorative facings in an automobile; trim state; haircut that neatens the existing style. **trimming** *n* decoration. ◆ *pl* usual accompaniments, e.g. *turkey with all the trimmings*.

trimaran [**trime**-a-ran] *n* three-hulled boat.

trinitrotoluene *n* full name of TNT.

trinity *n, pl* **-ties** group of three; (T-) *Christianity* union of three persons, Father, Son, and Holy Spirit, in one God.

trinket *n* small or worthless ornament or piece of jewellery.

trio *n, pl* **trios** group of three; piece of music for three performers.

trip *n* journey to a place and back, esp. for pleasure; stumble; switch on a mechanism; *Informal* hallucinogenic drug experience. ◆ *v* **tripping, tripped** (cause to) stumble; (often foll. by *up*) catch (someone) in a mistake; move or tread lightly; operate (a switch); *Informal* take a hallucinogenic drug. **tripper** *n* tourist.

tripe *n* stomach of a cow used as food; *Informal* nonsense.

triple *adj* having three parts; three times as great or as many. ◆ *v* increase threefold. **triplet** *n* one of three babies born at one birth. **triple jump** athletics event in which competitors make a hop, a step, and a jump as a continuous movement.

triplicate *adj* triple. ◆ *n* one of three copies. **in triplicate** in three copies.

tripod [**tripe**-pod] *n* three-legged stand, stool, etc.

tripos [**tripe**-poss] *n* final examinations for the degree of BA at Cambridge University.

triptych [**trip**-tick] *n* set of paintings or carvings on three hinged panels, often forming an altarpiece.

trite *adj* hackneyed or banal.

tritium *n* radioactive isotope of hydrogen.

triumph *n* (happiness caused by) victory or success. ◆ *v* be victorious or successful; rejoice over a victory. **triumphal** *adj* celebrating a triumph. **triumphant** *adj* feeling or showing triumph.

triumvirate [try-**umm**-vir-rit] *n* group of three people in joint control.

trivet [**triv**-vit] *n* metal stand for a pot or kettle.

trivial *adj* of little importance; everyday, trite. **trivially** *adv* **trivia** *pl n* trivial things or details. **triviality** *n* **trivialize** *v* make (something) seem less important than it is.

trod *v* past tense and a past participle of TREAD.

trodden *v* a past participle of TREAD.

troglodyte *n* cave dweller.

troika *n* Russian vehicle drawn by three horses abreast; group of three people in authority.

troll *n* giant or dwarf in Scandinavian folklore.

trolley *n* small wheeled table for food and drink; wheeled cart for moving goods. **trolley car** bus powered by electricity from an overhead wire but not running on rails.

trollop *n* promiscuous or slovenly woman.

trombone *n* brass musical instrument with a sliding tube. **trombonist** *n*

troop *n* large group; artillery or cavalry unit; Scout company. ◆ *pl* soldiers. ◆ *v* move in a crowd. **trooper** *n* cavalry soldier.

trope *n* figure of speech.

trophy *n, pl* **-phies** cup, shield, etc. given as a prize; memento of success.

tropic *n* either of two lines of latitude at 23½° N (**tropic of Capricorn**) or 23½° S (**tropic of Cancer**). ◆ *pl* part of the earth's surface between these lines. **tropical** *adj* of or in the tropics; (of climate) very hot.

trot *v* **trotting, trotted** move or cause (a horse) to move at a medium pace, lifting the feet in diagonal pairs; (of a person) move at a steady brisk pace. ◆ *n* trotting. **trotter** *n* pig's foot. **trot out** *v* repeat (old ideas etc.) without fresh thought.

troth [rhymes with **growth**] *n* pledge of fidelity, esp. a betrothal.

troubadour [troo-bad-oor] *n* medieval travelling poet and singer.

trouble *n* (cause of) distress or anxiety; disease or malfunctioning; state of disorder or unrest; care or effort. ◆ *v* (cause to) worry; cause inconvenience to; exert oneself. **troubled** *adj* **troublesome** *adj* **troubleshooter** *n* person employed to locate and deal with faults or problems.

trough [troff] *n* long open container, esp. for animals' food or water; narrow channel between two waves or ridges; *Meteorol* area of low pressure.

trounce *v* defeat utterly.

troupe [troop] *n* company of performers. **trouper** *n*

trousers *pl n* two-legged outer garment with legs reaching usu. to the ankles. **trouser** *adj* of trousers.

trousseau [troo-so] *n, pl* -**seaux**, -**seaus** bride's collection of clothing etc. for her marriage.

trout *n* game fish related to the salmon.

trowel *n* hand tool with a flat wide blade for spreading mortar, lifting plants, etc.

troy weight, troy *n* system of weights used for gold, silver, and jewels.

truant *n* pupil who stays away from school without permission. **play truant** stay away from school without permission. **truancy** *n*

truce *n* temporary agreement to stop fighting.

truck[1] *n* large vehicle for transporting loads by road. **trucker** *n* truck driver.

truck[2] *n* **have no truck with** refuse to be involved with.

truckle *v* (usu. foll. by *to*) yield weakly.

truculent [truck-yew-lent] *adj* aggressively defiant. **truculence** *n*

trudge *v* walk heavily or wearily. ◆ *n* long tiring walk.

true *adj* **truer, truest** in accordance with facts; faithful; exact; genuine. **truly** *adv* **truism** *n* self-evident truth.

truth *n* state of being true; something true. **truthful** *adj* honest; exact. **truthfully** *adv*

truffle *n* edible underground fungus; candy flavoured with chocolate.

trug *n* long shallow basket used by gardeners.

trump[1] *n, adj* (card) of the suit temporarily outranking the others. ◆ *v* play a trump card on (another card). ◆ *pl n* trump suit. **turn up trumps** turn out unexpectedly well. **trump up** *v* concoct.

trump[2] *n Lit* (sound of) a trumpet.

trumpet *n* valved brass instrument with a flared tube. ◆ *v* -**peting**, -**peted** (of an elephant) cry loudly; proclaim loudly. **trumpeter** *n*

truncate *v* cut short.

truncheon *n* small club carried by a policeman.

trundle *v* move heavily on wheels.

trunk *n* main stem of a tree; person's body excluding the head and limbs; large case or box for clothes etc.; elephant's long nose; space in an automobile for luggage. ◆ *pl* man's swimming shorts. **trunk call** long-distance telephone call. **trunk road** main road.

truss *v* tie or bind up. ◆ *n* device for holding a hernia in place; framework supporting a roof, bridge, etc.

trust *n* confidence in the truth, reliability, etc. of a person or thing; obligation arising from responsibility; charge or care; arrangement in which one person administers property, money, etc. on another's behalf; property held for another; group of companies joined to control a market. ◆ *v* believe in and rely on; expect or hope; consign to someone's care. **trustee** *n* person holding property on another's behalf. **trusteeship** *n* **trustful, trusting** *adj* inclined to trust. **trustworthy** *adj* reliable or honest. **trusty** *adj* reliable.

truth *n* see TRUE.

try *v* **trying, tried** make an effort or attempt; test or sample; put strain on, e.g. *he tries my patience*; investigate (a case); examine (a person) in a lawcourt. ◆ *n, pl* **tries** attempt or effort; *Rugby* score gained by touching the ball down over the opponent's goal line. **try it on** *Informal* try to deceive or fool someone. **trying** *adj* difficult or annoying.

tryst *n Old-fashioned* arrangement to meet.

tsar [zahr] *n Hist* Russian emperor.

tsetse [tset-see] *n* bloodsucking African fly whose bite transmits disease.

T-shirt *n* short-sleeved casual shirt or top.

tsp. teaspoon.

T-square *n* T-shaped ruler.

tsunami *n, pl* -**mis**, -**mi** tidal wave.

tub *n* open, usu. round container; bath. **tubby** *adj* (of a person) short and fat.

tuba [tube-a] *n* valved low-pitched brass instrument.

tube *n* hollow cylinder; flexible cylinder with a cap to hold pastes. **the tube** underground railway, esp. the one in London. **tubing** [tube-ing] *n* length of tube; system of tubes. **tubular** [tube-yew-lar] *adj* of or like a tube.

tuber [tube-er] *n* fleshy underground root of a plant such as a potato. **tuberous** [tube-er-uss] *adj*

tubercle [tube-er-kl] *n* small rounded swelling.

tuberculosis [tube-berk-yew-lohss-iss] *n* infectious disease causing tubercles, esp. in the lungs. **tubercular** [tube-berk-yew-lar] *adj* of tuberculosis. **tuberculin** *n* extract from a bacillus used to test for tuberculosis.

tuck *v* push or fold into a small space; stitch in folds. ♦ *n* stitched fold; *Informal* food. **tuck away** *v* store in a safe place.

Tudor *adj* of the English royal house ruling from 1485–1603; in an architectural style characterized by half-timbered buildings.

Tuesday *n* third day of the week.

tufa [tew-fa] *n* porous rock formed as a deposit from springs.

tuffet *n* small mound or seat.

tuft *n* bunch of feathers, grass, hair, etc. held or growing together at the base.

tug *v* **tugging, tugged** pull hard. ♦ *n* hard pull; small ship used to tow other vessels. **tug of war** contest in which two teams pull against one another on a rope.

tuition *n* instruction, esp. received

individually or in a small group.

tulip *n* plant with bright cup-shaped flowers.

tulle [tewl] *n* fine net fabric of silk etc.

tumble *v* (cause to) fall, esp. awkwardly or violently; roll or twist, esp. in play; rumple. ♦ *n* fall; somersault. **tumbler** *n* stemless drinking glass; acrobat; spring catch in a lock. **tumbledown** *adj* dilapidated. **tumble dryer, tumbler dryer** machine that dries laundry by rotating it in warm air. **tumble to** *v Informal* realize, understand.

tumbrel, tumbril *n* farm cart used during the French Revolution to take prisoners to the guillotine.

tumescent [tew-mess-ent] *adj* swollen or becoming swollen. **tumescence** *n*

tummy *n, pl* -**mies** *Informal* stomach.

tumour [tew-mer] *n* abnormal growth in or on the body.

tumult [tew-mult] *n* uproar or commotion. **tumultuous** [tew-mull-tew-uss] *adj*

tumulus [tew-mew-luss] *n, pl* -**li** burial mound.

tun *n* large beer cask.

tuna [tune-a] *n* large marine food fish.

tundra *n* vast treeless Arctic region with permanently frozen subsoil.

tune *n* (pleasing) sequence of musical notes; correct musical pitch, e.g. *she sang out of tune.* ♦ *v* adjust (a musical instrument) so that it is in tune; adjust (a machine) to obtain the desired performance. **tuneful** *adj* **tunefully** *adv* **tuneless** *adj* **tuner** *n* **tune in** *v* adjust (a radio or television) to receive (a station or programme).

tungsten *n* greyish-white metal.

tunic *n* close-fitting jacket forming part of some uniforms; loose knee-length garment.

tunnel *n* underground passage. ♦ *v* -**nelling, -nelled** make a tunnel (through).

tunny *n, pl* -**nies**, -**ny** same as TUNA.

tup *n* male sheep.

tupik, tupek *n* a traditional type of Inuit dwelling made of animal skins.

tuque [took] *n* knitted cap with tapering end.

turban *n* Muslim or Sikh man's headcovering made by winding cloth round the head.

turbid *adj* muddy, not clear. **turbidity** *n*

turbine *n* machine or generator driven by gas, water, etc. turning blades.

turbo- *combining form* of or powered by a turbine.

turbot *n* large European flatfish.

turbulence *n* confusion, movement, or agitation; atmospheric instability causing gusty air currents. **turbulent** *adj*

tureen *n* serving dish for soup.

turf *n, pl* **turfs, turves** short thick even grass; square of this with roots and soil attached. ◆ *v* cover with turf. **the turf** horse racing; racecourse. **turf accountant** bookmaker. **turf out** *v Informal* throw out.

turgid [tur-jid] *adj* swollen and thick; (of language) pompous.

turkey *n* large bird bred for food.

Turkish *adj* of Turkey, its people, or their language. ◆ *n* Turkish language. **Turkish bath** steam bath. **Turkish delight** jelly-like candy coated with icing sugar.

turmeric *n* yellow spice obtained from the root of an Asian plant.

turmoil *n* agitation or confusion.

turn *v* move around an axis, rotate; change the position or direction (of); (usu. foll. by *into*) change in nature or character; become sour; shape on a lathe; go round (a corner); reach or pass in age, time, etc., e.g. *she has just turned twenty*. ◆ *n* turning; direction or drift; opportunity to do something as part of an agreed succession; period or spell; short theatrical performance. **good, bad turn** helpful *or* unhelpful act. **turner** *n* **turning** *n* road or path leading off a main route. **turning point** moment when a decisive change occurs. **turncoat** *n* person who deserts one party or cause to join another. **turn down** *v* refuse or reject; reduce the volume or brightness (of). **turn in** *v* go to bed; hand in. **turn off** *v* stop (something) working by using a knob etc. **turn on** *v* start (something) working by using a knob etc.; become aggressive towards; *Informal* excite, esp. sexually. **turnout** *n* number of people appearing at a gathering; outfit. **turnover** *n* total sales made by a business over a certain period; rate at which staff leave and are replaced;

small pastry. **turnpike** *n* road where a toll is collected at barriers. **turnstile** *n* revolving gate for admitting one person at a time. **turntable** *n* revolving platform. **turn up** *v* arrive or appear; find or be found; increase the volume or brightness (of). **turn-up** *n* turned-up fold at the bottom of a trouser leg; *Informal* unexpected event.

turnip *n* root vegetable with orange or white flesh.

turpentine *n* (oil made from) the resin of certain trees. **turps** *n* turpentine oil.

turpitude *n* depravity.

turquoise *n* blue-green precious stone. ◆ *adj* blue-green.

turret *n* small tower; revolving gun tower on a warship or tank.

turtle *n* sea tortoise. **turn turtle** capsize. **turtledove** *n* small wild dove. **turtleneck** *n* (sweater with) a round high close-fitting neck.

tusk *n* long pointed tooth of an elephant, walrus, etc.

tussle *n, v* fight or scuffle.

tussock *n* tuft of grass.

tutelage [tew-till-lij] *n* tuition; guardianship. **tutelary** [tew-till-lar-ee] *adj*

tutor *n* person teaching individuals or small groups. ◆ *v* act as a tutor to. **tutorial** *n* period of instruction with a tutor.

tutu *n* short stiff skirt worn by ballerinas.

tuxedo *n, pl* **-dos** dinner jacket.

TV television.

twaddle *n* nonsense.

twain *n Obs* two.

twang *n* sharp ringing sound; nasal speech. ◆ *v* (cause to) make a twang.

tweak *v* pinch or twist sharply. ◆ *n* tweaking.

twee *adj Informal* too sentimental, sweet, or pretty.

tweed *n* thick woollen cloth. ◆ *pl* suit of tweed. **tweedy** *adj*

tweet *n, v* chirp. **tweeter** *n* loudspeaker reproducing high-frequency sounds.

tweezers *pl n* small pincer-like tool.

twelve *adj, n* two more than ten. **twelfth** *adj, n* (of) number twelve in a series.

twenty adj, n two times ten.
twenty-four-seven 24/7 adv Informal all the time. **twentieth** adj, n

twerp n Informal silly person.

twice adv two times.

twiddle v (foll. by with) fiddle (with). **twiddle one's thumbs** be bored, have nothing to do.

twig[1] n small branch or shoot.

twig[2] v **twigging, twigged** Informal realize or understand.

twilight n soft dim light just after sunset.

twill n fabric woven to produce parallel ridges.

twin n one of a pair, esp. of two children born at one birth. ◆ v **twinning, twinned** pair or be paired.

twine v twist or coil round. ◆ n string or cord.

twinge n sudden sharp pain.

twinkle v shine brightly but intermittently. ◆ n flickering brightness. **in the twinkling of an eye** in a very short time.

twirl v turn or twist around quickly; twiddle, esp. idly.

twirp n Informal same as TWERP.

twist v turn out of the natural position; wind or twine; distort or pervert. ◆ n twisting; twisted thing; unexpected development in the plot of a film, book, etc.; bend or curve; distortion. **twisted** adj (of a person) cruel or perverted. **twister** n Informal swindler. **twisty** adj

twit[1] v **twitting, twitted** taunt, esp. in jest.

twit[2] n Informal foolish person.

twitch v move spasmodically; pull sharply. ◆ n nervous muscular spasm; sharp pull.

twitter v (of birds) utter chirping sounds. ◆ n chirping.

two adj, n one more than one. **two-edged** adj (of a remark) having both a favourable and an unfavourable interpretation. **two-faced** adj deceitful, hypocritical. **twonie** n same as TOONIE. **two-time** v Informal deceive (a lover) by having an affair with someone else.

tycoon n powerful wealthy businessman.

tyke n Informal small cheeky child; small mongrel dog.

tympani pl n same as TIMPANI.

type n class or category; Informal person, esp. of a specified kind; block with a raised character used for printing; printed text. ◆ v print with a typewriter; typify; classify. **typist** n person who types with a typewriter.

typecast v continually cast (an actor or actress) in similar roles. **typewriter** n machine which prints a character when the appropriate key is pressed.

typhoid fever n acute infectious feverish disease.

typhoon n violent tropical storm.

typhus n infectious feverish disease.

typical adj true to type, characteristic. **typically** adv

typify v **-fying, -fied** be typical of.

typography n art or style of printing. **typographical** adj **typographer** n

tyrant n oppressive or cruel ruler; person who exercises authority tyrannically. **tyrannical** adj like a tyrant, oppressive. **tyrannically** adv **tyrannize** v exert power (over) oppressively or cruelly. **tyrannous** adj **tyranny** n tyrannical rule.

tyre n Brit tire.

tyro n, pl **-ros** novice or beginner.

U u

ubiquitous [yew-bik-wit-uss] adj being or seeming to be everywhere at once. **ubiquity** n

udder n large baglike milk-producing gland of cows, sheep, or goats.

UFO unidentified flying object.

ugly adj **uglier, ugliest** of unpleasant appearance; ominous or menacing. **ugliness** n

UHF ultrahigh frequency.

UK United Kingdom.

ukulele, ukelele [yew-kal-lay-lee] n small guitar with four strings.

ulcer n open sore on the surface of the skin or mucous membrane. **ulcerate** v make or become ulcerous. **ulceration** n

ulna n, pl **-nae, -nas** inner and longer of the two bones of the human forearm.

ulterior [ult-ear-ee-or] adj lying beyond what is revealed or seen, e.g. ulterior motives.

ultimate *adj* final in a series or process; highest or most significant. **ultimately** *adv* **ultimatum** [ult-im-**may**-tum] *n* final communication stating that action will be taken unless certain conditions are met.

ultra- *prefix* beyond a specified extent, range, or limit, e.g. *ultrasonic*; extremely, e.g. *ultramodern*.

ultrahigh frequency *n* radio frequency between 3000 and 300 megahertz.

ultramarine *adj* vivid blue.

ultrasonic *adj* of or producing sound waves with a higher frequency than the human ear can hear.

ultraviolet *adj, n* (of) light beyond the limit of visibility at the violet end of the spectrum.

ululate [**yewl**-yew-late] *v* howl or wail. **ululation** *n*

umber *adj* dark brown to greenish-brown.

umbilical [um-**bill**-ik-al] *adj* of the navel. **umbilical cord** long flexible tube of blood vessels that connects a fetus with the placenta.

umbrage *n* displeasure or resentment. **take umbrage** feel offended or upset.

umbrella *n* portable device used for protection against rain, consisting of a folding frame covered in material attached to a central rod; single organization, idea, etc. that contains or covers many different organizations.

umpire *n* official who rules on the playing of a game. ◆ *v* act as umpire in (a game).

umpteen *adj Informal* very many. **umpteenth** *n, adj*

UN United Nations.

un- *prefix* not, e.g. denoting reversal of an action, e.g. *untie*; denoting removal from, e.g. *unthrone*.

unable *adj* (foll. by *to*) lacking the necessary power, ability, or authority to (do something).

unaccountable *adj* that cannot be explained; (foll. by *to*) not answerable to. **unaccountably** *adv*

unadulterated *adj* with nothing added, pure.

unanimous [yew-**nan**-im-uss] *adj* in complete agreement; agreed by all. **unanimity** *n*

unarmed *adj* without weapons.

unassuming *adj* modest or unpretentious.

unaware *adj* not aware or conscious. **unawares** *adv* by surprise; without knowing.

unbalanced *adj* mentally deranged; biased or one-sided.

unbearable *adj* not able to be endured. **unbearably** *adv*

unbeknown *adv* (foll. by *to*) without the knowledge of (a person).

unbend *v Informal* become less strict or more informal in one's attitudes or behaviour. **unbending** *adj*

unbidden *adj* not ordered or asked.

unborn *adj* not yet born.

unbosom *v* relieve (oneself) of (secrets or feelings) by telling someone.

unbridled *adj* (of feelings or behaviour) not controlled in any way.

unburden *v* relieve (one's mind or oneself) of a worry by confiding in someone.

uncalled-for *adj* not fair or justified.

uncanny *adj* weird or mysterious. **uncannily** *adv* **uncanniness** *n*

unceremonious *adj* without ceremony; abrupt or rude. **unceremoniously** *adv*

uncertain *adj* not able to be accurately known or predicted; not able to be depended upon; changeable. **uncertainty** *n*

un-Christian *adj* not in accordance with Christian principles.

uncle *n* brother of one's father or mother; husband of one's aunt.

unclean *adj* lacking moral, spiritual, or physical cleanliness.

uncomfortable *adj* not physically relaxed; anxious or uneasy.

uncommon *adj* not happening often; in excess of what is normal. **uncommonly** *adv*

uncompromising *adj* not prepared to compromise.

unconcerned *adj* lacking in concern or involvement. **unconcernedly** *adv*

unconditional *adj* without conditions or limitations.

unconscionable *adj* having no principles, unscrupulous; excessive in amount or degree.

unconscious *adj* lacking normal awareness through the senses; not aware of one's actions or behaviour.

♦ *n* part of the mind containing instincts and ideas that exist without one's awareness. **unconsciously** *adv* **unconsciousness** *n*

uncooperative *adj* not willing to cooperate, unhelpful.

uncouth *adj* lacking in good manners, refinement, or grace.

uncover *v* remove the cap, top, etc. from; reveal or disclose.

unction *n* act of anointing with oil in sacramental ceremonies. **unctuous** *adj* pretending to be kind and concerned.

undeceive *v* reveal the truth to (someone previously misled or deceived).

undecided *adj* not having made up one's mind; (of an issue or problem) not agreed or decided upon.

undeniable *adj* indisputably true. **undeniably** *adv*

under *prep* on, to, or beneath the underside or base of; less than; subject to the supervision, control, or influence of; subject to (conditions). ♦ *adv* to a position underneath.

under- *prefix* below, e.g. *underground*; insufficient or insufficiently, e.g. *underrate*.

underage *adj* below the required or standard age.

underarm *Sport* ♦ *adj* denoting a style of throwing, bowling, or serving in which the hand is swung below shoulder level. ♦ *adv* in an underarm style.

undercarriage *n* landing gear of an aircraft; framework supporting the body of a vehicle.

underclass *n* class consisting of the most disadvantaged people, such as the long-term unemployed.

undercoat *n* coat of paint applied before the final coat.

undercover *adj* done or acting in secret.

undercurrent *n* current that is not apparent at the surface; underlying opinion or emotion.

undercut *v* charge less than (a competitor) to obtain trade.

underdog *n* person or team unlikely to win in a competition.

underdone *adj* not cooked enough.

underestimate *v* make too low an estimate of; not think highly enough of.

underfelt *n* thick felt laid under a carpet to increase insulation.

underfoot *adv* under the feet.

undergarment *n* any piece of underwear.

undergo *v* experience, endure, or sustain.

undergraduate *n* person studying in a university for a first degree.

underground *adj* occurring, situated, used, or going below ground level; secret. ♦ *n* movement dedicated to overthrowing a government or occupation forces; *Brit* subway.

undergrowth *n* small trees and bushes growing beneath taller trees in a wood or forest.

underhand *adj* sly, deceitful, and secretive.

underlie *v* lie or be placed under; be the foundation, cause, or basis of. **underlying** *adj* fundamental.

underline *v* draw a line under; state forcibly, emphasize.

underling *n* subordinate.

undermine *v* weaken gradually; (of the sea or wind) wear away the base of (cliffs).

underneath *prep, adv* beneath. ♦ *adj, n* lower (part or surface).

underpants *pl n* man's undergarment for the lower part of the body.

underpass *n* section of a road that passes under another road or a railway line.

underpin *v* give strength or support to.

underprivileged *adj* lacking the rights and advantages of other members of society.

underrate *v* underestimate. **underrated** *adj*

underseal *n* coating of tar etc. applied to the underside of a motor vehicle to retard corrosion.

underside *n* bottom or lower surface.

understand *v* know and comprehend the nature or meaning of; realize or grasp (something); assume, infer, or believe. **understandable** *adj* **understandably** *adv* **understanding** *n* ability to learn, judge, or make decisions; personal interpretation of a subject; mutual agreement, usu. an informal or private one. ♦ *adj* kind and sympathetic.

understate v describe or represent (something) in restrained terms; state that (something, such as a number) is less than it is. **understatement** n

understudy n actor who studies a part in order to be able to replace the usual actor if necessary. ◆ v act as an understudy for.

undertake v agree or commit oneself to (something) or (to do something); promise. **undertaking** n task or enterprise; agreement to do something.

undertaker n person whose profession is to prepare corpses for burial and organize funerals.

undertone n quiet tone of voice; underlying quality or feeling.

undertow n strong undercurrent flowing in a different direction from the surface current.

underwear n clothing worn under the outer garments and next to the skin.

underworld n criminals and their associates; *Greek & Roman myth* regions below the earth's surface regarded as the abode of the dead.

underwrite v accept financial responsibility for (a commercial project); sign and issue (an insurance policy), thus accepting liability. **underwriter** n

undesirable adj not desirable or pleasant, objectionable. ◆ n objectionable person. **undesirably** adv

undo v open, unwrap; reverse the effects of; cause the downfall of. **undone** adj **undoing** n cause of someone's downfall.

undoubted adj certain or indisputable. **undoubtedly** adv

undue adj greater than is reasonable, excessive. **unduly** adv

undulate v move in waves. **undulation** n

undying adj never ending, eternal.

unearth v dig up out of the earth; reveal or discover.

unearthly adj ghostly or eerie; ridiculous or unreasonable, e.g. *an unearthly hour.* **unearthliness** n

uneasy adj (of a person) anxious or apprehensive; (of a condition) precarious or uncomfortable. **uneasily** adv **uneasiness** n **unease** n

unemployed adj out of work.

unemployment n

unequivocal adj completely clear in meaning. **unequivocally** adv

unerring adj never mistaken, consistently accurate.

unexceptionable adj beyond criticism or objection.

unfailing adj continuous or reliable. **unfailingly** adv

unfair adj not right, fair, or just. **unfairly** adv **unfairness** n

unfaithful adj guilty of adultery; not true to a promise or vow. **unfaithfulness** n

unfeeling adj without sympathy.

unfit adj (foll. by *for*) unqualified or unsuitable; in poor physical condition.

unflappable adj *Informal* not easily upset. **unflappability** n

unfold v open or spread out from a folded state; reveal or be revealed.

unforgettable adj impossible to forget, memorable.

unfortunate adj unlucky, unsuccessful, or unhappy; regrettable or unsuitable. **unfortunately** adv

unfrock v deprive (a priest in holy orders) of his priesthood.

ungainly adj **-lier, -liest** lacking grace when moving. **ungainliness** n

ungodly adj wicked or sinful; *Informal* unreasonable or outrageous. **ungodliness** n

ungrateful adj not grateful or thankful. **ungratefully** adv **ungratefulness** n

unguarded adj not protected; incautious or careless.

unguent [ung-gwent] n ointment.

unhand v *Old-fashioned lit* release from one's grasp.

unhappy adj sad or depressed; unfortunate or wretched. **unhappily** adv **unhappiness** n

unhealthy adj likely to cause poor health; not fit or well; morbid, unnatural.

unhinge v derange or unbalance (a person or his or her mind).

uni- *combining form* of, consisting of, or having only one, e.g. *unicellular.*

unicorn n imaginary horselike creature with one horn growing from its forehead.

uniform n special identifying set of clothes for the members of an organization, such as soldiers. ◆ *adj* unvarying; alike or like. **uniformly** *adv* **uniformity** *n*

unify *v* **-fying, -fied** make or become one. **unification** *n*

unilateral *adj* made or done by only one person or group. **unilaterally** *adv*

unimpeachable *adj* completely honest and reliable.

uninterested *adj* having or showing no interest in someone or something.

union *n* uniting or being united; short for TRADE UNION; association of individuals or groups for a common purpose. **unionist** *n* member or supporter of a trade union. **unionize** *v* organize (workers) into a trade union. **unionization** *n* **Union Flag, Jack** national flag of the United Kingdom.

unique [yoo-**neek**] *adj* being the only one of a particular type; without equal or like. **uniquely** *adv*

unisex *adj* designed for use by both sexes.

unison *n* complete agreement; *Music* singing or playing the same notes at the same time.

unit *n* single undivided entity or whole; group or individual regarded as a basic element of a larger whole; fixed quantity etc., used as a standard of measurement. **unitary** *adj*

Unitarian *n* person who believes that God is one being and rejects the Trinity. **Unitarianism** *n*

unite *v* make or become an integrated whole; form an association or alliance. **unity** *n* state of being one; mutual agreement. **United Church** Canadian church formed by union of some Presbyterians and Methodists. **United Empire Loyalist** American colonist who settled in Canada in the War of American Independence through loyalty to Britain.

universe *n* whole of all existing matter, energy, and space; the world. **universal** *adj* of or typical of the whole of mankind or of nature; existing everywhere. **universally** *adv* **universality** *n*

university *n, pl* **-ties** institution of higher education having the authority to award degrees.

unkempt *adj* (of the hair) not combed; slovenly or untidy.

unknown *adj* not known; not famous.

◆ *n* unknown person, quantity, or thing.

unleaded *adj* (of gasoline) containing less tetraethyl lead, to reduce environmental pollution.

unless *conj* except under the circumstances that.

unlike *adj* dissimilar or different. ◆ *prep* not like or typical of **unlikely** *adj* improbable.

unload *v* remove (cargo) from (a ship, truck, or plane); get rid of; remove the ammunition from (a firearm).

unmask *v* remove the mask or disguise from; (cause to) appear in true character.

unmentionable *adj* unsuitable as a topic of conversation.

unmistakable, unmistakeable *adj* not ambiguous, clear. **unmistakably, unmistakeably** *adv*

unmitigated *adj* not reduced or lessened in severity, intensity, etc.; total and complete.

unmoved *adj* not affected by emotion, indifferent.

unnatural *adj* strange and frightening because not usual, e.g. *an unnatural silence*; not in accordance with accepted standards of behaviour.

unnerve *v* cause to lose courage, confidence, or self-control.

unnumbered *adj* countless; not counted or given a number.

unorthodox *adj* (of ideas, methods, etc.) not conventional and not generally accepted; (of a person) having unusual opinions or methods.

unpack *v* remove the contents of (a suitcase, trunk, etc.); take (something) out of a packed container.

unparalleled *adj* not equalled, supreme.

unpick *v* undo (the stitches) of (a piece of sewing).

unpleasant *adj* not pleasant or agreeable. **unpleasantly** *adv* **unpleasantness** *n*

unprintable *adj* unsuitable for printing for reasons of obscenity or libel.

unprofessional *adj* contrary to the accepted code of a profession; not belonging to a profession. **unprofessionally** *adv*

unqualified *adj* lacking the necessary qualifications; not modified.

unravel *v* **-elling, -elled** reduce (something knitted or woven) to separate strands; become unravelled; explain or solve.

unremitting *adj* never slackening or stopping.

unrest *n* rebellious state of discontent.

unrivalled *adj* having no equal.

unroll *v* open out or unwind (something rolled or coiled) or (of something rolled or coiled) become opened out or unwound

unruly *adj* **-lier, -liest** given to disobedience or indiscipline.

unsavoury *adj* distasteful or objectionable.

unscathed *adj* not harmed or injured.

unscrupulous *adj* unprincipled or without scruples.

unseat *v* throw or displace from a seat or saddle; depose from an office or position.

unsettled *adj* lacking order or stability; disturbed and restless; constantly changing or moving from place to place.

unsightly *adj* unpleasant to look at.

unsocial *adj* avoiding the company of other people; falling outside the normal working day, e.g. *unsocial hours.*

unsound *adj* unhealthy or unstable; not based on truth or fact.

unstable *adj* lacking stability or firmness; having abrupt changes of mood or behaviour.

unstudied *adj* natural or spontaneous.

unsuitable *adj* not right or appropriate for a particular purpose. **unsuitably** *adv*

unsuited *adj* not appropriate for a particular task or situation.

unswerving *adj* firm, constant, not changing.

unthinkable *adj* out of the question, inconceivable.

untidy *adj* not neat, slovenly. **untidily** *adv* **untidiness** *n*

untie *v* open or free (something that is tied); free from constraint.

until *conj* up to the time that. ◆ *prep* in or throughout the period before. **not until** not before (a time or event).

untimely *adj* occurring before the expected or normal time; inappropriate to the occasion.

unto *prep Old-fashioned* to.

untold *adj* incapable of description; incalculably great in number or quantity.

untouchable *adj* above reproach or suspicion; unable to be touched. ◆ *n* member of the lowest Hindu caste in India.

untoward *adj* causing misfortune or annoyance.

untruth *n* statement that is not true, lie.

unusual *adj* uncommon or extraordinary. **unusually** *adv*

unutterable *adj* incapable of being expressed in words. **unutterably** *adv*

unvarnished *adj* not elaborated upon.

unwieldy *adj* too heavy, large, or awkward to be easily handled.

unwind *v* (cause to) slacken, undo, or unravel; make or become relaxed.

unwitting *adj* not knowing or conscious; not intentional. **unwittingly** *adv*

unwonted *adj* out of the ordinary.

unworthy *adj* not deserving or worthy; (foll. by *of*) beneath the level considered befitting (to); lacking merit or value.

unwrap *v* remove the wrapping from (something) or (of something wrapped) have the covering removed

unwritten *adj* not printed or in writing; operating only through custom.

up *prep* indicating movement to a higher position; at a higher or further level or position in or on. ◆ *adv* to an upward, higher, or erect position; indicating readiness for an activity, e.g. *up and about*; indicating intensity or completion of an action; to the place referred to or where the speaker is. ◆ *adj* of a high or higher position; out of bed. ◆ *v* **upping, upped** increase or raise; *Informal* do something suddenly, e.g. *he upped and left.* **up against** having to cope with. **ups and downs** alternating periods of good and bad luck. **uptown** *n* the part of a city that is away from the centre. **what's up?** *Informal* what is wrong? **upward** *adj* directed or moving towards a higher place or level. ◆ *adv* (also **upwards**) from a lower to a higher place, level, or condition.

upbeat n Music unaccented beat.
♦ adj Informal cheerful and optimistic.

upbraid v scold or reproach.

upbringing n education of a person during the formative years.

update v bring up to date.

upend v turn or set or be turned or set on end.

upfront adj open and frank. ♦ adv, adj (of money) paid out at the beginning of a business arrangement.

upgrade v promote (a person or job) to a higher rank.

upheaval n strong, sudden, or violent disturbance.

uphill adj sloping or leading upwards; requiring a great deal of effort. ♦ adv up a slope.

uphold v maintain or defend against opposition; give moral support to. **upholder** n

upholster v fit (a chair or sofa) with padding, springs, and covering. **upholsterer** n **upholstery** n act of upholstering; soft covering on a chair or sofa.

upkeep n act, process, or cost of keeping something in good repair.

upland n area of high or relatively high ground. ♦ adj of or in an upland.

uplift v raise or lift up; raise morally or spiritually. ♦ n act, process, or result of lifting up. **uplifting** adj

upon prep on; up and on.

upper adj higher or highest in physical position, wealth, rank, or status. ♦ n part of a shoe above the sole.

uppermost adj highest in position, power, or importance. ♦ adv in or into the highest place or position. **upper-case** adj denoting capital letters as used in printed or typed matter. **upper class** highest social class. **upper-class** adj **upper crust** Informal upper class. **upper hand** position of control.

uppish, uppity adj Informal arrogant or presumptuous.

upright adj vertical or erect; honest or just. ♦ adv vertically. ♦ n vertical support, such as a post. **uprightness** n

uprising n rebellion or revolt.

uproar n disturbance characterized by loud noise and confusion. **uproarious** adj very funny; (of laughter) loud and boisterous. **uproariously** adv

uproot v pull up by or as if by the roots; displace (a person or people) from their native or usual surroundings.

upset adj emotionally or physically disturbed or distressed. ♦ v tip over; disturb the normal state or stability of; disturb mentally or emotionally; make physically ill. ♦ n unexpected defeat or reversal; disturbance or disorder of the emotions, mind, or body. **upsetting** adj

upshot n final result or conclusion.

upside down adj turned over completely; Informal confused or jumbled. ♦ adv in an inverted fashion; in a chaotic manner.

upstage adj at the back half of the stage. ♦ v Informal draw attention to oneself from (someone else).

upstairs adv up the stairs. ♦ n upper floor. ♦ adj situated on an upper floor.

upstanding adj of good character.

upstart n person who has risen suddenly to a position of power and behaves arrogantly.

upstream adv, adj in or towards the higher part of a stream.

upsurge n rapid rise or swell.

uptake n quick, slow on the uptake Informal quick or slow to understand or learn.

uptight adj Informal nervously tense, irritable, or angry.

up-to-date adj modern or fashionable.

upturn n upward trend or improvement; upheaval.

uranium [yew-rain-ee-um] n radioactive silvery-white metallic element, used chiefly as a source of nuclear energy.

Uranus n Greek god of the sky; seventh planet from the sun.

urban adj of or living in a city or town; denoting modern pop music of African-American origin, such as hip-hop. **urbanize** v make (a rural area) more industrialized and urban. **urbanization** n

urbane adj characterized by courtesy, elegance, and sophistication. **urbanity** n

urchin n mischievous child.

urethra [yew-reeth-ra] n, pl -thrae, -thras canal that carries urine from the bladder out of the body.

urge n strong impulse, inner drive, or

yearning. ◆ v plead with or press (a person to do something); advocate earnestly; force or drive onwards.

urgent adj requiring speedy action or attention. **urgency** n **urgently** adv

urine n pale yellow fluid excreted by the kidneys to the bladder and passed as waste from the body **uric** adj **urinal** n (place with) sanitary fitting(s) used by men for urination. **urinary** adj **urinate** v discharge urine. **urination** n

URL uniform resource locator: the address of a location on the Internet.

urn n vase used as a container for the ashes of the dead; large metal container with a tap, used for making and holding tea or coffee.

ursine adj of or like a bear.

us pron objective case of WE.

US, USA United States (of America).

use v put into service or action; take advantage of; consume or expend. ◆ n using or being used; ability or permission to use; usefulness or advantage; purpose for which something is used. **user** n **user-friendly** adj easy to familiarize oneself with, understand, and use. **usable** adj able to be used. **usability** n **usage** n regular or constant use; way in which a word is used in a language. **used** adj second-hand. **used to** adj accustomed to. ◆ v used as an auxiliary to express past habitual or accustomed actions, e.g. *I used to live there.* **useful** adj **usefully** adv **usefulness** n **useless** adj **uselessly** adv **uselessness** n

usher n official who shows people to their seats, as in a church. ◆ v conduct or escort. **usherette** n female assistant in a cinema who shows people to their seats.

USSR formerly, Union of Soviet Socialist Republics.

usual adj of the most normal, frequent, or regular type. **usually** adv most often, in most cases.

usurp [yewz-**zurp**] v seize (a position or power) without authority. **usurpation** n **usurper** n

usury n, pl -ries practice of lending money at an extremely high rate of interest. **usurer** [**yewz**-yoor-er] n

utensil n tool or container for practical use.

uterus [**yew**-ter-russ] n womb. **uterine** adj

utilitarian adj of utilitarianism; useful rather than beautiful. **utilitarianism** n doctrine that the right action is that which brings about the greatest good for the greatest number of people.

utility n, pl **-ties** usefulness; public service, such as gas. ◆ adj designed for use rather than beauty **utilize** v make practical use of. **utilization** n

utmost adj, n (of the) greatest possible degree or amount.

Utopia [yew-**tope**-ee-a] n any real or imaginary society, place, or state considered to be ideal. **Utopian** adj

utter¹ v express (something) audibly. **utterance** n something uttered; act or power of uttering.

utter² adj absolute. **utterly** adv

uttermost adj, n same as UTMOST.

U-turn n turn, made by a vehicle, in the shape of a U, resulting in a reversal of direction; complete change in policy.

UV ultraviolet.

uvula [**yew**-view-la] n, pl **-las, -lae** small fleshy part of the soft palate that hangs in the back of the throat. **uvular** adj

uxorious [ux-or-ee-uss] adj excessively fond of one's wife.

V v

V volt.

v. versus; very.

vacant adj (of a lavatory, room, etc.) unoccupied; without interest or understanding. **vacantly** adv **vacancy** n, pl **-cies** unfilled job; unoccupied room in a guesthouse; state of being unoccupied.

vacate v leave (a place or job). **vacation** n time when universities and law courts are closed; holiday.

vaccinate v inoculate with a vaccine. **vaccination** n **vaccine** n substance designed to cause a mild form of a disease to make a person immune to the disease itself.

vacillate [**vass**-ill-late] v waver in one's opinions. **vacillation** n

vacuous adj not expressing intelligent thought. **vacuity** n

vacuum n, pl **vacuums, vacua** empty space from which all or most air or gas has been removed. ◆ v clean with a vacuum cleaner. **vacuum cleaner** electrical appliance for removing dust by suction. **vacuum-packed** adj contained in packaging from which the air has been removed.

vagabond n person with no fixed home, esp. a beggar.

vagaries [vaig-a-reez] pl n unpredictable changes.

vagina [vaj-jine-a] n, pl -nas, -nae (in female mammals) passage from the womb to the external genitals. **vaginal** adj

vagrant [vaig-rant] n person with no settled home. ◆ adj wandering. **vagrancy** n

vague adj not clearly explained; unable to be seen or heard clearly; absent-minded. **vaguely** adv

vain adj excessively proud, esp. of one's appearance; bound to fail, futile. **in vain** unsuccessfully.

vainglorious adj Lit boastful. **vainglory** n

valance [val-lenss] n piece of drapery round the edge of a bed.

vale n Lit valley.

valediction [val-lid-dik-shun] n farewell speech. **valedictory** adj

valence [vale-ence] n molecular bonding between atoms.

valency n, pl -cies power of an atom to make molecular bonds.

valentine n (person to whom one sends) a romantic card on Saint Valentine's Day, 14th February.

valerian n herb used as a sedative.

valet n man's personal male servant.

valetudinarian [val-lit-yew-din-air-ee-an] n person with a long-term illness; hypochondriac.

valiant adj brave or courageous.

valid adj soundly reasoned; having legal force. **validate** v make valid. **validation** n **validity** n

valise [val-leez] n Old-fashioned travelling bag.

Valium n ® drug used as a tranquillizer.

valley n low area between hills, usu. with a river running through it.

valour n Lit bravery. **valorous** adj

value n importance, usefulness; monetary worth. ◆ pl moral principles. ◆ v **valuing, valued** assess the value of; have a high regard for. **valuable** adj having great worth. **valuables** pl n valuable personal property. **valuation** n assessment of worth. **valueless** adj **valuer** n **value-added tax** Brit see VAT. **value judgment** opinion based on personal belief.

valve n device to control the movement of fluid through a pipe; Anat flap in a part of the body allowing blood to flow in one direction only; Physics tube containing a vacuum, allowing current to flow from a cathode to an anode. **valvular** adj

vamoose v Slang go away.

vamp[1] n Informal woman who seduces men to her own advantage.

vamp[2] v (foll. by up) renovate; improvise an accompaniment to (a tune).

vampire n (in folklore) a corpse that rises at night to drink the blood of the living. **vampire bat** tropical bat that feeds on blood.

van[1] n motor vehicle for transporting goods; Brit railway carriage for goods in which the guard travels.

van[2] n short for VANGUARD.

vanadium n metallic element, used in steel.

vandal n person who deliberately damages property. **vandalism** n **vandalize** v

vane n flat blade on a rotary device such as a weathercock or propeller.

vanguard n unit of soldiers leading an army; most advanced group or position in a movement or activity.

vanilla n seed pod of a tropical climbing orchid, used for flavouring.

vanish v disappear suddenly or mysteriously; cease to exist.

vanity n, pl -ties (display of) excessive pride.

vanquish v Lit defeat (someone) utterly. **vanquisher** n

vantage n advantage. **vantage point** position that gives one an overall view.

vapid adj lacking character, dull. **vapidity** n

vapour n moisture suspended in air as steam or mist; gaseous form of something that is liquid or solid at room temperature. **vaporize** v **vaporizer** n **vaporous** adj

variable adj not always the same,

changeable. ◆ *n Math* expression with a range of values. **variability** *n*

variant *adj* different or alternative. ◆ *n* alternative form. **at variance** in disagreement.

variation *n* extent to which something varies; *Music* repetition in different forms of a basic theme. **variational** *adj*

varicose veins *pl n* knotted and swollen veins, esp. in the legs.

variegated *adj* having patches or streaks of different colours. **variegation** *n*

variety *n, pl* **-ties** state of being various; different things of the same kind; sort or kind; light entertainment composed of unrelated acts.

various *adj* of several kinds. **variously** *adv*

varlet *n Obs* rascal.

varnish *n* solution of oil and resin, put on a surface to make it hard and glossy. ◆ *v* apply varnish to.

vary *v* **varying, varied** change; cause differences in. **varied** *adj*

vascular *adj Biol* relating to vessels.

vas deferens *n, pl* **vasa deferentia** *Anat* sperm-carrying duct in each testicle.

vase *n* ornamental jar, esp. for flowers.

vasectomy *n, pl* **-mies** (operation for) the removal of part of the vas deferens, as a contraceptive method.

Vaseline *n* ® thick oily cream made from petroleum, used in skin care.

vassal *n Hist* man given land in return for allegiance to his lord.

vast *adj* extremely large. **vastly** *adv* **vastness** *n*

vat *n* large container for liquids.

VAT *Brit* value-added tax: tax on the difference between the cost of materials and the selling price.

Vatican *n* the Pope's palace.

vaudeville *n US* variety entertainment in a theatre.

vault[1] *n* secure room for storing valuables; underground burial chamber. **vaulted** *adj* having an arched roof.

vault[2] *v* jump over (something) by resting one's hand(s) on it. ◆ *n* such a jump.

vaunt *v* describe or display (success or possessions) boastfully. **vaunted** *adj*

VC Vice Chancellor; Victoria Cross.

VCR video cassette recorder.

VD venereal disease.

VDU visual display unit.

veal *n* calf meat.

vector *n Math* quantity that has size and direction, such as force; *animal,* usu. an insect, that carries disease.

veer *v* change direction suddenly.

vegan [vee-gan] *n* person who eats no meat, fish, eggs, or dairy products. ◆ *adj* suitable for a vegan. **veganism** *n*

vegetable *n* edible plant; *Informal* severely brain-damaged person. ◆ *adj* of or like plants or vegetables.

vegetarian *n* person who eats no meat or fish. ◆ *adj* suitable for a vegetarian. **vegetarianism** *n*

vegetate *v* live a dull uncreative life.

vegetation *n* plant life of a given place.

vehement *adj* expressing strong feelings. **vehemence** *n* **vehemently** *adv*

vehicle *n* machine, esp. with an engine and wheels, for carrying people or objects; means of communicating something. **vehicular** *adj*

veil *n* piece of thin cloth covering the head or face; something that conceals the truth, e.g. *a veil of secrecy.* ◆ *v* cover with a veil. **take the veil** become a nun. **veiled** *adj* disguised.

vein *n* tube that takes blood to the heart; line in a leaf or an insect's wing; layer of ore or mineral in rock; streak in marble; feature of someone's writing or speech, e.g. *a vein of humour*; mood, e.g. *in a lighter vein*. **veined** *adj*

Velcro *n* ® fastening consisting of one piece of fabric with tiny hooked threads and another with a coarse surface that adheres to it.

veld, veldt *n* high grassland in Southern Africa.

vellum *n* fine calfskin parchment; type of smooth paper.

velocity [vel-loss-it-ee] *n, pl* **-ties** speed of movement in a given direction.

velours, velour [vel-loor] *n* velvety fabric.

velvet *n* fabric with a thick pile. **velvety** *adj* soft and smooth. **velveteen** *n* cotton velvet.

venal [vee-nal] adj easily bribed; characterized by bribery.

vend v sell. **vendor** n **vending machine** machine that dispenses goods when coins are inserted.

vendetta n prolonged quarrel between families, esp. one involving revenge killings.

veneer n thin layer of wood etc. covering a cheaper material; superficial appearance, e.g. a veneer of sophistication.

venerable adj worthy of deep respect. **venerate** v hold (a person) in deep respect. **veneration** n

venereal disease [ven-ear-ee-al] n disease transmitted sexually.

Venetian blind n window blind made of horizontal slats that turn to let in more or less light.

vengeance n revenge. **vengeful** adj wanting revenge. **vengefully** adv

venial [veen-ee-al] adj (of a sin or fault) easily forgiven. **veniality** n

venison n deer meat.

venom n poison produced by snakes etc.; malice or spite. **venomous** adj

venous [vee-nuss] adj Anat of veins.

vent[1] n outlet releasing fumes or fluid. ◆ v express (an emotion) freely.

vent[2] n vertical slit in a jacket.

ventilate v let fresh air into; discuss (a complaint) openly. **ventilation** n **ventilator** n

ventral adj relating to the front of the body.

ventricle n Anat one of the four cavities of the heart or brain.

ventriloquist n entertainer who can speak without moving his or her lips, so that a voice seems to come from elsewhere. **ventriloquism** n

venture n risky undertaking, esp. in business. ◆ v do something risky; dare to express (an opinion); go to an unknown place. **venturesome** adj

venue n place where an organized gathering is held.

Venus n planet second nearest to the sun; Roman goddess of love. **Venus's flytrap, Venus flytrap** plant that traps and digests insects between hinged leaves.

veracious adj habitually truthful. **veracity** n

veranda, verandah n open porch attached to a house.

verb n word that expresses the idea of action, happening, or being. **verbal** adj spoken; of a verb. **verbally** adv **verbalize** v express (something) in words.

verbatim [verb-bait-im] adv, adj word for word.

verbena n plant with sweet-smelling flowers.

verbiage n excessive use of words.

verbose [verb-bohss] adj long-winded. **verbosity** n

verdant adj Lit covered in green vegetation.

verdict n decision of a jury; opinion formed after examining the facts.

verdigris [ver-dig-riss] n green film on copper, brass, or bronze.

verdure n Lit flourishing green vegetation.

verge n Brit grass border along a road. **on the verge of** having almost reached (a point or condition). **verge on** v be near to (a condition).

verger n Anglican church church caretaker.

verify v -ifying, -ified check the truth or accuracy of. **verifiable** adj **verification** n

verily adv Obs in truth.

verisimilitude n appearance of being real.

veritable adj rightly called, without exaggeration, e.g. a veritable feast. **veritably** adv

verity n, pl -ties true statement.

vermicelli [ver-me-chell-ee] n fine strands of pasta; tiny strands of chocolate.

vermiform adj shaped like a worm. **vermiform appendix** Anat same as APPENDIX.

vermilion adj orange-red.

vermin pl n animals, esp. insects and rodents, that spread disease or cause damage. **verminous** adj

vermouth [ver-muth] n wine flavoured with herbs.

vernacular [ver-nak-yew-lar] n most widely spoken language of a particular people or place.

vernal adj occurring in spring.

vernier [ver-nee-er] n movable scale on a graduated measuring instrument for taking readings in fractions.

veronica n plant with small flowers.

verruca [ver-roo-ka] n, pl -**cae**, -**cas** wart, usu. on the foot.

versatile adj having many skills or uses. **versatility** n

verse n group of lines in a song or poem; poetry as distinct from prose; subdivision of a book of the Bible. **versed in** knowledgeable about. **versify** v write in verse. **versification** n

version n form of something, such as a piece of writing, with some differences from other forms; account of an incident from a particular point of view.

verso n, pl -**sos** left-hand page of a book; back of a sheet of paper.

versus prep Sport, Law against; in contrast with.

vertebra [ver-tib-ra] n, pl **vertebrae** [ver-tib-ree] one of the bones that form the spine. **vertebral** adj **vertebrate** n, adj (animal) having a spine.

vertex n Math point on a geometric figure where the sides form an angle; highest point of a triangle.

vertical adj straight up and down. ♦ n vertical direction.

vertigo n dizziness when looking down from a high place. **vertiginous** adj

vervain n plant with spikes of blue, purple, or white flowers.

verve n enthusiasm or liveliness.

very adv more than usually, extremely. ♦ adj absolute, exact, e.g. the very top, the very man.

vesicle n Biol sac or small cavity, esp. one containing fluid.

vespers pl n RC Church (service of) evening prayer.

vessel n ship; Lit container for liquid; Biol tubular structure in animals and plants that carries body fluids, such as blood or sap.

vest n sleeveless garment worn under a jacket or coat; Brit undershirt. ♦ v (foll. by in or with) give (authority) to (someone). **vested interest** interest someone has in a matter because he or she might benefit from it. **vest-pocket** adj small enough to fit into a vest pocket.

vestibule n entrance hall.

vestige [vest-ij] n small amount or trace. **vestigial** [vest-ij-ee-al] adj

vestments pl n priest's robes.

vestry n, pl -**tries** room in a church used as an office by the priest or minister.

vet[1] n short for VETERINARY SURGEON. ♦ v **vetting**, **vetted** check the suitability of (a candidate).

vet[2] n military veteran.

vetch n climbing plant with a beanlike fruit used as fodder.

veteran n person with long experience in a particular activity, esp. military service. ♦ adj long-serving.

veterinary adj concerning animal health. **veterinary surgeon** medical specialist who treats sick animals.

veto [vee-toe] n, pl -**toes** official power to cancel a proposal. ♦ v -**toing**, -**toed** enforce a veto against.

vex v frustrate, annoy. **vexation** n something annoying; being annoyed. **vexatious** adj **vexed question** much debated subject.

VHF Radio very high frequency.

VHS ® Video Home System: format for recording on video.

via prep by way of.

viable adj able to be put into practice; Biol able to live and grow independently. **viability** n

viaduct n bridge over a valley.

Viagra (vie-ag-ra) n ® drug used to treat impotence in men.

vial n same as PHIAL.

viands pl n Obs food.

vibes pl n Informal emotional reactions between people, atmosphere of a place; short for VIBRAPHONE.

vibrant [vibe-rant] adj vigorous in appearance; (of a voice) resonant; (of a colour) strong and bright.

vibraphone n musical instrument with metal bars that resonate electronically when hit.

vibrate v move back and forth rapidly; (cause to) resonate. **vibration** n **vibrator** n device that produces vibratory motion, used for massage or as a sex aid. **vibratory** adj

vibrato n Music rapid fluctuation in the pitch of a note.

vicar n Anglican church clergyman in charge of a parish. **vicarage** n vicar's house.

vicarious [vick-air-ee-uss] adj felt indirectly by imagining what another person experiences; delegated. **vicariously** adv

vice[1] n immoral personal quality; minor imperfection in someone's character; criminal activities, esp. involving sex.

vice[2] n tool with a screw mechanism for holding an object while working on it.

vice[3] adj serving in place of.

vice chancellor n chief executive of a university.

viceroy n governor of a colony who represents the monarch. **viceregal** adj

vice versa [vie-see ver-sa] adv Latin conversely, the other way round.

vicinity [viss-in-it-ee] n surrounding area.

vicious adj cruel and violent. **viciously** adv **vicious circle** sequence of problems and solutions which always leads back to the original problem.

vicissitudes [viss-**iss**-it-yewds] pl n changes in fortune.

victim n person or thing harmed or killed; person or animal killed as a sacrifice. **victimize** v punish unfairly; discriminate against. **victimization** n

victor n person who has defeated an opponent, esp. in war or in sport. **victorious** adj **victory** n winning of a battle or contest.

Victoria Cross n Brit highest award for bravery.

Victorian adj of or in the reign of Queen Victoria (1837–1901); characterized by prudery or hypocrisy. ◆ n person who lived during Victoria's reign.

victuals [vit-als] pl n Old-fashioned food. **victual** v **victualling, victualled** supply with or obtain victuals. **victualler** n

vicuña [vik-koo-nya] n S American animal like the llama; fine cloth made from its wool.

video n short for VIDEO CASSETTE (RECORDER). ◆ v **videoing, videoed** record (a TV programme or event) on video. ◆ adj relating to or used in producing television images. **video cassette** cassette containing video tape. **video cassette recorder** tape recorder for recording and playing back TV programmes and films. **video tape** magnetic tape used to record video-frequency signals in TV

production; magnetic tape used to record programmes when they are broadcast. **videotape** v record (a TV programme) on video tape. **video tape recorder** tape recorder for vision signals, used in TV production. **videotext** n means of representing on a TV screen information that is held in a computer.

vie v **vying, vied** compete (with someone).

view n opinion; everything that can be seen from a given place; picture of this. ◆ v think of (something) in a particular way. **in view of** taking into consideration. **on view** exhibited to the public. **viewer** n person who watches television; hand-held device for looking at photographic slides. **viewfinder** n window on a camera showing what will appear in a photograph.

vigil [vij-ill] n night-time period of staying awake to look after a sick person, pray, etc. **vigilant** adj watchful in case of danger. **vigilance** n

vigilante [vij-ill-**ant**-ee] n person, esp. as one of a group, who takes it upon himself or herself to enforce the law.

vignette [vin-**yet**] n concise description of the typical features of something; small decorative illustration in a book.

vigour n physical or mental energy. **vigorous** adj **vigorously** adv

Viking n Hist seafaring raider and settler from Scandinavia.

vile adj very wicked; disgusting. **vilely** adv **vileness** n

vilify [vill-if-fie] v -**ifying, -ified** unjustly attack the character of. **vilification** n

villa n large house with gardens; house rented to holiday-makers.

village n small group of houses in a country area; rural community. **villager** n

villain n wicked person; main wicked character in a play. **villainous** adj **villainy** n

villein [vill-an] n Hist peasant bound in service to his lord.

vinaigrette n salad dressing of oil and vinegar.

vindicate v clear (someone) of guilt; justify (someone) whose behaviour has been challenged. **vindication** n

vindictive adj maliciously seeking

revenge. **vindictiveness** *n* **vindictively** *adv*

vine *n* climbing plant, esp. one producing grapes. **vineyard** [vinn-yard] *n* plantation of grape vines, esp. for making wine.

vinegar *n* acid liquid made from wine, beer, or cider. **vinegary** *adj*

vino [vee-noh] *n Informal* wine.

vintage *n* wine from a particular harvest of grapes. ♦ *adj* best and most typical. **vintage car** high-quality antique car.

vintner *n* dealer in wine.

vinyl [vine-ill] *n* type of plastic, used in mock leather and records.

viol [vie-oll] *n* early stringed instrument preceding the violin.

viola¹ [vee-oh-la] *n* stringed instrument lower in pitch than a violin.

viola² [vie-ol-la] *n* variety of pansy.

violate *v* break (a law or agreement); disturb (someone's privacy); treat (a sacred place) disrespectfully; rape. **violation** *n* **violator** *n*

violent *adj* using or marked by physical strength that is harmful or destructive; aggressively intense; using excessive force. **violence** *n* **violently** *adv*

violet *n* plant with bluish-purple flowers. ♦ *adj* bluish-purple.

violin *n* small four-stringed musical instrument played with a bow. **violinist** *n*

violoncello [vie-oll-on-chell-oh] *n, pl* **-los** same as CELLO.

VIP very important person.

viper *n* poisonous snake.

virago [vir-rah-go] *n, pl* **-goes, -gos** aggressive woman.

viral [vie-ral] *adj* of or caused by a virus.

virgin *n* person, esp. a woman, who has not had sexual intercourse. ♦ *adj* not having had sexual intercourse; not yet exploited or explored. **virginal** *adj* like a virgin. ♦ *n* rectangular keyboard instrument like a small harpsichord. **virginity** *n*

virile *adj* having the traditional male characteristics of physical strength and a high sex drive. **virility** *n*

virology *n* study of viruses.

virtual *adj* having the effect but not the form of; of or relating to virtual reality. **virtual reality** computer-generated environment that seems real to the user. **virtually** *adv* practically, almost.

virtue *n* moral goodness; positive moral quality; merit. **by virtue of** by reason of. **virtuous** *adj* morally good. **virtuously** *adv*

virtuoso *n, pl* **-sos, -si** person with impressive musical skill. **virtuosity** *n*

virulent [vir-yew-lent] *adj* extremely hostile; very infectious; violently harmful.

virus *n* microorganism that causes disease in animals and plants; *Computers* program that propagates itself, via disks and electronic networks, to cause disruption.

visa *n* permission to enter a country, granted by its government and shown by a stamp on one's passport.

visage [viz-zij] *n Lit* face.

vis-à-vis [veez-ah-vee] *prep* in relation to, regarding.

viscera [viss-er-a] *pl n* large abdominal organs. **visceral** *adj* instinctive; of or relating to the viscera.

viscid [viss-id] *adj* sticky. **viscidity** *n*

viscose *n* synthetic fabric made from cellulose.

viscount [vie-count] *n* British nobleman ranking between an earl and a baron. **viscountcy** *n*

viscountess [vie-count-iss] *n* wife or widow of a viscount; woman holding the rank of viscount in her own right.

viscous *adj* thick and sticky. **viscosity** *n*

visible *adj* able to be seen; able to be perceived by the mind. **visibly** *adv* **visibility** *n* clarity of vision.

vision *n* ability to see; mental image of something; hallucination; foresight. **visionary** *adj* showing foresight; idealistic but impractical. ♦ *n, pl* **-aries** visionary person.

visit *v* **-iting, -ited** go or come to see; stay temporarily with; (foll. by *upon*) *Lit* afflict. ♦ *n* instance of visiting; official call. **visitor** *n* **visitation** *n* formal visit or inspection; catastrophe seen as divine punishment.

visor [vize-or] *n* part of a helmet that moves up and down over the face; eyeshade, esp. in an automobile; peak on a cap.

vista *n* (beautiful) extensive view.

visual *adj* done by or used in seeing; designed to be looked at. **visualize** *v* form a mental image of. **visualization** *n* **visual display unit** device with a screen for displaying data held in a computer.

vital *adj* essential or highly important; lively; necessary to maintain life. **vitals** *pl n* body organs. **vitally** *adv* **vitality** *n* physical or mental energy. **vital statistics** statistics of births, deaths, and marriages; *Informal* woman's bust, waist, and hip measurements.

vitamin *n* one of a group of substances that are essential in the diet for specific body processes.

vitiate [vish-ee-ate] *v* spoil the effectiveness of. **vitiation** *n*

viticulture *n* cultivation of grape vines.

vitreous *adj* like or made from glass. **vitreous humour** gelatinous substance that fills the eyeball.

vitrify *v* **-ifying, -ified** change or be changed into glass or a glassy substance. **vitrification** *n*

vitriol *n* language expressing bitterness and hatred; sulfuric acid. **vitriolic** *adj*

vituperative [vite-tyew-pra-tiv] *adj* bitterly abusive. **vituperation** *n*

viva[1] *interj* long live (a person or thing).

viva[2] *n* examination in the form of an interview.

vivace [viv-vah-chee] *adv Music* in a lively manner.

vivacious *adj* full of energy and enthusiasm. **vivacity** *n*

vivarium *n, pl* **-iums, -ia** place where animals are kept in natural conditions.

viva voce [vive-a voh-chee] *adv* in spoken words. ◆ *n* same as VIVA[2].

vivid *adj* very bright; conveying images that are true to life. **vividly** *adv* **vividness** *n*

viviparous [viv-vip-a-russ] *adj* producing live offspring.

vivisection *n* performing surgical experiments on living animals. **vivisectionist** *n*

vixen *n* female fox; *Informal* spiteful woman. **vixenish** *adj*

viz. (introducing specified items) namely.

vizier [viz-zeer] *n* (formerly) Muslim high official.

vizor *n* same as VISOR.

vocabulary *n, pl* **-aries** all the words that a person knows; all the words in a language; specialist terms used in a given subject; list of words in another language with their translation.

vocal *adj* relating to the voice; outspoken. **vocals** *pl n* singing part of a piece of pop music. **vocally** *adv* **vocalist** *n* singer. **vocalize** *v* express with or use the voice. **vocalization** *n* **vocal cords** membranes in the larynx that vibrate to produce sound.

vocation *n* occupation that someone feels called to; profession or trade. **vocational** *adj* directed towards a particular profession or trade.

vociferous *adj* characterized by noisy shouting.

vodka *n* (Russian) spirit distilled from potatoes or grain.

vogue *n* popular style; period of popularity.

voice *n* (quality of) sound made when speaking or singing; expression of opinion by a person or group; property of verbs that makes them active or passive. ◆ *v* express verbally. **voiceless** *adj* **voice mail** electronic system for the storage of telephone messages. **voice-over** *n* film commentary spoken by someone off-camera.

void *n* lonely feeling; empty space. ◆ *adj* not legally binding; empty. ◆ *v* make invalid; empty.

voile [voyl] *n* light semitransparent fabric.

vol. volume.

volatile [voll-a-tile] *adj* liable to sudden change, esp. in behaviour; evaporating quickly. **volatility** *n*

vol-au-vent [voll-oh-von] *n* small puff-pastry case with a savoury filling.

volcano *n, pl* **-noes, -nos** mountain with a vent through which lava is ejected. **volcanic** *adj*

vole *n* small rodent.

volition *n* faculty of exercising the will. **of one's own volition** through one's own choice.

volley *n* simultaneous discharge of ammunition; burst of critical comments; *Sport* stroke or kick at a moving ball before it hits the ground. ◆ *v* discharge (ammunition) in a volley; *Sport* hit or kick (a ball) in a volley. **volleyball** n team game where a ball is hit with the hands over a high net.

volt n unit of electric potential. **voltaic** adj same as GALVANIC. **voltage** n electric potential difference expressed in volts. **voltmeter** n instrument for measuring voltage.

volte-face [volt-**fass**] n reversal of opinion.

voluble adj talking easily and at length. **volubility** n **volubly** adv

volume n size of the space occupied by something; amount; loudness of sound; control on a radio or TV for adjusting this; book, esp. one of a series. **voluminous** adj (of clothes) large and roomy; (of writings) extensive. **volumetric** adj relating to measurement by volume.

voluntary adj done by choice; done or maintained without payment; controlled by the will. ◆ n, pl -**taries** organ solo in a church service. **voluntarily** adv

volunteer n person who offers voluntarily to do something, esp. military service. ◆ v offer one's services; offer the services of (another person); give (information) willingly.

voluptuous adj (of a woman) sexually alluring through fullness of figure; sensually pleasurable. **voluptuary** n, pl -**aries** person devoted to sensual pleasures.

volute n spiral or twisting turn, form, or object.

vomit v -**iting**, -**ited** eject (the contents of the stomach) through the mouth. ◆ n matter vomited.

voodoo n religion involving ancestor worship and witchcraft.

voracious adj craving great quantities of food; insatiably eager. **voraciously** adv **voracity** n

vortex n, pl -**texes**, -**tices** whirlpool; whirling motion.

vote n choice made by a participant in a shared decision, esp. in electing a candidate; right to this choice; total number of votes cast; collective voting power of a given group, e.g. the Black vote. ◆ v make a choice by a vote; authorize (something) by vote. **voter** n

votive adj done to fulfil a vow.

vouch v (foll. by for) give one's

personal assurance about; (foll. by for) be proof of. **voucher** n ticket used instead of money to buy specified goods; record of a financial transaction, receipt.

vouchsafe v Old-fashioned give, entrust; agree graciously.

vow n solemn promise, esp. to a god or saint. ◆ v promise solemnly.

vowel n speech sound made without obstructing the flow of breath; letter representing this.

vox pop n interviews with members of the public on TV or radio.

vox populi n public opinion.

voyage n long journey by sea or in space. ◆ v make a voyage. **voyager** n **voyageur** [vwah-yah-**zher**] n guide or trapper in N regions.

voyeur n person who derives pleasure from watching people undressing or having sex.

vs versus.

V-sign n offensive gesture made by sticking up the index and middle fingers with the palm inwards; similar gesture, with the palm outwards, meaning victory or peace.

VTR video tape recorder.

vulcanize v strengthen (rubber) by treating it with sulfur. **vulcanization** n **vulcanite** n vulcanized rubber.

vulgar adj showing lack of good taste, decency, or refinement. **vulgarly** adv **vulgarity** n **vulgarian** n vulgar (rich) person. **vulgarism** n coarse word or phrase. **vulgar fraction** simple fraction.

Vulgate n fourth-century Latin version of the Bible.

vulnerable adj able to be physically or emotionally hurt; exposed to attack. **vulnerability** n

vulpine adj of or like a fox.

vulture n large bird that feeds on the flesh of dead animals.

vulva n woman's external genitals.

vying v present participle of VIE.

W w

W Chem tungsten; watt; Wednesday; west(ern).

wacky adj **wackier**, **wackiest** Informal

eccentric or funny. **wackiness** n

wad n small mass of soft material; roll or bundle. ◆ v **wadding, wadded** make into a wad; pad or stuff with wadding. **wadding** n soft material used for padding or stuffing.

waddle v walk with short swaying steps. ◆ n swaying walk.

wade v walk with difficulty through water or mud; proceed with difficulty. **wader** n long-legged water bird. ◆ pl angler's long waterproof boots.

wadi [wod-dee] n, pl -dies (in N Africa and Arabia) a watercourse which is dry except in the wet season.

wafer n thin crisp biscuit; thin disc of unleavened bread used at Communion; thin slice.

waffle[1] Informal ◆ v speak or write in a vague wordy way. ◆ n vague wordy talk or writing.

waffle[2] n square crisp pancake with a grid-like pattern.

waft v drift or carry gently through air or water. ◆ n something wafted.

wag v **wagging, wagged** move rapidly from side to side. ◆ n wagging; Informal humorous witty person. **waggish** adj **wagtail** n small long-tailed bird.

wage n (often pl.) payment for work done, esp. when paid weekly. ◆ v engage in (an activity).

wager n, v bet on the outcome of something.

waggle v wag. **waggly** adj

wagon, waggon n four-wheeled vehicle for heavy loads; railway freight truck. **wagoner, waggoner** n

waif n homeless child.

wail v cry out in pain or misery. ◆ n mournful cry.

wain n Poetic farm wagon.

wainscot, wainscoting, wainscotting n wooden lining of the lower part of the walls of a room.

waist n part of the body between the ribs and hips; narrow middle part. **waistband** n band of material sewn on to the waist of a garment to strengthen it. **waistcoat** n Brit vest. **waistline** n (size of) the waist of a person or garment.

wait v remain inactive in expectation (of something); be ready (for something); delay or be delayed; serve in a restaurant etc. ◆ n waiting. **waiter** n man who serves in a restaurant etc. **waitress** n fem

waive v refrain from enforcing (a law, right, etc.). **waiver** n (written statement of) this act.

wake[1] v **waking, woke, woken** rouse from sleep or inactivity. ◆ n vigil beside a corpse the night before burial. **waken** v wake. **wakeful** adj

wake[2] n track left by a moving ship. **in the wake of** following close behind.

walk v move on foot with at least one foot always on the ground; pass through or over on foot; escort or accompany on foot. ◆ n walking; distance walked; manner of walking; place or route for walking. **walk of life** occupation or career. **walker** n **walkabout** n informal walk among the public by royalty etc. **walkie-talkie** n portable radio transmitter and receiver. **walking stick** stick used as a support when walking. **walk into** v meet with unwittingly. **Walkman** n ® small portable cassette player with headphones. **walkout** n strike; act of leaving as a protest. **walkover** n Informal easy victory.

wall n structure of brick, stone, etc. used to enclose, divide, or support; something having the function or effect of a wall. ◆ v enclose or seal with a wall or walls. **wallflower** n fragrant garden plant; at a dance, a woman who remains seated for lack of a partner. **wallpaper** n decorative paper to cover interior walls.

wallaby n, pl -bies marsupial like a small kangaroo.

wallet n small folding case for paper money, documents, etc.

walleyed adj having eyes with an abnormal amount of white showing.

wallop Informal ◆ v -loping, -loped hit hard. ◆ n hard blow. **walloping** Informal ◆ n thrashing. ◆ adj large.

wallow v roll in liquid or mud; revel in an emotion. ◆ n wallowing.

wally n, pl -lies Slang stupid person.

walnut n edible nut with a wrinkled shell; tree it grows on; its wood.

walrus n, pl -ruses, -rus large sea mammal with long tusks.

waltz n ballroom dance; music for this. ◆ v dance a waltz; move in a relaxed confident way.

wampum [wom-pum] n shells woven

together, formerly used by N American Indians for money and ornament.

wan [rhymes with *swan*] *adj* **wanner, wannest** pale and sickly looking.

wand *n* thin rod, esp. one used in doing magic.

wander *v* move about without a definite destination or aim; go astray, deviate. ◆ *n* wandering. **wanderer** *n* **wanderlust** *n* great desire to travel.

wane *v* decrease gradually in size or strength; (of the moon) decrease in size. **on the wane** in decline.

wangle *v* *Informal* get by devious methods.

want *v* desire; lack. ◆ *n* wanting; thing wanted; lack; poverty. **wanted** *adj* sought by the police. **wanting** *adj* lacking; not good enough.

wanton *adj* dissolute or immoral; without motive; unrestrained.

wapiti [wop-pit-tee] *n*, *pl* **-tis** large N American and NZ deer.

war *n* fighting between nations; conflict or contest. ◆ *adj* of, like, or caused by war. ◆ *v* **warring, warred** make war. **warring** *adj* **warlike** *adj* of, for, or fond of war. **war crime** crime, such as killing, committed during a war in violation of accepted conventions. **war criminal** person who has committed war crimes. **warfare** *n* fighting or hostilities. **warhead** *n* explosive front part of a missile. **warmonger** *n* person who encourages war. **warship** *n* ship designed and equipped for naval combat.

warble *v* sing with trills. **warbler** *n* any of various small songbirds.

ward *n* room in a hospital for patients needing a similar kind of care; electoral division of a town; child under the care of a guardian or court. **warder** *n* prison officer. **wardress** *n* *fem* **ward off** *v* avert or repel (something unpleasant). **wardroom** *n* officers' quarters on a warship.

warden *n* person in charge of a building, institution, college etc.; official responsible for the enforcement of regulations. **wardenship** *n*

wardrobe *n* cupboard for hanging clothes in; person's collection of clothes; costumes of a theatrical company.

ware *n* articles of a specified type or

material, e.g. *silverware.* ◆ *pl* goods for sale. **warehouse** *n* building for storing goods prior to sale or distribution.

warlock *n* sorcerer.

warm *adj* moderately hot; providing warmth; affectionate; enthusiastic; (of a colour) predominantly yellow or red. ◆ *v* make or become warm. **warmly** *adv* **warmth** *n* mild heat; cordiality; intensity of emotion. **warm up** *v* make or become warmer; do preliminary exercises before a race or more strenuous exercise; make or become more lively. **warm-up** *n*

warn *v* make aware of possible danger or harm; caution or scold; inform (someone) in advance. **warning** *n* something that warns; scolding or caution. **warn off** *v* advise (someone) not to become involved with.

warp *v* twist out of shape; pervert. ◆ *n* state of being warped; lengthwise threads on a loom.

warrant *n* (document giving) official authorization. ◆ *v* guarantee; give authority or power to. **warranty** *n* (document giving) a guarantee. **warrant officer** officer in certain armed services with a rank between a commissioned and noncommissioned officer.

warren *n* series of burrows in which rabbits live; overcrowded building or part of a town with many narrow passages.

warrior *n* person who fights in a war.

wart *n* small hard growth on the skin. **wart hog** kind of African wild pig.

wary [ware-ree] *adj* **warier, wariest** watchful or cautious. **warily** *adv* **wariness** *n*

was *v* first and third person singular past tense of BE.

wash *v* clean (oneself, clothes, etc.) with water and usu. soap; be washable; flow or sweep over or against; *Informal* be believable or acceptable, e.g. *that excuse won't wash.* ◆ *n* washing; clothes washed at one time; thin coat of paint; trail of water left by a moving ship. **washable** *adj* **washer** *n* ring put under a nut or bolt or in a tap as a seal; *Informal* washing machine. **washing** *n* clothes to be washed. **wash away** *v* carry or be carried off by moving water. **washout** *n* *Informal* complete failure. **washroom** *n* lavatory. **wash up** *v* wash one's face and hands.

wasp *n* stinging insect with a slender black-and-yellow body. **waspish** *adj* bad-tempered.

waste *v* use pointlessly or thoughtlessly; fail to take advantage of; (foll. by *away*) lose one's health or strength. ◆ *n* wasting; something left over because in excess of requirements. ◆ *pl* desert. ◆ *adj* rejected as worthless or surplus to requirements; not cultivated or inhabited. **wastage** *n* loss by wear or waste; reduction in size of a workforce by not filling vacancies. **wasteful** *adj* extravagant. **wastefully** *adv* **waster, wastrel** *n* layabout. **wastepaper basket** container for discarded paper.

watch *v* look at closely; wait expectantly (for); guard or supervise. ◆ *n* portable timepiece for the wrist or pocket; (period of) watching; sailor's spell of duty. **watchable** *adj* **watcher** *n* **watchful** *adj* carefully observing everything that happens. **watchfully** *adv* **watchdog** *n* dog kept to guard property; person or group guarding against inefficiency or illegality. **watchman** *n* man employed to guard a building or property. **watchword** *n* slogan.

water *n* clear colourless tasteless liquid that falls as rain and forms rivers etc.; body of water, such as a sea or lake; level of the tide; urine. ◆ *v* put water on or into; (of the eyes) fill with tears; salivate. **watery** *adj* **water bed** waterproof mattress filled with water. **water buffalo** oxlike Asian animal. **water closet** *Old-fashioned* lavatory. **watercolour** *n* paint thinned with water; painting done in this. **watercourse** *n* stream or river. **watercress** *n* edible plant growing in clear ponds and streams. **water down** *v* dilute, make less strong. **waterfall** *n* place where the waters of a river drop vertically. **waterfront** *n* part of a town alongside a body of water. **water lily** water plant with large floating leaves. **watermark** *n* faint translucent design in a sheet of paper. **watermelon** *n* melon with green skin and red flesh. **water polo** team game played by swimmers with a ball. **waterproof** *adj* not letting water through. ◆ *v* make waterproof. ◆ *n* waterproof garment. **watershed** *n* line separating two river

systems; dividing line. **water-skiing** *n* sport of riding over water on skis towed by a speedboat. **watertight** *adj* not letting water through; with no loopholes. **water wheel** large wheel which is turned by flowing water to drive machinery.

watt [wott] *n* unit of power. **wattage** *n* electrical power expressed in watts.

wattle [wott-tl] *n* branches woven over sticks to make a fence; fold of skin hanging from the neck of certain birds.

wave *v* move the hand to and fro as a greeting or signal; move or flap to and fro. ◆ *n* moving ridge on water; curve (s) in the hair; gesture of waving; vibration carrying energy through a medium; prolonged spell of something. **wavy** *adj* **wavelength** *n* distance between the same points of two successive waves.

waver *v* hesitate or be irresolute; be or become unsteady. **waverer** *n*

wax[1] *n* solid shiny fatty or oily substance used for sealing, making candles, etc.; similar substance made by bees; waxy secretion of the ear. ◆ *v* coat or polish with wax. **waxen** *adj* made of or like wax. **waxy** *adj* **waxwing** *n* small songbird. **waxwork** *n* lifelike wax model of a (famous) person. ◆ *pl* place exhibiting these.

wax[2] *v* increase in size or strength; (of the moon) get gradually larger.

way *n* manner or method; route or direction; track or path; room for movement or activity, e.g. *you're in the way*; distance; passage or journey; characteristic manner; *Informal* state or condition. **wayward** *adj* erratic, selfish, or stubborn. **waywardness** *n* **wayfarer** *n* traveller. **waylay** *v* lie in wait for and accost or attack. **wayside** *adj*, *n* (situated by) the side of a road.

WC water closet.

we *pron* (used as the subject of a verb) the speaker or writer and one or more others; people in general; formal word for "I" used by editors and monarchs.

weak *adj* lacking strength; liable to give way; lacking flavour; unconvincing. **weaken** *v* make or become weak. **weakling** *n* feeble person or animal. **weakly** *adj* weak or sickly. ◆ *adv* feebly. **weakness** *n*

weal *n* raised mark left on the skin by a blow.

wealth n riches; abundance. **wealthy** adj **wealthiness** n

wean v accustom to food other than mother's milk; coax away from.

weapon n object used in fighting; anything used to get the better of an opponent. **weaponry** n weapons collectively.

wear v **wearing, wore, worn** have on the body as clothing or ornament; show as one's expression; (cause to) deteriorate by constant use or action; endure constant use; Informal tolerate. ◆ n wearing; things to wear, e.g. leisure wear; damage caused by use; ability to endure constant use. **wearer** n **wear off** v have a gradual decrease in intensity. **wear on** v (of time) pass slowly.

weary adj **-rier, -riest** tired or exhausted; tiring. ◆ v **-rying, -ried** make or become weary. **wearily** adv **weariness** n **wearisome** adj tedious.

weasel n small carnivorous mammal with a long body and short legs.

weather n day-to-day meteorological conditions of a place. ◆ v (cause to) be affected by the weather; come safely through. **under the weather** Informal slightly ill. **weather-beaten** adj worn, damaged, or (of skin) tanned by exposure to the weather. **weathercock, weathervane** n metal object on a roof showing which way the wind is blowing.

weave v **weaving, wove** or **weaved, woven** or **weaved.** make (fabric) by interlacing (yarn) on a loom; compose (a story); move from side to side while going forwards. **weaver** n

web n net spun by a spider; anything intricate, e.g. web of deceit; skin between the toes of a duck, frog, etc. **the Web** short for World Wide Web. **webbed** adj **webbing** n strong fabric woven in strips. **weblog** n person's online journal. **website** n group of connected pages on the World Wide Web.

wed v **wedding, wedded** or **wed.** marry; unite closely. **wedding** n act or ceremony of marriage. **wedlock** n marriage.

wedge n piece of material thick at one end and thin at the other. ◆ v fasten or split with a wedge; squeeze into a narrow space.

Wednesday n fourth day of the week.

wee adj small.

weed n plant growing where undesired; Informal thin ineffectual person. ◆ v clear of weeds. **weedy** adj Informal thin or weak; full of weeds. **weed out** v remove or eliminate (what is unwanted).

weeds pl n Obs widow's mourning clothes.

week n period of seven days, esp. one beginning on a Sunday; hours or days of work in a week. **weekly** adj, adv happening, done, etc. once a week. ◆ n, pl **-lies** periodical published once a week. **weekday** n any day of the week except Saturday or Sunday. **weekend** n Saturday and Sunday.

weep v **weeping, wept** shed tears; grieve or lament; ooze liquid. **weepy** adj **weeping willow** willow with drooping branches.

weevil n small beetle which eats grain etc.

weft n cross threads in weaving.

weigh v measure the weight of; have a specified weight; consider carefully; be influential; be burdensome. **weigh anchor** raise a ship's anchor or (of a ship) have its anchor raised.

weight n heaviness of an object; object of known mass used for weighing; unit of measurement of weight; heavy object; importance or influence. ◆ v add weight to; slant (a system) to favour one group. **weighting** n extra allowance paid in special circumstances. **weightless** adj **weightlessness** n **weighty** adj heavy; important; causing worry. **weightily** adv

weir n river dam.

weird adj unearthly or eerie; strange or bizarre. **weirdo** n Informal peculiar person.

welch v same as WELSH.

welcome adj received gladly; freely permitted. ◆ n kindly greeting. ◆ v **-coming, -comed** greet with pleasure; receive gladly.

weld v join (pieces of metal or plastic) by softening with heat; unite closely. ◆ n welded joint. **welder** n

welfare n wellbeing; help given to people in need. **welfare state** system in which the government takes responsibility for the wellbeing of its citizens.

well¹ *adv* **better, best** satisfactorily; skilfully; completely; prosperously; suitably; intimately; favourably; considerably. ◆ *adj* in good health; satisfactory. ◆ *interj* exclamation of surprise, interrogation, etc. **wellbeing** *n* state of being well, happy, or prosperous. **well-disposed** *adj* inclined to be friendly or sympathetic. **well-meaning** *adj* having good intentions. **well-spoken** *adj* speaking in a polite way. **well-worn** *adj* (of a word or phrase) having lost its meaning through overuse; so much used as to show signs of wear.

well² *n* hole sunk into the earth to reach water, oil, or gas; deep open shaft. ◆ *v* flow upwards or outwards.

wellingtons *pl n* high waterproof rubber boots.

welsh *v* fail to pay a debt or fulfil an obligation.

Welsh *adj* of Wales. ◆ *n* language or people of Wales. **Welsh rabbit, rarebit** dish of melted cheese on toast.

welt *n* raised or strengthened seam; weal. ◆ *v* provide with a welt.

welter *n* jumbled mass.

welterweight *n* boxer weighing up to 147lb (professional) or 67kg (amateur).

wen *n* cyst on the scalp.

wench *n Facetious* young woman.

wend *v* go or travel.

went *v* past tense of GO.

wept *v* past of WEEP.

were *v* form of the past tense of (be) used after *we, you, they,* or a plural noun; subjunctive of BE.

we're we are.

weren't were not.

werewolf *n* (in folklore) person who can turn into a wolf.

west *n* (direction towards) the point on the horizon where the sun sets; region lying in this direction; (**W-**) N America and western Europe. ◆ *adj* in, going towards, facing, or (of the wind) blowing from the west ◆ *adv* in or to the west. **westerly** *adj* in, towards, or (of the wind) blowing from the west. **western** *adj* of or in the west. ◆ *n* film or story about cowboys in the western US. **westerner** *n* **westernize** *v* adapt to

the customs and culture of the West. **westward** *adj, adv* **westwards** *adv* **West Coast** Pacific coast of N America.

wet *adj* **wetter, wettest** covered or soaked with water or another liquid; not yet dry, e.g. *wet paint; Informal* (of a person) feeble or foolish. ◆ *n* moisture or rain; *Informal* feeble or foolish person. ◆ *v* **wetting, wet** or **wetted**. make wet. **wet blanket** *Informal* person who has a depressing effect on others. **wetland** *n* area of marshy land. **wet nurse** woman employed to breast-feed another's child. **wet suit** close-fitting rubber suit worn by divers etc.

wether *n* castrated ram.

whack *v* strike with a resounding blow. ◆ *n* such a blow; *Informal* share; *Informal* attempt. **whacked** *adj* exhausted. **whacking** *adj Informal* huge.

whale *n* large fish-shaped sea mammal. **have a whale of a time** *Informal* enjoy oneself very much. **whaling** *n* hunting of whales. **whaler** *n* **whalebone** *n* horny substance hanging from the upper jaw of toothless whales.

wharf *n, pl* **wharves, wharfs** platform at a harbour for loading and unloading ships. **wharfage** *n* accommodation at or charge for use of a wharf.

what *pron* which thing; that which; request for a statement to be repeated. ◆ *adv* in which way, how much, e.g. *what do you care?* ◆ *interj* exclamation of surprise, anger, etc. **what for?** why? **whatever** *pron* anything that; no matter what. **whatnot** *n Informal* similar unspecified things. **whatsoever** *adj* at all.

wheat *n* grain used in making flour, bread, and pasta; plant producing this. **wheaten** *adj* **wheatear** *n* small songbird. **wheatmeal** *adj, n* (made with) brown, but not wholewheat, flour.

wheedle *v* coax or cajole.

wheel *n* disc that revolves on an axle; pivoting movement. ◆ *v* push or pull (something with wheels); turn as if on an axis; turn round suddenly. **wheeling and dealing** use of shrewd and sometimes unscrupulous methods to achieve success. **wheeler-dealer** *n*

wheelbarrow n shallow box for carrying loads, with a wheel at the front and two handles. **wheelbase** n distance between a vehicle's front and back axles. **wheelchair** n chair mounted on wheels for use by people who cannot walk.

wheeze v breathe with a hoarse whistling noise. ◆ n wheezing sound. **wheezy** adj

whelk n edible snail-like shellfish.

whelp n pup or cub; Offens youth. ◆ v produce whelps.

when adv at what time. ◆ conj at the time that; although; considering the fact that. ◆ pron at which time. **whenever** adv, conj at whatever time.

whence adv, conj Obs from what place or source.

where adv in, at, or to what place. ◆ pron in, at, or to which place. ◆ conj in the place at which. **whereabouts** adv at what place. ◆ n present position. **whereas** conj but on the other hand; considering that. **whereby** conj by which. **wherefore** Obs ◆ adv why. ◆ conj consequently. **whereupon** conj at which point. **wherever** adv at whatever place. **wherewithal** n necessary funds, resources, etc.

whet v **whetting, whetted** sharpen (a tool); increase (appetite or desire). **whetstone** n stone for sharpening tools.

whether conj used to introduce an indirect question or a clause expressing doubt or choice.

whey [way] n watery liquid that separates from the curd when milk is clotted.

which adj, pron used to request or refer to a choice from different possibilities. ◆ pron person or thing referred to. **whichever** adj, pron any out of several; no matter which.

whiff n puff of air or odour; trace.

Whig n member of a British political party of the 18th–19th centuries that sought limited reform.

while conj in the time that; despite the fact that; whereas. ◆ n period of time. **whilst** conj while. **while away** v pass (time) idly but pleasantly.

whim n sudden fancy. **whimsy, whimsey** n capricious idea; light or fanciful humour. **whimsical** adj fanciful; full of whims. **whimsicality** n

whimper v cry in a soft whining way. ◆ n soft plaintive whine.

whin n gorse.

whine n high-pitched plaintive cry; peevish complaint. ◆ v make such a sound. **whining** n, adj

whinge v complain. ◆ n complaint.

whinny v **-nying, -nied** neigh softly. ◆ n soft neigh.

whip n cord attached to a handle, used for beating animals or people; call made on members of Parliament to attend for important divisions; politician responsible for organizing and disciplining fellow party members; whipped dessert. ◆ v **whipping, whipped** hit with a whip; Informal pull, remove, or move quickly; beat (eggs or cream) to a froth; rouse into a particular condition; Informal steal. **whiplash injury** neck injury caused by a sudden jerk to the head, as in an automobile crash.

whippet n racing dog like a small greyhound.

whir, whirr n prolonged soft buzz. ◆ v **whirring, whirred** (cause to) make a whir.

whirl v spin or revolve; be dizzy or confused; drive or move at high speed. ◆ n whirling movement; confusion or giddiness; bustling activity. **whirlpool** n strong circular current of water. **whirlwind** n column of air whirling violently upwards in a spiral. ◆ adj much quicker than normal.

whisk v move or remove quickly; brush away lightly; beat (eggs or cream) to a froth. ◆ n light brush; egg-beating utensil.

whisker n any of the long stiff hairs on the face of a cat or other mammal. ◆ pl hair growing on a man's cheeks. **by a whisker** Informal only just.

whisky n, pl **-kies** strong alcoholic drink distilled from fermented cereals. **whiskey** n US or Irish whisky. **whiskyjack** n Canada jay.

whisper v speak softly, without vibration of the vocal cords; rustle. ◆ n soft voice; something whispered; rustling; Informal rumour.

whist n card game.

whistle v produce a shrill sound by forcing breath through pursed lips;

make a similar sound; signal by a whistle. ◆ *n* whistling sound; instrument blown to make a whistling sound. **blow the whistle on** *Informal* inform on or put a stop to. **whistling** *n, adj*

whit *n* **not a whit** not the slightest amount.

white *adj* of the colour of snow; pale; light in colour; (of coffee) served with milk. ◆ *n* colour of snow; clear fluid round the yolk of an egg; white part of the eyeball; (W-) member of the race of people with light-coloured skin. **whiten** *v* make or become white or whiter. **whiteness** *n* **whitish** *adj* **whitebait** *n* small edible fish. **white-collar** *adj* denoting nonmanual salaried workers. **white elephant** useless or unwanted possession. **white flag** signal of surrender or truce. **white-hot** *adj* very hot. **white lie** see LIE[1]. **white paper** report by the government, outlining its policy on a matter. **whitewash** *n* substance for whitening walls. ◆ *v* cover with whitewash; *Informal* conceal or gloss over faults. **white water** rapids.

whither *adv Obs* to what place.

whiting [white-ing] *n* edible sea fish.

Whitsun *n* week following Whit Sunday, the seventh Sunday after Easter.

whittle *v* cut or carve (wood) with a knife. **whittle down, away** *v* reduce or wear away gradually.

whizz, whiz *v* **whizzing, whizzed** move with a loud buzzing sound; *Informal* move quickly. ◆ *n, pl* **whizzes** loud buzzing sound; *Informal* person who is very good at something.

who *pron* which or what person; used to refer to a person or people already mentioned. **whoever** *pron* any person who; no matter who.

whodunnit [hoo-dun-nit] *n Informal* detective story, play, or film.

whole *adj* containing all the elements or parts; uninjured or undamaged; healthy; (of a number) not containing a fraction. ◆ *n* complete thing or system. **on the whole** taking everything into consideration. **wholly** *adv* **wholesome** *adj* physically or morally beneficial. **wholefood** *n* food that has been processed as little as possible. **wholehearted** *adj* sincere or enthusiastic. **whole note** musical note

four beats long. **wholesale** *adj, adv* of the business of selling goods in large quantities and at lower prices to retailers; on a large scale, e.g. *wholesale destruction of forests.* **wholesaler** *n* **wholewheat** *adj* (of flour) made from the whole wheat grain; made from wholewheat flour.

whom *pron* objective case of WHO.

whoop *n, v* shout or cry to express excitement.

whoopee *interj Informal* cry of joy.

whooping cough *n* infectious disease marked by convulsive coughing and noisy breathing.

whopper *n Informal* anything unusually large; huge lie. **whopping** *adj*

whore [hore] *n* prostitute.

whorl *n* ring of leaves or petals; one turn of a spiral; something coiled.

whose *pron* of who or which.

why *adv* for what reason. ◆ *pron* because of which.

wick *n* cord through a lamp or candle which carries fuel to the flame.

wicked *adj* morally bad; mischievous. **wickedly** *adv* **wickedness** *n*

wicker *adj* made of woven cane. **wickerwork** *n*

wicket *n* set of three cricket stumps and two bails; cricket pitch; small gate.

wide *adj* large from side to side; having a specified width; spacious or extensive; opened fully. ◆ *adv* to the full extent; over an extensive area; far from the target. **widely** *adv* **widen** *v* make or become wider. **width** *n* distance from side to side; quality of being wide. **widespread** *adj* affecting a wide area or a large number of people.

widgeon *n* same as WIGEON.

widow *n* woman whose husband is dead and who has not remarried. **widowed** *adj* **widowhood** *n* **widower** *n* man whose wife is dead and who has not remarried.

wield *v* hold and use (a weapon); have and use (power).

wife *n, pl* **wives** woman to whom a man is married.

wig *n* artificial head of hair. **wigged** *adj*

wigeon *n* duck found in marshland.

wiggle *v* move jerkily from side to

side. ◆ n wiggling movement. **wiggly** adj

wight n Obs person.

wigwam n N American Indian's tent.

wild adj (of animals or birds) not tamed or domesticated; (of plants) not cultivated; not civilized; lacking restraint or control; violent or stormy; Informal excited; without reason or substance; Informal furious. **wilds** pl n desolate or uninhabited place. **wildly** adv **wildness** n **wildcat** n European wild animal like a large domestic cat. ◆ adj (of a strike) sudden and unofficial. **wild-goose chase** search that has little chance of success. **wildlife** n wild animals and plants collectively.

wildebeest n gnu.

wilderness n uninhabited uncultivated region; state of no longer being in a prominent position.

wildfire n spread like wildfire spread quickly and uncontrollably.

wile n trick or ploy. **wily** adj crafty or sly.

wilful adj headstrong or obstinate; intentional. **wilfully** adv **wilfulness** n

will[1] v, past **would** used as an auxiliary to form the future tense or to indicate intention, ability, or expectation.

will[2] n faculty of deciding what one will do; directions written for disposal of one's property after death; desire or wish. ◆ v try to make (something) happen by wishing for it; wish or desire; leave (property) in one's will. **willing** adj ready or inclined (to do something); done or given readily. **willingly** adv **willingness** n **willpower** n ability to control oneself and one's actions.

will-o'-the-wisp n elusive person or thing; pale light sometimes seen over marshes at night.

willow n tree with thin flexible branches; its wood. **willowy** adj slender and graceful.

willy-nilly adv whether desired or not.

wilt v (cause to) become limp or lose strength.

wimp n Informal feeble ineffectual person.

wimple n garment framing the face, worn by medieval women and now by nuns.

win v **winning, won** come first in (a competition, fight, etc.); gain (a prize) in a competition; get by effort. ◆ n victory, esp. in a game. **winner** n **winning** adj gaining victory; charming. **winnings** pl n money won in gambling or in a competition. **win over** v gain the support or consent of (someone).

wince v draw back, as from pain. ◆ n wincing.

winceyette n cotton fabric with a raised nap.

winch n machine for lifting using a cable wound round a drum. ◆ v lift using a winch.

wind[1] n current of air; trend or tendency; breath; idle talk; flatulence; hint or suggestion. ◆ v make short of breath; make (a baby) bring up wind after feeding. **windy** adj **windward** adj, n (of or in) the direction from which the wind is blowing. **wind-chill factor** added chilling effect of wind on basic temperature. **windfall** n unexpected good luck; fallen fruit. **wind instrument** musical instrument played by blowing. **windmill** n machine for grinding or pumping driven by sails turned by the wind. **windpipe** n tube linking the throat and the lungs. **windscreen** n Brit windshield. **windshield** n front window of a motor vehicle. **windsock** n cloth cone on a mast at an airfield to indicate wind direction. **windsurfing** n sport of riding on water using a surfboard propelled and steered by a sail.

wind[2] v **winding, wound** coil or wrap around; tighten the spring of (a clock or watch); move in a twisting course. ◆ n winding; single turn or bend. **wind up** v bring to or reach an end; tighten the spring of (a clock or watch); Informal make tense or agitated.

windlass n winch worked by a crank.

window n opening in a wall or vehicle containing glass, which lets in light or air; glass pane or panes fitted in such an opening; display area behind the window of a shop; area on a computer screen that can be manipulated separately from the rest of the display area; period of unbooked time in a diary or schedule. **window-dressing** n arrangement of goods in a shop window; attempt to make something more attractive than it really is. **window-shopping** n looking at goods in shop windows without intending to buy.

wine n alcoholic drink made from fermented grapes; similar drink made from other fruits. ◆ adj of a dark purplish-red colour. **wine and dine** entertain or be entertained with fine food and drink.

wing n one of the limbs or organs of a bird, insect, or bat that are used for flying; one of the winglike supporting parts of an aircraft; projecting side part of a building; group within a political party; Brit fender; Sport (player on) either side of the field. ◆ pl sides of a stage. ◆ v move through the air; wound slightly in the wing or arm. **winged** adj **winger** n Sport player positioned on a wing.

wink v close and open (an eye) rapidly as a signal; twinkle. ◆ n winking; smallest amount of sleep.

winkle n shellfish with a cone-shaped shell. **winkle out** v Informal extract or prise out.

winnow v separate (chaff) from (grain); examine to select desirable elements.

winsome adj charming or winning.

winter n coldest season. ◆ v spend the winter. **wintry** adj of or like winter; cold or unfriendly. **winter sports** open-air sports held on snow or ice.

wipe v clean or dry by rubbing; erase (a tape). ◆ n wiping. **wiper** n (also **windshield wiper**) device that automatically wipes rain etc. from a windshield. **wipe out** v destroy completely; Slang kill.

wire n thin flexible strand of metal; length of this used to carry electric current; fencing made of wire; telegram. ◆ v provide with wires; send by telegraph. **wiring** n system of wires. **wiry** adj like wire; lean and tough. **wire-haired** adj (of a dog) having a stiff wiry coat.

wireless n Old-fashioned same as RADIO.

wise¹ adj possessing or showing wisdom. **wisely** adv **wisdom** n good sense and judgment; accumulated knowledge. **wisdom tooth** any of the four large molar teeth cut usu. after the age of twenty. **wiseacre** n person who wishes to seem wise. **wisecrack** Informal ◆ n flippant or sardonic remark. ◆ v make a wisecrack.

wise² n Obs manner.

wish v want or desire; feel or express a hope about someone's wellbeing, success, etc. ◆ n expression of a desire; thing desired. **wishful** adj too optimistic. **wishbone** n V-shaped bone above the breastbone of a fowl.

wishy-washy adj Informal insipid.

wisp n light delicate streak; small untidy bundle or tuft; slight trace. **wispy** adj

wisteria n climbing shrub with blue or purple flowers.

wistful adj sadly longing. **wistfully** adv

wit n ability to use words or ideas in a clever and amusing way; person with this ability; (sometimes pl.) ability to think and act quickly. **witty** adj **wittily** adv **witticism** n witty remark **wittingly** adv intentionally. **witless** adj foolish.

witch n person, usu. female, who practises (black) magic; ugly wicked woman; fascinating woman. **witchcraft** n use of magic. **witch doctor** (in certain societies) a man appearing to cure or cause injury or disease by magic. **witch-hunt** n campaign against people with unpopular views.

with prep by means of; in the company of; possessing; in relation to; in a manner characterized by; because of; understanding or agreeing with. **within** prep, adv in or inside. **without** prep not having, accompanied by, or using; Obs outside.

withdraw v -drawing, -drew, -drawn take or move out or away. **withdrawal** n **withdrawn** adj unsociable.

wither v wilt or dry up. **withering** adj (of a look or remark) scornful.

withers pl n ridge between a horse's shoulder blades.

withhold v -holding, -held refrain from giving.

withstand v -standing, -stood oppose or resist successfully.

witness n person who has seen something happen; evidence or testimony; person giving evidence in court. ◆ v see at first hand; give evidence; sign (a document) to certify that it is genuine.

wives n plural of WIFE.

wizard n magician; person with outstanding skill in a particular field. **wizardry** n

wizened [wiz-zend] *adj* shrivelled or wrinkled.

WMD weapon(s) of mass destruction.

wobble *v* move unsteadily; shake. ◆ *n* unsteady movement; shake. **wobbly** *adj*

wodge *n Informal* thick lump.

woe *n* grief. ◆ *pl* problems. **woeful** *adj* miserable; causing woe; pitiful. **woefully** *adv* **woebegone** *adj* looking miserable.

wok *n* bowl-shaped Chinese cooking pan, used esp. for frying.

woke *v* past tense of WAKE[1]. **woken** *v* past participle of WAKE[1].

wold *n* open downs.

wolf *n, pl* **wolves** wild predatory canine mammal. ◆ *v* eat ravenously. **cry wolf** raise a false alarm. **wolf whistle** whistle by a man indicating that he thinks a woman is attractive. **wolf willow** shrub with silvery leaves.

wolfram *n* tungsten.

wolverine *n* carnivorous mammal of Arctic regions.

woman *n, pl* **women** adult human female; women collectively. **womanhood** *n* **womanish** *adj* (of a man) looking like a woman. **womanly** *adj* having qualities traditionally associated with a woman. **womanizing** *n* (of a man) practice of having casual affairs with women. **womanizer** *n* **Women's Movement** movement for the removal of social and economic inequalities between women and men.

womb *n* hollow organ in female mammals where babies are conceived and develop.

wombat *n* small heavily-built burrowing Aust. marsupial.

won *v* past of WIN.

wonder *n* emotion caused by an amazing or unusual thing; wonderful thing. ◆ *v* be curious about; feel wonder. ◆ *adj* spectacularly successful, e.g. *a wonder drug.* **wonderful** *adj* very fine, e.g. *a wonderful job;* causing surprise or amazement. **wonderfully** *adv* **wonderment** *n* **wondrous** *adj Old-fashioned* wonderful; strange.

wonky *adj* **-kier, -kiest** *Informal* shaky or unsteady; not working properly.

wont [rhymes with **don't**] *n* custom. ◆ *adj* accustomed.

won't will not.

woo *v* try to persuade; *Old-fashioned* try to gain the love of.

wood *n* substance trees are made of, used in building and as fuel; (also pl.) area where trees grow. **wooded** *adj* covered with trees. **wooden** *adj* made of wood; without expression. **woody** *adj* **woodbine** *n* honeysuckle. **woodcock** *n* game bird. **woodcut** *n* engraved block of wood; print made from this. **woodland** *n* forest. **woodlouse** *n* small insect-like creature with many legs. **woodpecker** *n* bird which searches tree trunks for insects. **wood pigeon** large Eurasian pigeon. **woodwind** *adj, n* (of) a type of wind instrument made of wood. **woodworm** *n* insect larva that bores into wood.

woof[1] *n* cross threads in weaving.

woof[2] *n* barking noise made by a dog.

woofer *n* loudspeaker for reproducing low-frequency sounds.

wool *n* soft hair of sheep, goats, etc.; yarn spun from this. **woollen** *adj* **woolly** *adj* of or like wool; vague or muddled. ◆ *n* knitted woollen garment. **woolgathering** *n* daydreaming.

woozy *adj* **woozier, wooziest** *Informal* weak, dizzy, and confused.

word *n* smallest single meaningful unit of speech or writing; chat or discussion; brief remark; message; promise; command. ◆ *v* express in words. **wordy** *adj* using too many words. **wordiness** *n* **wording** *n* choice and arrangement of words. **word processor** keyboard, microprocessor, and VDU for electronic organization and storage of text. **word processing**

wore *v* past tense of WEAR.

work *n* physical or mental effort directed to making or doing something; paid employment; duty or task; something made or done; decoration of a specified kind, e.g. *needlework.* ◆ *pl* factory; total of a writer's or artist's achievements; *Informal* full treatment; mechanism of a machine. ◆ *v* (cause to) do work; be employed; (cause to) operate; cultivate (land); manipulate, shape, or process; (cause to) reach a specified condition; accomplish. ◆ *adj* of or for work. **work to rule** adhere strictly to all working regulations to reduce the rate of work as a protest. **work-to-rule** *n* **workable**

adj **worker** *n* **workaholic** *n* person addicted to work. **workhouse** *n Hist* institution where the poor were given food and lodgings in return for work. **working class** social class consisting of wage earners, esp. manual workers. **working-class** *adj* **working party** committee investigating a specific problem. **workman** *n* manual worker. **workmanship** *n* skill of a workman; skill exhibited in a finished product. **worktop** *n* surface in a kitchen, used for food preparation.

world *n* the planet earth; mankind; society; sphere of existence. ◆ *adj* of the whole world. **worldly** *adj* not spiritual; concerned with material things; wise in the ways of the world. **World Wide Web** global network of linked computer files.

worm *n* small limbless invertebrate animal; wretched or spineless person; shaft with a spiral thread forming part of a gear system; *Computers* type of virus. ◆ *pl* illness caused by parasitic worms in the intestines. ◆ *v* rid of worms; crawl; insinuate (oneself); extract (information) craftily. **wormy** *adj* **worm-eaten** *adj* eaten into by worms.

wormwood *n* bitter plant.

worn *v* past participle of WEAR.

worry *v* **-rying, -ried** (cause to) be anxious or uneasy; annoy or bother; (of a dog) bite repeatedly. ◆ *n, pl* **-ries** (cause) of anxiety or concern. **worried** *adj* **worrying** *adj, n*

worse *adj, adv* comparative of BAD or BADLY. ◆ *n* worse thing. **worst** *adj, adv* superlative of BAD or BADLY. ◆ *n* worst thing. **worsen** *v* make or grow worse.

worship *v* **-shipping, -shipped** show religious devotion to; love and admire. ◆ *n* worshipping; (W-) title for a mayor or magistrate. **worshipper** *n* **worshipful** *adj* worshipping; (in titles) honourable.

worsted [wooss-tid] *n* type of woollen yarn or fabric. ◆ *adj* made of worsted.

wort [wurt] *n* infusion of malt used to make beer.

worth *adj* having a value of; meriting or justifying. ◆ *n* value or price; excellence; amount to be had for a given sum. **worthless** *adj* **worthy** *adj* having value or merit; deserving. ◆ *n Informal* notable person. **worthily** *adv*

worthiness *n* **worthwhile** *adj* worth the time or effort involved.

would *v* used as an auxiliary to form the past tense or subjunctive mood of WILL[1], express a request, or describe a habitual past action. **would-be** *adj* wishing or pretending to be.

wouldn't would not.

wound[1] *n* injury caused by violence; injury to the feelings. ◆ *v* inflict a wound on.

wound[2] *v* past of WIND[2].

wove *v* a past tense of WEAVE. **woven** *v* a past participle of WEAVE.

wow *interj* exclamation of astonishment. ◆ *n Informal* astonishing person or thing.

wpm words per minute.

wrack *n* seaweed.

wraith *n* apparition of a person seen shortly before his or her death; ghost.

wrangle *v* argue noisily. ◆ *n* noisy argument.

wrap *v* **wrapping, wrapped** fold (something) round (a person or thing) so as to cover. ◆ *n* garment wrapped round the shoulders; sandwich made by wrapping a filling in a tortilla. **wrapper** *n* cover; loose dressing gown. **wrapping** *n* material used to wrap. **wrap up** *v* fold paper round; put warm clothes on; *Informal* finish or settle (a matter).

wrath [roth] *n* intense anger. **wrathful** *adj*

wreak *v* inflict (vengeance); cause (chaos).

wreath *n* twisted ring or band of flowers or leaves used as a memorial or tribute. **wreathed** *adj* surrounded (by), e.g. *wreathed in pipe smoke*; surrounded by a ring (of), e.g. *wreathed in geraniums*.

wreck *n* accidental destruction of a ship at sea; wrecked ship; remains of something destroyed; person in very poor condition. ◆ *v* cause the wreck of. **wrecker** *n* **wreckage** *n* wrecked remains.

wren *n* small brown songbird.

wrench *v* twist or pull forcefully; sprain. ◆ *n* forceful twist or pull; sprain; difficult or painful parting; adjustable spanner.

wrest *v* take by force; twist violently.

wrestle *v* fight, esp. as a sport, by grappling with and trying to throw down an opponent; struggle hard with. **wrestler** n **wrestling** n

wretch n despicable person; pitiful person. **wretched** [retch-id] adj miserable or unhappy; worthless. **wretchedly** adv **wretchedness** n

wrier adj a comparative of WRY. **wriest** adj a superlative of WRY.

wriggle v move with a twisting action; manoeuvre oneself by devious means. ◆ n wriggling movement.

wright n maker, e.g. playwright.

wring v wringing, wrung twist, esp. to squeeze liquid out of; clasp and twist (the hands); obtain by forceful means.

wrinkle n slight crease, esp. one in the skin due to age. ◆ v make or become wrinkled. **wrinkly** adj

wrist n joint between the hand and the arm. **wristwatch** n watch worn on the wrist.

writ n written legal command.

write v writing, wrote, written mark paper etc. with symbols or words; set down in words; be the author or composer of; communicate by letter. **writing** n **writer** n author; person who has written something specified. **write-off** n Informal something damaged beyond repair. **write-up** n published account of something.

writhe v twist or squirm in or as if in pain; be very embarrassed.

wrong adj incorrect or mistaken; immoral or bad; not intended or suitable; not working properly. ◆ adv in a wrong manner. ◆ n something immoral or unjust. ◆ v treat unjustly; malign. **wrongly** adv **wrongful** adj **wrongfully** adv **wrongdoing** n immoral behaviour.

wrote v past tense of WRITE.

wrought [rawt] v Lit past of WORK. ◆ adj (of metals) shaped by hammering or beating. **wrought iron** pure form of iron used for decorative work.

wrung v past of WRING.

wry adj wrier, wriest or wryer, wryest dryly humorous; (of a facial expression) contorted. **wryly** adv

wt. weight.

wuss n slang feeble person.

WWW World Wide Web.

wych-elm n elm with large rough leaves.

X x

X indicating an error, a choice, or a kiss; indicating an unknown, unspecified, or variable factor, number, person, or thing.

Xe Chem xenon.

xenon n colourless odourless gas found in very small quantities in the air.

xenophobia [zen-oh-**fobe**-ee-a] n fear or hatred of people from other countries.

Xerox [**zeer**-ox] n ® machine for copying printed material; ® copy made by a Xerox machine. ◆ v copy (a document) using such a machine.

Xmas [**eks**-mass] n Christmas.

x-ray n stream of radiation that can pass through some solid materials; picture made by sending x-rays through someone's body to examine internal organs. ◆ v photograph, treat, or examine using x-rays.

xylem [**zy**-lem] n plant tissue that conducts water and minerals from the roots to all other parts.

xylophone [**zile**-oh-fone] n musical instrument made of a row of wooden bars played with hammers.

Y y

yacht [yott] n large boat with sails or an engine used for racing or pleasure cruising. **yachting** n **yachtsman, yachtswoman** n

yak[1] n Tibetan ox with long shaggy hair.

yak[2] v yakking, yakked Slang talk continuously about unimportant matters.

yam n tropical root vegetable.

yank v pull or jerk suddenly. ◆ n sudden pull or jerk.

Yankee, Yank adj, n Slang (of) a person from the United States.

yap v yapping, yapped bark with a high-pitched sound; Informal talk continuously. ◆ n high-pitched bark.

yard[1] n unit of length equal to 36 inches or about 91.4 centimetres. **yardstick** n standard against which to judge other people or things.

yard² *n* enclosed area, usu. next to a building and often used for a particular purpose, e.g. *builder's yard.*

yarmulke [yar-mull-ka] *n* skullcap worn by Jewish men.

yarn *n* thread used for knitting or making cloth; *Informal* long involved story. **spin a yarn** tell an improbable story.

yarrow *n* wild plant with flat clusters of white flowers.

yashmak *n* veil worn by a Muslim woman to cover her face in public.

yaw *v* (of an aircraft or ship) turn to one side or from side to side while moving.

yawl *n* two-masted sailing boat.

yawn *v* open the mouth wide and take in air deeply, often when sleepy or bored; (of an opening) be large and wide. ◆ *n* act of yawning. **yawning** *adj*

yaws *n* infectious tropical skin disease.

yd. yard.

YDT Yukon Daylight Time.

ye [yee] *pron Obs* you.

year *n* time taken for the earth to make one revolution around the sun, about 365 days; twelve months from January 1 to December 31. **yearly** *adj, adv* (happening) every year or once a year. **yearling** *n* animal between one and two years old.

yearn *v* (foll. by *for*) want (something) very much. **yearning** *n, adj*

yeast *n* fungus used to make bread rise and to ferment alcoholic drinks. **yeasty** *adj*

yell *v* shout or scream in a loud or piercing way. ◆ *n* loud cry of pain, anger, or fear.

yellow *n* the colour of gold, a lemon, etc. ◆ *adj* of this colour; *Informal* cowardly. ◆ *v* make or become yellow. **yellow fever** serious infectious tropical disease. **yellowhammer** *n* European songbird with a yellow head and body. **yellow pages** telephone directory which lists businesses under the headings of the type of business or service they provide.

yelp *v, n* (give) a short, sudden cry.

yen¹ *n, pl* **yen** main unit of currency in Japan.

yen² *n Informal* longing or desire.

yeoman [yo-man] *n, pl* **-men** *Hist* farmer owning and farming his own

land. **yeoman of the guard** member of the ceremonial bodyguard of the British monarchy.

yes *interj* expresses consent, agreement, or approval; used to answer when one is addressed. **yes man** person who always agrees with his or her superior.

yesterday *adv, n* (on) the day before today; (in) the recent past.

yet *adv* up until then or now; still. ◆ *conj* nevertheless, still.

yeti *n* same as ABOMINABLE SNOWMAN.

yew *n* evergreen tree with needle-like leaves and red berries.

Yiddish *adj, n* (of or in) a language of German origin spoken by many Jews in Europe and elsewhere.

yield *v* produce or bear; give up control of, surrender; give in. ◆ *n* amount produced. **yielding** *adj* submissive; soft or flexible.

YMCA Young Men's Christian Association.

yodel *v* **-delling, -delled** sing with abrupt changes between a normal and a falsetto voice. ◆ *n* act or sound of yodelling.

yoga *n* Hindu method of exercise and discipline aiming at spiritual, mental, and physical wellbeing. **yogi** *n* person who practises yoga.

yoghurt, yogurt, yoghourt *n* slightly sour custard-like food made from milk that has had bacteria added to it, often sweetened and flavoured with fruit.

yoke *n* wooden bar put across the necks of two animals to hold them together; frame fitting over a person's shoulders for carrying buckets; *Lit* oppressive force, e.g. *the yoke of the tyrant*; fitted part of a garment to which a fuller part is attached. ◆ *v* put a yoke on; link.

yokel *n Offens* person who lives in the country and is usu. simple and old-fashioned.

yolk *n* yellow part of an egg that provides food for the developing embryo.

Yom Kippur *n* annual Jewish religious holiday.

yonder *adv* over there.

yore *n Lit* the distant past.

Yorkshire pudding *n* baked batter made from flour, milk, and eggs and often eaten with roast beef.

you *pron* refers to: the person or people addressed; an unspecified person or people in general.

young *adj* in an early stage of life or growth. ◆ *n* offspring, esp. young animals; young people in general. **youngster** *n* young person.

your *adj* of, belonging to, or associated with you; of, belonging to, or associated with an unspecified person or people in general. **yours** *pron* something belonging to you. **yourself** *pron*

youth *n* time or condition of being young; boy or young man; young people as a group. **youthful** *adj* **youthfulness** *n* **youth club** club that provides leisure activities for young people. **youth hostel** inexpensive lodging place for young people travelling cheaply.

yowl *v, n* (produce) a loud mournful cry.

yo-yo *n, pl* **-yos** toy consisting of a spool attached to a string, by which it is repeatedly spun out and reeled in.

YST Yukon Standard Time.

YT, Y.T. Yukon Territory.

yucca *n* tropical plant with spikes of white leaves.

yucky, yukky *adj* **yuckier, yuckiest** *or* **yukkier, yukkiest** *Slang* disgusting, nasty.

Yukon *see* Canadian Provincial Facts p631.

Yule *n Lit* Christmas.

Yuppie *n* young highly-paid professional person, esp. one who has a fashionable way of life. ◆ *adj* typical of Yuppies.

YWCA Young Women's Christian Association.

Z z

Zamboni *n* ® machine that repairs the surface of ice in a rink.

zany [zane-ee] *adj* **zanier, zaniest** comical in an endearing way.

zap *v* **zapping, zapped** *Slang* kill (by shooting); change television channels rapidly by remote control; move quickly.

zeal *n* great enthusiasm or eagerness.

zealot [zel-lot] *n* fanatic or extreme enthusiast. **zealous** [zel-luss] *adj* extremely eager or enthusiastic. **zealously** *adv*

zebra *n* black-and-white striped African animal of the horse family. **zebra crossing** pedestrian crossing marked by black and white stripes on the road.

zebu [zee-boo] *n* Asian ox with a humped back and long horns.

Zen *n* Japanese form of Buddhism that concentrates on learning through meditation and intuition.

zenith *n* highest point of success or power; point in the sky directly above an observer.

zephyr [zef-fer] *n* soft gentle breeze.

zeppelin *n Hist* large cylindrical airship.

zero *n, pl* **-ros, -roes** (symbol representing) the number 0; point on a scale of measurement from which the graduations commence; lowest point; nothing, nil. ◆ *adj* having no measurable quantity or size. **zero in on** *v* aim at; *Informal* concentrate on.

zest *n* enjoyment or excitement; interest, flavour, or charm; peel of an orange or lemon.

zigzag *n* line or course having sharp turns in alternating directions. ◆ *v* **-zagging, -zagged** move in a zigzag. ◆ *adj* formed in or proceeding in a zigzag. ◆ *adv* in a zigzag manner.

zinc *n* bluish-white metallic element used in alloys and to coat metal.

zing *n Informal* quality in something that makes it lively or interesting.

zinnia *n* garden plant with solitary heads of brightly coloured flowers.

Zionism *n* movement to found and support a Jewish homeland in Israel. **Zionist** *n, adj*

zip *n* fastener with two rows of teeth that are closed or opened by a small clip pulled between them; *Informal* energy, vigour; short whizzing sound. ◆ *v* **zipping, zipped** fasten with a zip; move with a sharp whizzing sound.

zircon *n* mineral used as a gemstone and in industry.

zither *n* musical instrument consisting of strings stretched over a flat box and plucked to produce musical notes.

Zn *Chem* zinc.

zodiac *n* imaginary belt in the sky

within which the sun, moon, and planets appear to move, divided into twelve equal areas, called signs of the zodiac, each named after a constellation.

zombie, zombi n person who appears to be lifeless, apathetic, or totally lacking in independent judgment; corpse brought back to life by witchcraft.

zone n area with particular features or properties; one of the divisions of the earth's surface according to temperature. ◆ v divide into zones.

zoo n, pl **zoos** place where live animals are kept for show.

zoology n study of animals. **zoologist** n **zoological** adj **zoological garden** zoo.

zoom v move or rise very rapidly; make or move with a buzzing or humming sound. **zoom lens** lens that can make the details of a picture larger or smaller while keeping the picture in focus.

zucchini [zoo-**keen**-ee] n, pl -**nis**, -**ni** small type of squash with green peel.

Zulu n member of a tall Black people of southern Africa; language of this people.

zygote n fertilized egg cell.

SUPPLEMENT

The information given on pages 4–10 has been reproduced by kind permission of Parks Canada, from **www.pc.gc.ca**.

CANADA – PROVINCIAL FACTS

Canada

Confederation: July 1, 1867   Capital: Ottawa
Area of land: 9 970 068 km^2 Population: 31 404 000

Alberta

Entered Confed.: Sept 1, 1905   Capital: Edmonton
Area of land: 661 198 km^2 Pop.: 3 113 600 (9.9% of Canada)
Provincial bird: Great horned owl   Provincial flower: Wild rose
Provincial tree: Lodgepole pine
Motto: Fortis et Liber – "Strong and free"

British Columbia

Entered Confed.: July 1, 1867   Capital: Victoria
Area of land: 947 806 km^2 Pop.: 4 141 300 (13% of Canada)
Provincial bird: Steller's jay   Provincial flower: Dogwood
Provincial tree: Western red cedar
Motto: Splendor Sine Occasu – "Splendour without diminishment"

Manitoba

Entered Confed.: July 15, 1870   Capital: Winnipeg
Area of land: 649 958 km^2 Pop.: 1 150 800 (3.7% of Canada)
Provincial bird: Great gray owl   Provincial flower: Prairie crocus
Provincial tree: White spruce
Motto: Gloriosus et Liber – "Glorious and free"

New Brunswick

Entered Confed.: July 20, 1871   Capital: Fredericton
Area of land: 73 452 km^2 Pop.: 756 700 (2.4% of Canada)
Provincial bird: Black-capped chickadee   Provincial flower: Purple violet
Provincial tree: Balsam fir
Motto: Spem Reduxit – "Hope was restored"

Newfoundland & Labrador

Entered Confed.: March 31, 1949   Capital: St John's
Area of land: 405 722 km^2 Pop.: 531 600 (1.7% of Canada)
Provincial bird: Atlantic puffin   Provincial flower: Pitcher plant
Provincial tree: Black spruce
Motto: Quaerite Prime Regnum Dei – "Seek ye first the kingdom of God"

Northwest Territories

Entered Confed.: July 15, 1870   Capital: Yellowknife
Area of land: 1 489 649 km^2 Pop.: 41 400 (0.1% of Canada)
Provincial bird: Gyrfalcon   Provincial flower: Mountain avens
Provincial tree: Tamarack
Motto: None

Nova Scotia

Entered Confed.: July 1, 1867
Area of land: 55 477 km^2
Provincial bird: Osprey
Provincial tree: Red Spruce

Capital: Halifax
Pop.: 944 800 (3.0% of Canada)
Provincial flower: Mayflower

Motto: Munit Haec et Altera Vincit – "One defends and the other conquers"

Nunavut

Entered Confed.: April 1, 1999
Area of land: 1 936 113 km^2
Provincial bird: Rock ptarmigan
Provincial tree: no official tree

Capital: Iqaluit
Pop.: 28 700 (0.1% of Canada)
Provincial flower: Purple saxifrage

Motto: Nunavut Sanginivut – "Nunavut, our strength"

Ontario

Entered Confed.: July 1, 1867
Area of land: 1 068 578 km^2
Provincial bird: Common loon
Provincial tree: Eastern white pine

Capital: Toronto
Pop.: 12 068 300 (38% of Canada)
Provincial flower: White trillium

Motto: Ut Incepit Fidelis Sic Permanet – "Loyal she began, loyal she remains"

Prince Edward Island

Entered Confed.: July 1, 1873
Area of land: 5 646 km^2
Provincial bird: Blue jay
Provincial tree: Red oak

Capital: Charlottetown
Pop.: 139 900 (0.5% of Canada)
Provincial flower: Lady's slipper

Motto: Parva sub Ingenti – "The small under the protection of the great"

Quebec

Entered Confed.: July 1, 1867
Area of land: 1 540 681 km^2
Provincial bird: Snowy owl
Provincial tree: Yellow birch

Capital: Quebec
Pop.: 7 455 200 (24.2% of Canada)
Provincial flower: Blue flag

Motto: Je me souviens – "I remember"

Saskatchewan

Entered Confed.: Sept 1, 1905
Area of land: 652 341 km^2
Provincial bird: Sharp-tailed grouse
Provincial tree: White birch

Capital: Regina
Pop.: 1 011 800 (3.3% of Canada)
Provincial flower: Prairie lily

Motto: Multibus e Gentibus Vires – "From many peoples strength"

Yukon Territory

Entered Confed.: July 13, 1898
Area of land: 483 447 km^2
Provincial bird: Raven
Provincial tree: Sub-alpine fir
Motto: None

Capital: Whitehorse
Pop.: 29 900 (0.1% of Canada)
Provincial flower: Fireweed

NATIONAL PARKS OF CANADA

–Alberta–

Banff NP	*Canada's first national park (created in 1885); UNESCO World Heritage Site*
Elk Island NP	*Plains oasis for rare and endangered species*
Jasper NP	*Glacial jewel of the Rockies; UNESCO World Heritage Site*
Waterton Lakes NP	*International Peace Park; where the Rocky Mountains meet the prairie*
Wood Buffalo NP	*UNESCO World Heritage Site crossing the borders of Alberta and Northwest Territories*

–British Columbia–

Glacier NP	*A mix of British Columbia's lush interior rainforests and permanent glaciers*
Gwaii Haanas NP Reserve	*Haida culture and coastal rainforest on Queen Charlotte Islands and Haïda heritage site*
Kootenay NP	*UNESCO World Heritage Site featuring the famous Radium Hot Springs*
Mount Revelstoke NP	*Rainforest of 1,000-year-old cedars and spectacular mountains*
Pacific Rim NP Reserve	*Pacific Coast Mountains make up this marine and forest environment*
Yoho NP	*UNESCO World Heritage Site in the Rockies*
Gulf Islands NP Reserve	*A series of protected islands in a heavily developed region*

–Manitoba–

Riding Mountain NP	*A mix of boreal forest, grasslands and eastern deciduous forest*
Wapusk NP	*One of the largest polar bear denning areas in the world*

–New Brunswick–

Fundy NP	*Atlantic sanctuary with the world's highest tides*
Kouchibouguac NP	*Intricate Acadian blend of coastal and inland habitats*

–Newfoundland and Labrador–

Gros Morne NP	*UNESCO World Heritage Site amid Newfoundland's wild natural beauty*
Terra Nova NP	*Remnants of Eastern Newfoundland's Ancient Appalachian Mountains*

–Northwest Territories–

Aulavik NP	*Over 12,000 km² of Arctic wilderness on Banks Island*
Nahanni NP Reserve	*UNESCO World Heritage Site known for its majestic river*
Tuktut Nogait NP	*Calving ground for the Bluenose caribou herd*

–Nova Scotia–

Cape Breton Highlands NP	*Home to Cabot Trail; a land blessed with spectacular cliffs*
Kejimkujik NP	*Nova Scotian inland with historic canoe routes and portages*

–Nunavut–

Auyuittuq NP	*Baffin Island landscapes containing northern extremity of Canadian Shield*
Quttinirpaaq (Ellesmere Island) NP	*Most remote, fragile, rugged and northerly lands in North America*
Sirmilik NP	*Northern Baffin Island landscape containing Eastern Arctic Lowlands and Lancaster Sound*
Ukkusiksalik NP	*Protecting 20,500km² of Central Tundra Natural Region*

–Ontario–

Bruce Peninsula NP	*Northern tip of Niagara Escarpment*
Georgian Bay Islands NP	*Captivating islands representing Lake Huron's landscape*
Point Pelee NP	*Most southern point on Canadian mainland*
Pukaskwa NP	*Ancient Canadian Shield landscape on Lake Superior's North Shore*
St. Lawrence Islands NP	*Canada's smallest national park*

–Prince Edward Island–

Prince Edward Island NP	*Sand dunes, a spectacular coast and Green Gables house*

–Quebec–

Forillon NP	*The "Jewel of the Gaspé", where land meets the sea*
La Mauricie NP	*Lakes winding through forested hills, excellent for canoe and portage activities*
Mingan Archipelago NP Reserve	*A magnificent string of islands carved out by the sea*

–Saskatchewan–

Grasslands NP	*Saskatchewan's rare prairie grasses, dinosaur fossils, and badlands*
Prince Albert NP	*Protects northern coniferous forest and wildlife*

–Yukon–

Ivvavik NP	*A protected calving ground for the Porcupine caribou herd*
Kluane NP and Reserve	*UNESCO World Heritage Site includes Canada's highest peak, Mt. Logan*
Vuntut NP	*Northern Yukon's unique non-glaciated landscape*

NATIONAL MARINE CONSERVATION AREAS OF CANADA

–Ontario–

Fathom Five National Marine Park	*The spectacular underwater of the Niagara Escarpment in Georgian Bay*

–Quebec–

Saguenay-St. Lawrence National Marine Park	*Whales, seals, plants and birds of all kinds can be found here*

NATIONAL HISTORIC SITES OF CANADA

–Alberta–

Abbot Pass Refuge Cabin National Historic Site: *Early stone cabin used by climbers (1922)*

Athabasca Pass National Historic Site: *Major fur trade transportation route*

Banff Park Museum National Historic Site: *Early natural history museum in rustic style (1902–03)*

Bar U Ranch National Historic Site: *Historic ranch found in the Alberta foothills (1883)*

Cave and Basin National Historic Site: *Hot springs, birthplace of national parks (1885)*

First Oil Well in Western Canada National Historic Site: *First commercially productive oil well in the West*

Frog Lake National Historic Site: *Site of Cree uprising (1885)*

Henry House National Historic Site: *Site of North West Company post (1811–1830s)*

Howse Pass National Historic Site: *First crossed by David Thompson in 1807*

Jasper House National Historic Site: *Archaeological remains of 1829 fur trade post*

Jasper Park Information Centre National Historic Site: *Picturesque fieldstone Park building in Rustic design (1913–14)*

Rocky Mountain House National Historic Site: *Rival Hudson's Bay Company and North West Company posts*

Skoki Ski Lodge National Historic Site: *Ski lodge in rustic vernacular style (1930–31)*

Sulphur Mountain Cosmic Ray Station National Historic Site: *Remains of high altitude geophysical laboratory*

Yellowhead Pass National Historic Site: *Transportation route through Rocky Mountains*

–British Columbia–

Chilkoot Trail National Historic Site: *Transportation route to Klondike goldfields; Tlingit trade route*

Fisgard Lighthouse National Historic Site: *First permanent lighthouse on Canada's West Coast (1859–60)*

Fort Langley National Historic Site: *Early 19th-century Hudson's Bay Company post*

Fort Rodd Hill National Historic Site: *Late 19th-century fort to defend Victoria-Esquimalt fortifications*

Fort St. James National Historic Site: *Fur trade post founded by Simon Fraser in 1806*

Gulf of Georgia Cannery National Historic Site: *Outstanding West Coast fish processing complex (1894)*

Kicking Horse Pass National Historic Site: *Traversed by Palliser expedition (1857–60)*

Kitwanga Fort National Historic Site: *18th-century fortified Tsimshian village*

Nan Sdins National Historic Site: *Remains of sacred Haïda longhouses and totem poles*

Rogers Pass National Historic Site: *Canadian Pacific Railway route through Selkirk Mountains*

Stanley Park National Historic Site: *Outstanding large urban park (1890s)*

Twin Falls Tea House National Historic Site: *Early rustic tea house in Yoho National Park (built 1923–24)*

–Manitoba–

Linear Mounds National Historic Site: *Aboriginal burial mounds from 1000–1200 AD*

Lower Fort Garry National Historic Site: *Major centre in 19th-century fur trade*

Prince of Wales Fort National Historic Site: *18th-century stone fur trade fort on Hudson Bay*

Riding Mountain Park East Gate Registration Complex National Historic Site: *Three rustic buildings built under depression relief programs*

Riel House National Historic Site: *Family home of Métis leader Louis Riel*

St. Andrew's Rectory National Historic Site: *Example of mid 19th-century Red River architecture*

The Forks National Historic Site: *Historic meeting place, junction of the Red and Assiniboine rivers*

York Factory National Historic Site: *Hudson's Bay Company's principal fur trade depot from 1684–1870s*

–New Brunswick–

Beaubears Island Shipbuilding National Historic Site: *Archaeological site associated with 19th-century shipbuilding*

Boishébert National Historic Site: *Acadian refugee settlement, 1756–59*

Carleton Martello Tower National Historic Site: *Fortification built to defend Saint John during War of 1812*

Fort Beauséjour National Historic Site: *Remnants of 1751 French fort*

Fort Gaspareaux National Historic Site: *Military ruins and cemetery of 1751 French fort*

Monument Lefebvre National Historic Site: *Multi-function building, symbol of Acadian cultural revival*

St. Andrews Blockhouse National Historic Site: *Restored wooden blockhouse from War of 1812*

–Newfoundland and Labrador–

Cape Spear National Historic Site: *Oldest surviving lighthouse in Newfoundland, 1836*

Castle Hill National Historic Site: *17th- and 18th-century French and British fortifications*

Hawthorne Cottage National Historic Site: *Picturesque cottage, home of Captain Bob Bartlett from 1875–1946*

Hopedale Mission National Historic Site: *Symbol of interaction between Labrador Inuit and Moravian Missionaries*

L'Anse aux Meadows National Historic Site: *Only authenticated Viking settlement in North America*

Port au Choix National Historic Site: *Pre-contact burial and habitation sites*

Red Bay National Historic Site: *16th-century Basque whaling industry complex*

Ryan Premises National Historic Site: *East Coast fishing industry complex*

Signal Hill National Historic Site: *Commemorates defence of St. John's; includes the Cabot Tower*

–Nova Scotia–

Alexander Graham Bell National Historic Site: *Commemorates famous inventor*

Canso Islands National Historic Site: *Site of fishing centre, 16th to 19th century*

Fort Anne National Historic Site: *Fortifications (1695–1708); seat of government of Acadia*

Fort Edward National Historic Site: *Oldest blockhouse in Canada (1750)*

Fort McNab National Historic Site: *Fort built in 1889 to defend Halifax Harbour*

Fortress of Louisbourg National Historic Site: *Reconstruction of 18th-century French fortress*

Georges Island National Historic Site: *Harbour fortification, part of Halifax defence complex*

Grand-Pré National Historic Site: *Commemorates Acadian settlement and expulsion*

Grassy Island Fort National Historic Site: *Site of thriving 18th-century New England fishery*

Halifax Citadel National Historic Site: *Restored British masonry fort (1828–56)*

Kejimkujik National Historic Site: *Important Mi'kmaq cultural landscape*

Marconi National Historic Site: *Site of first wireless station in Canada*

Melanson Settlement National Historic Site: *Pre-expulsion Acadian farm community (1664–1755)*

Port-Royal National Historic Site: *Reconstruction of 1605 French settlement*

Prince of Wales Tower National Historic Site: *Late 18th-century stone defence tower (1796–99)*

Scots Fort National Historic Site: *Site of Sir William Alexander's settlement, 1629–31*

St. Peters Canal National Historic Site: *Operational canal with structures dating from 19th century*

St. Peters National Historic Site: *French trading post and fort, 1650–1758*

York Redoubt National Historic Site: *Major seaward defences of Halifax Harbour until World War II*

–Ontario–

Battle of the Windmill National Historic Site: *American invasion mission foiled (1838)*

Battlefield of Fort George National Historic Site: *War of 1812; captured by Americans in May 1813*

Bellevue House National Historic Site: *Important Italianate villa (1840s); home of Sir John A. Macdonald, Prime Minister of Canada (1867–73, 1878–91)*

Bethune Memorial House National Historic Site: *Birthplace of Doctor Norman Bethune; of symbolic significance to the Chinese*

Bois Blanc Island Lighthouse National Historic Site: *Point of attack by American Patriots during the troubles of 1837–1838*

Butler's Barracks National Historic Site: *Complex represents 150 years of military history*

Cathcart Tower National Historic Site: *Mid 19th-century British imperial masonry fortification*

Fort George National Historic Site: *Reconstructed British fort from War of 1812*

Fort Henry National Historic Site: *British fort completed in 1836 to defend Rideau Canal*

Fort Malden National Historic Site: *First built in 1796 as Fort Amherstburg; rebuilt as Fort Malden in 1838–1840*

Fort Mississauga National Historic Site: *19th-century brick tower within star-shaped earthworks*

Fort St. Joseph National Historic Site: *British military outpost on western frontier (1796–1812)*

Fort Wellington National Historic Site: *Military remains of 1813–38 fortifications*

Glengarry Cairn National Historic Site: *Conical stone monument to the Glengarry and Argyle Regiment (1840)*

HMCS Haida National Historic Site: *Last of World War II tribal class destroyers*

Inverarden House National Historic Site: *Important 1816 Regency cottage with fur trade associations*

Laurier House National Historic Site: *Home of two prime ministers, Sir Wilfrid Laurier and William Lyon Mackenzie King; built in 1878*

Merrickville Blockhouse National Historic Site: *Part of lock system of Rideau Canal; built in 1832–33*

Mississauga Point Lighthouse National Historic Site: *Site of first lighthouse on Great Lakes, 1804*

Mnjikaning Fish Weirs National Historic Site: *Aboriginal fishing site*

Murney Tower National Historic Site: *Mid 19th-century British imperial masonry fortification*

Navy Island National Historic Site: *Archaeological remains related to shipbuilding*

Peterborough Lift Lock National Historic Site: *World's highest hydraulic lift lock (built 1896–1904)*

Point Clark Lighthouse National Historic Site: *Imperial tower and lightkeeper's house (1859)*

Queenston Heights National Historic Site: *Site of 1812 Battle of Queenston Heights*

Rideau Canal National Historic Site: *Operational canal; 202km route with forty-five locks*

Saint-Louis Mission National Historic Site: *Site of Huron village destroyed by Iroquois in 1649*

Sault Ste. Marie Canal National Historic Site: *First electrically-powered lock in the world*

Shoal Tower National Historic Site: *Mid 19th-century British imperial masonry fortification*

Sir John Johnson House National Historic Site: *House of famous Loyalist (1780s)*

Southwold Earthworks National Historic Site: *Site of Attiwandaronk Indian village, circa 1500 AD*

Trent–Severn Waterway National Historic Site: *Operational canal; 386 km route with forty-five locks*

Woodside National Historic Site: *Boyhood home of William Lyon Mackenzie King, Prime Minister of Canada (1921–26, 1926–30, 1936–48)*

–Prince Edward Island–

Ardgowan National Historic Site: *Residence of Father of Confederation William Henry Pope, circa 1850*

Dalvay-by-the-Sea Hotel National Historic Site: *Queen Anne Revival style summer home, built 1896–99*

Port-la-Joye–Fort Amherst National Historic Site: *Remains of British and French forts*

Province House National Historic Site: *Neoclassical architecture; birthplace of Confederation*

–Quebec–

Battle of the Châteauguay National Historic Site: *Site of 1813 battle in defence of Lower Canada*

Battle of the Restigouche National Historic Site: *Site of last naval battle in Seven Years' War*

Carillon Barracks National Historic Site: *Early 19th-century stone military building*

Carillon Canal National Historic Site: *Operational canal; site of two earlier canals, 1826–33*

Cartier-Brébeuf National Historic Site: *Wintering place of Jacques Cartier (1535–36)*

Chambly Canal National Historic Site: *Operational canal with nine locks and swing bridges*

Coteau-du-Lac National Historic Site: *18th-century transportation and defence structures*

Forges du Saint-Maurice National Historic Site: *Remains of Canada's first industrial village*

Fort Chambly National Historic Site: *Restored stone fort dating from 1709*

Fort Lennox National Historic Site: *Outstanding example of early 19th-century fortifications*

Fort Témiscamingue National Historic Site: *Remains of French fur trading post*

Fortifications of Québec National Historic Site: *World Heritage City surrounded by 4.6km network of walls, gates and squares*

Grosse Île and the Irish Memorial National Historic Site: *Quarantine station for immigrants from 1832–1937*

Lachine Canal National Historic Site: *Operational canal with five locks, railway and road bridges*

Lévis Forts National Historic Site: *Part of Québec fortification system*

Louis S. St. Laurent National Historic Site: *Childhood home of Louis S. St. Laurent, Prime Minister of Canada, 1948–57*

Louis-Joseph Papineau National Historic Site: *Stone house built in 1785, associated with Louis-Joseph Papineau*

Maillou House National Historic Site: *Fine example of 18th-century Quebec town architecture, 1736*

Manoir Papineau National Historic Site: *19th-century manor, home of Patriot leader Louis-Joseph Papineau*

Montmorency Park National Historic Site: *Site of bishop's palace; Parliament of Canada 1851–55*

Pointe-au-Père Lighthouse National Historic Site: *Early reinforced concrete lighthouse at strategic location*

Québec Garrison Club National Historic Site: *Private military club, 1879*

Saint-Louis Forts and Châteaux National Historic Site: *Integral part of Québec's defence system*

Saint-Ours Canal National Historic Site: *Operational canal on Richelieu River (opened in 1849)*

Sainte-Anne-de-Bellevue Canal National Historic Site: *Operational canal; site of earlier 1843 canal*

Sir George-Étienne Cartier National Historic Site: *Double house of prominent 19th-century politician, 1830s*

Sir Wilfrid Laurier National Historic Site: *House interprets life of Sir Wilfrid Laurier, Prime Minister (1896–1911)*

The Fur Trade at Lachine National Historic Site: *Stone warehouse used as depot (1803)*

–Saskatchewan–

Batoche National Historic Site: *Métis village; site of 1885 Battle of Batoche*

Battle of Fish Creek National Historic Site: *Site of battle between Métis and Canadian forces (1885)*

Fort Battleford National Historic Site: *North West Mounted Police headquarters (1876)*

Fort Espérance National Historic Site: *Remains of two North West Company fur trade posts*

Fort Livingstone National Historic Site: *Original headquarters of North West Mounted Police*

Fort Pelly National Historic Site: *Remains of Hudson's Bay Company fur trade post*

Fort Walsh National Historic Site: *Early North West Mounted Police post*

Frenchman Butte National Historic Site: *Site of 1885 battle between Cree and Canadian troops*

Motherwell Homestead National Historic Site: *Farm of William Richard Motherwell, noted politician and scientific farmer (1882)*

–Yukon Territory–

Dawson Historical Complex National Historic Site: *Important collection of buildings from the Klondike Gold Rush*

Dredge No. 4 National Historic Site: *Symbolizes importance of dredging operations in the Klondike (1899–1966)*

S.S. Keno National Historic Site: *Wooden steamboat built 1922*

S.S. Klondike National Historic Site: *Largest and last Yukon commercial steamboat*

COUNTRIES, CAPITALS AND CURRENCIES

Country	Capital	Currency
Afghanistan	Kabul	afghani
Albania	Tirana	lek
Algeria	Algiers	dinar
Andorra	Andorra la Vella	euro
Angola	Luanda	kwanza
Antigua and Barbuda	St John's	East Caribbean dollar
Argentina	Buenos Aires	peso
Armenia	Yerevan	dram
Australia	Canberra	Australian dollar
Austria	Vienna	euro
Azerbaijan	Baku	manat
Bahamas	Nassau	Bahamian dollar
Bahrain	Manama	dinar
Bangladesh	Dhaka	taka
Barbados	Bridgetown	Barbados dollar
Belarus	Minsk	rouble
Belau	Koror	US dollar
Belgium	Brussels	euro
Belize	Belmopan	Belize dollar
Benin	Porto Novo	CFA franc
Bhutan	Thimphu	ngultrum
Bolivia	Sucre/La Paz	boliviano
Bosnia and Herzegovina	Sarajevo	euro
Botswana	Gaborone	pula
Brazil	Brasília	real
Brunei	Bandar Seri Begawan	Brunei dollar
Bulgaria	Sofia	lev
Burkina-Faso	Ouagadougou	CFA franc
Burundi	Bujumbura	Burundi franc
Cambodia	Phnom Penh	riel
Cameroon	Yaoundé	CFA franc
Canada	Ottawa	Canadian dollar
Cape Verde	Praia	escudo
Central African Republic	Bangui	CFA franc
Chad	Ndjaména	CFA franc
Chile	Santiago	peso
China	Beijing	yuan
Colombia	Bogotá	peso
Comoros	Moroni	Comorian franc
Congo (Republic of)	Brazzaville	CFA franc
Congo (Democratic Republic of)	Kinshasa	Congolese franc
Costa Rica	San José	colón
Côte d'Ivoire	Yamoussoukro	CFA franc
Croatia	Zagreb	kuna
Cuba	Havana	peso
Cyprus	Nicosia	pound
Czech Republic	Prague	koruna

Country	Capital	Currency
Denmark	Copenhagen	krone
Djibouti	Djibouti	Djibouti franc
Dominica	Roseau	East Caribbean dollar
Dominican Republic	Santo Domingo	peso
East Timor	Dili	US dollar
Ecuador	Quito	US dollar
Egypt	Cairo	pound
El Salvador	San Salvador	cólon
Equatorial Guinea	Malabo	CFA franc
Eritrea	Asmara	nakfa
Estonia	Tallinn	kroon
Ethiopia	Addis Ababa	birr
Fiji	Suva	Fiji dollar
Finland	Helsinki	euro
France	Paris	euro
Gabon	Libreville	CFA franc
Gambia	Banjul	dalasi
Georgia	Tbilisi	lari
Germany	Berlin	euro
Ghana	Accra	cedi
Greece	Athens	euro
Grenada	St George's	East Caribbean dollar
Guatemala	Guatemala City	quetzal
Guinea	Conakry	Guinea franc
Guinea-Bissau	Bissau	CFA franc
Guyana	Georgetown	Guyana dollar
Haiti	Port-au-Prince	gourde
Honduras	Tegucigalpa	lempira
Hungary	Budapest	forint
Iceland	Reykjavik	króna
India	Delhi	rupee
Indonesia	Jakarta	rupiah
Iran	Tehran	rial
Iraq	Baghdad	dinar
Ireland	Dublin	euro
Israel	Tel Aviv/Jerusalem	shekel
Italy	Rome	euro
Jamaica	Kingston	Jamaican dollar
Japan	Tokyo	yen
Jordan	Amman	dinar
Kazakhstan	Akmola	tenge
Kenya	Nairobi	shilling
Kiribati	Tarawa	Australian dollar
Kuwait	Kuwait	dinar
Kyrgyzstan	Bishkek	som
Laos	Vientiane	kip
Latvia	Riga	lats
Lebanon	Beirut	pound
Lesotho	Maseru	loti

Country	Capital	Currency
Liberia	Monrovia	Liberian dollar
Libya	Tripoli	dinar
Liechtenstein	Vaduz	Swiss franc
Lithuania	Vilnius	litas
Luxembourg	Luxembourg	euro
Macedonia	Skopje	denar
Madagascar	Antananarivo	Malagasy franc
Malawi	Lilongwe	kwacha
Malaysia	Kuala Lumpur	ringgit
Maldives	Malé	rufiyaa
Mali	Bamako	CFA franc
Malta	Valletta	lira
Marshall Islands	Majuro	US dollar
Mauritania	Nouakchott	ouguiya
Mauritius	Port Louis	rupee
Mexico	Mexico City	peso
Micronesia	Palikir	US dollar
Moldova	Kishinev	leu
Monaco	Monaco-Ville	euro
Mongolia	Ulan Bator	tugrik
Morocco	Rabat	dirham
Mozambique	Maputo	metical
Myanmar	Yangon	kyat
Namibia	Windhoek	Namibian dollar
Nauru	Yaren	Australian dollar
Nepal	Kathmandu	rupee
Netherlands	Amsterdam/The Hague	euro
New Zealand	Wellington	New Zealand dollar
Nicaragua	Managua	córdoba
Niger	Niamey	CFA franc
Nigeria	Abuja	naira
North Korea	Pyongyang	won
Norway	Oslo	krone
Oman	Muscat	rial
Pakistan	Islamabad	rupee
Panama	Panama City	balboa
Papua New Guinea	Port Moresby	kina
Paraguay	Asunción	guaraní
Peru	Lima	new sol
Philippines	Manila	peso
Poland	Warsaw	zloty
Portugal	Lisbon	euro
Qatar	Doha	riyal
Romania	Bucharest	leu
Russia	Moscow	rouble
Rwanda	Kigali	Rwanda franc
St Kitts and Nevis	Basseterre	East Caribbean dollar
St Lucia	Castries	East Caribbean dollar
St Vincent & the Grenadines	Kingstown	East Caribbean dollar

Country	Capital	Currency
Samoa	Apia	tala
San Marino	San Marino	euro
São Tomé and Príncipe	São Tomé	dobra
Saudi Arabia	Riyadh	riyal
Senegal	Dakar	CFA franc
Serbia and Montenegro	Belgrade	new dinar and euro
Seychelles	Victoria	rupee
Sierra Leone	Freetown	leone
Singapore	Singapore	Singapore dollar
Slovakia	Bratislava	koruna
Slovenia	Ljubljana	tolar
Solomon Islands	Honiara	Solomon Islands dollar
Somalia	Mogadishu	shilling
South Africa	Pretoria/Cape Town	rand
South Korea	Seoul	won
Spain	Madrid	euro
Sri Lanka	Colombo	rupee
Sudan	Khartoum	dinar
Suriname	Paramaribo	guilder
Swaziland	Mbabane	lilangeni
Sweden	Stockholm	krona
Switzerland	Bern	Swiss franc
Syria	Damascus	pound
Taiwan	Taipei	Taiwan dollar
Tajikistan	Dushanbe	somoni
Tanzania	Dodoma	shilling
Thailand	Bangkok	baht
Togo	Lomé	CFA franc
Tonga	Nuku'alofa	pa'anga
Trinidad and Tobago	Port of Spain	Trinidad and Tobago dollar
Tunisia	Tunis	dinar
Turkey	Ankara	lira
Turkmenistan	Ashkhabad	manat
Tuvalu	Funafuti	Australian dollar
Uganda	Kampala	shilling
Ukraine	Kiev	hryvna
United Arab Emirates	Abu Dhabi	dirham
United Kingdom	London	pound sterling
United States of America	Washington DC	US dollar
Uruguay	Montevideo	peso
Uzbekistan	Tashkent	sum
Vanuatu	Port Vila	vatu
Vatican City	Vatican City	euro
Venezuela	Caracas	bolívar
Vietnam	Hanoi	dong
Yemen	San'a	Riyal
Zambia	Lusaka	kwacha
Zimbabwe	Harare	Zimbabwe dollar

GRAMMAR – Plurals of nouns

Plurals are formed by adding –s except in the following cases:

1. When a word ends in –ch, –s, –sh, –ss or –x, the plural is formed by adding –es (e.g. *benches, gases, dishes, crosses, taxes*).

2. When a word ends in –y preceded by a consonant, the plural form is –ies (e.g. *parties, bodies, policies*). When a word ends in –y preceded by a vowel, the plural is formed by adding –s (e.g. *trays, joys, keys*).

3. When a word ends in –o, the more common plural ending is –oes (e.g. *cargoes, potatoes, heroes*). In many less familiar words or when the final –o is preceded by a vowel, the plural ending is –os (e.g. *avocados, armadillos, studios, cameos*).

4. When a word ends in –f, the plural is formed either by adding –s (e.g. *beliefs, cuffs, whiffs*) or by changing the –f to –v and adding –es (e.g. *wives, thieves, loaves*). Some words may take both forms (e.g. *scarf, hoof, wharf*).

5. When a word ends in –ex or –x, the more formal plural ending is –ices. In more general contexts –es is used (e.g. *appendices, appendixes; indices, indexes*).

6. When a word from Latin ends in –is, the plural form is –es (e.g. *crises, analyses*).

7. With compound words (like mother-in-law) it is usually the more important part that is made plural (e.g. *mothers-in-law, brigadier generals*).

8. In certain cases the plural form of a word is the same as the singular (e.g. *deer, sheep, grouse*) and in some words both forms end in –s (e.g. *measles, corps*).

Note: There are two main types of plurals that take either singular or plural verbs:
   a. words like *media* and *data*. These are in common use as singular nouns although strictly, this is incorrect.
   b. words ending in –ics. Generally, these are treated as plural when the word relates to an individual person or thing (e.g. *your statistics are out-of-date; the hall's acoustics are good*) and as singular when the word is regarded more strictly as a science (e.g. *statistics is an important subject*).

Forms of adjectives

Adjectives can be used in three different forms: the basic word (e.g. *strong*), the comparative (e.g. *stronger*), and the superlative (e.g. *strongest*). The comparative is regularly formed by adding –er to the basic word and the superlative by adding –est.

1. Adjectives that end in a consonant plus –e regularly drop the –e before adding –er and –est (e.g. *fine, finer, finest*).

2. Adjectives ending in –y, such as pretty, regularly change the –y to –i before adding –er or –est (*prettier, prettiest*).

3. Adjectives ending in –ey usually change the –ey to –i (e.g. *dicey, dicier, diciest*).

4. Short adjectives (of one syllable and with a short vowel sound) that end in a consonant double the consonant before adding –er or –est (e.g. *fat, fatter, fattest*).

Note: A different way of expressing the comparative and superlative of an adjective is to use *more* for the comparative and *most* for the superlative before the adjective. This is done with longer adjectives, such as some which have two syllables and all that have three or more syllables (e.g. *faithful, more faithful, most faithful* and *beautiful, more beautiful, most beautiful*). This form is also used with adjectives like *afraid* or *alone* and with those adjectives that come from past participles (e.g. *tired, refined*). Sometimes the sound of an adjective makes this form more suitable (e.g. *eager, bizarre, correct*).

Forms of verbs

Most verbs in English have four different forms. Some have five. The forms are:

a. the **base form**, e.g. *talk, expect, grow, think, swim.*

b. the **third person present singular**, e.g. *talks, expects, grows, thinks, swims.*

c. the **present participle**, e.g. *talking, expecting, growing, thinking, swimming.*

d. the **past tense**, e.g. *talked, expected, grew, thought, swam.*

e. the **past participle**, e.g. *talked, expected, grown, thought, swum.*

Notice that the past tense and the past participle are identical for many verbs, but for a few, e.g. *grew/grown* and *swam/swum*, they are different. The past tense is used as in *He grew some prize vegetables*. The past participle is used for the perfect tenses, as in *He has grown some prize vegetables*, and for the passive voice, as in *Some prize vegetables were grown*.

1. Forming the third person singular of verbs

The third person singular form of English verbs ends in –s (e.g. *expects*), and the rules for forming it are generally the same as for the plural of nouns. An exception to this is *knife*, where the third person singular is *knifes*, but the plural of the corresponding noun is *knives*.

2. Forming the present participle of verbs

The present participle is regularly formed by adding –ing to the base form (e.g. *walk, walking*; *invent, inventing*). Verbs that end in a consonant plus –e regularly drop the final –e before the addition of –ing (e.g. *locate, locating*; *snare, snaring*).

Verbs that end in a single consonant double that consonant before the addition of –ing (e.g. *pin, pinning*; *submit, submitting*). Exceptions to this are verbs of more than one syllable with no stress on the last syllable, such as *rivet, gather* (*rivet, riveting*; *gather, gathering*) but this does not apply to verbs ending in –l, such as *label, revel*, which double the l (*label, labelling*; *revel, revelling*).

3. Forming the past tense and past participle of verbs

Verbs that end in a consonant plus –e regularly drop the final –e before the addition of –ed (e.g. *locate, located*; *snare, snared*).

Verbs that end in a consonant plus –y regularly change the –y to an –i before the addition of –ed (e.g. *pity, pitied*).

Verbs that end in a single consonant double that consonant before the addition of –ed (e.g. *pin, pinned*; *submit, submitted*). Exceptions to this are verbs with two vowels before the final consonant, (e.g. *train, trained*) or verbs of more than one syllable with no stress on the last syllable, such as *rivet, gather* (*rivet, riveted*; *gather, gathered*) but this does not apply to verbs ending in –l, such as *label, revel* which double the l (*label, labelled*; *revel, revelled*).

Punctuation

Punctuation mark	Examples

. Period

1. Ends a sentence that is not a question or an exclamation. — *I live in Victoria.*
2. Follows most abbreviations. — *abbrev., e.g., i.e.*
3. Used after a person's initials. — *Franklin D. Roosevelt*
4. Used after an indirect question. — *He asked me if I live in Halifax.*

? Question Mark

1. Ends a question. — *Where is your birthday cake?*
2. Indicates uncertainty. — *Geoffrey Chaucer (?1340–1400) was a poet.*

! Exclamation Mark

1. Ends a sentence that expresses strong emotion. — *Watch out!*
2. Should be used sparingly. — *Don't write like this!!!!!!!*

, Comma

1. Separates main clauses joined by a coordinating conjunction. — *Eve looked for the cake, but it was gone.*
2. Sets off an introductory expression that precedes the main clause. — *In the afternoon, the skateboarders arrive.*
3. Sets off mild interjections, transitional expressions, and conjunctive adverbs. — *Ah, now I understand.* / *The best songs, I think, include long drum solos.* / *At night, after my parents go to sleep, I dance in the kitchen.*
4. Separates three or more words, phrases, or clauses in a series. — *Chris wore red, pink, and orange clothes yesterday.*
5. Separates coordinate adjectives. — *Zoë is a slick, stylish girl.*
6. Used in direct address. — *Dear Mr. Pringle,*
7. Used in dates and addresses. — *August 12, 2004* / *10 Downing Street, Regina, Saskatchewan*
8. Introduces a direct quotation. — *John said, "Nobody told me."*

; Semicolon

1. Separates long or confusing items in a complex list. — *She drove through Brandon, Manitoba; Lethbridge, Alberta; and Kamloops, B.C.*
2. Separates long clauses in a compound sentence. — *Stewart may have bought an instruction book; he may have taken many lessons; he may have practiced for hours; yet he still can't play the musical saw.*
3. Joins two independent clauses in the place of a conjunction. — *Some people can dance; others just can't do it.*

: Colon

1. Introduces a long list, an explanation, or a long quotation.

The competition was between three people: Bob, Alice, and Phil.
I called the police: the man had a gun.
Boris Pasternak said it best: "Man is born to live, not to prepare for life."

2. Used to separate numerals and in book titles.

I'll come over at 8:30 p.m. tonight.
Shakespeare's Macbeth: A Magical Tale

– Dash

1. Indicates a short pause, an afterthought, or an informal break in a sentence.

Hi, it's me – Bobby McGee.
No one can jump that high – not even you.
I don't believe it – the dog is here!

2. Indicates a range of numbers.

1939–1945

- Hyphen

1. Joins compound words.

U-turn, X-ray, father-in-law, bling-bling

2. Joins phrases used as compound adjectives.

This was a once-in-a-lifetime concert.

3. Used in compound numerals and fractions.

twenty-one, three-quarters

( ) Parentheses

1. Indicates words, phrases, or clauses that are not central to the main point of a sentence.

My cat Nelly (the one with the sharp fangs) is at the vet's office today.
The CIA (Central Intelligence Agency) is studying the evidence.

' Apostrophe

1. Shows that something belongs to someone.

That is Cameron's bike.

2. Used in shortened forms of words to show that one or more letters are missing.

That's the bike.

" " Quotation Marks

1. Indicate direct speech.
2. Highlight a particular word or phrase.

David said, "What about me?"
He said he was a "grifter", whatever that is.

NAMES AND SYMBOLS OF METRIC UNITS

Quantity	Name of Unit	Value	Symbol
LENGTH	metre	base unit	m
	centimetre	0.01 m	cm
	millimetre	0.001 m	mm
	micrometre	0.000 001 m	μm (or um)
	kilometre	1 000 m	km
	international nautical mile (for navigation)	1 852 m	n mile
MASS (weight)	kilogram	base unit	kg
	milligram	0.000 001 kg	mg
	gram	0.001 kg	g
	tonne	1 000 kg	t
TIME	second	base unit	s
	minute	60 s	min
	hour	60 min	h
	day	24 h	d
AREA	square metre	SI unit	m²
	square millimetre	0.000 001 m²	mm²
	square centimetre	0.000 1 m²	cm²
	hectare	10 000 m²	ha
	square kilometre	1 000 000 m²	km²
VOLUME	cubic metre	SI unit	m³
	cubic centimetre	0.000 001 m³	cm³
VOLUME (for fluids)	litre	0.001 m³	l
	millilitre	0.001 l	ml
	kilolitre	1 000 l (1 m³)	kl
VELOCITY	metre per second	SI unit	m/s
	kilometre per hour	0.27 m/s	km/h
	knot	1 n mile/h or 0.514 m/s	kn
FORCE	newton	SI unit	N
	kilonewton	1 000 N	kN
	meganewton	1 000 000 N	MN
ENERGY	joule	SI unit	J
	kilojoule	1 000 J	kJ
	megajoule	1 000 000 J	MJ

POWER	watt	SI unit	W
	kilowatt	1 000 W	kW
	megawatt	1 000 000 W	MW

DENSITY	kilogram per cubic metre	SI unit	kg/m^3
	tonne per cubic metre	1 000 kg/m^3	t/m^3
	gram per cubic metre	0.0001 kg/m^3	g/m^3

DENSITY (for fluids)	kilogram per litre	1 000 kg/m^3	kg/l

PRESSURE	pascal	SI unit (N/m^2)	Pa
	kilopascal	1 000 Pa	kPa
	megapascal	1 000 000 Pa	MPa

PRESSURE (for meteorology)	millibar	100 Pa	mb

ELECTRIC CURRENT	ampere	base unit	A
	milliampere	0.001 A	mA

POTENTIAL DIFFERENCE	volt	SI unit	V
	microvolt	0.000 001 V	μV
	millivolt	0.001 V	mV
	kilovolt	1 000 V	kV
	megavolt	1 000 000 V	MV

ELECTRICAL RESISTANCE	ohm	SI unit	Ω
	microhm	0.000 001 Ω	μΩ
	megohm	1 000 000 Ω	MΩ

FREQUENCY	hertz	SI unit	Hz
	kilohertz	1 000 Hz	kHz
	megahertz	1 000 000 Hz	MHz
	gigahertz	1 000 000 000 hz	GHz

TEMPERATURE	kelvin	SI unit	K
	degree Celsius	K-273.15	°C

METRIC/IMPERIAL CONVERSION FACTORS

Imperial to Metric Units   **Metric to Imperial Units**

LENGTH

1 in	= 25.4 mm	1 cm	= 0.394 in
1 ft	= 30.5 cm	1 m	= 3.28 ft
1 yd	= 0.914 m	1 m	= 1.09 yd
1 mile	= 1.61 km	1 km	= 0.621 mile

MASS

1 oz	= 28.35 g	1 g	= 0.0353 oz
1 lb	= 454 g	1 kg	= 2.20 lb
1 ton	= 1.02 tonne	1 tonne	= 0.984 ton

AREA

1 in^2	$= 6.45 \text{ cm}^2$	1 cm^2	$= 0.155 \text{ in}^2$
1 ft^2	$= 929 \text{ cm}^2$	1 m^2	$= 10.8 \text{ ft}^2$
1 yd^2	$= 0.836 \text{ m}^2$	1 m^2	$= 1.20 \text{ yd}^2$
1 ac	= 0.405 ha	1 ha	= 2.47 ac
1 sq mile	= 259 ha	1 km^2	= 247 ac

VOLUME

1 in^3	$= 16.4 \text{ cm}^3$	1 cm^3	$= 0.0610 \text{ in}^3$
1 ft^3	$= 0.0283 \text{ m}^3$	1 m^3	$= 35.3 \text{ ft}^3$
1 yd^3	$= 0.765 \text{ m}^3$	1 m^3	$= 1.31 \text{ yd}^3$
1 bushel	$= 0.364 \text{ m}^3$	1 m^3	= 27.5 bushels

VOLUME (fluids)

1 fl oz	= 28.4 ml	1 ml	= 0.0352 fl oz
1 pint	= 568 ml	1 litre	= 1.76 pint
1 gallon	= 4.55 litre	1 m^3	= 220 gallons

FORCE

1 lbf (pound-force)	= 4.45 N	1N (newton)	= 0.225 lbf

PRESSURE

1 psi (lb/sq in)	= 6.89 kPa	1kPa (kilopascal)	= 0.145 psi

VELOCITY

1 mph	= 1.61 km/h	1km/h	= 0.621 mph

TEMPERATURE

$$°C = \frac{5}{9}(°F - 32)$$ $$°F = \frac{(9 \times °C)}{5} + 32$$

ENERGY

1 Btu	= 1.06 kJ	1 kJ	= 0.948 Btu
(British thermal unit)			

POWER

1 hp	= 0.746 kW	1 kW	= 1.34 hp

FUEL CONSUMPTION

$$\text{mpg} = \frac{282}{(\text{litres}/100 \text{ km})}$$ $$\text{litres}/100 \text{ km} = \frac{282}{\text{mpg}}$$

www.collinslanguage.com

Free Trial Terms and Conditions